PRENTICE HALL

DDC Publishing

Stepping Through Office XP

With Business Applications

INTRODUCTORY

Backspace

Enter

Shift

PEARSON

Prentice Hall DDC

Upper Saddle River, New Jersey
Needham, Massachusetts

Components

Student Edition
Teacher's Edition with Student Data Files CD-ROM
Solutions Key with Teacher's Solutions Files CD-ROM
Assessment and Certification Manual with Computerized Test Bank CD-ROM
Presentation Pro CD-ROM
Companion Web site

** The DDC banner design is a registered trademark of Pearson Education, Inc.

**Microsoft, Microsoft Internet Explorer logo, Windows, PowerPoint, and Outlook are either registered trademarks or trademarks of Microsoft Corporation in the United States and/or other countries.

**Microsoft and the Microsoft Office Logo are trademarks or registered trademarks of Microsoft Corporation in the United States and/or other countries, and the Microsoft Office Specialist Logo is used under license from owner.

Acknowledgments

Microsoft Corporation
"Screen shot(s) reprinted by permission from Microsoft Corporation."

America Online, Inc.
"AOL screenshots © 2002 America Online, Inc. Used with permission."

National Park Service
"September 3rd, 2002, screenshot used with permission."

ISBN: 0-13-036301-4
4 5 6 7 8 9 10   07 06 05 04

Program Advisors

The program advisors provided ongoing input throughout the development of Prentice Hall's *Stepping Through Office XP*. Their sensitivity to the needs of students and teachers helps ensure that these needs are addressed within this textbook. Many thanks to each of the following individuals:

Martha L. Behrends
Auburn High School
Auburn, Illinois

James Thomas Davis
A.C. Mosley High School
Lynn Haven, Florida

Ann Godfrey
Cherokee Technology Center
Gaffney, South Carolina

Cathy Jinkerson
Washington High School
Washington, Missouri

Sondra S. Mangan
Emerald Ridge High School
South Hill, Washington

Maria N. Negro
Portsmouth High School
Portsmouth, Rhode Island

Steven Shell
White Plains High School
White Plains, New York

Gail Swain
Peach County High School
Fort Valley, Georgia

Using Your Text

Stepping Through Office XP – Introductory

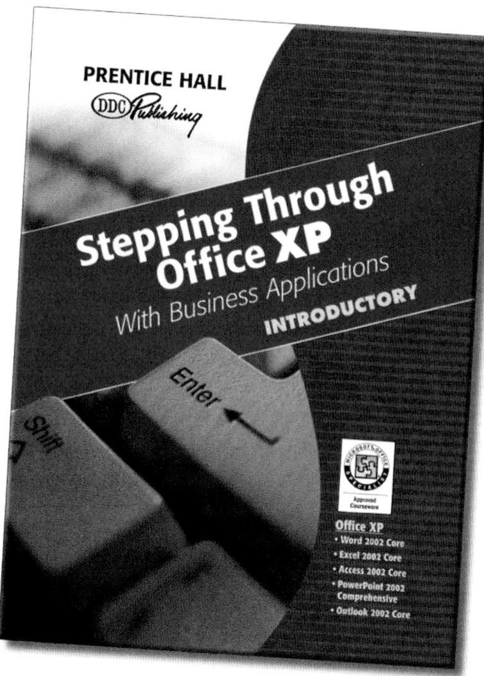

Stepping Through Office XP – Introductory presents the basic concepts and skills of Microsoft Office XP (Microsoft Word, Microsoft Excel, Microsoft Access, Microsoft PowerPoint®, and Microsoft Outlook®) and also introduces fundamental computer concepts.

Through a learn-by-doing approach, you are challenged to master Microsoft Office concepts and skills within a business context. Additional features throughout the book also provide insight into how the skills you are learning apply in other areas of school and in the business world.

The book is organized into six units with two or more lessons in each unit:

- **Business Communications (Word)**
- **Business Financials (Excel)**
- **Business Databases (Access)**
- **Business Presentations (PowerPoint)**
- **Business Telecommunications (Outlook)** and
- **Operating Systems, Utilities, and Networks (Systems)**.

Stepping Through Office XP – Introductory will prepare you to take the following Microsoft Office Specialist certification exams: Word 2002 Core, Excel 2002 Core, Access 2002, PowerPoint 2002 comprehensive, and Outlook 2002 Core. These certifications are an important credential to add to your resumé whether you are looking for a job or applying for college. You will see the objectives for the exams identified throughout the text. For more information about Microsoft Office Specialist certification objectives, see Appendix B.

Lesson Overview

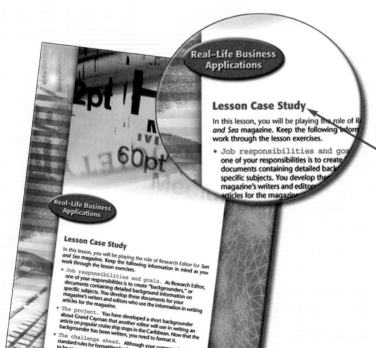

Lesson Objectives

Each lesson begins with a list of the tasks you will perform, key terms, and the Microsoft Office Specialist objectives that are covered.

Lesson Case Studies

Lessons are presented within the context of a unique case study that sets the stage for you to learn Office skills in a business setting.

Lesson Overview (cont'd)

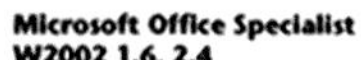

Microsoft Office Specialist
W2002 1.6, 2.4

Exercise 1 Overview:
Apply Paragraph and Charact

Formatting means changing the way a d
style is a named set of formatting chara
styles lets you format individual cha
paragraphs with just a few mouse clic
give a consistent look to different
Paragraph styles can be appl
paragraphs. **Character styles**
characters, such as a word or a le

When you open a template, Word makes predetermined styles available. Some templates feature a wide variety of styles, and each one has a specific use. Styles are easy to apply. Just select the text you want to format, and then select the style. Word applies the formatting. You can select styles in two ways: from the Style list on the Formatting toolbar or from the Styles and Formatting task pane. Both show you all the styles in use in the document as well as other available styles.

Once you have applied a style to a paragraph or to some characters, you can use Word's Format Painter to *paint* the formatting onto another piece of text. The Format Painter

Need Help?
Type: styles

Word

Lesson Exercise Overview

Brief overviews introduce the concepts, skills, and vocabulary.

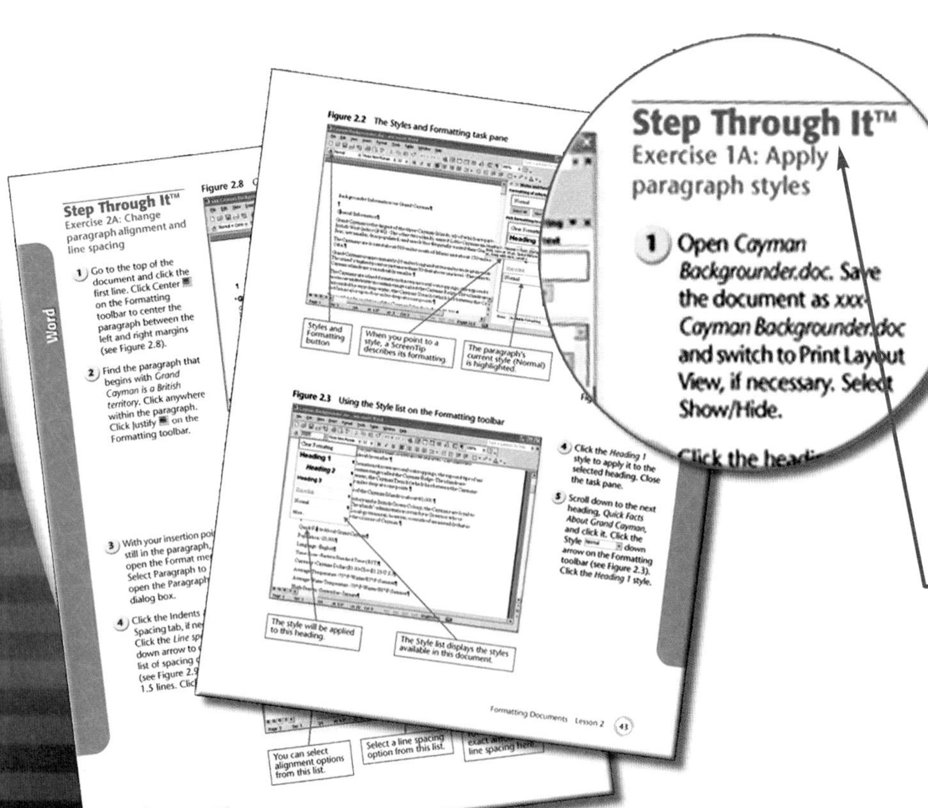

Step Through It™

Introductory exercises provide a step-by-step visual guide to the Office XP feature you are learning.

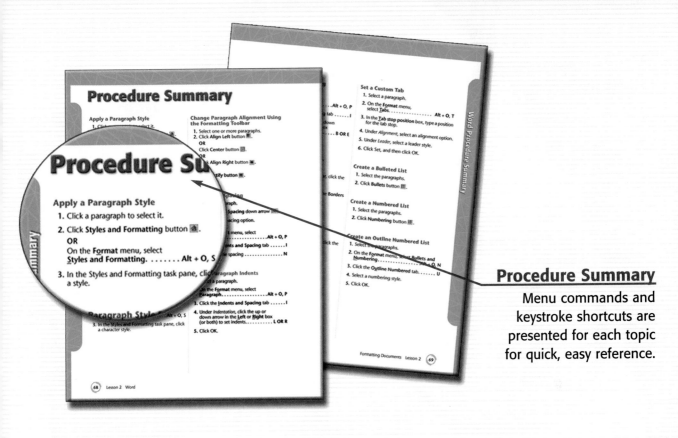

Procedure Summary

Menu commands and keystroke shortcuts are presented for each topic for quick, easy reference.

Review and Reinforce Office XP Skills

At the end of each lesson, you will review the concepts you have learned and reinforce your skills with additional exercises that will progressively challenge your skills.

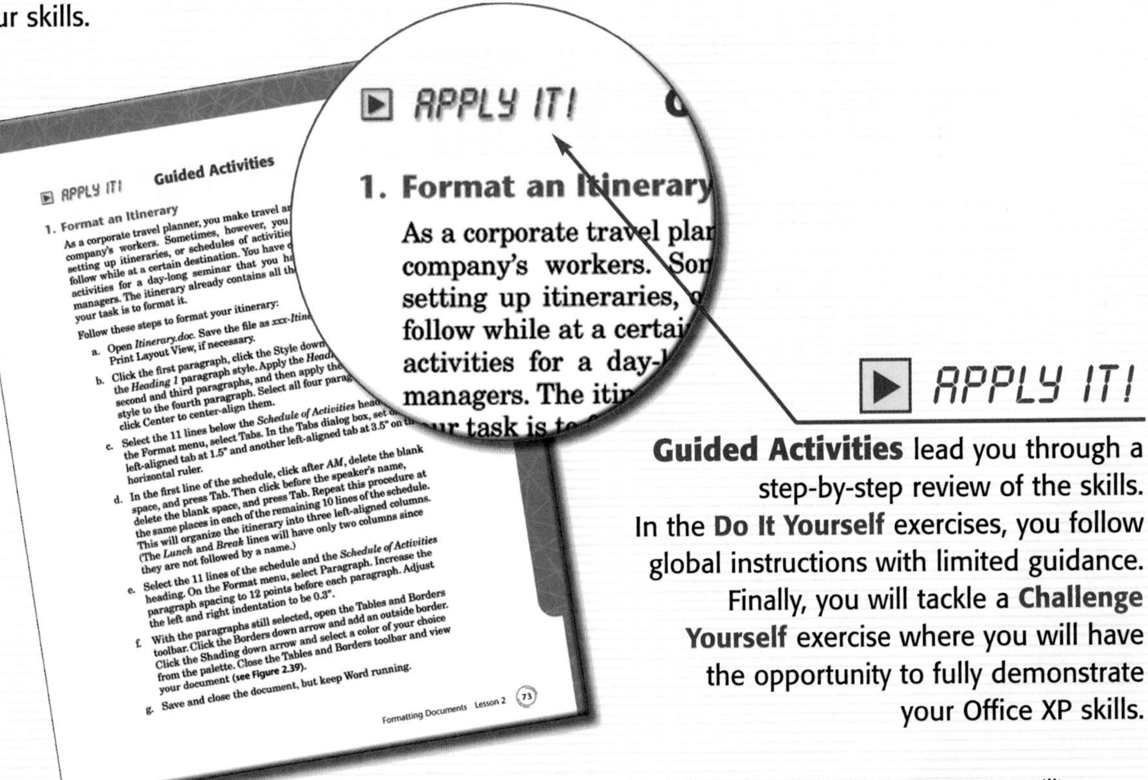

APPLY IT!

Guided Activities lead you through a step-by-step review of the skills. In the **Do It Yourself** exercises, you follow global instructions with limited guidance. Finally, you will tackle a **Challenge Yourself** exercise where you will have the opportunity to fully demonstrate your Office XP skills.

Lesson Overview (cont'd)

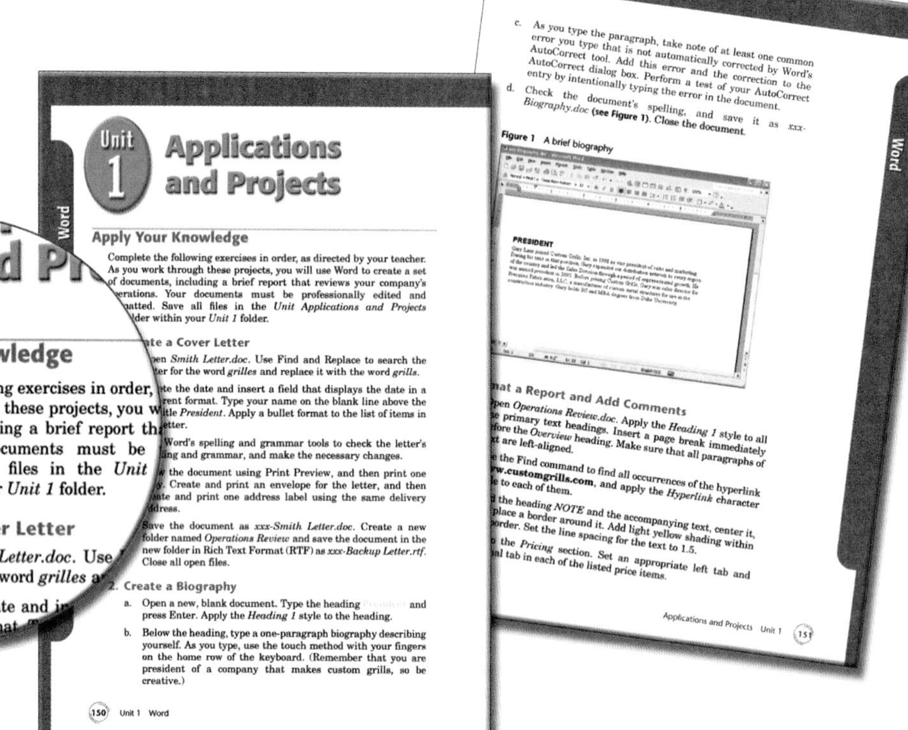

Unit 1 Applications and Projects
Word
Apply Your Knowledge
Complete the following exercises in order, as directed by your teacher. As you work through these projects, you will use Word to create a set of documents, including a brief report that reviews your company's operations. Your documents must be professionally edited and formatted. Save all files in the Unit Applications and Projects subfolder within your Unit 1 folder.
1. Create a Cover Letter
a. Open Smith Letter.doc. Use Find and Replace to search the letter for the word grilles and replace it with the word grills.
b. Delete the date and insert a field that displays the date in a different format.
2. Create a Biography
a. Open a new, blank document. Type the heading President and press Enter. Apply the Heading 1 style to the heading.
b. Below the heading, type a one-paragraph biography describing yourself. As you type, use the touch method with your fingers on the home row of the keyboard. (Remember that you are president of a company that makes custom grills, so be creative.)
150 Unit 1 Word
c. As you type the paragraph, take note of at least one common error you type that is not automatically corrected by Word's AutoCorrect tool. Add this error and the correction to the AutoCorrect dialog box. Perform a test of your AutoCorrect entry by intentionally typing the error in the document.
d. Check the document's spelling, and save it as xxx-Biography.doc (see Figure 1). Close the document.
Figure 1 A brief biography
Applications and Projects Unit 1 151

Unit Applications and Projects

Each unit ends with activities designed to provide critical thinking and reinforcement, including:

- **Apply Your Knowledge** – challenging, comprehensive projects.
- **What's Wrong With This Picture?** – layout and design activities.
- **Cross-Curriculum Projects** – integrate Office XP skills into other academic subjects.
- **Companion Web Site** – provides additional resources for both students and teachers. Go to **www.PHSchool.com** and enter Web code **GBK 0001**.

Special Features

Business Connections Discover other skills demonstrated by successful business professionals and how they relate to Office applications you are learning.

Business Connections

Effective Business Writing and Editing

Creative, journalistic, and technical writing are just a few examples of the many different styles of writing. Each style follows its own set of rules just like business writing does. If you plan to create documents for use in business—such as memos, letters, and reports—then you need to learn the appropriate style.

In business, effective documents follow these simple rules:

- **They are as brief as possible.** Good business writers make their point quickly and stick to it without adding a lot of fluff.
- **They focus on facts.** Unless your document's purpose is to convey an opinion, you should leave it out. If you venture an opinion, support it with specific information, and incorporate references.
- **They provide important data.** In addition to the basic facts, business people often need to see data supporting the facts. This data may take the form of charts, diagrams, or simple explanatory text.
- **They use simple, active language.** Strong writers avoid using the passive voice unless it can help make a point. They use short, direct sentences and avoid the overuse of adjectives.
- **They are well organized.** Long documents should be divided into sections, each focusing on a specific subject. This makes it easier for the reader to locate and interpret information. Short documents may be organized into lists or bulleted points.

Organization

- Logic is essential to business writing, so good organization is important. That's why business writers often begin with detailed outlines to make sure that their topics and ideas flow logically and sequentially. This keeps the reader's attention focused and makes the document easier to understand.
- In addition, many reports begin with a summary instead of ending with one. This feature is sometimes called an executive summary because it is designed for busy managers who don't have time to read a lot of information.
- Lastly, accuracy is everything. You'll learn why if you give your boss a report filled with errors! Experienced business writers carefully research every bit of information that goes into their documents.

CRITICAL THINKING

1. **Applying the Active Voice** It's preferable to use the active voice rather than the passive voice. Write three sentences in passive voice and then make them active. Describe the differences in the tone of the sentences.
2. **Research Writing Style Guides** Have you ever used a style guide? Why do you think style guides are so important in writing effectively? Take a look at some of the style guides commonly used by business writers.

Formatting Documents Lesson 2 55

Special Features (cont'd)

Career Corner provides information on various career paths and fields that relate to the lesson topic.

Tech Talk investigates topics and trends in technology.

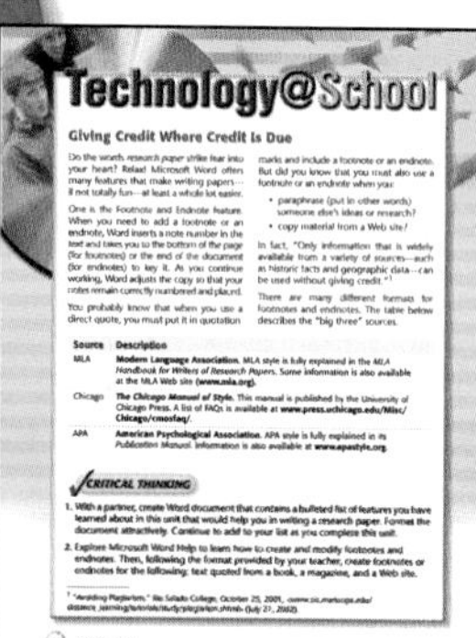

Technology@School presents ways you can apply what you are learning to other areas of school.

Microsoft Office Specialist Certification

What does this logo mean?

It means this courseware has been approved by the Microsoft® Office Specialist Program to be among the finest available for learning Microsoft Word 2002, Microsoft Excel 2002, Microsoft PowerPoint® 2002, Microsoft Access 2002, and Microsoft Outlook® 2002. It also means that upon completion of this courseware, you may be prepared to take an exam for Microsoft Office Specialist qualification.

What is a Microsoft Office Specialist?

A Microsoft Office Specialist is an individual who has passed exams for certifying his or her skills in one or more of the Microsoft Office desktop applications such as Microsoft Word, Microsoft Excel, Microsoft PowerPoint, Microsoft Outlook, Microsoft Access, or Microsoft Project. The Microsoft Office Specialist Program typically offers certification exams at the "Core" and "Expert" skill levels. The Microsoft Office Specialist Program is the only program approved by Microsoft for testing proficiency in Microsoft Office desktop applications and Microsoft Project. This testing program can be a valuable asset in any job search or career advancement.

More Information:

To learn more about becoming a Microsoft Office Specialist, visit **www.microsoft.com/officespecialist**

To learn about other Microsoft Specialist approved courseware from Pearson Education visit **www.PHSchool.com**

*The availability of Microsoft Office Specialist certification exams varies by application, application version, and language. Visit **www.microsoft.com/officespecialist** for exam availability.

Table of Contents

Unit 1: WORD

Unit 2: EXCEL

Unit 3: ACCESS

Unit 4: POWERPOINT

Business Presentations....................474

Unit 5: OUTLOOK

Unit 6: SYSTEMS

Word

Unit 1 Business Communications

Unit Contents

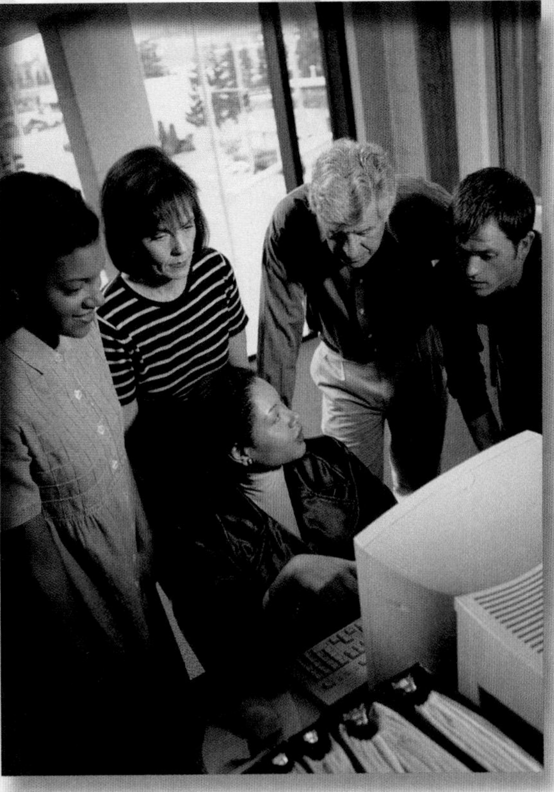

Unit Objectives

1. Enter and edit text and save a document
2. Preview and print a document
3. Create a new document
4. Use Cut, Copy, and Paste
5. Find and replace document text
6. Use the AutoCorrect feature
7. Use the Spelling and Grammar tools and the Thesaurus
8. Apply paragraph and character styles
9. Modify paragraph formats
10. Set tabs in a document
11. Apply bullets, numbering, and outline numbering to lists
12. Apply character formats
13. Create and modify a header and footer
14. Insert a page break and page number
15. Apply highlights and text effects
16. Create, modify, and format tables
17. Insert graphics into a document
18. Apply and modify newsletter columns
19. Print a letter, an envelope, and a label
20. Use the Comments feature
21. Share a document online
22. Insert and modify a date/time field

Word

Lesson 1

Introducing Word

Lesson Exercise Objectives

After completing this lesson, you'll be able to do the following tasks:

1. Enter and edit text
2. Save a document
3. Preview and print a document
4. Create a new document using Word
5. Use Cut, Copy, and Paste
6. Find and replace document text
7. Use the AutoCorrect feature
8. Use the Spelling and Grammar tools and the Thesaurus

Key Terms

- AutoCorrect (p. 26)
- Clipboard (p. 20)
- Copy (p. 20)
- Cut (p. 20)
- documents (p. 6)
- edit (p. 6)
- file (p. 9)
- file type (p. 9)
- Find (p. 24)
- Grammar checker (p. 27)
- insertion point (p. 6)
- Insert mode (p. 6)
- Overtype mode (p. 6)
- Paste (p. 20)
- placeholders (p. 14)
- Replace (p. 24)
- save (p. 9)
- Spelling checker (p. 27)
- template (p. 14)
- Thesaurus (p. 27)

Microsoft Office Specialist Activities

W2002: 1.1, 1.3, 3.5, 4.1, 4.2, 4.3

Real-Life Business Applications

Lesson Case Study

In this lesson, you will play the role of the Managing Editor for *Sun and Sea*, a magazine devoted to cruise ship travel and vacationing. Keep the following information in mind as you work through the lesson exercises.

- `Job responsibilities and goals.` As Managing Editor, one of your responsibilities is to screen applicants for jobs in the Editorial Department. Your goal is to choose the best candidate for the position of Research Editor.
- `The project.` You have reviewed dozens of resumes from people applying for the Research Editor position. Since you have selected a candidate for the job, you will communicate your choice to others within your organization. Then you will offer the job to the applicant.
- `The challenge ahead.` You need to create a professional memo telling your managers that you have chosen the right person for the Research Editor job. Then you need to create a letter offering the job to that applicant.

Microsoft Office Specialist W2002 1.1

Word

Exercise 1 Overview:
Enter and Edit Text

Microsoft Word is a word processing program that you can use to create **documents** such as letters, resumes, or newsletters. A document can contain text alone; however, it can also include graphics, tables, and other features. A document can be as short as a few words or hundreds of pages in length.

Word lets you create a new document from scratch, sort of like writing on a blank sheet of paper. You can create new documents in two ways, as you will learn later in this lesson.

You can also use Word to **edit**, or make changes to, an existing document. Whether you are creating or editing a document, you need to enter text. Editing can also mean moving or deleting text or adding, moving, and deleting graphics or other items.

Word displays a blinking vertical line called the **insertion point** to show you where the next character will be inserted in the document. As you type, the insertion point moves across the screen and each letter you type appears right behind it.

You can enter text in two ways. In **Insert mode** (Word's default mode), you enter new text within existing text. The old text is pushed to the right as you type the new characters. In **Overtype mode**, you type over existing text, replacing it with new text.

In the following exercise, you will open an existing memo to your boss, and you will edit it.

Figure 1.1 The OVR button on the status bar

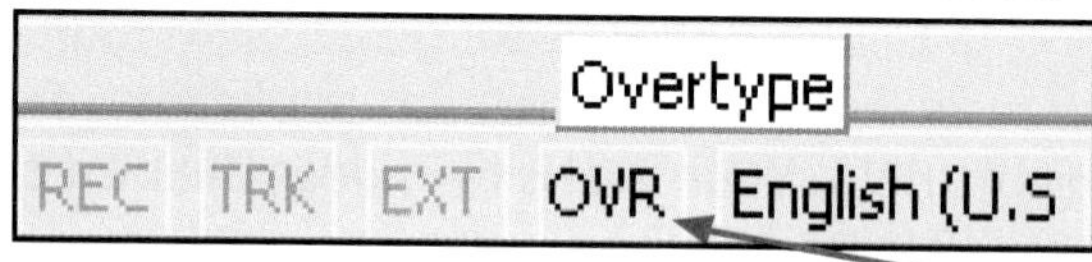

Double-click OVR on the status bar to switch between Overtype and Insert mode

Before you begin Exercise 1, check with your teacher regarding where your data files are located and where you should save your solutions.

Figure 1.2 Editing a memo in Word

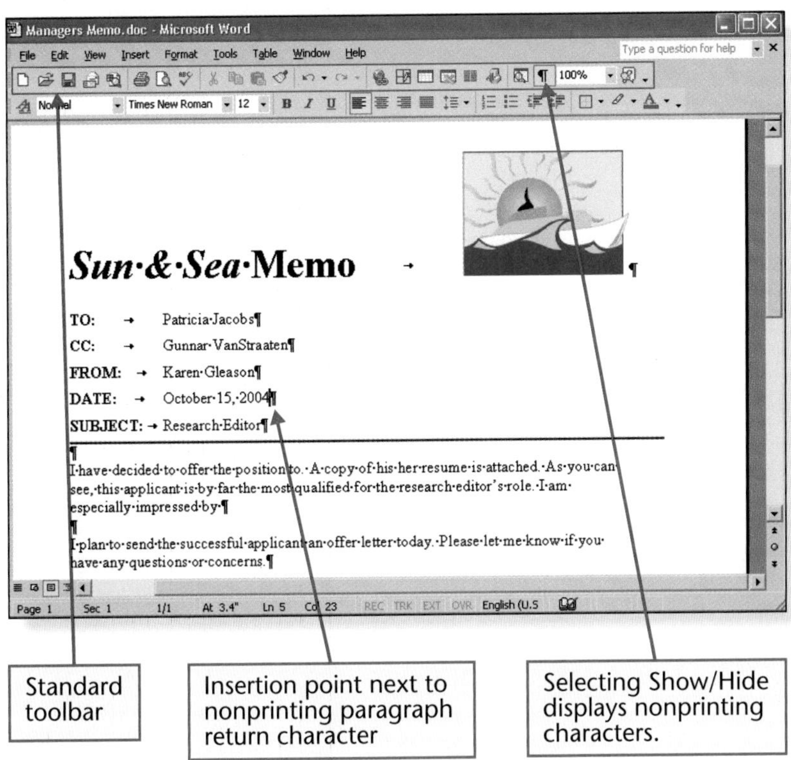

Step Through It™

Exercise 1: Enter and edit document text

1. Open *Managers Memo.doc.*
2. If necessary, select Show/Hide ¶ on the Standard toolbar to display nonprinting characters.
3. Click at the end of the memo's *Date* line (before the paragraph return). When the insertion point appears there, type today's date (see Figure 1.2).

Figure 1.3 Entering and deleting text

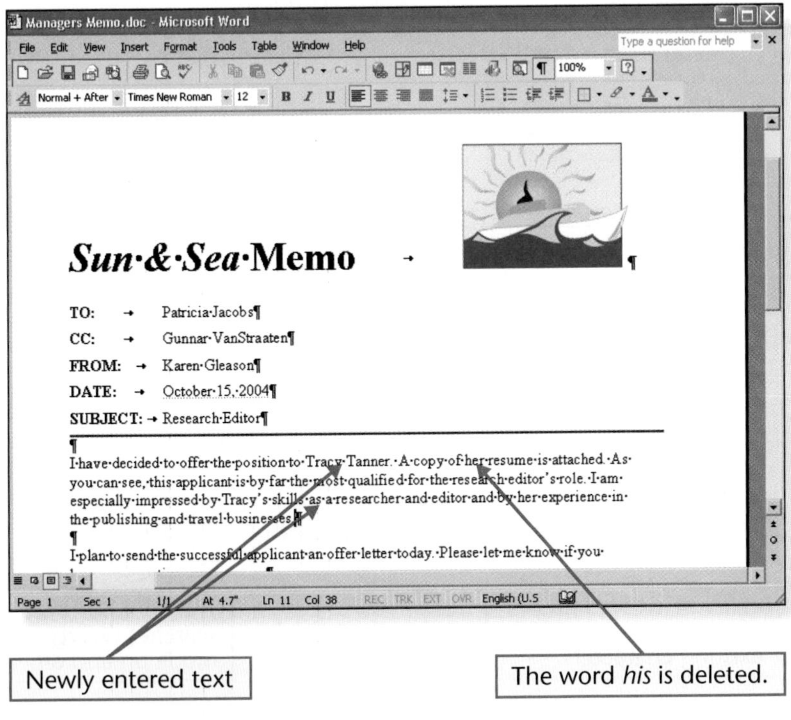

4. In the first paragraph, click at the end of the first sentence. Press the spacebar and type Tracy Tanner. In the next sentence, click before the word *his* and press Delete repeatedly to delete the word.
5. Go to the end of the first paragraph and type Tracy's skills as a researcher and editor and by her experience in the publishing and travel businesses. (See Figure 1.3.)

6 Press Enter twice, and type the text shown in Figure 1.4. Press Enter twice after the first sentence.

Figure 1.4 A new paragraph

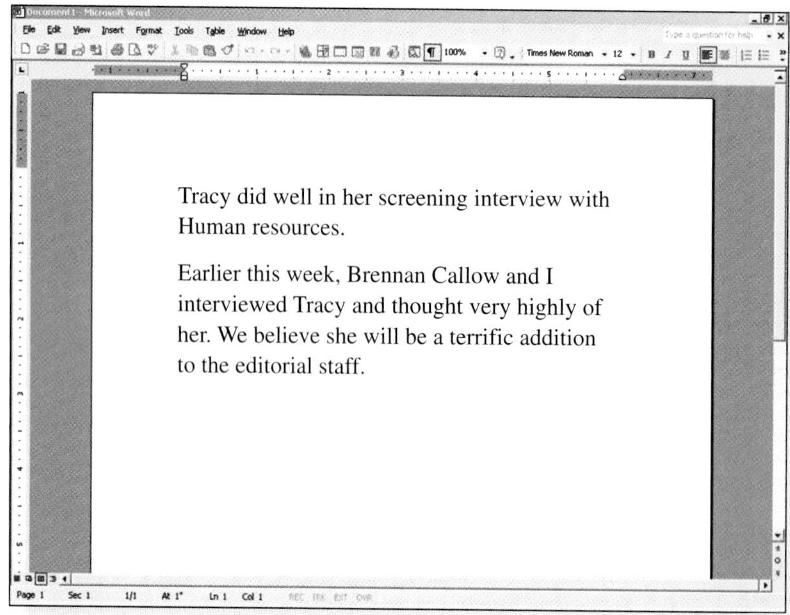

7 Click before the word *businesses* at the end of the first paragraph. Double-click the OVR button on the status bar, and type industries. Double-click OVR again to return to Insert mode.

8 In the last paragraph, click after the word *applicant*. Press Backspace to delete the words *the successful applicant*. Type Tracy (see Figure 1.5).

Figure 1.5 The edited memo

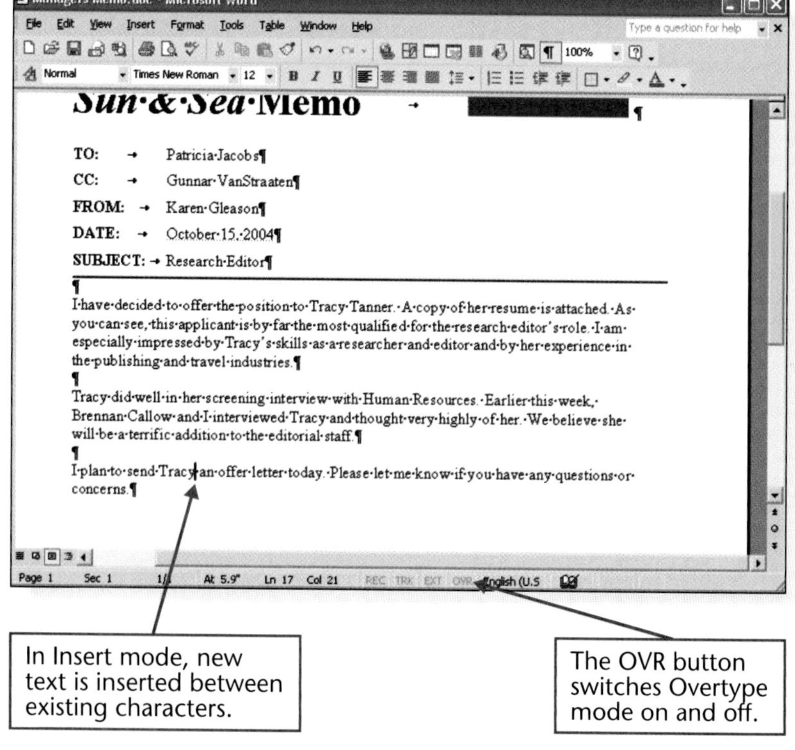

Exercise 2 Overview: Save a Document

Microsoft Office Specialist W2002 4.1, 4.3

Whenever you work on a document, you should **save** it; that is, tell your computer to store it permanently on a disk. When you save a document for the first time, you must give it a meaningful name so you can recognize it among other documents. A saved document with a unique name is called a **file**.

After you save a file the first time, you should resave it every few minutes as you work on it. When you do this, Word overwrites the last version of the file with the most recent version so your changes are preserved. This protects your data from being lost if the power goes out or you have a computer problem.

Word lets you save an existing file under a different name (preserving the original file); save it in a different location on a disk; or even save it as a different **file type** that can be used in a different program. For example, you can save a Word file as a WordPerfect file type; that way, you can share it with someone who uses that program instead of Word. Each different file type has a unique file name extension. For example, Word document files have the extension *.doc*; Excel workbooks have the extension *.xls*.

In the following exercises, you will save *Managers Memo.doc* with a new name. You will then save the same document in a new folder and change the file type.

Type: save a document in the Ask a Question box at the right end of the menu bar

Figure 1.6 The *Save as type* list

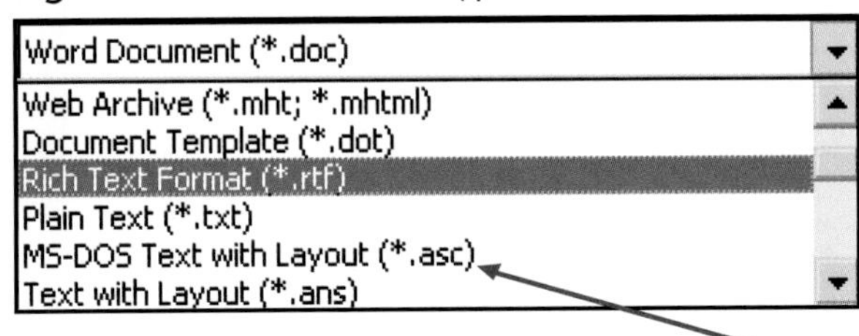

The *Save as type* list in the Save As dialog box provides many file type options.

Warning

Before you start the following exercises, confirm with your teacher how you should name your files and where you should create your new folder.

Step Through It™
Exercise 2A: Save a file with a new name

1. On the File menu, select Save As to open the Save As dialog box.
2. Click the *Save in* down arrow and select the drive where your data files are located.
3. Navigate to the *Lesson 1* subfolder within your *Unit 1* folder.
4. In the *File name* box, select the file's current name, and type xxx-Managers Memo replacing *xxx* with your initials (see Figure 1.7).
5. Click Save.

Figure 1.7 Saving the edited memo under a different name

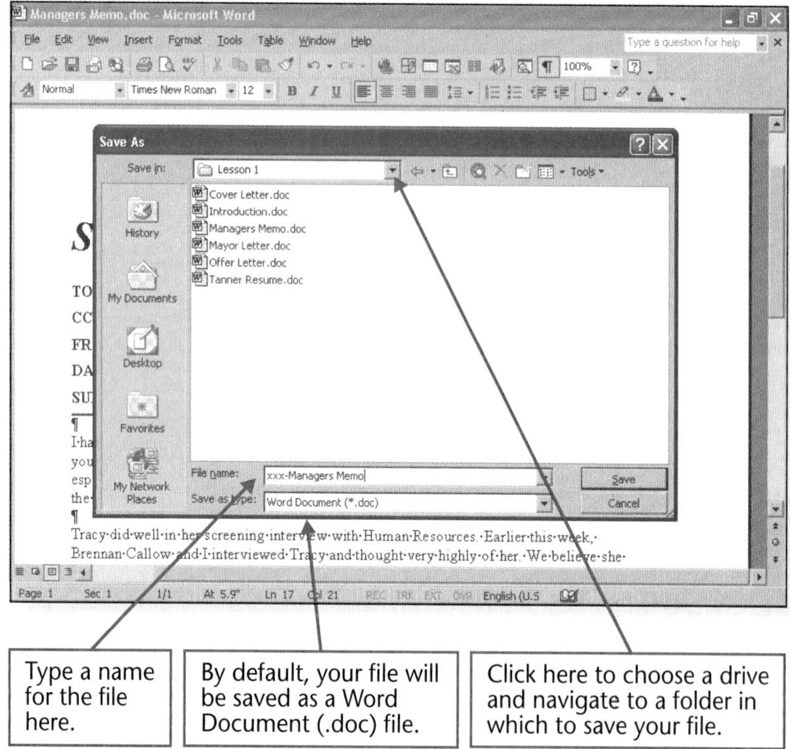

Type a name for the file here.
By default, your file will be saved as a Word Document (.doc) file.
Click here to choose a drive and navigate to a folder in which to save your file.

Step Through It™
Exercise 2B: Save a file in a new folder

1. Open the Save As dialog box. Click the Create New Folder button.
2. In the New Folder dialog box, type Copies as the new folder name (see Figure 1.8). Click OK.
3. Click Save to save your open document in the new folder.

Figure 1.8 Saving the file in a newly created folder

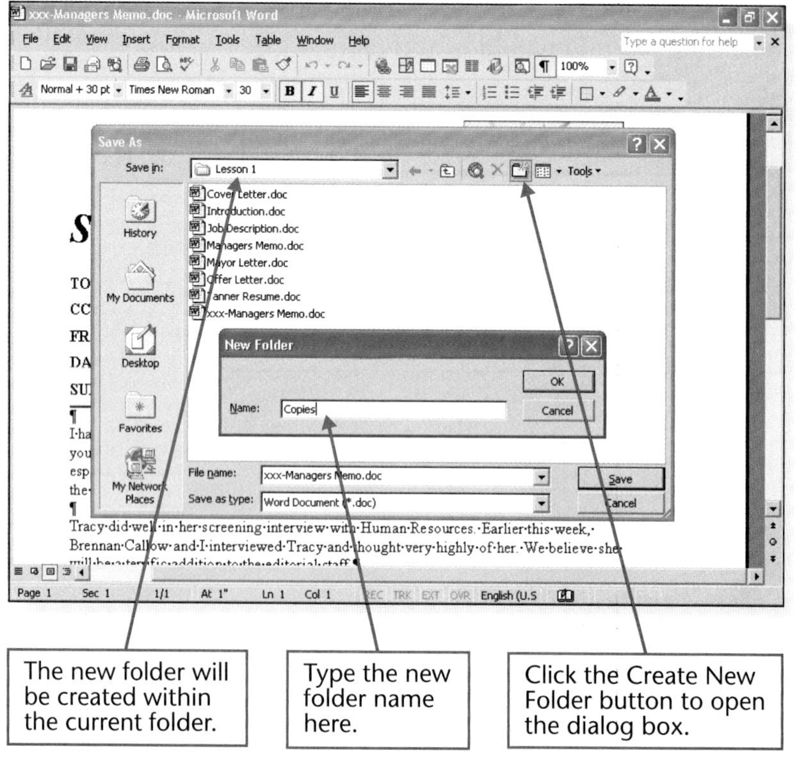

The new folder will be created within the current folder.

Figure 1.9 Choosing a different file type

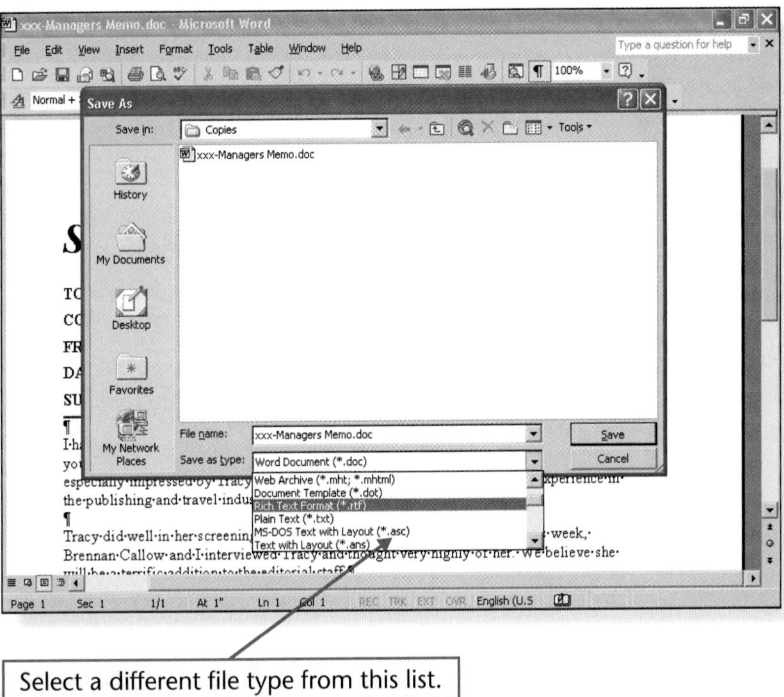

Step Through It™

Exercise 2C: Change the file type

1. Open the Save As dialog box. In the *Save in* box, navigate to the *Copies* folder you just created, if necessary.
2. Click the *Save as type* down arrow to see a list of available file types.
3. Scroll through the list and click Rich Text Format (see Figure 1.9).
4. Click Save.
5. Close all open files, but do not exit the Word program.

Word

Exercise 3 Overview: Preview and Print a Document

Microsoft Office Specialist W2002 3.5

It is easy to print any document you create in Word. Before printing a document, however, you should use Word's Print Preview feature to see how the pages will look. Viewing a document in Print Preview mode provides some unique advantages.

Print Preview Toolbar

Button	Purpose
Print	Sends the document directly to the printer
Magnifier	Magnifies any part of the document
One Page	Presents one page of the document
Multiple Pages	Presents up to six pages of the document
Close Close Preview	Closes the Print Preview window

For example, Print Preview gives you a big picture view of the document and lets you decide whether you need to change its layout or formatting before printing. This helps you save time and paper by avoiding wasted print jobs. The table on the previous page illustrates some of the commonly used buttons on the Print Preview toolbar.

When you are ready to print a document, you can use Word's Print dialog box to set printing options. For example, you can set the number of copies to print, select certain pages for printing, select a printer, and set other options.

Type: print a document

In the following exercises, you will preview and print the resume for Tracy Tanner.

Step Through It™

Exercise 3A: Preview a document

1. Open *Tanner Resume.doc.*
2. Switch to Print Layout View, if necessary (see Figure 1.10).
3. Click Print Preview on the Standard toolbar.

Figure 1.10 Viewing a resume in Print Layout View

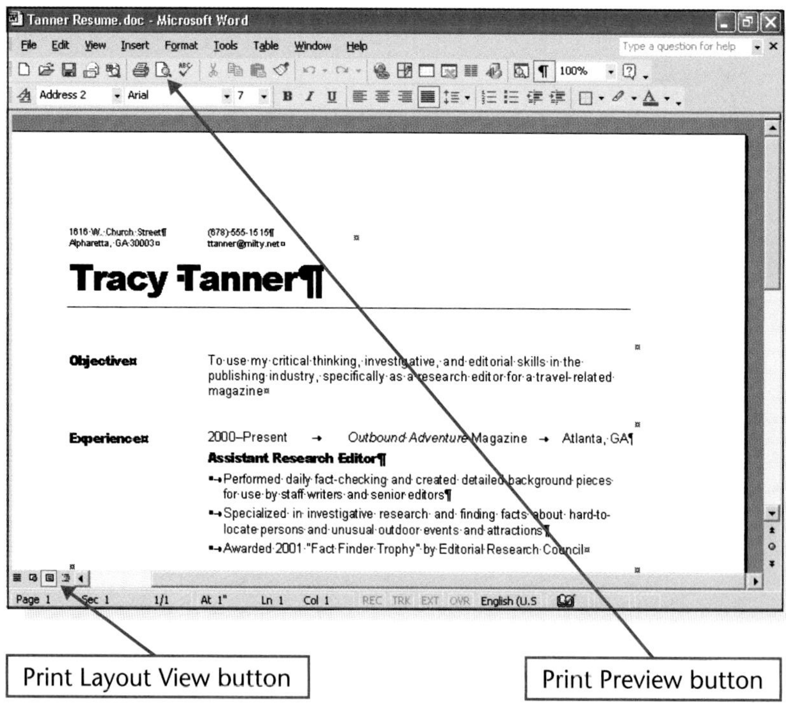

If you know your document is ready to print and you don't want to change any print options, click the Print button on the Standard toolbar to print one copy.

Figure 1.11 The Print Preview window

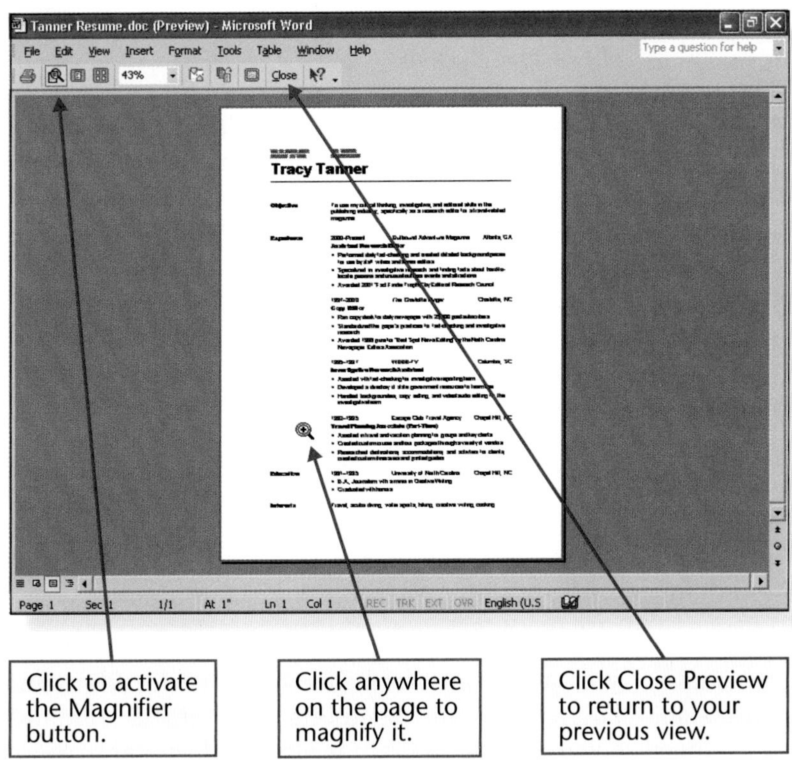

Click anywhere on the page to magnify it.

4. In the Print Preview window, select the Magnifier button, if necessary (see Figure 1.11).

5. Click an area of the document to magnify it. Click the document again to view the full page.

6. Click Close Preview to return to Print Layout View.

Word

Figure 1.12 The Print dialog box

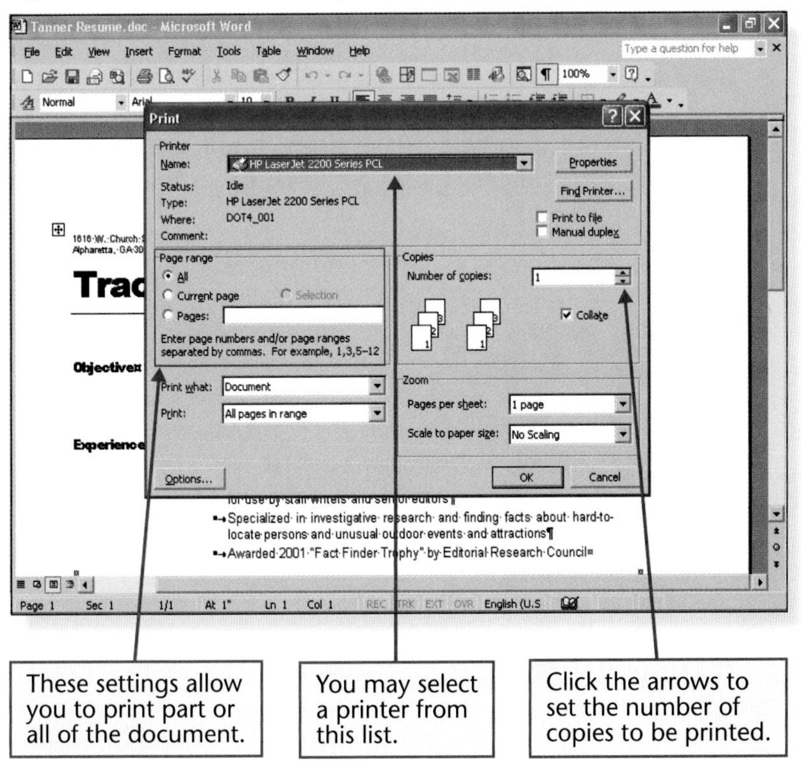

These settings allow you to print part or all of the document.
You may select a printer from this list.
Click the arrows to set the number of copies to be printed.

Step Through It™

Exercise 3B: Print a document

1. On the File menu, select Print to open the Print dialog box (see Figure 1.12).

2. Make sure the *Page range* is set to All and the *Number of copies* is set to 1 (these are the default settings). Click OK to close the dialog box and print one copy of the resume.

3. Close the document without saving it, but leave Word running.

Microsoft Office Specialist
W2002 4.2

Exercise 4 Overview:
Create a New Document Using Word

The easiest way to create a new document is to click the New Blank Document button on the Standard toolbar. Word will then display a new, blank document in which you can begin to type your text. You can format the document any way you like and then print or save it. You also can create a new document by using one of Word's templates. A **template** is a special type of file that already contains some text and which is already formatted. Word has many built-in templates that you can use to create letters, memos, resumes, and other types of documents.

Need Help?
Type: template

Most templates are easy to use. Some templates feature formatted lines of text called **placeholders** that you replace with specific items such as your name, address, or phone number. Just select a placeholder and enter your text. This process is called *customizing* the template.

A document that was started from a template will be saved automatically as a normal Word file with the *.doc* file name extension. This way, the template file itself remains unchanged so you can use it again for future documents. Word protects templates by storing them in a special folder and giving them a different file name extension (*.dot*).

In the following exercises, you will open a Word template and use it to create a fax cover sheet. You need this sheet because you must fax your memo and Tracy Tanner's resume to one of your bosses who is visiting your company's office in Dallas. After that, you will create a new, blank document and type a job description for use later in this lesson.

Figure 1.13 Placeholders in a memo template

Memo

To: [Click **here** and type name]

From: [Click **here** and type name]

How to Use This Memo Template

Select the text you would like to replace, and type your memo.

When you click the New Blank Document button, the blank document is based on a Word template called the Normal template.

Figure 1.14 Choosing a template

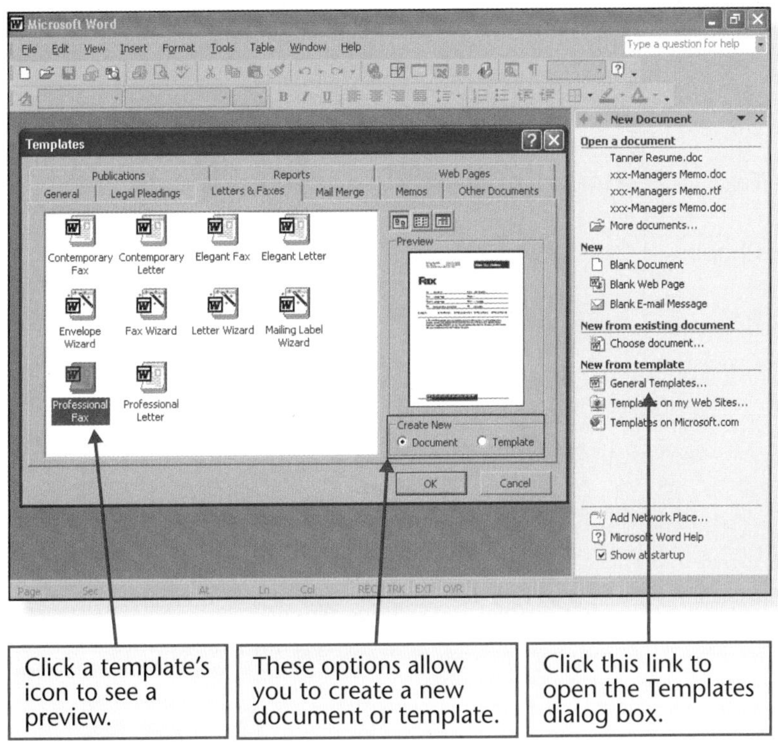

Click a template's icon to see a preview.

Step Through It™

Exercise 4A: Open a Word template

1. On the File menu, select New to open the New Document task pane.
2. Click the **General Templates** link to open the Templates dialog box. Click the Letters & Faxes tab.
3. Click the Professional Fax icon (see Figure 1.14), and click OK.

Word

Figure 1.15 Customizing a template

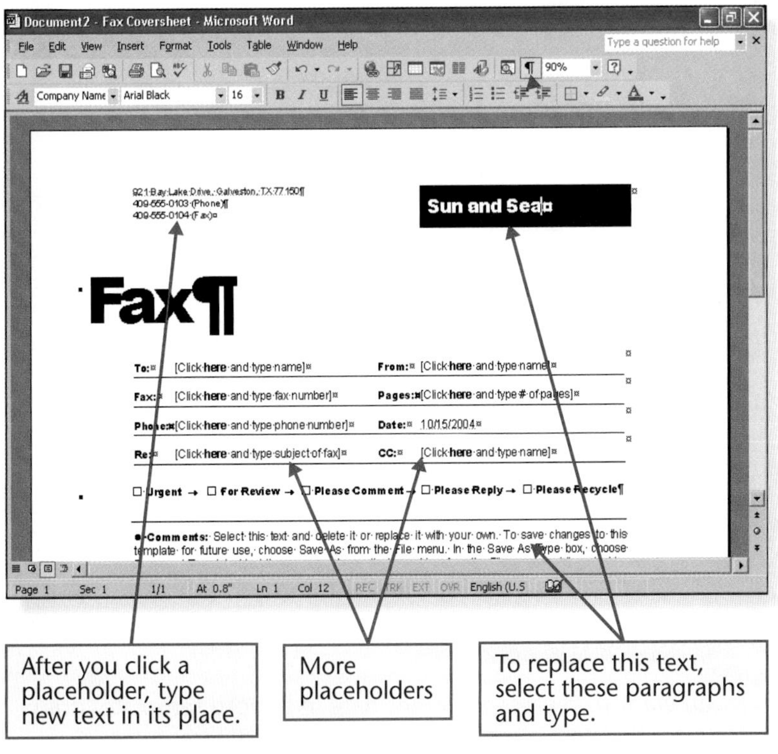

After you click a placeholder, type new text in its place.
More placeholders
To replace this text, select these paragraphs and type.

Step Through It™

Exercise 4B: Customize a Word template

1. Click the placeholder labeled *Click here and type return address and phone and fax numbers.*
2. Type 921 Bay Lake Drive, Galveston, TX 77150, and press Enter. Type 409-555-0103 (Phone), press Enter, and type 409-555-0104 (Fax).
3. Drag to select *Company Name Here* and then type Sun and Sea (see Figure 1.15).

4 Beneath the *Fax* heading, click each placeholder, and then type the information shown in Table 1.1. (The current date will already appear in the template.)

5 Double-click the *For Review* check box to place a check mark in it.

Table 1.1

	Type This:		Type This:
To:	Patricia Jacobs	From:	Karen Gleason
Fax:	214-555-0188	Pages:	3
Phone:	214-555-0138	Date:	*Current Date*
Re:	Research Editor	CC:	File

6 Select the entire *Comments* placeholder paragraph and type I have decided to offer the Research Editor position to Tracy Tanner. See the following memo and resume for more information. Call me if you have any questions. (See Figure 1.16.)

7 Print one copy, and then save the document as *xxx-TannerFax.doc.* Close the file, but leave Word running.

Figure 1.16 The completed fax cover sheet

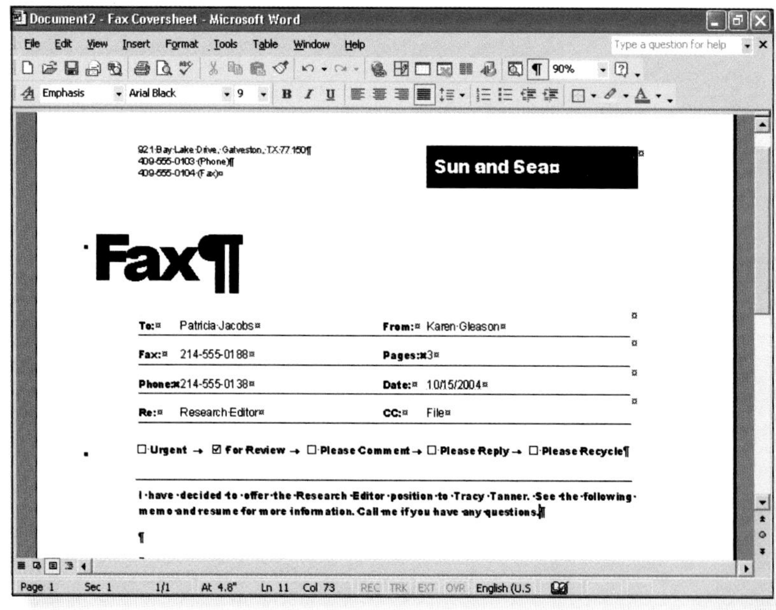

Quick Tip

If you want to replace a current date in a Word template, drag to select the date, press Delete, and type a different date.

Figure 1.17 Opening a new, blank document

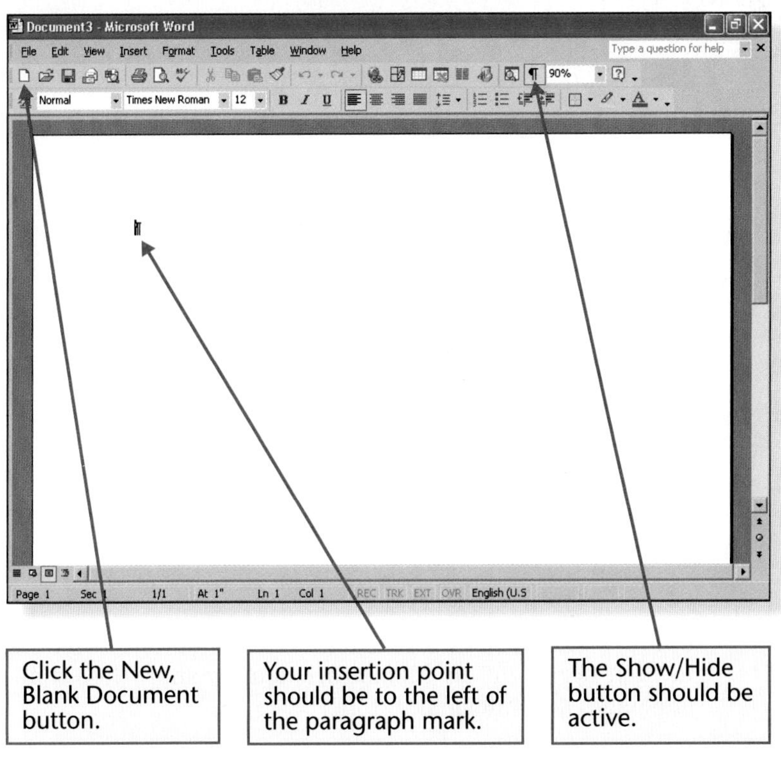

Step Through It™

Exercise 4C: Open a new, blank document

1. Click New Blank Document on the Standard toolbar to open a new document (see Figure 1.17).
2. If necessary, click the Show/Hide button to display nonprinting characters.

Figure 1.18 Job description

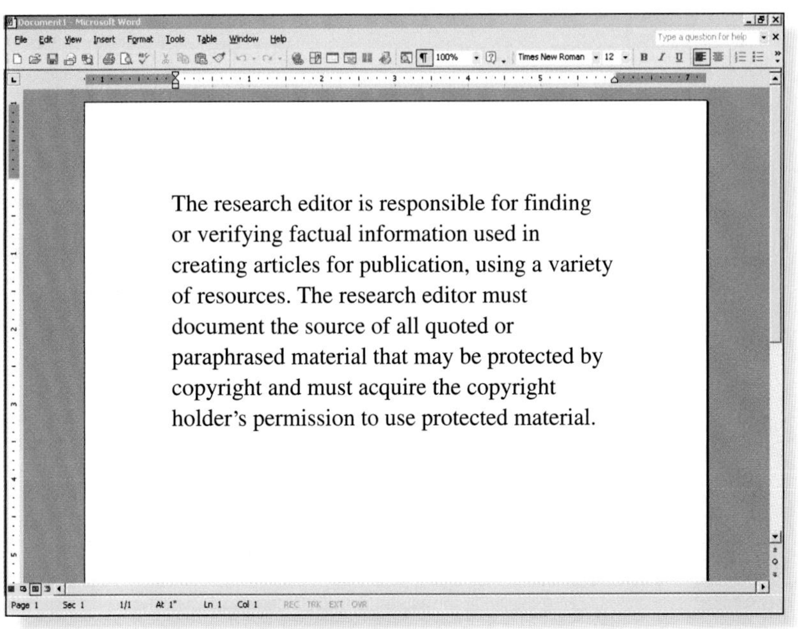

Document1 - Microsoft Word
File Edit View Insert Format Tools Table Window Help
100%
Times New Roman
12
The research editor is responsible for finding or verifying factual information used in creating articles for publication, using a variety of resources. The research editor must document the source of all quoted or paraphrased material that may be protected by copyright and must acquire the copyright holder's permission to use protected material.
Page 1 Sec 1 1/1 At 1" Ln 1 Col 1 REC TRK EXT OVR

3. With the insertion point before the document's only paragraph mark, type the text shown in Figure 1.18.
4. Print one copy of the document, and then save the file as *xxx-Job Description.doc*.
5. Close the document, but leave Word running.

Word

APPLY IT! After finishing Exercises 1–4, you may test your skills by completing Apply It! Guided Activity 1, Create a Resume.

Business Connections

Standard Business Documents

When computers began appearing on desks everywhere, a few people imagined a "paperless society." The notion was that, thanks to computers, people wouldn't need to use printed documents any longer.

In fact, the opposite is true. People now print more documents than ever. In business, it's easy to see why. Documents are the lifeblood of many companies, carrying all sorts of information from person to person. Most of them are variations of one of the following types:

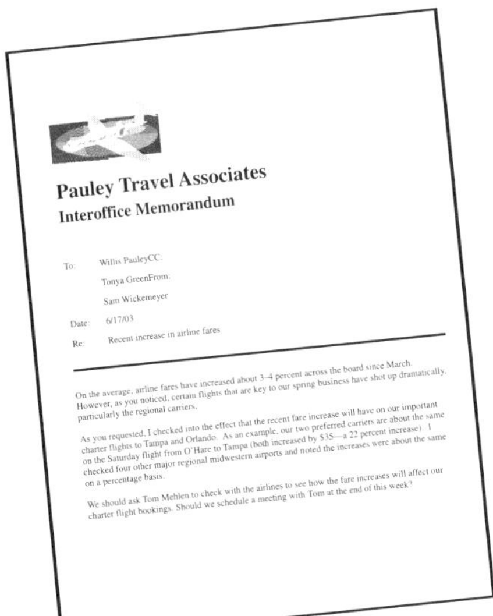

Pauley Travel Associates
Interoffice Memorandum

To: Willis PauleyCC:
Tonya GreenFrom:
Sam Wickemeyer
Date: 6/17/03
Re: Recent increase in airline fares

On the average, airline fares have increased about 3–4 percent across the board since March. However, as you noticed, certain flights that are key to our spring business have shot up dramatically, particularly the regional carriers.

As you requested, I checked into the effect that the recent fare increase will have on our important charter flights to Tampa and Orlando. As an example, our two preferred carriers are about the same on the Saturday flight from O'Hare to Tampa (both increased by $35—a 22 percent increase). I checked four other major regional midwestern airports and noted the increases were about the same on a percentage basis.

We should ask Tom Mehlen to check with the airlines to see how the fare increases will affect our charter flight bookings. Should we schedule a meeting with Tom at the end of this week?

- **Memos.** People use memos to share information with others in their organization. Memos are usually short (less than one page) and informal in tone.
- **Letters.** Letters carry information to people outside the company. Business letters should be kept as brief as possible, and they should always be written in a professional tone.
- **Newsletters.** Many businesses regularly send newsletters to customers or stockholders to provide information and make special offers. Most newsletters are informally written, have a layout with multiple columns, and use plenty of graphics.

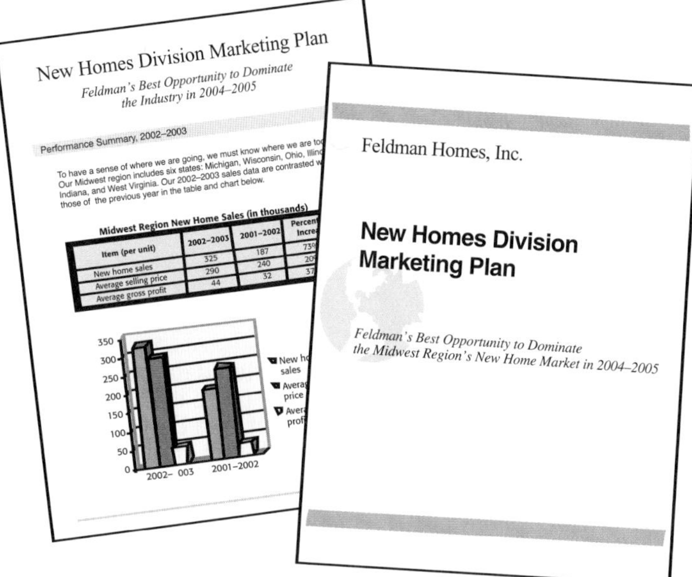

New Homes Division Marketing Plan

Feldman's Best Opportunity to Dominate the Industry in 2004–2005

Performance Summary, 2002–2003

To have a sense of where we are going, we must know where we are to
Our Midwest region includes six states: Michigan, Wisconsin, Ohio, Illin
Indiana, and West Virginia. Our 2002–2003 sales data are contrasted w
those of the previous year in the table and chart below.

Midwest Region New Home Sales (in thousands)

Item (per unit)	2002–2003	2001–2002	Percent Increa
New home sales	325	187	73%
Average selling price	290	240	20
Average gross profit	44	32	37

Feldman Homes, Inc.

New Homes Division Marketing Plan

Feldman's Best Opportunity to Dominate the Midwest Region's New Home Market in 2004–2005

- **Reports.** A business report can be very short or very long, depending on the nature of the information it contains. Reports often include data tables, charts, diagrams, and other graphics in addition to text.

1231 Pin Oak Lane
Batavia, OH 45103
Jason Anders

Phone: 513.555.3535
Jason_Anders@myemail.com

Objective

Seeking Vice President, Sales position that would utilize my successful sales management background and extensive sales experience.

Employment

1997–2002 **Leland Products** **Leland, SC**

National Sales Manager

- Increased Plastics division sales by 350 percent to $44 million
- Expanded sales territories from 12 to 32 states
- Advised on 43 new products that increased sales by $12 million
- President of the Southwestern Plastics Manufacturing Association, 2001–2002
- Developed "Ideas for Tomorrow," a new product advisory team composed of representatives from the functional areas of Sales, Marketing, Manufacturing, and Finance. This advisory team was responsible for the creation or improvement of 33 products and increased levels of customer satisfaction, as determined by our marketing surveys.
- Lifetime member of National Management Association
- Helped negotiate successful union settlement, 2001

1993–1997 **Kelsey Manufacturing** **Cypress, LA**

Sales Representative

- Developed new south-central sales territory, which increased sales by 170 percent in two years
- Received Superseller award (1994) for reaching $2 million sales goal
- Responsible for training 12 new sales representatives

Education

1988–1993 **Northwest State University** **Nigel, OH**

- B.A., Business Administration
- Graduated magna cum laude
- Editor-in-chief of school newspaper, *The Titan*
- Track team: 400-meter relay
- President, American history club

References

Upon request, I would be happy to provide excellent references from a number of industry professionals in both the sales and manufacturing areas.

- **Resumes.** Many individuals use resumes to sell their skills and abilities to prospective employers. A company may review dozens or hundreds of resumes to find the right person for a job.

Note: To learn more about these and other types of common business documents, refer to Appendix C.

Many businesses have standard formats for their documents. While many organizations use word processing templates as the basis for their documents, others design their memos, letterhead, and envelopes from scratch. Most businesses want their documents to reflect the company's identity or personality.

CRITICAL THINKING

1. **Creating a Document** Suppose you run a small catering business named Catering Plus. What would you want your company's letterhead to look like?
2. **Using a Template** What information would you include in your resume right now? Use one of Word's resume templates to get started.

Microsoft Office Specialist W2002 1.1

Exercise 5 Overview: Use Cut, Copy, and Paste

The **Cut**, **Copy**, and **Paste** commands let you copy or remove text (as well as graphics and other items) from a document and use them elsewhere. If you need to reverse any of these actions (or any other edit you just made), click the Undo button. These buttons appear on the Standard toolbar and are illustrated in the following table.

Standard Toolbar

Button		Purpose
	Cut	Lets you remove selected data from a document and then paste it elsewhere in the same document, in a different document, or in a different application
	Copy	Makes a copy of the selected data (instead of removing it from the document) so you can then paste the copied data elsewhere
	Paste	Inserts cut or copied data into the same document or into a different document
	Undo	Reverses your last action such as the text you just typed or text you just pasted into a document

The Cut, Copy, and Paste commands use a special area of your computer's memory called the **Clipboard** to store data that you cut or copy. The data you cut or copy remains on the Clipboard as long as your computer is running or until it is overwritten by another piece of cut or copied data.

Type: clipboard

In the following exercises, you will use the Cut, Copy, and Paste commands to edit a letter in which you will offer the Research Editor position to Tracy Tanner.

Quick Tip

One of the benefits of using a word processing program is the ability to reuse data from other documents. Editing existing text can be much faster than creating new text from scratch.

Figure 1.19 Selecting text to copy

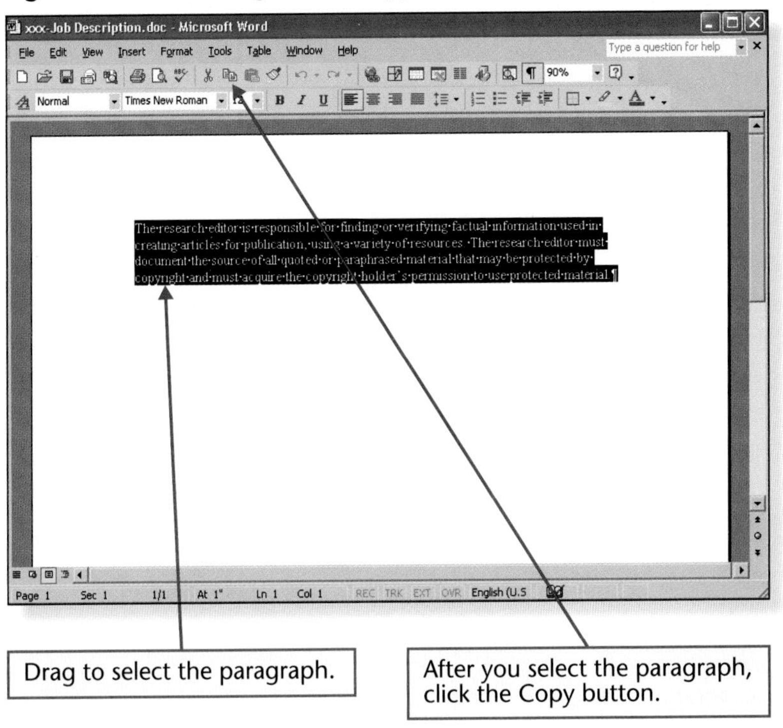

Figure 1.20 Pasting the copied paragraph into the letter

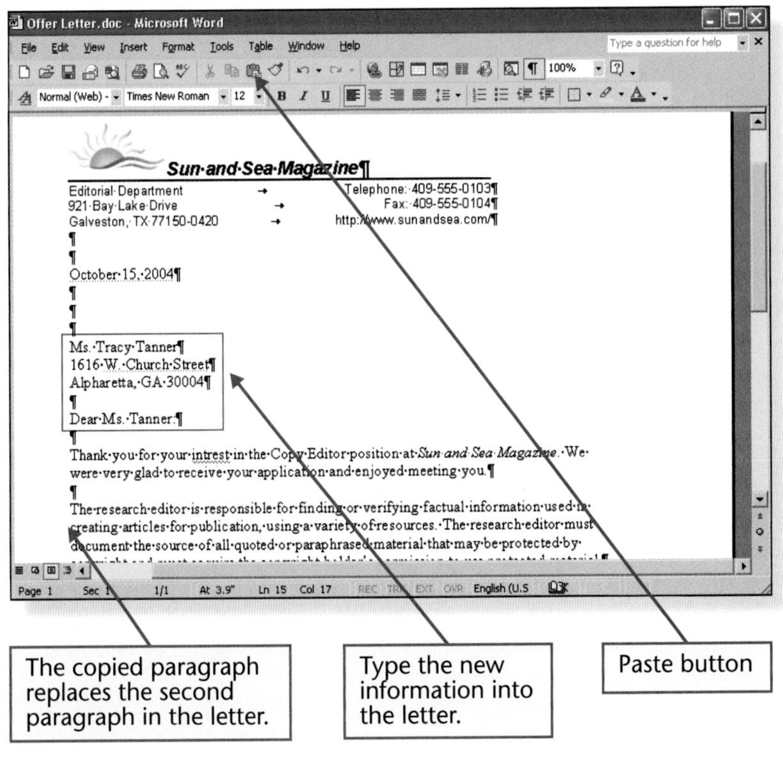

The copied paragraph replaces the second paragraph in the letter.
Type the new information into the letter.
Paste button

Step Through It™

Exercise 5A: Copy and Paste text

1. Open *xxx-Job Description.doc.*
2. Drag to select the entire paragraph.
3. Click Copy on the Standard toolbar (see Figure 1.19).
4. Close the document without saving it.
5. Open *Offer Letter.doc.* Select the second paragraph of letter text and press Delete.
6. Click Paste on the Standard toolbar.
7. Scroll to the top of the letter, and replace the date with the current date.
8. Replace the three inside address lines with Ms. Tracy Tanner 1616 W. Church Street Alpharetta, GA 30004.
9. Select the salutation and type Dear Ms. Tanner: (See Figure 1.20.)

Step Through It™
Exercise 5B: Cut and Paste text

1. Scroll to the third paragraph. Select the entire paragraph as well as the paragraph mark below it (see Figure 1.21).

2. Click Cut on the Standard toolbar to remove the selected text from the letter and place it on the Clipboard.

Figure 1.21 Selecting text for Cut and Paste

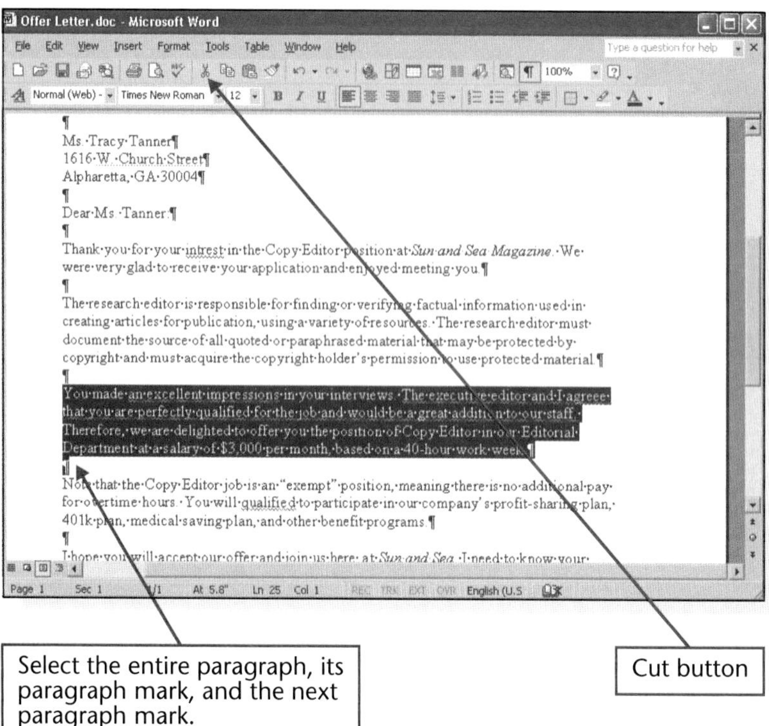

Offer Letter.doc - Microsoft Word
Select the entire paragraph, its paragraph mark, and the next paragraph mark.
Cut button

3. Place the Insertion point at the beginning of the second paragraph (just before the word *The*), and click Paste to paste the cut text from the Clipboard.

4. In the second paragraph, select the dollar amount *$3,000* and type $3,500.

5. Scroll to the last paragraph in the letter, select the date *January 16, 2004*, and type a new date that is one week later than the current date (see Figure 1.22).

Figure 1.22 Moving a paragraph with Cut and Paste

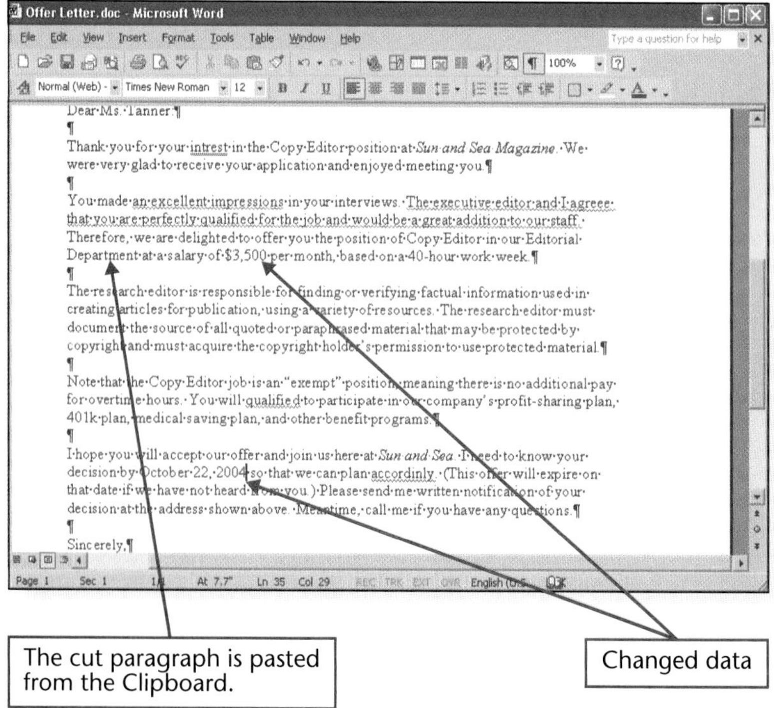

Offer Letter.doc - Microsoft Word
The cut paragraph is pasted from the Clipboard.
Changed data

Career Corner

Engineering Your Future

How can a bridge reach so far across the water and carry all those cars without falling down? How can a roller coaster put you through so many wild loops, turns, and drops and still be safe?

Somebody had to design them to be strong enough, to move or bend in the wind (but not too much!), and to make lots of parts work together. The people who do that are civil engineers.

Civil engineers design skyscrapers, stadiums, tunnels, roads, dams, airports, highways, and water and sewer systems. Virtually any structure created by humans—from a shopping mall to a zoo—was probably designed by a civil engineer.

Civil engineers begin their work by meeting with clients and visiting a site. They think about a structure's intended use and the requirements it must meet, and they draw sketches, take notes, and talk with team members. Then they make detailed plans using computer-aided design (CAD) software. During construction, civil engineers visit the site and talk with the builders to solve problems and make sure the work is done correctly. They also inspect older structures, even climbing to the tops of bridges to check for rust, cracks, and weak spots.

Civil engineers generally need a four-year degree, and their starting pay averages over $40,000 a year. Many civil engineers have specific areas of expertise, such as structural, water resources, environmental, construction, transportation, and even entertainment.

Interested? You can start right now! Take a few minutes to really look at the structures you see every day, such as bridges and skateboard parks, and try to figure out how they are put together.

CRITICAL THINKING

1. Sometimes we hear about an engineering failure, like a bridge collapse. What are some reasons for these failures? How can engineers prevent them in the future?
2. Choose a famous structure like the Brooklyn Bridge, Channel Tunnel, or Panama Canal, and use Word to write a report on how it was designed. Include a picture with your story.

Microsoft Office Specialist W2002 1.1

Word

Exercise 6 Overview: Find and Replace Document Text

Word's Find and Replace commands let you quickly locate specific text in a document, and they are especially helpful when you need to find text in a long document. The **Find** command searches for text you specify; when Word finds the text, it stops and highlights the text in the document window. The **Replace** command lets you search for specific text and replace it with different text. You can use these commands to locate a single word, a phrase, a combination of letters, numbers, or even special characters and formatting.

In the following exercises, you will use the Find and Replace commands to edit the offer letter to Tracy Tanner.

Step Through It™

Exercise 6A: Find specific text

1. Press Ctrl + Home to move the insertion point to the top of the document.
2. On the Edit menu, select Find to open the Find and Replace dialog box.
3. Type 401k in the *Find what* box, and click Find Next. Word jumps to the text (see Figure 1.23).
4. Close the dialog box. Edit the term *401k* so it reads *401(k)*.

Figure 1.23 Finding specific text in a document

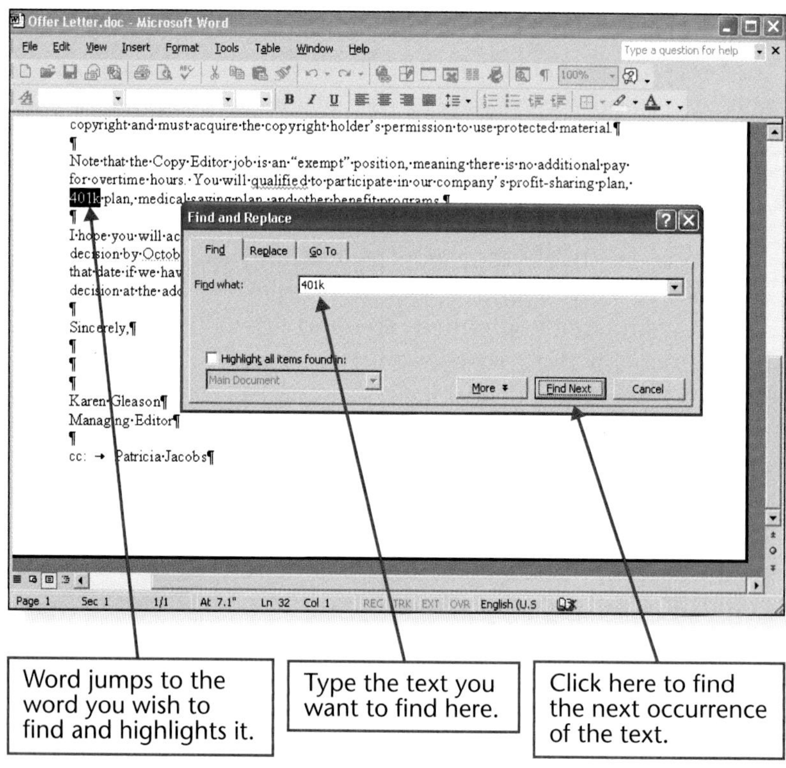

The Go To tab in the Find and Replace dialog box allows you to instantly jump to a specific element of your document such as a page, a line, or a heading.

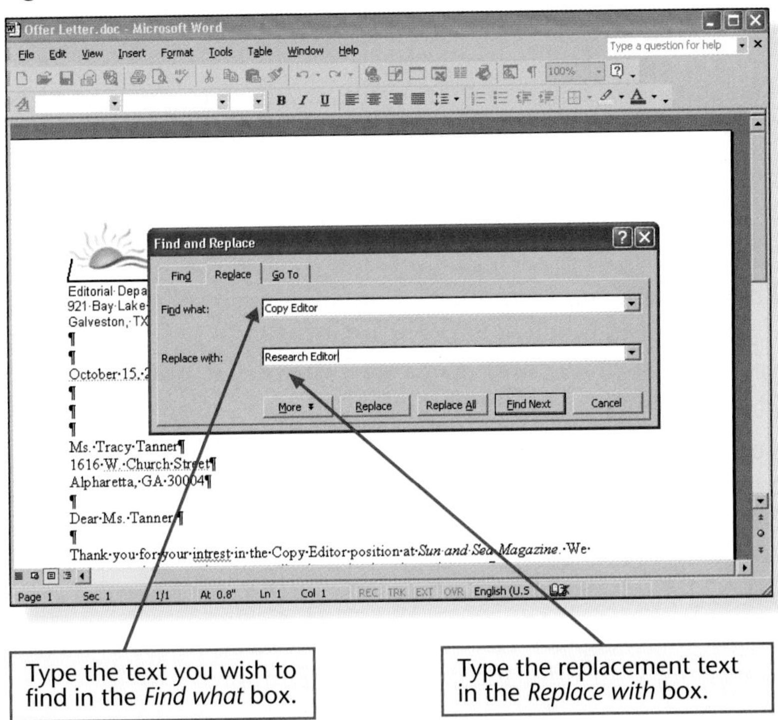
Find and Replace
Find what: Copy Editor
Replace with: Research Editor
Type the text you wish to find in the *Find what* box.
Type the replacement text in the *Replace with* box.

Figure 1.24 Finding and replacing text

Step Through It™

Exercise 6B: Find and replace words or phrases

1. Go to the top of the document. On the Edit menu, select Replace to open the Find and Replace dialog box with the Replace tab active.
2. Type **Copy Editor** in the *Find what* box.
3. Click in the *Replace with* box and type **Research Editor**. (See Figure 1.24.)
4. Click Find Next. When Word finds and highlights the first occurrence of the text, click Replace. Word makes the replacement and then highlights the next occurrence of the search text.
5. Click Replace All to replace all the remaining occurrences of the text. Word displays a message telling you how many replacements have been made (see Figure 1.25).
6. Close the message box, and then close the Find and Replace dialog box.

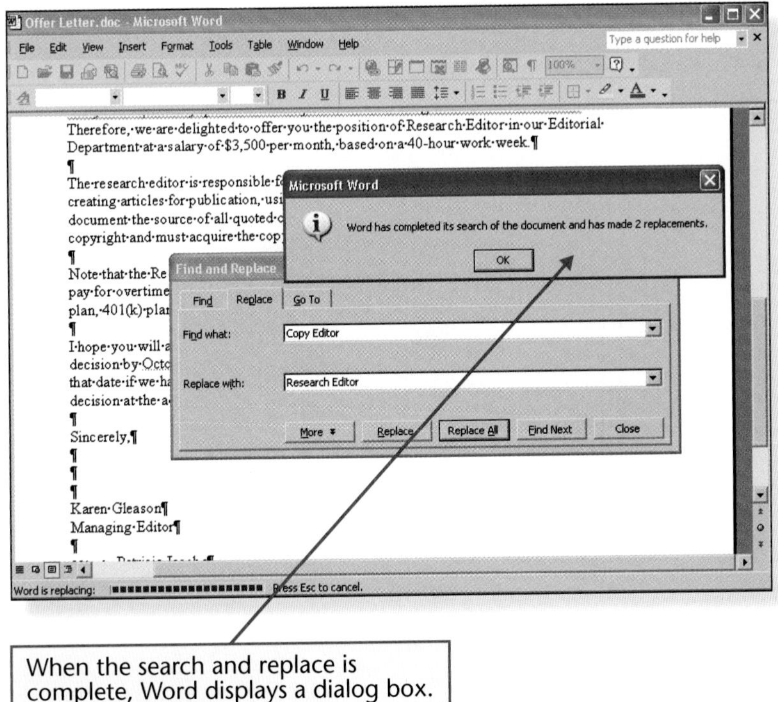
Microsoft Word
Word has completed its search of the document and has made 2 replacements.
OK
When the search and replace is complete, Word displays a dialog box.

Figure 1.25 The completed Replace All command

Microsoft Office Specialist
W2002 1.1

Exercise 7 Overview: Use the AutoCorrect Feature

The **AutoCorrect** feature enables Word to spot and fix many typing mistakes as soon as you make them.

For example, if you commonly type "hte" when you mean to type "the," AutoCorrect can fix the word so you don't have to.

This feature can also insert symbols for you. For instance, if you need to insert a copyright symbol (©) in a document, you can type "(c)" and Word will convert it automatically to the symbol.

You can customize AutoCorrect to suit your needs. For example, you can add your own unique typing errors to AutoCorrect, and it will then fix them for you automatically. You can also delete items from the AutoCorrect list.

In the following exercise, you will use AutoCorrect as an aid in writing your offer letter to Tracy Tanner.

Step Through It™
Exercise 7: Use AutoCorrect

1. On the Tools menu, select AutoCorrect Options to open the AutoCorrect dialog box.
2. Make sure all the check boxes are selected. (The *Correct keyboard setting* check box should not be checked.)
3. Type lsat in the *Replace* box and press Tab. Type last in the *With* box (see Figure 1.26).
4. Click Add and click OK.

Figure 1.26 The AutoCorrect dialog box

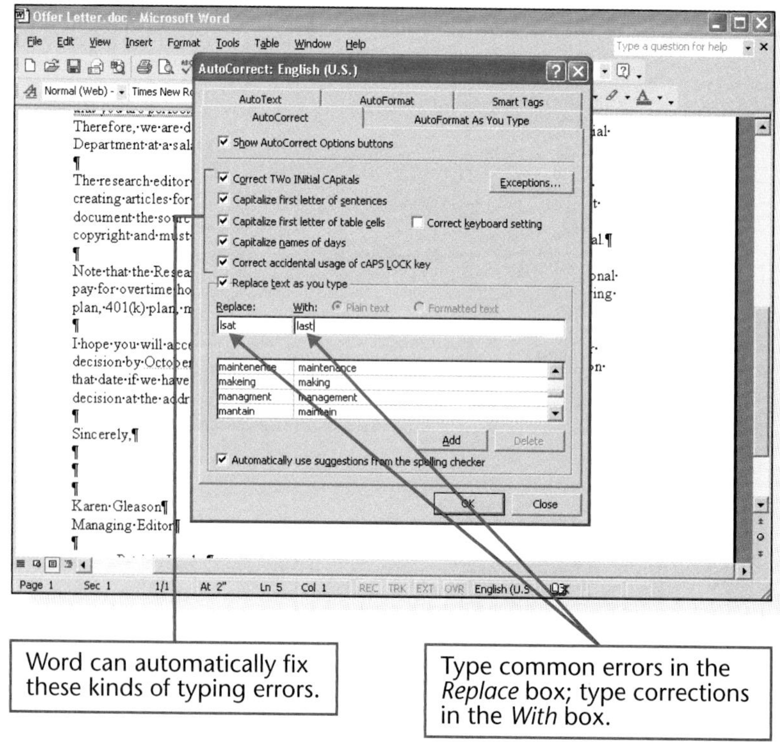
AutoCorrect: English (U.S.)
Word can automatically fix these kinds of typing errors.
Type common errors in the Replace box; type corrections in the With box.

Figure 1.27 Replacing text with AutoCorrect

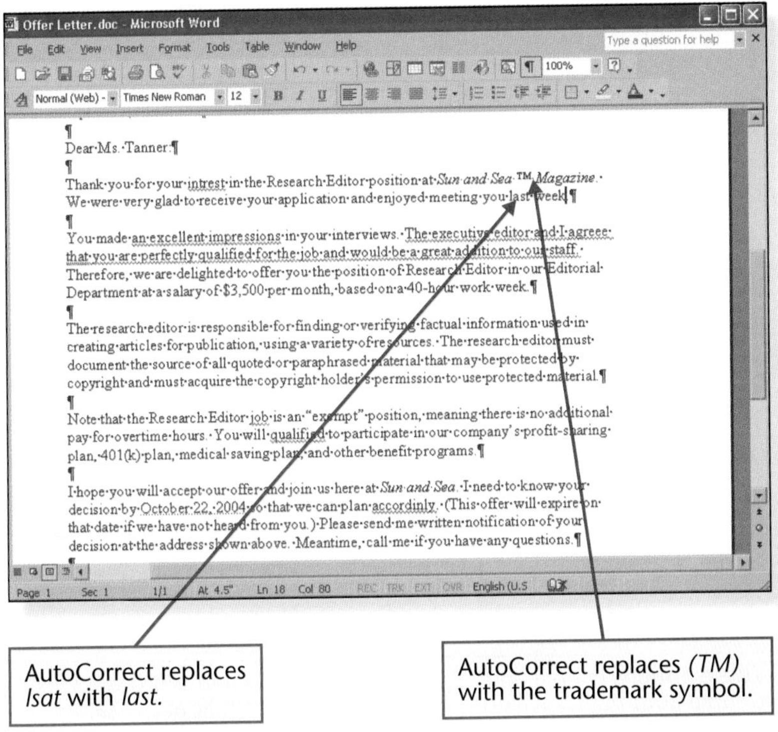
AutoCorrect replaces *lsat* with *last.*
AutoCorrect replaces *(TM)* with the trademark symbol.

5. In the first paragraph of the letter, click immediately after the word *Sea* and press the spacebar. Type (TM) to automatically insert a trademark symbol.

6. At the end of the first paragraph, click after the word *you* and before the period. Press the spacebar once, type lsat, press the spacebar again, and type week. The word *lsat* is automatically corrected (see Figure 1.27).

Word

Exercise 8 Overview: Use the Spelling and Grammar Tools and the Thesaurus

Microsoft Office Specialist W2002 1.3

Word's Spelling and Grammar tools can help you check and correct your documents. Word's Thesaurus provides instant access to alternative word choices as you write.

The Spelling and Grammar Checker

Word's **Spelling checker** and **Grammar checker** do exactly what their names imply: they find possible spelling and grammar errors and then suggest ways to fix them. You can check the spelling of a single word or an entire document. Similarly, you can check your grammar in one sentence or throughout a document.

Need Help?
Type: spelling

The Thesaurus

Like a printed thesaurus, Word's **Thesaurus** tool can help you make better word choices. Overusing words is a common problem. If you select a word and launch the Thesaurus, Word suggests several other words that have similar meanings. This can add more variety and punch to your writing. In the following exercises, you will use the Spelling and Grammar tools and the Thesaurus as you finish your offer letter to Tracy Tanner.

Step Through It™

Exercise 8A: Check spelling and grammar

Word

1. On the Tools menu, select Options to open the Options dialog box. On the Spelling & Grammar tab, clear the *Check spelling as you type* and *Check grammar as you type* check boxes, if necessary.

2. Make sure that the *Check grammar with spelling* check box contains a check mark (see Figure 1.28). Click OK.

Figure 1.28 Setting spelling and grammar options

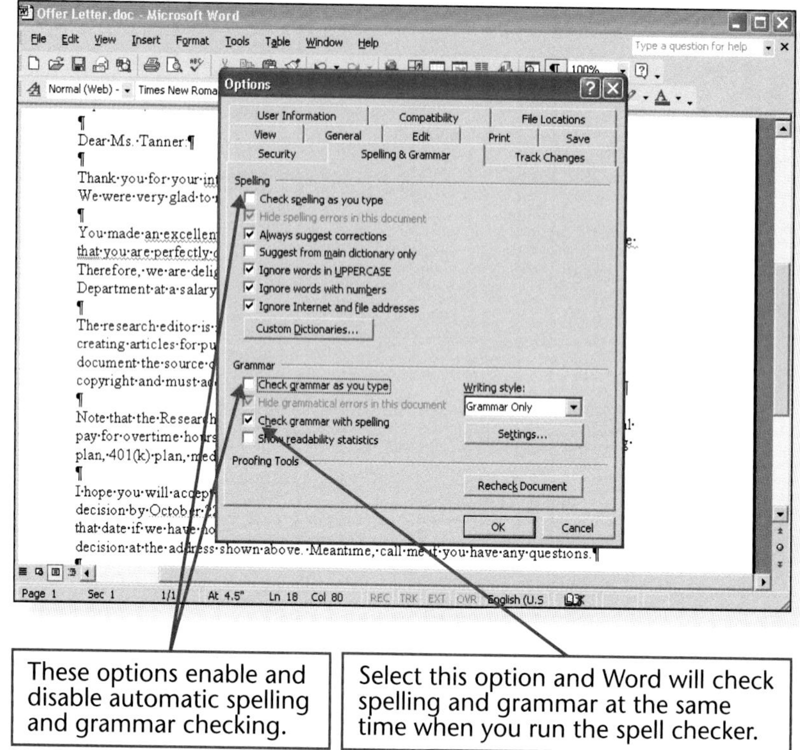

These options enable and disable automatic spelling and grammar checking.
Select this option and Word will check spelling and grammar at the same time when you run the spell checker.

3. Go to the beginning of the document. Click Spelling and Grammar on the Standard toolbar to open the Spelling and Grammar dialog box.

4. The word *intrest* appears in color in the *Not in Dictionary* box. In the *Suggestions* list, the word *interest* is highlighted (see Figure 1.29). Click Change.

5. Word identifies a grammar problem with the phrase *an excellent impressions*. Click *an excellent impression* in the *Suggestions* list and click Change.

Figure 1.29 The Spelling and Grammar dialog box

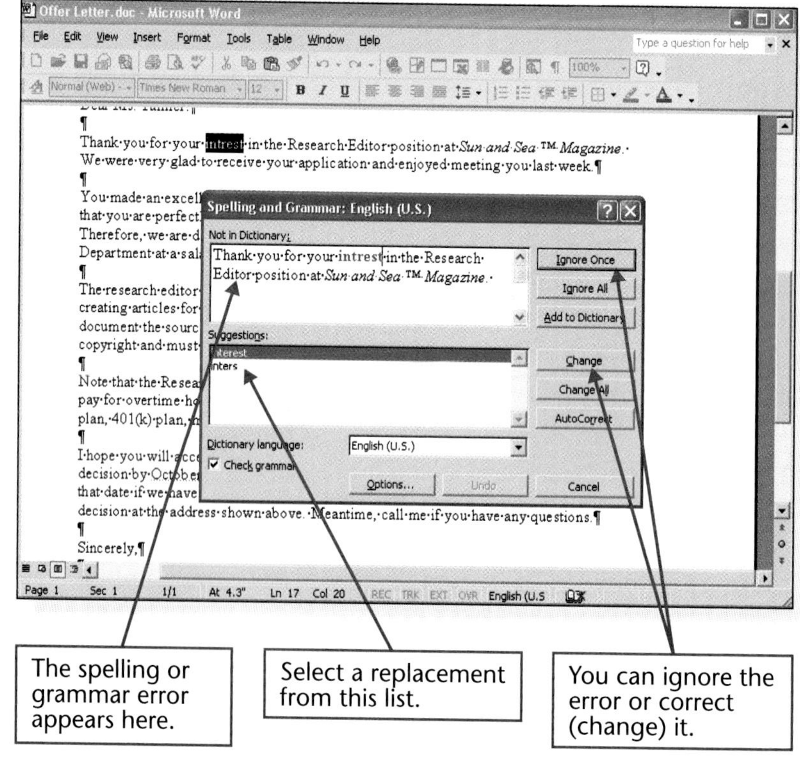

The spelling or grammar error appears here.
Select a replacement from this list.
You can ignore the error or correct (change) it.

Figure 1.30 Correcting a grammar error by replacing a word

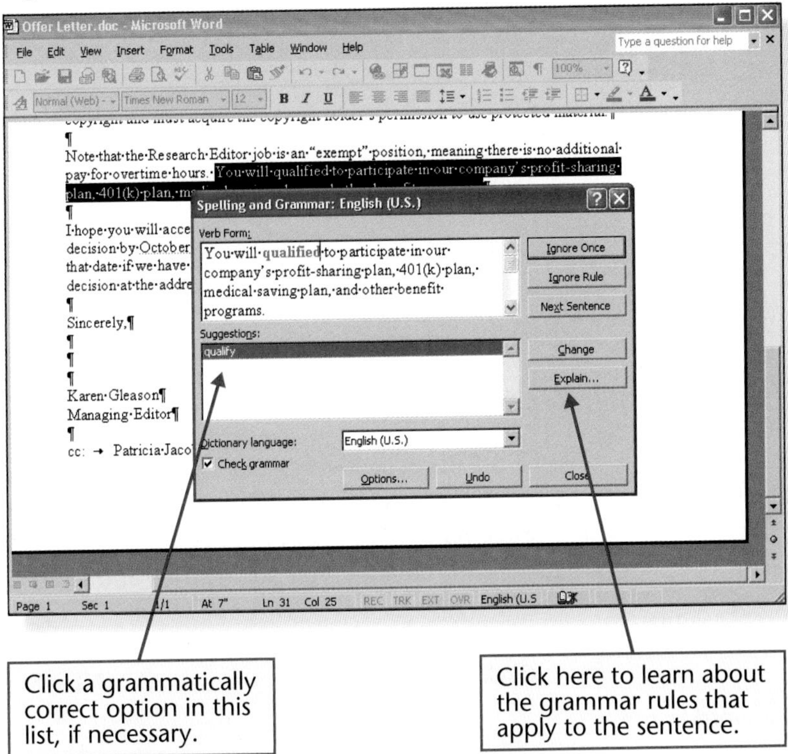

Click a grammatically correct option in this list, if necessary.
Click here to learn about the grammar rules that apply to the sentence.

6. Click Change to replace *agreee* with *agree*.
7. Word suggests that *job* be replaced with *Job*; click Ignore Once.
8. Word displays the grammatically incorrect *qualified* (see Figure 1.30). Click Change to substitute *qualify*.
9. Click Change to correct the misspelled word *accordinly*.
10. When Word displays a message stating that the spelling and grammar check is complete, click OK.

Figure 1.31 The Thesaurus dialog box

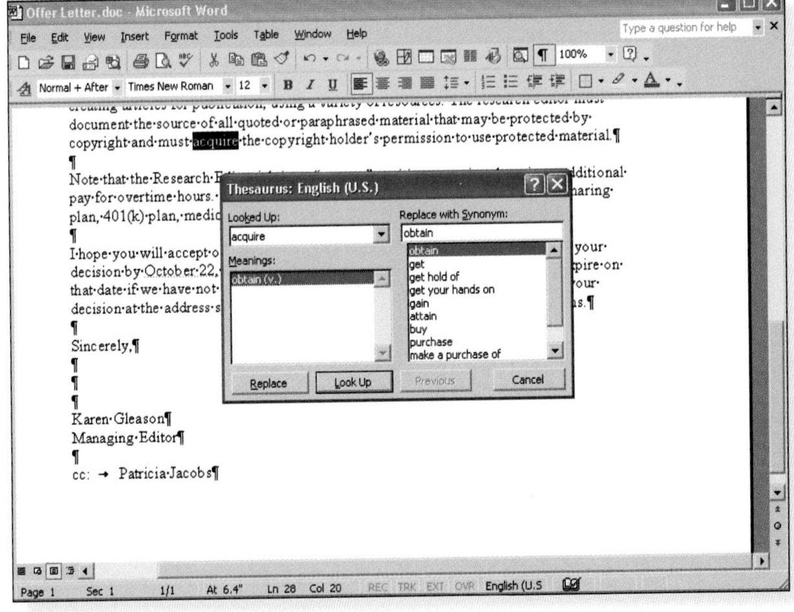

Step Through It™

Exercise 8B: Use the Thesaurus

1. In the third paragraph, select the word *acquire*. On the Tools menu, point to Language, and select Thesaurus to open the Thesaurus dialog box (see Figure 1.31).
2. Click Replace to replace the word *acquire* with the synonym *obtain*.
3. Save the document as *xxx-Offer Letter.doc*. Print one copy of the document, and then close it. Leave Word running.

APPLY IT! After finishing Exercises 5–8, you may test your skills by completing Apply It! Guided Activity 2, Check Your Spelling and Grammar.

Procedure Summary

Word Procedure Summary

Enter Text

1. Select **Show/Hide** button ¶ to display paragraph marks and spaces in your document.
2. Click an insertion point where you want the new text to be located, and then type.
3. Double-click OVR on the status bar to switch between Overtype mode and Insert mode.
   OR
   Press Insert to switch between Overtype and Insert mode.

Delete Text

Press Delete to delete a single character to the right of the insertion point.
OR
Press Ctrl + Delete to delete an entire word to the right of the insertion point.
OR
Press Backspace to delete a single character to the left of the insertion point.
OR
Press Ctrl + Backspace to delete an entire word to the left of the insertion point.
OR
Select text, and then press Delete.

Save a File With a Different Name

1. On the **File** menu, select **Save As**. . . . . **Alt + F, A**
2. In the Save As dialog box, click the **Save in** down arrow and select a drive. . . . . . **Alt + I**
3. Navigate to the folder where you wish to save your file.
4. Select the file's current name in the **File name** box, and type a new file name. . . . . **Alt + N**
5. Click **Save**. **Alt + S**

Save a File in a New Folder

1. On the **File** menu, select **Save As** . . . . **Alt + F, A**
2. In the Save As dialog box, click the **Save in** down arrow and select a drive . . . . . . **Alt + I**
3. Navigate to the location where you wish to place your new folder.
4. In the Save As dialog box, click **Create New Folder** button.
5. In the New Folder dialog box, type a folder name and click OK.
6. Click **Save** . . . . **Alt + S**

Save a File as a Different File Type

1. On the **File** menu, select **Save As** . . . . **Alt + F, A**
2. Click the **Save as type** down arrow and select a file type.
3. Type a new file name, if necessary.
4. Click **Save** . . . . **Alt + S**

Use Print Preview

1. Click **Print Preview** button.
   OR
   On the **File** menu, select **Print Preview**. . . . . **Alt + F, V**
2. Select **Magnifier** button to activate the Magnifier tool.
3. Click any part of the document to magnify it.
4. Click **Close**. . . . . **Alt + C OR Esc**

Print a Document

1. On the **File** menu, select **Print** . . . . **Alt + F, P OR Ctrl + P**
2. In the Print dialog box, click the **Name** down arrow and select a printer. . . . . **Alt + N**
3. In the *Page range* section, select an option.
4. Click the **Number of copies** up or down arrow to set the number of copies to print. . . . . **Alt + C**
5. Click OK.
   OR
   Click **Print** button to send a document directly to the printer.

Create a New Document From a Template

1. On the **File** menu, select **New**. . . **Alt + F, N**
2. In the New Document task pane, click General Templates.
3. In the Templates dialog box, click a tab and then select a template icon.
4. Click OK.

Open a New, Blank Document

1. Click New **Blank Document** button . . . . **Ctrl + N**

Copy and Paste Text

1. Select the text.
2. Click **Copy** button.
   OR
   On the **Edit** menu, select **Copy**. . . . . **Alt + E, C OR Ctrl + C**
3. Click where the text should be pasted.
4. Click **Paste** button.
   OR
   On the **Edit** menu, select **Paste** . . . . **Alt + E, P OR Ctrl + V**

Cut and Paste Text

1. Select the text.
2. Click **Cut** button.
   OR
   On the **Edit** menu, select **Cut** . . . . **Alt + E, T OR Ctrl + X**
3. Click where the text should be pasted.
4. Click **Paste** button.
   OR
   On the **Edit** menu, select **Paste** . . . . **Alt + E, P OR Ctrl + V**

Find Text in a Document

1. Click **Find** button.
   OR
   On the **Edit** menu, select **Find** . . . . **Alt + E, F OR Ctrl + F**
2. Type the text in the **Find what** box.
3. Click **Find Next**. . . . . **Alt + F**

Find and Replace Text in a Document

1. On the **Edit** menu, click **Replace**. . . . .**Alt + E, E OR Ctrl + H**
2. Type the text you wish to replace in the **Find what** box.
3. Type the replacement text in the **Replace with** box.
4. Click **Find Next**. . . . . **Alt + F**
5. Click **Replace** to replace each occurrence individually or click **Replace All** to replace all occurrences. . . . . **Alt + R OR Alt + A**

Use AutoCorrect

1. On the **Tools** menu, click **AutoCorrect Options**. **Alt + T, A**
2. Click in the **Replace** box and type a commonly misspelled word.
3. Click in the **With** box and type the correction. . . . .**Alt + W**
4. Click **Add**. . . . . **Alt + A**
5. Click OK.

Check Spelling and Grammar

1. Click **Spelling and Grammar** button.
   OR
   On the **Tools** menu, select **Spelling and Grammar**. . . . . **Alt + T, S OR F7**
2. When Word highlights an error, select a replacement, and then click **Change**. . . . . **Alt + C**
   OR
   Click **Ignore Once** to leave the text unchanged . . . .**Alt + I**

Use the Thesaurus

1. Select a word.
2. On the **Tools** menu, select **Language** and then **Thesaurus** . . . **Alt + T, L, T OR Shift F7**
3. Select a synonym.
4. Click **Replace**. . . . . **Alt + R**

Word

Lesson Review and Exercises

Summary Checklist

- ☑ Can you enter and edit document text using both Insert and Overtype modes?
- ☑ Can you save a file with a meaningful name?
- ☑ Can you save a file in a new folder and as a different file type?
- ☑ Can you preview and print a document?
- ☑ Can you create a new document by opening a Word template or a new, blank document?
- ☑ Can you edit a document by cutting, copying, and pasting text?
- ☑ Can you use Find and Replace commands to locate and replace words or phrases?
- ☑ Can you customize the AutoCorrect feature and use it to automatically correct common typing mistakes?
- ☑ Can you improve your writing by using the Spelling and Grammar checker and by working with the Thesaurus to find different words?

Key Terms

- AutoCorrect (p. 26)
- Clipboard (p. 20)
- Copy (p. 20)
- Cut (p. 20)
- documents (p. 6)
- edit (p. 6)
- file (p. 9)
- file type (p. 9)
- Find (p. 24)
- Grammar checker (p. 27)
- insertion point (p. 6)
- Insert mode (p. 6)
- Overtype mode (p. 6)
- Paste (p. 20)
- placeholders (p. 14)
- Replace (p. 24)
- save (p. 9)
- Spelling checker (p. 27)
- template (p. 14)
- Thesaurus (p. 27)

APPLY IT! Guided Activities

1. Create a Resume

You want to apply for a summer job as an intern reporter for one of your local newspapers. Although you don't have direct work experience as a reporter, you have worked on your school's newspaper for two years. You also have good writing skills and can use a camera. Use one of Word's resume templates to create a new resume for yourself so you can highlight your skills and experience.

Follow these steps to open the template and create your resume:

a. On the File menu, select New to open the New Document task pane. Click the General Templates link.

b. In the Templates dialog box, click the Other Documents tab (the Document option button should be selected). Click the *Professional Resume* icon, and then click OK.

c. Fill in the resume template with information about yourself. To do this, select and delete the placeholders and other information in the template (see the example in **Figure 1.32**). In the *Experience* section, type your actual work experiences. Start with your most recent job, and list your past jobs in reverse order. If you don't have any journalism experience, make up this information. (This resume is just for practice. Make sure your real resume includes only true information!)

Figure 1.32 A customized resume template

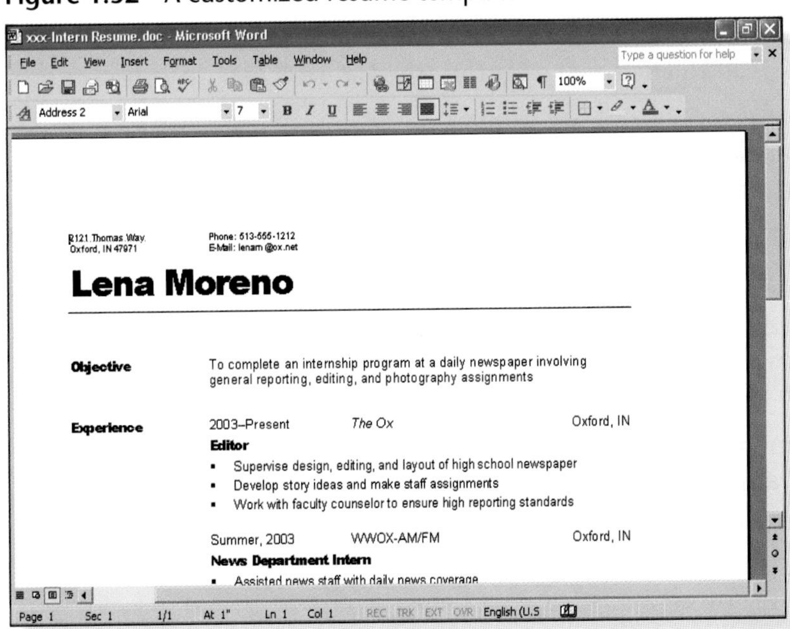

Word

d. In the last line of the resume template, select the word *Tips* and type Activities, and then list two or three activities in which you participate at school.

e. When you have completed the resume, carefully proofread it. Correct any errors you find, preview the resume, and then print one copy.

f. On the File menu, select Save As. Navigate to the *Lesson 1* subfolder within your *Unit 1* folder. Click the Create New Folder button and create a new folder named *Resumes* within your *Lesson 1* folder. Save the document as *xxx-Intern Resume.doc* in your new *Resumes* folder.

g. Close the document, but leave Word running.

2. Check Your Spelling and Grammar

As Assistant Director of your area's Tourism and Travel Commission, one of your jobs is to think of ways to promote tourism in your town. You have written a letter to the mayor of a large town in your area inviting him to attend several events that are aimed at getting business owners and community leaders involved in the tourism effort. The letter just needs some finishing touches. Follow these steps:

a. Open *Mayor Letter.doc*. Save the document as *xxx-Mayor Letter.doc*. Move the insertion point to the beginning of the document, and then click the Spelling and Grammar button to open the Spelling and Grammar dialog box.

b. Proceed to check spelling and grammar throughout the document and make appropriate changes. ***Note:*** Word will highlight the mayor's last name as a spelling error, so add it to the dictionary by clicking the Add to Dictionary button **(see Figure 1.33)**.

c. When the Spelling and Grammar dialog box highlights the *[Your Name]* placeholder text at the end of the document, replace it with your own name.

d. When the spelling and grammar checks are completed, close the dialog box.

e. Return to the top of the document. On the Edit menu, select Find to open the Find and Replace dialog box. Find the word *select*, and then close the dialog box.

f. On the Tools menu, point to Language and select Thesaurus. Choose a new adjective in the *Meanings* box, and click Replace.

g. Proofread the letter and make any necessary changes. Preview the letter, and then print one copy. Save and close the document, but leave Word running.

Figure 1.33 Checking spelling and grammar in a business letter

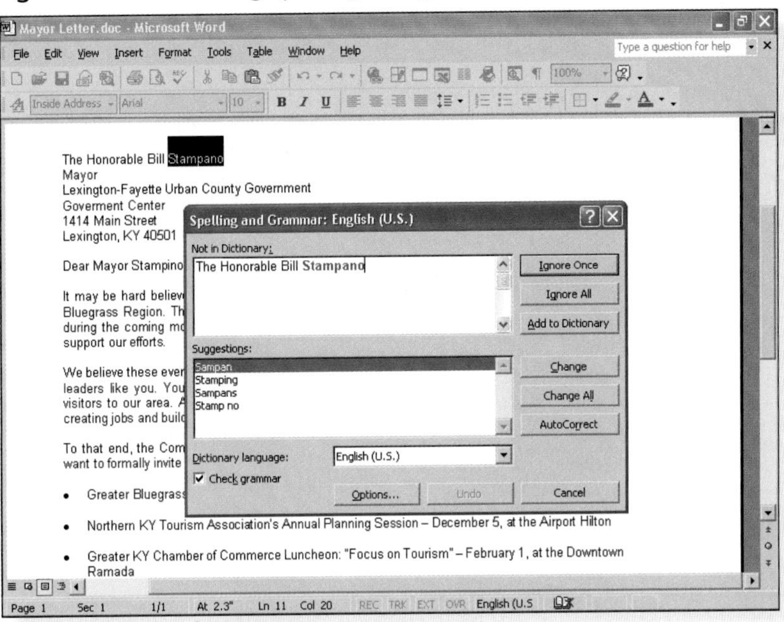

Do It Yourself

1. Create a Better Letter

As the General Manager of a construction company, one of your jobs is to award promotions to your employees. Because promotions are a special occasion, you take great care in preparing these letters. In this activity, you will open a template and customize it to create a promotion letter. To create the letter, do the following:

a. Open the *Promotion Letter.dot* template **(see Figure 1.34)**. (***Note:*** In the Open dialog box, select All Files on the *Files of type* list, if necessary.) Replace the date, and then replace the three placeholders for the inside address with the following information:

Martha Mason
2386 Kingsford Way
Mahwah, NJ 07430

b. Complete the letter by promoting the employee to the position of office manager at a salary of $50,000. She is now eligible to participate in the company's bonus and profit-sharing plans.

Figure 1.34 The *Promotion Letter.dot* template

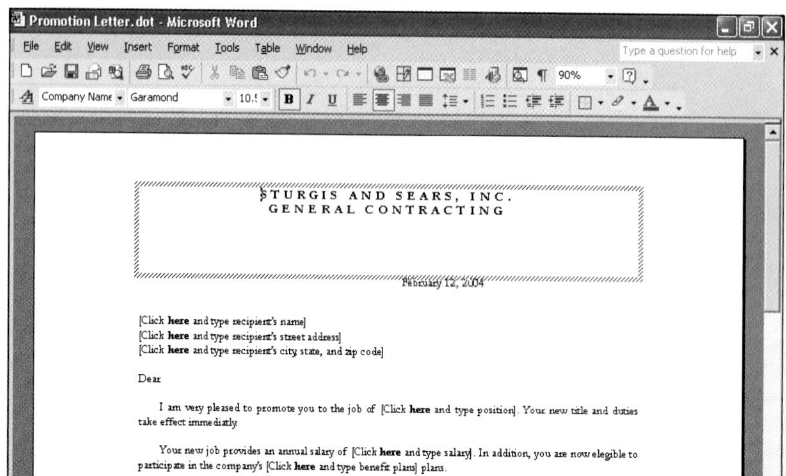

c. Use Word's AutoCorrect feature as follows to correct typographical errors. Click the blank line above *Sincerely*, and type the following sentence, including the errors: You hvae done outstanding work in yuor previous role as bookkeeper. Your experience adn skill will serve you well in your nwe position.

d. Select the third paragraph of body text (beginning with *I join the*). Use the Cut and Paste commands to make it the last paragraph in the letter.

e. Use Find and Replace to search for the word *job* and replace it with the word *position*. In the letter's last sentence, select the word *staff* and use the Thesaurus to select a good replacement for it.

f. Check the document with Word's Spelling and Grammar tools, and make the necessary corrections. Carefully proofread the document and correct any additional errors.

g. Use Print Preview to see how the letter will appear when printed, and then print one copy.

h. Save the document as *xxx-Promotion Letter.doc*. Create a new folder named *Promotions* in the *Lesson 1* subfolder within your *Unit 1* folder. Save the document again with the same name but in the new folder in Rich Text Format.

2. Write a Memo

Vacation season is coming up, and you need to write a memo to your manager requesting some time off. To create the memo, do the following:

a. Create a new document using a memo template. Choose any memo template you like.

b. Complete the memo by replacing placeholder text with appropriate information that you can make up. Request two separate weeks of vacation time. Write the memo in a professional tone. Assure your boss that your work is caught up, that a work associate will help cover for you in your absence, and that your clients will be informed of your time away.

c. Check the document's spelling and grammar, and proofread it carefully. Print one copy of the memo, and then save it as *xxx-Vacation Memo.doc*.

3. Introduce Yourself

You have just taken a new job as a software trainer at an insurance company. Your boss wants to circulate a memo that introduces you to the staff. He has given you an old memo that he used to introduce another employee named Sherry Smith. He wants you to update it with information about yourself. In the following steps, you'll customize the old memo and then save the file as a different type, as requested by your boss. To create the memo, do the following:

a. Open a new, blank document, and then type one brief paragraph of information about yourself. Include information such as your school and your interests or hobbies. Save the document as *xxx-My Information.doc*. Leave the document open.

b. Open *Introduction.doc*, the old memo that you need to update. Use the Find and Replace commands to find the other employee's name (search for *Sherry* as well as *Sherry Smith*) in the document, and replace it with your own.

c. Delete the memo's second paragraph that contains information about Sherry Smith. Review the memo carefully, and make any other changes that might be needed.

d. Switch to the document named *xxx-My Information.doc*. Copy the paragraph to the Clipboard, and then close that document. Paste the copied information into the *Introduction.doc* memo in the appropriate location.

e. Using the Save As command, create a new folder named *Updated Memo* in the *Lesson 1* subfolder within your *Unit 1* folder. Save the file in the new folder as *xxx-Introduction.doc*. Now save it for your boss as a *Plain Text (.txt)* file type with the file name *xxx-Introduction.txt* in the same folder. (If a File Conversion dialog box appears, click OK.)

f. Close all documents, but leave Word running.

Word

4. Choose Your Words Carefully

You have a friend who is looking for a job as a hardware technician in the Information Technology Services department of a large bank. He has written a resume and is working on a cover letter to go with it. He asks you to review the letter, and you find that the writing could be improved. Its tone is too casual, and your friend has tried to use some fancy-sounding language to impress the manager. Your job is to revise the letter and make it sound more professional. Use Word's Spelling and Grammar tools and the Thesaurus to help you revise the cover letter. To revise the letter, do the following:

a. Open *Cover Letter.doc* and read the letter carefully. Save the document as *xxx-Cover Letter.doc*.

b. Now, go through the letter and look for pretentious words and phrases. Select these words one at a time, open the Thesaurus, and pick a down-to-earth replacement for each. ***Note:*** If you can't find some words in Word's Thesaurus, pick up a dictionary or a printed thesaurus to find a replacement.

c. Look for opportunities to reduce the letter's wordiness. For example, where your friend has written that he wants to *initiate a dialog* with the employer, it might be better to say *talk* or *interview*. Use your best judgment, but try to revise the letter so it is written in a more natural way and is easier to understand.

d. Give the letter a more professional tone. Look for sentences that seem too casual or friendly and replace them.

e. When you are finished, spell check the letter **(see Figure 1.35)**, and then carefully proofread it. (Don't depend on Word to find all the mistakes or to improve the letter's tone.) Preview the letter, and then print one copy.

f. Save and close the document, but leave Word running.

Figure 1.35 Editing a cover letter

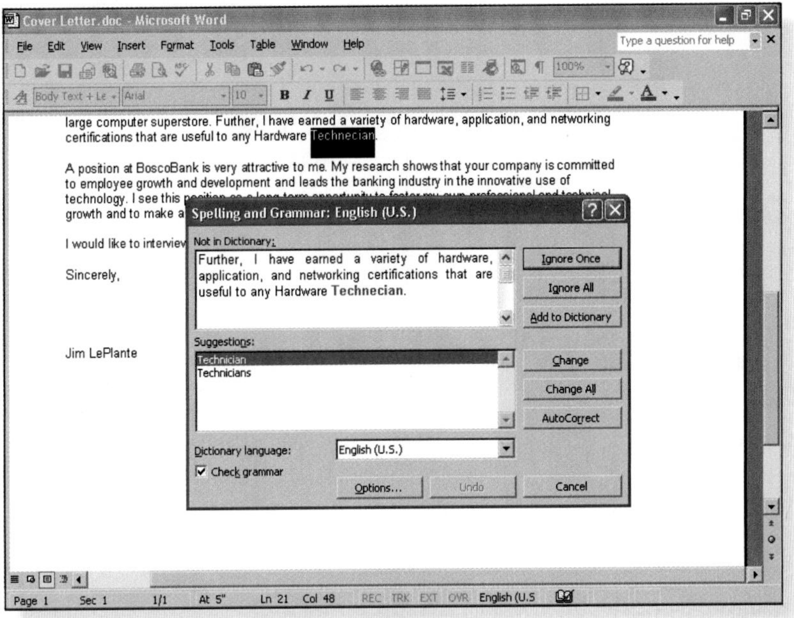

Challenge Yourself

Find Templates on the Web

You have had the opportunity to use a few templates that were installed on your computer along with the Word program. However, there is a greater selection of templates available at the Microsoft Office Template Gallery Web site. ***Note:*** Your computer must have a browser and an Internet connection to access this Web site. To visit this online gallery, open Word's New Document task pane and click the Templates on Microsoft.com link. When you reach the gallery, do the following:

- Imagine that you are a sales professional who works for a small company that sells dental instruments and supplies to dentists. Search for a letter template that could help you introduce your company and your product to a new customer. Download and save the template as *xxx-Customer Letter.doc*.
- Suppose you want to advance within your company so you can move beyond your current job selling dental supplies. You have applied within your company for a job as the assistant to the vice-president of marketing. Search for a resume template that may help you get the new job. Download and save the template as *xxx-Resume.doc.*
- Customize the two documents to suit each situation. Be creative in inventing realistic information for each document. Save your changes.

Lesson 2

Formatting Documents

Lesson Exercise Objectives

After completing this lesson, you'll be able to do the following tasks:

1. Apply paragraph and character styles
2. Modify paragraph formats
3. Set tabs in a document
4. Apply bullets, numbering, and outline numbering to lists
5. Apply character formats
6. Create and modify a header and footer
7. Insert a page break and page number

Key Terms

- alignment (p. 47)
- border (p. 47)
- bullet (p. 56)
- character style (p. 42)
- font (p. 59)
- font style (p. 59)
- footer (p. 63)
- formatting (p. 42)
- header (p. 63)
- indent (p. 47)
- line spacing (p. 47)
- page break (p. 66)
- paragraph (p. 47)
- paragraph spacing (p. 47)
- paragraph style (p. 42)
- point (p. 47)
- shading (p. 47)
- style (p. 42)
- tab (p. 51)

Microsoft Office Specialist Activities

W2002: 1.2, 1.6, 2.1, 2.2, 2.3, 2.4, 3.1, 3.3

Real-Life Business Applications

Lesson Case Study

In this lesson, you will be playing the role of Research Editor for *Sun and Sea* magazine. Keep the following information in mind as you work through the lesson exercises.

- `Job responsibilities and goals.` As Research Editor, one of your responsibilities is to create "backgrounders," or documents containing detailed background information on specific subjects. You develop these documents for your magazine's writers and editors who use the information in writing articles for the magazine.
- `The project.` You have developed a short backgrounder about Grand Cayman that another editor will use in writing an article on popular cruise ship stops in the Caribbean. Now that the backgrounder has been written, you need to format it.
- `The challenge ahead.` Although your company has no standard rules for formatting backgrounders, the document needs to be as neat and professional looking as possible. Another goal of formatting is to make the document easy to read and use.

Microsoft Office Specialist
W2002 1.6, 2.4

Exercise 1 Overview:
Apply Paragraph and Character Styles

Formatting means changing the way a document looks. A **style** is a named set of formatting characteristics. Using styles lets you format individual characters or entire paragraphs with just a few mouse clicks. Styles help you give a consistent look to different parts of a document. **Paragraph styles** can be applied to one or more entire paragraphs. **Character styles** can be applied to individual characters, such as a word or a letter.

When you open a template, Word makes a group of predetermined styles available. Some templates feature a wide variety of styles, and each one has a specific use. Styles are easy to apply. Just select the text you want to format, and then select the style. Word applies the formatting. You can select styles in two ways: from the Style list on the Formatting toolbar or from the Styles and Formatting task pane. Both show you all the styles in use in the document as well as other available styles.

Type: styles

Once you have applied a style to a paragraph or to some characters, you can use Word's Format Painter to *paint* the formatting onto another piece of text. The Format Painter is a great time saver because it lets you copy formatting from one text selection and apply it to another.

In the following exercises, you will apply paragraph and character styles.

Figure 2.1 The Style list

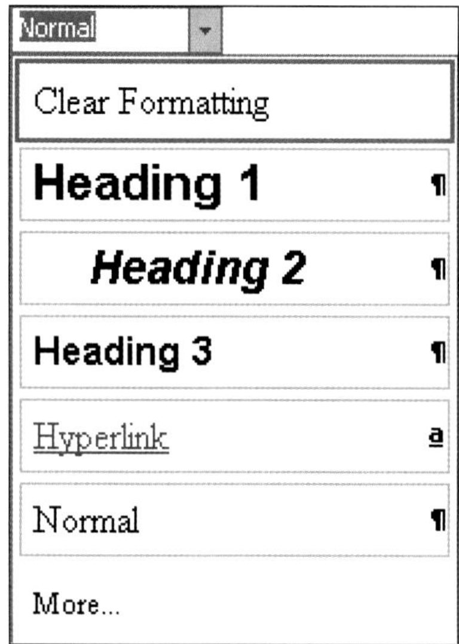

Figure 2.2 The Styles and Formatting task pane

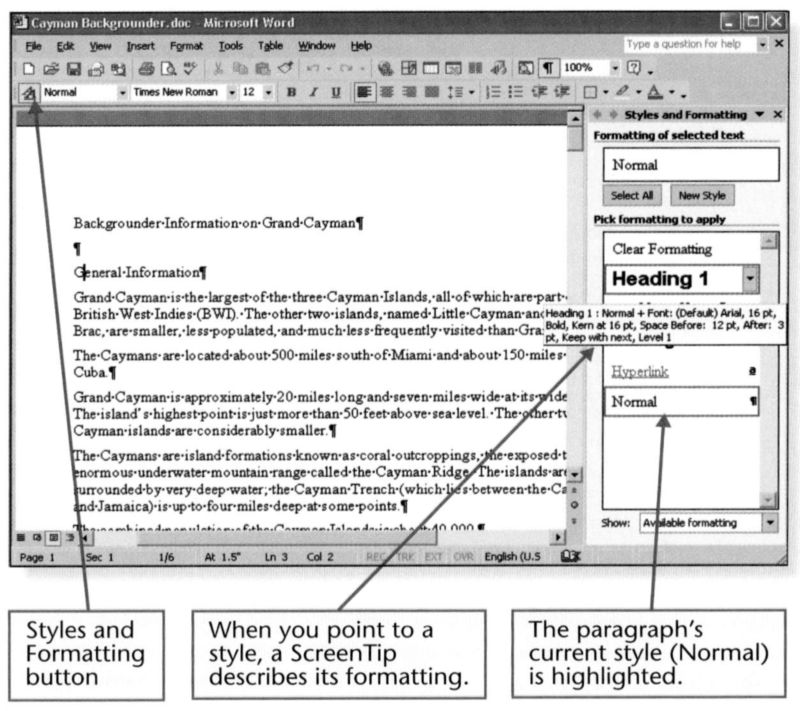

Styles and Formatting button
When you point to a style, a ScreenTip describes its formatting.
The paragraph's current style (Normal) is highlighted.

Step Through It™

Exercise 1A: Apply paragraph styles

1. Open *Cayman Backgrounder.doc*. Save the document as *xxx-Cayman Backgrounder.doc* and switch to Print Layout View, if necessary. Select Show/Hide, if necessary.
2. Click the heading *General Information*. Click Styles and Formatting on the Formatting toolbar.
3. Point to the *Heading 1* style. A ScreenTip describes the style's formatting characteristics (see Figure 2.2).

Figure 2.3 Using the Style list on the Formatting toolbar

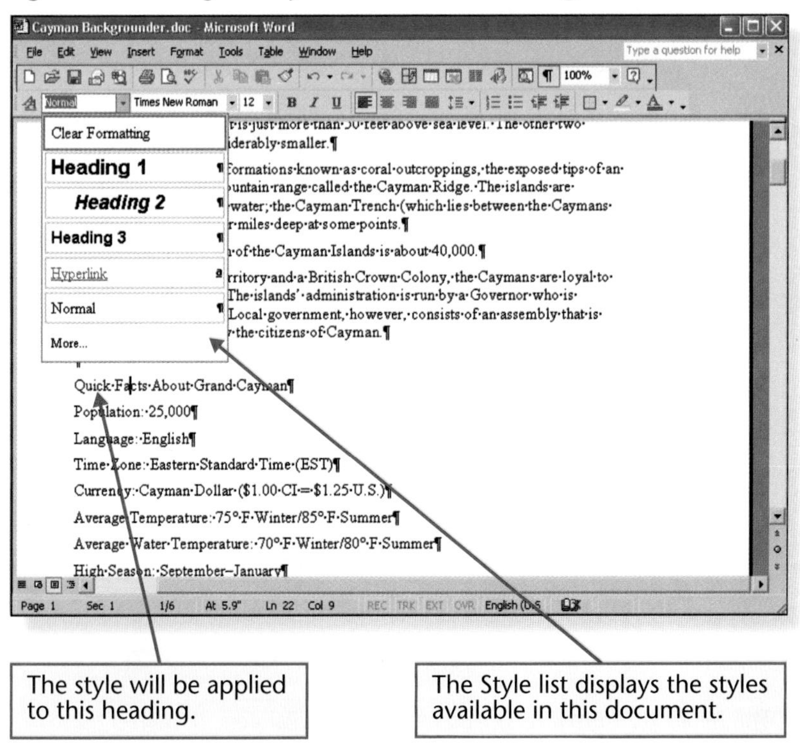

The style will be applied to this heading.
The Style list displays the styles available in this document.

4. Click the *Heading 1* style to apply it to the selected heading. Close the task pane.
5. Scroll down to the next heading, *Quick Facts About Grand Cayman*, and click it. Click the Style Normal down arrow on the Formatting toolbar (see Figure 2.3). Click the *Heading 1* style.

Word

6. Scroll down and apply the *Heading 1* style to each of the eight remaining primary headings. ***Note:*** As with the *Quick Facts About Grand Cayman* heading, each primary heading is preceded by a blank paragraph mark.

7. Find the subheading *Shore Snorkeling* and apply the *Heading 2* style. With the heading still selected, click Format Painter on the Standard toolbar. The pointer changes to a paintbrush (see Figure 2.4).

Figure 2.4 Copying a format with Format Painter

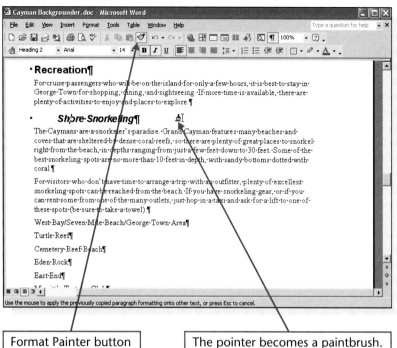

Format Painter button

The pointer becomes a paintbrush.

8. Scroll down to find the subhead *Snorkeling Excursions*. Drag the paintbrush across the heading to apply the Heading 2 format (see Figure 2.5).

9. Using the Format Painter, copy the formatting from *Snorkeling Excursions* and apply it to the next subhead, *Scuba Diving*.

Figure 2.5 Applying a format with Format Painter

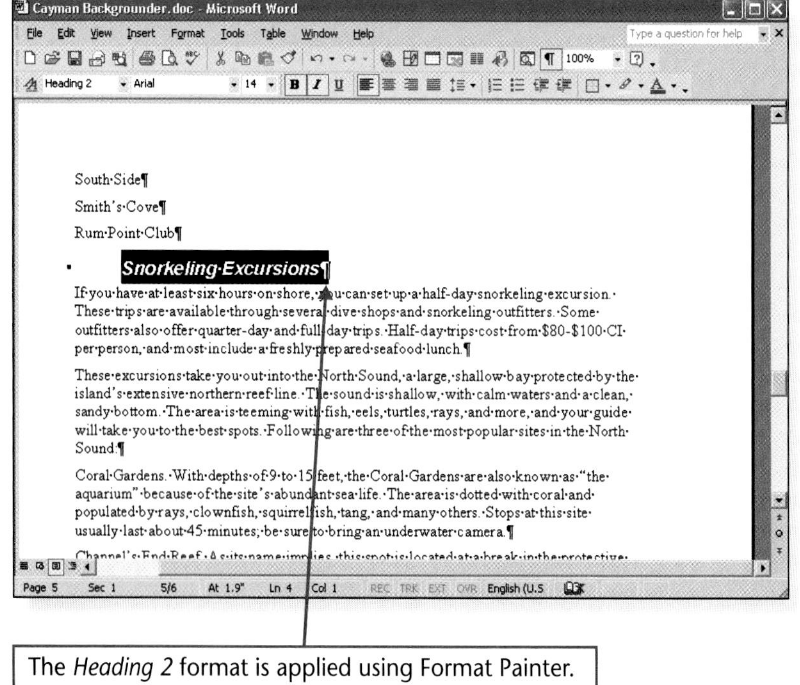

Figure 2.6 Selecting a character style

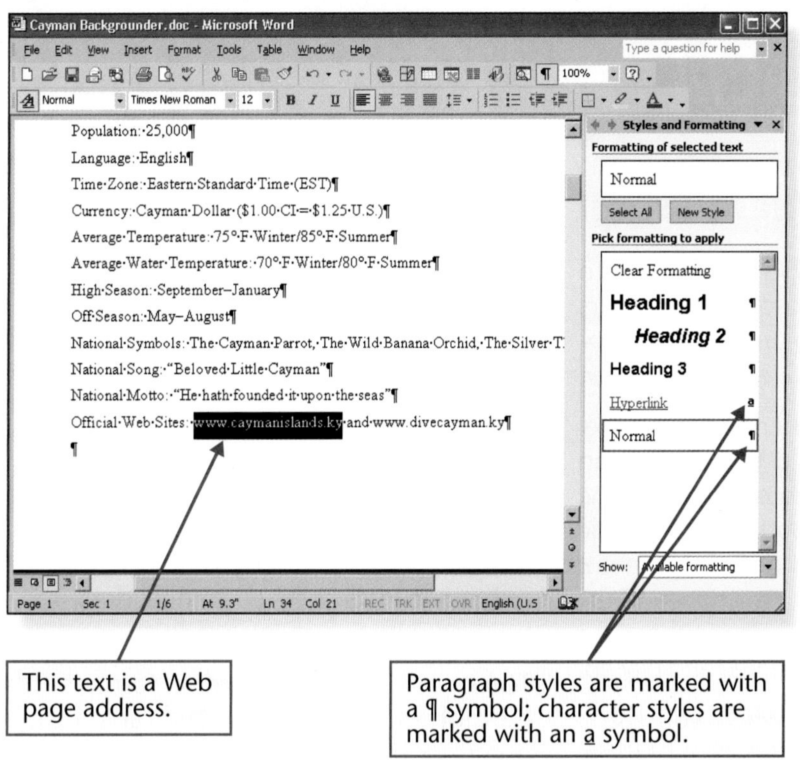

Step Through It™
Exercise 1B: Apply character styles

1. Find and select the text *www.caymanislands.ky.* Open the Styles and Formatting task pane (see Figure 2.6).
2. Click the *Hyperlink* style to apply it to the selected text. Close the task pane.

Figure 2.7 Copying the Hyperlink style

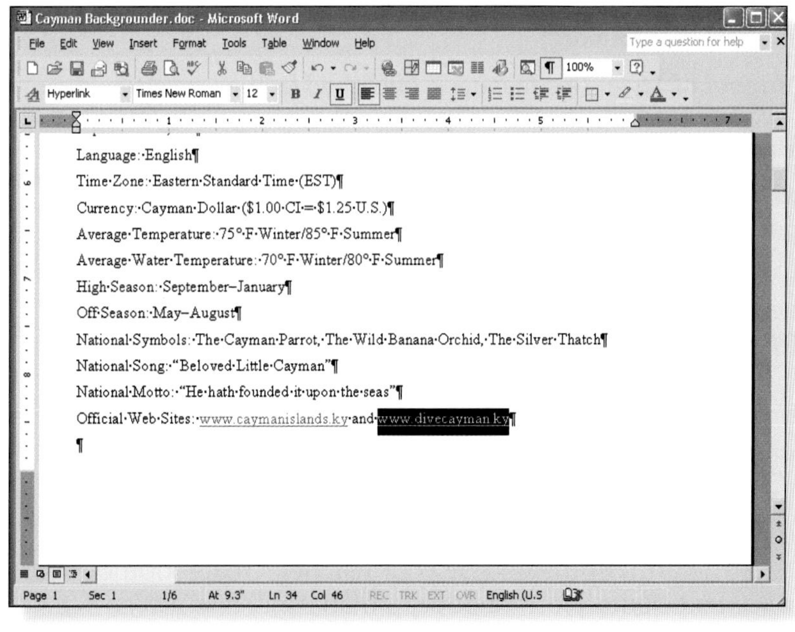

3. With the text still selected, click Format Painter. Drag the paintbrush pointer over the text *www.divecayman.ky* (see Figure 2.7).
4. Save your changes.

Technology@School

Giving Credit Where Credit Is Due

Do the words *research paper* strike fear into your heart? Relax! Microsoft Word offers many features that make writing papers—if not totally fun—at least a whole lot easier.

One is the Footnote and Endnote feature. When you need to add a footnote or an endnote, Word inserts a note number in the text and takes you to the bottom of the page (for footnotes) or the end of the document (for endnotes) to key it. As you continue working, Word adjusts the copy so that your notes remain correctly numbered and placed.

You probably know that when you use a direct quote, you must put it in quotation marks and include a footnote or an endnote. But did you know that you must also use a footnote or an endnote when you:

- paraphrase (put in other words) someone else's ideas or research?
- copy material from a Web site?

In fact, "Only information that is widely available from a variety of sources—such as historic facts and geographic data—can be used without giving credit."[1]

There are many different formats for footnotes and endnotes. The table below describes the "big three" sources.

Source	Description
MLA	**Modern Language Association.** MLA style is fully explained in the *MLA Handbook for Writers of Research Papers*. Some information is also available at the MLA Web site **(www.mla.org)**.
Chicago	***The Chicago Manual of Style.*** This manual is published by the University of Chicago Press. A list of FAQs is available at **www.press.uchicago.edu/Misc/Chicago/cmosfaq/**.
APA	**American Psychological Association**. APA style is fully explained in its *Publication Manual*. Information is also available at **www.apastyle.org**.

CRITICAL THINKING

1. With a partner, create Word document that contains a bulleted list of features you have learned about in this unit that would help you in writing a research paper. Format the document attractively. Continue to add to your list as you complete this unit.
2. Explore Microsoft Word Help to learn how to create and modify footnotes and endnotes. Then, following the format provided by your teacher, create footnotes or endnotes for the following: text quoted from a book, a magazine, and a Web site.

---

[1] "Avoiding Plagiarism," Rio Salado College, October 25, 2001, <www.rio.maricopa.edu/distance_learning/tutorials/study/plagiarism.shtml> (July 21, 2002).

Exercise 2 Overview:
Modify Paragraph Formats

Microsoft Office Specialist
W2002 2.1

A **paragraph** is any text that is followed by a paragraph mark (¶). There are a number of different ways that you can format paragraphs. These include changing the alignment, line spacing, paragraph indents, and paragraph spacing. **Alignment** is a paragraph's relationship to the page's right and left margins. **Line spacing** is the amount of vertical space between the lines within a paragraph. The amount of space between a paragraph and the right or left margin is called an **indent**. When you reset the amount of spacing before and after a paragraph you are changing the **paragraph spacing**. Paragraph spacing is measured in **points**. One point equals 1/72 inch.

Type: paragraph spacing

You can change paragraph formats using buttons on the Formatting toolbar or through the Paragraph dialog box (Format menu). Some of the more commonly used buttons for the alignment and spacing of paragraphs are shown in the following table.

Formatting Toolbar

Button		Purpose
	Align Left	Aligns all lines of the paragraph flush with the left margin
	Center	Centers all lines horizontally between the left and right margins
	Align Right	Aligns all lines of the paragraph flush with the right margin
	Justify	Aligns all lines of the paragraph flush vertically at both the left and right margins
	Line Spacing	Provides options for changing the vertical spacing between lines in a paragraph
	Decrease Indent	Moves an indented paragraph left to the next default tab stop
	Increase Indent	Moves an indented paragraph right to the next default tab stop

You can apply borders and shading to any paragraph or group of paragraphs. A **border** is a line you place around a paragraph or along any one or more of its sides. **Shading** appears as a gray or colored background behind the paragraph.

Step Through It™

Exercise 2A: Change paragraph alignment and line spacing

1. Go to the top of the document and click the first line. Click Center on the Formatting toolbar to center the paragraph between the left and right margins (see Figure 2.8).

2. Find the paragraph that begins with *Grand Cayman is a British territory*. Click anywhere within the paragraph. Click Justify on the Formatting toolbar.

3. With your insertion point still in the paragraph, open the Format menu. Select Paragraph to open the Paragraph dialog box.

4. Click the Indents and Spacing tab, if necessary. Click the *Line spacing* down arrow to open the list of spacing options (see Figure 2.9). Select 1.5 lines. Click OK.

Figure 2.8 Centering a paragraph

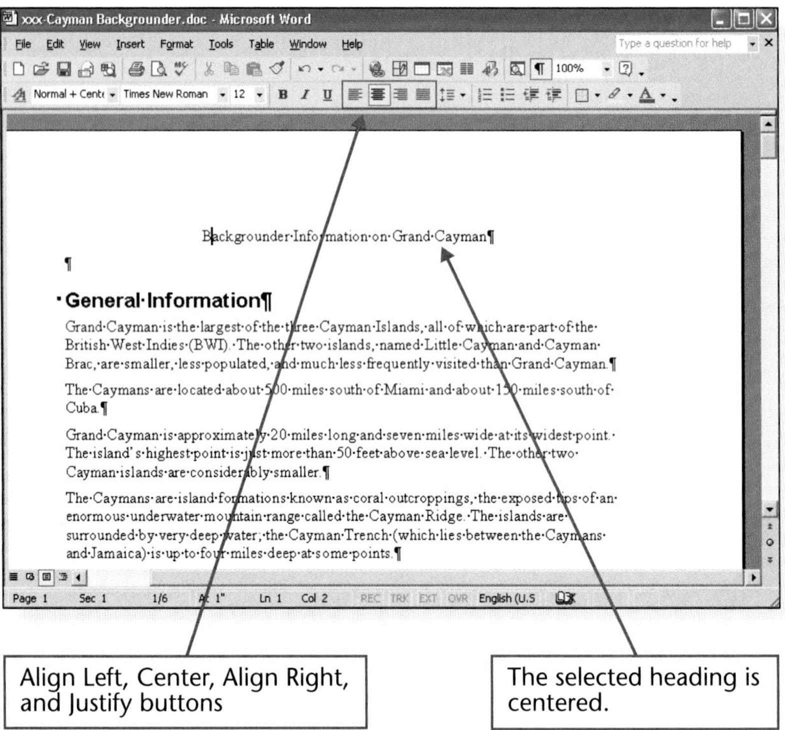

Figure 2.9 Changing a paragraph's line spacing

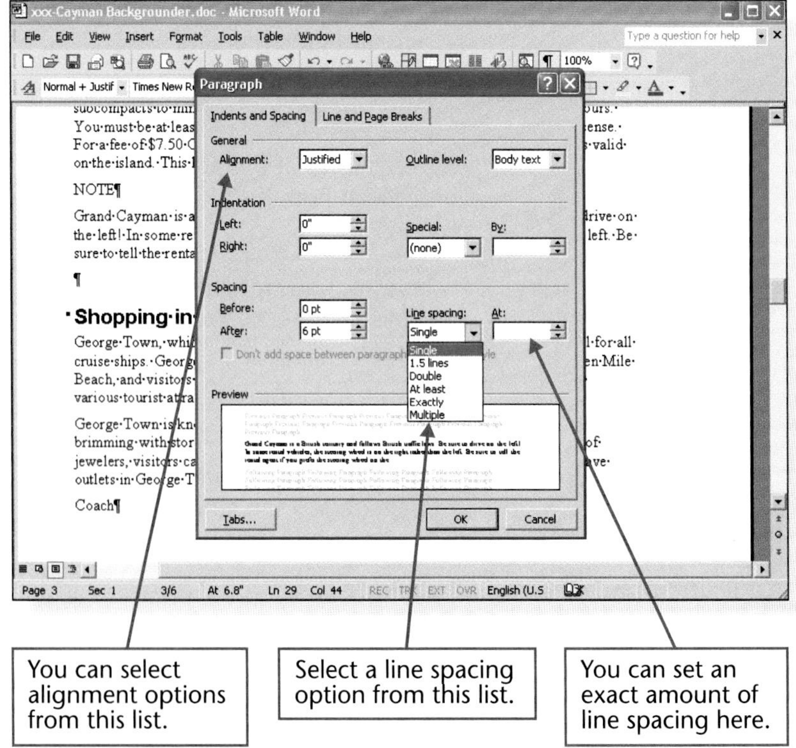

You can select alignment options from this list.
Select a line spacing option from this list.
You can set an exact amount of line spacing here.

Word

Figure 2.10 Changing indents and paragraph spacing

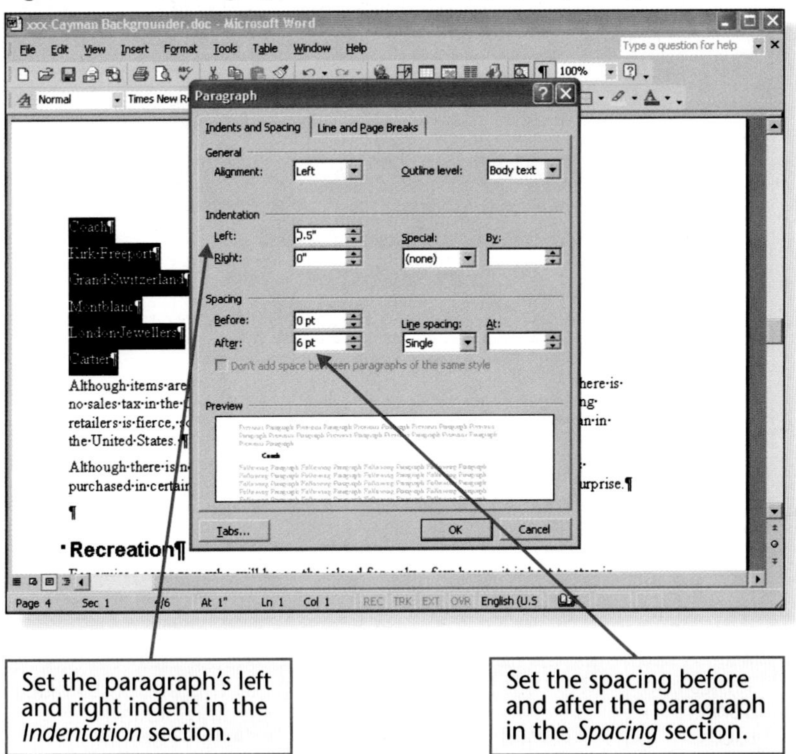

Set the paragraph's left and right indent in the *Indentation* section.
Set the spacing before and after the paragraph in the *Spacing* section.

Step Through It™

Exercise 2B: Change indents and paragraph spacing

1. Find the section entitled *Shopping in George Town*. Select the list of stores starting with *Coach* and ending with *Cartier*.
2. Open the Paragraph dialog box. Under *Indentation*, click the *Left* up arrow to indent the selected paragraphs one-half inch (0.5") from the left margin (see Figure 2.10).
3. Under *Spacing*, click the *After* down arrow to read zero points (0 pt). Click OK. The selected paragraphs are now indented and the paragraph spacing is changed.
4. Click within the next paragraph of body text (starting with *Although items are*), and then open the Paragraph dialog box.
5. Under *Spacing*, click the *Before* up arrow to increase the amount of space before the paragraph to six points (6 pt). Click OK (see Figure 2.11).

Figure 2.11 The list with modified indents and spacing

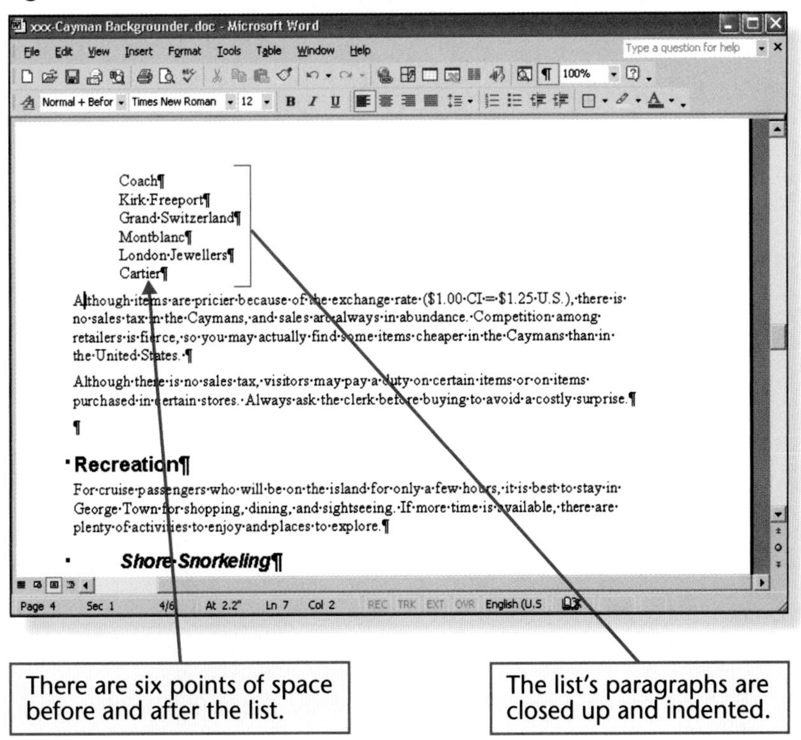

There are six points of space before and after the list.
The list's paragraphs are closed up and indented.

Word

Word

Step Through It™

Exercise 2C: Apply a border and shading

1. Scroll up to the bottom of the previous page. Select the word *NOTE* and the following paragraph.

2. On the View menu, point to Toolbars and select Tables and Borders. The Tables and Borders toolbar appears (see Figure 2.12).

3. Click the Borders down arrow, and then click Outside Border to place a border around the selected paragraphs.

4. Click the Shading Color down arrow. On the color palette, click Gray-20% to place shading behind the selected paragraphs.

5. Click the Close the Tables and Borders toolbar, and then click to view your changes (see Figure 2.13).

6. Save your changes.

Figure 2.12 The Tables and Borders toolbar

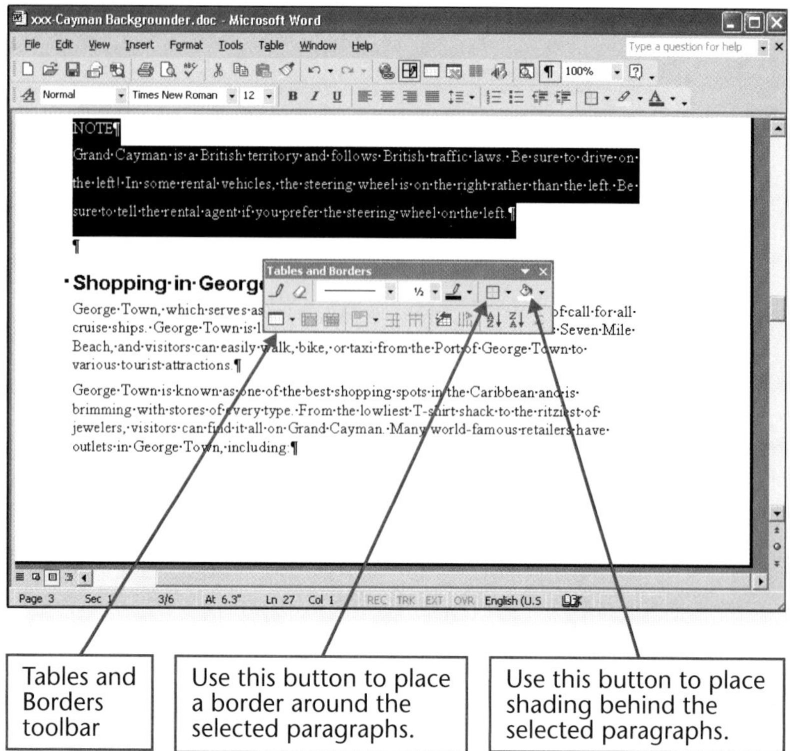
Tables and Borders toolbar
Use this button to place a border around the selected paragraphs.
Use this button to place shading behind the selected paragraphs.

Figure 2.13 The paragraphs with a border and shading

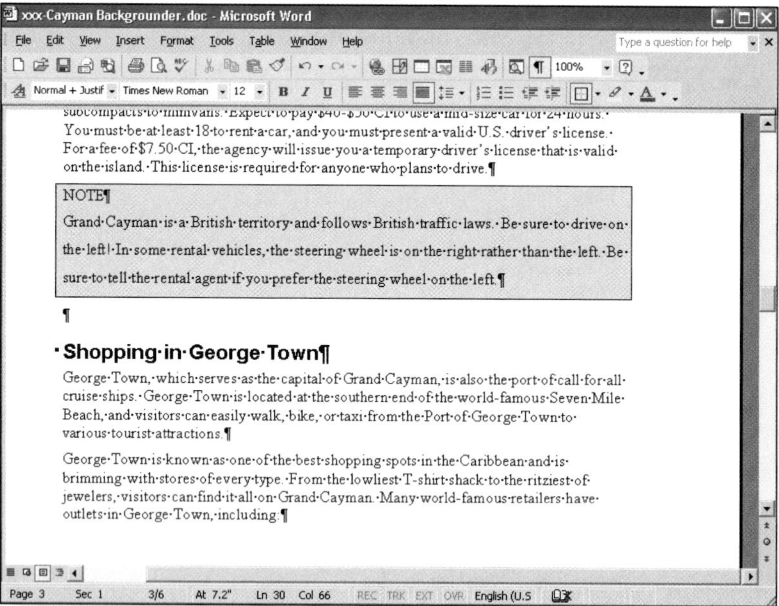

Another Way

You can apply borders and shading by using the Borders and Shading dialog box. On the Format menu, select Borders and Shading.

Exercise 3 Overview:
Set Tabs in a Document

Microsoft Office Specialist W2002 2.2

In word processing, a **tab** (also called a *tab stop*) is an amount of space by which text is indented from the left margin. You can use tabs to align text in various ways. For example, if you place a tab stop one-half inch from the left margin and then press the Tab key, your text will be aligned at that point.

You can use multiple tabs in a single paragraph to align text in columns; for example, if you set tabs at the 1", 3", and 5" marks on the horizontal ruler, you can align your text in three columns. If you apply the same tabs to several paragraphs, your text will be aligned like a table.

You can set several different kinds of tabs, each represented by a different character. (Tab characters appear on the horizontal ruler.)

The most common type of tab is the left tab, which left-aligns text at a specified point on the ruler. You can also use tabs to right-align and center-align text. Another type of tab, called the decimal tab, aligns a column of numbers vertically on their decimal point.

Word has a left-aligned default tab every one-half inch along every line in a document. Like other types of paragraph formatting, tabs apply only to selected paragraphs. You can set different tab stops for different paragraphs.

In the following exercise, you will set tabs in your document.

Type: tab

Figure 2.14 Tabs set on the horizontal ruler

Before starting the following exercise, make sure your ruler is active: On the View menu, select Ruler, if necessary.

Word

Step Through It™

Exercise 3: Set and modify tabs

Word

1. Find the section of the document entitled *Postal Rates*. Select the two paragraphs of text below the heading.

2. On the Format menu, select Tabs to open the Tabs dialog box.

3. In the *Tab stop position* box, type .75". Under *Alignment*, select Left. Under *Leader*, select None. Click Set (see Figure 2.15).

Figure 2.15 Setting custom tabs

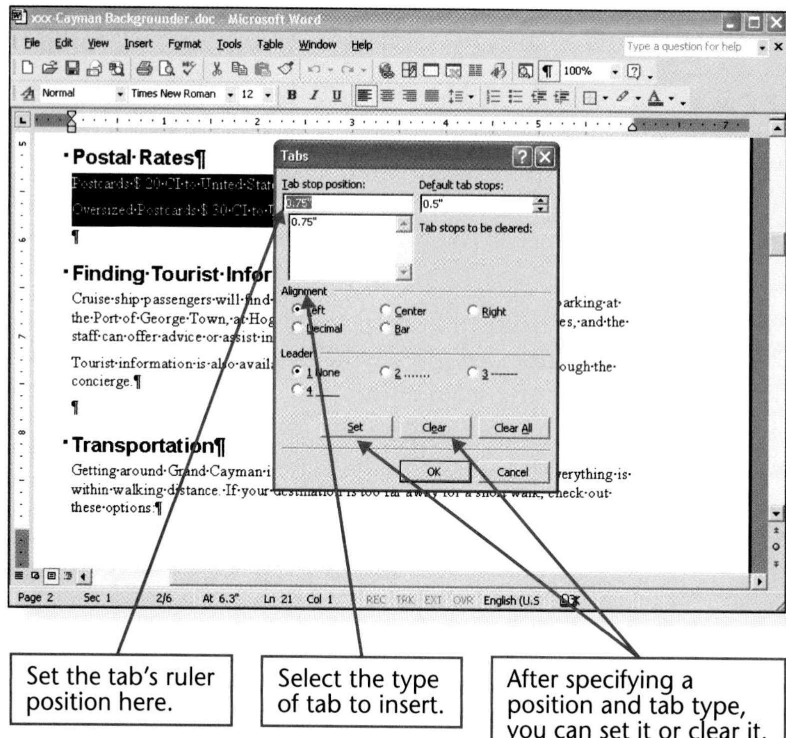

Set the tab's ruler position here.
Select the type of tab to insert.
After specifying a position and tab type, you can set it or clear it.

4. In the *Tab stop position* box, type 2.5". Under *Alignment*, select Decimal. Click Set.

5. In the Tab stop position box, type 5.5". Under *Alignment*, select Right. Click Set. Click OK.

6. Click before *Postcards* in the first paragraph. Press Tab. Click before the dollar sign ($) in the same sentence, and press Tab. Click before the word *to* and press Tab again.

7. Insert tabs in the same positions in the next paragraph (see Figure 2.16).

Figure 2.16 Using tabs to align text in columns

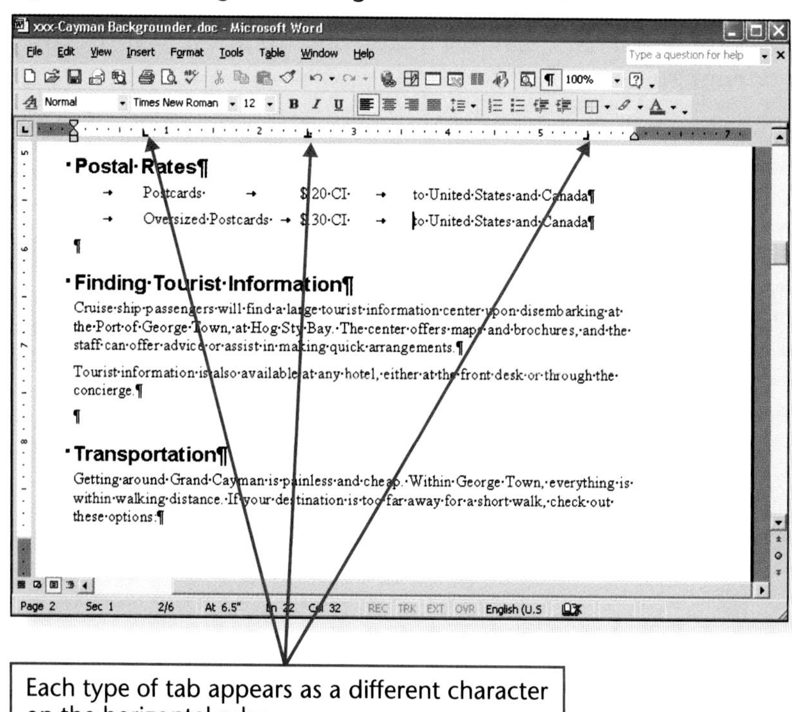

Each type of tab appears as a different character on the horizontal ruler.

Figure 2.17 Dragging a tab on the ruler

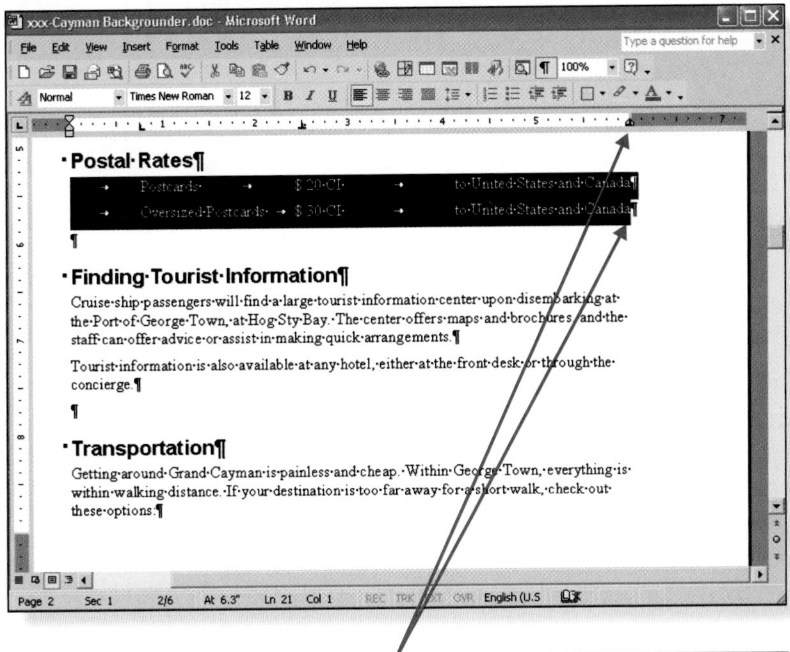

The third column of text moves to the 6" mark when the right tab marker is dragged to the right.

8. Select both paragraphs containing the tabs. On the ruler, click the right tab at the 5.5" mark, and then drag it over to the 6" mark. The third column of text moves to the right (see Figure 2.17).

Figure 2.18 Dragging the decimal tab

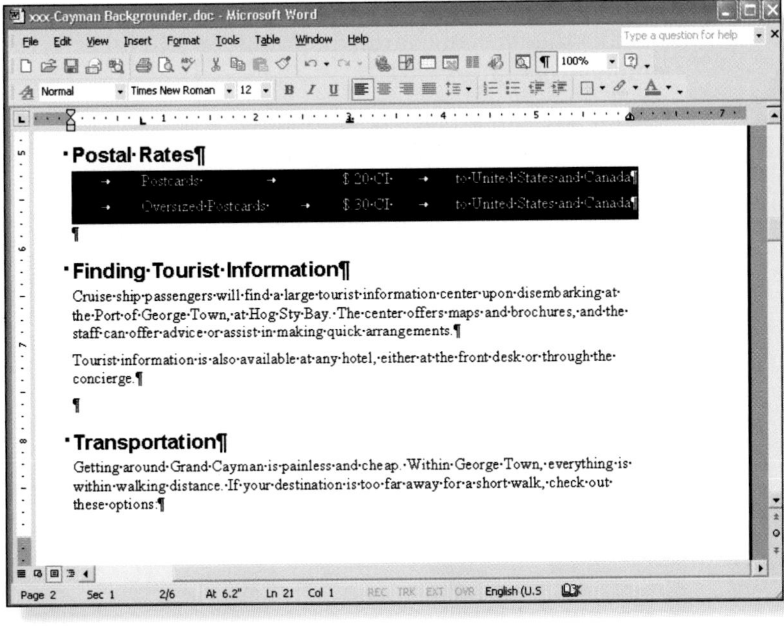

9. Click the decimal tab at the 2.5" mark and drag it to the 3" mark. The second column of text moves to the right (see Figure 2.18).

10. Save your changes.

APPLY IT! After finishing Exercises 1–3, you may test your skills by completing Apply It! Guided Activity 1, Format an Itinerary.

Business Connections

Effective Business Writing and Editing

Creative, journalistic, and technical writing are just a few examples of the many different styles of writing. Each style follows its own set of rules just like business writing does. If you plan to create documents for use in business—such as memos, letters, and reports—then you need to learn the appropriate style.

In business, effective documents follow these simple rules:

- **They are as brief as possible.** Good business writers make their point quickly and stick to it without adding a lot of fluff.
- **They focus on facts.** Unless your document's purpose is to convey an opinion, you should leave it out. If you venture an opinion, support it with specific information, and incorporate references.
- **They provide important data.** In addition to the basic facts, business people often need to see data supporting the facts. This data may take the form of charts, diagrams, or simple explanatory text.
- **They use simple, active language.** Strong writers avoid using the passive voice unless it can help make a point. They use short, direct sentences and avoid the overuse of adjectives.

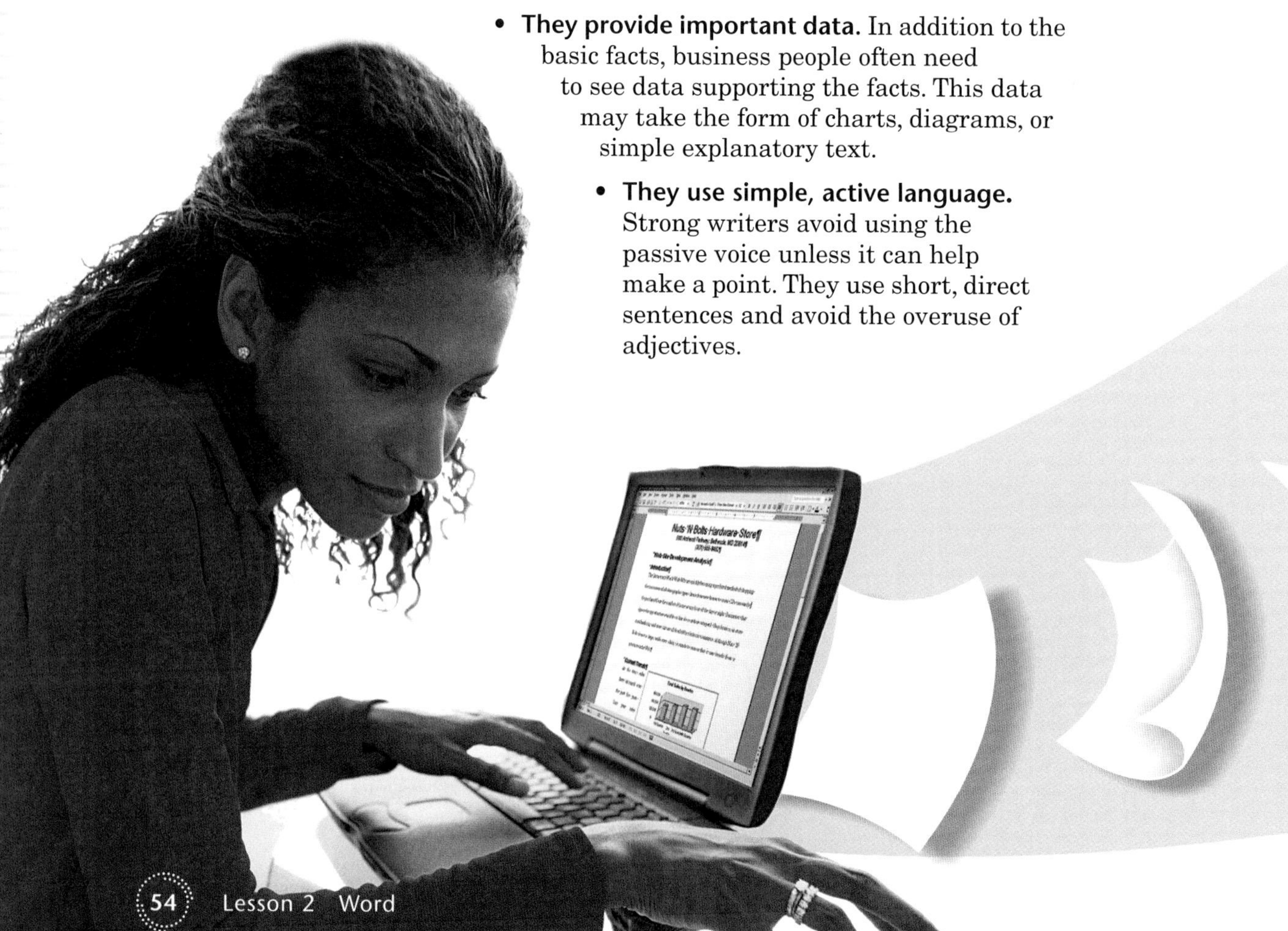

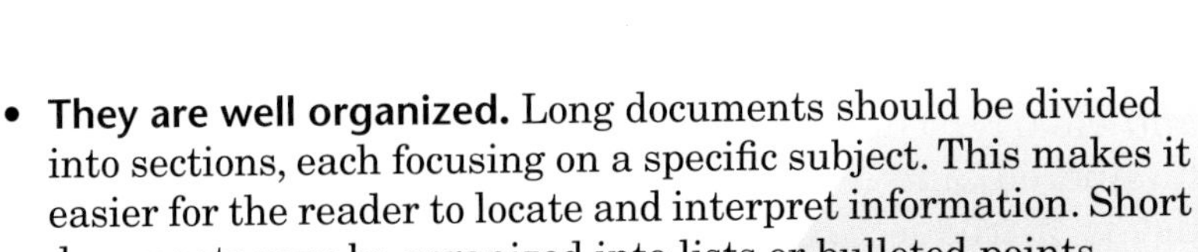

- **They are well organized.** Long documents should be divided into sections, each focusing on a specific subject. This makes it easier for the reader to locate and interpret information. Short documents may be organized into lists or bulleted points.

Organization

- Logic is essential to business writing, so good organization is important. That's why business writers often begin with detailed outlines to make sure that their topics and ideas flow logically and sequentially. This keeps the reader's attention focused and makes the document easier to understand.
- In addition, many reports begin with a summary instead of ending with one. This feature is sometimes called an executive summary because it is designed for busy managers who don't have time to read a lot of information.
- Lastly, accuracy is everything. You'll learn why if you give your boss a report filled with errors! Experienced business writers carefully research every bit of information that goes into their documents.

EXECUTIVE SUMMARY

ANNUAL REPORT

MARKETING SURVEY RESULTS

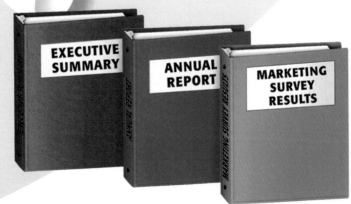

CRITICAL THINKING

1. **Applying the Active Voice** It's preferable to use the active voice rather than the passive voice. Write three sentences in passive voice and then make them active. Describe the differences in the tone of the sentences.
2. **Research Writing Style Guides** Have you ever used a style guide? Why do you think style guides are so important in writing effectively? Take a look at some of the style guides commonly used by business writers.

Microsoft Office Specialist
W2002 2.3

Exercise 4 Overview:
Apply Bullets, Numbering, and Outline Numbering to Lists

Lists allow you to organize facts, ideas, and steps quickly and clearly. There are three basic kinds of lists: bulleted, numbered, and outline numbered. Each item in a bulleted list is introduced by a small graphic called a **bullet**. By default, Word uses a small dot as the bullet. You should use a bulleted list when the order of items is not significant, such as the items in a grocery list.

In a numbered list, items are introduced by a numeral. By default, Word uses Arabic numerals (1, 2, 3, and so on) in numbered lists. You should use a numbered list when the order of items is significant, such as the steps in a procedure.

Type: list

An outline numbered list has multiple levels and indicates a hierarchy—the kind you would find in a book outline. Word uses a different introductory character and indent to show each level in the list.

In the following exercises, you will apply different types of list formats to your document.

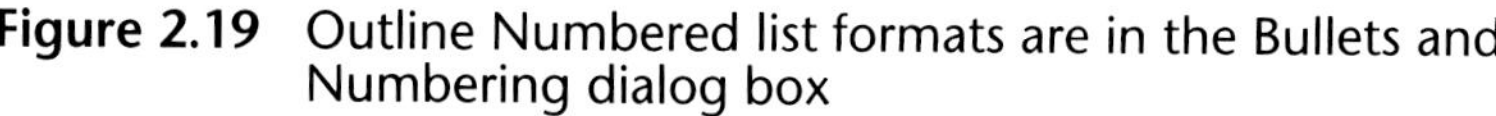

Figure 2.19 Outline Numbered list formats are in the Bullets and Numbering dialog box

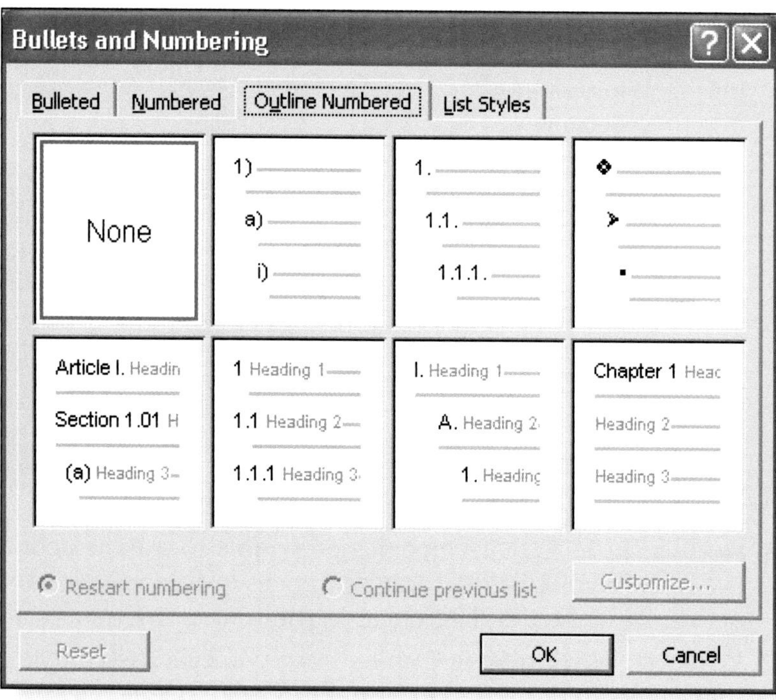

Figure 2.20 Creating a bulleted list

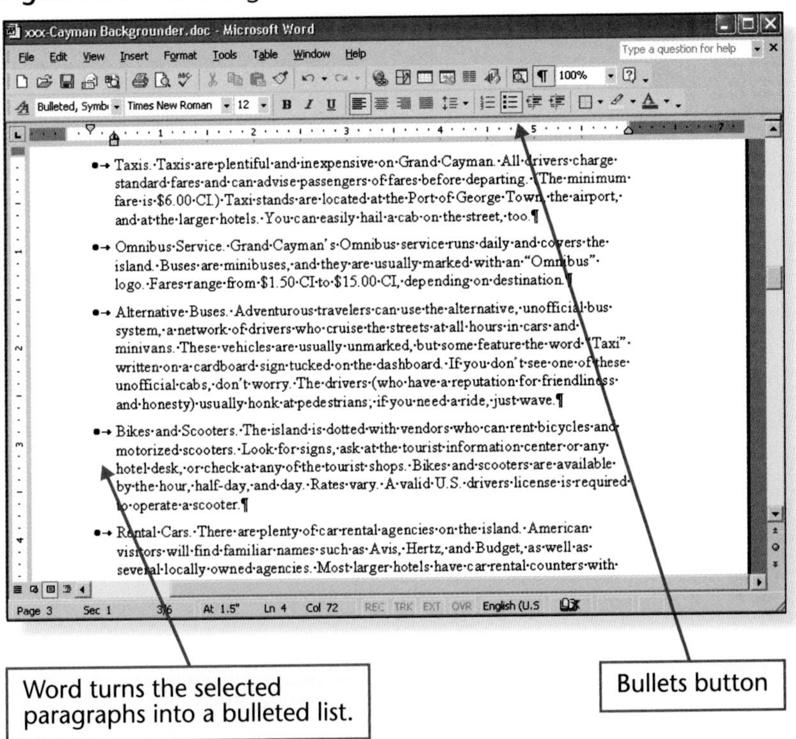

Word turns the selected paragraphs into a bulleted list.
Bullets button

Step Through It™
Exercise 4A: Apply bullets and numbering

1 Find the section of your document entitled *Transportation.* (This section contains six paragraphs followed by a note.) Select the second through the sixth paragraph of text.

2 Click Bullets on the Formatting toolbar to apply a bullet format to the selected paragraphs. Click anywhere in the list to deselect it (see Figure 2.20).

Figure 2.21 Creating a numbered list

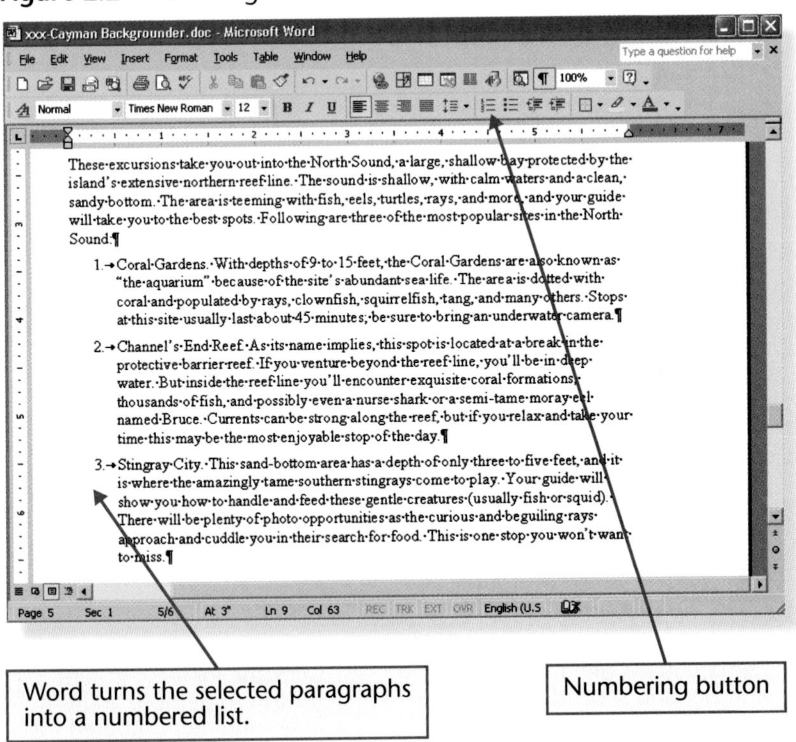

Word turns the selected paragraphs into a numbered list.
Numbering button

3 Find the section entitled *Snorkeling Excursions* and select the last three paragraphs of text in the section.

4 Click Numbering on the Formatting toolbar to apply a numbered list format. Click anywhere in the document to deselect the list (see Figure 2.21).

Step Through It™

Exercise 4B: Create an outline numbered list

1. Find the list that begins with the text *West Bay.*

2. Select all the items in the list (starting with *West Bay* and ending with *Rum Point Club*). On the Format menu, select Bullets and Numbering to open the Bullets and Numbering dialog box. Click the Outline Numbered tab (see Figure 2.22).

3. Click the numbering style that uses the scheme *1), a), i).* Click OK.

Figure 2.22 The Bullets and Numbering dialog box

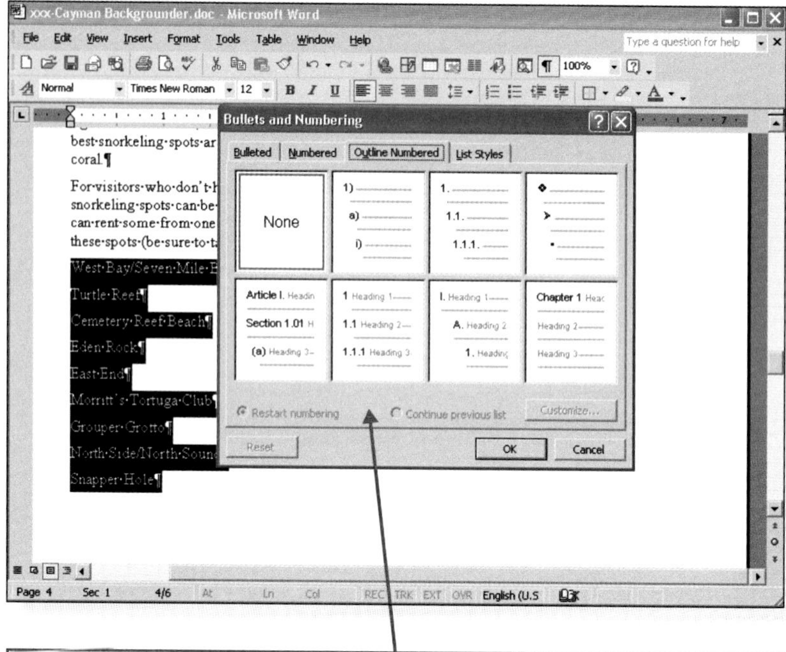

Select a style of outline numbering from the Outline Numbered tab.

4. Click the text *Turtle Reef,* and then click Increase Indent on the Formatting toolbar. The item is demoted and gets the secondary numbering *a).*

5. Select each of the following items and click Increase Indent to demote them (see Figure 2.23):
   Cemetery Reef Beach
   Eden Rock
   Morritt's Tortuga Club
   Grouper Grotto
   Snapper Hole
   Ghost Mountain
   Smith's Cove
   Rum Point Club

Figure 2.23 An outline numbered list

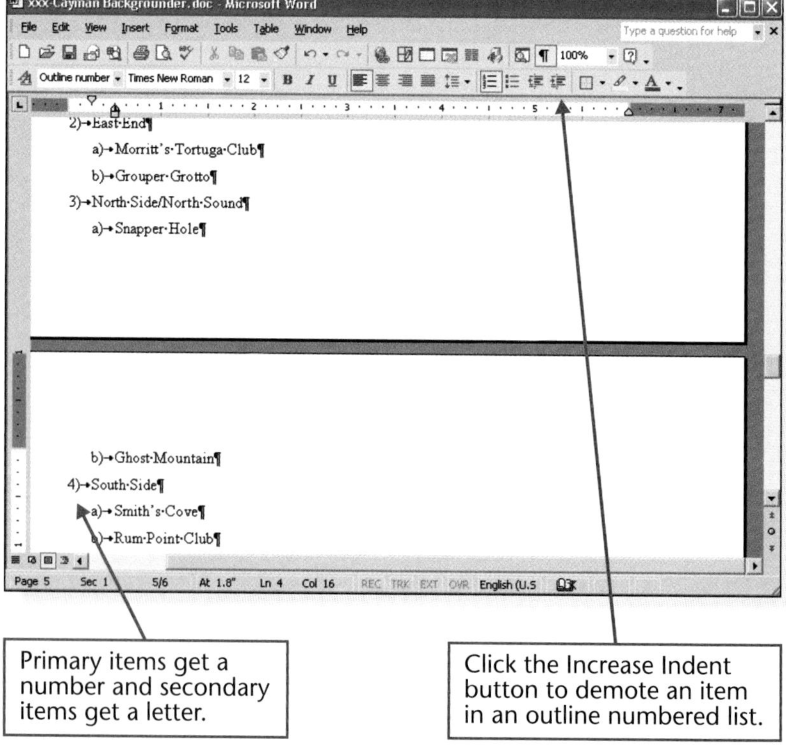

Primary items get a number and secondary items get a letter.

Click the Increase Indent button to demote an item in an outline numbered list.

Exercise 5 Overview: Apply Character Formats

Microsoft Office Specialist
W2002 1.2

Word

Good text formatting is essential in a professional-looking document. Consistency is important when formatting your text. This means that body text should be uniformly formatted throughout the document, as should headings, lists, tables, and other elements. This consistent look and feel makes a document easier to read.

The first step in formatting text is selecting a font. In word processing, a **font** is a complete set of alphabetical characters (including the letters, numbers, punctuation marks, and symbols) based on the same, unique design. Fonts have names such as Times, Helvetica, and Tahoma. Some people use the term *typeface* when referring to a font.

Like many programs, Word features a number of built-in fonts that you can apply to any text in a document. Every font is available in a wide variety of sizes, and you can use different sizes of fonts throughout a document. Font sizes are expressed in points. Standard font sizes are 10 to 12 points for body text and 14 to 18 points for most headings.

You can also apply different colors and font styles to document text. The most commonly used **font styles** are bold, italic, and underline. These styles are easy to apply by using toolbar buttons.

Type: font, color

In the following exercises, you will change the font, font size, font color, and font styles in your document.

Figure 2.24 Changing the font and the font styles

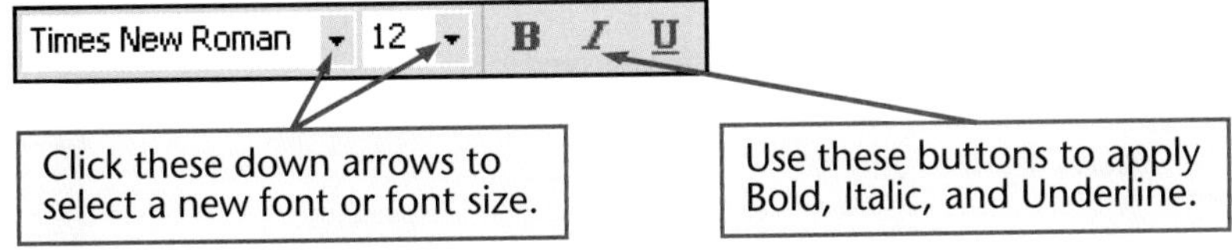

To ensure that Word displays actual fonts, select Customize on the Tools menu. On the Options tab, select the *List font names in their font* check box, and click OK.

Step Through It™

Exercise 5A: Change the font, font size, and font color

1. Go to the top of the document and select the *Backgrounder Information on Grand Cayman* main heading.
2. Click the Font [Times New Roman] down arrow on the Formatting toolbar to see a list of available fonts (see Figure 2.25).
3. Scroll through the list, if necessary. Select Arial to change the title from Times New Roman to Arial.

Figure 2.25 Changing the font of selected text

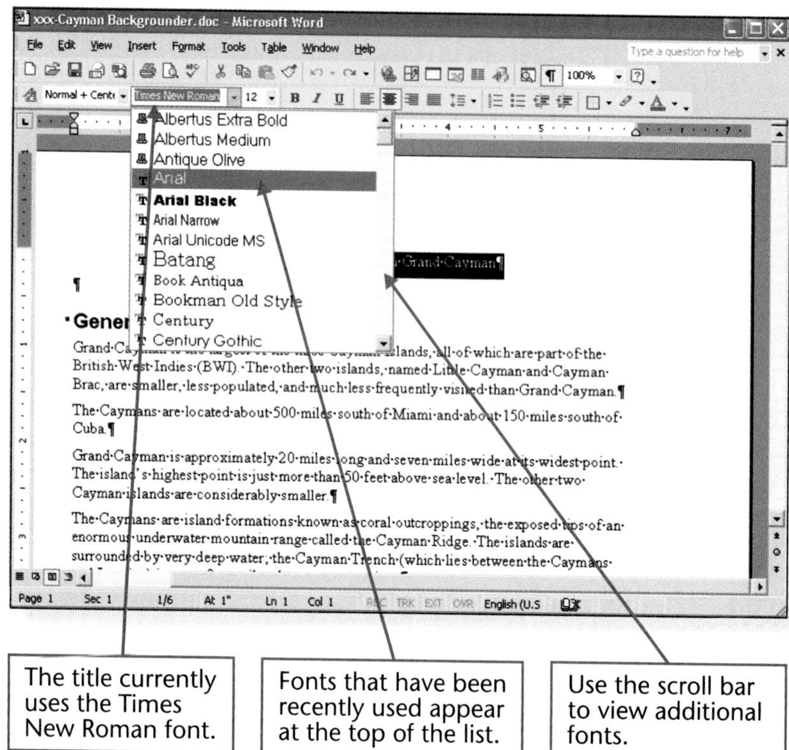

The title currently uses the Times New Roman font.
Fonts that have been recently used appear at the top of the list.
Use the scroll bar to view additional fonts.

4. With the title still selected, click the Font Size [12] down arrow on the Formatting toolbar to see a list of available font sizes (see Figure 2.26).
5. Select 18 to enlarge the font of the title to 18 point Arial.

Figure 2.26 Changing the title's font size

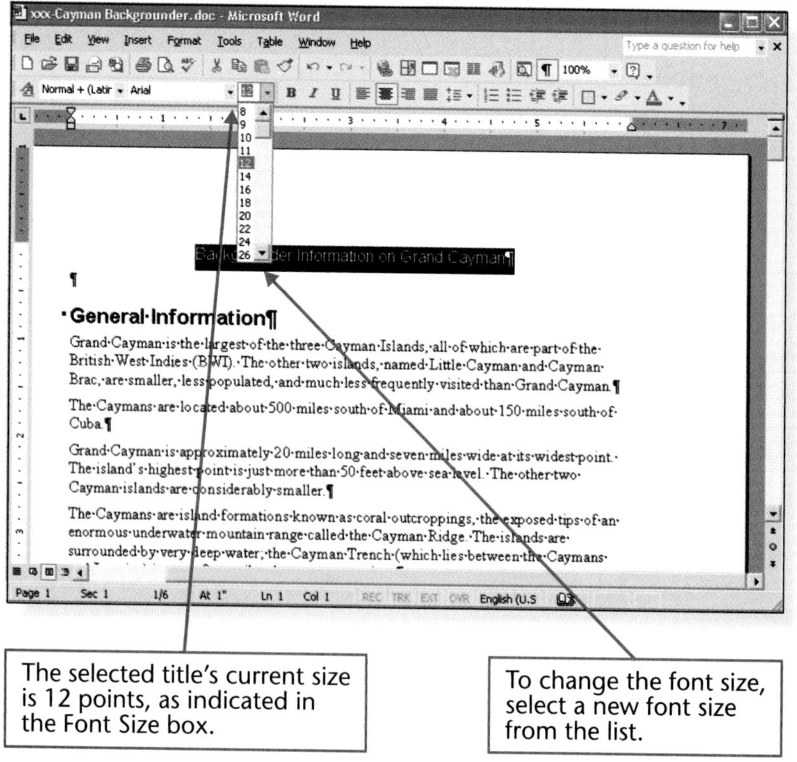

The selected title's current size is 12 points, as indicated in the Font Size box.
To change the font size, select a new font size from the list.

Figure 2.27 Changing the title's color

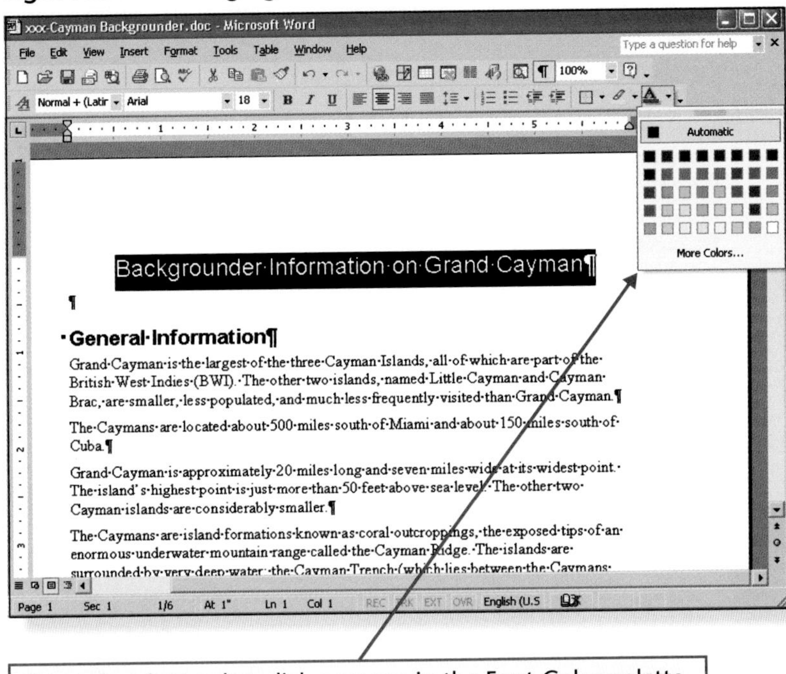

6. With the document's title still selected, click the Font Color down arrow on the Formatting toolbar (see Figure 2.27).

7. When the color palette appears, click the Blue color box (the sixth box from the left in the second row) to apply that color to the selected text.

Word

Figure 2.28 Making text italic

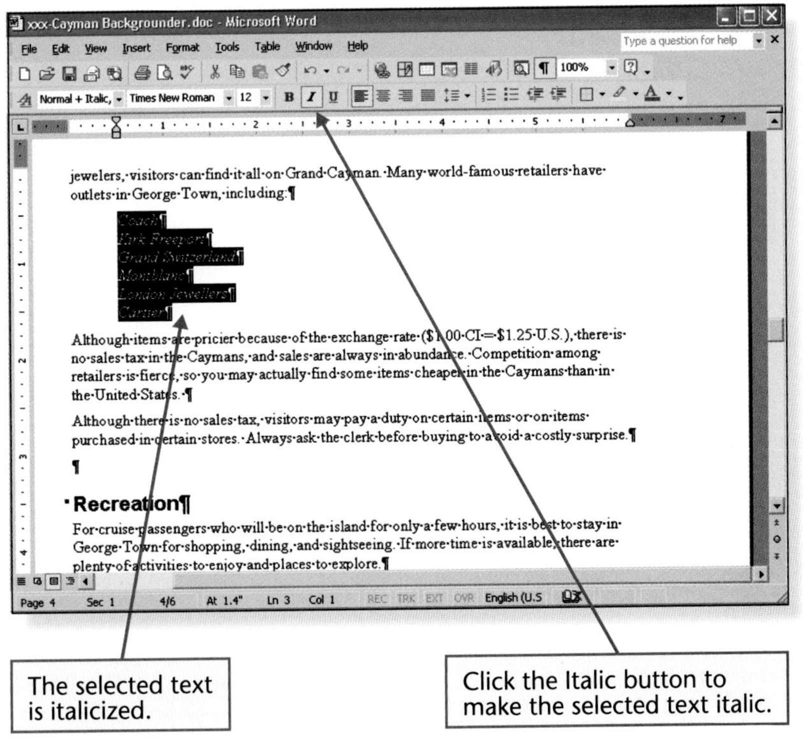

Step Through It™

Exercise 5B: Apply bold, italic, and underline

1. Find the section entitled *Shopping in George Town*, and select the six-line list of stores beginning with *Coach* and ending with *Cartier*.

2. Click Italic on the Formatting toolbar (see Figure 2.28).

Word

3 Find the section of the document entitled *Museums and Sights*. In the second paragraph, select *Cayman Islands National Museum.* (Select the period, too.)

4 Click Underline on the Formatting toolbar to underline the museum's name (see Figure 2.29).

Figure 2.29 Underlining text

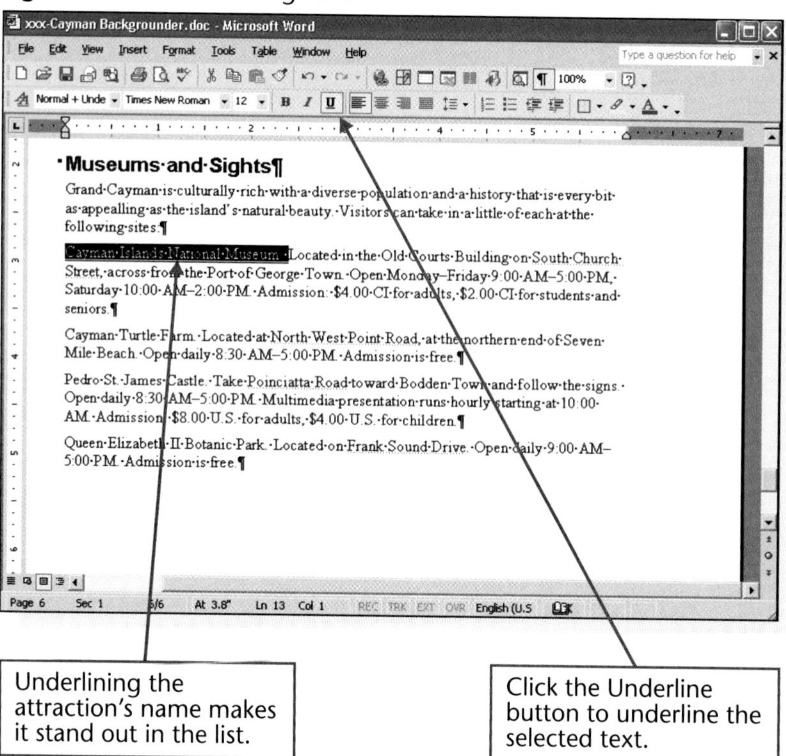

5 In the next three paragraphs, select each attraction's name (*Cayman Turtle Farm, Pedro St. James Castle,* and *Queen Elizabeth II Botanic Park*) and underline it.

6 Go to the top of the document and again select the main title. Click Bold on the Formatting toolbar.

7 Scroll through the document and click before each empty paragraph mark and press Delete (see Figure 2.30). Save your changes.

Figure 2.30 Making the document's title bold

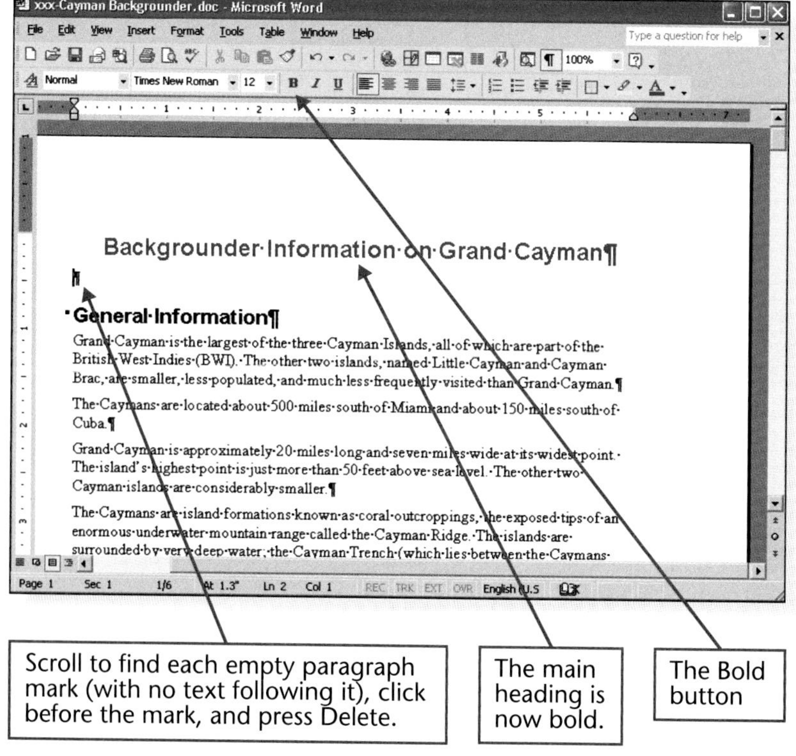

Exercise 6 Overview: Create and Modify a Header and Footer

Microsoft Office Specialist W2002 3.1

In long documents, it is often helpful to add repeating information (such as the document's title or page numbers) to every page. This information makes the document easier to read and navigate and can help the reader locate items of interest.

The most effective way to add repeating information to a document is by adding a header or a footer to each of its pages. A **header** is a line of text that appears at the top of each page in a document; a **footer** is a line of text that appears at the bottom of each page.

Type: header, footer

Word lets you create headers and/or footers in any document and provides tools for inserting various kinds of information in them, such as the date and time the document was last saved, the file's name, the page number, and so on. You can also type information into a header or footer and format it any way you want.

Because it is common practice to omit the header and footer from a document's first page, Word also provides this option.

In the following exercises, you will add a header and footer to your document.

Figure 2.31 Creating a header with the Header and Footer toolbar

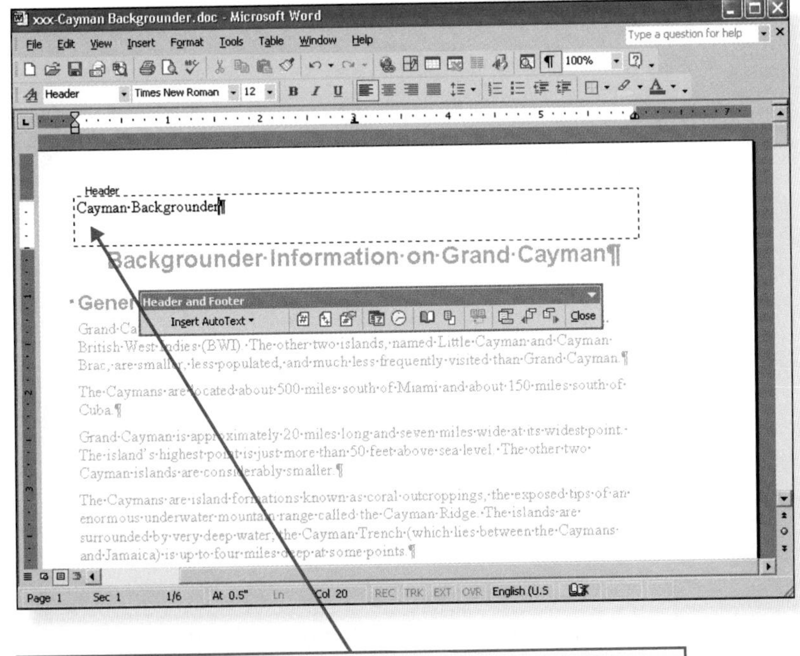

The header text appears at the left side of the header area.

Step Through It™

Exercise 6A: Create a header and footer

1. Go to the top of the document. On the View menu, select Header and Footer to open the Header and Footer toolbar.
2. With the insertion point visible at the left end of the header area, type Cayman Backgrounder (see Figure 2.31).

Word

3 On the Header and Footer toolbar, click Switch Between Header and Footer to move to the footer area at the bottom of the page.

4 Type Sun and Sea Confidential and press Tab twice to move the insertion point to the right end of the footer area.

5 Click Insert Date to insert today's date. Press the spacebar and click Insert Time (see Figure 2.32). Click Close on the Header and Footer toolbar.

Figure 2.32 Creating a footer

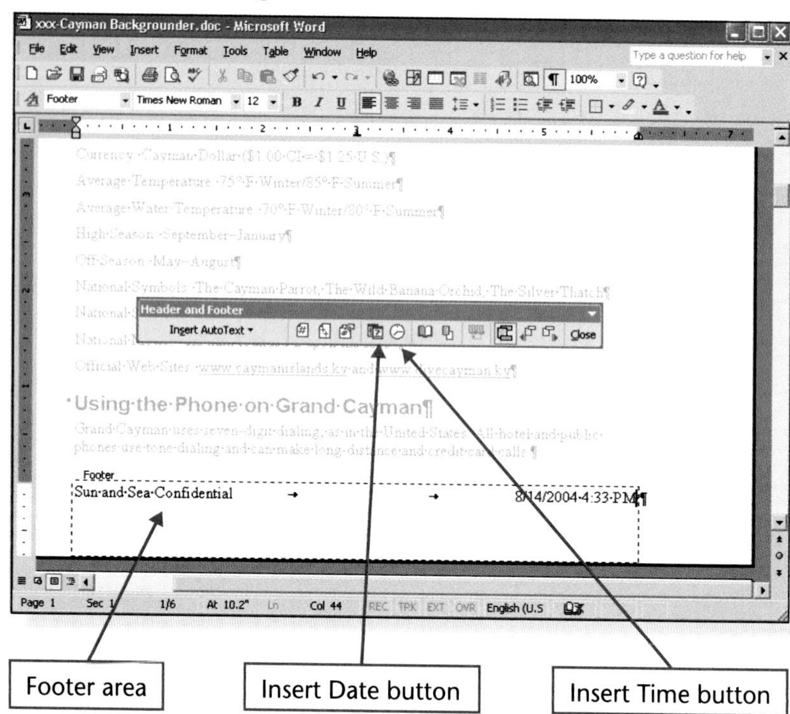

Step Through It™

Exercise 6B: Modify a header and footer

1 Go to the top of the document. Double-click the header area to activate the Header and Footer toolbar.

2 At the beginning of the header, type Grand, to make the header read *Grand Cayman Backgrounder.*

3 Select the header and change the font to Arial and the font size to 10 (see Figure 2.33).

Figure 2.33 Modifying a header

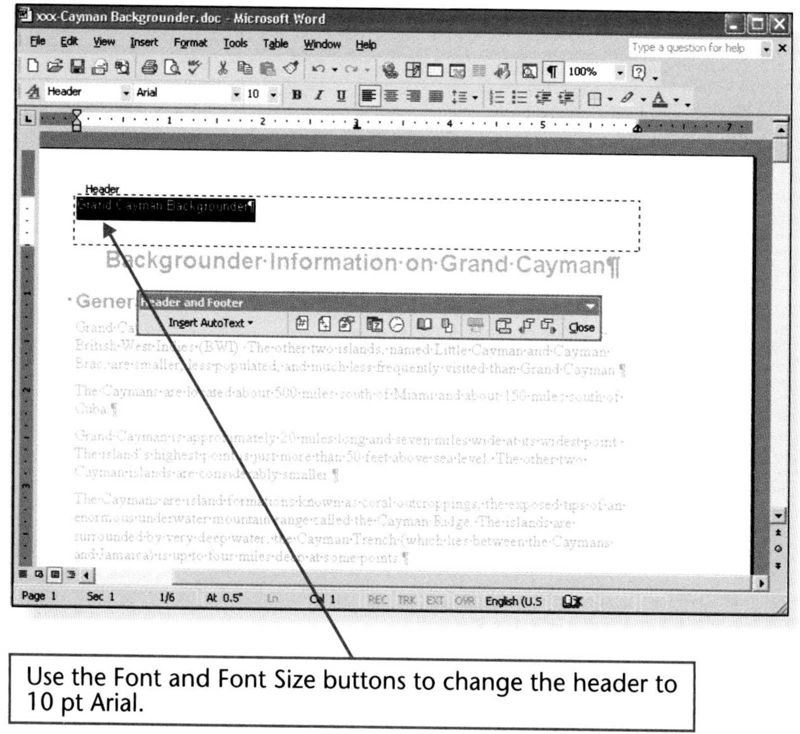

Figure 2.34 Formatting a footer

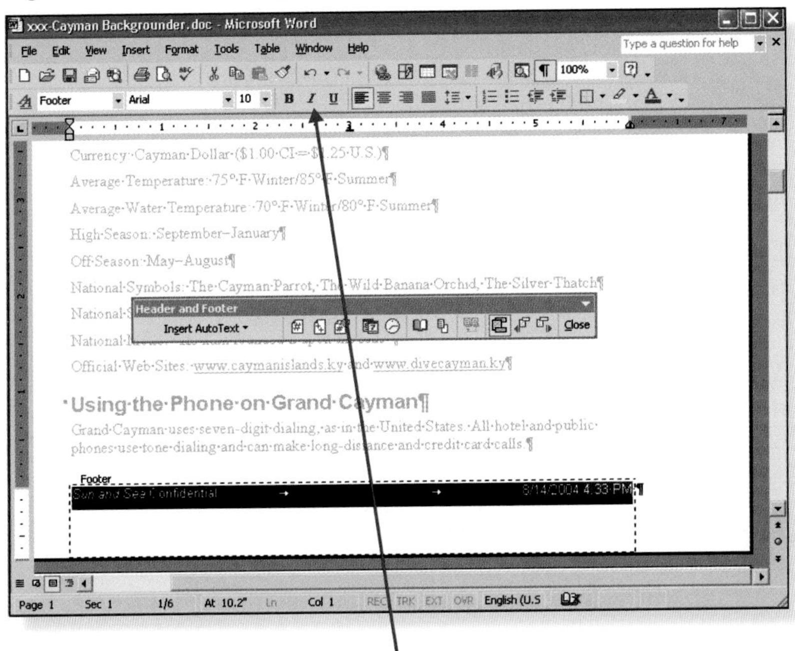

Use the standard tools on the Formatting toolbar (such as the Italic button) to format text in a header or footer.

4) Switch to the footer area. Select the words *Sun and Sea*, and make them italic.

5) Select the entire footer and change the font and font size to 10 point Arial (see Figure 2.34). Close the Header and Footer toolbar.

Figure 2.35 The Page Setup dialog box

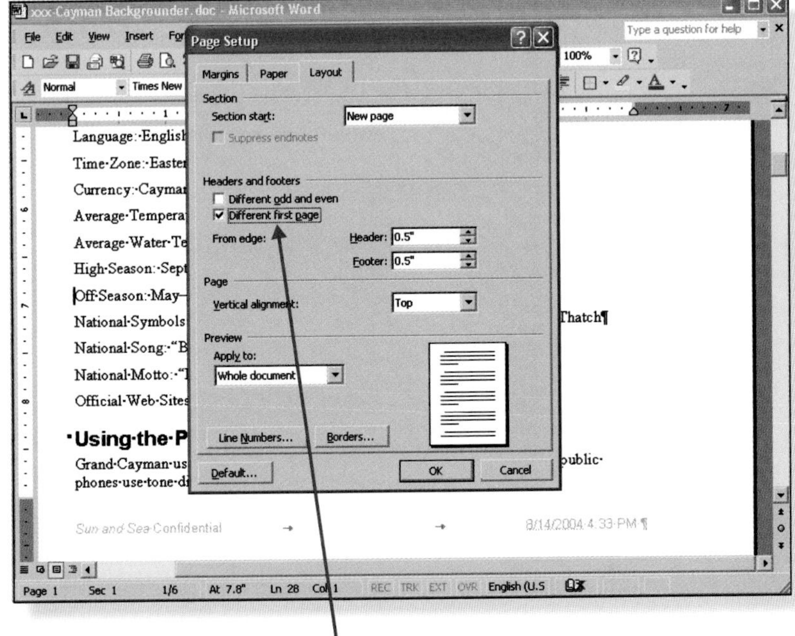

Select this option to omit the header and footer from the document's first page.

6) On the File menu, select Page Setup to open the Page Setup dialog box.

7) On the Layout tab, select the *Different first page* check box (see Figure 2.35). Click OK.

8) Scroll through the document to view the headers and footers. There is no longer a header or footer on the document's first page.

9) Save your changes.

Microsoft Office Specialist W2002 3.3

Exercise 7 Overview:
Insert a Page Break and Page Number

As you type, Word automatically inserts a page break at the end of each page you fill with text. A **page break** is a marker that indicates the end of the current page and the start of a new one.

Depending on how much text you have typed on the current page, the break may occur in the middle of a paragraph or between paragraphs.

You can insert a page break manually at any point in a document. This is convenient when you want certain types of material to stay together on the same page.

Word can add page numbers to your document. It is a good idea to add page numbers to any document that is more than two or three pages long. Word lets you choose the location and style for page numbers and gives you the option of omitting the page number from the document's first page.

In the following exercises, you will insert a page break and page numbers into your document.

Step Through It™
Exercise 7A: Insert a page break

1. Find the section entitled *Transportation*. Click the insertion point before the *T* in the section title.
2. On the Insert menu, select Break to open the Break dialog box.
3. Under *Break types*, select Page break (see Figure 2.36). Click OK.
4. Insert page breaks before the section titles *Shopping in George Town* and *Scuba Diving*.

Figure 2.36 Inserting a page break

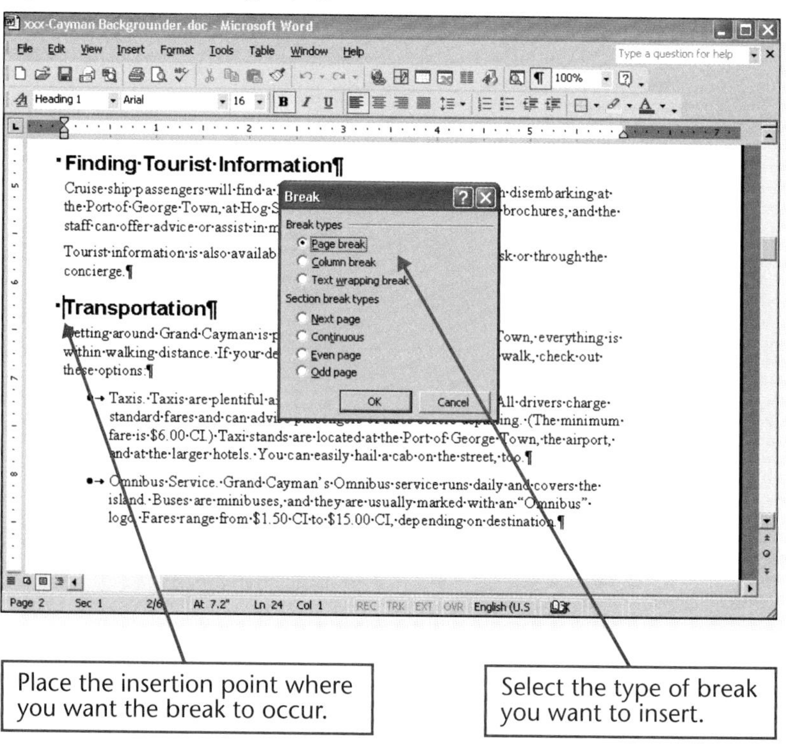

Figure 2.37 Inserting a page number

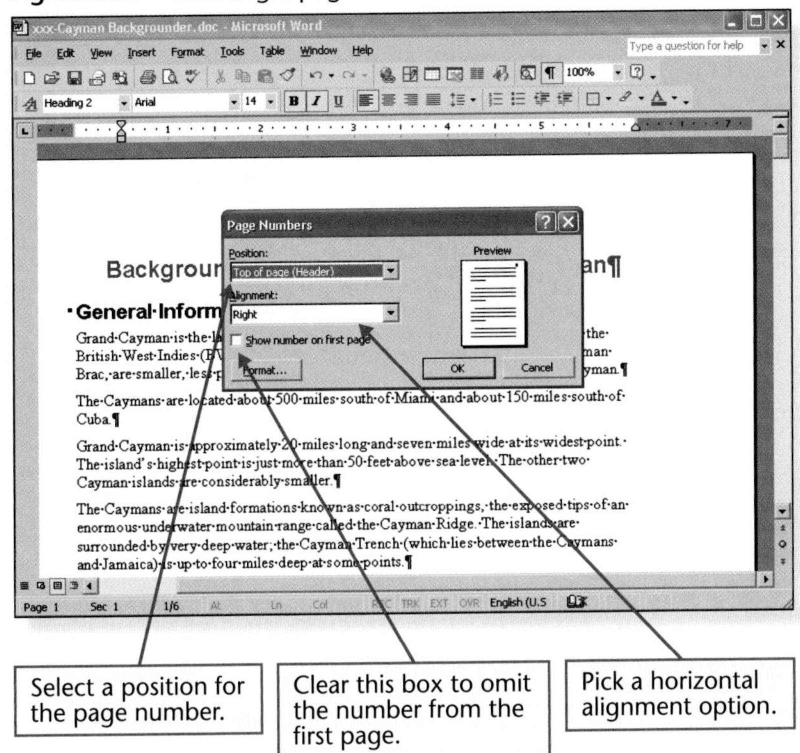

Select a position for the page number.
Clear this box to omit the number from the first page.
Pick a horizontal alignment option.

Step Through It™

Exercise 7B: Insert a page number

1. Go to the top of the document. On the Insert menu, select Page Numbers to open the Page Numbers dialog box.

2. Click the *Position* down arrow, and then click Top of page (Header). Click the *Alignment* down arrow and click Right.

3. Clear the *Show number on first page* check box, if necessary (see Figure 2.37). Click OK.

Word

Figure 2.38 Formatting the page number

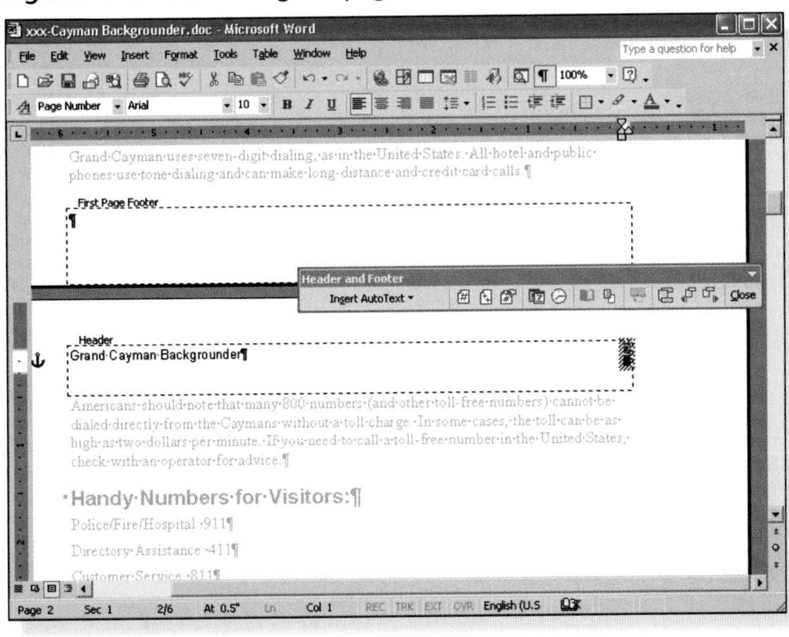

4. Open the Header and Footer toolbar and scroll to page 2. Select the page number. The number is surrounded by a box. Change the font size and font to 10 point Arial (see Figure 2.38).

5. Close the Header and Footer toolbar and save your changes. Close the document but leave Word running.

APPLY IT! After finishing Exercises 4–7, you may test your skills by completing Apply It! Guided Activity 2, Format a Long Memo.

Procedure Summary

Apply a Paragraph Style

1. Click a paragraph to select it.
2. Click **Styles and Formatting** button.
   OR
   On the **Format** menu, select
   Styles and Formatting. . . . . **Alt + O, S**
3. In the Styles and Formatting task pane, click a style.

Apply a Paragraph Style From the Style List

1. Click a paragraph to select it.
2. Click the **Style** down arrow Normal, and then click a style.

Copy Formatting

1. Select the text with the formatting you want to copy.
2. Click **Format Painter** button.
3. Drag the pointer across the text that will receive the copied formatting.

Apply a Character Style

1. Select one or more characters of text.
2. Click **Styles and Formatting** button.
   OR
   On the **Format** menu, select
   Styles and Formatting . . . . **Alt + O, S**
3. In the Styles and Formatting task pane, click a character style.

Change Paragraph Alignment Using the Formatting Toolbar

1. Select one or more paragraphs.
2. Click **Align Left** button.
   OR
   Click **Center** button.
   OR
   Click **Align Right** button.
   OR
   Click **Justify** button.

Change Line Spacing

1. Select a paragraph.
2. Click the **Line Spacing** down arrow.
3. Select a line spacing option.
   OR
   On the **Format** menu, select
   Paragraph. . . . .**Alt + O, P**
4. Click the **Indents and Spacing** tab . .**Alt + I**
5. Select the line spacing . . . . **Alt + N**

Change Paragraph Indents

1. Select a paragraph.
2. On the **Format** menu, select
   Paragraph. . . . .**Alt + O, P**
3. Click the **Indents and Spacing** tab . .**Alt + I**
4. Under *Indentation*, click the up or down arrow in the **Left** or **Right** box (or both) to set indents. . **Alt + L OR Alt + R**
5. Click OK.

Change Paragraph Spacing

1. Select a paragraph.
2. On the **Format** menu, select **Paragraph** . . . . **Alt + O, P**
3. Click the **Indents and Spacing** tab . . **Alt + I**
4. Under *Spacing*, click the up or down arrow in the **Before** or **After** box (or both) to set spacing . . . . **B OR E**
5. Click OK. . . . . **Alt + B OR Alt + E**

Add a Border to a Paragraph

1. Select a paragraph.
2. On the Tables and Borders toolbar, click the **Borders** down arrow.

   OR

   On the Formatting toolbar, click the **Borders** down arrow.
3. Select a border style.

Add Shading to a Paragraph

1. Select a paragraph.
2. On the Tables and Borders toolbar, click the **Shading Color** down arrow.
3. Select a shading color.

Set a Custom Tab

1. Select a paragraph.
2. On the **Format** menu, select **Tabs**. . . . . **Alt + O, T**
3. In the **Tab stop position** box, type a position for the tab stop.
4. Under *Alignment*, select an alignment option.
5. Under *Leader*, select a leader style.
6. Click Set, and then click OK.

Create a Bulleted List

1. Select the paragraphs.
2. Click **Bullets** button.

Create a Numbered List

1. Select the paragraphs.
2. Click **Numbering** button.

Create an Outline Numbered List

1. Select the paragraphs.
2. On the **Format** menu, select **Bullets and Numbering**. . . . .**Alt + O, N**
3. Click the **Outline Numbered** tab. . . **Alt + U**
4. Select a numbering style.
5. Click OK.

Procedure Summary

Change the Font

1. Select the text.
2. Click the **Font** down arrow Times New Roman.
3. Select a font.

   OR

1. On the **Format** menu, select **Font**. . . . . **Alt + O, F**
2. Click the **Font** tab and select the **Font**. . . . . **Alt + N, Alt + F**

Change the Font Size

1. Select the text.
2. Click the **Font Size** down arrow 12.
3. Select a font size.

   OR

1. On the **Format** menu, select **Font**. . . . . **Alt + O, F**
2. Click the **Font** tab and select the **Size**. . . . . **Alt + N, Alt + S**

Change the Font Color

1. Select the text.
2. Click the **Font Color** down arrow.
3. Select a font color.

   OR

1. On the **Format** menu, select **Font**. . . . . **Alt + O, F**
2. Click the **Font** tab and select the **Font color** . . . . **Alt + N, Alt + C**

Apply a Character Format

1. Select the text.
2. Click **Bold** button.

   OR

   Click **Italic** button.

   OR

   Click **Underline** button.

Add a Header

1. On the **View** menu, select **Header and Footer** .... **Alt + V, H**
2. Type text in the header area.

Add a Footer

1. On the **View** menu, select **Header and Footer** .... **Alt + V, H**
2. Click **Switch Between Header and Footer** button.
3. Type text in the footer area.

Add the Date and Time to a Header or Footer

1. On the **View** menu, select **Header and Footer** .... **Alt + V, H**
2. Position the insertion point at the desired place in the header or footer.
3. Click **Insert Date** button.

   OR

   Click **Insert Time** button.

Insert a Page Break

1. Click where you wish the page break to occur.
2. Press Ctrl + Enter.

   OR

   On the **Insert** menu, select **Break**, select **Page break**, and then click OK. . **Alt + I, B, P**

Insert Page Numbers

1. On the **Insert** menu, select **Page Numbers** .... **Alt + I, U**
2. Click the **Position** down arrow and select a position for the number. . . . .**P**
3. Click the **Alignment** down arrow and select an alignment option .... **Alt + A**
4. Select or clear the **Show number on first page** check box. . . . . **Alt + S**
5. Click OK.

Lesson Review and Exercises

Summary Checklist

- ☑ Can you apply styles to paragraphs and characters?
- ☑ Can you change the line spacing in a paragraph?
- ☑ Can you change paragraph alignment, indents, and paragraph spacing?
- ☑ Can you add a border and shading to a paragraph?
- ☑ Can you align text in different ways using tabs?
- ☑ Can you create a bulleted list, a numbered list, and an outline numbered list?
- ☑ Can you change the font, font size, and color of text?
- ☑ Can you apply font styles such as bold, italic, or underlining?
- ☑ Can you create or modify a header or a footer?
- ☑ Can you insert page breaks?
- ☑ Can you add page numbers to a document?

Key Terms

- alignment (p. 47)
- border (p. 47)
- bullet (p. 56)
- character style (p. 42)
- font (p. 59)
- font style (p. 59)
- footer (p. 63)
- formatting (p. 42)
- header (p. 63)
- indent (p. 47)
- line spacing (p. 47)
- page break (p. 66)
- paragraph (p. 47)
- paragraph spacing (p. 47)
- paragraph style (p. 42)
- point (p. 47)
- shading (p. 47)
- style (p. 42)
- tab (p. 51)

APPLY IT! Guided Activities

1. Format an Itinerary

As a corporate travel planner, you make travel arrangements for your company's workers. Sometimes, however, you are responsible for setting up itineraries, or schedules of activities, that workers must follow while at a certain destination. You have created an itinerary of activities for a day-long seminar that you have set up for senior managers. The itinerary already contains all the needed information; your task is to format it.

Follow these steps to format your itinerary:

a. Open *Itinerary.doc.* Save the file as *xxx-Itinerary.doc.* Switch to Print Layout View, if necessary.

b. Click the first paragraph, click the Style down arrow, and apply the *Heading 1* paragraph style. Apply the *Heading 2* style to the second and third paragraphs, and then apply the *Heading 3* style to the fourth paragraph. Select all four paragraphs and click Center to center-align them.

c. Select the 11 lines below the *Schedule of Activities* heading. On the Format menu, select Tabs. In the Tabs dialog box, set one left-aligned tab at 1.5" and another left-aligned tab at 3.5" on the horizontal ruler.

d. In the first line of the schedule, click after *AM*, delete the blank space, and press Tab. Then click before the speaker's name, delete the blank space, and press Tab. Repeat this procedure at the same places in each of the remaining 10 lines of the schedule. This will organize the itinerary into three left-aligned columns. (The *Lunch* and *Break* lines will have only two columns since they are not followed by a name.)

e. Select the 11 lines of the schedule and the *Schedule of Activities* heading. On the Format menu, select Paragraph. Increase the paragraph spacing to 12 points before each paragraph. Adjust the left and right indentation to be 0.3".

f. With the paragraphs still selected, open the Tables and Borders toolbar. Click the Borders down arrow and add an outside border. Click the Shading down arrow and select a color of your choice from the palette. Close the Tables and Borders toolbar and view your document **(see Figure 2.39)**.

g. Save and close the document, but keep Word running.

Figure 2.39 A formatted itinerary

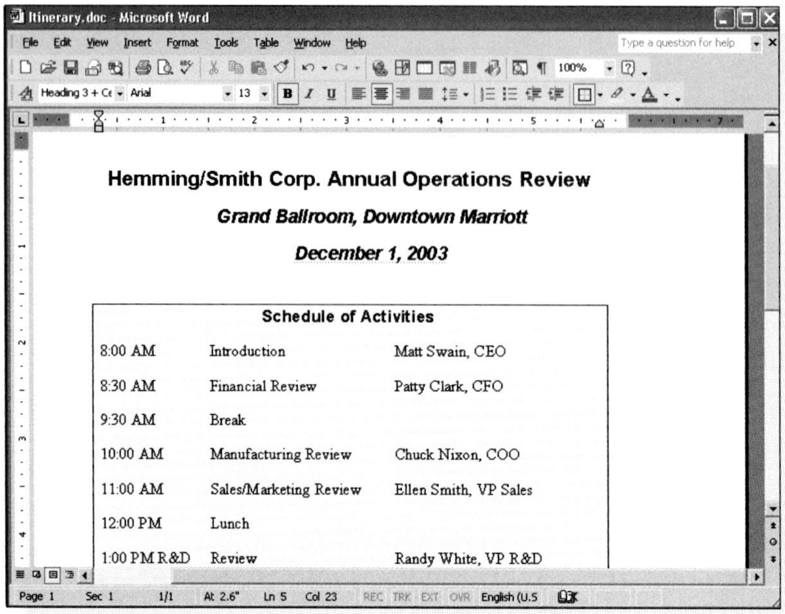
Itinerary.doc - Microsoft Word
File Edit View Insert Format Tools Table Window Help
Type a question for help
Hemming/Smith Corp. Annual Operations Review
Grand Ballroom, Downtown Marriott
December 1, 2003
Schedule of Activities
8:00 AM Introduction Matt Swain, CEO
8:30 AM Financial Review Patty Clark, CFO
9:30 AM Break
10:00 AM Manufacturing Review Chuck Nixon, COO
11:00 AM Sales/Marketing Review Ellen Smith, VP Sales
12:00 PM Lunch
1:00 PM R&D Review Randy White, VP R&D
Page 1 Sec 1 1/1 At 2.6" Ln 5 Col 23 REC TRK EXT OVR English (U.S

2. Format a Long Memo

As the purchasing director for Hugo Corporation (an auto parts manufacturer), one of your jobs is to streamline the process that vendors follow when bidding for your company's business. You have written a memo for your department's purchasing agents outlining some new procedures. You still need to format the memo and add some other finishing touches.

Follow these steps:

a. Open *Bid Memo.doc.* Save your document as *xxx-Bid Memo.doc.* Select the three paragraphs of body text that list three types of forms. (The paragraphs begin with *Bidder Identification and Authorization*, *Guarantee of Availability*, and *Price and Specification List*). Click Bullets to make this a bulleted list.

b. In the paragraph following the bulleted list, select *www.hugoautoparts.com*, open the Style list, and apply the *Hyperlink* character style.

c. Click to the left of the heading *Rules for Vendors*. On the Insert menu, select Break and insert a page break. Scroll to the bottom of page 2, click to the left of the heading *Purchasing Timetable*, and insert another page break.

d. Under the *Rules for Vendors* heading, select the second through sixth paragraphs of text (the five rules). Click the Numbering button to make this a numbered list.

e. Find and select the paragraph beginning with the word *NOTE*. Change the font to Arial and the font size to 11. Select *NOTE:* and click Bold; select the text of the note and click Italic.

f. Select the last nine lines of text in the document (under *Purchasing Timetable*). On the Format menu, select Bullets and Numbering. On the Outline Numbered tab, select the *1) a) i)* outline format and click OK. Select items 2 and 3 under *30 days before bidding* and click Increase Indent to make them secondary items. Follow the same procedure for the items below *15 days before bidding* and 7 *days before bidding* **(see Figure 2.40)**.

g. On the View menu, click Header and Footer. Click Switch Between Header and Footer to view the footer area. At the left side of the footer area, type New Bidding Procedures and close the Header and Footer toolbar. On the Insert menu, click Page Numbers. Insert a right-aligned page number at the bottom of the page (show the number on the first page).

h. Save and close the document, but keep Word running.

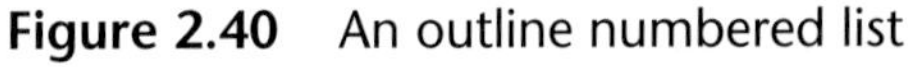

Figure 2.40 An outline numbered list

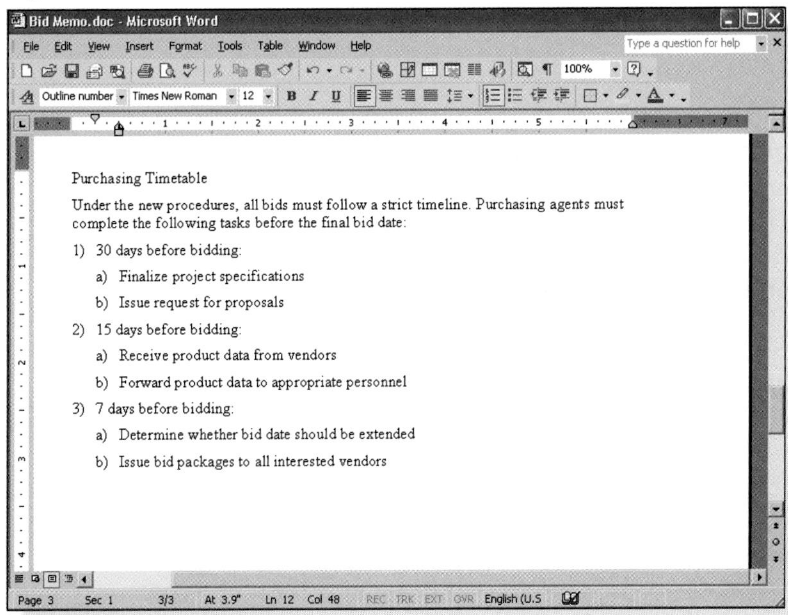

Word

Do It Yourself

1. Finish a Letter to a Customer

As the Sales Manager at a large auto dealership, one of your responsibilities is to respond to complaints from customers. Recently, you received a long letter from a customer who is very unhappy with a truck he just purchased. Before you send your reply, you need to do some formatting to make your correspondence look professional.

To finish the letter, do the following:

a. Open *Truck Complaint.doc.* Save the file as *xxx-Truck Complaint.doc.* Insert a page break to move the last paragraph to the second page.

b. On the first page, format each of the three main points so they appear in a numbered list. Decrease the list indent so the numbers are flush with the left margin. Within the numbered list, apply italic to the first sentence in each item.

c. Create a header. Type the customer's name at the left end of the header, insert a page number in the center of the header, and insert today's date at the right end of the header. (***Note:*** Click Insert Page Number on the Header and Footer toolbar to insert the page number.) Make sure the header does not appear on the letter's first page.

d. Save and close the document, but keep Word running.

2. Format a Recall Memo

You are the general manager of a chain of candy stores. You just learned that a maker of a brand of peppermint candy that you sell is recalling one of its products. You need to send a memo to your store managers advising them to remove the product from the shelves. The memo includes a quotation from the candy maker, and you want to format the paragraph to set it off.

To complete your memo, do the following:

a. Open the file *Candy Recall.doc.* Save the file as *xxx-Candy Recall.doc.* Type your name at the right end of the *From* line.

b. Indent the direct quotation from the manufacturer one-half inch from both the left and right margins.

c. Change the font and font size of the direct quotation to 10-point Courier New. (***Note:*** If you don't have the Courier font, choose another.) Underline the entire paragraph and set line spacing to 1.5 lines **(see Figure 2.41)**.

d. Save and close the document, but keep Word running.

Figure 2.41 The formatted quotation

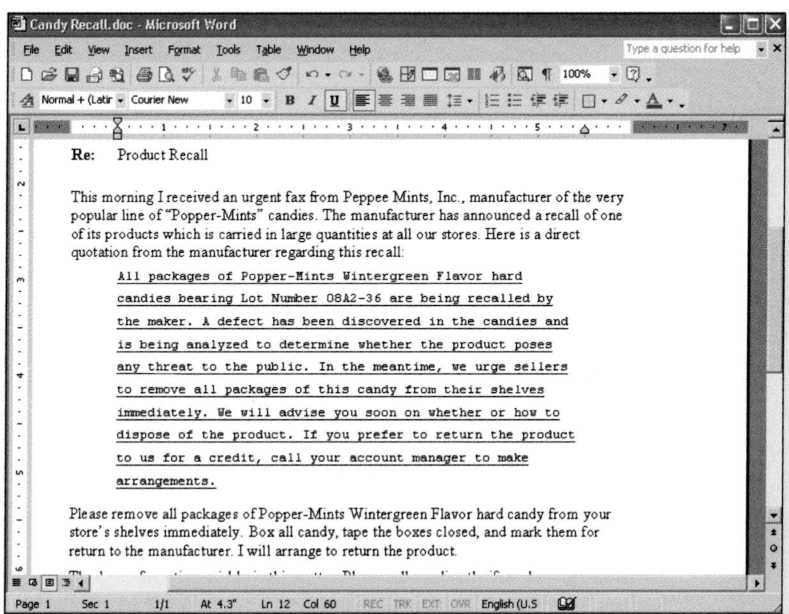

Re: Product Recall

This morning I received an urgent fax from Peppee Mints, Inc., manufacturer of the very popular line of "Popper-Mints" candies. The manufacturer has announced a recall of one of its products which is carried in large quantities at all our stores. Here is a direct quotation from the manufacturer regarding this recall:

> All packages of Popper-Mints Wintergreen Flavor hard candies bearing Lot Number 08A2-36 are being recalled by the maker. A defect has been discovered in the candies and is being analyzed to determine whether the product poses any threat to the public. In the meantime, we urge sellers to remove all packages of this candy from their shelves immediately. We will advise you soon on whether or how to dispose of the product. If you prefer to return the product to us for a credit, call your account manager to make arrangements.

Please remove all packages of Popper-Mints Wintergreen Flavor hard candy from your store's shelves immediately. Box all candy, tape the boxes closed, and mark them for return to the manufacturer. I will arrange to return the product.

3. Prepare an Itinerary for a Seminar

As the Assistant to the Director of Human Resources, you have been asked to set the agenda for a seminar for HR professionals. Take these steps to finish formatting your itinerary:

a. Open *TelCon Itinerary.doc.* Save the file as *xxx-TelCon Itinerary.doc.* Below the title the itinerary is broken into three sections listing the speakers, the schedule of activities, and the panel discussions. Make the three introductory sentences (above each of the three parts of the itinerary) 11-point Arial, italic.

b. Make the list below *Today's special guest speakers* into a bulleted list.

c. Using tabs, format the schedule of activities as a two-column list. Keep the time for each event flush left. Move each event description to a second column at a left-aligned tab stop at the 1.75" mark on the ruler.

d. Format the list of discussion panelists as an outline numbered list using the titles as the primary items and the participants' names as the secondary items.

e. Save and close the document, but keep Word running.

4. Red-Hot Giveaway

You are the General Manager of an FM radio station. One of your clients has given you four tickets to next year's Kentucky Derby. You want to give the tickets to some of your employees, so you invite all of them to enter their names in a drawing. You have created a memo containing a fun entry form and you need to finish formatting it. Follow these steps:

a. Open *Drawing.doc.* Save your document as *xxx-Drawing.doc.* Type your name at the right end of the *From* line.

b. Select the paragraph *Let's Have a Drawing!*, center it, change its font size to 16 points, and change the font to Arial. Change the font color to red.

c. Select the line *Cut Here* and all the material below it. Place a border around all four sides. Place yellow shading behind the boxed paragraphs **(see Figure 2.42)** .

d. Save and close the document, but keep Word running.

Figure 2.42 Formatting a fun entry form

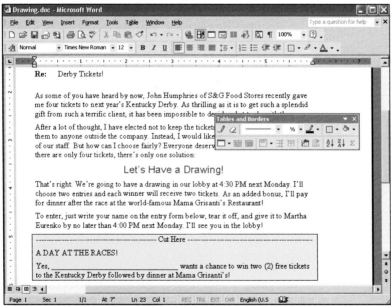

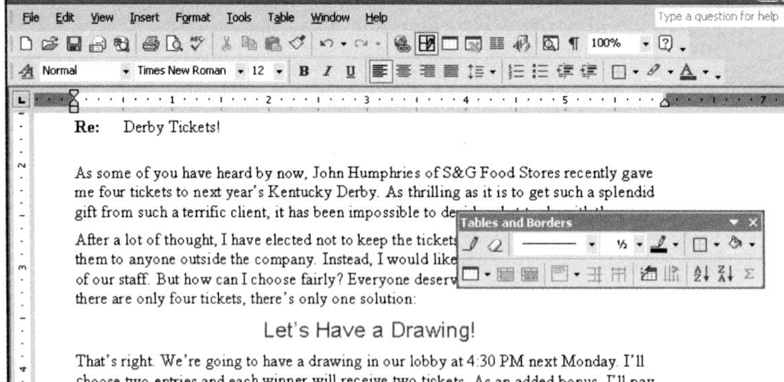

Challenge Yourself

Polish Up a Research Paper

You are the archivist (corporate historian) for a large consumer products company. The most important part of your job is working with your company's public relations department to help reinforce the appropriate corporate image with various consumer groups and organizations. You do this by attending all kinds of events, often as a guest speaker.

You have been asked to prepare a short research paper to present at a seminar entitled Capitalism and Social Responsibility. Your role is to present some basic facts about the industrial revolution in England to serve as a starting point for discussion. Your paper must be brief and to the point and focus on basic facts. It is time to complete your paper so you can have copies made for the seminar.

- Open *Industrial Revolution.doc.* Type your name at the appropriate location after the title. Separate the title page (which shows the paper's name and your name) from the rest of the document by inserting a page break. Center the title page text horizontally. Make the title italic.
- With the exception of the title page, endnotes, and bibliography, change line spacing for all text to 1.5 and add six points of space after each paragraph. The endnotes and bibliography entries should be single-spaced but should have six points of space after each paragraph.
- Except for the title page, add a page number in the upper-right corner of each page. Add a footer to the document: at the left side of the footer, type the paper's title; at the right side of the footer, insert the date. Format the footer as 10-point Arial, and make the title italic. (The footer should not be visible on the title page.)
- Insert page breaks to make sure *Endnotes* and *Bibliography* appear on separate pages.
- Find the two long block-style quotations that are introduced by colons. Delete the quotation marks around them. Indent the block-style quotations one-half inch from both the right and left margins. They should be single-spaced.
- Find the list that begins with *5.8 million*. Apply a bullet format to the list.
- Change all text to 12-point Times New Roman. Remove the underline format in the bibliography titles and change them to italic. Save the document as *xxx-Industrial Revolution.doc.* Close the document.

Lesson 3

Working With Tables, Graphics, and Columns

Lesson Exercise Objectives

After completing this lesson, you'll be able to do the following tasks:

1. Apply highlights and text effects
2. Create and modify tables
3. Format a table
4. Insert graphics into a document
5. Apply and modify newsletter columns
6. Print a letter, an envelope, and a label

Key Terms

- cell (p. 84)
- character effect (p. 82)
- chart (p. 96)
- clip art (p. 96)
- datasheet (p. 96)
- diagram (p. 96)
- highlight (p. 82)
- landscape orientation (p. 106)
- margin (p. 106)
- merge (p. 84)
- organization chart (p. 96)
- portrait orientation (p. 106)
- split (p. 84)
- table (p. 84)
- text effect (p. 82)

Microsoft Office Specialist Activities

W2002: 1.1, 1.4, 3.2, 3.3, 3.4, 3.5, 5.1, 5.2

Real-Life Business Applications

Lesson Case Study

In this lesson, you will play the role of the subscriber service director for *Sun and Sea*, a magazine devoted to cruise ship travel and vacationing. Keep the following information in mind as you work through the lesson exercises.

- **Job responsibilities and goals.** As subscriber service director, you deal with subscribers to your magazine. You are responsible for attracting new subscribers, tracking subscription activity and revenues, creating special promotions for subscribers, and ensuring that subscription-related problems are solved.
- **The project.** You have three projects to complete. First, you need to finish a report for your company's editorial board summarizing subscription sales for the past quarter. Second, you need to format a newsletter that you send to travel agents. Finally, you'll create and print a letter, envelope, and mailing label.
- **The challenge ahead.** All the tasks in this lesson require you to use some of Word's most powerful and specialized tools. When you're finished, your documents need to appear professional.

Microsoft Office Specialist W2002 1.4

Exercise 1 Overview: Apply Highlights and Text Effects

Have you ever used a colored highlighting pen to mark a word or a line of text in a book? Word lets you do the same thing in a document. Using the **Highlight** feature, you can make selected text stand out by giving it a colored background.

In addition to highlighting, Word provides two other kinds of effects: animated text effects and nonanimated character effects. Animated (moving) **text effects**, that may include sparkling text or a moving border, can only be viewed on screen.

Need Help?
Type: text effects

Nonanimated **character effects**—such as superscript, subscript, or strikethrough—can serve many different purposes. If you are editing someone else's document, for example, you can format a passage with the strikethrough effect to show that the text should be deleted.

In the following exercises, you will add highlighting and text and character effects to a document.

Step Through It™

Exercise 1A: Highlight words and phrases

1. Open *Subscription Activity.doc.* Save the document as *xxx-Subscription Activity.doc.*
2. Scroll to the *Summary* section. In the first line of the bulleted list, select *increased 11%.*
3. Click the Highlight down arrow (see Figure 3.1).
4. Click the yellow box.
5. In the last line of the bulleted list, select *up 12%* and click the Highlight button (*not* the down arrow) to apply a yellow highlight.

Figure 3.1 Highlighting selected text

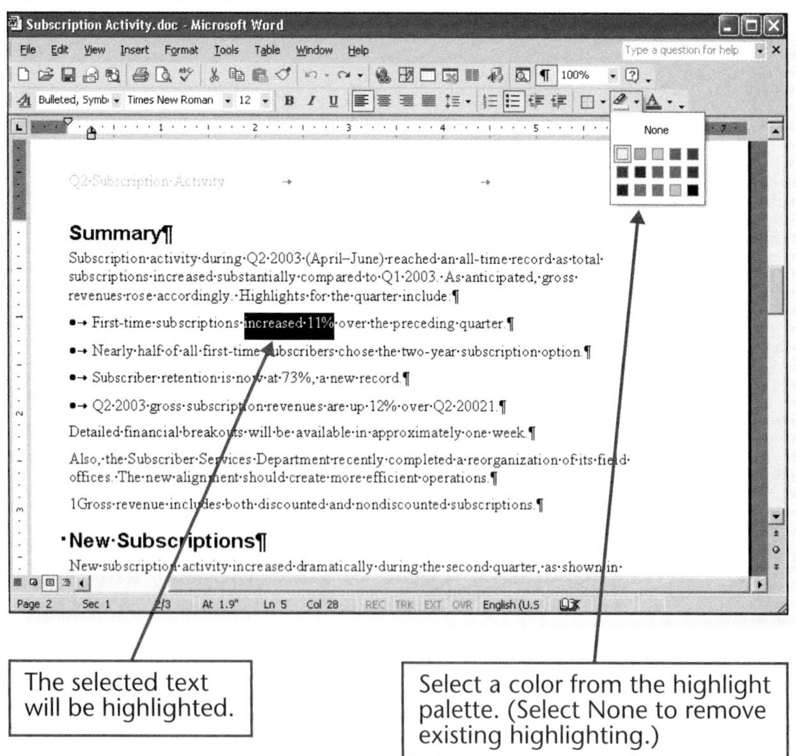

Figure 3.2 Selecting an animated text effect

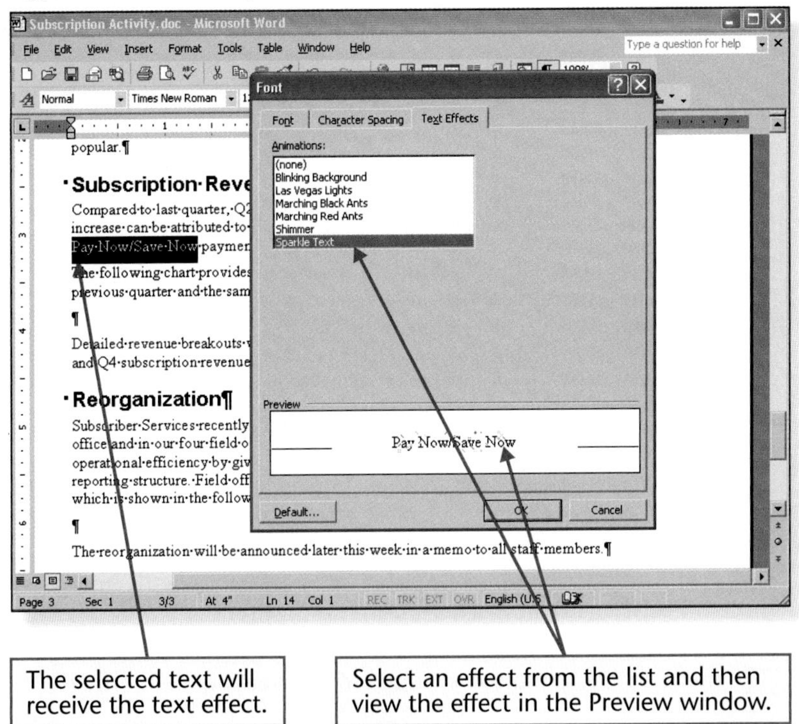

The selected text will receive the text effect.
Select an effect from the list and then view the effect in the Preview window.

Step Through It™

Exercise 1B: Apply text effects

1. Find the *Subscription Revenues* section. In the third line of the first paragraph, select *Pay Now/Save Now.*
2. On the Format menu, select Font to open the Font dialog box. Click the Text Effects tab.
3. In the *Animations* list, click Sparkle Text and preview the effect (see Figure 3.2). Click OK. Click the document to view the effect.
4. Save the document.

Word

Figure 3.3 Selecting a character effect

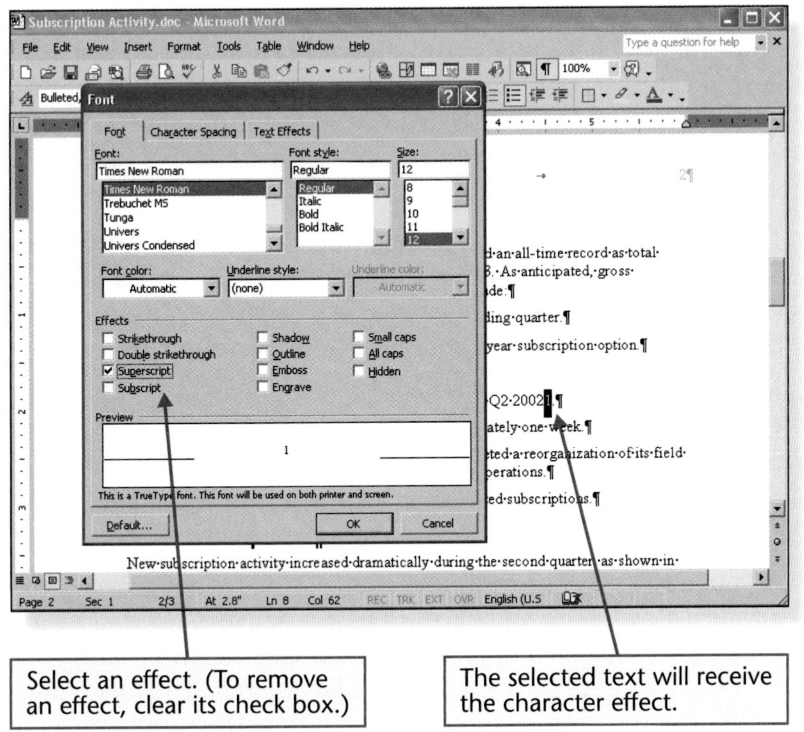

Select an effect. (To remove an effect, clear its check box.)
The selected text will receive the character effect.

Step Through It™

Exercise 1C: Apply character effects

1. Go to the *Summary* section. In the last bulleted line of the section, select *1* at the end of the sentence.
2. On the Format menu, select Font to open the Font dialog box. Click the Font tab.
3. In the *Effects* section, select the *Superscript* check box (see Figure 3.3). Click OK to apply the superscript character effect.

Word

4. In the *Summary* section, select *1* at the beginning of the last sentence. Press F4 to format the number as a superscript. *Note:* Pressing F4 repeats the last command.

5. Set the footnote text to italic.

6. Save your document.

Figure 3.4 Superscript number in a footnote

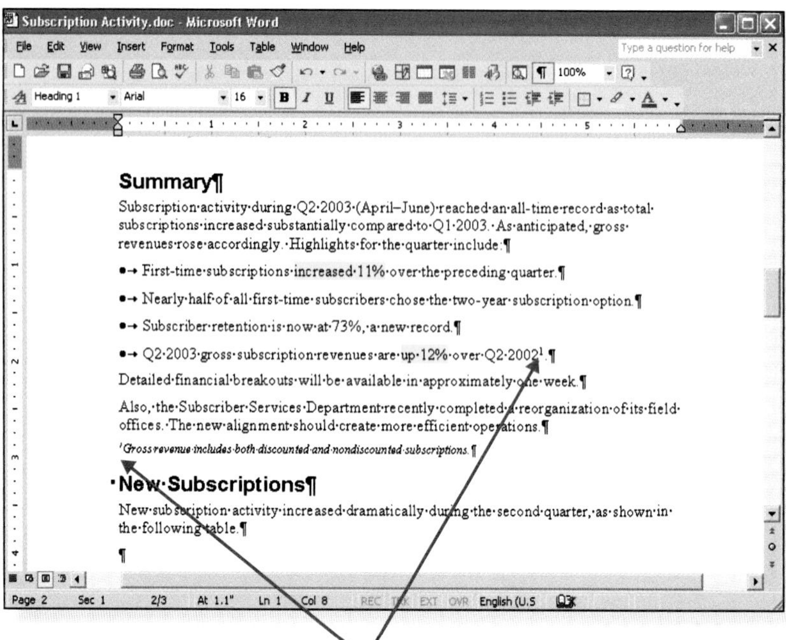

The numbers are formatted as superscripts, creating an informal footnote.

Microsoft Office Specialist W2002 3.4

Exercise 2 Overview: Create and Modify Tables

Sometimes the best way to display information is by putting it in a table. A **table** is a grid made up of horizontal rows and vertical columns. When a row and column intersect, the resulting box is called a **cell.** A cell is the part of a table that actually stores information.

Tables are commonly used in business reports to show sales figures for products by month, quarter, or another period of time. Tables are useful because they organize data in a way that makes the information easy to understand.

Type: table

A table can have any number of rows or columns, although you may need to limit a table's size. You can add rows or columns to a table, if necessary. You can **merge** multiple cells by joining them together and creating one large cell or **split** a cell by dividing it into two or more cells.

If you have a lot of numbers to type, learn how to use the numeric keypad on your keyboard. Press Num Lock, position your thumb on the 0 key, your little finger on Enter, and your first three fingers on the 4, 5, and 6 keys. Press Tab to advance across the row from cell to cell as you type the numbers.

In the following exercises, you will create and modify tables.

Figure 3.5 Creating a table

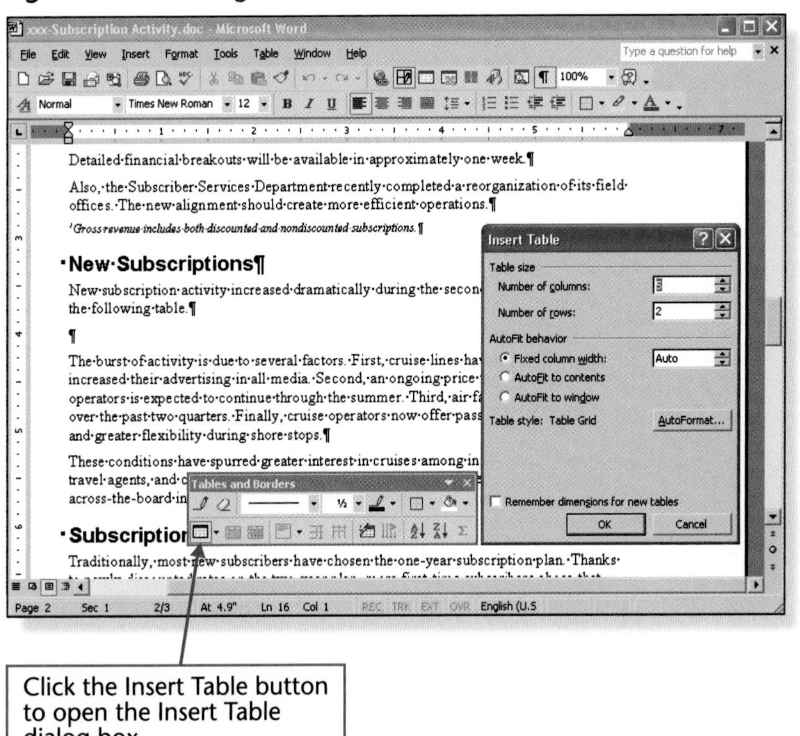

Step Through It™

Exercise 2A: Create a table

1. Find the *New Subscriptions* section. Click the blank line between the first two paragraphs.
2. Click Tables and Borders on the Standard toolbar to activate the Tables and Borders toolbar. Click Insert Table on the toolbar to open the Insert Table dialog box (see Figure 3.5).

Figure 3.6 The newly inserted table

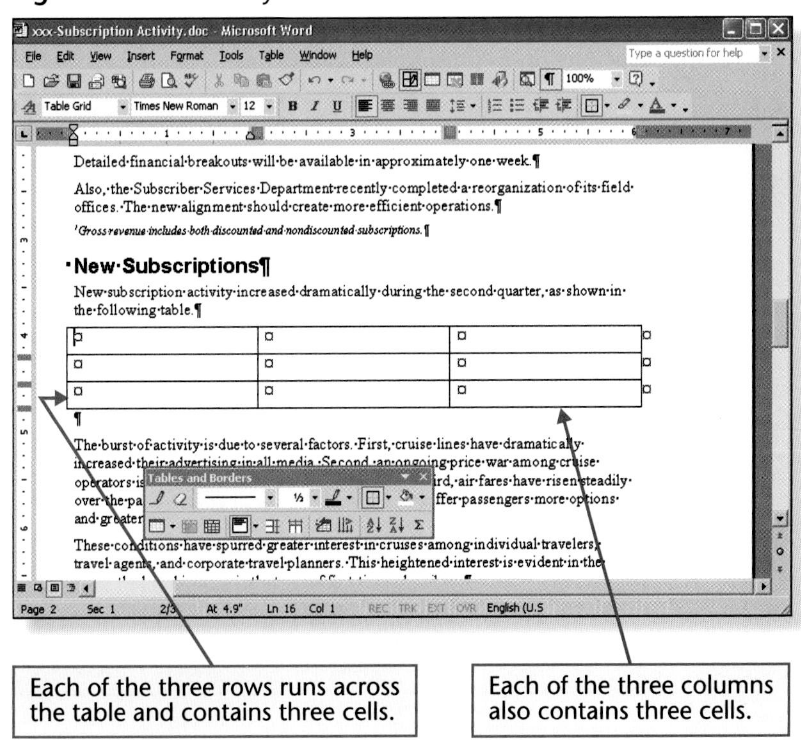

Each of the three rows runs across the table and contains three cells.
Each of the three columns also contains three cells.

3. In the *Number of columns* box, set the number of columns to 3.
4. In the *Number of rows* box, set the number of rows to 3.
5. Select the *Fixed column width* option, and select *Auto* in the *Fixed column width* box. Click OK.
6. Word inserts a table containing three columns and three rows (see Figure 3.6).

Word

7. With the insertion point in the table cell to the upper left, type the word Type and press Tab.

8. Type the data shown in the table in Figure 3.7. Activate Num Lock and use the numeric keypad to type the numbers. ***Note:*** You can navigate through a table by clicking in a cell, pressing the Tab key, or pressing the arrow keys.

9. Delete the empty paragraph mark below the table.

10. With the insertion point in the paragraph that follows the table, add six points of paragraph spacing between the paragraph and the table (see Figure 3.7).

Figure 3.7 The table with newly entered data

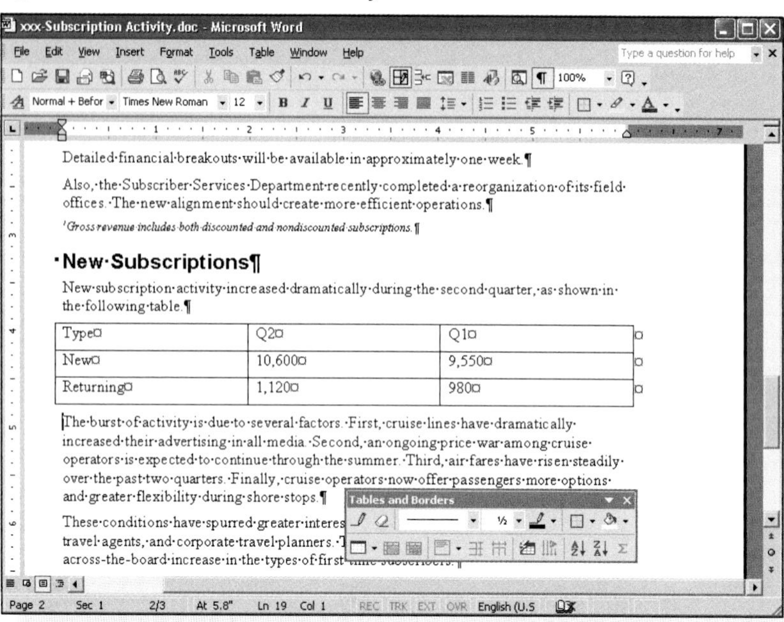

Step Through It™

Exercise 2B: Insert a column or row

1. Click anywhere in the table's third row. On the Tables and Borders toolbar, click the Insert Table down arrow to open a menu of options (see Figure 3.8).

Figure 3.8 Options on the Insert Table button

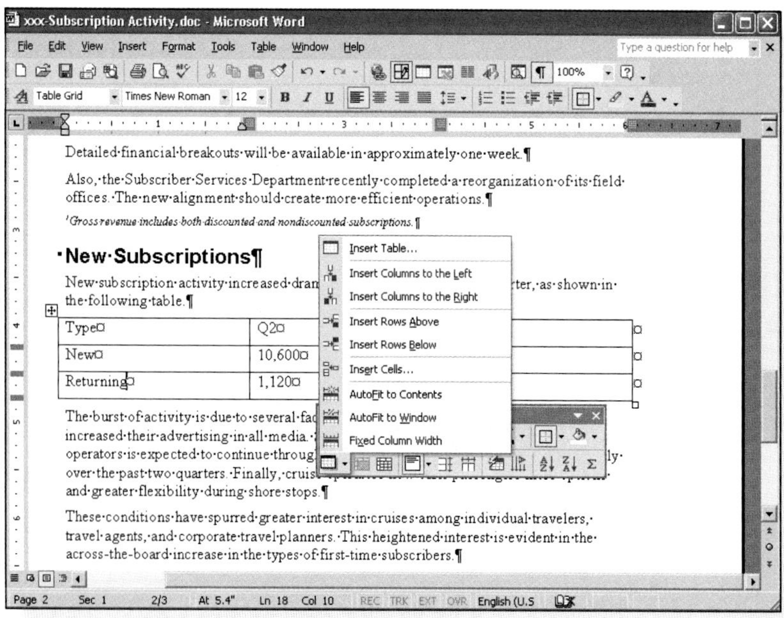

Figure 3.9 The table with a new column

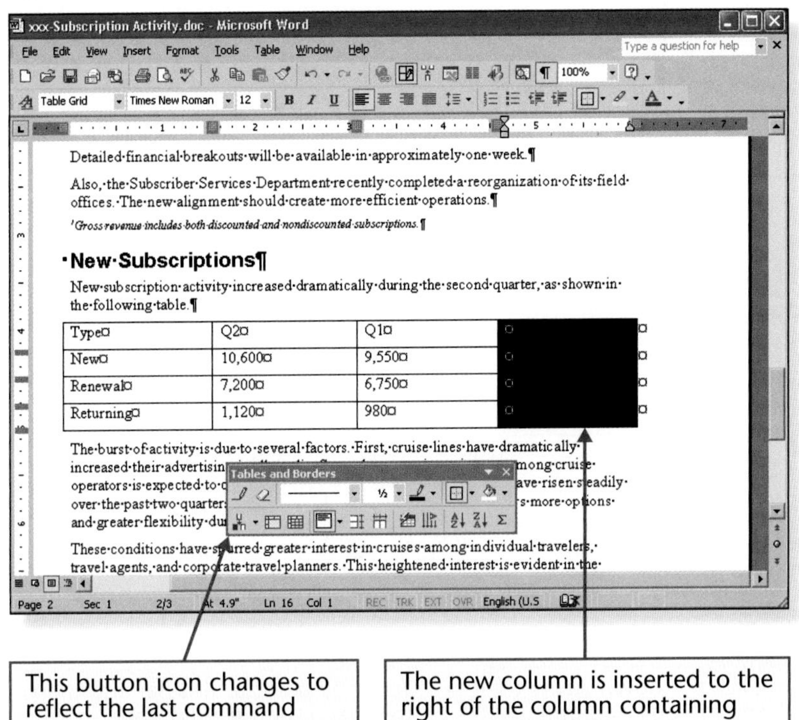

2. Select *Insert Rows Above* to insert a new, blank row above the row containing the insertion point.
3. Click in the new row's first cell and type Renewal. Press Tab and type 7,200. Press Tab and type 6,750 in the last cell.
4. With the insertion point in the table's last column, click the Insert Rows Above down arrow. On the menu, select *Insert Columns to the Right* to add a new column to the table (see Figure 3.9).

Figure 3.10 The new column with data

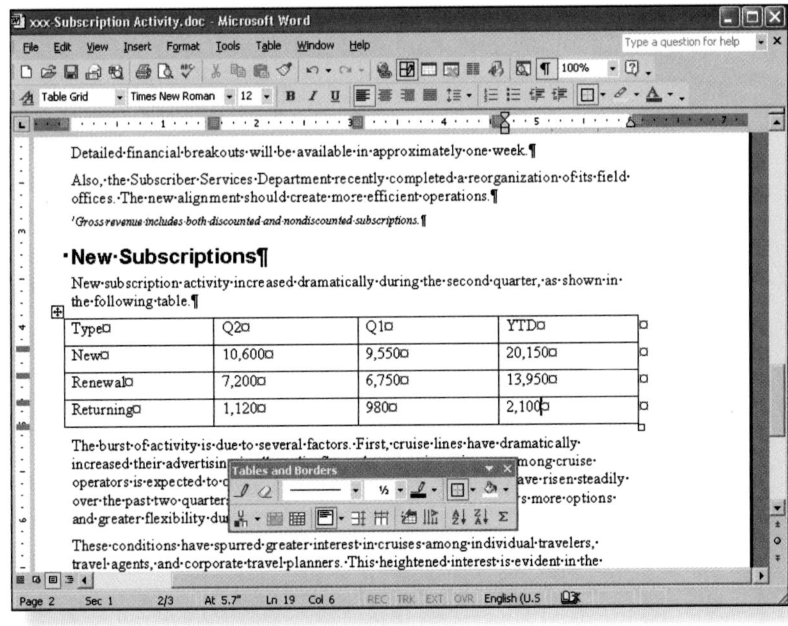

5. Click in the new column's top cell and type YTD (for Year to Date).
6. In the column's second cell, type 20,150. In the third cell, type 13,950. In the last cell, type 2,100. (See Figure 3.10.)
7. Save your changes.

To delete a row or column, click the row or column. On the Table menu, point to Delete and click Rows or Columns.

Step Through It™

Exercise 2C: Change text alignment

1. Point to the margin at the left of the table's first row. When the pointer changes to an arrow, click to select the entire first row of the table.
2. On the Tables and Borders toolbar, click the Align Top Left down arrow to open the Cell Alignment menu (see Figure 3.11).

Figure 3.11 Accessing the cell-alignment tools

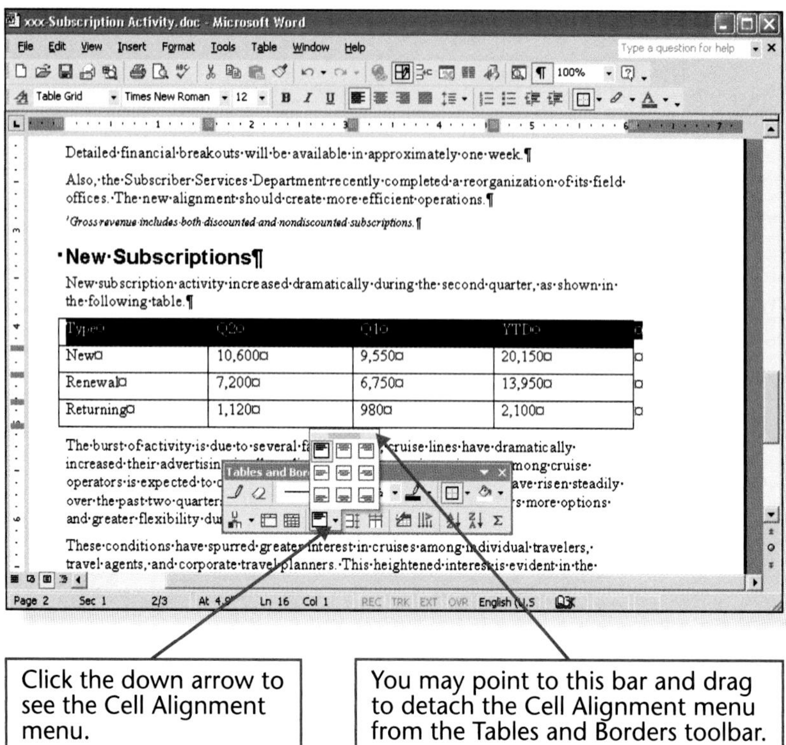

3. Point to the bar at the top of the menu and then drag the menu away from the toolbar.
4. On the floating menu, click Align Center.
5. Drag to select all the cells with numbers, starting with the cell containing *10,600* and ending with the cell containing *2,100*.
6. Click Align Center Right (see Figure 3.12).
7. Click the table to deselect the cells. Close the Cell Alignment menu.

Figure 3.12 Changing cell alignment

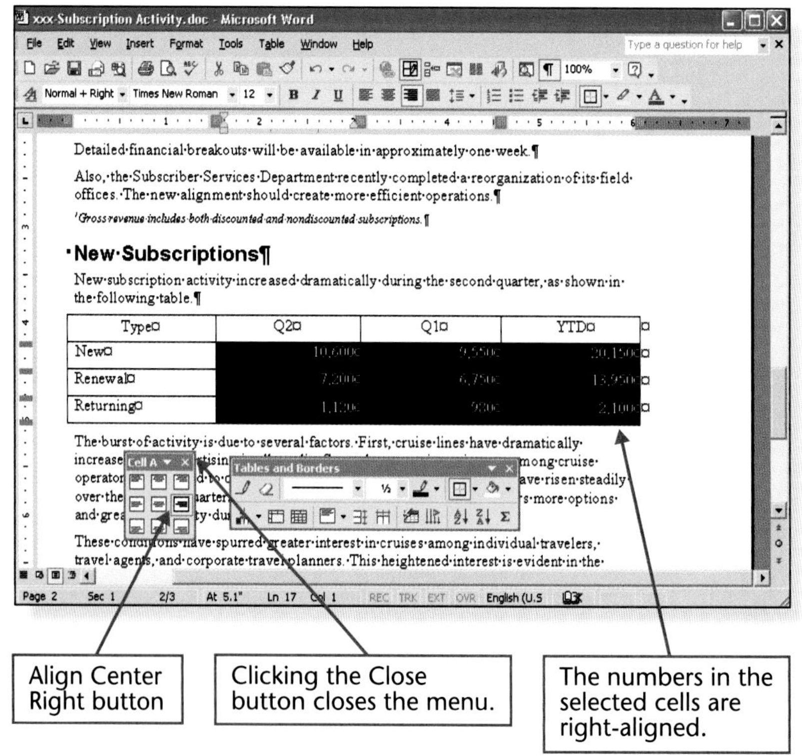

Align Center Right button
Clicking the Close button closes the menu.
The numbers in the selected cells are right-aligned.

Word

Figure 3.13 The Split Cells dialog box

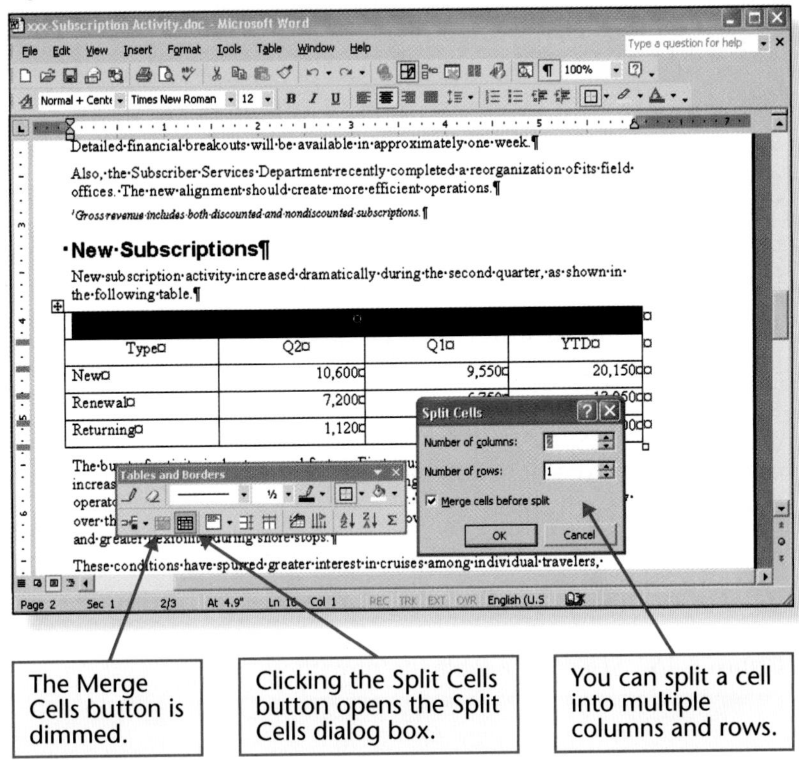

Figure 3.14 Data entered in the split cell

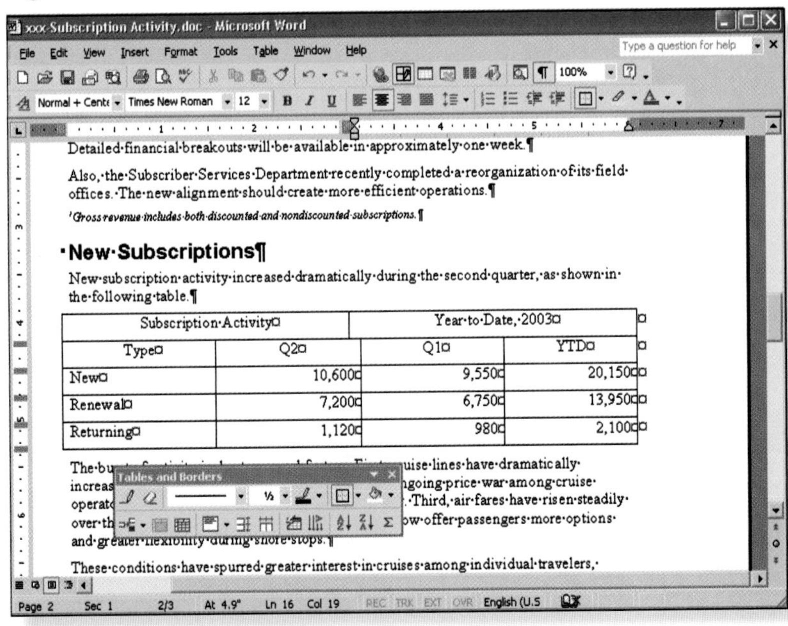

Step Through It™

Exercise 2D: Merge and split cells

1. Add a new row to the top of the table.
2. With the new row selected, click Merge Cells on the Tables and Borders toolbar. The four selected cells are merged together creating one cell.
3. With the first row still selected, click Split Cells on the Tables and Borders toolbar to open the Split Cells dialog box (see Figure 3.13).
4. In the Split Cells dialog box, set the number of columns to 2 and the number of rows to 1.
5. Click OK to split the selected cell.
6. In the first cell in the top row, type Subscription Activity. In the second cell, type Year to Date, 2003 (see Figure 3.14).
7. Save your changes.

Word

You may drag a row or column border to increase or decrease the column width or row height.

Microsoft Office Specialist W2002 3.4

Exercise 3 Overview:
Format a Table

You can format a table in a number of ways to enhance its appearance. For instance, you can place borders around cells or between rows or columns, or you can add shading. You can use multiple fonts in the same table—for example, you could use Arial for column labels and Times New Roman for the data.

You can manually format a table by using the tools available on the Tables and Borders toolbar and the Formatting toolbar. If you are in a hurry, Word's Table AutoFormat tool can automatically do the job for you by adding attractive borders, shading, fonts, and other design features to your table.

In the following exercises, you will format a table.

Step Through It™
Exercise 3A: Apply an AutoFormat

1. Scroll down and insert a page break just before the *Subscription Plans* heading.
2. Point to the table in the *Subscription Plans* section. A move handle appears at the table's upper-left corner (see Figure 3.15). Click the move handle to select the entire table.

Figure 3.15 Selecting a table for formatting

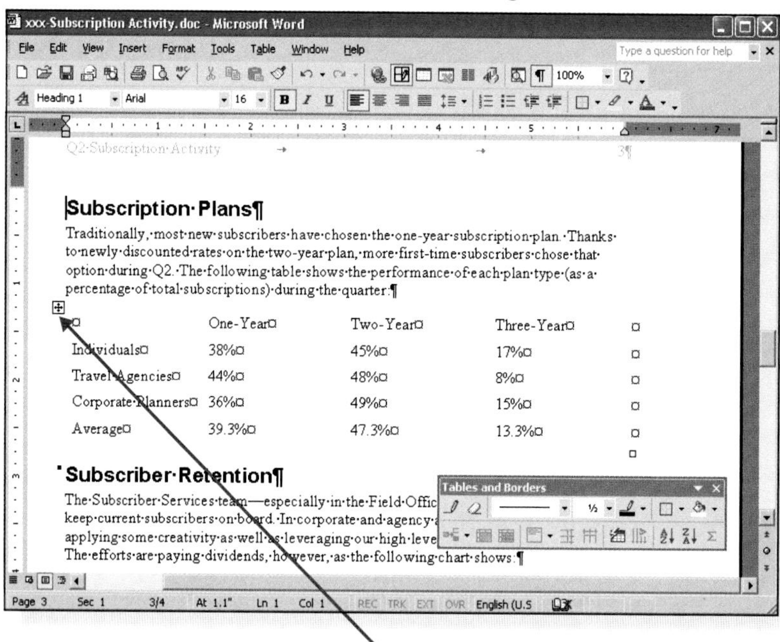

A move handle appears when you point to the table. Click the move handle to select the entire table.

You can number the cells in a table by selecting the cells and clicking the Numbering button on the Formatting toolbar.

Figure 3.16 Selecting AutoFormat options

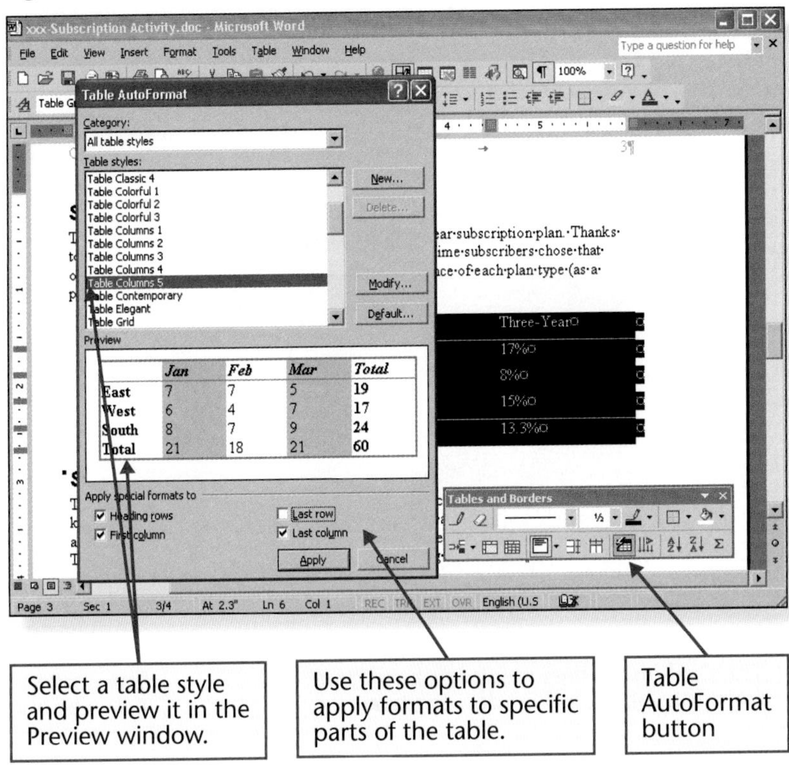

Select a table style and preview it in the Preview window.
Use these options to apply formats to specific parts of the table.
Table AutoFormat button

3. Click Table AutoFormat on the Tables and Borders toolbar to open the Table AutoFormat dialog box.
4. In the *Table styles* list, select *Table Columns 5*. Clear the *Last row* check box to remove special formatting from the table's last row.
5. Preview the table style in the Preview window (see Figure 3.16). Click Apply.

Word

Figure 3.17 The formatted table

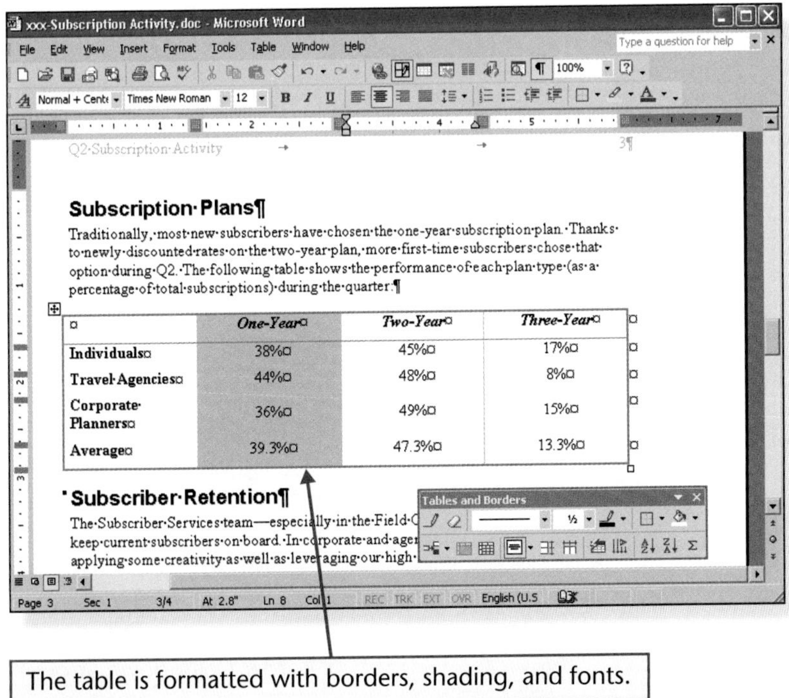

The table is formatted with borders, shading, and fonts.

6. Select the data in the four cells below the *Three-Year* column label and click Bold to remove the bold formatting.
7. Point to the top border of the table's second column. When a down arrow appears, drag to select the second, third, and fourth columns. Center the data in the selected cells. Click the table to view your changes (see Figure 3.17).

Step Through It™
Exercise 3B: Add borders

1. Find the table within the *New Subscriptions* section. Select the table's first row. On the Table menu, point to Delete and select Rows.

2. Drag to select *Type* in the table's first cell and press Delete.

3. Select the entire table. On the Tables and Borders toolbar, click the Outside Border down arrow. Point to the bar at the top of the Borders menu and drag the menu away from the toolbar (see Figure 3.18).

Figure 3.18 The floating Borders menu

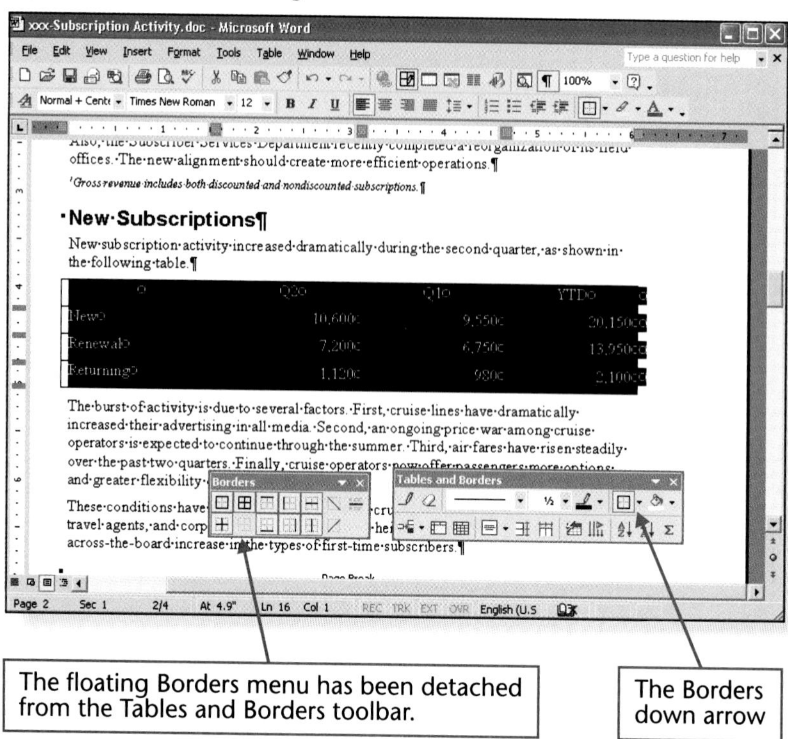

The floating Borders menu has been detached from the Tables and Borders toolbar.
The Borders down arrow

4. Click No Border. Click the Line Style down arrow and select the solid line at the top of the menu.

5. Click the Line Weight down arrow and select *1 1/2 pt.* Click the Border Color down arrow and select *Gray-50%.*

6. On the Borders menu, click Outside Border. Click the table to view it (see Figure 3.19).

7. Select the table's first row and change the line weight to 1/2 pt. On the Borders menu, click Bottom Border.

Figure 3.19 Adding a custom outside border

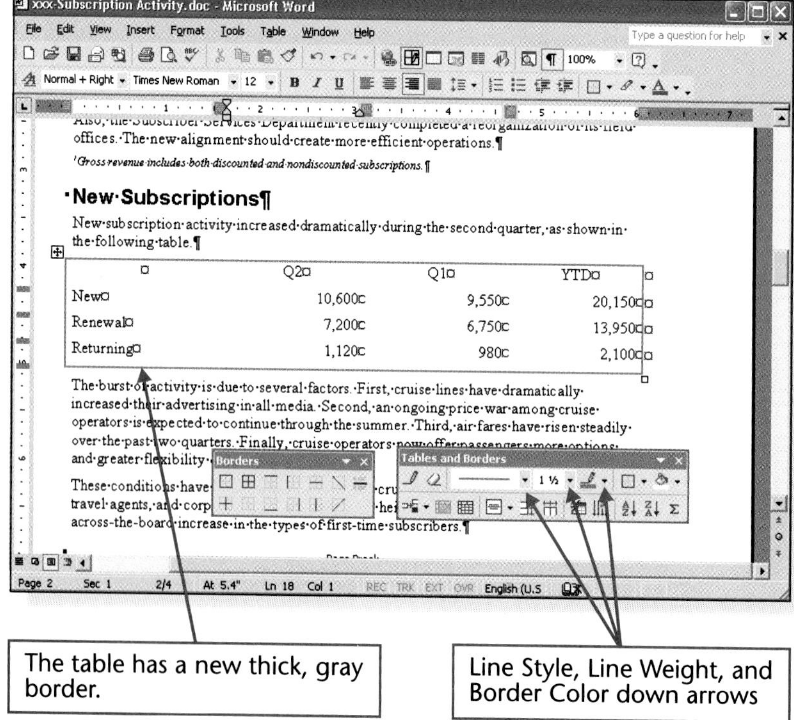

The table has a new thick, gray border.
Line Style, Line Weight, and Border Color down arrows

Figure 3.20 The table with custom borders and shading

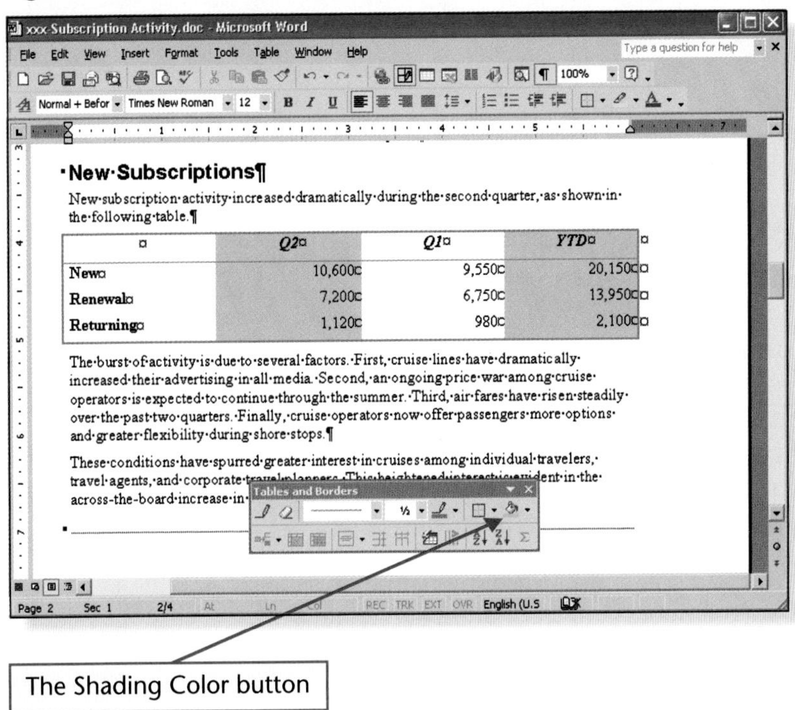

Figure 3.21 The formatted Subscription Plans table

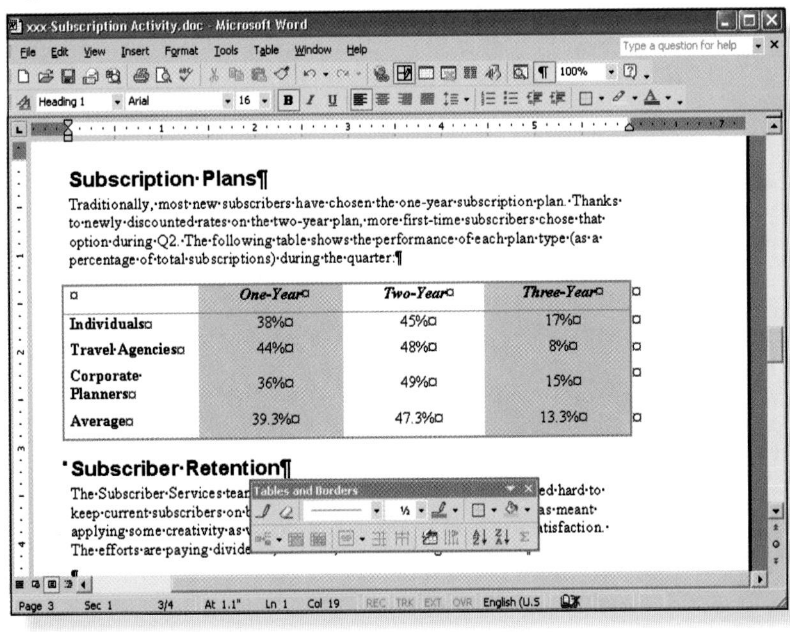

Step Through It™

Exercise 3C: Add shading

1. Close the floating Borders menu. Select the table's second column. Click the Shading Color down arrow and click *Gray-25%* to add gray shading to the column.

2. Select the table's last column and click Shading Color (*not* the down arrow) to apply the same shading to that column. Apply bold and italic to the top row, and apply bold to the first column. Click to view the table (see Figure 3.20).

3. Scroll to the table in the *Subscription Plans* section. Select its last column and click Shading Color to apply the *Gray-25%* shading. Click to view the table (see Figure 3.21). The two tables now have similar formatting.

4. Close the Tables and Borders toolbar.

5. Save the document.

Word

APPLY IT! After finishing Exercises 1–3, you may test your skills by completing Apply It! Guided Activity 1, Format a Table in a Letter.

Business Connections

Standard Business Graphics

Graphics are a great addition to nearly any document. Just imagine reading a textbook or magazine that didn't have any illustrations! The same is true of business documents, especially long, formal documents, suh as business reports. Sometimes even a short memo or letter needs a graphic element such as a table, chart, or clip art to help illustrate a point. Graphics serve two important purposes. First, they can help you explain facts or ideas more clearly. Second, graphics can greatly improve the appearance of any document.

Charts

Charts enable you to display numeric data visually, and they can be easier to understand than numbers alone. There are many kinds of charts, and each type has a specific use.

Tables

Tables allow you to organize information in a logical way. When you use a table, you have the luxury of simply laying out the facts in order.

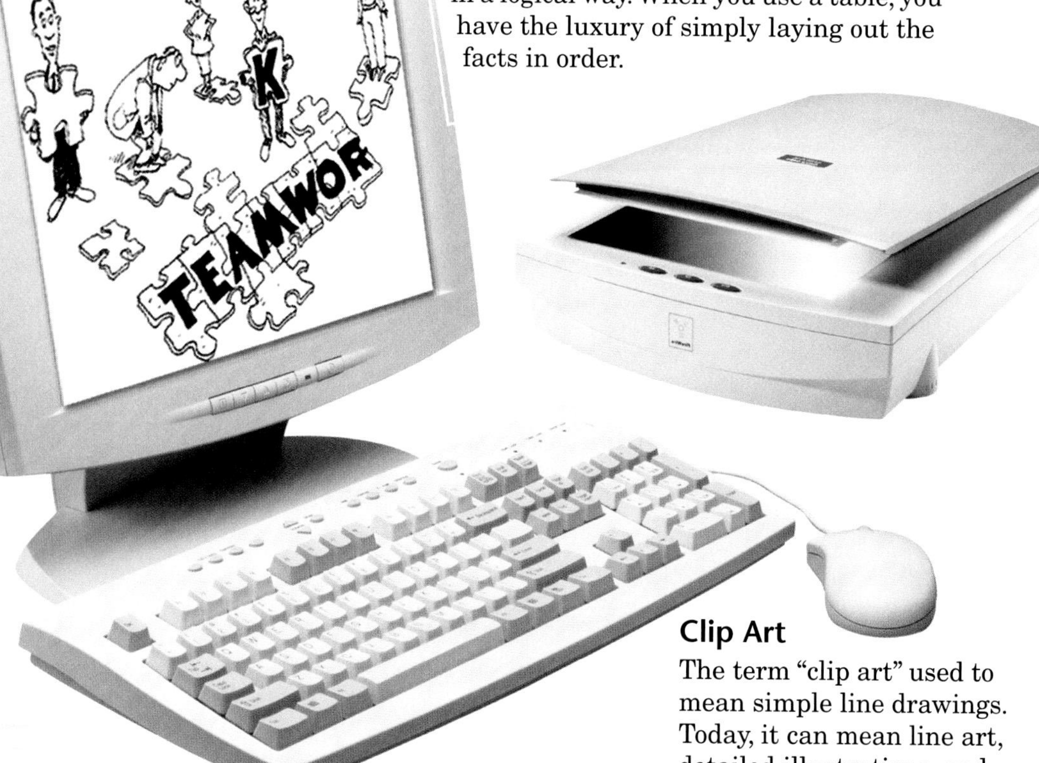

Clip Art

The term "clip art" used to mean simple line drawings. Today, it can mean line art, detailed illustrations, and even photos.

Diagrams

Diagrams are widely used in business for a variety of purposes. One of the most common types of diagrams is the organization chart, which shows how a company's departments or personnel are organized.

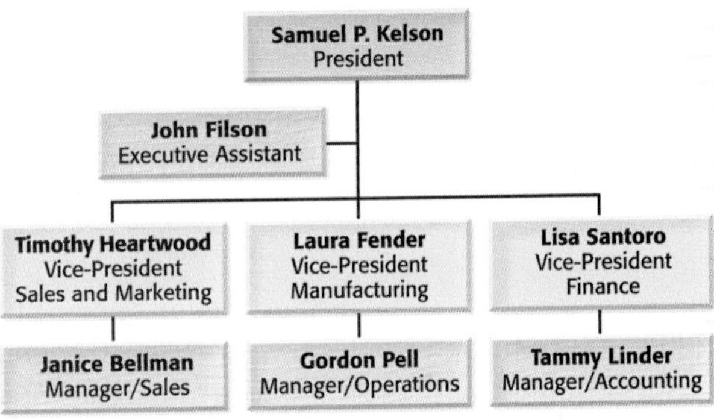

Microsoft Word has built-in tools that let you add all these kinds of graphics to a document. You can use these tools to create custom tables, charts, and diagrams from scratch, format them, and insert them anywhere in a document. Word's clip art tools give you access to thousands of pieces of clip art.

Of course, if you have a drawing program, a digital camera, or a scanner, you can create your own illustrations and add them to a document.

But if you plan to use these tools, never use graphics that someone else created without first checking the conditions under which you may legally use them since illustrations of all types are protected by copyright.

CRITICAL THINKING

1. **Visually Representing Data** Describe a business or personal situation involving data that would be best represented in a pie chart
2. **Inserting a Diagram** View the Diagram Gallery by selecting Diagram on the Insert menu. What type of diagram would best represent a series of steps toward a goal?

Microsoft Office Specialist
W2002 1.1, 5.1, 5.2

Word

Exercise 4 Overview:
Insert Graphics Into a Document

An easy way to spice up a page of ordinary text is to use some of the clip art images that are built into Microsoft Office. **Clip art** images (such as line drawings, colorful illustrations, or photographs) are organized in categories that you can search or browse. Clip art graphics (sometimes called *clips*) are usually license-free, meaning you can freely use them in any document that you do not plan to sell.

Another important type of graphic is the chart. A **chart** is a graphic that visually presents numerical data. For example, suppose you want to compare the monthly sales data for three of your company's products. A chart lets you do this easily, and it enables the reader to understand the data instantly.

To build a chart, you enter numeric data in a special table called a **datasheet.** Word uses this data to construct the chart.

If you already have a chart in one document, you can easily reuse it in another document by linking the chart data from the first document to the second. To do this, you simply copy the chart and then use Word's Paste Special command (*not* the Paste command) to insert the chart into the second document.

Another special type of graphic is the **diagram,** which lets you illustrate conceptual information rather than numeric information. Word provides tools that let you build diagrams from scratch. One of the most common types of business diagrams is the **organization chart,** which shows how a company's departments or staff are structured.

In the following exercises, you will insert graphics into your document.

Figure 3.22 A chart represents numerical data

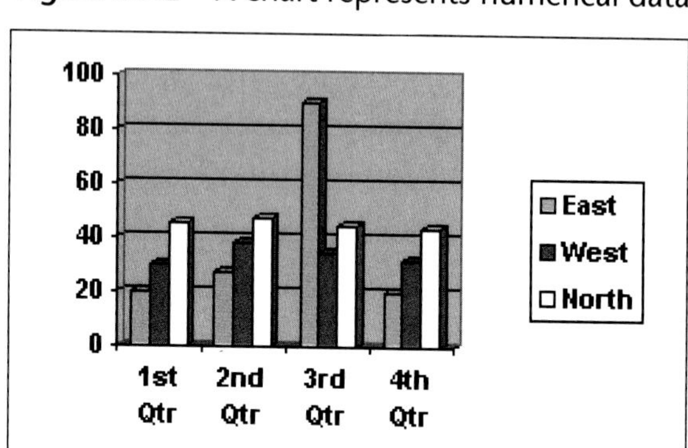

Figure 3.23 Searching for clip art

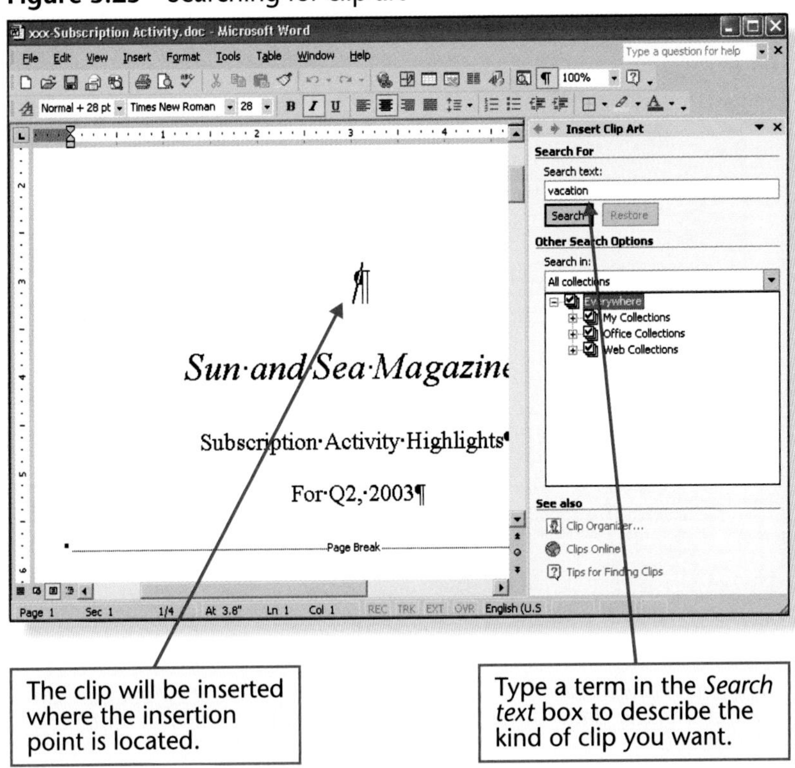

The clip will be inserted where the insertion point is located.
Type a term in the *Search text* box to describe the kind of clip you want.

Step Through It™

Exercise 4A: Insert clip art

1. Press Ctrl + Home to move to the top of the document.
2. On the Insert menu, point to Picture and select Clip Art to open the Insert Clip Art task pane.
3. In the *Search text* box, type vacation. Click the *Search in* down arrow and make sure that the *Everywhere* check box is selected in the collections list (see Figure 3.23). Click the down arrow again to close the list.

Figure 3.24 The clip art search results and inserted clip

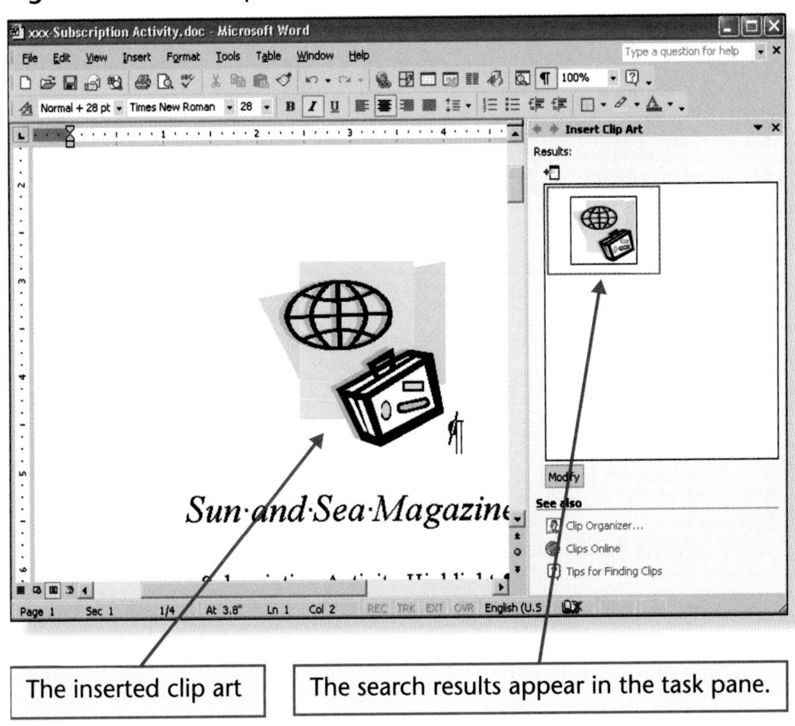

4. Click the *Results should be* down arrow, and make sure that the *All media types* check box is selected in the media file types list. Close the list.
5. Click Search to find clips that match your search criteria. ***Note***: The results of your search may vary from Figure 3.24 depending upon the clips installed on your system.
6. Point to a clip, click the down arrow, and then click Insert to insert the clip (see Figure 3.24). Close the task pane. Save the document.

Word

Step Through It™

Exercise 4B: Create and modify a chart

1. Find the *Subscriber Retention* section. Click an insertion point on the blank line between the first and second paragraphs.

2. On the Insert menu, point to Picture and click Chart. A sample chart appears in the document along with a datasheet in which you insert numeric data (see Figure 3.25).

Figure 3.25 A chart and datasheet with sample data

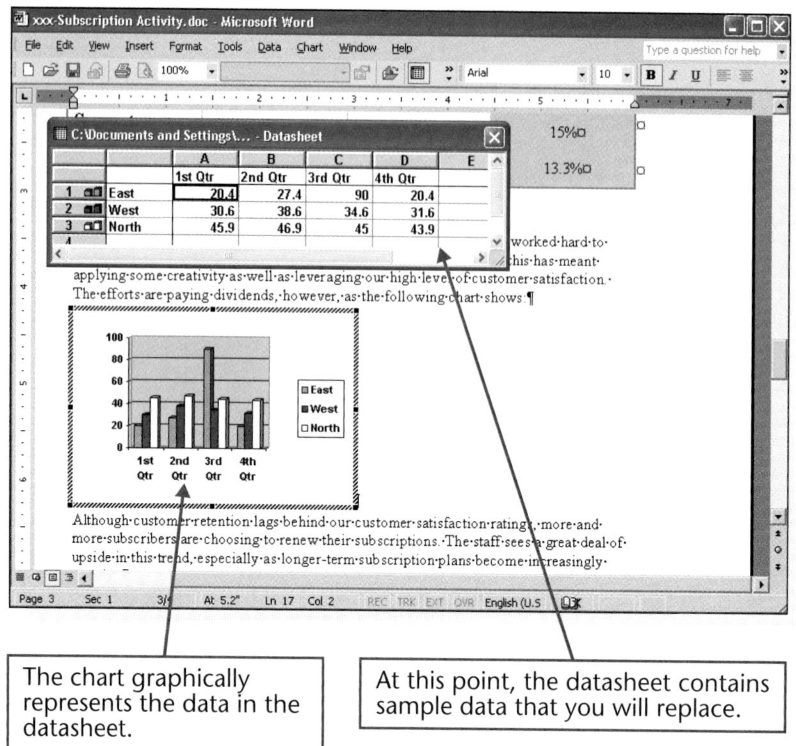

The chart graphically represents the data in the datasheet.
At this point, the datasheet contains sample data that you will replace.

3. Click the gray box in the upper-left corner of the datasheet to select the sample data. Press Delete.

4. In the datasheet's cells, type the data shown in Figure 3.26 and then close the datasheet.

5. Point to the sizing handle at right-side center. When the pointer becomes a two-headed arrow, widen the chart by dragging it to the right margin.

Figure 3.26 Modifying a chart

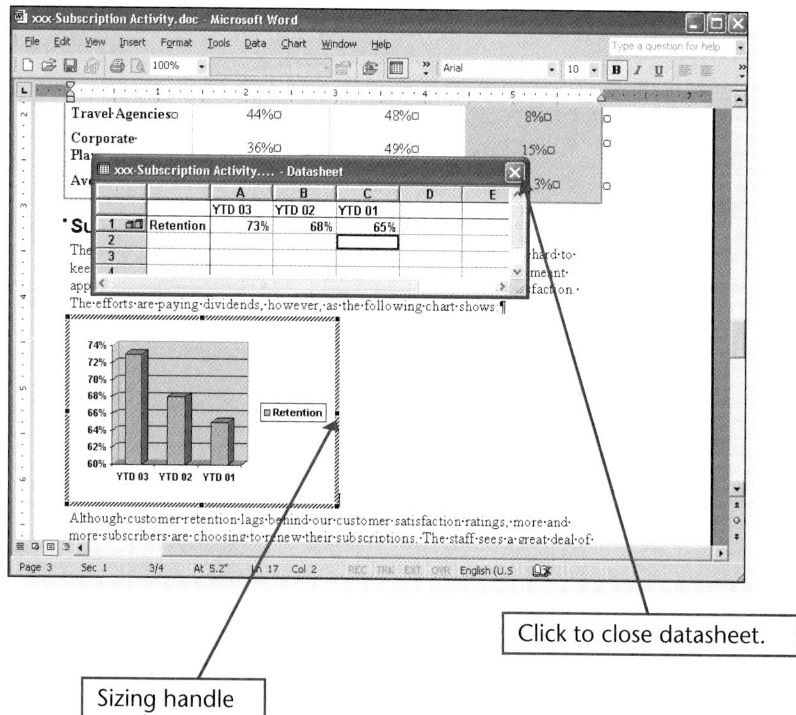

Click to close datasheet.

Figure 3.27 Adding a chart title

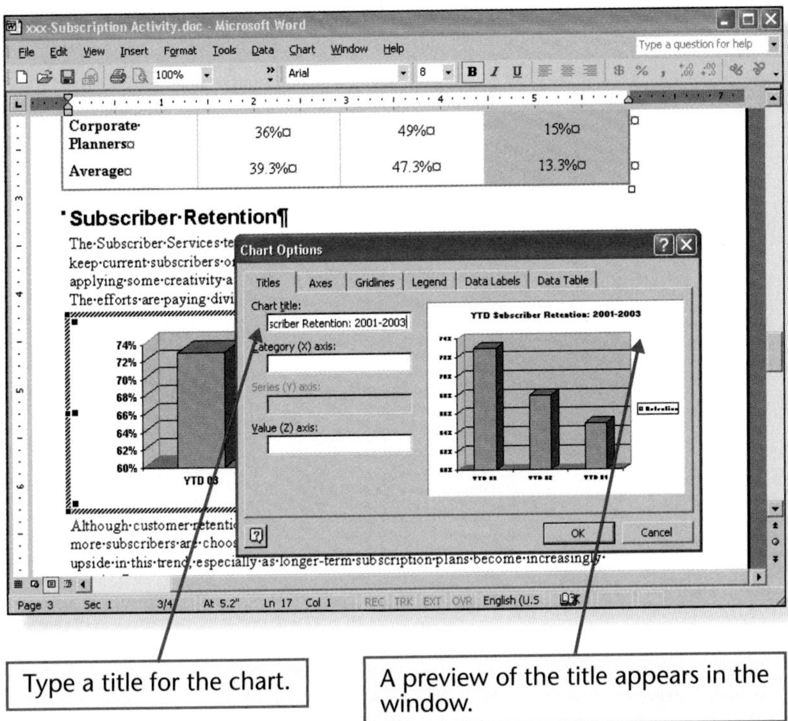

6. Click Chart Options on the Chart menu to open the Chart Options dialog box. Click the Titles tab.

7. In the *Chart title* box, type **YTD Subscriber Retention: 2001–2003**. The title appears in the preview window (see Figure 3.27). Click OK.

Word

Figure 3.28 Varying the column colors

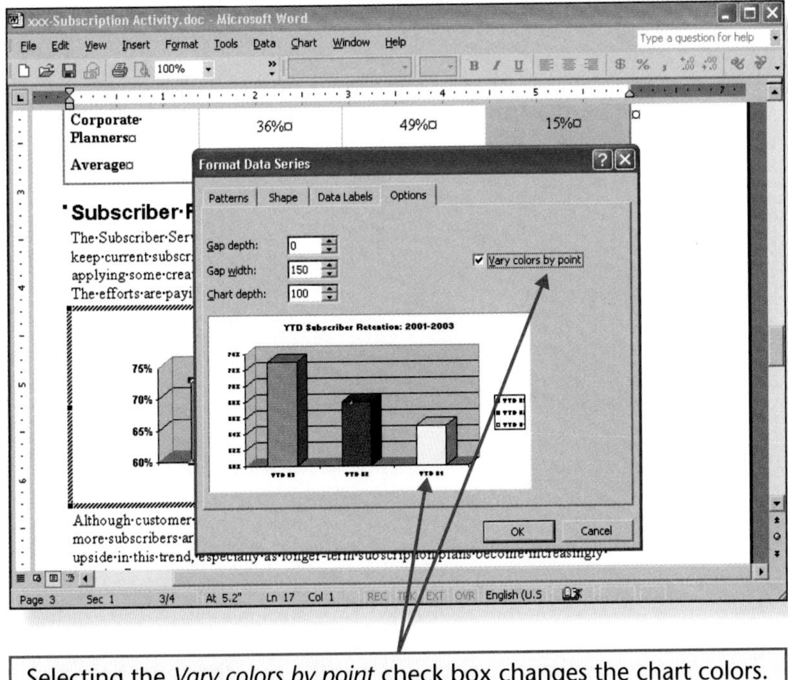

8. Click a bar in the chart. On the Format menu, select Selected Data Series to open the Format Data Series dialog box.

9. Click the Options tab. Select the *Vary colors by point* check box. The bar colors change in the preview window (see Figure 3.28). Click OK.

10. Click the chart's legend (the box at the right side of the chart) and press Delete to remove it from the chart.

11. Click anywhere outside the chart to deselect it.

Step Through It™
Exercise 4C: Link a chart With Paste Special

Word

1. In the *Subscription Revenues* section, click the blank line between the second and third paragraphs. Open *Q2 Revenues.doc*, click the chart, and click Copy.
2. Switch to *xxx-Subscription Activity.doc*. On the Edit menu, click Paste Special to open the Paste Special dialog box.
3. In the *As* list, select Microsoft Graph Chart Object. Select the *Paste link* option. The *Display as icon* check box should be cleared (see Figure 3.29). Click OK.
4. Switch to *Q2 Revenues.doc*, and double-click the chart.
5. Click the last cell that contains data (*151,000*). Type 125,000 and press Enter. Close the datasheet. Save the document as *xxx-Q2 Revenues.doc*, and then close it.
6. In *xxx-Subscription Activity.doc*, the last column is at $125,000 reflecting the change you made in *Q2 Revenues.doc*. This shows that the charts are linked (see Figure 3.30).
7. Save your changes.

Figure 3.29 The Paste Special dialog box

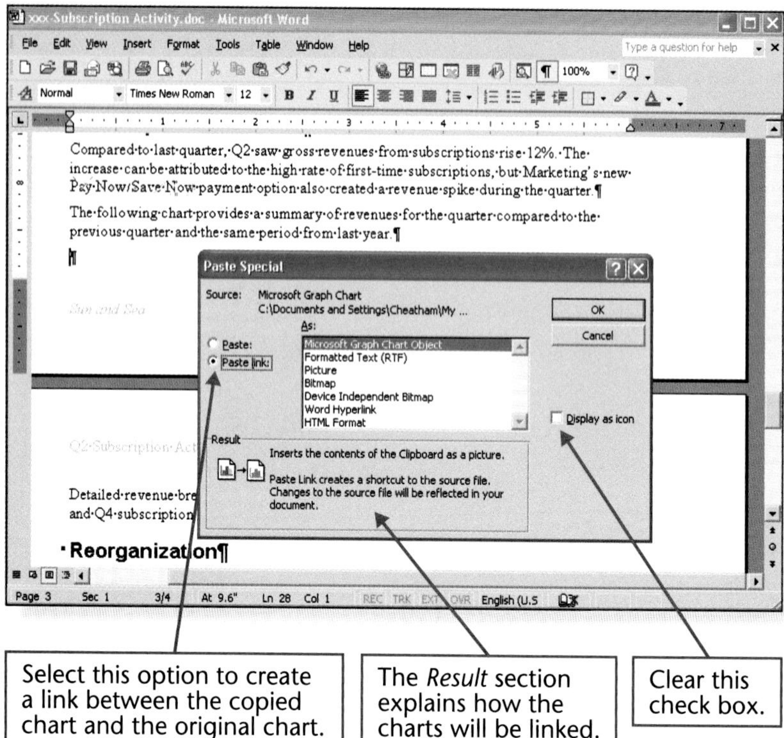

Figure 3.30 The updated, linked chart

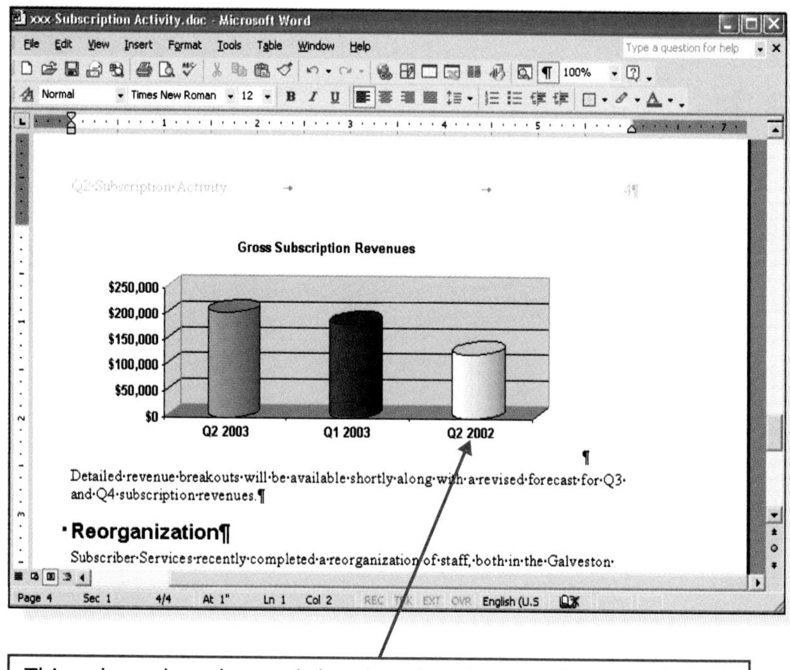

Figure 3.31 A blank organization chart

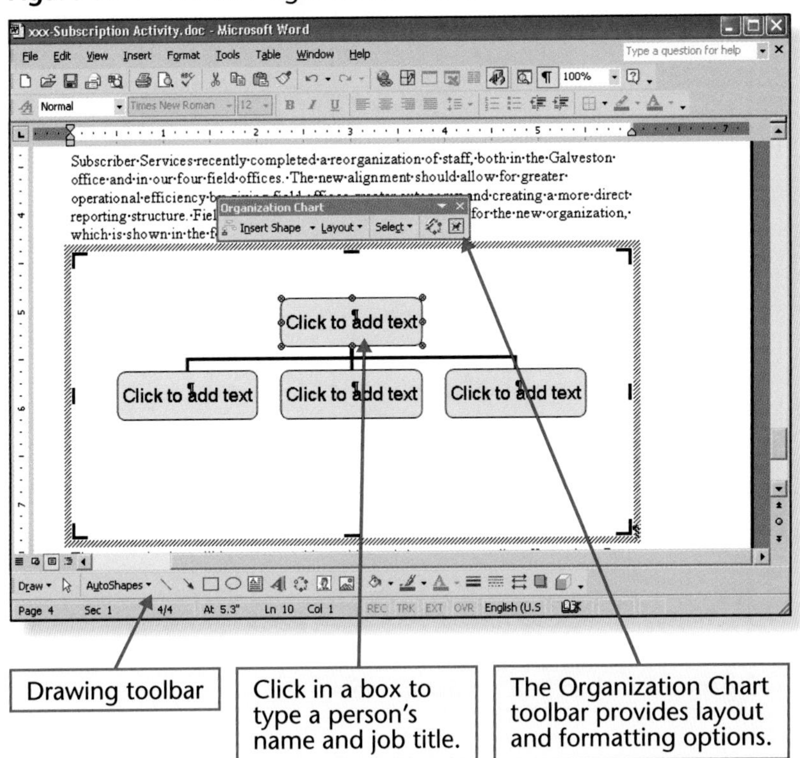

Step Through It™

Exercise 4D: Create and modify a diagram

1. Go to the *Reorganization* section and click the blank line after the reference to *the following chart*.
2. On the Insert menu, point to Picture and select Organization Chart. A blank organization chart and drawing tools appear in your document (see Figure 3.31).
3. Click in the top box of the chart and type your name. Press Enter and type Director.

Figure 3.32 Adding text to an organization chart

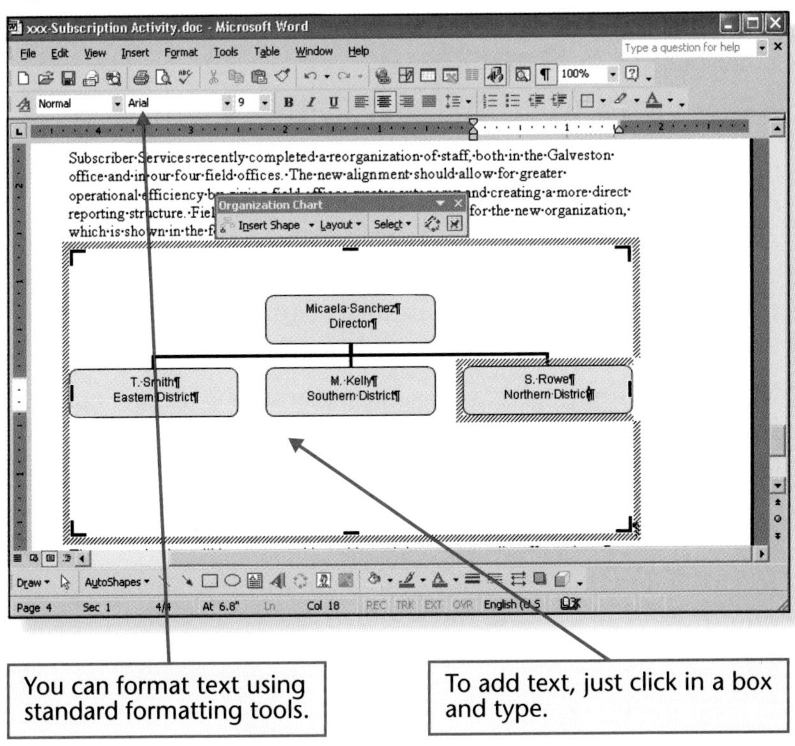

4. Select the text in the top box. Change the font to Arial and the font size to 9. Set the paragraph spacing to 0 pt before and after. Click each of the boxes in the second row and change the settings to match the top box.
5. In the first box of the second row, type T. Smith. Press Enter and type Eastern District. In the second box, type M. Kelly, press Enter, and type Southern District. In the third box, type S. Rowe, press Enter, and type Northern District (see Figure 3.32).

Word

Word

6. Click the top box. On the Organization Chart toolbar, click the Insert Shape down arrow, and select Assistant.

7. Format the new box to match the others. With the insertion point in the box, type D. Sprague, press Enter, and type Associate.

8. Click outside the chart to deselect it (see Figure 3.33).

9. On the View menu, point to Toolbars and select Drawing to hide the toolbar.

10. Save and then close your document.

Figure 3.33 The finished organization chart

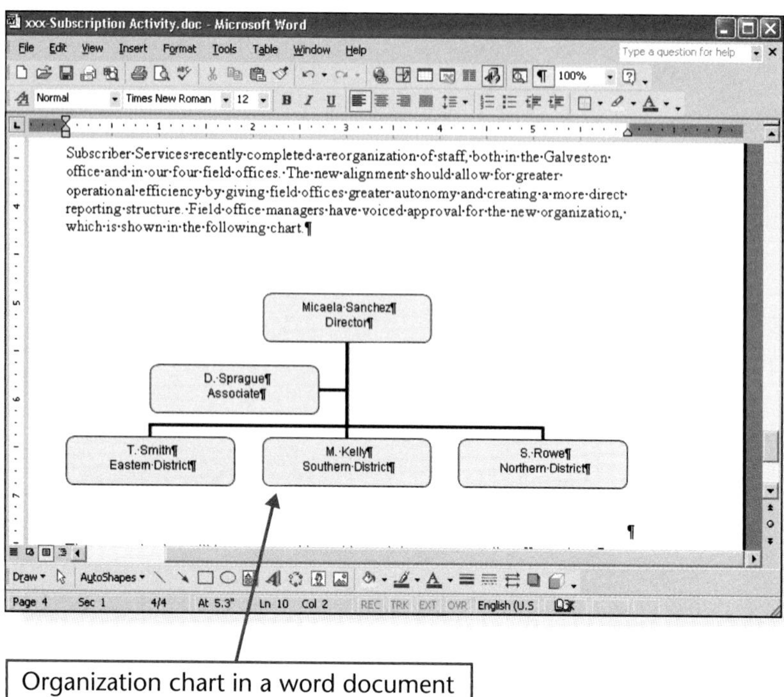

Microsoft Office Specialist W2002 3.2

Exercise 5 Overview: Apply and Modify Newsletter Columns

So far, you have worked with documents that use a single-column layout. Documents such as newsletters, however, are often designed in a multiple-column layout. Multiple columns can make a document easier to read since most people can read narrow columns of text much faster than they can read a single, page-wide column.

Multiple columns give you some interesting design options. For example, you can use two, three, or more columns depending on the amount of text and space you have to work with. Word lets you place thin vertical lines between columns, if you want, or you can make some columns wider than others.

In the following exercises, you will work with newsletter columns.

Figure 3.34 The Columns dialog box

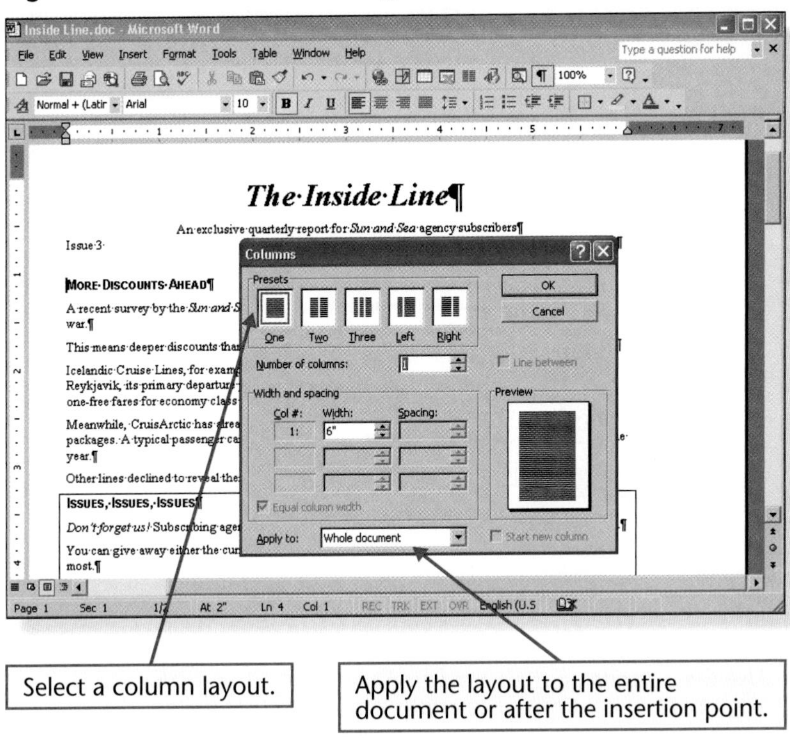

Select a column layout.
Apply the layout to the entire document or after the insertion point.

Step Through It™

Exercise 5A: Apply newsletter columns

1. Open *Inside Line.doc*. Save the file as *xxx-Inside Line.doc*.
2. Switch to Print Layout View, if necessary.
3. Click an insertion point to the left of the heading *More Discounts Ahead*. Select Columns on the Format menu to open the Columns dialog box (see Figure 3.34).
4. Under *Presets*, click the *Left* box. Click the *Apply to* down arrow, and select *This point forward*. Click OK. Word applies the selected format to all the text following the insertion point (see Figure 3.35).

Figure 3.35 The newsletter, formatted with columns

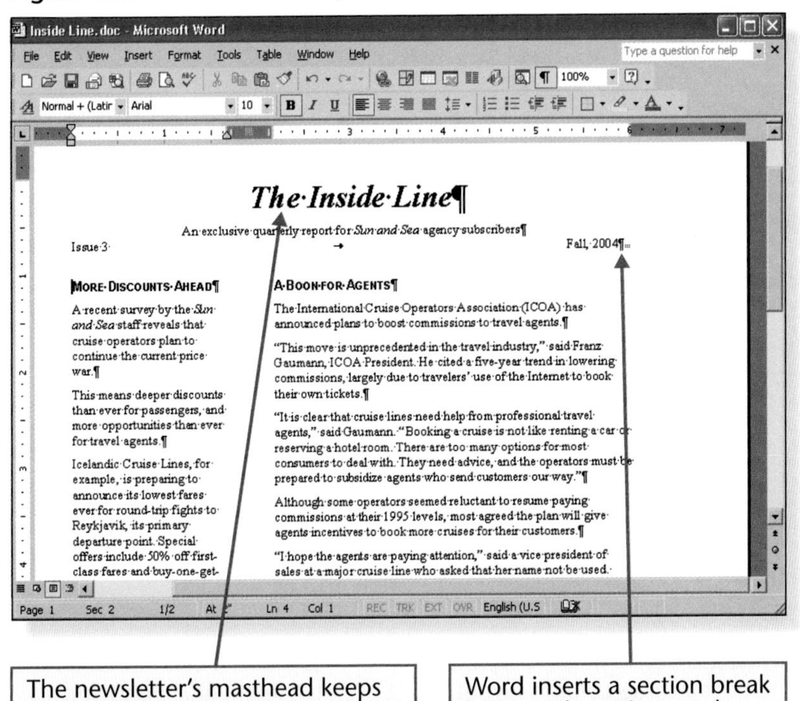

The newsletter's masthead keeps its full-page width since it is above the insertion point.
Word inserts a section break here; each section can be formatted differently.

Word

Step Through It™
Exercise 5B: Modify column alignment

1. Go to the bottom of the first page. In the boxed section in the first column, select the three paragraphs of text below the heading.
2. Click Justify on the Formatting toolbar to justify the text within the box (see Figure 3.36).
3. Go to the second page. Select the paragraph of text below the heading *Next Time*. Click Align Right and Italic on the Formatting toolbar.

Figure 3.36 Changing text alignment in a column

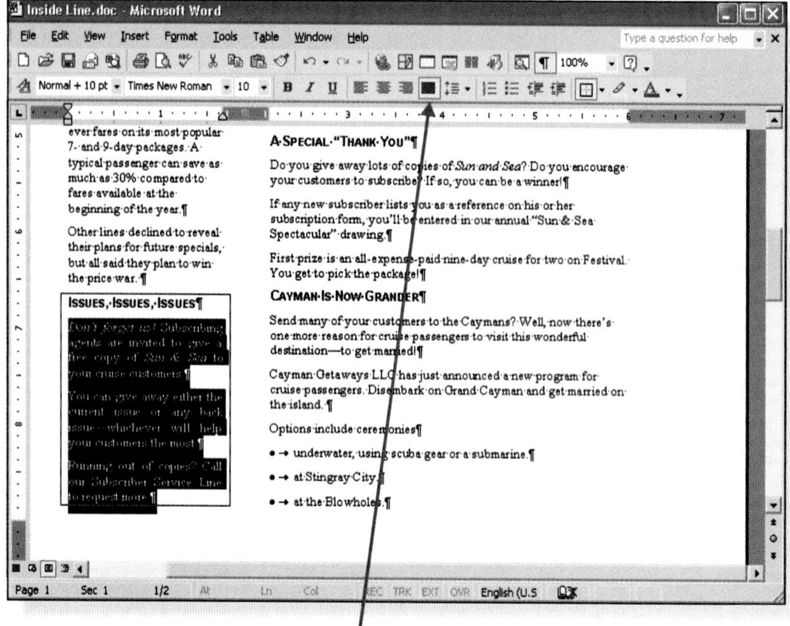

Use the buttons on the Formatting toolbar to change the text alignment of columns or to apply formats such as italic.

Step Through It™
Exercise 5C: Revise the column layout

1. Go to the newsletter's first page and click one of the columns. Open the Columns dialog box.
2. Click the *Three* box. Make sure that the *Equal column width* check box is selected (see Figure 3.37). Click OK.
3. Scroll through the newsletter to view the three-column format.
4. Save the newsletter. Close the document.

Figure 3.37 Changing the column layout

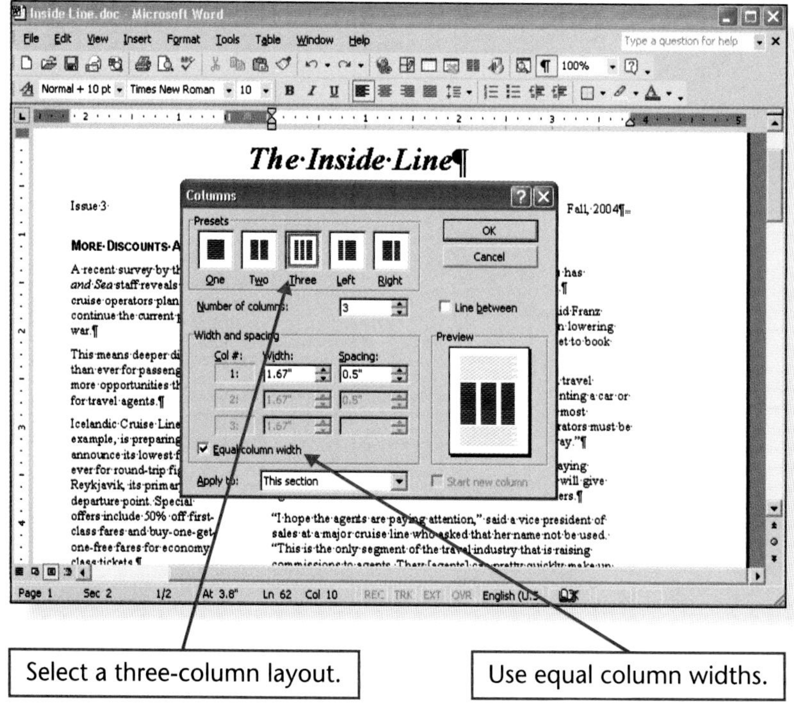
Select a three-column layout.
Use equal column widths.

Tech Talk

Desktop Publishing

Desktop publishing has had a dramatic impact on the way that many businesses prepare documents intended for wide distribution—documents such as marketing brochures, newsletters, and company reports. In the not-too-distant past, most businesses had to work with a typesetter at a local quick-print shop to develop such publications. With desktop publishing, however, professional-looking printed materials can be typed, designed, and printed on a personal computer and output on a high-volume printer.

To create effective desktop publications, you not only need the proper hardware and software but also a good eye for design and attention to detail. Desktop publishing programs integrate text, photographs, and other graphics. You can create publications with word processing software such as Microsoft Word. Longer and more complex documents may require the use of programs such as QuarkXPress, Adobe PageMaker, or Microsoft Publisher.

Simple graphics can be created using Microsoft Paint; more complex graphics can be created using programs like Adobe Illustrator. If the image you want to use is on paper, a scanner is ideal for converting it into digital form.

Creating desktop publications requires a variety of skills and attention to detail and may require employees to work together in teams. You must work with others to develop the design, verify information, and make sure the tone and direction of the publication is appropriate for your audience. The finished publication must be carefully examined for consistent and effective use of fonts, spacing, and overall appearance. And don't leave your editing and proofreading skills behind—you'll need them!

CRITICAL THINKING

1. Assume you are in charge of managing the publication of a school newsletter that will contain graphics, photos, and a complex layout. What programs besides Microsoft Word might you use? Explain why.
2. Name four different types of publications that a business may need to produce using desktop publishing technology. Describe their purpose.

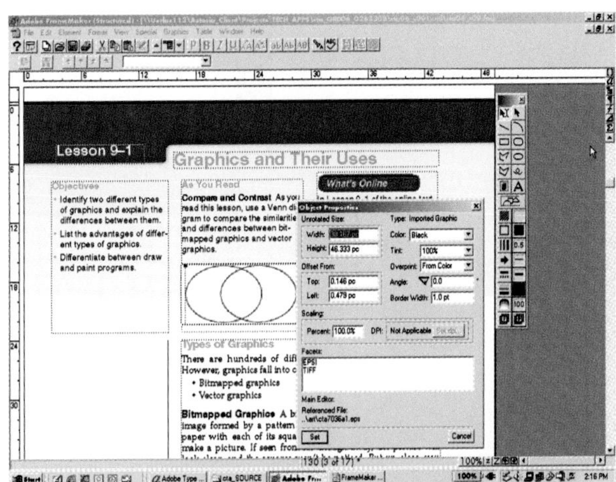

Word

Exercise 6 Overview:
Print a Letter, an Envelope, and a Label

Before you print a document, you need to decide its orientation. *Orientation* refers to the direction in which text is printed on a page. The usual orientation for a business letter is **portrait orientation** where text is printed across the shorter dimension of the page. Some documents, however, may look best in **landscape orientation** where information prints across the wider dimension of the page.

Every document has **margins,** or blank space along the page's top, bottom, right, and left edges, where text cannot be printed (with the exception of headers, footers, and page numbers). In Word, most documents have default top and bottom margins of 1 inch and default left and right margins of 1.25 inch. You can set each margin to a different width, if necessary.

Need Help?
Type: margins

When printing a letter for mailing, you may also need to print an envelope. Word makes it easy to print envelopes and address labels.

In the following exercises, you will change page setup options and print a letter, an envelope, and a label.

Figure 3.38 Word makes it easy to print an envelope

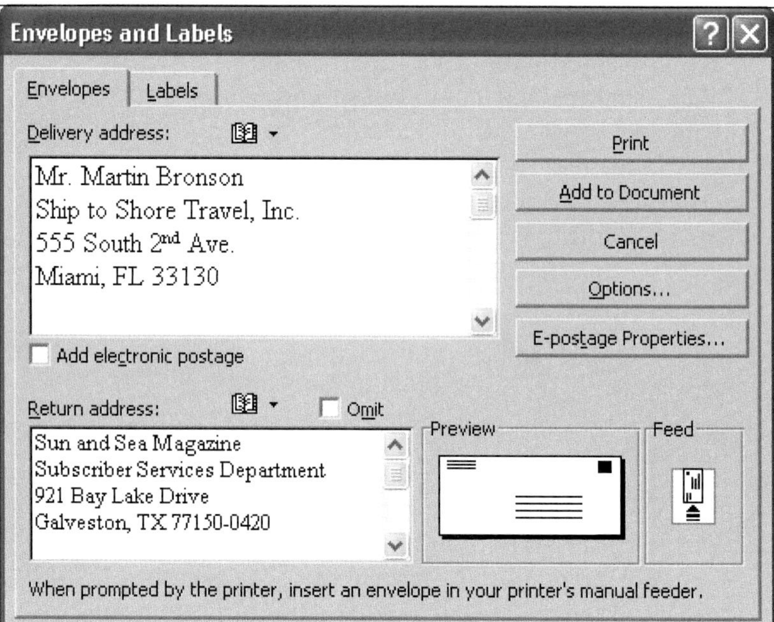

Figure 3.39 Changing orientation for one page of a document

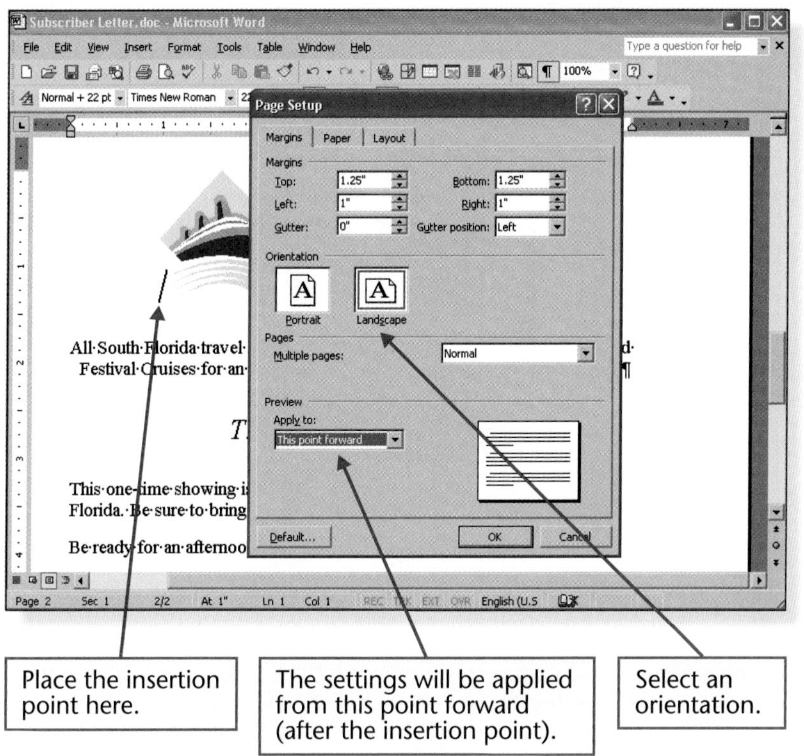

Place the insertion point here.
The settings will be applied from this point forward (after the insertion point).
Select an orientation.

Figure 3.40 Setting margins for the second page

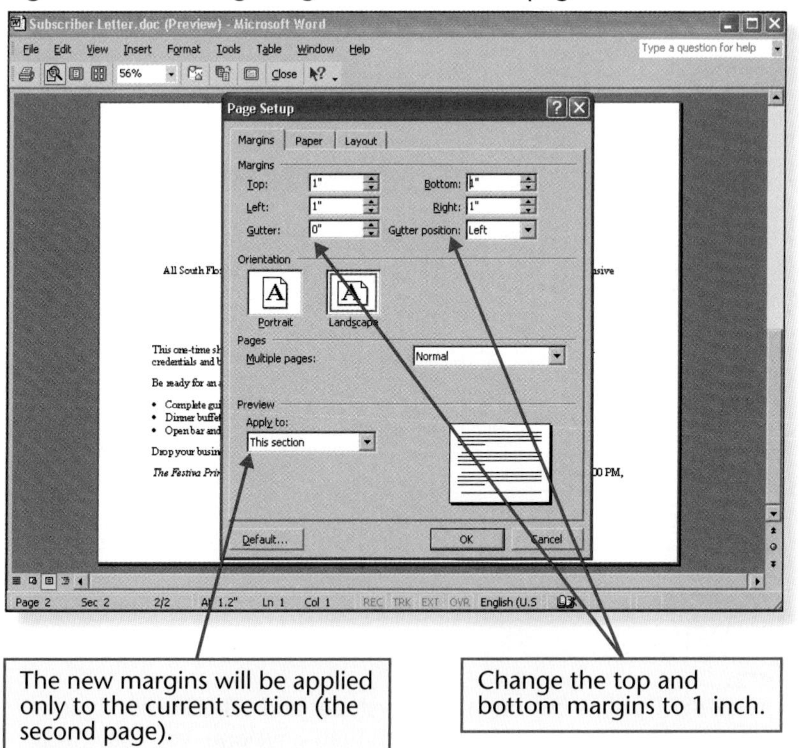

The new margins will be applied only to the current section (the second page).
Change the top and bottom margins to 1 inch.

Step Through It™

Exercise 6A: Change page orientation and margins

Word

1. Open *Subscriber Letter.doc*. Save the document as *xxx-Subscriber Letter. doc.* Scroll to the document's second page, which is an invitation.
2. Click an insertion point to the left of the first clip art image on the first line. On the File menu, select Page Setup to open the Page Setup dialog box.
3. Click the Margins tab. Under *Orientation*, click Landscape. Click the *Apply to* down arrow and select *This point forward* (see Figure 3.39). Click OK.
4. Click Print Preview on the Standard toolbar. Open the Page Setup dialog box. Change the top and bottom margins to 1 inch (see Figure 3.40). Click OK. Close Print Preview.
5. Click at the end of the first item in the bulleted list and press Enter. Type **Individual meetings with ship staff and travel planners**.
6. Click Print on the Standard toolbar to send your document to the printer.

Word

Step Through It™

Exercise 6B: Print an envelope

1. Go to the first page. Drag the scroll bar to position the *Sun and Sea* letterhead so it is at the very top of the window. Select all four lines of the inside address.

2. On the Tools menu, point to Letters and Mailings. Select Envelopes and Labels to open the Envelopes and Labels dialog box.

3. Click the Envelopes tab. If necessary, click in the *Delivery address* window to view the address (see Figure 3.41).

4. Drag the title bar of the dialog box, down to better view the magazine address.

5. Clear the *Add electronic postage* and *Omit* check boxes. If necessary, edit the default address in the *Return address* window so it is the same as at the top of the letter (see Figure 3.42).

6. Click Print to print one copy of the envelope. If Word prompts you to save the return address, click No.

Figure 3.41 The Envelopes and Labels dialog box

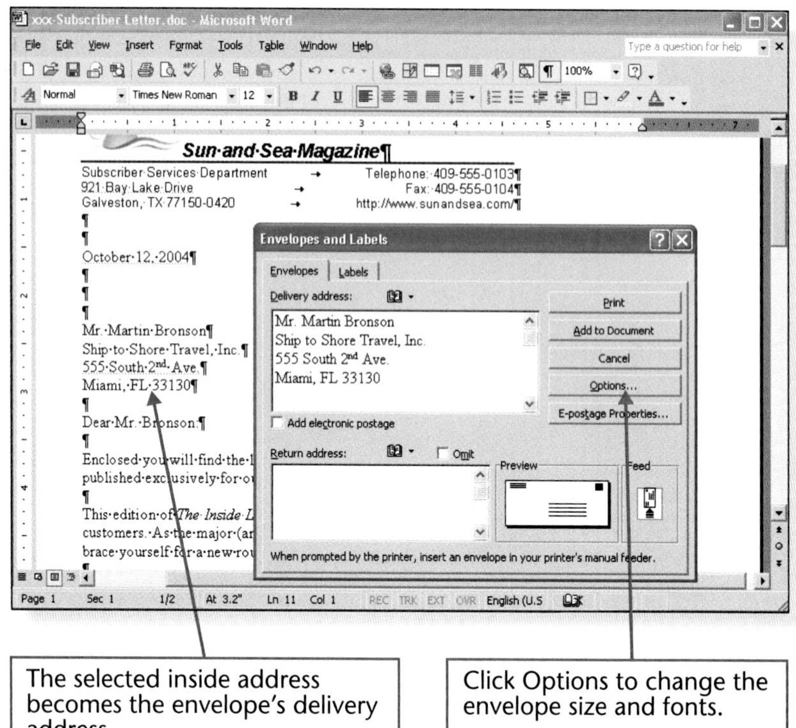

Figure 3.42 Adding the return address

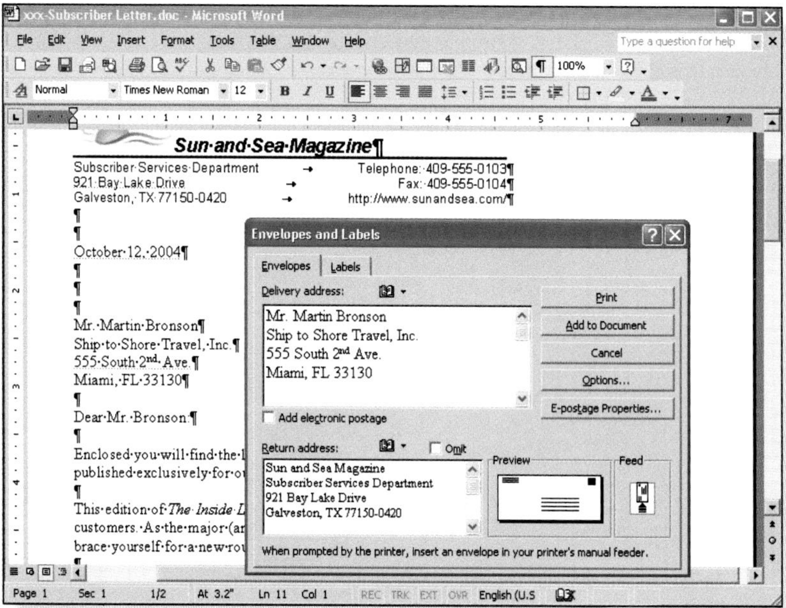

Warning

Click the Options button in the Envelopes and Labels dialog box to change the envelope size. If you print an envelope, you may need to manually feed it into the printer.

Figure 3.43 Creating an address label

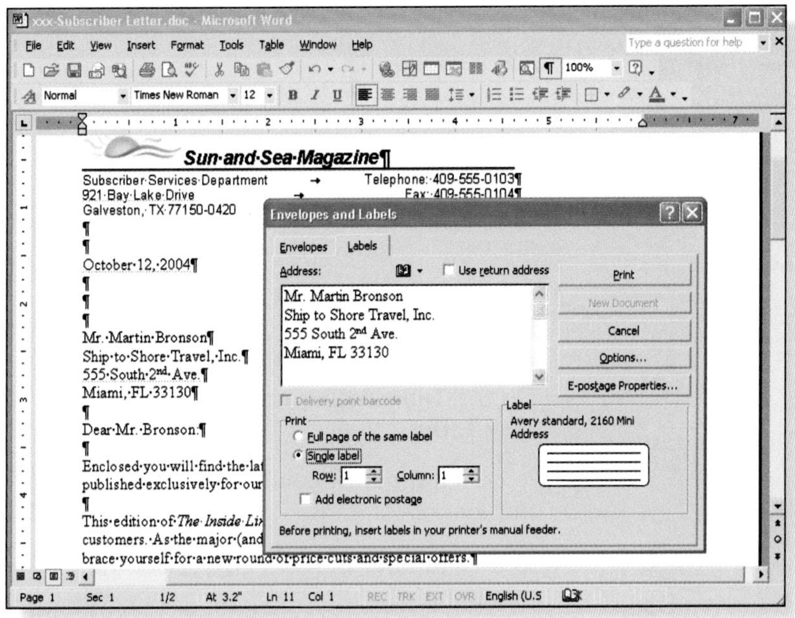

Step Through It™

Exercise 6C: Print an address label

1. With the inside address selected, open the Envelopes and Labels dialog box. Click the Labels tab.

2. Under *Print*, select *Single label*, and select Row 1 and Column 1 (see Figure 3.43).

Figure 3.44 The Label Options dialog box

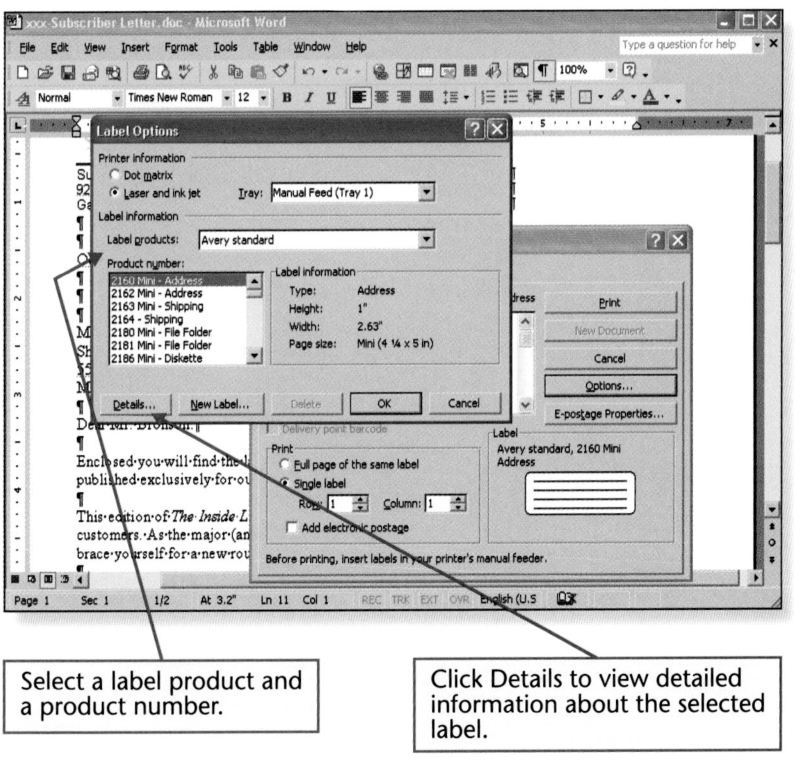

3. Click Options to open the Label Options dialog box (see Figure 3.44). Select a label product and a label product number. Click OK.

4. Click Print. Save and close the document.

APPLY IT! After finishing Exercises 4–6, you may test your skills by completing Apply It! Guided Activity 2, Complete a Newsletter.

Procedure Summary

Highlight Text

1. Select the text.
2. Click the **Highlight** down arrow.
3. Select a highlight color.

Apply a Text Effect

1. Select the text.
2. On the **Format** menu, select **Font**. . . . . **Alt + O, F**
3. Click the **Text Effects** tab. . . . . **Alt + X**
4. In the **Animations** list, select an effect. . . . . **Alt + A**
5. Click OK.

Apply a Character Effect

1. Select the text.
2. On the **Format** menu, select **Font**. . . . . **Alt + O, F**
3. Click the **Font** tab. . . . . **Alt + N**
4. Select one or more effects.
5. Click OK.

Create a Table

1. Place the insertion point where the table will appear.
2. Click **Insert Table** on the Tables and Borders toolbar.
   OR
   On the **Table** menu, point to **Insert** and click **Table**. . . . . **Alt + A, I, T**
3. In the **Number of columns** box, select the number of columns. . . . . **Alt + C**
4. In the **Number of rows** box, select the number of rows. . . . . **Alt + R**
5. Click OK.

Add a Row to a Table

1. Click a table row.
2. On the Tables and Borders toolbar, click the **Insert Table** down arrow.
3. Click Insert Rows Above.
   OR
   Click Insert Rows Below.

Add a Column to a Table

1. Click a table column.
2. On the Tables and Borders toolbar, click the **Insert Table** down arrow.
3. Click Insert Columns to the Left.
   OR
   Click Insert Columns to the Right.

Change Text Alignment in a Table

1. Select one or more table cells.
2. On the Tables and Borders toolbar, click the **Align** down arrow.
3. Select a cell alignment.

Merge Table Cells

1. Select the cells to merge.

   Click **Merge Cells** on the Tables and Borders toolbar.

   OR
2. On the **Table** menu, select **Merge Cells** . . . . Alt + A, M

Split Table Cells

1. Select a cell.
2. Click **Split Cells** on the Tables and Borders toolbar.

   OR

   On the **Table menu,** select **Split Cells** . . . . Alt + A, P
3. In the **Number of columns** box, select the number of columns. . . . . Alt + C
4. In the **Number of rows** box, select the number of rows. . . . . Alt + R
5. Click OK.

Use Table AutoFormat

1. Select the table.
2. On the Tables and Borders toolbar, click Table AutoFormat.

   OR
3. On the **Table** menu, select **Table AutoFormat** . . . . Alt + A, F
4. In the **Table styles** list, select a table style . . . . Alt + T
5. Click **Apply** . . . . Alt + A

Add Borders to a Table

1. Select the table.
2. On the Tables and Borders toolbar, click the **Borders** down arrow.

   OR

   On the Formatting toolbar, click the **Borders** down arrow.
3. Select a border type.

Procedure Summary

Format Table Borders

1. Select the cells you want to format.
2. On the Tables and Borders toolbar, click the **Line Style** down arrow and select a line style.
3. Click the **Line Weight** down arrow ½ and select a line weight.
4. Click the **Border Color** down arrow and select a border color.
5. Click the **Borders** down arrow and select a border.

   OR
6. On the **Format** menu, select **Borders and Shading** and make selections on the **Borders** tab . . . . . **Alt + O, B, Alt + B**

Add Shading to a Table

1. Select the cells you want to shade.
2. On the Tables and Borders toolbar, click the Shading **Color** down arrow and select a fill color.

   OR

   On the **Format** menu, select **Borders and Shading** and make selections on the **Shading** tab. . . . . **Alt + O, B, Alt + S**

Insert Clip Art

1. Place the insertion point where the clip art should appear.
2. On the **Insert** menu, point to **Picture** and click **Clip Art** . . . . . **Alt + I, P, C**
3. In the *Search text* box, type a term describing the clip art you want.
4. Set the search options and click Search.
5. In the search results, click a clip to insert it into your document.

Insert a Chart

1. Place the insertion point where the chart should appear.
2. On the **Insert** menu, point to **Picture** and click **Chart**. . . . . **Alt + I, P, H**
3. Type your data in the datasheet.
4. Close the datasheet.

Insert an Organization Chart or Diagram

1. Click an insertion point in the document.
2. On the **Insert** menu, point to **Picture** and click **Organization Chart** . . . . **Alt + I, P, O**

   OR

   On the **Insert** menu, select **Diagram**, click the Organization Chart icon, and click OK. . . . . **Alt + I, G**
3. Type your information in each box.

Apply Newsletter Columns

1. Place the insertion point where the columns should begin.
2. On the **Format** menu, select **Columns** . . . . **Alt + O, C**
3. Select the **One, Two, Three, Left,** or **Right** column layout . . . . **Alt + O, Alt + W, Alt + T, Alt + L, Alt + R**
4. Make a selection in the **Apply to** list. **Alt + A**
5. Click OK.

Change Margins and Page Orientation

1. On the **File** menu, select **Page Setup** . . . . **Alt + F, U**
2. Click the Margins tab.
3. Change the **Top, Bottom, Left,** or **Right** margin settings **Alt + T, Alt + B, Alt + L, OR Alt + R**
4. Select **Portrait** or **Landscape** orientation . . . . **Alt + P OR Alt + S**
5. Click OK.

Create and Print an Envelope

1. Select the inside address in your letter.
2. On the **Tools** menu, point to **Letters and Mailings** and click **Envelopes and Labels**. . . . . **Alt + T, E, E**
3. Click the **Envelopes** tab . . . . **Alt + E**
4. Type your address in the **Return address** window . . . . **Alt + R**
5. Click **Options** to change the envelope size and click OK . . . . **Alt + O**
6. Click **Print** . . . . **Alt + P**

Create and Print an Address Label

1. Select the inside address in your letter.
2. On the **Tools** menu, point to **Letters and Mailings** and click **Envelopes and Labels**. . . . . **Alt + T + E + E**
3. Click the **Labels** tab . . . . **Alt + L**
4. Select the number of labels to print.
5. Click **Options** to select a label product and number. Click OK . . . . **Alt + O**
6. Click **Print** . . . . **Alt + P**

Lesson Review and Exercises

Summary Checklist

- ☑ Can you apply highlighting, text effects, and character effects?
- ☑ Can you create a table and then modify it by adding rows or columns, aligning text, or merging and splitting cells?
- ☑ Can you format a table using Table AutoFormat?
- ☑ Can you format a table by adding borders and shading?
- ☑ Can you insert clip art into a document?
- ☑ Can you create a chart and then modify its appearance?
- ☑ Can you use Paste Special to link a chart from one Word document to another?
- ☑ Can you create and modify a diagram such as an organization chart?
- ☑ Can you apply newsletter-style columns to a document and then modify column alignment or layout?
- ☑ Can you change the orientation and margins of a page?
- ☑ Can you print a letter, an envelope, and a label?

Key Terms

- cell (p. 84)
- character effect (p. 82)
- chart (p. 96)
- clip art (p. 96)
- datasheet (p. 96)
- diagram (p. 96)
- highlight (p. 82)
- landscape orientation (p. 106)
- margin (p. 106)
- merge (p. 84)
- organization chart (p. 96)
- portrait orientation (p. 106)
- split (p. 84)
- table (p. 84)
- text effect (p. 82)

APPLY IT! Guided Activities

1. Format a Table in a Letter

You want to add some formatting touches to a letter you are sending a client. The customer will view it on his computer, so you can use color and text effects if you wish. Follow these steps:

a. Open *Schedule Letter.doc*. Save your document as *xxx-Schedule Letter.doc*. Select your company's name at the top of the letter, and select Font on the Format menu. On the Font tab, change the character effect to small caps.

b. In the first sentence of the second paragraph, select *no more than six months*. Click the Highlight down arrow on the Formatting toolbar and apply a yellow highlight.

c. Click the first row of the table. On the Tables and Borders toolbar, click the Insert Table down arrow and add a new row to the top of the table. In the first cell of the new row, type Phase; in the remaining cells, type Starts and Duration.

d. Apply the *Table List 5* AutoFormat, accepting all the default settings. ***Note:*** If the table becomes misaligned, point to the left table and drag it to the right to align it with the left margin. Drag the borders between the columns to position the column text attractively **(see Figure 3.45)**.

Figure 3.45 Formatting a table in a letter

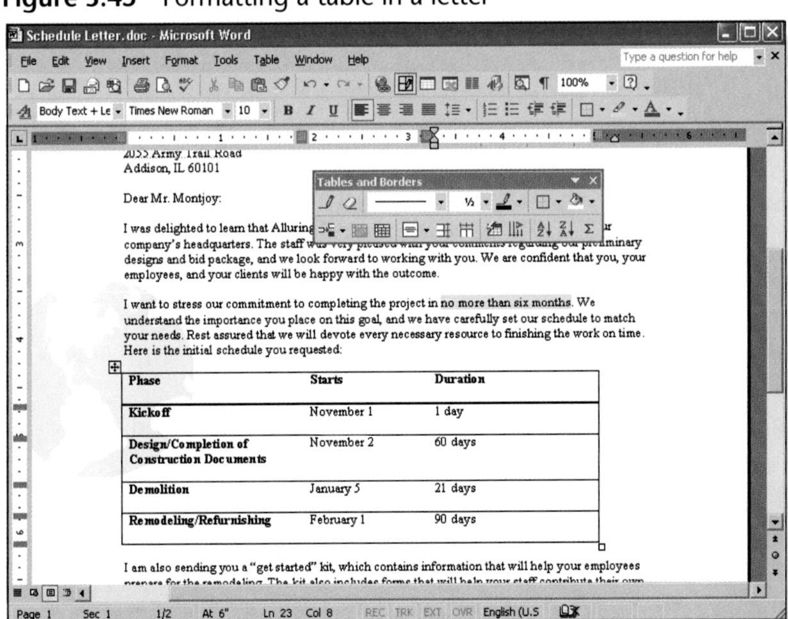

e. Select the table. On the Tables and Borders toolbar, click the Line Style down arrow, and select a distinctive line style. Click the Line Weight down arrow and select a line weight to make a thick border. Click the Border Color down arrow and select Gray-50%. On the Borders menu, select Outside Border.

f. With the table still selected, click the Shading Color down arrow and select the light green fill color. Select *Phase* in the first row, open the Cell Alignment menu, and select Align Center.

g. In table row 2, select the word *Kickoff*. On the Format menu, click Font and click the Text Effects tab. Apply the Blinking Background animation.

h. Type your name at the bottom of the letter on the blank line above the job title. Save the document. Close the document, but keep Word running.

2. Complete a Newsletter

As a reading instructor for a large school system, you publish a newsletter for all the reading teachers in the district. You need to format your latest issue to look like a newsletter and add a chart to it. You must print and mail the newsletter to a colleague for review before you can distribute it. Follow these steps:

a. Open *Notes & Such.doc*. Save the document as *xxx-Notes & Such.doc*. With the insertion point at the top of the document, select Columns on the Format menu. Select a three-column format with equal column widths. Clear the *Line between* check box and click OK.

b. Open the Columns dialog box again. Select the *Right* layout and select the *Line between* check box. Click OK. Go to the bottom of the first column. In the boxed area, center the *Help!* heading and the text below it.

c. Click an insertion point above the first heading in the second column. On the Insert menu, point to Picture and click Clip Art. In the Insert Clip Art task pane, search for clips using *book* as the search text. Insert an appropriate clip **(see Figure 3.46)**. Close the task pane.

d. Go to the top of page 2 and select the two rows in the table. On the Insert menu, point to Picture and click Chart to insert a chart under the table. Close the datasheet. Click the legend and press Delete. Click outside the chart to deselect it.

e. Press Ctrl + Home. On the File menu, click Page Setup and click the Margins tab. Change the left and right margins to 1 inch and click OK.

f. To prepare an envelope for Mark Young, select his name and address above the *Help!* box. On the Tools menu, point to Letters and Mailings and click Envelopes and Labels. On the Envelopes tab, clear the Omit box, if necessary, and type the return address: Notes & Such, 1212 Park St., Rockwell, NC 28138. Click Options and change the envelope size, if necessary. Print the envelope (do not save the return address).

g. Print the newsletter.

h. Save the document. Close the document, but keep Word running.

Figure 3.46 Formatting a newsletter

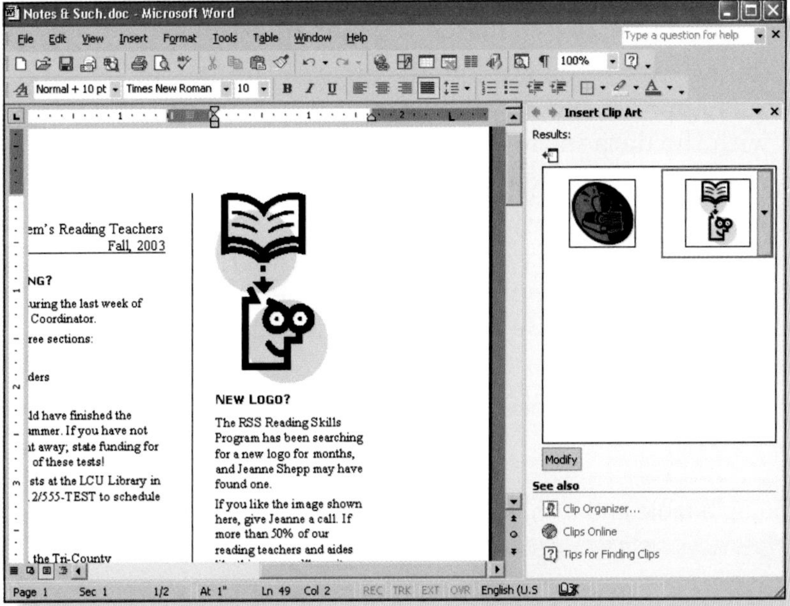

Do It Yourself

1. Price Patrol

As general manager of a car detailing service, you need to let your service technicians know when you change the prices of your services. You have created a memo, and now you need to finish it by inserting a table with the price information. Follow these steps:

a. Open *Price Changes.doc*. Save the document as *xxx-Price Changes.doc*. Type your name at the right end of the *From* line.

b. Find the sentence in the letter that mentions *the following table*. Select the four lines of table data containing the service and price information. Click Insert Table to place this data in a table format.

c. Center the column labels in the first row. Center all the prices.

d. Add a new row to the bottom of the table and merge its cells. In this new row, type a note stating that the new prices will take effect on November 15. Left-align the note and make it italic.

e. Save the document. Close the document, but keep Word running.

Word

2. A Greeting Card Report Card

As Sales Director, it's your job to report sales activity. You need to complete your monthly report. Follow these steps:

a. Open *Monthly Sales.doc*. Save it as *xxx-Monthly Sales.doc*. Add a thick, light gray outside border to the table. (Don't add borders between the columns or rows inside the table.) Add a light gray shading to the table's first row to match the outside border.

b. Split the last (blank) row into four equally spaced columns. In the four new cells, type Misc., 11,800, 11,100, and 10,860. Align the new data with the data in the cells above.

c. Find *the following chart*, and click an insertion point on the blank line following that paragraph. Open *Channel Performance.doc*. Copy the chart and paste it as a Microsoft Graph Chart Object into the *Monthly Sales* document using Paste Special **(see Figure 3.47)**. Be sure to link the copied chart. Close *Channel Performance.doc*.

d. Save the document. Close the document, but keep Word running.

Figure 3.47 Setting up a table and a chart

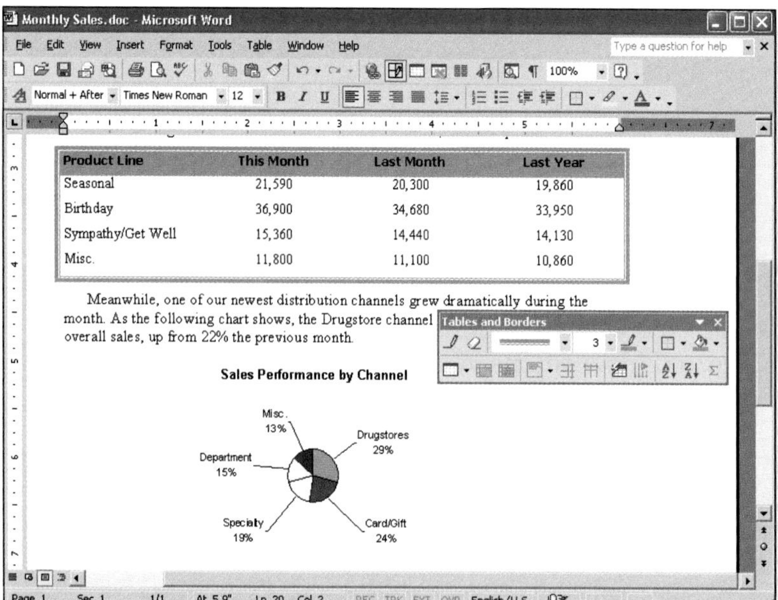

3. Print an Organization Chart

You are the president of a private accounting practice in search of investors. One investor is very interested in your company's structure and has asked to see your "org chart." You have set up an organization chart as part of a letter to this investor, but it needs some work. Follow these steps:

a. Open the file *Organization.doc*. Save the document as *xxx-Organization.doc* and move the insertion point to the beginning of the second page.

b. Change the second page only to landscape orientation. Change all margins for the second page to one inch.

c. Type your name in the letter's signature line and in the top box of the organization chart.

d. Preview and then print the letter and chart, and then print an envelope with the correct delivery and return addresses.

e. Save the document. Close the document, but keep Word running.

4. Chart Employee Turnover

As human resources director for a bank, you are very concerned about employee turnover (the rate at which employees quit). Alarmed by a recent increase in resignations, you are preparing a memo to the bank's president describing the problem. To finish the memo, you need to create a chart to present the statistics. Follow these steps:

a. Open *Turnover.doc*. Save the file as *xxx-Turnover.doc*. Type your name at the right end of the *From:* line. Find the paragraph that refers to *the following chart*. Click the blank line following that paragraph, and insert a chart.

b. Use the default chart type. Delete all the data in the chart's datasheet, and replace it with the information shown in Table 3.3. When you are done, close the datasheet.

Table 3.3

	Headquarters	Branches
Professional	15%	17%
Administrative	17%	21%
Clerical	21%	24%

c. Resize the chart as necessary to best fit the page. Create a title for the chart, using the text Employee Turnover, Year to Date (see **Figure 3.48**).

d. Save and close the document, but keep Word running.

Figure 3.48 Inserting a chart

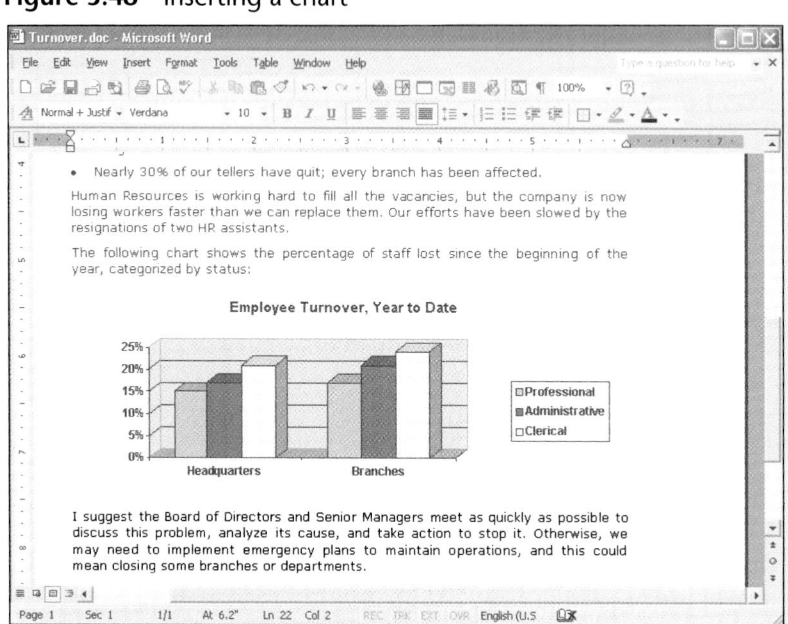

Challenge Yourself

Create an Instructional Manual

As the assistant to the vice president of operations for a chain of ice-cream stores, you are helping to develop and desktop publish training materials. You have been working on an instructional manual for new employees. To finish it, do the following:

- Open *Instruction Manual.doc*. Save the document as *xxx-Instruction Manual.doc*. Read the entire document to understand its purpose.
- Under *To prepare a milk shake*, add at least three steps instructing a new server how to make a milkshake. Be creative. Under *Opening the Store*, add a list of at least three tasks that must be performed when the store is opened every morning.
- Go to the end of the document and type the heading Professionalism, Dependability, and Punctuality. Write a short introductory paragraph explaining the importance of team success to customer satisfaction

and company success. In a bulleted list below the paragraph, list at least four expectations that the company has for individual team members that will help ensure team success.

- Open the file *Upselling.doc*. Copy all the text in the document, and then close the document. In *xxx-Instruction Manual.doc*, paste the text as the last paragraph under *Greeting Customers and Taking Orders*.
- Open *Processing Purchases.doc*. This document contains a large flowchart graphic. Select the entire graphic, copy it, and then close the document. At the end of *Instruction Manual.doc*, insert a page break. Paste the flowchart on the new page. Create a new heading for the flowchart **(see Figure 3.49)**.
- Format the entire document. This includes formatting the titles as headings (levels 1 and 2), lists, and other text. Insert a footer, including the document's title and a page number; however, omit the footer from the first page. Insert page breaks as needed.
- On the first page insert an appropriate clip art image.
- Format the document's table by adding borders, shading, and changing formats and alignment as necessary.
- Spell check and proofread on the document. Print one copy.
- Save and close the document.

Figure 3.49 Copying and pasting a flowchart

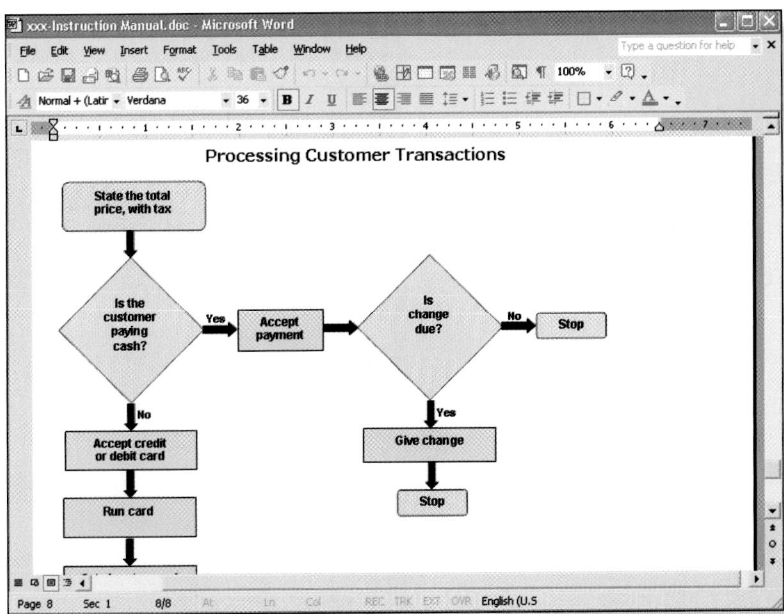

Lesson 4

Collaborating with Others

Lesson Exercise Objectives

After completing this lesson, you'll be able to do the following tasks:

1. Use the Comments feature
2. Share a document online
3. Insert and modify a date/time field

Key Terms

- comment (p. 124)
- field (p. 137)
- field code (p. 137)
- Hypertext Markup Language (HTML) (p. 132)
- Internet (p. 132)
- intranet (p. 132)
- Web browser (p. 132)
- Web page (p. 132)
- World Wide Web (WWW) (p. 132)

Microsoft Office Specialist Activities

W2002: 1.5, 6.1, 6.2, 6.3

Real-Life Business Applications

Lesson Case Study

In this lesson, you will play the role of the Promotions Director for *Sun and Sea*. Keep the following information in mind as you work through the lesson exercises.

- `Job responsibilities and goals.` As Promotions Director, one of your responsibilities is designing special promotional campaigns that encourage people to subscribe or renew their subscriptions.
- `The project.` You are working on a special letter to send to former subscribers. You will use Word's document-review features to add comments to the letter, and then you will merge them with comments and changes from another reviewer. Next, you will use Word to create a page for your company's Web site. Finally, you will finish a memo to your manager by adding date and time fields to it.
- `The challenge ahead.` In today's workplace, it is common for people to work in groups. This can involve sharing documents through a Web site or a company's intranet. To successfully share and manage documents in a work group, you need to master Word's collaboration features.

Microsoft Office Specialist
W2002 6.1, 6.2

Word

Exercise 1 Overview:
Use the Comments Feature

Did you ever review a document that was written by someone else? If so, you may have used a pen or pencil to write comments on a paper document, suggesting ways the writer could change or improve it.

Word's Comments feature lets you do the same thing on screen. **Comments** are small boxes called *balloons* that hold your remarks or suggestions. When you add a comment to a document, Word displays the Reviewing toolbar that has tools for working with comments and tracking changes that are made to the document. The following table illustrates some of the commonly used buttons on the Reviewing toolbar.

Reviewing Toolbar

Button	Purpose
Previous Comment	Moves the insertion point to the previous comment
Next Comment	Moves the insertion point to the next comment
Accept Change	Accepts the selected change or comment
Reject Change/ Delete Comment	Deletes the selected change or comment
New Comment	Inserts a new comment balloon in the document
Track Changes	Turns Track Changes on or off
Reviewing Pane	Displays the Reviewing Pane at the bottom of the document

If you want several people to review a document, you can send each person a copy (by e-mail, for example). Each reviewer can add comments and return his or her commented file to you. You can then merge all their comments together into a single copy of the document.

Type: comments

In addition to inserting comments, reviewers can make changes to the document, such as editing and formatting text. Word can track changes made to a document so you can see what changes the reviewers made.

In the following exercises, you will insert and edit comments and compare and merge documents.

Figure 4.1 Inserting a comment

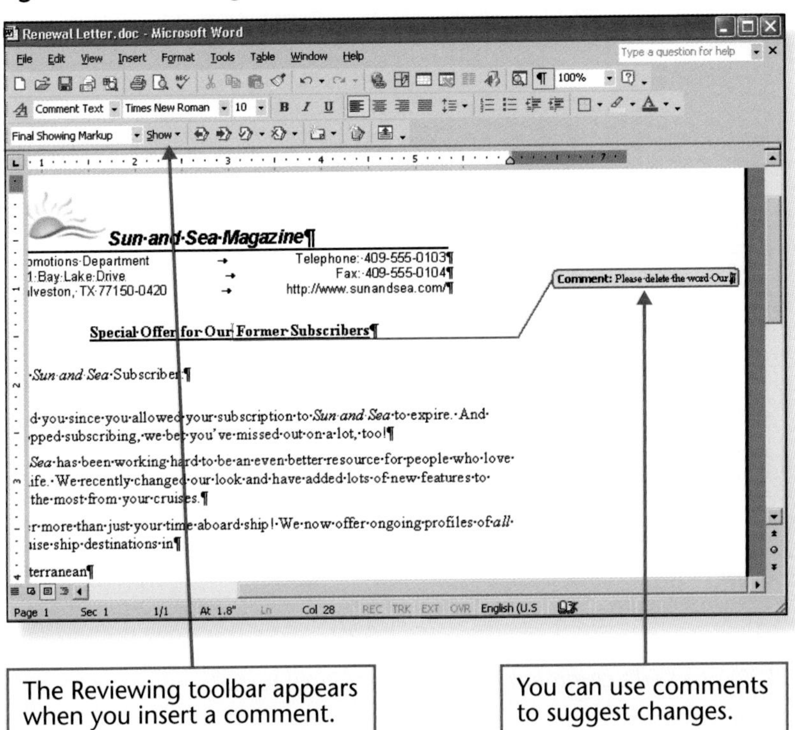

The Reviewing toolbar appears when you insert a comment.
You can use comments to suggest changes.

Step Through It™

Exercise 1A: Insert and edit comments

1. Open *RenewalLetter.doc.* Save the file as xxx-*Renewal Letter.doc.*
2. Click after *Our* in the underlined text at the beginning of the document.
3. On the Insert menu, select Comment to activate the Reviewing toolbar and create a new comment balloon. In the comment balloon, type Please delete the word Our. (See Figure 4.1.)

Figure 4.2 Editing text with Track Changes active

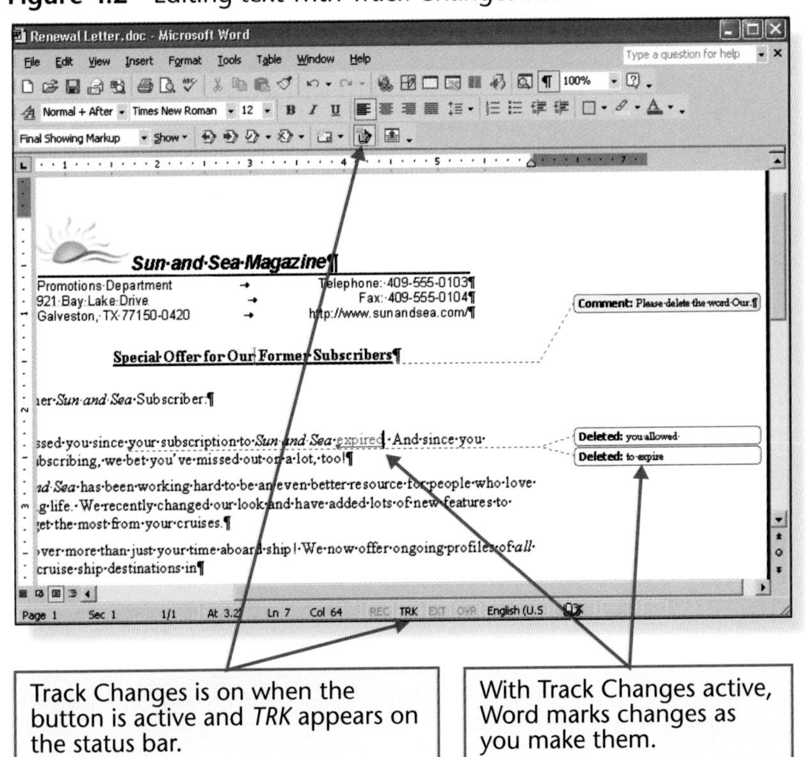

Track Changes is on when the button is active and *TRK* appears on the status bar.
With Track Changes active, Word marks changes as you make them.

4. On the Reviewing toolbar, select Track Changes to mark the changes you will make.
5. In the first line of text following the letter's greeting, select *you allowed* and press Delete.
6. In the same line, select the words *to expire* and type the word expired (see Figure 4.2).

Word

7. Scroll down to the second bulleted list and click after *$42.95*.

8. Click New Comment . When the new comment balloon appears, type This should be $41.95.

9. Scroll up to the document's first comment and click at the right end of the balloon. Press the spacebar once, and then type Increase the font size of this line to 14 points. (See Figure 4.3.)

Figure 4.3 Editing a comment

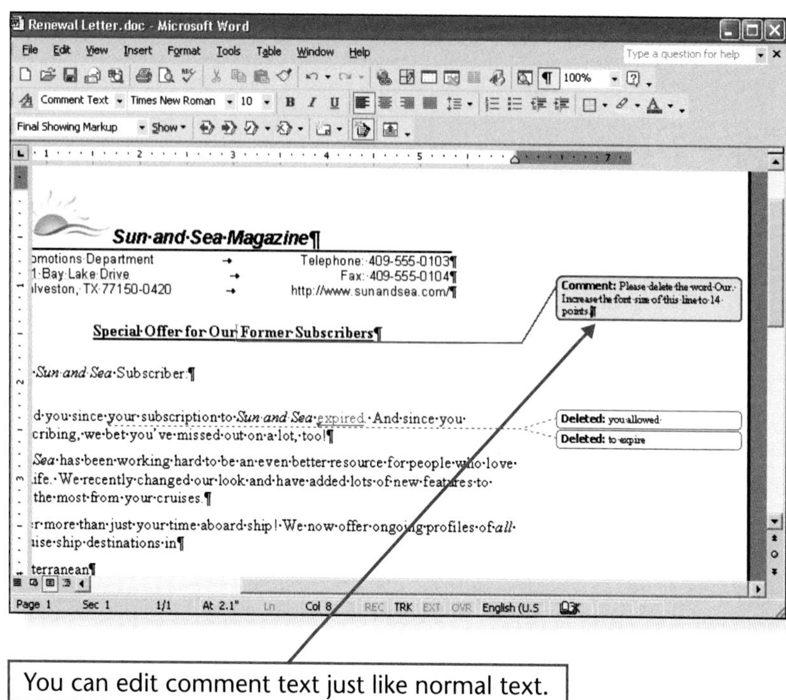

10. Scroll to the last comment in the document. Click Reviewing Pane to open the Reviewing pane at the bottom of the document.

11. In the Reviewing pane, scroll to the last comment and edit the amount *$41.95* to read *$41.99* (see Figure 4.4).

12. Click the Reviewing Pane button to close the Reviewing pane. Click Track Changes to turn off the Track Changes feature. Save the document.

Figure 4.4 Using the Reviewing pane

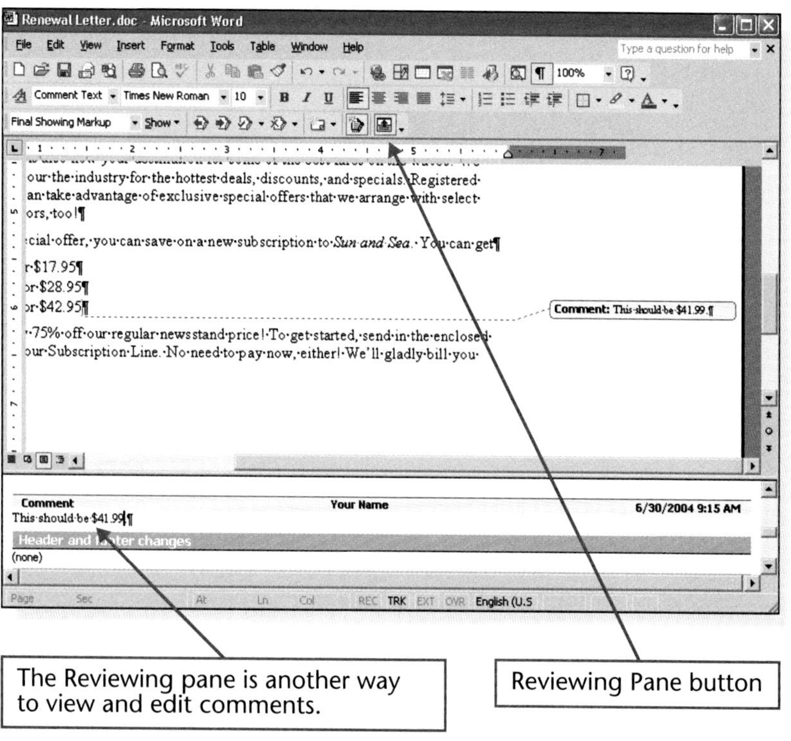

Figure 4.5 Merging comments and changes

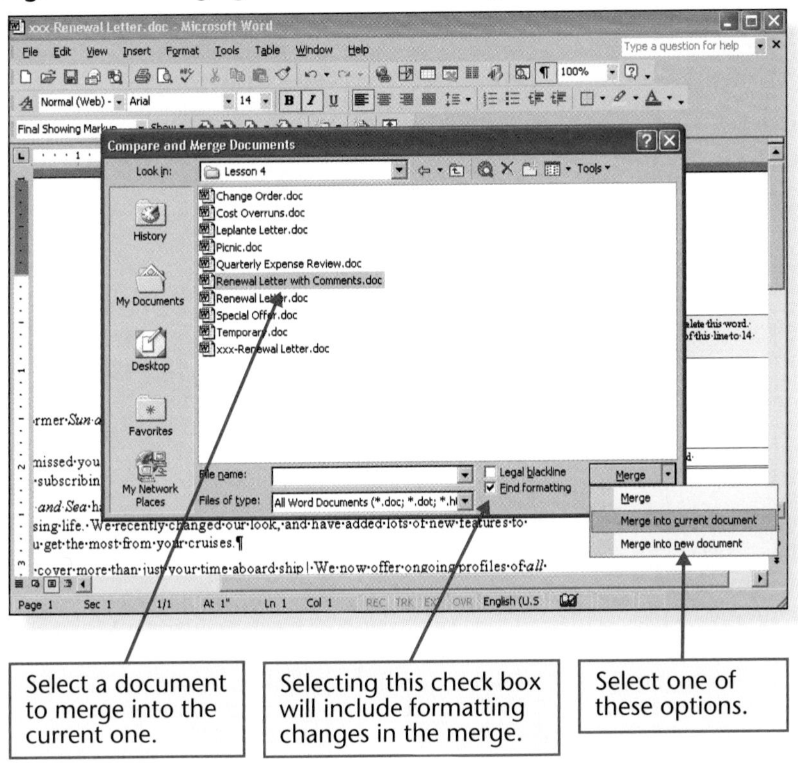

Select a document to merge into the current one.
Selecting this check box will include formatting changes in the merge.
Select one of these options.

Step Through It™

Exercise 1B: Compare and merge documents

1. Press Ctrl + Home. On the Tools menu, select Compare and Merge Documents to open the Compare and Merge Documents dialog box.
2. Navigate to the *Lesson 4* subfolder in your *Unit 1* folder. Select *Renewal Letter with Comments.doc.*
3. Click the Merge down arrow (see Figure 4.5). Click *Merge into current document* to combine the comments from both documents.

Figure 4.6 The merged documents

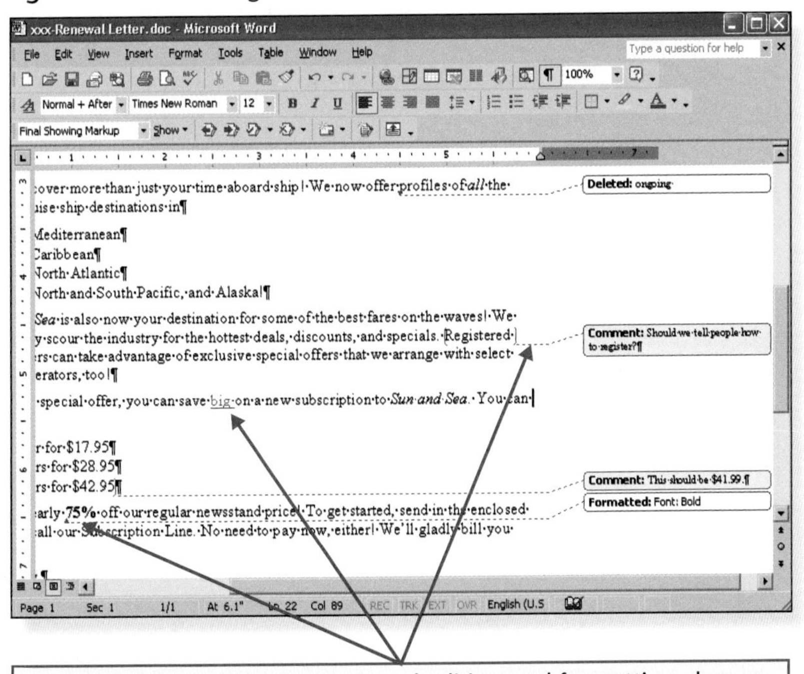

The other reviewer's comments and editing and formatting changes have been merged.

4. Scroll through the letter and you'll see one new comment and additional changes with your own (see Figure 4.6). The other reviewer has made three changes to the document's text.
5. Save the document.

Step Through It™

Exercise 1C: Working with merged comments and changes

1. With the insertion point at the top of the document, click Next to select the first comment balloon (see Figure 4.7).

2. Click Reject Change/ Delete Comment to delete the comment.

3. Within the line of underlined text, delete the word *Our* and change the font size of the entire line to 14.

Figure 4.7 Selecting a comment

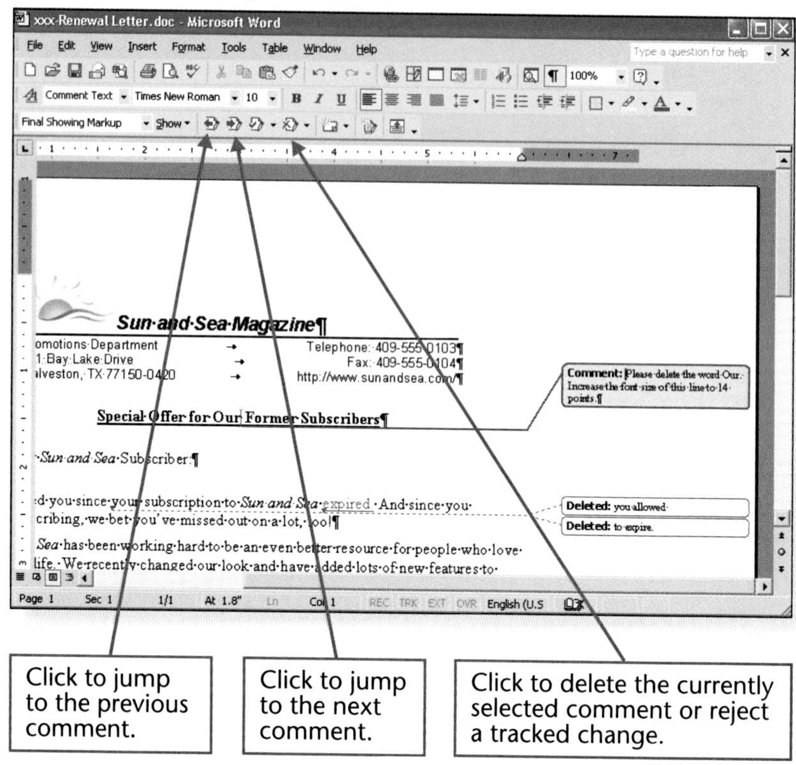

Click to jump to the previous comment.
Click to jump to the next comment.
Click to delete the currently selected comment or reject a tracked change.

4. Click Next to move to the next balloon, which shows that the words *you allowed* were deleted.

5. Click Accept Change to accept this change and remove its comment balloon (see Figure 4.8).

6. Click Next. Click Accept Change to clear the balloon. Click Accept Change again to accept the word *expired*.

7. Click Next. This balloon shows the other reviewer deleted *ongoing* from the document. Accept this change.

Figure 4.8 Accepting a change

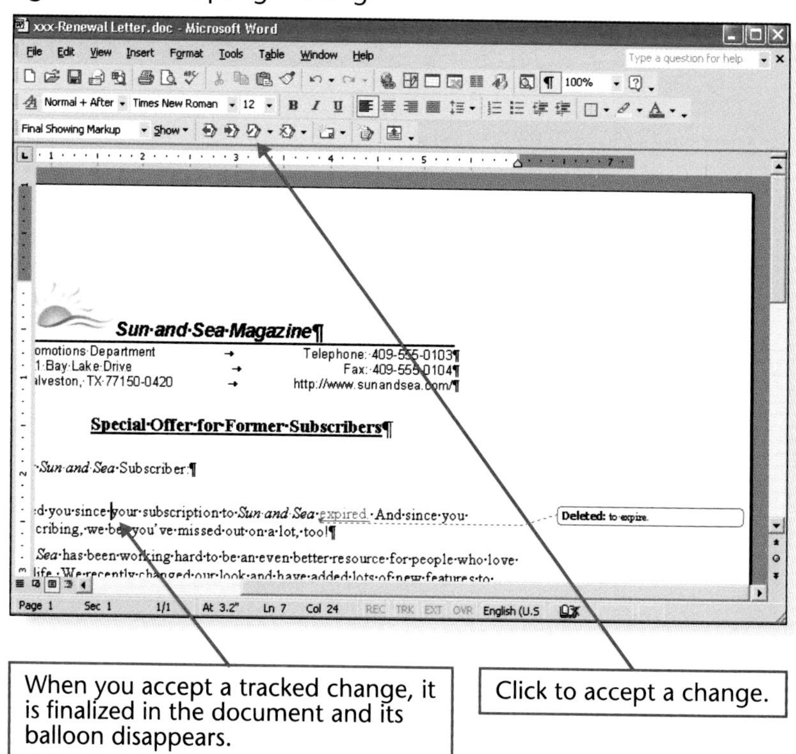

When you accept a tracked change, it is finalized in the document and its balloon disappears.
Click to accept a change.

Figure 4.9 Accepting text added by another reviewer

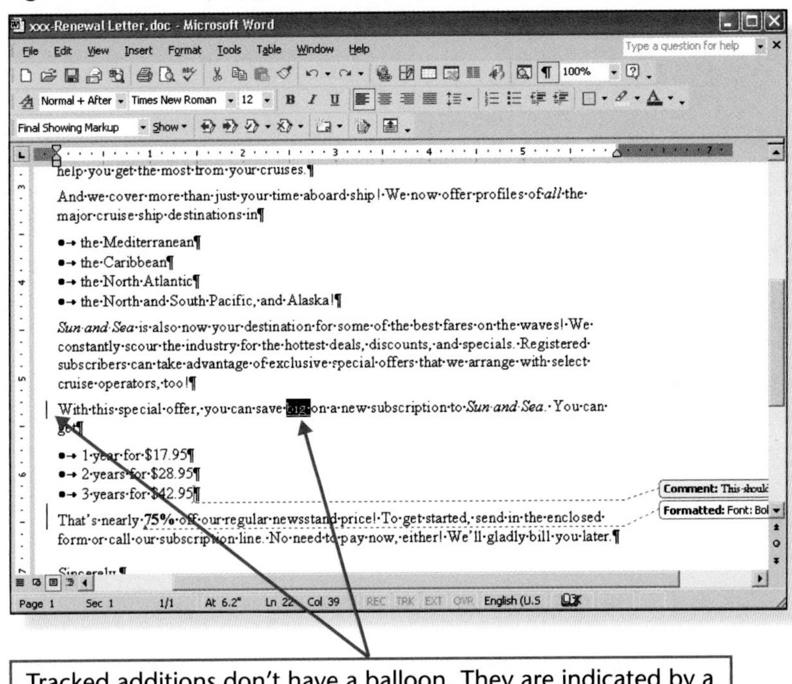

Tracked additions don't have a balloon. They are indicated by a revision mark in the left margin.

8 Click Next, and then click Reject Change/ Delete Comment.

9 Click Next. The word *big* is highlighted showing that it was added to the document (see Figure 4.9). Accept this change and click Next.

Word

Figure 4.10 The edited subscription price

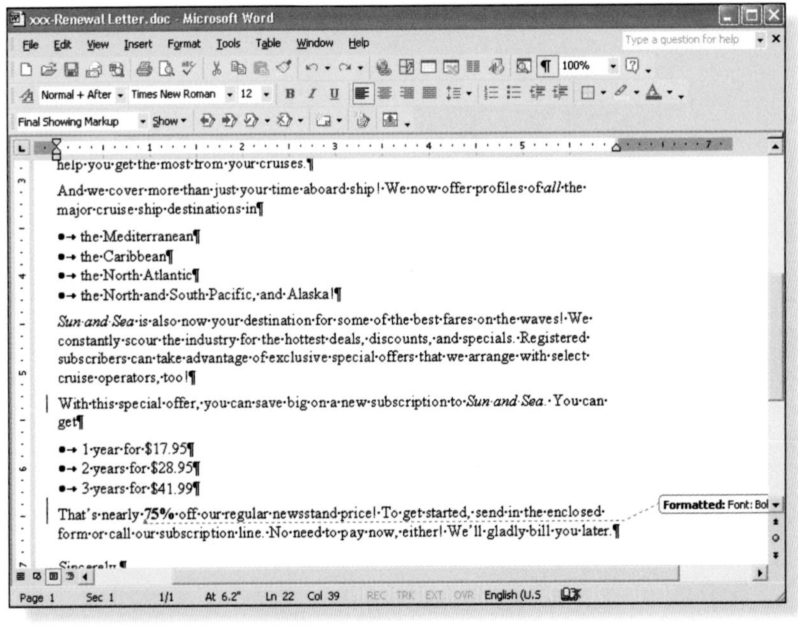

10 Delete the comment and change the amount *$42.95* to *$41.99* (see Figure 4.10).

11 Click Next and click Accept Change.

12 Close the Reviewing toolbar.

13 Save and close your document.

APPLY IT! After finishing Exercise 1, you may test your skills by completing Apply It! Guided Activity 1, Review a Document.

Business Connections

Teams in the Workplace

More than ever before, today's businesses rely on teams to get jobs done. Teamwork is an especially effective approach when each team member brings special skills to a project. By allowing each worker to focus on one aspect of a project, teams often produce higher-quality work than is possible when one person tries to do everything.

In the past, teams needed to be together much of the time. This isn't the case today because workers can use computers and communications technologies like the following:

- **Electronic mail (e-mail).** Using computers and a network or the Internet, workers can use e-mail software to exchange messages. They can attach files (such as word processing documents) to messages to share information.

- **File transfer.** Special file-transfer protocol (FTP) software gives users common access to files over a network or Internet connection.
- **Videoconferencing.** Special software, such as Microsoft NetMeeting, allows users to see and hear one another on screen. In a videoconference, users can work in a "chat" window by typing messages for one another to see. Some conferencing systems allow users to share and edit documents together during a conference.

Team Productivity

Long-distance collaboration requires that workers know how to locate and retrieve information using various methods.

Team members must be able to interpret information effectively. This ability reduces the amount of time workers spend "figuring things out" or asking questions.

Team members have to depend on each other; otherwise, the team cannot achieve its goals. For this reason, productive work habits—such as dependability and punctuality—are essential in each team member. Anyone who does not demonstrate these basic work habits threatens the entire team's success.

CRITICAL THINKING

1. **Providing for Distance Collaboration** List two ways that team members may collaborate from a distance, and identify the kind of software they might use to support this collaboration.
2. **What Makes a Team Player?** List two qualities that successful team members have in addition to their technical skills or knowledge. Put your findings in a table.

Microsoft Office Specialist W2002 6.3

Word

Exercise 2 Overview:
Share a Document Online

Increasingly, people share documents by publishing them on the Internet or a corporate intranet. The **Internet** is a worldwide system that connects thousands of individual networks together. These connections allow a computer on one network to communicate with virtually any other computer on any other network.

The **World Wide Web (WWW)** is the most popular service of the Internet. It allows people to publish colorful documents that include text, images, and other kinds of content; Web documents can be linked together, too. To be published on the Web, documents are usually saved in **Hypertext Markup Language (HTML)** format. Documents published on the Web are called **Web pages**. HTML is the underlying code that determines how Web documents look and behave when viewed in a special software tool called a **Web browser**. (Microsoft Internet Explorer is an example of a Web browser.)

An **intranet** is a small, private network that is set up to function like the Internet. An intranet enables users to communicate and access files as though they were using the Internet with an e-mail program and a Web browser.

Word can convert documents into Web pages so you can publish them on a Web site or an intranet. The process is as simple as saving the file; however, Word provides some special options when you save a document as a Web page.

Figure 4.11 The code within a Web page

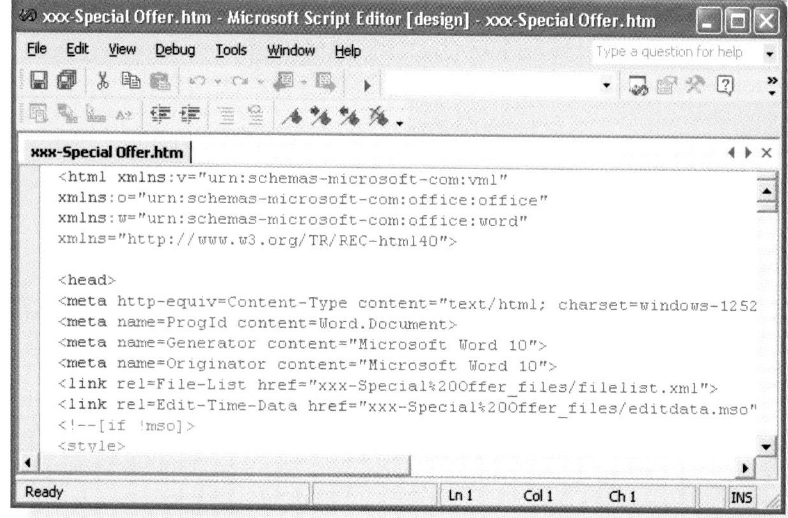

Figure 4.12 A document in Web Layout View

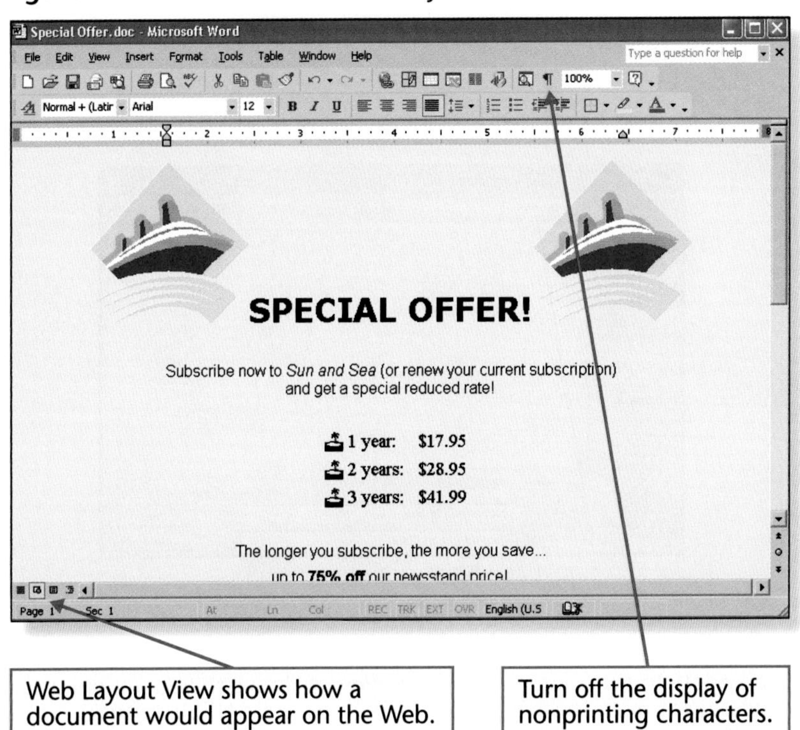

Step Through It™

Exercise 2A: Preview a document as a Web page

1. Open *Special Offer.doc*. Turn off Show/Hide to hide paragraph marks and other nonprinting characters.
2. Scroll through the document to view its formatting. The document should appear in Web Layout View (see Figure 4.12).

Figure 4.13 The document in Internet Explorer

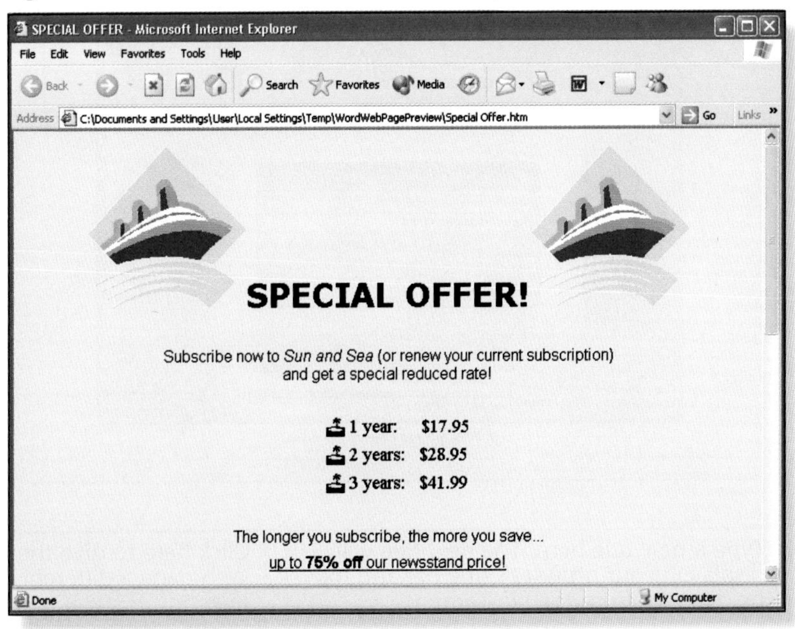

3. On the File menu, select Web Page Preview to open the document in your Microsoft Internet Explorer browser (see Figure 4.13).
4. Scroll through the document in your browser. Select Close on the File menu to close your browser.

Step Through It™

Exercise 2B: Save a document as a Web page

1. With the document in the Word window, select Save as Web Page on the File menu to open the Save As dialog box.
2. In the *Save in* box, navigate to the *Lesson 4* subfolder in your *Unit 1* folder, if necessary.
3. In the *File name* box, change the file name to *xxx-Special Offer.htm* (see Figure 4.14).

Figure 4.14 Saving a document as a Web page

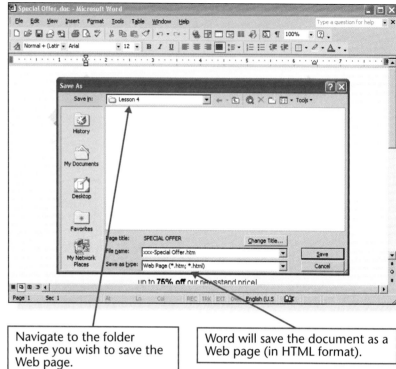

Navigate to the folder where you wish to save the Web page.

Word will save the document as a Web page (in HTML format).

4. Click Change Title to open the Set Page Title dialog box.
5. In the *Page title* box, type **Special Subscription Offer!** (see Figure 4.15). Click OK.
6. In the Save As dialog box, click Save.

Figure 4.15 Giving the Web page a different title

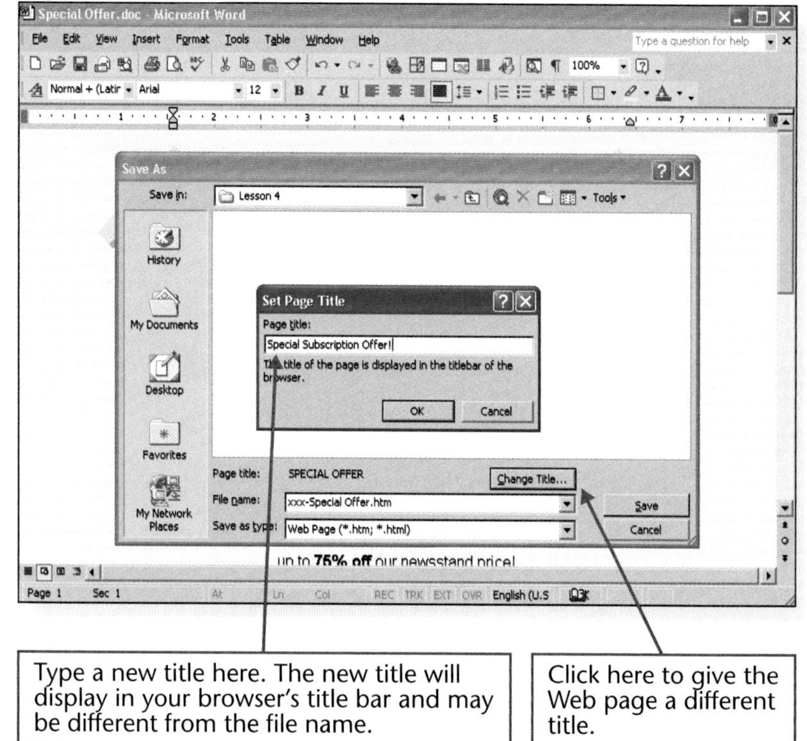

Figure 4.16 Opening a Web page in Internet Explorer

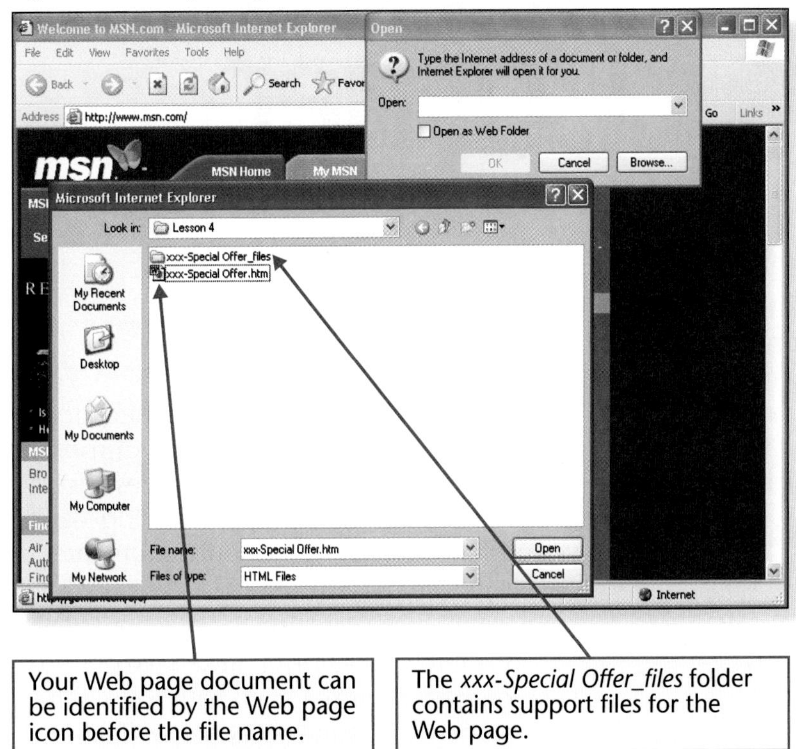

Your Web page document can be identified by the Web page icon before the file name.
The *xxx-Special Offer_files* folder contains support files for the Web page.

7. Close the document, and then minimize the Word window. Launch Internet Explorer.

8. In the browser window, click Open on the File menu. Click Browse in the Open dialog box, and navigate to the *Lesson 4* subfolder in your *Unit 1* folder (see Figure 4.16). ***Note:*** The *xxx-Special Offer_files* folder contains support files for your Web page—do not move or delete any of the files within this folder.

Figure 4.17 The finished Web page

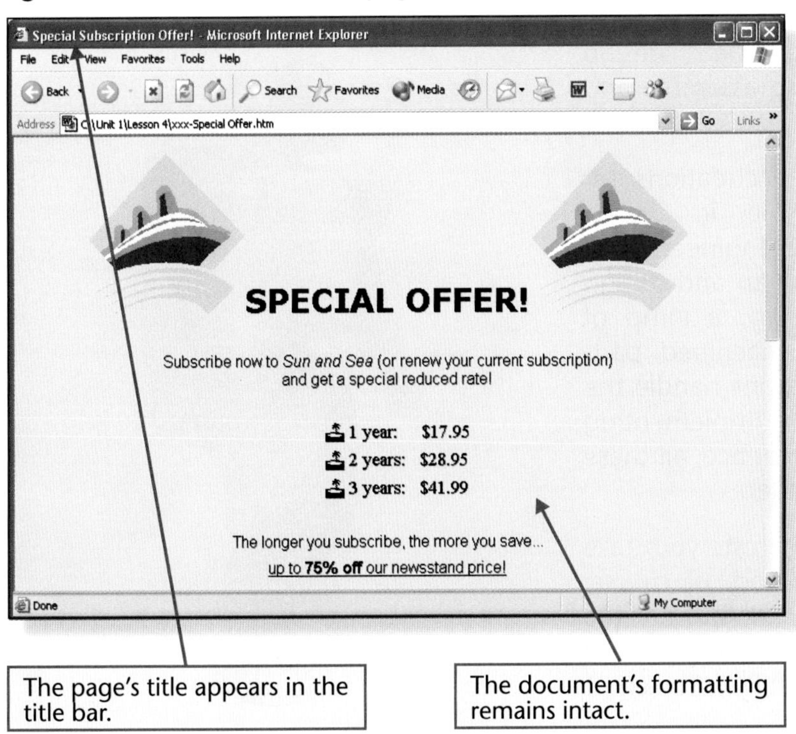

9. Select *xxx-Special Offer.htm* and click Open. Click OK in the Open dialog box to launch the Web page in your browser (see Figure 4.17).

10. Scroll to view the Web page.

11. Close the browser, and then maximize the Word window.

Word

Career Corner

Robots at Work

Do you like BattleBots, battle droids, and R2–D2? Wouldn't it be great to have a droid help you clean your room or mow the grass? Having your own personal droid is still only a vision for the future, but there are robots at work among us today.

Robots do many different kinds of jobs too dangerous or wearying for people. They crawl the surface of Mars, detonate bombs, and clean up hazardous spills. They work on assembly lines, doing welding, painting, cutting, loading—even running factories.

When a robot is the answer, the task falls to robotics technologists to create robots that are specially designed to perform the work. Robotics technologists design robots using computer-aided design (CAD) software. They also assemble and test the robots.

There are many other occupations for creative, inventive people in manufacturing. Manufacturing engineers look at the big picture. They plan and design the process that turns, say, a lump of metal into a smoothly machined part. Technologists and technicians handle the nuts-and-bolts details of implementing the engineer's vision. In practice, all these people work closely together.

If one of these careers interests you, take classes in math, physics, and, of course, computers. Take things apart (but not the toaster or anything essential!) and put them back together again (hopefully!). Tinker!

CRITICAL THINKING

1. Robots with artificial intelligence, or AI, are becoming a reality. Think of robots in movies and on TV. How does what they do reflect what is promising—and what people fear—about robots that can think on their own?
2. If you created a robot, what would it do? Explore space? Fight fires? Take out the garbage? Form a team with some other students. Use the collaborative features of Word you are learning about in this lesson to plan a robot. Don't forget to include a drawing or model! Present your robot to the class.

Exercise 3 Overview:
Insert and Modify a Date/Time Field

Sometimes it is important to know when a document was created or when it was last modified or printed. In business, for example, some documents such as reports or financial statements are very time sensitive. Managers want to know they are looking at the most recent version of the document.

You can insert a field to display the date or time. A **field** is a special placeholder for changeable information such as the date or time, the date the document was last modified or printed, the file name, the author's name, and other kinds of information. The underlying code that enables this information to change is called a **field code** [?].

Word fields are predefined, meaning you simply select the kind of field you need from a menu. However, you can customize fields in several ways. You can set a field to update its information automatically (whenever a file is opened or printed, for example), and you can modify some kinds of fields to change their appearance or the way they function.

In the following exercises, you will insert a field into a document and modify the underlying field code.

Microsoft Office Specialist W2002 1.5

Word

Need Help?

Type: field

Figure 4.18 The Field dialog box

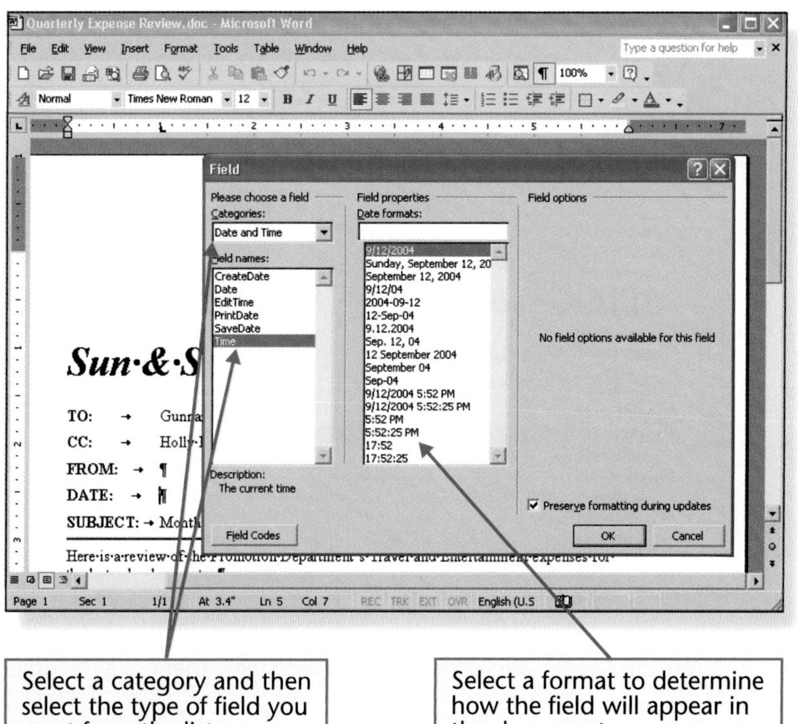

Select a category and then select the type of field you want from the list.
Select a format to determine how the field will appear in the document.

Step Through It™
Exercise 3A: Insert a time field

1. Open *Quarterly Expense Review.doc*. Save the file as *xxx-Quarterly Expense Review.doc*.
2. Select Show/Hide to display nonprinting characters, if necessary. Place the insertion point at the right end of the *Date:* line.
3. On the Insert menu, select Field to open the Field dialog box.
4. Click the *Categories* down arrow and click Date and Time. In the *Field names* list, click Time (see Figure 4.18).

Word

5. In the *Date formats* list, click the field that appears in the format *h:mm:ss am/pm* (4:10:50 PM, for example).

6. Click OK to insert this time field into the document.

7. Click the time field (see Figure 4.19). ***Note:*** If the codes appear in your document instead of the time of day, select Options on the Tools menu. In the Options dialog box (View tab), clear the *Field codes* check box and click OK.

Figure 4.19 The time field inserted into the document

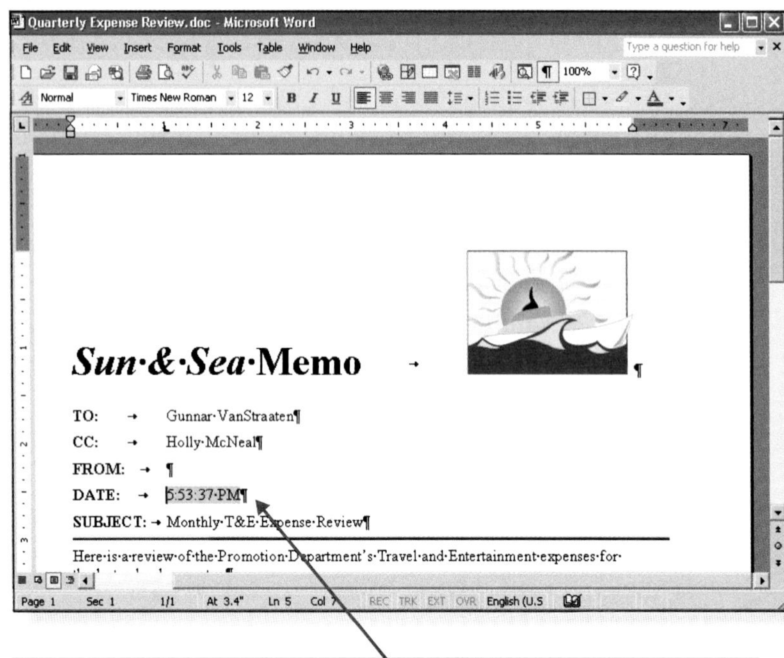

Step Through It™

Exercise 3B: Edit a field format to display the date

1. Right-click the time field you just inserted. On the shortcut menu, click *Update Field* to update the field to the current time.

2. Right-click the field again and click *Toggle Field Codes* on the shortcut menu. Word now displays the field's underlying code (see Figure 4.20).

Figure 4.20 Viewing a field code

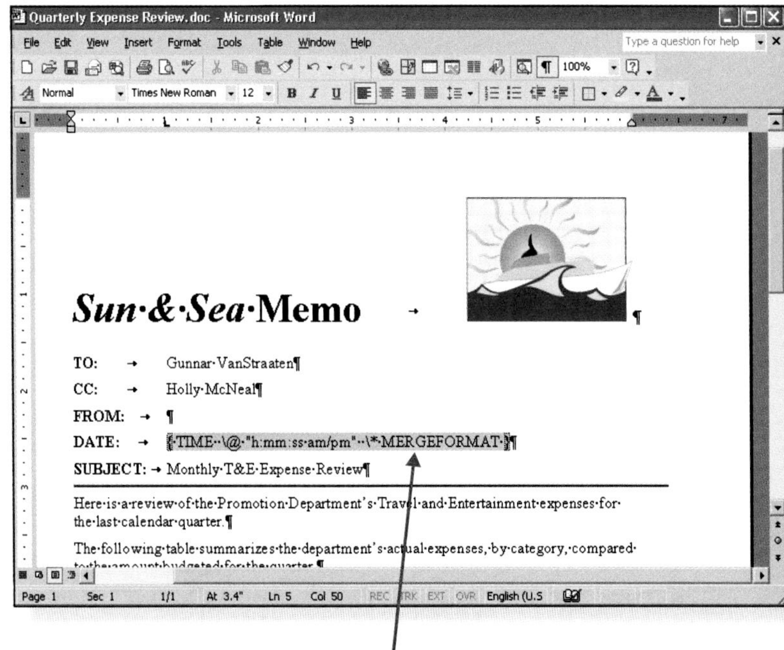

Figure 4.21 Editing a field code

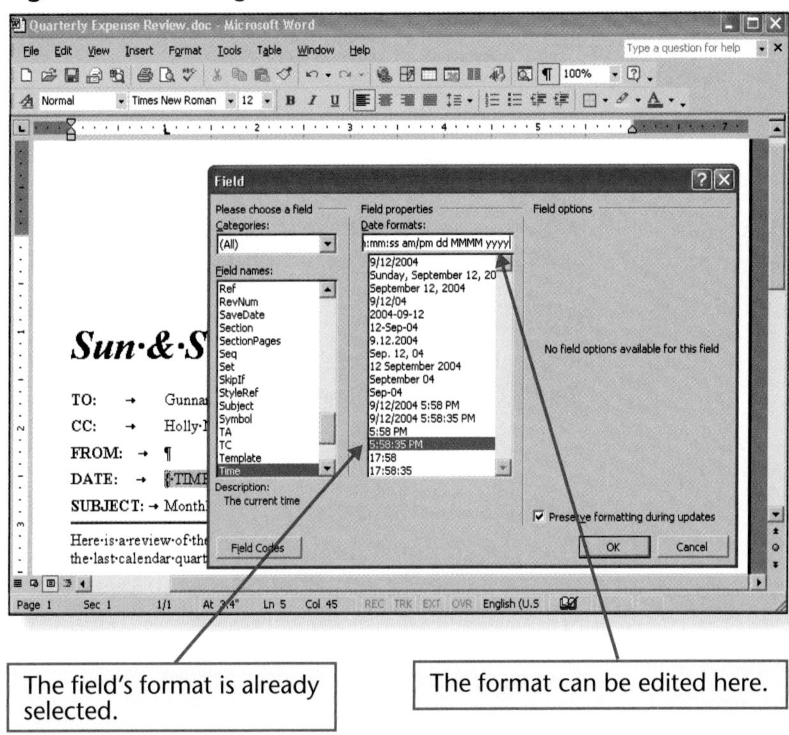
The field's format is already selected.
The format can be edited here.

3 Right-click the field code and click *Edit Field* on the shortcut menu to open the Field dialog box. The dialog box opens with the field's format selected.

4 Click at the right end of the code within the *Date formats* box and press the spacebar. Type dd MMMM yyyy (see Figure 4.21).

Word

Figure 4.22 The modified field

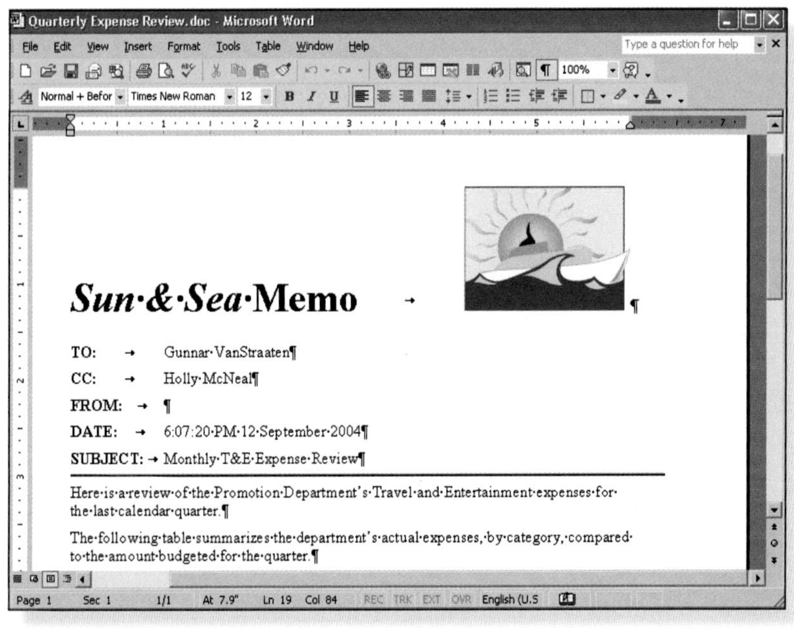

5 Click OK to close the dialog box. The modified field now displays the time and the date (see Figure 4.22).

6 Click at the right end of the *From:* line and type your name.

7 Save the file.

8 Close the document.

APPLY IT! After finishing Exercise 3, you may test your skills by completing Apply It! Guided Activity 2, Create a Web Page.

Procedure Summary

Word Procedure Summary

Insert a Comment

1. Click an insertion point where you want to comment.
2. Click **New Comment** button on the Reviewing toolbar.

   OR

   On the **Insert** menu, click **Comment**. . . . .**Alt + I, M**
3. Type a comment in the balloon.

Activate or Deactivate Track Changes

Click **Track Changes** button on the Reviewing toolbar.
OR
On the **Tools** menu, click **Track Changes**. . . . . **Alt + T, T**
OR . . . .**Ctrl + Shift + E**

Open or Close the Reviewing pane

On the Reviewing toolbar, click **Reviewing Pane** button .

Review Comments in a Document

1. Click an insertion point at the top of the document.
2. Click **Next** button on the Reviewing toolbar.

Reject a Change/Delete a Comment

With the comment balloon or text change selected, click **Reject Change/Delete Comment** button .
OR
Right-click the change and click Reject Insertion, Reject Deletion, or Reject Format Change.

Accept a Change

With the comment balloon or text change selected, click **Accept Change** button .
OR
Right-click the change and select Accept Insertion, Accept Deletion, or Accept Format Change.

Edit a Comment

1. Click in the comment balloon.

   OR

   Click the comment in the Reviewing pane.
2. Add, delete, edit, or format text.

Merge Documents

1. On the **Tools** menu, select **Compare and Merge Documents**. . . . . **Alt + T, D**
2. Select a file to merge into the current document.

3. Click **Merge**. . . . . **Alt + M**

   OR

   Click the Merge down arrow, and select Merge into current document or Merge into new document.

Preview a Document as a Web Page

1. Open the document.
2. On the **File** menu, select **Web Page Preview** . . . . **Alt + F, B**
3. Close the browser window.

Save a Document as a Web Page

1. On the **File** menu, select **Save as Web Page**. . . . . **Alt + F, G**
2. Select a folder in which to store the Web page.
3. Type a name in the **File name** box. . . . **Alt + N**
4. Click **Change Title**, if necessary. . . . . . **Alt + C**
5. Type a new page title and click OK.
6. Click **Save**. . . . . **Alt + S**

Insert a Time Field

1. Click where the field should be inserted.
2. On the **Insert** menu, select **Field**. . . **Alt + I, F**
3. In the **Categories** list, select Date and Time. **Alt + C**
4. In the **Field names** list, select Date . **Alt + F**
5. In the **Date formats** list, select a format . . . . **Alt + D**
6. Click OK.

OR

On the **Insert** menu, select **Date and Time**, select a time format, and click OK.. . . . . **Alt + I, T**

Update a Time Field

1. Right-click the field.
2. Select Update Field.

Display Field Codes

1. Right-click the field.
2. Select Toggle Field Codes.

Edit a Field Code

1. Right-click the field.
2. Click Edit Field.
3. Type your changes in the *Date formats* box.
4. Click OK.

Lesson Review and Exercises

Word

Summary Checklist

- ☑ Can you insert comments into a document?
- ☑ Can you edit the comments?
- ☑ Can you track the changes you make in a document?
- ☑ Can you merge documents together to see comments and changes from multiple reviewers?
- ☑ Can you accept comments and changes?
- ☑ Can you reject comments and changes?
- ☑ Can you preview a document as a Web page?
- ☑ Can you save a document as a Web page?
- ☑ Can you insert a date/time field?
- ☑ Can you modify a date/time field format?

Key Terms

- comment (p. 124)
- field (p. 137)
- field code (p. 137)
- Hypertext Markup Language (HTML) (p. 132)
- Internet (p. 132)
- intranet (p. 132)
- Web browser (p. 132)
- Web page (p. 132)
- World Wide Web (WWW) (p. 132)

APPLY IT! Guided Activities

1. Review a Document

As an interior designer, you sometimes have the unpleasant task of telling a client that a project will cost more than expected. Your assistant has prepared a draft of the letter and has sent it to you for review. While you are reviewing the letter, he will try one more time to persuade the suppliers to hold their prices.

Follow these steps:

a. Open *Cost Overruns.doc.* In the first line of the letter, click after the word *Sadly,* and then select Comment on the Insert menu. Type This word is too gloomy. How about Regretfully? in the comment balloon.

b. Turn on Track Changes. In the second line of the first paragraph, select the number *3* and type the word three. Make sure Word tracks the change.

c. In the last sentence above the table, click after *$8,680.* Click New Comment and type Please double-check this figure.

d. Within your first comment, select the word *Regretfully* and type Regrettably. Turn off Track Changes. Save the document as *xxx-Cost Overruns.doc.* **(See Figure 4.23.)**

e. Your assistant tells you that he just placed a version of the letter (with additional comments) in your folder on the shared drive of the corporate network. Press Ctrl + Home. On the Tools menu, select Compare and Merge Documents. Navigate to the *Lesson 4* subfolder in your *Unit 1* folder. Select *Cost Overruns with Comments.doc,* click the Merge down arrow, and select *Merge into current document.*

f. Review all the comments in the document, including your own. Make the appropriate changes in the document based on your best judgment in order to finalize it so it is ready to mail to your client. Rewrite the first paragraph and revise the table as necessary. Save your changes.

g. Close the document, but leave Word running.

Figure 4.23 Adding comments and changes to a letter

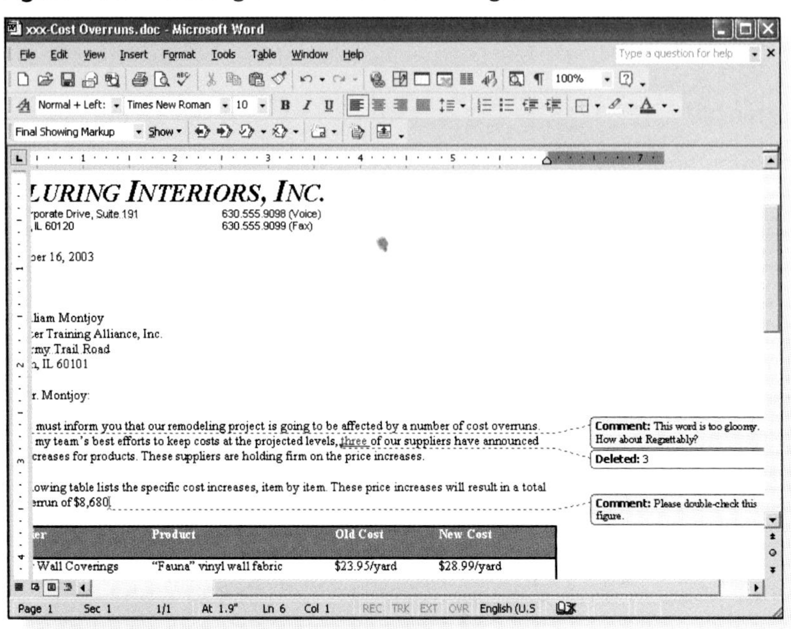

2. Create a Web Page

As personnel director for a construction company, you get to plan the annual company picnic. This year, in addition to posting invitations on the office bulletin boards, you want to publish an invitation on the company's intranet. You have created an invitation in Word, and now you need to convert it to a Web page.

Follow these steps to create your Web page:

a. Open *Picnic.doc.* Scroll to view the document.

b. On the File menu, select Web Page Preview to see how the invitation will look in your Web browser. Close the browser.

c. Click below the last line in the document and press Enter. On the Insert menu, select Date and Time. Select the date and time that appears in the format *M/d/yyyy h:mm:ss am/pm* (example: 9/17/2003 8:19:27 AM). Clear the *Update automatically* check box, and click OK. Change the date/time font to Arial and the font size to 11. Click before the date and type Created **(see Figure 4.24)**.

d. On the File menu, select Save as Web Page. In the Save As dialog box, navigate to the *Lesson 4* subfolder in your *Unit 1* folder.

e. Click Change Title and change the page title to Company Picnic Invitation.

f. Save your Web page as xxx-Picnic.htm. On the File menu, select Open. Click xxx-Picnic.htm and click open. Preview your Web page in your browser to check the new page title, and then close your browser. Close your document.

Figure 4.24 Inserting the date and time in a Web page

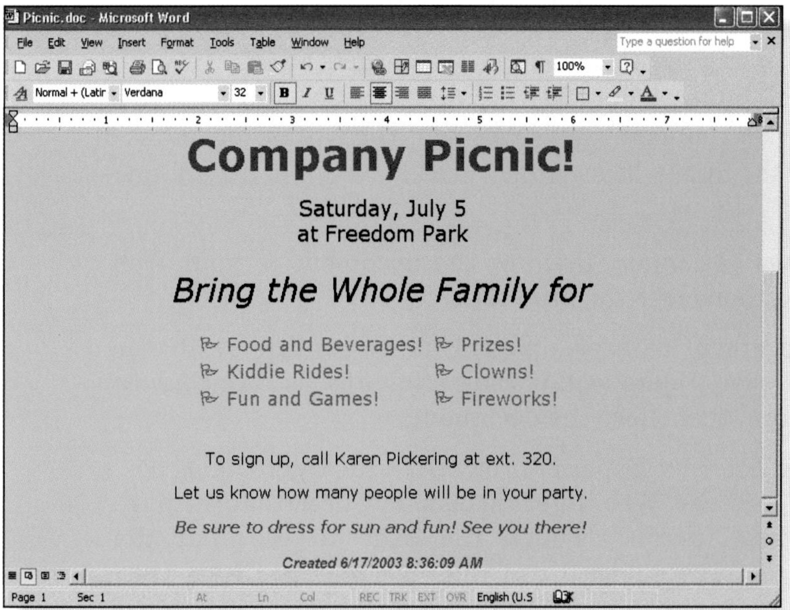

Do It Yourself

1. Insert the Date and Time in a Memo

You work in the accounting department of a large computer manufacturing company. Your boss is very interested in knowing how many temporary workers are being used each day. You have created a report that you update every day, print, and place in his mailbox. To assure him that the report is always current, you want to add a field that shows the date and time. Follow these steps to add the field to your document:

a. Open *Temporary.doc*. Type your name on the *From* line. Place the insertion point on the *Date / Time* line.

b. Insert a field that shows the time but *not* the date. Right-click the field and select Edit Field. With the field code visible in the Field dialog box, edit the field's format to display the date in addition to the time: Place the date before the time using the format *dd MMMM yyyy* followed by a comma and a blank space.

c. Save the file as *xxx-Temporary.doc.* Close the document, but keep word running.

Word

2. Create an Online Change Order

You are a manager for a large printing company with several out-of-town locations. You need to give your designers and account managers an easy way to deal with changes to their projects. You have decided to create a form called a change order and post it on your company's Web site. Then users, regardless of their location, can print the form whenever they need it and fill in the information. Follow these steps:

a. Open *Change Order.doc.* Preview the document in your Web browser and then close the browser.

b. Save the document as a Web page. Change its title to Change Order Form **(see Figure 4.25)**. Save the file as *xxx-Change Order.htm*, and then close the document.

c. Launch your Internet Explorer browser. In the Open dialog box, navigate to your new Web page and open it. Check that the page title is correct. Scroll through the page to see that the formatting is acceptable. Print the document. Close your browser.

Figure 4.25 Changing the Web page title

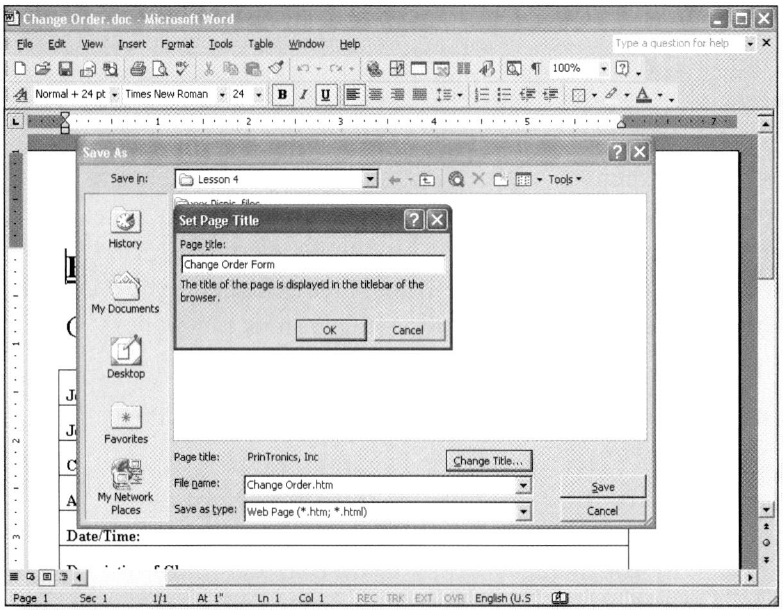

3. Add and Edit Comments

As the assistant manager of a popular, family-owned restaurant, one of your jobs is to make sure the menu is properly updated. You need to review the newest lunch menu, which was created by the restaurant's chef. It has already been reviewed by your manager (the restaurant's owner). After reviewing the menu, you'll need to pass it on for further review to the owner's daughter, so all the comments need to be easy to understand. Follow these steps:

a. Open *New Menu.doc*, and make sure that the Reviewing toolbar is visible.

b. Read the entire menu, including the comments that were inserted by the restaurant's owner. You will find errors in two of the comments—correct these mistakes. Do not make any other changes to the document.

c. Now you must insert new comments of your own at the appropriate locations in the menu:

- Remind the owner that chicken will not work for the Fettuccini alla Bono—the chef tried that last year and the results were not pleasing.
- Mention to the owner that Bono's Combo is your best-selling lunch item at the current price. Ask if he will reconsider the suggestion of dropping the price.

d. Save the document as *xxx-New Menu.doc.*

4. Accept and Reject Comments and Changes

As a travel agent, you have many clients who want to visit Caribbean islands. To make their travels easier, you have created a document that provides simple instructions for getting through customs when visiting an island. You have asked a fellow agent to review it before you start giving it to your clients. He made a number of changes and added several comments. You must now decide whether to accept or reject his comments and changes. Follow these steps:

a. Open *Customs Tips.doc.* Make sure the Reviewing toolbar is visible, and turn off the Track Changes feature.

b. Read through the entire document without making any changes. Look closely at each change and comment **(see Figure 4.26)**.

c. Starting at the beginning of the document, advance to each change and comment using the Reviewing toolbar. Accept or reject each change. If you agree with one of the comments, follow the suggestion described in the comment before deleting the comment.

d. After you finish working with comments and changes, save the completed document as *xxx-Customs Tips.doc*.

e. Close the document, but keep Word running.

Figure 4.26 Working with changes and comments

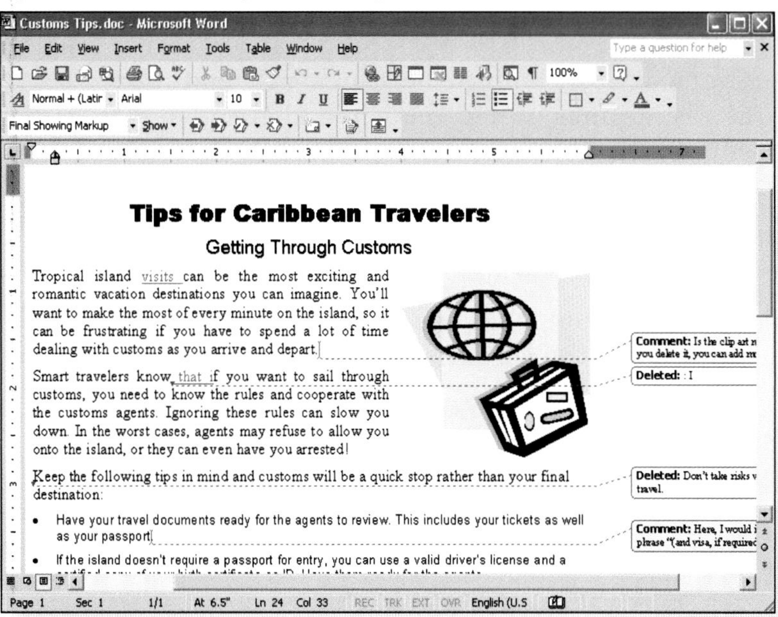

Challenge Yourself

1. Work With Comments and Tracked Changes

You are the assistant director of human resources for a medium-size printing company. A few days ago, you wrote the draft of a memo that will be distributed to all of the company's employees. The memo's purpose is to announce improved benefits that will take effect at the beginning of the new year. The director has already reviewed the memo and just returned it with changes and comments. You need to work with those comments and changes to complete the document. Here's what to do:

- Open *Benefits Memo.doc*. Make sure that the Reviewing toolbar is visible and that the Track Changes feature is turned off.

- Read the entire memo and all changes and comments. At this point, do not make any changes.
- Starting at the beginning of the document, move to each tracked change using the Reviewing toolbar. Accept or reject each tracked change as you think best; however, leave all comments intact for now.
- Review each of the director's comments. Make changes to the document as suggested by the comments. As you finish your revisions, remove each comment from the document when you no longer need it for reference.
- Add an appropriate header to the document including the subject matter of the document, the current date, and the page number. The header should not show on the first page. Format the header in an appropriate font and font size.
- Closely proofread the document and make any necessary changes. At this point, your document should no longer contain comments or tracked changes.
- When you are finished, save your document as *xxx-Benefits Memo.doc* **(see Figure 4.27)**. Close the document.

Figure 4.27 The finished document

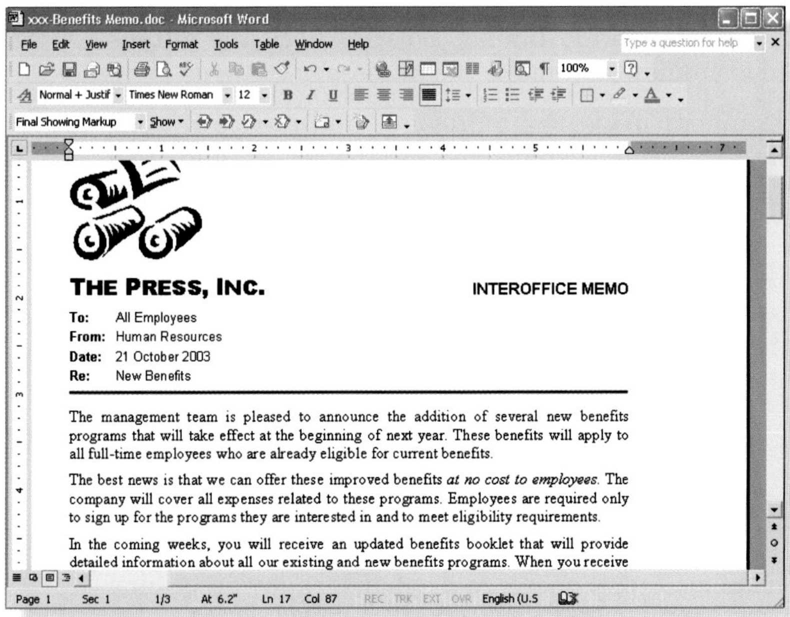

THE PRESS, INC. INTEROFFICE MEMO

To: All Employees
From: Human Resources
Date: 21 October 2003
Re: New Benefits

The management team is pleased to announce the addition of several new benefits programs that will take effect at the beginning of next year. These benefits will apply to all full-time employees who are already eligible for current benefits.

The best news is that we can offer these improved benefits *at no cost to employees*. The company will cover all expenses related to these programs. Employees are required only to sign up for the programs they are interested in and to meet eligibility requirements.

In the coming weeks, you will receive an updated benefits booklet that will provide detailed information about all our existing and new benefits programs. When you receive

Word

Unit 1 Applications and Projects

Apply Your Knowledge

Complete the following exercises in order, as directed by your teacher. As you work through these projects, you will use Word to create a set of documents, including a brief report that reviews your company's operations. Your documents must be professionally edited and formatted. Save all files in the *Unit Applications and Projects* subfolder within your *Unit 1* folder.

1. Create a Cover Letter

a. Open *Smith Letter.doc*. Use Find and Replace to search the letter for the word *grilles* and replace it with the word *grills*.

b. Delete the date and insert a field that displays the date in a different format. Type your name on the blank line above the job title *President*. Apply a bullet format to the list of items in the letter.

c. Use Word's spelling and grammar tools to check the letter's spelling and grammar, and make the necessary changes.

d. View the document using Print Preview, and then print one copy. Create and print an envelope for the letter, and then create and print one address label using the same delivery address.

e. Save the document as *xxx-Smith Letter.doc*. Create a new folder named *Operations Review* and save the document in the new folder in Rich Text Format (RTF) as *xxx-Backup Letter.rtf*. Close all open files.

2. Create a Biography

a. Open a new, blank document. Type the heading **President** and press Enter. Apply the *Heading 1* style to the heading.

b. Below the heading, type a one-paragraph biography describing yourself. As you type, use the touch method with your fingers on the home row of the keyboard. (Remember that you are president of a company that makes custom grills, so be creative.)

c. As you type the paragraph, take note of at least one common error you type that is not automatically corrected by Word's AutoCorrect tool. Add this error and the correction to the AutoCorrect dialog box. Perform a test of your AutoCorrect entry by intentionally typing the error in the document.

d. Check the document's spelling, and save it as *xxx-Biography.doc* (see Figure 1). Close the document.

Figure 1 A brief biography

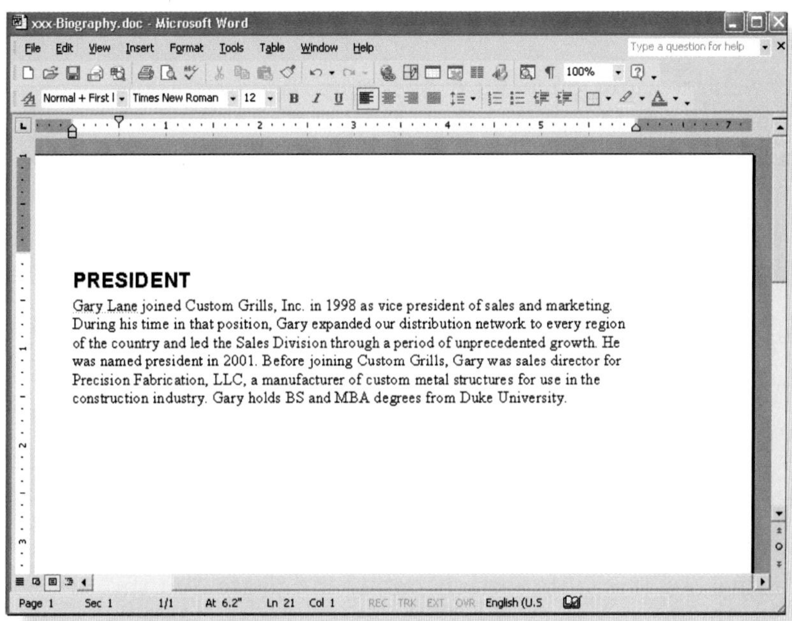

3. Format a Report and Add Comments

a. Open *Operations Review.doc*. Apply the *Heading 1* style to all the primary text headings. Insert a page break immediately before the *Overview* heading. Make sure that all paragraphs of text are left-aligned.

b. Use the Find command to find all occurrences of the hyperlink **www.customgrills.com**, and apply the *Hyperlink* character style to each of them.

c. Find the heading *NOTE* and the accompanying text, center it, and place a border around it. Add light yellow shading within the border. Set the line spacing for the text to 1.5.

d. Go to the *Pricing* section. Set an appropriate left tab and decimal tab in each of the listed price items.

Word

e. Go to the *Sales* heading. Insert a comment to your assistant Pat asking him to double-check the adjusted total revenue figures for the last quarter of 2002.

f. Add a footer to the document: Put the name of the report on the left and the word *Confidential* on the right. Format the footer in 10 point Arial; apply italic to the word *Confidential*. Omit the footer from the first page. Add a page number to the upper-right corner of each page with the exception of the first page.

g. Save your document as *xxx-Operations Review.doc*.

4. Work With Text

a. In the *Overview* section, click after the word *ArcSpot*. Type **(TM)** to insert the trademark symbol. Find the word *reputed* and use the Thesaurus to replace it with a different word.

b. Open *xxx-Biography.doc*, copy the entire document, and then close it. Paste the copied text before the heading *Management Team*. Adjust the formatting and spacing of the copied text as necessary. Apply the *Heading 2* paragraph style to the headings *President* and *Management Team*.

c. Go to the *Testimonials* section. Indent the three paragraphs of text in quotation marks one-half inch from the right and left margins. Select the line after each indented paragraph that begins with a person's name, right-align it, and format it in italic.

d. Select the entire *Testimonials* section, cut it, and paste it at the end of the document.

e. Go to the title on the document's first page. Change the title to 26 point Arial, bold, dark blue, centered.

f. Go to the *Sales* section and apply a yellow highlight to *increased 12%*. In the table title, select the number *1* and make it superscript. Go to the note below the table, select the number *1,* and make it superscript. Save your changes.

5. Add Clip Art, Tables, Charts, Lists

a. Select the three paragraphs below the heading *Management Team* and make them a bulleted list. In the *Markets* section, apply a numbered list format to the last four paragraphs. In the *New Distributors* section, make the list of states and business names into an outline numbered list.

b. In the *Sales* section, add a new row to the bottom of the table. Type **Modifications**, **$264,000**, and **$287,000** in the row's three cells. Apply the Table Contemporary AutoFormat. Select the second row of the table, center the cells, and apply italic.

c. At the end of the *Sales* section, insert a new table with three columns and five rows. Select the first row and merge the cells together. Fill in the cells with the following data.

Sales By Unit		
Style	2001	2002
Freestanding	10,740	12,550
Built-in	9,230	10,890
Combination	3,760	4,260

d. Manually format the new table to match the document's first table (do *not* use AutoFormat) **(see Figure 2)**.

Figure 2 Formatting a table

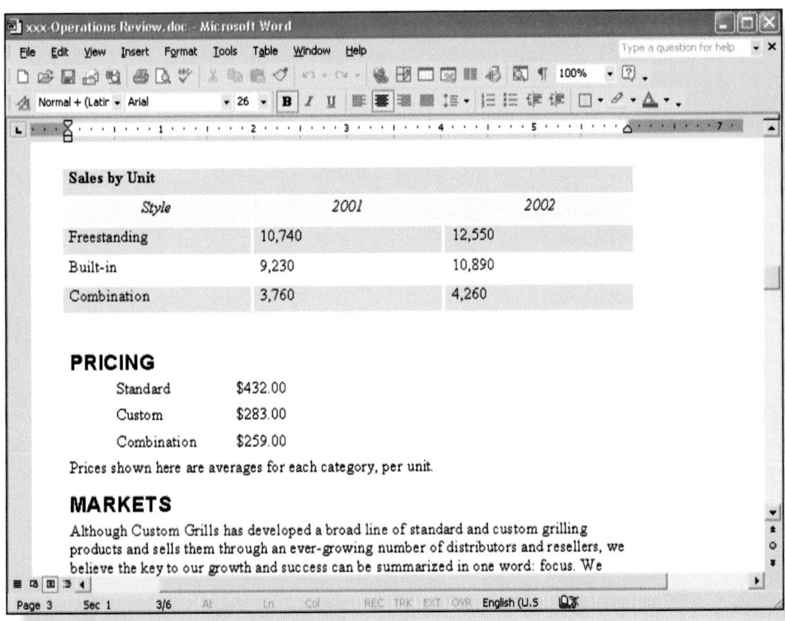

e. Go to the first page and insert a blank line after the report title. Search for appropriate clip art, and insert a clip below the title. (Go to Clips Online, if necessary, to find your clip.)

f. At the end of the *New Distributors* section, insert a simple column chart. Set up the datasheet as shown below.

		A	B
		2001	2002
1	North	36	55
2	South	48	74

g. Go to the end of the *Management Team* section and insert a blank line. Open *Headcount.doc*, copy the chart, and close the document. Paste the chart as a Microsoft Graph Chart Object using Paste Special. Resize the chart in the *New Distributors* section to be roughly the same size, and add the title *New Distributors* to it.

h. On a blank line after the Headcount Growth chart, create an organization chart showing your company's management. Create a box for yourself (President) and a box for each of the managers under the *Management Team* heading. Resize the organization chart **(see Figure 3)**.

Figure 3 The organization chart

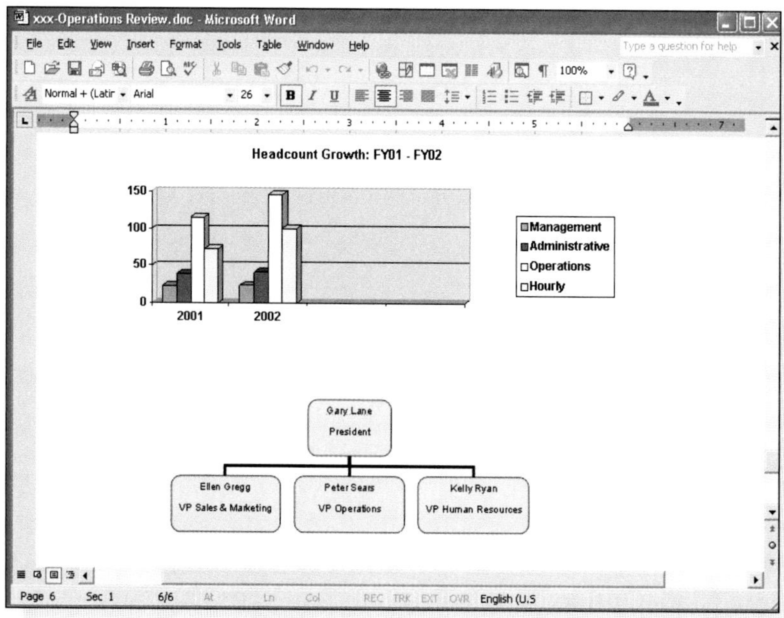

i. Scroll through the document and insert page breaks where necessary. Check the document's spelling and grammar, and then save your changes.

j. Close the document.

6. Create a Newsletter

a. Open *Grilling News.doc*. Change the document's page orientation to portrait, and make sure that the top, bottom, left, and right margins are all set to one inch.

b. Click before the first heading of the newsletter (*ArcSpot Patent Approved*). Apply the left-column layout to the document from that point forward.

c. Change to a three-column layout with equal column widths and with a line between the columns **(see Figure 4)**. If necessary, make sure that the document fits on a single page by editing the text.

Figure 4 Formatting a newsletter

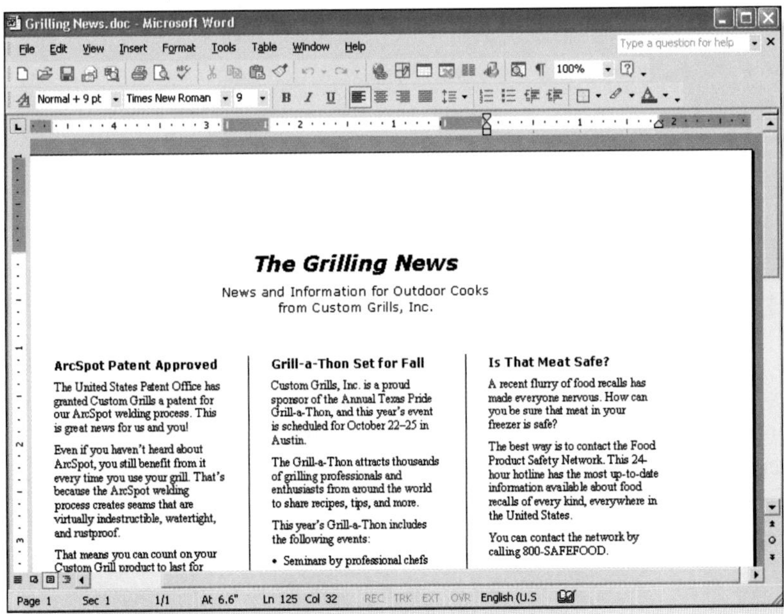

d. Check the document's spelling, and then save it as *xxx-Grilling News.doc*. Close the document.

What's Wrong With this Picture?

The document shown in **Figure 5** contains six mistakes. Some are easy to find, but others are not. Using what you have learned about creating and formatting documents in Word, try to find at least four of the errors in this document. On a sheet of paper, identify each mistake you find, and describe how you would fix it using Word's tools.

Figure 5 This document has many flaws. How many can you find?

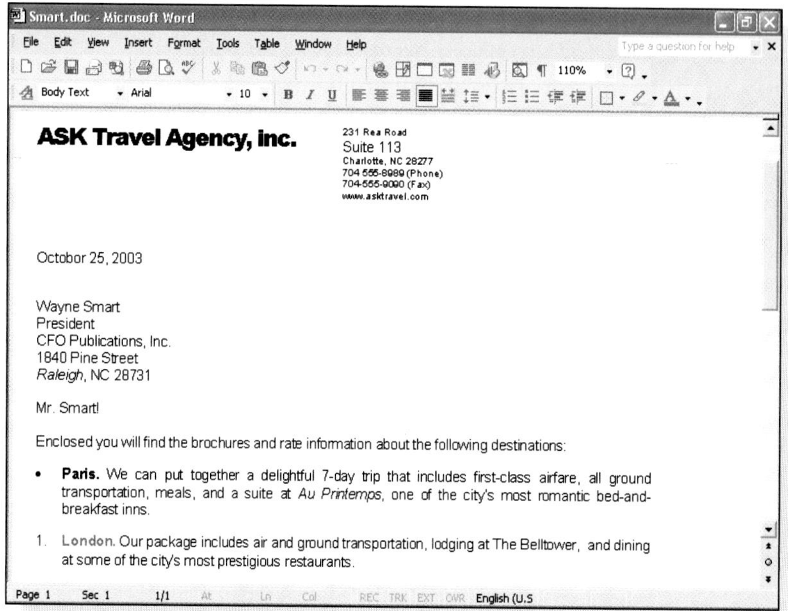

ASK Travel Agency, inc.

231 Rea Road
Suite 113
Charlotte, NC 28277
704 555-8989 (Phone)
704-555-9090 (Fax)
www.asktravel.com

Octobor 25, 2003

Wayne Smart
President
CFO Publications, Inc.
1840 Pine Street
Raleigh, NC 28731

Mr. Smart!

Enclosed you will find the brochures and rate information about the following destinations:

- **Paris.** We can put together a delightful 7-day trip that includes first-class airfare, all ground transportation, meals, and a suite at *Au Printemps*, one of the city's most romantic bed-and-breakfast inns.

1. London. Our package includes air and ground transportation, lodging at The Belltower, and dining at some of the city's most prestigious restaurants.

Cross-Curriculum Project

Assume that your History/Social Studies teacher has asked you to create a report about the life and presidency of Franklin Delano Roosevelt. With your assigned team members, conduct appropriate research on the Web and in printed publications to learn more about Roosevelt. Select one of the following topics for your paper:

- Childhood
- Education
- Marriage and family
- Eleanor Roosevelt
- Early political career
- Presidential elections
- Presidency
- The Great Depression
- The New Deal
- World War II
- Health Problems
- Death

Word

In addition to any research you do online, be sure to check with local resources. For example, your local newspaper may have a "morgue" containing issues of the paper (either in print or on microfilm) dating back several decades. You may know several people who lived through one or more of Roosevelt's presidential terms; these individuals may tell interesting stories about the period or about Roosevelt's impact on their lives.

Using the results of your research, develop a paper that includes at least 10 pages of text; headings and subheadings; bulleted lists; numbered lists; clip art; a table; a chart; an organization chart; and page numbers.

Your teacher may ask you to include headers, footers, footnotes, endnotes, or a bibliography. If so, ask your teacher how to properly format these items.

One team member should write a first draft of the paper and distribute it to the other team members. Each team member should review the document with Track Changes on. Working together, the team should compare and merge all versions of the document and review all edits and comments.

Working together, the team should use a Word memo template to compose a memo containing a brief description of the project **(see Figure 6)**.

Check your spelling and grammar. Use Word's Thesaurus as necessary. Use the Print Preview feature to check your documents before printing them. You may need to insert page breaks to help the text flow smoothly.

Figure 6 Using a Word memo template

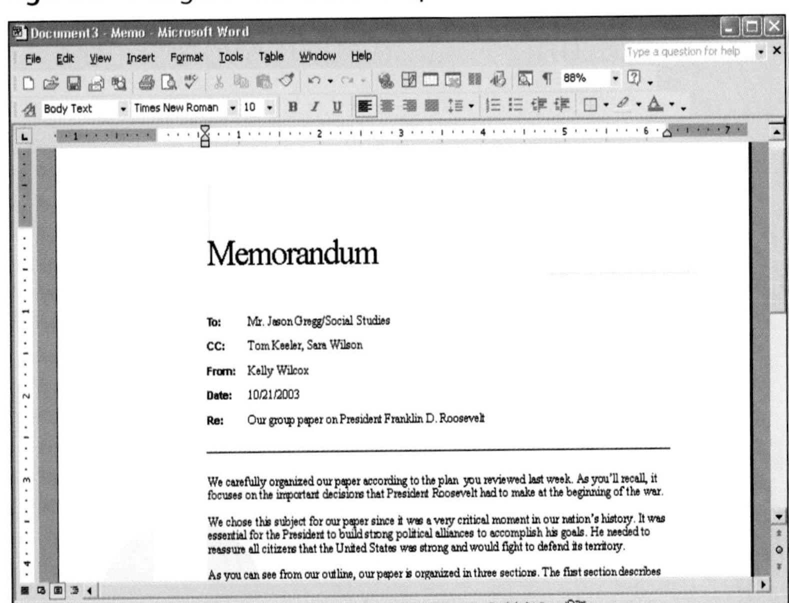

Excel

Unit 2

Business Financials

Unit Contents

Unit Objectives

1. Manage workbooks
2. Navigate and edit a worksheet
3. Change number formats and copy and move data
4. Check and correct cell data and formats
5. Manipulate rows and columns
6. Apply and modify cell formats
7. Apply styles and AutoFormats
8. Modify the page setup
9. Preview and print worksheets
10. Analyze a subset of data
11. Create and revise formulas
12. Understand absolute and relative references
13. Add functions to formulas
14. Create a workbook from a template
15. Create and modify charts and graphics
16. Provide feedback on a worksheet
17. Share a worksheet online
18. Rearrange cells in a worksheet
19. Rearrange worksheets in a workbook
20. Share data among worksheets
21. Create hyperlinks in a workbook

Excel

Lesson 1

Introducing Excel

Lesson Exercise Objectives

After completing this lesson, you'll be able to do the following tasks:

1. Manage workbooks
2. Navigate and edit a worksheet
3. Change number formats and copy and move data
4. Check and correct cell data and formats

Key Terms

- active cell (p. 165)
- cell (p. 164)
- column (p. 164)
- formula (p. 165)
- label (p. 165)
- range (p. 170)
- row (p. 164)
- value (p. 165)
- workbook (p. 162)
- worksheet (p. 162)

Microsoft Office Specialist Activities

EX2002: 1.1, 1.2, 1.3, 1.4, 2.1, 2.3

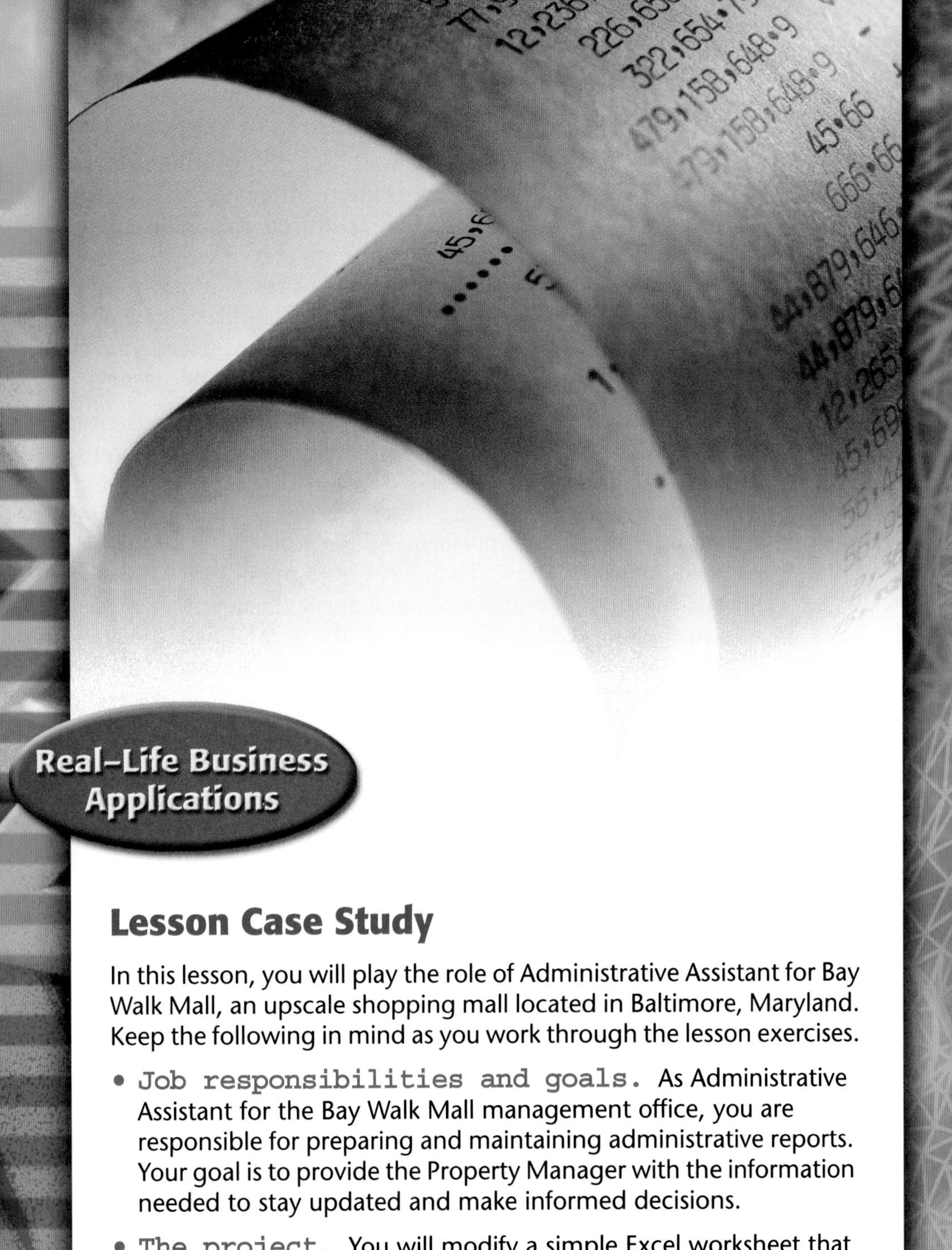

Real-Life Business Applications

Lesson Case Study

In this lesson, you will play the role of Administrative Assistant for Bay Walk Mall, an upscale shopping mall located in Baltimore, Maryland. Keep the following in mind as you work through the lesson exercises.

- `Job responsibilities and goals.` As Administrative Assistant for the Bay Walk Mall management office, you are responsible for preparing and maintaining administrative reports. Your goal is to provide the Property Manager with the information needed to stay updated and make informed decisions.
- `The project.` You will modify a simple Excel worksheet that summarizes general site information for the mall. You need to ensure that the data presented are accurate and well organized.
- `The challenge ahead.` You'll add text and numbers to a basic mall information worksheet and use common Excel procedures to edit, organize, and check the data and formats.

Microsoft Office Specialist EX2002 2.1, 2.3

Excel

Exercise 1 Overview: Manage Workbooks

Microsoft Excel is a spreadsheet program that enables you to organize and analyze related information. The information you enter in Excel is stored in a file called a **workbook**. Each workbook contains one or more pages, or worksheets. A **worksheet** is a grid of rows and columns in which you enter and edit data. By default, a new Excel workbook contains three worksheets; however, you can insert or delete worksheets in a workbook as necessary.

When working with Excel (as with any program), you should create a logical structure of folders and subfolders in which to save your files. You should assign meaningful names to your folders and files so you can quickly find them. Although you can perform folder and file management tasks using Windows Explorer (see Appendix A), often you will create a new folder or save a workbook with a new file name using Excel. You can easily accomplish these and other folder and file management tasks through the Save As dialog box.

You can use the Save As dialog box to save a workbook in a different file format. Excel workbook files use the *.xls* file name extension. Other file types use different extensions. For example, an Excel template uses the *.xlt* file extension.

Figure 1.1 Use the New Folder dialog box to create folders and subfolders

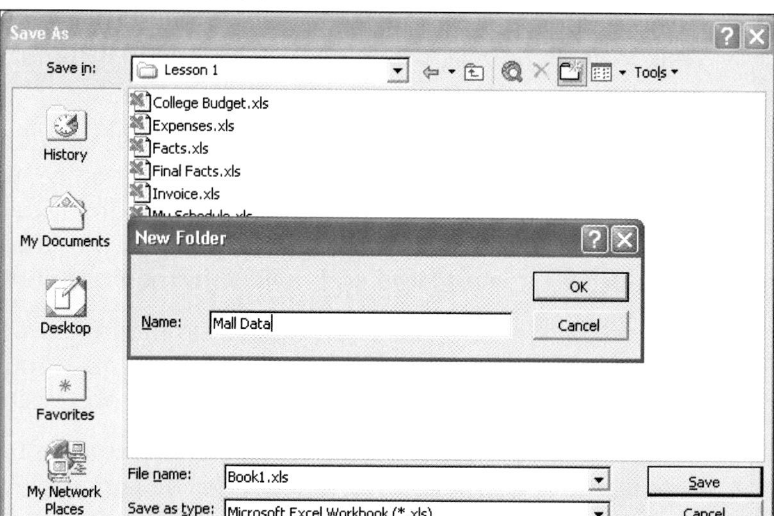

Figure 1.2 Creating a new folder

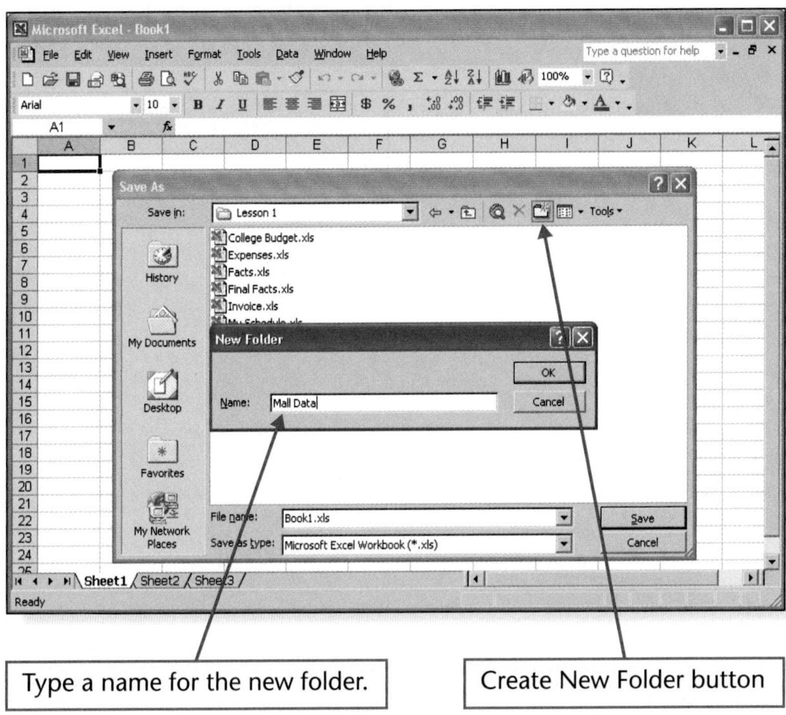
Type a name for the new folder.
Create New Folder button

Step Through It™
Exercise 1A: Create a folder for saving workbooks

1. If necessary, click New to display a new, blank workbook.
2. On the File menu, select Save As.
3. In the *Save in* box, navigate to the *Lesson 1* subfolder within your *Unit 2* folder. Click Create New Folder in the Save As dialog box.
4. In the *Name* box, type Mall Data (see Figure 1.2) and click OK. Close the Save As dialog box.

Figure 1.3 Saving a workbook with a new name

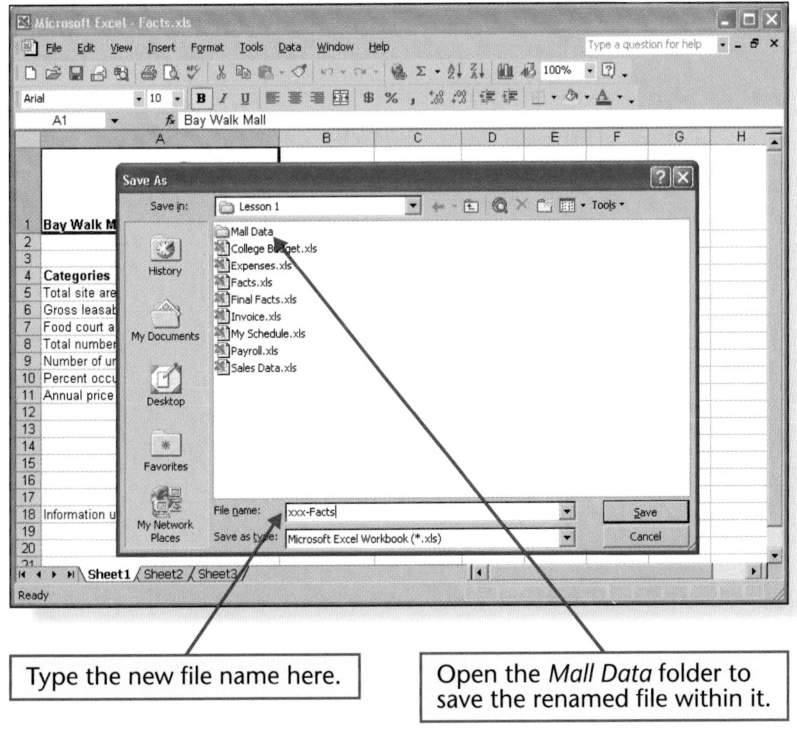
Type the new file name here.
Open the *Mall Data* folder to save the renamed file within it.

Step Through It™
Exercise 1B: Save a workbook with a new name

1. On the File menu, select Open. Click the *Look in* down arrow and navigate to the *Lesson 1* subfolder within your *Unit 2* folder. Open *Facts.xls*.
2. Open the Save As dialog box. In the *File name* box, type ***xxx-Facts*** (replacing *xxx* with your initials). (See Figure 1.3.)
3. Double-click the *Mall Data* folder to open it. Click Save to save the renamed file in the new folder.

4. Open the Save As dialog box, and click the *Save as type* down arrow. Scroll down the list to view the available file formats (see Figure 1.4), and select Template.

5. In the *Save in* box, navigate to the *Mall Data* folder and click Save to save the workbook as a template file type. ***Note:*** Templates are covered in Lesson 3.

6. Close the template, but leave Excel running.

Figure 1.4 Changing the file type

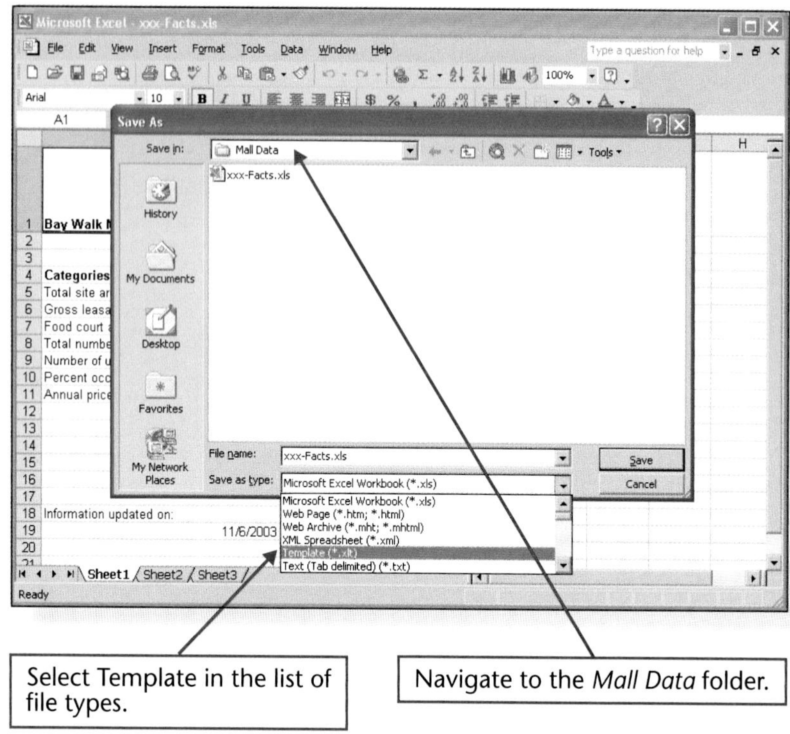
Select Template in the list of file types.
Navigate to the *Mall Data* folder.

Microsoft Office Specialist
EX2002 1.2, 2.3

Exercise 2 Overview:
Navigate and Edit a Worksheet

All worksheets in an Excel workbook consist of rows and columns. Each **row** is numbered consecutively from 1 to 65,536. Each **column** is assigned an alphabetic label ranging from A to Z, then AA to AZ, BA to BZ, and so on, up to column IV, the 256th column. The intersection of a row and a column forms a **cell**. Individual cells are identified by their column letter followed by their row number. The intersection of column C and row 7, for example, is referred to as *cell C7*.

In Excel, you enter all worksheet data into cells. First, you select the cell to contain the data, and then you type the data and press Enter, Tab, or an arrow key to finalize the entry.

The cell that is selected is called the **active cell**. In an active cell, you can enter a **label** (text), a **value** (number), or a **formula** (calculation). To select the cell in which you want to enter data, you can simply *click* the cell. If you don't see the cell, you can navigate to it by using the techniques listed in Table 1.1.

Table 1.1

Key(s)	Moves the Active Cell
Arrow keys (up, down, left, right)	One cell in the direction of the arrow
Tab	One cell to the right
Shift + Tab	One cell to the left
Page Down	Down one screen
Page Up	Up one screen
Alt + Page Down	Right one screen
Alt + Page Up	Left one screen
Home	To the first cell in the current row
Ctrl + Home	To cell A1

When entering long columns of numbers, it is often easier to use the numeric keypad available on the right side of most keyboards. Press the Num Lock key before typing the data.

If you make a mistake while entering data, or if you want to change data that you've already entered in a cell, you can easily edit the cell's contents.

To edit an existing cell entry, double-click the cell (or press F2 with the cell selected) to activate Edit mode. Use the normal editing keys (left and right arrow keys, Delete, and Backspace) to navigate through the cell and modify its contents.

To remove the entire contents of a cell, click the cell and press Delete.

Step Through It™

Exercise 2: Enter and edit text and numbers in cells

1. Open *xxx-Facts.xls* in the *Mall Data* subfolder within your *Lesson 1* folder.
2. Click cell A2 to make it the active cell. Type Facts and Figures and press Enter. The entry appears in cell A2, and cell A3 is now the active cell (see Figure 1.5).

Figure 1.5 Entering text in a cell

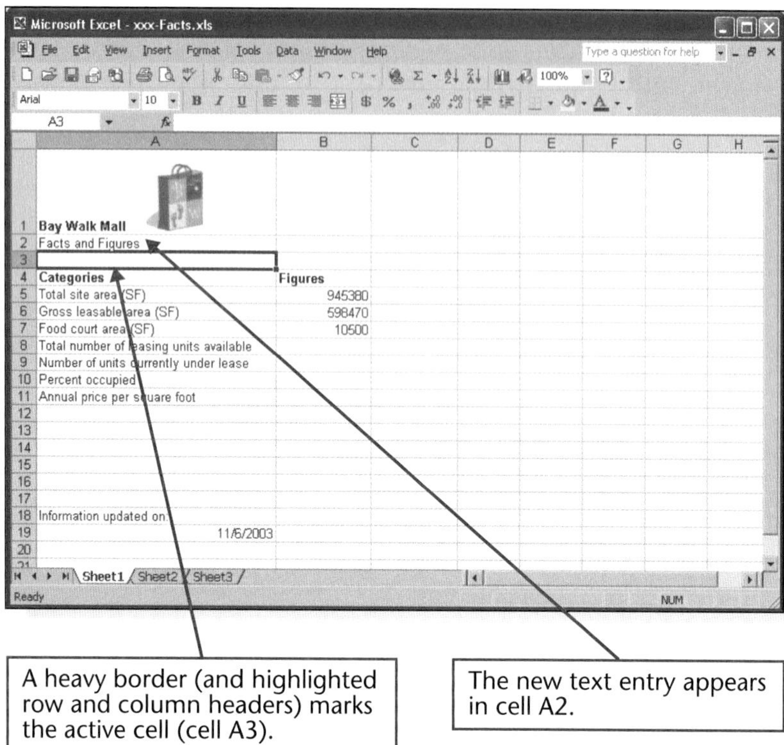

A heavy border (and highlighted row and column headers) marks the active cell (cell A3).
The new text entry appears in cell A2.

3. Click cell B8. Type 160, and press Enter. Cell B9 is now the active cell. Type 152, and press Enter.
4. In cell B10, type 0.95 and press Enter. Type 20 in cell B11, and press Enter (see Figure 1.6).

Figure 1.6 Entering numbers in cells

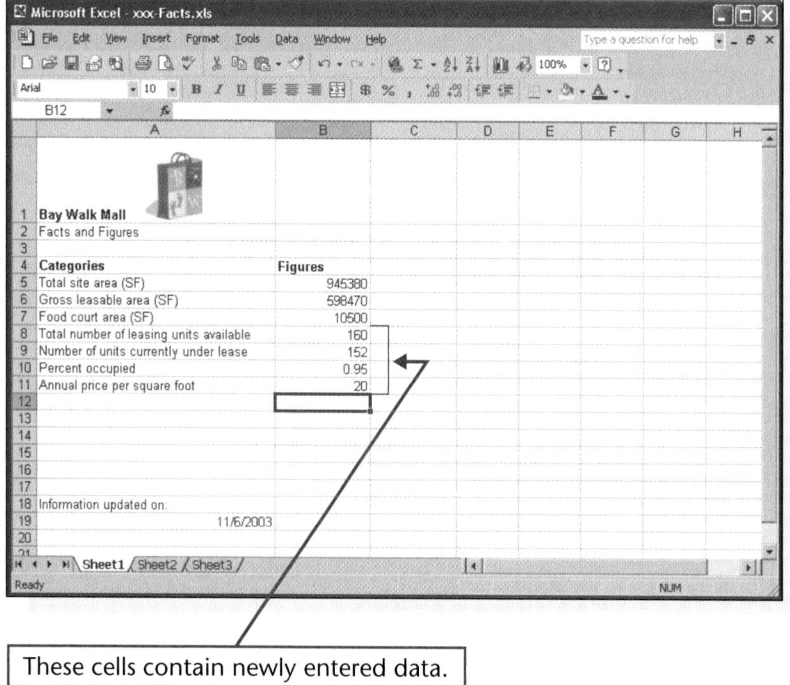

These cells contain newly entered data.

Excel

Figure 1.7 Adding two more categories to the worksheet

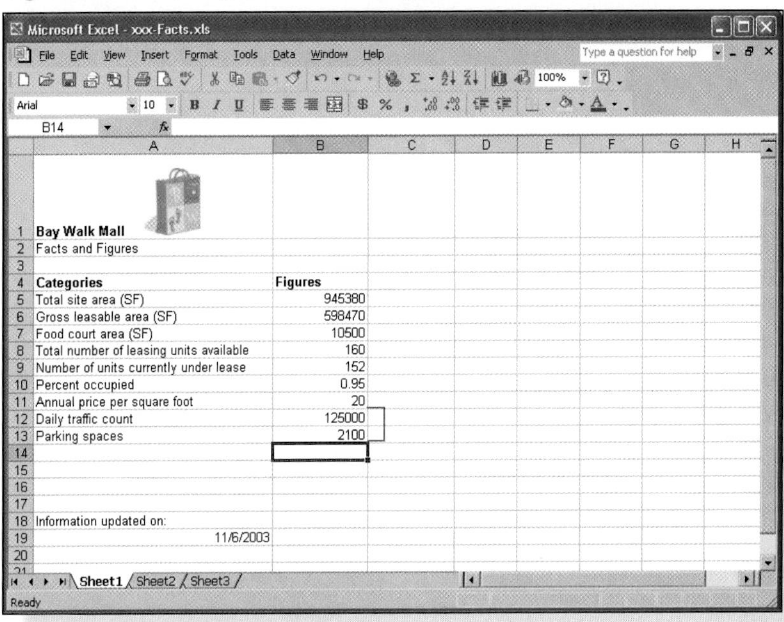

5. Click cell A12, type **Daily traffic count**, and press Tab. The cell to the right (cell B12) becomes the active cell.

6. Type the number **125000**, and press Enter.

7. In cell A13, type **Parking spaces**, and press the right arrow key to move to cell B13. Type **2100** and press Enter (see Figure 1.7).

Excel

Figure 1.8 Editing worksheet data

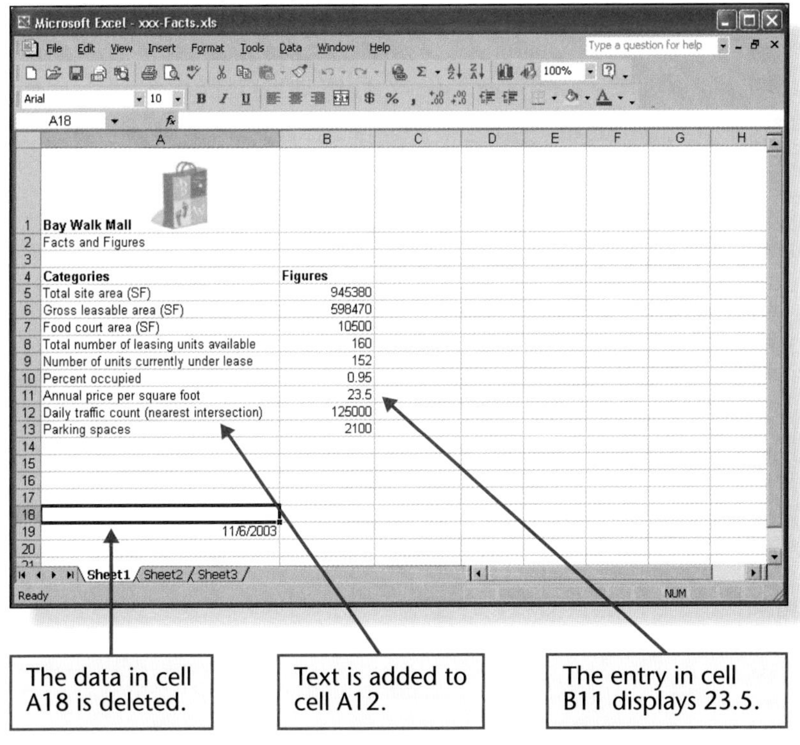

8. Double-click cell A12 to activate Edit mode. A blinking cursor appears in the cell. Press End, if necessary, to move to the end of the entry.

9. Press the spacebar, type **(nearest intersection)**, and press Enter.

10. Click cell B11 and press F2. While in Edit mode, press Backspace to delete the last number in the cell. Type **3.5**, and press Enter.

11. Select cell A18 and press Delete to clear the contents of the cell (see Figure 1.8). Save your workbook.

APPLY IT! After finishing Exercises 1–2, you may test your skills by completing Apply It! Guided Activity 1, Enter Text and Numbers in a Payroll Worksheet.

Business Connections

It's All in the Math

Excel provides a variety of mathematical tools that businesses use to perform simple calculations as well as to analyze more complex data. Nearly all worksheets you use will include calculations of some sort. Therefore, it is important to understand how Excel uses arithmetic operators in formulas and the order in which Excel performs the operations.

Arithmetic Operators

Arithmetic operators can be used with both values and cell references in Excel formulas. The following table lists common arithmetic operators and examples of their use.

Operator	Function	Example
+ (plus sign)	Addition	2+6=8
– (minus sign)	Subtraction	7–3=4
* (asterisk)	Multiplication	5X2=10
/ (slash)	Division	8÷4=2
^ (caret)	Exponentiation	2^3=8

Order of Operations

Excel evaluates a formula from left to right, but certain operators take precedence over others if you include multiple operators within a single formula. For example, exponentiation is calculated before multiplication and division, and multiplication and division are calculated before addition and subtraction. You can modify this order by using parentheses in a formula to indicate which portion should be evaluated first. In the formula =2*(5+4), Excel adds 5 and 4 and then multiplies that result by 2. Without the parentheses, Excel would first multiply 2 by 5 and then add 4 to the result.

Predicting Data Patterns

Trend analysis graphs are used to forecast business cycles and analyze prediction problems. Various Excel chart types (such as column, bar, and line charts) support trendlines, which project future patterns based on existing data. Several types of trendlines are available, such as linear, exponential, and moving average. The type of data you are working with determines which trendline you should use.

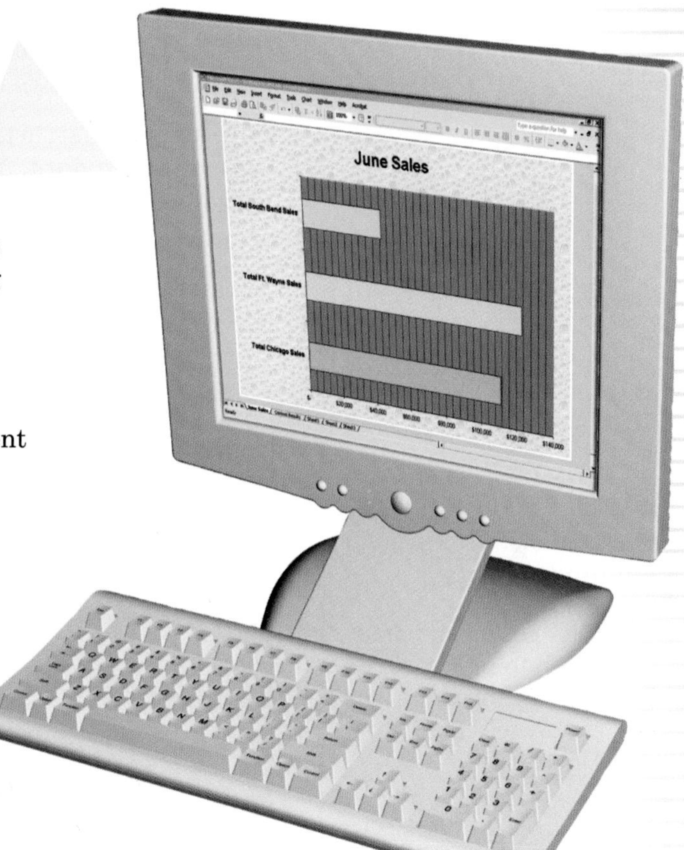

Estimation Tools

Because you can easily manipulate values in Excel, it is an excellent tool for creating and evaluating *what-if* scenarios. You can perform best case, worst case, and likely case scenarios for common business problems such as projecting quarterly revenues. Excel enables you to save different scenarios, or sets of values, and switch among the scenarios as needed to view the different results. You also can print a scenario report that enables you to compare the various scenarios in one printout.

CRITICAL THINKING

1. **Calculating Formulas** Use Excel's order of operations to determine the result of the following formula without typing the formula in the worksheet: =8+2*3/(6-4)
2. **Understanding Trend Analysis** Use Excel's Help feature to locate additional information on using trendlines. What types of Excel charts support trendlines? List and briefly describe two types of trendlines.

Microsoft Office Specialist
EX2002 1.1, 1.2

Excel

Exercise 3 Overview:

Change Number Formats and Copy and Move Data

Using the Formatting toolbar, you can apply a format to numbers entered in a worksheet, including the currency, percent, or comma style formats. You can customize these formats by adjusting the number of decimal places.

A **range** is a group of two or more cells that may or may not be contiguous (adjoining). The advantage of selecting a range is that you can apply one or more actions at once (such as formatting) to all cells in the range. A range of contiguous cells is expressed by the first and last cell in the range (for example, *B5:B7* or *A1:B5*). The upper-left cell in the range appears before the colon, and the lower-right cell in the range follows the colon.

As you are constructing a worksheet, you also may want to copy or move data. You can use the Cut, Copy, and Paste buttons on the Standard toolbar. In addition, you can copy or move data by dragging the data.

In the following exercises, you will add text and numbers to the *xxx-Facts.xls* worksheet.

Step Through It™

Exercise 3A: Change number formats

1. Click cell B5 and drag down to select cells B6 and B7. The range B5:B7 is now selected (see Figure 1.9).

Figure 1.9 Selecting a range of cells

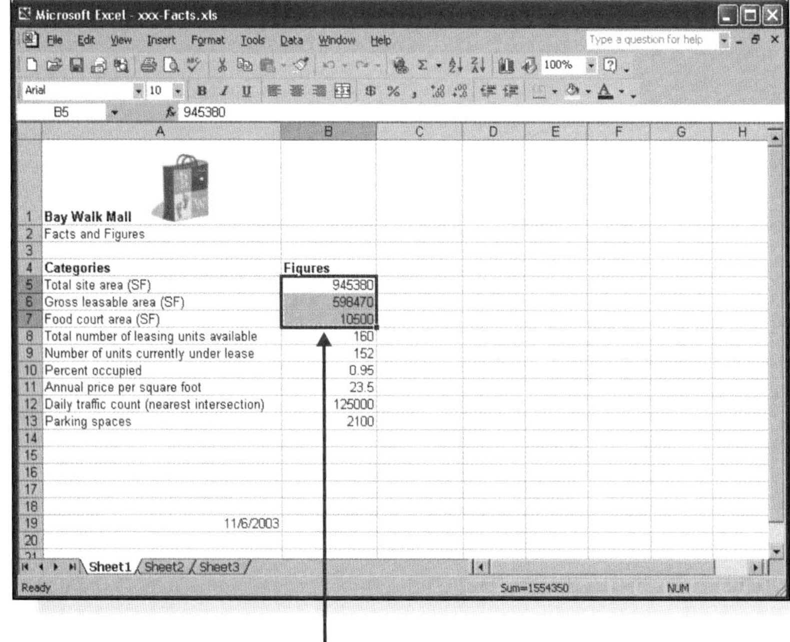

Click cell B5 and drag down to select the range B5:B7.

Figure 1.10 Applying number formats

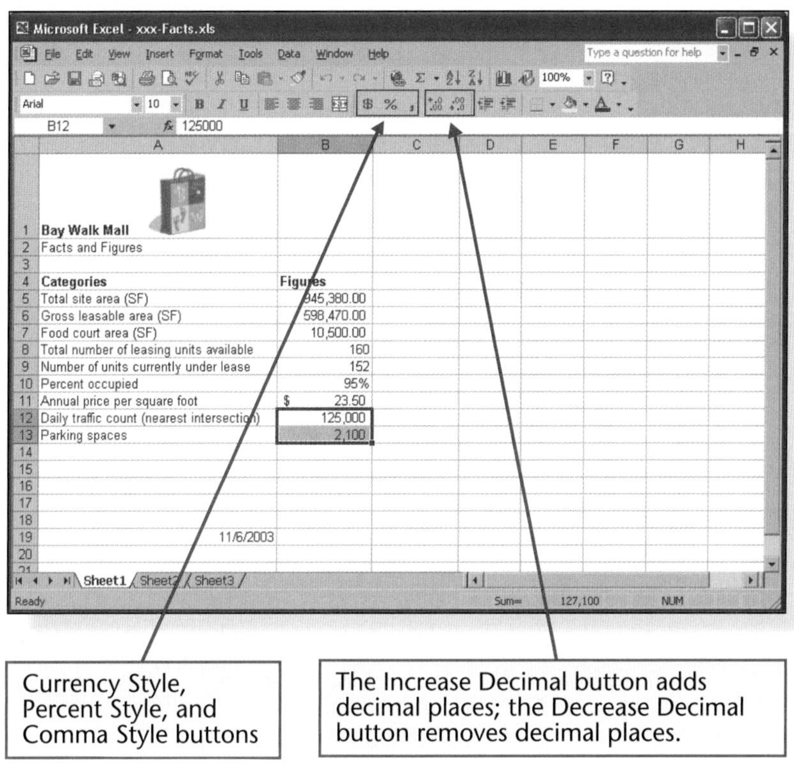

2. Click Comma Style on the Formatting toolbar.
3. Click cell B10, and then click Percent Style on the Formatting toolbar. Select cell B11, and click Currency Style on the Formatting toolbar.
4. Select the range B12:B13 and click Comma Style. Click Decrease Decimal on the Formatting toolbar two times to remove both decimal places (see Figure 1.10).
5. Save the workbook.

Excel

Figure 1.11 Copying cell data to the Clipboard

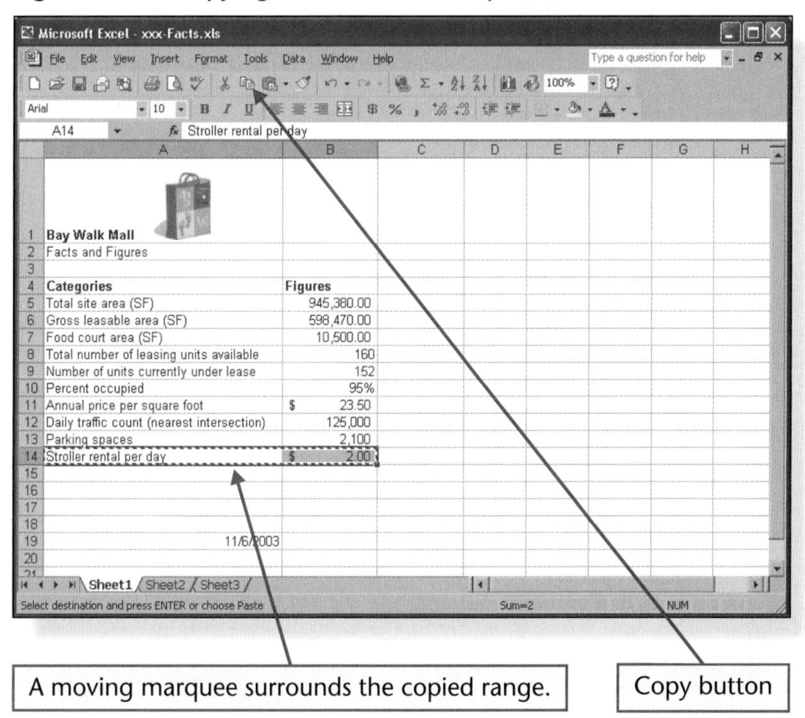

A moving marquee surrounds the copied range.
Copy button

Step Through It™

Exercise 3B: Copy and move cell data

1. Type **Stroller rental per day** in cell A14, press Tab, and type **2** in cell B14. Select cell B14 and click Currency Style.
2. Click cell A14, and then drag to the right to select cell B14.
3. Click Copy to copy the cell data to the Clipboard (see Figure 1.11).

4. Select cell A15 and click Paste. The cell data in row 14 is pasted into row 15 (see Figure 1.12).

5. Press Esc to remove the moving marquee.

Figure 1.12 Pasted data

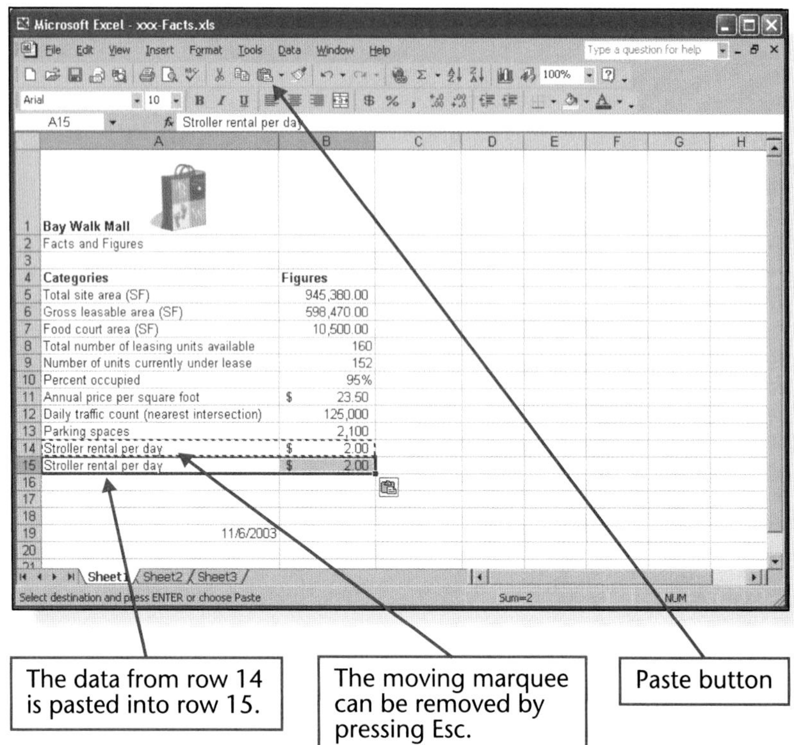

6. In cell A15, change the word *Stroller* to **Wheelchair**.

7. Click cell A19, and point to the cell's border. When the mouse pointer becomes a four-headed arrow, drag the border to cell B1 and release the mouse button. The date in cell A19 is moved to cell B1 (see Figure 1.13).

8. Save and then close the workbook.

Figure 1.13 Moving cell data by dragging

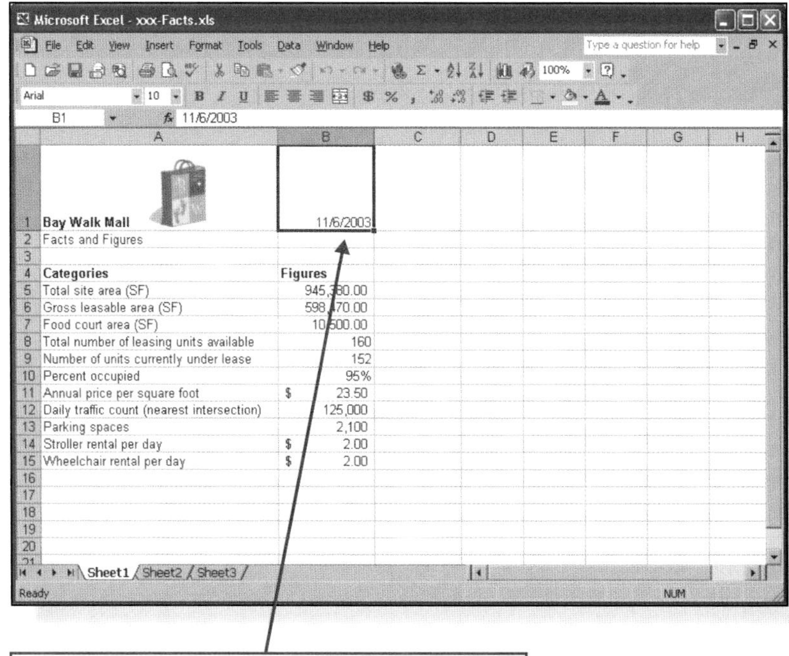

Career Corner

Doing Good, Doing Well

Billy has been living on the street for three months. Now he's sitting in Jenna's office.

As Billy talks, Jenna enters his personal information in an Excel worksheet. Later, when she's able to place him in housing, Jenna will use Excel to track case-worker visits, GED classes, and other services she arranges for him. Her agency is funded by grants, so a lot of what she does has to be documented.

Jenna is a social and human services assistant. People like her handle a wide range of responsibilities in many different jobs with the common purpose of helping people.

Social work is a related occupation. Social workers counsel people facing illness or problems like unemployment, substance abuse, or family conflict. They help clients identify their concerns, consider solutions, and find resources.

You do not need a four-year college degree to be a social and human services assistant. But employers look for relevant work experience or education beyond high school—a certificate or an associate's degree in social work, human services, or a related area. Social workers need a bachelor's or master's degree in social work or a related field. They must also be licensed, certified, or registered by their state. Knowledge of a foreign language is an asset in both occupations.

Social and human services assistants must be responsible. They also need good communication and time-management skills. Patience, understanding, and a desire to help others are valuable qualities.

Social workers should be emotionally mature, objective, and sensitive to people and their problems. They must be able to handle responsibility and have good people skills.

A great way to explore social work is to volunteer. Go to **www.volunteermatch.org** for volunteer opportunities in your area, or search the Web using the keyword *volunteer*. Sign up today!

CRITICAL THINKING

1. Social and human services work can be stressful. What are some ways that people can reduce or cope with job-related stress?
2. Interview a social and human services assistant or social worker. Find out what this person does in his or her job. Report to the class on what you learn.

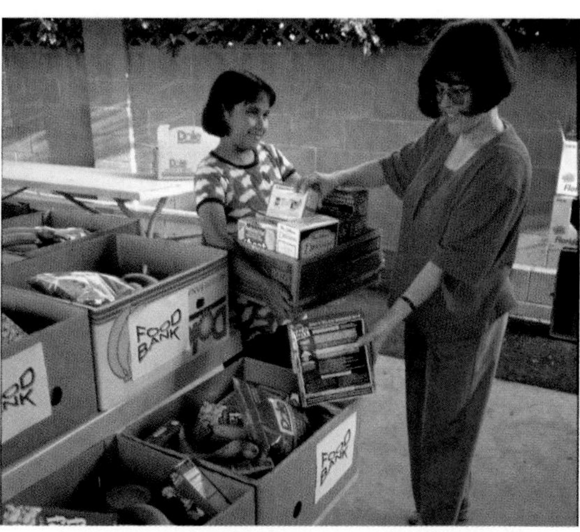

Microsoft Office Specialist EX2002 1.3, 1.4

Excel

Exercise 4 Overview:
Check and Correct Cell Data and Formats

The procedure for using the spelling checker in Excel is similar to that of the Spelling and Grammar feature provided in Word. However, Excel's spelling checker does not look for grammatical errors.

If you want to check the spelling of only a portion of a worksheet, select the cells you want to check before you run the spell check. If you want to perform a spell check on the entire worksheet, first click cell A1.

You may find it helpful to use the Find and Replace commands to find and/or replace existing cell contents. Although this feature is similar to using Find and Replace in Word, you can also find and replace specific number formats within Excel. For example, you can replace all numbers that use two decimal places with zero decimal places.

Need Help?

Type: find and replace in the Ask a Question box at the right end of the menu bar.

In the following exercises, you will run a spell check on a worksheet. Then you will use the Find and Replace feature to replace cell data and number formats.

Step Through It™

Exercise 4A: Check spelling

1. Open *Final Facts.xls*. Save your workbook as *xxx-Final Facts.xls*.
2. Click the Spelling button.
3. The Spelling dialog box opens and identifies the first possible spelling error. The cell containing the error is highlighted, and a list of suggested changes is provided (see Figure 1.14).
4. Click Ignore Once since *leasable* is spelled correctly.

Figure 1.14 Spell checking a worksheet

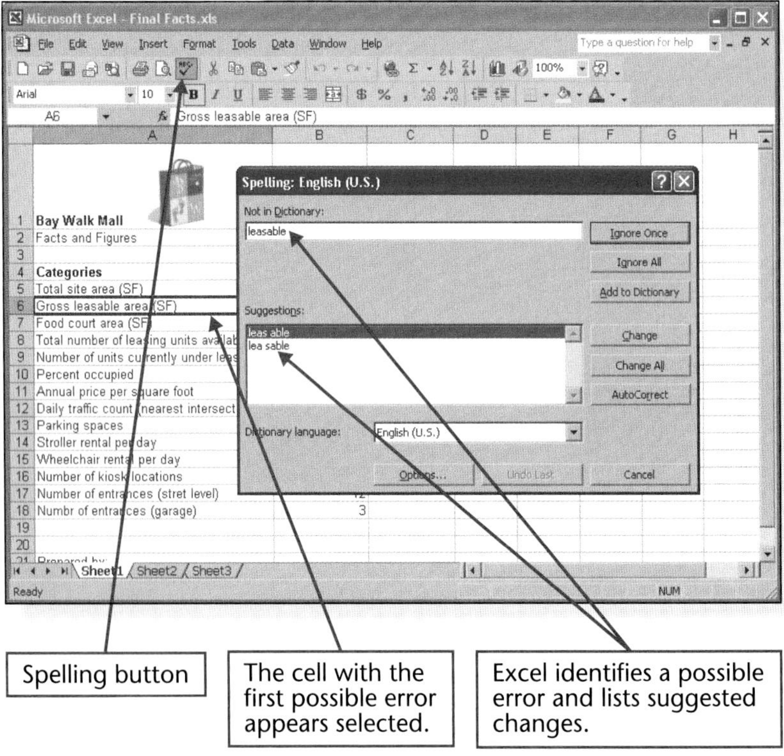

Figure 1.15 The completed spell check

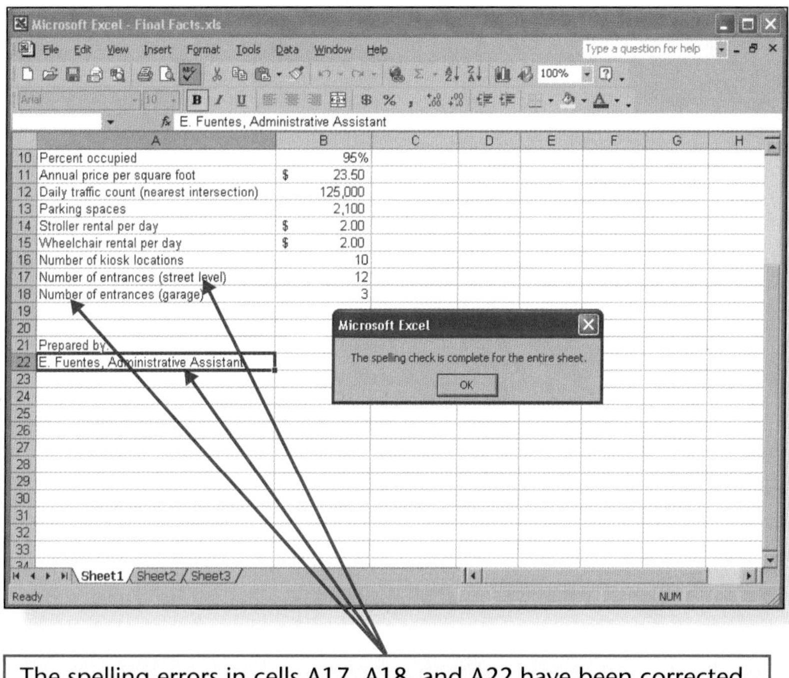

The spelling errors in cells A17, A18, and A22 have been corrected.

5. Complete the remainder of the spell check. Click Change to correct each of the remaining errors.
6. When your spell check is complete, a dialog box appears (see Figure 1.15).
7. Close the dialog box.

Excel

Figure 1.16 Using the Go To dialog box to move to a cell

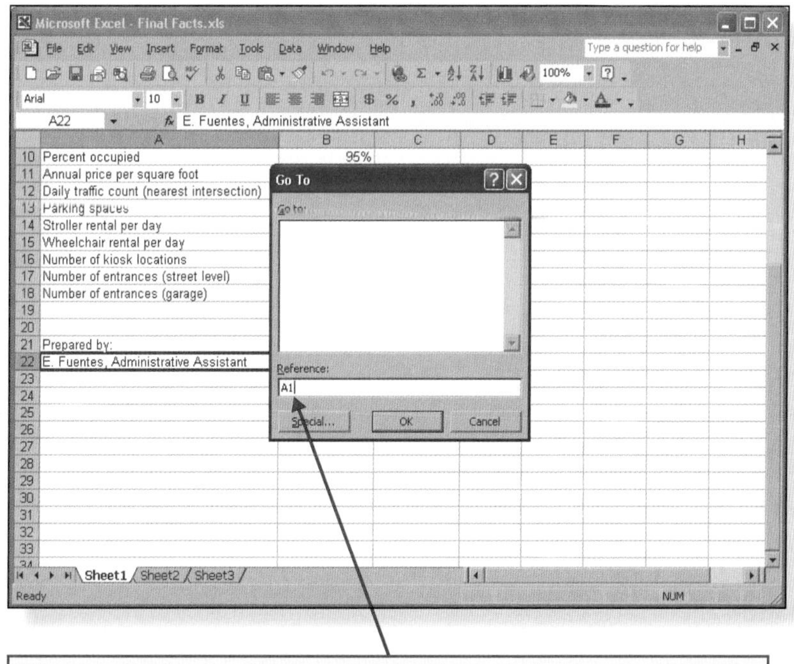

Type a cell reference here and click OK to quickly jump to that cell.

Step Through It™

Exercise 4B: Find and replace cell data and formats

1. Press F5 to display the Go To dialog box. Type A1 in the *Reference* box (see Figure 1.16). Click OK. Excel jumps to cell A1, which appears as the active cell.

2 On the Edit menu, select Replace. Type SF in the *Find what* box, and type sq. ft. in the *Replace with* box. Click Options to expand the dialog box and display additional settings.

3 Select the *Match case* check box, and click the Find Next button. Excel jumps to cell A5, the first cell that contains the search text (see Figure 1.17).

Figure 1.17 Finding and replacing cell data

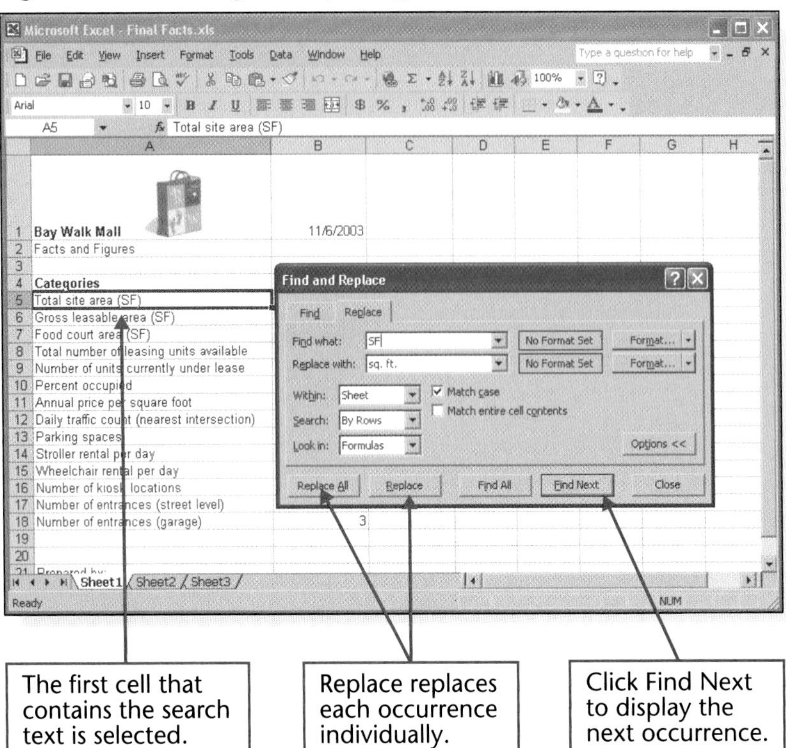
The first cell that contains the search text is selected.
Replace replaces each occurrence individually.
Click Find Next to display the next occurrence.

4 Click Replace. Excel makes the replacement and jumps to the next occurrence of the text in cell A6.

5 Click Replace All to replace all remaining occurrences. A dialog box appears stating that two additional replacements were made (see Figure 1.18). Click OK.

6 Close the Find and Replace dialog box.

Figure 1.18 The replaced cell data

All three occurrences of "SF" have been replaced with "sq. ft."

A dialog box appears when the Replace All operation is complete.

Figure 1.19 Specifying the Find Format options

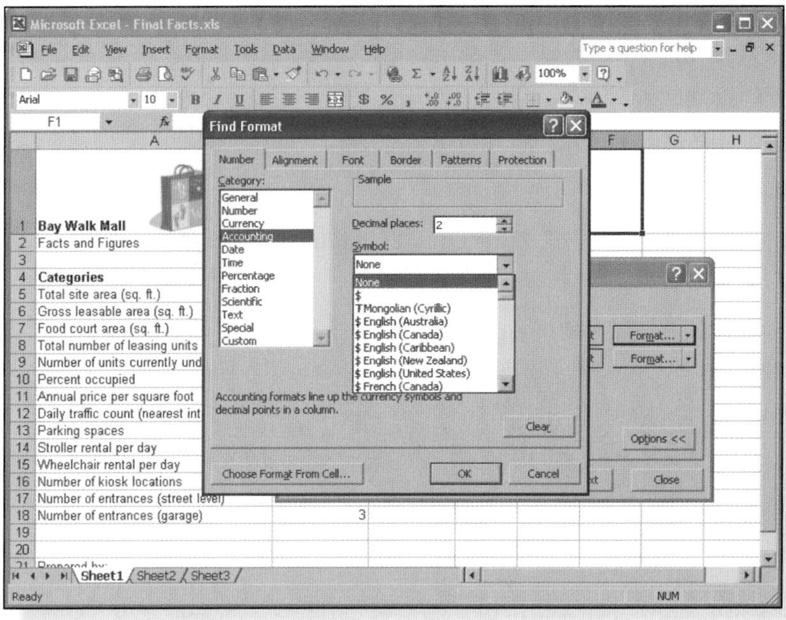

7. Press Ctrl + Home. On the Edit menu, select Replace. Delete the text in the *Find what* and *Replace with* text boxes, and clear the check mark in the *Match case* check box.

8. Click the *Find what* Format button to display the Find Format dialog box. Click the Number tab, if necessary.

9. In the *Category* box, select Accounting. Make sure 2 appears in the *Decimal places* box, and change the *Symbol* setting to None (see Figure 1.19). Click OK.

Figure 1.20 Replacing cell formats

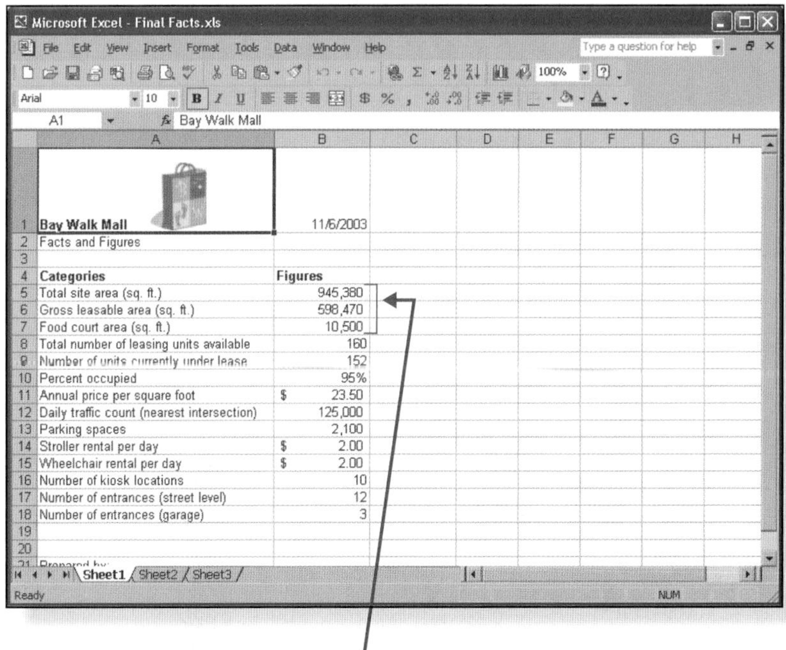

The number formats in the range B5:B7 have been replaced to remove the decimal places.

10. Click the *Replace with* Format button to display the Replace Format dialog box.

11. Select Accounting in the *Category* box. Change the decimal places to 0, and change the symbol setting to None. Click OK.

12. Click Replace All. Close the dialog box that appears after the replacements have been made. Close the Find and Replace dialog box. The decimal places have been removed in B5:B7 (see Figure 1.20).

13. Save your workbook and close the workbook.

Excel

After finishing Exercises 3–4, you may test your skills by completing Apply It! Guided Activity 2, Edit an Expenses Worksheet Using Find and Replace.

Procedure Summary

Enter Data in a Blank Cell

1. Select the cell.
2. Type the data.
3. Press Enter.
   OR
   Press Tab.
   OR
   Press an arrow key.

Edit Data in a Cell

1. Select the cell containing the data you want to edit.
2. Double-click the cell to activate Edit mode.
   OR
   Press F2.
3. Modify the cell's contents.
4. Press Enter.

Clear the Contents of a Cell

1. Select the cell containing the data you want to delete.
2. Press Delete.
   OR
   On the **Edit** menu, point to **Clear** and select **Contents**. . . . . **Alt + E, A, C**

Create a New Folder

1. If a workbook is not open, click **New** button to open a new, blank workbook.
2. On the **File** menu, select **Save As** . . . . **Alt + F, A**
3. In the **Save in** box, navigate to the location where you wish to place the new folder . . . . **Alt + I**
4. Click **Create New Folder** button.
5. In the New Folder dialog box, type a folder name and click OK.

Save a Workbook With a Different Name

1. On the **File** menu, select **Save As**. **Alt + F, A**
2. In the Save As dialog box, click the **Save in** down arrow and select a drive . . . . . . **Alt + I**
3. Navigate to the folder where you wish to save your file.
4. Select the file's current name in the **File name** box, and type a new file name . . . . **Alt + N**
5. Click **Save** . . . . **Alt + S**

Save a Workbook as a Different File Type

1. On the **File** menu, select **Save As** . . . . **Alt + F, A**
2. In the Save As dialog box, click the **Save in** down arrow and select a drive . . . . . . **Alt + I**
3. Navigate to the folder where you wish to save your file.
4. Click the **Save as type** down arrow and select a file type. **Alt + T**
5. Click **Save** . . . . **Alt + S**

Apply Numeric Formats

1. Select the cells.
2. Click **Currency Style**, **Percent Style**, or **Comma Style**.
3. Click the **Increase Decimal** button or **Decrease Decimal** button as necessary.
   OR
   Select the cells.
   On the **Format** menu, select **Cells** . . . . **Alt + O, E OR Ctrl + 1**
   On the Number tab, select a **Category**. **Alt + C**
   Set the number of **Decimal** places and click OK. . . . . **Alt + D**

Copy and Paste Cell Data

1. Select the cells you wish to copy.
2. Click **Copy** button.
   OR
   On the **Edit** menu, select **Copy** . . . . **Alt + E, C OR Ctrl + C**

3. Click the location where the text should be pasted.
4. Click **Paste** button.
   OR
   On the **Edit** menu, select
   Paste . . . . **Alt + E, P OR Ctrl + V**

Cut and Paste Cell Data

1. Select the cells you wish to cut.
2. Click **Cut** button.
   OR
   On the **Edit** menu, select
   Cut . . . . **Alt + E, T OR Ctrl + X**
3. Click the location where the data should be pasted.
4. Click **Paste** button.
   OR
   On the **Edit** menu, select
   Paste . . . . **Alt + E, P OR Ctrl + V**

Copy Cell Data by Dragging

1. Select the cells you wish to copy.
2. Hold Ctrl and point to a border of the selected cell or range.
3. Click and drag the selection to a new location.

Move Cell Data by Dragging

1. Select the cells you wish to move.
2. Point to a border of the selected cell or range.
3. When the pointer becomes a four-headed arrow, click and drag the selection to another location.

Check Spelling in a Worksheet

1. Move to cell A1.
2. Click **Spelling** button.
   OR
   On the **Tools** menu, select
   Spelling . . . . **Alt + T, S OR F7**
3. When Excel highlights an error, select a replacement, and click **Change** . . . . **Alt + C**
   OR
   Click **Ignore Once** to leave the text unchanged . . . . **Alt + I**

Go to a Specific Cell

1. On the **Edit** menu, click
   Go To . . . . **Alt + E, G OR F5 OR Ctrl + G**
2. Type the cell reference and click OK.

Find and Replace Cell Data

1. On the **Edit** menu, select
   Replace. . . . .**Alt + E, E OR Ctrl + H**
2. In the **Find what** box, type the data you wish to replace . . . . **Alt + N**
3. In the **Replace with** box, type the replacement data. . . . . **Alt + E**
4. Click **Find Next**. . . . . **Alt + F**
5. Click **Replace** to replace each occurrence individually. **Alt + R**
   OR
   Click **Replace All** to replace all occurrences at once . . . . **Alt + A**

Find and Replace Cell Formats

1. On the **Edit** menu, select
   Replace. . . . .**Alt + E, E OR Ctrl + H**
2. Clear the *Find what* and *Replace with* text boxes, if necessary.
3. Click the **Options** button to expand the dialog box. **Alt + T**
4. Click the *Find what* Format button, specify the format, and click OK.
5. Click the *Replace with* Format button, specify the format, and click OK.
6. Click **Find Next** . . . . **Alt + F**
7. Click **Replace** or **Replace All** . . . **Alt + R OR Alt + A**

Lesson Review and Exercises

Summary Checklist

- ☑ Can you create a new folder for workbook storage?
- ☑ Can you save a workbook with a new name that describes its contents in a location where you can easily find it?
- ☑ Can you navigate a worksheet using the keyboard?
- ☑ Can you navigate a worksheet using the scroll bars?
- ☑ Can you navigate a worksheet using the Go To dialog box?
- ☑ Can you enter and edit data within a worksheet and clear the contents of a cell?
- ☑ Can you apply numeric formats?
- ☑ Can you adjust decimal places?
- ☑ Can you copy and move data in a worksheet to better organize it and make the data easier to comprehend?
- ☑ Can you perform a spell check on a worksheet and correct the errors you find?
- ☑ Can you find and replace cell data?
- ☑ Can you find and replace formats?

Key Terms

- active cell (p. 165)
- cell (p. 164)
- column (p. 164)
- formula (p. 165)
- label (p. 165)
- range (p. 170)
- row (p. 164)
- value (p. 165)
- workbook (p. 162)
- worksheet (p. 162)

APPLY IT! **Guided Activities**

1. Enter Text and Numbers in a Payroll Worksheet

You are the assistant manager of an appliance store. The owner asks you to enter information into a new payroll worksheet that she has started. So far, the worksheet includes only titles and column headings. You will enter text and numbers from employee time cards and apply appropriate number formatting.

Follow these steps to modify the worksheet:

a. Open *Payroll.xls*.

b. On the File menu, select Save As. Navigate to the *Lesson 1* subfolder within your *Unit 2* folder. Click Create New Folder and create a new folder named *Weekly Payroll*. Save your workbook within the new folder as *xxx-Payroll.xls*.

c. Select cell A4, press F2, and enter the current date (Saturday of the current week).

d. Beginning in row 7, enter the employee names, hourly rates, and total hours shown in **Table 1.2**. Use the keyboard to navigate among cells. Press Tab to move one cell to the right; Home to move to the first cell in a row; Shift + Tab to move one cell to the left; and the arrow keys to move cell by cell in any direction.

Table 1.2

Employee Name	Hourly Rate	Total Hours
Brown, Julia	8.25	23
Cho, Tim	10.5	18
Grant, John	7.5	35
Filmore, Karen	12	40
Sanchez, Susan	9.75	27
Williams, Matthew	11.5	40

e. After entering the data, you recall that Karen Filmore's name has changed to Karen Jennings. Navigate to the appropriate cell and edit the data.

f. You notice that Matthew Williams has mistakenly turned in a time card (he is now a salaried employee). Select and clear the contents of the appropriate cells. Save the workbook.

g. Your boss has an older version of Excel and has asked you to provide the workbook in a compatible file type. Open the Save As dialog box. (Make sure that the *Weekly Payroll* folder appears within the *Save in* box.) Click the *Save as type* down arrow, scroll down the list, and select the Microsoft Excel 4.0 Workbook (.xlw) file type **(see Figure 1.21)**.

h. Save and close the workbook.

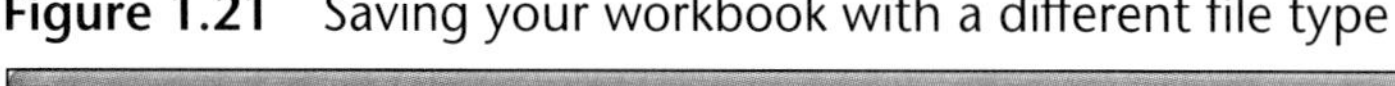

Figure 1.21 Saving your workbook with a different file type

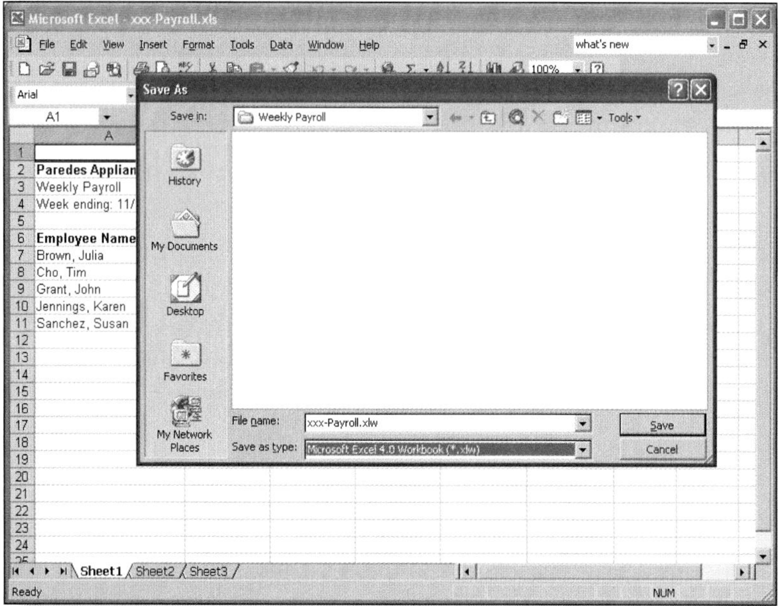

2. Edit an Expenses Worksheet Using Find and Replace

You are an independent marketing consultant. Since your clients will reimburse you for your business expenses, it is important to maintain accurate records. You need to edit your expenses workbook for the month of February.

a. Open *Expenses.xls*. Save your workbook as *xxx-Expenses.xls*.

b. A client's name has recently changed. On the Edit menu, select Replace. Replace all occurrences of *Software Today* with *Jones Computing*.

c. Press F5 and use the Go To dialog box to jump to cell A29. Select the range A29:E29 and click Cut. Select A25 and click Paste. Select cell E25, type 325.70, and apply the currency style to that cell.

d. You decide to format all the numbers in the Expense column with a dollar sign and two decimal places. Press Ctrl + H. In the Find and Replace dialog box, delete the contents of the *Find what* and *Replace with* boxes. Expand and view the options. Click the *Find what* Format button. On the Number tab, select the General category, if necessary, and click OK.

e. Click the *Replace with* Format button. On the Number tab, select the Accounting category. Select 2 in the *Decimal places* box; select the dollar sign in the *Symbol* box; and click OK. Click Replace All.

f. Copy and paste A16:E16 to the range A26:E26 **(see Figure 1.22)**. Select cell A25, press Ctrl, and drag the cell border to copy its contents to cell A26. Select C18 and drag its border down to move it to C19. Type Hotel in C18.

g. Press Ctrl + Home. Perform a spell check of your worksheet and make the appropriate changes. Save your finished workbook, and close the workbook.

Figure 1.22 Editing the expenses worksheet

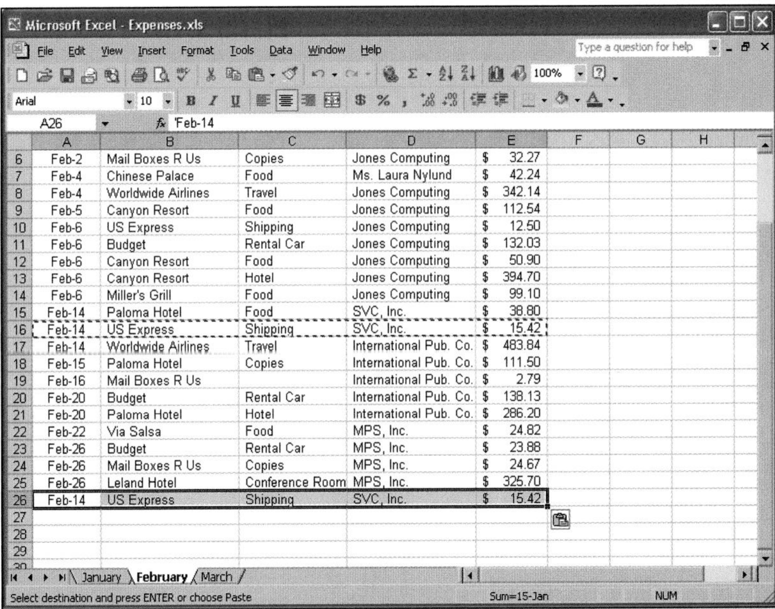

	A	B	C	D	E
6	Feb-2	Mail Boxes R Us	Copies	Jones Computing	$ 32.27
7	Feb-4	Chinese Palace	Food	Ms. Laura Nylund	$ 42.24
8	Feb-4	Worldwide Airlines	Travel	Jones Computing	$ 342.14
9	Feb-5	Canyon Resort	Food	Jones Computing	$ 112.54
10	Feb-6	US Express	Shipping	Jones Computing	$ 12.50
11	Feb-6	Budget	Rental Car	Jones Computing	$ 132.03
12	Feb-6	Canyon Resort	Food	Jones Computing	$ 50.90
13	Feb-6	Canyon Resort	Hotel	Jones Computing	$ 394.70
14	Feb-6	Miller's Grill	Food	Jones Computing	$ 99.10
15	Feb-14	Paloma Hotel	Food	SVC, Inc.	$ 38.80
16	Feb-14	US Express	Shipping	SVC, Inc.	$ 15.42
17	Feb-14	Worldwide Airlines	Travel	International Pub. Co.	$ 483.84
18	Feb-15	Paloma Hotel	Copies	International Pub. Co.	$ 111.50
19	Feb-16	Mail Boxes R Us		International Pub. Co.	$ 2.79
20	Feb-20	Budget	Rental Car	International Pub. Co.	$ 138.13
21	Feb-20	Paloma Hotel	Hotel	International Pub. Co.	$ 286.20
22	Feb-22	Via Salsa	Food	MPS, Inc.	$ 24.82
23	Feb-26	Budget	Rental Car	MPS, Inc.	$ 23.88
24	Feb-26	Mail Boxes R Us	Copies	MPS, Inc.	$ 24.67
25	Feb-26	Leland Hotel	Conference Room	MPS, Inc.	$ 325.70
26	Feb-14	US Express	Shipping	SVC, Inc.	$ 15.42

Do It Yourself

1. Create a College Budget

Your parents have asked you to help develop a simple budget plan that estimates your basic expenses for your first year in college. With

Excel

their help, you have created a basic worksheet listing the major expense categories. In another section of the worksheet you have estimated your income based on the various jobs you've had over the last year. Now you need to estimate how much you will spend on each major expense category (books, clothing, dormitory, entertainment, food, transportation, and tuition). Gather expense information from various sources such as the school library, the Internet, from friends who have attended college, or provide your own estimates. Follow these steps:

a. Open *College Budget.xls*.
b. Create a new folder named *College Costs* in the *Lesson 1* subfolder within your *Unit 2* folder. Save the workbook as *xxx-College Budget.xls* in the new folder.
c. Enter the dollar amounts from your research into column B opposite the categories. ***Note:*** Formulas have already been entered into D7:D13 and B14:D14 so that totals will appear in these cells after you enter the expense amounts.
d. Format all numbers in the worksheet with the currency format with zero decimal places since your figures are estimated.
e. Run a spell check on the worksheet and make appropriate corrections.
f. Save and close the workbook.

2. Create and Modify a Sales Worksheet

As the owner of Canyon Gifts, you need to enter some quarterly sales data for four store locations for each month of the first quarter.

a. Open *Sales Data.xls*. Save your workbook as *xxx-Sales Data.xls*. Enter the data in the following table.

Table 1.3

Location	January	February	March
Flagstaff	3497.65	5708.3	5530.28
Phoenix	7312.73	7068.83	8126.44
Tucson	6061.64	7443.91	4778.25
Mesa	4153.46	6778.61	6563.95

b. Format B6:D9 using the comma style format (with two decimal places, but with no currency symbol). Format the column and row totals (B10:E10 and E6:E9) using currency style. Format

F6:F9 using the percent style and then add two decimal places **(see Figure 1.23)**.

c. Perform a spell check on the worksheet and make appropriate changes. Save and close the workbook.

Figure 1.23 The quarterly sales worksheet

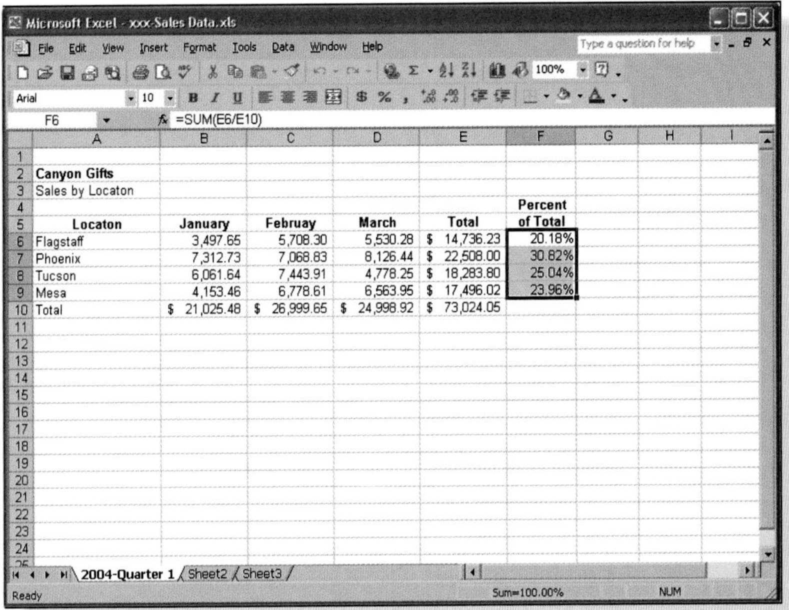

	A	B	C	D	E	F
1						
2	**Canyon Gifts**					
3	Sales by Locaton					
4						**Percent**
5	**Locaton**	**January**	**Februay**	**March**	**Total**	**of Total**
6	Flagstaff	3,497.65	5,708.30	5,530.28	$ 14,736.23	20.18%
7	Phoenix	7,312.73	7,068.83	8,126.44	$ 22,508.00	30.82%
8	Tucson	6,061.64	7,443.91	4,778.25	$ 18,283.80	25.04%
9	Mesa	4,153.46	6,778.61	6,563.95	$ 17,496.02	23.96%
10	Total	$ 21,025.48	$ 26,999.65	$ 24,998.92	$ 73,024.05	

3. Create a Personal Schedule

As a new student at a large university, you are a little overwhelmed by your schedule. While juggling work and school, you have recently missed two classes and have often been late for work. To get better organized, you have typed your schedule into an Excel worksheet. However, you are not totally satisfied with the organization of the worksheet. You have already started a new section to create a daily schedule you can follow from the beginning to the end of each day. Follow these steps to revise the worksheet:

a. Open *My Schedule.xls* and examine the general layout. Save the workbook as *xxx-My Schedule.xls*

b. To complete the new Daily Schedule section of your worksheet, copy and paste the data from the Time column (E5:E9) into the corresponding cells of the Daily Schedule section.

c. Copy and paste the information from the Work section of the worksheet (B13:F14) into the corresponding cells of the Daily Schedule section.

d. Carefully check that you have copied and pasted the data into the correct cells of the Daily Schedule section.

e. Save and close the workbook.

4. Discover Excel's New Features

As a technology coordinator for a large school district, you have just upgraded to Excel 2002 and have been asked by teachers what new features are provided in this version. Follow these steps:

a. Open a new, blank workbook. Type what's new in the Ask a Question box, press Enter, and navigate to the What's New page.

b. Click the links for each of the Microsoft Excel topics on the What's New page, and read the information. In the blank worksheet, make written notes briefly describing at least three features that are new to Excel 2002 **(see Figure 1.24)**.

c. Close the Help window. Save your workbook as *xxx-What's New.xls* and close the workbook.

Figure 1.24 The new features in Excel 2002

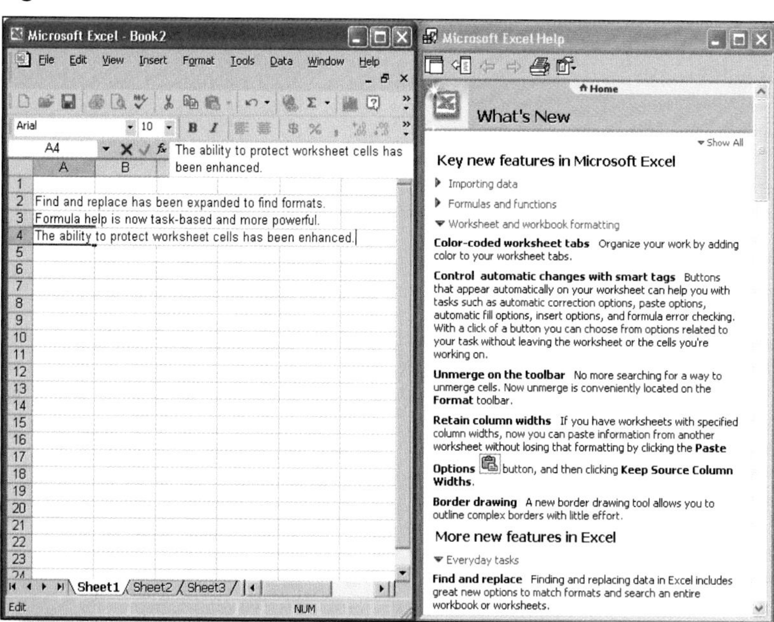

Challenge Yourself

Complete a Sales Invoice

You are the owner of a small sporting goods store. Your success has come from providing quality service, including prompt delivery of goods, to local sports teams. Providing good service is only one part of making your business successful; it is also important for you to keep revenue flowing in so you can pay your suppliers and employees. You use an Excel worksheet to prepare invoices. This has increased your efficiency by reducing the time required to get your invoices out to customers.

Follow these steps to complete a sales invoice worksheet:

- Open *Invoice.xls*. Save the workbook as *xxx-Invoice.xls.* ***Note:*** Certain cells in this workbook are protected to prevent you from overwriting existing cell data or formulas.
- Referring to the table below for information, complete the invoice worksheet by clicking the appropriate cell in the invoice and typing the data. Press Tab or use the arrow keys to navigate the invoice after each entry.

Table 1.4

Name	Mrs. Paula Mackey, Manager/Prescott Titans	
Address	2322 Tumbleweed Dr.	
City	Prescott	
State	AZ	
ZIP	85555	
Phone	(555) 555-2345	
Date	(*Type current date*)	
Order No.	104293	
Qty	**Description**	**Unit Price**
26	Custom caps	18.22
22	Embroidered jerseys	62.80
3	Fielder's gloves	74.99
1	Sports drink cooler (stainless)	104.12
1	First aid kit	53.44

- Scroll down the worksheet and notice that the invoice total has already been calculated.
- Go to cell M3 using the Go To dialog box and revise the order number to read SSG-14258.
- Save and then close the workbook.

Lesson 2

Formatting and Printing Worksheets

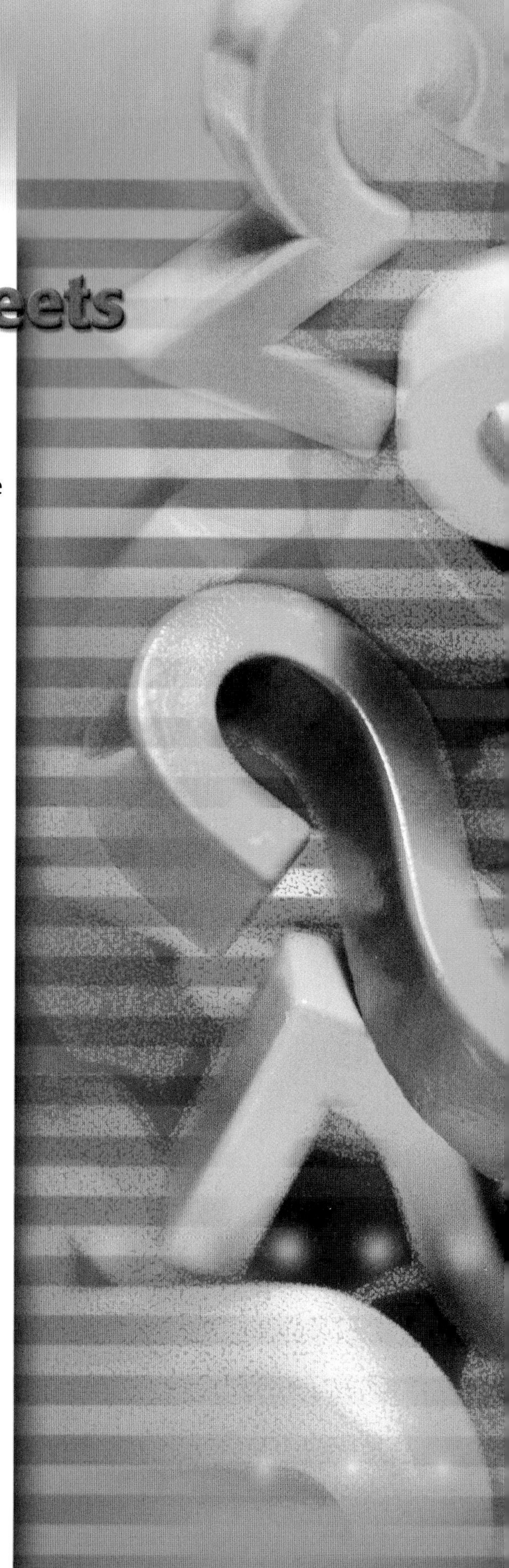

Lesson Exercise Objectives

After completing this lesson, you'll be able to do the following tasks:

1. Manipulate rows and columns
2. Apply and modify cell formats
3. Apply styles and AutoFormats
4. Modify the page setup
5. Preview and print worksheets

Key Terms

- freeze panes (p. 190)
- print titles (p. 206)

Microsoft Office Specialist Activities

EX2002: 3.1–3.7

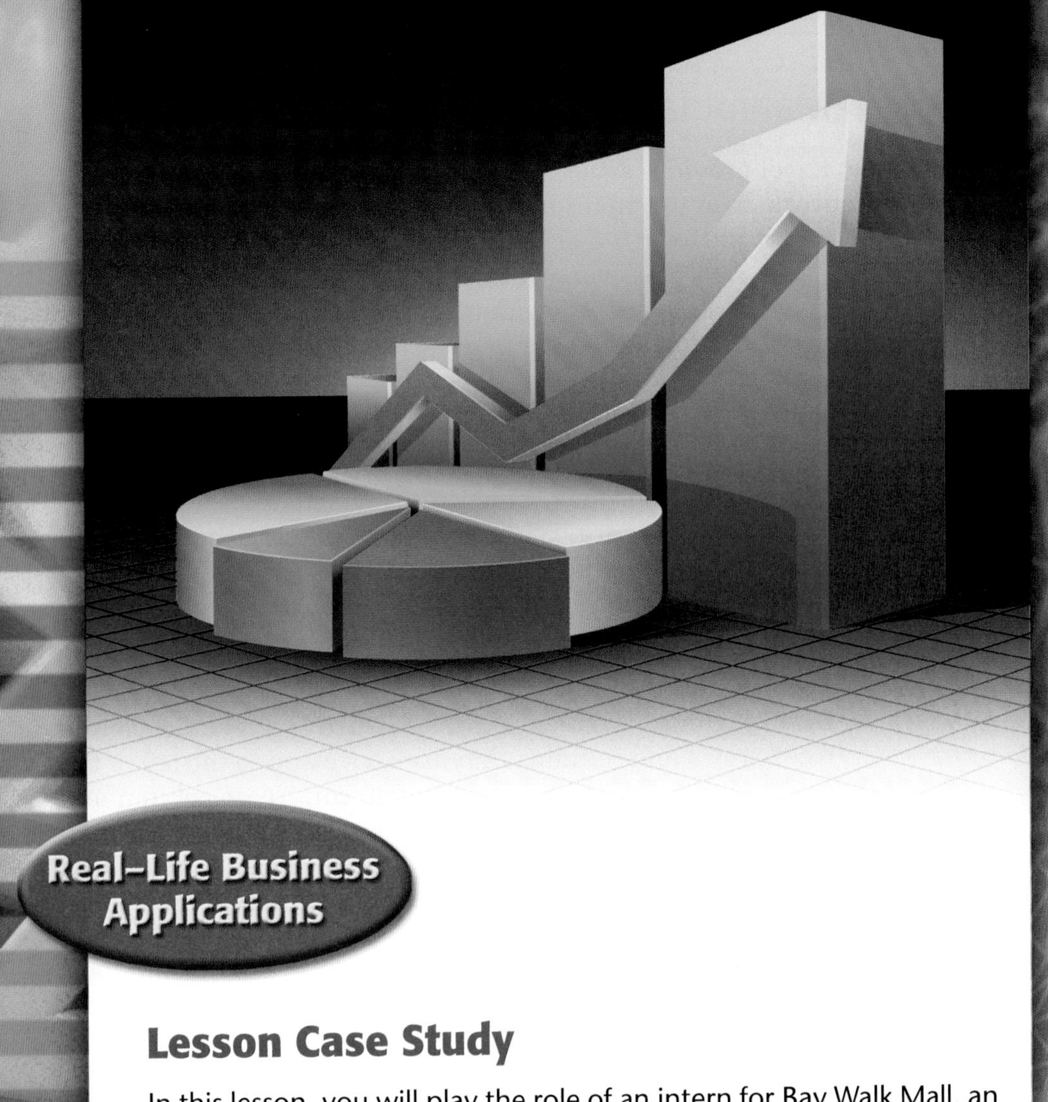

Real-Life Business Applications

Lesson Case Study

In this lesson, you will play the role of an intern for Bay Walk Mall, an upscale shopping mall located in Baltimore, Maryland. Keep the following information in mind as you work through the lesson exercises.

- **Job responsibilities and goals.** You have been asked to assist the Property Manager with formatting and printing worksheets. Your goal is to produce effective, eye-catching reports while also impressing the staff with your skills in Excel.
- **The project.** You will modify the structure of an existing employee information worksheet, format and print the worksheet, and apply styles.
- **The challenge ahead.** Although most of the data has been entered in the worksheets you will be using, you need to improve their appearance and readability.

Microsoft Office Specialist
EX2002 3.2, 3.3

Excel

Exercise 1 Overview:
Manipulate Rows and Columns

Excel provides several ways to modify the structure of your worksheet by manipulating rows and columns. You can insert entire rows or columns, for example, if you need to make room for more data or you need to add more space between areas of the worksheet. You can delete entire rows or columns, if necessary.

You also can temporarily hide information in rows or columns so that it doesn't appear on screen or when printed. This feature is helpful if you need to print a worksheet for others and you don't want to print sensitive information such as salary data. When you hide rows or columns, you'll notice that the affected row numbers or column letters appear to be missing. The hidden data is still contained in the worksheet, however, and can be redisplayed whenever you choose.

Excel includes a **freeze panes** feature that enables you to freeze rows and columns that are above and to the left of the selected cell. Using this feature, you can freeze column and row headings so they are still visible as you move through large worksheets and enter additional data. If your data doesn't fit in a cell, you can easily adjust individual column widths and row heights so that the data displays in its entirety. The easiest way to do so is to drag the boundary between the row numbers or column letters.

In the following exercises, you'll use these techniques to modify an employee information worksheet.

Figure 2.1 Rows 9 and 10 are hidden in this worksheet

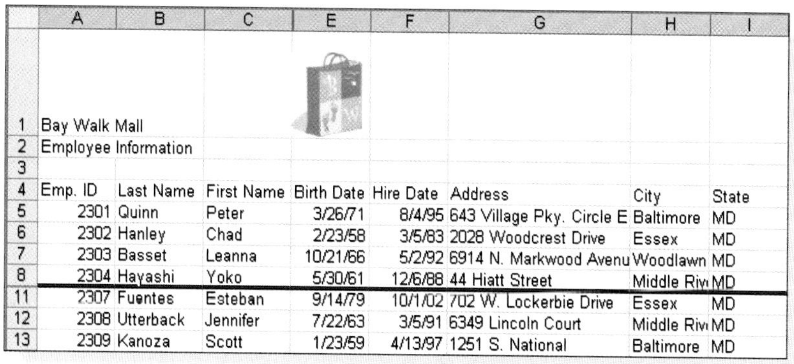

	A	B	C	E	F	G	H	I
1	Bay Walk Mall							
2	Employee Information							
3								
4	Emp. ID	Last Name	First Name	Birth Date	Hire Date	Address	City	State
5	2301	Quinn	Peter	3/26/71	8/4/95	643 Village Pky. Circle E	Baltimore	MD
6	2302	Hanley	Chad	2/23/58	3/5/83	2028 Woodcrest Drive	Essex	MD
7	2303	Basset	Leanna	10/21/66	5/2/92	6914 N. Markwood Avenu	Woodlawn	MD
8	2304	Hayashi	Yoko	5/30/61	12/6/88	44 Hiatt Street	Middle Riv	MD
11	2307	Fuentes	Esteban	9/14/79	10/1/02	702 W. Lockerbie Drive	Essex	MD
12	2308	Utterback	Jennifer	7/22/63	3/5/91	6349 Lincoln Court	Middle Riv	MD
13	2309	Kanoza	Scott	1/23/59	4/13/97	1251 S. National	Baltimore	MD

Figure 2.2 Inserting a row

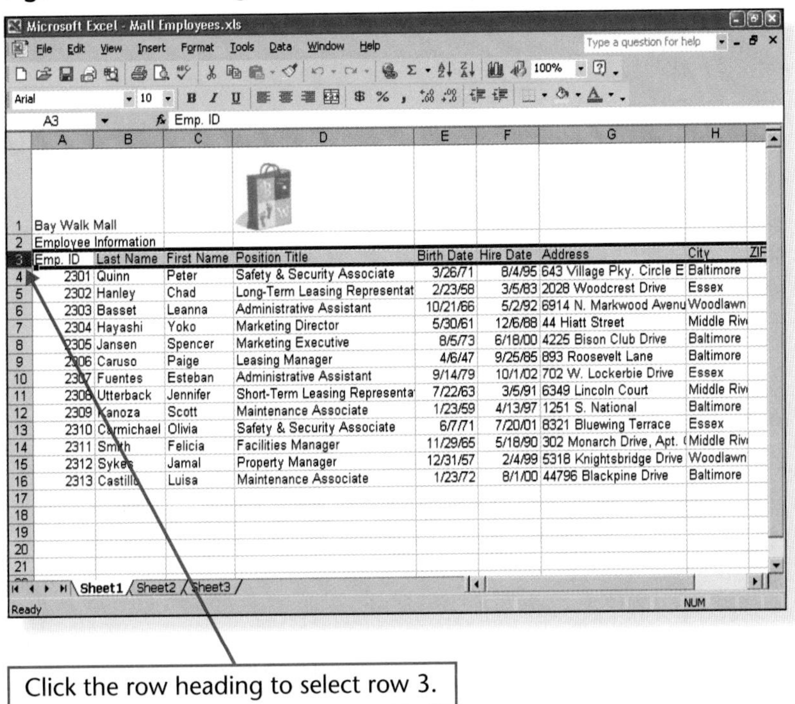
Click the row heading to select row 3.

Step Through It™

Exercise 1A: Insert and delete rows and columns

1. Open *Mall Employees.xls*. Save it as *xxx-Mall Employees.xls*. Click the row heading to select row 3 (see Figure 2.2).
2. On the Insert menu, select Rows. A new, blank row is inserted above the selected row, and all rows below the inserted row are moved down.

Figure 2.3 Deleting two rows

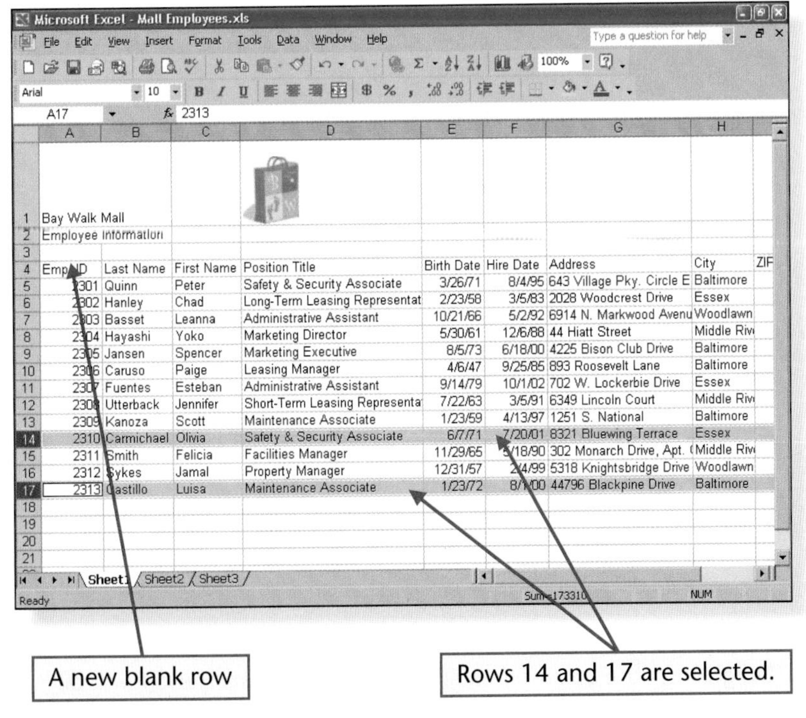
A new blank row
Rows 14 and 17 are selected.

3. Click the row 14 heading.
4. Hold Ctrl and click the row 17 heading. Rows 14 and 17 are selected (see Figure 2.3).
5. On the Edit menu, select Delete. The rows containing data for *Olivia Carmichael* and *Luisa Castillo* are deleted. The remaining rows shift up to fill the empty space.

6) Scroll to the right and select column I by clicking the column heading.

7) On the Insert menu, select Columns. A blank column is inserted to the left of the selected column, and all remaining columns are moved to the right.

8) Type State in cell I4. Type MD in cell I5, and press Enter. Select cell I5 and click Copy. Drag to select I6:I15 and click Paste. Press F2, and then click a blank cell to view the column (see Figure 2.4).

Figure 2.4 Inserting a column

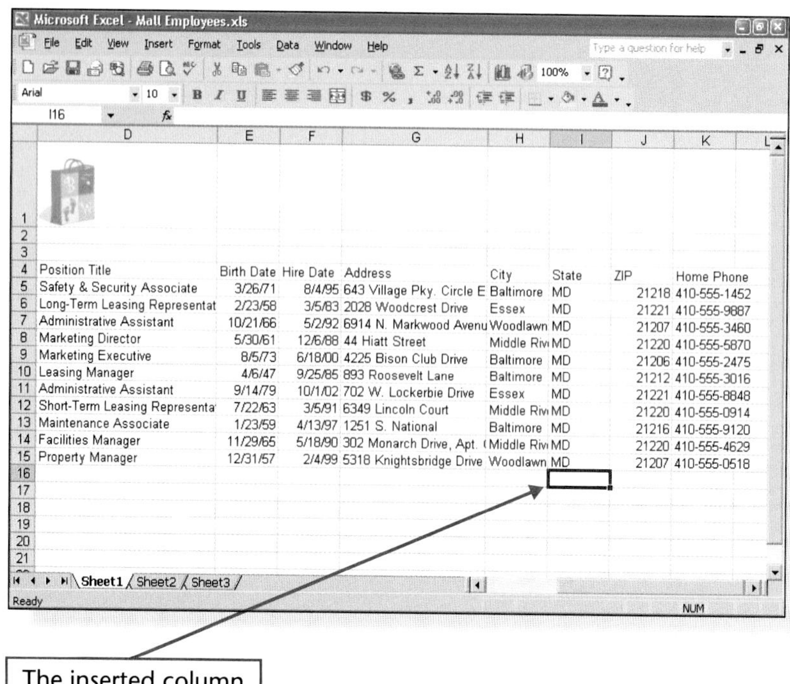

The inserted column

9) Click column heading E and then drag to the right to select column F. Both columns appear selected (see Figure 2.5).

10) On the Edit menu, select Delete. Columns E and F are deleted and the remaining columns shift to the left.

11) Click Undo to reverse this action and restore the deleted columns. Press Ctrl + Home.

12) Save your changes.

Figure 2.5 Deleting columns

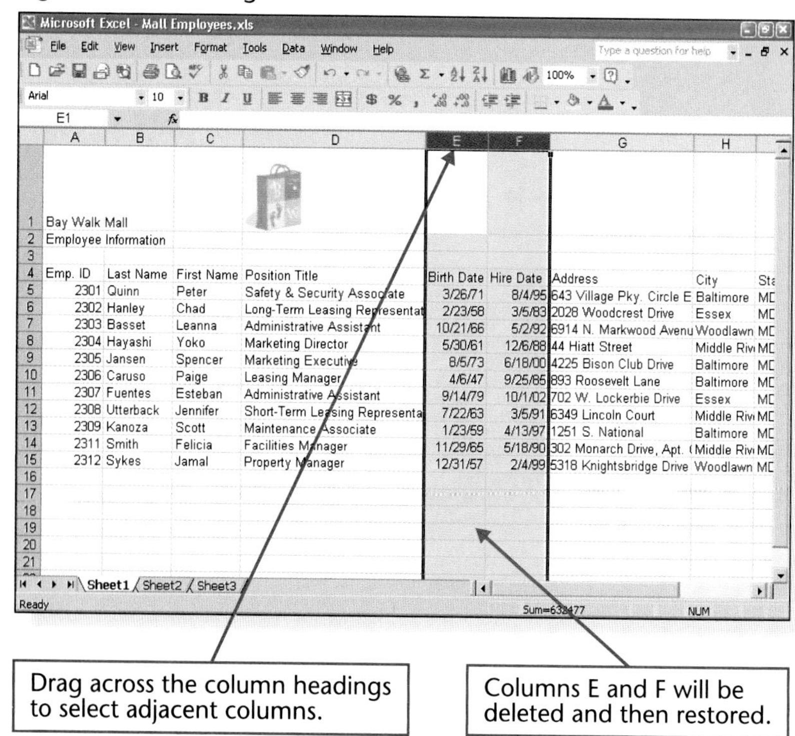

Drag across the column headings to select adjacent columns.

Columns E and F will be deleted and then restored.

Figure 2.6 Hiding column and row data

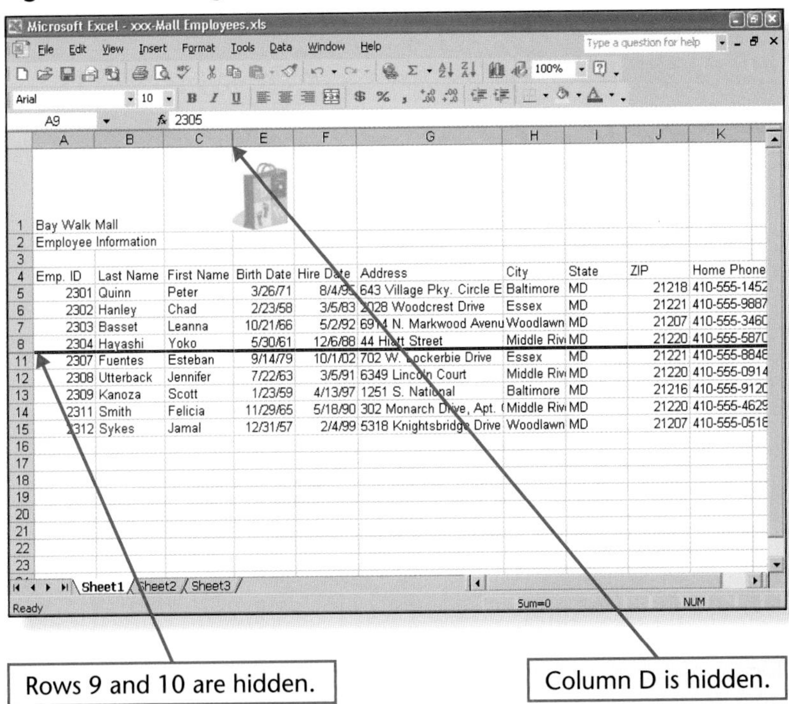
Rows 9 and 10 are hidden.
Column D is hidden.

Step Through It™

Exercise 1B: Hide and display rows and columns

1. Click column heading D to select the column.
2. On the Format menu, point to Column and click Hide. Column D is now hidden.
3. Select rows 9 and 10. Right-click anywhere inside the selected rows, and select Hide on the shortcut menu. The employee information for rows 9 and 10 is hidden (see Figure 2.6).

Excel

Figure 2.7 Redisplaying column and row data

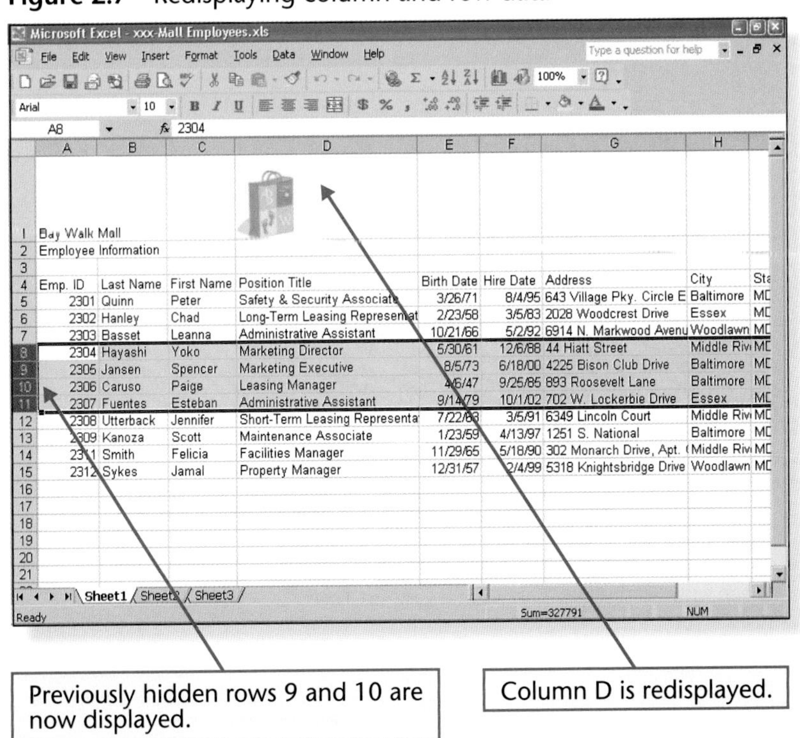
Previously hidden rows 9 and 10 are now displayed.
Column D is redisplayed.

4. Drag across column headings C and E. (This also selects the hidden column D.) On the Format menu, point to Column and click Unhide to redisplay column D.
5. Drag across rows 8 and 11. Right-click inside the selected rows and select Unhide. Rows 9 and 10 redisplay (see Figure 2.7).

Step Through It™

Exercise 1C: Freeze and unfreeze rows and columns

1. Select cell D5.
2. On the Window menu, select Freeze Panes. Excel freezes the rows above and the columns to the left of the selected cell. Horizontal and vertical black lines display in the worksheet to show which rows and columns are frozen (see Figure 2.8).

Figure 2.8 Freezing rows and columns

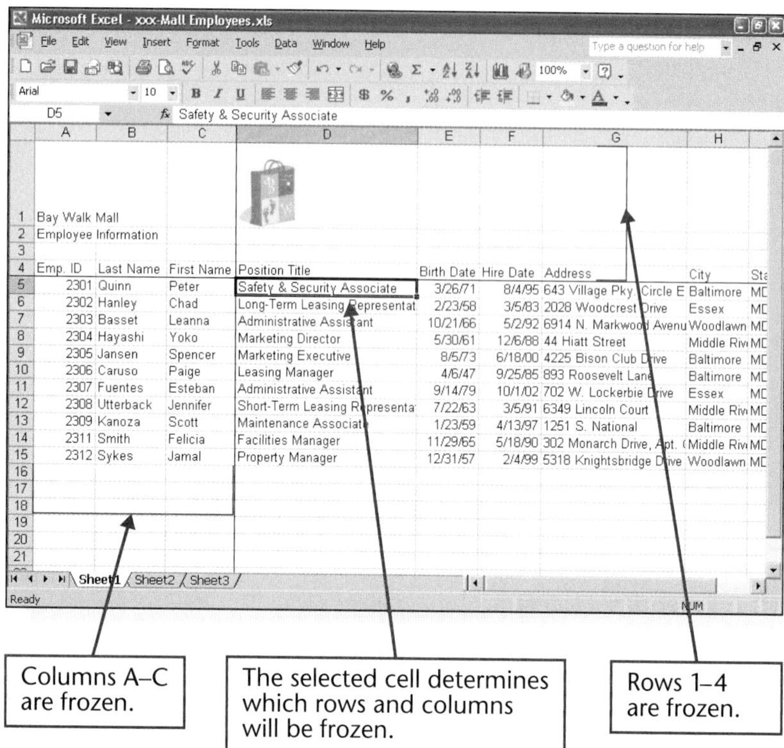

Columns A–C are frozen.

Rows 1–4 are frozen.

3. Press the right arrow key eight times. Columns A through C remain in view.
4. Click the down arrow on the vertical scroll bar four times. Rows 1 through 4 remain in view as you scroll down the worksheet (see Figure 2.9).
5. Press Ctrl + Home.
6. On the Window menu, click Unfreeze Panes.
7. Save your changes.

Figure 2.9 Scroll the worksheet to view more rows and columns

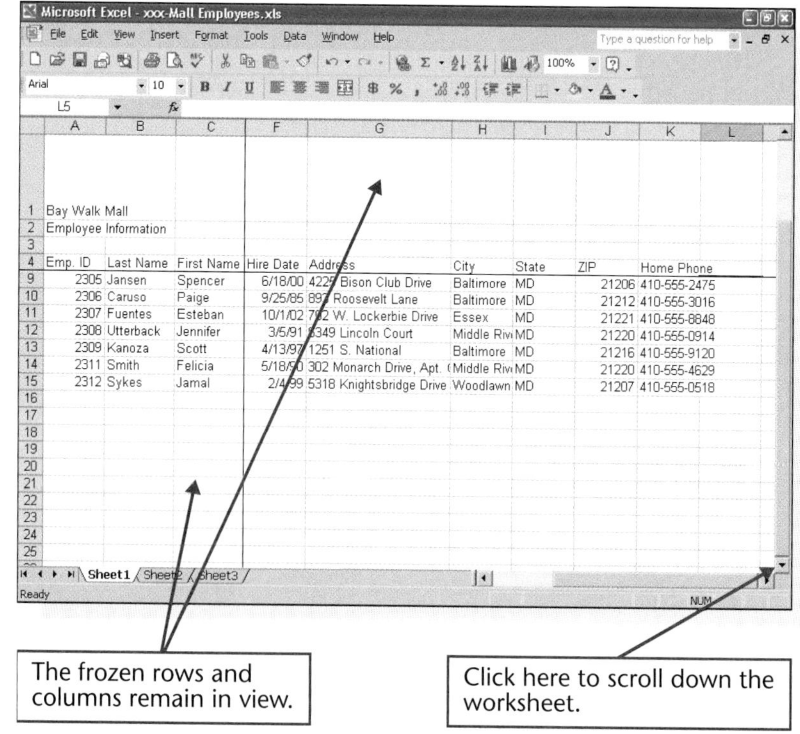

The frozen rows and columns remain in view.
Click here to scroll down the worksheet.

Figure 2.10 Fitting columns to the longest entry

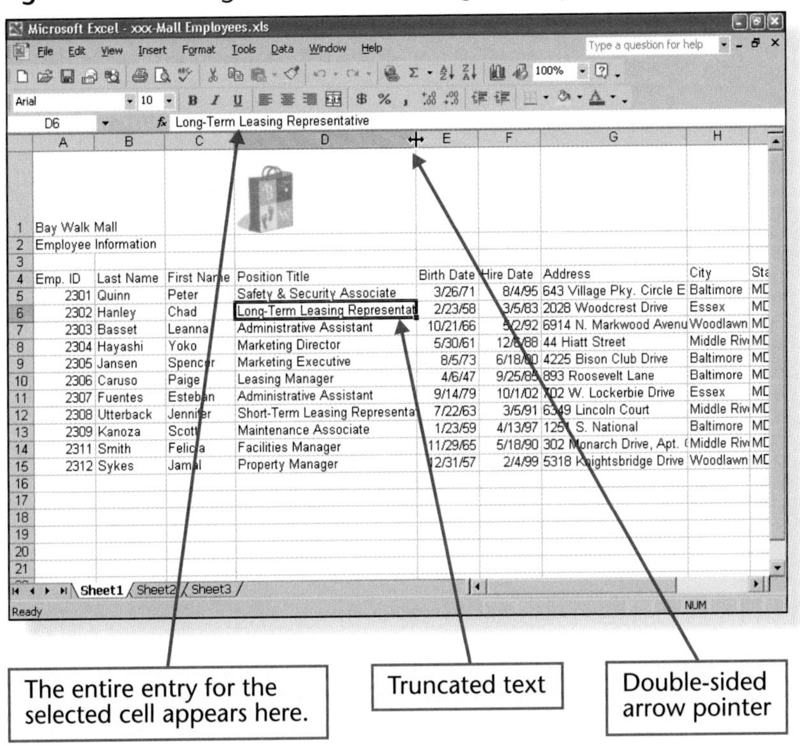

Step Through It™

Exercise 1D: Change row heights and column widths

1. Select cell D6. The text in this cell is truncated (cut off) because the cell to the right contains an entry.

2. Point to the border between the column D and E headings. The pointer displays as a double-sided arrow (see Figure 2.10).

Figure 2.11 The column widths have been adjusted

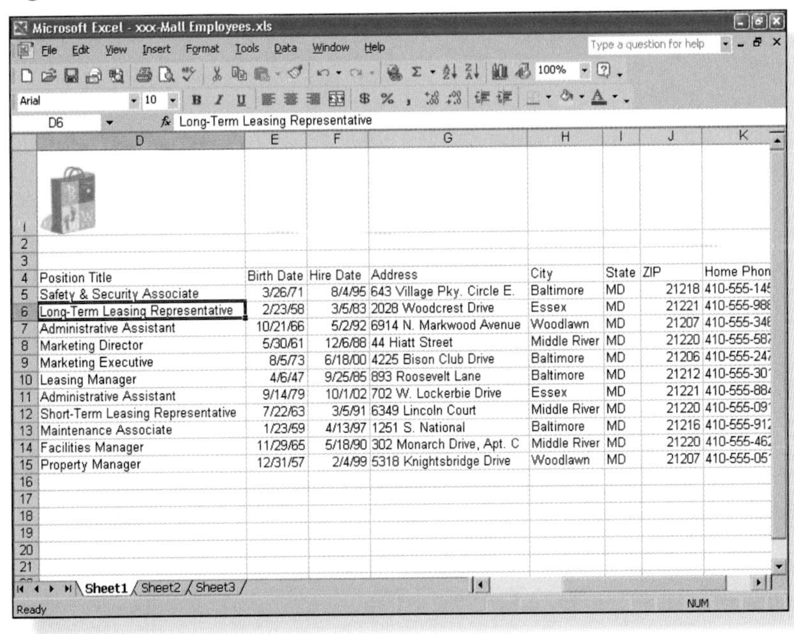

3. With the double-sided arrow still visible, double-click the line between the column headings. Column D automatically resizes to fit the longest entry.

4. Use this same technique (following steps 2 and 3) to resize columns G, H, I, and K. The columns are adjusted to the width of the longest entry. The width of column I is reduced in size, while the other columns have increased in size (see Figure 2.11).

5 Select columns I and J. On the Format menu, point to Column and select Width to display the Column Width dialog box.

6 Type 7 in the *Column width* box (see Figure 2.12). Click OK. Both columns are resized.

Figure 2.12 Using the Column Width dialog box

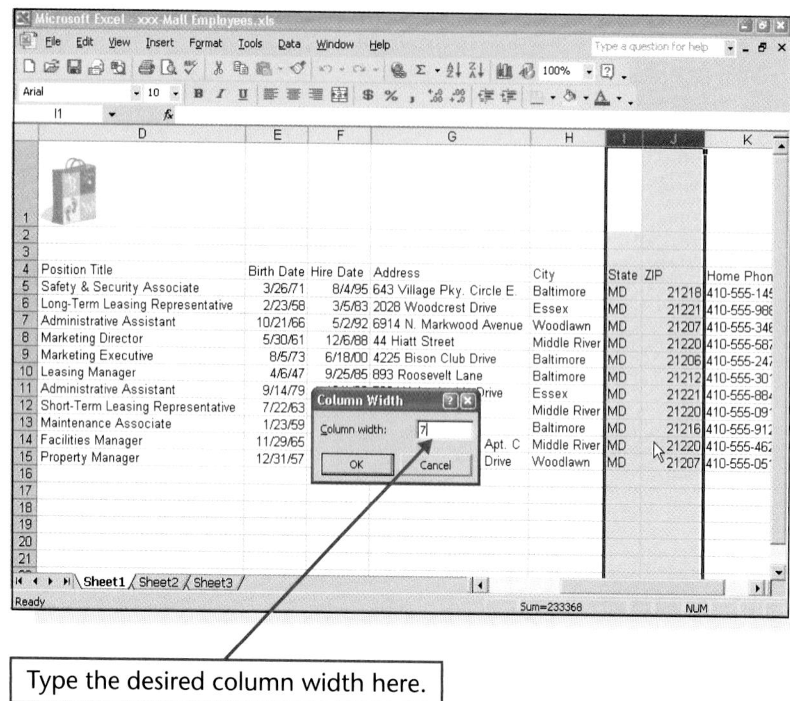

7 Press Home and then point to the border between the row 1 and 2 headings. A double-sided arrow displays.

8 Click the border between the row 1 and 2 headings and slowly drag downward. As you drag, a ScreenTip displays the current row height (see Figure 2.13). Release the mouse button when the label displays *Height: 72.00 (96 pixels)*.

Figure 2.13 Adjusting the height of a row

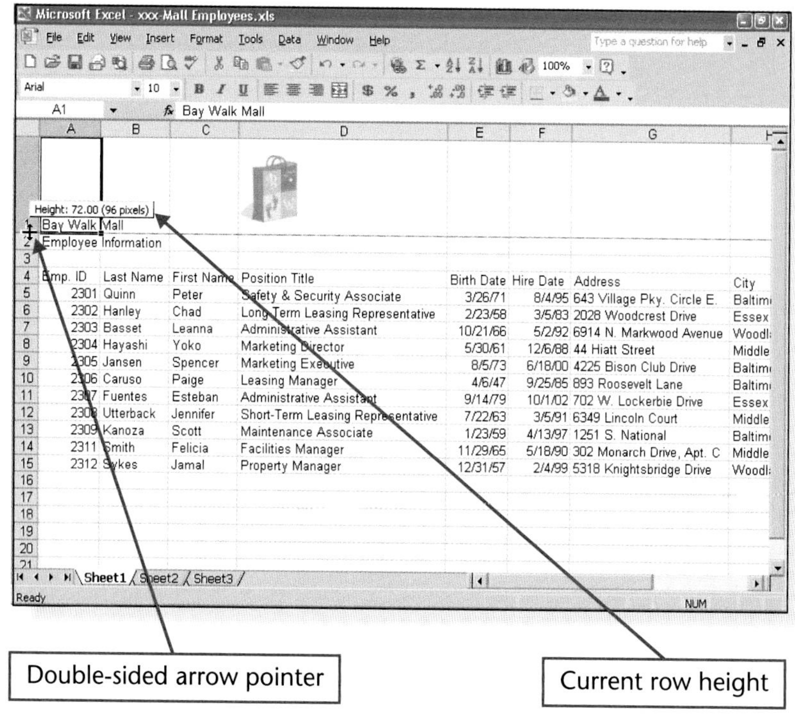

Excel

Figure 2.14 Using the Row Height dialog box

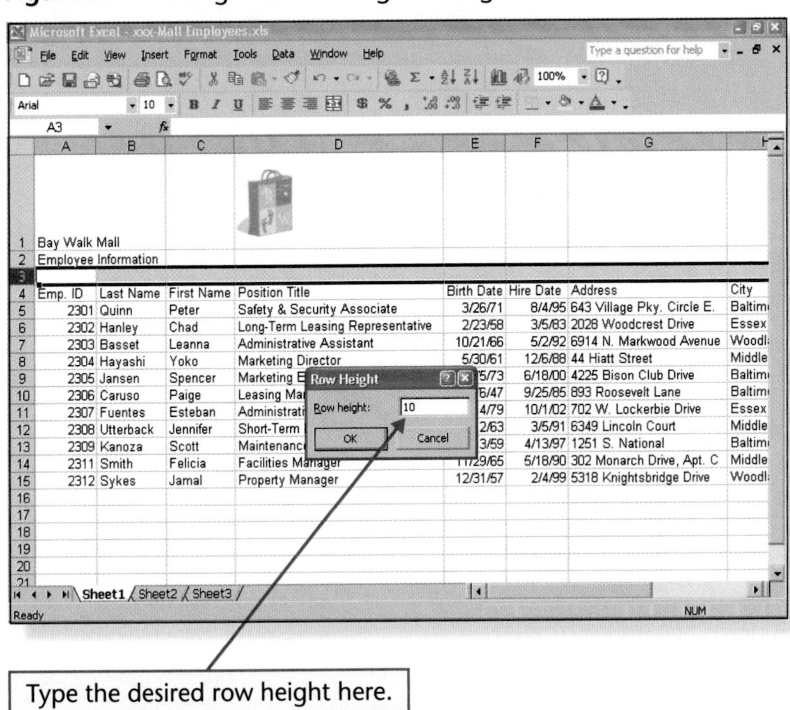

Type the desired row height here.

9. Click the row 3 heading. On the Format menu, point to Row and select Height to display the Row Height dialog box.

10. Type 10 in the *Row height* box (see Figure 2.14). Click OK. The height of row 3 decreases.

Figure 2.15 Symbols (#) in the Birth Date column

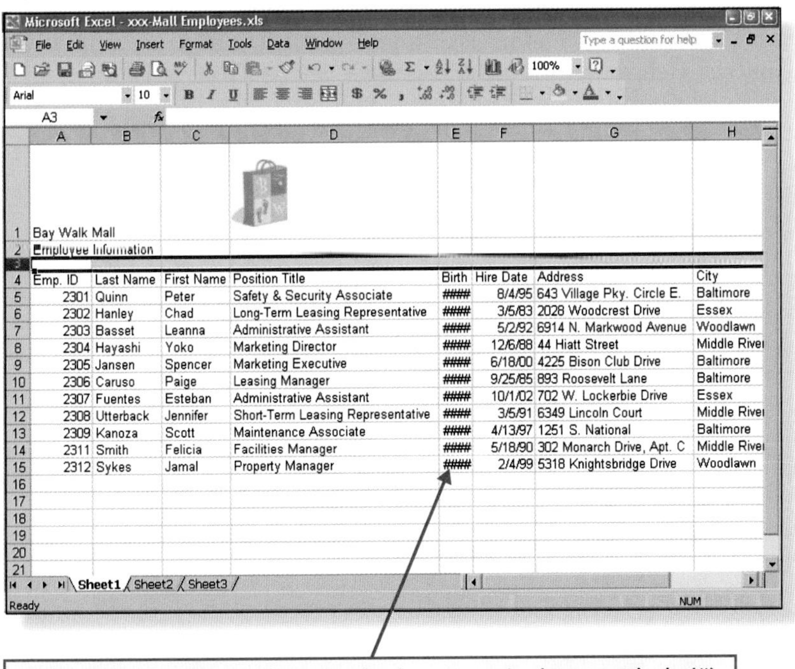

If the column is too narrow to display numeric data, symbols (#) signs are displayed.

11. Point to the border between the column E and F headings. Drag to the left until the column width is reduced by about half. Symbols (#) display because the column is too narrow to display the dates (see Figure 2.15).

12. Double-click the border of the Column E heading to restore the column width.

13. Save your changes.

Business Connections

Converting Currencies

Many professions in the financial services industry—such as those relating to banking, investments, financial planning, and insurance services—require knowledge of current currency conversion rates. Many Web sites contain currency converters. Use your favorite search engine to search for them. Be aware that these rates are constantly changing.

Changing to Euros

On January 1, 2002, euro notes and coins were put into circulation in a dozen European countries. The European Union (EU) members that initially adopted the euro include Austria, Belgium, Finland, France, Germany, Greece, Ireland, Italy, Luxembourg, the Netherlands, Portugal, and Spain.

The euro was introduced primarily to provide a common currency that could be used among European countries to avoid the need to convert from one currency to another. This benefits manufacturers that buy or sell products or services within the countries because they no longer have to incur the costs of changing money.

Using Excel's Currency Tools

Excel 2002 includes a Euro Currency Tools add-in that you can use to convert euro member currencies to euro currency. To access the add-in, select Add-Ins on the Tools menu. Select the Euro Currency Tools check box and click OK. The following tools are then available to you within Excel:

- The EuroValue toolbar, which includes a drop-down list of the available conversions and enables you to view converted values.
- A Euro Conversion button on the Standard toolbar (and a command on the Tools menu), which enables you to convert values or formulas to and from the euro and between euro member currencies.
- A Euro button on the Formatting toolbar that enables you to apply the euro numeric format (and symbol) to selected cells.

Excel also provides a EUROCONVERT worksheet function to assist you with conversions. Refer to Excel Help for detailed information on how to use these tools.

1. **Using Keyboard Shortcuts** What keys do you use to manually type the euro currency symbol in an Excel worksheet? Test the keystrokes on your keyboard. (***Hint:*** Type euro in Excel Help.)
2. **Converting Currencies** Locate a Web site that provides a currency converter and convert a U.S. dollar to a euro. In what situations might this information be useful to you?

Microsoft Office Specialist EX2002 3.1, 3.3

Exercise 2 Overview:
Apply and Modify Cell Formats

Common formatting attributes such as bold, italic, and underline are available by clicking the appropriate buttons on the Formatting toolbar. You also can use the Formatting toolbar to change the font, font size, font color, and fill color. Additional formatting options are available through the Format menu.

When you enter data in a cell, Excel automatically aligns text entries on the left side of a cell and numeric entries on the right side of a cell. You can change this horizontal alignment by using the alignment buttons on the Formatting toolbar. Through the Format menu, you can change the vertical alignment of cell data, wrap multiple lines of text within a cell, and even rotate text.

When you are done formatting a cell, you can use the Format Painter button on the Standard toolbar to copy the formatting to other cells. This time-saving feature helps to ensure that data is formatted consistently.

In the following exercises, you will format cells in the *Mall Employees* worksheet.

Step Through It™
Exercise 2A: Change the font, font color, and size

1. Select cell A1. Click the Font down arrow. Scroll through the list and select *Monotype Corsiva*. If you don't have this font, select another decorative font.

2. Click the Font Size down arrow and select *24* from the list (see Figure 2.16).

Figure 2.16 Changing the font and font size

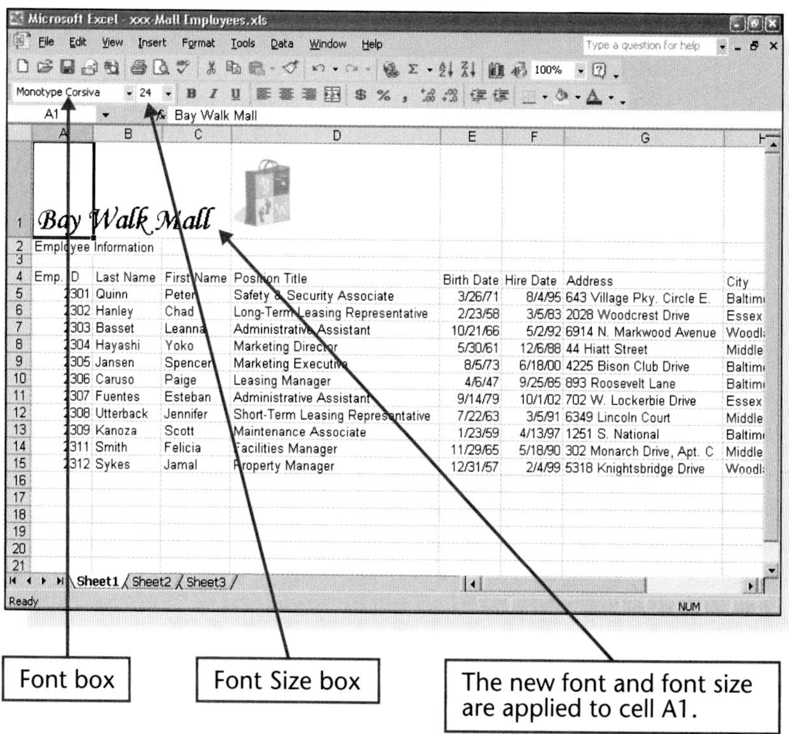

Figure 2.17 Changing the font color

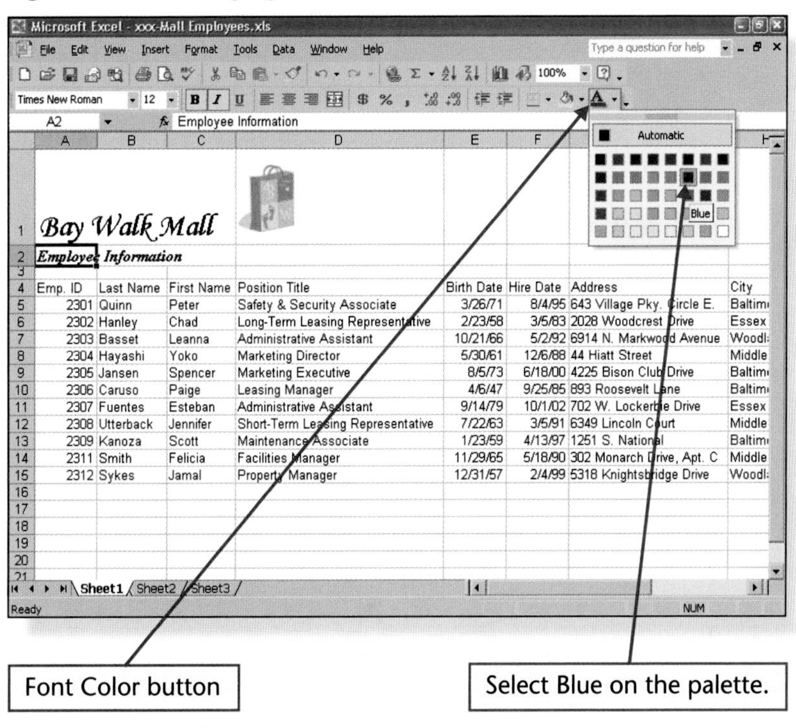

3. Select cell A2. Change the font to Times New Roman and the font size to 12.

4. On the Formatting toolbar, click Bold and then click Italic.

5. Click the Font Color down arrow and point to the Blue color square (see Figure 2.17). Click the Blue color square to apply the color to cell A2.

Figure 2.18 Aligning data in cells

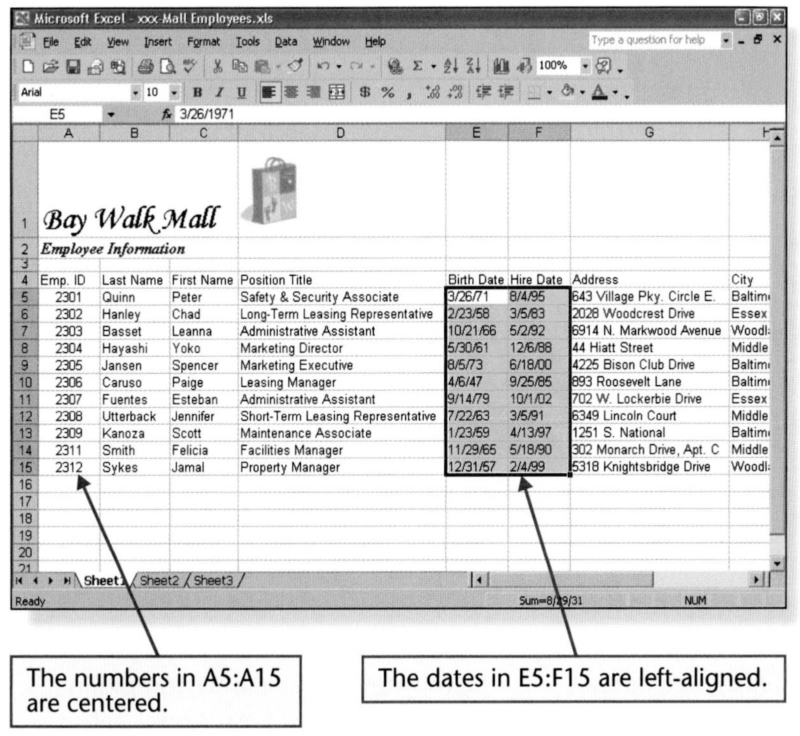

Step Through It™

Exercise 2B: Change alignment in cells

1. Select the range A5:A15. Click Center on the Formatting toolbar. The data is centered horizontally within the cells.

2. Center the data in the range I5:J15 (the *State* and *ZIP* columns).

3. Select E5:F15 and then click Align Left on the Formatting toolbar (see Figure 2.18).

Step Through It™

Exercise 2C: Copy formats with Format Painter

1. Select cell A4. Click Bold, click Center, and then change the font size to 9.
2. Click the Fill Color down arrow on the Formatting toolbar and select Blue.
3. Click the Font Color down arrow and select White (see Figure 2.19).

Figure 2.19 Applying formats to copy

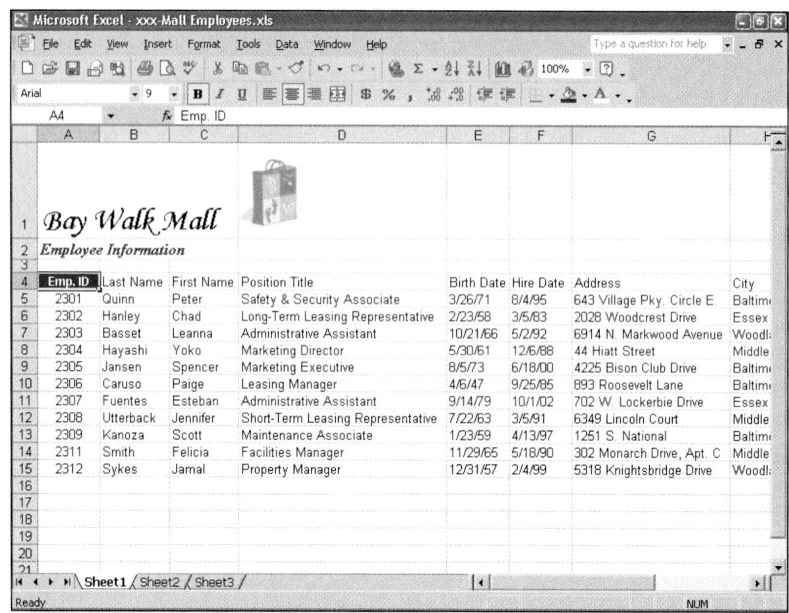

4. With cell A4 still selected, click Format Painter on the Standard toolbar. The pointer changes to a paintbrush.
5. Click cell B4 and drag across the row to cell K4. The formats from A4 are applied to B4:K4 (see Figure 2.20).
6. Save and close the workbook.

Figure 2.20 Copying formats with Format Painter

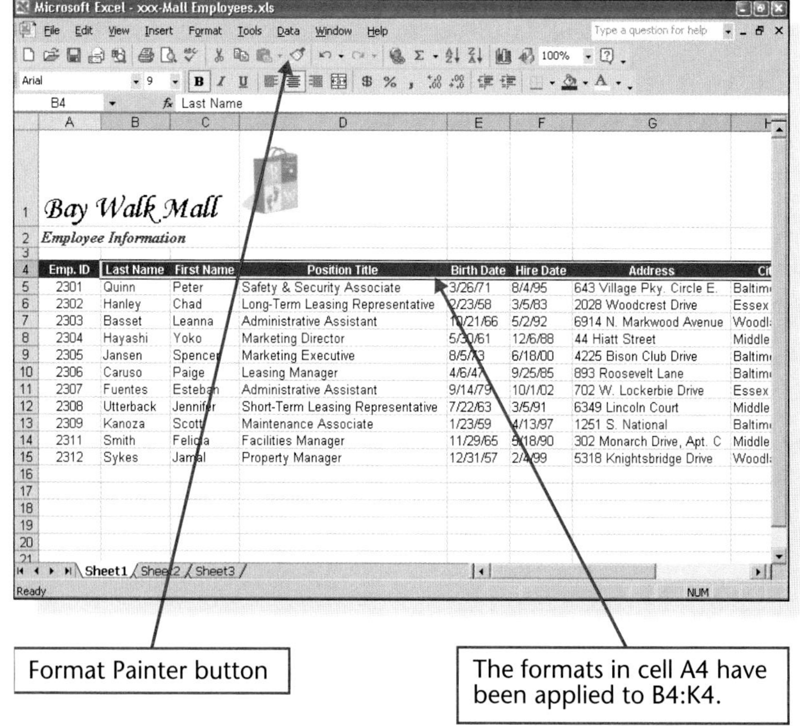

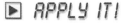

APPLY IT! After finishing Exercises 1–2, you may test your skills by completing Apply It! Guided Activity 1, Format a Profit and Loss Worksheet.

Exercise 3 Overview:
Apply Styles and AutoFormats

Microsoft Office Specialist
EX2002 3.4, 3.5

Excel

You can use styles in Excel to apply a set of formats to existing data in a single step. Using styles can help you save time and ensure consistent formatting in your worksheets. Although Excel includes a few predefined styles, you may want to define your own styles that reflect formats you use often.

When you initially define a style, you apply to a single cell all the formats that you want to save in the style. These formats include the font, font size, font color, alignment, borders, shading, number formats, and attributes such as bold, italic, and underline.

Excel includes an AutoFormat feature that enables you to quickly format an entire list or table with a set of predefined formats. You can choose among 16 different AutoFormats each of which provides a different look for a table.

In the following exercises, you will define a style and then apply the new style. Then, you will apply an AutoFormat to a table of data.

Type: styles

Figure 2.21 Applying formats for a new style

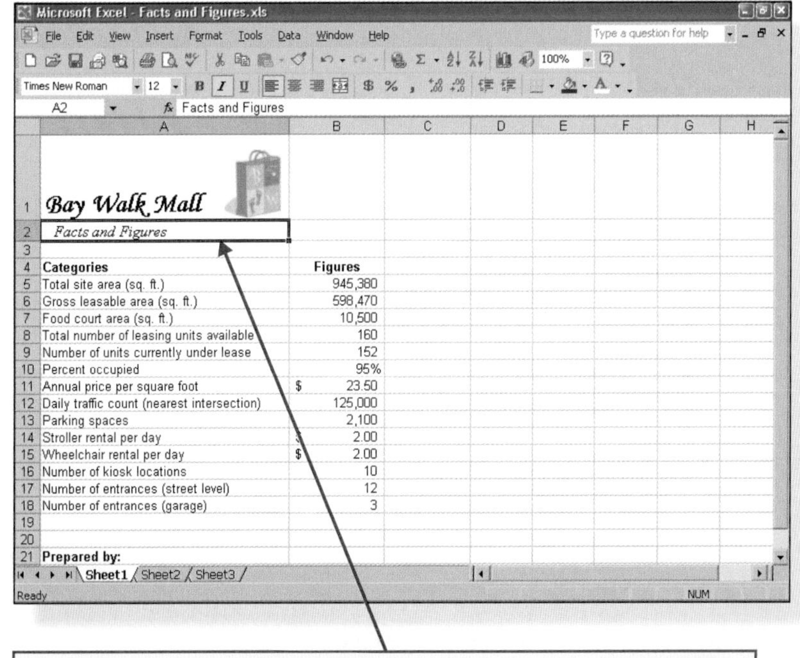

The formats applied to this cell will be used to define a new style.

Step Through It™
Exercise 3A: Apply styles

1. Open *Facts and Figures.xls*. Save it as *xxx-Facts and Figures.xls*.
2. Click cell A2. Change the font to *Times New Roman* and the font size to 12.
3. Click Italic and then click Increase Indent (see Figure 2.21).

4. With cell A2 selected, select Style on the Format menu to display the Style dialog box.

5. Type Subtitle in the *Style name* box. The options in the lower portion of the dialog box change to reflect the formats in the selected cell (see Figure 2.22).

6. Click OK to define the new style.

Figure 2.22 Defining the style

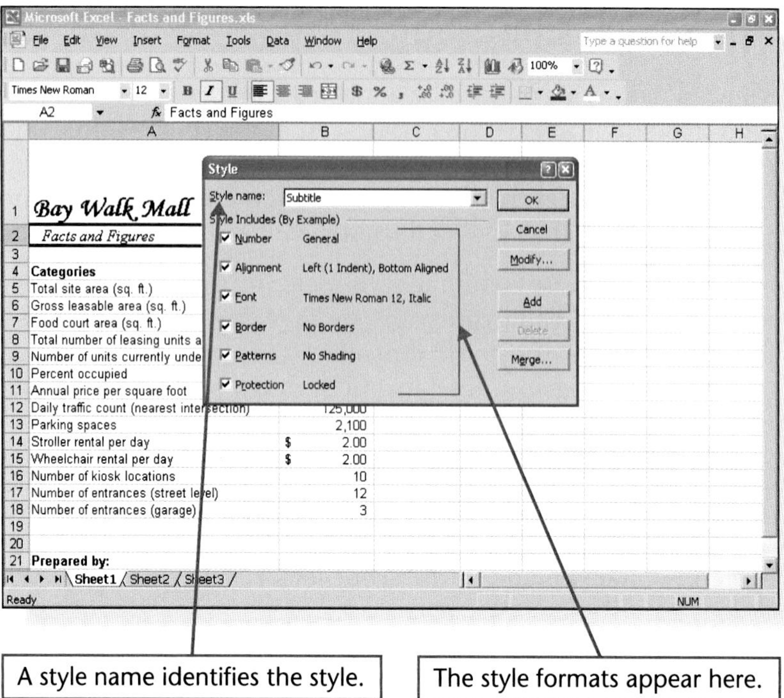

A style name identifies the style.
The style formats appear here.

7. Click cell A22. On the Format menu, select Style. Click the *Style name* down arrow, select *Subtitle*, and click OK. The new style is applied to cell A22 (see Figure 2.23).

Figure 2.23 Applying the new style to another cell

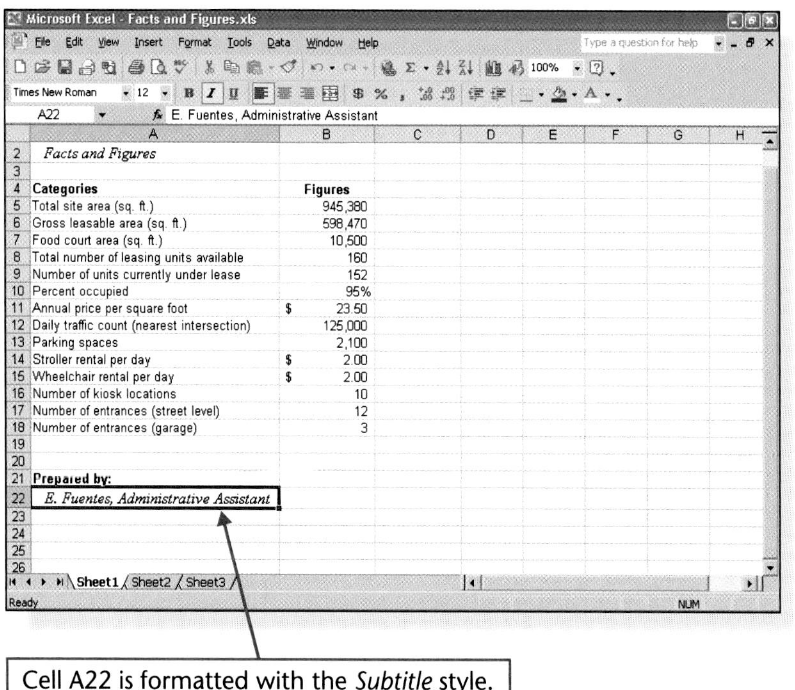

Cell A22 is formatted with the *Subtitle* style.

Figure 2.24 Choosing the AutoFormat options

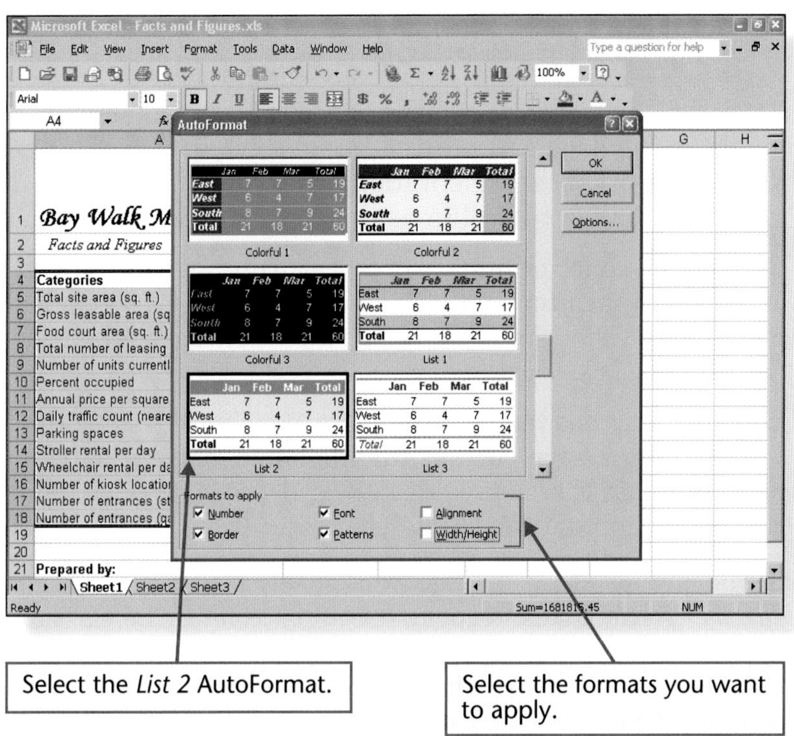

Step Through It™

Exercise 3B: Apply AutoFormats

1. Select the range A4:B18. On the Format menu, select AutoFormat.
2. Scroll down the list and select the *List 2* AutoFormat.
3. Click the Options button. Clear the *Alignment* and *Width/ Height* check boxes to retain your alignment and column width settings (see Figure 2.24).

Figure 2.25 The table with an AutoFormat

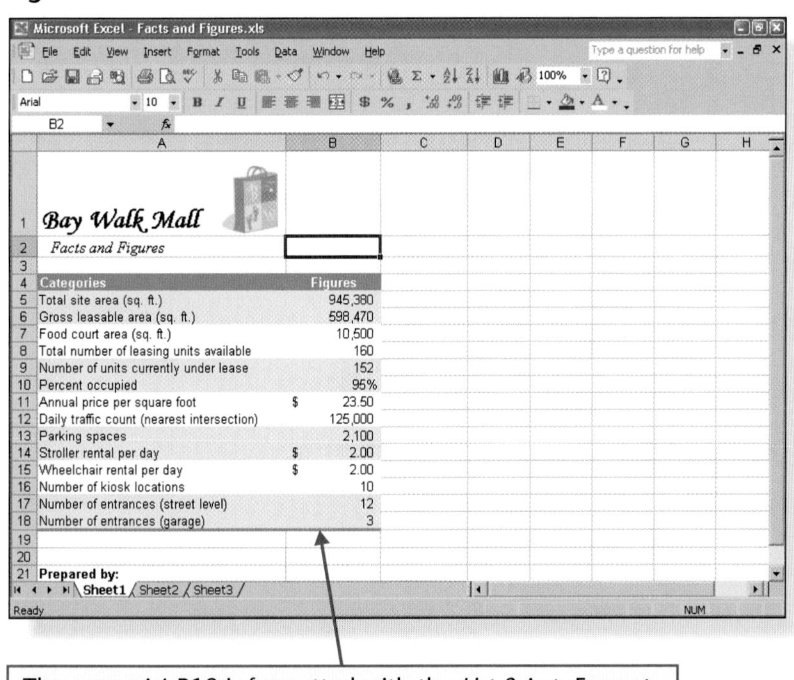

4. Click OK, and then click outside the table to view the new table format (see Figure 2.25).
5. Save your changes.
6. Close the workbook.

Excel

Microsoft Office Specialist
EX2002 3.6

Excel

Exercise 4 Overview:
Modify the Page Setup

Before you are ready to print your worksheet, you may need to adjust the page setup by defining or modifying settings such as worksheet orientation, margins, headers and footers, and rows and columns that repeat on each page.

By default, Excel prints a worksheet using portrait orientation with 1-inch top and bottom margins and 0.75-inch left and right margins. You can change these settings in the Page Setup dialog box, if necessary.

You can add headers or footers to your worksheets that include information such as the file name, current date, or page number. Excel provides several predefined headers and footers, or you can create your own.

Need Help?

Type: headers and footers

If you are printing a large worksheet, you may want to specify **print titles**—repeated row or column labels that appear on each page—to make the printout easier to read. You also can specify whether or not you want to print worksheet gridlines and the row and column headers that identify row numbers and column letters for the printed data.

In the following exercises, you will change page setup options.

Step Through It™
Exercise 4A: Modify worksheet orientation and margins

1. Open *Employee Info.xls*. Save it as *xxx-Employee Info.xls*. On the File menu, select Page Setup to display the Page Setup dialog box.
2. Click the Page tab. In the *Orientation* section, select the *Landscape* option.
3. In the *Scaling* section, select the *Fit to* option. Keep the default settings of *1 page wide by 1 tall* (see Figure 2.26).

Figure 2.26 Specifying orientation and scaling options

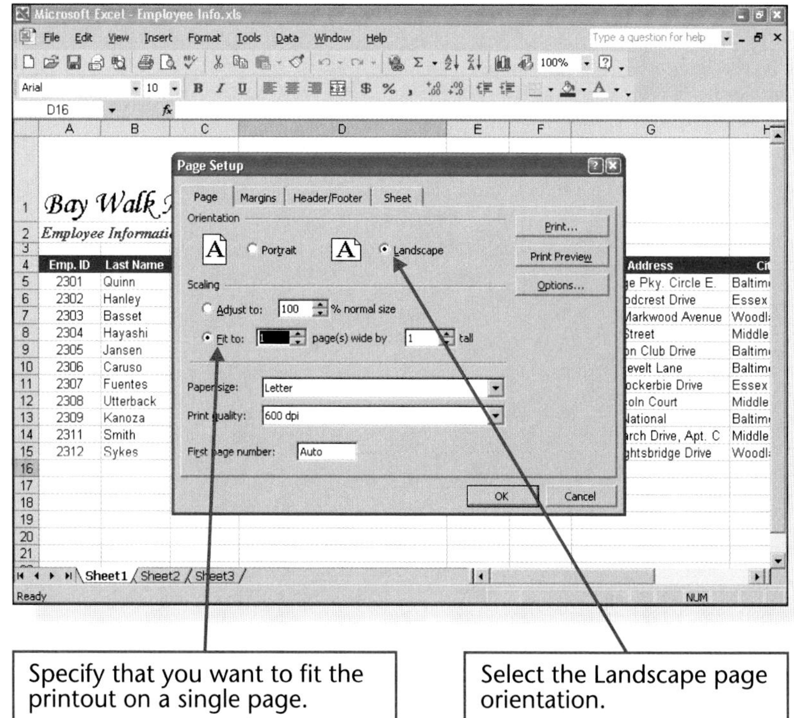

Figure 2.27 Adjusting the margins and centering options

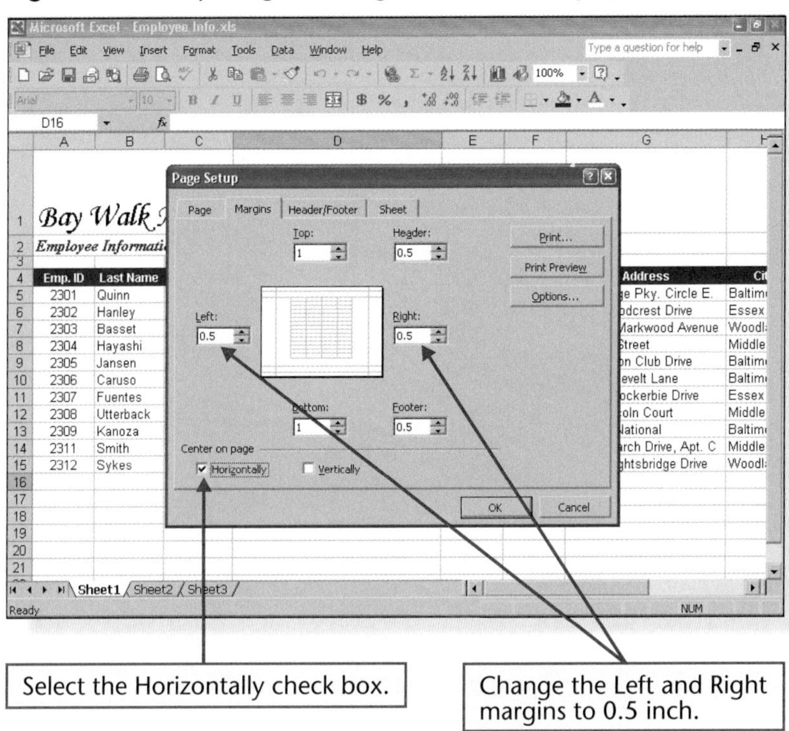

Select the Horizontally check box.
Change the Left and Right margins to 0.5 inch.

4. Click the Margins tab. In the *Left* box, reduce the left margin setting to 0.5 inch. In the *Right* box, also reduce the right margin setting to 0.5 inch.
5. In the *Center on page* section, select the *Horizontally* check box to center the printout horizontally (see Figure 2.27). Click OK to close the dialog box.
6. Save your changes.

Excel

Figure 2.28 Specifying a header and footer

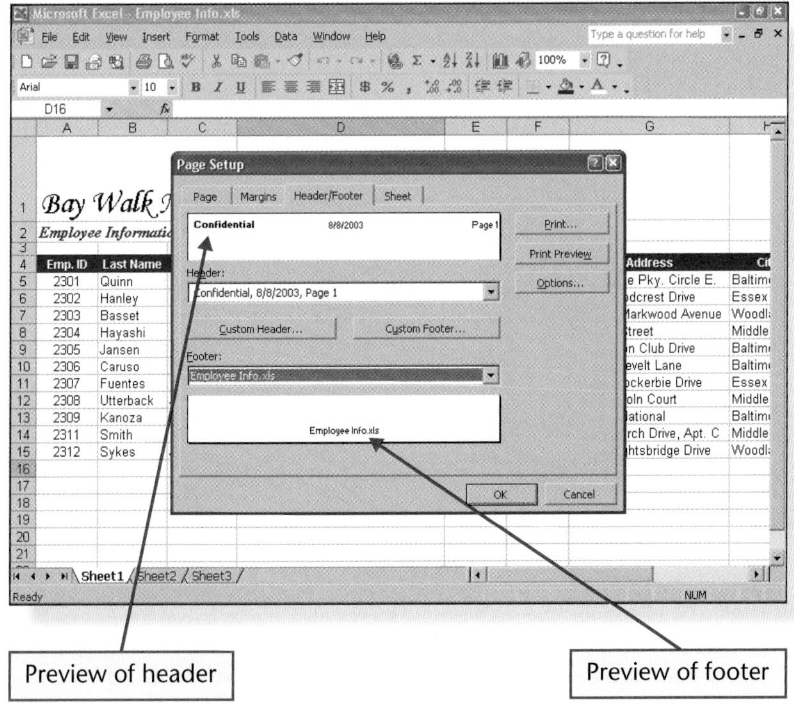

Preview of header
Preview of footer

Step Through It™

Exercise 4B: Add a header and footer

1. On the View menu, select Header and Footer.
2. Click Custom Header. In the *Left section*, type **Confidential** and press Tab. Click Insert Date and press Tab. Click Insert Page Number and click OK.
3. Click the *Footer* down arrow, and select the option that displays the file name (see Figure 2.28). Click OK.

Step Through It™

Exercise 4C: Set rows and columns to repeat

Excel

1. On the File menu, select Page Setup. Click the Sheet tab.

2. Beside the *Rows to repeat at top* box, click the Collapse Dialog button (see Figure 2.29). The dialog box collapses to enable you to make a selection in the worksheet.

Figure 2.29 Specifying the rows to repeat

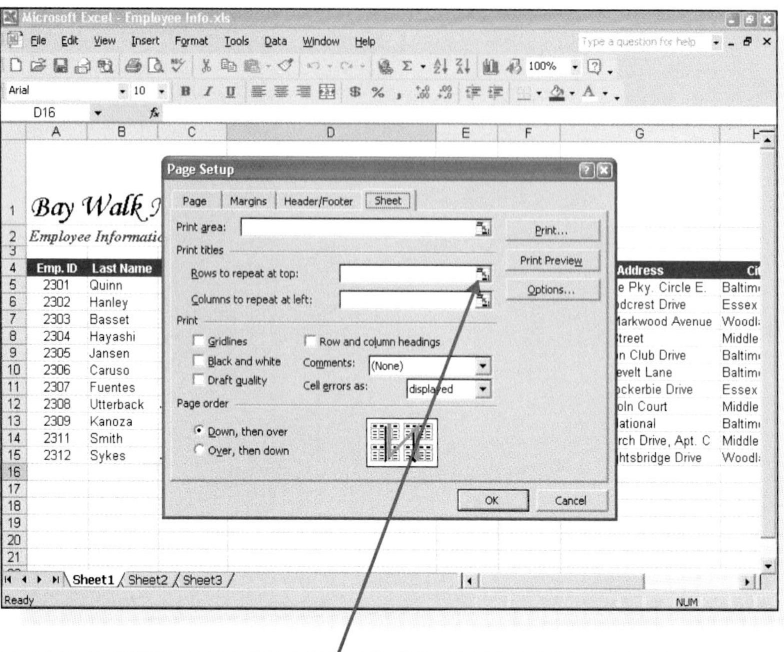

Click this Collapse Dialog button to specify rows to repeat.

3. Click and drag to select row headings 1 through 4. A moving border surrounds rows 1 through 4. These rows are now set to repeat on each printed page.

4. Click the Expand Dialog button (see Figure 2.30). The Page Setup dialog box expands. The row settings display in the dialog box. Click OK.

5. Save your changes.

Figure 2.30 The selected rows to repeat

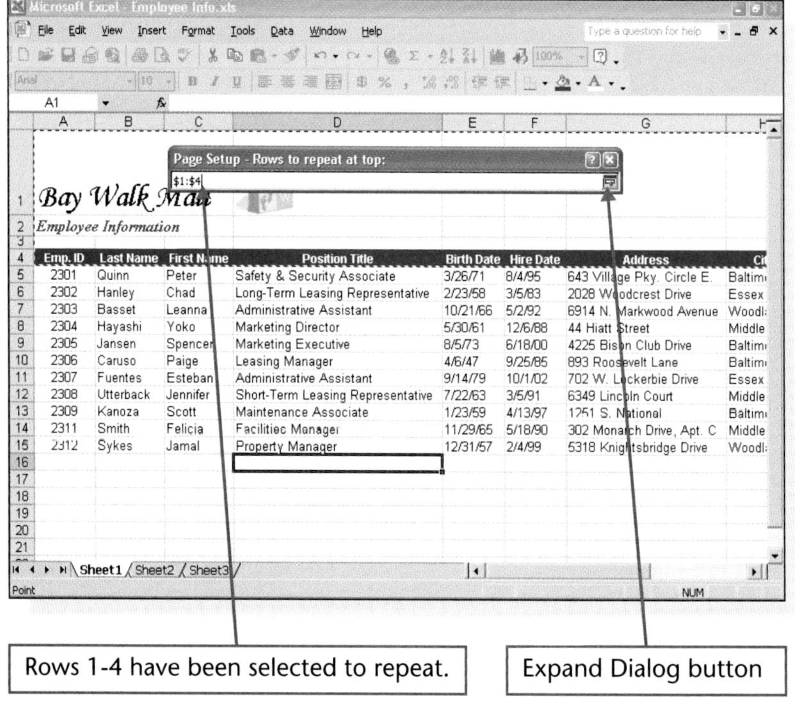

Rows 1-4 have been selected to repeat.

Expand Dialog button

Tech Talk

Managing Financial Data Online

Businesses and consumers are increasingly using the Web and special software tools to manage their finances. This quiet revolution in the banking, investment, and insurance industries has transformed the way that we shop for loans, pay our bills, or invest in the stock market.

An online service can pay your bills and integrate your online bank account (a history of your deposits and withdrawals) into a current statement showing your financial picture. Account information is usually available to you through the service company's Web site.

Specialized finance software such as Quicken and Microsoft Money can keep track of your financial data. This software can retrieve information from your bank and automate the management of business and personal accounts, such as savings, checking, credit cards, and even stocks and bonds. In addition, many banks provide proprietary software that allows you to connect to the bank's own network to retrieve information. These tools provide you with the current financial information you need to make decisions about your personal finances or your business.

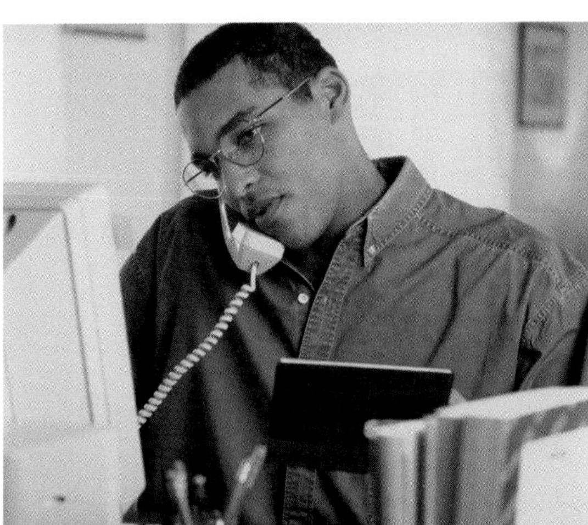

Excel has features that help you to manage specific types of financial data. For example, using Excel's Smart Tags feature you can instantly retrieve current stock information from the Web. Learn more about how to enable and use this feature by searching on *smart tags* in Excel Help.

CRITICAL THINKING

1. Perform a Web search using *online banking* as the search text, and visit the Web sites of at least three companies that provide these services (you will revisit these sites for the next question, so save them as Favorites). Based on what you find, name three advantages of using online banking services to pay bills and monitor your accounts.
2. The Web sites of some financial services firms provide free tools with which to plan your finances. These may include spending analysis tools, savings calculators, and retirement, tax, and debt reduction planners. Locate at least one of these tools, determine how it works, and report this information to the class.

Microsoft Office Specialist EX2002 3.6, 3.7

Exercise 5 Overview:
Preview and Print Worksheets

After you've modified the page setup for your worksheet, it should be previewed. Previewing a worksheet will show you how the worksheet will look when printed. This helps you catch problems with the layout and make needed adjustments.

You can print any portion of a worksheet, including nonadjacent ranges—you don't have to print the entire worksheet. If you typically print only a portion of a large worksheet, you can define that print area and save it with the worksheet so that you don't need to redefine the print area each time you print.

If you are printing a large worksheet that won't easily fit on a single page, you can specify where in the worksheet you want page breaks to occur. You can set a horizontal page break or a vertical page break. If you want to view the worksheet with all page break locations displayed, select Page Break Preview (View menu). In this view, you can drag page break lines to different locations to adjust them.

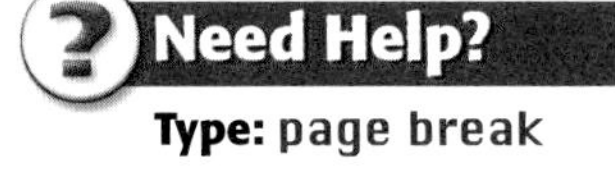

Type: page break

In the following exercises, you will work with print areas and preview and print your worksheet.

Figure 2.31 Print Preview shows how a worksheet will look when printed

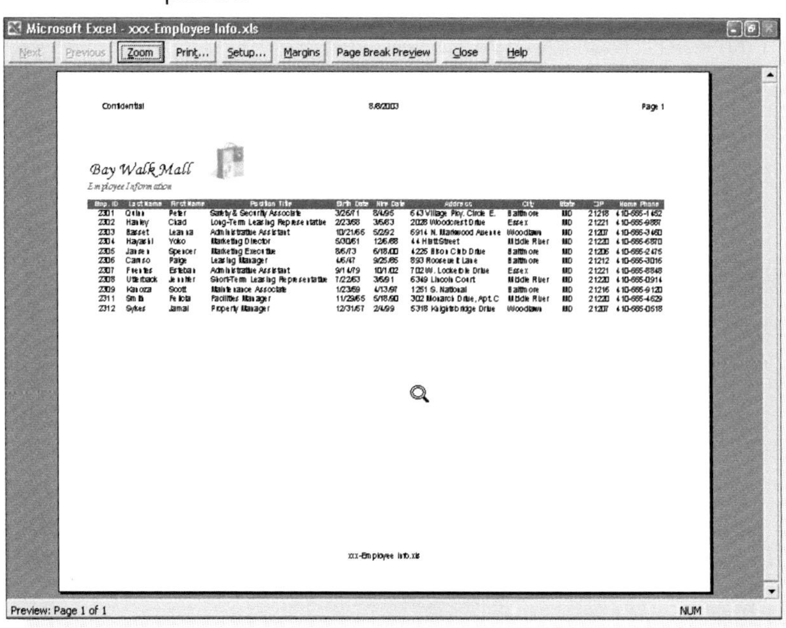

Figure 2.32 Setting a print area

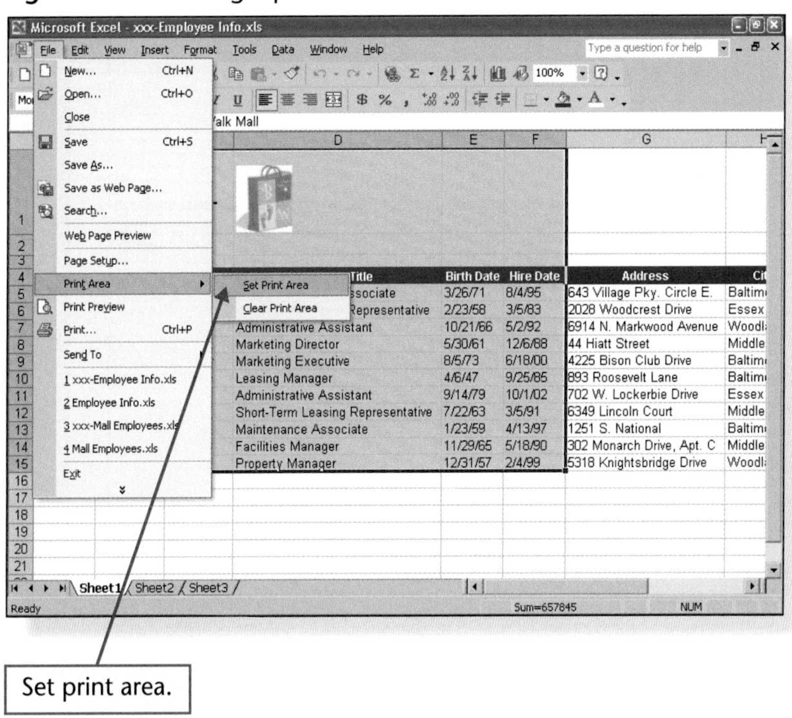

Step Through It™

Exercise 5A: Set, print, and clear a print area

1. Select the range A1:F15.
2. On the File menu, point to Print Area and select Set Print Area (see Figure 2.32).

Figure 2.33 The Print dialog box

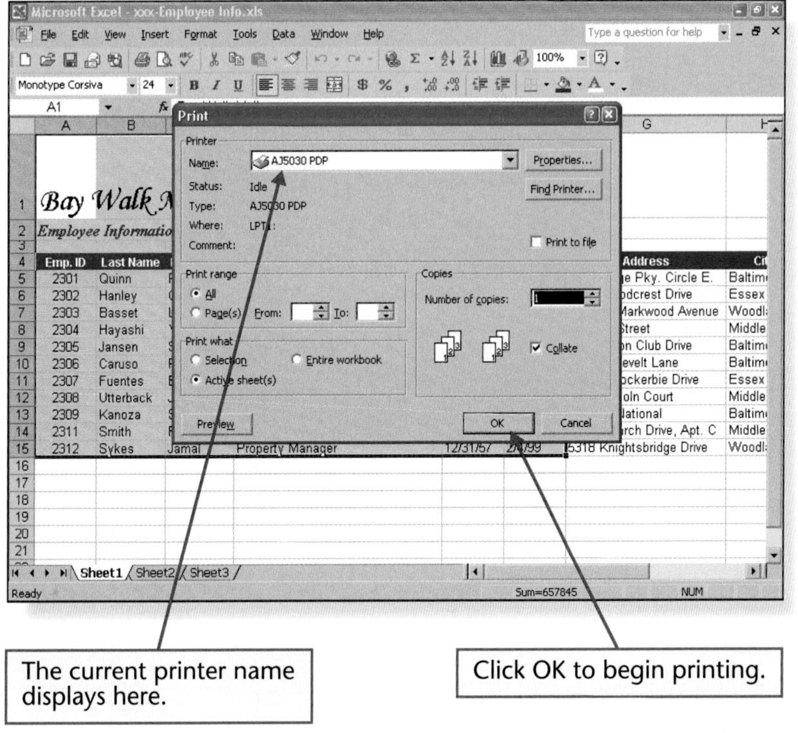

The current printer name displays here.
Click OK to begin printing.

3. On the File menu, select Print. The Print dialog box displays (see Figure 2.33).
4. Click OK to print your worksheet.
5. On the File menu, point to Print Area and select Clear Print Area to reset the print area to include the entire worksheet.
6. Click cell A1 to deselect the range.

Excel

Step Through It™

Exercise 5B: Preview and print nonadjacent portions of a worksheet

Excel

1. Click Print Preview on the Standard toolbar. The entire worksheet displays in Print Preview mode (see Figure 2.34).

2. Select Zoom, if necessary. Point to the worksheet. When the pointer changes to a magnifying glass, click once to zoom in on the display. Click again to return to the previous view.

3. Click the Close button in the Print Preview toolbar.

4. On the File menu, select Page Setup. Click the Sheet tab. Click the *Print area* Collapse Dialog button.

5. Select the range A5:C15 and type a comma. Select the range G5:J15 and press Enter. The Page Setup dialog box redisplays (see Figure 2.35).

Figure 2.34 The Print Preview window

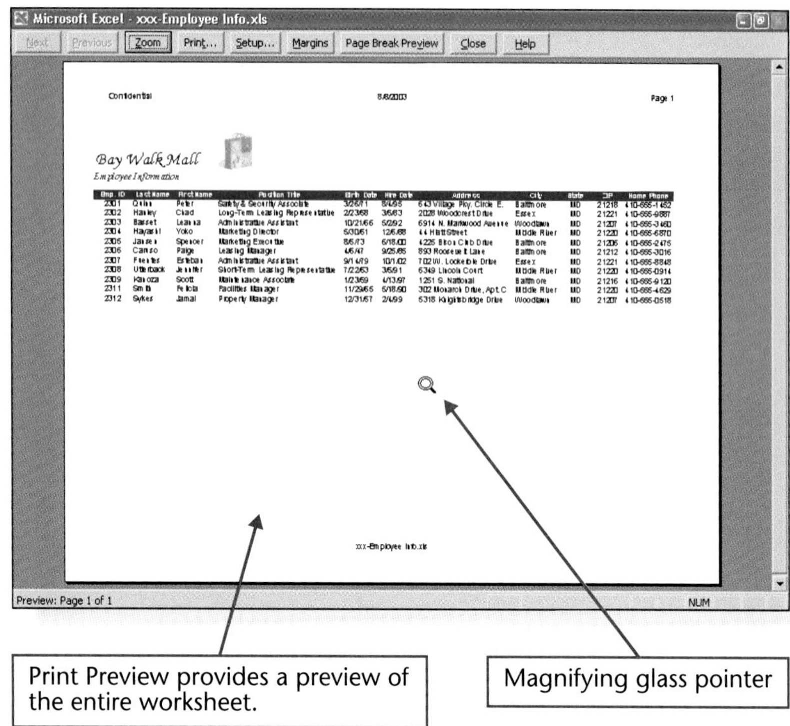

Figure 2.35 Specifying nonadjacent print ranges in the worksheet

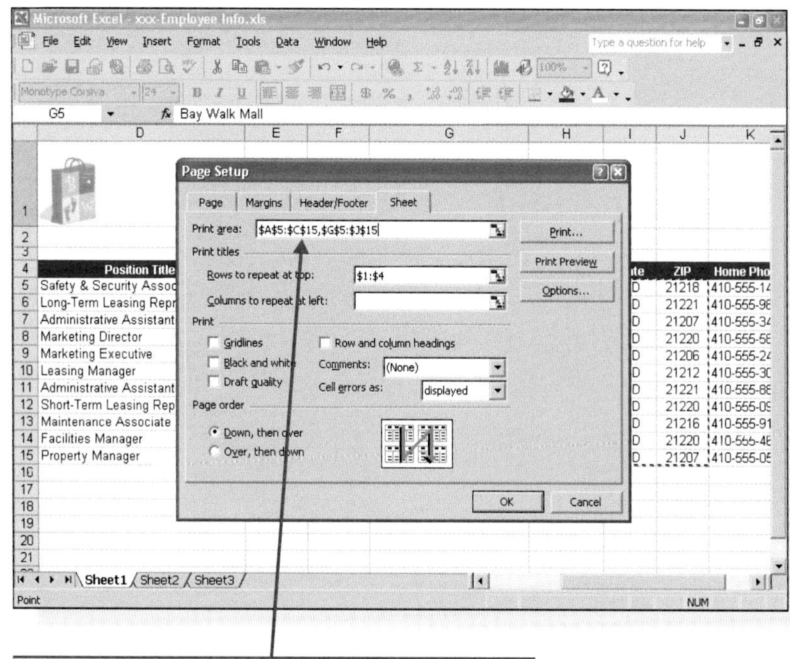

Figure 2.36 Previewing the first page in the print range

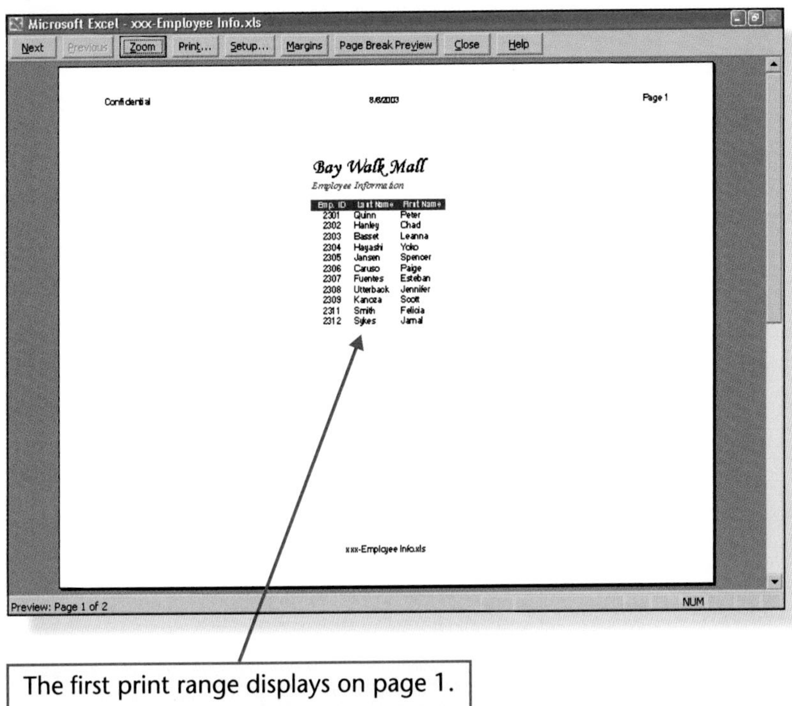

6 Click Print Preview in the Page Setup dialog box. The first page of the printout displays in the Print Preview window (see Figure 2.36).

Figure 2.37 Previewing the second page in the print range

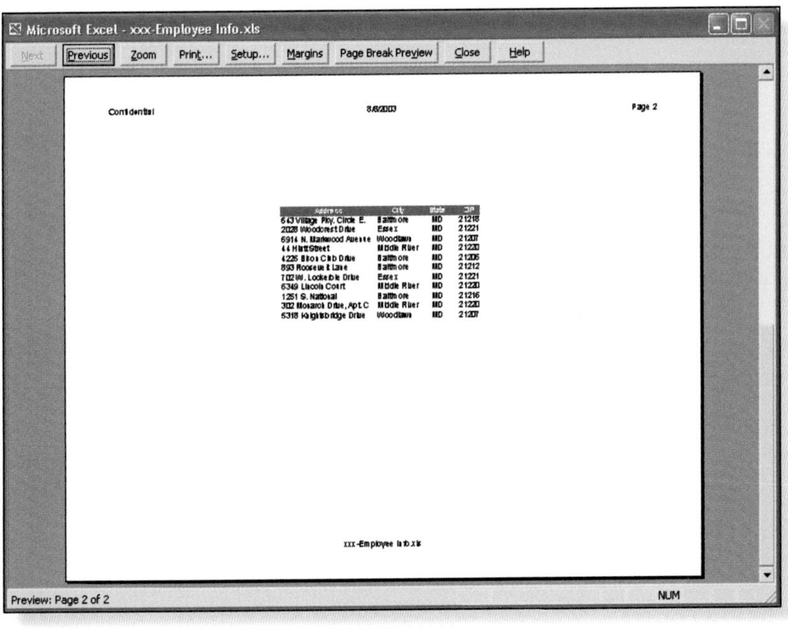

7 Click Next to see the second page (see Figure 2.37). Click Close on the Print Preview toolbar. Press Ctrl + Home.

8 Click the Print button on the Standard toolbar to print the worksheet with the current settings.

9 Clear the print area, and then save and close the workbook.

Excel

APPLY IT! After finishing Exercises 3–5, you may test your skills by completing Apply It! Guided Activity 2, Apply an AutoFormat and Print a Worksheet.

Procedure Summary

Excel Procedure Summary

Insert a Row

1. Select the row below where you want to insert the new row.
2. On the **Insert** menu, select **Rows** . . . . **Alt + I, R**

Insert a Column

1. Select the column to the right of where you want to insert the new column.
2. On the **Insert** menu, select **Columns** . . . . **Alt + I, C**

Delete Rows or Columns

1. Select the rows or columns.
2. On the **Edit** menu, select **Delete** . . . . **Alt + E, D**

Hide Rows or Columns

1. Select the rows or columns.
2. On the **Format** menu, point to **Row** or **Column** and select **Hide** . . . . **Alt + O, R OR C, H**

OR

Right-click the selected rows or columns and select Hide on the shortcut menu.

Unhide Rows or Columns

1. Select the rows or columns that border the hidden area.
2. On the **Format** menu, point to **Row** or **Column** and select **Unhide** . . . . **Alt + O, R OR C, U**

OR

Right-click the selected rows or columns and click Unhide on the shortcut menu.

Freeze and Unfreeze Rows and Columns

1. Click the cell below and to the right of where you want to freeze rows and columns.
2. On the **Window** menu, select **Freeze Panes**. . . . . **Alt + W, F**
3. On the **Window** menu, select **Unfreeze Panes** to restore the previous view. . . . . **Alt + W, F**

Change the Row Height

1. Select the rows.
2. On the **Format** menu, point to **Row** and click **Height** . . . . **Alt + O, R, E**
   OR
   Right-click the selected row and select Row Height on the shortcut menu.
3. Type the row height and click OK.

Change the Column Width

1. Select the columns.
2. On the **Format** menu, point to **Column** and click **Width** . . . . **Alt + O, C, W**
   OR
   Right-click the selected columns and select **Column Width** on the shortcut menu.
3. Type the column width and click OK.

Format Cells

1. Select the cells.
2. Click the **Font** down arrow and click the desired font Arial.
3. Click the **Font Size** down arrow and click the desired size 10.

4. Click the **Font Color** down arrow and click the desired color.
5. Click font attribute buttons, as desired.
6. Click the **Borders** down arrow and click the desired border.
7. Click the **Fill Color** down arrow and click a desired fill color.
8. Click the indent buttons, as desired.

OR

1. Select the cells.
2. On the **Format** menu, select **Cells**. . . . . **Alt + O, E OR Ctrl + 1**
3. Make selections on the Alignment, Font, Border, and Patterns tabs.

Change Alignment in Cells

1. Select the cells.
2. Click the desired alignment button.

Copy Formats with Format Painter

1. Click the cell that has the formatting you wish to copy.
2. Click **Format Painter** button.
3. Drag the across the cells you wish to format.

Define and Apply a Style

1. Apply specific formats to a cell and then select it.
2. On the **Format** menu, select **Style**. . . . . **Alt + O, S**
3. In the Style dialog box, type a style name and click OK.
4. Click a cell you wish to format with the new style.
5. On the **Format** menu, select **Style**. . . . . **Alt + O, S**
6. Click the **Style name** down arrow, select the style, and click OK. . . . . **Alt + S**

Apply an AutoFormat

1. Select the cells.
2. On the **Format** menu, select **AutoFormat**. . . . . **Alt + O, A**
3. Click the desired AutoFormat.
4. Click the **Options** button. . . . . **Alt + O**
5. Select or deselect the formats to apply, and then click OK.

Modify the Page Setup

1. On the **File** menu, select **Page Setup**. . . . . **Alt + F, U**
2. In the Page Setup dialog box, select or change options, as desired, and click OK.

Preview and Print a Worksheet

1. Click the **Print Preview** button.
   OR
   On the **File** menu, select **Print Preview**. . . . . **Alt + F, V**
2. Click the **Close** button. . . . . **C**
3. Click the **Print** button.
   OR
   On the **File** menu, select **Print**, change the settings as desired, and click OK. . . . . **Alt + F, P OR Ctrl + P**

Excel Procedure Summary

Lesson Review and Exercises

Summary Checklist

- ☑ Can you insert rows or columns?
- ☑ Can you delete rows or columns?
- ☑ Can you hide rows or columns containing sensitive data that shouldn't be printed or viewed by others?
- ☑ Can you freeze and unfreeze rows or columns and change row heights and column widths?
- ☑ Can you apply and modify cell formats such as the font, font attributes (bold, italic, underline), alignment, color, and borders?
- ☑ Can you copy and apply formats using Format Painter?
- ☑ Can you apply styles to cells or tables in a worksheet?
- ☑ Can you apply AutoFormats to cells or tables in a worksheet?
- ☑ Can you modify the page setup?
- ☑ Can you modify orientation, margins, and rows and columns to repeat in order to improve the appearance of the printout?
- ☑ Can you add headers to a worksheet?
- ☑ Can you add footers to a worksheet?
- ☑ Can you set and clear a print area and print nonadjacent portions of a worksheet?
- ☑ Can you preview a worksheet before printing?

Key Terms

- freeze panes (p. 190)
- print titles (p. 206)

▶ APPLY IT! Guided Activities

1. Format a Profit and Loss Worksheet

You work at the home office for an investment firm and have been asked to improve the appearance of the company's profit and loss statement. All of the data has been entered, but the worksheet needs some formatting to make it look more professional.

Follow these steps:

a. Open *Profit and Loss.xls*. Save it as *xxx-Profit and Loss.xls*.

b. Select cell B1, click the Font down arrow, and select *Monotype Corsiva*. Click the font size down arrow and select 20. In cells B2 and B3, change the font to *Times New Roman*. Change the font size in cell B2 to 14.

c. Select row 2, right-click the row, and select Row Height on the shortcut menu. Change the row height to 27. Click a cell in row 4 and select Rows on the Insert menu to insert a new row. Select row 4, point to Row on the Format menu, and select Height. Change the height to 7.50.

d. Select column D and then select Delete on the Edit menu. Select column E, right-click the column, and click Column Width on the shortcut menu. Change the width to 16. Click cell E5 and click Align Right.

e. Select B1:B3 and click Bold. Apply bold to E5, B6, B11, B13, B18, B20, B22, B37, and B39.

f. Select B1:F4, click the Fill Color down arrow, and apply the light yellow fill color. Apply the Light Turquoise fill color to B5:F5.

g. Select the range B1:F1 and click the Merge and Center button on the Formatting toolbar. Repeat this step for the ranges B2:F2 and B3:F3.

h. Select cell A6. On the Window menu, select Freeze Panes.

i. Select B20:F20, click the Borders down arrow, and apply a thick bottom border. Apply the same border to the B39:F39. On the Window menu, select Unfreeze Panes, and then press Ctrl + Home **(see Figure 2.38)**.

j. Save and close the workbook.

Figure 2.38 The formatted profit and loss worksheet

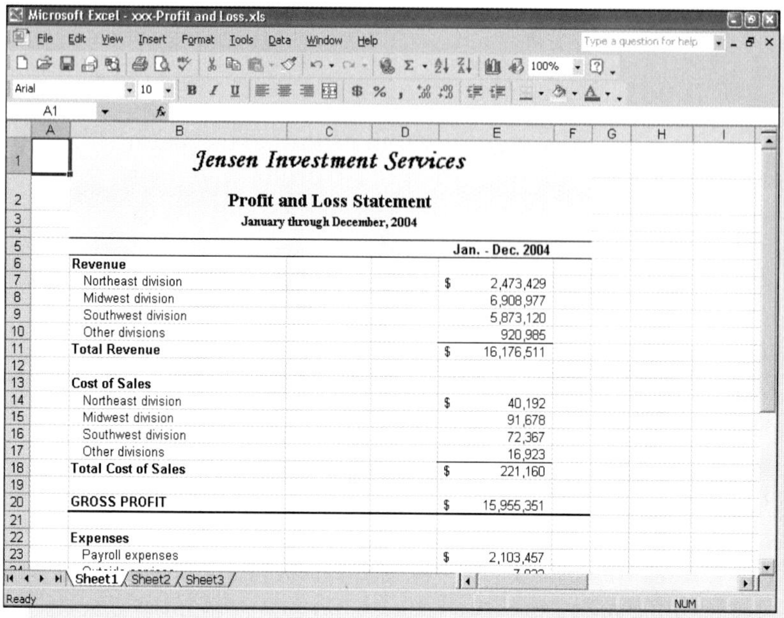
Microsoft Excel - xxx-Profit and Loss.xls
Jensen Investment Services
Profit and Loss Statement
January through December, 2004
Jan. - Dec. 2004
Revenue
Northeast division $ 2,473,429
Midwest division 6,908,977
Southwest division 5,873,120
Other divisions 920,985
Total Revenue $ 16,176,511
Cost of Sales
Northeast division $ 40,192
Midwest division 91,678
Southwest division 72,367
Other divisions 16,923
Total Cost of Sales $ 221,160
GROSS PROFIT $ 15,955,351
Expenses
Payroll expenses $ 2,103,457
Sheet1 Sheet2 Sheet3
Ready
NUM

2. Apply an AutoFormat and Print a Worksheet

You have already entered your business expense data in a worksheet for the month of March. Now you want to enhance the appearance of the worksheet by applying styles and an AutoFormat. You also need to make some adjustments to the page setup before you print the worksheet. Follow these steps:

a. Open *Expense Summary.xls*. Save it as *xxx-Expense Summary.xls*.

b. Select the range E5:E56. On the Format menu, select Style. Click the *Style name* down arrow, select *Currency*, and click OK.

c. Press Home. On the Format menu, select AutoFormat. Click the *Colorful 2* format, and then click the Options button. Clear the *Width/Height* check box and click OK **(see Figure 2.39)**.

d. On the File menu, select Page Setup. On the Margins tab, select the option to center the worksheet horizontally on the page. On the Header/Footer tab, click the *Footer* down arrow and select the footer that displays the file name and page number. Click OK.

e. On the File menu, click Print Preview. Scroll to view the second page of the worksheet. Click the Setup button. In the *Scaling* section (on the Page tab), select *Fit to 1 page wide by 1 tall* so that the worksheet will print on one page. Click OK. Close Print Preview, and then print the worksheet.

f. On the File menu, select Page Setup and click the Sheet tab. Click in the *Rows to repeat at top* box and type $1:$4. Click in the *Print area* box and type $A17:$E24, $A33:$E38. Click Print Preview to view the two areas that will print, and then print the worksheet. Clear the print area.

g. Save and close the workbook.

Figure 2.39 Formatted expense summary worksheet

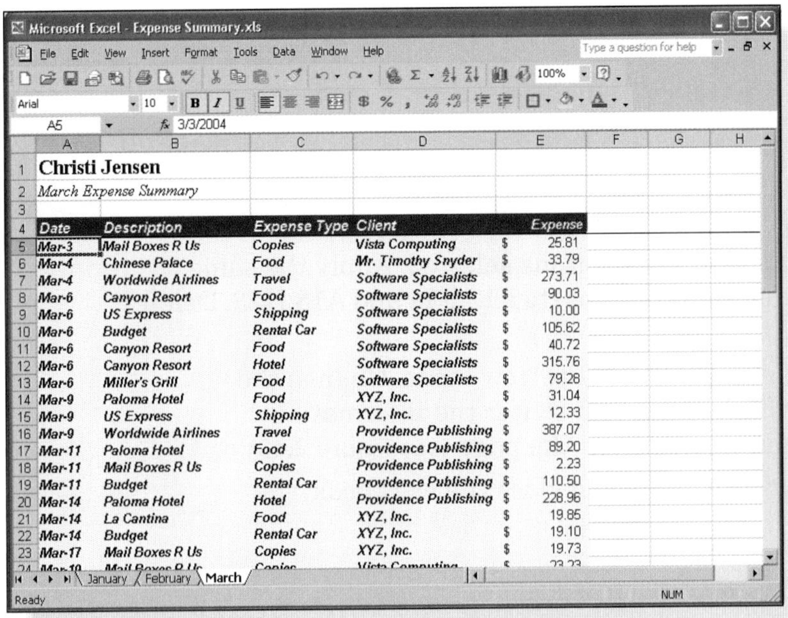
Microsoft Excel - Expense Summary.xls
File Edit View Insert Format Tools Data Window Help
Type a question for help
100%
Arial
10
A5
3/3/2004
Christi Jensen
March Expense Summary
Date Description Expense Type Client Expense
Mar-3 Mail Boxes R Us Copies Vista Computing $ 25.81
Mar-4 Chinese Palace Food Mr. Timothy Snyder $ 33.79
Mar-4 Worldwide Airlines Travel Software Specialists $ 273.71
Mar-6 Canyon Resort Food Software Specialists $ 90.03
Mar-6 US Express Shipping Software Specialists $ 10.00
Mar-6 Budget Rental Car Software Specialists $ 105.62
Mar-6 Canyon Resort Food Software Specialists $ 40.72
Mar-6 Canyon Resort Hotel Software Specialists $ 315.76
Mar-6 Miller's Grill Food Software Specialists $ 79.28
Mar-9 Paloma Hotel Food XYZ, Inc. $ 31.04
Mar-9 US Express Shipping XYZ, Inc. $ 12.33
Mar-9 Worldwide Airlines Travel Providence Publishing $ 387.07
Mar-11 Paloma Hotel Food Providence Publishing $ 89.20
Mar-11 Mail Boxes R Us Copies Providence Publishing $ 2.23
Mar-11 Budget Rental Car Providence Publishing $ 110.50
Mar-14 Paloma Hotel Hotel Providence Publishing $ 228.96
Mar-14 La Cantina Food XYZ, Inc. $ 19.85
Mar-14 Budget Rental Car XYZ, Inc. $ 19.10
Mar-17 Mail Boxes R Us Copies XYZ, Inc. $ 19.73
January February March
Ready
NUM

Do It Yourself

1. Modify and Format a College Budget Worksheet

As a student preparing for college next year, you have decided to present your college budget worksheet to your school guidance counselor. First you need to update the information and format the worksheet.

Follow these steps:

a. Open *College Budget2.xls*. Save it as *xxx-College Budget2.xls*.

b. Adjust the width of column D so you can read all the data. Select A5:D6. Apply the violet font color, change the font size to 9, and add a light yellow fill color and a thick box border. Apply the same formats to A16:B17.

c. Apply italic to the *Year 1 Estimated College Expenses* heading. Below row 18, insert a new row and add the item *Painting $275*.

d. Hide rows 16–25 so your counselor doesn't see your income information. Preview the worksheet, and then change the worksheet orientation to Landscape. Center the data horizontally on the page and print the worksheet. Unhide the hidden rows.

e. Save and close the workbook.

2. Apply an AutoFormat to a Class Schedule

Now that you've learned some formatting skills, you want to format your class schedule worksheet. Follow these steps:

a. Open *My Schedule2.xls*. Save it as *xxx-My Schedule2.xls.*

b. Apply a distinctive font of your choice to the title in row 1. Increase the font size to 18 points, and apply the teal font color to the title.

c. Select A4:F9. Apply the *Classic 3* AutoFormat with just the *Border, Font*, and *Patterns* options selected. Apply the same AutoFormat (and same options) to A12:F14 and A18:H23. Delete the blank row 17.

d. View the worksheet in Print Preview mode. Change the orientation to Landscape, and center the information horizontally and vertically on the page **(see Figure 2.40)**.

e. Print the worksheet. Save and close the workbook.

Figure 2.40 The formatted class schedule

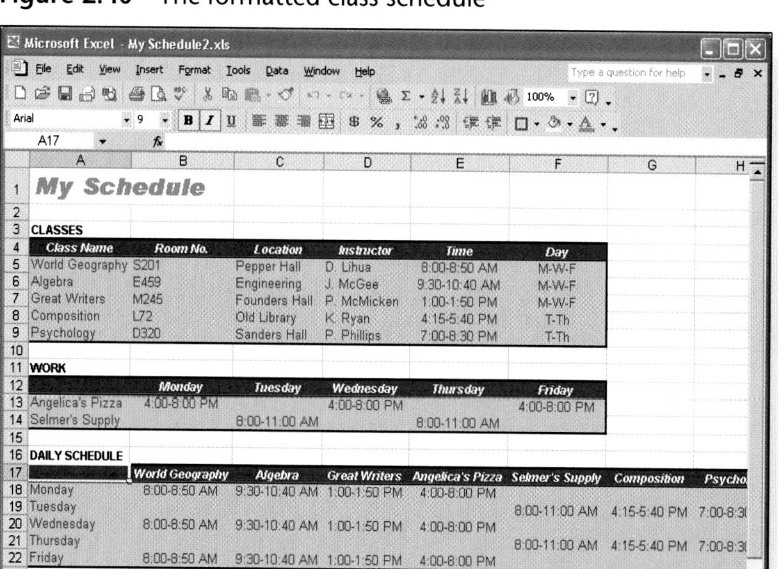

3. Create and Format a CD Inventory Worksheet

You are the manager of McCall's Gift Shop. You have decided to list your small inventory of audio CDs in a new worksheet. After entering the data into the worksheet, you intend to modify the structure of the worksheet, apply an AutoFormat, and print the results. Follow these steps:

a. Open a new, blank workbook. Save it as *xxx-Inventory.xls*.

b. Enter data for at least five or six CDs. (***Note:*** If time allows, collect the data from your personal CD collection. If this isn't practical, use your best guess for the required data.)

c. Enter data for at least five or six CDs. (***Note:*** If time allows, collect the data from your personal CD collection. If this isn't practical, use your best guess for the required data.)

d. Resize the rows and columns so that all data is visible in the worksheet.

e. Type the gift shop name and date at the top of the worksheet and format it in an appropriate font, font size, and color. Apply an AutoFormat of your choice to the column labels and columns of data. You may wish to experiment with different AutoFormats and AutoFormat options to see which looks best with your data **(see Figure 2.41)**.

f. Set a print area for your data, view the worksheet in Print Preview mode, and print the worksheet. Save and close the workbook.

Figure 2.41 A sample CD inventory worksheet

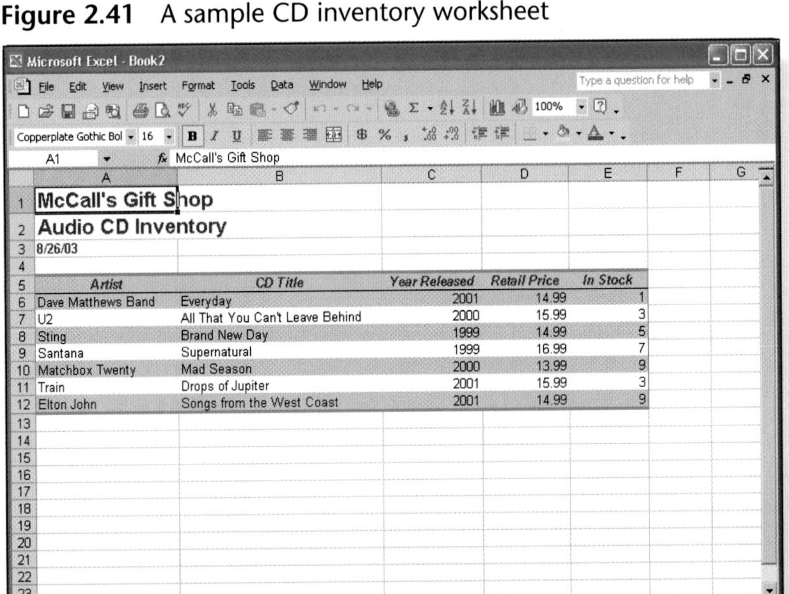

Artist	CD Title	Year Released	Retail Price	In Stock
Dave Matthews Band	Everyday	2001	14.99	1
U2	All That You Can't Leave Behind	2000	15.99	3
Sting	Brand New Day	1999	14.99	5
Santana	Supernatural	1999	16.99	7
Matchbox Twenty	Mad Season	2000	13.99	9
Train	Drops of Jupiter	2001	15.99	3
Elton John	Songs from the West Coast	2001	14.99	9

4. Format and Print a Balance Sheet

The financial analyst for your firm has presented you with the latest balance sheet worksheet for the company and has asked you to spruce up the formatting before you print the data for final review.

a. Open *Balance Sheet.xls*. Save it as *xxx-Balance Sheet.xls*.

b. Select the range B5:F40 (this range includes the blank column F). Apply the *Accounting 2* AutoFormat; however, do not apply the *Font* and *Width/Height* format options. ***Note:*** If the results aren't what you expect, click Undo and try again.

c. At the top of the worksheet, apply a distinctive font and a larger font size to the company name. Select B1:F1 and merge and center the company name. Follow the same procedure to merge and center the title and date information in rows 2 and 3. Apply a tan fill color to B1:F4 **(see Figure 2.42)**.

d. View the worksheet in Print Preview mode to make sure it fits on one page. Center the worksheet data horizontally on the page. Change the top margin to 1.25 and the bottom margin to .75.

e. Add a custom footer that includes the text *Prepared by:* followed by your name, centered at the bottom of the page. ***Note:*** If necessary, consult Excel Help to create the custom footer. Print the document.

f. Save and close the workbook.

Figure 2.42 A sample balance sheet

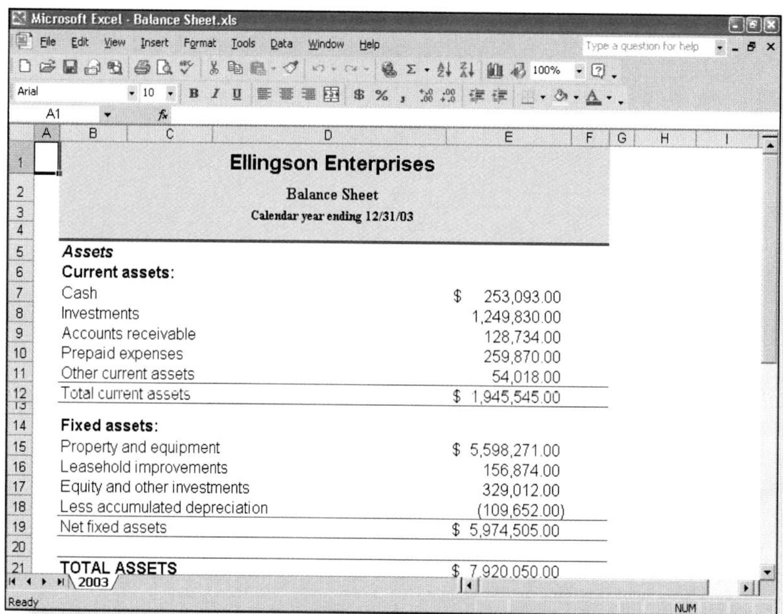

Challenge Yourself

Research Foreign Currencies and Converter Tools

You are planning a business trip to France. This will be your first trip since France switched to the euro currency. You need to find information on current conversion rates and available currency converters. In addition, you need to explore the available conversion tools provided with Excel 2002.

Note: Before proceeding with these steps, ask your teacher for permission to load the Euro Currency Tools add-in.

Follow these steps:

- Create a new, blank workbook. Save it as *xxx-Currency Rates.xls*.
- On the Tools menu, click Add-Ins. In the Add-Ins dialog box, select the Euro Currency Tools option and click OK. In a moment, the Euro Currency Tools add-in will be installed. (You may need your Office XP CD to install the Add-In.)
- Note these changes upon completion of the installation: The EuroValue toolbar appears in the worksheet area; the Euro Conversion button now appears on the Standard toolbar; and a Euro button appears on the Formatting toolbar. (To identify these buttons, point to various buttons on the Standard and Formatting toolbars and read the ScreenTips.)
- Close the EuroValue toolbar. In your worksheet, type euro in cell A1; type French franc in cell B1. Type 1 in cell A2. With A2 selected, click the Euro Conversion button to open the Euro Conversion dialog box. The *Source range* (A2) is already selected. Click in the *Destination range* box and click cell B2. In the *Currency conversion* section, click the *From* down arrow and select *Euro*; click the *To* down arrow and select *French Franc*. Click OK.

EuroValue Toolbar

Button	Purpose
Euro Conversion	Opens the Euro Conversion dialog box to convert selected data
Euro	Applies the euro currency format

- Type U.S. dollar in cell C1. Launch your browser. Using your search engine, search using the keywords *currency converters* and *currency rates* and then browse the search results. When you find the current conversion rate from 1 euro to 1 dollar, enter it in your worksheet.
- Save and close the workbook.

Lesson 3

Tapping the Power of Excel

Lesson Exercise Objectives

After completing this lesson, you'll be able to do the following tasks:

1. Analyze a subset of data
2. Create and revise formulas
3. Understand absolute and relative references
4. Add functions to formulas
5. Create a workbook from a template
6. Create and modify charts and graphics
7. Provide feedback on a worksheet
8. Share a worksheet online

Key Terms

- absolute reference (p. 232)
- arguments (p. 235)
- AutoFilter (p. 226)
- discussion comments (p. 252)
- discussion server (p. 252)
- fill handle (p. 232)
- filter (p. 226)
- Formula Bar (p. 229)
- function (p. 235)
- relative reference (p. 232)
- syntax (p. 235)
- thread (p. 253)
- wizard (p. 246)

Microsoft Office Specialist Activities

EX2002: 1.2, 1.5, 2.2, 5.1, 5.2, 6.1, 6.2, 7.1, 7.3

Real-Life Business Applications

Lesson Case Study

In this lesson, you will play the role of Research Analyst for Jackson-Drake Properties, Inc., a mall management company. Keep the following information in mind as you work through the lesson exercises.

- **Job responsibilities and goals.** You are responsible for preparing and analyzing reports that summarize data for multiple mall locations. Your goal is to learn about some of the more advanced features of Excel so you can improve your analytical skills and apply this knowledge to the reports you create.
- **The project.** You will use formulas and functions, filter data, create a workbook based on a template, work with graphics, provide feedback on worksheets, and share a worksheet online.
- **The challenge ahead.** Your reports will be distributed to upper management, so it is critical that you develop a good understanding of these features and ensure that the data you present is accurate.

Microsoft Office Specialist EX2002 1.5

Exercise 1 Overview:
Analyze a Subset of Data

The **AutoFilter** feature in Excel enables you to **filter**, or display a subset of data, in an Excel list. When you select this command, each column label in the list displays a gray filter arrow. You can click the arrow in the column that contains the data you want to filter and then choose the criteria you want to display from the drop-down list. For example, in a *City* column, you could choose to display only rows that contain a particular city contained in the list, such as *Baltimore*. All rows that don't meet the criteria you specify are hidden from view but not removed from the worksheet.

After you filter a list, you can choose (All) from the filter list to redisplay all columns, or you can apply an additional filter in another column to further refine the list. Columns that contain active filters display blue (instead of black) filter arrows. If you choose the (Custom...) option from the list, you can use the Custom AutoFilter dialog box to specify more complex criteria.

Type: AutoFilter

In the following exercise, you will filter a list in a worksheet containing job data.

Step Through It™
Exercise 1: Use AutoFilter to filter a list

1. Open *Job Openings.xls*.
2. Select cell A4. On the Data menu, point to Filter, and select AutoFilter. Black filter arrows display beside the column labels.
3. Click the filter arrow beside the *Location* column label (see Figure 3.1). Select *Field*.

Figure 3.1 Filtering the list by job location

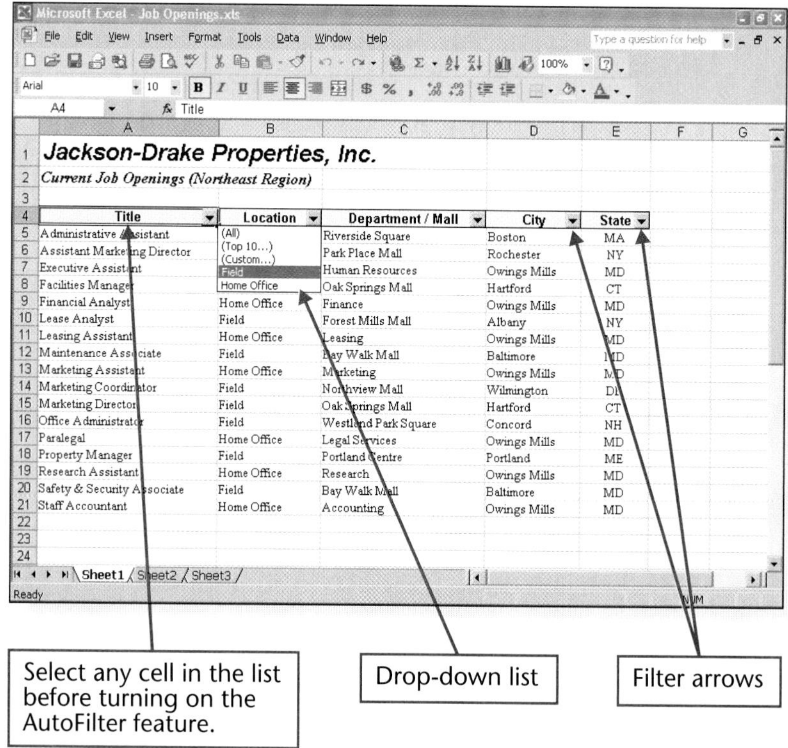

Figure 3.2 Displaying all data in the list

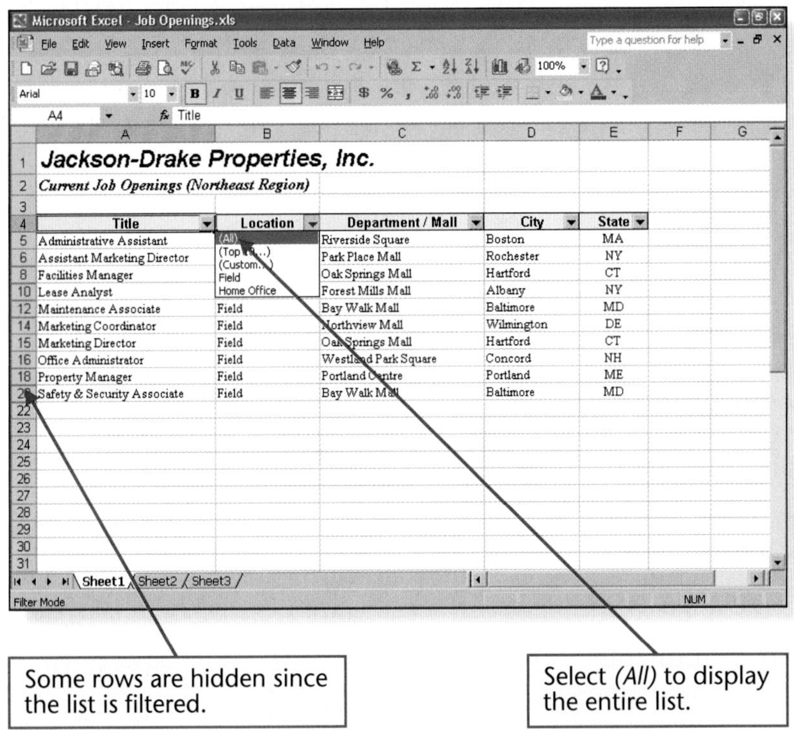

4. The filtered list now displays only job openings for field positions (no home office positions are displayed). The filter arrow appears in color, indicating it is active.
5. Click the filter arrow beside the *Location* column label (see Figure 3.2). Select *(All)*. All rows are again displayed.

Excel

Figure 3.3 The list filtered by state

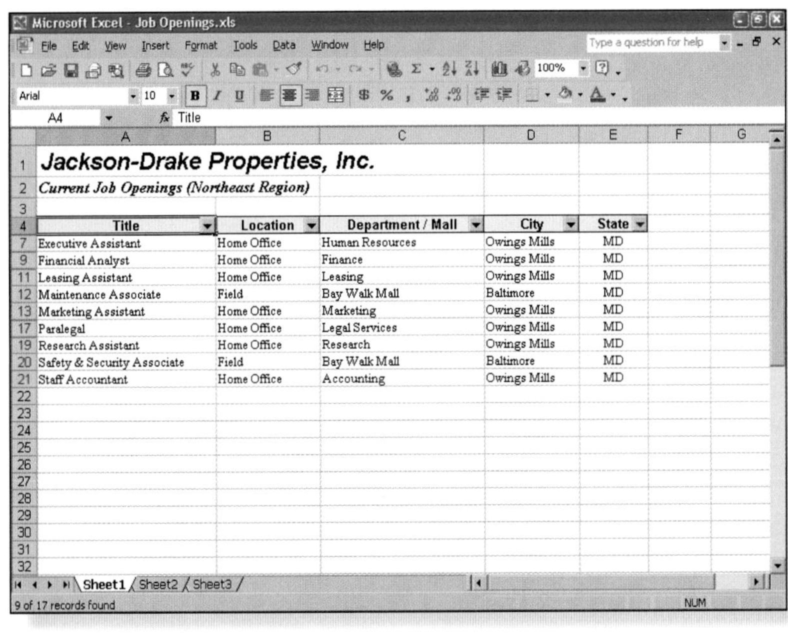

6. Click the filter arrow beside the *State* column label, and click *MD* in the list. All job openings in the state of Maryland are displayed (see Figure 3.3).
7. Click the filter arrow beside the *State* column label again, and select *(All)* to redisplay all rows.
8. On the Data menu, point to Filter and select AutoFilter to turn off the feature.
9. Close the workbook without saving it.

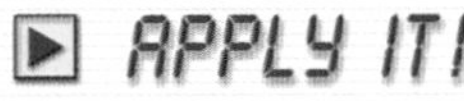

After finishing Exercise 1, you may test your skills by completing Apply It! Guided Activity 1, Filter Data in an Expenses Worksheet.

Career Corner

Making It All Add Up

Do your friends turn to you to figure out how to split the check, float a loan, or help with math homework? Does the world of finance interest you? How about working on Wall Street or helping others (and yourself!) achieve their financial goals?

A good entry-level job in finance is as close as your nearest bank. Financial services sales agents sell bank services to customers, such as loans, certificates of deposit, lines of credit, and investments. Such a job can give you a wide knowledge of business and a lot of experience working with clients. A related occupation is insurance agent—selling insurance to businesses and people.

When people want to buy or sell stocks and bonds, they turn to brokers. You see them on TV, swarming around the trading floor of a stock exchange, shouting out orders. Stockbrokers also trade by computer and give financial advice. Many work for large securities and investment banking firms headquartered in New York City. About a quarter are self-employed.

There are also a lot of opportunities in the field of financial planning. Financial planners help people save money for retirement, children's college education, and other financial needs. Most work for companies, but about a quarter have their own businesses.

A bachelor's degree with business courses is good preparation for any of these occupations. However, many employers consider sales ability and good interpersonal and communication skills more important than educational background.

CRITICAL THINKING

1. In a book by Somerset Maugham, one of the characters says, "Money is like a sixth sense without which you cannot make a complete use of the other five. Without an adequate income half the possibilities of life are shut off." (*Of Human Bondage*, Penguin, New York, 1992.) Do you agree? Why or why not?
2. Pretend you have $1,000 to invest. Using the Internet or the financial pages of a newspaper, "buy" three to five stocks that interest you. Create a worksheet to track your profit or loss over the next month and a chart that shows your stocks' performance.

Exercise 2 Overview:
Create and Revise Formulas

Microsoft Office Specialist
EX2002 1.2, 5.1

A formula is an equation that performs a calculation. All Excel formulas begin with an equal sign (=), and they may include arithmetic operators (see Table 3.1).

Type: operators

Table 3.1

Operator	Meaning	Example
+ (plus sign)	Addition	= 7+1
- (minus sign)	Subtraction (or negation)	= A3-6
* (asterisk)	Multiplication	= 2*C5
/ (forward slash)	Division	= B2/8
^ (caret)	Exponentiation	= 4^2

After you enter a formula, the cell stores the formula and displays the *result*. If you click the cell containing a formula, you can view or edit the formula in the **Formula Bar**—the bar that displays above the column headings.

Type: formulas

Figure 3.4 The result of entering a formula

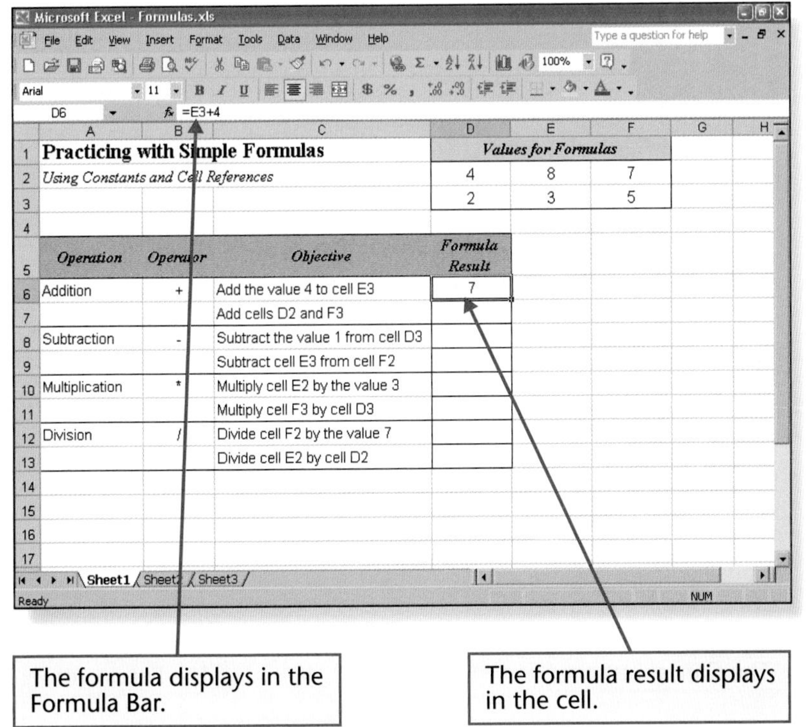

Step Through It™
Exercise 2A: Create a formula using the keyboard

1. Open *Formulas.xls*. Save the workbook as *xxx-Formulas.xls*.
2. Click cell D6. As stated in cell C6, you will type a formula here that adds the value 4 to the contents of cell E3.
3. In cell D6, type =E3+4 and press Enter.
4. Click cell D6, and examine the formula in the Formula Bar (see Figure 3.4).

5. Click cell D7, and type =D2+F3 (but don't press Enter). Notice that Excel uses different colors to highlight cell references as you are creating the formula (see Figure 3.5).

6. Press Enter to complete the formula.

7. In cell D8, type =D3-1 and press Enter.

8. In cell D9, type =F2-E3 and press Enter.

Figure 3.5 Highlighted cell references

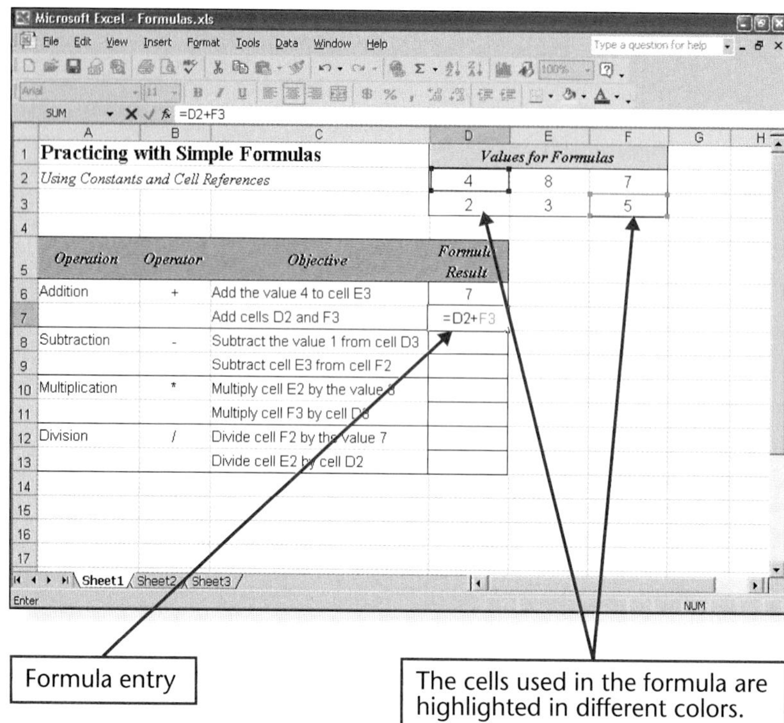

Formula entry
The cells used in the formula are highlighted in different colors.

Step Through It™

Exercise 2B: Create and edit a formula using the Formula Bar

1. With cell D10 selected, click inside the Formula Bar and type =E2*3.

2. Point to the Enter button (the green check mark) to the left of the Formula Bar to identify it (see Figure 3.6). Click the Enter button.

Figure 3.6 Entering a formula using the Formula Bar

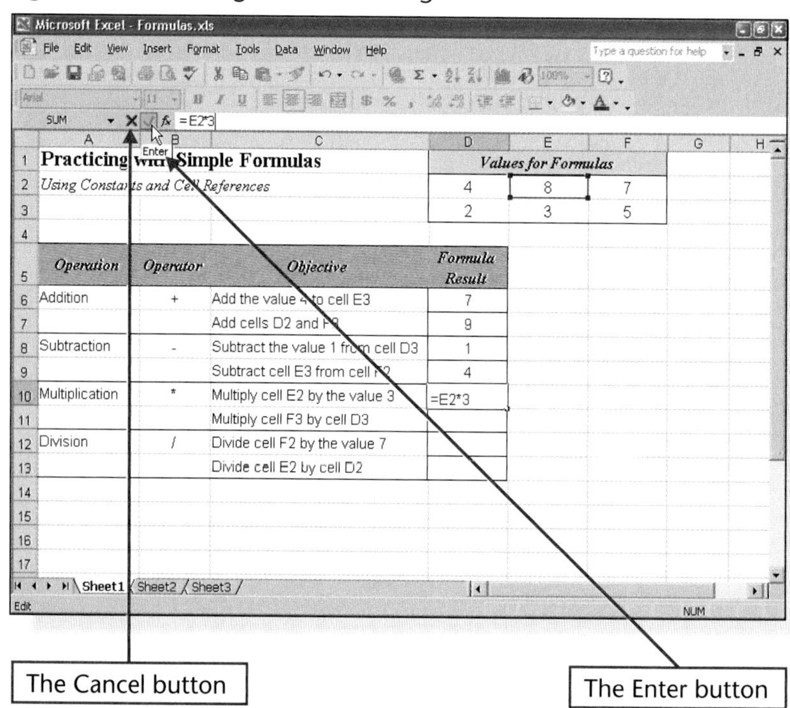

Figure 3.7 Editing a formula in the Formula Bar

Drag over the part of the formula you want to edit in the Formula Bar, and then type your edits.

3. Click cell D11. In the Formula Bar, type =F3*G4 and click the Enter button.
4. Click inside the Formula Bar, and drag to select the G4 cell reference (see Figure 3.7).
5. Type D3 and click the Enter button to enter the formula correction.

Excel

Figure 3.8 Entering a formula by pointing to cells

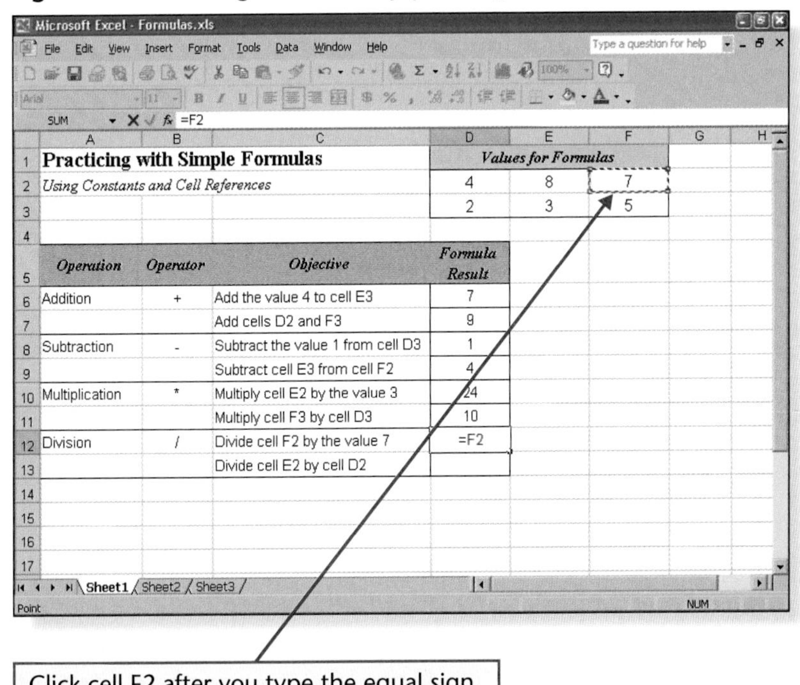

Click cell F2 after you type the equal sign.

Step Through It™

Exercise 2C: Create a formula by pointing to cells

1. Click cell D12.
2. Type = and click cell F2 (see Figure 3.8).
3. Type /7 (the slash followed by the number 7), and then press Enter.

4. In cell D13, type = and then click cell E2. Type / and click cell D2.

5. Press Enter to complete the formula (see Figure 3.9).

6. Save the workbook and close the workbook.

Figure 3.9 The completed worksheet

Microsoft Excel - Formulas.xls

	A	B	C	D	E	F
1	**Practicing with Simple Formulas**			*Values for Formulas*		
2	*Using Constants and Cell References*			4	8	7
3				2	3	5
4						
5	*Operation*	*Operator*	*Objective*	*Formula Result*		
6	Addition	+	Add the value 4 to cell E3	7		
7			Add cells D2 and F3	9		
8	Subtraction	-	Subtract the value 1 from cell D3	1		
9			Subtract cell E3 from cell F2	4		
10	Multiplication	*	Multiply cell E2 by the value 3	24		
11			Multiply cell F3 by cell D3	10		
12	Division	/	Divide cell F2 by the value 7	1		
13			Divide cell E2 by cell D2	2		

Microsoft Office Specialist EX2002 5.1

Exercise 3 Overview: Understand Absolute and Relative References

When you copy a formula that contains cell references, you typically want the cell references to adjust to the new location. This type of cell reference, which automatically adjusts when you copy it, is called a **relative reference**. New formulas use relative references by default.

On the other hand, if you want a cell reference in a formula to always refer to the same cell when you copy the formula, you should use an **absolute reference** in the formula. You can indicate an absolute reference by typing a dollar sign ($) in front of the column letter and the row number, for example C5. (If you press the F4 key after typing a cell reference as you create a formula, Excel inserts the dollar signs for you.)

Type: absolute reference

You can use the fill handle to copy a value or formula into adjacent cells. The **fill handle** is the small black square located in the lower-right corner of a selected cell or range.

In the following exercise, you will enter absolute and relative references in formulas to analyze tenant information.

Figure 3.10 Entering a formula with two relative references

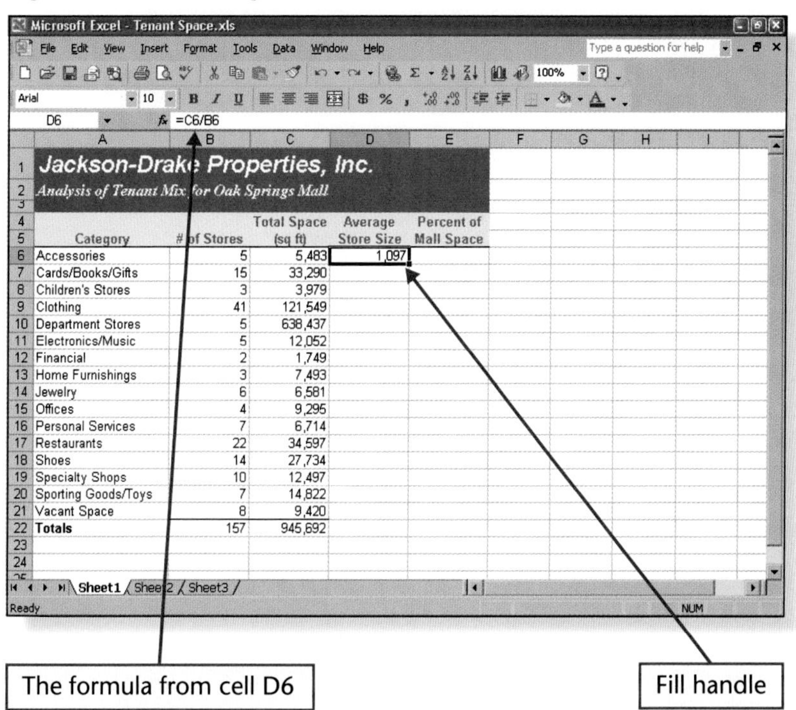

	Category	# of Stores	Total Space (sq ft)	Average Store Size	Percent of Mall Space
1	Jackson-Drake Properties, Inc.				
2	Analysis of Tenant Mix for Oak Springs Mall				
6	Accessories	5	5,483	1,097	
7	Cards/Books/Gifts	15	33,290		
8	Children's Stores	3	3,979		
9	Clothing	41	121,549		
10	Department Stores	5	638,437		
11	Electronics/Music	5	12,052		
12	Financial	2	1,749		
13	Home Furnishings	3	7,493		
14	Jewelry	6	6,581		
15	Offices	4	9,295		
16	Personal Services	7	6,714		
17	Restaurants	22	34,597		
18	Shoes	14	27,734		
19	Specialty Shops	10	12,497		
20	Sporting Goods/Toys	7	14,822		
21	Vacant Space	8	9,420		
22	Totals	157	945,692		

Step Through It™

Exercise 3: Use absolute and relative references

1. Open *Tenant Space.xls.* Save the workbook as *xxx-Tenant Space.xls.*

2. Click cell D6, type =C6/B6, and press Enter.

3. Click cell D6 again. Notice that the formula displays in the Formula Bar, while the formula result displays in the cell (see Figure 3.10).

Excel

Figure 3.11 Using Auto Fill to fill the range with formulas

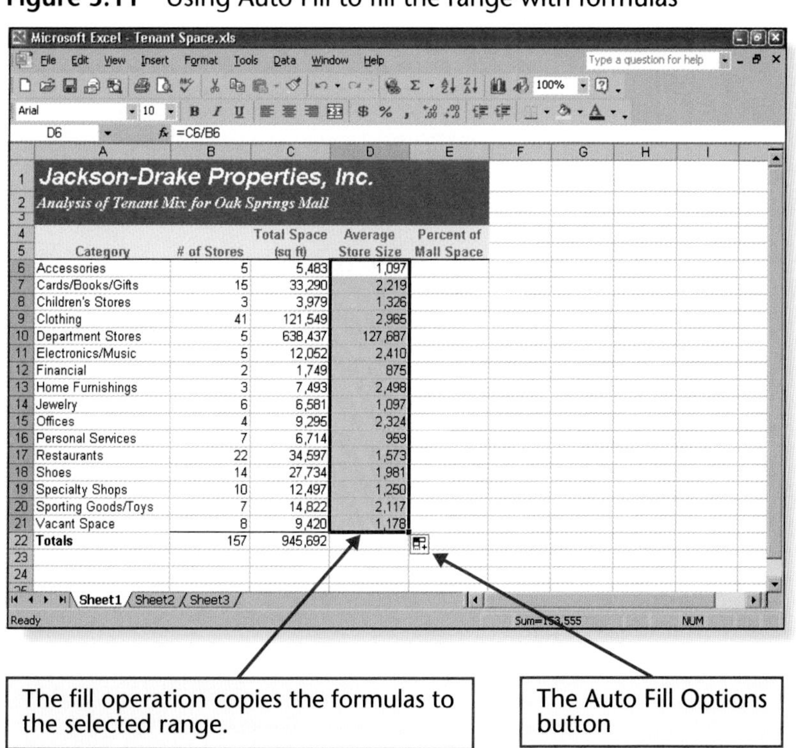

	Category	# of Stores	Total Space (sq ft)	Average Store Size	Percent of Mall Space
1	Jackson-Drake Properties, Inc.				
2	Analysis of Tenant Mix for Oak Springs Mall				
6	Accessories	5	5,483	1,097	
7	Cards/Books/Gifts	15	33,290	2,219	
8	Children's Stores	3	3,979	1,326	
9	Clothing	41	121,549	2,965	
10	Department Stores	5	638,437	127,687	
11	Electronics/Music	5	12,052	2,410	
12	Financial	2	1,749	875	
13	Home Furnishings	3	7,493	2,498	
14	Jewelry	6	6,581	1,097	
15	Offices	4	9,295	2,324	
16	Personal Services	7	6,714	959	
17	Restaurants	22	34,597	1,573	
18	Shoes	14	27,734	1,981	
19	Specialty Shops	10	12,497	1,250	
20	Sporting Goods/Toys	7	14,822	2,117	
21	Vacant Space	8	9,420	1,178	
22	Totals	157	945,692		

4. Point to the fill handle in the lower-right corner of cell D6. When the pointer changes to a plus sign, drag down to cell D21 and release the mouse button. The formula in cell D6 is copied to the range D7:D21 and the results display in all cells in the range (see Figure 3.11).

5. Click cell E6.
6. Type =, and then click cell C6. Type / and then click cell C22.
7. Press F4 to insert dollar signs before the column letter and row number, indicating an absolute reference (see Figure 3.12). Press Enter.

Figure 3.12 Entering a formula with an absolute reference

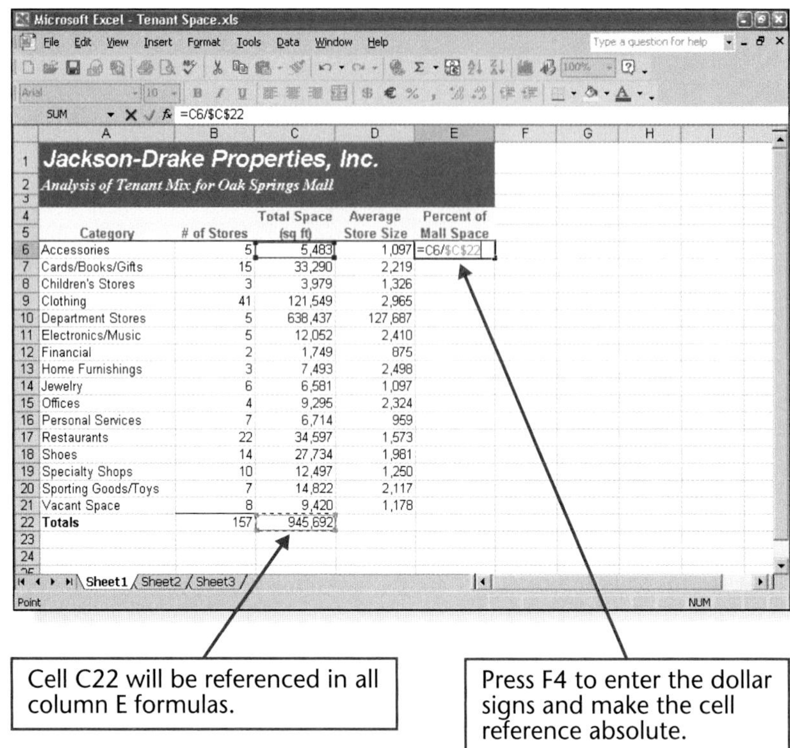

8. Click cell E6, and use the fill handle to copy the formula to E7:E21 (see Figure 3.13).
9. Click several cells in the range E6:E22, and examine the formula in the Formula Bar. The absolute cell reference (C22) is the same throughout the range. However, the first reference in each cell in the range (a relative reference) has adjusted to its new location.
10. Save and close the workbook.

Figure 3.13 The formula copied with Auto Fill

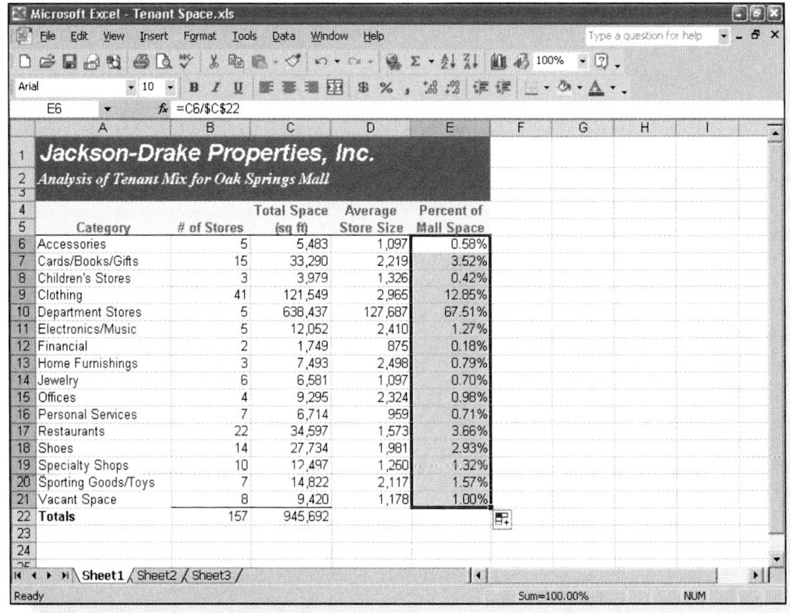

Exercise 4 Overview:
Add Functions to Formulas

Microsoft Office Specialist
EX2002 1.2, 5.1, 5.2

A **function** is a predefined formula in Excel that performs a specific, built-in operation, such as determining a loan payment amount. Functions return values based on **arguments** which must be specified in a certain order. Table 3.2 shows the structure, or **syntax**, of some of the most commonly used functions.

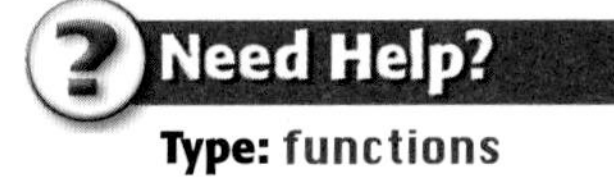

Type: functions

Table 3.2

Function	Description
=SUM (*cells*)	Adds all the numbers in the specified cells
=MIN (*cells*)	Returns the smallest value in the specified cells
=MAX (*cells*)	Returns the largest value in the specified cells
=DATE (*year,month,day*)	Returns a number that represents the specified date
=NOW ()	Returns a number that represents the current date and time (uses no arguments)
=PMT (*rate,nper,pv,fv,type*)	Calculates the payment for a loan
=IF (*logical_test,value_if_true value_if_false*)	Performs a conditional test

Figure 3.14 Typing the SUM function into a cell

Microsoft Excel - Qtr1 Sales.xls

SUM =SUM(B6:B13)

Jackson-Drake Properties, Inc.
Northeast Region
First Quarter Sales by Mall

Mall	January	February	March	Total
Bay Walk Mall	$ 2,093,015	$ 1,783,845	$ 1,978,352	
Forest Mills Mall	1,515,410	1,360,977	1,425,696	
Northview Mall	1,038,362	1,694,652	1,641,932	
Oak Springs Mall	1,736,770	1,678,845	1,930,027	
Park Place Mall	1,754,685	2,154,815	1,611,330	
Portland Centre	921,106	976,025	889,531	
Riverside Square	778,768	1,270,987	1,231,450	
Westland Park Square	2,064,900	2,101,635	1,984,325	
Totals	=SUM(B6:B13)			
Minimum				
Maximum				
Prepared on:				

Step Through It™
Exercise 4A: Use the SUM function

1. Open *Qtr1 Sales.xls*. Save the workbook as *xxx-Qtr1 Sales.xls*.
2. Click cell B14. Type =SUM(B6:B13). (See Figure 3.14.) Press the right arrow key. The total sales for January displays in cell B14. Cell C14 is now the active cell.

3) In cell C14, type =SUM(and then drag to select the range C6:C13 (see Figure 3.15).

4) Type the closing parenthesis, and press the right arrow key to move to cell D14.

Figure 3.15 Entering a range by dragging

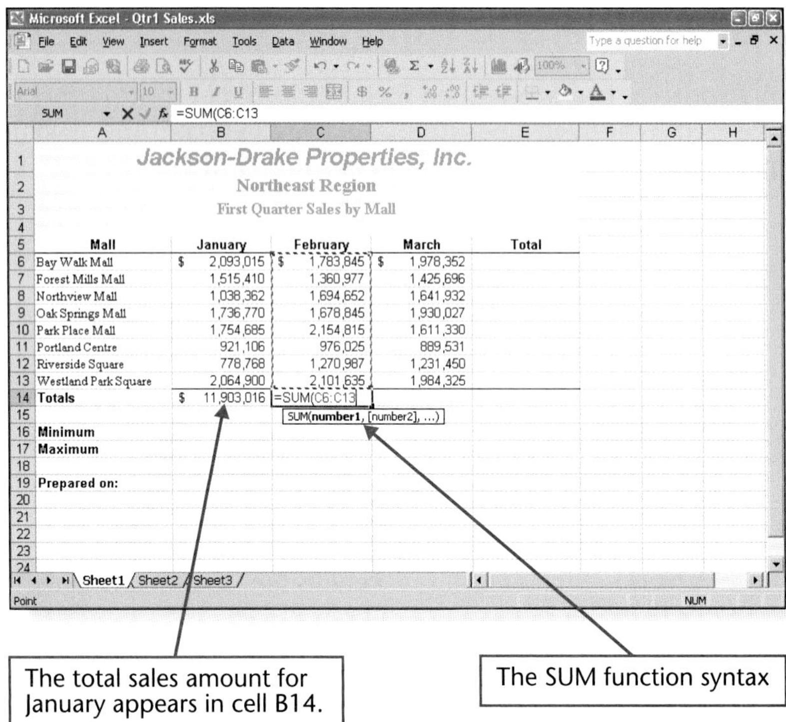

The total sales amount for January appears in cell B14.
The SUM function syntax

5) With D14 as the active cell, click the AutoSum button Σ on the Standard toolbar. ***Note:*** Excel guesses which cells you want to include in the formula, so you must check the range. In this example, the selected range is correct.

6) Press Enter to accept the suggested formula.

7) Select the range E6:E14 and click the AutoSum button to enter the SUM function in these cells (see Figure 3.16).

Figure 3.16 Using AutoSum to enter the SUM function

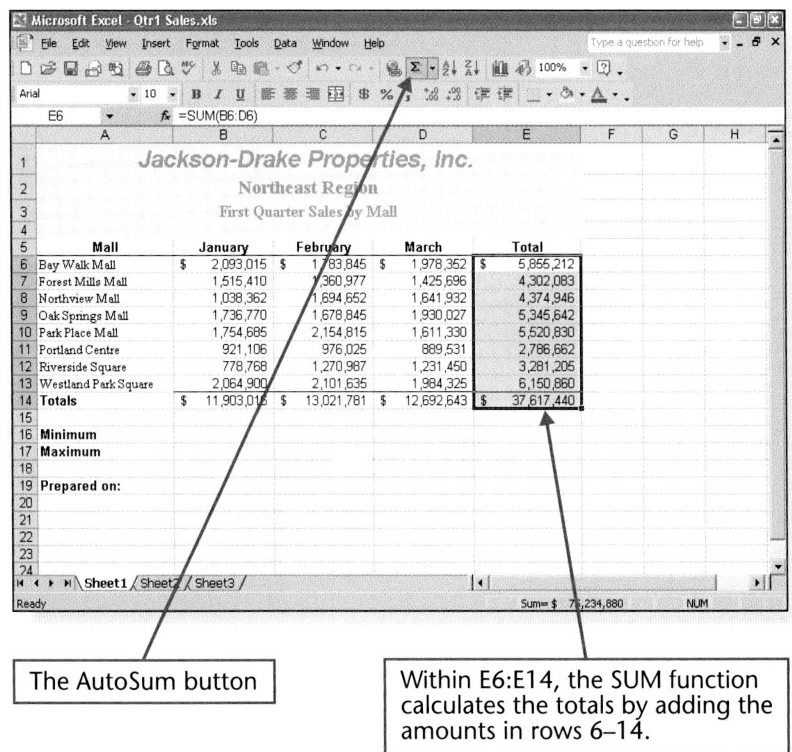

The AutoSum button
Within E6:E14, the SUM function calculates the totals by adding the amounts in rows 6–14.

Excel

Figure 3.17 Entering the MIN and MAX functions

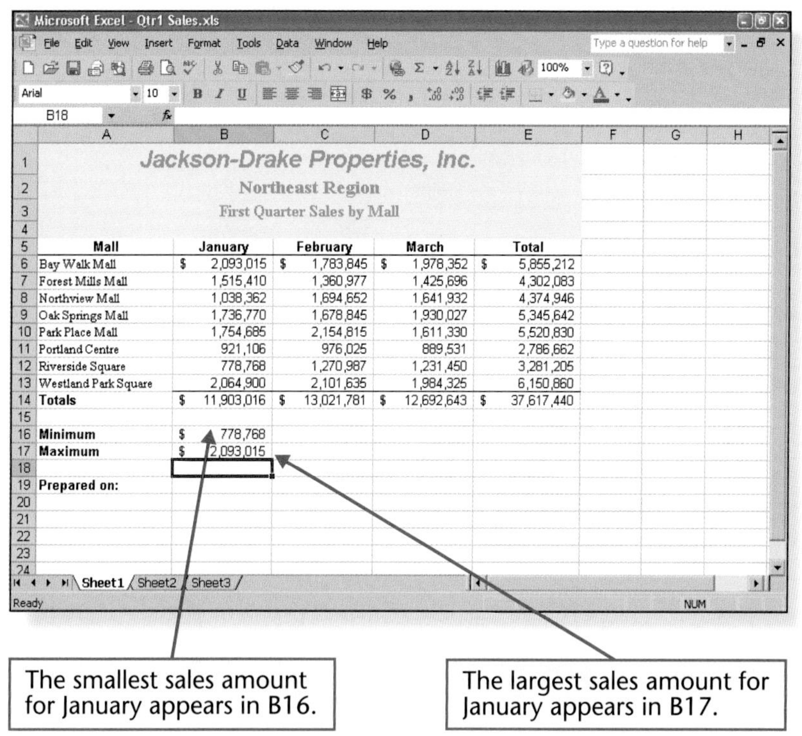

Step Through It™

Exercise 4B: Use the MIN and MAX functions

1. Click cell B16. Type =MIN(B6:B13) and press Enter. Cell B16 displays the minimum sales amount for the month of January.

2. With B17 as the active cell, type =MAX(and then drag to select the range B6:B13. Type the closing parenthesis and press Enter to complete the formula (see Figure 3.17).

Figure 3.18 Copying the MIN and MAX functions

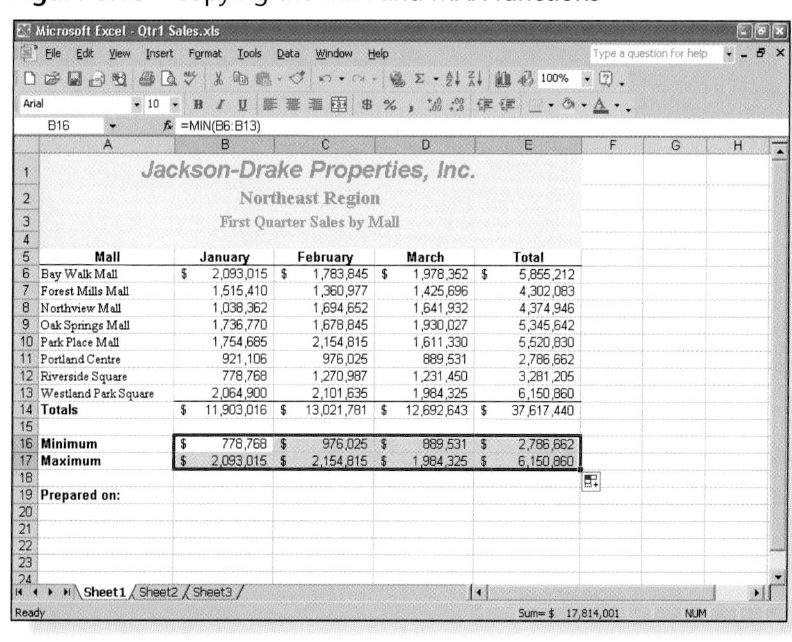

3. Select the range B16:B17.

4. Drag the fill handle right to column E, and release the mouse button (see Figure 3.18). Excel copies the MIN and MAX functions to columns C, D, and E and displays the formula results for February, March, and the quarterly totals.

5. Save the workbook.

Step Through It™
Exercise 4C: Use the DATE and NOW functions

Excel

1. Click cell B19 and type =DATE(. Examine the function syntax displayed by Excel (see Figure 3.19).

2. To complete the function with a specified date, type 2003,5,2) and press Enter. Excel displays the date in the format *m/d/yyyy*.

Figure 3.19 Entering the DATE function

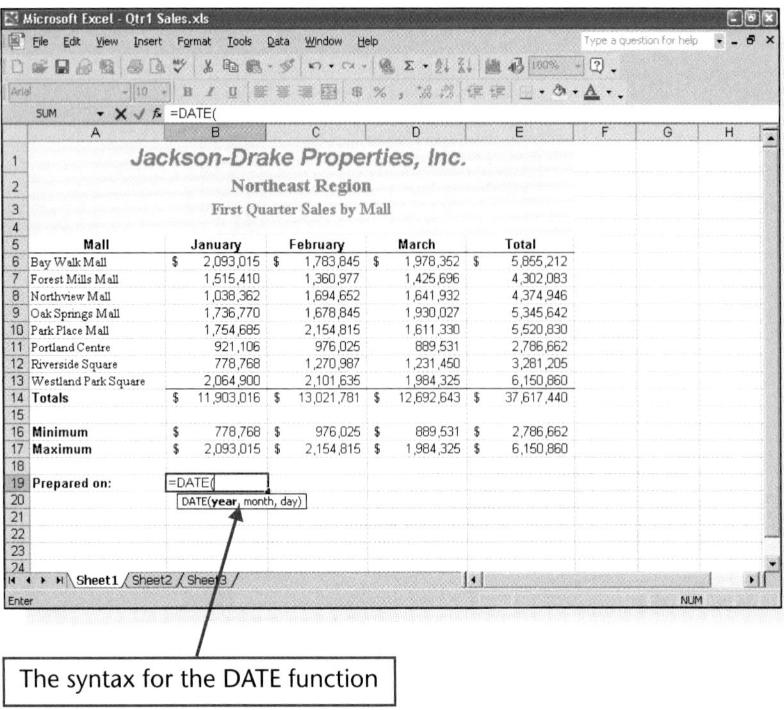

3. In cell B20, type =NOW() and press Enter. Notice that the NOW function uses no arguments. Excel displays today's date and time (see Figure 3.20).

4. Save and close the workbook.

Figure 3.20 Entering the NOW function

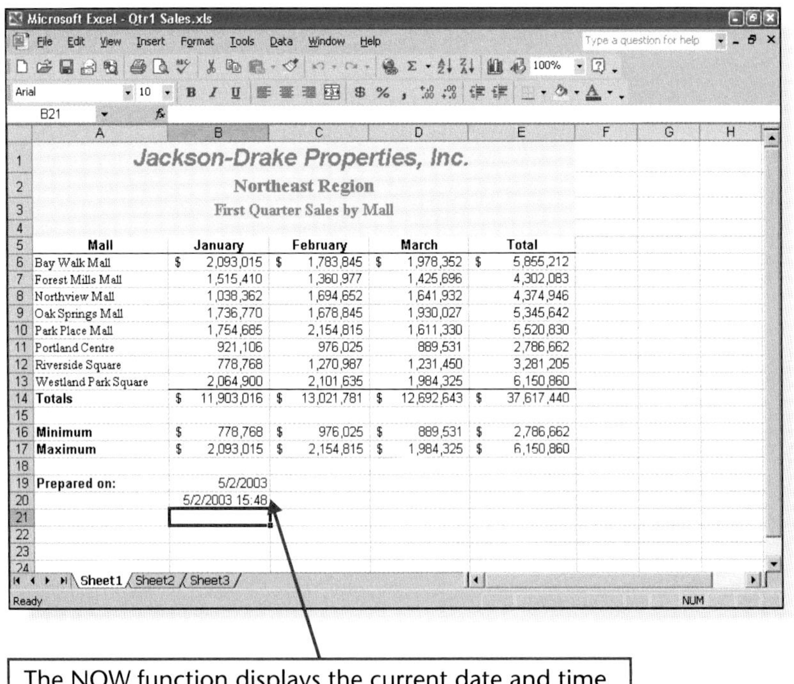

The NOW function displays the current date and time.

Figure 3.21 Selecting a function in the Insert Function dialog box

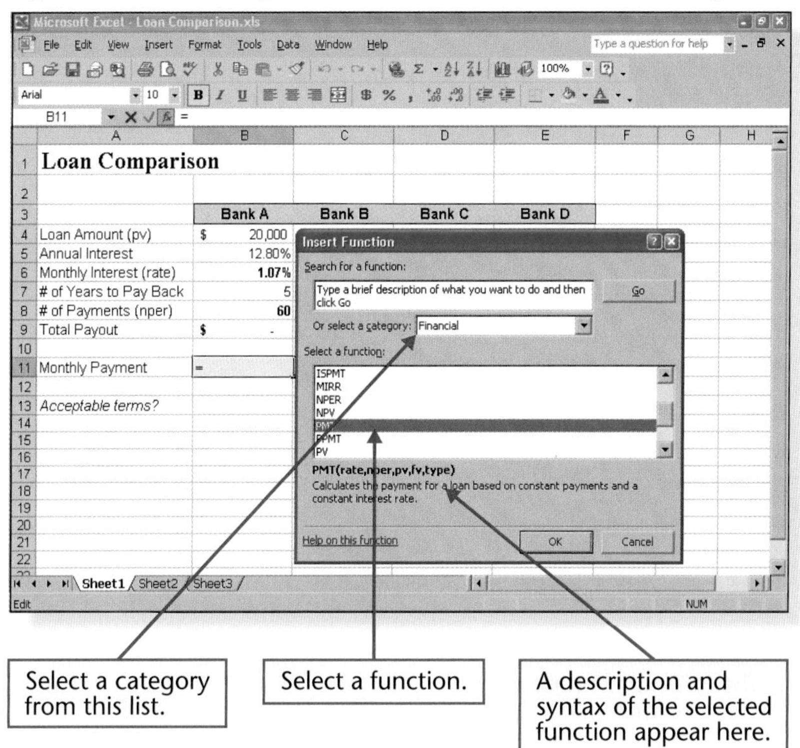

Step Through It™

Exercise 4D: Use the PMT function

1. Open *Loan Comparison.xls*. Save the workbook as *xxx-Loan Comparison.xls*.
2. Click cell B11.
3. On the Insert menu, select Function. The Insert Function dialog box displays.
4. Click the *Or select a category* down arrow, and select *Financial*. Scroll down the *Select a function* list, and select *PMT* (see Figure 3.21).

Figure 3.22 Entering arguments for the PMT function

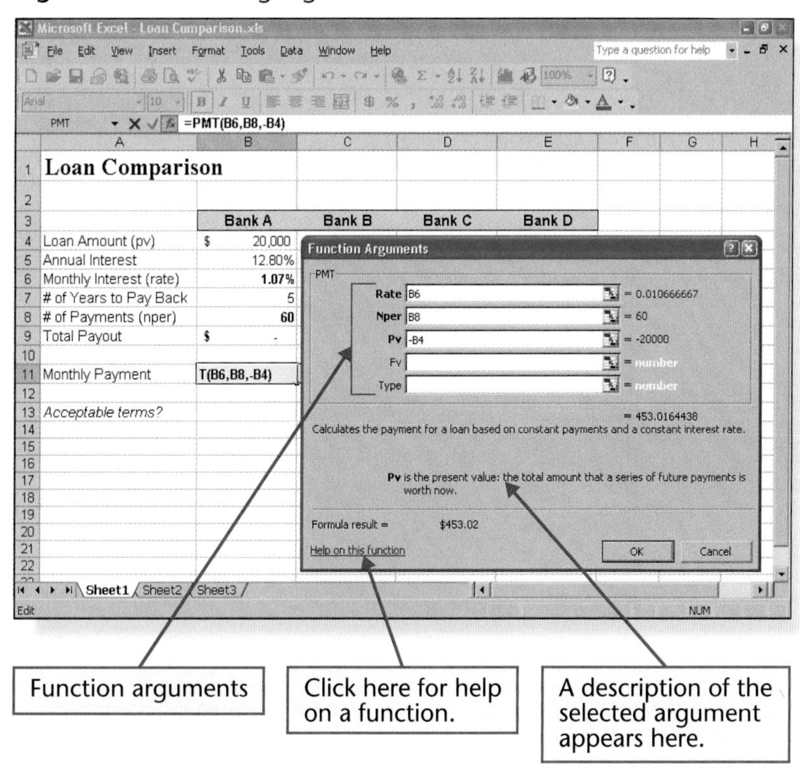

Function arguments
Click here for help on a function.
A description of the selected argument appears here.

5. Click OK. A description of the first argument, *Rate*, displays at the bottom of the dialog box.
6. Drag the title bar of the dialog box to the right so you can view column B. Click cell B6 containing the monthly interest rate for the loan.
7. Click inside the *Nper* box. Click cell B8 (the number of payments for the loan).
8. Press Tab to move to the *Pv* argument (the present value of the loan), and type –B4. (See Figure 3.22.)

Excel

9) Click OK. The function result displays in cell B11.

10) Use the fill handle to copy the formula to cells C11:E11 (see Figure 3.23).

Figure 3.23 The resulting payment amounts for the loans

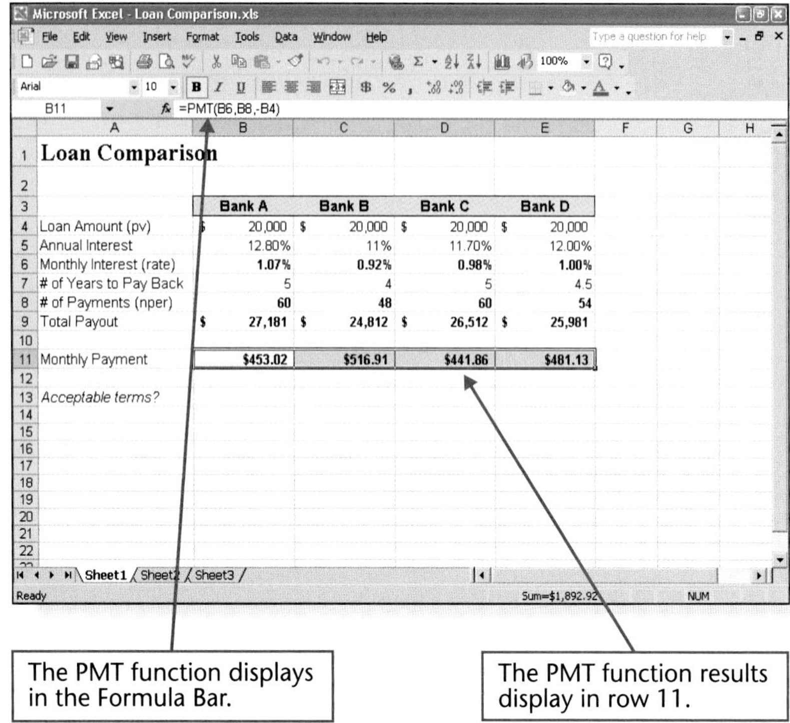

The PMT function displays in the Formula Bar.
The PMT function results display in row 11.

Figure 3.24 The Insert Function dialog box

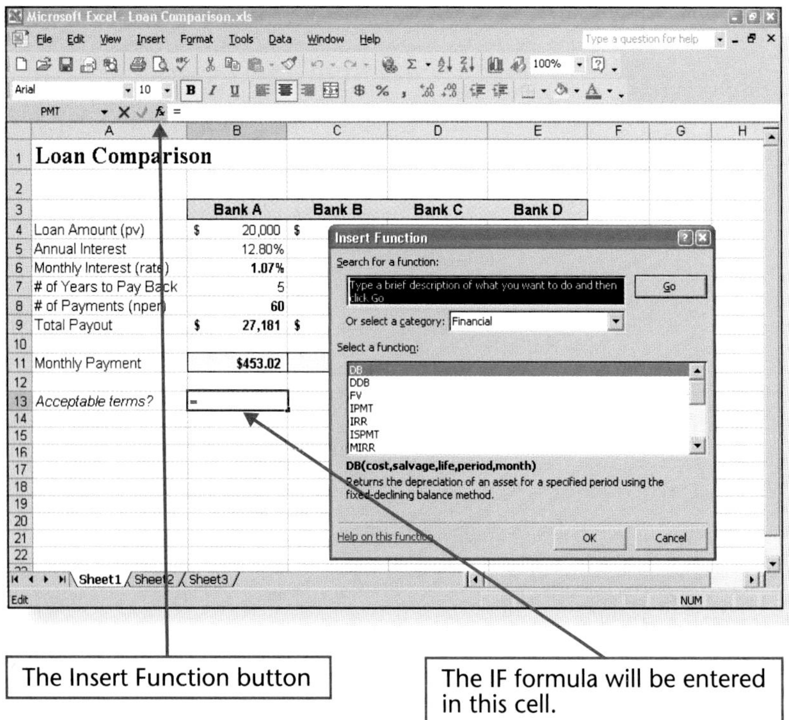

The Insert Function button
The IF formula will be entered in this cell.

Step Through It™

Exercise 4E: Use the IF function

1) Click cell B13. ***Note:*** In this cell, you will enter an IF function that examines the result in cell B11 and returns the text *No* if the payment amount is too high or *Yes!* if the payment amount is acceptable.

2) Click the Insert Function button just to the left of the Formula Bar. The Insert Function dialog box displays (see Figure 3.24).

Figure 3.25 Specifying the IF function arguments

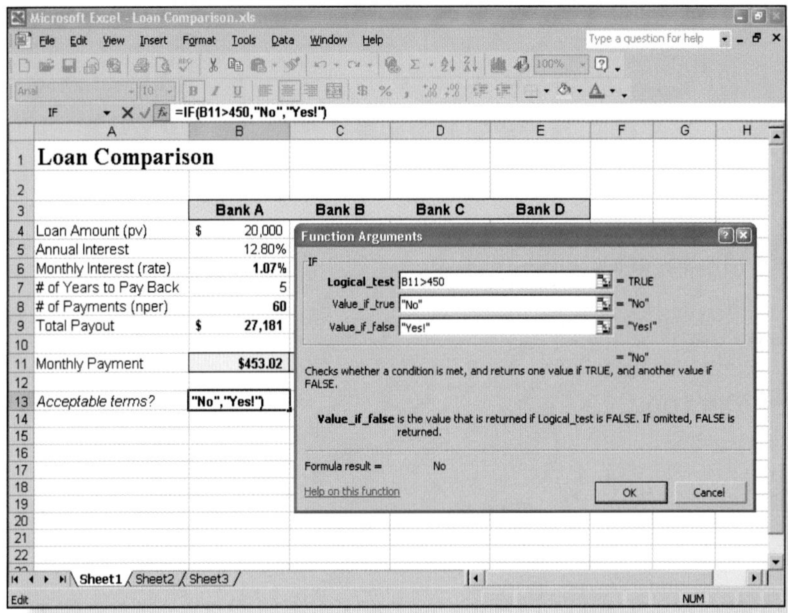

3. Click the *Or select a category* down arrow and select *Logical*. Select *IF* in the *Select a function* list. Click OK to open the Function Arguments dialog box.

4. In the *Logical_test* box, type B11>450 and press Tab to test whether the monthly payment amount exceeds $450.

5. In the *Value_if_true* box, type "No" and press Tab.

6. In the *Value_if_false* box, type "Yes!" (See Figure 3.25.)

Figure 3.26 The IF function results

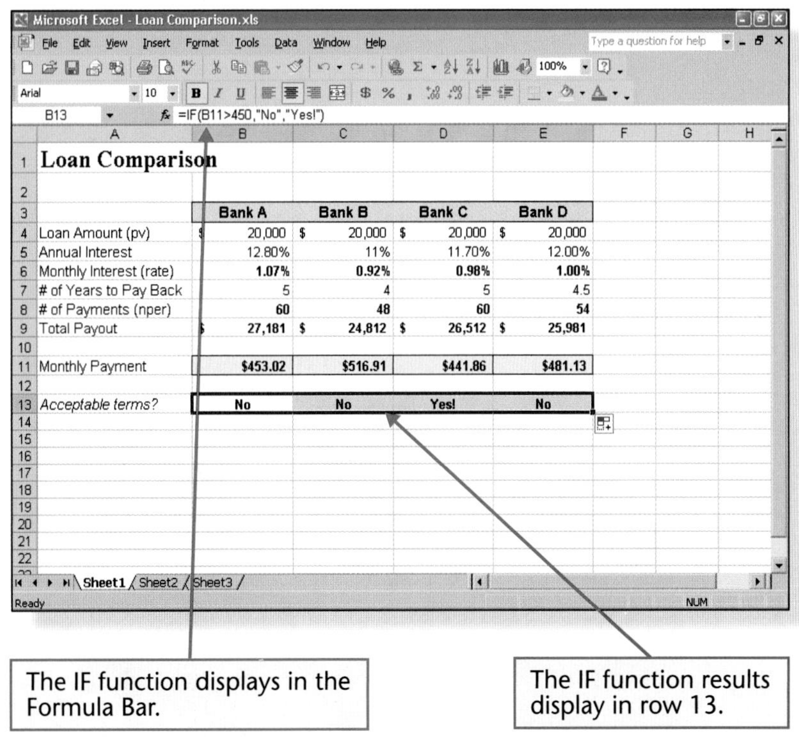
The IF function displays in the Formula Bar.
The IF function results display in row 13.

7. Click OK. The function result displays in cell B13.

8. Using the fill handle, copy the formula to cells C13:E13 (see Figure 3.26).

9. Save and close the workbook.

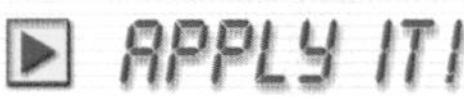
APPLY IT!

After finishing Exercises 2–4, you may test your skills by completing Apply It! Guided Activity 2, Enter Formulas and Functions in a Payroll Worksheet.

Business Connections

Business Financial Statements

Businesses of all types prepare reports that summarize the company's financial activity or position for a specified period of time. Two common reports that businesses prepare on a regular basis are the profit-and-loss statement and the balance sheet.

- A profit-and-loss statement summarizes totals for all of the income and expense accounts for a business over a specified period resulting in a net income amount (total income minus total expenses).
- A balance sheet measures the value of a business as of a certain date—usually the date that the report is prepared. The total assets listed in a balance sheet must equal the sum of liabilities and owner's equity (net worth).

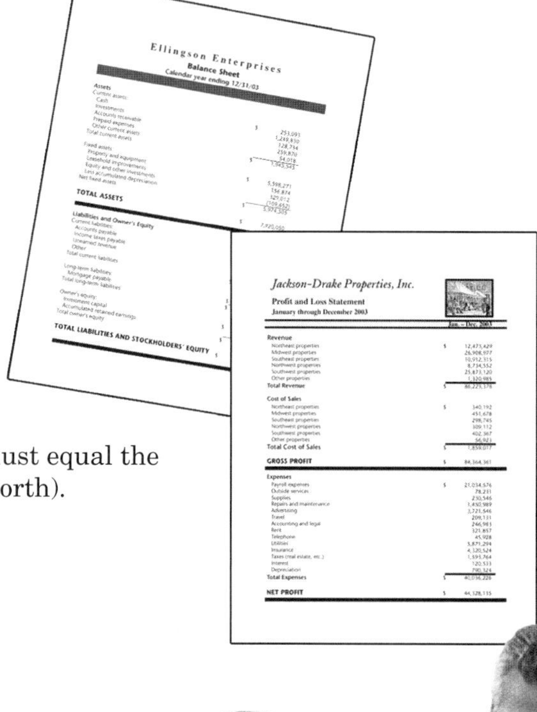

Ellingson Enterprises
Balance Sheet
Calendar year ending 12/31/03

Assets		
Current assets:		
Cash	$	253,093
Investments		1,249,830
Accounts receivable		128,734
Prepaid expenses		259,870
Other current assets		54,018
Total current assets	$	1,945,545
Fixed assets:		
Property and equipment	$	5,598,271
Leasehold improvements		156,874
Equity and other investments		329,012
Less accumulated depreciation		(109,652)
Net fixed assets	$	5,974,505
TOTAL ASSETS	$	7,920,050
Liabilities and Owner's Equity		
Current liabilities:		
Accounts payable		
Income taxes payable		
Unearned revenue		
Other		
Total current liabilities		
Long-term liabilities:		
Mortgage payable		
Total long-term liabilities		
Owner's equity:		
Investment capital		
Accumulated retained earnings		
Total owner's equity		
TOTAL LIABILITIES AND STOCKHOLDERS' EQUITY	$	

Jackson-Drake Properties, Inc.
Profit and Loss Statement
January through December 2003

		Jan. – Dec. 2003
Revenue		
Northeast properties	$	12,473,429
Midwest properties		26,908,977
Southeast properties		10,932,315
Northwest properties		8,734,552
Southwest properties		25,873,120
Other properties		1,320,985
Total Revenue	$	86,223,378
Cost of Sales		
Northeast properties	$	340,192
Midwest properties		451,678
Southeast properties		298,745
Northwest properties		309,112
Southwest properties		402,367
Other properties		56,923
Total Cost of Sales	$	1,859,017
GROSS PROFIT	$	84,364,361
Expenses		
Payroll expenses	$	21,034,576
Outside services		78,233
Supplies		230,546
Repairs and maintenance		1,450,989
Advertising		3,721,546
Travel		209,133
Accounting and legal		246,983
Rent		321,857
Telephone		45,928
Utilities		3,871,294
Insurance		4,320,524
Taxes (real estate, etc.)		1,593,764
Interest		120,533
Depreciation		790,324
Total Expenses	$	40,036,226
NET PROFIT	$	44,328,115

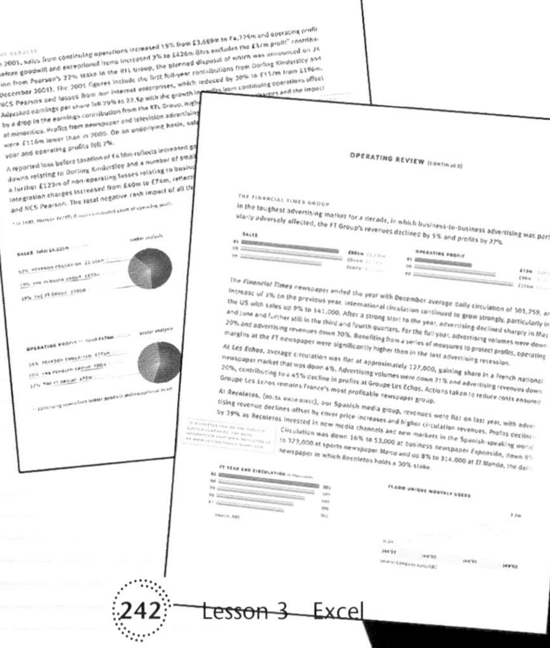

OPERATING REVIEW

OPERATING REVIEW (CONTINUED)

Excel includes many built-in business templates that you can use to create a new workbook. Included are balance sheet, expense statement, loan amortization, sales invoice, and timecard templates. Refer to Exercise 5 in this lesson for details on how to access and use these templates.

- ***Note:*** If you don't see these templates on the Spreadsheet Solutions tab of the Templates dialog box, you may need to install them. Ask your instructor if you need help.

You can find additional templates online that are designed for tasks such as planning your personal finances. The Microsoft Template Gallery includes an extensive collection of templates for both business and personal needs. Follow these instructions to browse the templates:

- On the File menu, click New.
- In the New Workbook task pane, click the General Templates link to open the Templates dialog box.
- Click the Templates on Microsoft.com link to launch your browser and explore the Microsoft Office Template Gallery Web site.

Other online sites provide templates that you can download, although some may charge a fee for their use. Use a search engine to search on "templates" or "business templates."

1. **Using Templates** Review each of Excel's Spreadsheet Solutions templates. Name some common uses for three of these templates.
2. **Assessing Usability** Go to www.Microsoft.com and locate additional templates. List and describe two Excel templates found there. What types of businesses or individuals might find these templates useful?

Microsoft Office Specialist EX2002 2.2

Exercise 5 Overview:
Create a Workbook From a Template

Excel includes several predefined workbook templates that you can use as the basis for a new workbook. These templates include common forms such as a balance sheet, an expense statement, and a sales invoice.

You can modify an existing template to fit your needs or create your own custom templates. As you have learned, an Excel template file uses the *.xlt* file extension.

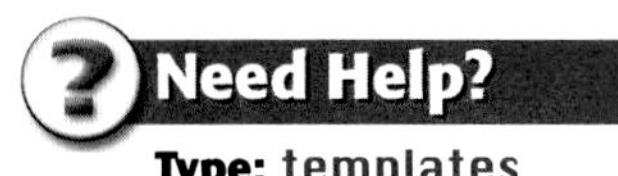

Type: templates

The Microsoft Template Gallery Web site includes a standard balance sheet template, a profit and loss template, and many other financial templates. Therefore, if you can't find the template you need in Excel, you can find more templates online. Access the Microsoft Template Gallery by clicking the Templates on Microsoft.com link in the New Workbook task pane.

In the following exercise, you'll use the Balance Sheet template provided with Excel. This template enables you to list specific transactions and includes a running total balance (similar to a checkbook register).

Step Through It™
Exercise 5: Use a template to create a balance sheet

1. On the File menu, select New.
2. In the New Workbook task pane, click the General Templates link to open the Templates dialog box.
3. Click the Spreadsheet Solutions tab to view the templates supplied with Excel (see Figure 3.27).

Figure 3.27 The Templates dialog box

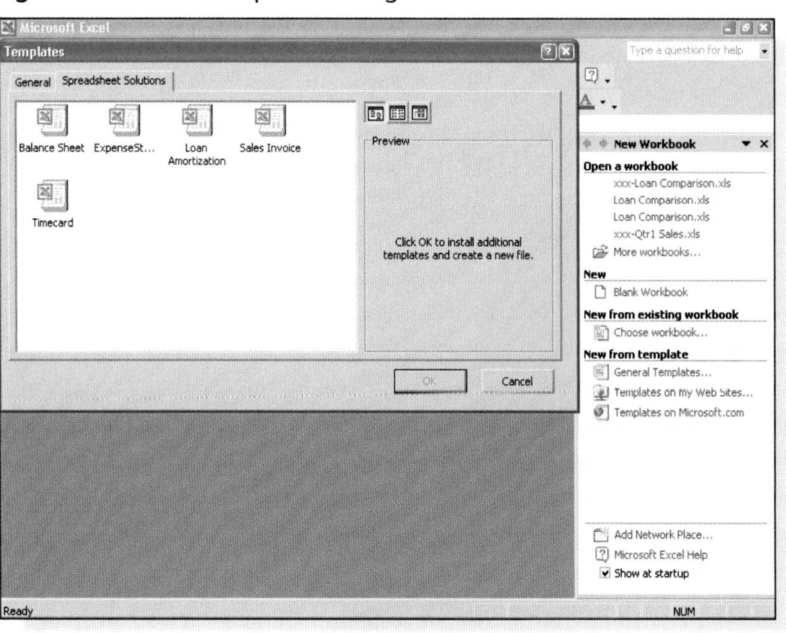

Figure 3.28 The Balance Sheet template

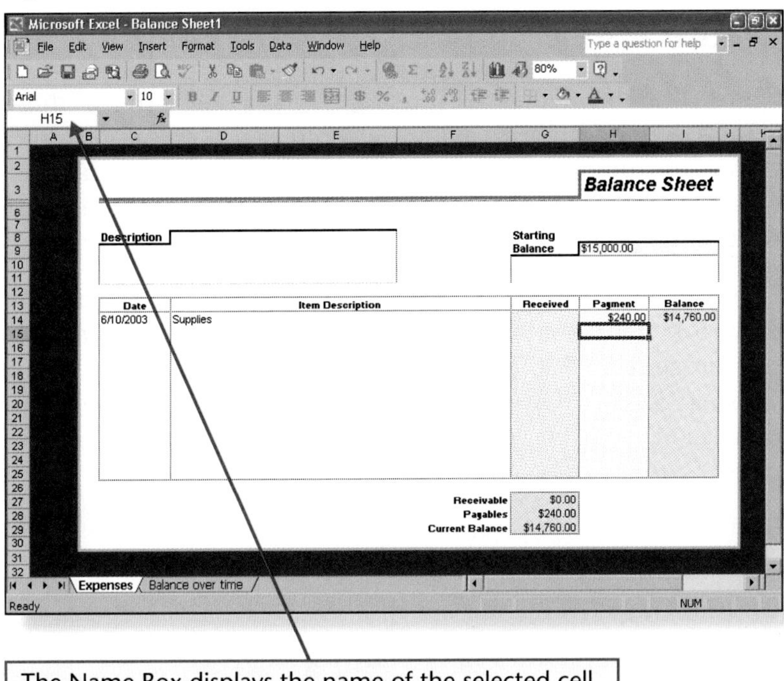

4. Click the Balance Sheet icon, and click OK. A blank, preformatted Balance Sheet template displays.

5. Click cell H9. Type 15000 as the starting balance. ***Note:*** Refer to the Name Box (at the left of the Formula Bar) to confirm that you have selected the correct cell.

6. Click cell C14, type 6/10/03, and press Tab. In D14, type Supplies, and press Tab twice. In H14, type 240, and press Enter (see Figure 3.28).

Figure 3.29 Adding data to the Balance Sheet template

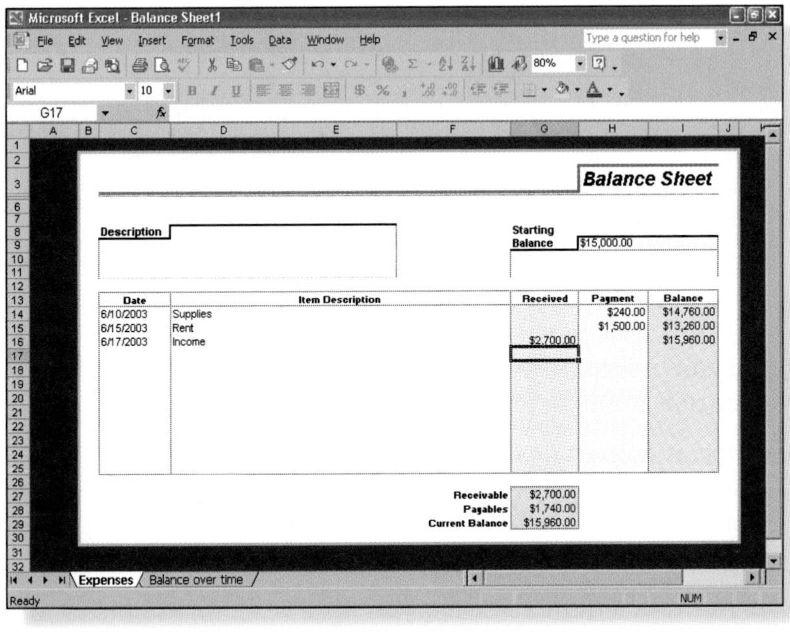

7. Enter the following data: C15: 6/15/03; D15: Rent; H15: 1500.

8. Enter the following data: C16: 6/17/03; D16: Income; G16: 2700. Column I is updated as you enter each item, and the running totals display at the bottom of the balance sheet (see Figure 3.29).

9. Save the workbook as *xxx-Balance Sheet2.xls* and close the workbook.

After finishing Exercise 5, you may test your skills by completing Apply It! Guided Activity 3, Use a Template to Calculate Loan Payments.

Microsoft Office Specialist
EX2002 6.1, 6.2

Exercise 6 Overview:
Create and Modify Charts and Graphics

Type: charts

Charts enable you to illustrate your worksheet data graphically making it easier for you to see comparisons and trends in numbers. When you make changes to the data on which a chart is based, the chart automatically updates to reflect those changes.

Excel also provides a **wizard** to simplify chart creation. A wizard is an automated tool that helps you perform a task by presenting step-by-step content and organization choices. Excel's Chart Wizard will lead you through the process of creating your chart one step at a time.

Figure 3.30 The Chart Wizard Leads you through the process of creating a chart

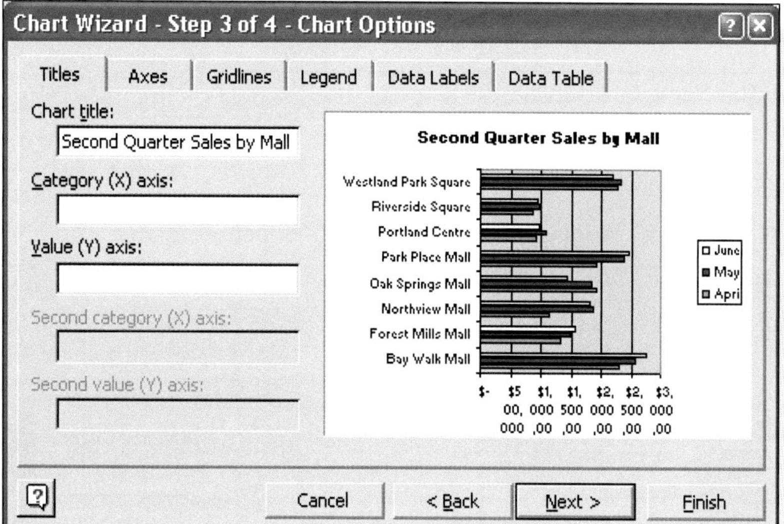

You can insert graphic elements in your worksheets to draw attention to important items or add visual interest.

You can import graphics created in another application, insert clip art objects, or use the Drawing toolbar to create graphic objects such as arrows, rectangles, or AutoShapes (such as banners and stars).

In the following exercises, you will work with charts and graphics.

Figure 3.31 The Chart Type window of the Chart Wizard dialog box

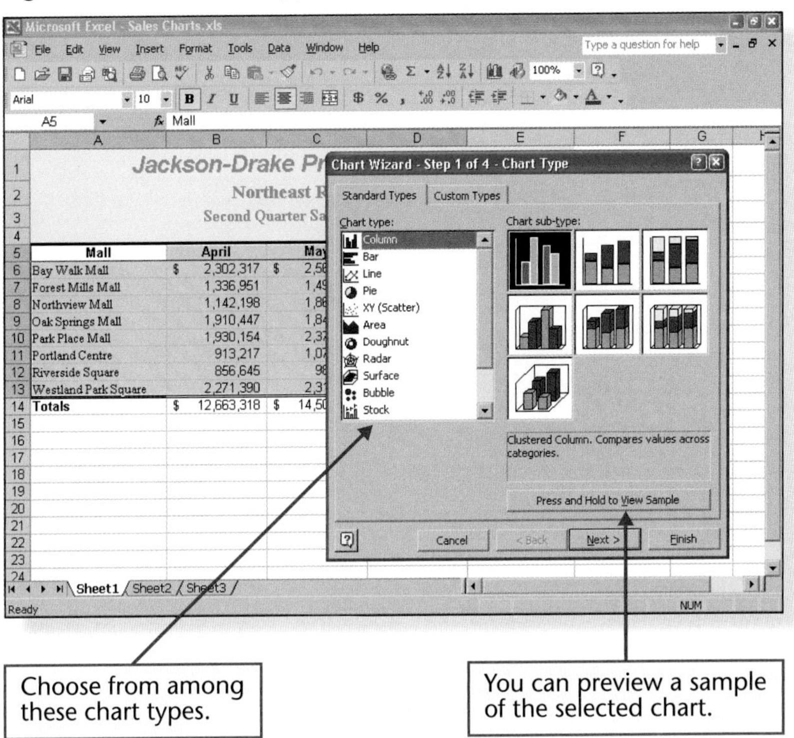
Chart Wizard - Step 1 of 4 - Chart Type
Choose from among these chart types.
You can preview a sample of the selected chart.

Step Through It™

Exercise 6A: Create a bar chart

1. Open *Sales Charts.xls*. Save the workbook as *xxx-Sales Charts.xls*.
2. Select the range A5:D13. ***Note:*** Do not select the totals data.
3. On the Insert menu, select Chart. The Chart Wizard dialog box, Step 1 of 4, displays (see Figure 3.31).

Figure 3.32 Specifying the chart options

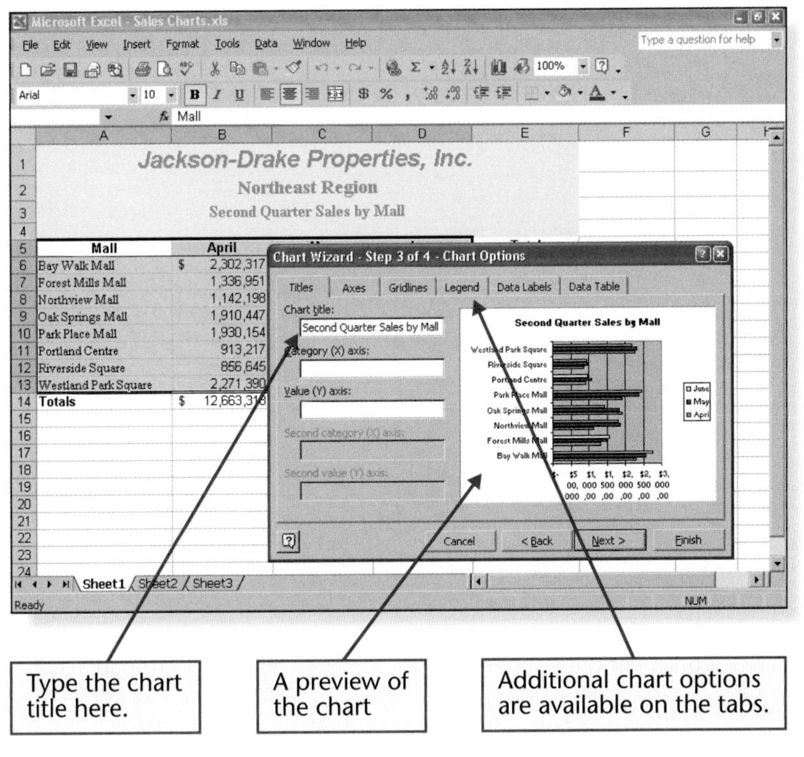
Chart Wizard - Step 3 of 4 - Chart Options
Type the chart title here.
A preview of the chart
Additional chart options are available on the tabs.

4. In the *Chart type* list, select *Bar*. Click the Next button.
5. Step 2 of the wizard allows you to specify the chart source data. The current selection is correct, so click Next to continue.
6. Step 3 of the wizard allows you to specify the chart options. In the *Chart title* box, type Second Quarter Sales by Mall. (See Figure 3.32.)

Excel

Excel

7) Click Next to continue. Step 4 of 4 of the Chart Wizard allows you to specify where to place the chart—in a new sheet, or as an object in the current worksheet.

8) Select the *As new sheet* option button, and then click Finish. The bar chart displays in a separate chart sheet in the workbook (see Figure 3.33).

9) Save the workbook.

Figure 3.33 A bar chart displayed as a separate sheet

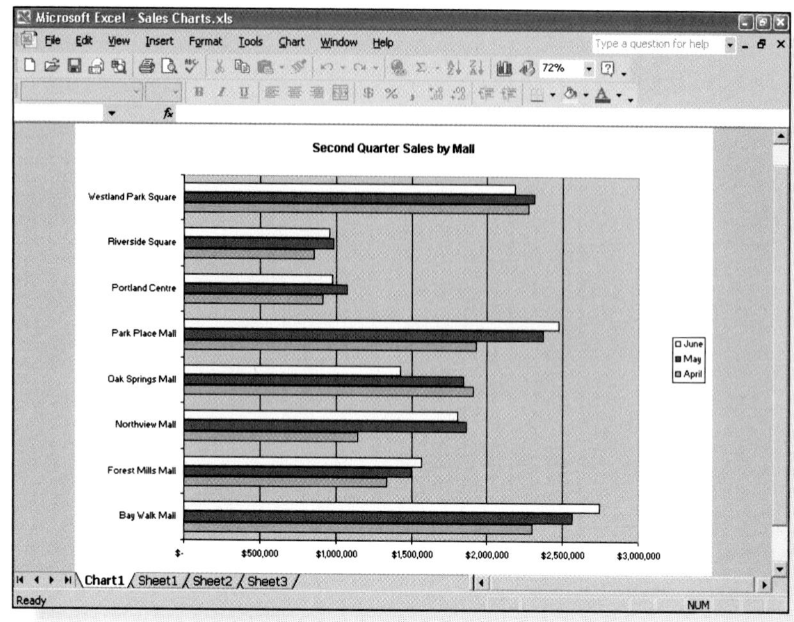

Step Through It™

Exercise 6B: Create a pie chart

1) Click the *Sheet1* tab at the bottom of the worksheet to display the worksheet data again.

2) Select the range A6:A13, hold Ctrl, and select the range E6:E13 (see Figure 3.34).

Figure 3.34 Selecting nonadjacent ranges for the pie chart

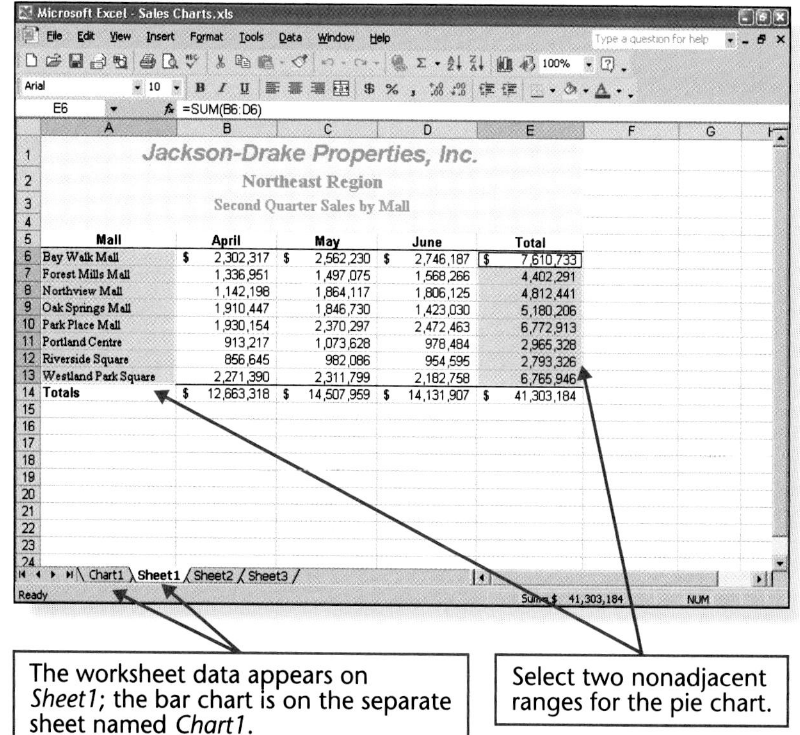

Microsoft Excel - Sales Charts.xls

E6 =SUM(B6:D6)

Jackson-Drake Properties, Inc.

Northeast Region

Second Quarter Sales by Mall

Mall	April	May	June	Total
Bay Walk Mall	$ 2,302,317	$ 2,562,230	$ 2,746,187	$ 7,610,733
Forest Mills Mall	1,336,951	1,497,075	1,568,266	4,402,291
Northview Mall	1,142,198	1,864,117	1,806,125	4,812,441
Oak Springs Mall	1,910,447	1,846,730	1,423,030	5,180,206
Park Place Mall	1,930,154	2,370,297	2,472,463	6,772,913
Portland Centre	913,217	1,073,628	978,484	2,965,328
Riverside Square	856,645	982,086	954,595	2,793,326
Westland Park Square	2,271,390	2,311,799	2,182,758	6,765,946
Totals	$ 12,663,318	$ 14,507,959	$ 14,131,907	$ 41,303,184

Figure 3.35 A pie chart displayed as an object in the worksheet

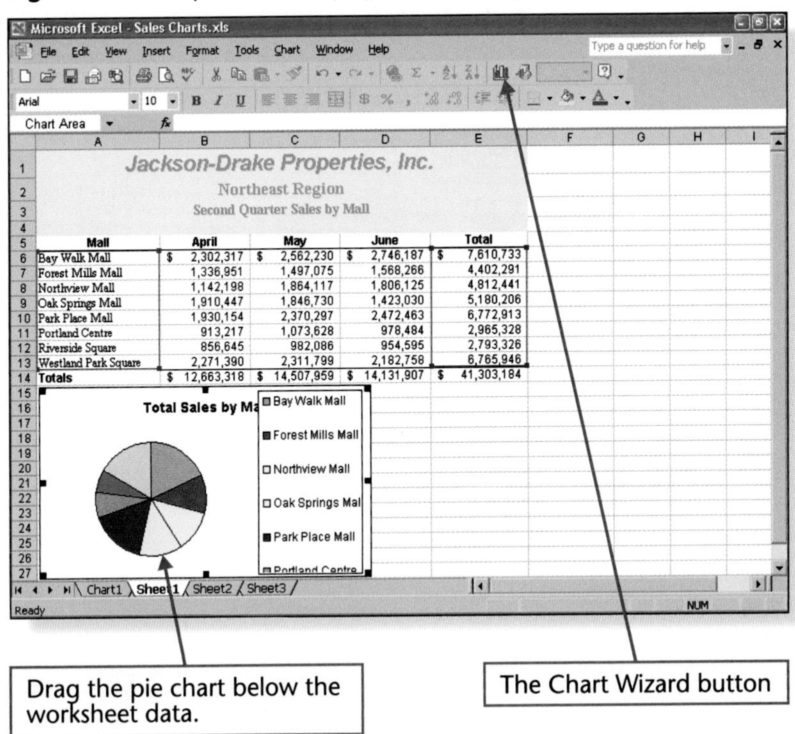

3. Click the Chart Wizard button on the Standard toolbar.
4. In the *Chart type* list, select *Pie* and click Next.
5. Click Next again to advance to Step 3 of 4. Type **Total Sales by Mall** in the *Chart title* box.
6. Click Next. In Step 4 of 4, select *As object in*, and click Finish. Click a blank area of the chart and drag to position it below the worksheet data (see Figure 3.35).
7. Save the workbook.

Excel

Figure 3.36 Adding data label percentages to a pie chart

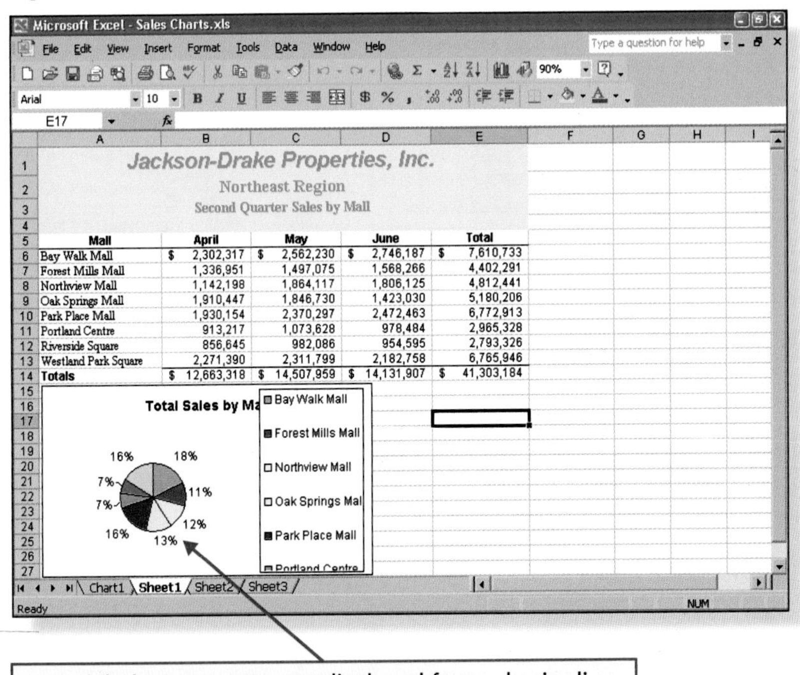

Step Through It™

Exercise 6C: Format a chart

1. Click the pie within the chart to select it. On the Format menu, select Selected Data Series to display the Format Data Series dialog box.
2. On the Data Labels tab, select the *Percentage* check box and click OK.
3. Click outside the chart. The pie chart now displays data labels that show the percentage allotted to each pie slice (see Figure 3.36).

4) Right-click inside the legend, and select Format Legend on the shortcut menu. The Format Legend dialog box displays.

5) On the Font tab, select 8 in the *Size* list. Click OK, and then click outside the chart. The legend now has room to display all of the mall names (see Figure 3.37).

6) Save and close the workbook.

Figure 3.37 Modifying the format of the legend

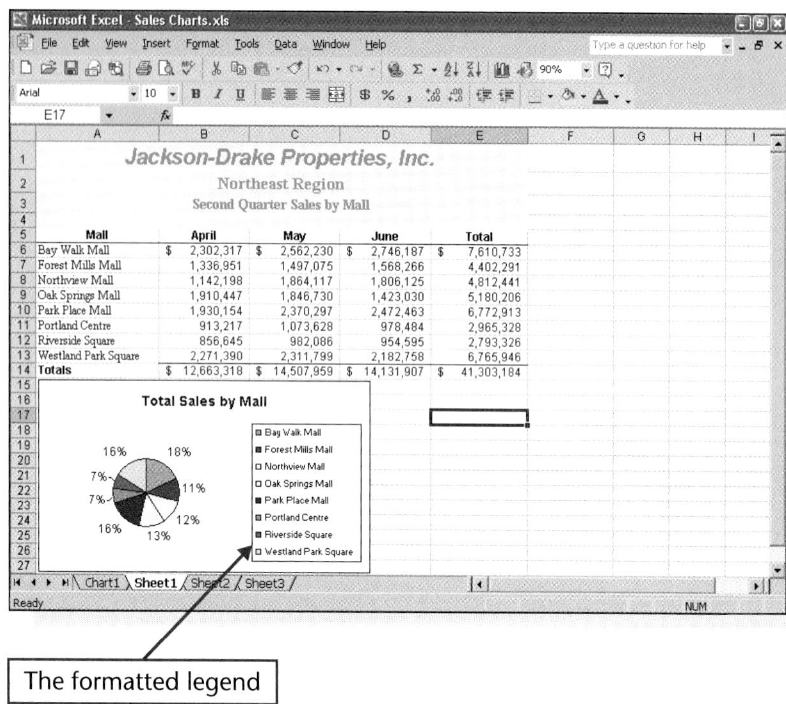

Step Through It™
Exercise 6D: Insert and position a graphic

1) Open *Qtr2 Sales.xls*. Save it as *xxx-Qtr2 Sales.xls*. Cell A1 should be selected.

2) On the Insert menu, point to Picture, and select Clip Art. Type trees in the *Search text* box and click Search.

3) Click an appropriate image in the search results to insert it into the worksheet (see Figure 3.38). ***Note:*** If necessary, click Modify and perform a new search using different search text.

Figure 3.38 Importing a graphic file

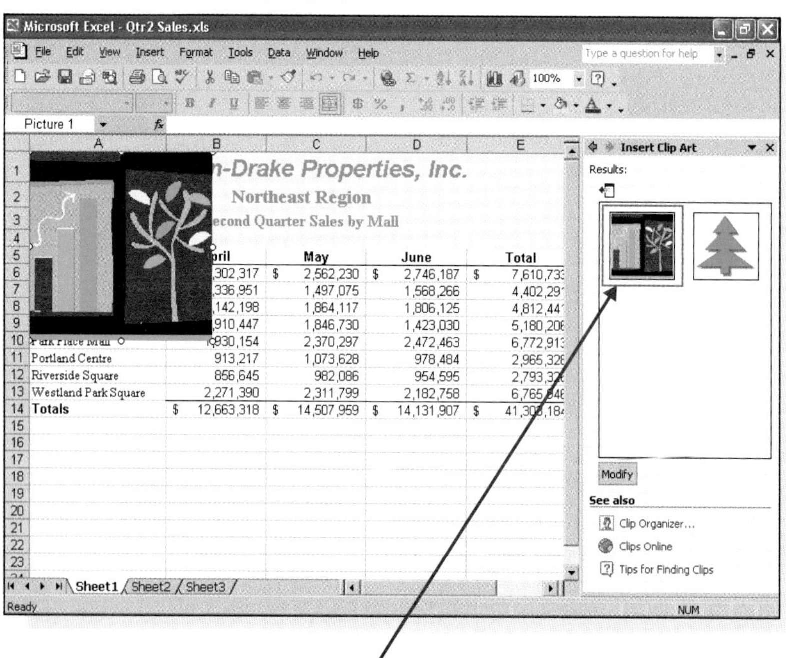

Figure 3.39 Positioning and resizing a graphic

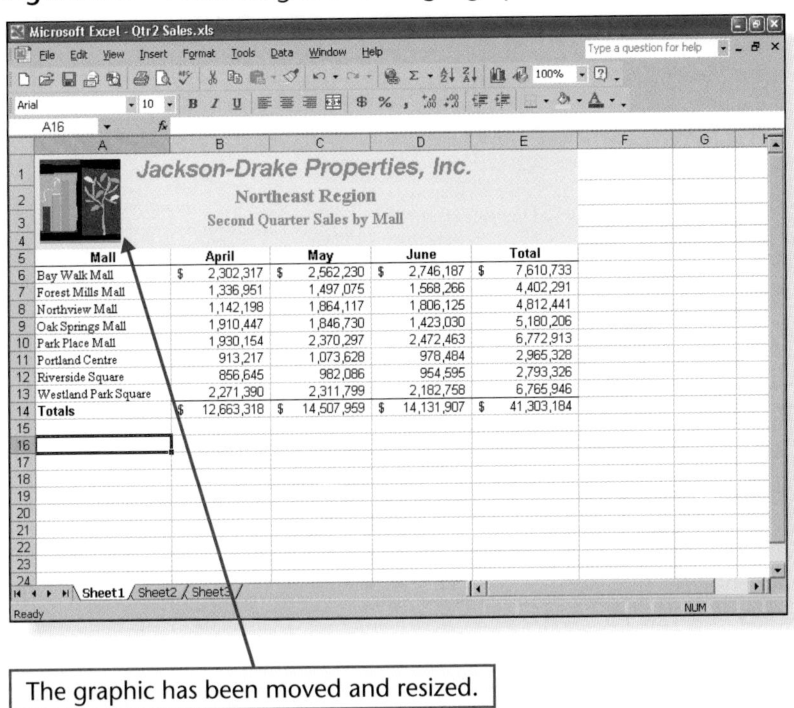
The graphic has been moved and resized.

4. Close the task pane. Click the graphic to select it, if necessary.

5. Drag the lower-right handle of the graphic toward the upper left to reduce its size. The image should fit within the first four rows and should not obscure text or data in the worksheet. Click outside the graphic (see Figure 3.39). ***Note:*** If necessary, you can drag the graphic to reposition it so that it appears in the position shown in Figure 3.39.

6. Save the workbook.

Figure 3.40 Selecting an AutoShape

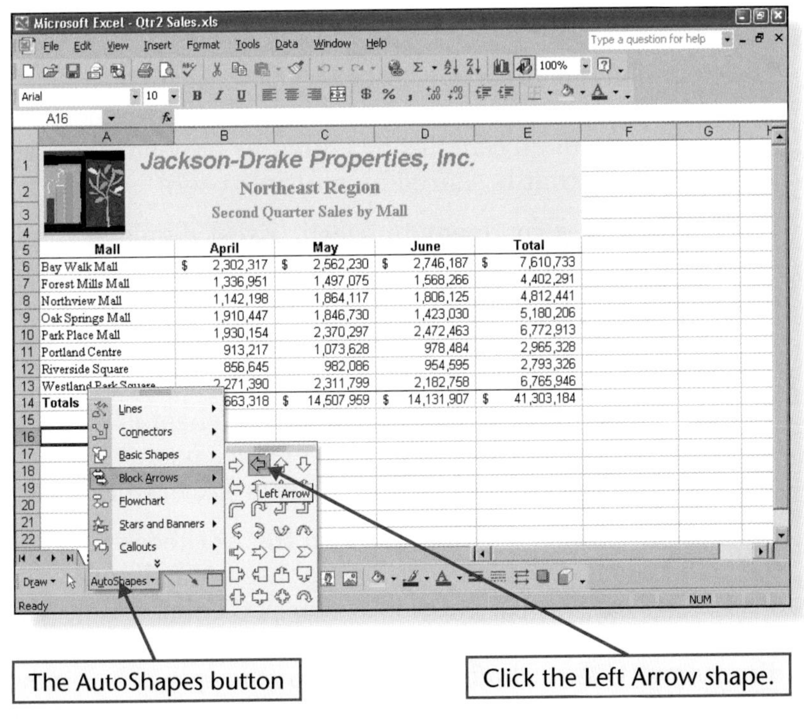
The AutoShapes button
Click the Left Arrow shape.

Step Through It™

Exercise 6E: Create and modify a graphic

1. Click the Drawing button on the Standard toolbar to display the Drawing toolbar.

2. Click the AutoShapes button on the Drawing toolbar and point to Block Arrows (see Figure 3.40). Click the Left Arrow shape. The pointer changes to a plus sign.

3. Click cell F14 to insert the AutoShape. Right-click the AutoShape and select Add Text.

4. Type Grand Total. Click the outside border of the AutoShape. On the Format menu, select AutoShape to open the Format AutoShape dialog box.

5. On the Font tab, change the Color to red and the Font Size to 12. On the Colors and Lines tab, select a light yellow fill color and click OK.

6. Drag the border of the selected AutoShape to position it so it points to cell E14. Click outside the AutoShape (see Figure 3.41).

7. Save and close the workbook.

Figure 3.41 The modified AutoShape

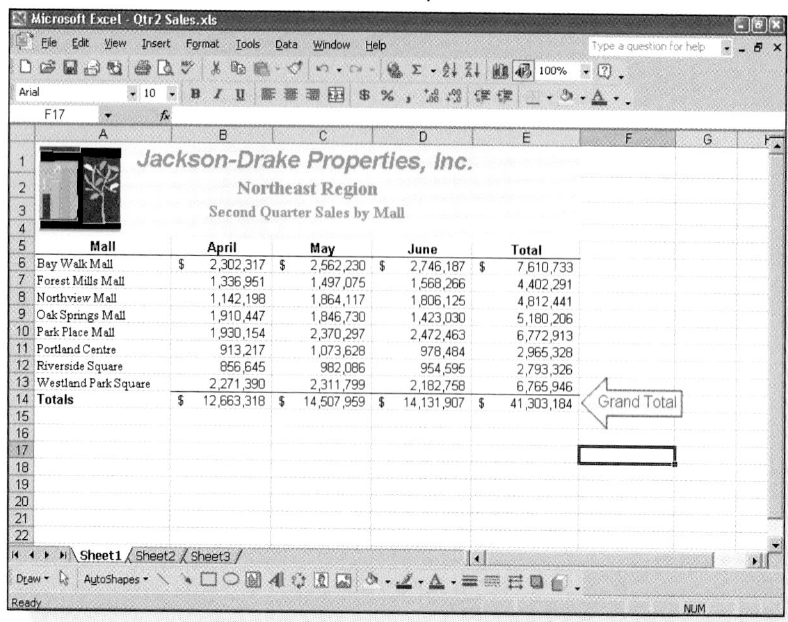

Microsoft Office Specialist EX2002 7.3

Exercise 7 Overview:
Provide Feedback on a Worksheet

The Comments feature in Excel enables you to attach notes to cells. You can use comments to emphasize important information, explain complex formulas, or provide feedback in a worksheet that is shared by multiple users.

When you add a comment to a cell, Excel displays a red triangle in the upper-right corner of the cell. If you point to this indicator, the comment displays in a yellow pop-up box with the author's name preceding the comment. You can edit, print, and delete comments attached to cells.

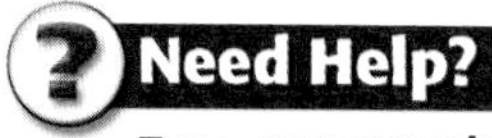

Type: comments

Another way to provide feedback in a worksheet is through the Web Discussions feature, which enables users to attach **discussion comments** to a Web page or Excel workbook.

Discussion comments display within the workbook file, but the text is actually stored in a database on a **discussion server**, which is a computer that stores the discussion text and information about the location of the file you are discussing. Users who have access to this server can view and reply to the comments, resulting in a discussion

thread that groups comments in hierarchical order. You can then review the responses and make changes to the workbook as necessary.

Note: You need access to a discussion server to complete Exercise 7B. Check with your teacher to ensure that you have the permissions needed to use the Web Discussions feature so that you are able to view and respond to discussion comments.

Consider trading comments with another student as you work through Exercise 7B.

Excel

Figure 3.42 Inserting a comment

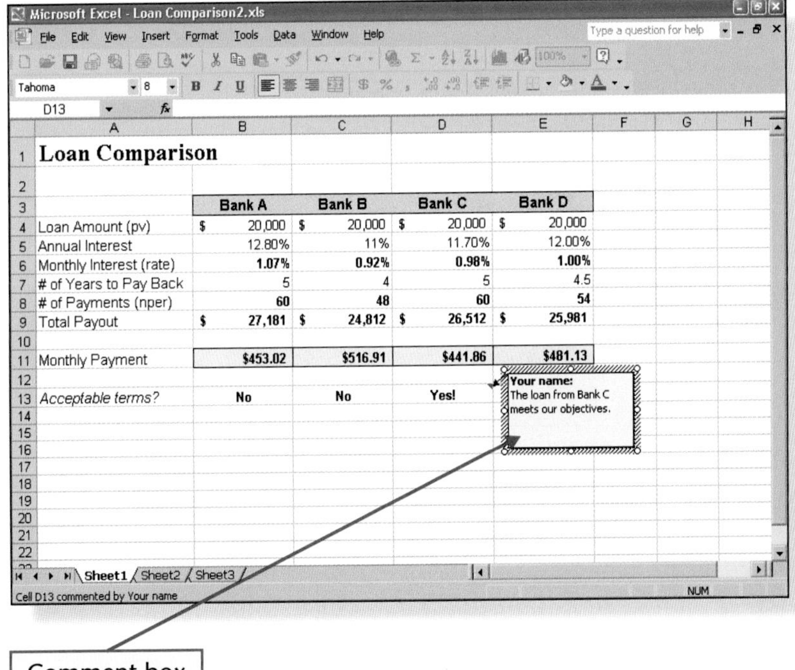

	A	B	C	D	E
1	Loan Comparison				
2					
3		Bank A	Bank B	Bank C	Bank D
4	Loan Amount (pv)	$ 20,000	$ 20,000	$ 20,000	$ 20,000
5	Annual Interest	12.80%	11%	11.70%	12.00%
6	Monthly Interest (rate)	1.07%	0.92%	0.98%	1.00%
7	# of Years to Pay Back	5	4	5	4.5
8	# of Payments (nper)	60	48	60	54
9	Total Payout	$ 27,181	$ 24,812	$ 26,512	$ 25,981
10					
11	Monthly Payment	$453.02	$516.91	$441.86	$481.13
12					
13	Acceptable terms?	No	No	Yes!	

Step Through It™

Exercise 7A: Insert and edit comments in a worksheet

1. Open *Loan Comparison2.xls*. Save the workbook as *xxx-Loan Comparison2.xls*.
2. Click cell D13. On the Insert menu, select Comment. A yellow comment box displays in the worksheet.
3. Type the following text in the comment box: The loan from Bank C meets our objectives. (See Figure 3.42.)

Quick Tip

Comments identifying each reviewer are inserted into a *shared workbook*. A shared workbook is set up on a network to provide access for multiple reviewers who can make changes and see the changes made by others.

4. Click outside the comment box to close the box.

5. Click cell D13. On the Insert menu, select Edit Comment. Type the following text at the end of the existing comment: Let's apply today.

6. Click outside the comment box and then point to cell D13 to view the comment (see Figure 3.43).

7. Save and close the workbook.

Figure 3.43 Viewing an edited comment

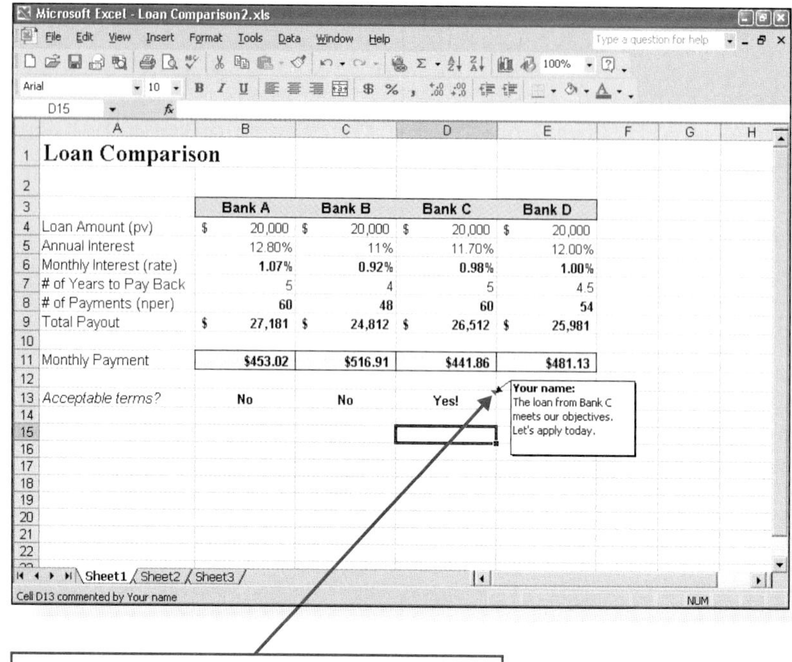

Loan Comparison

	Bank A	Bank B	Bank C	Bank D
Loan Amount (pv)	$ 20,000	$ 20,000	$ 20,000	$ 20,000
Annual Interest	12.80%	11%	11.70%	12.00%
Monthly Interest (rate)	1.07%	0.92%	0.98%	1.00%
# of Years to Pay Back	5	4	5	4.5
# of Payments (nper)	60	48	60	54
Total Payout	$ 27,181	$ 24,812	$ 26,512	$ 25,981
Monthly Payment	$453.02	$516.91	$441.86	$481.13
Acceptable terms?	No	No	Yes!	

Step Through It™

Exercise 7B: Create and respond to discussion comments

1. Open *Qtr2 Sales.xls.* Save the file as *xxx-Qtr2 Sales.xls.*

2. On the Tools menu, point to Online Collaboration, and select Web Discussions. The Web Discussions toolbar displays (see Figure 3.44).

3. Click the Insert Discussion about the Workbook button on the Web Discussions toolbar. The Enter Discussion Text dialog box displays.

Figure 3.44 The Web Discussions toolbar

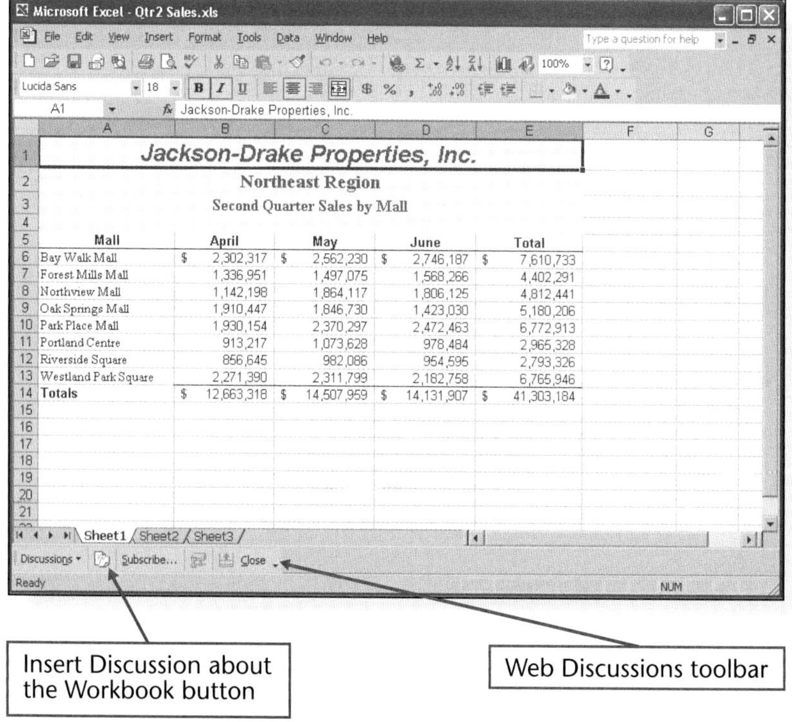

Jackson-Drake Properties, Inc.
Northeast Region
Second Quarter Sales by Mall

Mall	April	May	June	Total
Bay Walk Mall	$ 2,302,317	$ 2,562,230	$ 2,746,187	$ 7,610,733
Forest Mills Mall	1,336,951	1,497,075	1,568,266	4,402,291
Northview Mall	1,142,198	1,864,117	1,806,125	4,812,441
Oak Springs Mall	1,910,447	1,846,730	1,423,030	5,180,206
Park Place Mall	1,930,154	2,370,297	2,472,463	6,772,913
Portland Centre	913,217	1,073,628	978,484	2,965,328
Riverside Square	856,645	982,086	954,595	2,793,326
Westland Park Square	2,271,390	2,311,799	2,182,758	6,765,946
Totals	$ 12,663,318	$ 14,507,959	$ 14,131,907	$ 41,303,184

Figure 3.45 Enter Discussion Text dialog box

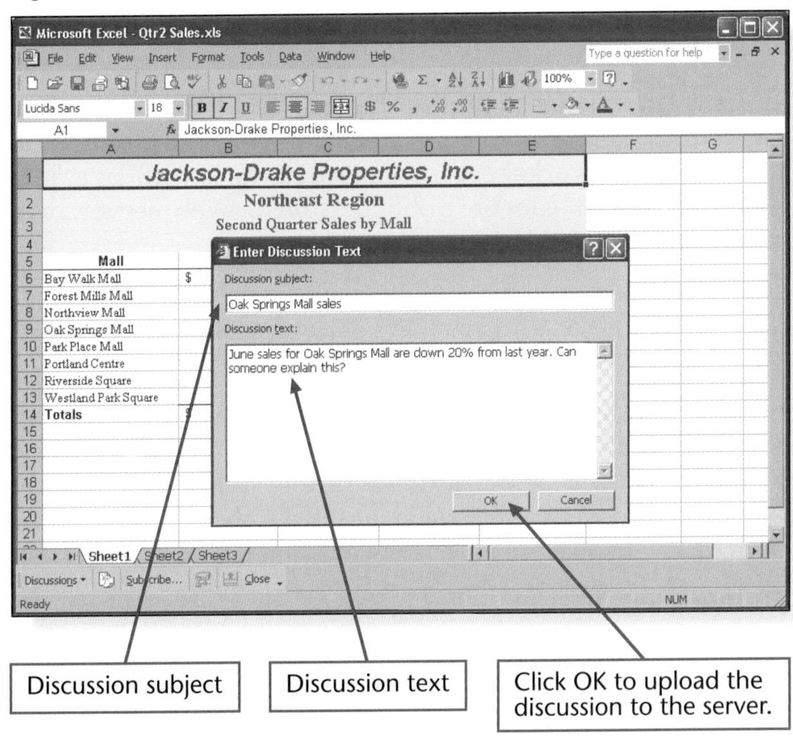

4. Type **Oak Springs Mall sales** in the *Discussion subject* box.

5. Type the following in the *Discussion text* box: **June sales for Oak Springs Mall are down 20% from last year. Can someone explain this?** (See Figure 3.45.)

6. Click OK. The discussion text is uploaded to the server. The Discussion pane displays the discussion text below the worksheet.

Figure 3.46 A threaded discussion

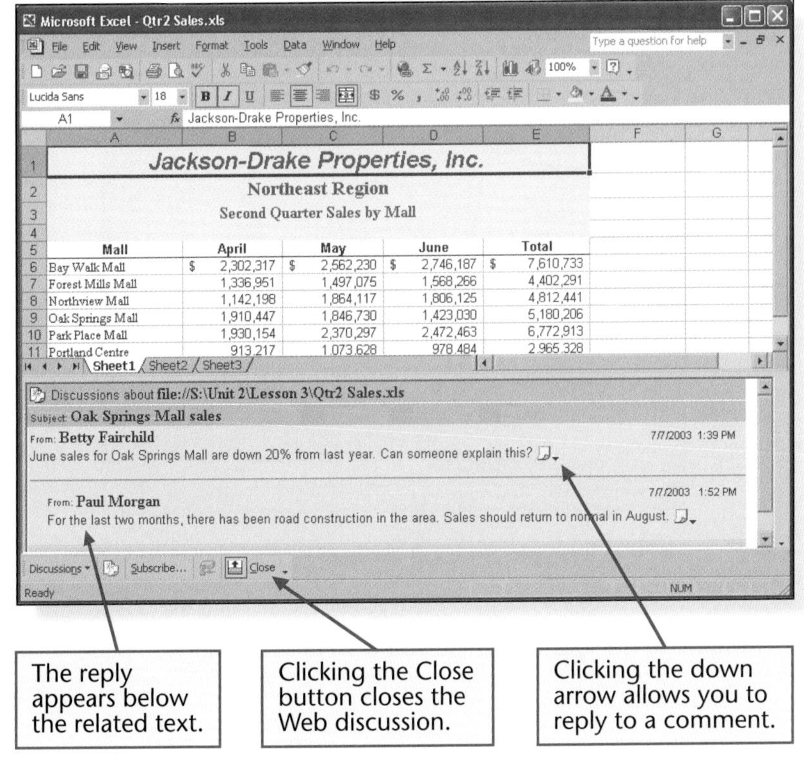

7. Click the down arrow at the end of the discussion text, and click Reply.

8. Type the following reply in the *Discussion text* box: **For the last two months, there has been road construction in the area. Sales should return to normal in August.** Click OK. The reply text displays below the original comment in the Discussion pane (see Figure 3.46).

9. Click Close on the Web Discussions toolbar. Close the workbook.

Exercise 8 Overview: Share a Worksheet Online

In Unit 1, you learned how to share a Word document online by saving it as a Web page. You can use a similar process to save an Excel worksheet (or an entire workbook) as a Web page so that it can be published on a Web server or a network server and viewed by others.

Excel enables you to preview a worksheet in your Web browser before or after you save it as a Web page.

When you save the worksheet as a Web page, you can specify whether or not you want others to be able to change formatting or data in the published worksheet. If you publish the worksheet *without* interactivity (the default setting), users can view the worksheet's data and formatting but cannot use the worksheet.

In this exercise, you will save a worksheet as a Web page, without interactivity, and view the page in a browser.

Step Through It™

Exercise 8: Convert a worksheet into a Web page

1. Open *Job Openings.xls*.
2. On the File menu, select Save as Web Page to display the Save As dialog box.
3. Click the *Save in* down arrow and navigate to the *Lesson 3* subfolder within your *Unit 2* folder, if necessary (see Figure 3.47).

Figure 3.47 Navigating to a location in the Save As dialog box

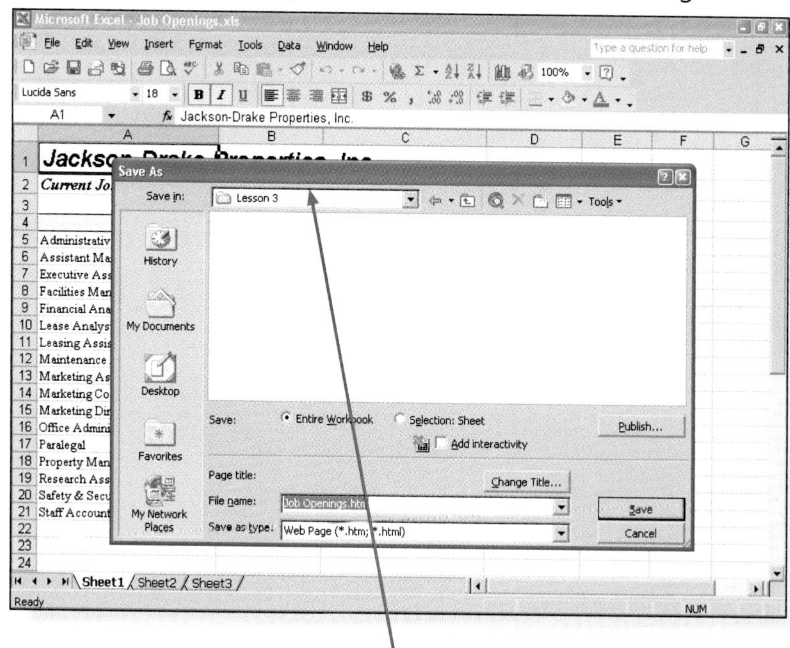

Navigate to the location where you wish to save your web page.

Figure 3.48 Saving a worksheet as a Web page

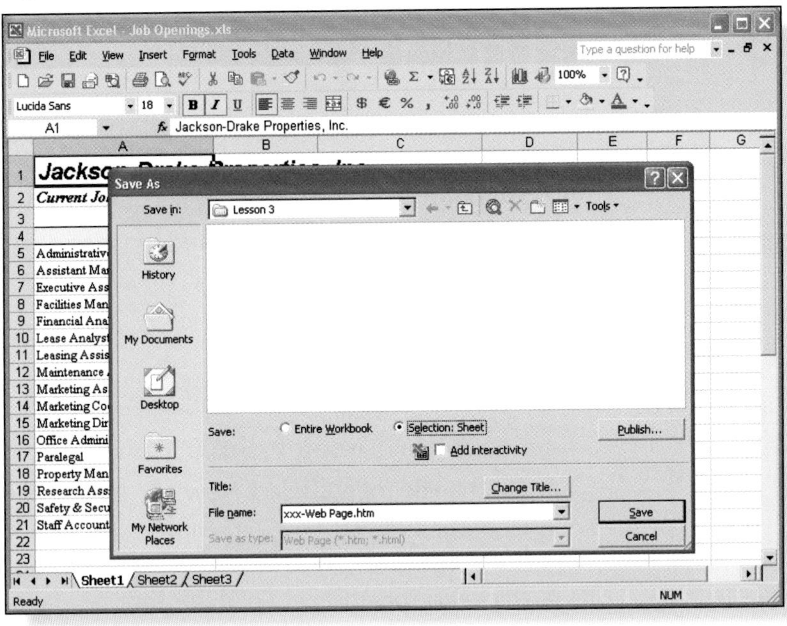

4. Type xxx-Web Page.htm in the *File name* box.
5. Select the *Selection: Sheet* option button (see Figure 3.48). Click Save. The worksheet is saved as a Web page.

Figure 3.49 Previewing the worksheet in a Web browser

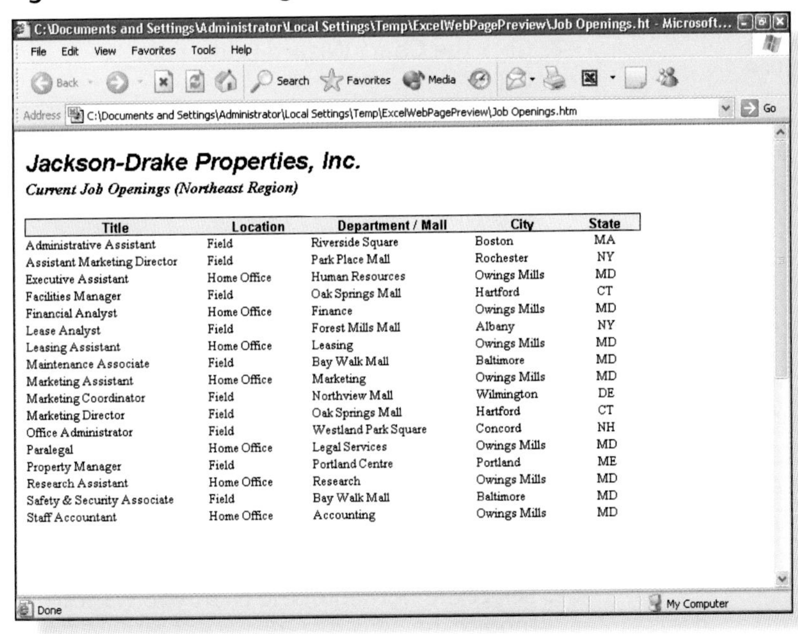

Jackson-Drake Properties, Inc.

Current Job Openings (Northeast Region)

Title	Location	Department / Mall	City	State
Administrative Assistant	Field	Riverside Square	Boston	MA
Assistant Marketing Director	Field	Park Place Mall	Rochester	NY
Executive Assistant	Home Office	Human Resources	Owings Mills	MD
Facilities Manager	Field	Oak Springs Mall	Hartford	CT
Financial Analyst	Home Office	Finance	Owings Mills	MD
Lease Analyst	Field	Forest Mills Mall	Albany	NY
Leasing Assistant	Home Office	Leasing	Owings Mills	MD
Maintenance Associate	Field	Bay Walk Mall	Baltimore	MD
Marketing Assistant	Home Office	Marketing	Owings Mills	MD
Marketing Coordinator	Field	Northview Mall	Wilmington	DE
Marketing Director	Field	Oak Springs Mall	Hartford	CT
Office Administrator	Field	Westland Park Square	Concord	NH
Paralegal	Home Office	Legal Services	Owings Mills	MD
Property Manager	Field	Portland Centre	Portland	ME
Research Assistant	Home Office	Research	Owings Mills	MD
Safety & Security Associate	Field	Bay Walk Mall	Baltimore	MD
Staff Accountant	Home Office	Accounting	Owings Mills	MD

6. On the File menu, select Web Page Preview. Your Web browser opens and displays the worksheet as a Web page (see Figure 3.49).
7. Close the browser, and then close *Job Openings.xls* without saving changes.

After finishing Exercises 6–8, you may test your skills by completing Apply It! Guided Activity 4, Adding Charts and a Comment to a College Budget Worksheet.

Procedure Summary

Use AutoFilter to Filter a List

1. Select any cell in the list.
2. On the **Data** menu, point to **Filter** and select **AutoFilter**. . . . . .Alt + D, F, F
3. Click the filter arrow above the column you want to filter, and select the desired filter option.
4. On the **Data** menu, point to **Filter**, and select **AutoFilter** to turn off the feature. . . . . .Alt + D, F, F

Enter a Formula

1. Select the cell to contain the formula.
2. Type = (equal sign) to begin the formula.
3. Type the remainder of the formula, using values, cell references, and arithmetic operators as desired.
4. Press Enter.

Create an Absolute Reference in a Formula

1. After entering the cell reference to the cell, press F4.
2. Type the remainder of the formula.
3. Press Enter.

Enter a Function Manually

1. Select the cell to contain the function.
2. Type = (equal sign) and the function name, such as SUM.
3. Type an opening parenthesis, enter the arguments, and type the closing parenthesis.
4. Press Enter.

Enter a Function Using a Dialog Box

1. Select the cell to contain the function.
2. Click **Insert Function** button on the Formula Bar.
   OR
   On the **Insert** menu, select **Function** .Alt + I, F
3. Select the desired category and function.
4. Click OK.
5. Enter the function arguments.
6. Click OK.

Create a Workbook From a Template

1. On the **File** menu, select **New** . . . Alt + F, N
2. Click the General Templates link in the New Workbook task pane.
3. Click the Spreadsheet Solutions tab.
4. Select the template.
5. Click OK.

Create a Chart

1. Select the data you want to chart.
2. Click the **Chart Wizard** button .
   OR
   On the **Insert** menu, select **Chart**. . . . . Alt + I, H
3. In Step 1 of 4, select the chart type and sub-type.
4. In Step 2 of 4, select the chart data options.
5. In Step 3 of 4, make the various title, legend, and label selections.
6. In Step 4 of 4, select *As new sheet* or *As object in* to place the object on a new sheet or embed it within the worksheet.
7. Click **Finish**.

Format a Chart

1. Select the portion of the chart you want to modify.
2. Select the desired command on the **Format** menu . . . . .Alt + O, E
3. Make the desired changes in the dialog box.
4. Click OK.

Modify the Content of a Chart

1. Select any part of the chart.
2. On the **Chart** menu, select **Chart Type** to change the chart type . . Alt + C, ↓, Y
   OR
   Select **Source Data** to modify the data or data series . . . . S
   Select **Chart Options** to modify the titles, axes, gridlines, legend, labels, or to add a data table I
   Select **Location** to change the chart location L
   Select **Add Data** to add data to the chart . . . . A
   Select **Add Trendline** to add a trendline to the chart . . . . R
3. Make desired selections in the dialog box and click OK.

Insert and Position Clip Art

1. On the **Insert** menu, point to **Picture** and select **Clip Art**. . . . . Alt + I, P, C
2. Type your search text into the *Search text* box.
3. In the search results, click the image to insert it into the file.
4. Drag the graphic to the desired position and drag a handle to resize it, if necessary.

Insert a Picture From a File

1. On the **Insert** menu, point to **Picture** and select **From File** . . . . Alt + I, P, F
2. In the Insert Picture dialog box, navigate to the location of your picture file.
3. Click the picture file and click **Insert** .Alt + S
4. Drag the graphic to the desired position and drag a handle to resize it, if necessary.

Create and Modify a Graphic

1. Click the **Drawing** button to display the Drawing toolbar.
   OR
   On the **View** menu, point to **Toolbars** and select **Drawing** . . . . Alt + V, T
2. Select a shape or an AutoShape from the Drawing toolbar.
3. Click in the worksheet to insert the graphic.
4. With the graphic selected, open the **Format** menu and select **AutoShape** . . . .Alt + O, O
5. In the Format AutoShape dialog box, make the desired changes and click OK.

Insert a Comment

1. Select the cell in which you want to add a comment.
2. On the **Insert** menu, select **Comment** . . . . Alt + I, M
3. Type the comment text.
4. Click outside the comment to close the comment box.

Edit a Comment

1. Select the cell that contains the comment you want to edit.
2. On the **Insert** menu, select **Edit Comment** . . . . .Alt + I, E
3. Edit the comment, as desired.
4. Click outside the comment to close the comment box.

Save a Worksheet as a Web Page

1. On the **File** menu, select **Save as Web Page** . . . . Alt + F, G
2. In the **Save in** list, navigate to the folder where you wish to save your file. . . .Alt + I
3. Type a name for the file in the **File name** box . . . . Alt + N
4. Click **Change Title** to add a new title . . . . Alt + C
5. Click **Save** . . . . Alt + S
6. Open the **File** menu and select **Web Page Preview** to preview the Web page . . . . Alt + F, B

Lesson Review and Exercises

Summary Checklist

- ☑ Can you use the AutoFilter feature to view a subset of data in an Excel list?
- ☑ Can you use relative or absolute cell references in your formulas?
- ☑ Can you verify the accuracy of formulas by checking the formula results displayed in cells?
- ☑ Can you use the proper structure when entering functions?
- ☑ Can you create a new worksheet based on a template provided with Excel?
- ☑ Can you insert a chart that best reflects the type of data used in your worksheet?
- ☑ Can you insert a graphic object in your worksheet and then move or resize it?
- ☑ Can you add helpful comments to a worksheet that is shared online with others?
- ☑ Can you preview a worksheet and check it for accuracy before converting it to a Web page?

Key Terms

- absolute reference (p. 232)
- arguments (p. 235)
- AutoFilter (p. 226)
- discussion comments (p. 252)
- discussion server (p. 252)
- fill handle (p. 232)
- filter (p. 226)
- Formula Bar (p. 229)
- function (p. 235)
- relative reference (p. 232)
- syntax (p. 235)
- thread (p. 253)
- wizard (p. 246)

APPLY IT! Guided Activities

1. Filter Data in an Expenses Worksheet

After creating and formatting an expense worksheet that summarizes your business expenses for the month of March, you need to use the AutoFilter feature to view subsets of the data. Follow these steps:

a. Open *Expense Summary2.xls*. Click cell A4. On the Data menu, point to Filter and select AutoFilter.

b. Click the filter arrow in the *Expense Type* column, and select *Travel*. Click the filter arrow in the *Client* column, and select *Providence Publishing*. On the Data menu, point to Filter, and select Show All to redisplay the entire list.

c. Click the filter arrow in the *Expense* column, and select *(Custom)*. Click the *equals* down arrow and select *is greater than*. Press Tab, type 150, and click OK. Excel displays only those records in which the expense is more than $150.

d. On the Data menu, point to Filter and select AutoFilter to turn off the AutoFilter. Close the workbook without saving it.

2. Enter Formulas and Functions in a Payroll Worksheet

As the owner of a sporting goods store, you need to enter formulas and functions in a payroll worksheet to calculate gross pay, deductions, net pay, and percent of total hours. Follow these steps:

a. Open *Payroll2.xls*. Save the workbook as *xxx-Payroll2.xls*.

b. In cell D7, type =B7*C7 and press Enter. Click cell E7. Click in the Formula Bar, type =D7*0.25, and click the Enter button. In the Formula Bar, change 0.25 to 0.28, and press Enter.

c. In cell F7, enter the formula =D7-E7. Select D7:F7, and use the fill handle to copy the formulas down to row 12.

d. Click cell C13, click the AutoSum button, and press Enter to accept the suggested range. Click cell D13. Type =SUM(and drag to select the range D7:D12. Press Enter. ***Note:*** Excel automatically enters totals in cells D13:F13.

e. Click G7, type =C7/C13, and press F4. Copy G7 to G8:G12.

f. Click G13, type =G7+G8+G9+G10+G11+G12, and press Enter. Select the range G7:G13, and then apply the percent format with two decimal places.

g. Click G3. Type =DATE(2003,7,25) and press Enter.

h. In cell B15, enter the formula =MIN(B7:B12). In cell B16, type the formula =MAX(B7:B12). **(See Figure 3.50.)**

i. Save the workbook and then close it.

Figure 3.50 Entering formulas and functions in a payroll worksheet

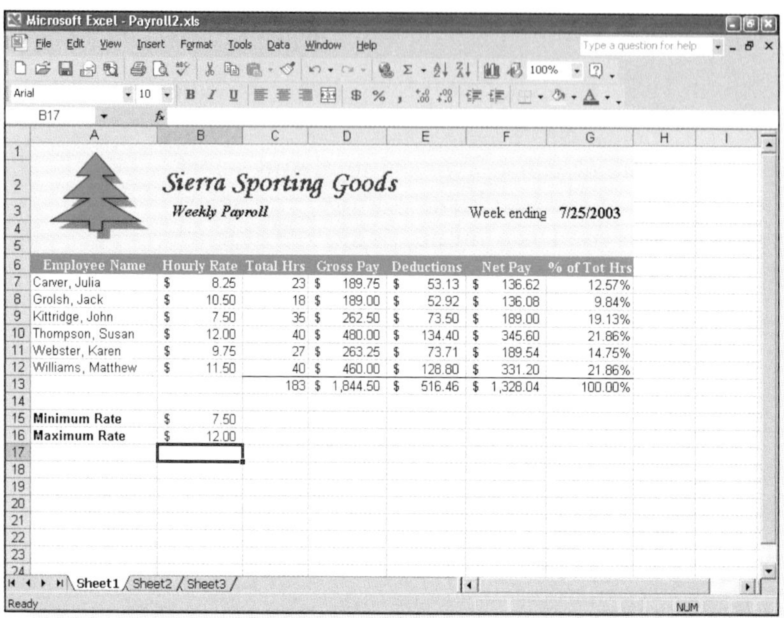

Employee Name	Hourly Rate	Total Hrs	Gross Pay	Deductions	Net Pay	% of Tot Hrs
Carver, Julia	$ 8.25	23	$ 189.75	$ 53.13	$ 136.62	12.57%
Grolsh, Jack	$ 10.50	18	$ 189.00	$ 52.92	$ 136.08	9.84%
Kittridge, John	$ 7.50	35	$ 262.50	$ 73.50	$ 189.00	19.13%
Thompson, Susan	$ 12.00	40	$ 480.00	$ 134.40	$ 345.60	21.86%
Webster, Karen	$ 9.75	27	$ 263.25	$ 73.71	$ 189.54	14.75%
Williams, Matthew	$ 11.50	40	$ 460.00	$ 128.80	$ 331.20	21.86%
		183	$ 1,844.50	$ 516.46	$ 1,328.04	100.00%
Minimum Rate	$ 7.50					
Maximum Rate	$ 12.00					

3. Use a Template to Calculate Loan Payments

You are preparing to buy a car and would like to use Excel to determine the monthly payment schedule for a car loan. Excel provides a loan amortization template that you can use. Follow these steps:

a. On the File menu, select New. In the New Workbook task pane, click the General Templates link. On the Spreadsheet Solutions tab, double-click the *Loan Amortization* template.

b. Enter the following data: D6:18000; D7: 7; D8: 4; D9: 12; D10: 9/1/03. Leave cell D11 blank. Scroll down the worksheet and notice that the last payment will be made in September, 2007.

c. You remember that the trade-in value of your car is about $6,000. Therefore, you only need to borrow $12,000 for the new car. Also, you found a dealer who is willing to offer you a financing rate of 5.5%. To determine how this will affect the loan payment, type 12000 in cell D6, and 5.5% in cell D7. Notice that the scheduled monthly payment drops from $431.03 to $279.08.

d. Save the workbook as *xxx-Loan Amortization.xls* and close it.

4. Adding Charts and a Comment to a College Budget Worksheet

After entering the expense and income data into your college budget worksheet, you decide to add charts to illustrate the data. You also want to enter a comment, add a graphic, and save and preview the worksheet as a Web page. Follow these steps:

a. Open *College Budget3.xls*. Save it as *xxx-College Budget3.xls*.

b. Select A5:B14, and click the Chart Wizard button. Select the *Pie* chart type, and then select the *Pie with a 3-D visual effect* chart sub-type. Advance to the step 3 of 4 (Chart Options) without making changes. On the Titles tab, type Expenses as the chart title. Click Finish.

c. Move and resize the Expenses pie chart so that it displays in the range D1:H12. Click the legend and press Ctrl + 1 to open the Format Legend dialog box. Change the font size to 8.

d. Select A18:B21, and click the Chart Wizard button. Select the *Pie* chart type, and the *Pie with a 3-D visual effect* chart sub-type. Advance through the wizard and type Income as the chart title. Click Finish.

e. Move and resize the Income pie chart so that it displays in the range D13:H22. Right-click the *Income* chart title and select Format Chart Title on the shortcut menu. Change the font size to 12. Click outside the chart.

f. Click cell B5. On the Insert menu, select Comment. Type the following text: This amount is an estimate, based on a 5% increase over the previous year. Click outside the comment box. Right-click cell B5 and select Edit Comment. Change 5% to 10% and click outside the comment.

g. Click the Drawing button in the Standard toolbar. Click the Arrow button on the Drawing toolbar, and then draw an arrow from the Loans amount in cell B21 to the Loans pie slice in the Income chart. Right-click the arrow and select Format AutoShape. Change the Color to blue and the Weight to 2 pt. Click cell A1. Click the Drawing button to close the Drawing toolbar. Save the workbook.

h. On the File menu, select Save as Web Page. Click the *Save in* down arrow and navigate to the *Lesson 3* subfolder within your *Unit 2* folder. The name *xxx-College Budget3.htm* displays in the *File name* box. Click Save. On the File menu, select Web Page Preview **(see Figure 3.51)**. Close the browser, and then close the workbook.

Figure 3.51 The college budget worksheet displayed as a Web page

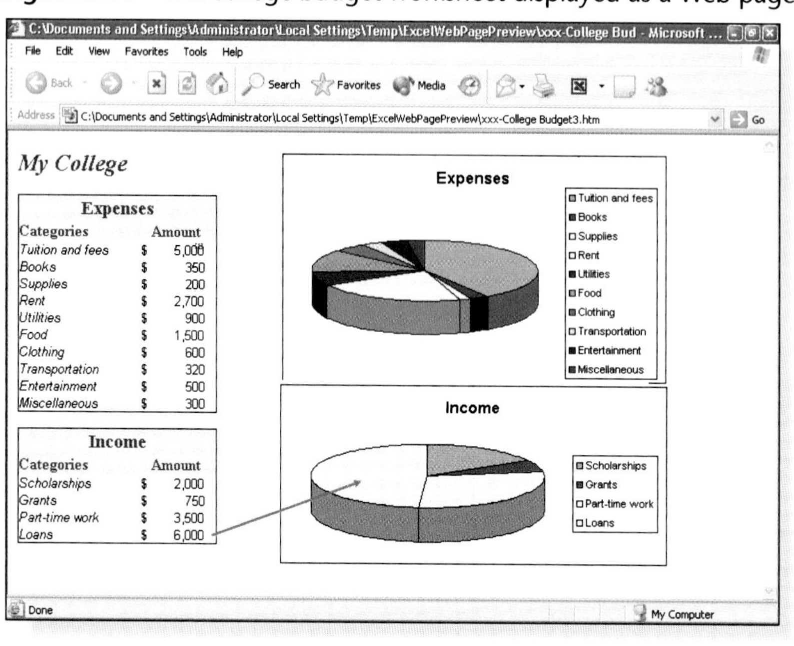

Do It Yourself

1. Controlling the Order of Operations in Formulas

In this exercise, you will enter formulas that use simple arithmetic operators. The formulas use parentheses to control the order of operations—remember that in Excel, all calculations within parentheses are calculated first. After verifying that your results are correct, you'll copy the formulas and then edit them to remove the parentheses so that you can see the changes in the formula results.

a. Open a new workbook. Type the formulas shown in **Table 3.3**. Ensure that your formula results match the results reflected in the last column of the table.

Table 3.3

Cell	Formula	Result
B4	= 1+2*(3+4)-5	10
B5	= (1+2)*5+4-7	12
B6	= 2+3*(8-4)/2+7	15
B7	= (2+3)*((5-4)+18/2)	50

b. Copy the formulas in cells B4:B7 to the range C4:C7.

c. Edit the formulas in the range C4:C7 by removing all parentheses in the formulas (don't make any other adjustments to the formulas). Notice that the results of the formulas in column C vary from the formula results in column B.

d. Save the workbook as *xxx-Order of Operations.xls* and then close the workbook.

2. Add Formulas and Functions to a Sales Worksheet

As the owner of a chain of gift shops, you need to analyze the sales figures for the first quarter to determine if your stores are performing according to expectations. To do so, you will enter formulas and functions in your sales worksheet. ***Note:*** Step f of this activity involves the use of a discussion server. If you are not set up to use the Web Discussions feature, skip step e and f. Follow these steps:

a. Open *Sales Data2.xls*. Save it as *xxx-Sales Data2.xls*.

b. Click cell F5 and enter a formula that will display the percentage of total sales for the Flagstaff location. Remember to include an absolute reference in the formula.

c. Copy the formula in cell F5 to F6:F8. Use any method to enter a SUM function in cell F9. Use the Format Cells dialog box to format the data in column F as percentages with one decimal place.

d. In B10:E10, enter functions that compute the average of the data in rows 5–8. (Don't calculate the average for the % of Total data.)

e. In B12:B13, enter functions that calculate the maximum and minimum sales amounts for the data in the range B5:D8 **(see Figure 3.52)**. Save the workbook.

f. Using the Web Discussions feature, enter discussion text directed to your Flagstaff store manager asking if sales projections look brighter for the second quarter. ***Note:*** Ask another student to reply to your message so that you may create a threaded discussion. When you are finished, close all files and close the Web Discussions toolbar.

Figure 3.52 Adding formulas and functions to the sales worksheet

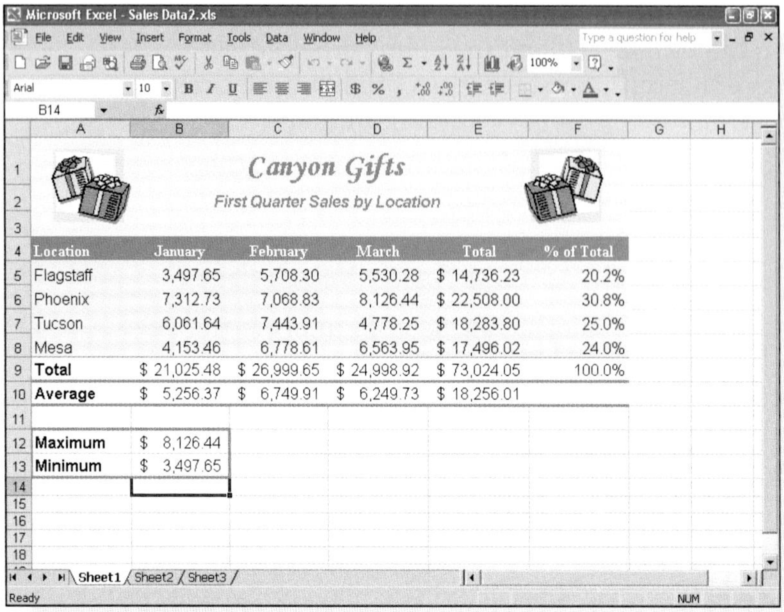

Microsoft Excel - Sales Data2.xls

	A	B	C	D	E	F
1		Canyon Gifts				
2		First Quarter Sales by Location				
3						
4	Location	January	February	March	Total	% of Total
5	Flagstaff	3,497.65	5,708.30	5,530.28	$ 14,736.23	20.2%
6	Phoenix	7,312.73	7,068.83	8,126.44	$ 22,508.00	30.8%
7	Tucson	6,061.64	7,443.91	4,778.25	$ 18,283.80	25.0%
8	Mesa	4,153.46	6,778.61	6,563.95	$ 17,496.02	24.0%
9	Total	$ 21,025.48	$ 26,999.65	$ 24,998.92	$ 73,024.05	100.0%
10	Average	$ 5,256.37	$ 6,749.91	$ 6,249.73	$ 18,256.01	
11						
12	Maximum	$ 8,126.44				
13	Minimum	$ 3,497.65				

3. Format a 3-D Chart and Save the Chart as a Web Page

You need to prepare and format a 3-D bar chart based on your company's payroll worksheet. You want to create a chart that summarizes the gross pay by employee for the week and then save the chart as a separate sheet. You will make several changes to the format to enhance the appearance of the chart. Finally, you will save the chart as a Web page. Follow these steps:

a. Open *Payroll3.xls*. Save the workbook as *xxx-Payroll3.xls*.

b. Create a clustered bar chart with a 3-D visual effect based on the ranges A7:A12 and D7:D12. Type the chart title Gross Pay for Week of 7/25/2003. Place the chart as a new sheet.

c. Choose a new font for the chart title and change font size to 18. Delete the chart legend.

d. Right-click one of the bars and select Format Data Series. On the Patterns tab, click Fill Effects. On the Gradient tab, select the *Preset* option in the *Colors* section. Select *Ocean* on the *Preset colors* list.

e. Right-click the Walls area of the chart, select Format Walls, and select a light yellow pattern.

f. With the chart selected, select Chart Options on the Chart menu. On the Data Labels tab of the Chart Options dialog box, add data labels representing the value of each bar. Right-click a label, select Format Data Labels, and apply boldface to the data labels. Drag each label inside the right edge of each bar.

g. Save the workbook. Then, save only the chart (not the entire workbook) as a Web page with the name *xxx-Payroll3.htm*. Preview *xxx-Payroll3.htm* in your Web browser. Close the browser and the workbook.

Challenge Yourself

Use a Trendline to Predict Patterns of Data

As a financial analyst, you are responsible for preparing reports that predict future sales revenues based on existing data. You will create a column chart that includes first quarter sales data for one store location. You will then add a trendline to the chart that will project sales estimates for the second quarter. ***Note:*** If you need help with this activity, type trend analysis in the *Ask a Question* box and read the related topics.

- Open *Sales Projections.xls*. Save the workbook as *xxx-Sales Projections.xls*.
- Create a clustered column chart as an object in your worksheet based on the range A6:B11. Add an appropriate chart title. Type the following as the *Category (X) axis* title: *Includes projections for the second quarter.
- Move and resize the chart so that it displays beside the sales data in the worksheet. Delete the chart legend. Adjust the font size and style of the various titles as needed.
- Select the data series by clicking one of the bars in the chart. On the Chart menu, select Add Trendline. In the Add Trendline dialog box, select *Linear* in the *Trend/Regression type* section and click OK to add the trendline to the chart. Right-click the trendline and click Format Trendline. Change the trendline's color to yellow and applying a thicker line weight. Change the color of the data series (the bars) to green.
- Save and close the workbook.

Lesson 4

Manipulating Cells, Worksheets and Workbooks

Lesson Exercise Objectives

After completing this lesson, you'll be able to do the following tasks:

1. Rearrange cells in a worksheet
2. Rearrange worksheets in a workbook
3. Share data among worksheets
4. Create hyperlinks in a workbook

Key Terms

- 3-D cell reference (p. 279)
- hyperlink (p. 281)
- merge (p. 270)
- split (p. 270)
- tab scrolling buttons (p. 274)
- tab split bar (p. 274)

Microsoft Office Specialist Activities

EX2002: 1.1, 3.7, 4.1, 4.2, 4.3, 7.2

Lesson Case Study

In this lesson, you will play the role of Leasing and Sales Representative for Jackson-Drake Properties, Inc., a mall management company located in Owings Mills, Maryland. Keep the following information in mind as you work through the lesson exercises.

- **Job responsibilities and goals.** One of your responsibilities is to maintain worksheets that summarize leasing and sales information. Your goal is to update and reorganize workbooks so that they can be used by others.
- **The project.** You will edit multiple-sheet workbooks. The edited workbooks must be accurate and well organized.
- **The challenge ahead.** You need to manipulate cells in a worksheet, rearrange sheets in a workbook, add 3-D cell references, and insert a hyperlink.

Microsoft Office Specialist EX2002 1.1

Excel

Exercise 1 Overview: Rearrange Cells in a Worksheet

You have already learned how to insert or delete entire rows or columns in a worksheet. Sometimes you may only need to insert or delete one cell or a range of cells. You can insert new, blank cells or delete existing cells anywhere in the worksheet. If you delete cells, you delete the contents of the cells as well as the actual cells themselves. Excel automatically updates formulas in other cells that are affected by the insertion or deletion procedure.

Excel provides a Merge and Center button on the Formatting toolbar that enables you to center data (such as a title) over multiple columns. Type your data within the cell furthest to the left in the range, select the range of cells, and click the Merge and Center button. The **merge** combines the selected cells into a single cell and centers the data within the larger cell. At this point, you can change the alignment of text in the cell or **split** the merged cell back into individual cells. To split the cell, select the merged cell and click the Merge and Center button.

Type: merge and center

Step Through It™

Exercise 1A: Insert and delete cells

1. Open *Leasing Info.xls.* Save the workbook as *xxx-Leasing Info.xls.*
2. While entering data, you realize that you skipped over the figures for *Park Place Mall.*
3. Select F9:H9. On the Insert menu, select Cells. The Insert dialog box displays (see Figure 4.1).

Figure 4.1 Preparing to insert cells

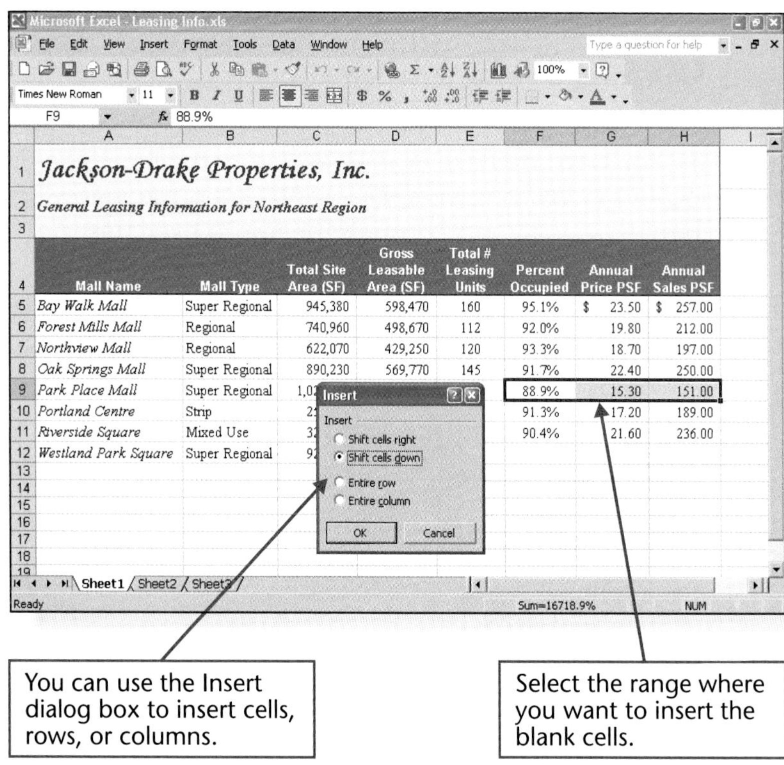

Figure 4.2 Inserting cells in a worksheet

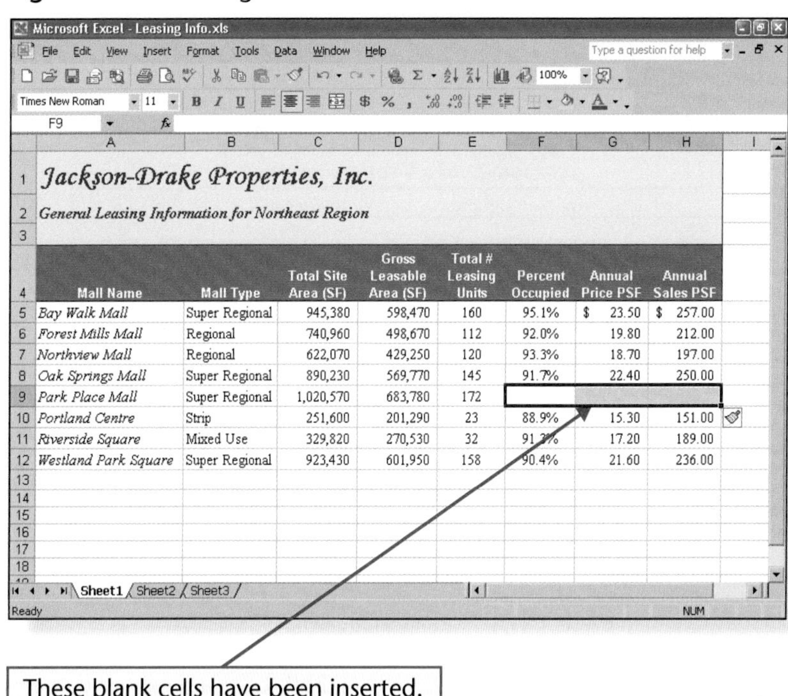

	Mall Name	Mall Type	Total Site Area (SF)	Gross Leasable Area (SF)	Total # Leasing Units	Percent Occupied	Annual Price PSF	Annual Sales PSF
5	Bay Walk Mall	Super Regional	945,380	598,470	160	95.1%	$ 23.50	$ 257.00
6	Forest Mills Mall	Regional	740,960	498,670	112	92.0%	19.80	212.00
7	Northview Mall	Regional	622,070	429,250	120	93.3%	18.70	197.00
8	Oak Springs Mall	Super Regional	890,230	569,770	145	91.7%	22.40	250.00
9	Park Place Mall	Super Regional	1,020,570	683,780	172			
10	Portland Centre	Strip	251,600	201,290	23	88.9%	15.30	151.00
11	Riverside Square	Mixed Use	329,820	270,530	32	91.3%	17.20	189.00
12	Westland Park Square	Super Regional	923,430	601,950	158	90.4%	21.60	236.00

4. Select *Shift cells down* and click OK to move the data in F9:H9 down one row. Three blank cells are inserted in the selected range (see Figure 4.2).

5. In the blank cells F9:H9, enter the following values for Park Place Mall: 96.5, 25.7, and 283.

Figure 4.3 Deleting cells in a worksheet

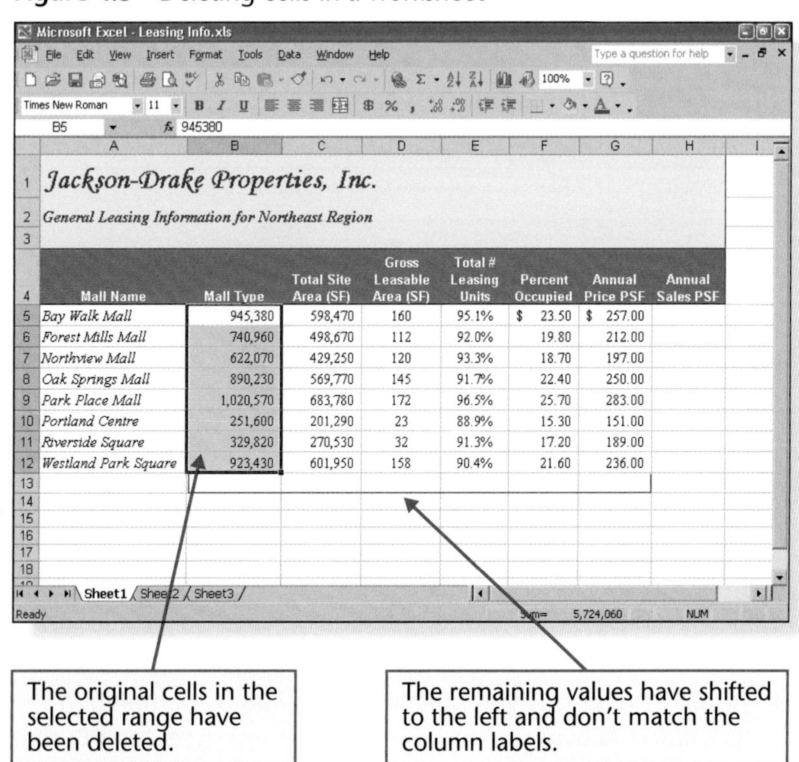

	Mall Name	Mall Type	Total Site Area (SF)	Gross Leasable Area (SF)	Total # Leasing Units	Percent Occupied	Annual Price PSF	Annual Sales PSF
5	Bay Walk Mall	945,380	598,470	160	95.1%	$ 23.50	$ 257.00	
6	Forest Mills Mall	740,960	498,670	112	92.0%	19.80	212.00	
7	Northview Mall	622,070	429,250	120	93.3%	18.70	197.00	
8	Oak Springs Mall	890,230	569,770	145	91.7%	22.40	250.00	
9	Park Place Mall	1,020,570	683,780	172	96.5%	25.70	283.00	
10	Portland Centre	251,600	201,290	23	88.9%	15.30	151.00	
11	Riverside Square	329,820	270,530	32	91.3%	17.20	189.00	
12	Westland Park Square	923,430	601,950	158	90.4%	21.60	236.00	

6. Select the range B5:B12.

7. On the Edit menu, select Delete. In the Delete dialog box, select *Shift cells left* and click OK. All of the values to the right of column B shift to the left (see Figure 4.3).

8. Click Undo on the Standard toolbar to restore the deleted cells.

Excel

Step Through It™

Exercise 1B: Merge and split cells

1. Select the range A1:H1.
2. Click the Merge and Center button on the Formatting toolbar to center the company name within the selected range.
3. Select the range A2:H2 and click Merge and Center (see Figure 4.4).

Figure 4.4 Centering titles over multiple columns

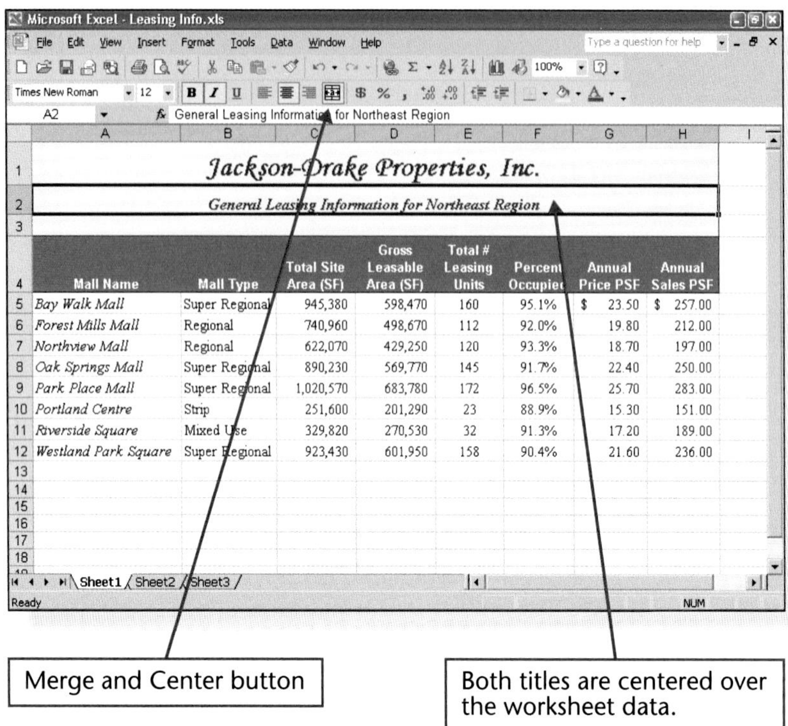

Mall Name	Mall Type	Total Site Area (SF)	Gross Leasable Area (SF)	Total # Leasing Units	Percent Occupied	Annual Price PSF	Annual Sales PSF
Bay Walk Mall	Super Regional	945,380	598,470	160	95.1%	$ 23.50	$ 257.00
Forest Mills Mall	Regional	740,960	498,670	112	92.0%	19.80	212.00
Northview Mall	Regional	622,070	429,250	120	93.3%	18.70	197.00
Oak Springs Mall	Super Regional	890,230	569,770	145	91.7%	22.40	250.00
Park Place Mall	Super Regional	1,020,570	683,780	172	96.5%	25.70	283.00
Portland Centre	Strip	251,600	201,290	23	88.9%	15.30	151.00
Riverside Square	Mixed Use	329,820	270,530	32	91.3%	17.20	189.00
Westland Park Square	Super Regional	923,430	601,950	158	90.4%	21.60	236.00

4. Select cell A1, which now spans columns A through H. Click Merge and Center to split the single cell into multiple cells (see Figure 4.5).
5. Click Undo to restore the merged cell.
6. Save the workbook and close the workbook.

Figure 4.5 Splitting a merged cell

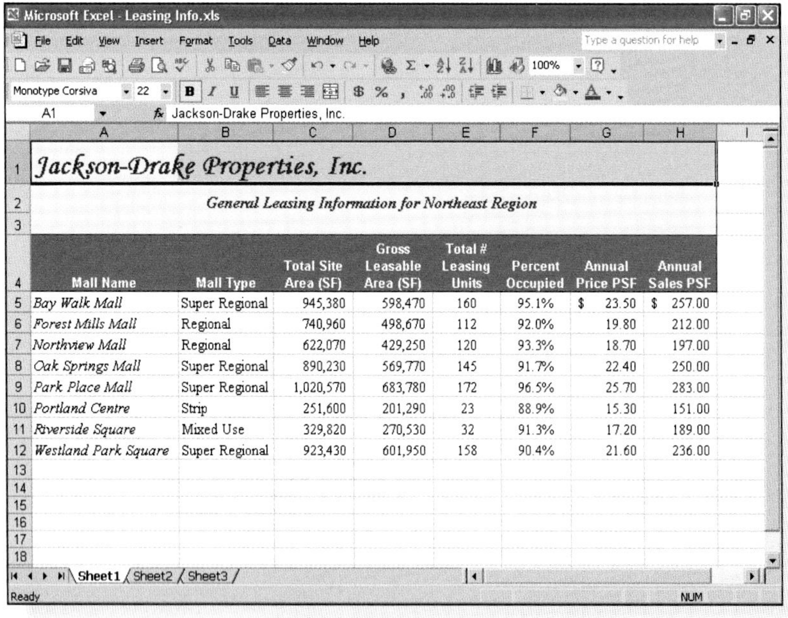

Mall Name	Mall Type	Total Site Area (SF)	Gross Leasable Area (SF)	Total # Leasing Units	Percent Occupied	Annual Price PSF	Annual Sales PSF
Bay Walk Mall	Super Regional	945,380	598,470	160	95.1%	$ 23.50	$ 257.00
Forest Mills Mall	Regional	740,960	498,670	112	92.0%	19.80	212.00
Northview Mall	Regional	622,070	429,250	120	93.3%	18.70	197.00
Oak Springs Mall	Super Regional	890,230	569,770	145	91.7%	22.40	250.00
Park Place Mall	Super Regional	1,020,570	683,780	172	96.5%	25.70	283.00
Portland Centre	Strip	251,600	201,290	23	88.9%	15.30	151.00
Riverside Square	Mixed Use	329,820	270,530	32	91.3%	17.20	189.00
Westland Park Square	Super Regional	923,430	601,950	158	90.4%	21.60	236.00

APPLY IT! After finishing Exercise 1, you may test your skills by completing Apply It! Guided Activity 1, Modify a Budget Worksheet for a Business.

Technology@School

Excelling in Class

In this unit, you've learned how useful Excel can be in preparing financial documents. In fact, spreadsheet software is one of the most popular types of business software, and not just for financial applications. Spreadsheets make working with all kinds of numerical data easier. Architects and engineers use spreadsheets in designing structures. Scientists and historians use them in research. People in all kinds of occupations use spreadsheet software, including legal assistants, urban planners, nutritionists, and economists.

Excel can be useful to you in almost any class. Here are two ways Excel can help you in math (for more examples, see the table below):

- You can enter formulas in a workbook and then use the formulas to solve algebra problems.
- You can make estimates, record the actual amounts, and graph your results.

CRITICAL THINKING

1. Create a workbook that could help you in school or in your personal life.
2. With a partner, poll 20 people on a question of your choice. You might give them a list of cookies and ask which they like best. Create a workbook to record responses. Then use Excel to analyze them. For example, what percentages of those surveyed liked the different kinds of cookies? Make a chart or graph of your results and explain them to the class.

Table 4.1

Class	How You Can Use Excel
Math	You can use the Convert function to convert numbers from one measurement system to another (miles to kilometers, for example).
Science	Excel can be very helpful in science experiments and projects. Entering data in a workbook, arranging the data, performing calculations, and making charts of the results can help you see relationships and interpretthe data more easily.
Physical Education/ Health	How much farther and faster can you run? How many more sit-ups can you do? You can use Excel to track and chart your progress in physical fitness.
Social Studies	A worksheet or chart makes a good illustration for a report. You can create a worksheet or chart in Excel, format it attractively, and import it into a social studies paper you create in Word.

Microsoft Office Specialist
EX2002 4.1, 4.2

Exercise 2 Overview:
Rearrange Worksheets in a Workbook

Excel enables you to use multiple worksheets within a single workbook to store related information. A new workbook contains three worksheets by default; however, you can insert or delete worksheets in a workbook as needed. After you set up one worksheet using a desired layout and format, you can easily create a copy of that worksheet within the workbook.

You can easily switch between worksheets in a workbook by clicking the desired sheet tab. In a new workbook, the worksheets are named *Sheet1*, *Sheet2*, and *Sheet3* by default. You can assign your own descriptive name to any worksheet, and you can also reposition worksheets in a workbook.

If a workbook contains many worksheets and some tabs are hidden, you can drag the **tab split bar** to the right to display them. In addition, you can use the **tab scrolling buttons** (to the left of the sheet tabs) to move to the first, previous, next, or last worksheet in a workbook. You can also assign various colors to the tabs.

Type: worksheet tabs

Figure 4.6 You can move or copy worksheets using the Move or Copy dialog box

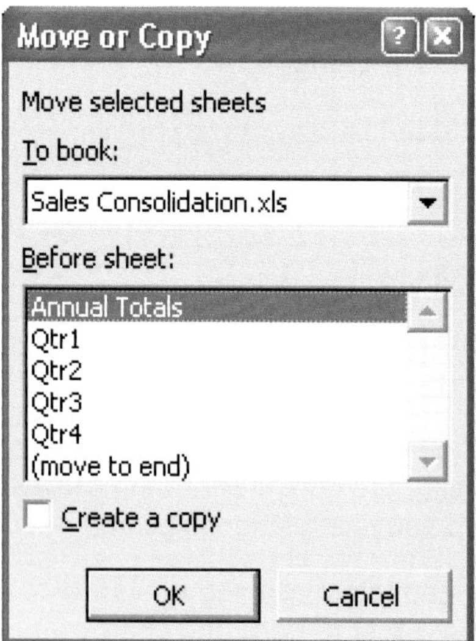

Figure 4.7 Multiple worksheets within a workbook

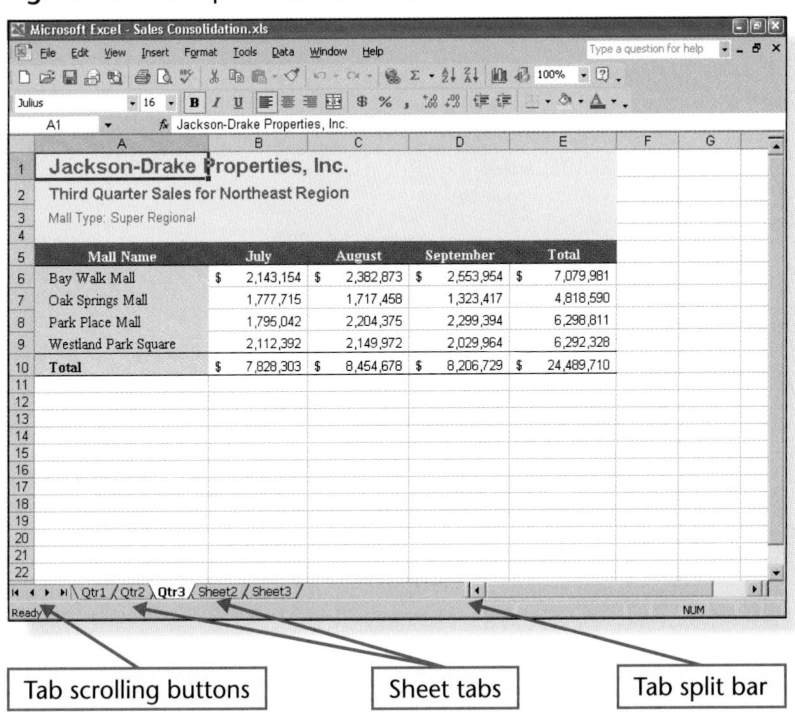

Step Through It™

Exercise 2A: Insert and delete worksheets

1. Open *Sales Consolidation.xls*. Save the workbook as *xxx-Sales Consolidation.xls*. This workbook contains sales data for the first three quarters of the year.

2. Click the *Qtr2* sheet tab at the bottom of the workbook. Click the *Qtr3* sheet tab. Notice that all three worksheets share the same layout and format even though they contain different data (see Figure 4.7).

Excel

Figure 4.8 Copying the *Qtr3* worksheet

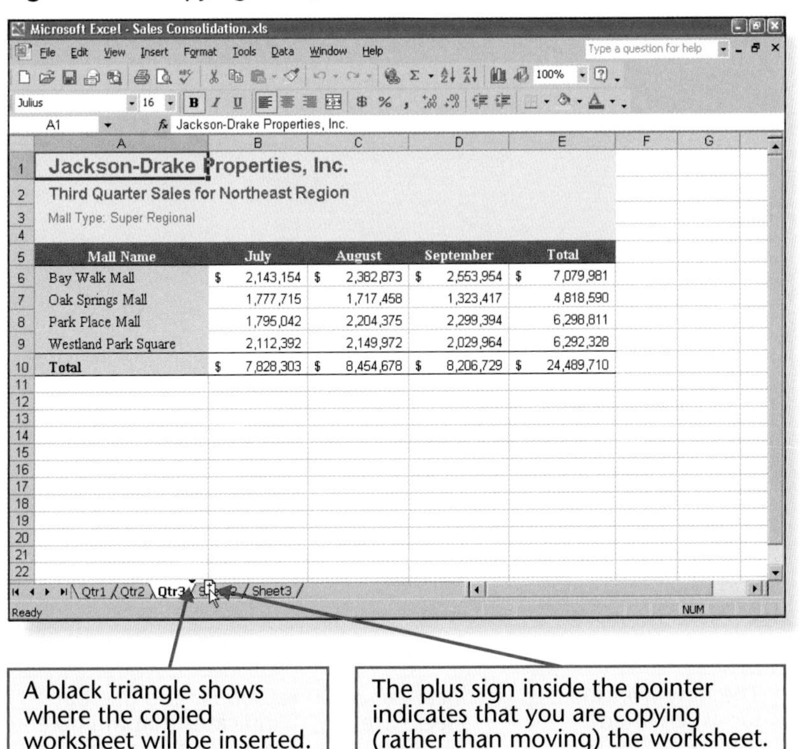

3. Position the pointer over the active *Qtr3* sheet tab, hold Ctrl, and drag the pointer slightly to the right so the black triangle points between the *Qtr3* and *Sheet2* tabs (see Figure 4.8).

4. Release the mouse button and release Ctrl. Excel inserts a copy of the *Qtr3* worksheet, which is named *Qtr3 (2)*.

5) Right-click the *Qtr3 (2)* sheet tab and select Rename on the shortcut menu.

6) Type Qtr4 and press Enter to rename the worksheet.

7) On the *Qtr4* worksheet, select *Third* in cell A2 and type Fourth. Edit cells B5:D5 to read October, November, and December.

8) Delete the contents of the range B6:D9 (see Figure 4.9).

Figure 4.9 Editing the *Qtr4* worksheet

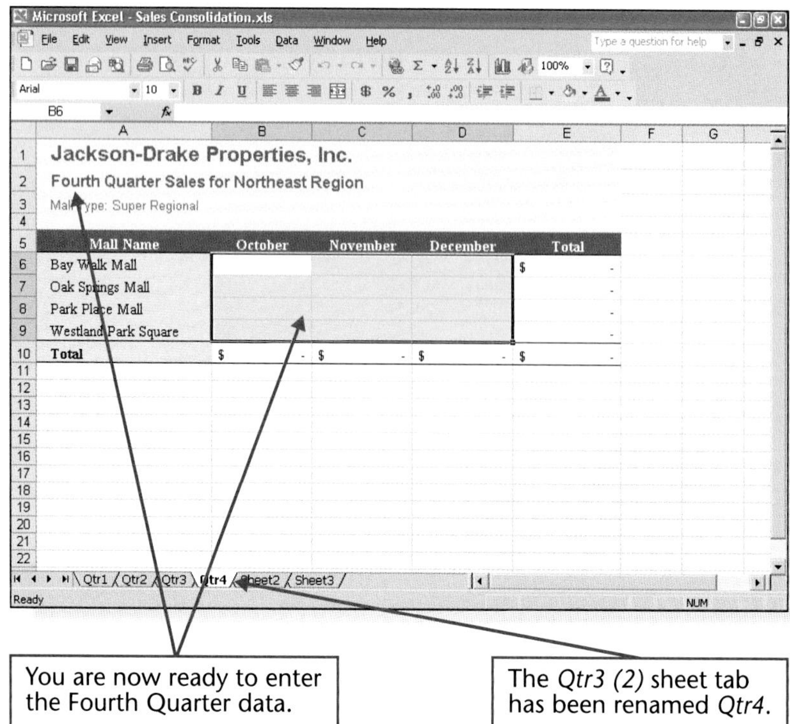

You are now ready to enter the Fourth Quarter data.
The *Qtr3 (2)* sheet tab has been renamed *Qtr4*.

9) Click the *Qtr1* sheet tab. On the Insert menu, select Worksheet. A new worksheet named *Sheet1* is inserted to the left of the *Qtr1* worksheet.

10) Double-click the *Sheet1* sheet tab and type Annual Totals.

11) Click the *Sheet2* sheet tab, hold Ctrl, and click the *Sheet3* sheet tab (see Figure 4.10).

12) On the Edit menu, select Delete Sheet. Both the selected sheets are deleted.

13) Save the workbook.

Figure 4.10 Inserting and deleting worksheets

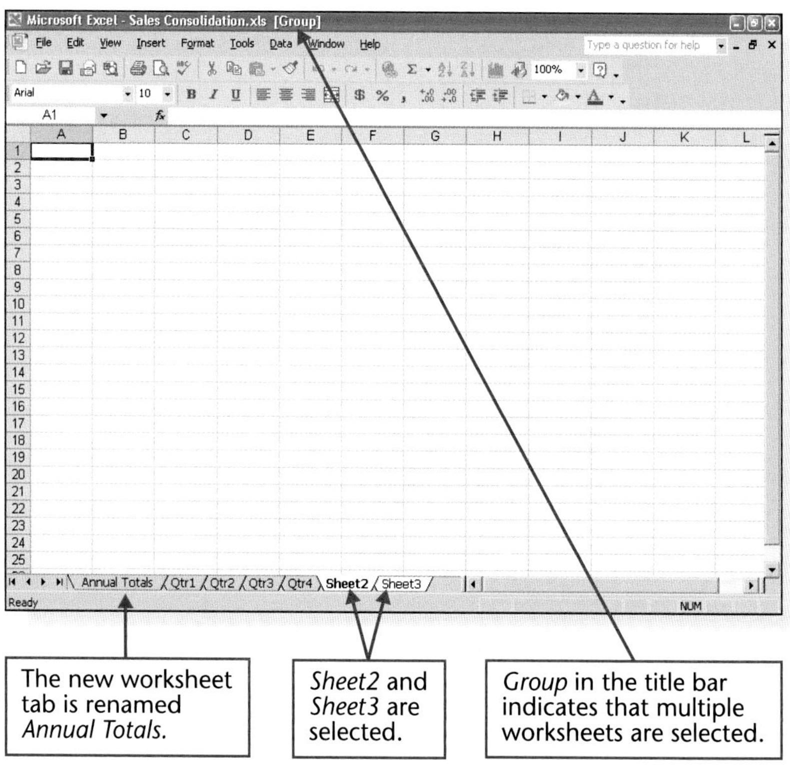

Figure 4.11 The Move or Copy dialog box

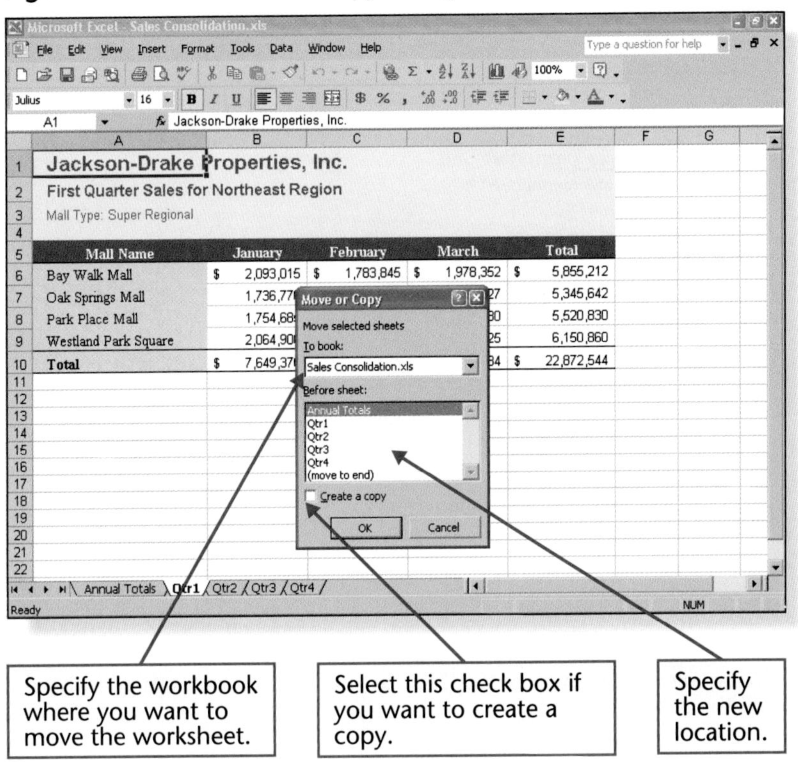

Specify the workbook where you want to move the worksheet.
Select this check box if you want to create a copy.
Specify the new location.

Step Through It™

Exercise 2B: Reposition worksheets in a workbook

1. Right-click the *Qtr1* sheet tab and select *Move or Copy*. The Move or Copy dialog box displays (see Figure 4.11).

2. In the *Before sheet* list, select *(move to end)* and click OK. The *Qtr1* sheet displays after the *Qtr4* sheet.

Figure 4.12 Repositioning the sheet tabs

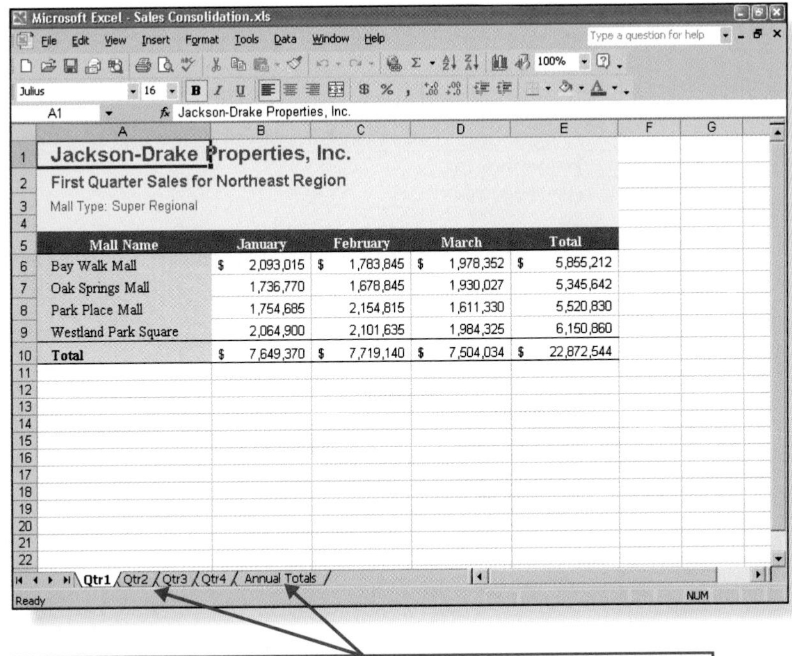

The five sheet tabs should appear in numerical order with the *Annual Totals* tab at the end.

3. Click the *Annual Totals* sheet tab and drag it to the right of the *Qtr1* sheet.

4. Drag the *Qtr1* sheet tab to the left of the *Qtr2* sheet (see Figure 4.12).

Excel

Step Through It™

Exercise 2C: Format worksheet tabs

1. With the *Qtr1* sheet tab selected, hold Shift and click the *Qtr4* sheet tab. Sheets *Qtr1* through *Qtr4* are selected.

2. Right-click any of the selected sheet tabs and select Tab Color. The Format Tab Color dialog box displays (see Figure 4.13).

Figure 4.13 The Format Tab Color dialog box

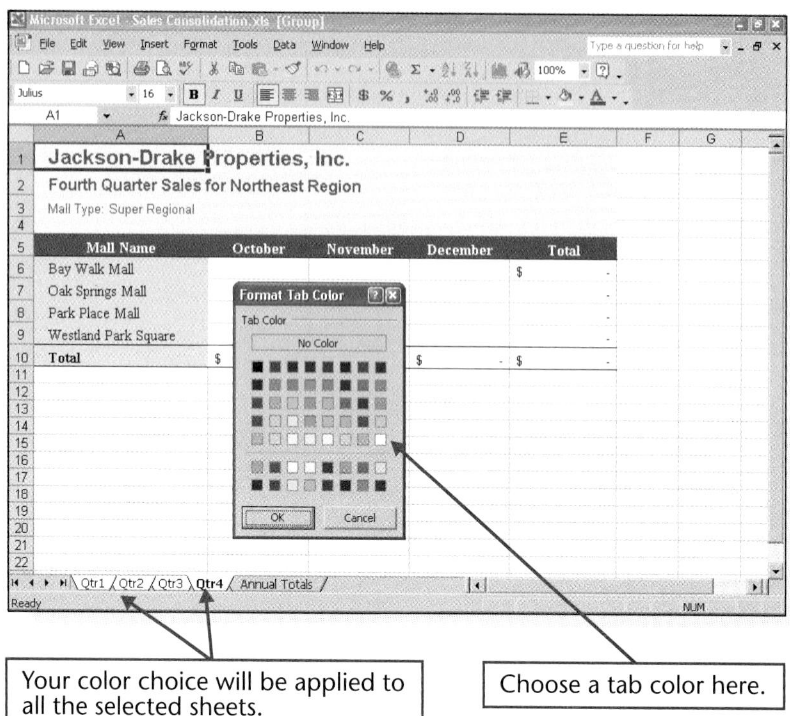

Your color choice will be applied to all the selected sheets.
Choose a tab color here.

3. Select a purple color box on the palette and click OK.

4. Apply yellow to the *Annual Totals* sheet tab. Click the *Qtr1* sheet tab (see Figure 4.14).

5. Save and close the workbook.

Figure 4.14 Applying colors to the sheet tabs

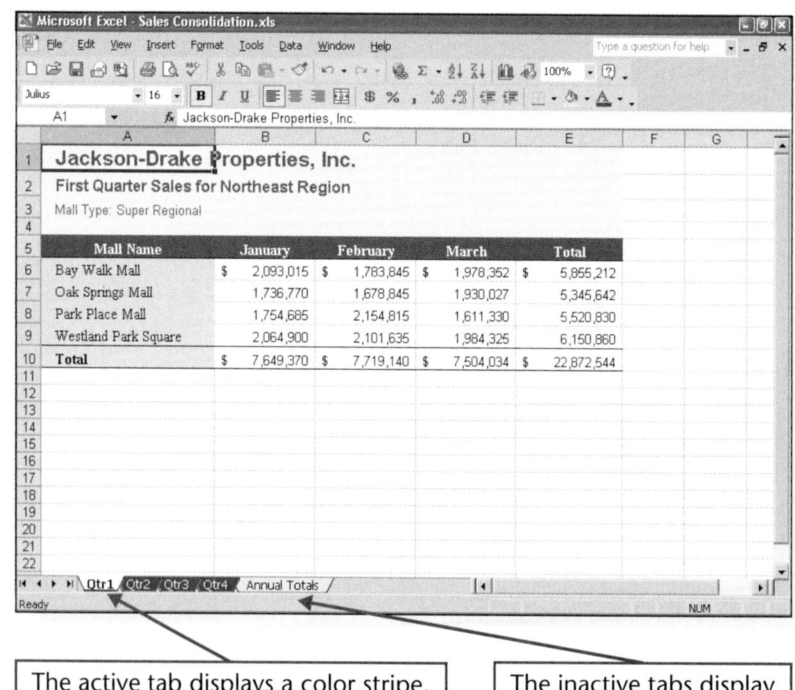

The active tab displays a color stripe.
The inactive tabs display colored backgrounds.

Exercise 3 Overview: Share Data Among Worksheets

In a workbook that contains multiple worksheets, you can link data among the worksheets using a **3-D cell reference**. To ensure that Excel knows which worksheet contains the cell you want to reference, you must include a sheet reference in the formula. If you want to refer to cell E6 in another worksheet named *Qtr1*, for example, you would type Qtr1!E6 in the formula. Use an exclamation mark (!) to separate the sheet name from the cell reference.

In a workbook that includes worksheets with the same structure, you can use the SUM function to total the same cell in multiple worksheets. To do so, type a colon (:) between the range of sheet names, followed by the exclamation mark and cell reference within the function, such as =SUM(Qtr1:Qtr4!E6).

Excel

Figure 4.15 A formula with 3-D references

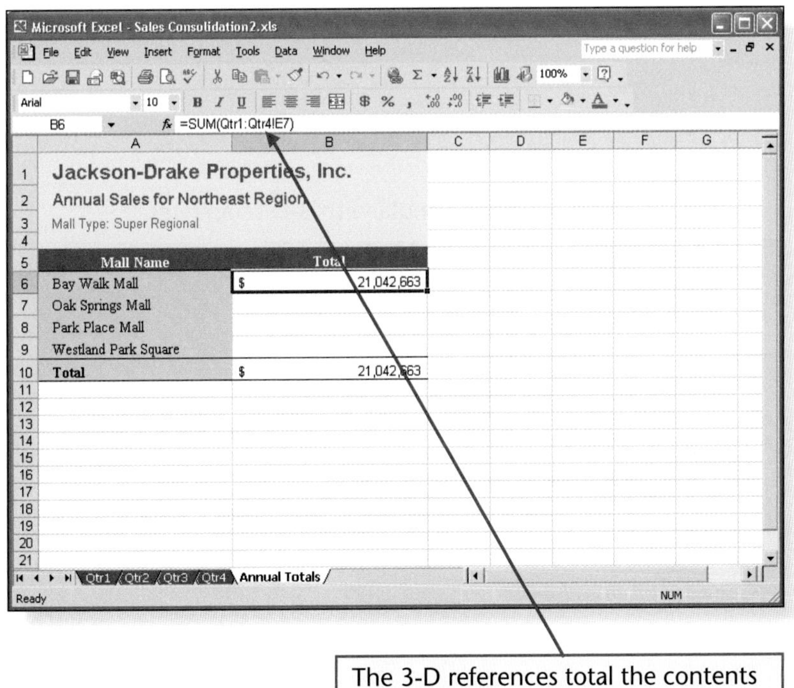

The 3-D references total the contents of cell E7 within the four other sheets in the workbook.

Step Through It™

Exercise 3: Use 3-D cell references in formulas

1. Open *Sales Consolidation2.xls*. Save the workbook as *xxx-Sales Consolidation2.xls*.

2. Click the *Annual Totals* sheet tab.

3. Click cell B6. Type =SUM(and click the *Qtr1* sheet tab. Hold Shift and click the *Qtr4* sheet tab.

4. Click cell E6 (see Figure 4.16), and press Enter. This formula sums all of the totals in cell E6 resulting in a grand total for *Bay Walk Mall*.

Figure 4.16 Entering formulas with 3-D references

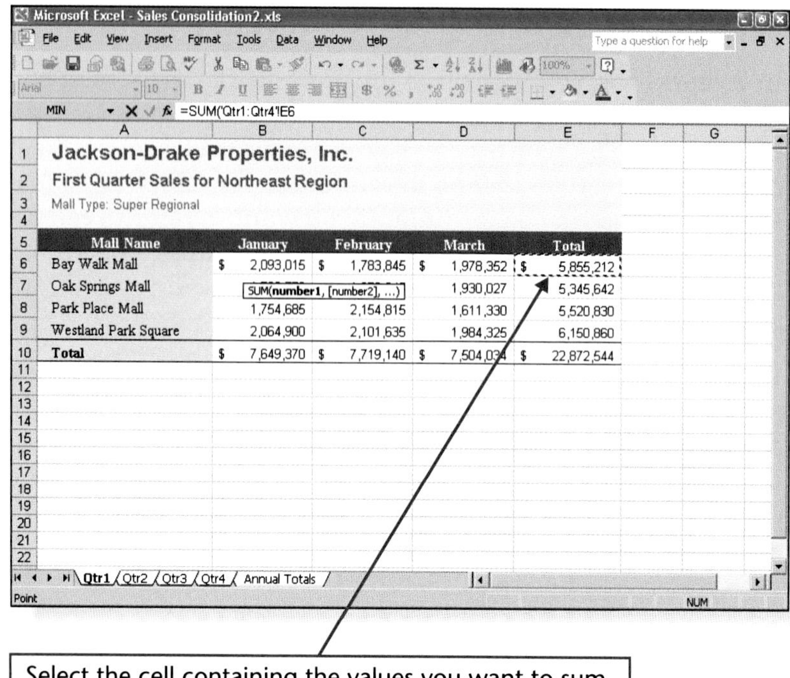

Select the cell containing the values you want to sum.

5. In cell B7, type the formula =SUM(Qtr1:Qtr4!E7) and press Enter.

6. Click cell B7, and drag the fill handle down to cell B9 to copy the formula. The remaining results display in the worksheet (see Figure 4.17).

7. Press Ctrl + Home.

Figure 4.17 Copying the formula with 3-D references

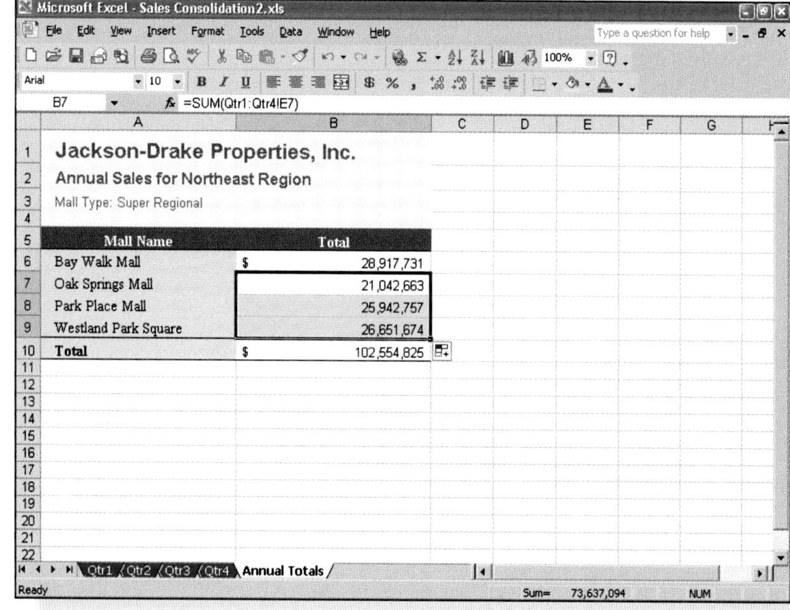

Excel

Figure 4.18 Previewing ranges in multiple worksheets

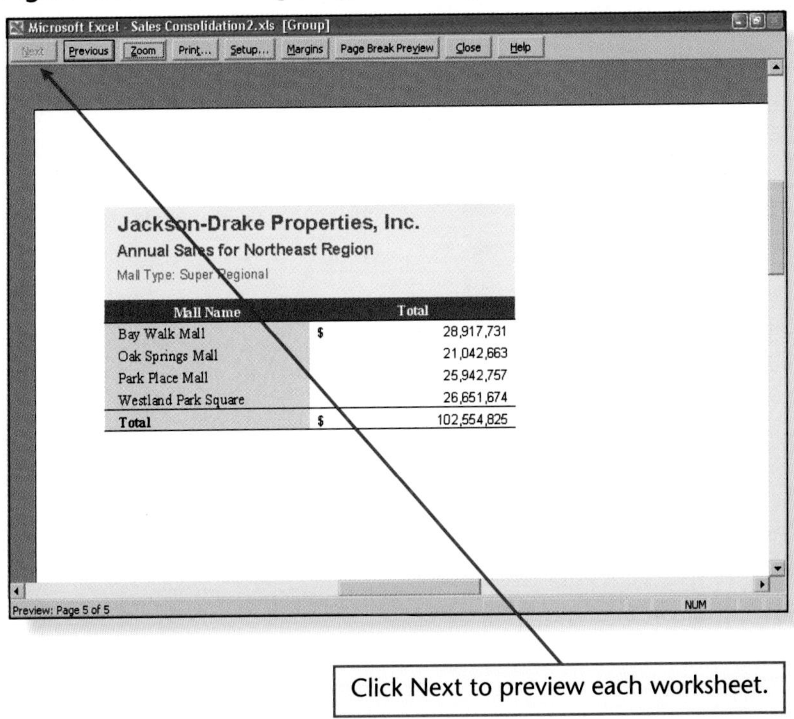

8. Select all the sheet tabs in the workbook. Click the Print Preview button. Click Next to preview all five pages (see Figure 4.18). Each worksheet in the workbook displays on a separate page.
9. Close the Print Preview window and print the workbook. Click the *Qtr1* sheet tab to deselect the worksheets.
10. Save the workbook.

Excel

Exercise 4 Overview:
Create Hyperlinks in a Workbook

Microsoft Office Specialist EX2002 7.2

In an Excel workbook, you can insert a **hyperlink** that enables you to quickly jump to another workbook, an Office file, an e-mail address, or an Internet or intranet site. You can designate text or a picture to use as the hyperlink.

When you point to a hyperlink, the pointer changes to a hand. Click the hyperlink to move to the location you specified when you inserted the hyperlink.

You can edit the hyperlink at any time to change the link information, such as the hyperlink text or the link destination. You also can remove the hyperlink.

Quick Tip

Refer to Appendix A for more information on using Internet Explorer and accessing Web sites.

Step Through It™

Exercise 4: Insert and edit hyperlinks

1. In the *xxx-Sales Consolidation2.xls* workbook, click cell A14 on the *Qtr1* worksheet.

2. Type the text Leasing Info in the cell and press Enter.

3. Select cell A14 and click the Insert Hyperlink button on the Standard toolbar. The Insert Hyperlink dialog box displays (see Figure 4.19).

Figure 4.19 The Insert Hyperlink dialog box

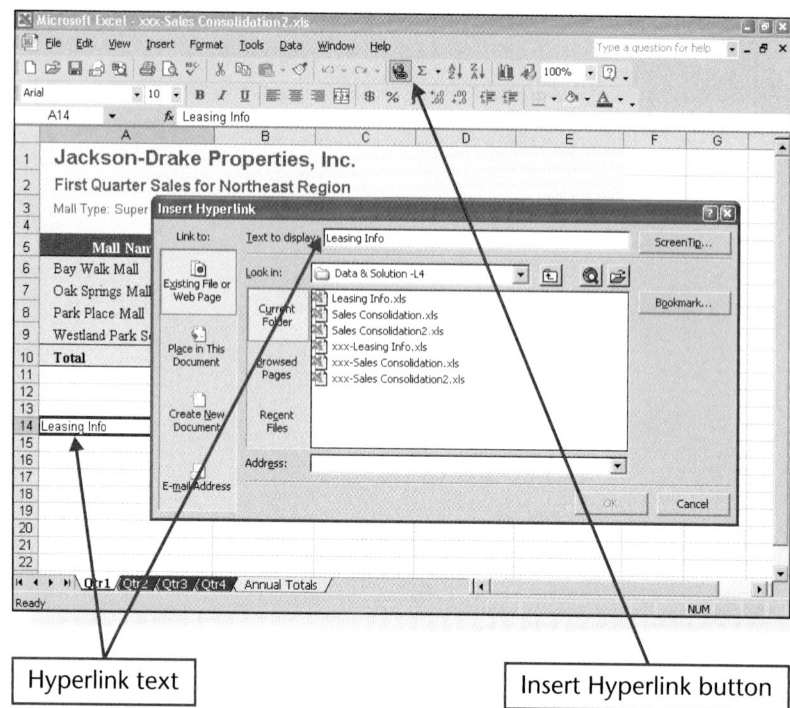

4. In the *Link to* section, click *Existing File or Web Page*. In the *Look in* list, navigate to the *Lesson 4* subfolder within your *Unit 2* folder, if necessary.

5. With the Current Folder button selected to the left of the files list, select *xxx-Leasing Info.xls* and click OK. The text in cell A14 changes color and is underlined, indicating that it is a hyperlink.

6. Point to the hyperlink. The pointer becomes a hand and a ScreenTip displays the path to the destination file (see Figure 4.20).

Figure 4.20 The hyperlink and its ScreenTip

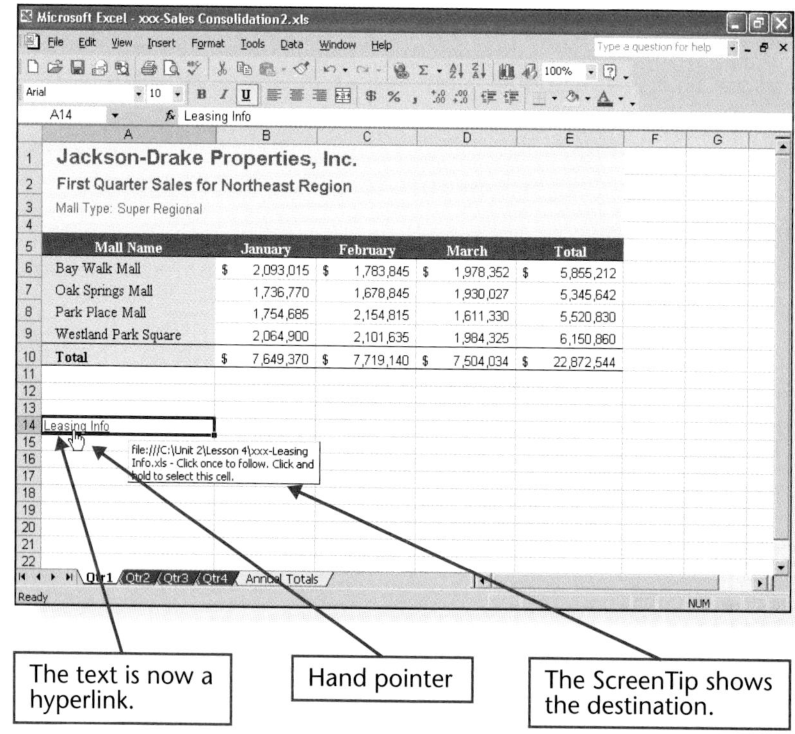

The text is now a hyperlink.
Hand pointer
The ScreenTip shows the destination.

Excel

Figure 4.21 Editing a hyperlink

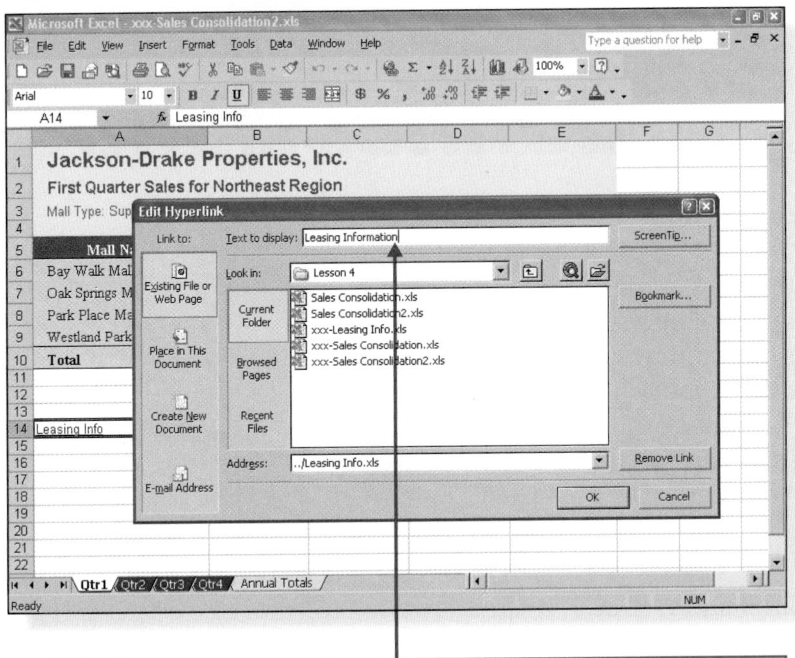

Edit the hyperlink text in the dialog box. The new text will display in the worksheet.

7. Click the hyperlink. The *xxx-Leasing Info.xls* workbook opens and the Web toolbar displays beneath the Formatting toolbar.

8. Close *xxx-Leasing Info.xls*, and then close the Web toolbar. Right-click the hyperlink in cell A14 and select Edit Hyperlink. The Edit Hyperlink dialog box displays.

9. In the *Text to display* box, edit the text by changing *Info* to **Information** (see Figure 4.21). Click OK.

Figure 4.22 Removing the link

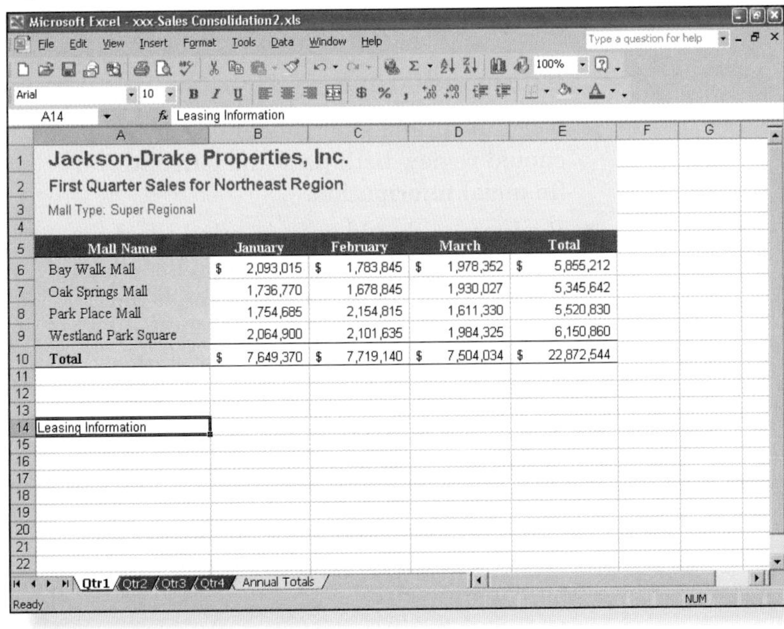

	Mall Name	January	February	March	Total
1	Jackson-Drake Properties, Inc.				
2	First Quarter Sales for Northeast Region				
3	Mall Type: Super Regional				
6	Bay Walk Mall	$ 2,093,015	$ 1,783,845	$ 1,978,352	$ 5,855,212
7	Oak Springs Mall	1,736,770	1,678,845	1,930,027	5,345,642
8	Park Place Mall	1,754,685	2,154,815	1,611,330	5,520,830
9	Westland Park Square	2,064,900	2,101,635	1,984,325	6,150,860
10	Total	$ 7,649,370	$ 7,719,140	$ 7,504,034	$ 22,872,544
14	Leasing Information				

10. Select Hyperlink on the Insert menu. In the Edit Hyperlink dialog box, click the Remove Link button. The formatting is removed from the hyperlink (see Figure 4.22), and the link no longer works.

11. Click Undo to restore the hyperlink.

12. Save your changes and close the workbook.

APPLY IT! After finishing Exercises 2–4, you may test your skills by completing Apply It! Guided Activity 2, Consolidate Data in a Real Estate Worksheet.

Business Connections

Maintaining a Budget

Planning, preparing, and maintaining a budget is essential to your financial success. Creating a personal budget can help you to review your income and expenses, compare them to your expectations, and make any necessary adjustments in your spending habits. Likewise, a business must also effectively manage individual budgets throughout the organization since they are tied to the financial success of the company.

Expecting the Unexpected

- When preparing a budget, you must always plan for necessary spending. In addition, you should allow for the occasional expenses that you might not expect, such as car repairs and medical or dental bills.
- One way to address unexpected expenses is to ensure that you maintain a reasonable amount of money in savings that can be easily converted to cash.

Creating a Budget

- When planning a personal budget, you should review both past and current financial information.
- Businesses should keep in mind their historical data on revenues and expenses, the past and current market conditions, the state of the economy, and the demand for their company's products or services.
- Using a budget can help you establish and maintain a good credit history. Why is this important? If you don't use credit responsibly, you may find it extremely difficult to buy a home in the future, obtain a car loan, or even to be accepted for a credit card.
- Your payment history is usually reflected in your credit report. Several agencies keep credit reports that reflect your payment history over the last seven years.

Applying for Credit

- When you apply for a new loan or credit card, banks and credit card companies first check your credit history to see if you meet their qualifications.
- A history of late payments will almost ensure that you will be turned down.
- It is important for businesses to establish and maintain a good credit history so that they can maintain good relations with their vendors.

Using Financial Templates

- Search online for Excel budget templates and many other templates and resources that are useful for planning your business and personal finances. Check the Microsoft Template Gallery, where you'll find a variety of helpful templates. Microsoft frequently adds new templates that are available for you to download.

Account Summary

ACCOUNT NUMBER
880DF00293-93044

POSTING DATE	TRANSACTION DESCRIPTION	TRANSACTION AMOUNT	NEW BALANCE
05/04	Primary Savings balance forward		754.39
05/06	Deposit branch transfer	310.11	1064.50
05/07	Withdrawal at ATM #78394	-60.00	1004.50
05/09	Club draft	-125.00	879.50
05/10	Check 001935 Harvest Market	-33.14	846.36
05/11	Withdrawal transfer to Share 01	-200.00	646.36
05/13	Deposit	250.00	896.36
05/14	Withdrawal at ATM #78394	-60.00	836.36
05/04	Check 001936 Gas and Electric	-96.03	740.33

CRITICAL THINKING

1. **Establishing a Credit History** Why is it important to maintain a good credit history? What problems might you encounter if you don't establish and use credit responsibly?

2. **Tracking Expenses** Which Excel templates can you use to help track your budget? What other sources provide help information or tools to help you create and maintain a budget?

Procedure Summary

Insert Cells

1. Select the cells where you want to insert the blank cells.
2. On the **Insert** menu, select **Cells** . . Alt + I, E
3. Select **Shift cells right** or **Shift cells down** . . . . I OR D
4. Click OK.

Delete Cells

1. Select the cells you want to delete.
2. On the **Edit** menu, select **Delete**. . . . . Alt + E, D
3. Select **Shift cells left** or **Shift cells up**. . . . . L OR U
4. Click OK.

Merge Cells

1. Type text in the cell which is the furthest to the left within the range you want to merge.
2. Select the cells you want to merge.
3. Click the **Merge and Center** button on the Formatting toolbar.

Split a Merged Cell

1. Select the merged cell you want to split.
2. Click the **Merge and Center** button on the Formatting toolbar.

Insert a New Worksheet

1. Select the worksheet tab that you want to appear after the new worksheet.
2. On the **Insert** menu, select **Worksheet** . . . . Alt + I, W

OR

1. Right-click the worksheet tab that you want to appear after the new worksheet.
2. Select Insert on the shortcut menu.
3. In the Insert dialog box (General tab), select the Worksheet icon and click OK.

Delete a Worksheet

1. Select the worksheet tab that you want to delete.
2. On the **Edit** menu, select **Delete Sheet**. . . . . Alt + E, L

OR

1. Right-click the worksheet tab that you want to delete.
2. Click Delete on the shortcut menu.

Move a Worksheet in a Workbook

1. Select the sheet tab you want to move.
2. On the **Edit** menu, select **Move or Copy Sheet**. . . . . .Alt + E, M
3. In the **Before sheet** list, select the desired position and click OK . . . . Alt + B

OR

1. Right-click the sheet tab you want to move.
2. Select Move or Copy on the shortcut menu.
3. In the **Before sheet** list, select the desired position and click OK . . . . . . Alt + B

OR

Drag the sheet tab to the desired position.

Copy a Worksheet in a Workbook

1. Select the sheet tab you want to copy.
2. On the **Edit** menu, select **Move or Copy Sheet**. . . . . Alt + E, M
3. In the **Before sheet** list, select the desired position . . . . Alt + B
4. Select **Create a copy** and click OK . Alt + C

OR

1. Right-click the sheet tab you want to copy.
2. Select **Move or Copy** on the shortcut menu.
3. In the **Before sheet** list, select the desired position. . . . . Alt + B
4. Select the **Create a copy** check box . . . . Alt + C
5. Click OK.

OR

Hold the Ctrl key and drag a copy of the sheet tab to the desired position.

Format a Worksheet Tab

1. Select the sheet tab that you want to format.
2. On the **Format** menu, point to **Sheet** and select **Tab Color** . . Alt + O, H, T
3. Click the desired color and click OK.

OR

1. Right-click the sheet tab you want to format.
2. Select **Tab Color** on the shortcut menu.
3. Click the desired color and click OK.

Use 3-D References to Total a Cell in Multiple Sheets

1. Type =SUM(in your totals worksheet.
2. Click the sheet tab containing the first cell you want to reference.
3. Hold Shift, click the cell, and then click each sheet tab containing the same cell reference.
4. Press Enter.

Insert a Hyperlink to Another Workbook

1. Type the text (or insert the graphic) that you want to use as the hyperlink.
2. Select the cell containing the text (or the graphic).
3. Click the **Insert Hyperlink** button on the Standard toolbar.

   OR

   On the **Insert** menu, select **Hyperlink** . . . . .Alt + I, I OR Ctrl + K
4. In the *Link to* section, select **Existing File or Web Page** . . . . Alt + X
5. In the **Look in** box, navigate to the file you want to link to and click OK. . . . . . . Alt + L
6. Click the hyperlink to jump to the specified file.

Edit a Hyperlink

1. Click and hold to select the hyperlink.
2. On the **Insert** menu, select **Hyperlink** . . . . .Alt + I, I OR Ctrl + K
3. Edit the hyperlink as desired and click OK.

OR

1. Right-click the hyperlink and select Edit Hyperlink on the shortcut menu.
2. Edit the hyperlink as desired and click OK.

Remove a Hyperlink

1. Click and hold to select the hyperlink.
2. On the **Insert** menu, select **Hyperlink** . . . . .Alt + I, I OR Ctrl + K
3. Click **Remove Link** and click OK . . . Alt + R

OR

Right-click the hyperlink and select **Remove Hyperlink** on the shortcut menu.

Lesson Review and Exercises

Summary Checklist

- ☑ Can you insert blank cells?
- ☑ Can you delete selected cells?
- ☑ Can you merge cells to center text over a worksheet?
- ☑ Can you split a merged cell?
- ☑ Can you insert a new worksheet into a workbook?
- ☑ Can you delete an existing worksheet?
- ☑ Can you move or copy worksheets within a workbook by dragging the sheet tabs?
- ☑ Can you format worksheet tabs by changing their color?
- ☑ Can you create a formula with 3-D references by either typing the formula or pointing in the worksheet?
- ☑ Can you insert a hyperlink that links to another workbook?
- ☑ Can you edit an existing hyperlink by changing the hyperlink text displayed in a cell?
- ☑ Can you remove a hyperlink so that the link no longer works?

Key Terms

- 3-D cell reference (p. 279)
- hyperlink (p. 281)
- merge (p. 270)
- split (p. 270)
- tab scrolling buttons (p. 274)
- tab split bar (p. 274)

APPLY IT! Guided Activities

1. Modify a Budget Worksheet for a Business

In this activity, you will work with a budget worksheet for a business that sells office products. Follow these steps:

a. Open *Budget.xls*. Save the workbook as *xxx-Budget.xls*.

b. Click cell F19. On the Insert menu, select Cells. Select *Shift cells down* and click OK.

c. Remove the fill color within cell F19 so that it appears white.

d. Select the range A16:F16. Right-click the selected range and select Delete on the shortcut menu. Select *Shift cells up* and click OK.

e. Select the range A1:F1 and click Merge and Center. Select A2:F2 and click Merge and Center.

f. Select cell A5 and click Merge and Center to split the merged cell. Repeat this operation in cell A13. Click cell A1 **(see Figure 4.23)**.

g. Save and close the workbook.

Figure 4.23 The modified budget worksheet

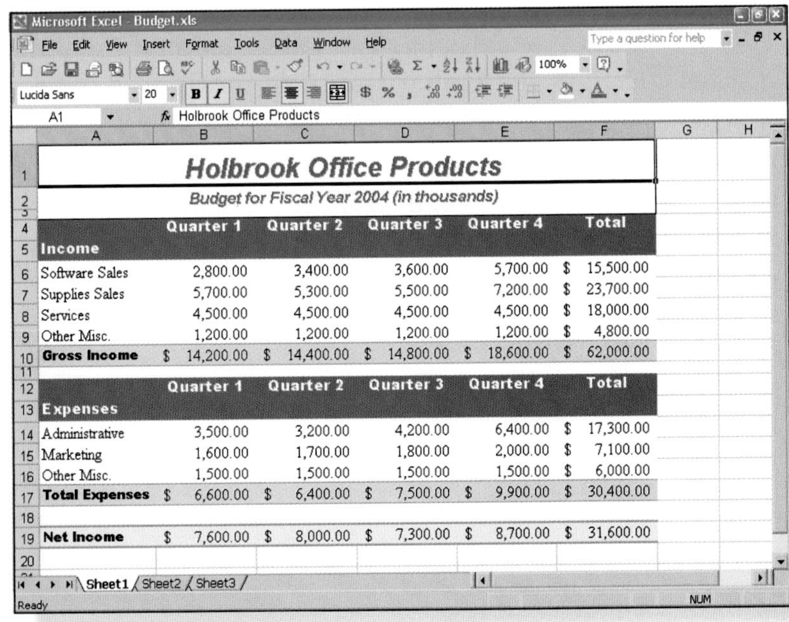

	Quarter 1	Quarter 2	Quarter 3	Quarter 4	Total
Holbrook Office Products					
Budget for Fiscal Year 2004 (in thousands)					
Income					
Software Sales	2,800.00	3,400.00	3,600.00	5,700.00	$ 15,500.00
Supplies Sales	5,700.00	5,300.00	5,500.00	7,200.00	$ 23,700.00
Services	4,500.00	4,500.00	4,500.00	4,500.00	$ 18,000.00
Other Misc.	1,200.00	1,200.00	1,200.00	1,200.00	$ 4,800.00
Gross Income	$ 14,200.00	$ 14,400.00	$ 14,800.00	$ 18,600.00	$ 62,000.00
	Quarter 1	**Quarter 2**	**Quarter 3**	**Quarter 4**	**Total**
Expenses					
Administrative	3,500.00	3,200.00	4,200.00	6,400.00	$ 17,300.00
Marketing	1,600.00	1,700.00	1,800.00	2,000.00	$ 7,100.00
Other Misc.	1,500.00	1,500.00	1,500.00	1,500.00	$ 6,000.00
Total Expenses	$ 6,600.00	$ 6,400.00	$ 7,500.00	$ 9,900.00	$ 30,400.00
Net Income	$ 7,600.00	$ 8,000.00	$ 7,300.00	$ 8,700.00	$ 31,600.00

Excel

2. Consolidate Data in a Real Estate Worksheet

You are an assistant to a real estate executive who has given you information on the number of new homes sold for the month of January.

You've already entered the January data into a worksheet. You now need to add worksheets to the workbook that you will update with sales data as it becomes available. You will also use 3-D references in formulas and insert a hyperlink. Follow these steps:

a. Open *Homes Sold.xls*. Save the workbook as *xxx-Homes Sold.xls*.

b. Delete the *Sheet2* and *Sheet3* worksheets.

c. Hold Ctrl and drag the January sheet tab to the right to make a copy of the worksheet. Right-click the *January (2)* sheet tab, click Rename, and type February as the new sheet name. Make a copy of the February worksheet and change the *February (2)* sheet name to March.

d. On the Insert menu, select Worksheet. Drag the *Sheet1* tab to the left of the *January* tab and change the name to Quarter1.

e. Click the *January* sheet tab and copy the range A1:G14. Click the *Quarter1* sheet tab, select cell A1, and paste the copied cells.

f. In the *Quarter1* worksheet, delete the data in B6:G14. In cell B6, enter the formula =SUM(January:March!B6).

g. Using the fill handle, copy the formula to C6:G6. Use the fill handle to copy B6:G6 down to B7:G14.

h. Right-click the *Quarter1* sheet tab and select Tab Color. Select a blue tab color and click OK. Click the January tab, hold the Shift key, and click the March tab. Apply the color pink to the three selected tabs.

i. Click the *Quarter1* sheet tab and select cell A17. On the Insert menu, select Hyperlink. Select *E-mail Address* in the *Link to* section. Type your own e-mail address (or any other e-mail address) in the *E-mail address* box, and click OK to create a hyperlink in the worksheet **(see Figure 4.24)**.

j. Save and close the workbook.

Figure 4.24 Consolidated data for the *Homes Sold* workbook

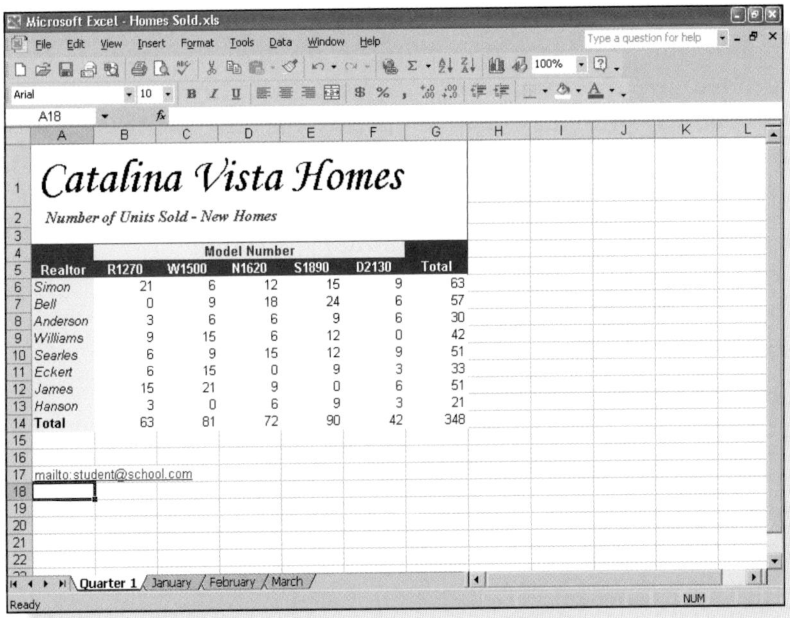

Microsoft Excel - Homes Sold.xls

Catalina Vista Homes

Number of Units Sold - New Homes

Realtor	R1270	W1500	N1620	S1890	D2130	Total
	Model Number					
Simon	21	6	12	15	9	63
Bell	0	9	18	24	6	57
Anderson	3	6	6	9	6	30
Williams	9	15	6	12	0	42
Searles	6	9	15	12	9	51
Eckert	6	15	0	9	3	33
James	15	21	9	0	6	51
Hanson	3	0	6	9	3	21
Total	63	81	72	90	42	348

mailto:student@school.com

Quarter 1 / January / February / March

Do It Yourself

1. Modify a Travel Worksheet

A friend has given you a travel worksheet that you can use to plan an upcoming vacation. (Your friend has modified a version of a travel itinerary template found at Microsoft's Template Gallery.) You will make some further modifications to the worksheet and enter your vacation information. Follow these steps:

a. Open *Itinerary.xls*. Save the workbook as *xxx-Itinerary.xls*.

b. Merge and center the title in cells A1:G1. Select A3:A9 and click Merge and Center. Following this procedure, merge and center the rest of the category titles in column A (for example, A11:A15, A17:A21, and so on).

c. Delete *Sheet2* and *Sheet3*. Type Travel as the name of the remaining worksheet. Apply a purple color to the sheet tab.

d. Fill in the worksheet, using data for an upcoming vacation (or your most recent trip). Supply fictitious data, if necessary. You don't need to fill in data for all categories.

e. Save and close the workbook.

2. Organize Data for Income Tax Preparation

You are a computer consultant who runs your business out of a home office. As tax time approaches, you are preparing to finalize the tax worksheets that you have set up to help itemize your deductions for tax purposes. You will create a summary of your utilities expenses with information that your accountant needs to help prepare Form 8829, *Expenses For Business Use of Your Home*. Follow these steps:

a. Set up a worksheet that lists the months January through December as row labels in column A and utilities (such as electric, gas, and water) as column labels. Add title(s) to identify the contents of the worksheet.

b. Supply data (you can use estimates) for the utilities expenses for each month, add row and column totals, and include a grand total for all utilities for the year combined.

c. Format the worksheet as desired. Enter the name Form 8829 in the sheet tab and apply a tab color of your choice.

d. Below the worksheet, insert a hyperlink to the IRS Web site: **www.irs.gov**.

e. Save the workbook as *xxx-Tax Data.xls* **(see Figure 4.25)** and close the workbook.

Figure 4.25 A utilities worksheet for use in tax preparation

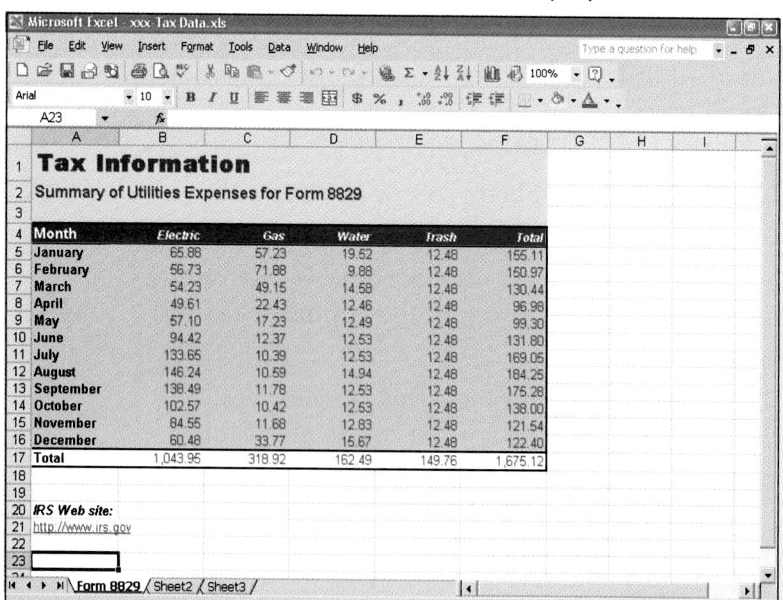

Tax Information

Summary of Utilities Expenses for Form 8829

Month	Electric	Gas	Water	Trash	Total
January	65.88	57.23	19.52	12.48	155.11
February	56.73	71.88	9.88	12.48	150.97
March	54.23	49.15	14.58	12.48	130.44
April	49.61	22.43	12.46	12.48	96.98
May	57.10	17.23	12.49	12.48	99.30
June	94.42	12.37	12.53	12.48	131.80
July	133.65	10.39	12.53	12.48	169.05
August	146.24	10.59	14.94	12.48	184.25
September	138.49	11.78	12.53	12.48	175.28
October	102.57	10.42	12.53	12.48	138.00
November	84.55	11.68	12.83	12.48	121.54
December	60.48	33.77	15.67	12.48	122.40
Total	1,043.95	318.92	162.49	149.76	1,675.12

IRS Web site:
http://www.irs.gov

3. Create a Multiple-Sheet Workbook That Calculates Grade Averages

You have been asked by your instructor to update a worksheet on grade averages for her class with data from the spring semester. In addition, you need to create a worksheet that uses 3-D cell references to summarize data from both the fall and spring semesters. Follow these steps:

a. Open *Grade Averages.xls*. Save the workbook as *xxx-Grade Averages.xls*.

b. Create two copies of *Sheet1*. Delete the blank worksheets named *Sheet2* and *Sheet3*.

c. Rename the three sheets (from left to right) as *Fall, Spring*, and *Summary*. Move the *Summary* worksheet so it appears as the first sheet tab on the left.

d. In the *Spring* worksheet, edit the title in cell A2 to be consistent with the sheet tab name. Cut and paste the data from B18:D25 into B6:D13. Delete the text in B17. Edit the formula in E6 to display the average exam score from B6:D6 and then copy the formula to E7:E13. Edit the formula in B14 to display the average of B6:B13 and copy the formula to C14:D14.

e. In the *Fall* and *Summary* sheets, delete B17:D25. In the *Summary* sheet, edit cell A2 to read *Final Grade Summary* and delete column C. In the same sheet, edit cells B5 and C5 to read *Fall* and *Spring*. In columns B6:C13, enter formulas that reference the averages from the *Fall* and *Spring* worksheets. (***Hint:*** In cell B6, the formula should be =Fall!E6).

f. Format the range B6:C13 with one decimal place. Merge and center the worksheet titles in cells A2 and A3.

g. Save and close the workbook.

4. Customizing a Personal Budget Worksheet

You have downloaded a personal budget template that you would like to personalize. Now you need to rework it to fit your needs.

a. Open *Personal Budget.xls*. Save the workbook as *xxx-Personal Budget.xls*.

b. Scroll down the worksheet to view the structure and categories included in the worksheet.

c. Copy the worksheet. Delete columns so that January through June appear on the first worksheet and July through December appear on the second sheet (keep the Total column in each sheet).

d. Edit the sheet tabs to read *Jan-June* and *July-Dec*. Check the formulas in the Total column in each sheet to ensure they are correct.

e. Copy the *Jul-Dec* sheet placing it as the tab furthest to the right. Name the new sheet *Grand Total*. Assign a different color to each tab.

f. Delete all the month columns in the *Grand Total* sheet and edit the Total column formulas keeping the SUM function and adding 3-D references. For example, click the formula in the Wages row. In the Formula Bar, select #REF! and press Delete, click the *Jan-June* sheet, click the Wages total, hold Shift and click the *July-Dec* sheet tab, and press Enter. Enter sample data in the Wages row in the *Jan-June* and *July-Dec* sheets to check your formula in the *Grand Total* sheet.

g. Copy and paste the edited formula to the appropriate cells in the Total column. To avoid having to reformat cells, click the Paste Options button that appears below the pasted cells and select Match Destination Formatting **(see Figure 4.26)**. Do not copy the formula to cell C9 or C99.

h. Enter your income and expense data into the worksheets and check to ensure that the formulas are correct.

i. Save and close the workbook.

Figure 4.26 The Paste Options button

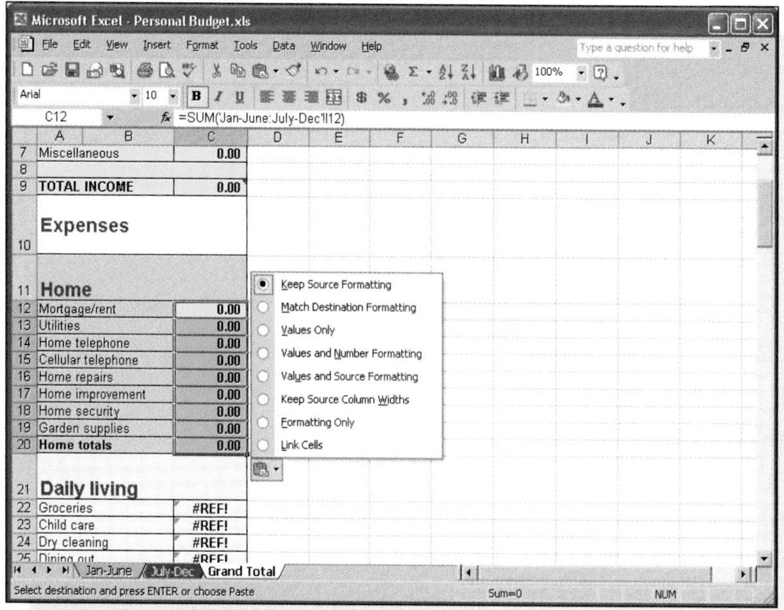

Challenge Yourself

Work With What-If Scenarios

In this activity, you will use the Scenario Manager feature in Excel to create a *Best Case* and *Worst Case* scenario for a travel store to help examine what the net income might be at the end of the year. Excel saves each set of changing values (revenue and expenses, in this example) as a scenario with a name that you specify. Scenarios are one of the what-if analysis tools provided with Excel that can help you see what an outcome would be if you change values that affect the outcome. If you need additional help with this exercise, search Excel Help using the word *scenario* or ask your instructor. Follow these steps:

- Open *Scenarios.xls*. Save the workbook as *xxx-Scenarios.xls*.
- On the Tools menu, select Scenarios. Click the Add button to display the Add Scenario dialog box.
- Type the name Best Case in the *Scenario name* box. In the *Changing cells* box, type B5:B6 and click OK.
- In the Scenario Values dialog box, type 175000 in the first text box and 50000 in the second text box. These are the values you want to use for the new scenario.
- Click OK. The new scenario displays in the Scenario Manager dialog box. Notice that this dialog box also includes options to delete, edit, and merge scenarios.
- Click Add to create another scenario. Type Worst Case in the *Scenario name* box. Ensure that B5:B6 is specified in the *Changing cells* box, and click OK.
- In the Scenario Values dialog box, type 120000 in the first text box and 65000 in the second text box. Click OK to create the second scenario.
- In the Scenario Manager dialog box, click the Summary button. Select *Scenario summary* as the report type. Check that cell B7 appears in the *Result cells* box. Click OK to create the report.
- Examine the data in the Scenario Summary report. Notice that the current values in the changing cells are displayed in column D; the *Best Case* and *Worst Case* values are displayed in columns E and F. The *Best Case* result (Net Income) would be $125,000; the *Worst Case* result would be $55,000.
- Save and close the workbook.

Excel

Unit 2 Applications and Projects

Apply Your Knowledge

Complete the following exercises in order, as directed by your teacher. As you work through these projects, you will create four quarterly worksheets, a summary worksheet for annual data, and a chart sheet. Save all files within the *Unit Applications and Projects* subfolder within your *Unit 2* folder.

1. Enter Revenue Data and Formulas in a Worksheet

a. Open a new workbook and save it as *xxx-Piano1.xls*.

b. Enter the data in the following table. Begin to enter data in cell A1 and leave row 3 blank. The *Total* row label should appear in cell A10.

Northstar Piano Sales and Service

First Quarter Revenues				
	January	February	March	Total
Piano Sales	61500	55000	58300	
Organ Sales	27300	31300	23800	
Rentals	3400	5200	6700	
Service	17900	15100	16200	
Lessons	8500	8700	7900	
Total				

c. Using the SUM function, enter formulas in the appropriate cells to total the columns and rows.

d. To the right of the Total column, add a Percentage column. In the Percentage column (including cell F10), enter formulas that display the total sales for each category as a percent of the grand total for all categories. Each formula should contain one relative reference and one absolute reference.

e. Save the workbook.

2. Improve the Appearance of the Worksheet

a. Change the width of all columns with data to 14, and center the column labels. Change the height of row 1 to 34.5.

b. Apply the accounting format with two decimal places to the revenue data. Remove the currency symbols from all values except those in the first row and the Total row. Apply the percent format with one decimal place to the percentage formulas.

c. Merge and center the labels in cells A1 and A2 over the worksheet. Apply the titles in cells A1 and A2 by choosing an appropriate font and font size.

d. Apply the *Classic 2* AutoFormat to the range A4:F10 without changing the existing alignment or width/height settings. Apply a light yellow fill color to the range A1:F3.

e. Locate and import a clip art image of a piano. Place the image in the upper-left corner.

f. Save the workbook as *xxx-Piano2.xls* **(see Figure 1)**.

Figure 1 The formatted worksheet

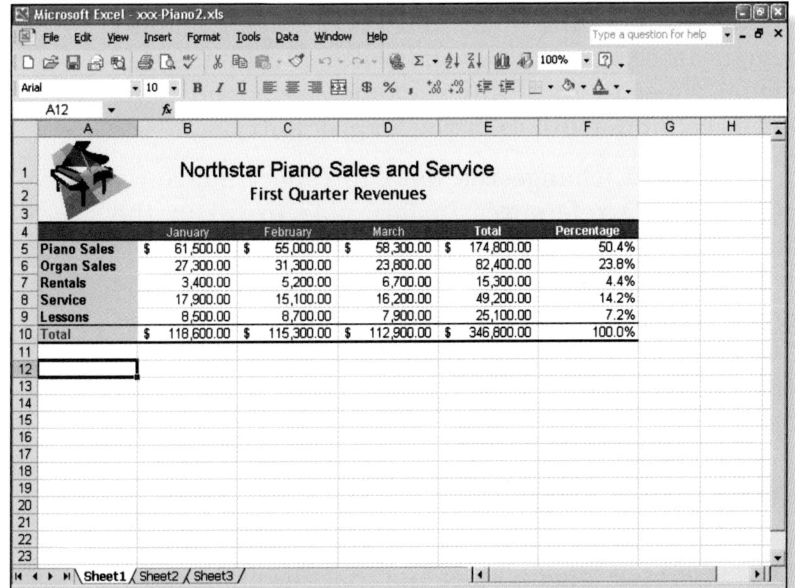

Excel

3. Copy, Insert, and Delete Worksheets

a. Delete the *Sheet2* and *Sheet3* worksheets. Rename the *Sheet1* tab as *1st Quarter* and apply yellow to the tab. Place three copies of the worksheet immediately following the *1st Quarter* worksheet. Edit the new worksheet tabs so they read *2nd Quarter, 3rd Quarter*, and *4th Quarter*.

b. In the *2nd Quarter, 3rd Quarter*, and *4th Quarter* sheets, edit the titles and column labels so that they reflect the appropriate quarter, and delete the sales data. ***Note:*** Be careful not to delete any of the formulas.

c. Enter new revenue data in the *2nd Quarter, 3rd Quarter*, and *4th Quarter* sheets. (Use numbers in a similar range as those in the *1st Quarter* worksheet.)

d. Save the workbook as *xxx-Piano3.xls*.

4. Prepare the Summary Worksheet

a. Make a copy of the *4th Quarter* sheet, and rename the new sheet tab as *Summary*. Apply the color purple to the sheet tab. Position the *Summary* sheet so that it is the first sheet in the workbook.

b. On the *Summary* sheet, edit the subtitle to read Annual Revenues. Insert a new column just after column B. Edit the column labels over the four revenue columns so that they match the sheet tabs (1st Quarter through 4th Quarter).

c. On the *Summary* sheet, add a formula to total the 2d Quarter column. Check the remaining Total and Percentage formulas and edit them, if necessary. Change the width of columns A-G in the *Summary* sheet to 12. If any cells display pound signs (###), adjust the column width to fit the longest entry.

d. In the *Summary* sheet, change the data to reflect quarterly revenues by using 3-D references in formulas to fill in the quarterly totals for each category. Each of these formulas should refer to the appropriate cell in the Total column of the corresponding quarterly sheet. If necessary, adjust the number formatting in the *Summary* sheet to make it consistent with the other sheets.

e. Save the workbook as *xxx-Piano4.xls*.

5. Create and Format Charts

a. Create a 3-D Pie chart based on the percent of total revenue by category in the *Summary* sheet. Place the chart as an object in the *Summary* sheet.

b. Add a title to the pie chart, and then add data labels that show the values on which each pie slice is based. Move and resize the chart as necessary so that it displays below the worksheet data on the *Summary* sheet.

c. On a separate chart sheet, create a stacked column chart with a 3-D visual effect that displays the quarterly revenue data by category (from the *Summary* sheet). Add a descriptive chart title, and display the legend at the bottom of the chart.

d. Move the *Chart1* sheet to the end of the workbook, and change the color of the sheet tab to blue. Save the workbook as *xxx-Piano5.xls* **(see Figure 2)**.

Figure 2 The stacked column chart displayed on a separate chart sheet

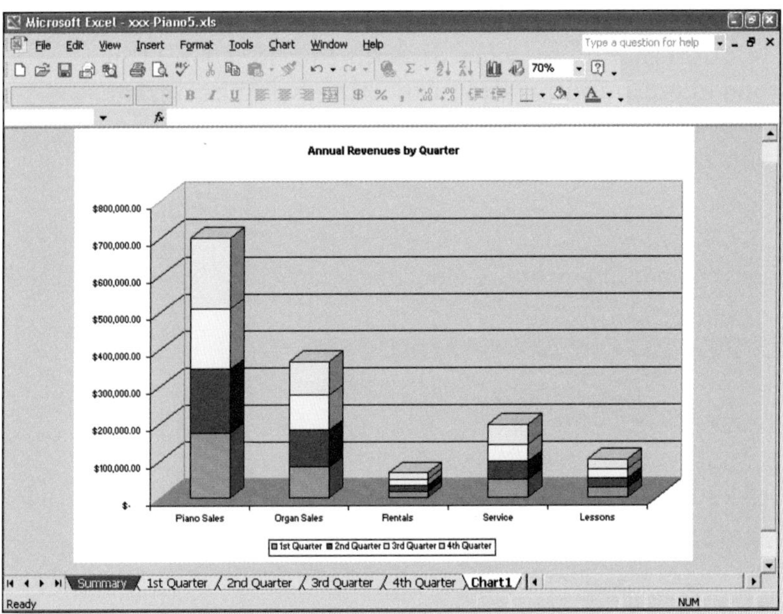

6. Preview and Print Your Data

a. On the *Summary* sheet, add an appropriate header and footer. Change the page orientation to landscape.

b. Change the page setup so that the data is centered on the page horizontally. Adjust the scaling, if necessary, so that the data fits on one page. Preview the worksheet, and then print the *Summary* sheet only (including the pie chart).

c. On the *Summary* sheet, simultaneously select the 1st Quarter and 3rd Quarter sales data and set a print area. Preview and print these nonadjacent areas of the worksheet. Clear the print area.

d. Save the workbook as *xxx-Piano6.xls*.

7. Save and Preview the Workbook as a Web Page

a. Save the entire workbook as a Web page, with interactivity. Use the file name *xxx-Piano7.htm*.

b. Use Web Page Preview to preview the workbook in your browser. Click the tab near the bottom of the window, and display the different worksheets in the workbook.

c. Close the browser window. Close the *xxx-Piano6.xls* workbook without saving it.

What's Wrong With This Picture?

The workbook shown in **Figure 3** contains ten mistakes. Some of the errors are obvious, but others may be more difficult to find. Using the skills you have learned about building and formatting worksheets, try to find at least seven of these mistakes. On a sheet of paper, identify each of the errors you find and describe how you would fix it using Excel's tools.

Figure 3 This worksheet contains many errors. How many can you find?

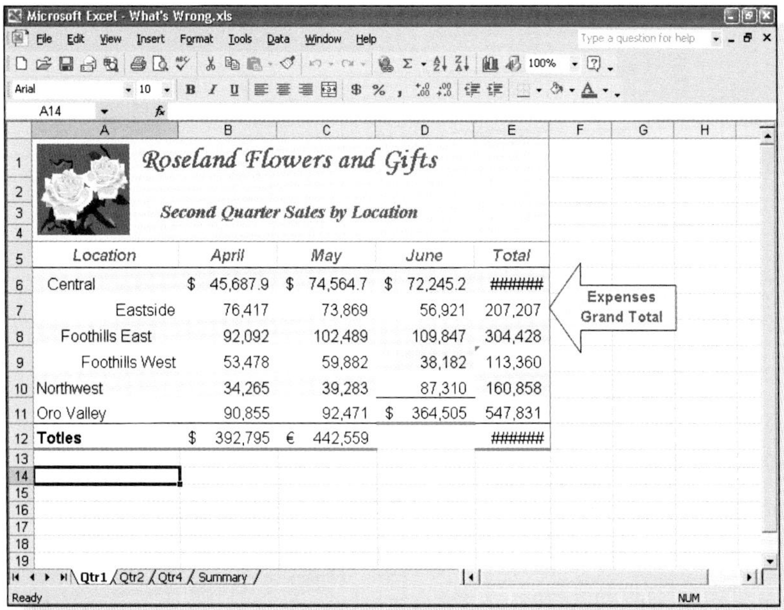

Cross-Curriculum Project

Your Business Communications teacher has challenged you to develop a worksheet that compares current interest rates and other key provisions for five major credit card companies. See the following list as a general guide for the type of information you may collect and compare:

- Annual percentage rate (APR)
- Grace period for payments
- Annual fee, late fee, and over the limit fee
- Minimum payment (this may be a formula rather than a specific amount)

Form a team to complete this project. Check with friends and family to get their recommendations on credit card companies to research. You may also start your research on the Web at **www.bankrate.com**.

After you finish conducting your research, prepare the basic worksheet and enter the data. Then, do the following:

- Include descriptive worksheet title(s) and column labels and apply attractive fonts. Format the numeric data as appropriate.
- Adjust column widths, row heights, and font sizes.
- Apply an AutoFormat, or use Excel's formatting features to devise your own format.
- Insert one or more clip art images.
- Add functions that calculate the minimum and maximum APR.
- Create a chart that compares the APR for the five companies. Be sure to choose a chart type that fits the data, and format the chart to enhance its appearance and readability (include the interest rates as data labels).
- Add a graphic arrow to the chart that draws attention to the credit card company that looks the most attractive to you and your team.
- Preview the worksheet and chart, and make any necessary adjustments such as changing the page orientation or centering the data on the page. Include your team name in a footer.

When you're finished, review and discuss the information and make any necessary changes. Verify that you've entered the data correctly and that all formulas are correct. Perform a spell check and then print the worksheet.

Access

Unit 3 Business Databases

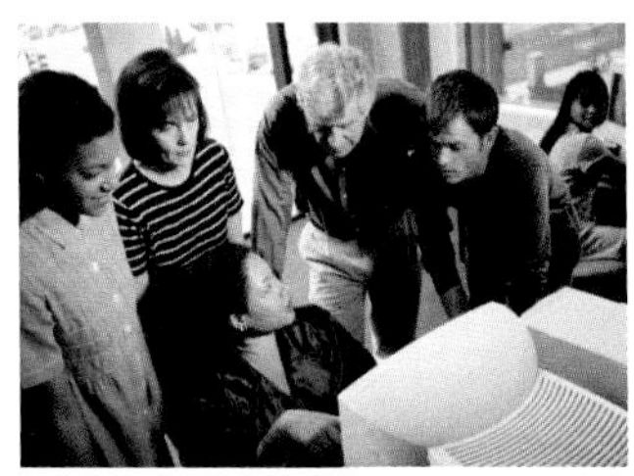

Unit Contents

- **Lesson 1:** Introducing Access
- **Lesson 2:** Creating, Modifying, and Relating Tables
- **Lesson 3:** Working With Datasheets and Queries
- **Lesson 4:** Working With Forms, Reports, and Data Access Pages
- **Unit Applications and Projects**

Unit Objectives

1. Start Access and explore the Database window.
2. Explore database objects.
3. Navigate records in a datasheet.
4. Enter, edit, and delete records in a datasheet.
5. Enter, edit, and delete records in a form.
6. Create a database.
7. Create tables.
8. Modify table design.
9. Create an input mask.
10. Import, export, and link Access data.
11. Define relationships and enforce referential integrity.
12. Create a Lookup field.
13. Sort records in a datasheet.
14. Search for data in a datasheet.
15. Filter records in a datasheet.
16. Create and modify select queries.
17. Create special queries using wizards.
18. Format a datasheet.
19. Create simple forms.
20. Create business reports.
21. Modify forms and reports in Design view.
22. Create a simple data access page.

Access

Lesson 1

Introducing Access

Lesson Exercise Objectives

After completing this lesson, you'll be able to do the following tasks:

1. Start Access and explore the Database window
2. Explore database objects
3. Navigate records in a datasheet
4. Enter, edit, and delete records in a datasheet
5. Enter, edit, and delete records in a form
6. Create a database

Key Terms

- database (p. 306)
- database object (p. 306)
- Database window (p. 306)
- datasheet (p. 312)
- Datasheet view (p. 307)
- Design view (p. 307)
- field (p. 312)
- form (p. 307)
- Form view (p. 307)
- Print Preview (p. 307)
- query (p. 307)
- record (p. 312)
- record selector (p. 315)
- relational database (p. 306)
- report (p. 307)
- table (p. 307)

Microsoft Office Specialist Activities

AC2002: 1.1, 1.2, 1.3, 5.1, 7.3

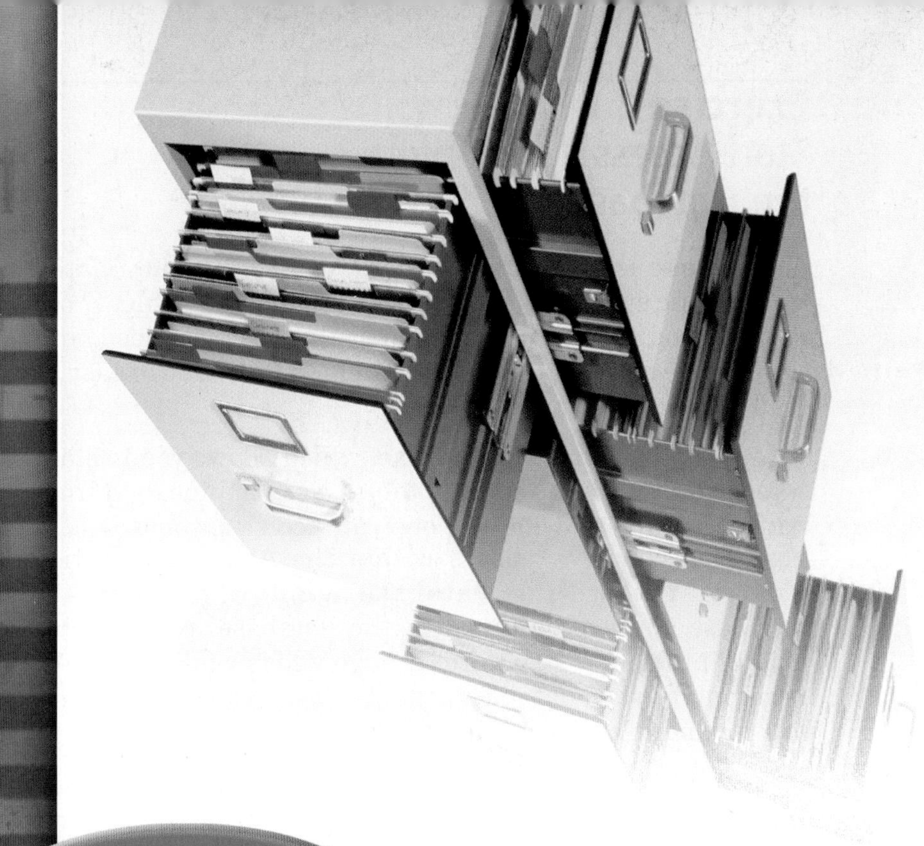

Real-Life Business Applications

Lesson Case Study

In this lesson, you will play the role of a student intern in the information systems department at Saburo Sporting Goods, a sporting goods wholesaler located in Wheat Ridge, Colorado. Keep the following information in mind as you work through the lesson exercises.

- `Job responsibilities and goals.` As a student intern, you need to develop a basic working knowledge of Microsoft Access so that you can work effectively with the company's Access database.
- `The project.` You will learn about the various objects that comprise the company database; you will enter, edit, and delete data in the database; and you will create a new database.
- `The challenge ahead.` Access and database programs are new to you, and you need to learn about them from the ground up in order to develop the database expertise that the company needs.

Access

Exercise 1 Overview: Start Access and Explore the Database Window

A **database** is a collection of data, or information, related to a specific subject and kept together in a single file. From this file, you can retrieve the particular data you need, and summarize and present many details so that they're easy to read and understand.

Access is a **relational database,** which allows you to store categories of data in separate tables, yet combine data from any of the tables. When you open an Access database file, a Database window appears within the Access application window. You use the **Database window** to access the database objects contained in the database. A **database object** provides a structure through which you can store or manipulate your data. Tables, queries, forms, and reports are common database objects.

Need Help?

Type: ways to get started in the Ask a Question box at the right end of the menu bar

Access objects are grouped by type in the Objects bar on the left side of the Database window. When you click the name of an object in the Objects bar, the objects in that group are displayed in the right pane of the Database window.

Step Through It™

Exercise 1: Explore the Database window

1. Start Access, and open the *Saburo Sample.mdb* database (see Figure 1.1).
2. Click Queries in the Objects bar to display the queries in the database.
3. Click Forms in the Objects bar to display the queries in the database.
4. Click Reports in the Objects bar.
5. Click Tables in the Objects bar.

Figure 1.1 The *Saburo Sample* Database window

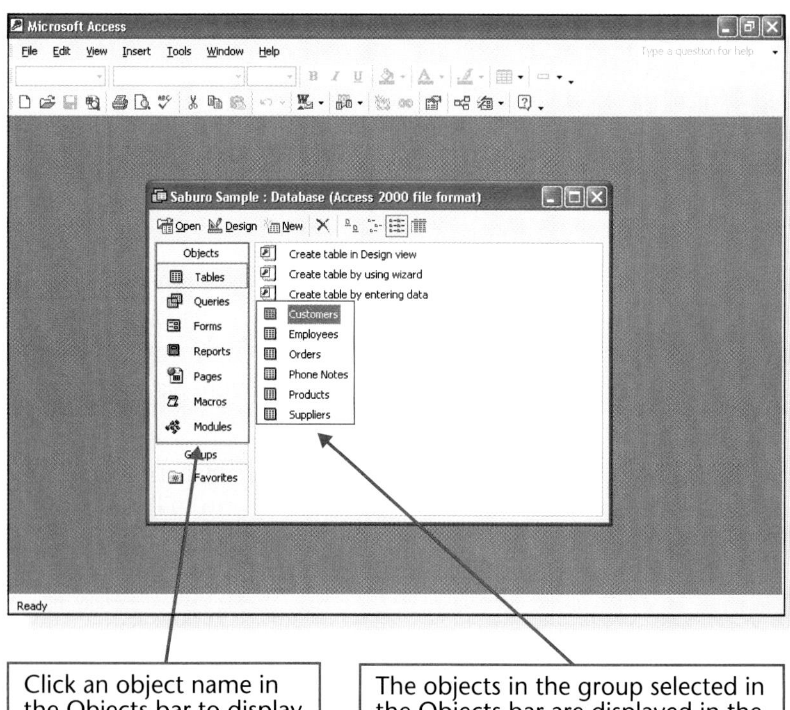

Exercise 2 Overview:
Explore Database Objects

Microsoft Office Specialist
AC2002 1.2

The most common database objects are tables, queries, forms, and reports. A **table** is the only object in an Access database that actually contains data. All the data in a database are contained in one or more tables. A **query** looks like a table, but it doesn't contain any data itself; instead, it displays only specific data from tables based on criteria you supply. A **form** is a window into the data in one or more tables. A form is primarily used to enter and edit data. A **report** is a professional-looking printout of database data that usually contains summary information.

Understanding Views

Access allows you to examine and manipulate the data or the objects in your database in many different views.

You use **Datasheet view** to add, modify, or delete data in a table or query. In Datasheet view, the data are displayed in a row-and-column format that resembles an Excel worksheet.

While you can also use Datasheet view to work with data in forms, **Form view** is more commonly used because it allows you to view the fields for only one record at a time. (You'll learn more about fields and records in the next section.)

Datasheet view is not available for reports because you cannot directly manipulate data in a report. Instead, use **Print Preview** to see how the data will look when you print a report.

You use **Design view** to set or change the structure of any object. In Design view, you do not see any actual data. Instead, you see the structure of the object, which includes elements such as field names, data types, controls, properties, and areas for headers, footers, and data details.

Working With Toolbars

Access provides a unique toolbar for each view. Every time you open an object or switch views, the appropriate toolbar is displayed automatically. Every toolbar contains a View button that allows you to switch views. The View button is a toggle button, which means you click the same button to toggle, or switch, between object views. (The graphic on the button changes depending on which view is displayed, but it's the same button.)

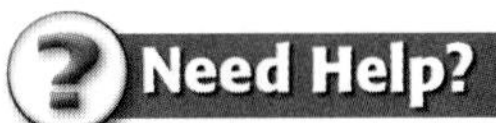

Type: switch between views of a database object

In the following exercises, you will open various objects in the *Saburo Sample.mdb* database and explore them in different views.

Step Through It™

Exercise 2A: Explore a table

1. In the Database window, click Tables in the Objects bar.
2. Double-click the Employees table Database window. The Employees table opens in Datasheet view by default (see Figure 1.2).
3. Click the Maximize button in the table window.
4. Drag the horizontal scroll box to the right. Then drag the horizontal scroll box back to the left.

Figure 1.2 The Employees table in Datasheet view

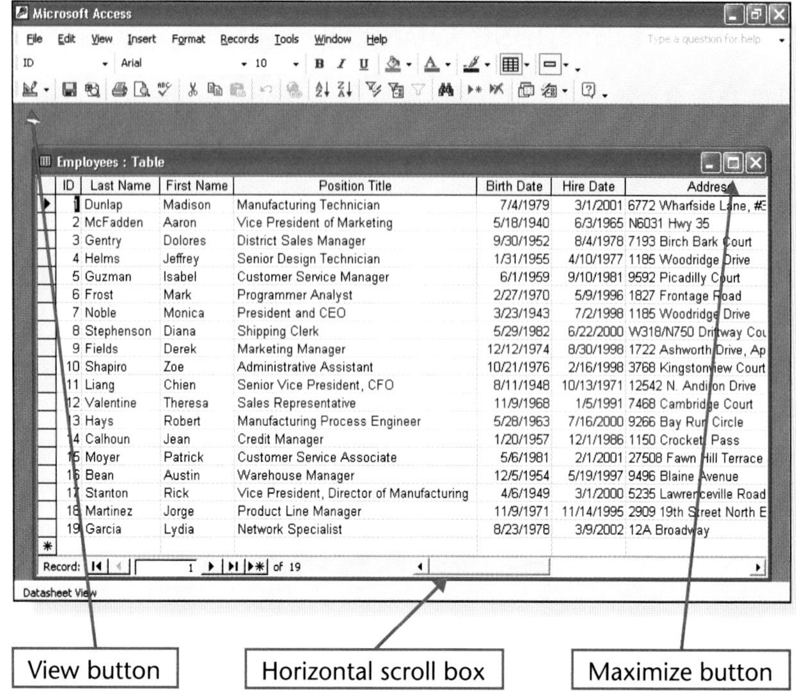
View button
Horizontal scroll box
Maximize button

5. Click the View button. The table switches to Design view (see Figure 1.3). Notice that the table design window is divided into an upper pane and a lower pane. You'll work with tables in Design view in Lesson 2.
6. Click the View button. (Notice that the graphic on the View button changed.) The table switches back to Datasheet view.
7. Click the Close Window button in the upper-right corner of the table to close it and return to the Database window.

Figure 1.3 The Employees table in Design view

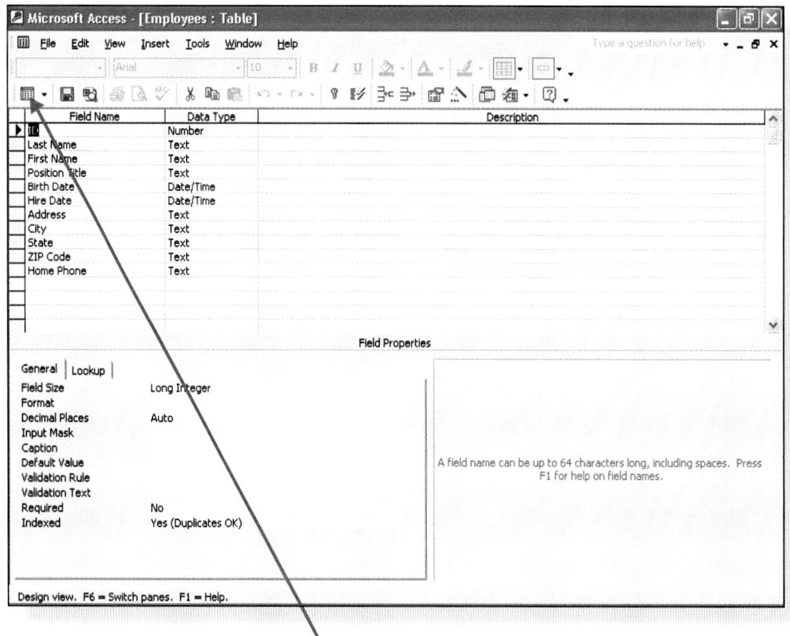
The View button is a toggle button. The graphic on the View button changes depending on your view.

Access

Figure 1.4 The Employee Critical Information query in Datasheet view

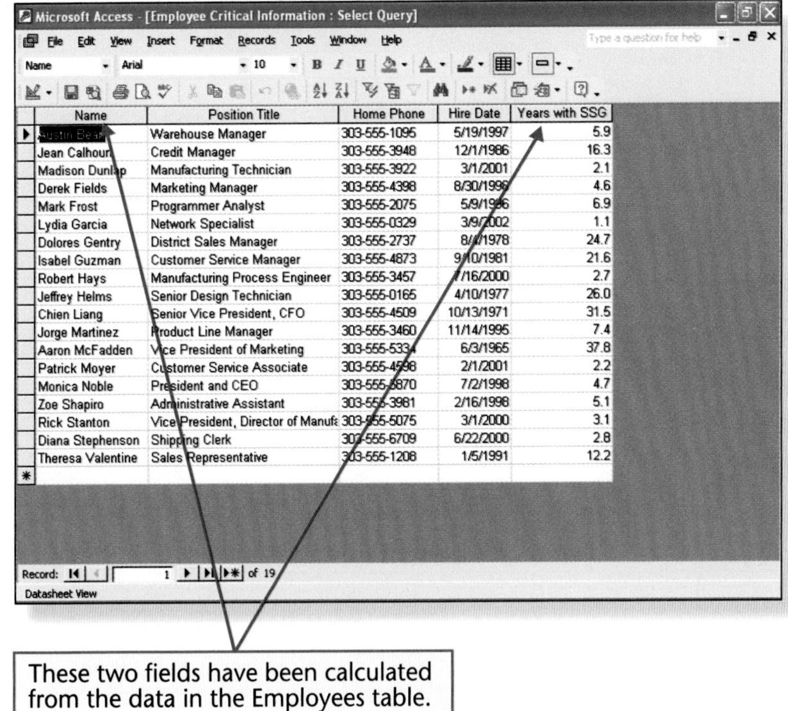

Name	Position Title	Home Phone	Hire Date	Years with SSG
Austin Bean	Warehouse Manager	303-555-1095	5/19/1997	5.9
Jean Calhoun	Credit Manager	303-555-3948	12/1/1986	16.3
Madison Dunlap	Manufacturing Technician	303-555-3922	3/1/2001	2.1
Derek Fields	Marketing Manager	303-555-4398	8/30/1996	4.6
Mark Frost	Programmer Analyst	303-555-2075	5/9/1996	6.9
Lydia Garcia	Network Specialist	303-555-0329	3/9/2002	1.1
Dolores Gentry	District Sales Manager	303-555-2737	8/4/1978	24.7
Isabel Guzman	Customer Service Manager	303-555-4873	9/10/1981	21.6
Robert Hays	Manufacturing Process Engineer	303-555-3457	7/16/2000	2.7
Jeffrey Helms	Senior Design Technician	303-555-0165	4/10/1977	26.0
Chien Liang	Senior Vice President, CFO	303-555-4509	10/13/1971	31.5
Jorge Martinez	Product Line Manager	303-555-3460	11/14/1995	7.4
Aaron McFadden	Vice President of Marketing	303-555-5334	6/3/1965	37.8
Patrick Moyer	Customer Service Associate	303-555-4598	2/1/2001	2.2
Monica Noble	President and CEO	303-555-5870	7/2/1998	4.7
Zoe Shapiro	Administrative Assistant	303-555-3981	2/16/1998	5.1
Rick Stanton	Vice President, Director of Manufa	303-555-5075	3/1/2000	3.1
Diana Stephenson	Shipping Clerk	303-555-6709	6/22/2000	2.8
Theresa Valentine	Sales Representative	303-555-1208	1/5/1991	12.2

Step Through It™

Exercise 2B: Explore a query

1. In the Database window, click Queries in the Objects bar.
2. Double-click the Employee Critical Information query. The query opens in Datasheet view.
3. Compare your screen with the Employees table in Figure 1.2 on page 308. The query is based on the data in the Employees table, but the query only displays some of the data in the table. Other data have been calculated by the query (see Figure 1.4).

Figure 1.5 The Employee Critical Information query in Design view

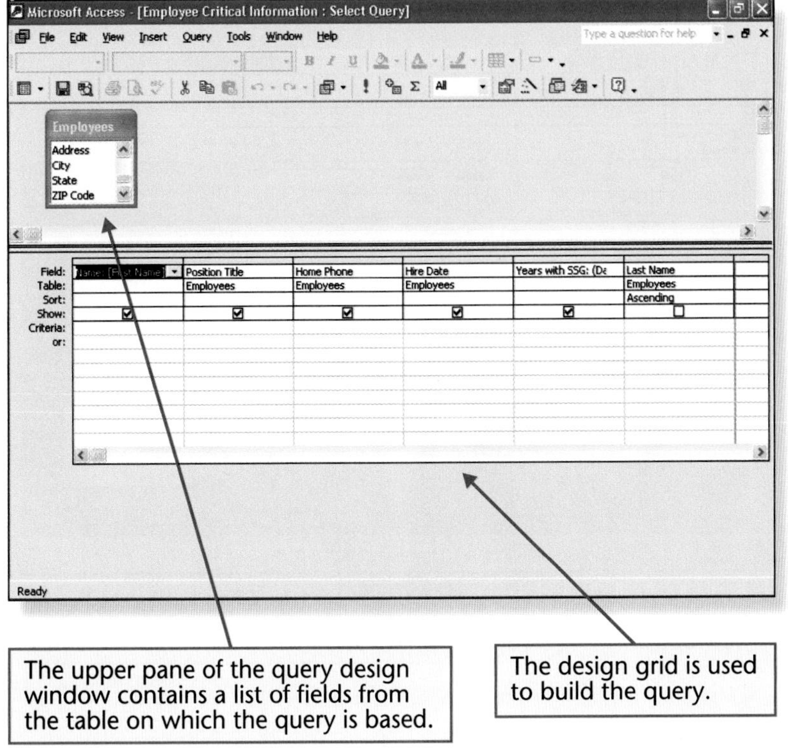

4. Click the View button on the Query Datasheet toolbar. The query switches to Design view (see Figure 1.5). You see an upper pane displays the list of fields from the table on which the query is based, and you see a design grid, where you build the query.
5. Click the View button on the Query Design toolbar. The query switches back to Datasheet view.
6. Close the query and return to the Database window.

Step Through It™

Exercise 2C: Explore a form

Access

1. Click the Restore Window button at the right end of the menu bar to return the Database window to its smaller size.

2. In the Database window, click Forms in the Objects bar.

3. Double-click the Employees form. (See Figure 1.6.) This form displays the same data you saw in the Employees table; however, it displays only one record at a time in an easy-to-read format.

Figure 1.6 The Employees form in Form view

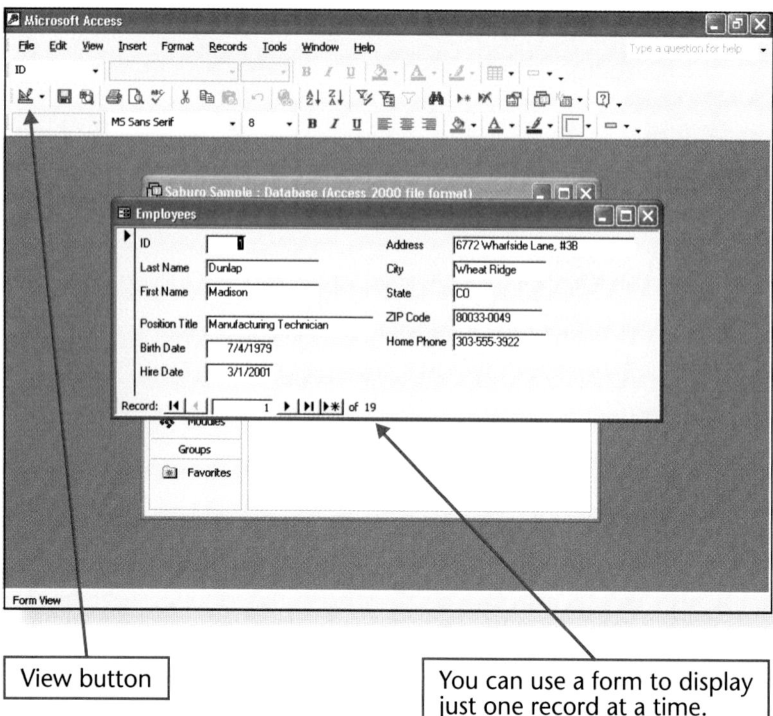

View button
You can use a form to display just one record at a time.

4. Click the View button on the Form View toolbar. The form switches to Design view. Maximize the form design window (see Figure 1.7). You can create or modify a form in Design view.

5. Click the View button on the Form Design toolbar. The form switches back to Form view.

6. Click the Close Window button in the upper-right corner of the menu bar to close the form and return to the Database window.

Figure 1.7 The Employees form in Design view

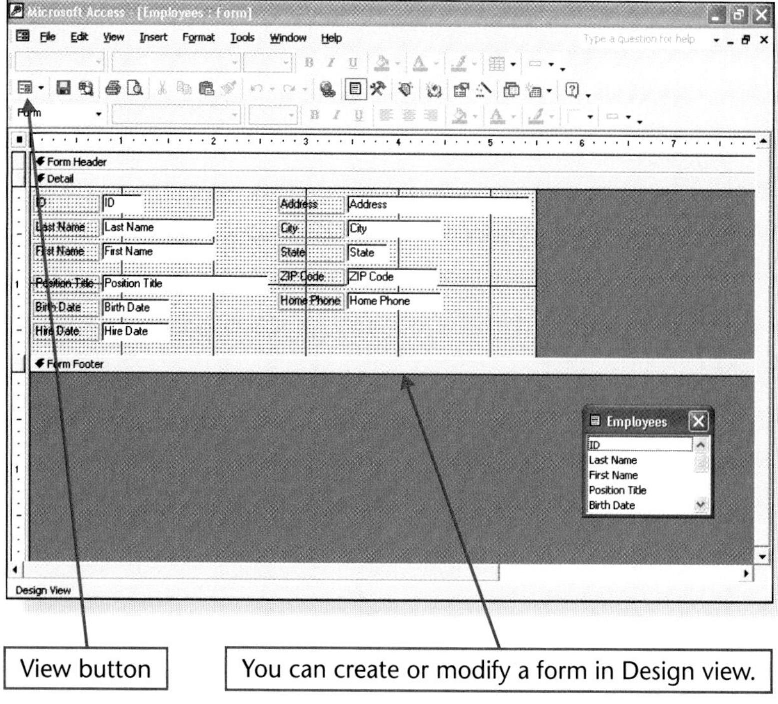

View button
You can create or modify a form in Design view.

Figure 1.8 The Employee Quick Reference report in Print Preview

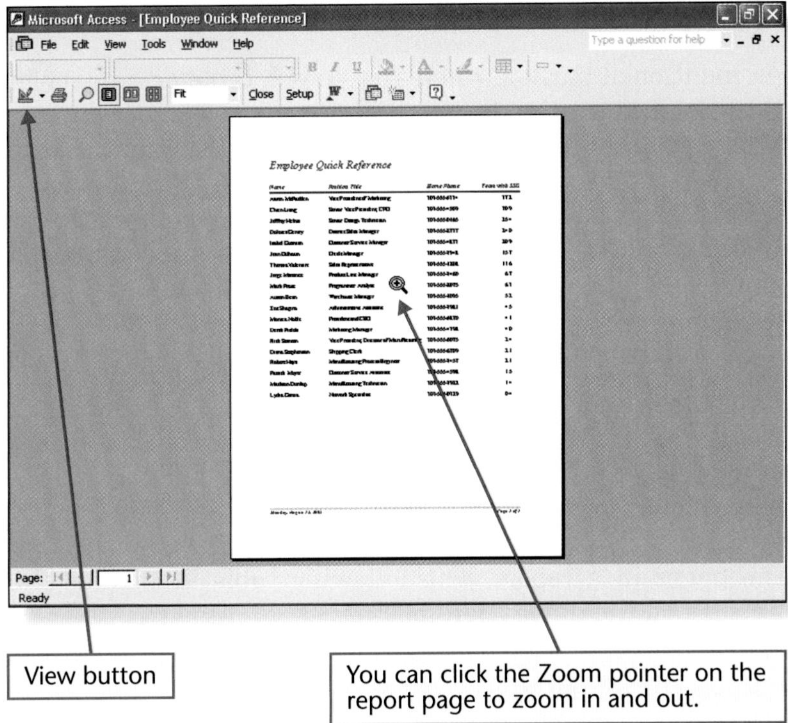

View button
You can click the Zoom pointer on the report page to zoom in and out.

Step Through It™

Exercise 2D: Explore a report

1. In the Database window, click Reports in the Objects bar.
2. Double-click the Employee Quick Reference report. The report opens in Print Preview (see Figure 1.8).
3. Compare the report to the Employee Critical Information query shown in Figure 1.4 on page 309. The data in the report are the same data as in the query, on which the report is based.

Figure 1.9 The Employee Quick Reference report in Design view

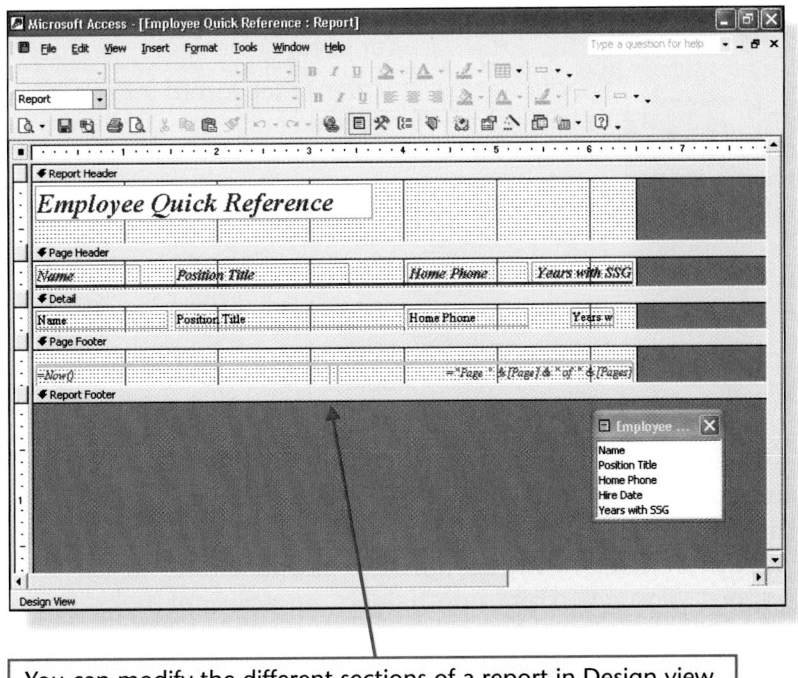

You can modify the different sections of a report in Design view.

4. Click the View button on the Print Preview toolbar. Maximize the window by clicking the Maximize button in the upper-right corner. The report switches to Design view (see Figure 1.9). You see different sections of the report page, and in each section there are controls for data or labels.
5. Click the View button on the Report Design toolbar. The report switches back to Print Preview.
6. Click the Close Window button in the upper-right corner of the menu bar. Then click the Restore Window button to return the Database window to its smaller size.

Microsoft Office Specialist
AC2002 1.3

Access

Exercise 3 Overview:
Navigate Records in a Datasheet

As mentioned earlier, when you view a table or a query in Datasheet view, the data is laid out in rows and columns. This row-and-column format is called a **datasheet.** Every row is a unique **record** that contains all the data for a particular item, and every column is a **field** that contains a specific piece of data for each record. For example, a table of employee data contains a record for each employee, and each employee record contains a field for last name, a field for first name, a field for phone number, and so on.

As you can imagine, if a table contains a lot of records, it would be difficult to move around in the datasheet efficiently. Access provides a navigation toolbar at the bottom of every object window to help you navigate quickly among the records in a table, query, or form, and through the pages in a report. The following table illustrates the buttons on the navigation toolbar.

Need Help?

Type: move between records or fields

Navigation Toolbar

Button		Purpose
	First Record	Moves to the first record (or page) in an object
	Previous Record	Moves to the previous record (or page) in an object
1	Specific Record (a box, not a button)	Moves to the record (or page) specified in the Specific Record box
	Next Record	Moves to the next record (or page) in an object
	Last Record	Moves to the last record (or page) in an object
	New Record	Moves to a new record in an object

In addition to using the navigation toolbar to move around in a datasheet, you can also use standard keyboard actions, such as Ctrl + Home to move to the first field in the first record or Ctrl + End to move to the last field in the last record. To move from one field to an adjacent field, press Tab or use the appropriate arrow keys.

Review Appendix A if you need help navigating a file.

In the following exercise, you will open the Employees table in the *Saburo Sample.mdb* database and move among the records in the datasheet.

Figure 1.10 Moving to a specific record in a datasheet

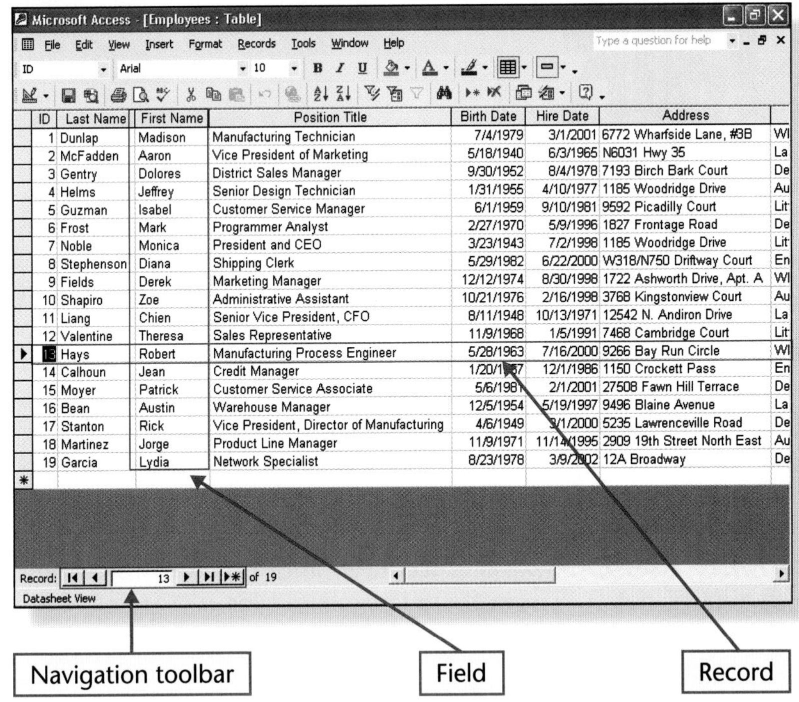

Figure 1.11 Moving to the last field in the last record

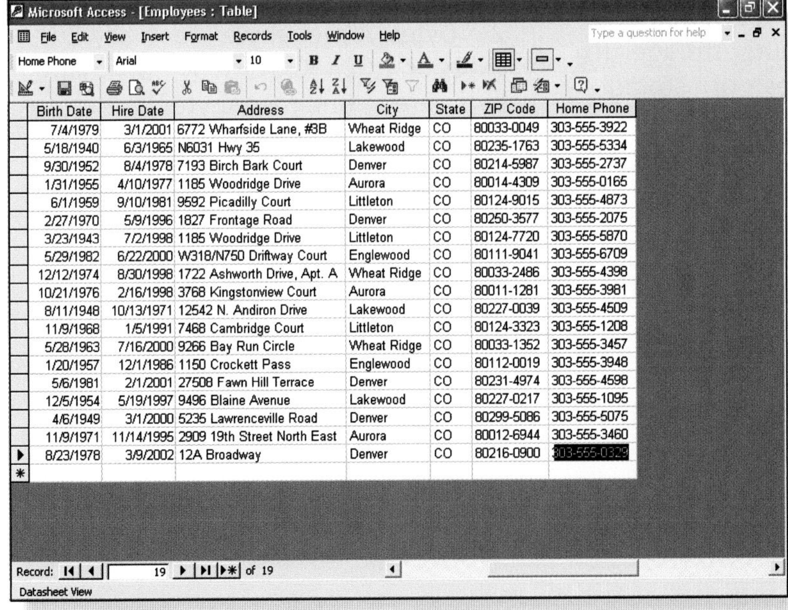

Step Through It™

Exercise 3: Move among records in a datasheet

1. In the *Saburo Sample.mdb* database, open the Employees table (in Datasheet view) and maximize the window.
2. Click the Next Record button ▶ on the navigation toolbar.
3. Double-click in the Specific Record box on the navigation toolbar, type 13, and press Enter (see Figure 1.10).
4. Press Tab repeatedly to navigate to the Home Phone field for Robert Hays (record 13).
5. Click the First Record button ⏮ to jump to the Home Phone field in the first record.
6. Press Tab to move to the first field in the next record.
7. Click the Last Record button ⏭ to move to the ID field in the last record.
8. Press Ctrl + End to move to the last field in the last record (see Figure 1.11).
9. Press Ctrl + Home to move to the first field in the first record.
10. Close the Employees table.

APPLY IT! After finishing Exercises 1–3, you may test your skills by completing Apply It! Guided Activity 1, Examine Objects in Different Views and Navigate Records.

Tech Talk

Take a Big Byte of Data!

No matter what an organization's "core" business is—whether it's manufacturing products, constructing buildings, providing medical services, or any other type of business—all organizations continually gather and track data—data about products, data about processes, data about customers, and a host of other things. The larger the organization, the more data it collects, which can add up to a lot of data. But how much is a lot of data? And once you gather a lot of data, where do you put it?

To understand data and data storage, let's start with the fundamental unit of measure for data storage—the *byte*. Each character of data (a letter, a number, a symbol, etc.) takes up one byte of computer storage. To describe larger quantities of storage, prefixes are added to the term *byte*. For example, the prefix *kilo*, which means 1,000, is added to the term byte to represent 1,000 bytes. The table below lists the terms used to describe large quantities of data and computer storage.

Even though today's hard drives can hold gigabytes of data, eventually even the largest hard drives will reach their capacity. Then what? Many organizations with massive storage needs use data silos, which are like gigantic databases. A data silo can hold thousands of terabytes, or *petabytes*, of data. A technique called data mining is used to find and extract information from these large databases. Access and Excel are often used to create custom applications to extract accurate and timely information from these large data silos.

CRITICAL THINKING

1. A kilobyte is technically 1,024 bytes or 2^{10} bytes. A megabyte is actually 2^{20} bytes or 1,024 KB. Exactly how many bytes are in one megabyte?
2. The terms *exabyte*, *zettabyte*, and *yottabyte* describe quantities of data and computer storage that are even larger than a petabyte. Research the definitions of these terms. In your opinion, what are the advantages of accumulating massive amounts of data? What are the disadvantages?

Term (Abbreviation)	Approximate Number of Bytes	How much data is that?
Kilobyte (K or KB)	1 thousand bytes (10^3)	One page of text
Megabyte (M or MB)	1 million bytes (10^6) or 1,000 KB	A large book
Gigabyte (G or GB)	1 billion bytes (10^9) or 1,000 MB	One thousand books
Terabyte (T or TB)	1 trillion bytes (10^{12}) or 1,000 GB	Ten libraries of books

Exercise 4 Overview:
Enter, Edit, and Delete Records in a Datasheet

Microsoft Office Specialist AC2002 5.1

Access

Information in a database is constantly changing. You will always need to add new records, modify existing records, and delete obsolete records. You can enter, edit, and delete records in a datasheet—that is, in a table using Datasheet view. ***Note:*** You can also enter, edit, and delete records in most (but not all) query datasheets and also in a form using Datasheet view (but forms are used in Datasheet view only in special circumstances).

To the left of each record in a datasheet is a small, gray box called a **record selector.** You can select an entire record by clicking the record selector. Access displays various symbols in the record selector to show the status of the record (see table below).

Record Selector Symbols

Symbol	Meaning
▶	Indicates that this is the current record and the record has been saved
✎	Indicates that the record is being edited and the changes have not been saved
*	Indicates that this is a new record into which you can enter information

When you click anywhere in a datasheet or use the keyboard to move the cursor to new fields, a triangle appears in the record selector. The triangle indicates that the record is the current record and that the data it contains has been saved.

When you begin to enter or edit data in a record, the triangle in the record selector changes to a pencil icon. The pencil icon indicates that the record is being edited and the changes have not yet been saved. When you move the cursor, by any means, to another record, the edited record is automatically saved, and the pencil icon disappears.

Type: add or edit data

To delete a record in a datasheet, click the record selector to select the entire record, and then press the Delete key. Access will display a message asking if you're sure you want to delete the record. If you respond Yes to the message, Access will delete the record.

In the next exercise, you'll enter a new record in the Employees table of the *Saburo Sample.mdb* database, then you'll edit the record, and then you'll delete the record.

Step Through It™

Exercise 4: Manipulate records using a datasheet

1. In the *Saburo Sample.mdb* database, open the Employees table. Notice that the triangle appears in the record selector for the first record, and the first field in the first record is selected.

2. Click the New Record button ▸* on the navigation toolbar. Now the triangle appears in the record selector for the new record at the bottom of the datasheet, and the insertion point is positioned in the first field (ID field) in the new record (see Figure 1.12).

Figure 1.12 Adding a new record

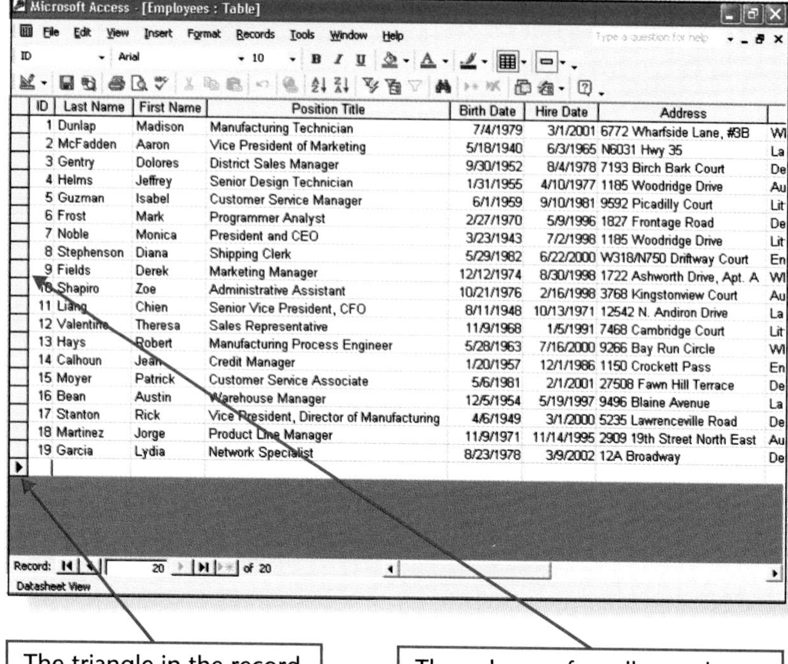

ID	Last Name	First Name	Position Title	Birth Date	Hire Date	Address	
1	Dunlap	Madison	Manufacturing Technician	7/4/1979	3/1/2001	6772 Wharfside Lane, #3B	Wi
2	McFadden	Aaron	Vice President of Marketing	5/18/1940	6/3/1965	N6031 Hwy 35	La
3	Gentry	Dolores	District Sales Manager	9/30/1952	8/4/1978	7193 Birch Bark Court	De
4	Helms	Jeffrey	Senior Design Technician	1/31/1955	4/10/1977	1185 Woodridge Drive	Au
5	Guzman	Isabel	Customer Service Manager	6/1/1959	9/10/1981	9592 Picadilly Court	Lit
6	Frost	Mark	Programmer Analyst	2/27/1970	5/9/1996	1827 Frontage Road	De
7	Noble	Monica	President and CEO	3/23/1943	7/2/1998	1185 Woodridge Drive	Lit
8	Stephenson	Diana	Shipping Clerk	5/29/1982	6/22/2000	W318/N750 Driftway Court	En
9	Fields	Derek	Marketing Manager	12/12/1974	8/30/1998	1722 Ashworth Drive, Apt. A	Wi
10	Shapiro	Zoe	Administrative Assistant	10/21/1976	2/16/1998	3768 Kingstonview Court	Au
11	Liang	Chien	Senior Vice President, CFO	8/11/1948	10/13/1971	12542 N. Andiron Drive	La
12	Valentine	Theresa	Sales Representative	11/9/1968	1/5/1991	7468 Cambridge Court	Lit
13	Hays	Robert	Manufacturing Process Engineer	5/28/1963	7/16/2000	9266 Bay Run Circle	Wi
14	Calhoun	Jean	Credit Manager	1/20/1957	12/1/1986	1150 Crockett Pass	En
15	Moyer	Patrick	Customer Service Associate	5/6/1981	2/1/2001	27508 Fawn Hill Terrace	De
16	Bean	Austin	Warehouse Manager	12/5/1954	5/19/1997	9496 Blaine Avenue	La
17	Stanton	Rick	Vice President, Director of Manufacturing	4/6/1949	3/1/2000	5235 Lawrenceville Road	De
18	Martinez	Jorge	Product Line Manager	11/9/1971	11/14/1995	2909 19th Street North East	Au
19	Garcia	Lydia	Network Specialist	8/23/1978	3/9/2002	12A Broadway	De

The triangle in the record selector indicates that this is the current record.

The column of small, gray boxes to the left of the records are the record selectors.

3. Type 20 in the ID field and press Tab to move to the Last Name field. Notice that the symbol in the record selector changes to a pencil icon.

4. Type the data provided in Table 1.1 into the record, pressing Tab after each entry.

Table 1.1

Field	Data to be Typed
Last Name	Krause
First Name	Cheryl
Position Title	Recruiting Manager
Birth Date	7/11/1962
Hire Date	*(enter current date in m/d/yyyy format)*
Address	4436 Deer Stone Lane
City	Denver
State	CO
ZIP Code	80223-2385

Figure 1.13 The record for Cheryl Krause has been entered

Microsoft Access - [Employees : Table]

ID	Last Name	First Name	Position Title	Birth Date	Hire Date	Address	
1	Dunlap	Madison	Manufacturing Technician	7/4/1979	3/1/2001	6772 Wharfside Lane, #3B	Wi
2	McFadden	Aaron	Vice President of Marketing	5/18/1940	6/3/1965	N6031 Hwy 35	La
3	Gentry	Dolores	District Sales Manager	9/30/1952	8/4/1978	7193 Birch Bark Court	De
4	Helms	Jeffrey	Senior Design Technician	1/31/1955	4/10/1977	1185 Woodridge Drive	Au
5	Guzman	Isabel	Customer Service Manager	6/1/1959	9/10/1981	9592 Picadilly Court	Lit
6	Frost	Mark	Programmer Analyst	2/27/1970	5/9/1996	1827 Frontage Road	De
7	Noble	Monica	President and CEO	3/23/1943	7/2/1998	1185 Woodridge Drive	Lit
8	Stephenson	Diana	Shipping Clerk	5/29/1982	6/22/2000	W318/N750 Driftway Court	En
9	Fields	Derek	Marketing Manager	12/12/1974	8/30/1998	1722 Ashworth Drive, Apt. A	Wi
10	Shapiro	Zoe	Administrative Assistant	10/21/1976	2/16/1998	3768 Kingstonview Court	Au
11	Liang	Chien	Senior Vice President, CFO	8/11/1948	10/13/1971	12542 N. Andiron Drive	La
12	Valentine	Theresa	Sales Representative	11/9/1968	1/5/1991	7468 Cambridge Court	Lit
13	Hays	Robert	Manufacturing Process Engineer	5/28/1963	7/16/2000	9266 Bay Run Circle	Wi
14	Calhoun	Jean	Credit Manager	1/20/1957	12/1/1986	1150 Crockett Pass	En
15	Moyer	Patrick	Customer Service Associate	5/6/1981	2/1/2001	27508 Fawn Hill Terrace	De
16	Bean	Austin	Warehouse Manager	12/5/1954	5/19/1997	9496 Blaine Avenue	La
17	Stanton	Rick	Vice President, Director of Manufacturing	4/6/1949	3/1/2000	5235 Lawrenceville Road	De
18	Martinez	Jorge	Product Line Manager	11/9/1971	11/14/1995	2909 19th Street North East	Au
19	Garcia	Lydia	Network Specialist	8/23/1978	3/9/2002	12A Broadway	De
20	Krause	Cheryl	Recruiting Manager	7/11/1962	8/13/2002	4436 Deer Stone Lane	De

Record: 21 of 21

Datasheet View

After you press Tab in the last field, Access moves to a new record, and the record you just entered is automatically saved.

5. In the Home Phone field, (the last field in the record), type **303-555-7743** and press Tab. The insertion point moves to the first field in the next record, and the Krause record is automatically saved (see Figure 1.13).

6. Suppose you just received information that Ms. Krause's birth date should be 7/11/1965. Click in the Birth Date field in the record you just entered, and position the insertion point between the *6* and the *2*.

7. Press Delete and type **5**. The pencil icon appears in the record selector, indicating that there is new, unsaved data in the record.

Figure 1.14 Selecting a record in a datasheet

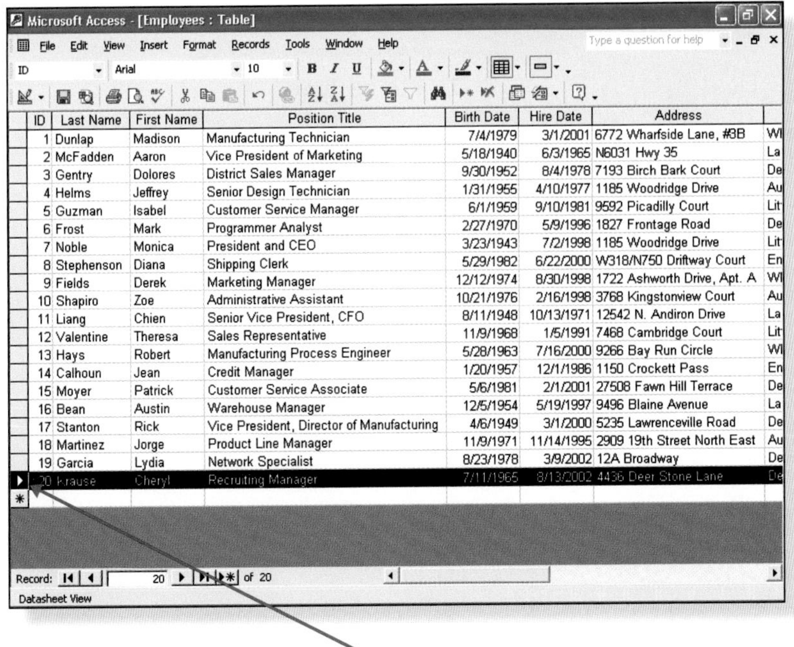

Microsoft Access - [Employees : Table]

ID	Last Name	First Name	Position Title	Birth Date	Hire Date	Address	
1	Dunlap	Madison	Manufacturing Technician	7/4/1979	3/1/2001	6772 Wharfside Lane, #3B	Wi
2	McFadden	Aaron	Vice President of Marketing	5/18/1940	6/3/1965	N6031 Hwy 35	La
3	Gentry	Dolores	District Sales Manager	9/30/1952	8/4/1978	7193 Birch Bark Court	De
4	Helms	Jeffrey	Senior Design Technician	1/31/1955	4/10/1977	1185 Woodridge Drive	Au
5	Guzman	Isabel	Customer Service Manager	6/1/1959	9/10/1981	9592 Picadilly Court	Lit
6	Frost	Mark	Programmer Analyst	2/27/1970	5/9/1996	1827 Frontage Road	De
7	Noble	Monica	President and CEO	3/23/1943	7/2/1998	1185 Woodridge Drive	Lit
8	Stephenson	Diana	Shipping Clerk	5/29/1982	6/22/2000	W318/N750 Driftway Court	En
9	Fields	Derek	Marketing Manager	12/12/1974	8/30/1998	1722 Ashworth Drive, Apt. A	Wi
10	Shapiro	Zoe	Administrative Assistant	10/21/1976	2/16/1998	3768 Kingstonview Court	Au
11	Liang	Chien	Senior Vice President, CFO	8/11/1948	10/13/1971	12542 N. Andiron Drive	La
12	Valentine	Theresa	Sales Representative	11/9/1968	1/5/1991	7468 Cambridge Court	Lit
13	Hays	Robert	Manufacturing Process Engineer	5/28/1963	7/16/2000	9266 Bay Run Circle	Wi
14	Calhoun	Jean	Credit Manager	1/20/1957	12/1/1986	1150 Crockett Pass	En
15	Moyer	Patrick	Customer Service Associate	5/6/1981	2/1/2001	27508 Fawn Hill Terrace	De
16	Bean	Austin	Warehouse Manager	12/5/1954	5/19/1997	9496 Blaine Avenue	La
17	Stanton	Rick	Vice President, Director of Manufacturing	4/6/1949	3/1/2000	5235 Lawrenceville Road	De
18	Martinez	Jorge	Product Line Manager	11/9/1971	11/14/1995	2909 19th Street North East	Au
19	Garcia	Lydia	Network Specialist	8/23/1978	3/9/2002	12A Broadway	De
20	Krause	Cheryl	Recruiting Manager	7/11/1965	8/13/2002	4436 Deer Stone Lane	De

Record: 20 of 20

Datasheet View

Click the record selector to select (highlight) the entire record.

8. Press the up arrow key to move to the previous record. The edited data is saved, and the pencil icon disappears.

9. Now you receive a memo that Ms. Krause won't be an employee at Saburo Sporting Goods after all. Click the record selector for Ms. Krause's record. The entire record is selected (see Figure 1.14).

10. Press Delete. When the message asking if you want to delete the record appears, click Yes.

11. Close the table.

Microsoft Office Specialist
AC2002 5.1

Access

Exercise 5 Overview:
Enter, Edit, and Delete Records in a Form

You can also enter, edit, and delete data using a form. In a form, you see the fields for only one record at a time instead of the whole datasheet of records and fields. You use the form's navigation toolbar to move to different records and add new records.

In a form, the record selector is a single vertical gray bar down the left side of the form. Just like in the table, there is a triangle in the record selector until you begin to edit. Then the triangle changes to a pencil icon, indicating that the record is being changed and the new data has not been saved. After you make your changes and move to a new record, the edited record is automatically saved.

Entering data in a form is just like entering data in a table, except there's no chance of entering data in the wrong record because only one record is displayed at a time.

In the following exercise, assume that Ms. Krause changed her mind and decided to take the position at Saburo Sporting Goods. You need to enter her data in the Employees table again. This time, however, you'll enter the data using the Employees form instead of directly in the table.

Step Through It™
Exercise 5: Manipulate records using a form

1. Restore the Database window to its smaller size, and then open the Employees form. Click the New Record button on the navigation toolbar. You see all the empty fields you saw in the Employees table, but on the form you can see all the fields at the same time, and only the fields for this record.

2. Type the data provided in Table 1.2 into the record, pressing Tab after each entry.

Table 1.2

Field	Data to be Typed
ID	20
Last Name	Krause
First Name	Cheryl
Position Title	Recruiting Manager
Birth Date	7/11/1965
Hire Date	*(enter current date in m/d/yyyy format)*
Address	4436 Deer Stone Lane
City	Denver
State	CO
ZIP Code	80223-2385
Home Phone	303-555-7743

Figure 1.15 Editing the City field in the Krause record

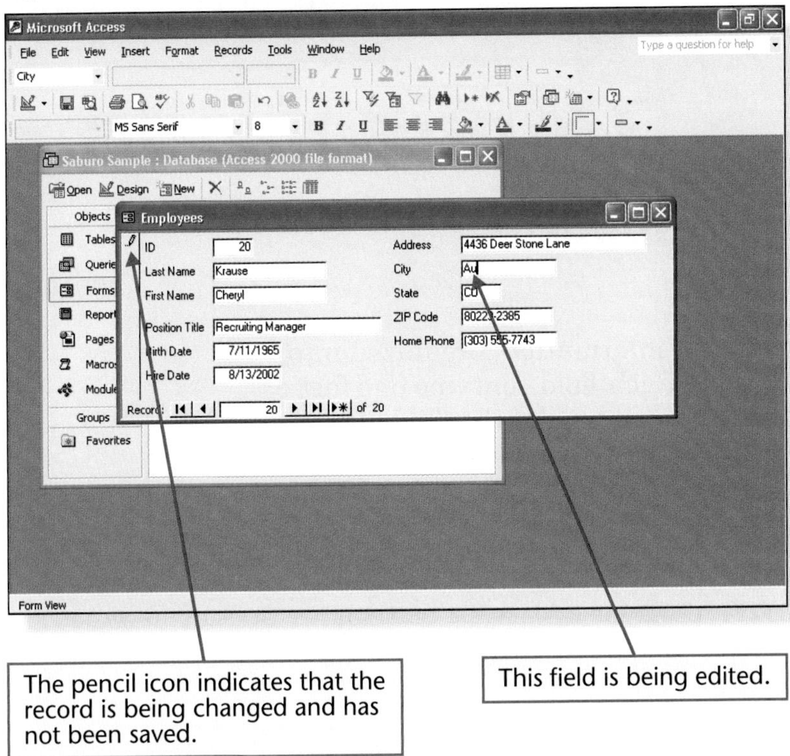
The pencil icon indicates that the record is being changed and has not been saved.
This field is being edited.

3 After you type data in the last field and press Tab, the record is saved, and a new record is displayed.

4 You just received information that Ms. Krause's address is incorrect—the city should be Aurora. Click the Previous Record button ◄ to redisplay the Krause record.

5 Press Tab to move forward until the City field is selected, and type Aurora to replace Denver (see Figure 1.15).

6 Click any button on the navigation toolbar to move to a different record—Access saves the data you edited.

Figure 1.16 Deleting a record in a form

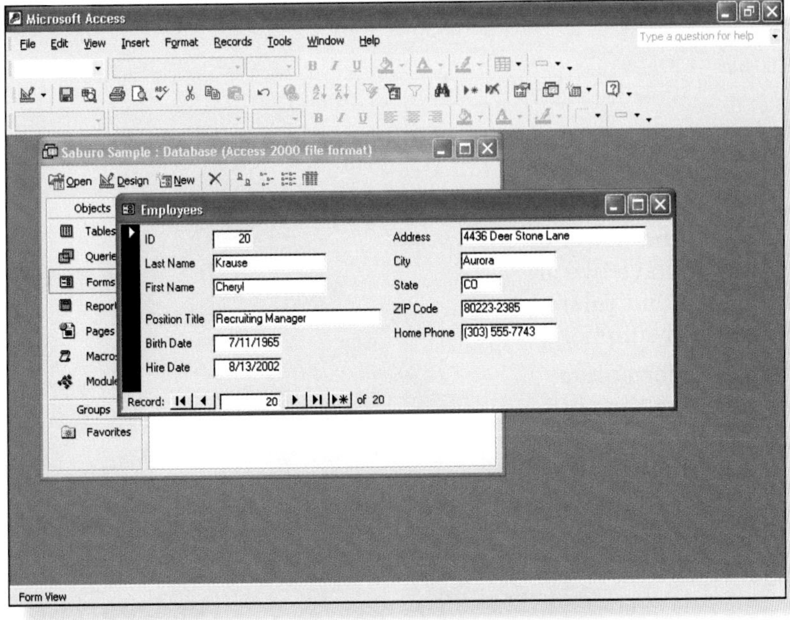

7 Ms. Krause decided not to work at Saburo after all. Click the Last Record button to display the Krause record.

8 Click the record selector. The record selector turns black, indicating that the entire record is selected (see Figure 1.16).

9 Press Delete. When Access asks if you are sure you want to delete the record, click Yes.

10 Close the form and close the database, but do not exit the Access program.

APPLY IT! After finishing Exercises 4–5, you may test your skills by completing Apply It! Guided Activity 2, Manipulate Records Using a Datasheet and a Form.

Business Connections

The Power of a Relational Database

As you know, a database is a body of information, organized into columns (fields) and rows (records). Each field contains one fact or piece of information about a particular item. All the fields for a particular item compose a record. A database can be as simple as one list of records, such as a list of parts and suppliers, with a field for part names, a field for supplier names, and fields for other supplier information (such as contact name, phone number, and so forth). A simple list such as this is called a flat-file database. In fact, when you worked with Word tables in Unit 1 or Excel worksheets in Unit 2, you were working with flat-file databases.

The Supplier ID field is used to relate these two tables.

PARTS

Part	Supplier ID
RAM 52	51
RAM 64	51
RAM 128	51
HD 6 GB	51
HD 12 GB	51
USB Port	52

SUPPLIERS

Supplier ID	Supplier Name	Contact	Phone Number
51	Parts-R-Us	Marty Lenowski	555-2061
52	USB Int'l	Chris Stevens	555-3758

Access at Work

A relational database such as Access is much more versatile than a flat-file database. The advantage and power of a relational database are clear when you have two or more lists of data that are about different but related subjects, such as the example of parts and suppliers.

- In a relational database, one type of information, such as part names, is recorded only one time in one list and never duplicated.
- Another type of different, yet related information, such as supplier names, contacts, and phone numbers, is recorded only one time in another list and never duplicated.
- Then you create a relationship between the two lists based on a field that is common to both lists.

Usually a common field is some type of ID field, such as a supplier ID number. Access uses that common field to "match up" the information in the two lists. You can then retrieve related information from the two lists and combine the information from both lists in new ways. Because the data in each list are not duplicated in the other list, you save storage space. Also, updating the information in the lists is easier and more accurate because you only need to update one occurrence of the data, instead of multiple occurrences.

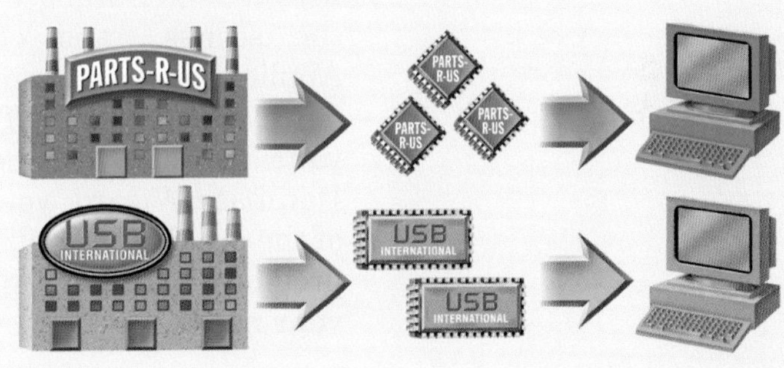

Access Objects Overview

As you learned in this lesson, an Access database contains database objects that you use to store and manipulate data.

- All data in a relational database are stored in tables, and none of the data is duplicated.
- The data in related tables are retrieved using queries.

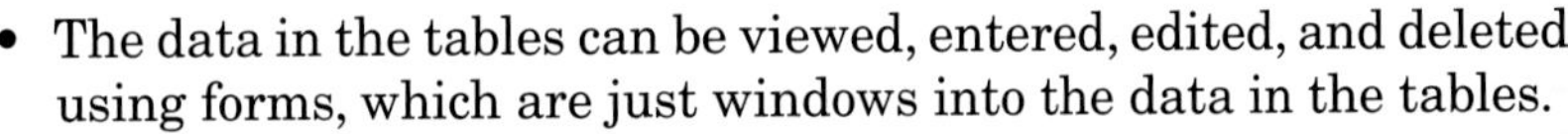

- The data in the tables can be viewed, entered, edited, and deleted using forms, which are just windows into the data in the tables.
- The data in the tables can be combined and presented for easy reading in reports, which are ready for printing.

Tables, queries, forms, and reports are called database objects. All the database objects that pertain to a specific enterprise (a company or a division) are kept in a single database file.

CRITICAL THINKING

1. **Summarizing Access Terms** Explain the differences between a field, a record, a database object, and a database file.
2. **Relational vs. Flat-File** What is one major advantage of a relational database over a flat-file database?

Microsoft Office Specialist
AC2002 1.1

Exercise 6 Overview:
Create a Database

So far in this lesson you've worked with data in an existing database. But that database had to be built before you could use it. There are two ways to create an Access database: (1) by using the Database Wizard, which creates a pre-defined database from a template, and (2) by creating a new, blank database from scratch.

Need Help?

Type: create an Access database

Microsoft Access provides several different wizards to help you accomplish complex procedures easily. The Database Wizard can quickly build a new database that's filled with objects and ready to use. The advantages of using the Database Wizard are that it automatically creates the various objects within the database, it's fast, and you can start using the database immediately. The disadvantage is that you don't know how the database is constructed, because the Database Wizard creates the database "behind the scenes," and often uses VBA (Visual Basic for Applications) programming code to make parts of the database functional. Thus, customizing the database to suit your purposes can be difficult. Also, when you use the Database Wizard, you must select your database from one of the pre-defined database templates that Microsoft Access provides, and there may not be a template that is right for your needs.

When you build a database from scratch, you create each object you need separately, based on the data you want to store in the database and what you want to do with that data. Customizing a database you build yourself is much easier than customizing a database created by the Database Wizard, and you'll have a greater understanding of Microsoft Access when you create a new, blank database and the objects in it.

In the following exercises, you will use the Database Wizard to create a database, and then you will create a new, blank database.

Quick Tip

You can find and download more database templates on the Microsoft Web site. To go to the Web site, open the New File task pane and click the Templates on Microsoft.com link.

Figure 1.17 Choosing a database template

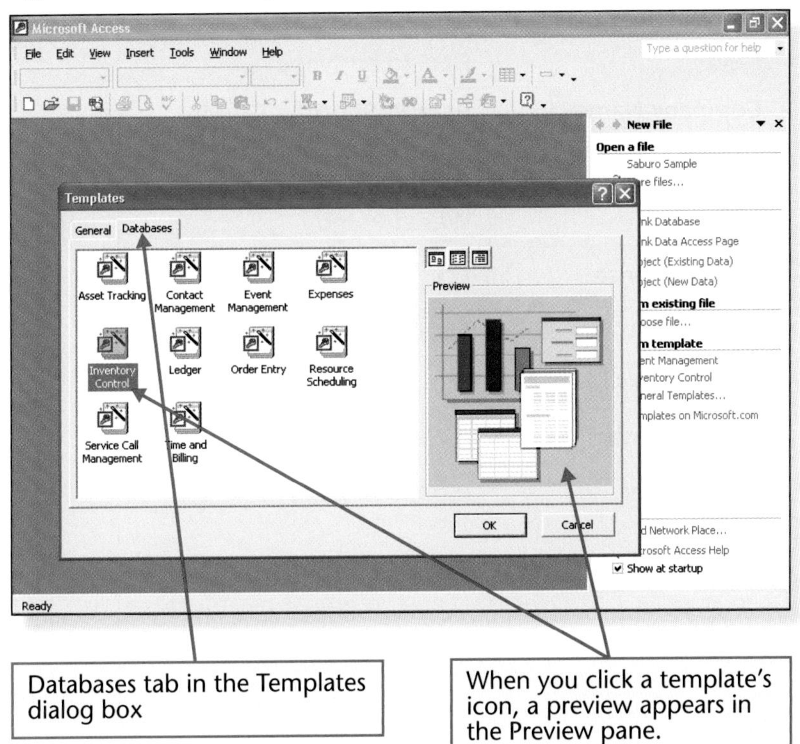

When you click a template's icon, a preview appears in the Preview pane.

Step Through It™

Exercise 6A: Create a database using the Database Wizard

1. On the Database toolbar, click the New button to open the New File task pane.
2. In the *New from template* section of the New File task pane, click the General Templates link to open the Templates dialog box.
3. Click the Databases tab, and then click the Inventory Control icon (see Figure 1.17). Then click OK.

Figure 1.18 Using the Database Wizard

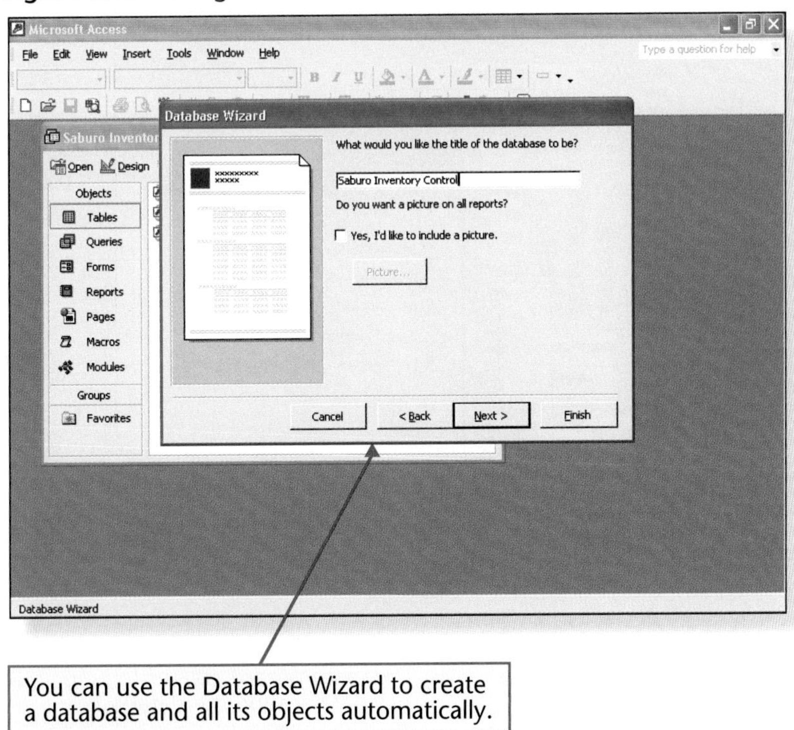

You can use the Database Wizard to create a database and all its objects automatically.

4. In the File New Database dialog box, type the name Saburo Inventory Control for the new database, and select the *Lesson 1* subfolder in the *Unit 3* folder in the *Save in* box. Then click Create.
5. Follow the steps in the wizard. For each step (dialog box) in the wizard, read the step, accept the default settings, and click Next to move to the next step (dialog box).
6. When the wizard asks what you would like the title of the database to be, type the name Saburo Inventory Control. (See Figure 1.18.)

Access

Access

7. Click Next, and then click Finish. The wizard creates the database using your selections.

8. Access displays a message prompting you to enter your company name, address, and related information. Click OK to close the message box.

9. In the My Company Information form that appears, enter the data provided in Table 1.3, pressing Tab after each entry.

Table 1.3

Field	Data to be Typed
Company Name	Saburo Sporting Goods
Address	5588 Cardinal Avenue
City	Wheat Ridge
State/Province	CO
Postal Code	80033
Country/Region	USA
Phone Number	(303) 555-3984
Fax Number	(303) 555-4975

10. Close the form (see Figure 1.19).

11. Select some of the options on the Main Switchboard. (Do not choose the *Exit this database* option.) Then close the Main Switchboard form.

12. Click the Restore Up button on the minimized Database window to display it. Select the various object groups in the Objects bar to display the numerous objects in the right pane of the Database window.

13. Close the *Saburo Inventory Control.mdb* database.

Figure 1.19 The new database created by the wizard

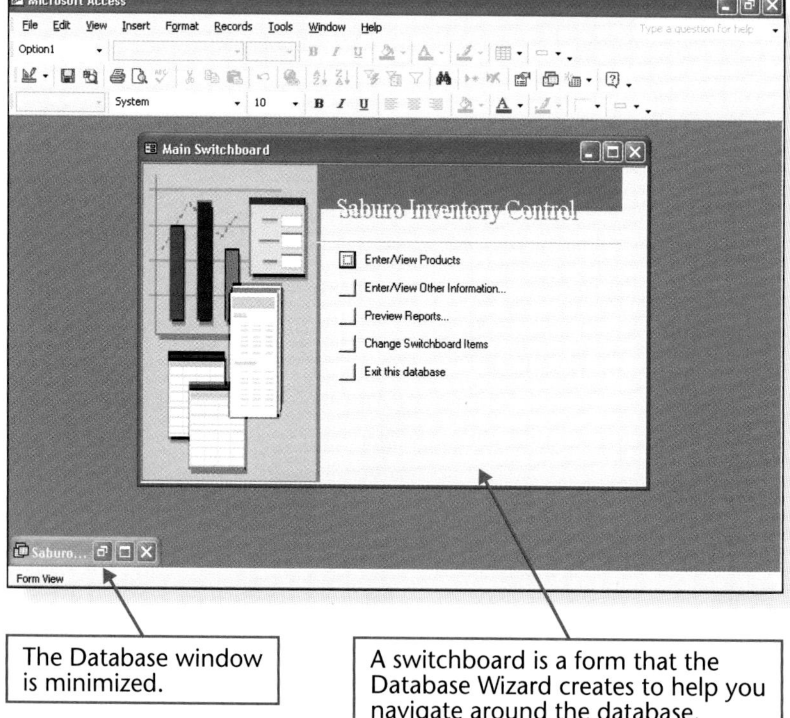

Figure 1.20 New File task pane in the Access application window

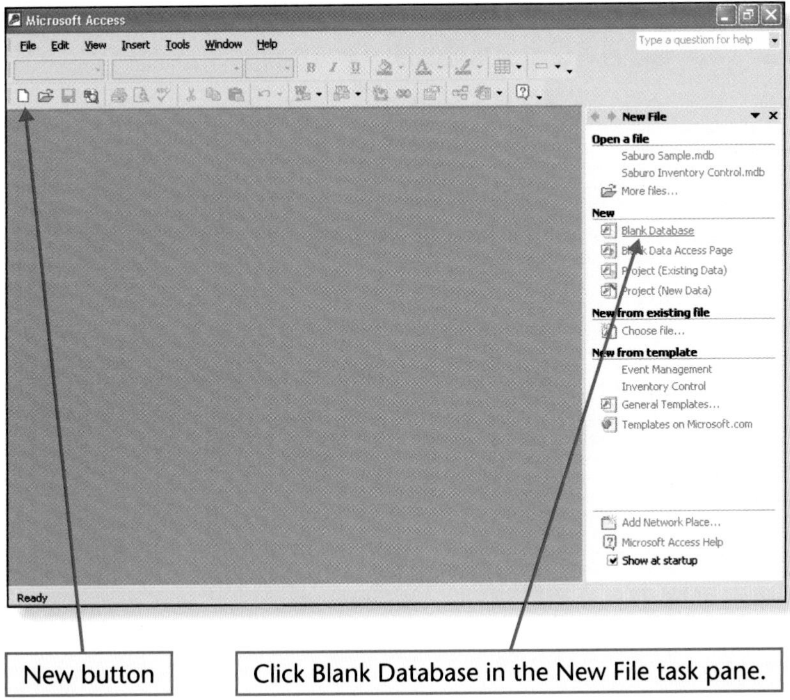
New button
Click Blank Database in the New File task pane.

Figure 1.21 Creating a new, blank database

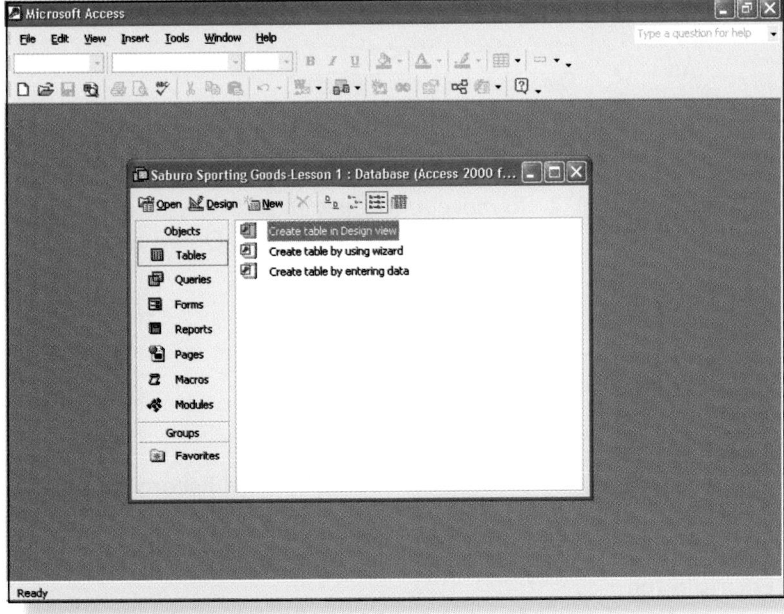

Step Through It™

Exercise 6B: Create a new, blank database

1. Click the New button on the Database toolbar to open the New File task pane.
2. In the *New* section of the New File task pane, click Blank Database (see Figure 1.20).
3. In the Save in text box of the File New Database dialog box, navigate to the *Lesson 1* subfolder in the *Unit 3* folder. Type **Saburo Sporting Goods-Lesson 1** in the *File name* box, and then click Create. A new, blank Database window appears (see Figure 1.21).
4. Click the various object groups in the Objects bar. Notice that there are no objects displayed in the right pane of the Database window; there are only options to create new objects. You'll create the database objects (tables, forms, queries, reports, and data access pages) as you work through the remaining lessons in this unit.
5. Click the Close button in the upper-right portion of the Database window to close the *Saburo Sporting Goods-Lesson 1.mdb* database.

APPLY IT!

After finishing Exercise 6B, you may test your skills by completing Apply It! Guided Activity 3, Create a New, Blank Database.

Procedure Summary

Display the Objects in an Access Database

1. Open an Access database file.
2. In the Database window, click the name of an object group in the Objects bar.
   OR
   Click **View** . . . . **Alt + V**
   Point to **Database Objects** . . . . **J**
   Select the name of the object.
3. View the objects in the selected group in the right pane of the Database window.

Open a Table (Datasheet view)

1. In the Database window, click **Tables** in the Objects bar.
2. Double-click the table name in the right pane of the Database window.
   OR
   Select the table name in the right pane of the Database window and click **Open** . . . . **Alt + O**

Open a Query (Datasheet view)

1. In the Database window, click **Queries** in the Objects bar.
2. Double-click the query name in the right pane of the Database window.
   OR
   Select the query name in the right pane of the Database window and click **Open** . . . . **Alt + O**

Open a Form (Form view)

1. In the Database window, click **Forms** in the Objects bar.
2. Double-click the form name in the right pane of the Database window.
   OR
   Select the form name in the right pane of the Database window and click **Open** . . . . **Alt + O**

Open a Report (Print Preview)

1. In the Database window, click **Reports** in the Objects bar.
2. Double-click the report name in the right pane of the Database window.
   OR
   Select the report name in the right pane of the Database window and click **Preview** . . . . **Alt + P**

Switch to Design View

1. Open an object in an Access database.
2. Click **View** . . . . **Alt + V, D**

Navigate Records in a Datasheet or Form

1. *To move to a previous record:*
   Click **Previous Record** . . . .**Up arrow key**
2. *To move to the next record:*
   Click **Next Record** . . . **Down arrow key**
3. *To move to the first record:*
   Click **First Record** . . . .**Ctrl + Home**
4. *To move to the last record:*
   Click **Last Record** . . . . **Ctrl + End**

To move to a specific record:

5. Double-click in the Specific Record box . .**F5**
6. Type the desired record number.
7. Press Enter.

Navigate Fields in a Datasheet or Form

1. *To move to the next field in a record:*
   Click in the desired field . . . . . **Tab OR Right arrow key**

2. *To move to the previous field in a record:* Click in the desired field. . . . . . . **Shift + Tab OR Left arrow key**

3. *To move to the first field in a record:* Click in the desired field. . . . . **Home**

4. *To move to the last field in a record:* Click in the desired field. . . . . **End**

Add a Record in a Datasheet or Form

1. Click **New Record** ▸✱.
   OR
   Click **Insert**. . . . . **Alt + I**
   Click **New Record**. . . . . **W**
2. Type the data in the first field.
3. Press Tab.
4. Type the data in the next field.
5. Repeat steps 3 and 4 until all data for the record are entered.

Edit Data in a Datasheet or Form

1. Navigate to the record you want to edit.
2. Click in the field to position the insertion point.
3. Delete incorrect text, if necessary.
4. Type correct text.

OR

1. Navigate to the record you want to edit.
2. Select (highlight) the data you want to edit.
3. Type new data to replace the selected data.

Delete a Record in a Datasheet or Form

1. Click the record selector of the record you wish to delete.
2. Press Delete.

OR

1. Click anywhere in the record you wish to delete.
2. Click **Delete Record**.

OR

1. Click anywhere in the record you wish to delete.
2. Click **Edit**. . . . . **Alt + E**
3. Click **Delete Record**. . . . . **R**

Create a Database Using the Database Wizard

1. Click **New**.
   OR
   Click **File**. . . . . **Alt + F**
   Click **New**. . . . . **N**
2. In the *New from template* section of the New File task pane, click General Templates.
3. In the Templates dialog box, click the Databases tab.
4. Select the desired template icon.
5. Click OK.
6. In the File New Database dialog box, type the name of the database file and navigate to the folder where you wish to save the file.
7. Click Create.
8. Follow the steps in the wizard to create the database.

Create a New, Blank Database

1. Click **New**.
   OR
   Click **File** . . . . **Alt + F**
   Click **New** . . . . **N**
2. In the *New* section of the New File task pane, click Blank Database.
3. In the File New Database dialog box, type the name of the database file and navigate to the folder where you wish to save the file.
4. Click Create.

Lesson Review and Exercises

Access

Summary Checklist

- ☑ Can you start Access and display the various database objects in the Database window?
- ☑ Do you know the four most common database objects and the purpose of each?
- ☑ Do you understand the differences between Datasheet view, Form view, Print Preview, and Design view?
- ☑ Can you open a database object and switch views?
- ☑ Do you understand the difference between a record and a field?
- ☑ Can you navigate among records in a datasheet?
- ☑ Can you add, edit, and delete a record in a datasheet and in a form?
- ☑ Can you create a database using the Database Wizard?
- ☑ Can you create a new, blank database?

Key Terms

- database (p. 306)
- database object (p. 306)
- Database window (p. 306)
- datasheet (p. 312)
- Datasheet view (p. 307)
- Design view (p. 307)
- field (p. 312)
- form (p. 307)
- Form view (p. 307)
- Print Preview (p. 307)
- query (p. 307)
- record (p. 312)
- record selector (p. 315)
- relational database (p. 306)
- report (p. 307)
- table (p. 307)

Access

APPLY IT! Guided Activities

1. Examine Objects in Different Views and Navigate Records

Three friends are partners in LawnMowers, a small lawn-mowing business. They're considering using Access to store and maintain the records for the business. However, before they commit to using Access, they've asked you to show them a sample database for a similar business. Follow these steps:

a. Open the *LawnMowers Sample.mdb* database.

b. Using the Objects bar in the Database window, display the objects contained in the database **(see Figure 1.22)**.

c. Do the following for each table and query in the database:

   (1) Open the object in Datasheet view and maximize the window, if necessary.

   (2) Use the appropriate buttons on the navigation toolbar to move among the records.

   (3) Switch to Design view and examine the object's design.

   (4) Return to Datasheet view.

   (5) Close the object.

Figure 1.22 Use the Objects bar to display the various objects in a database

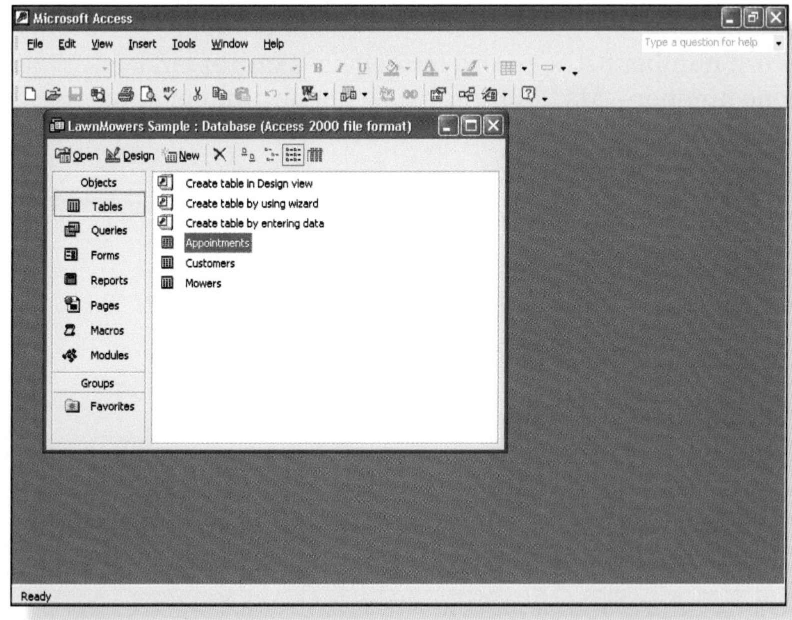

Access

d. Restore the Database window to its smaller size, and open the Customers form in Form view. Use the appropriate buttons on the navigation toolbar to examine each record. Switch to Design view to examine the form's design. (Use the scroll bars or maximize the window to view the entire form.) Then return to Form view and close the form.

e. Open the Mower Appointments report in Print Preview. Switch to Design view to examine the report's design. (Use the scroll bars or maximize the window to view the entire report.) Then return to Print Preview and close the report.

f. Close the *LawnMowers Sample.mdb* database.

2. Manipulate Records Using a Datasheet and a Form

To further demonstrate how to use an Access database to the three partners in the lawn-mowing business, you offer to enter, edit, and delete a few records in the sample database. Follow these steps:

a. Open the *LawnMowers Sample.mdb* database.

b. Open the Customers form and enter the following data in a new record:
Customer ID: 9
Last Name: Adkins
First Name: David
Street Address: 725 Sibcy Road
City: Denver
State: CO
ZIP Code: 80210-2783
Phone Number: 303-555-3704

c. Navigate to record number 8, the record for Felicia Ramirez, and correct the phone number—Ms. Ramirez's new phone number is 303-555-6390.

d. Navigate to record number 3, the record for Carl Yust, and delete the record. Then close the Customers form.

e. Open the Customers table and examine it. Notice that the changes you just made using the Customers form are reflected in the Customers table **(see Figure 1.23)**.

Figure 1.23 Changes made to the data using the Customers form are reflected in the Customers table

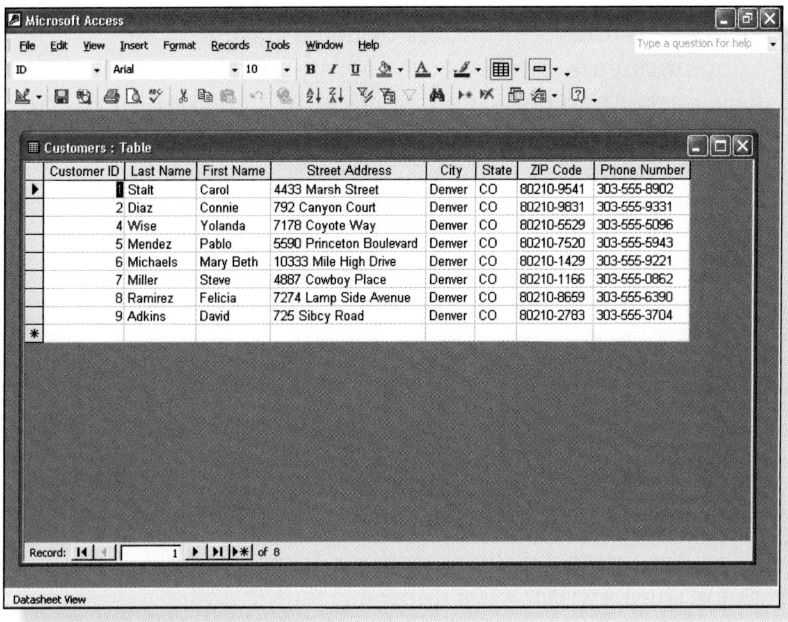

Customer ID	Last Name	First Name	Street Address	City	State	ZIP Code	Phone Number
1	Stalt	Carol	4433 Marsh Street	Denver	CO	80210-9541	303-555-8902
2	Diaz	Connie	792 Canyon Court	Denver	CO	80210-9831	303-555-9331
4	Wise	Yolanda	7178 Coyote Way	Denver	CO	80210-5529	303-555-5096
5	Mendez	Pablo	5590 Princeton Boulevard	Denver	CO	80210-7520	303-555-5943
6	Michaels	Mary Beth	10333 Mile High Drive	Denver	CO	80210-1429	303-555-9221
7	Miller	Steve	4887 Cowboy Place	Denver	CO	80210-1166	303-555-0862
8	Ramirez	Felicia	7274 Lamp Side Avenue	Denver	CO	80210-8659	303-555-6390
9	Adkins	David	725 Sibcy Road	Denver	CO	80210-2783	303-555-3704

f. Enter the following data in a new record in the Customers table datasheet:
Customer ID: 10
Last Name: Flora
First Name: Susan
Street Address: 4665 Pleasant View Drive
City: Denver
State: CO
ZIP Code: 80210-7721
Phone Number: 303-555-2036

g. Examine the record you just entered and correct any data entry errors, if necessary.

h. Close the Customers table.

i. Close the *LawnMowers Sample.mdb* database.

3. Create a New, Blank Database

The three partners have decided that they should use Access to store and maintain their business records. They want to use a database to track lawn-mowing appointments with customers, provide an appointments list for each partner, and maintain customer information so that the partners can periodically mail informational flyers to their customers. The partners have asked you to create and maintain the database for their business.

Follow these steps to create a new, blank database for LawnMowers:

a. Click the New button on the Database toolbar. In the New File task pane, click Blank Database.

b. Name the new database LawnMowers-Lesson 1, and save it in the *Lesson 1* subfolder in the *Unit 3* folder **(see Figure 1.24)**. Then click Create to build the database.

c. Close the *LawnMowers-Lesson 1.mdb* database.

Note: In the Guided Activities for the next three lessons, you'll create the objects for the LawnMowers database, enter and import data, and make the database completely functional.

Figure 1.24 Creating a new, blank database

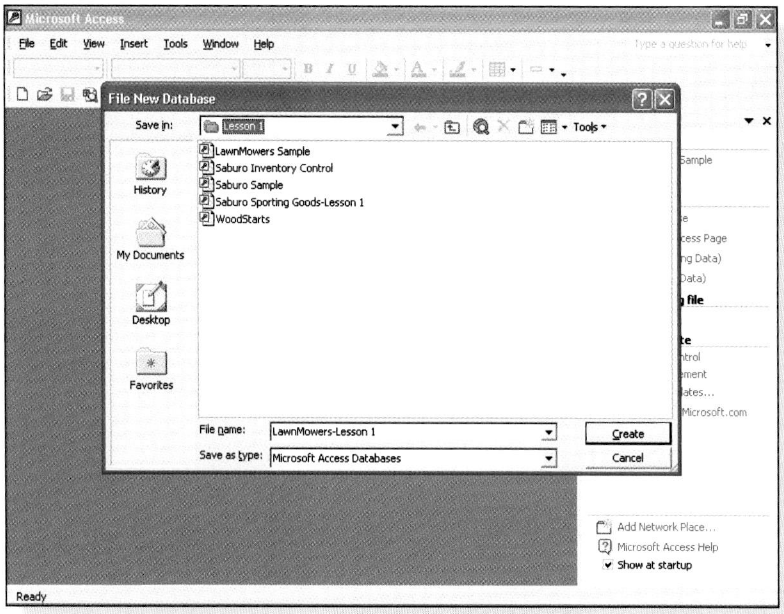

Do It Yourself

1. Examine a Database

You have recently been hired as the database manager for WoodStarts, a small woodshop business. WoodStarts makes wood blanks for trophy manufacturers to use in wall plaques and trophies. The shaped wood blanks are made in three sizes (small, medium, and large), and in three different woods (pine, oak, and walnut).

The business has four employees, who are paid an hourly wage, and eight wholesale customers (trophy manufacturers). The database you will be managing is used to store and track customer and employee data.

a. Open the *WoodStarts.mdb* database.

b. Open the Employees table and maximize the window. Scroll the datasheet horizontally to view all the fields. Examine the table in Design view, and then close it.

c. Open the Products table and examine it in both Datasheet view and Design view. Then close the table.

d. Open the Product Information query, examine it in both Datasheet view and Design view, and then close the query.

e. Open the Employees form, restore the window to its smaller size, and navigate the records in Form view.

f. Switch to Design view, maximize the window, and examine the form's design. Then close the form.

g. Open the Products form, restore the window to its smaller size, and navigate the records in Form view.

h. Switch to Design view, maximize the window, and examine the form's design. Then close the form.

i. Open the List of Products and Prices report and examine it in Print Preview. Switch to Design view and examine the report's design. Then close the report.

j. Close the *Woodstarts.mdb* database.

2. Manipulate Database Records

One of the employees at Woodstarts, Arthur Hemingway, is off to college out of state, and won't be able to continue with WoodStarts. You need to delete his record from the Employees table. A new employee has been hired to replace Arthur Hemingway, and you need to enter the new employee information using the Employees form. To perform these tasks, do the following:

a. Open the *Woodstarts.mdb* database.

b. Open the Employees table and locate the Hemingway record. Delete the Hemingway record **(see Figure 1.25)**. Then close the Employees table.

Figure 1.25 Deleting the Hemingway record

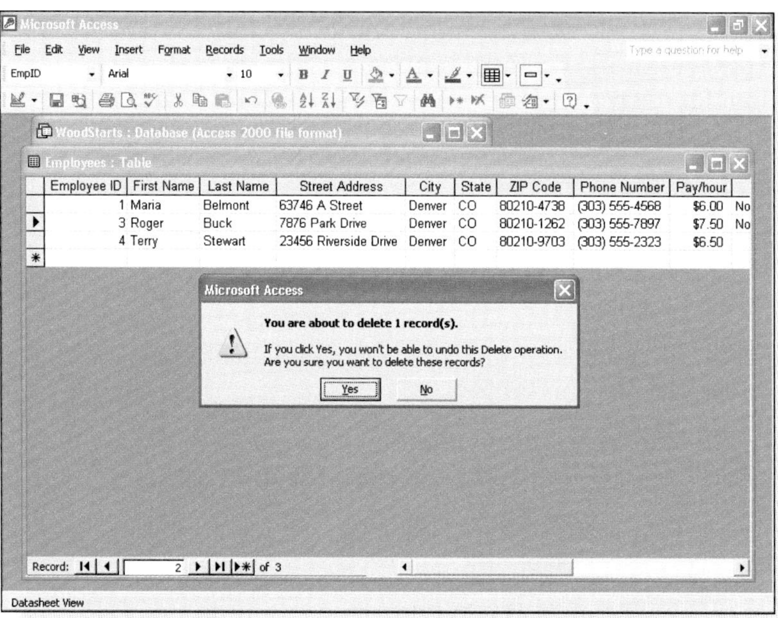

c. Open the Employees form, and enter the following data in a new record **(see Figure 1.26)**:
Employee ID: 5
First Name: Andrew
Last Name: Smith
Street Address: 124 Oakton Street
City: Denver
State: CO
ZIP Code: 80210-4728
Phone Number: (303) 555-6374
Pay/hour: $6.50
Notes: Available weekends

Figure 1.26 The Employees form in the *WoodStarts* database

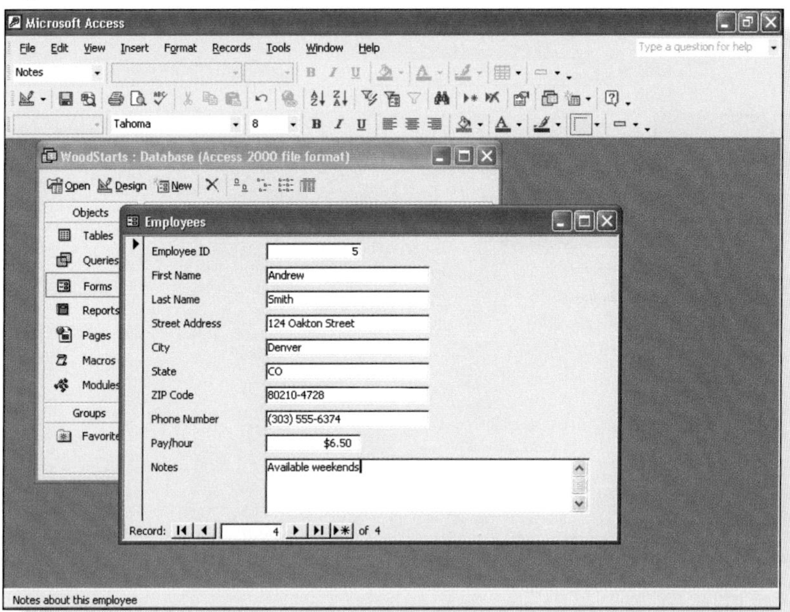

d. Close the Employees form.

e. Another employee, Maria Belmont, has changed her phone number. Open the Employees table, and change Maria Belmont's phone number to (303) 555-7774. Then close the Employees table.

f. Close the *WoodStarts.mdb* database.

3. Create a New Database From an Access Template

As your community service project, you have volunteered to help organize a fund-raising event for a local charity. You are responsible for creating a database to track and maintain all the data for the event. Follow these steps to create an Event Management database using the Database Wizard:

a. Click New on the Database toolbar. In the New File task pane, click General Templates.

b. On the Databases tab in the Templates dialog box, double-click the Event Management icon.

c. In the File New Database dialog box, name the new database Fund-raising Event, and save it in the *Lesson 1* subfolder of the *Unit 3* folder.

d. Follow the wizard steps. Select the Blends style for screen displays and the Casual style for printed reports **(see Figure 1.27)**.

Figure 1.27 Selecting a style for printed reports

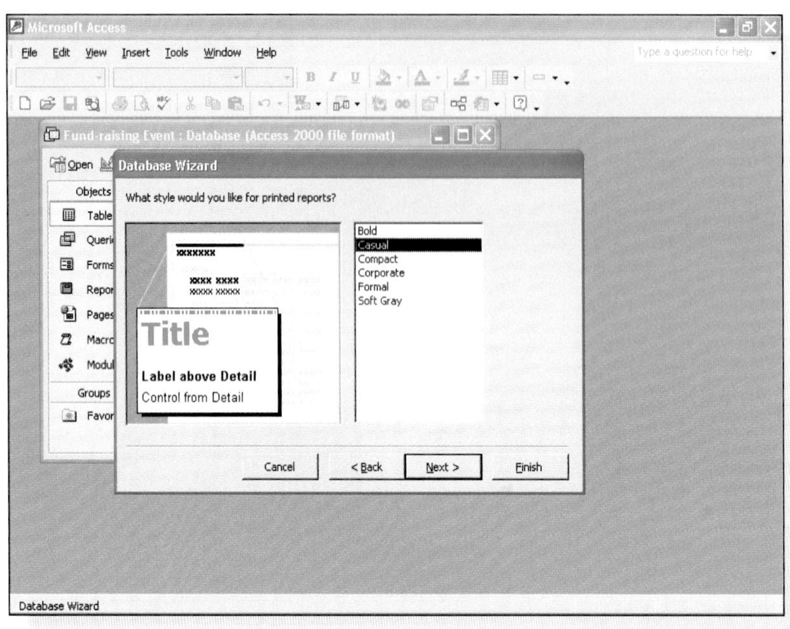

e. Type Fund-raising Event as the title for the database, and then finish the database. You do not need to complete the My Company Information form—just close that form when it appears.

f. Explore the various objects in the database **(see Figure 1.28)**. Then click the *Exit this database* option.

Figure 1.28 Creating a database using the Database Wizard

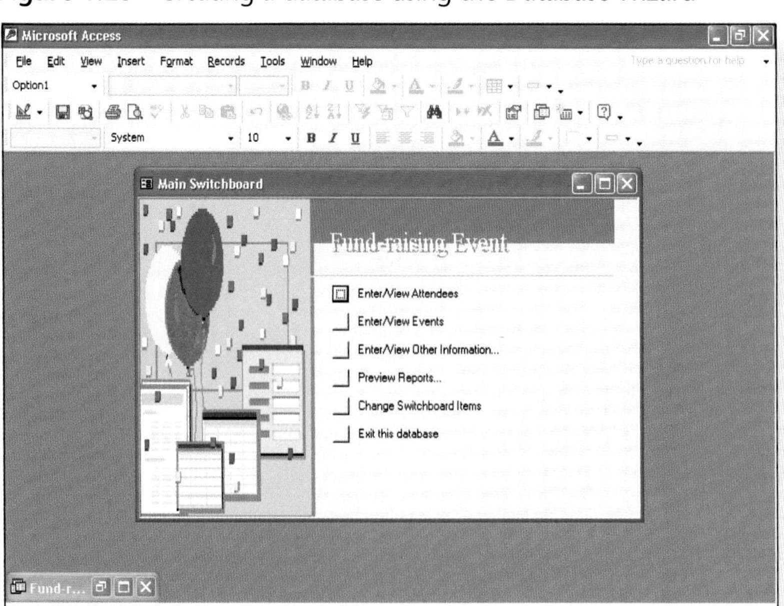

Challenge Yourself

Check Your Spelling

In order to maintain the integrity of a database, users must enter correct data. As you'll learn later in this unit, Access offers several sophisticated methods to help ensure accurate data entry. However, you should already know how to use one of the basic data-entry tools that Access offers—the Spelling tool.

The Spelling tool in Access works the same way as the Spelling tool in the other Microsoft Office programs you've learned about thus far. You can check spelling in tables, queries, and forms. You cannot check spelling directly in reports, so you must make sure the data in the table or query on which your report is based are spelled correctly.

Open the Products table in the *Saburo Sample.mdb* database and maximize the window. Use the Spelling tool to check the spelling in the datasheet. There are three ways to activate the Spelling tool: You can select Spelling on the Tools menu, you can press F7 on the keyboard, or you can simply click the Spelling button on the Table Datasheet toolbar. If a word is spelled incorrectly, highlight the correct spelling in the Spelling dialog box and click Change **(see Figure 1.29)**. If Access highlights a word that is spelled correctly, click Ignore or click Add to add the word to the dictionary. After you've finished checking the spelling and making any corrections, close the Products table and close the *Saburo Sample.mdb* database.

Figure 1.29 Checking the spelling in a datasheet

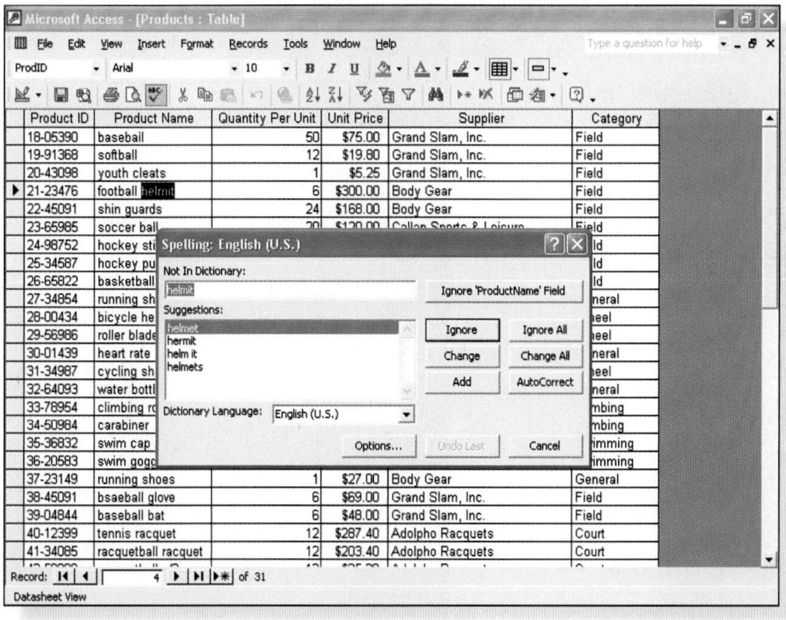

Lesson 2

Designing a Presentation

Lesson Exercise Objectives

After completing this lesson, you'll be able to do the following tasks:

1. Create tables
2. Modify table design
3. Create an input mask
4. Import, export, and link Access data
5. Define relationships and enforce referential integrity
6. Create a Lookup field

Key Terms

- data type (p. 346)
- export (p. 356)
- field name (p. 345)
- field property (p. 346)
- import (p. 354)
- input mask (p. 349)
- junction table (p. 362)
- link (p. 357)
- Lookup field (p. 369)
- many-to-many relationship (p. 362)
- one-to-many relationship (p. 362)
- one-to-one relationship (p. 363)
- orphan (p. 364)
- primary key (p. 340)
- primary table (p. 362)
- referential integrity (p. 364)
- related table (p. 362)
- relationship (p. 361)
- subdatasheet (p. 365)

Microsoft Office Specialist Activities

AC2002: 2.1, 2.2, 2.3, 2.4, 6.1, 6.2, 8.1, 8.2

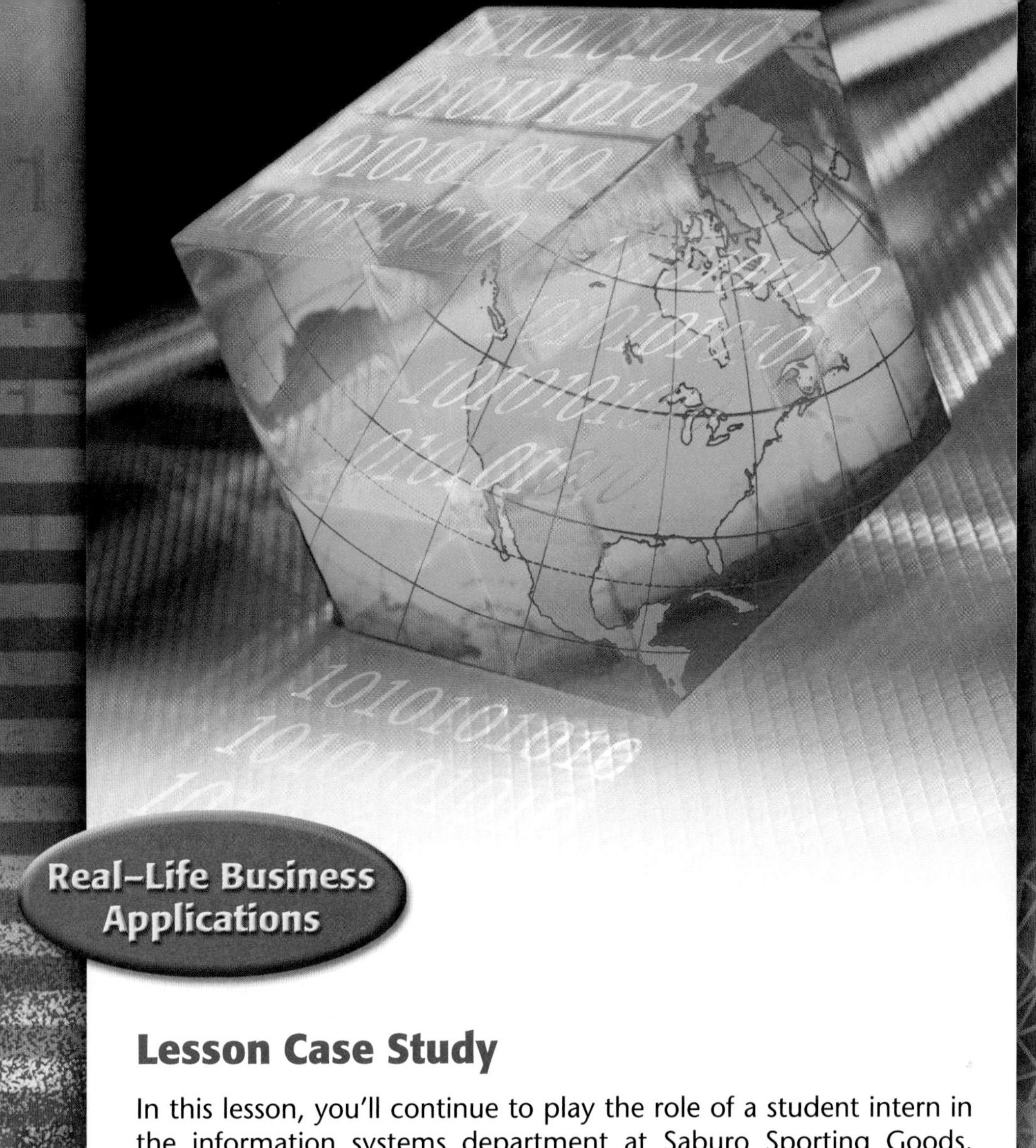

Real-Life Business Applications

Lesson Case Study

In this lesson, you'll continue to play the role of a student intern in the information systems department at Saburo Sporting Goods. During this phase of your internship, you will create and modify tables in an Access database. Keep the following information in mind as you work through this lesson.

- **Job responsibilities and goals.** You now know how to enter, edit, and delete data in an existing database, and you know how to create a new database. The next step in building a database is to create the tables that will store the data.
- **The project.** You will create and modify some tables in the Saburo Sporting Goods database. You will also create relationships that join the tables so that the data in related records in different tables can be manipulated and combined in new, useful ways. You will also import, export and link Access data.
- **The challenge ahead.** In Lesson 1, you created the basic Saburo Sporting Goods database shell. Now you must create and modify the database tables and establish relationships, in order to make the database truly functional and useful.

Microsoft Office Specialist AC2002 2.1

Access

Exercise 1 Overview: Create Tables

All data in a database are stored in tables. In Lesson 1, you entered, modified, and deleted data in an existing table; in this lesson, you'll actually create some tables.

When you create a table, one of the important decisions you'll need to make is whether to include a primary key, and if so, which field should be the primary key. A **primary key** is a field that uniquely identifies each record in a table. There cannot be two identical entries in a table's primary key field. So, after you've designated a field as the primary key, Access won't allow you to enter a duplicate entry in that field.

Need Help?

Type: about primary keys

If a table has a field that always contains unique data for every record, such as a field that contains part numbers or social security numbers, that field would make an ideal primary key. When you create a new table, you can either allow Access to add the primary key, or you can set your own primary key in one of the table's existing fields. You can identify the field that has been designated as the primary key when you view a table in Design view (see Figure 2.1).

Figure 2.1 Identifying the primary key in Design view

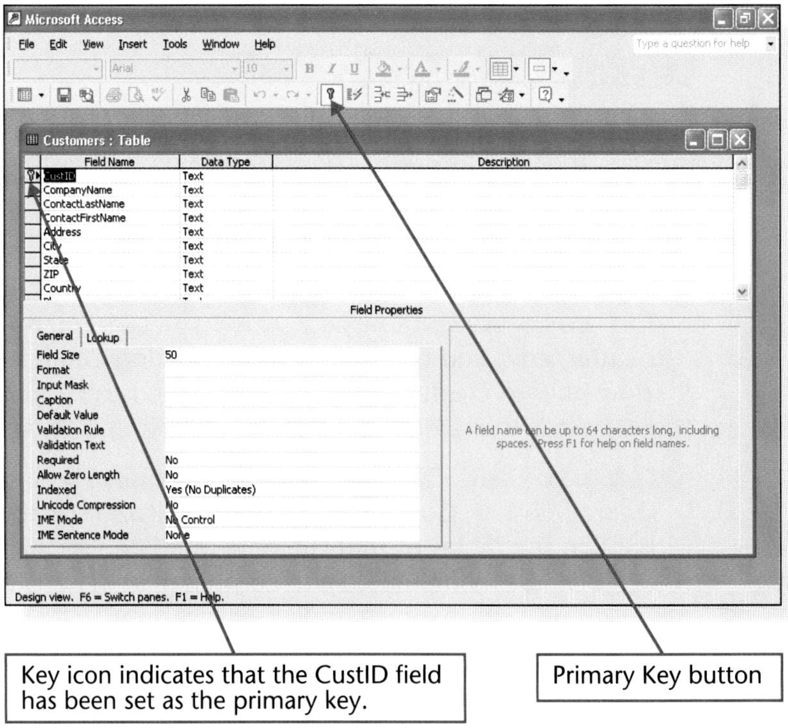

Key icon indicates that the CustID field has been set as the primary key.

Primary Key button

Create a Table Using the Table Wizard

In Lesson 1 you used a wizard (specifically the Database Wizard) to guide you through the process of creating a database. In the following exercise, you will use the Table Wizard to create a new table. Access will build a table based on the options you choose in each Table Wizard step.

The *Saburo Sporting Goods-Lesson 2.mdb* database that you will be working with in this lesson already contains some tables. However, another table is needed to store information about Saburo's suppliers. In the following exercise, you will create a Suppliers table using the Table Wizard. The table will contain fields for the supplier company name, the contact name in that company, the contact's phone number, and some informational notes about the company and what it supplies.

Type: create a table

Access

Figure 2.2 Starting the Table Wizard

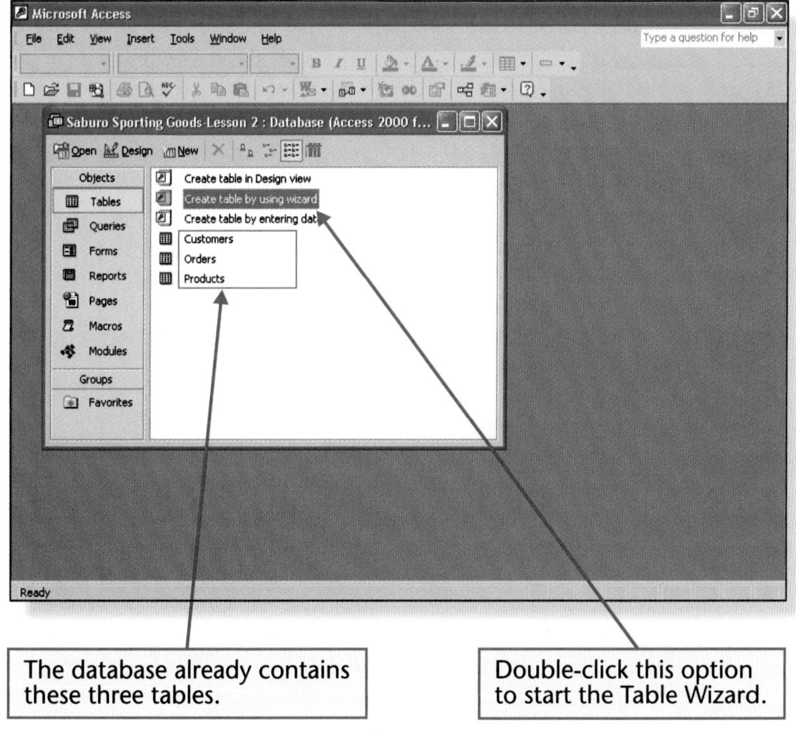

The database already contains these three tables.

Double-click this option to start the Table Wizard.

Step Through It™

Exercise 1A: Create a table using the Table Wizard

1. Open the *Saburo Sporting Goods-Lesson 2.mdb* database.
2. In the Database window, click Tables in the Objects bar, if it's not already selected. The database already contains three tables: Customers, Orders, and Products.
3. Double-click *Create table by using wizard* in the right pane of the Database window (see Figure 2.2). The Table Wizard starts.

Another Way

To start the Table Wizard, you can also click New on the Database window toolbar, and double-click Table Wizard in the NewTable dialog box.

Access

4 In the first Table Wizard step, click the Business option, if it's not already selected. Then scroll down the *Sample Tables* list and click Suppliers.

5 In the *Sample Fields* list, double-click SupplierID, SupplierName, ContactName, PhoneNumber, and Notes. All of these fields are added to the *Fields in my new table* list (see Figure 2.3). Then click Next.

Figure 2.3 Choosing a sample table and sample fields in the Table Wizard

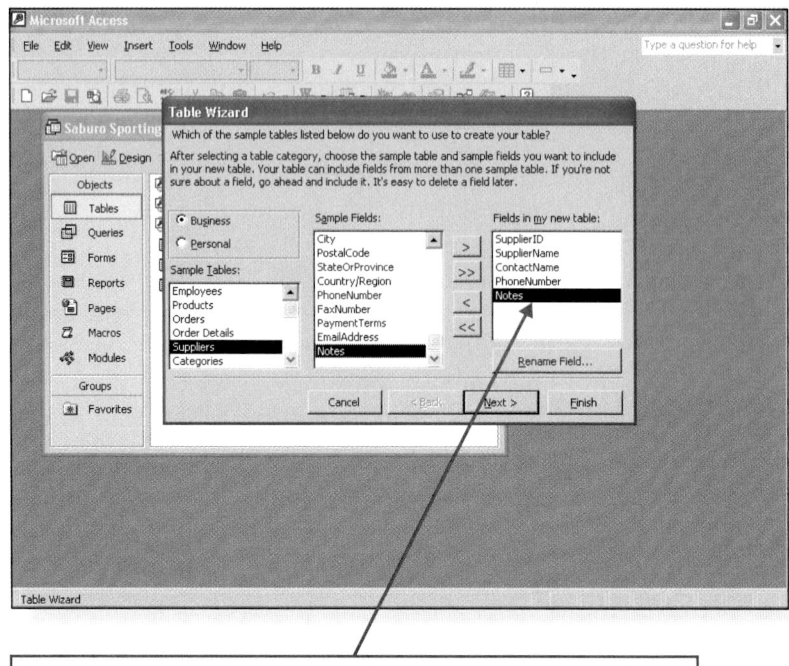

The sample fields are added to the *Fields in my new table* list.

6 Accept the table name Access suggests, *Suppliers*. Also, verify that the *Yes, set a primary key for me* option is selected. Click Next.

7 The next step asks about relationships. Click Next to skip this step, because you'll set up your own relationships later.

8 In the last step, click the *Enter data directly into the table* option (if necessary), and click Finish. The finished table opens in Datasheet view (see Figure 2.4).

Figure 2.4 The new Suppliers table in Datasheet view

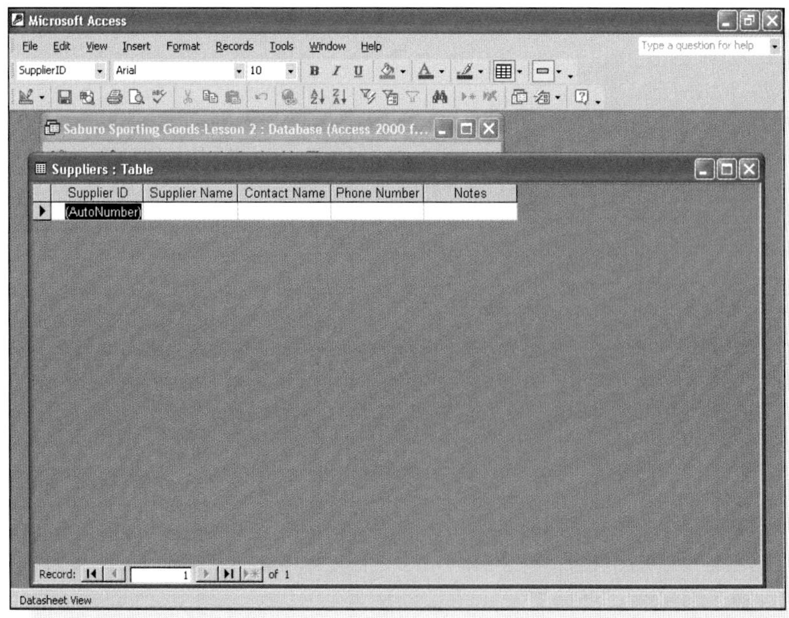

Figure 2.5 The new Suppliers table in Design view

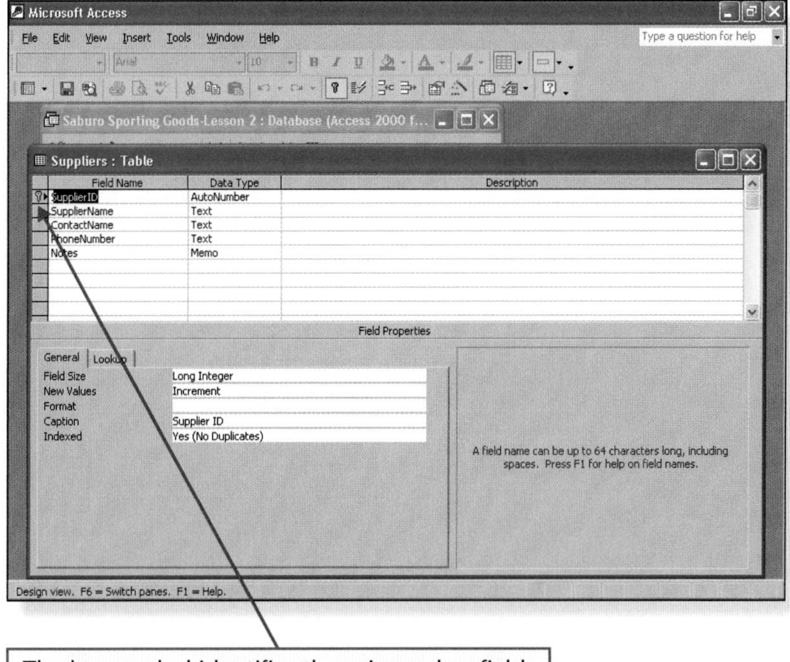

9) Switch to Design view. Access entered all of the table design information based on the options you chose in the Table Wizard. Notice that a key symbol appears to the left of the SupplierID field, indicating that the SupplierID field is the primary key field (see Figure 2.5).

10) Close the Suppliers table.

Create a Table Using Design View

While creating a table using the Table Wizard is relatively easy, you often need to modify the table design later because the Table Wizard automatically makes some decisions regarding the structure of the table that may not suit your needs.

A more effective way to create a table is in Design view. Using Design view to create a table may seem a bit more difficult than using the Table Wizard at first, but the table will better suit your needs and require less modification later.

Because Saburo is a sporting goods wholesaler, the Saburo employees spend a considerable amount of time on the phone with both suppliers and customers. The employees could use a table to record notes of phone conversations with suppliers and customers, so that transaction details and concerns can be recorded and tracked.

In the following exercise, you will create a Phone Notes table in Design view that contains fields for name, company, phone, and date, and also a field for typing notes of the conversation.

Access

Step Through It™
Exercise 1B: Create a table in Design view

1. In the Database window, double-click *Create table in Design view*. A new table opens in Design view. The cursor is blinking in the first cell in the Field Name column.

2. Type Name as the first field name, and then press Tab. The default data type *Text* is automatically entered in the Data Type column, which is the appropriate data type for this field (see Figure 2.6).

3. Press Tab twice. Type Company, and then press Tab twice to accept the Text data type for this field. Press Tab.

4. In the third row, type Phone in the Field Name column, and then press Tab three times.

5. In the fourth row, type Date for the field name and press Tab. In the Data Type column, select Date/Time (see Figure 2.7). Then press Tab twice.

6. For the last field, type the field name Notes, and select Memo as the data type.

Figure 2.6 Entering a field name and assigning a data type in Design view

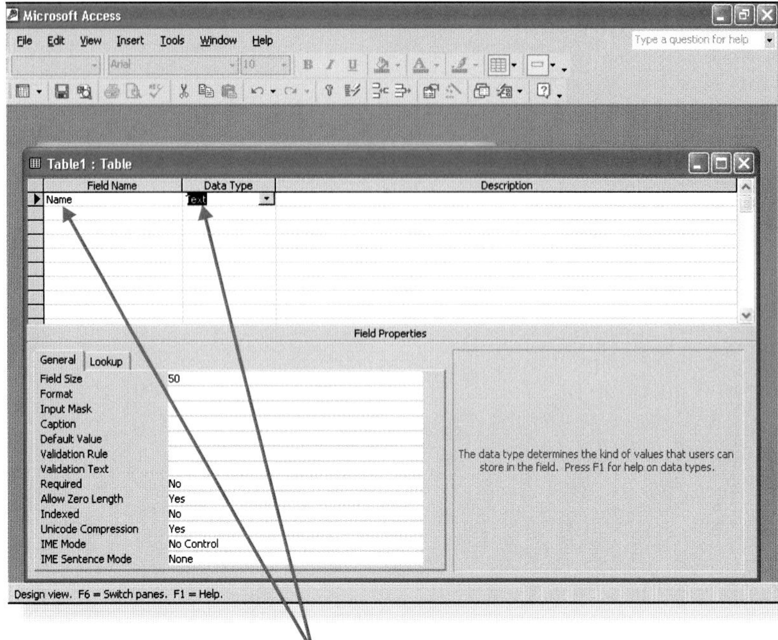

When creating a table, you must provide a field name and assign a data type for every field in the table.

Figure 2.7 Assigning a data type to a field

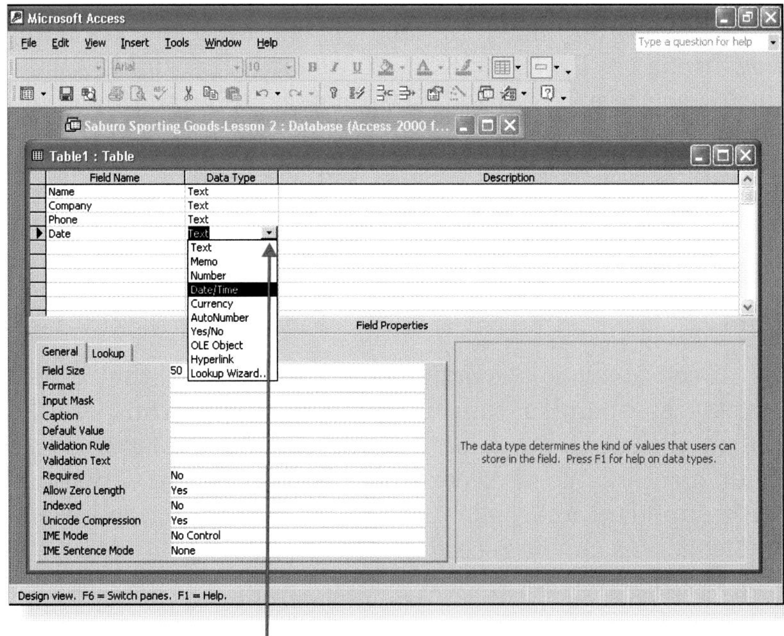

Click the down arrow in the Data Type column and select an appropriate data type.

Figure 2.8 The new Phone Notes table in Datasheet view

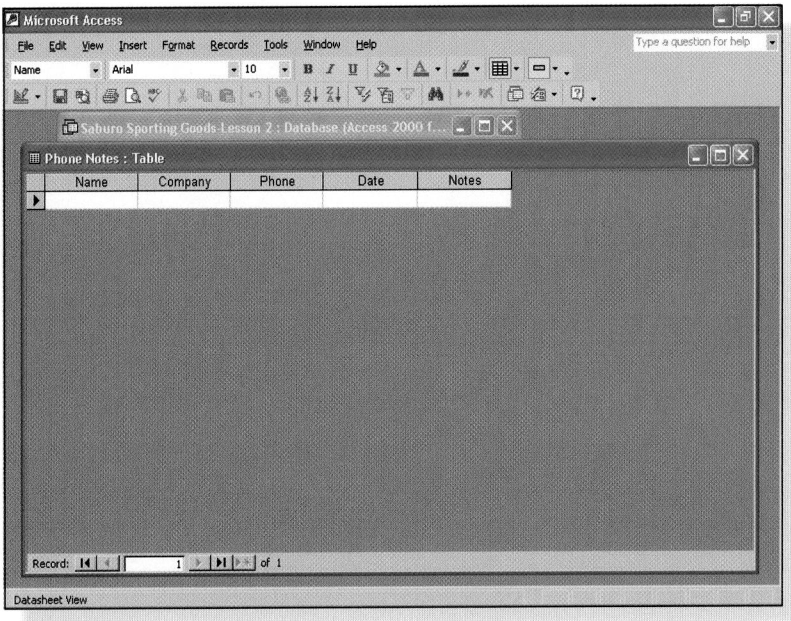

7. Click the Save button on the Table Design toolbar, and type Phone Notes in the Save As dialog box. When asked if you want to create a primary key for this table, click No.

8. Switch to Datasheet view and examine the datasheet (see Figure 2.8). Now anyone who has a phone conversation with a supplier or a customer can type the pertinent data in each field, and keep a record of all that was discussed or agreed upon during that conversation.

9. Close the table.

Access

Exercise 2 Overview: Modify Table Design

Microsoft Office Specialist AC2002 2.1, 2.4

In order to change how a table looks or functions, you must first understand a bit about data types and field properties. Refer to Figure 2.9 as you read the following discussion.

The upper pane of the table design window contains the field definitions—the names, data types, and descriptions for every field in the table. You must provide a field name and assign a data type for every field in a table, as you did in the previous exercise.

A **field name** is just that—the name of a field. However, it is important to understand that Access locates fields by their field names, so if a field name is modified in one location (such as in a table), but not in another (such as in a report based on the table), Access won't be able to find the field. When assigning field names, it is good database practice to make them descriptive without including any spaces.

Access

Figure 2.9 Examining the table design window

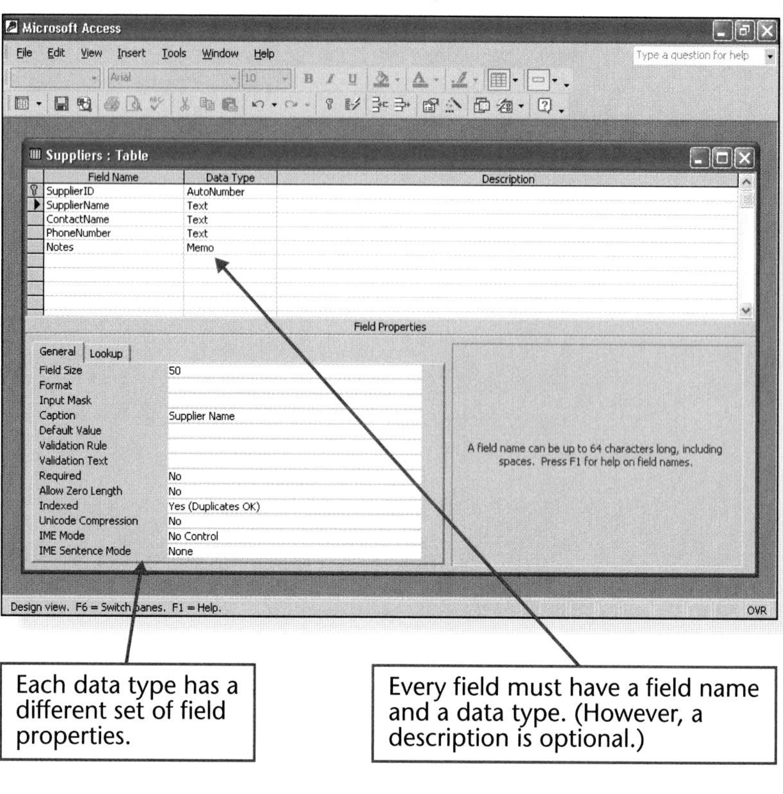

Need Help?
Type: about data types and field sizes

When you assign a **data type** to a field, you are telling Access what kinds of data can be stored in the field, such as a number, a date, or alphanumeric data. For example, if you assign a Number data type to a field, Access will not permit you to enter any alphabetic letters in the field.

You don't have to enter a description in the Description column, but any text you type in the Description column will appear in the Access status bar when data is being entered in that field. (So it's a good place for brief, helpful data entry tips.)

The lower pane of the table design window is called the Field Properties pane. It displays all the **field properties**, or attributes, for whatever field is selected in the upper pane. Fields with different data types have different properties.

When you assign a data type, Access automatically assigns some default field properties; however, you can modify those field properties to change how a field looks or behaves in Datasheet view. In Exercise 2A, you will examine some data types and field properties. Then in Exercise 2B, you will modify a few field properties in the Suppliers table to make the table more user friendly, and to ensure that the data are entered correctly.

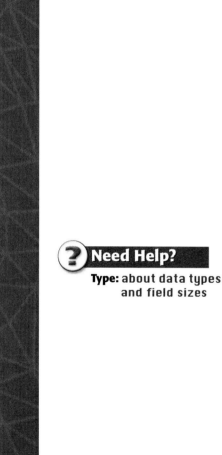

Figure 2.10 Examining data types and field properties in Design view

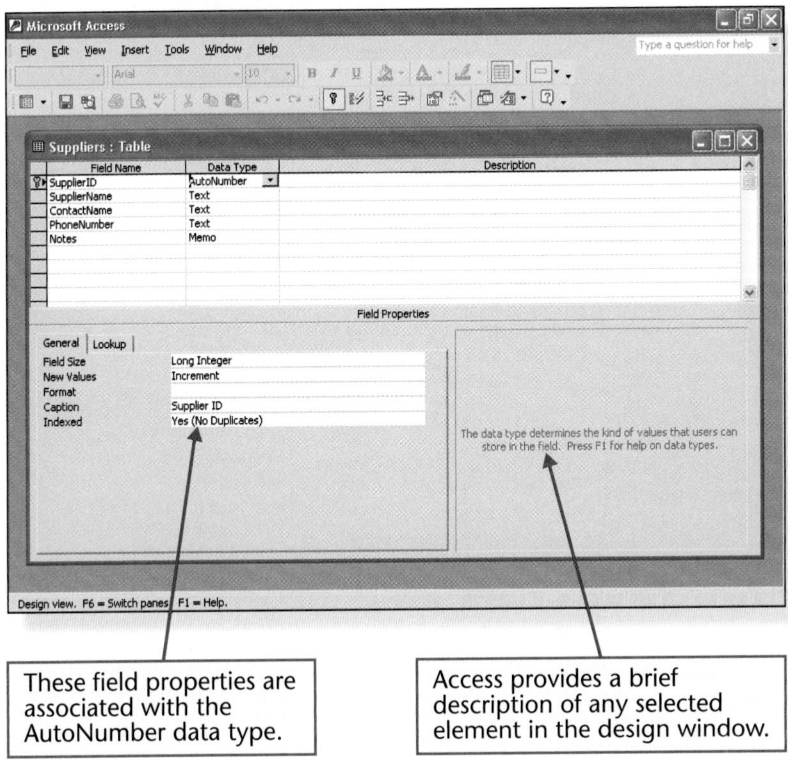

Step Through It™

Exercise 2A: Examine data types and field properties

1. Open the Suppliers table in Design view. Click in the Data Type cell for the SupplierID field in the upper pane.
2. Read the description for data type (the blue text) in the lower right corner of the window, and examine the field properties associated with the AutoNumber data type (see Figure 2.10).

Figure 2.11 Learning more about data types using Microsoft Access Help

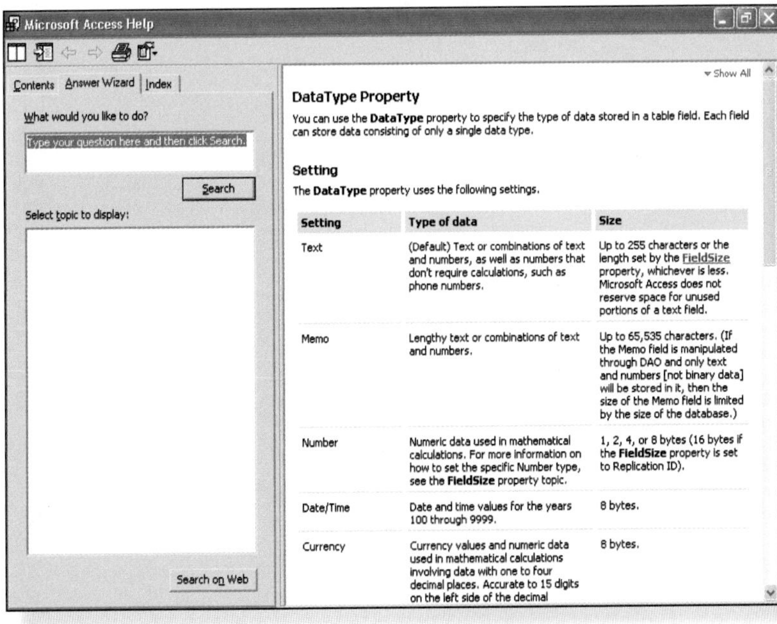

3. Click in the Data Type cells for the remaining fields in the upper pane and examine the field properties for the Text and Memo data types.
4. Press F1 to open the Help window. Maximize the Help window (see Figure 2.11).
5. Scroll down the Help window and read the information about data types. Then close the Help window.

Access

Step Through It™

Exercise 2B: Modify field properties

1. Click in the SupplierName field in the upper pane.
2. Press F6 to jump to the Field Properties pane. Navigate to the Caption property box and change the caption *Supplier Name* to Company.
3. Navigate to the Required property box, click the arrow that appears on the right end of the box, and select Yes (see Figure 2.12).

Figure 2.12 Changing field properties in the Suppliers table

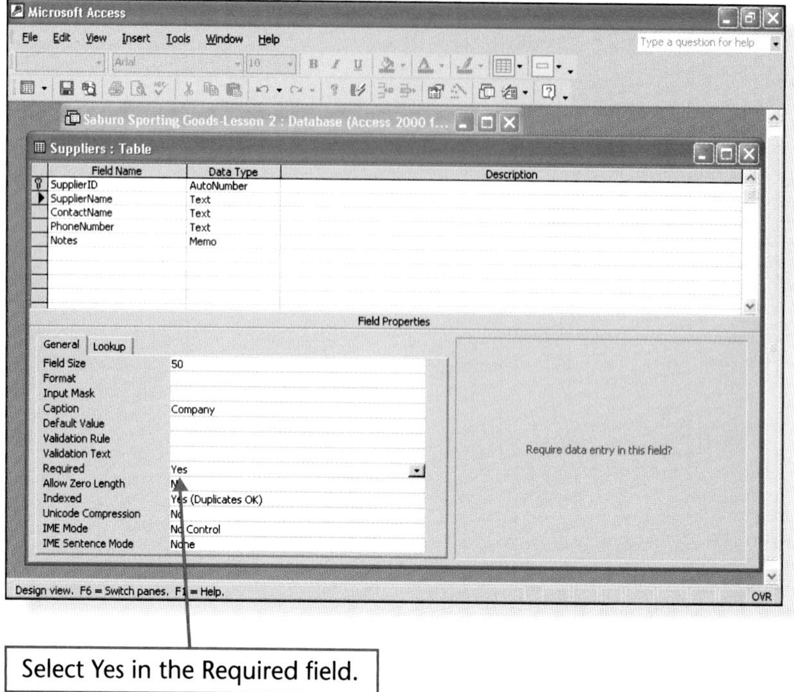

Select Yes in the Required field.

4. Press F6 to jump to the upper pane, and click anywhere in the PhoneNumber field row.
5. Press F6 to jump to the Field Properties pane. Click in the Required property box, click the down arrow that appears, and select Yes.
6. Click Save on the Table Design toolbar to save the changes to the table design.
7. Switch to Datasheet view and look at the SupplierName field caption (see Figure 2.13).

Figure 2.13 The modified Suppliers table

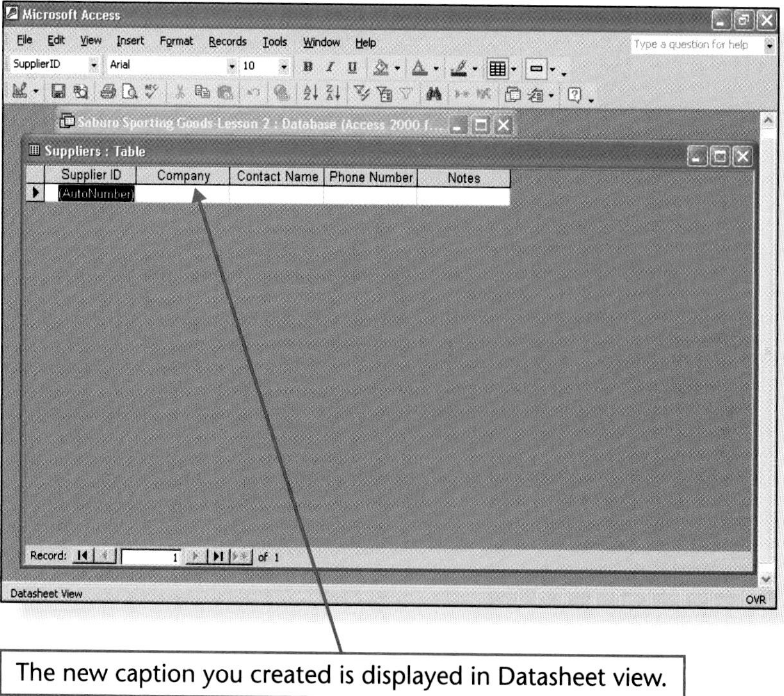

The new caption you created is displayed in Datasheet view.

Exercise 3 Overview:
Create an Input Mask

Microsoft Office Specialist
AC2002 2.2

By changing the Required property of the PhoneNumber field in the previous exercise to Yes, you made the phone number a required entry. Thus, if you attempt to enter a record without a phone number, Access won't accept the record. But you can still enter a phone number that's missing a digit, which would be just as useless as no number at all. To prevent that from happening, you can create an input mask. An **input mask** is a field property that allows only a specific number and type of characters to be entered into a field, and automatically formats those characters correctly.

Access

Access helps you create common input masks with the Input Mask Wizard. The wizard can create input masks for phone numbers, social security numbers, ZIP Codes, time entries, dates, and more.

In the next exercise, you'll create an input mask for the PhoneNumber field in the Suppliers table. Then in the following exercise, you will test your modified field properties by entering data for four suppliers in the new Suppliers table.

Figure 2.14 Modifying the Input Mask field property

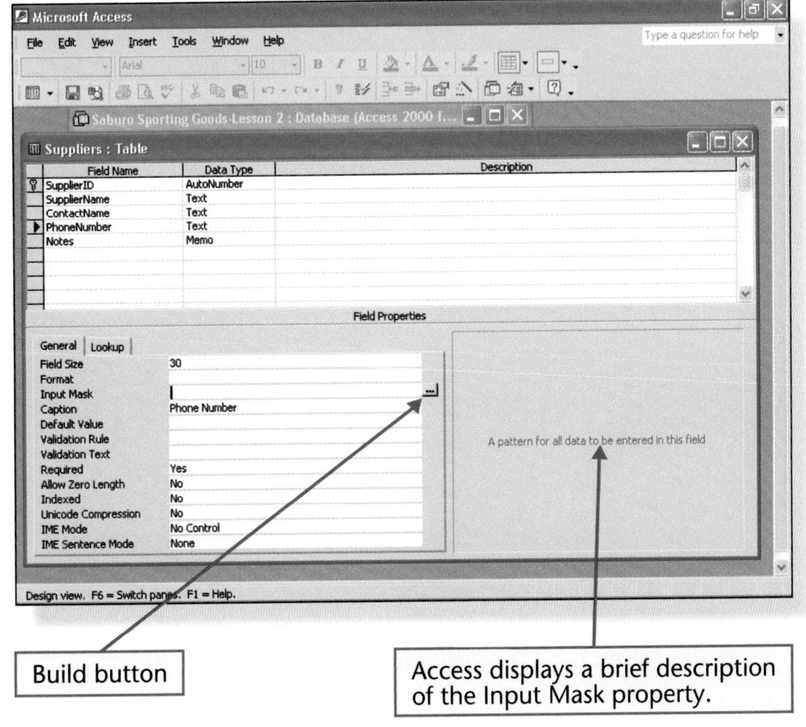

Step Through It™
Exercise 3A: Use the Input Mask Wizard

1. With the Suppliers table still open, switch to Design view. If necessary, click in the PhoneNumber field in the upper pane, and press F6 to jump to the Field Properties pane.
2. Click in the Input Mask property box. A Build button appears on the right side of the property box (see Figure 2.14).

3) Click the Build button to start the Input Mask Wizard. (If Access asks if you want to save the table first, click Yes).

4) In the first Input Mask Wizard step, click the Phone Number mask if it is not already selected (see Figure 2.15). Then click Next.

Figure 2.15 Using the Input Mask Wizard

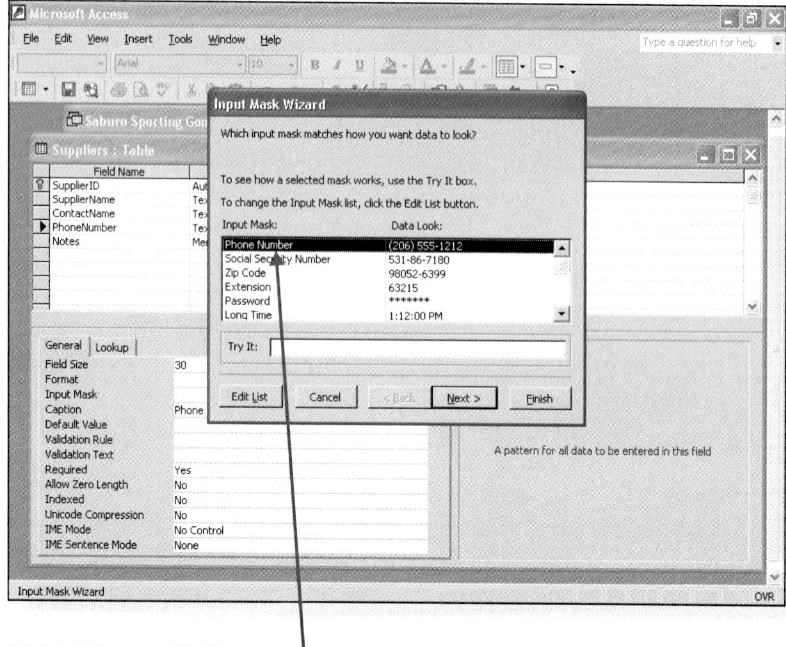

The Input Mask Wizard provides several common masks, such as a mask for entering phone numbers.

5) In the second step, the wizard shows you the default pattern for the mask. Click Next to accept the default.

6) In the third wizard step, click the *With the symbols in the mask* option, and click Next.

7) In the last wizard step, click Finish. Look at the Input Mask property box—the wizard has entered the encoding for the phone number input mask (see Figure 2.16).

8) Save the changes to the table design.

Figure 2.16 The Input Mask property for the PhoneNumber field

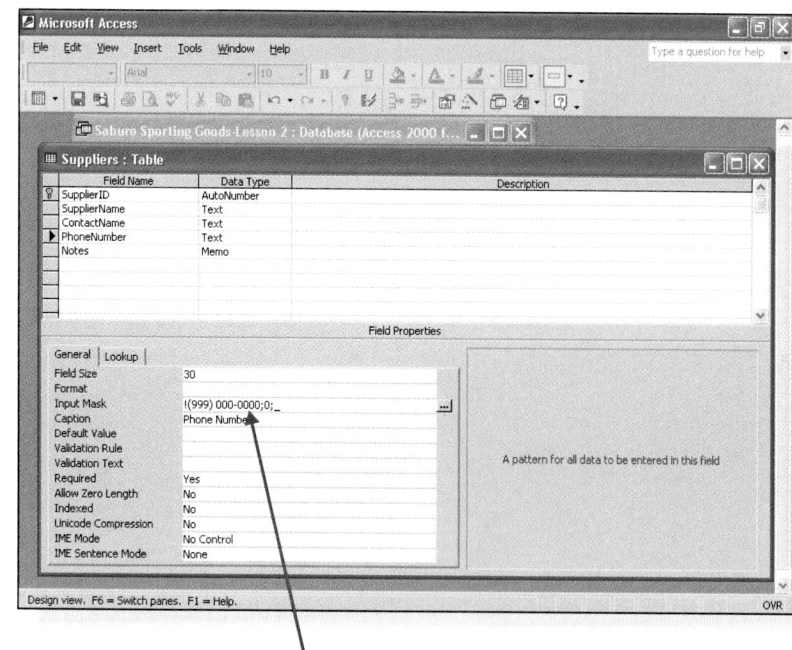

The Input Mask Wizard creates the input mask and places it in the Input Mask field property box.

Table 2.1

Company	Contact Name	Phone Number	Notes
Body Gear	Laura Buchanan	318-555-4810	Manufactures lightweight, durable clothing for sports, including team uniforms and sports clothing for individuals. Also supplies protective equipment, such as helmets, goggles, shin and wrist guards, etc.
Grand Slam, Inc.	Mario Ramirez	813-555-3792	Specializes in all types of baseball and softball equipment, such as baseballs, bats, gloves, helmets, cleats, etc. Very responsive; consistently supplies items within one week of placing an order.
Adolpho Racquets	Michi Okano	650-555-4617	Manufactures racquets for tennis, racquetball, squash, badminton, etc. Also carries high-quality line of tennis balls, racquetball balls, and badminton shuttlecocks.
Outdoor Outfitters Unlimited	Ben Moore	509-555-7250	Produces gear and equipment for rock climbing and spelunking. Most orders ship within 2 business days; overnight shipping available on request.
Callan Sports & Leisure	Rochelle Davis	812-555-7529	Supplies all types of game balls and other game equipment. Also carries a small line of sports novelty items. Out-of-stock problems are frequent; check on availability before placing orders.

Step Through It™

Exercise 3B: Populate the new table with data

1. Switch to Datasheet view.
2. You need to make the Notes field bigger for easier data entry. Click in the Notes field, and then click Column Width on the Format menu.
3. Type 60 in the Column Width text box. Click OK.
4. Click Row Height on the Format menu, type 50 in the Row Height text box, and click OK.
5. Click in the Supplier ID field. Because this is an AutoNumber field, Access will assign a Supplier ID number automatically. Press Tab to move to the next field, and then enter the records provided in Table 2.1.
   Note: Because you created an input mask for the Phone Number field, you do not need to enter any special characters, such as the parentheses or hyphens.
6. Save the changes to the table design. Then close the Suppliers table.

Access

APPLY IT! After finishing Exercises 1–3, you may test your skills by completing Apply It! Guided Activity 1, Create and Modify Tables.

Garbage In, Garbage Out

One of the main reasons for keeping data in a database is so you can find it again when you need it. But if you can't find it again, what's the point? Often data can't be found again because it was entered in error—perhaps it was spelled wrong or entered as text instead of calculable numbers or entered in the wrong field. Stringent, accurate data entry is extremely important—and the larger the database, the more important accurate data entry is. No database program can ensure completely error-proof data, but Access has features that vastly reduce the chance of inaccurate data entry.

Data Types

A data type sets the kind of value that can be stored in a field. For example, if a field requires date entries, the Date/Time data type will accept only date or time entries, and will format those entries so that they are consistent.

Data Validation

You can create data validation rules for fields in a table to set restrictions on the data that can be entered. For example, if a field is supposed to contain a number greater than zero, you can create a data validation rule that will display an error message if someone tries to enter a number that is zero or less.

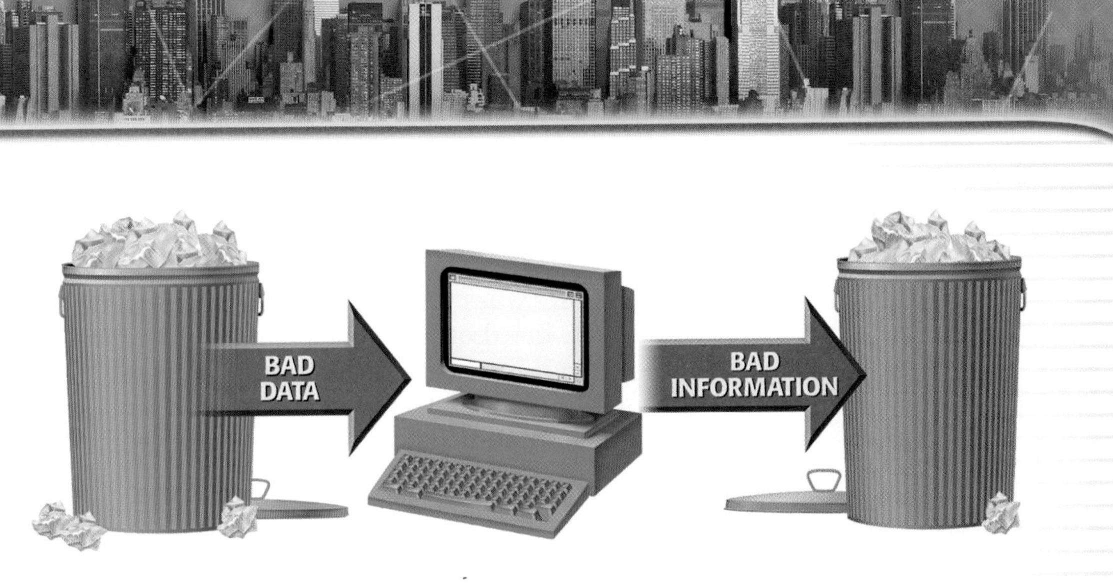

ıput masks

ıput masks are good for entries that must have a ɔnsistent format, such as phone numbers and postal codes. .ccess supplies the necessary punctuation automatically.

ookup Fields

ookup fields don't require any typing (and possible ıisspelling) of entries. Instead, you select the entry from a st of pre-determined entries for that field. Lookup fields peed up data entry, and the resulting entries are ompletely consistent and correct.

eferential Integrity

eferential integrity is a system of rules that Access uses ɔ ensure that relationships between records in related ables are valid, and that you don't accidentally delete or hange related data.

CRITICAL THINKING

. **Adding Input Masks** Access provides a number of pre-defined input masks that you can select using the Input Mask Wizard, but you can also create your own custom input masks. What situations can you think of that might require a custom input mask in a field?

. **Using Referential Integrity** Referential integrity is available for all table relationships, but you are free to use it or not, depending on the situation. What data relationships can you think of in which referential integrity would be critical? What data relationships can you think of in which referential integrity would be unnecessary or even counterproductive?

Access

Microsoft Office Specialist AC2002 8.1, 8.2

Exercise 4 Overview: Import, Export, and Link Access Data

One of the tremendous advantages of using computers to store information is that once information has been entered in an electronic file, it doesn't have to be entered again. And, when you are using Access, it doesn't matter if that information was captured electronically in an Excel worksheet, in a Lotus spreadsheet, or in another database file—you can just import the data from those files directly into Access. This not only saves a lot of time, it prevents inaccuracies due to data being mistyped.

You can **import** existing data into an Access database from most list- or database-type files, such as Excel, Lotus 1-2-3, Paradox, dBase, other Access databases, SQL, FoxPro, and others. Excel files are particularly easy to import.

Need Help?

Type: import or link data and objects

Until now, the Saburo Sporting Goods employee information was maintained by the human resources department as an Excel file, but you want to import it into the company database in order to streamline the company's recordkeeping process. In the following exercise, you'll import employee data from an Excel file into the *Saburo Sporting Goods-Lesson 2.mdb* database.

Step Through It™

Exercise 4A: Import structured data into a table

1. Close any open database objects, so that only the *Saburo Sporting Goods-Lesson 2.mdb* Database window is visible in your Access application window.
2. On the File menu, point to Get External Data, and then select Import.
3. In the Import dialog box, navigate to the *Lesson 2* subfolder in the *Unit 3* folder, and then select Microsoft Excel in the Files of type box (see Figure 2.17).

Figure 2.17 Choosing a file to import

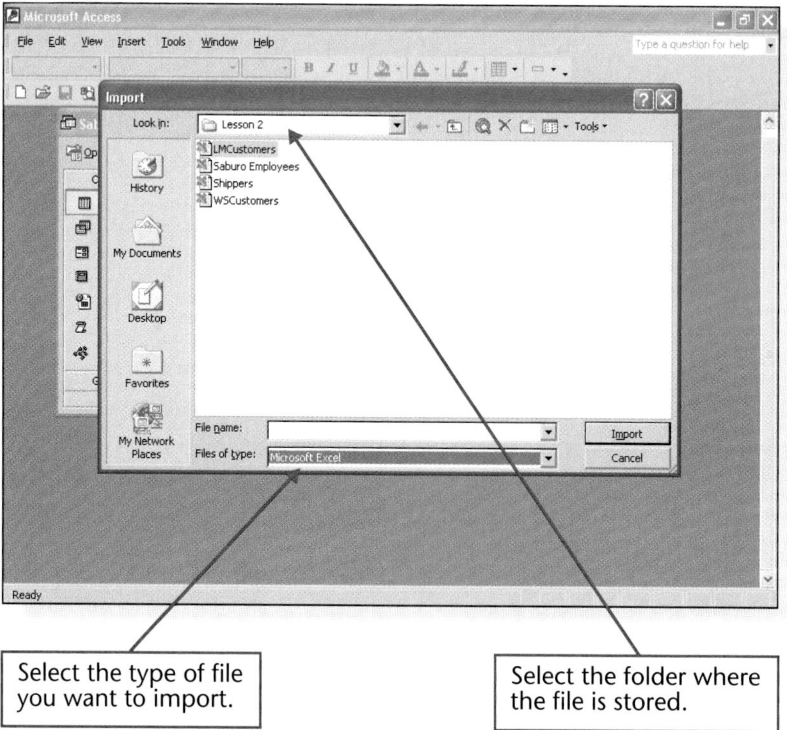

Figure 2.18 Using the Import Spreadsheet Wizard

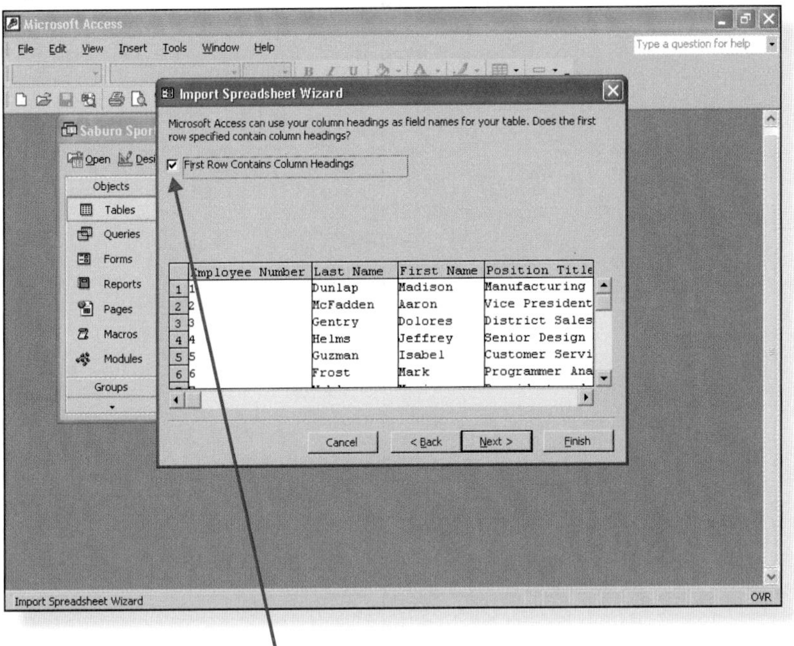

If the first row of the worksheet contains column headings, this option must be selected.

4. Double-click the *Saburo Employees.xls* file. The Import Spreadsheet Wizard starts.

5. In the first wizard step, be sure the *Show Worksheets* option is selected. The sample data window in the wizard shows you how the data in the worksheet are divided into fields. Click Next.

6. In the next wizard step, be sure the *First Row Contains Column Headings* option is selected (see Figure 2.18). Then click Next.

Figure 2.19 Check the data type for each field

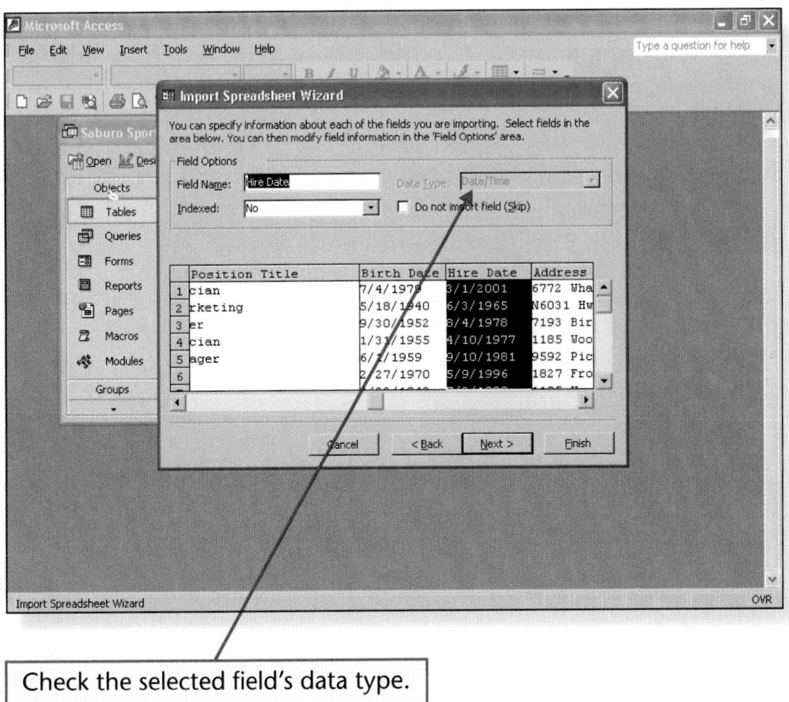

Check the selected field's data type.

7. In the next wizard step, verify that the *In a New Table* option is selected, and click Next.

8. In the next wizard step, click in each field in the sample data pane, and examine the data type in the Data Type box. In this table, every field should have a Text data type except the Employee Number field, which is assigned the Double data type (a specific type of the Number data type), and the Birth Date and Hire Date fields, which are both assigned the Date/Time data type (see Figure 2.19). Then click Next.

9 Select the *Choose my own primary key* option (see Figure 2.20). The wizard automatically selects the Employee Number field for you, which is correct. Then click Next.

10 In the last wizard step, Access suggests the name *Employees* for the table, which is an appropriate name. Click Finish to accept the name and import the data.

11 Click OK when Access displays the message that it has finished importing the data. The Employees table appears in the Database window.

Figure 2.20 Choosing a primary key

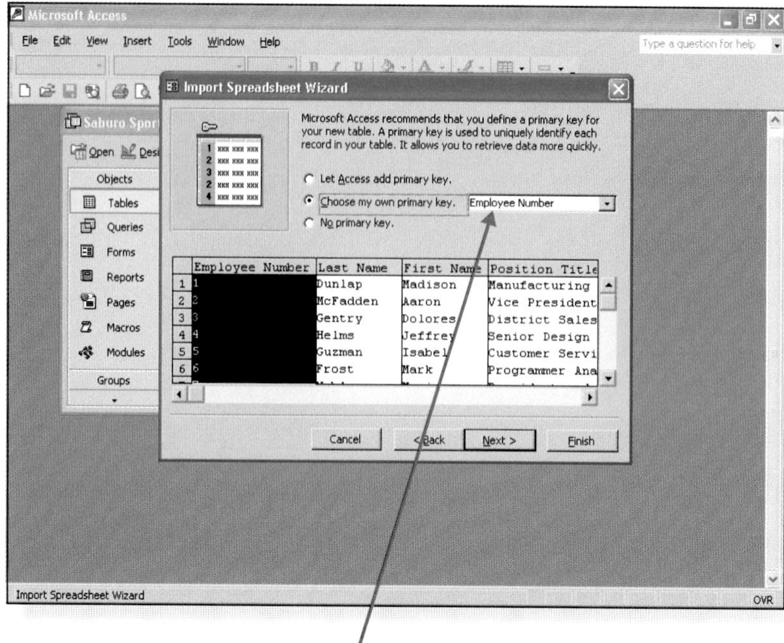

The Employee Number field is designated as the primary key.

Exporting Data From an Access Database

What if YOU have data in your Access database that someone else needs? Not only can you import data into an Access database, you can also **export** the data in any Access table to a file outside the database.

You can export an Access table to many different file types, including all the list- or database-type files mentioned previously, and as a Rich Text Format (.rtf) file that most word processing programs can open.

If you need to do large-scale or intricate mathematical manipulations on the data in a table or a query, it's often much easier to export a copy of the data to an Excel file and do your calculations in Excel.

In the following exercise, you'll export the Products table to an Excel file.

Type: export data or database objects

Figure 2.21 Exporting an Access table

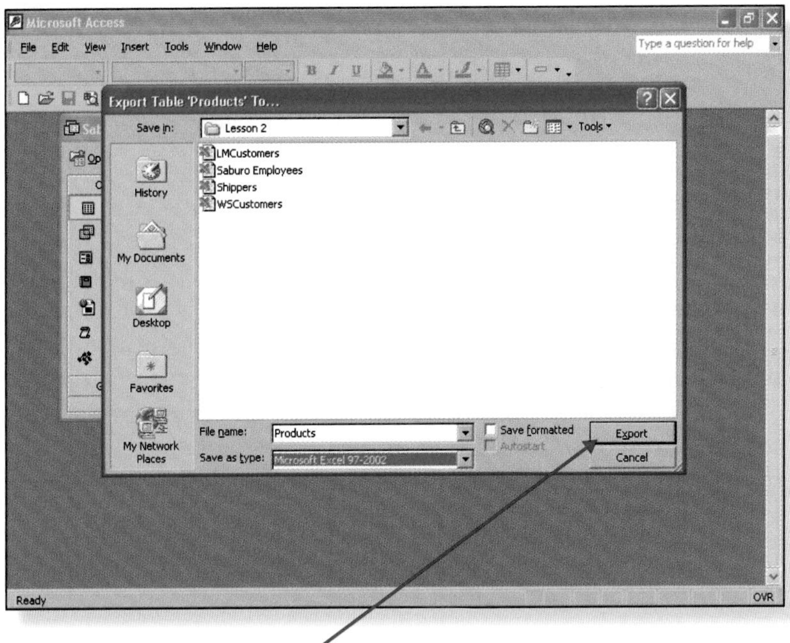

Click this button to export the data after you've selected the appropriate file type and folder location.

Linking Data to an Access Database

Suppose that someone in another division in your company is maintaining a file with data that you need to use in your database. You could import the file; however, if the other division makes changes to the file, your data would be out of date until someone in the other division told you, and you re-imported the (updated) data.

The best way to ensure that the data in your database is current when you don't maintain the data is to **link** to the file where the current data are maintained. In a linked table, Access reaches out to use the data located outside of the database, but it doesn't keep a copy of that data in the database.

Another Way

An even faster way to export data as an Excel file is to use the OfficeLinks button on the Database toolbar. In the Database window, click the name of the table or query you want to export, then click the OfficeLinks down arrow and select Excel. The table opens immediately in a saved Excel file, and is ready to work with.

Step Through It™

Exercise 4B: Export data from a table

1. Close all open objects (if necessary). In the Database window, select, but do not open, the Products table.
2. On the File menu, select Export.
3. In the Export Table 'Products' To dialog box, navigate to the *Lesson 2* subfolder in the *Unit 3* folder.
4. In the Save as type box, select Microsoft Excel 97-2002 (see Figure 2.21). Then click the Export button.
5. Launch Excel and navigate to and open the *Products.xls* file. Then close the workbook and exit Excel.

Access

A linked table is very similar to an Access table you create; however, you cannot alter the structure (design) of the table from within Access. You can, however, open, edit, and delete any data in a linked table; (however, it is not wise to do this since you are not responsible for that data).

? Need Help?

Type: about importing and linking data and database objects

The shipping department at Saburo Sporting Goods keeps an eye on the costs to ship orders with various companies, and always ships with the company that offers the lowest rates. Since the shipping cost information changes often, the shipping department maintains the list of current shipping companies in an Excel file on their computer. But when someone places an order, the salesperson taking the order is using the company database. If the customer wants to know about the shipping options, the salesperson needs to have current data promptly available.

In the following exercise, you will link your *Saburo Sporting Goods-Lesson 2.mdb* database to the shipping department's Excel file.

Step Through It™

Exercise 4C: Link to data in an Excel file

1. Close all open database objects (if necessary). On the File menu, point to Get External Data, and click Link Tables.
2. In the Link dialog box, navigate to the *Lesson 2* subfolder in the *Unit 3* folder. Then select Microsoft Excel in the Files of type box. The Excel files in the *Lesson 2* subfolder appear.
3. Double-click the *Shippers.xls* file. The Link Spreadsheet Wizard starts (see Figure 2.22).

Figure 2.22 Starting the Link Spreadsheet Wizard

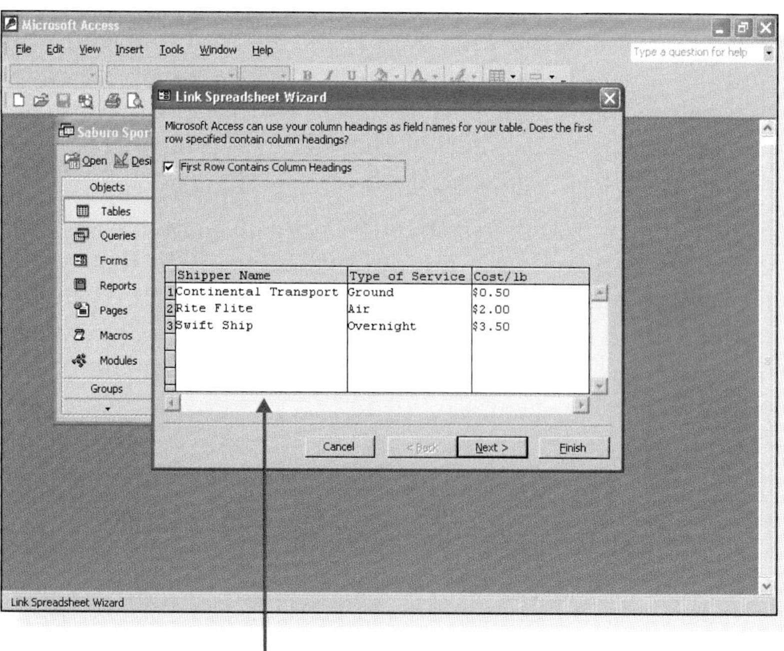

The Link Spreadsheet Wizard displays the data in the Excel file in a column-and-row format.

Figure 2.23 A linked table in the database

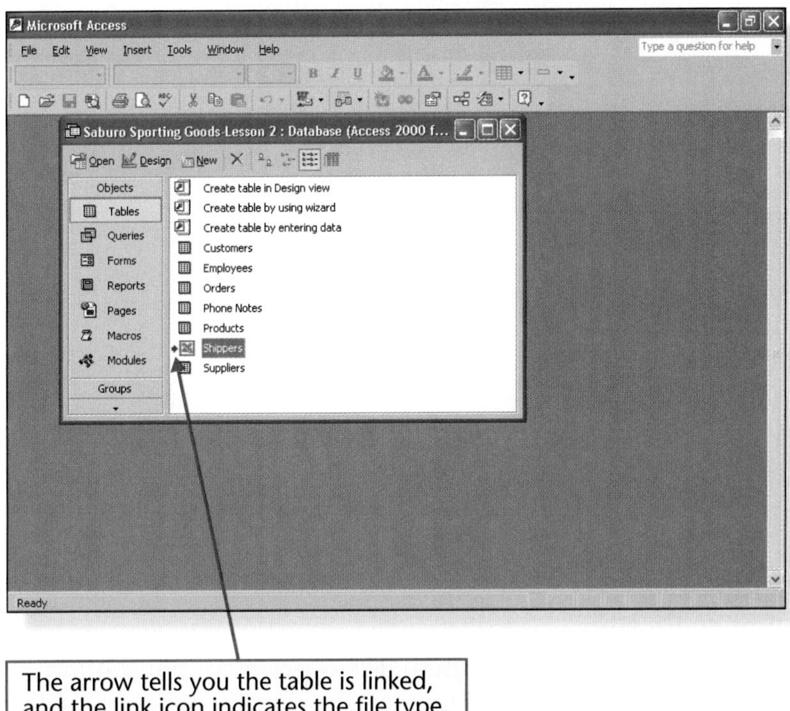

The arrow tells you the table is linked, and the link icon indicates the file type.

4. In the first wizard step, make sure the *First Row Contains Column Headings* option is selected, and click Next.

5. In the next wizard step, Access suggests the name *Shippers* as the linked table name. Click Finish to accept the name and link the table.

6. When Access displays the message indicating that it's finished linking the table, click OK. The Shippers linked table icon appears in the Database window (see Figure 2.23).

Access

Figure 2.24 Using a linked table to view data in an Excel file

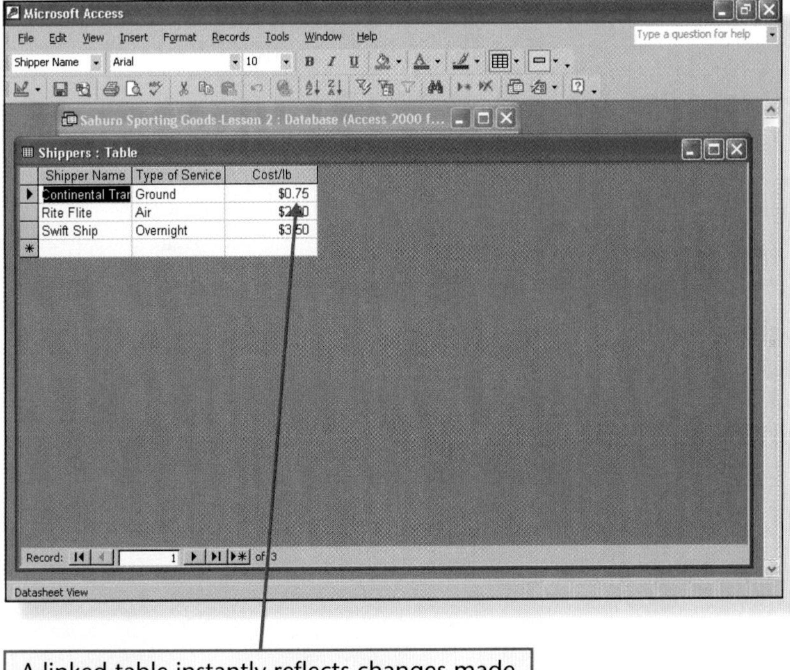

A linked table instantly reflects changes made in the file to which the table is linked.

7. Double-click the Shippers linked table to open it. Review the information in the table; then close the table.

8. Launch Excel and open the *Shippers.xls* file. Change the cost per pound for Continental Transport to $.75.

9. Reopen the Shippers linked table in Access to verify that the change you just made is reflected in the linked table (see Figure 2.24). Close the Shippers linked table.

10. Close the *Shippers.xls* file without saving the change. Exit Excel.

Career Corner

The Wide World of Sports

If you really like sports, you've probably wished sometimes that you could make it a career. You could play professionally, if you're good enough, or you could coach or referee. What else could you do? You could approach the field of sports from another angle—a career in exercise science!

Exercise scientists work in fitness clubs, hospitals, employee health programs, and professional and amateur sports, including pro teams and Olympic training centers. Some set up and run exercise programs, using a database program to track participants' progress. Others do research. Some work with people one-on-one.

There are many good jobs in exercise science. Sports medicine technicians work with doctors to evaluate and treat sports injuries. They also help athletes prevent injuries and help people train and get in shape. Other jobs include fitness trainer, aerobics instructor, sport nutritionist, equipment tester, weight-loss counselor, and physical therapist.

For most exercise science jobs, you need a bachelor's degree in exercise science or a related area. A few require an associate's degree or certification. Starting pay ranges from $18,000 to $30,000 per year.

If any of these jobs sounds good to you, you can get started now by playing sports, helping a school or local athletic team, and trying different kinds of exercise. Take courses in science (especially anatomy and physiology), math, and computers. People are getting into physical fitness, sports, and health all the time. So take a look! There's plenty of room for you!

CRITICAL THINKING

1. Americans say they want to be healthy. Yet many do things they know are bad for them, like overeating, not getting enough exercise, and smoking. Why do you think this is so?
2. Suppose you ran a fitness center or cardiac rehab program. Design a database that would help you in your work. What tables would it have? What fields would each table contain?

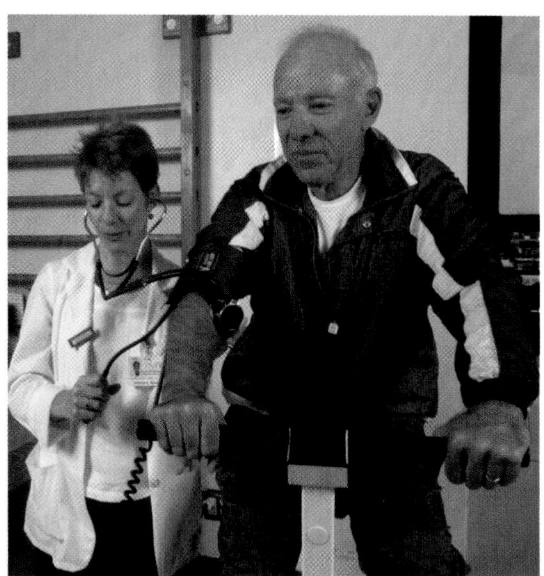

Exercise 5 Overview:
Define Relationships and Enforce Referential Integrity

Microsoft Office Specialist AC2002 6.1, 6.2

A **relationship** is an association you can create between common fields in two tables. When two tables are "connected" in a relationship, you can create other database objects, such as queries and forms, that contain data from both tables. That's why Access is called a relational database.

Relationships between tables are created and displayed in the Relationships window. To open the Relationships window, you simply press the Relationships button on the Database toolbar. To create a relationship between two tables, you must first display a field list for each table in the Relationships window. Then you "relate" the two tables by dragging the common field from one field list and placing it on the corresponding common field in the other field list. Access inserts a relationship line between the two fields to indicate the relationship. Figure 2.25 shows the relationship between the Suppliers table and the Products table in the Saburo Sporting Goods database.

Type: about relationships in an Access database

Figure 2.25 Examining the relationship between two tables

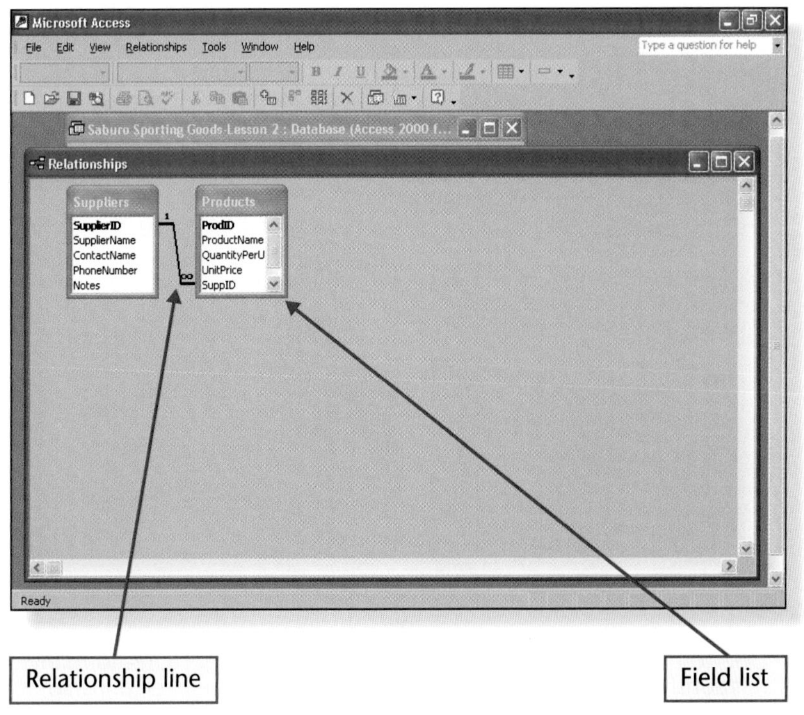

Access

There are three types of relationships: one-to-one, one-to-many, and many-to-many. The Suppliers-to-Products relationship shown in Figure 2.25 (which you'll create in the next exercise) is a **one-to-many relationship**, because there is one supplier for many products. In a one-to-many relationship, the "one" table is called the **primary table**, and the "many" table is called the **related table**. A one-to-many relationship is the most common type of relationship.

The next most common relationship is the **many-to-many relationship**, in which each record in each table has many related records in the other table. However, a many-to-many relationship cannot exist as a direct relationship. Instead, a many-to-many relationship is broken into a pair of one-to-many relationships, and a **junction table** is created as the go-between for the two tables. Each of the two tables in a many-to-many relationship has a one-to-many relationship with the junction table. You can look up related information between the two "many" tables when they are related through the junction table.

Figure 2.26 illustrates a many-to-many relationship: the Customers and Products tables are related through the Orders table (the junction table), which also contains important additional information about each customer-product order.

Figure 2.26 A many-to-many relationship requires a junction table

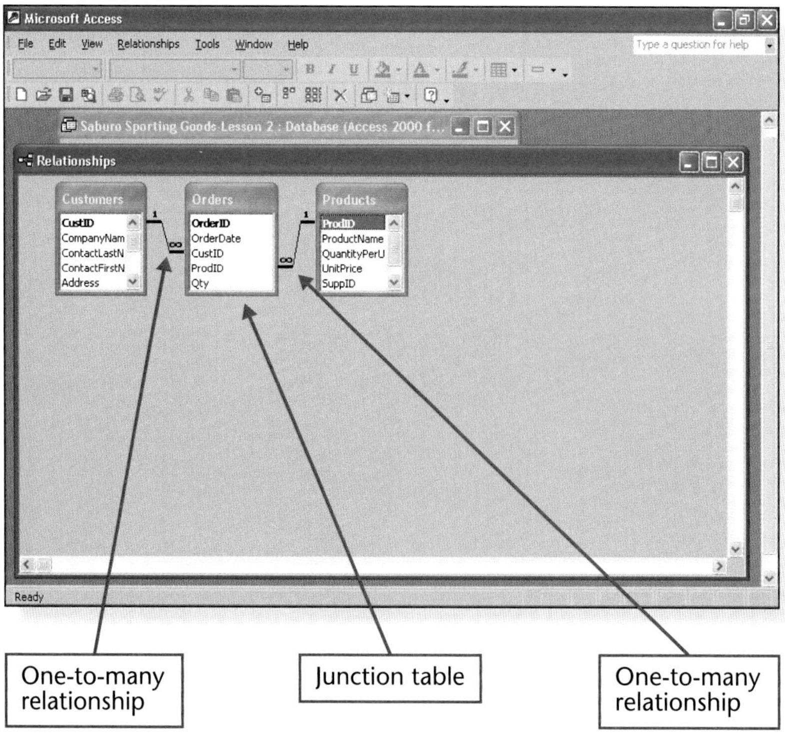

One-to-many relationship

Junction table

One-to-many relationship

The least common type of relationship is a **one-to-one relationship**. In a one-to-one relationship, each record in one table is related to a single record in the other table as illustrated in Figure 2.27. (It's as if a single table has been separated into two tables.)

Figure 2.27 A one-to-one relationship

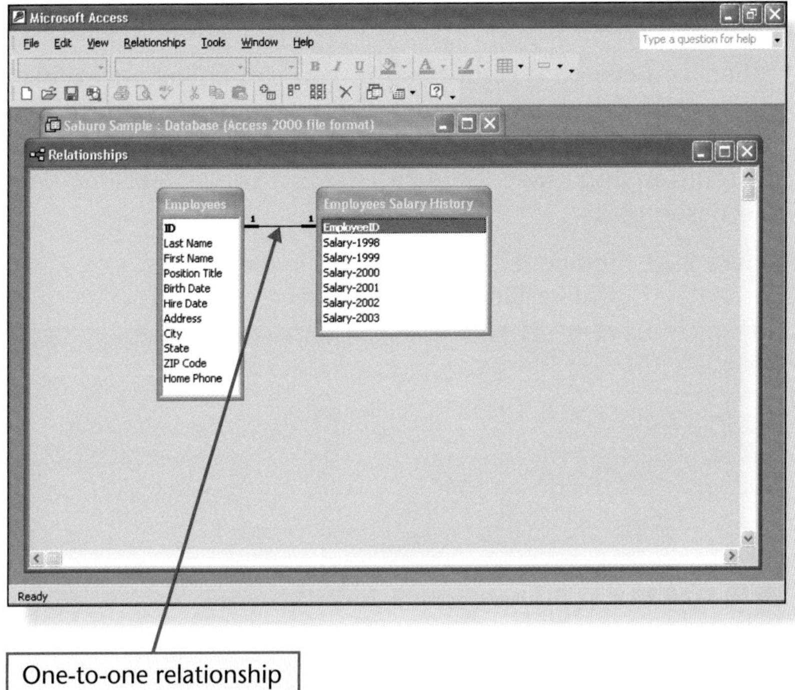

A one-to-one relationship might be used when a table contains sensitive data that shouldn't be available to everyone using the database. The fields of sensitive data can be kept in a separate table that's less accessible, but the one-to-one relationship that exists between the two tables allows users who can access both tables to pull up the data they need from either table.

To make a table less accessible, you can hide it. To hide a database object, right-click the object name in the Database window, click Properties, and then select the Hidden option. To show hidden objects, select Options on the Tools menu, and then select the Hidden Objects option on the View tab.

Access

Understanding Referential Integrity

A database is constantly changing—records are added, others are modified, and still others are deleted. When tables in a database are related, it's very easy to destroy the integrity of the data if changes made to one table are not "followed through" in the related table. **Referential integrity** is a set of rules Access uses to maintain the accuracy of a database as time passes and changes are made to the data.

When you create a relationship, you can choose to enforce referential integrity or not. There are three referential integrity options that you can choose to set when you create a relationship (see Figure 2.28). These options are discussed below.

Figure 2.28 Setting referential integrity in the Edit Relationships dialog box

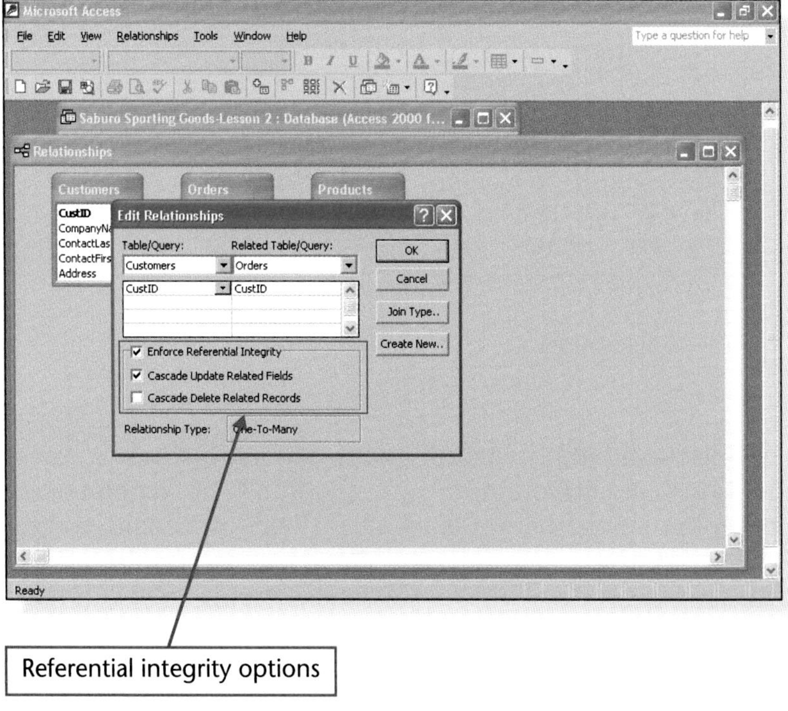

Enforce Referential Integrity. When you select this option without selecting either of the two options below it, Access imposes strict limitations on your ability to manipulate the data in related tables. When referential integrity is enforced, Access will not allow you to change the value in the primary key field in the "one" table, because changing it would leave all the related records in the "many" table unmatched. Also, Access will not allow you to delete a record in the "one" table, because that would **orphan** all the related records in the "many" table. If you attempt to make these types of changes,

Access displays a message similar to the one shown in Figure 2.29.

Figure 2.29 Access enforces referential integrity

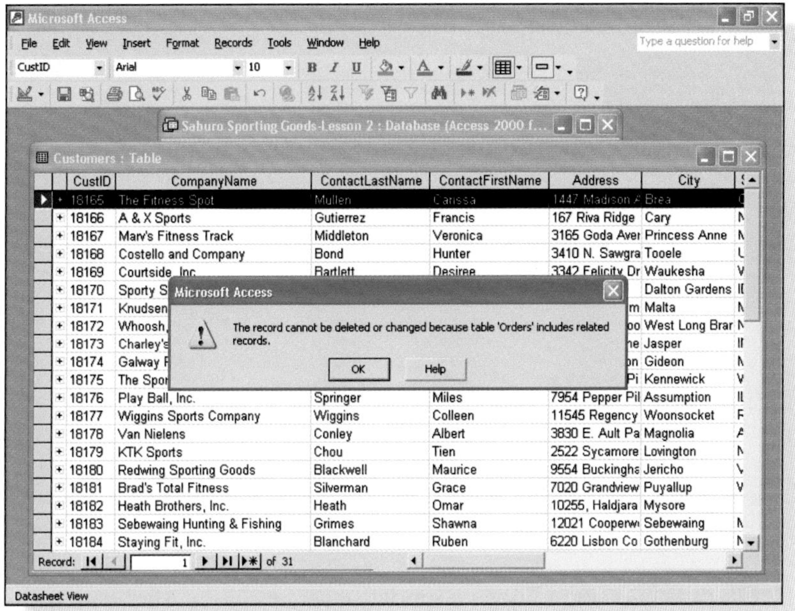

Cascade Update Related Fields. If you select this option and then change a value in the primary key field in the primary table (the "one" table), Access automatically updates that value in all the related records in the related table (the "many" table).

Cascade Delete Related Records. If you select this option and then delete a record in the primary table, Access automatically deletes all the related records in the related table instead of leaving them orphaned. Be very cautious about using this option—you can inadvertently lose a lot of data that you didn't intend to lose!

What Are Subdatasheets?

After you have established a relationship between two tables, you can open the primary table (the "one" table) and use **subdatasheets** to view and manipulate records in the related table (the "many" table) without actually opening the related table.

When you open a table that is the primary table in a relationship, you'll see a column of plus symbols on the left side of the table. If you click a plus symbol, a subdatasheet of the related records in the related table opens (see Figure 2.30). You can then enter, edit, and delete data in the subdatasheet, just as you can in the open table.

Type: about subdatasheets

Figure 2.30 A subdatasheet displays the related records from another table

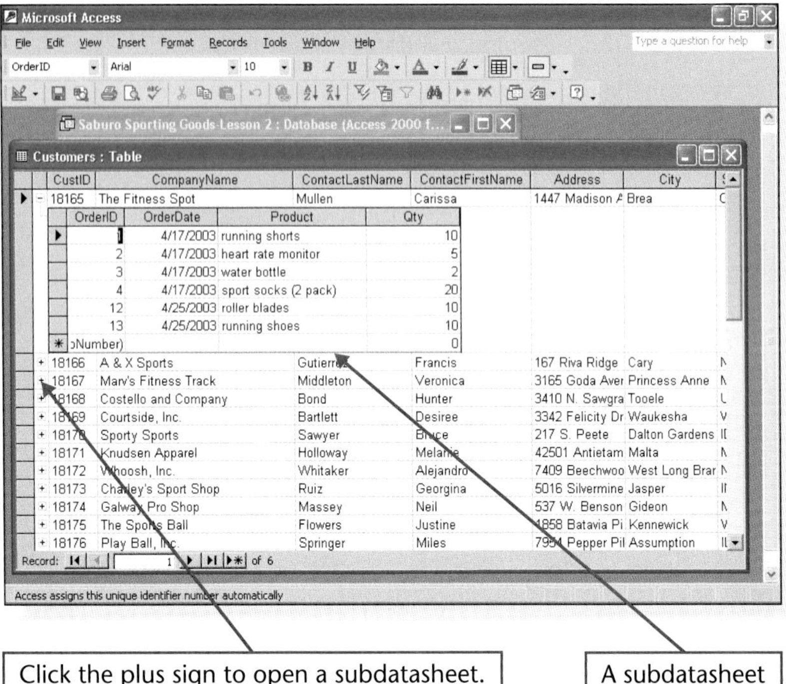

In the following exercises, you will create a one-to-many relationship between the Suppliers table and the Products table in the *Saburo Sporting Goods-Lesson 2.mdb* database, and then you will enforce referential integrity between the two tables. To join these two tables in a relationship, you must first be able to answer *Yes* to the following three questions:

- Do the two tables have a one-to-many relationship?
- Is there a common field in each table that can be used to relate the tables?
- Do the common fields have matching data types?

The Suppliers and Products tables do have a one-to-many relationship (one supplier to many products), but they don't have a common field you can use to create the relationship. Therefore, you must first create a field in the Products table that contains the same data as the SupplierID field in the Suppliers table, and assign it a data type that is compatible with the data type of the SupplierID field in the Suppliers table. Then you can create the relationship based on those common fields.

Figure 2.31 Adding a common field to the Products table

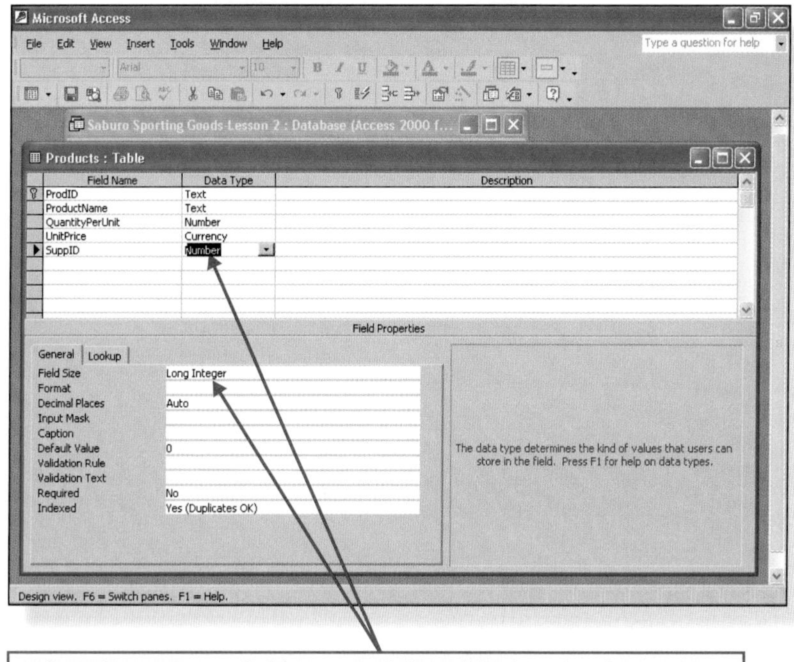

When the common field in one of the tables has the data type AutoNumber, the common field in the other table *must* have the data type Number, with a Field Size property of Long Integer.

Step Through It™

Exercise 5A: Create a one-to-many relationship

1. Open the Suppliers table in Design view and look at the data type in the SupplierID field (AutoNumber).
2. Close the Suppliers table and open the Products table in Design view.
3. Click in the Field Name cell below the UnitPrice row and type **SuppID**. Then choose the Number data type.
4. If Field Size property doesn't read *Long Integer*, then click in the Field Size property box and select Long Integer (see Figure 2.31).

Access

Figure 2.32 Adding tables in the Relationships window

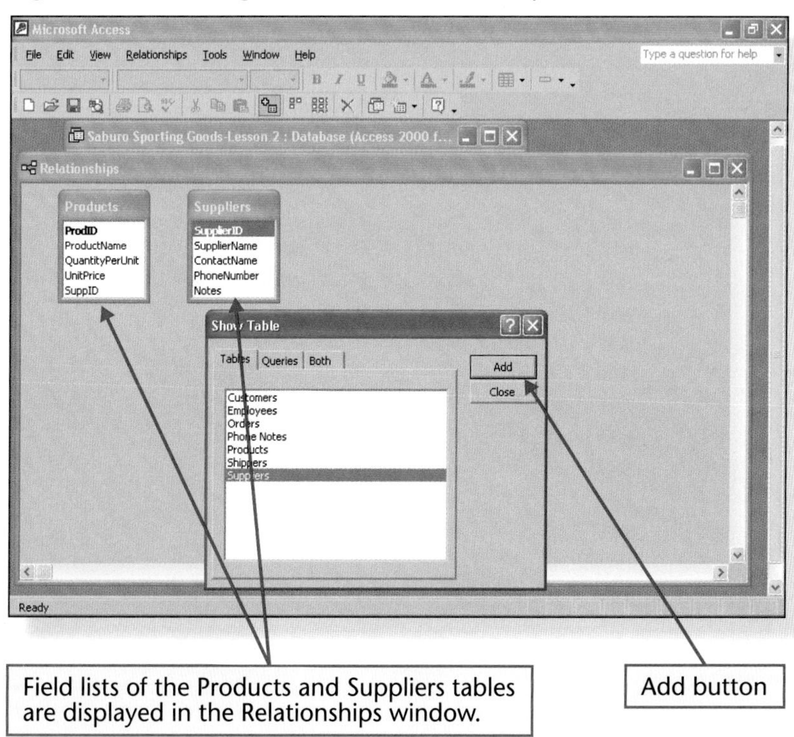

Field lists of the Products and Suppliers tables are displayed in the Relationships window.

Add button

5. Save and close the Products table.
6. Close any open database objects, if necessary. Then click Relationships on the Database toolbar to open the Relationships window.
7. If the Relationships window is blank, click Show Table on the Database toolbar.
8. In the Show Table dialog box, select Products on the Tables tab and click Add. Then select Suppliers and click Add (see Figure 2.32). Close the Show Table dialog box.

Access

9. Select the SuppID field in the Products table field list, drag it onto the SupplierID field in the Suppliers table field list, and release the mouse button. The Edit Relationships dialog box appears (see Figure 2.33).

10. Click the Create button. The dialog box closes, and a relationship line appears between the related fields.

Figure 2.33 The Edit Relationships dialog box

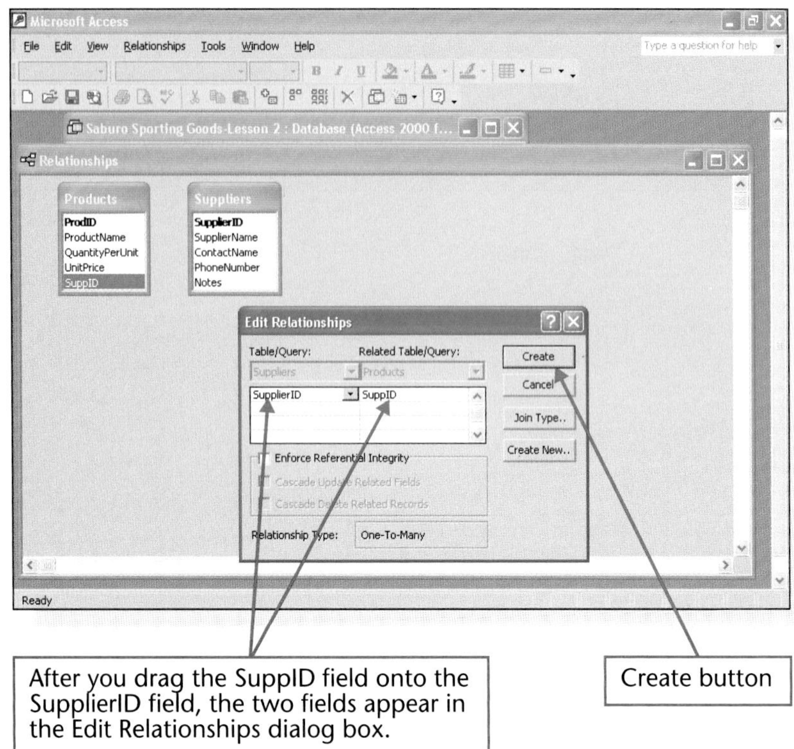

Step Through It™

Exercise 5B: Enforce referential integrity

1. Double-click the relationship line. The Edit Relationships dialog box reappears.

2. Click to select the *Enforce Referential Integrity* option.

3. Click to select the *Cascade Update Related Fields* option. Click OK (see Figure 2.34).

4. Close the Relationships window. Click Yes to save changes to the layout of 'Relationships'.

Figure 2.34 A one-to-many relationship with referential integrity enforced

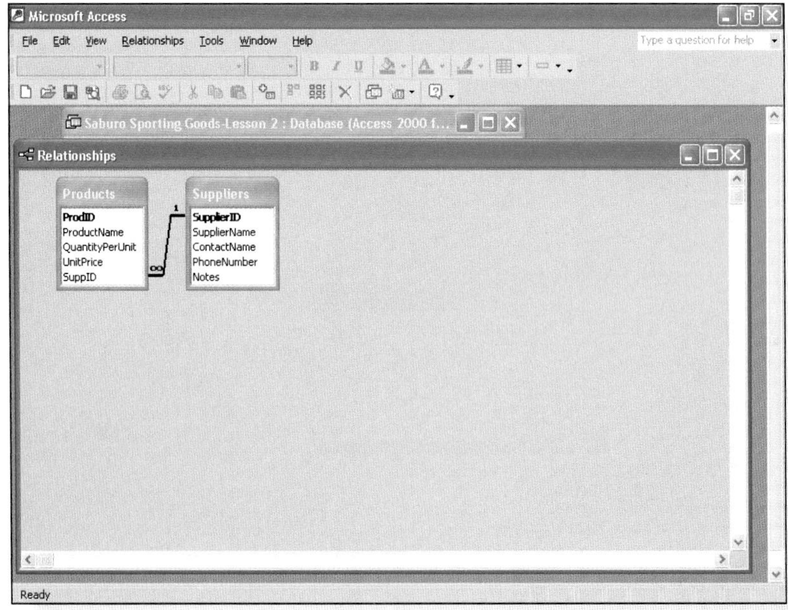

Exercise 6 Overview:
Create a Lookup Field

Microsoft Office Specialist
AC2002 2.3

Access

One of the most common ways that "bad" data get into a database is through typing errors. An important goal of most database managers is to eliminate as much typing by database users as possible. One way to do this is to designate fields as Lookup fields. A **Lookup field** displays a list of values from which you or other database users can choose, or "look up" data, instead of typing a value—which, in addition to ensuring data accuracy, also saves time.

There are two kinds of lists associated with Lookup fields: (1) a Lookup list, which is a dynamic list that looks up entries in a different table, and (2) a value list, which is a static list of values that you enter when you create the Lookup field. In a Lookup (dynamic) list, when the data in the "lookup" table change, the data in the Lookup list change, too.

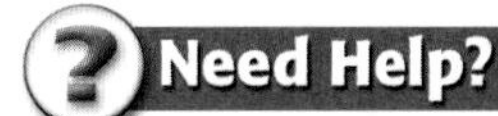

Type: create a field that looks up or lists values in tables

You can change an existing field into a Lookup field, or you can designate a new field as a Lookup field. However, if you want to change a field into a Lookup field, and the field you want to change serves as the common field in a relationship, you must first delete the relationship. (Access will automatically reestablish the relationship after the Lookup field has been created.)

As with most multi-step processes, Access provides a wizard—aptly named the Lookup Wizard—to help you create a Lookup field. To start the Lookup Wizard, you select Lookup Wizard as the data type for the field in table Design view. Then you respond to the prompts in each of the wizard steps to create a Lookup field.

In the following exercises, you will create and use Lookup fields. In the first exercise, you will create a Lookup field in the Products table that looks up supplier names in the Suppliers table. In the next exercise, you will create a new Lookup field, Categories, that contains a value list. Finally, you will use the Lookup fields to enter data into the table.

Quick Tip

In Exercise 6A, you will be changing the SupplierID field in the Products table to a Lookup field. Because the SupplierID field is designated as the common field in the Products–Suppliers relationship, you must delete the relationship before you create the Lookup field.

Step Through It™

Exercise 6A: Use the Lookup Wizard to create a Lookup list

1. Close any open tables, if necessary, and then open the Relationships window.

2. In the Relationships window, click the relationship line between the Products and Suppliers tables to select it (see Figure 2.35). Then press Delete. When asked if you're sure you want to permanently delete the selected relationship, click Yes.

Figure 2.35 Deleting a relationship before creating a Lookup field

When selected, the relationship line is bold.

3. Close the Relationships window and open the Products table in Design view.

4. Click in the Data Type column of the SuppID field row and click the down arrow that appears. Select Lookup Wizard in the data type list (see Figure 2.36). The Lookup Wizard starts.

Figure 2.36 Choose the Lookup Wizard from the data type list

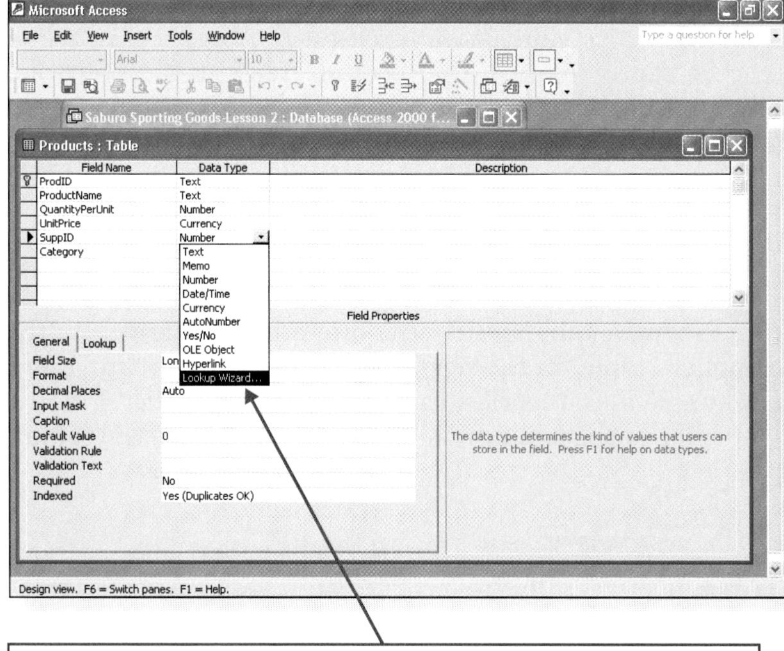

Select Lookup Wizard as the data type to start the Lookup Wizard.

Figure 2.37 Selecting the table from which to look up data

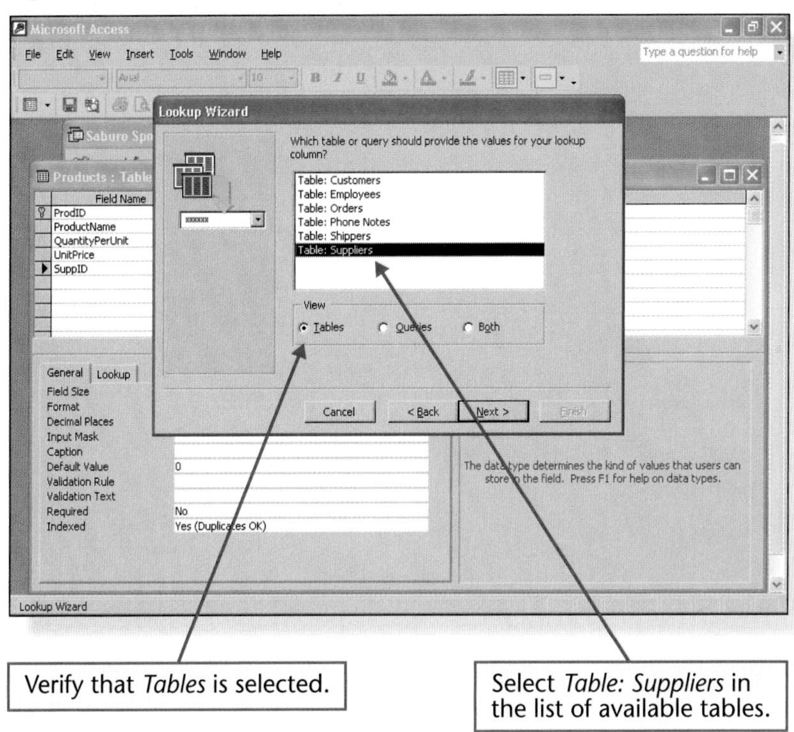

5. In the first wizard step, select the *I want the lookup column to look up the values in a table or query* option. Click Next.

6. In the next wizard step, be sure the Tables option is selected in the View section, and click Table: Suppliers in the list (see Figure 2.37). Click Next.

Access

Figure 2.38 Using the Lookup Wizard—step 4

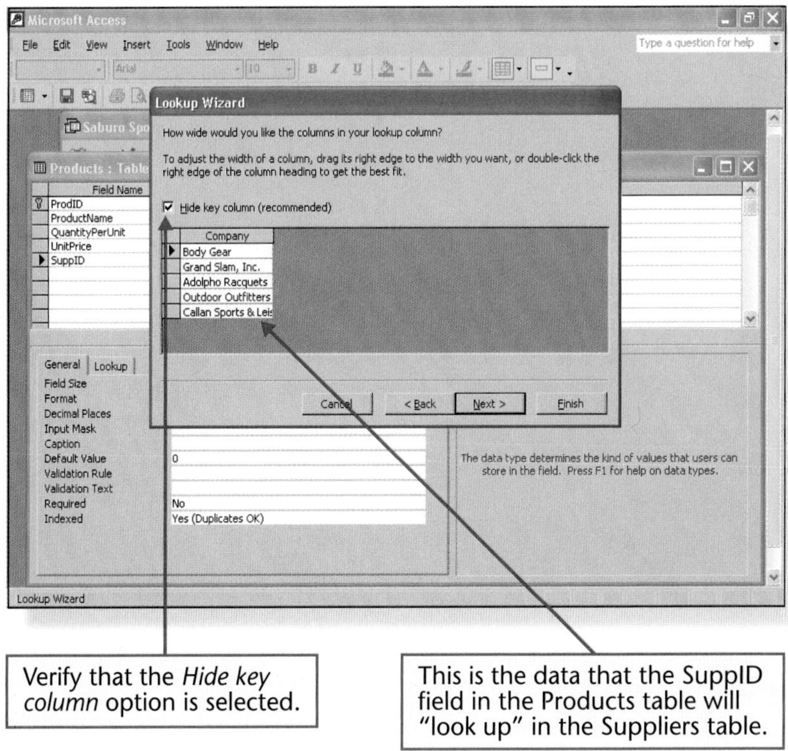

7. In the next wizard step, double-click SupplierName in the Available Fields list, and then click Next.

8. In the fourth wizard step, be sure the *Hide key column* option is selected (see Figure 2.38). Then click Next.

9. In the last wizard step, click Finish to accept the suggested label *SuppID* and close the wizard. In the message that asks you to save the table, click Yes. The Lookup field is created.

Step Through It™

Exercise 6B: Use the Lookup Wizard to create a value list

1. Be sure the Products table is in Design view.

2. In the upper pane of the table design window, add a new field named Category below the SuppID field.

3. In the Data Type column, select Lookup Wizard in the data type list (see Figure 2.39).

Figure 2.39 Starting the Lookup Wizard

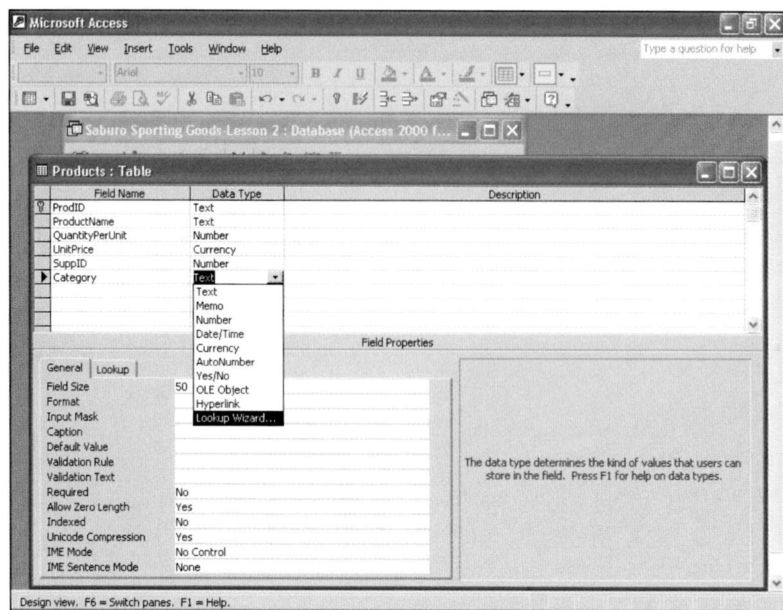

4. In the first wizard step, select the *I will type in the values that I want* option, and then click Next.

5. In the second wizard step, type Field in the first Col1 cell and press Tab. Type the following entries, pressing Tab after each one: Indoor, Court, Swimming, Climbing, Wheel, and General (see Figure 2.40). Then click Next.

6. In the last wizard step, click Finish to accept the suggested label *Category* and close the wizard. Then save the table.

Figure 2.40 Type the entries in your value list

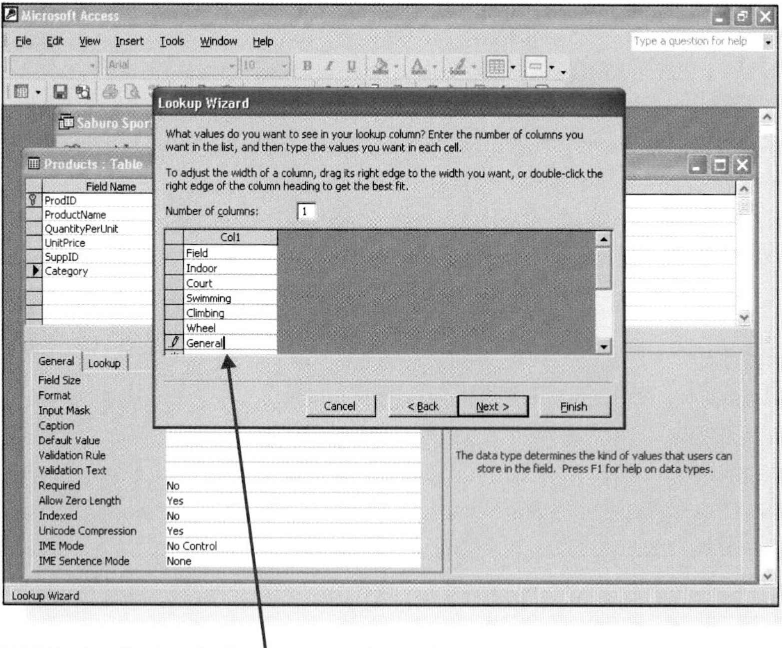

Type an entry, and then press Tab—a new cell appears for the next entry.

Table 2.2

Product Name	Supplier	Category
softball	Grand Slam, Inc.	Field
youth cleats	Grand Slam, Inc.	Field
football helmet	Body Gear	Field
shin guards	Body Gear	Field
soccer ball	Callan Sports & Leisure	Field
hockey stick	Callan Sports & Leisure	Field
hockey puck	Callan Sports & Leisure	Field
basketball	Callan Sports & Leisure	Field
running shorts	Body Gear	General
bicycle helmet	Body Gear	Wheel
roller blades	Body Gear	Wheel
heart rate monitor	Body Gear	General
cycling shorts	Body Gear	Wheel
water bottle	Outdoor Outfitters Unlimited	General
climbing rope	Outdoor Outfitters Unlimited	Climbing
carabiner	Outdoor Outfitters Unlimited	Climbing
swim cap	Outdoor Outfitters Unlimited	Swimming
swim goggles	Outdoor Outfitters Unlimited	Swimming
running shoes	Body Gear	General
baseball glove	Grand Slam, Inc.	Field
baseball bat	Grand Slam, Inc.	Field
tennis racquet	Adolpho Racquets	Court
racquetball racquet	Adolpho Racquets	Court
racquetballs (3 per can)	Adolpho Racquets	Court
volleyball	Callan Sports & Leisure	Field
squash racquet	Adolpho Racquets	Court
ping pong paddle	Adolpho Racquets	Indoor
sport socks (2 pack)	Adolpho Racquets	General
bowling shoes	Body Gear	Indoor
bowling ball	Callan Sports & Leisure	Indoor

Step Through It™

Exercise 6C: Test the Lookup fields

1. Switch to Datasheet view.
2. Navigate to the SuppID field for the first record. Click the down arrow that appears and select Grand Slam, Inc. on the Lookup list.
3. Press Tab, click the down arrow in the Category field, and select Field from the value list.
4. Enter the supplier and category data provided in Table 2.2 for the remaining records.
5. Close the Products table and close the *Saburo Sporting Goods-Lesson 2.mdb* database

APPLY IT! After finishing Exercises 4–6, you may test your skills by completing Apply It! Guided Activity 2, Import Data, Define Relationships, and Create a Lookup Field.

Procedure Summary

Create a Table Using the Table Wizard

1. In the Database window, click Tables in the Objects bar.
   OR
   Click **View** .... Alt + V
   Point to **Database Objects** .... J
   Select **Tables** .... T
2. Double-click *Create table by using wizard* in the right pane of the Database window.
   OR
   Click **New** .... Alt + N
   Select Table Wizard in New Table dialog box.
   Click OK.
3. In the first wizard step, select a table category (Business or Personal), and then select a sample table and sample fields for the table.
4. In the second wizard step, enter a table name and select an appropriate option regarding setting the primary key.
5. In subsequent wizard steps, enter appropriate responses to the wizard prompts.

Create a Table in Design View

1. In the Database window, click Tables in the Objects bar.
   OR
   Click **View** .... Alt + V
   Point to **Database Objects** .... J
   Select **Tables** .... T
2. Double-click *Create table in Design view* in the right pane of the Database window.
   OR
   Click **New** .... Alt + N
   Select Design View in New Table dialog box.
   Click OK.
3. In the upper pane of the table design window, enter field names and select data types for each field in the table.
4. If desired, click in the field you want to set as the primary key, and click **Primary Key**.
5. Save and name the table.

Modify Field Properties

1. Open a table in Design view.
2. In the upper pane of the table design window, click in the row of the field whose properties you want to change.
3. Click in the Field Properties pane F6
4. Navigate to the appropriate field property and modify it.
5. Save the changes to the table design.

Create an Input Mask

1. Open a table in Design view.
2. In the upper pane of the table design window, click in the row of the field whose properties you want to change.
3. Click in the Input Mask property box.
4. Click **Build** at the right end of the Input Mask property box to start the Input Mask Wizard.
5. Enter appropriate responses to the wizard prompts.
6. Save the changes to the table design.

Import Data Into an Access Table

1. Click **File** .... Alt + F
2. Point to **Get External Data** .... G
3. Select **Import** I
4. In the Import dialog box, navigate to the correct folder, and select the correct file type.
5. Double-click the file name.
   OR
   Click the file name.
   Click **Import** .... Alt + M
6. Enter appropriate responses to the wizard prompts.

Export Data From an Access Table

1. In the Database window, click the table name to select it.
2. Click **File** . . . . Alt + F
3. Select **Export** . . . . E
4. In the Export Table dialog box, navigate to the location where you want to export the data, and select the appropriate file type.
5. Click **Export** . . . . Alt + X

Link to Data Outside an Access Database

1. Click **File** . . . . Alt + F
2. Point to **Get External Data** . . . . G
3. Click **Link Tables** L
4. In the Link dialog box, navigate to the location where the file you wish to link to is stored, and select the appropriate file type.
5. Double-click the file to which you want to link.
   OR
   Click the file name.
   Click **Link** . . . . Alt + K
6. Enter appropriate responses to the wizard prompts.

Create a Relationship

1. Click **Relationships** .
   OR
   Click **Tools** . . . . Alt + T
   Click **Relationships** . . . . R
2. In the Relationships window, click **Show Tables** .
   OR
   Click **Relationships** . . . . Alt + R
   Click **Show Table** . . . . T
3. In the Show Tables dialog box, double-click the tables you want to relate.
   OR
   Select each table you want to relate, clicking Add after each selection.
4. Close the Show Tables dialog box.
5. Drag the common field from one table and drop it onto the common field in the other table.
6. In the Edit Relationships dialog box, click Create.
7. Close the Relationships window.
8. Click Yes in the message box that prompts you to save changes to the relationships layout.

Enforce Referential Integrity

1. Click **Relationships** .
   OR
   Click **Tools** . . . . Alt + T
   Click **Relationships** . . . . R
2. Double-click the relationship line between the two tables.
   OR
   Click **Relationships** . . . . Alt + R
   Click **Edit Relationship** . . . . R
3. In the Edit Relationships dialog box, click to select the *Enforce Referential Integrity* option.
4. If desired, click to select the *Cascade Update Related Fields* or *Cascade Delete Related Records* options.

Create a Lookup Field

1. Open a table in Design view.
2. In the upper pane of the table design window, choose the Lookup Wizard data type for the field you wish to designate as a Lookup field.
3. Enter appropriate responses to the wizard prompts.
4. Save the changes to the table design.

Lesson Review and Exercises

Summary Checklist

- ☑ Can you create a table using the Table Wizard?
- ☑ Can you create a table in Design view?
- ☑ Do you understand data types?
- ☑ Do you understand field properties?
- ☑ Can you modify a field property?
- ☑ Can you create an input mask using the Input Mask Wizard?
- ☑ Can you import data into an Access table?
- ☑ Can you export data from an Access table?
- ☑ Can you link data to an Access database?
- ☑ Do you understand the value of defining relationships?
- ☑ Do you understand referential integrity?
- ☑ Can you create a relationship?
- ☑ Can you enforce referential integrity?
- ☑ Can you use the Lookup Wizard to create a Lookup list and a value list?

Key Terms

- data type (p. 346)
- export (p. 356)
- field name (p. 345)
- field property (p. 346)
- import (p. 354)
- input mask (p. 349)
- junction table (p. 362)
- link (p. 357)
- Lookup field (p. 369)
- many-to-many relationship (p. 362)
- one-to-many relationship (p. 362)
- one-to-one relationship (p. 363)
- orphan (p. 364)
- primary key (p. 340)
- primary table (p. 362)
- referential integrity (p. 364)
- related table (p. 362)
- relationship (p. 361)
- subdatasheet (p. 365)

APPLY IT! Guided Activities

1. Create and Modify Tables

At the end of Lesson 1, you created a new, blank database for LawnMowers, a small lawn-mowing business. Now you will create two of the tables for the database—a table that contains data about the mower-partners and a table that contains appointment data. Follow these steps to create the tables:

a. Open the *LawnMowers-Lesson 2.mdb* database and start the Table Wizard. Select the Business option (if necessary), and choose Employees as the sample table. Add the FirstName, LastName, and HomePhone fields to the table. Click Next.

b. Name the table Mowers, and tell the wizard to set a primary key for you. Finish and close the table.

c. Create a table in Design view. Add fields for Mowers (data type *Number*), Customers (data type *Number*), and Date (data type *Date/Time*). Save the table as Appointments. You do not need to set a primary key.

d. In the Appointments table, create an input mask for the Date field. Choose the Short Date (9/27/1969) mask **(see Figure 2.41)**. Save and close the Appointments table.

Figure 2.41 The Appointments table in Design view

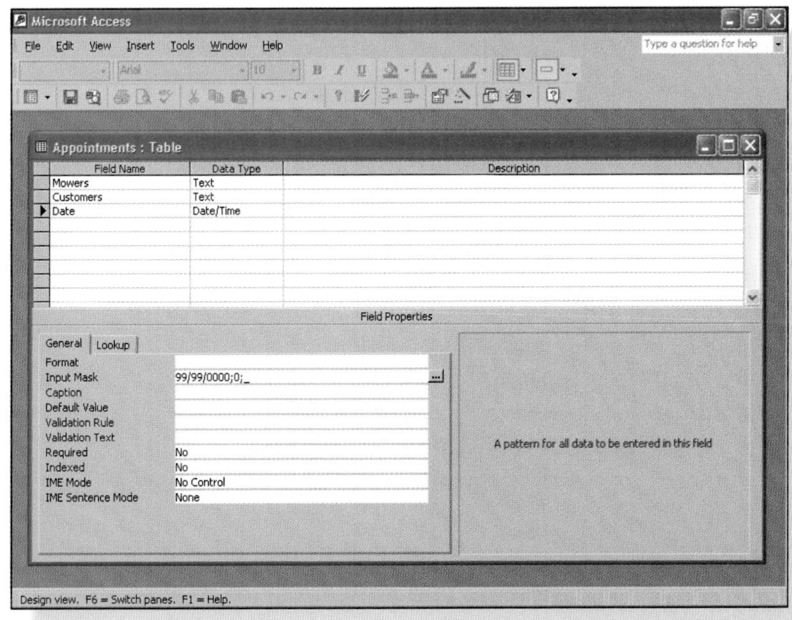

Access

e. Open the Mowers table in Design view, and create an input mask for the HomePhone field. In the Input Mask Wizard, choose the option to include the punctuation symbols in the mask. Also, change the caption for the HomePhone field to **Phone**, and change the HomePhone field's Required property to Yes.

f. Save the changes to the table design and switch to Datasheet view. Enter the data contained in **Table 2.3** into the Mowers table. Then close the Mowers table.

Table 2.3

First Name	Last Name	Home Phone
Lon	Miller	303-555-0271
Juan	Guiterrez	303-555-6459
Alicia	Gerrard	303-555-1818

2. Import Data, Define Relationships, and Create a Lookup Field

One of the business partners has the LawnMowers customer list stored in an Excel workbook. First you will import that customer information into a table in the LawnMowers database. Then you will define relationships between the three tables and enforce referential integrity. Finally, you will create Lookup fields to make data entry easier, and then enter appointments. Follow these steps:

a. Import the *LMCustomers.xls* Excel file from the *Lesson 2* subfolder in the *Unit 3* folder into a new table named Customers. As you progress through the Import Spreadsheet Wizard steps, determine if the first row contains column headings, verify the data types to be sure they're appropriate for each field, and let Access add the primary key.

b. Open the Relationships window and, if necessary, show the Customers, Appointments, and Mowers tables. Define a one-to-many relationship between the Customers table and Appointment table. Enforce referential integrity and select the option to *Cascade Update Related Fields*. Then define a one-to-many relationship between the Appointments table and the Mowers table, also enforcing referential integrity and selecting the option to *Cascade Update Related Fields*. Close the Relationship window and save changes to the relationship layout.

c. Now you want to modify the Customers and Mowers fields in the Appointments table into Lookup fields. Open the Appointments table in Design view and try to create a Lookup field for the

Mowers field. Then try to create a Lookup field for the Customers field. Because these two fields are common fields used in relationships, you must first delete the relationships before you can create the Lookup fields. Close the Appointments table (without saving changes), open the Relationships window, and delete the relationships you created earlier. Then close the Relationships window.

d. Reopen the Appointments table in Design view. Modify the Mowers field to look up the FirstName and HomePhone fields in the Mowers table. Then modify the Customers field to look up the Last, First, and Phone fields in the Customers table.

e. Switch the Appointments table to Datasheet view and use the Lookup fields you just created to enter the appointments provided in **Table 2.4**. Then close the table and the database.

Table 2.4

Mowers	Customers	Date
Lon	Wise	06/06/2003
Juan	Mendez	06/06/2003
Alicia	Ramirez	06/10/2003
Lon	Diaz	06/12/2003
Lon	Miller	06/15/2003
Juan	Mendez	07/06/2003
Juan	Mendez	08/06/2003
Juan	Mendez	09/06/2003
Lon	Diaz	07/12/2003
Lon	Diaz	08/12/2003
Alicia	Ramirez	07/15/2003
Alicia	Stalt	06/25/2003
Alicia	Michaels	07/02/2003

Do It Yourself

1. Import and Modify a Table

As the database manager for WoodStarts, a small woodshop business, you decide that, in addition to the existing Employees and Products tables, the company database needs a table to store customer information. The owner of the business had been storing the customer information in an Excel file, which you want to import into a table in your database. Then you want to modify the table to make it more useful.

a. Open the *WoodStarts-Lesson 2.mdb* database and import the data in the *WSCustomers.xls* Excel file (located in the *Lesson 2* subfolder in the *Unit 3* folder) into a new table named Customers. Include the column headings. Allow Access to add a primary key field for you.

b. Examine the new Customers table in Design view. Notice that the new primary key field is named *ID* and has a data type of AutoNumber.

c. Since the field name *ID* is not very descriptive, add the caption Customer ID.

d. Add an input mask to the Zip field, and then add the caption ZIP Code.

e. Add an input mask to the Phone field, and then add the caption Phone Number.

f. Save and close the Customers table.

g. The company salesperson would like a list of the customers saved in a format that can be opened in Microsoft Word. Export the Customers table in Rich Text Format, and then save it in the *Lesson 2* subfolder in the *Unit 3* folder.

2. Create a Table and Establish Relationships

You decide that the WoodStarts database would be more useful if you could use it to store order information. Follow these steps to create an Orders table in Design view and establish relationships between the tables in the database.

a. Create a new table in Design view. Include the fields provided in Table 2.5.

Table 2.5

Field Name	Data Type
CustomerID	Number
Date	Date/Time
ProductID	Number
Quantity	Number
OrderID	AutoNumber

b. Click in the OrderID row (if necessary) and click the Primary Key button on the Table Design toolbar to designate the OrderID field as the primary key field **(see Figure 2.42)**. Save the table as Orders, and then close the table.

c. Create a relationship between the Customers and Orders tables; do not enforce referential integrity. Then create a relationship between the Orders and Products tables; again, do not enforce referential integrity.

Figure 2.42 Designate the OrderID field as the primary key

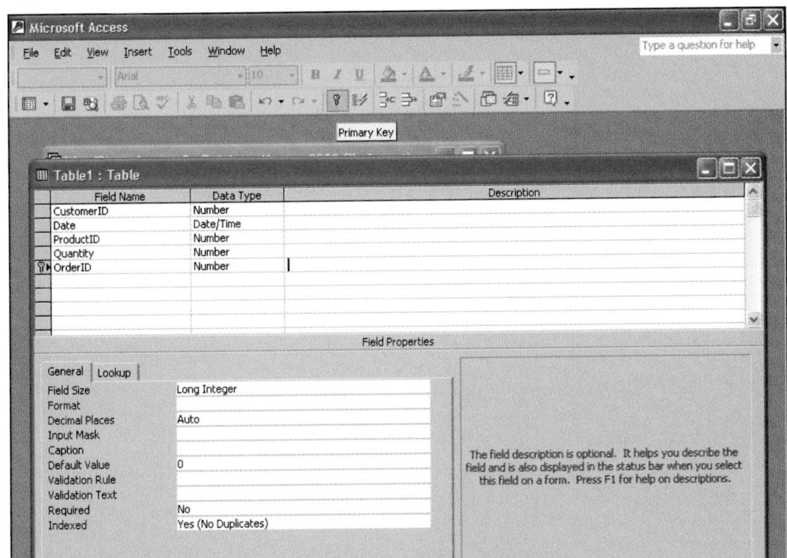

3. Modify Field Properties and Enter Data

Because many of the WoodStarts employees don't know the ID numbers assigned to the customers or the products, they asked if you could modify the Orders table so they could just pick the customer names and products from Lookup lists. They also wondered if you could modify the Date field to make entering the date easier. Follow these steps to make the requested modifications:

a. Examine the table relationships. Since the CustomerID and Product fields are common fields used in the table relationships, you must delete the relationships before you can change the fields into Lookup fields.

b. Change the CustomerID field in the Orders table to a Lookup field that looks up the Company field in the Customers table. Change the label of the lookup column to Customer.

c. Change the ProductID field to a Lookup field that looks up the Product field in the Products table. Change the label of this lookup column to Products.

d. Create an input mask for the Date field using the Short Date mask.

e. Save the design changes to the Orders table, and then test your modifications by entering the order information provided in **Table 2.6**. Then close the table and close the *WoodStarts-Lesson 2.mdb* database.

Table 2.6

Customer	Date	Product	Quantity
Trophies'r'Us	07/03/2003	Medium oak	20
Trophies'r'Us	07/03/2003	Medium pine	20
Trophies'r'Us	07/03/2003	Medium walnut	30
BigWin Trophies	07/15/2003	Large oak	50
Blue and Silver Co.	08/03/2003	Small oak	10
Blue and Silver Co.	08/03/2003	Small pine	10
Blue and Silver Co.	08/03/2003	Small walnut	10

Challenge Yourself

Create a Table by Entering Data

In this lesson, you have created tables using the Table Wizard, and you've created tables in Design view. You can also create a table using yet another method—by simply entering data.

Experiment with this third method for creating a table. Open the *WoodStarts-Lesson 2.mdb* database. With the Table objects displayed in the Database window, double-click the *Create table by entering data* option. An empty datasheet is displayed **(see Figure 2.43)**.

Figure 2.43 Creating a table by entering data

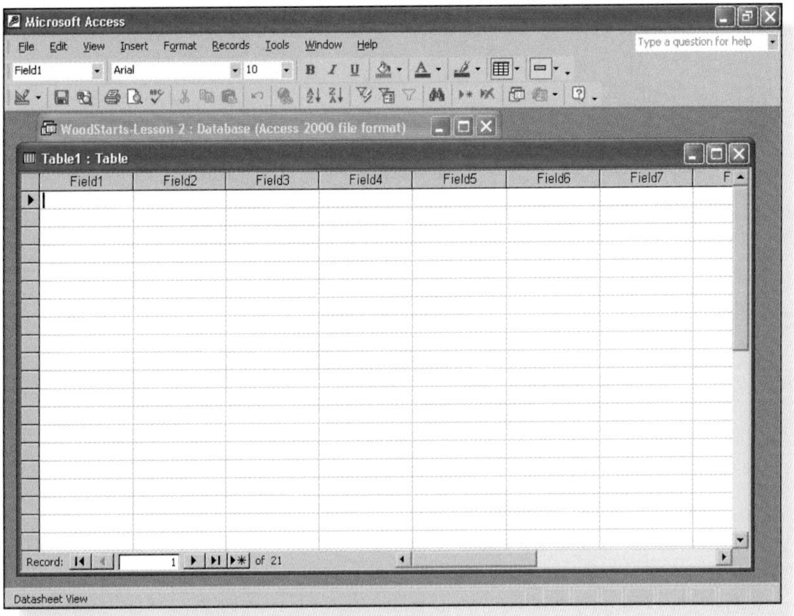

Double-click the first field selector—the gray box above the first record that contains the label *Field1*—and change it to ShipperName. Change the *Field2* field selector to TypeofService, and change the *Field3* field selector to Cost/lb.

Then enter the shipping data provided in **Table 2.7** into the empty datasheet. As you enter data in the datasheet, Access assigns data types to the fields based on the kind of data you type.

Table 2.7

Shipper Name	Type of Service	Cost/lb
Continental Transport	Ground	$0.50
Rite Flite	Air	$2.00
Swift Ship	Overnight	$3.50

Save the table as Shippers. (You do not need to create a primary key.) Switch to Design view and examine the data types that Access assigned to the fields. Add captions to the fields as appropriate. Examine the table in Datasheet view. Then close the table, close the database, and exit Access.

Lesson 3

Working With Datasheets and Queries

Lesson Exercise Objectives

After completing this lesson, you'll be able to do the following tasks:

1. Sort records in a datasheet
2. Search for data in a datasheet
3. Filter records in a datasheet
4. Create and modify select queries
5. Create special queries using wizards
6. Format a datasheet

Key Terms

- ascending sort (p. 386)
- calculated field (p. 401)
- concatenation (p. 398)
- criteria (p. 388)
- descending sort (p. 386)
- expression (p. 401)
- filter (p. 388)
- Filter By Form (p. 390)
- Filter By Selection (p. 389)
- select query (p. 396)

Microsoft Office Specialist Activities

AC2002: 1.4, 3.1, 3.2, 5.2, 5.3, 5.4

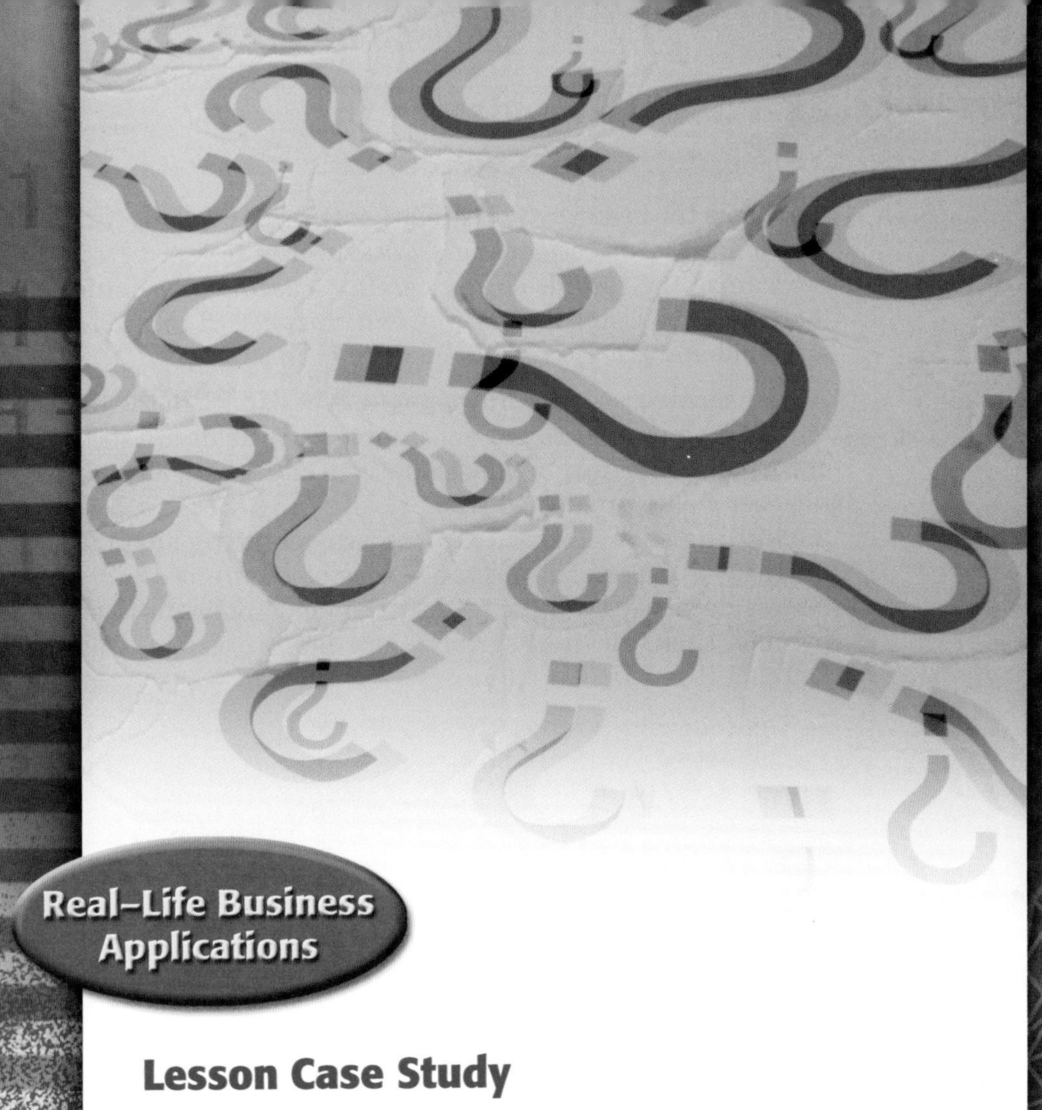

Real-Life Business Applications

Lesson Case Study

In this lesson, you will continue in your role as a student intern in the information systems department at Saburo Sporting Goods. Keep the following information in mind as you work through this lesson.

- **Job responsibilities and goals.** You know how to create tables, add data to your tables, and create relationships between tables so that you can work with combined, related data. During this phase of your internship, you will learn how to locate and organize data within tables and create queries, so that you can quickly find the specific information you need.
- **The project.** You will learn how to sort, search, and filter a datasheet in order to locate specific information. You will also learn how to create queries to extract specific records from a table, and format a datasheet.
- **The challenge ahead.** You know how to get data into a database. The next challenge is to learn how to extract information from a database in an organized form.

Microsoft Office Specialist AC2002 5.3

Access

Exercise 1 Overview:
Sort Records in a Datasheet

Sorting is the best way to begin organizing data of any kind. The main reason for sorting a datasheet is to temporarily reorganize the records so you can find specific information more quickly. Using Access, you can quickly sort records on any field and see the results instantly.

Need Help?

Type: about sorting records

Access sorts records according to the type of data in the field on which you are sorting. For example, date fields are sorted chronologically, text fields are sorted alphabetically, and number fields are sorted numerically. Any sort can be an **ascending sort** (A–Z or 1–10), or a **descending sort** (Z–A or 10–1). To perform a simple sort of the records in an Access datasheet, you just select the field you want to sort by and click the appropriate Sort button on the Table Datasheet toolbar.

In the following exercise, you will sort the records in the Products table in the *Saburo Sporting Goods-Lesson 3.mdb* database.

Step Through It™
Exercise 1: Sort records

1. Open the Products table in the *Saburo Sporting Goods-Lesson 3.mdb* database in Datasheet view.
2. Click in the ProductName field, and click Sort Ascending. The entire table is sorted with the product names in alphabetical order.
3. Click in the UnitPrice field, and click Sort Descending. The entire table is sorted with the prices in descending order (see Figure 3.1).

Figure 3.1 The sorted Products table

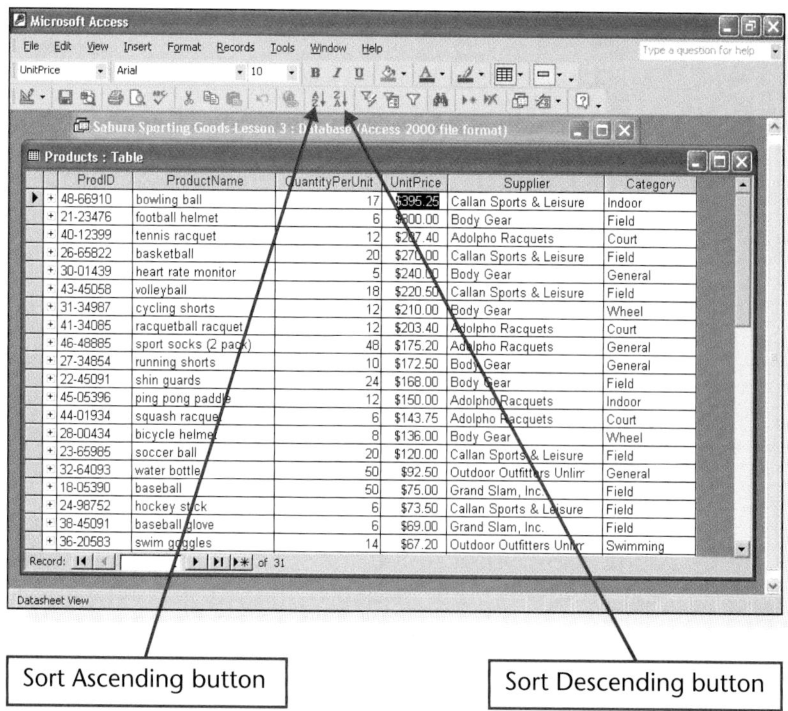

Exercise 2 Overview:
Search for Data in a Datasheet

The primary reason for sorting records is to reorganize them so that you can more easily locate specific information. Another way to locate specific information in a datasheet is to use the Find feature. Using the Find feature in Access is very similar to using the Find feature in Word or Excel.

If you know just a portion of the entry you're looking for, you can use the Find feature to search for all entries that contain those characters. The easiest way to activate the Find feature in Access is to click the Find button on the Table Datasheet toolbar. When you activate the Find feature, Access displays the Find tab of the Find and Replace dialog box. In this dialog box, you can specify exactly what you want to find, where you want Access to look (in either an entire table or a specific field), and whether you want Access to match your search criteria to a whole field or just part of a field.

In the following exercise, you will search the Products table for product name entries that contain the characters *ball*.

Type: find or replace a value in a field

Access

Figure 3.2 Using the Find feature

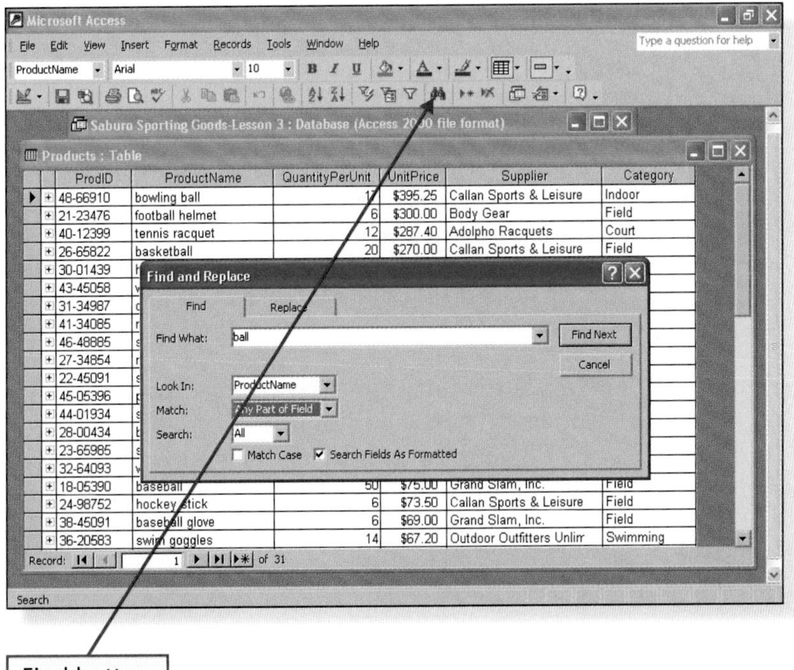

Step Through It™
Exercise 2: Search for specific data

1. In the Products datasheet, click anywhere in the ProductName field.
2. On the Table Datasheet toolbar, click Find.
3. In the Find What box, type ball. Be sure the Look In box displays *ProductName*. In the Match box, select *Any Part of Field* (see Figure 3.2).

4. Click the Find Next button. The first entry containing *ball* is found and highlighted. Continue to click Find Next to locate other entries containing *ball*.

5. Click OK when Access indicates that it has finished the search (see Figure 3.3).

6. Close the Find and Replace dialog box, and then close the Products table without saving changes.

Figure 3.3 Access displays a message indicating that it has finished the search

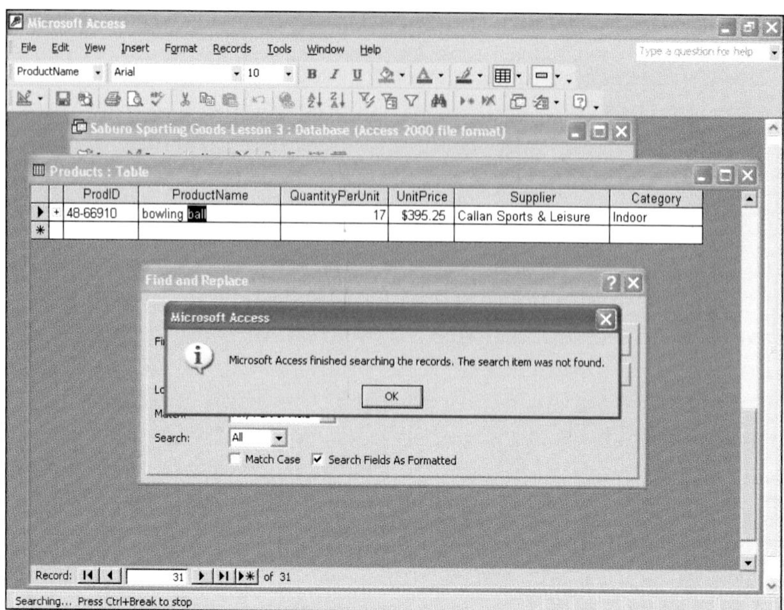

Microsoft Office Specialist AC2002 5.4

Exercise 3 Overview:
Filter Records in a Datasheet

You use a **filter** to isolate a subset of records in a datasheet. When you apply a filter to a datasheet, Access "screens out" records that don't meet your **criteria**, and displays only those records that do meet your criteria. This allows you to work with a limited set of records that have the data you need. For example, suppose you want to send a special mailing to all the customers who live in the USA. You can apply a filter using USA as your criterion, and Access will display records for only those customers who live in the USA.

Type: about filters

Filters can be simple and straightforward or fairly complex, depending on the criteria you supply. A simple filter might find records that meet a single criterion, but a more complex filter might look for records that satisfy multiple criteria.

Filter criteria can consist of entire entries (such as "Indoor" in the Category field), or partial entries (such as "ball" in the ProductName field), or they can be calculated (such as UnitPrice < $100).

Using the Filter By Selection Method

You can quickly apply a simple filter using the **Filter By Selection** method. With this method, you select an entry or a partial entry in a field, and then click the Filter By Selection button on the Table Datasheet toolbar to filter the table and display only the records that share the entry or partial entry you selected.

In the following exercise, you will use the Filter by Selection method in the Products table of the *Saburo Sporting Goods-Lesson 3.mdb* database to answer three different questions:

- Which orders were placed on April 18, 2003?
- Which orders were placed in the month of April?
- Which orders included any kind of racquet product?

Figure 3.4 Filtered datasheet displays only the records for orders placed on April 18, 2003

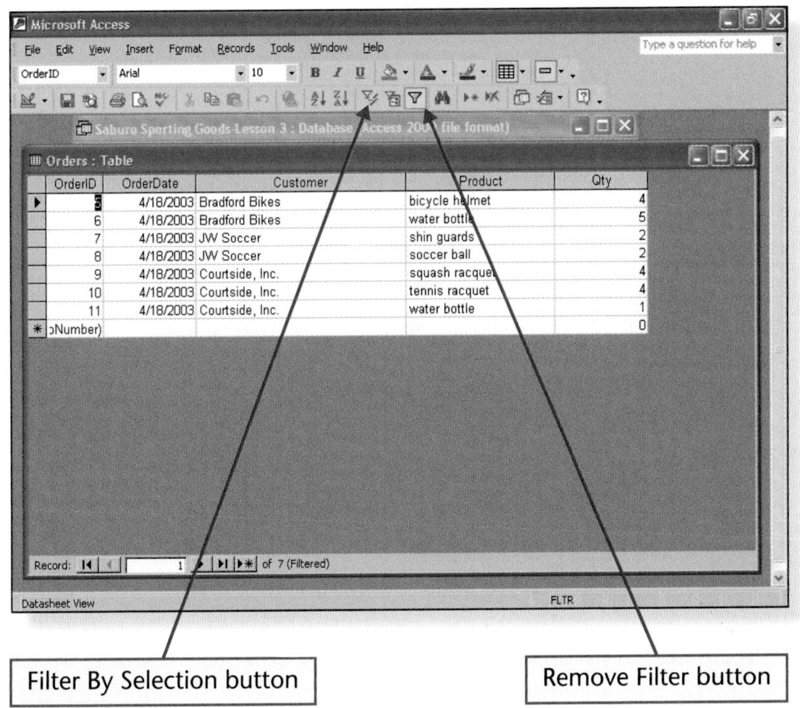

Step Through It™

Exercise 3A: Use Filter By Selection

1. Open the Orders table.
2. In the OrderDate field, click in any cell that contains the entry *4/18/2003.*
3. On the Table Datasheet toolbar, click Filter By Selection. Only the records for orders placed on April 18, 2003 are displayed (see Figure 3.4).
4. On the Table Datasheet toolbar, click Remove Filter. The filter is removed, and all the records are displayed.

5 Highlight the *4/* characters in an OrderDate cell, and click Filter By Selection. Only the records for orders placed in April are displayed.

6 Click Remove Filter.

7 In the Product field, double-click the word *racquet,* and then right-click the selected word. On the shortcut menu, select Filter By Selection (see Figure 3.5). Only the records for orders for racquets are displayed.

8 Click Remove Filter. Then close the Orders table without saving changes.

Figure 3.5 Selecting the Filter By Selection option on the shortcut menu

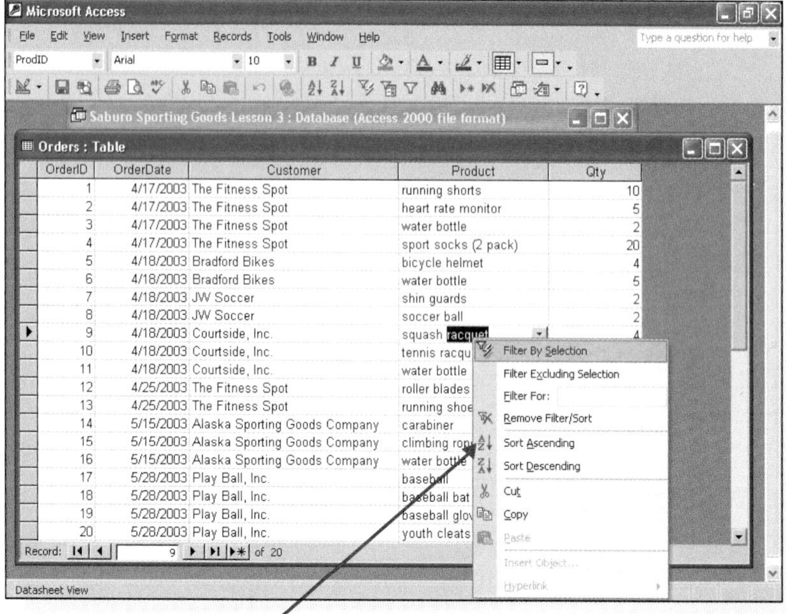

You can also select filtering (and sorting) options from the shortcut menu.

Using the Filter By Form Method

Use **Filter By Form** when you need to apply a filter that contains a criterion (such as product prices greater than $100), an OR condition, or an AND condition.

When you instruct Access to locate records that meet either one criterion *or* another criterion, that is referred to as an OR condition. These two (or more) criteria can be in the same field, or in different fields. For example, in the Saburo Products table, a filter that looks for any records that have either "Wheel" or "General" as entries in the Category field would be an OR condition. Records meeting either of those criteria would be displayed by the filter.

You can also apply a filter that specifies an AND condition. A filter with an AND condition looks for records that meet both a specific criterion in one field *and* a specific criterion in another field. For example, a filter to find products with "ball" in the ProductName field and with "Indoor" in the Category field is an AND condition. Only records meeting both criteria would be displayed by the filter.

In the following exercise, you will use the Filter By Form method to display subsets of records.

Figure 3.6 The Filter By Form window

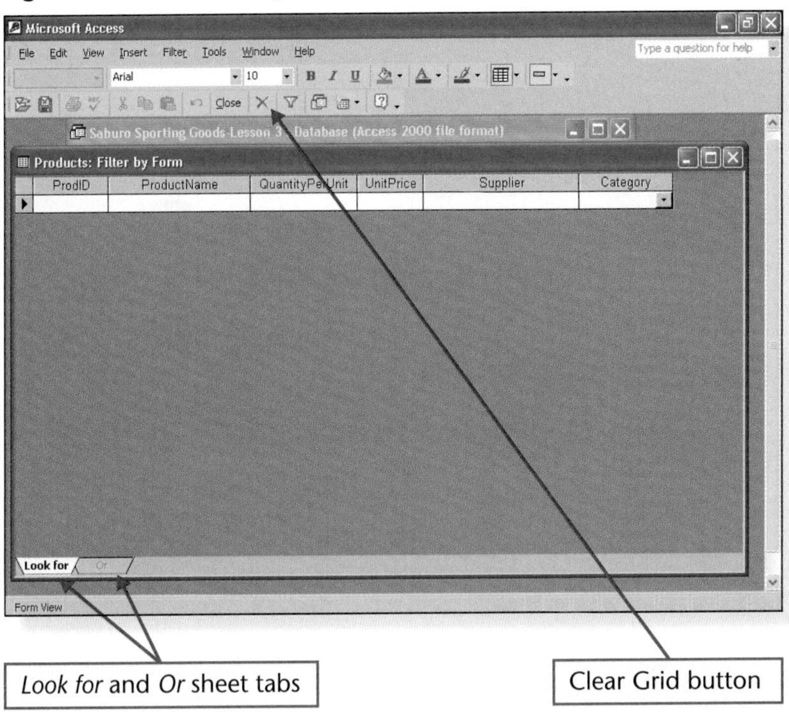

Figure 3.7 Creating a filter using the Filter By Form method

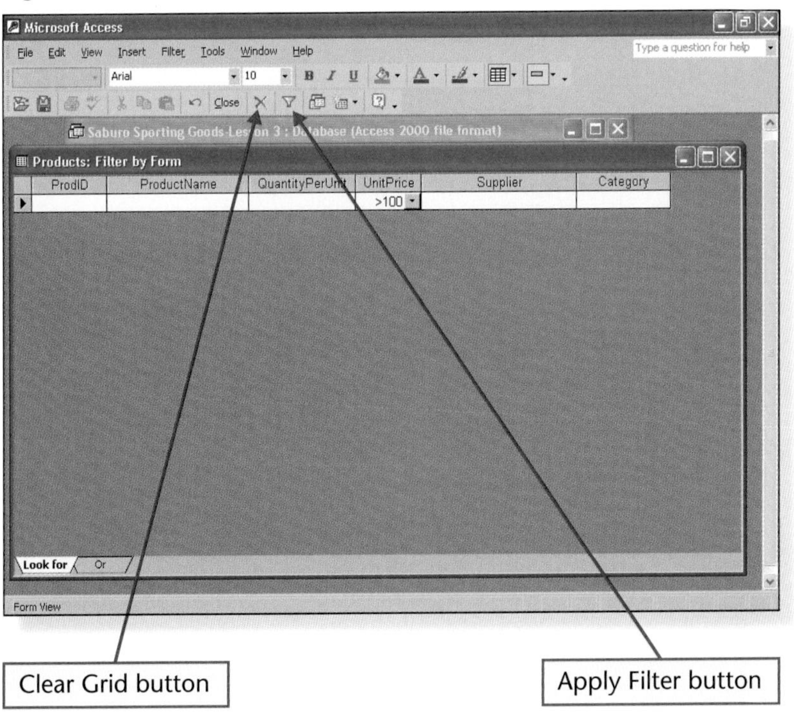

Step Through It™

Exercise 3B: Use Filter By Form

1. Open the Products table and click Filter By Form on the Table Datasheet toolbar. A Filter By Form window opens that contains a single cell for each field and two sheet tabs labeled *Look for* and *Or*, respectively.
2. Click Clear Grid on the Filter/Sort toolbar to clear any previous filter entries (see Figure 3.6).
3. Click in the UnitPrice cell and type >100 (see Figure 3.7). Then click Apply Filter on the Filter/Sort toolbar. The table is filtered to show only the products priced at more than $100.
4. Click in the UnitPrice field and click Sort Descending to sort the filtered datasheet on the UnitPrice field.
5. Click Remove Filter.
6. On the Table Datasheet toolbar, click Filter By Form. Then click Clear Grid to clear the previous filter.

7) Click in the Supplier cell. Then click the down arrow that appears and select Body Gear.

8) Click the *Or* sheet tab at the bottom of the Filter By Form window. Another Filter By Form window opens, and another *Or* sheet tab appears.

9) In the Category cell, select General (see Figure 3.8). Now you've entered the criteria for the OR condition, and Access will display records that contain either Body Gear in the Supplier field or General in the Category field.

Figure 3.8 Entering an OR condition in the Filter By Form window

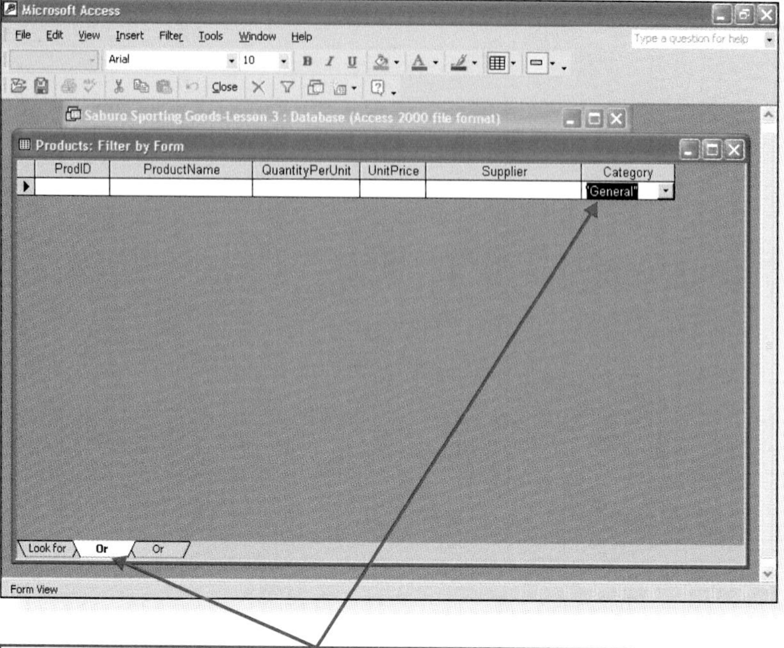

Click the *Or* sheet tab and enter the second criterion of an OR condition in another Filter By Form window.

10) Click Apply Filter. The filter is applied, and only those records that meet either one condition (Body Gear) or the other condition (General) are displayed.

11) Click anywhere in the Supplier field and click Sort Ascending. The filtered datasheet is sorted alphabetically by supplier (see Figure 3.9)

Figure 3.9 Filtered and sorted datasheet displays records that satisfy an OR condition

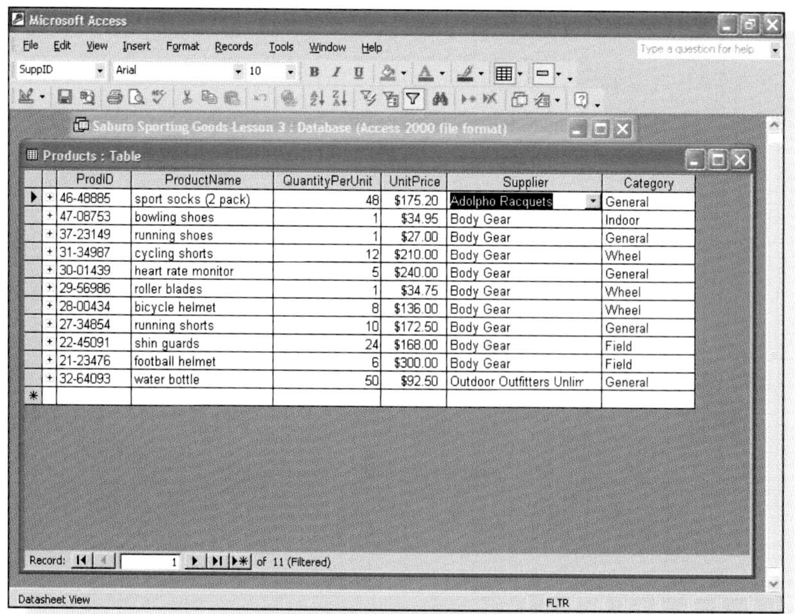

ProdID	ProductName	QuantityPerUnit	UnitPrice	Supplier	Category
46-48885	sport socks (2 pack)	48	$175.20	Adolpho Racquets	General
47-08753	bowling shoes	1	$34.95	Body Gear	Indoor
37-23149	running shoes	1	$27.00	Body Gear	General
31-34987	cycling shorts	12	$210.00	Body Gear	Wheel
30-01439	heart rate monitor	5	$240.00	Body Gear	General
29-56986	roller blades	1	$34.75	Body Gear	Wheel
28-00434	bicycle helmet	8	$136.00	Body Gear	Wheel
27-34854	running shorts	10	$172.50	Body Gear	General
22-45091	shin guards	24	$168.00	Body Gear	Field
21-23476	football helmet	6	$300.00	Body Gear	Field
32-64093	water bottle	50	$92.50	Outdoor Outfitters Unlim	General

Figure 3.10 Entering an AND condition in the Filter By Form window

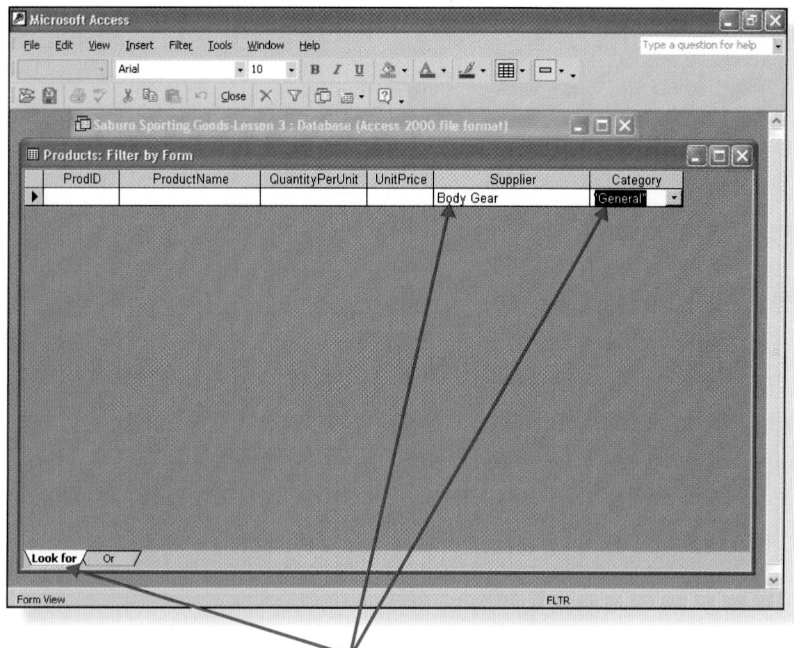

To filter for an AND condition, you must enter two (or more) criteria on the *Look for* tab in the Filter By Form window.

12) Click Filter By Form on the Table Datasheet toolbar, and then click Clear Grid.

13) Now you will filter for an AND condition. Click in the Supplier cell and select Body Gear again.

14) Click in the Category cell and select General. Because both of these criteria are on the Look up tab, Access must retrieve only those records that contain both of these criteria (see Figure 3.10).

Figure 3.11 Filtered datasheet displays records that satisfy an AND condition

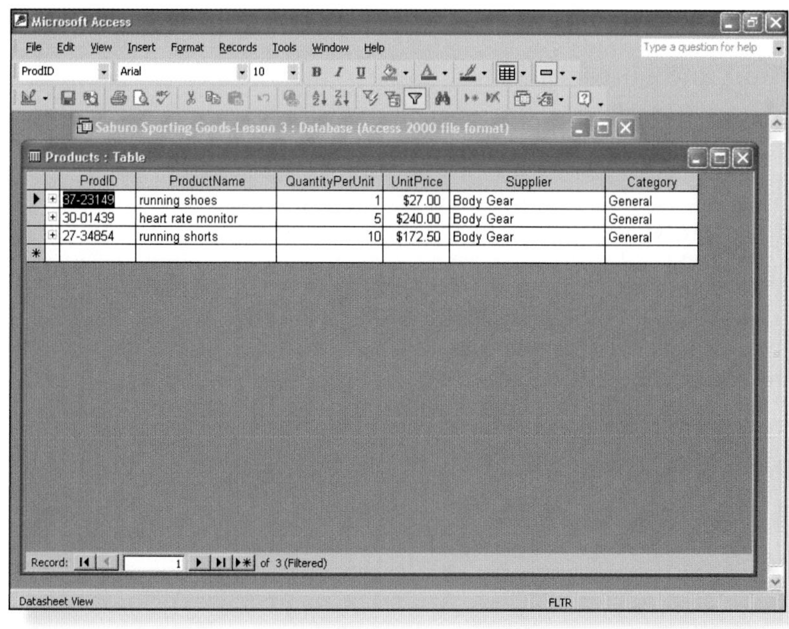

15) Click Apply Filter. The filter is applied, and only those records that meet both conditions (Body Gear in Supplier field and General in Category field) are displayed (see Figure 3.11).

16) Click Remove Filter to remove the filter and redisplay all the records in the Products table.

17) Close the table without saving changes.

After finishing Exercises 1–3, you may test your skills by completing Apply It! Guided Activity 1, Sort, Search, and Filter a Datasheet.

Business Connections

Empowered Employees Provide Increased Customer Satisfaction

Have you ever been frustrated talking with a company's representative on the phone or in person because he or she could not answer your questions or provide information? Suppose that representative is you—how can you possibly be prepared for every question that may arise, and be ready to provide quick help to customers or coworkers who need it?

If you master the skills to locate information in database, you can find the answers you need much more quickly; and when you can find quick, correct answers, both you and your customers will be happier.

Locating Information by Sorting and Filtering

- How you find the information you need depends on what type of information you are looking for.
- Sometimes the fastest way to find an answer is to open a table or query in Datasheet view and **sort** the records based on the field that has the answer you need.
- When data have been entered accurately, all the records with the field entries you're looking for are instantly sorted into the same area in the datasheet.
- Filters provide another fast way to locate information. By using the Filter By Selection method, you can instantly find and display a group of records that meets your filtering criteria.
- Or, you can use the Filter By Form method to quickly apply a more complex filter, such as a filter that looks for the records of all products with a unit price greater than $100.

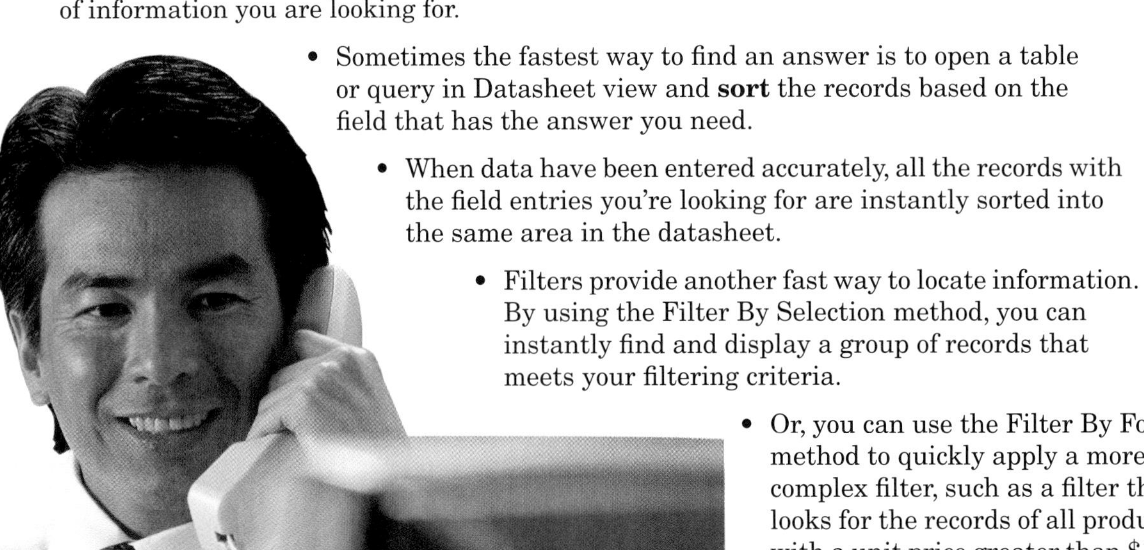

- In addition, you can use the **Find** feature to locate an entry or partial entry in a Access table.

Using Queries

- Queries are another level of filtering Access data to extract specific information.
- One advantage of creating a query is that you can save ones that answer commonly asked questions, and then every time you run those queries you will be able to quickly access current answers to those questions.

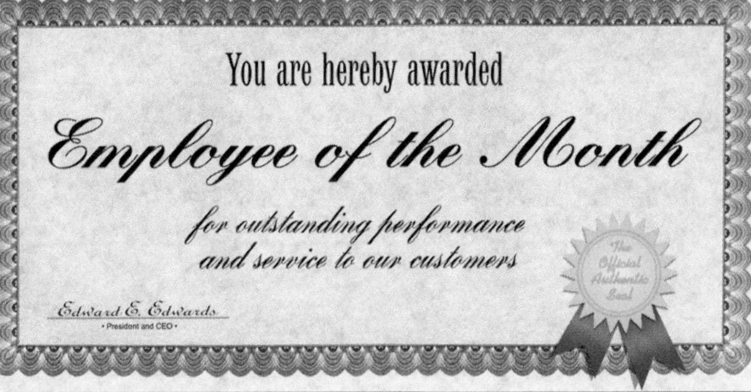

Mastering Your Skills

You should practice using all of the sort, filter, find, and query features available in Access. The more practiced you are at finding data, the more knowledgeable and helpful you will be—which will boost your personal and professional success!

CRITICAL THINKING

1. **Providing Good Customer Service** Suppose you are a customer service representative who answers customer questions over the phone. What are some things you can do to have answers to common questions ready at hand?
2. **Communicating Effectively** When you are trying to get answers from someone else, either a customer service representative or another employee in your company, what can you do to help that person find the answers you need more easily?

Microsoft Office Specialist
AC2002 3.1, 3.2, 5.2

Access

Exercise 4 Overview: Create and Modify Select Queries

A query is like a filter, but it is much more powerful. With a query, you can examine your data in any way you can think of. You can choose the tables, records, and fields that contain the data you want to see; you can organize, summarize, and calculate the data; and you can create forms and reports based on a query.

The most common type of query in Access is a **select query**. You can create a select query either by using the Simple Query Wizard or in Design view.

Need Help?

Type: about select and crosstab queries

Using the Simple Query Wizard is similar to using the Table Wizard. The wizard leads you through several dialog boxes in which you choose options, such as selecting the table (or tables) on which you want to base your query and choosing the fields you want displayed in the query results. Usually after creating a basic query with the Simple Query Wizard, you must modify the query in Design view.

Whenever you run a query, the resulting records that are displayed are always up to date because the records are not contained in the query—they are contained in table(s) on which the query is based. Queries can be saved, so you don't need to recreate a query every time you need a particular set of records.

Before creating a query, you need to define the question that you want the query to answer. For example, in the Products table of the Saburo Sporting Goods database, the products are listed with unit prices. Suppose you want to know the answer to the question "What is the individual item price for each of Saburo's products?"

In the following exercise, you will use the Simple Query Wizard to create the basic query that begins to answer the above question. Then in the following sections, you will learn how to modify the query in Design view to complete the query.

Quick Tip

Remember, if you make a mistake when using a wizard, you can click the Back button to "back up" and change your selection in a previous wizard dialog box.

Figure 3.12 The New Query dialog box

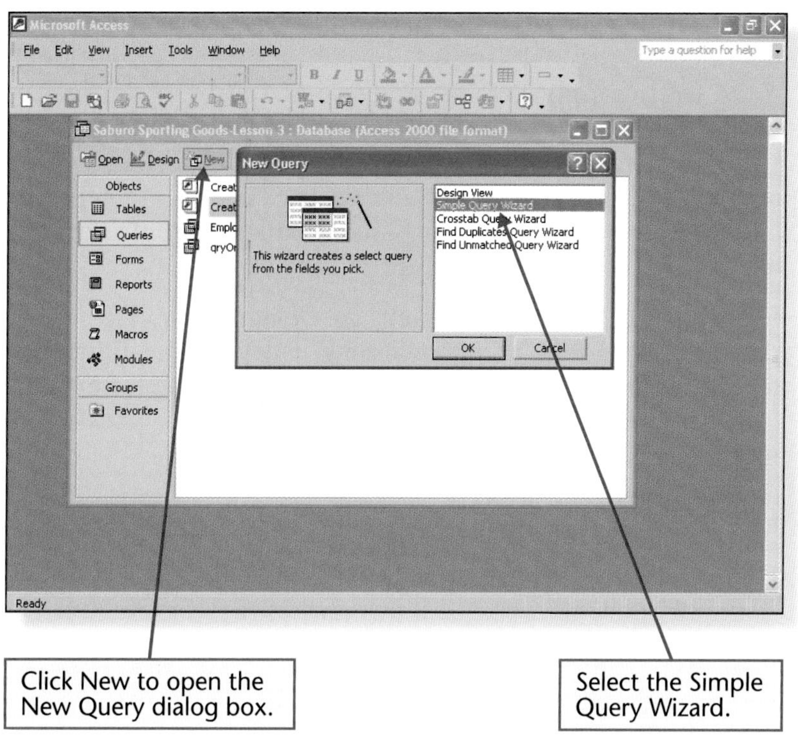
Click New to open the New Query dialog box.
Select the Simple Query Wizard.

Step Through It™
Exercise 4A: Use the Simple Query Wizard

1. In the *Saburo Sporting Goods-Lesson 3*.mdb Database window, click Queries in the Objects bar.
2. Click New on the Database window toolbar to open the New Query dialog box (see Figure 3.12).
3. In the New Query dialog box, click Simple Query Wizard and click OK.

Figure 3.13 Using the Simple Query Wizard

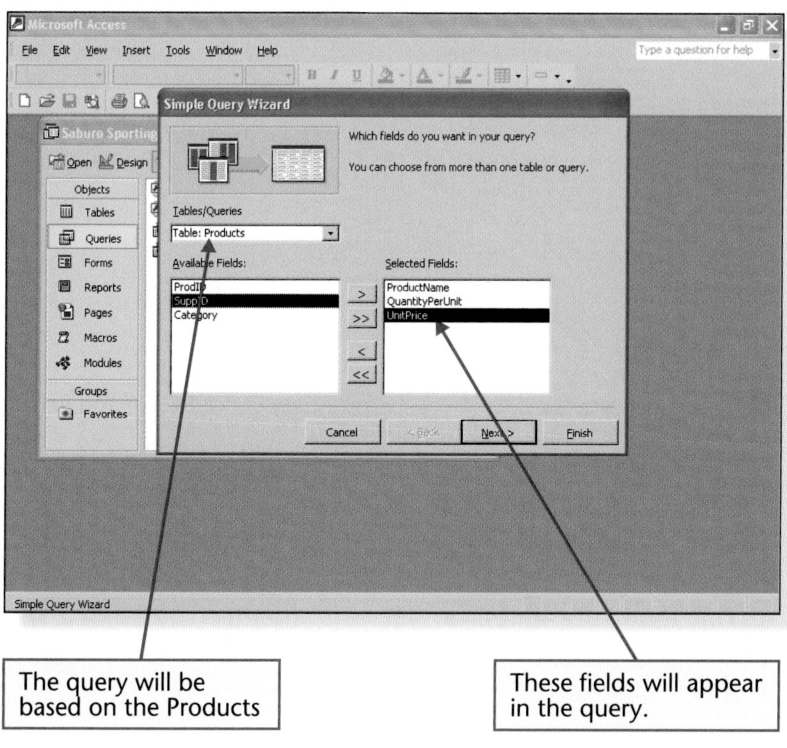
The query will be based on the Products
These fields will appear in the query.

4. In the first wizard step, select Table: Products in the Tables/Queries box.
5. In the Available Fields list, double-click ProductName, QuantityPerUnit, and UnitPrice (see Figure 3.13). Then click Next.
6. In the next step, select the *Detail (shows every field of every record)* option, and click Next.
7. In the last wizard step, type the title Item Price in the text box, and then click Finish. The query runs and displays the query results.

Modifying a Query in Design View

The Item Price query you just created works just fine, but it is not particularly useful. In fact, a query can do much more than simply display a group of records from one or more tables. You can modify a query in Design view to sort the query results in a particular order, to perform mathematical calculations on the data it retrieves, to link the entries in two fields into a text string (called **concatenation**), and to do many other data manipulations.

Figure 3.14 illustrates a query in Design view. The upper pane of the query design window contains the field lists from the tables on which the query is based. The lower pane contains the design grid, which is where you make modifications to the query.

Type: about designing a query

Figure 3.14 A sample query in Design view

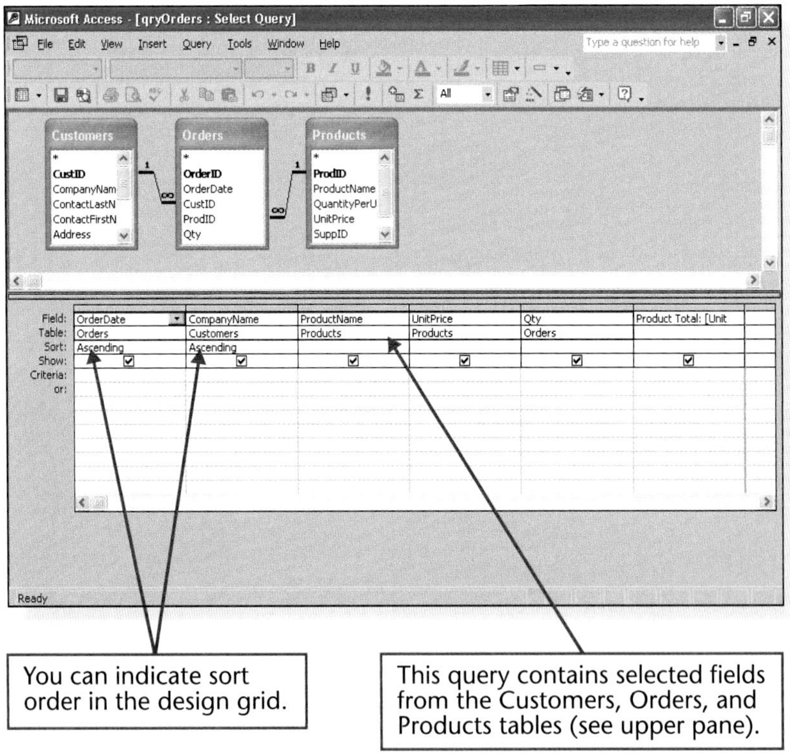

You can indicate sort order in the design grid.

This query contains selected fields from the Customers, Orders, and Products tables (see upper pane).

In the following exercise, you will modify the Item Price query you created in the previous exercise to make it more useful.

Figure 3.15 Adding a field to the design grid

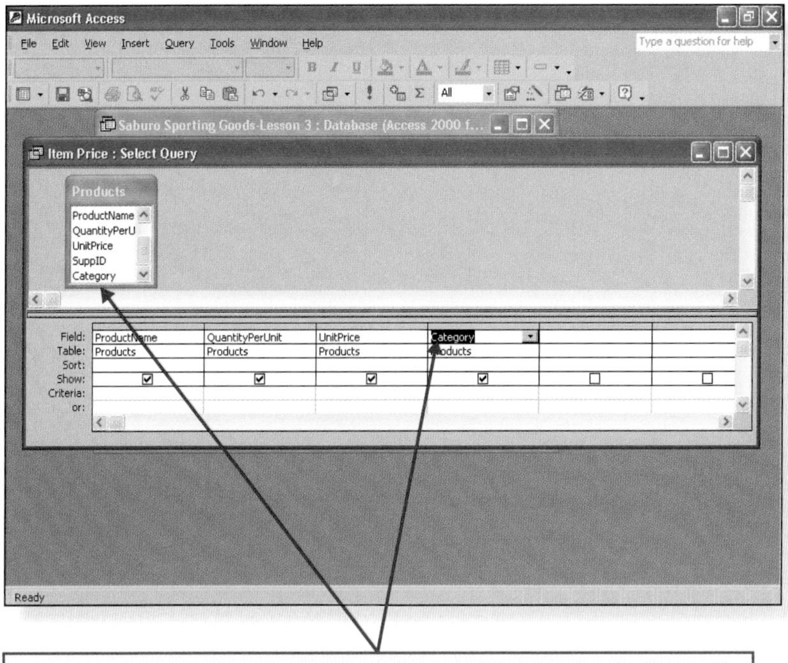

Step Through It™
Exercise 4B: Modify a query in Design view

1. With the Item Price query still open, switch to Design view.
2. Scroll down the Products table field list in the upper pane, and double-click Category to add it to the design grid (see Figure 3.15).
3. Point to the gray bar above the Category column in the design grid. When the pointer changes to a black down arrow, click to select the Category column.

Figure 3.16 Moving a field and adding a caption to a query

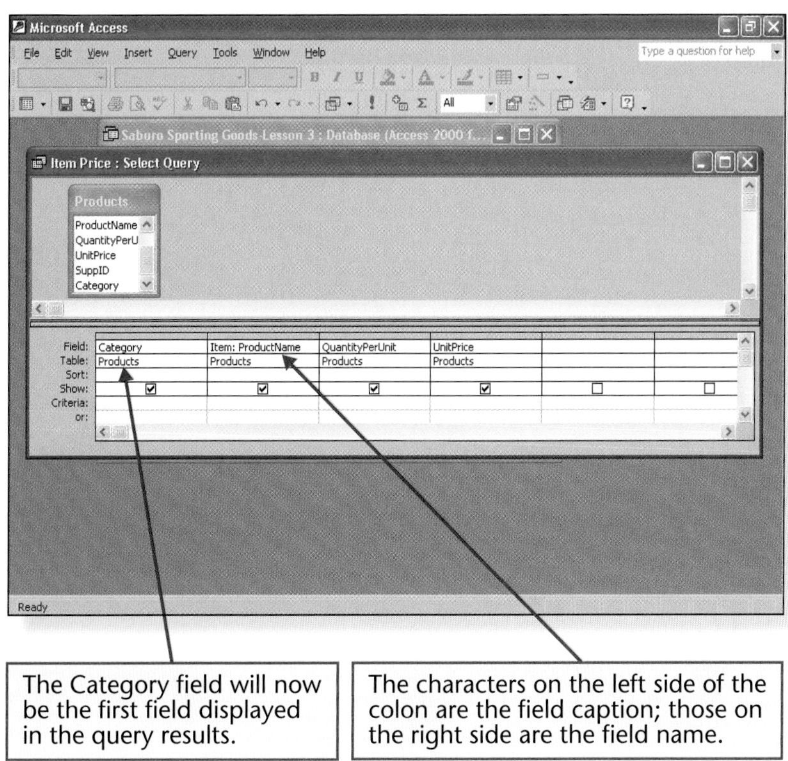

The Category field will now be the first field displayed in the query results.
The characters on the left side of the colon are the field caption; those on the right side are the field name.

4. Click and hold the mouse button and drag the entire Category column to the left (before the ProductName column). Release the mouse button. The Category field is now the first field in the query.
5. In the design grid, click at the beginning of the ProductName field, type Item:, and then click away from the cell (see Figure 3.16).
6. Click in the Sort cell in the Category field, click the down arrow that appears, and select Ascending.

Access

Access

7. Click in the Sort cell in the Item: ProductName field and select Ascending.

8. In the Criteria cell of the Category field, type **field** and press Tab to move from the cell. Access displays the word you typed in quotation marks, indicating that it recognizes your criterion as valid (see Figure 3.17).

9. Switch to Datasheet view to display the query results. Only the records for the Field category are displayed.

Figure 3.17 Sorting fields and adding criteria to a query

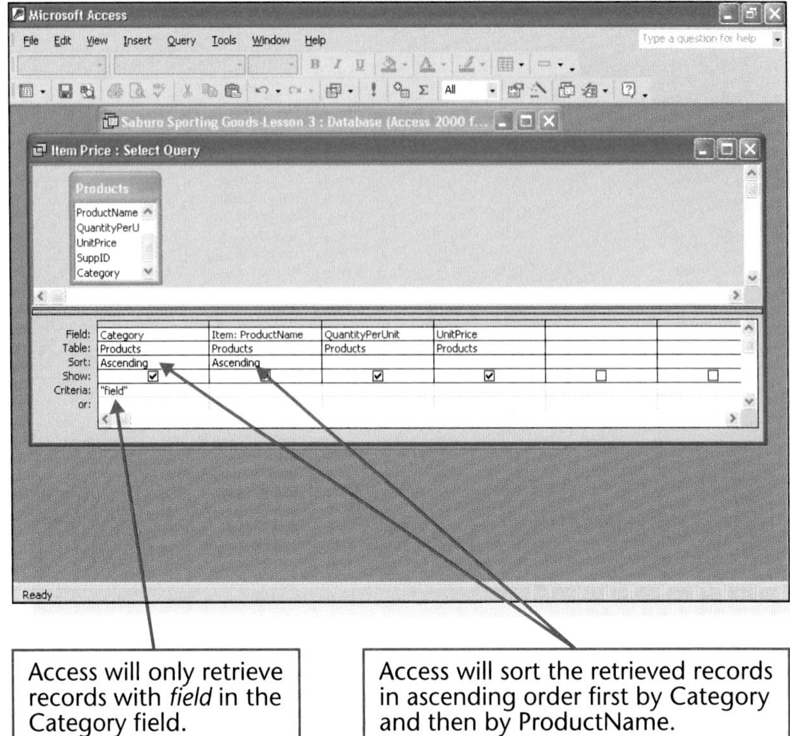

10. Switch to Design view and delete the criterion "field."

11. Click the Run button on the Query Design toolbar to run the query. Maximize the query datasheet window (see Figure 3.18).

12. Save and close the query. Restore the Database window to its smaller size.

Figure 3.18 Running the query

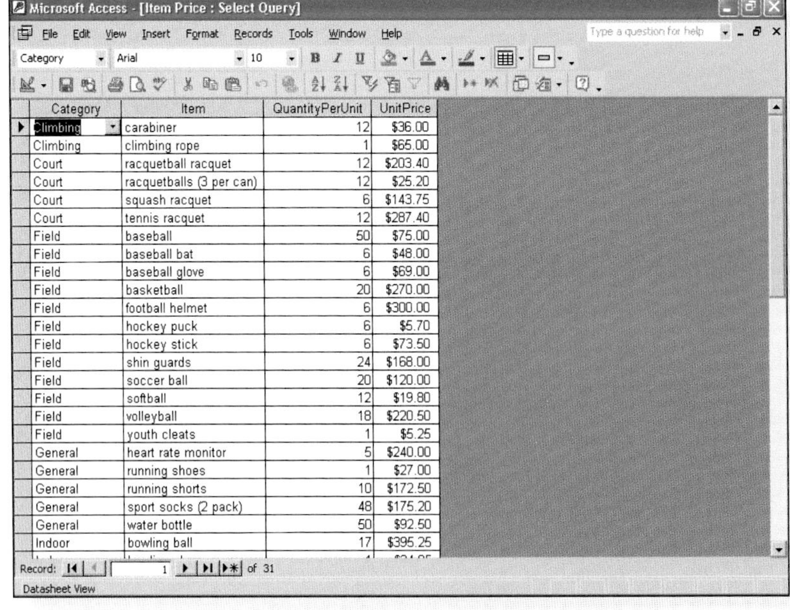

Category	Item	QuantityPerUnit	UnitPrice
Climbing	carabiner	12	$36.00
Climbing	climbing rope	1	$65.00
Court	racquetball racquet	12	$203.40
Court	racquetballs (3 per can)	12	$25.20
Court	squash racquet	6	$143.75
Court	tennis racquet	12	$287.40
Field	baseball	50	$75.00
Field	baseball bat	6	$48.00
Field	baseball glove	6	$69.00
Field	basketball	20	$270.00
Field	football helmet	6	$300.00
Field	hockey puck	6	$5.70
Field	hockey stick	6	$73.50
Field	shin guards	24	$168.00
Field	soccer ball	20	$120.00
Field	softball	12	$19.80
Field	volleyball	18	$220.50
Field	youth cleats	1	$5.25
General	heart rate monitor	5	$240.00
General	running shoes	1	$27.00
General	running shorts	10	$172.50
General	sport socks (2 pack)	48	$175.20
General	water bottle	50	$92.50
Indoor	bowling ball	17	$395.25

Adding a Calculated Field to a Query and Formatting the Results

One of the most useful and powerful features of queries is the ability to perform calculations.

To perform calculations in a query, you must create a **calculated field** in the query design grid. The calculated field contains a mathematical **expression** that performs calculations on other fields in a query.

Type: about

When you run the query, the results of the calculated field are displayed in the query results; however, they are not stored in the table on which the query is based. Instead, whenever the query is run, Access recalculates the field; thus the results are always based on the most up-to-date data in the table.

Earlier in this lesson, you began building the Item Price query to answer the question "What is the individual item price for each of Saburo's products?" In the following exercise, you will add a calculated field to the Item Price query to answer that question. Then you will format the results of the calculated field.

Access

Figure 3.19 Creating a calculated field

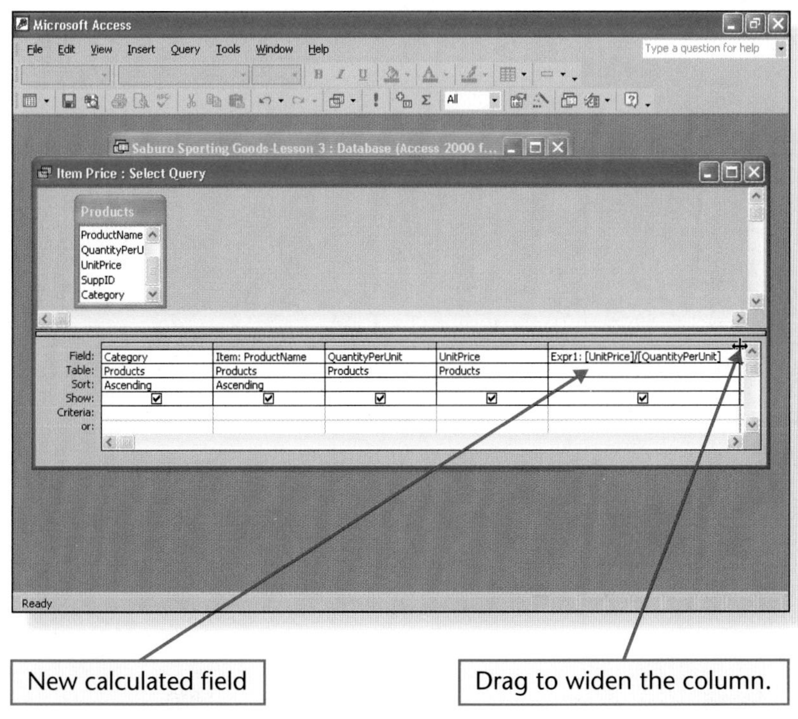

Step Through It™

Exercise 4C: Add a calculated field to a query and format the results

1. Open the Item Price query in Design view.
2. In the first empty Field cell on the right end of the design grid, type the expression [UnitPrice]/[QuantityPerUnit], and then click in any empty cell below the Field cell.
3. Position the pointer on the right edge of the gray bar above the calculated field. When the pointer changes shape, drag to widen the column (see Figure 3.19).

Access

4 Switch to Datasheet view to display the query results. While the new field contains the correct calculation, it is difficult to understand.

5 Switch to Design view to format the calculated field.

6 Right-click anywhere in the new calculated field column in the design grid, and click Properties on the shortcut menu.

7 On the General tab, click in the Format box. Then click the down arrow that appears in the box and select Currency (see Figure 3.20).

Figure 3.20 Formatting the calculated field

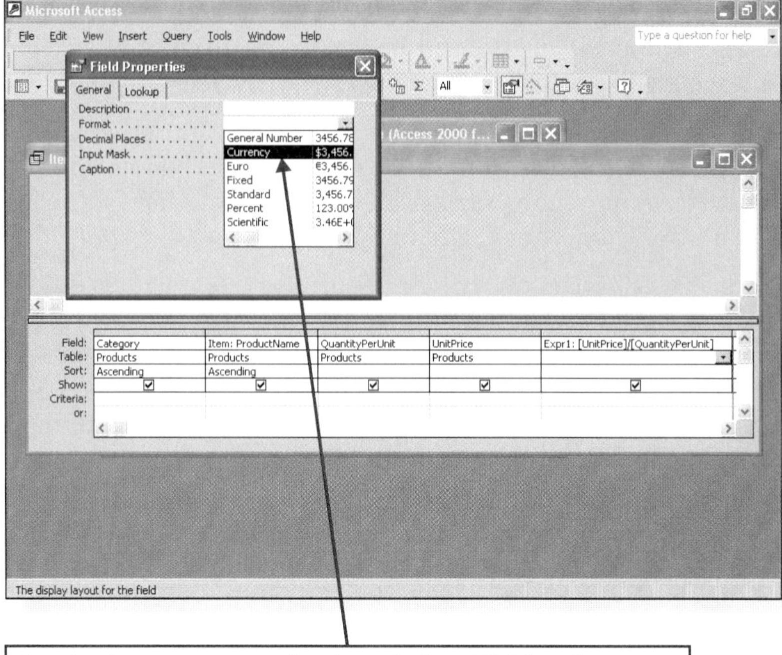

Set the Format property for the calculated field to Currency.

8 Navigate to the Caption field property box and type Item Price. Then close the Field Properties window.

9 Switch to Datasheet view. The Item Price field is now easy to read and understand (see Figure 3.21).

10 Save and close the Item Price query.

Figure 3.21 The formatted calculated field is now displayed in the query result

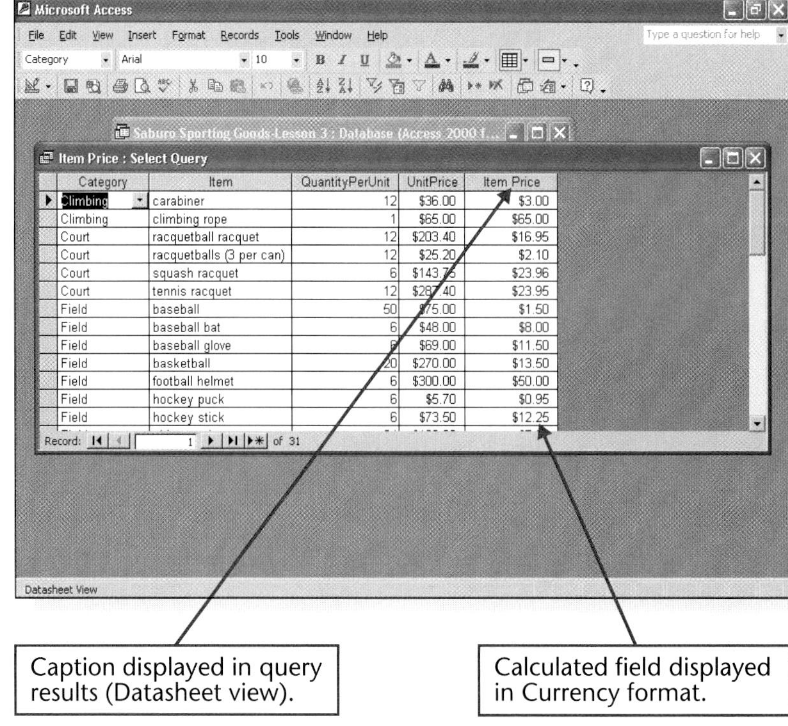

Caption displayed in query results (Datasheet view).

Calculated field displayed in Currency format.

Exercise 5 Overview: Create Special Queries Using Wizards

Microsoft Office Specialist AC2002 5.2

In addition to the select query, such as the one you created and modified in Exercise 4, there are other types of queries you can create for specific purposes. Table 3.1 contains brief descriptions of some of the other types of queries you can create. Most of these queries can be created directly in Design view; however, there are some queries that you can create only by using a wizard—the Crosstab, Find Duplicates, and Find Unmatched queries.

Type: about types of queries

Table 3.1

Query Type	Wizard Required?	Description
Action	No	You use an action query to make changes to or move several records in one operation. There are four types of action queries: Delete, Update, Append, and Make Table.
Crosstab	Yes	Displays the query results in a spreadsheet-type format with fields across the top of the table and down the side of the table (like a loan chart or a logarithm table).
Find Duplicates	Yes	Finds records that have duplicate entries in the fields you specify.
Find Unmatched	Yes	Finds records in one table that have no related records in another table.
Parameter	No	Similar to a select query, but prompts you for information (criteria), and then displays the query results based on the information you supply.
SQL (pronounced *sequel*)	No	You must write *SQL statements* using Structured Query Language to build a SQL query, instead of building it in Design view.

In the following exercise, you will use the Find Duplicates Query Wizard to locate duplicate entries in the Employees table of the *Saburo Sporting Goods-Lesson 3.mdb* database. The table contains 21 employee records, but you are pretty sure there are only 20 employees at Saburo Sporting Goods. In a table this small, you could search for the duplicates by sorting the Last Name field and quickly scanning the table, but if the table contained hundreds of records it would be more efficient to use the Find Duplicates Query Wizard.

Step Through It™

Exercise 5: Use the Find Duplicates Query Wizard

Access

1. Be sure the Queries group is displayed in the *Saburo Sporting Goods-Lesson 3.mdb* Database window.

2. Click New [New] on the Database Window toolbar. In the New Query dialog box, double-click *Find Duplicates Query Wizard.*

3. In the first wizard step, select Table: Employees (see Figure 3.22). Click Next.

Figure 3.22 Using the Find Duplicates Query Wizard

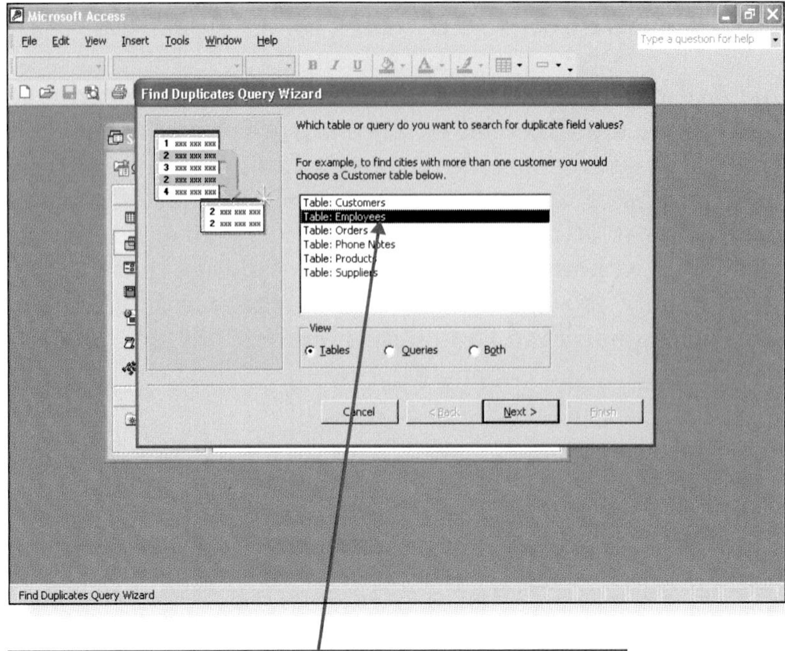

4. In the second wizard step, double-click Last Name and First Name. Click Next.

5. In the third wizard step, double-click Birth Date, Hire Date, and Address. Click Next.

6. In the last wizard step, accept the suggested query name by clicking Finish. Then review the query results (see Figure 3.23).

7. Delete one of the duplicate records. Then close the query.

Figure 3.23 Query results show one duplicate record in the Employees table

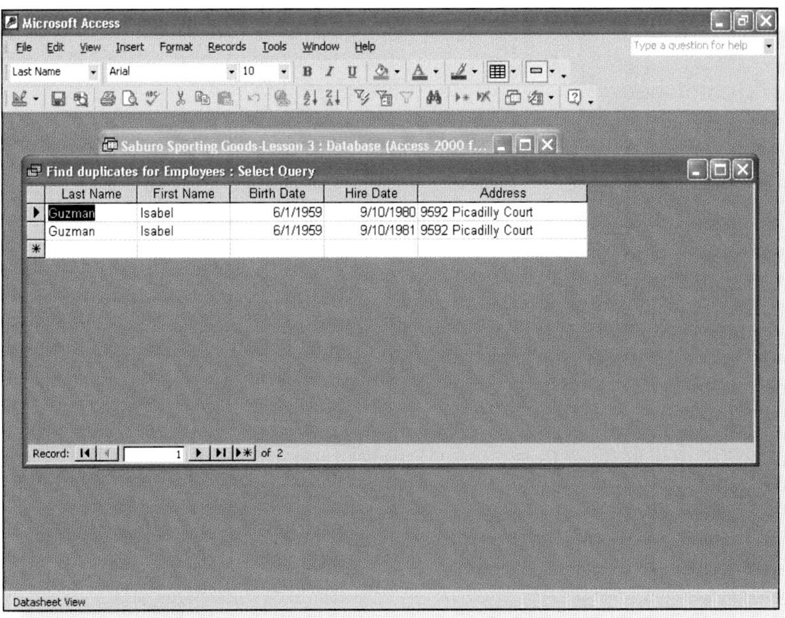

Tech Talk

Standardized Queries

To extract information from a database, you have to pose a question (a *query statement*) in language that the database understands. There is one query language that works with databases created by many different vendors. It is also used or supported by most relational database management software, including Access, Sybase, Ingres, Oracle, and SQL Server—Structured Query Language, or SQL (pronounced *sequel*).

For most queries, Access automatically supplies a SQL version when you create the query. You can look at or edit it by clicking the View button and choosing SQL View.

Different software includes variations on the basic SQL standards, but the essential commands are the same. You can see some of these commands in Table 3.2.

One of the most frequently used SQL commands is SELECT. Suppose you have a database table named *Contacts*, with fields called *Name* and *Address*. The SELECT statement to display the addresses of all contacts with the name *Mary* would read as follows:

```
SELECT ADDRESS
    FROM CONTACTS
    WHERE NAME = 'Mary'
```

CRITICAL THINKING

1. What would the SQL statement be to find the names of customers whose ZIP Code is 60647 in a table called *Customers*? (Table fields include *Names* and *ZIPCode*.)
2. Form a team to learn more about a SQL command. Give your class a lesson on how to use it. Include an exercise asking them for sample commands.

Table 3.2

Command	Use
SELECT	Retrieve data from one or more tables
UPDATE	Make changes to records
DELETE	Remove records
CREATE TABLE	Build a new table
INSERT	Add records
DROP TABLE	Remove a table and all its records

Microsoft Office Specialist
AC2002 1.4

Access

Exercise 6 Overview:
Format a Datasheet

Any datasheet, whether from a query or a table, can be formatted in a number of ways for easier reading. For example, you can:

- change column widths and row heights fully.
- hide columns that you don't need to see.
- freeze specific columns so that they remain in view while you scroll horizontally through the rest of the columns.
- change gridline layout and color.
- switch page orientation for printing.
- change margins.

The formatting techniques you used in Word and Excel also apply to formatting an Access datasheet. One difference, however, is that when you format an Access datasheet, the formatting is applied to the entire datasheet, not just a single cell.

You can use several different methods to format a datasheet. You can use the mouse to manually change column widths and row heights; you can right-click in a datasheet and access formatting commands on the shortcut menu; or you can use the Formatting (Datasheet) toolbar. Table 3.3 illustrates some of the commonly used buttons on the Formatting (Datasheet) toolbar. (You will use these buttons in one of the following exercises.)

Table 3.3

Button	Purpose
B	Makes all text bold in the datasheet.
	Applies color to the background of a datasheet.
A	Applies color to all text in a datasheet.
	Applies color to the gridlines in a datasheet.

In the following exercises, you will practice several of these formatting procedures, and then print the Customers table datasheet in the *Saburo Sporting Goods-Lesson 3.mdb* database.

Figure 3.24 Changing the width of a column

Microsoft Access - [Customers : Table]

CustID	CompanyName	ContactLastN	ContactFirstN	Address	City
18165	The Fitness Spot	Mullen	Carissa	1447 Madison Avenue	Brea
18166	A & X Sports	Gutierrez	Francis	167 Riva Ridge Court	Cary
18167	Marv's Fitness Track	Middleton	Veronica	3165 Goda Avenue	Princess Anne
18168	Costello and Company	Bond	Hunter	3410 N. Sawgrass Lane	Tooele
18169	Courtside, Inc.	Bartlett	Desiree	3342 Felicity Drive	Waukesha
18170	Sporty Sports	Sawyer	Bruce	217 S. Peete	Dalton Gardens
18171	Knudsen Apparel	Holloway	Melanie	42501 Antietam Boulevard	Malta
18172	Whoosh, Inc.	Whitaker	Alejandro	7409 Beechwood Avenue	West Long Bra
18173	Charley's Sport Shop	Ruiz	Georgina	5016 Silvermine Court	Jasper
18174	Galway Pro Shop	Massey	Neil	537 W. Benson	Gideon
18175	The Sports Ball	Flowers	Justine	1858 Batavia Pike	Kennewick
18176	Play Ball, Inc.	Springer	Miles	7954 Pepper Pike	Assumption
18177	Wiggins Sports Company	Wiggins	Colleen	11545 Regency Square	Woonsocket
18178	Van Nielens	Conley	Albert	3830 E. Ault Park Avenue	Magnolia
18179	KTK Sports	Chou	Tien	2522 Sycamore Road	Lovington
18180	Redwing Sporting Goods	Blackwell	Maurice	9554 Buckingham Road	Jericho
18181	Brad's Total Fitness	Silverman	Grace	7020 Grandview Lane	Puyallup
18182	Heath Brothers, Inc.	Heath	Omar	10255, Haldjara Complex, P.O. Box 582	Mysore
18183	Sebewaing Hunting & Fishing	Grimes	Shawna	12021 Cooperwood Lane	Sebewaing
18184	Staying Fit, Inc.	Blanchard	Ruben	6220 Lisbon Court	Gothenburg
18185	Captain Cook Outfitters	O'Donnell	Kiara	333 Hilltop Lane	Captain Cook
18186	Product Number	Russo	Dane	8593 Stonebridge Drive	Nutter Fort
18187	Alaska Sporting Goods Compar	Baxter	Janelle	6305 S. Riehle Road	Wasilla
18188	Jaxton's	Wyatt	Perry	7999 Secretariat Court	Grovetown

Record: 1 of 31

Datasheet View

When the pointer changes shape, drag to the right to widen the column.

Step Through It™

Exercise 6A: Adjust column widths and row heights

1. Open the Customers table in the *Saburo Sporting Goods-Lesson 3.mdb* database and maximize the view.
2. Point to the right border of the column header in the Address field. When the pointer changes shape, drag the border a few characters to the right to widen the column width (see Figure 3.24).

Figure 3.25 Hiding a column

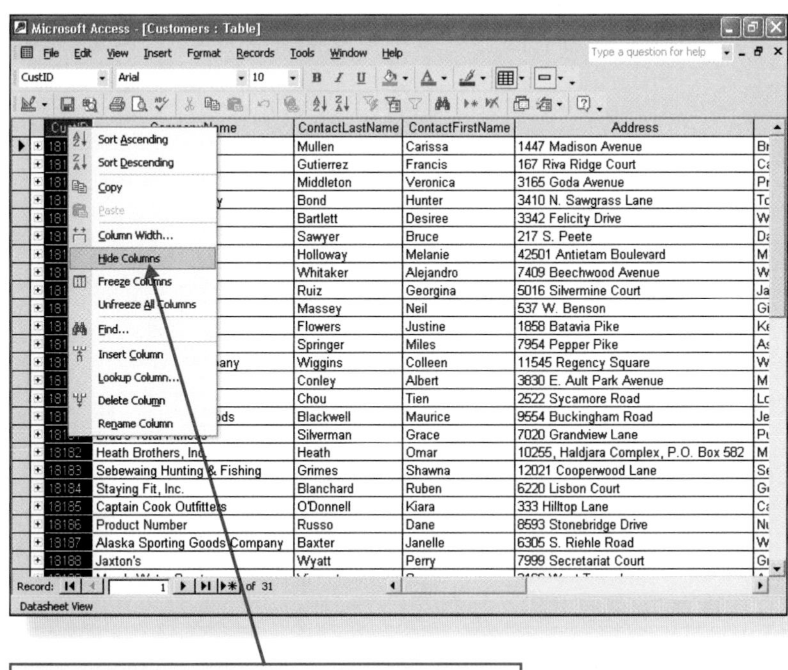

Select Hide Columns on the shortcut menu.

3. Repeat step 2 to adjust the column widths of the remaining fields.
4. Right-click the CustID column header, and select Hide Columns on the shortcut menu (see Figure 3.25). The column is hidden from view.

Access

5. Point to the border between any two row selectors. When the pointer changes shape, drag the border down to approximately two line heights. The heights of all the rows change (see Figure 3.26).

6. Right-click the CompanyName column header, and click Freeze Columns. Scroll to the right—the CompanyName column remains in view as you scroll.

Figure 3.26 Datasheet with hidden CustID column and modified row heights

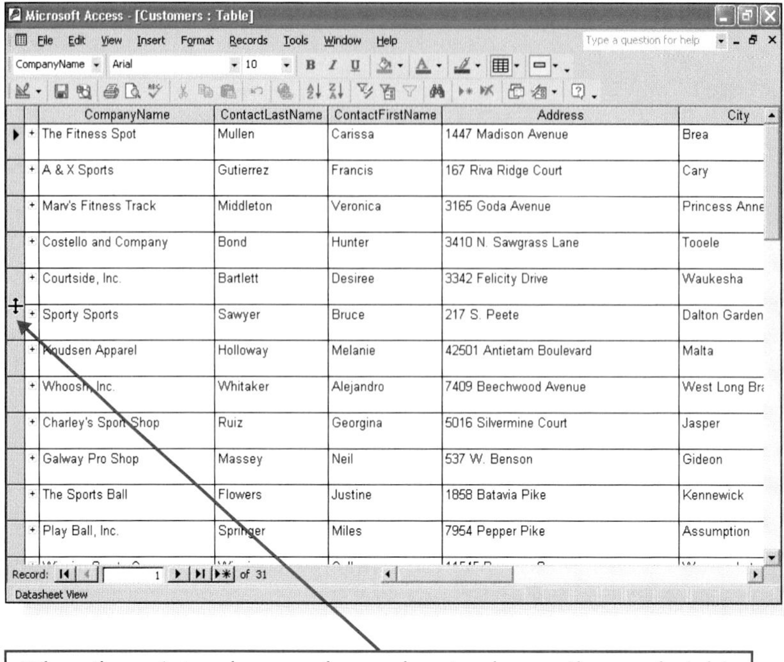
When the pointer changes shape, drag to change the row height.

Step Through It™

Exercise 6B: Use the Formatting toolbar

1. If the Formatting (Datasheet) toolbar is not displayed, right-click the menu bar or any displayed toolbar and then click Formatting (Datasheet).

2. Click Bold on the Formatting toolbar. The bold format is applied to the entire datasheet.

3. Click the Fill/Back Color down arrow and select the pale green color for the background (see Figure 3.27).

Figure 3.27 Datasheet with bold formatting and background color applied

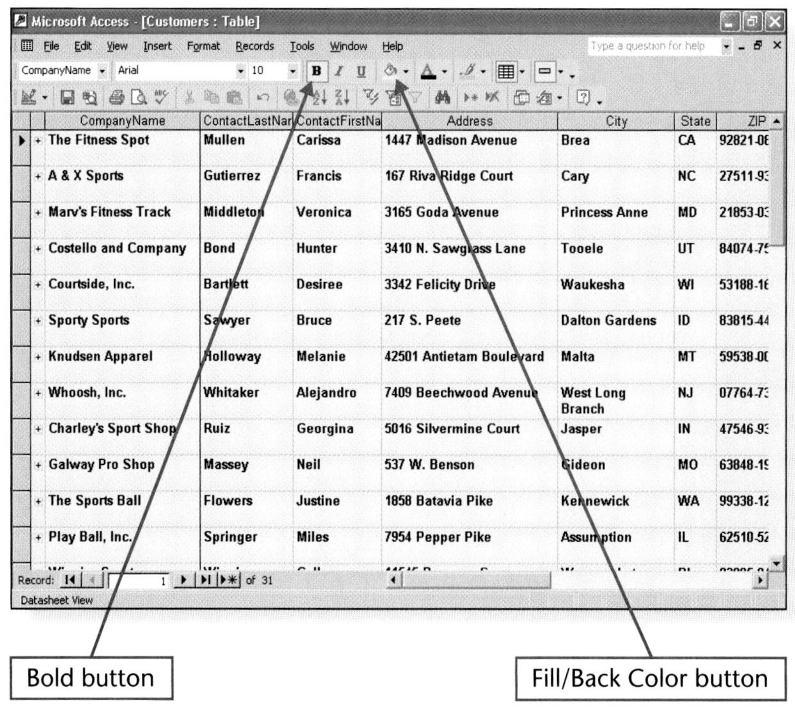
Bold button
Fill/Back Color button

Figure 3.28 Modifying settings in the Page Setup dialog box

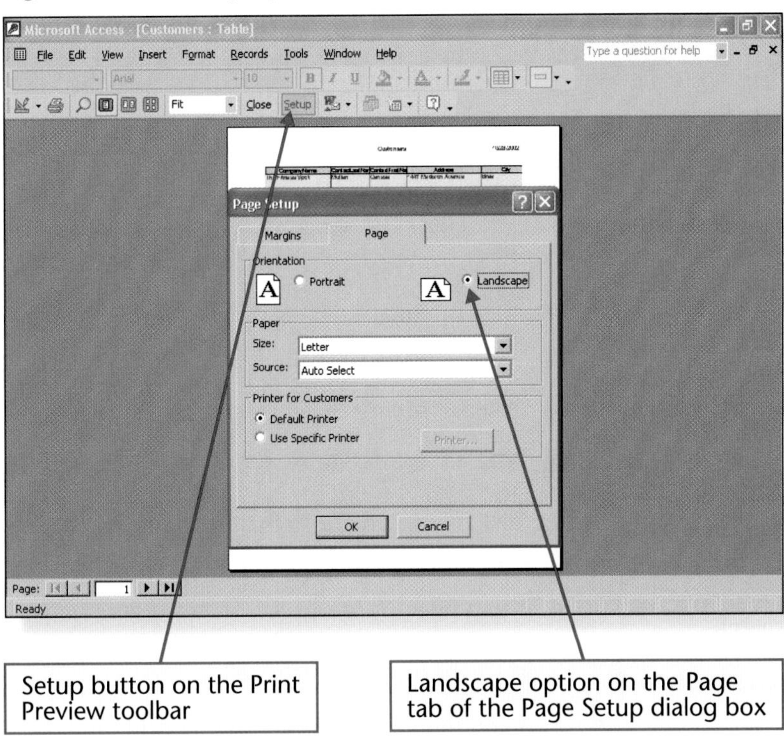

4) Click the Font/Fore Color down arrow and select a dark blue color.

5) Click the Line/Border Color down arrow and select a dark green color.

6) Click Print Preview on the Table Datasheet toolbar.

7) On the Print Preview toolbar, click the Setup button.

8) On the Margins tab, change the Left and Right margin settings to 0.5. On the Page tab, select the Landscape option (see Figure 3.28). Then click OK.

Access

Figure 3.29 Print preview of the Customers table (page 1)

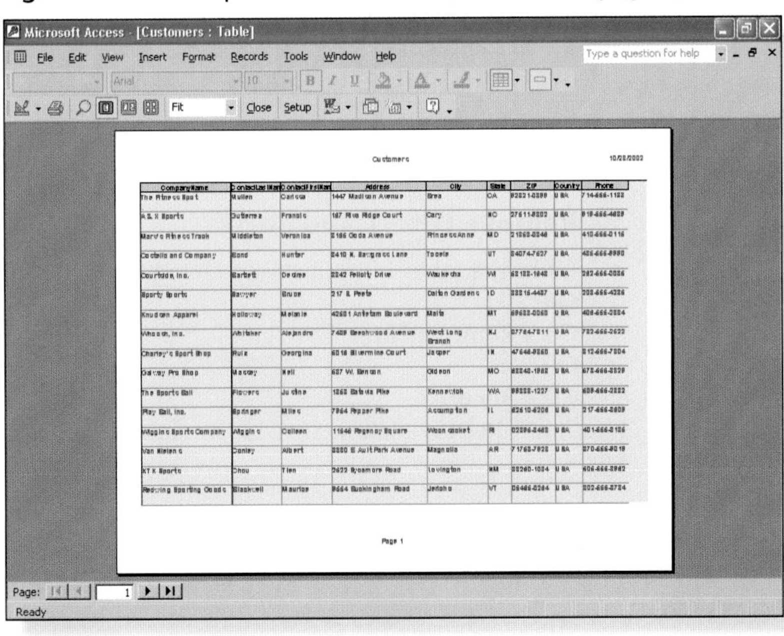

9) If all the columns do not fit on one page, close the print preview and adjust the column widths to compress the table horizontally.

10) Click Print Preview to verify that all the columns on the datasheet fit on one page (see Figure 3.29).

11) Click the Print button to print the table. Then save your changes and close the table.

APPLY IT! After finishing Exercises 4–6, you may test your skills by completing Apply It! Guided Activity 2, Create, Modify, and Format a Query.

Procedure Summary

Sort Records in a Datasheet

1. Click in the field by which you want to sort.
2. Click **Sort Ascending** or **Sort Descending**.
   OR
   Click **Records** . . . . Alt + R
   Point to **Sort** . . . . S
   Select **Sort Ascending** or **Sort Descending**. . . . . A or D

Search for Data in a Datasheet

1. Click in the field you want to search.
2. Click **Find** . . . . Ctrl + F
   OR
   Click **Edit**. . . . . Alt + E
   Select **Find** . . . . F
3. On the Find tab in the *Find What:* box, type the search characters, and select the appropriate *Match:* setting for the search.
4. Click **Find Next** . . . . .Alt + F

Use Filter By Selection

1. Select the entry or characters for which you want to filter.
2. Click **Filter By Selection**.
   OR
   Click **Records** . . . . Alt + R
   Point to **Filter** . . . . F
   Select **Filter By Selection** . . . . S

Use Filter By Form

1. Click **Filter By Form**.
   OR
   Click **Records**. . . . . Alt + R
   Point to **Filter** . . . . F
   Select **Filter By Form** . . . . F
2. Click **Clear Grid**.
3. Type a criterion in the appropriate field cell.
   OR
   Click the down arrow that appears and select the criterion from the list.
4. If you need to create an OR condition, click the *Or* sheet tab, and type another criterion in the appropriate field cell.
5. If you need to create an AND condition, type another criterion in the appropriate field cell on the *Look for* tab.
6. Click **Apply Filter**.
   OR
   Click **Records**. . . . . Alt + R
   Select **Apply Filter/Sort**. . . . . Y

Remove Filters and Sorts

Close the table without saving changes.
OR
Click **Remove Filter**.
OR
Click **Records**. Alt + R
Select **Remove Filter/Sort** . . . . R

Use the Simple Query Wizard

1. Open the Queries group in the Database window.
2. Double-click *Create query by using wizard.*
   OR
   Click **New** . . . . **Alt + N**
   Select **Simple Query Wizard**.
   Click **OK**.
   OR
   Click **Insert** . . . . **Alt + I**
   Select **Query** . . . . **Q**
   Select **Simple Query Wizard**.
   Click **OK**.
3. Enter appropriate responses to the wizard prompts.

Add a Field to a Query

1. Select a query in the Database window.
2. Click **Design** . . . . **Alt + D**
3. Double-click the desired field in the field list in the upper pane of the query design window.
   OR
   Select the desired field in the field list in the upper pane of the query design window.
   Drag the field to an empty column in the design grid.

Move Fields in a Query

1. Select a query in the Database window.
2. Click **Design** . . . . **Alt + D**
3. In the design grid, point to the gray bar above the field you wish to move.
4. When the pointer changes to a black down arrow, click to select the column.
5. Click and hold the mouse button and drag the entire column to the desired location.
6. Release the mouse button.

Add a Caption to a Query

1. Select a query in the Database window.
2. Click **Design** . . . . **Alt + D**
3. In the design grid, click at the beginning of the field in which you want to add a caption.
4. Type the caption, followed by a colon (:)

OR

1. Select a query in the Database window.
2. Click **Design** . . . . **Alt + D**
3. In the design grid, right-click in the field to which you want to add a caption.
4. Click **Properties** on the shortcut menu.
5. Modify the Caption property.
6. Close the Field Properties window.

Procedure Summary

Access Procedure Summary

Set a Sort Order in a Query

1. Select a query in the Database window.
2. Click **Design** . . . . **Alt + D**
3. Click in the Sort cell in the field by which you wish to sort.
4. Click the down arrow that appears.
5. Select Ascending or Descending.

Add a Criterion to a Query

1. Select a query in the Database window.
2. Click **Design** . . . . **Alt + D**
3. Click in the Criteria cell in the field to which you want to add a criterion.
4. Type the criterion.
5. Press Tab to move away from the cell.

Run a Query

From the Database window:

1. Select a query in the Database window.
2. Click **Open**.

   From the query design window:
   Switch to Datasheet view.
   OR
   Click Run.
   OR

1. Click **Query** . . . . **Alt + Q**
2. Click **Run** . . . . **R**

Add a Calculated Field to a Query and Format the Results

1. Select a query in the Database window.
2. Click **Design** . . . . **Alt + D**
3. In an empty Field cell in the design grid, type an expression for the calculated field, enclosed in brackets.
4. Right-click in the calculated field column in the design grid.
5. Click **Properties** on the shortcut menu.
6. Modify the Format property.
7. Modify the Caption property.
8. Close the Field Properties window.

Use a Special Query Wizard

1. Open the Queries group in the Database window.
2. Click **New** . . . . **Alt + N**
   OR
   Click **Insert**. **Alt + I**
   Select **Query**. . . . . **Q**
   Select the type of query wizard you want to use.
3. Double-click the type of query wizard you want to use.
4. Click **OK**.
5. Enter appropriate responses to the wizard prompts.

Format a Datasheet

1. Click **Format**. . . . . **Alt + O**
2. Select the desired option from the menu or submenu.
   OR
   Click the appropriate button(s) on the Formatting (Datasheet) toolbar.

Preview and Print a Datasheet

1. Click **Print Preview** .
   OR
   Click **File**. . . . . **Alt + F**
   Select **Print Preview**. . . . . **V**
2. On the Print Preview toolbar, click the Setup button to make any changes to page margins or page orientation.
   OR
   Click **File**. . . . . **Alt + F**
   Select **Page Setup**. . . . . **U**
3. Click **Print** . . . . **Ctrl + P**

Lesson Review and Exercises

Summary Checklist

- ☑ Can you sort records in a datasheet?
- ☑ Can you search for a specific entry in a datasheet?
- ☑ Can you filter records using Filter By Selection?
- ☑ Can you filter records using Filter By Form?
- ☑ Can you create a Select query using the Simple Query Wizard?
- ☑ Can you modify a query in Design view?
- ☑ Can you add a calculated field to a query?
- ☑ Can you format the results?
- ☑ Can you create a query using one of the special query wizards?
- ☑ Can you format a datasheet for better data display?
- ☑ Can you preview a datasheet?
- ☑ Can you print a datasheet?

Key Terms

- ascending sort (p. 386)
- calculated field (p. 401)
- concatenation (p. 398)
- criteria (p. 388)
- descending sort (p. 386)
- expression (p. 401)
- filter (p. 388)
- Filter By Form (p. 390)
- Filter By Selection (p. 389)
- select query (p. 396)

APPLY IT! Guided Activities

1. Sort, Search, and Filter a Datasheet

One of the LawnMowers partners, Juan Gutierrez, is on the phone and wants to know the customer names and dates for his next three appointments. He also wants to know who else is mowing for the customer Carl Yust. Follow these steps:

a. Open the *LawnMowers-Lesson 3.mdb* database, and then open the Appointments table.

b. Use the Filter By Selection method to display all of Juan's appointments: Click in a cell in the Mowers field that contains the entry *Juan*, and click Filter By Selection.

c. Sort the filtered records by date in ascending order: Click anywhere in the Date field and click Sort Ascending. Tell Juan when his next three appointments are and for whom. The filtered, sorted table should look like **Figure 3.30**.

Figure 3.30 The filtered and sorted Appointments table

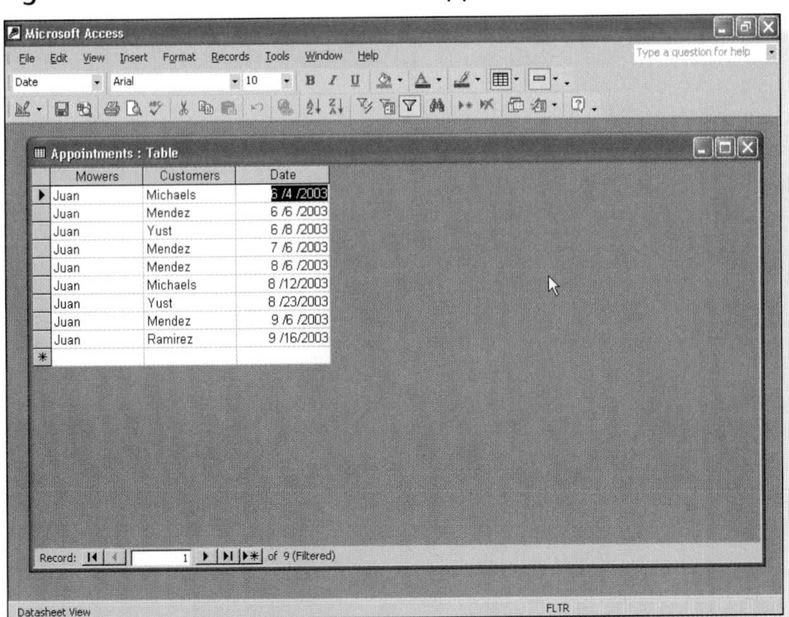

d. Remove the filter. Then use the Find feature to search for *Yust* in the Appointments table: Click Find, type Yust in the Find What text box, and select Appointments: Table in the Look In text box. Click Find Next repeatedly to find all the Yust records. Tell Juan who else, if anyone, is mowing for Mr. Yust.

e. Close the table without saving changes.

2. Create, Modify, and Format a Query

Each of the LawnMowers partners would like an up-to-date list of his or her appointments that includes customer names, dates, and phone numbers. To provide them with the information they need, you decide to create three queries based on selected fields from the Mowers table, the Appointments table, and the Customers table. The first query will display only the appointments for one of the LawnMowers partners. Then you will modify the query to display the appointments for each of the other two. Follow these steps:

a. Double-click *Create query by using wizard* in the Database window. In the first wizard step, select the Mowers table and include the FirstName field. Then, while still in the first wizard step, select the Appointments table and include the Date field in the query. Finally, select the Customers table and include the First, Last, and Phone fields in that order **(see Figure 3.31)**.

Figure 3.31 Selecting the fields for the query

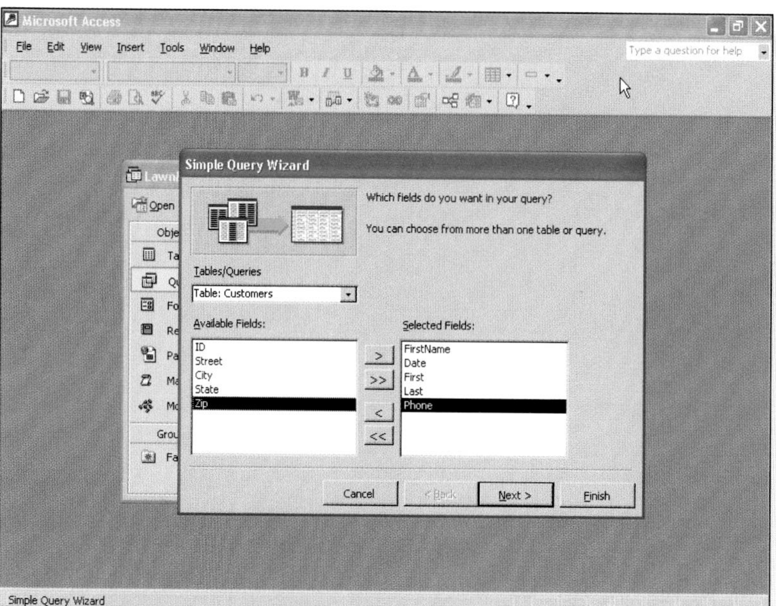

b. In the second wizard step, indicate that you would like a detail query. In the last wizard step, name the query Appointments for Alicia, and select the option to modify the query design.

c. In the design grid, type Alicia in the Criteria cell of the FirstName field, and then run the query.

d. You decide that the query would be more useful if the appointments were sorted by date. Return to Design view. In the design grid, select Ascending in the Sort cell of the Date field. Then run the query again.

e. To make the query results easier to read, you decide to create a calculated field that concatenates the customers' first and last names into full names. Switch to Design view. In the design grid, click in the empty Field cell to the right of the Phone column. Then type the expression [First]&" "&[Last]. Click in any empty cell below the Field cell. Widen the column so the entire expression is visible **(see Figure 3.32)**.

Figure 3.32 Entering an expression in a calculated field

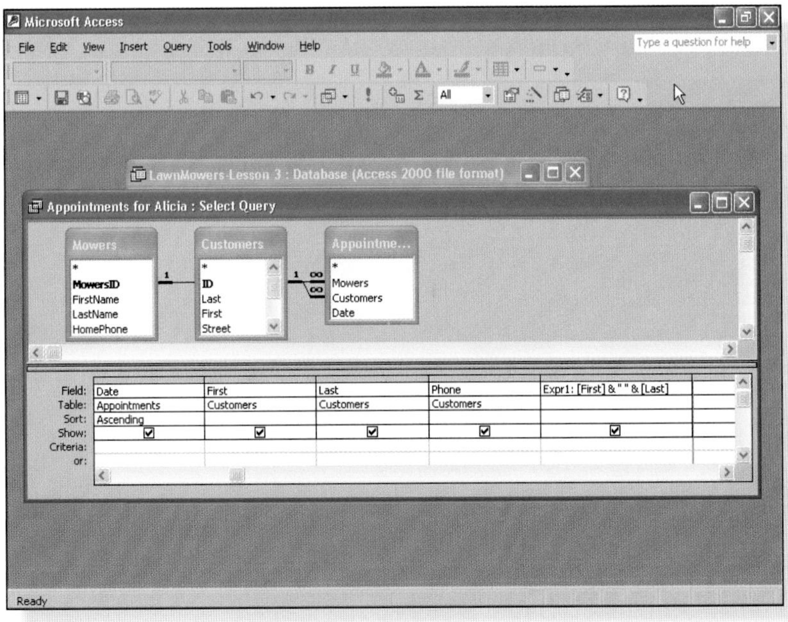

f. Run the query. While the query results contain the information you need, you notice that the name fields (*First* and *Last*) from the Customers table are no longer necessary because you added the calculated field. Switch to Design view. In the design grid, point to the gray bar above the First field cell; when the pointer changes to a black down arrow, click to select the entire First column, and then press Delete. Follow the same procedure to delete the Last column from the design grid.

g. You also decide to add a caption to the calculated field that is more descriptive than the field name *Expr1*. Right-click anywhere in the calculated field column and select Properties on the shortcut menu. Type Customer Name in the Caption property box, and then close the Field Properties window.

h. Now you want to move the Phone field so that it appears as the last field in the query results. To move the Phone field, point to the gray bar above the Phone field cell; when the pointer changes to a black down arrow, click to select the entire Phone column. Then click and drag the Phone column to the right, and drop it immediately after the calculated field.

i. Run the query. Adjust the column widths as necessary so that all the data are visible. Apply a pale yellow background color to the datasheet **(see Figure 3.33)**. Preview and print the datasheet. Then save and close the query.

Figure 3.33 Modified and formatted query

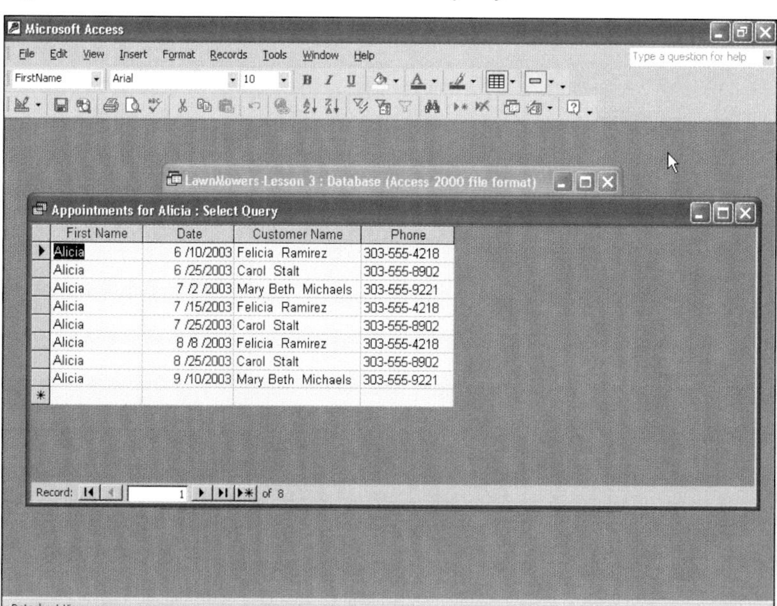

j. Open the Appointments for Alicia query in Design view. Change the criteria in the FirstName field to Juan. Save the query as Appointments for Juan. Run the query. Change the background color to a pale blue; then preview and print the datasheet. Save and close the query.

k. Open the Appointments for Alicia query in Design view. Change the criteria in the FirstName field to Lon. Save the query as Appointments for Lon. Run the query. Change the background color to a pale green; then preview and print the datasheet. Save and close the query.

l. Close the *LawnMowers-Lesson 3.mdb* database.

Do It Yourself

1. Use Sort and Filter Techniques to Retrieve Data

The WoodStarts database contains an Hours table in which employees' work hours are logged each day. Oftentimes the Payroll Supervisor must sort and filter the table to retrieve specific data.

a. Open the Hours table in the *WoodStarts-Lesson 3.mdb* database.

b. Sort the datasheet in ascending order by employee name.

c. Sort the datasheet in descending order by date.

d. Use the Filter By Form method to retrieve only the records for employees who worked more than 6.5 hours on 4/24/2003 **(see Figure 3.34)**.

Figure 3.34 Filtered Hours datasheet

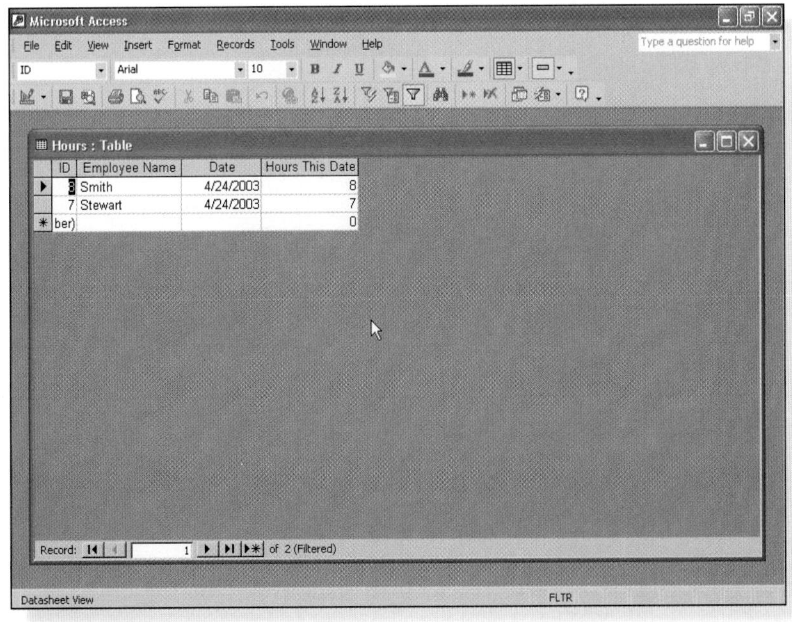

e. Use the Filter By Form method to retrieve only the records for employees who worked less than 6 hours in a day or who worked on 4/29/2003. Sort the filtered datasheet in alphabetical order by employee name. Remove both the filter and the sort.

f. Use the Filter By Selection method to retrieve the records for Terry Stewart.

g. Close the Hours table without saving any changes.

2. Create a Find Duplicates Query

The Payroll Supervisor believes that there may be some duplicate records in the Hours table. In order to locate the duplicate entries, you will create a Find Duplicates query.

a. Start the Find Duplicates Query Wizard. Search for duplicate entries in both the Employee Name and Date fields in the Hours table. Include the Hours field in the query results.

b. Accept the name *Find duplicates for Hours* for the query and view the query results **(see Figure 3.35)**.

Figure 3.35 Duplicate records in the Hours table

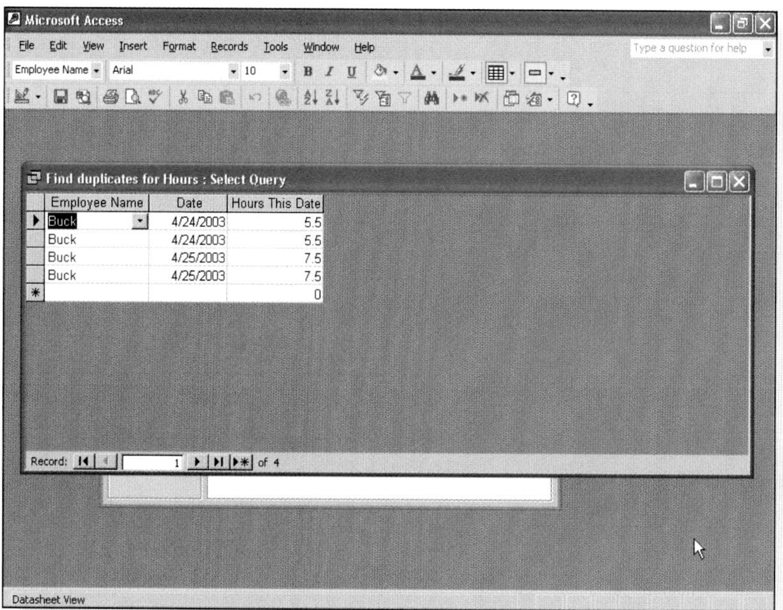

c. Delete the duplicate records from the query results, and then close the query.

d. Open the Hours table and apply a filter to display only the records for Buck. Sort the filtered datasheet in ascending order by date. Verify that the duplicate records have been deleted from the Hours table.

e. Close the Hours table without saving changes to the table design.

3. Create and Modify a Select Query

The WoodStarts Shop Manager needs to determine how much of each type of wood will be needed to fill the August orders. You need to create a query that answers the question "How many products of each wood type were ordered in August?"

a. Create the query using the Simple Query Wizard. Base the query on the Orders table, and include the Date, Product, and Quantity fields in the query. Click Next. If necessary, select Detail.

b. Name the query Wood Types Ordered in August and view the query design.

c. Type the criterion between 7/31/03 and 9/1/03 in the Criteria cell of the Date field so that the query only retrieves records that contain an August date.

d. Sort the query by the Product field, in ascending order.

e. Run the query. Format the datasheet attractively **(see Figure 3.36)**.

f. Save changes to the query design and close the query. Then close the *Woodstarts-Lesson 3.mdb* database.

Figure 3.36 The completed query

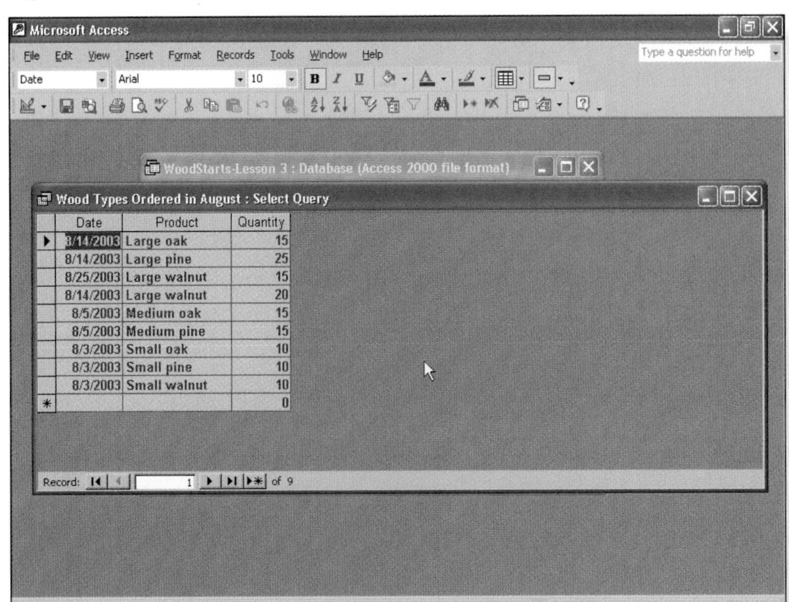

Challenge Yourself

Create and Modify a Query in Design View

In this lesson, you created queries using the Simple Query Wizard, and then modified those queries in Design view. As you become more proficient using Access, you will probably forego using the Simple Query Wizard and create your queries "from scratch" in Design view. In this exercise, you will create a query in Design view that calculates a total for each Saburo Sporting Goods customer order placed in April.

Open the *Saburo Sporting Goods-Lesson 3.mdb* database. With the Queries objects displayed in the Database window, double-click *Create query in Design view*. An empty query design window appears, along with the Show Table dialog box **(see Figure 3.37)**. (You may remember the Show Table dialog box when you created relationships between tables in Lesson 2.) ***Note:*** If the Show Table dialog box is not displayed, click the Show Table button on the Query Design toolbar.

Figure 3.37 The empty query design window and the Show Table dialog box

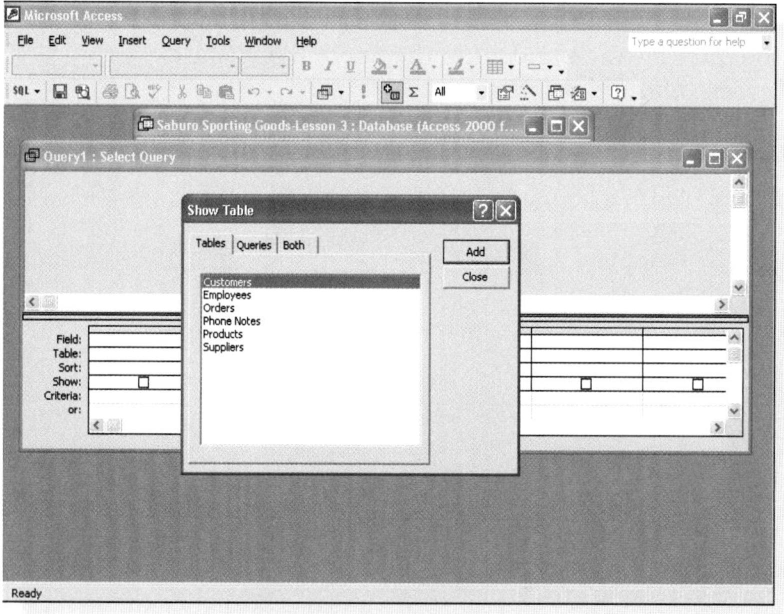

This query will be based on fields from three tables in the database—the Customers table, the Orders table, and the Products table.

Click Customers in the Show Table dialog box and click Add to add the Customers field list to the upper pane of the query design window. Then add the Orders table and the Products table and close the Show Table dialog box.

Double-click each of the following fields from the appropriate field list to add it to the design grid: CompanyName, OrderDate, ProductName, UnitPrice, Qty. (Add the fields in the order listed.) Run the query and analyze the results.

Return to Design view and add a criterion in the appropriate cell that limits the query to only those orders for April. Sort the query in ascending order first by company name and then by order date. Run the query and analyze the results. Save the query as April Orders.

Return to Design view and create a calculated field that multiplies the unit price by the quantity. Add the caption *Subtotal* to the calculated field and format the field for currency **(see Figure 3.38)**. Run the query and analyze the results. Save the changes to the query design.

Close the query, close the database, and exit Access.

Figure 3.38 The completed query in Design view

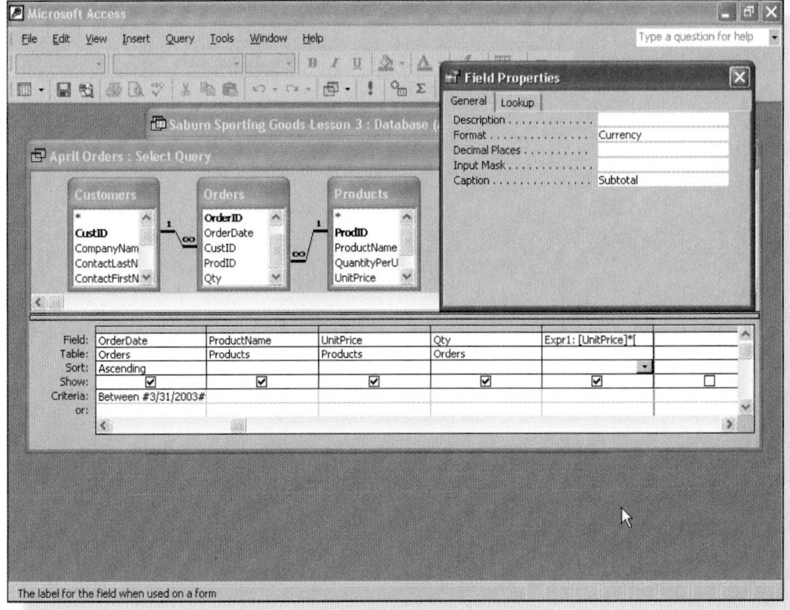

Lesson 4

Working With Forms, Reports, and Data Access Pages

Lesson Exercise Objectives

After completing this lesson, you'll be able to do the following tasks:

1. Create simple forms
2. Create business reports
3. Modify forms and reports in Design view
4. Create a simple data access page

Key Terms

- AutoForm (p. 427)
- bound control (p. 435)
- calculated control (p. 435)
- controls (p. 435)
- main form (p. 426)
- main/subform (p. 426)
- sections (p. 434)
- subform (p. 426)
- tab order (p. 436)
- toolbox (p. 439)
- unbound control (p. 435)

Microsoft Office Specialist Activities

AC2002: 4.1, 4.2, 7.1, 7.2, 7.3, 8.3

Real-Life Business Applications

Lesson Case Study

In this lesson, you will continue in your role as a student intern in the information systems department at Saburo Sporting Goods. Keep the following information in mind as you work through this lesson:

- **Job responsibilities and goals.** During this final phase of your internship, you will create and modify forms for data entry, create and modify professional-looking business reports, and create a simple data access page to allow users to view and modify the data in the database from a remote location.
- **The project.** You will learn how to create forms and reports, and then modify them to make them easier to use and more visually appealing. You will also learn how to create data access pages to allow users access to the database using a Web browser.
- **The challenge ahead.** You know the basics of managing data in an Access database. The next challenge is to learn how to make data entry easier and more efficient, generate useful reports, and make the database more accessible to users in remote locations.

Microsoft Office Specialist AC2002 4.1

Access

Exercise 1 Overview: Create Simple Forms

A form is a window into the data in your tables that is used primarily for entering and editing data. You can create a form to display whatever data you want the user to see, in any layout you choose. Forms can be very elegant and artistic, but it is important to remember that they must be easy to read and use.

A form can display the data from a single table or query, or it can display data from two or more related tables or queries. For example, the form in Figure 4.1 displays the data in a single record from the Customers table in the **main form**, which is the top portion of the form. All the related records from the Orders table are displayed in the **subform**, which is the bottom portion of the form. This is called a **main/subform** combination. A main/subform combination often makes data entry much more efficient, because all the fields in which data must be entered are displayed in a single form, even though the fields are from different tables or queries.

Figure 4.1 A main/subform combination

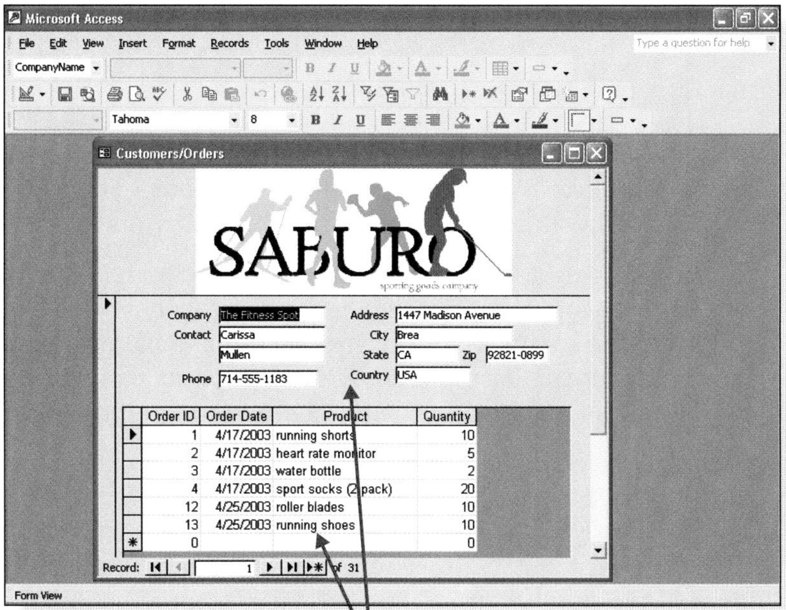

When you use a main/subform combination, you can enter data into two tables using the same form.

If you base a form on a query, the form can only display fields from the query. Thus, you cannot add another field to the form from a table unless you first add the field to the query. However, you can display a calculated field from the query that would not be available if the form was based on a table.

There are three methods you can use to create a form: You can use one of the AutoForms, you can use the Form Wizard, or you can create a form "from scratch" in Design view. In this section, you will use AutoForms and the Form Wizard to create forms, which are the two most widely used methods for creating forms. Then later in this lesson, you will modify a form in Design view.

Access

Type: create a form

Creating an AutoForm

Using an AutoForm is the quickest way to create a form. An **AutoForm** contains all of the fields from the table or query on which it is based, and can be created simply by clicking a button. It is important to note, however, that an AutoForm can only be based on a single table or query.

There are several types of AutoForms available in Access. For example, one type of AutoForm creates a main/subform combination if the underlying table on which the AutoForm is based is related to other tables. Other types of AutoForms display data in specific layouts, such as columnar or tabular.

The best way to learn about the differences between the various types of AutoForms is to try each one. In the following exercise, you will create four different types of AutoForms based on the Suppliers table in the *Saburo Sporting Goods-Lesson 4.mdb* database.

Note: Because the Suppliers table is the primary table in a relationship with the Products table, the first AutoForm you create will display both a main form (a supplier record from the Suppliers table) and a subform (the related product records for the supplier record).

Quick Tip

In the following exercise, you must be sure to select *but not open* the table upon which you are basing your AutoForms.

Access

Step Through It™

Exercise 1A: Create different AutoForms

1. Open the *Saburo Sporting Goods-Lesson 4.mdb* database. Display the Tables group in the Database window.

2. Select the Suppliers table (but do not open it).

3. On the Database toolbar, Click the New Object down arrow, and then click AutoForm from the list. Access creates a main form that includes all the fields in the Suppliers table and a subform that shows related records from the Products table (see Figure 4.2).

4. Close the new form without saving changes.

5. With the Suppliers table still selected, click the New Object down arrow, and then select Form from the list of objects. The New Form dialog box opens.

6. Double-click AutoForm: Columnar.

7. Using the same methods you used in steps 5 and 6, create Tabular and Datasheet AutoForms (see Figure 4.3).

8. Compare the new forms, and then close them without saving changes.

Figure 4.2 This AutoForm is a main/subform combination

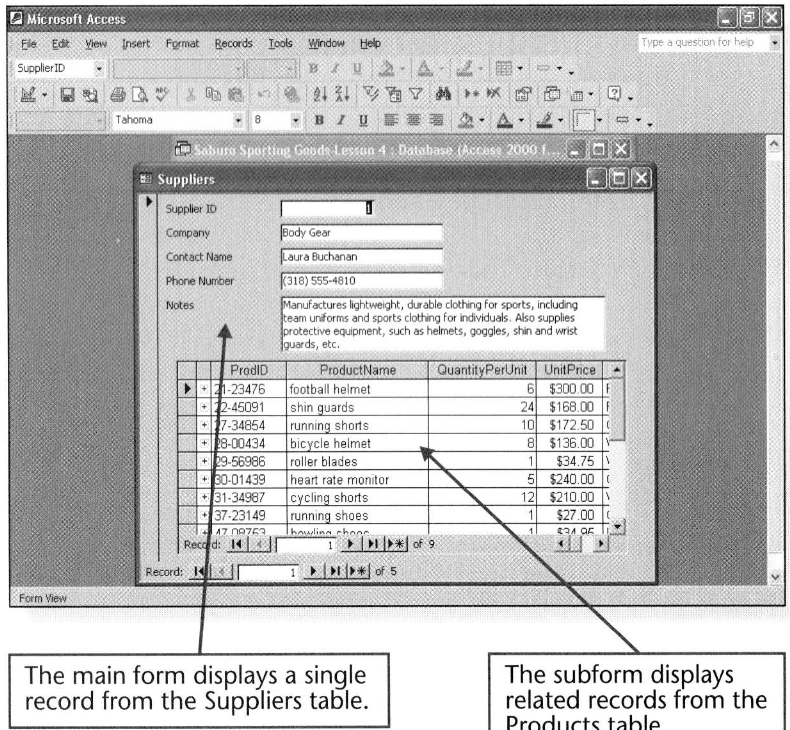
The main form displays a single record from the Suppliers table.
The subform displays related records from the Products table.

Figure 4.3 Different types of AutoForms based on the Suppliers table

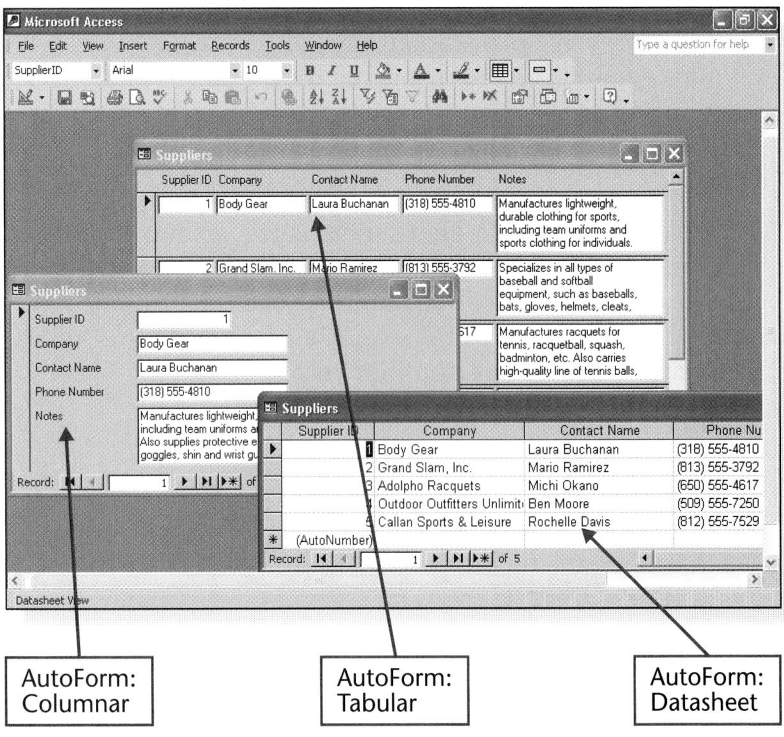
AutoForm: Columnar
AutoForm: Tabular
AutoForm: Datasheet

Creating a Form Using the Form Wizard

While creating an AutoForm is definitely easy, you have more flexibility and control over the content of a form if you use the Form Wizard. The Form Wizard is the most effective way to create a form, because you can tell the wizard exactly which fields contain the data you want the form to display, and the wizard does all the background work for you. Even without further modification, a form created by the Form Wizard is quite functional.

When you use the Form Wizard, you can select specific fields from one or more tables or queries to display in the form. You can choose a number of other options as well. For example, if you include a related table in a wizard-created form, you can also choose which fields to display from the related records in the subform.

In the following exercise, you will use the Form Wizard to create a main/subform based on the Suppliers table in the *Saburo Sporting Goods-Lesson 4.mdb* database.

Figure 4.4 Selecting the fields to include on the form

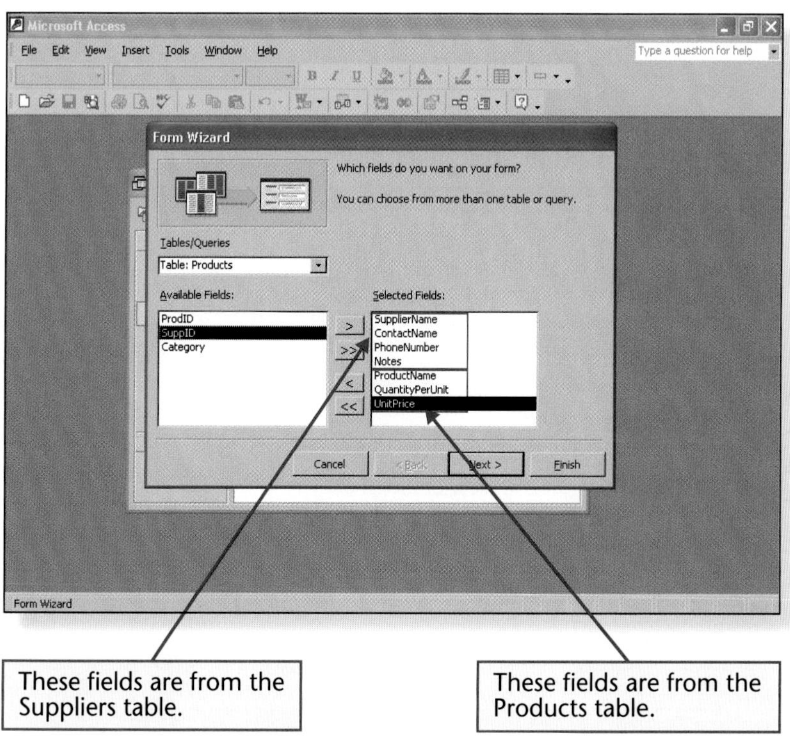

Another Way

You can also add fields from the Available Fields list to the Selected Fields list by selecting the field you want to add and clicking the Add Field button between the two lists.

Step Through It™

Exercise 1B: Use the Form Wizard

1. Display the Forms group, and double-click the *Create form by using wizard* option.
2. Select Table: Suppliers in the Tables/Queries box. Then add all the fields *except* SupplierID to the selected Fields list.
3. Now select Table: Products in the Tables/ Queries box, and add ProductName, QuantityPerUnit, and UnitPrice to the *bottom* of the Selected Fields list (see Figure 4.4). Then click Next.

4. Because the Suppliers and Products tables are related, you must tell the wizard if you want a main/subform combination. Select *by Suppliers*, and select the *Form with subform*(s) option (see Figure 4.5). Then click Next

5. In the third wizard step, select Datasheet as the layout and click Next.

Figure 4.5 Determining how you want to view the data in the form

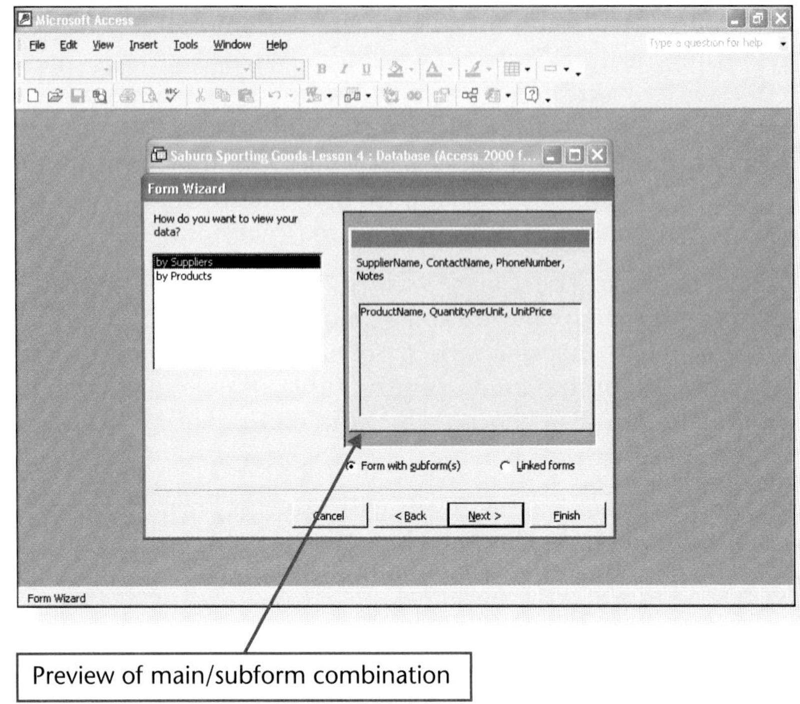

6. In the fourth wizard step, select Standard as the style and click Next.

7. In the last wizard step, accept the suggested form and subform names by clicking Finish. Use the navigation toolbars to display the records in the main form and subform (see Figure 4.6).

8. Close the Suppliers form. (The wizard already saved it for you.)

Figure 4.6 The finished Suppliers form

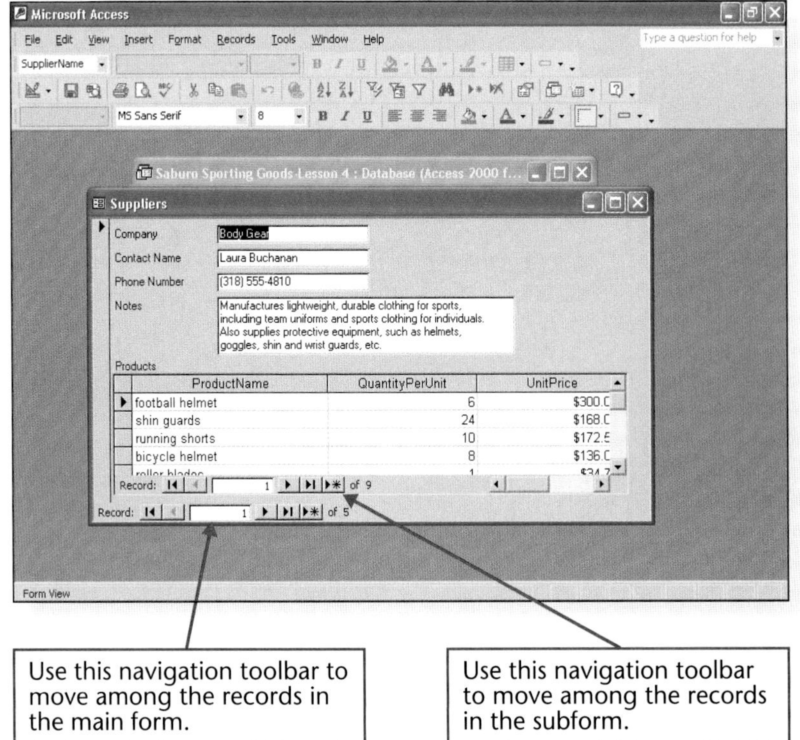

Exercise 2 Overview: Create Business Reports

Microsoft Office Specialist AC2002 7.1

The primary purpose of an Access report is to effectively present data from the database in a printed format. In a report, the data details are usually grouped and summarized to make the information easier to understand and analyze. You can also add extra elements, such as logos, to customize a report.

Before you create a report, you should first plan in writing exactly which fields you want to include in the report, and create a query that contains only those fields. Then build the report based on the query.

The most efficient way to create a report is to use the Report Wizard to build a basic report, and then modify it in Design view by moving, resizing, aligning, and formatting report elements, and adding calculated fields and graphics. (You will modify a report in Design view in the next section.)

Saburo Sporting Goods would like to generate customer invoices based on information contained in the company database. In the following exercise, you will use the Report Wizard to create a customer invoices report.

Figure 4.7 Selecting the fields for the report

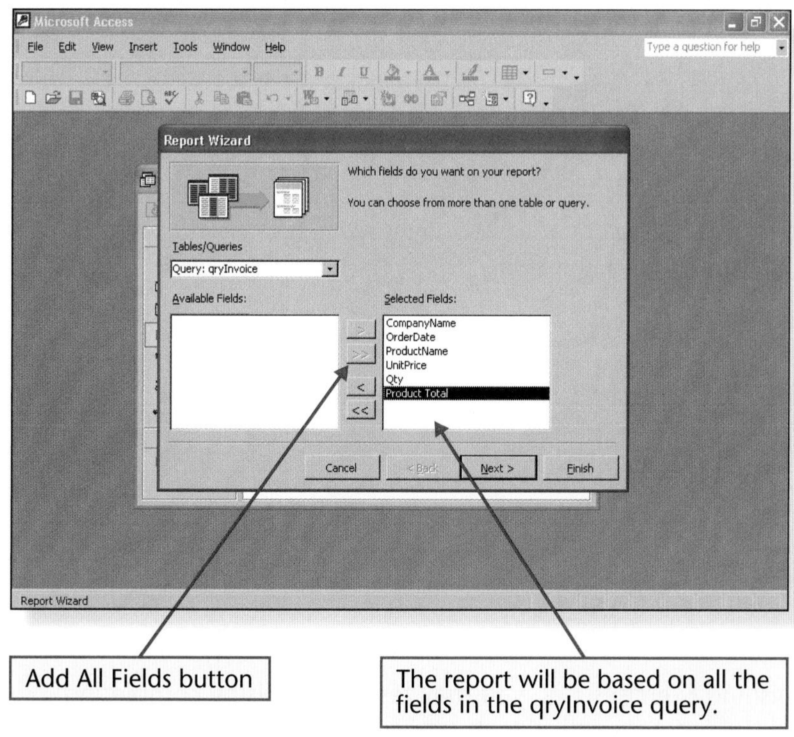

Access

Step Through It™

Exercise 2: Create a report

1. Open the Reports group in the Database window.
2. Double-click the *Create report by using wizard* option. The Report Wizard opens.
3. In the first wizard step, select Query: qryInvoice from the Tables/Queries box. Click the Add All Fields button >> between the Available Fields and Selected Fields lists to add all the query fields to the Selected Fields list (see Figure 4.7). Then click Next.

4 Double-click CompanyName in the list on the left to group the report on the CompanyName field. Then click Next.

5 In the next wizard step, click the down arrow to the right of the first box and select OrderDate. In the second box, select ProductName. The buttons next to both boxes should read *Ascending* (see Figure 4.8).

6 Click the Summary Options button. In the dialog box, check the Sum box in the Product Total row. Select the *Detail and Summary* option, and click OK. Then click Next.

Figure 4.8 Indicating the sort order for the detail records in the report

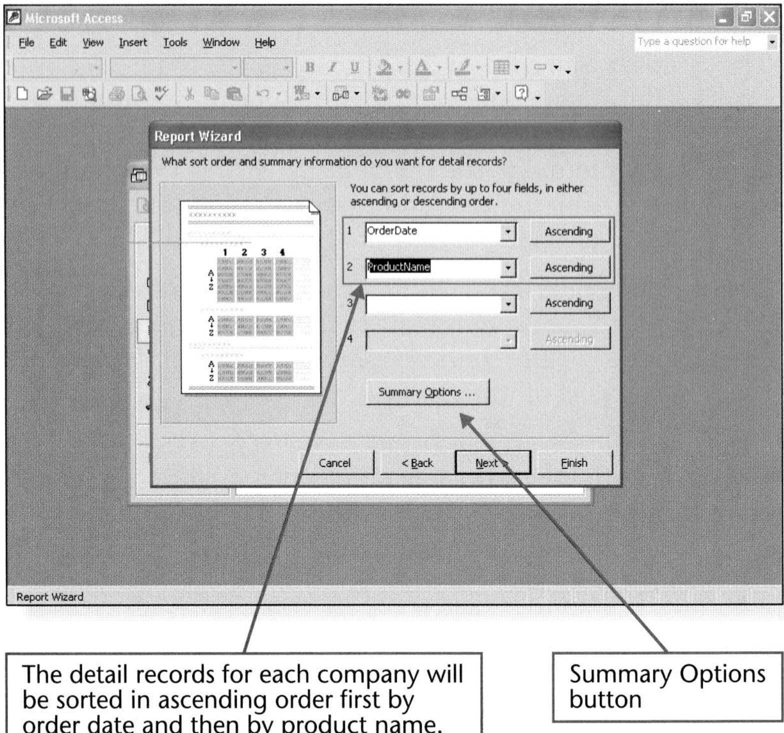

7 In the next wizard step, select Stepped layout and Portrait orientation, and click Next.

8 Select Corporate style, and click Next.

9 In the last wizard step, type Invoices for the title, and click Finish. The report opens in Print Preview (see Figure 4.9).

10 Maximize the window and examine both pages of the report. Then close the report. (The wizard already saved it for you.)

Figure 4.9 The new Invoices report

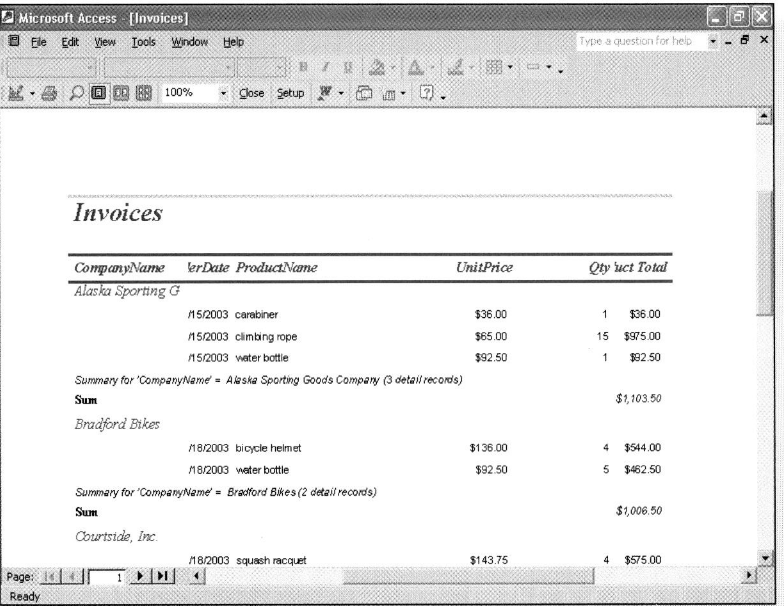

▶ APPLY IT! After finishing Exercises 1–2, you may test your skills by completing Apply It! Guided Activity 1, Create a New Form and Report.

Technology@School

Accessing Information

Databases are everywhere. Information about you is probably in more databases than you realize. For example, schools use them to track class schedules and grades. Do you have a library card, driver's license, or Social Security number? Do you work, have a bank account, and pay taxes? Do you see a doctor or dentist? Do you have an e-mail account? In each of these instances, information about you is stored in a database.

Not only are you already *in* databases, but you also already *use* them. When you search a computerized library card catalog or the Internet, or when you scan an item in your part-time job as a salesclerk, you are working with some type of database.

Learning Access does not just provide you with a valuable skill, it also helps you recognize and appreciate how databases have become an integral (and sometimes intrusive!) part of our everyday lives.

CRITICAL THINKING

1. Form a team with some other students. Visit your library to find out what databases it offers. Create a presentation on what you learn. Include a handout that lists and describes the databases and explains how to use them.
2. Explore the Microsoft Office Template Gallery (**www.officeupdate.microsoft.com/templategallery**) for a database template you can use in your school or personal life. Create a database based on the template. Then create and print a report based on the data in your database.

Database Uses	Examples
School and public libraries	Need good, up-to-date, reliable information for a school paper? Explore the databases at your school or public library. Libraries offer databases on any subject you can think of, from science to music to health. You can also access newspapers, magazines, biographies, dictionaries, encyclopedias, and more.
The Internet	The Internet gives you access to more databases than any other source. Search engines themselves are databases of Internet addresses. When you search for a product at an online retailer, you are actually querying a database of its inventory.
On your own	Can't think of how you might use databases on your own? Think again! How about cataloging your music or baseball card collection? Access can help you track sales for a fund-raising event, run your lawn-mowing, tutoring, or babysitting business, and organize data you collect for a history or science project.

Microsoft Office Specialist AC2002 4.2, 7.2, 7.3

Access

Exercise 3 Overview: Modify Forms and Reports in Design View

As you've no doubt noticed, while the forms and reports created by the wizards are functional, they are not very attractive. They usually need some modifications to make them more effective and visually appealing. Before you can modify forms and reports, however, you need to become familiar with the structure, or design, of these two database objects.

Understanding Sections

Both forms and reports are divided into **sections**, which are areas that contain a particular type of information, and are visable in Design view. There is always a Detail section, where data details are displayed. There may also be Header and Footer sections, where general and summary data are displayed (see Figure 4.10).

Forms have Form Header and Form Footer sections that contain information that is not linked to the records in the underlying tables, such as a logo or a title. Reports have Page Header and Page Footer sections, which contain information that is displayed at the top and bottom of every page in a report. Reports also have Report Header and Report Footer sections, which contain information that is displayed at the beginning and end of a report.

Figure 4.10 Examining the sections of a report in Design view

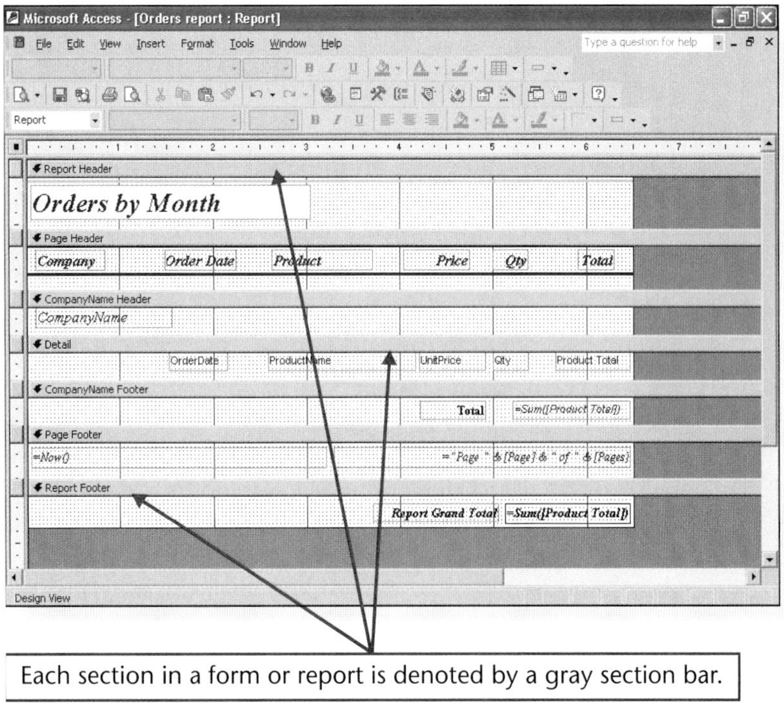

Microsoft Access - [Orders report : Report]

Report Header

Orders by Month

Page Header

Company | Order Date | Product | Price | Qty | Total

CompanyName Header

CompanyName

Detail

OrderDate | ProductName | UnitPrice | Qty | Product Total

CompanyName Footer

Total | =Sum([Product Total])

Page Footer

=Now() | ="Page " & [Page] & " of " & [Pages]

Report Footer

Report Grand Total | =Sum([Product Total])

Design View

Each section in a form or report is denoted by a gray section bar.

Understanding Controls

Controls are the elements in forms and reports where data is displayed. Two of the more common controls are labels and text boxes. A label is a control that displays descriptive text or elements, such as a caption, a title, or a decorative rule. Oftentimes a label is attached to (and describes) another control, such as a text box. A text box is a control that displays data from a field in the underlying table or query or accepts data entered by the user (see Figure 4.11).

Controls in a form are usually interactive (buttons to push, check boxes to mark or clear, and so forth) so that the user can enter, edit, and delete data in the underlying table. However, controls in a report are not interactive—they only display ready-to-print data.

Controls can be bound, unbound, or calculated. A **bound control** displays data from an underlying table or query, and is therefore *bound* to that data. Oftentimes a text box is a bound control (but not always). An **unbound control** is a control that is not bound to underlying data. A label is always an unbound control. A **calculated control** displays the result of an expression on a form or report, and is similar to a calculated field in a query, which you learned about in Lesson 3.

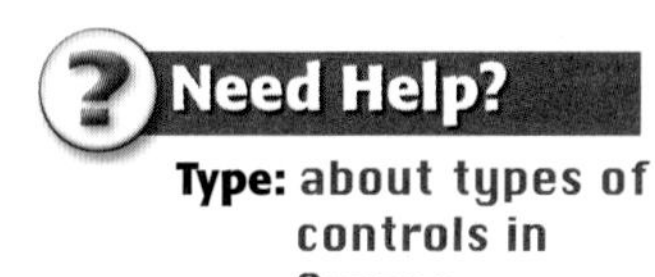

Type: about types of controls in Access

Figure 4.11 Examining the controls in a report in Design view

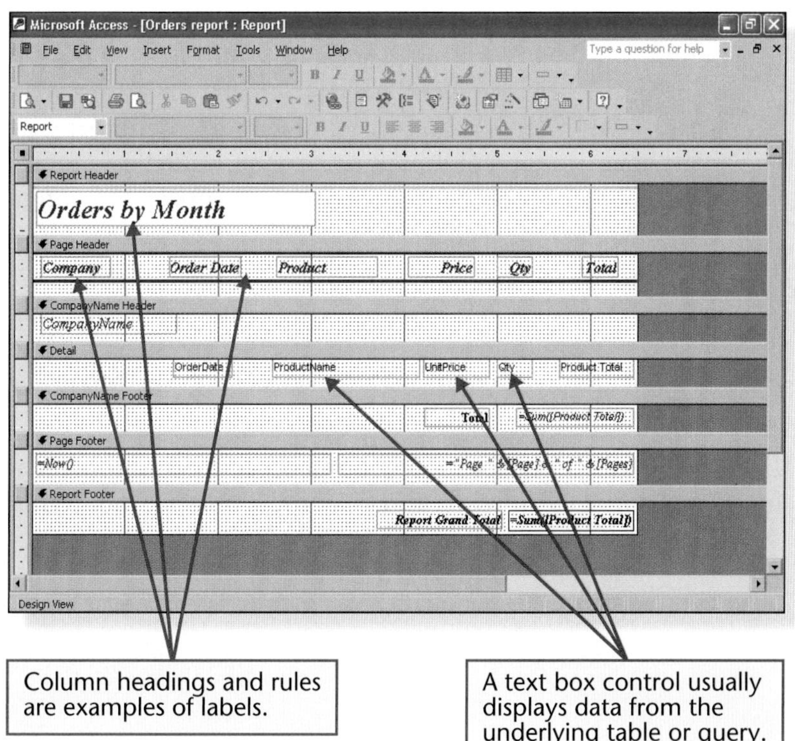

Moving and Resizing Controls, Rearranging Tab Order, and Modifying Properties

To maximize the effectiveness and readability of a form or a report, controls often need to be moved or resized. When you click a control, Access places selection handles around it. As you move your pointer over a selected control, the pointer will change into various shapes. Each of these pointer shapes allows you to manipulate the control in a certain way as described in Table 4.1.

Table 4.1

Pointer Shape	Purpose
[hand icon]	Allows you move a control. If the control is attached to another control, both controls will move.
[pointing hand icon]	Allows you to move an attached control independently.
[↔]	Allows you to resize a control horizontally.
[↕]	Allows you to resize a control vertically.
[↗↙]	Allows you to resize a control proportionally, both horizontally and vertically.

Remember when you changed the properties of fields in tables and queries? You can also modify the properties of a form or report. Every element on a form or report has properties—whether it's a control, a section, a subform, or the entire form or report. You use a property sheet to modify the properties of an element on a form or report to change how it looks or behaves.

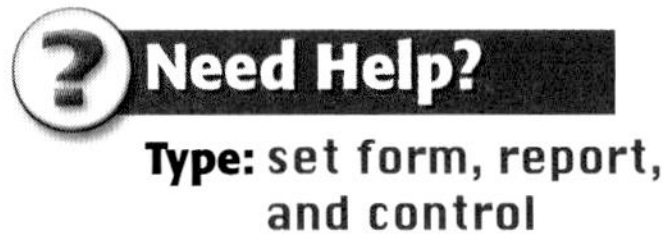

Type: set form, report, and control properties

Since forms are primarily used for data entry, it is important that the **tab order**—the order in which the cursor moves from field to field when a user presses the Tab key—is logical and efficient for the user. Often the tab order needs to be modified to make a form more user-friendly.

In the following exercise, you will modify the Suppliers form in Design view by moving and resizing controls, modifying properties, and rearranging the tab order.

Figure 4.12 Moving a text box control and its attached label

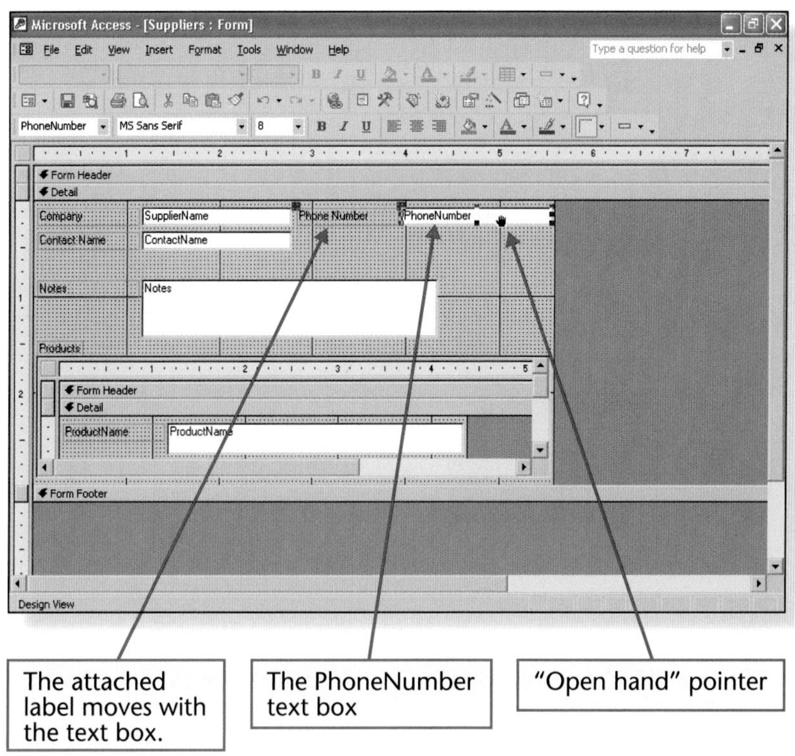

Step Through It™

Exercise 3A: Modify a form

1. Open the Suppliers form, switch to Design view.
2. Click the PhoneNumber text box. Move your pointer slowly over the selected control until it changes to the shape of an open hand. Then drag the PhoneNumber text box into the upper-right corner of the form grid and align it horizontally with the SupplierName text box (see Figure 4.12). Notice that the text box and its attached label control move together.

Figure 4.13 Moving a label control independently of its attached text box control

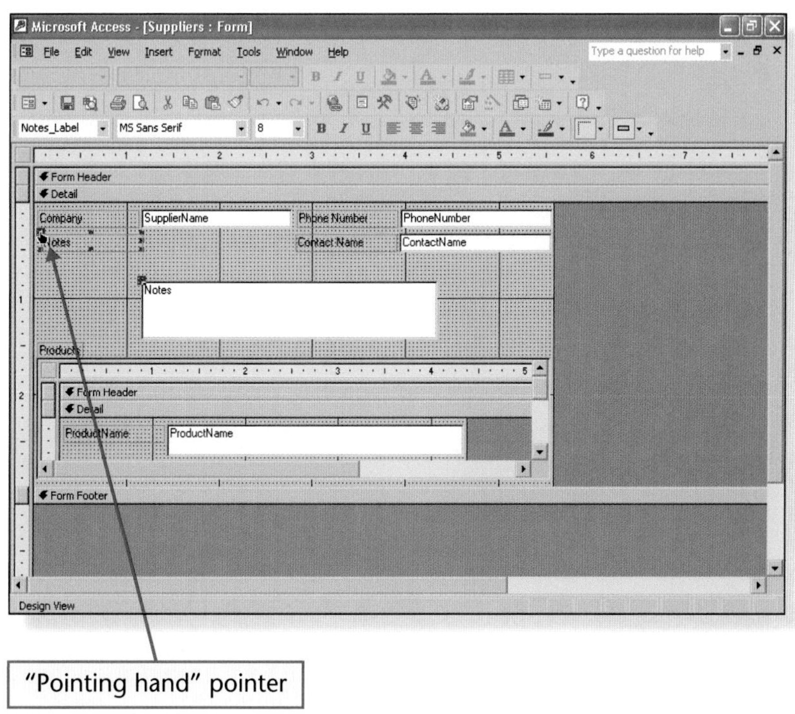

3. Using the same technique you used in step 2, drag the ContactName text box (with its attached label) under the PhoneNumber text box.
4. Click the Notes. Move your pointer slowly over the selection handle in the upper-left corner of the label until it changes to the shape of a pointing hand. Drag the Notes label (without moving the text box) up under the Company label, and align it horizontally with the Contact Name label (see Figure 4.13).

5 Click the Notes text box and point to the handle on the top center of the box. When the pointer changes to a double arrow, drag the top of the box upward to make it a bit taller. Then move only the Notes text box (not the Notes label) to the left and position it under the Notes label.

6 Click the gray square in the upper-left corner of the subform. A small, black square appears. Click the Properties button on the Form Design toolbar. The property sheet should read *Form* in the title bar and in the box above the tabs (see Figure 4.14).

Figure 4.14 Opening the property sheet for the subform

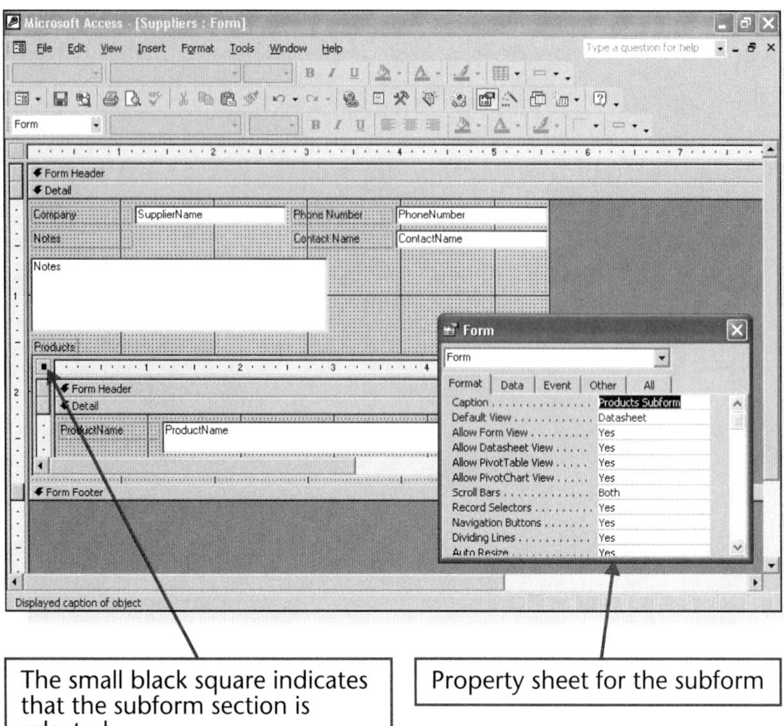

7 Click the Format tab in the property sheet, click in the Navigation Buttons box, and change the property to No. Then close the property sheet.

8 Switch to Form view. Restore the window to its original size (see Figure 4.15).

9 Examine the form. Press Tab three times and note the order in which the cursor moves from field to field in the main form.

10 Switch back to Design view.

Figure 4.15 The modified Suppliers form in Form view

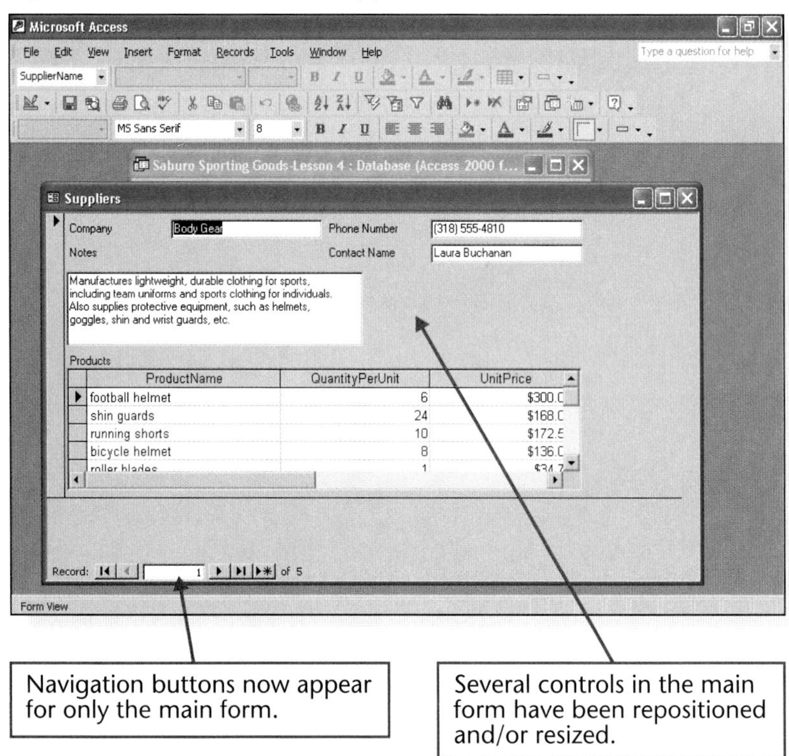

Figure 4.16 Changing the tab order

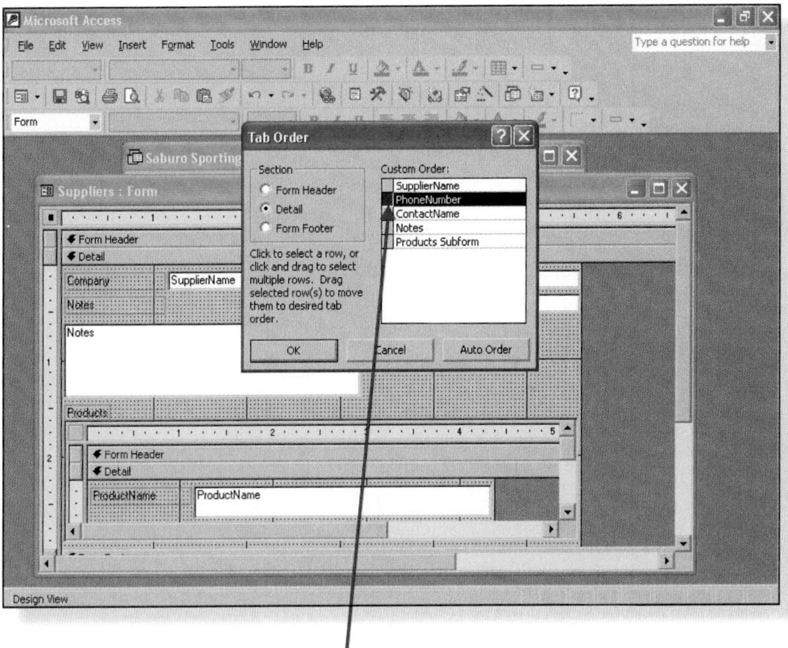

Click the selection box to select the row, and then drag the row to the desired location to rearrange the tab order.

11 On the View menu, select Tab Order. Be sure the Detail option is selected under *Section.* Under *Custom Order,* click the gray selection box to the left of PhoneNumber to select it.

12 With the PhoneNumber row selected, point to the selection box (which is now black) and drag the row up to position it between the SupplierName and ContactName rows (see Figure 4.16). Click OK.

13 Switch to Form view. Press Tab to move through the main form fields in a more orderly pattern. Then save and close the Suppliers form.

Working With the Grid, the Rulers, and the Toolbox

If you look closely at the Design view window for either forms or reports, you will notice that all the controls are positioned on a grid composed of horizontal and vertical lines and tiny dots. You can use the grid to help you align controls in the design window. You can also use the horizontal and vertical rulers to help you align controls. The lines in the grid appear at 1" intervals and correspond with the inch marks on the rulers.

To add a control to a form or report in Design view, you use the **toolbox**, which is a set of tools that you use to add a control, such as a label, a text box, or an image, to a form or report. The toolbox usually opens when you switch a form or report to Design view. However, you can display (or hide) it by clicking the Toolbox button on the Form Design and Report Design toolbars. Figure 4.17 illustrates the grid, the rulers, and the toolbox in Design view for a report.

Access

Figure 4.17 Examining the grid, the rulers, and the toolbox

Rulers

Grid

Toolbox

In the next three exercises, you will modify the Invoices report to make it more useful and visually appealing.

Step Through It™

Exercise 3B: Modify a report

1. Open the Invoices report in Design view. Maximize the window.
2. In the Page Header section, click in the CompanyName label, drag to select the text and type Customer. Then click away from the label to deselect it.
3. Using the same technique you used in step 2, change the remaining Page Header labels to Date, Item, Price, Quantity, and Total, respectively (see Figure 4.18).

Figure 4.18 Modifying the text in a label control

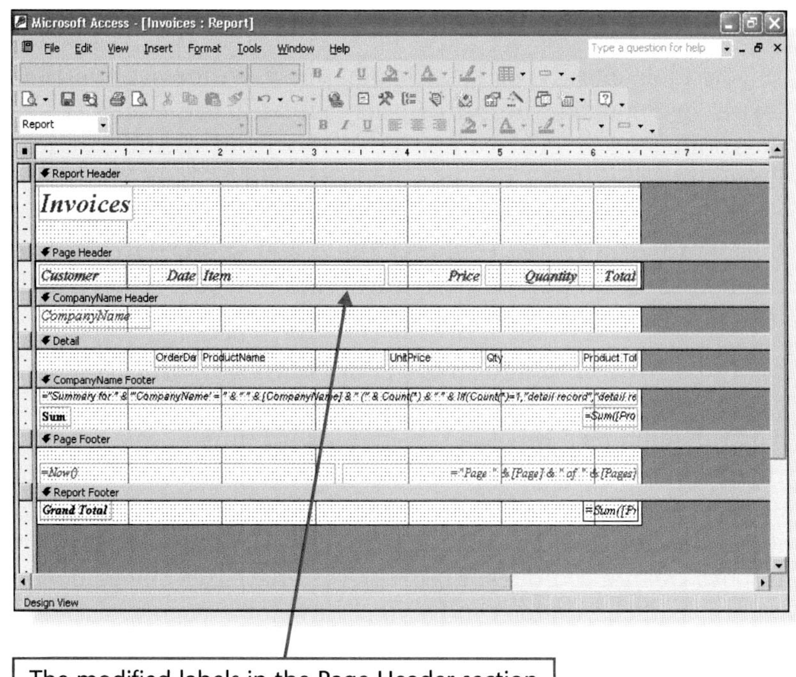

Figure 4.19 Examining the results of the modifications in Print Preview

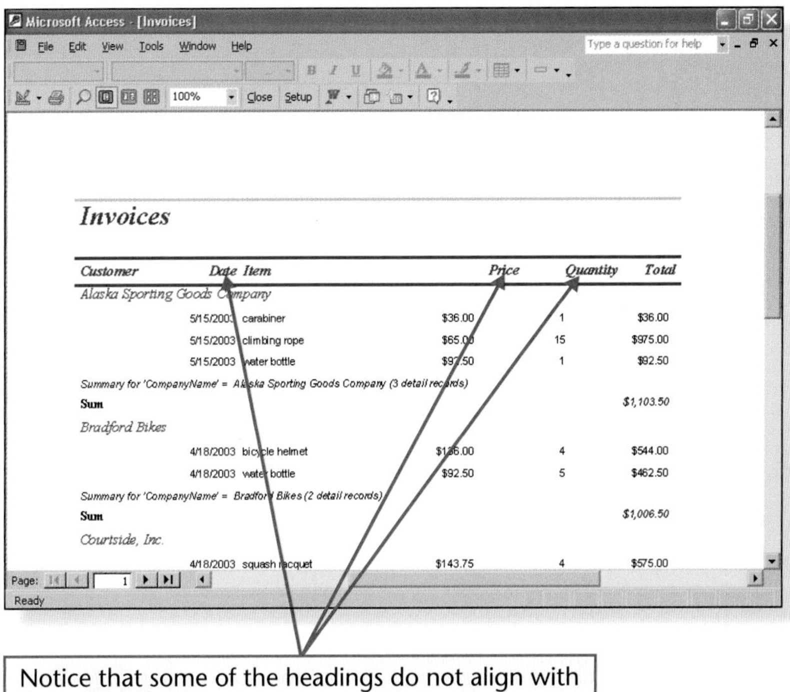

Notice that some of the headings do not align with the report details.

4 In the Page Header section, click the Customer label, and hold Shift while you select the five other labels. Point to Size on the Format menu, and select To Fit.

5 In the CompanyName header section, select the CompanyName text box. Drag the right center handle to widen the text box to the 2.5" mark on the horizontal ruler.

6 In the Detail section, widen the OrderDate text box, and make the UnitPrice and Qty text boxes narrower. Then switch to Print Preview (see Figure 4.19).

Figure 4.20 Making additional design changes to the Invoices report

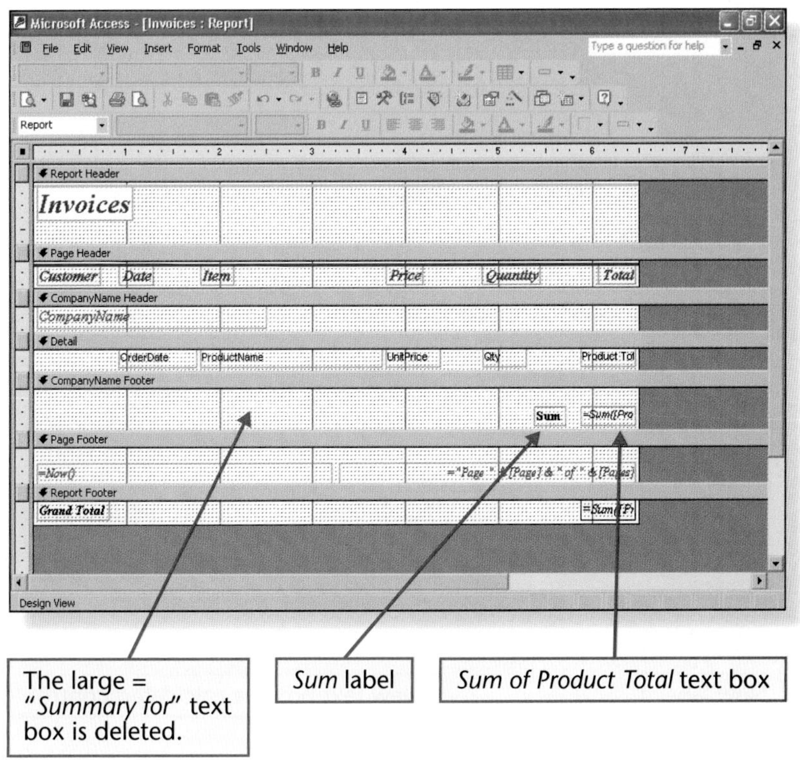

7 Switch to Design view. Move some of the labels in the Page Header section as necessary to align them over the appropriate text boxes in the Detail section.

8 In the CompanyName Footer section, click the = *"Summary for"* text box to select it, and press Delete. Then drag the Sum label to the right and position it next to the Sum Of Product Total text box (see Figure 4.20).

9 In the Report Footer section, select and delete the Grand Total label and the Product Total Grand Total Sum text box. Save your changes, and then examine the report in Print Preview.

Access

Step Through It™

Exercise 3C: Add calculated controls to a report

Access

1 Switch to Design view. Point to the gray section bar above the Page Footer section. When the pointer becomes a double arrow, drag the bar down about 1" to lengthen the CompanyName Footer section.

2 If the toolbox isn't displayed, click Toolbox on the Report Design toolbar to display it (see Figure 4.21).

Figure 4.21 Lengthening a report section and displaying the toolbox

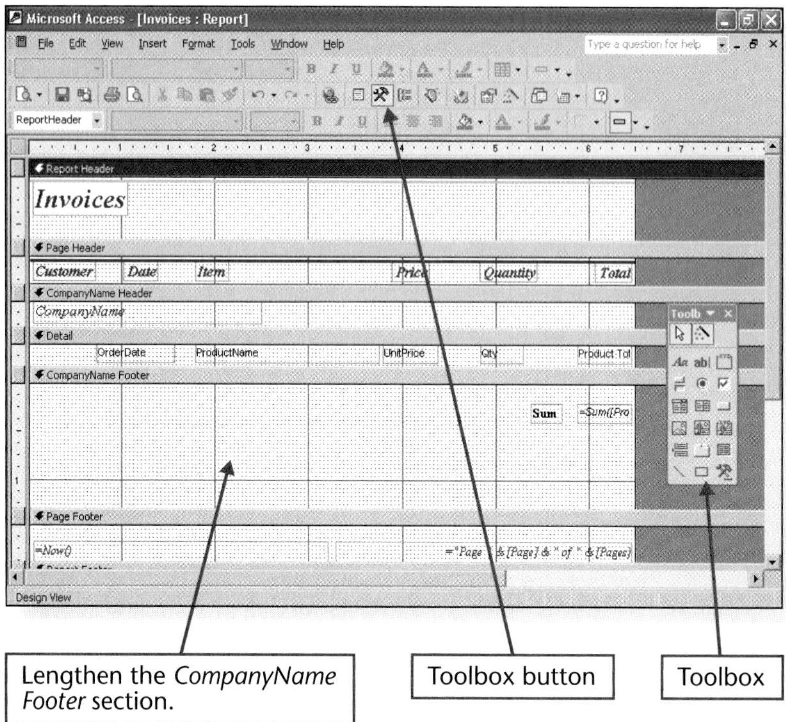

3 Click the Text Box tool, and then click anywhere in the blank area of the CompanyName Footer section.

4 Click in the new label, drag to select its text, and type Shipping. The label widens to fit the text you type.

5 Select the new text box and drag the right handle to make it about two inches long. Then click in the text box and type =[Sum of Product Total]*0.02 (see Figure 4.22).

Figure 4.22 Creating a calculated control

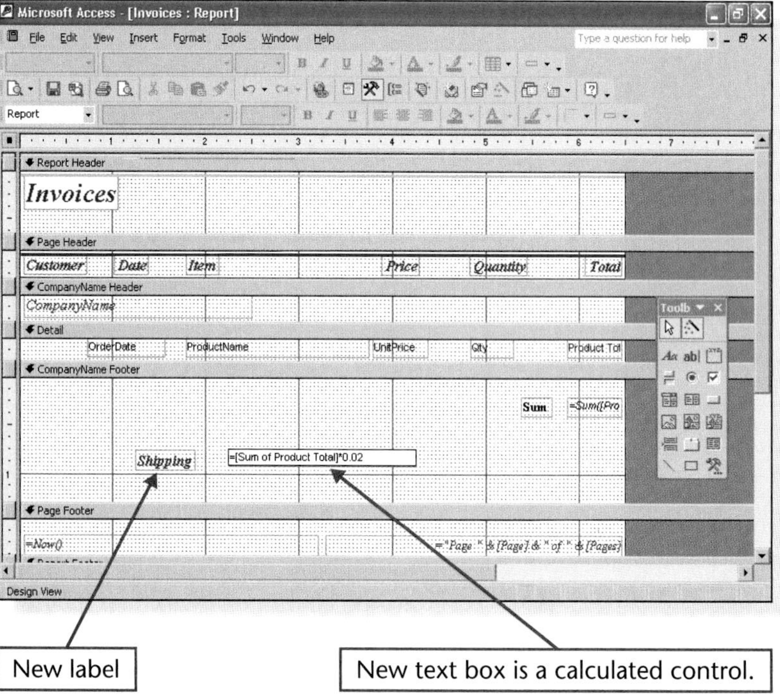

Figure 4.23 Changing the properties of the calculated control

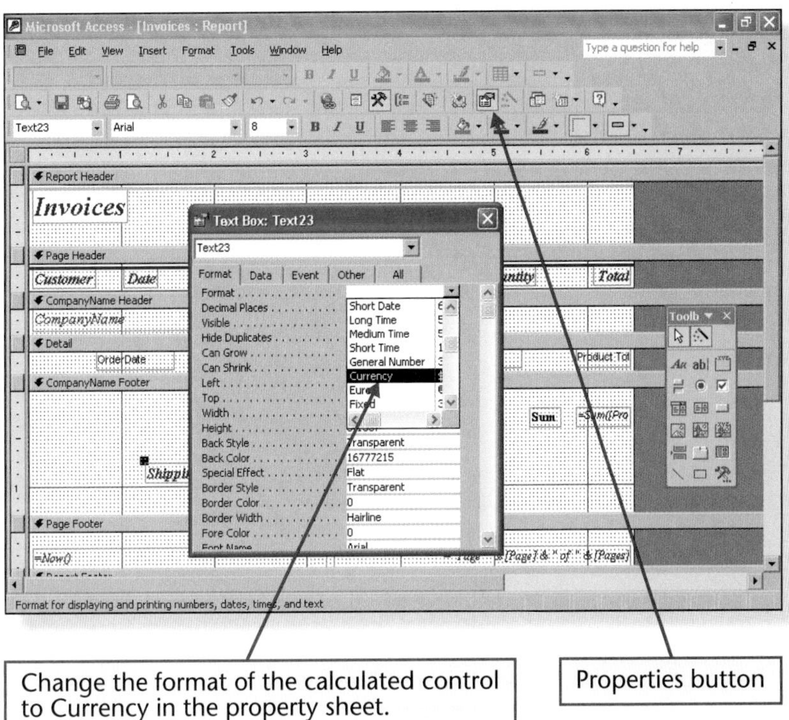

6. Switch to Print Preview and examine the new calculated control and label. Then return to Design view.

7. Select the new calculated control, if necessary, and click Properties on the Report Design toolbar. On the Format tab of the Text Box property sheet, click in the Format box and select Currency (see Figure 4.23).

8. Click the Other tab in the property sheet, delete the characters in the Name box, and type ShipCost. Close the property sheet.

Access

Figure 4.24 Resizing and repositioning the calculated control and label

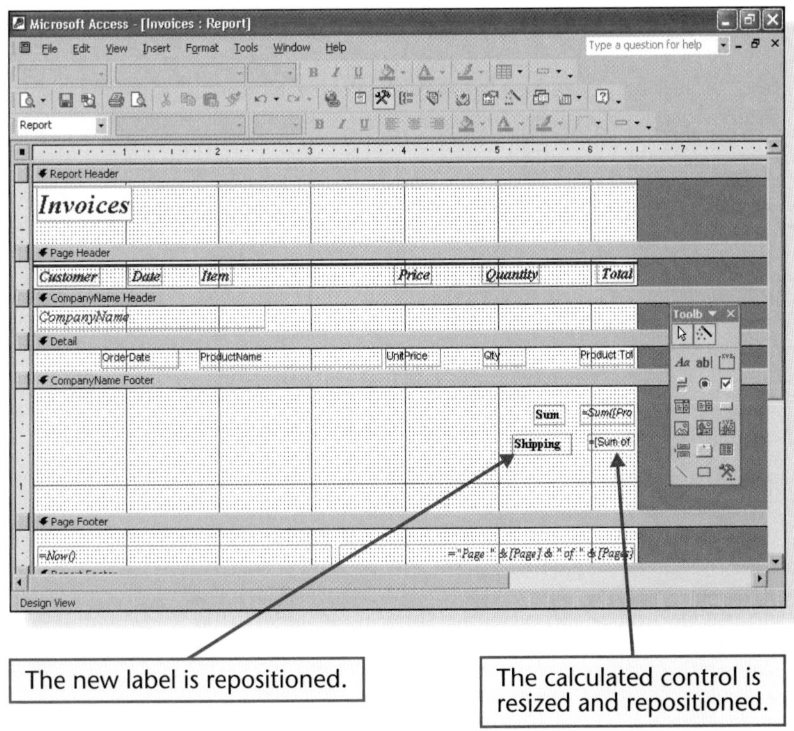

The new label is repositioned.
The calculated control is resized and repositioned.

9. To quickly format the Shipping label to match the existing Sum label, click the Sum label, click Format Painter on the Report Design toolbar, and click the Shipping label.

10. Resize the text box to approximately 0.5″. Move the new text box independently and align it under the Sum of Product Total text box. Then align the Shipping label under the Sum label, and click away to deselect the label (see Figure 4.24).

11 Create another text box and attached label in the CompanyName Footer section. Type **Total Due** in the new label and the expression **=[Sum of Product Total]+[ShipCost]** in the new text box.

12 Format the calculated control as Currency. Reformat the Total Due label to match the Shipping label. Then align the label and text box under the Sum and Shipping controls, resizing as necessary.

13 Save the design changes, and then examine the results in Print Preview (see Figure 4.25).

Figure 4.25 The modified Invoices report in Print Preview

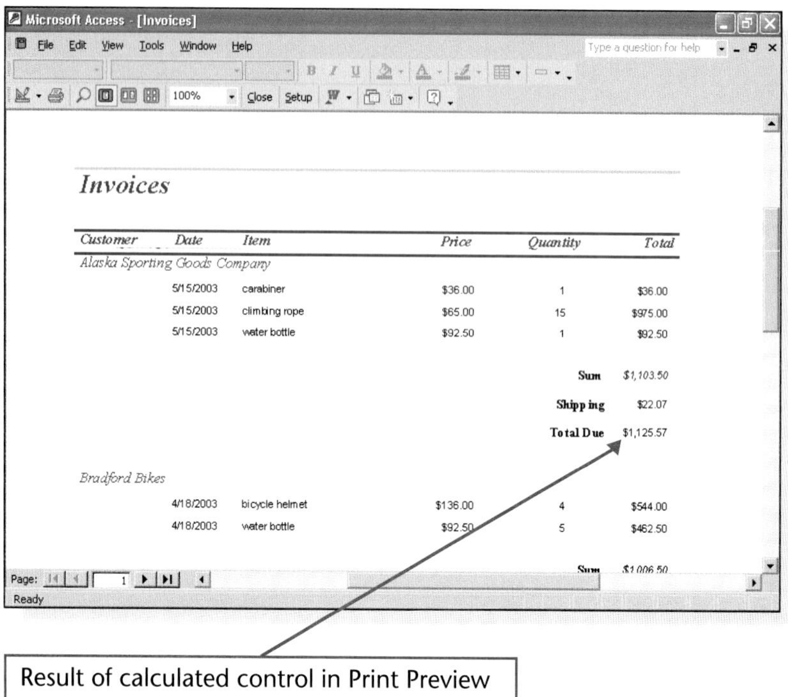

Step Through It™

Exercise 3D: Preview and print a report

1 Examine the report. In order to send an invoice to each customer, you need to modify the report to print only one invoice per page.

2 Switch to Design view. Right-click the CompanyName Header section bar, and click Properties. On the Format tab, select Before Section in the Force New Page property box (see Figure 4.26). Then close the property sheet.

Figure 4.26 Changing the Force New Page property

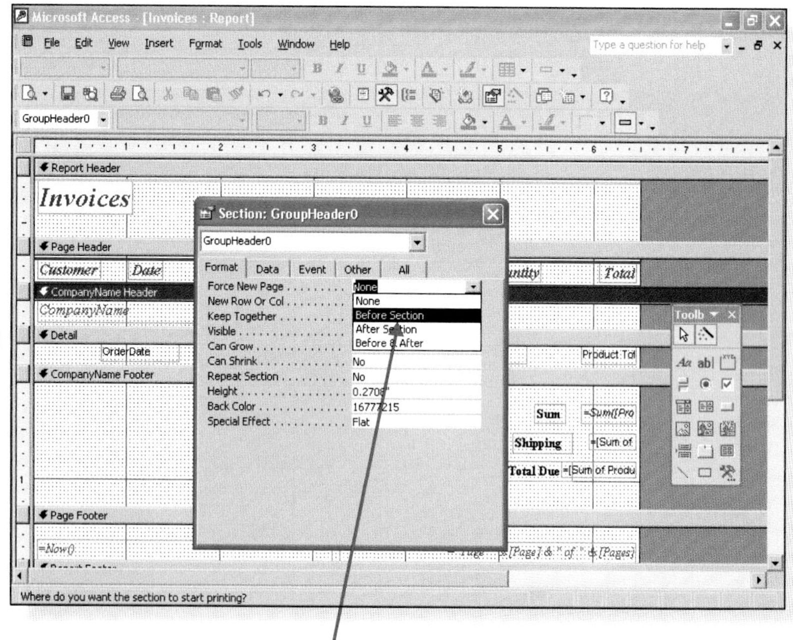

Figure 4.27 Deleting labels in the Report Header section and hiding the section grid

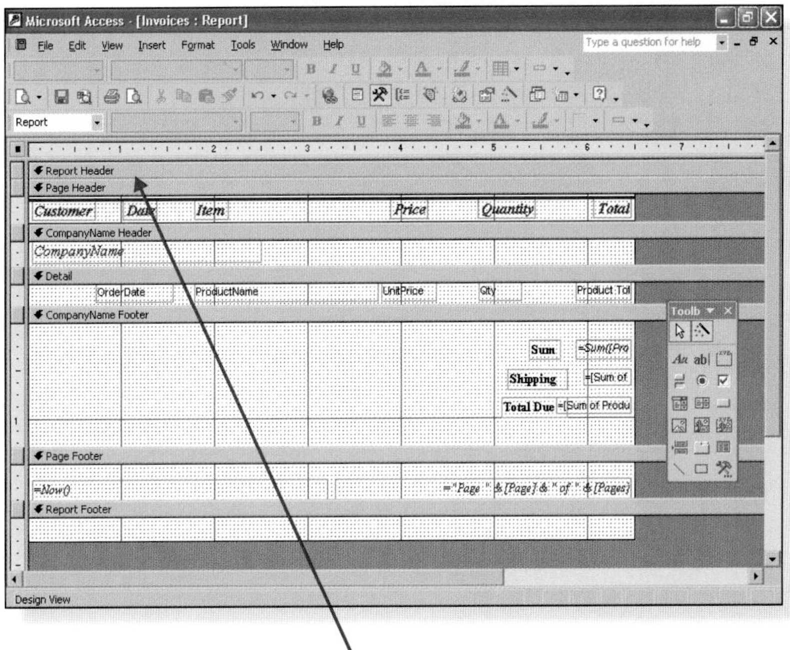

The Report Header section is "closed up" because you won't need a report header on the first page of the Invoices report.

3 Switch to Print Preview and navigate the report. Notice that each page contains invoice data for a single customer.

4 Switch back to Design view. Now you will add the company logo to the Invoices report.

5 In the Report Header section, select and delete the large *Invoices* label and the gray rule above it. Then drag the top of the Page Header section bar upward to hide the grid in the Report Header section (see Figure 4.27).

Figure 4.28 Expanding and modifying the Page Header section

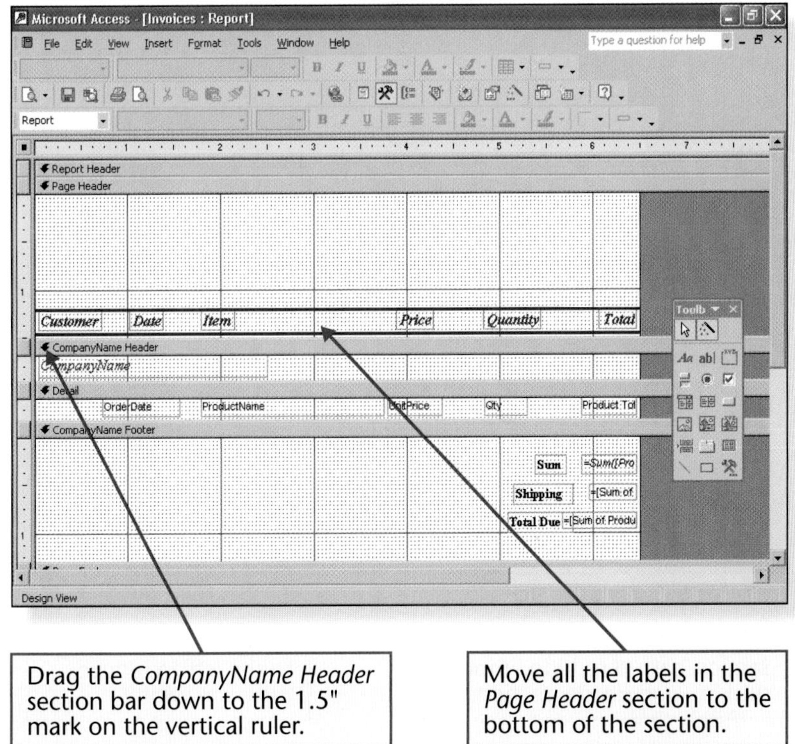

Drag the *CompanyName Header* section bar down to the 1.5" mark on the vertical ruler.

Move all the labels in the *Page Header* section to the bottom of the section.

6 Drag the top of the CompanyName Header section bar down to the 1.5" mark on the vertical ruler to create room for the company logo in the Page Header section.

7 Press and hold Shift and select all the labels in the Page Header section, including the two blue rules.

8 Drag the entire set of controls to the bottom of the section to make room for the logo. Then click away to deselect the controls (see Figure 4.28).

9. In the toolbox, click the Image tool. Then click in the left corner of the empty area in the *Page Header* section.

10. In the Insert Picture dialog box, navigate to the *Lesson 4* folder, and double-click the *Saburo.jpg* file. The logo is inserted in the section.

11. With the logo selected, click the Properties button. On the Format tab of the property sheet, change the Size Mode property to Zoom (see Figure 4.29). Then close the property sheet.

Figure 4.29 Changing the Size Mode property of an image

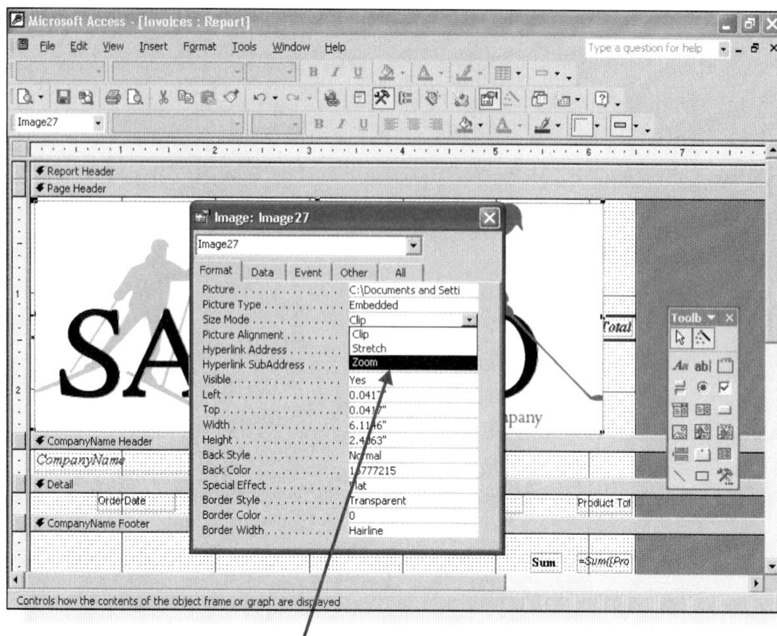

By changing the Size Mode property to *Zoom*, you will be able to resize the image proportionately.

12. Drag a corner handle of the selected image to resize the logo proportionally. Resize the image to be approximately 1" tall. Click and drag the image to center it horizontally over the labels. Move up the CompanyName Header section bar to hide the empty grid above it.

13. Scroll to the left, if necessary, and check the width of the design grid. In order for the report to print properly, the width of the grid must be less than or equal to 6.5". Drag the right side of the grid to the left to resize it (see Figure 4.30).

Figure 4.30 The logo control, resized and centered

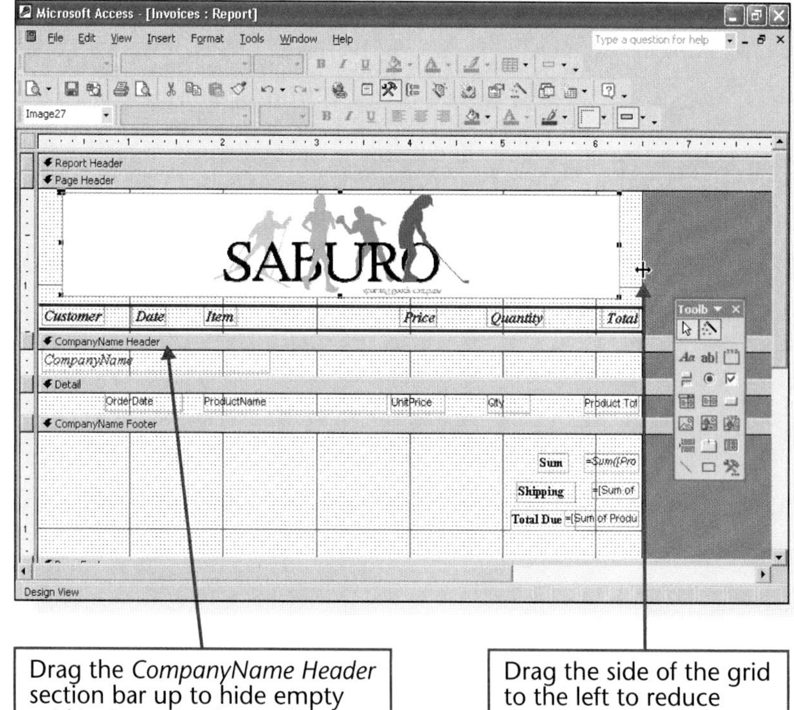

Drag the *CompanyName Header* section bar up to hide empty grid in *Page Header* section.

Drag the side of the grid to the left to reduce the page width.

Figure 4.31 The final Invoices report

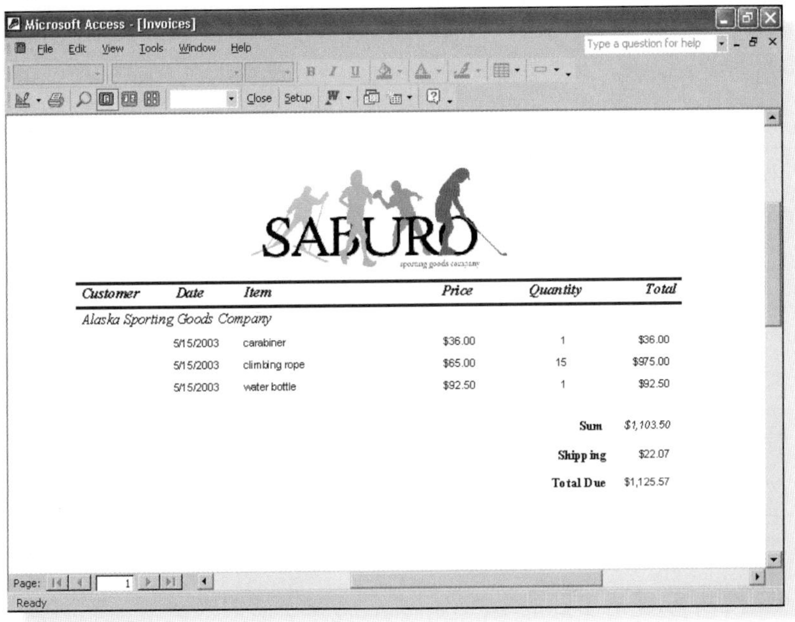

14 Switch to Print Preview and navigate the report (see Figure 4.31). If there are any blank pages, switch to Design view, drag the right side of the grid a bit more to the left, and then return to Print Preview.

15 Click Print on the Print Preview toolbar to print the Invoices report.

16 Return to Design view, save your design changes, and close the Invoices report.

APPLY IT! After finishing Exercise 3, you may test your skills by completing Apply It! Guided Activity 2, Modify a Form and Report.

Exercise 4 Overview: Create a Simple Data Access Page

Microsoft Office Specialist AC2002 8.3

A data access page is a special type of database object that is saved as a Web page. It can be posted on a Web server or a network server, and authorized users who have the appropriate Web browser and Office program components can open the data access page to view and modify the data in the database.

There are different ways to create a data access page; however, the most common method is to use the Page Wizard, which you will do in the following exercise. After you create a data access page, you can use Web Page Preview to see how it will look when viewed using a Web browser.

In the following exercise, you will create a data access page using selected fields from the Customers table in the *Saburo Sporting Goods-Lesson 4.mdb* database. The company sales representatives will then be able to use the data access page to access up-to-date customer information while they are on the road.

Step Through It™
Exercise 4: Create a data access page

1. Restore the Database window to its smaller size and click Pages in the Objects bar. Then double-click the *Create data access page by using wizard* option. The Page Wizard opens.

2. In the first wizard step, select Table: Customers in the Tables/Queries box. Click the Add All Fields button >> to select all the fields. Then double-click the CustID field to move it back to the Available Fields list (see Figure 4.32).

Figure 4.32 Creating a data access page using the Page Wizard

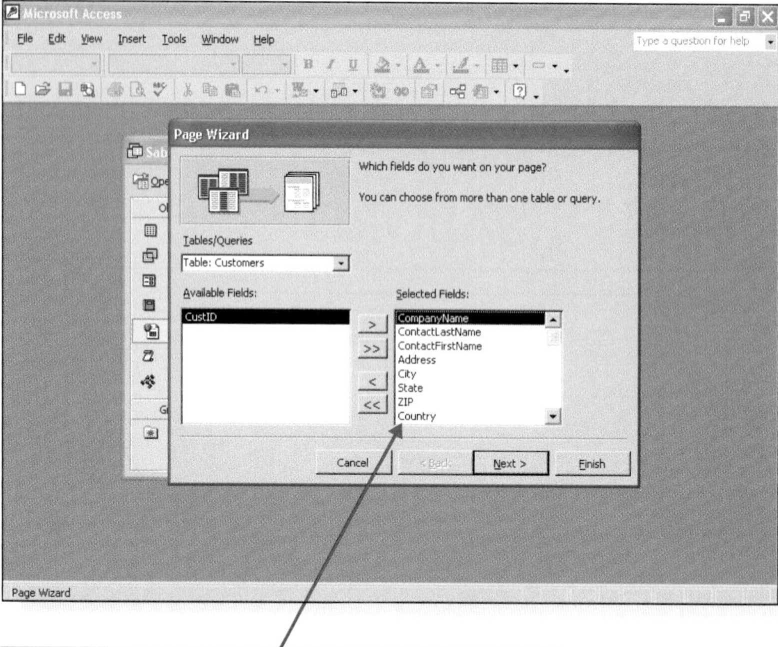

3. In the next wizard step, you do not need grouping levels, so click Next.

4. Click the down arrow in the first text box and select CompanyName for the sorting field. Then click Next.

5. In the last wizard step, change the title to Customer Information. Select the *Open the page* option, and click Finish. The data access page opens in Page view.

6. Use the buttons to view all the records (see Figure 4.33).

Figure 4.33 The Customer Information data access page in Page view

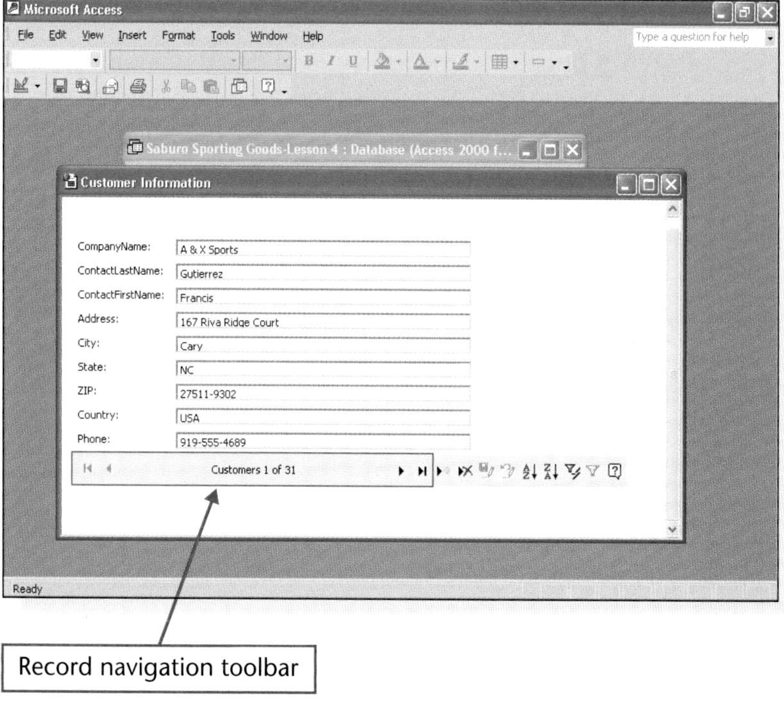

Figure 4.34 Saving a data access page

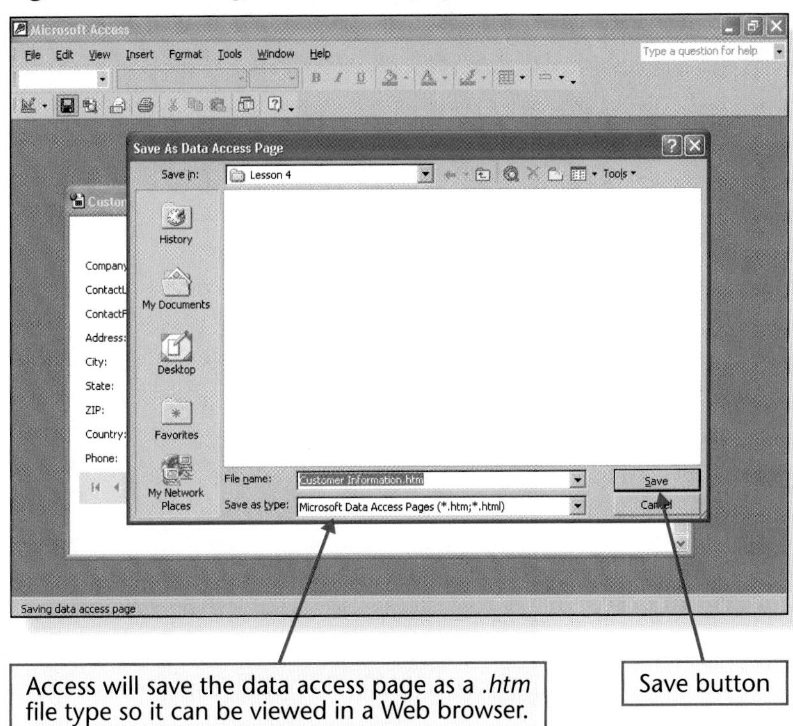

7 Click Save on the Page View toolbar. In the Save As Data Access Page dialog box, accept the file name *Customer Information.htm,* and be sure the page will be saved in the *Lesson 4* folder (see Figure 4.34). Then click Save in the dialog box.

8 If a message box appears indicating that the connection string of the page refers to an absolute path, click OK.

Figure 4.35 Viewing the Customer Information data access page in the Web browser

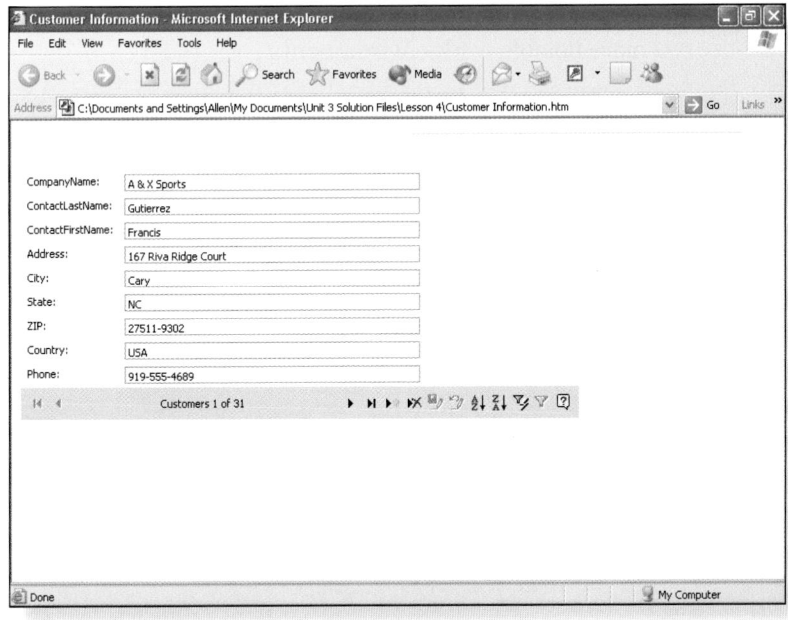

9 Click the View down arrow on the Page View toolbar and select Web Page Preview.

10 You are now viewing the data access page in your Web browser (see Figure 4.35). Use the buttons on the record navigation toolbar to view each record.

11 Close your Web browser. Then close the data access page and the *Saburo Sporting Goods-Lesson 4.mdb* database.

Access

After finishing Exercise 4, you may test your skills by completing Apply It! Guided Activity 3, Create a Data Access Page.

Business Connections

Tapping the Power of a Distributed Workforce

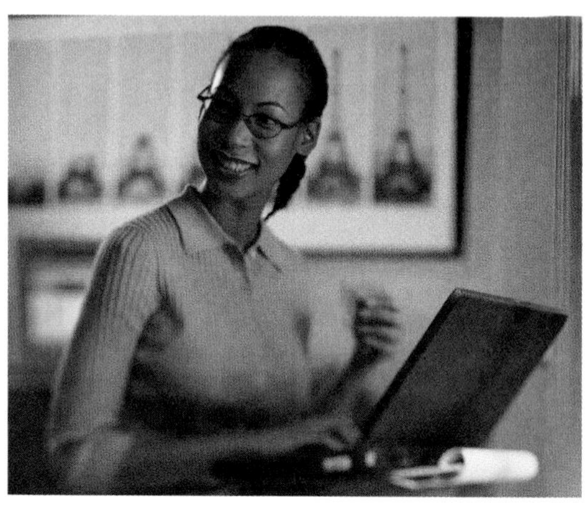

In the "old days," most people worked in a central company building, where they were under the direct surveillance of their supervisor. A daily work schedule was set and adhered to, including a specific time period for lunch. Time off for personal appointments had to be approved by the supervisor. And, regular paychecks were distributed on scheduled days.

Flexible Work Environments

- As computer, network, and communications technologies evolve, more and more businesses are moving toward more flexible work environments.
- New technologies have made distributed networks possible, in which employees can connect computers at home or on the road to the company's network, just as if they were in the same building.
- These changes have helped to develop a distributed workforce in which many more people are working at home, or taking their work on the road with them.

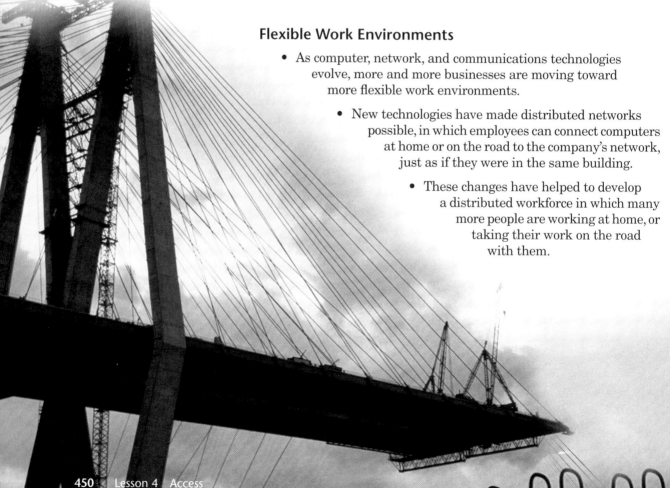

Data Access Pages

- One way Access helps this kind of distributed workforce to function is through data access pages, which are database objects, such as tables and forms that are created as Web pages. By opening a data access page in a Web browser, employees can update database information from any remote location, as long as they can connect to the Internet.

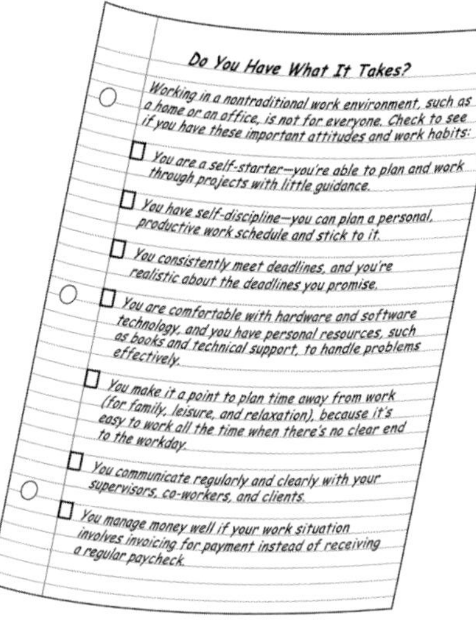

Do You Have What It Takes?

Working in a nontraditional work environment, such as a home or an office, is not for everyone. Check to see if you have these important attitudes and work habits:

- ☐ You are a self-starter—you're able to plan and work through projects with little guidance.
- ☐ You have self-discipline—you can plan a personal, productive work schedule and stick to it.
- ☐ You consistently meet deadlines, and you're realistic about the deadlines you promise.
- ☐ You are comfortable with hardware and software technology, and you have personal resources, such as books and technical support, to handle problems effectively.
- ☐ You make it a point to plan time away from work (for family, leisure, and relaxation), because it's easy to work all the time when there's no clear end to the workday.
- ☐ You communicate regularly and clearly with your supervisors, co-workers, and clients.
- ☐ You manage money well if your work situation involves invoicing for payment instead of receiving a regular paycheck.

Do You Have What It Takes?

- To make working off-site beneficial to both the employee and the employer, a strong set of personal work habits and a good attitude are required.
- The employer must be willing to trust the employee, and the employee must work to build and maintain that trust.

- Working remotely is not ideal for everyone—some employees prefer a more structured environment and clearly defined work hours.
- But, if you are willing to develop the important work habits and attitudes, and a distributed workforce suits the industry in which you work, it may just be the right thing for you!

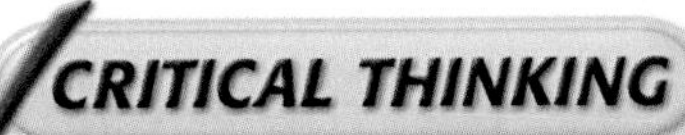

1. **Exaimining Advantages and Disadvantages** What would be some advantages, both to employees and employers, to having employees work away from the central workplace? What would be some disadvantages?
2. **Working Remote** What businesses are likely to benefit from a distributed workforce? What businesses are likely to find a distributed workforce inefficient or impossible to implement?

Procedure Summary

Access Procedure Summary

Create an AutoForm

1. Select the table or query on which you want to base your form.
2. Click the **New Object** down arrow, and select AutoForm from the list.
   OR
   Click **Insert** .... **Alt + I**
   Select **AutoForm** .... **O**
   To create a different type of AutoForm, select Form from the New Object list, and then double-click the type of AutoForm in the New Form dialog box.

Create a Form Using the Form Wizard

1. Open the Forms group in the Database window.
2. Double-click *Create form by using wizard.*
   OR
   Click **New** New.
   Select **Form Wizard**.
   Click **OK**.
   OR
   Click **Insert** .... **Alt + I**
   Select **Form** .... **F**
   Select **Form Wizard**.
   Click **OK**.
3. Enter appropriate responses to the wizard prompts.

Create a Report Using the Report Wizard

1. Open the Reports group in the Database window.
2. Double-click *Create report by using wizard.*
   OR
   Click **New** New.
   Select **Report Wizard**.
   Click **OK**.
   OR
   Click **Insert** .... **Alt + I**
   Select **Report** .... **R**
   Select **Report Wizard**.
   Click **OK**.
3. Enter appropriate responses to the wizard prompts.

Modify Text in a Control

1. Open a form or report in Design view.
2. Maximize the Design view window.
3. Click to select the control.
4. Drag to select the existing text.
5. Type new text.
6. Click away from the control to deselect it.

Move a Control

1. Open a form or report in Design view.
2. Maximize the Design view window.
3. Click to select the control.
4. Move pointer slowly over control until it changes to shape of open hand.
5. Drag control to new location.
6. Click away from control to deselect it.

Move an Attached Control Independently

1. Open a form or report in Design view.
2. Maximize the Design view window.
3. Click to select the control.
4. Move pointer over upper-left selection handle until it changes to shape of a pointing hand.
5. Drag control to new location.
6. Click away from control to deselect it.

Resize a Control

1. Open a form or report in Design view.
2. Maximize the Design view window.
3. Click to select the control.
4. Move pointer over appropriate selection handle until it changes to shape of a double-headed arrow.
5. Drag in appropriate direction to resize.
6. Click away from control to deselect it.

Delete a Control

1. Open a form or report in Design view.
2. Maximize the Design view window.
3. Click to select the control.
4. Press Delete.
   OR
   Click **Edit**. . . . . **Alt + E**
   Select **Delete**. . . . . **D**

Procedure Summary

Access Procedure Summary

Modify Control Properties

1. Open a form or report in Design view.
2. Maximize the Design view window.
3. Click to select the control.
4. Click **Properties** F4
   OR
   Right-click and select Properties from shortcut menu.
   OR
   Click **View** . . . . Alt + V
   Select **Properties** . . . . P
5. Change the appropriate property in the property sheet.
6. Close the property sheet.

Change the Tab Order on a Form

1. Open a form in Design view.
2. Click **View** . . . . Alt + V
3. Select **Tab Order** . . . . B
4. Drag field names to different positions in the tab order.
5. Click **OK**.

Resize a Section

1. Open a form or report in Design view.
2. Maximize the Design view window.
3. Position pointer at top of section bar.
4. When pointer changes shape, drag to resize section.

Create a Calculated Control

1. Open a form or report in Design view.
2. Maximize the Design view window.
3. Click **Toolbox**.
   OR
   Click **View** . . . . Alt + V
   Select **Toolbox** X
4. Select **Text Box**.
5. Click anywhere in blank area of appropriate section.
6. Click in text box and type expression.

Format a Calculated Control

1. Open a form or report in Design view.
2. Maximize the Design view window.
3. Click to select the control.
4. Click Properties.
   OR
   Right-click and select Properties from shortcut menu.
   OR
   Click **View**. **Alt + V**
   Select **Properties** . . . . **P**
5. Change the appropriate property in the property sheet.
6. Close the property sheet.

Insert an Image in a Form or Report

1. Open a form or report in Design view.
2. Maximize the Design view window.
3. Click **Toolbox**.
   OR
   Click **View**. **Alt + V**
   Select **Toolbox** . . . . **X**
4. Select **Image**.
5. Click anywhere in blank area of appropriate section.

Preview and Print a Report

1. Open a report in Print Preview.
2. Click . . . . **Ctrl + P**
   OR
   Click **File** . . . . **Alt + F**
   Select **Print** . . . . **P**

Create a Data Access Page Using the Page Wizard

1. Open the Pages group in the Database window.
2. Double-click *Create data access page by using wizard.*
   OR
   Click **New**.
   Select **Page Wizard**.
   Click **OK**.
   OR
   Click **Insert** . . . . **Alt + I**
   Select **Page** . . . . **P**
   Select **Page Wizard**.
   Click **OK**.

Lesson Review and Exercises

Summary Checklist

- ☑ Can you create different types of AutoForms?
- ☑ Can you create a new form using the Form Wizard?
- ☑ Can you create a new report using the Report Wizard?
- ☑ Do you understand the difference between a label control and a text box control?
- ☑ Do you understand the difference between a bound, unbound, and calculated control?
- ☑ Can you resize and reposition controls in a form or report?
- ☑ Can you change the tab order of the controls in a form?
- ☑ Can you modify control properties?
- ☑ Can you create a calculated control?
- ☑ Can you add an image to a report?
- ☑ Can you preview and print a report?
- ☑ Can you create a data access page?

Key Terms

- AutoForm (p. 427)
- bound control (p. 435)
- calculated control (p. 435)
- controls (p. 435)
- main form (p. 426)
- main/subform (p. 426)
- sections (p. 434)
- subform (p. 426)
- tab order (p. 436)
- toolbox (p. 439)
- unbound control (p. 435)

APPLY IT! **Guided Activities**

1. Create a New Form and Report

The business partners for LawnMowers, a small lawn-mowing business, would like you to create an easy-to-use form for entering appointments and new customer data. In the current database, the Customers table is related to the Appointments table. Thus, you can use an AutoForm to quickly create a main/subform combination that will allow the partners to enter and edit data in both the Customers table and the Appointments table using a single form.

The partners would also like you to create a report that lists all the LawnMowers appointments, grouped by mower. The All Appointments query, which has already been created for you, can be used as the underlying data source for the report. Both the mower names and customer names have been concatenated into full names, and the query results are sorted by mower name and then by appointment date. Follow these steps to create a new form and report:

a. Open the *LawnMowers-Lesson 4.mdb* database.

b. In the Tables group, click the Customers table to select it (but do not open it).

c. Using the New Object button on the Database toolbar, click AutoForm **(see Figure 4.36)**.

Figure 4.36 The newly created AutoForm

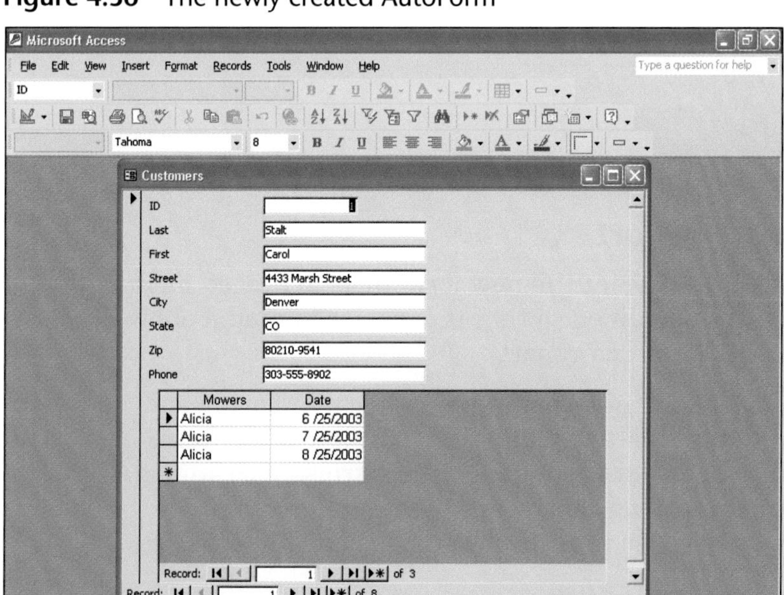

Access

d. Save the new form as Customers and Appointments, and then close it.

e. In the Reports group, double-click *Create report by using wizard*.

f. Base the report on the All Appointments query, and include all four fields in the report.

g. Select the options to view the data by appointments and group the data by mower.

h. Sort the detail records in ascending order by date, and choose a Stepped layout, Portrait orientation, and a Corporate style. Name the report LawnMowers Appointments and preview the report **(see Figure 4.37)**. Then close the report.

Figure 4.37 The LawnMowers Appointments report

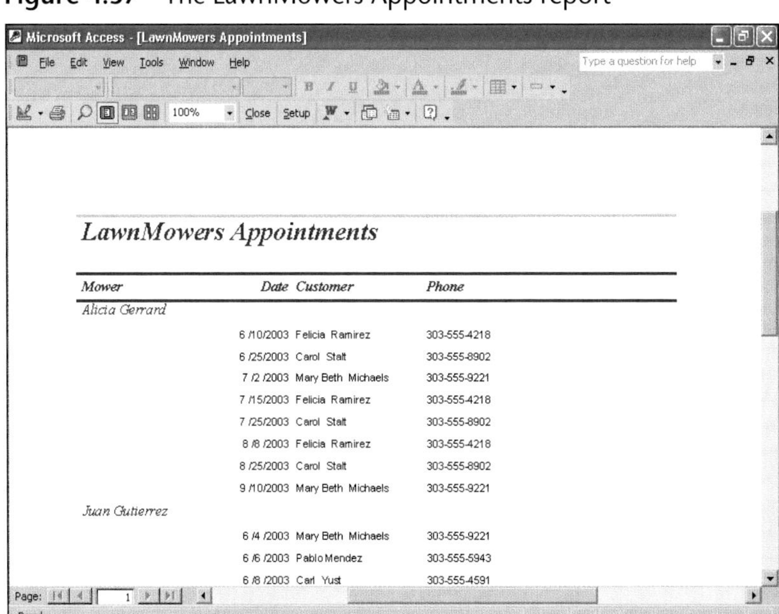

2. Modify a Form and Report

The partners of LawnMowers want the new form to be arranged more neatly and the report to be modified so that it is easier to read. Follow these steps to modify the form and report:

a. Examine the Customers and Appointments form in Form view. The changes you would like to make to the design of the form include: deleting the ID label and text box controls, rearranging and resizing the remaining controls in the main form, and shortening the subform so that the two navigation toolbars are farther apart.

b. Switch to Design view and maximize the form design window.

c. Select the ID label and text box and delete them.

d. Rearrange the remaining fields in the main form to look like **Figure 4.38**. (Switch frequently between Design view and Form view to check the results of your changes.)

Figure 4.38 The modified Customers and Appointments form

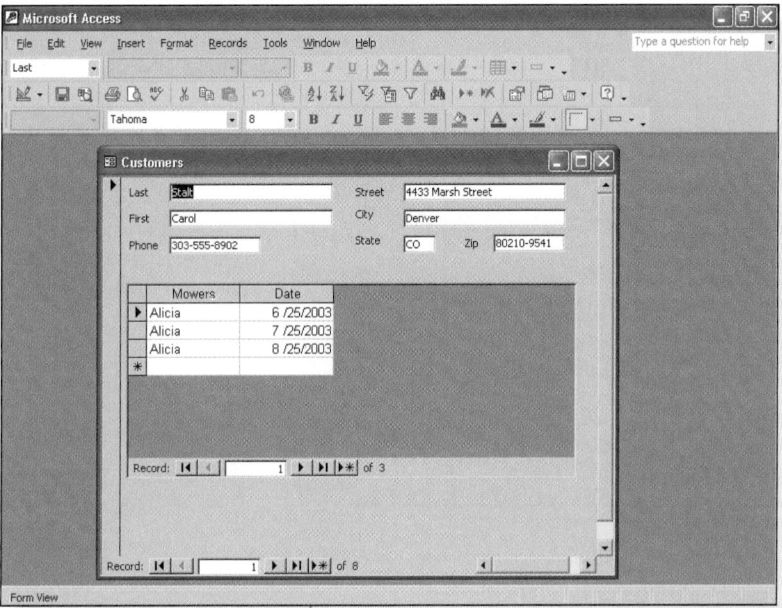

e. Move up the subform so that its navigation bar is positioned closer to the subform data. (You use the same techniques to move the subform as you do to move label and text box controls.)

f. Switch to Form view and check the tab order in the main form. Return to Design view and change the tab order so that the cursor jumps to the Phone field after the First field when you tab through the fields on the main form. Return to Form view and test the new tab order.

g. Save the design changes and close the form.

h. Examine the LawnMowers Appointments report in Print Preview. The overall design of the report is pretty good; you just need to resize and reposition some controls to improve the report's appearance.

i. Switch to Design view and make the Date text box in the Detail section a bit wider by dragging the left handle to the left. Then move the Date text box to the left, away from the Customer text box.

j. If necessary, move the Date label in the Page Header section to the left, to align it over the Date details (check your changes in Print Preview as you work).

k. Shorten the Phone label and text box, and then move them to the right.

l. Move the Customer label and text box to the right to create well-separated columns on the report.

m. Examine the design changes in Print Preview **(see Figure 4.39)**.

Figure 4.39 The modified LawnMowers Appointments report

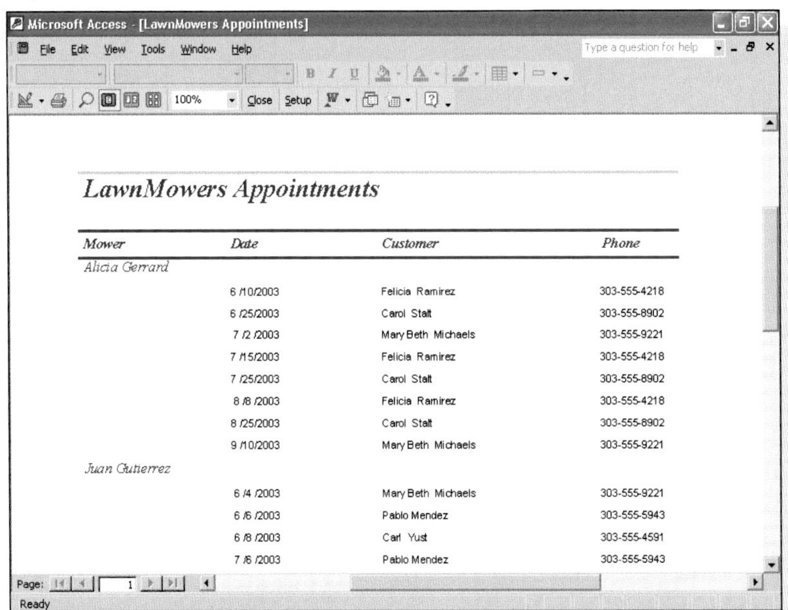

n. The partners would like you to modify the report so that each partner's appointments print on a separate page. Return to Design view. Move down the Mower Header section bar in order to lengthen the Page Header section. Then reposition all the labels (including the rules) at the top of the Page Header section to the bottom of the Page Header section.

o. Move the LawnMowers Appointments label and the gray rule from the top-left corner of the Report Header section to the top-left corner of the Page Header section. Then move up the Page Header section to hide the Report Header section grid.

p. Click the Mower Header section bar and click Properties. Change the Force New Page property to Before Section. Save your design changes.

q. Preview the report and then print it. Then close the report.

3. Create a Data Access Page

Since LawnMowers is just a small summer business, each of the partners works from home. The partners would like to be able to view and modify the database from home using their Web browsers. Follow these steps to create a data access page:

a. In the Pages group, double-click *Create data access page by using wizard.*

b. Base the data access page on the All Appointments query and include all fields in the data access page.

c. Do not add any grouping levels to the data access page, and sort the page first by mower and then by date.

d. When the wizard asks you to select the table you wish to update, choose Appointments.

e. Name the data access page LM Appointments and open the page in Page view **(see Figure 4.40)**. Navigate the records in the data access page.

Figure 4.40 The LM Appointments data access page

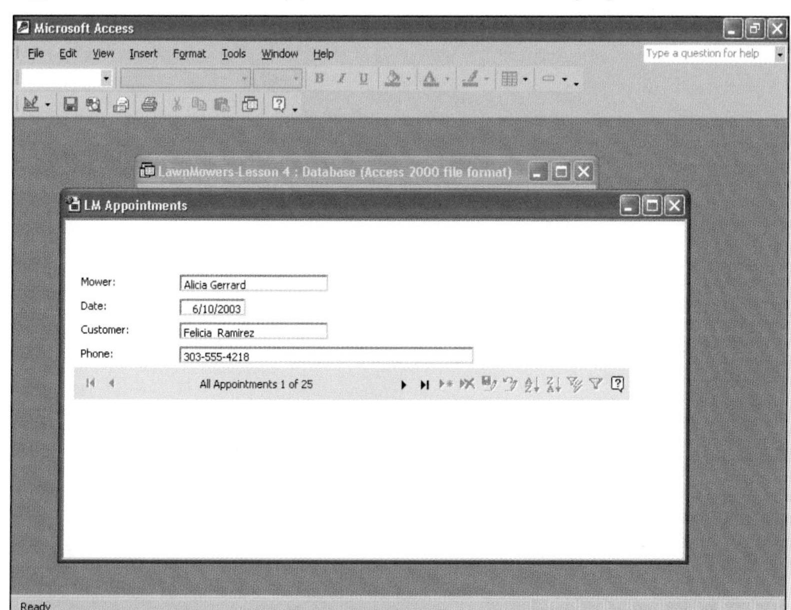

f. Save the data access page in the *Lesson 4* folder of your *Unit 3* folder. Accept the file name that Access suggests, *LM Appointments.htm*. (If necessary, click OK when Access displays the message box about the connection string.)

g. Switch to Web Page Preview and view the data access page in your Web browser.

h. Close your Web browser and close the data access page. Then close the *LawnMowers-Lesson 4.mdb* database.

Do It Yourself

1. Create a Form

As the database manager for WoodStarts, a small woodshop business, you feel it is necessary to add a form to the database that employees can use to enter the dates and number of hours they worked.

a. Open the *WoodStarts-Lesson 4.mdb* database.

b. Create a new form using the Form Wizard. Build the form based on the Hours table, and include all fields except the ID field **(see Figure 4.41)**.

Figure 4.41 Creating a form using the Form Wizard

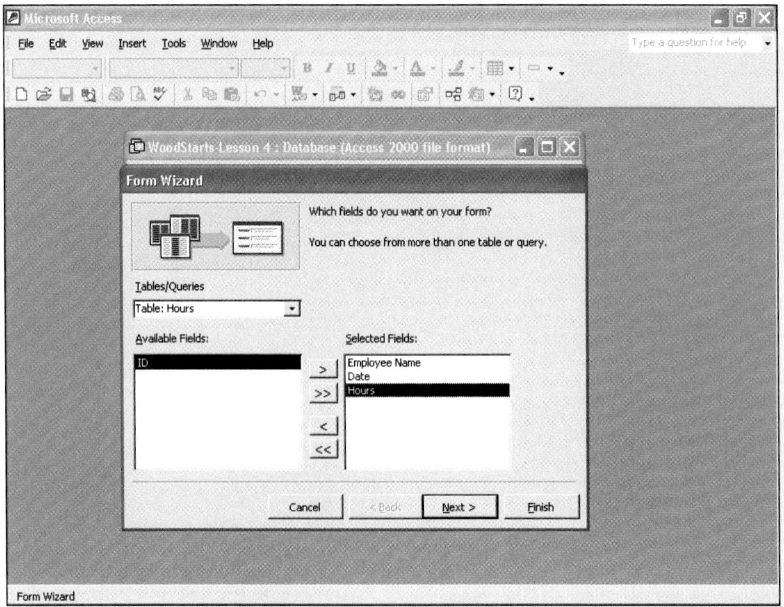

c. Use a Columnar layout and a Standard style. Name the form Hours Worked.

d. Examine the form in Form view. Then switch to Design view and make the Hours text box narrower (just wide enough to display 3 digits).

e. Switch to Form view to check your changes. Then save and close the form.

2. Create a Report

In addition to the new form, you also want to add a new report to the database for the accountant who calculates each employee's pay.

a. Use the Report Wizard to build a report based on the Payroll Hours query, and include all the fields in the report.

b. View the data by Employees and group the data by the LastName field.

c. Sort the detail records in ascending order by date.

d. In the Summary Options dialog box, select Sum for the Hours field.

e. Use a Stepped layout, Portrait orientation, and a Corporate style.

f. Name the report Payroll Information, and then preview it **(see Figure 4.42)**.

Figure 4.42 The Payroll Information report

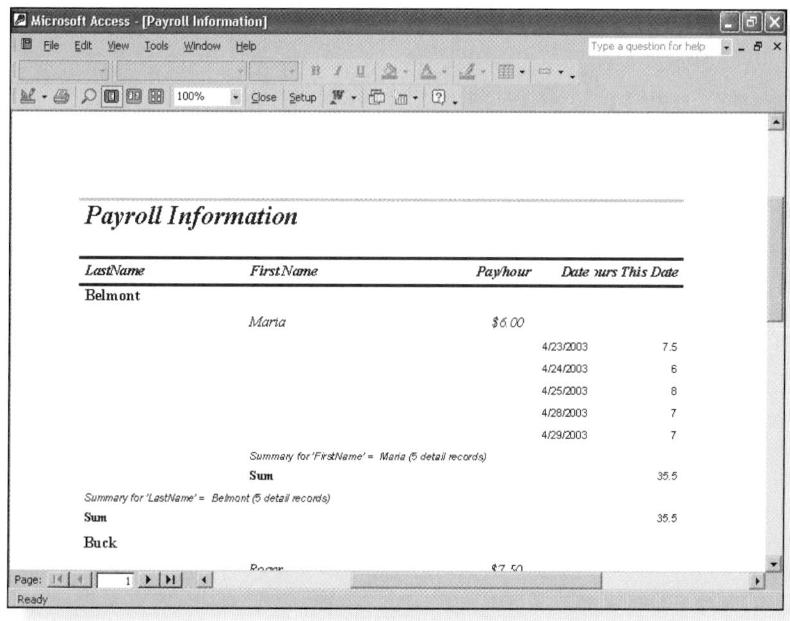

Access

3. Modify and Print a Report

Now that you have created the new report for the accountant, you want to make sure it is easy to read and contains all the necessary information. Therefore, you must make some modifications in Design view.

a. Edit the LastName label in the Page Header section to add a space between the words *Last* and *Name*.

b. Change the Hours This Date label in the Page Header section to Hours.

c. Move the FirstName and Pay/hour text boxes from the FirstName Header section to the LastName Header section.

d. Use the Format Painter to match the format of the FirstName and Pay/hour text boxes to the LastName text box.

e. Move up the Detail section to hide the FirstName Header section.

f. Delete the long *"= Summary for ..."* text boxes in the FirstName Footer and LastName Footer sections.

g. In the FirstName Footer section, change the text of the Sum label to Total Hours. Then move the Total Hours label to the right and position it next to the *=Sum([Hours])* text box.

h. In the LastName Footer section, delete the Sum label and the calculated control.

i. Lengthen the FirstName Footer section, and add a text box (and attached label). Type Gross Pay in the new label. Lengthen the new text box and type the expression =Sum([Hours]*[Pay/hour]). Change the Format property of the new text box to Currency.

j. Position the new controls under the Total Hours label and the *=Sum([Hours])* text box. Use the Format Painter to match the format of all the controls in the FirstName Footer section to the Total Hours label **(see Figure 4.43)**.

k. In the Report Footer section, move the Grand Total label to the right and position it next to the text box. Edit the expression in the text box to read =Sum([Hours]*[Pay/hour]). Change the Format property of the calculated control to Currency. Then use the Format Painter to match the format (type style and font size) of the calculated control to the format of the Grand Total label.

Figure 4.43 Adding a calculated control

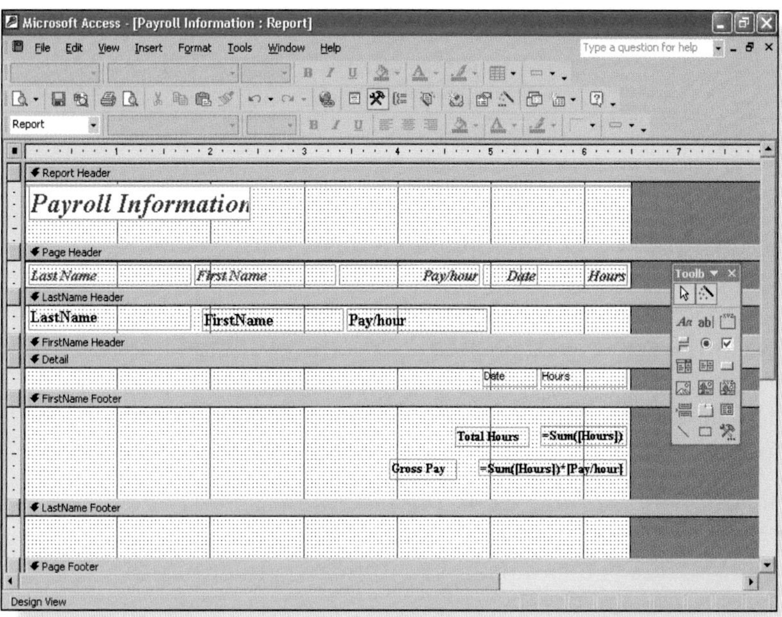

1. Move, align, and resize labels and text boxes as necessary to make the report attractive and easy to read. Switch to Print Preview and analyze both the content and design of the entire report **(see Figure 4.44)**.

Figure 4.44 The modified Payroll Information report

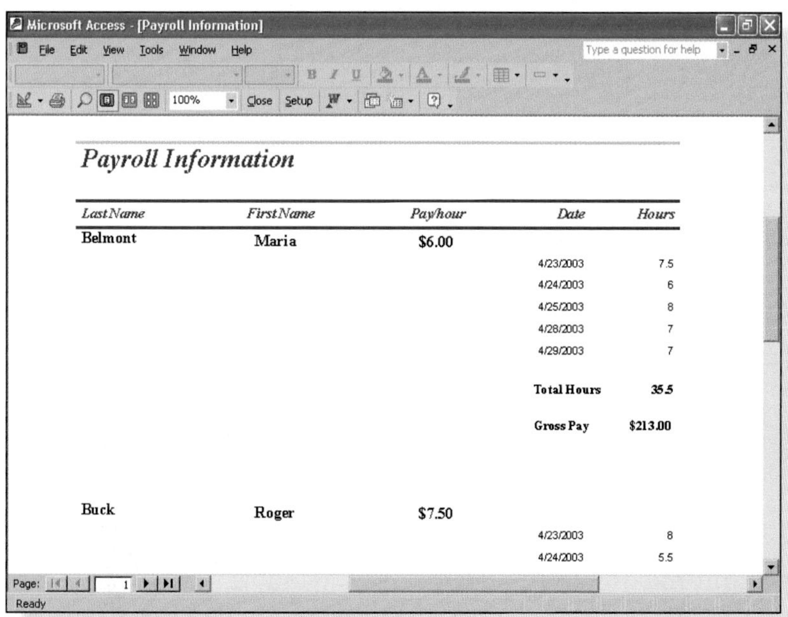

m. Print the report. Then save the design changes and close the report. Close the *Woodstarts-Lesson 4.mdb* database.

Challenge Yourself

Modify a Form

In this lesson, the only modifications you made to a form were to move and resize controls and modify the tab order. However, there are many other changes you can make to enhance the appearance or usefulness of a form. In fact, the different types of modifications you made to reports can also be applied to forms. In addition, the formatting techniques you applied to datasheets in Lesson 3 can also be applied to both forms and reports.

Open the Suppliers form in the *Saburo Sporting Goods-Lesson 4.mdb* database and examine it in Form view **(see Figure 4.45)**. The form is certainly functional as it is, but you can easily customize it to enhance its appearance and usefulness.

Figure 4.45 Suppliers form in Form view before design modifications

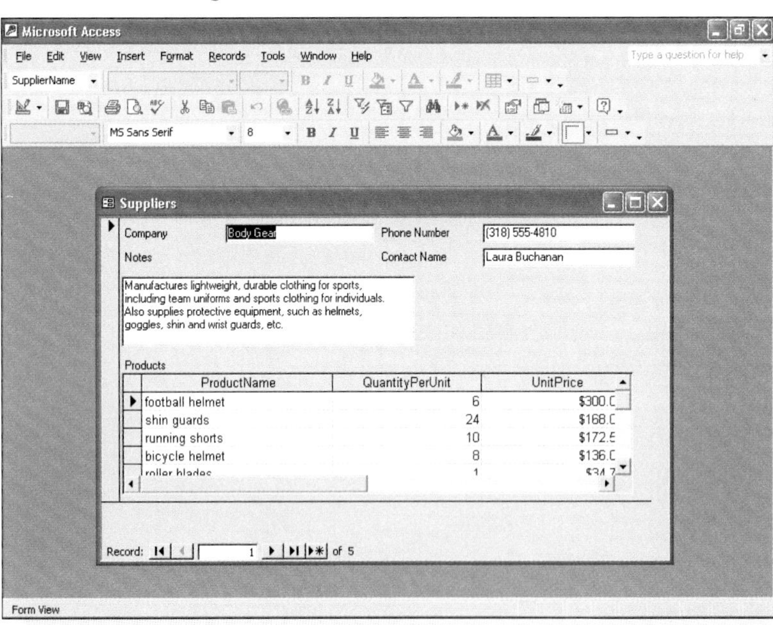

Switch to Design view and maximize the design view window. Using the techniques you learned in this and previous lessons, make the

following modifications to the form. Remember to switch frequently between Design view and Form view to see the results of your changes.

Expand the Form Header section and insert the Saburo company logo (the *Saburo.jpg* file stored in the *Lesson 4* subfolder in the *Unit 3* folder). Change the Size Mode property to Zoom, and then size and position the logo attractively.

Now change all the labels in the main form to a different type style and type size. Select the Company label and change the font to 11-point Times New Roman and apply bold formatting. Change all the labels in the main form to match the Company label, and then resize the labels to fit. Adjust the spacing between the labels and text boxes in the main form as necessary.

Change the background color of the Form Header section to white, and change the background color of the Detail section to light blue. Expand the Detail section and reposition and resize the subform control as necessary. Modify the Caption property for the labels in the subform to add spaces between the words in the labels.

Your finished form should resemble **Figure 4.46**. Save your design changes. Then close the form, close the database, and exit Access.

Figure 4.46 Suppliers form in Form view after design modifications

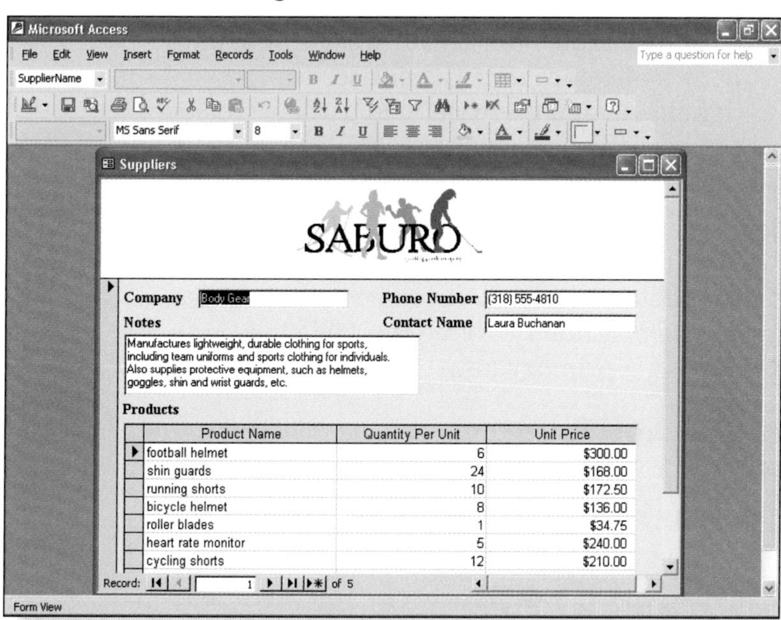

Access

Unit 3 Applications and Projects

Apply Your Knowledge

Your school offers a business class in retail sales, and one of the class projects is to help manage the Snack Shack near the cafeteria from 11 a.m. to 1 p.m. every day. The Snack Shack is staffed by volunteer workers for class credit, and it sells snack items to students during the lunch period. Your project in this class is to use your Access database skills to create a data management system to track daily profits.

1. Create a Database and Create Tables

a. Launch Access and create a new, blank database. Name the database Snack Shack, and save it in the *Unit Applications and Projects* subfolder in your *Unit 3* folder.

b. A list of snack items, with prices and costs, has been kept in an Excel file named *Items.xls* (located in the *Unit Applications and Projects* subfolder in the *Unit 3* folder). Import the data in the Items worksheet into a new table named Items. Check the data before you import it, to make sure that the entries are appropriate for each field. Assign the Item field as the primary key field. After you import the data, make sure the Price field and the Cost field each have the data type Currency.

c. Using Design view, create a table to store the daily beginning and ending inventory quantities for each item. Create the following fields in the table and assign appropriate data types: ItemName, Date, BeginQty, EndQty. Name the table Inventory. You do not need to assign a primary key.

2. Define Relationships and Enforce Referential Integrity

a. Establish a one-to-many relationship between the Items and Inventory tables.

b. Enforce referential integrity, but do not choose any cascading options.

3. Modify Table Design

a. Create appropriate captions for the ItemName, BeginQty, and EndQty fields in the Inventory table.

b. Create an input mask for the Date field in the Inventory table so that the field will only accept data typed in the Short Date format.

c. To reduce errors in recording the daily inventory, you decide to make the ItemName field in the Inventory table a Lookup field that looks up the items in the Items table. Use the Lookup Wizard to change the ItemName field into a Lookup field.

4. Import Data and Format a Datasheet

a. One of the other Snack Shack volunteers recorded the inventory data for the last few days in an Excel file named *Inventory.xls* (located in the *Unit Applications and Projects* subfolder in the *Unit 3* folder). Import that data into the Inventory table in your Snack Shack database.

b. Examine the Inventory table datasheet. Apply bold formatting and change the font color to royal blue. Change the background color to pale yellow and adjust the column widths as appropriate **(see Figure 1)**.

Figure 1 The formatted Inventory table datasheet

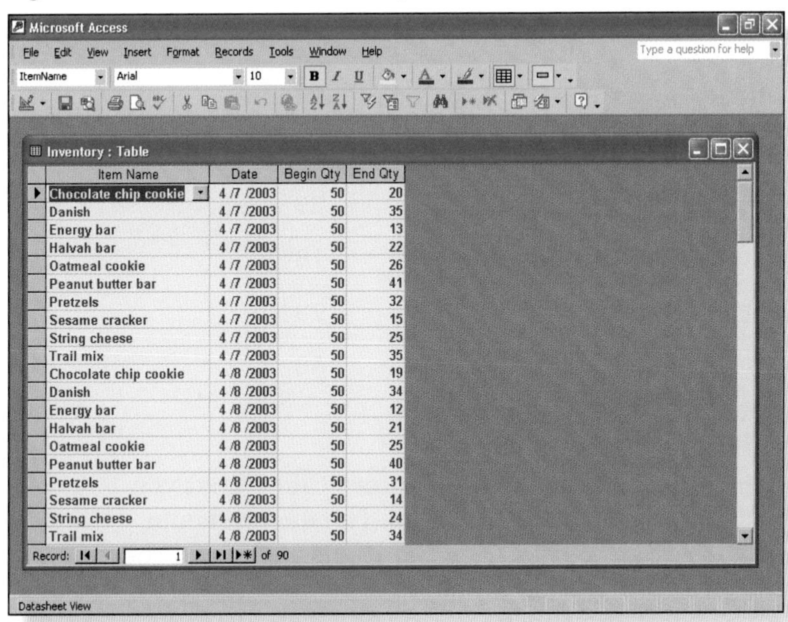

Item Name	Date	Begin Qty	End Qty
Chocolate chip cookie	4 /7 /2003	50	20
Danish	4 /7 /2003	50	35
Energy bar	4 /7 /2003	50	13
Halvah bar	4 /7 /2003	50	22
Oatmeal cookie	4 /7 /2003	50	26
Peanut butter bar	4 /7 /2003	50	41
Pretzels	4 /7 /2003	50	32
Sesame cracker	4 /7 /2003	50	15
String cheese	4 /7 /2003	50	25
Trail mix	4 /7 /2003	50	35
Chocolate chip cookie	4 /8 /2003	50	19
Danish	4 /8 /2003	50	34
Energy bar	4 /8 /2003	50	12
Halvah bar	4 /8 /2003	50	21
Oatmeal cookie	4 /8 /2003	50	25
Peanut butter bar	4 /8 /2003	50	40
Pretzels	4 /8 /2003	50	31
Sesame cracker	4 /8 /2003	50	14
String cheese	4 /8 /2003	50	24
Trail mix	4 /8 /2003	50	34

5. Enter Records in a Datasheet and Create and Use a Form

a. Enter the inventory records shown in **Table 1** into the Inventory table.

Table 1

Item Name	Date	Begin Qty	End Qty
Chocolate chip cookie	4/18/2003	50	23
Danish	4/18/2003	50	38
Energy bar	4/18/2003	50	16
Halvah bar	4/18/2003	50	29
Oatmeal cookie	4/18/2003	50	25

b. One of the other Snack Shack volunteers just handed you some more inventory data to be entered, but the data are not in the same sequence as the fields in the Inventory table. You decide it will be easier to input the data if you use a form. Create a columnar AutoForm, and rearrange the controls so that they appear in the same order as in **Table 2**. Change the tab order as necessary to make data entry more efficient. Save the form as Inventory Form, and then enter the records shown in **Table 2**.

Table 2

Date	Item Name	Begin Qty	End Qty
4/18/2003	Peanut butter bar	50	44
4/18/2003	Pretzels	50	35
4/18/2003	Sesame cracker	50	18
4/18/2003	String cheese	50	28
4/18/2003	Trail mix	50	38

6. Create a Query

a. Create a query from the Items and Inventory tables that you can use to calculate the daily item profits. The query should display the item, cost, and price from the Items table, and the date, beginning inventory, and ending inventory from the Inventory table. Name the query Snack Shack Profits.

b. Sort the query first by date and then by item. (*Hint:* Access performs multiple sorts from left to right in the order the fields appear in the query design grid. Therefore, you may need to move the Date field in the design grid so that it appears before the Item field.)

c. To determine the daily profits, you must add several calculated fields to the query. In the first calculated field, you want to determine the quantity sold for each item each day. Add a calculated field to the query that subtracts the ending inventory from the beginning inventory. The expression is QtySold:=[BeginQty]-[EndQty].

d. In the next calculated field, you want to determine the revenue earned for each item each day. Add a calculated field that multiplies the quantity sold by the price. The expression is Revenue:=[Qty Sold]*[Price].

e. Now you want to determine the cost of each item sold each day, or the cost of goods sold (COGS). Add a calculated field that multiples the quantity sold by the cost. The expression is COGS:=[QtySold]*[Cost].

f. Finally, you want to determine the profit realized for each item sold each day. Add a calculated field that subtracts the cost of goods sold from the revenue. The expression is Profit:=[Revenue]-[COGS].

g. If necessary, format the Revenue, COGS, and Profit fields to be Currency. (Access may have already done this for you.)

7. Create and Modify a Report

a. Use the Report Wizard to create a report of Snack Shack daily profits. Base the report on the Snack Shack Profits query, and include only the Date, Item, and Profit fields.

b. Since you want a report of daily profits, you must group the report by Date. Notice however, that Access automatically assumes you want a monthly report. To group the data in the report by day instead of month, click the Grouping Options button and select Day in the Grouping intervals box.

c. Sort the detail records in the report first by Date and then by Item. Add a summary option of Sum to the Profit field.

d. Select the Stepped layout and the Corporate style. Name the report Snack Shack Daily Profits.

e. Examine the report. Modify the report controls and properties as necessary to model your report after the one shown in **Figure 2**. After making the design changes, preview and print the report. Then close the report and close the *Snack Shack.mdb* database.

Figure 2 The Snack Shack Daily Profits report

Microsoft Access - [Snack Shack Daily Profits]

File Edit View Tools Window Help

Snack Shack Daily Profits

Date	*Item*	*Profit*
Monday, April 07, 2003		
	Chocolate chip cookie	$15.00
	Danish	$15.00
	Energy bar	$27.75
	Halvah bar	$8.40
	Oatmeal cookie	$12.00
	Peanut butter bar	$3.15
	Pretzels	$3.60
	Sesame cracker	$7.00
	String cheese	$12.50
	Trail mix	$10.50
	Sum	*$114.90*
Tuesday, April 08, 2003		
	Chocolate chip cookie	$15.50
	Danish	$16.00

Page: 1

Ready

What's Wrong With This Picture?

The report shown in **Figure 3** was created using the Report Wizard. Using what you've learned about creating reports, list all the flaws you find, and describe how you would avoid or fix the problems.

Figure 3 This report has many flaws. How many can you find?

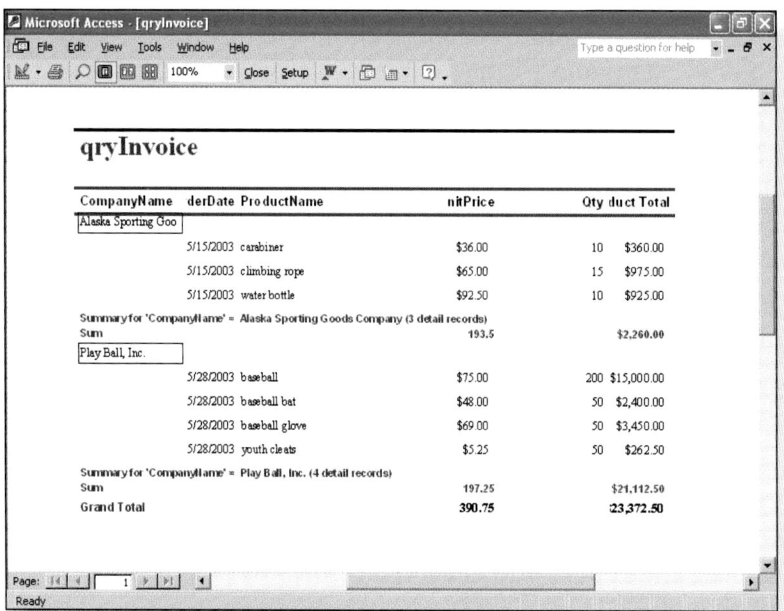

Microsoft Access - [qryInvoice]

File Edit View Tools Window Help

qryInvoice

CompanyName	derDate	ProductName	nitPrice	Qty	duct Total
Alaska Sporting Goo					
	5/15/2003	carabiner	$36.00	10	$360.00
	5/15/2003	climbing rope	$65.00	15	$975.00
	5/15/2003	water bottle	$92.50	10	$925.00
Summary for 'CompanyName' = Alaska Sporting Goods Company (3 detail records)					
Sum			193.5		$2,260.00
Play Ball, Inc.					
	5/28/2003	baseball	$75.00	200	$15,000.00
	5/28/2003	baseball bat	$48.00	50	$2,400.00
	5/28/2003	baseball glove	$69.00	50	$3,450.00
	5/28/2003	youth cleats	$5.25	50	$262.50
Summary for 'CompanyName' = Play Ball, Inc. (4 detail records)					
Sum			197.25		$21,112.50
Grand Total			390.75		23,372.50

Page: 1

Ready

Cross-Curriculum Project

Assume that the Honors Society at your school runs a tutoring service. Tutors get extra credit for tutoring in their strongest subjects, and students who need help can schedule free tutoring sessions.

Working either on a team or individually, create a database named Tutoring Service to track the tutors, their subjects, their availability, and their hours spent tutoring, and to make appointments for students with specific tutors.

Tables. You'll need three tables in the Tutoring Service database: (1) a Tutors table to store data about the students who tutor; (2) a Students table to store data about the students who sign up for tutoring; and (3) an Appointments table (junction table) to store appointment data. Be sure to include a primary key in both the Tutors and the Students tables; however, do not assign a primary key in the Appointments table. The fields and relationships between the tables in the database should look similar to the ones shown in **Figure 4**.

Figure 4 Sample fields and relationships in Tutoring Service database

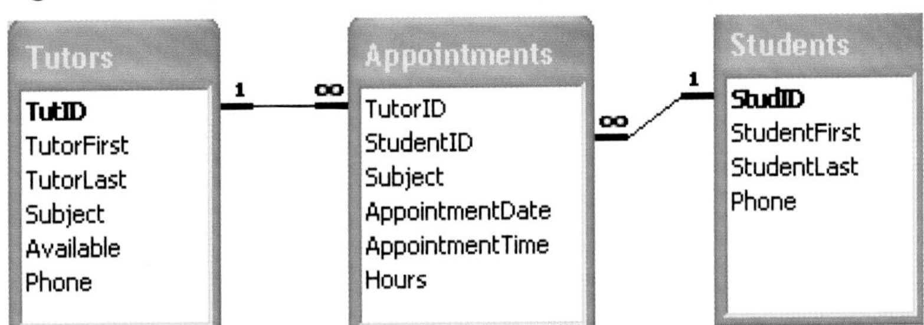

Forms. You'll need to add some data to all three tables. Add at least 4 records to the Tutors table; 8 records to the Students table; and 15–20 records to the Appointments table. Data entry will be easier if you create a main/subform that shows tutor records in the main form and that tutor's scheduled appointments in the subform.

Queries and Reports. After you have entered data in the tables, create two reports: (1) a Tutoring Hours for Extra Credit report that contains detail and summary information regarding the hours spent tutoring, grouped by tutor, and (2) a Tutor Appointments report that lists each tutor's appointments (with student name, date, time, hours, and subject for each appointment). It's easier to create reports if you first create queries upon which to base the reports.

PowerPoint®

Business Presentations

Unit Contents

PowerPoint

Unit Objectives

1. Navigate PowerPoint views and slide shows.
2. Manage files and folders.
3. Preview and print presentation components.
4. Create a presentation using the AutoContent Wizard.
5. Insert, edit, and modify text.
6. Manipulate slides.
7. Create hyperlinks.
8. Create a presentation using a design template and customize a design template and a slide layout.
9. Create a presentation from a blank presentation and by importing text from Word.
10. Insert and modify clip art and a bit-mapped image.
11. Create and customize a table, a chart, and OfficeArt elements.
12. Insert sound effects and movies.
13. Manage slide masters.
14. Animate your presentation.
15. Set up and deliver a presentation.
16. Prepare a presentation for delivery on another computer.
17. Set up a review cycle and manage a reviewed presentation.
18. Publish a presentation to the Web.
19. Set up and schedule an online broadcast.

Lesson 1

Introducing PowerPoint

Lesson Exercise Objectives

After completing this lesson, you'll be able to do the following tasks:

1. Navigate PowerPoint views and slide shows
2. Manage files and folders
3. Preview and print presentation components
4. Create a presentation using the AutoContent Wizard
5. Insert, edit, and modify text
6. Manipulate slides
7. Create hyperlinks

Key Terms

- AutoContent Wizard (p. 488)
- boilerplate text (p. 488)
- demote (p. 494)
- indent level (p. 494)
- object (p. 481)
- object area (p. 481)
- placeholder (p. 481)
- presentation (p. 478)
- promote (p. 494)
- Rich Text Format (RTF) (p. 483)
- splitter bar (p. 479)
- subtitle (p. 481)
- text area (p. 481)
- thumbnail (p. 479)
- title (p. 481)
- title area (p. 481)
- title slide (p. 481)

Microsoft Office Specialist Activities

PP2002: 1.1, 1.2, 2.2, 4.1, 4.8, 4.10, 5.1, 6.4, 7.3

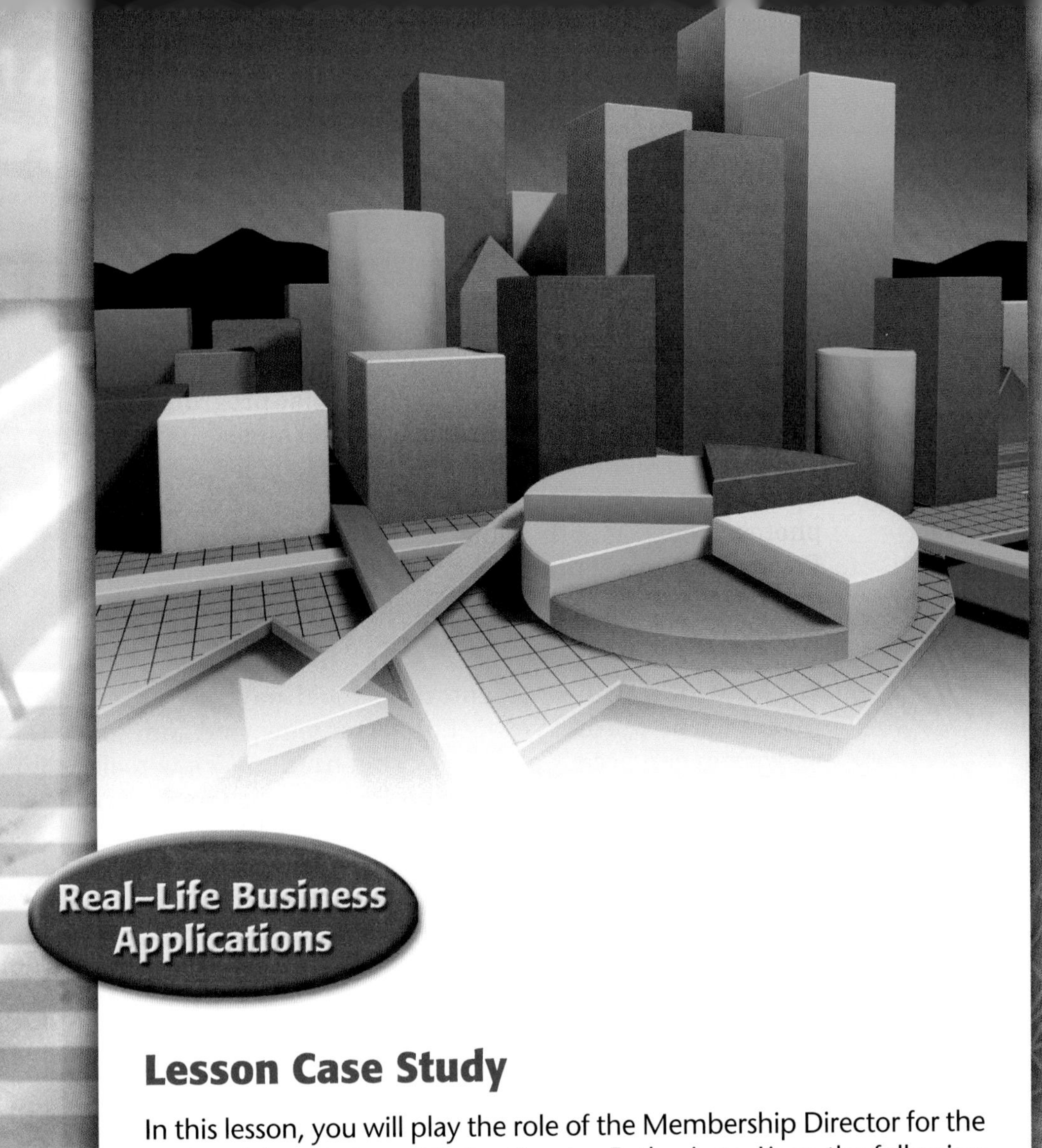

Real-Life Business Applications

Lesson Case Study

In this lesson, you will play the role of the Membership Director for the National Association of Roller Coaster Enthusiasts. Keep the following information in mind as you work through the lesson exercises.

- **Job responsibilities and goals.** As Membership Director, you are responsible for membership drives and for regular contact with members. Your goals are (1) to brief members of various civic and professional organizations about the benefits of membership in NARCE and (2) to inform new members about the organization, its history, and membership benefits.
- **The project.** You are preparing a series of presentations for welcoming new members as well as for marketing the organization to potential members. Each presentation may be used alone or with others in the series, depending on the occasion and the information you need to provide. You may include some of the same information in more than one presentation for use on different occasions.
- **The challenge ahead.** You will create, edit, and view your presentations to ensure they are appropriate for your audiences.

Exercise 1 Overview: Navigate PowerPoint Views and Slide Shows

In a work environment, employees often attend training sessions and company or professional meetings that consist of presentations. A **presentation** is a formal or an informal report, usually given orally, sometimes called a "speech" or a "talk." Microsoft PowerPoint is a popular program you can use to create presentations in the form of slides that may be viewed on a computer, projected onto a screen, or printed. Speakers can add notes, charts, tables, clip art, drawings, photographs, sounds, and even movie clips to their PowerPoint presentations in order to make them more interesting and/or explain difficult material more easily.

Views and Panes

While working on a presentation, you'll navigate through three views—normal view, slide sorter view, and slide show view. You can access all these views from the View toolbar in the bottom-left corner of the PowerPoint window. You can see three panes in normal view (see Figure 1.1): the slide pane is the main working area of the screen, and it displays one slide at a time; the notes pane displays notes that you type; and the left pane consists of the Slides tab and the Outline tab.

Need Help?

Type: about PowerPoint views in the Ask a Question box at the right end of the menu bar

Figure 1.1 The PowerPoint Window

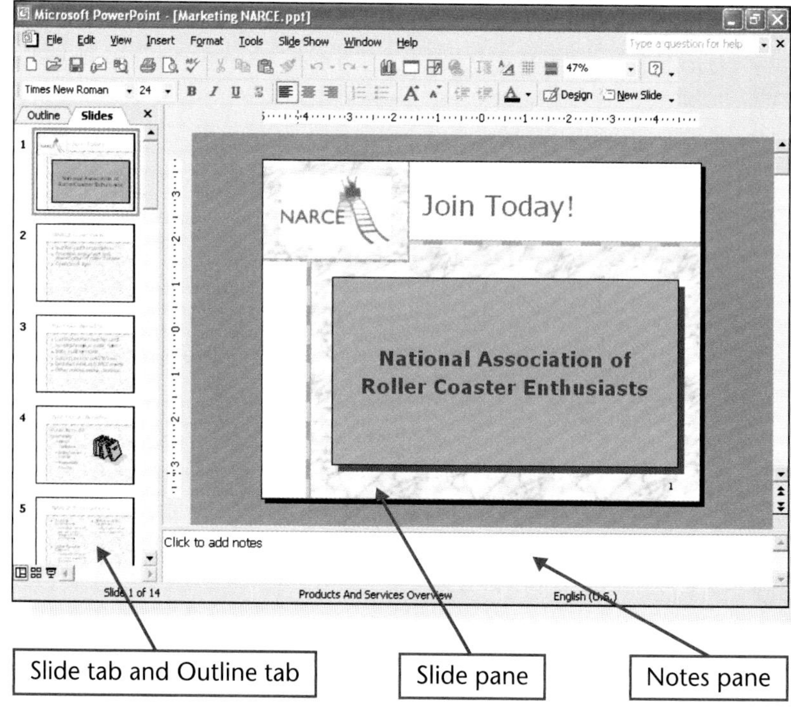

The Slides tab contains small-size views, called **thumbnails**, of all slides in the presentation. The Outline tab shows the slides in outline format. You can type an outline on the Outline tab, and PowerPoint will automatically create the presentation. At times you will use the task pane as well.

You may type a few notes into the notes pane, to use as reminders to yourself or to mention to an audience during a presentation. You may also print notes. You might ask others to review your slides and make comments to improve your presentation. You can print those comments, too. You will learn more about comments in Lesson 4 of this unit.

Horizontal or vertical bars, called **splitter bars**, separate the left, slide, and notes panes in normal view. You can drag the splitter bars to customize the sizes of these panes.

Slide sorter view displays thumbnails of the entire presentation. Slide show view is the view you use when you actually deliver the presentation. You can switch to slide show view periodically while preparing a presentation to see how the slides will look to an audience.

In the following exercise, you will navigate panes, views, and slides in a presentation that promotes NARCE.

Figure 1.2 Normal view with Slides tab on top

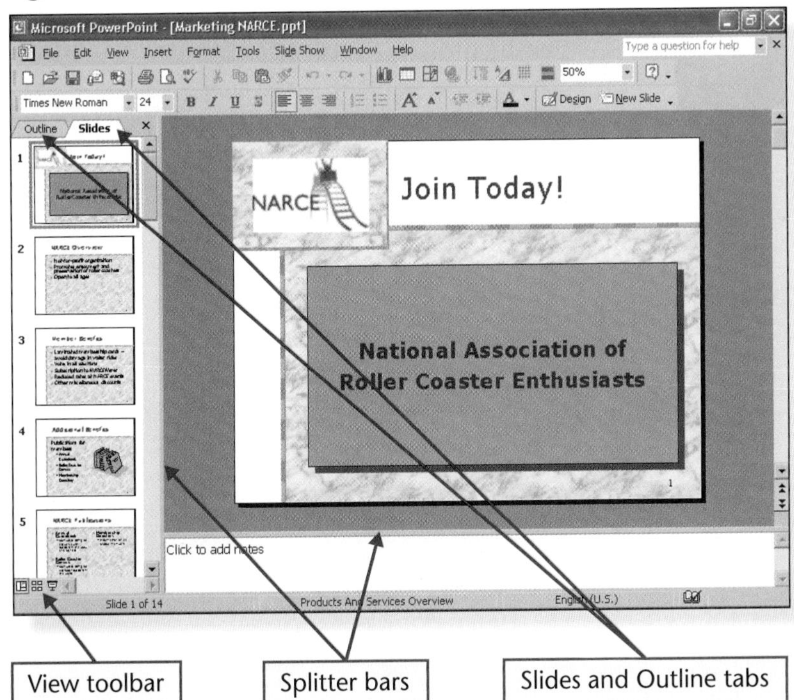

Step Through It™

Exercise 1A: Explore PowerPoint views

1. Open *Marketing NARCE.ppt*, which opens in normal view with the first slide in the slide pane (see Figure 1.2). On the Slides tab, click the second thumbnail to view the second slide.

2. Click each thumbnail. Point to the vertical splitter bar; when the pointer changes to a double-headed arrow, drag the bar in either direction to change the size of the thumbnails.

PowerPoint®

3 Click the Outline tab. If necessary, use the scroll bar to see slide 1.

4 Click the slide 2 icon (see Figure 1.3).

5 Click the remaining slide icons. For each slide, compare the outline material with the slide in the slide pane. Resize the panes as needed.

Figure 1.3 Normal view with Outline tab on top

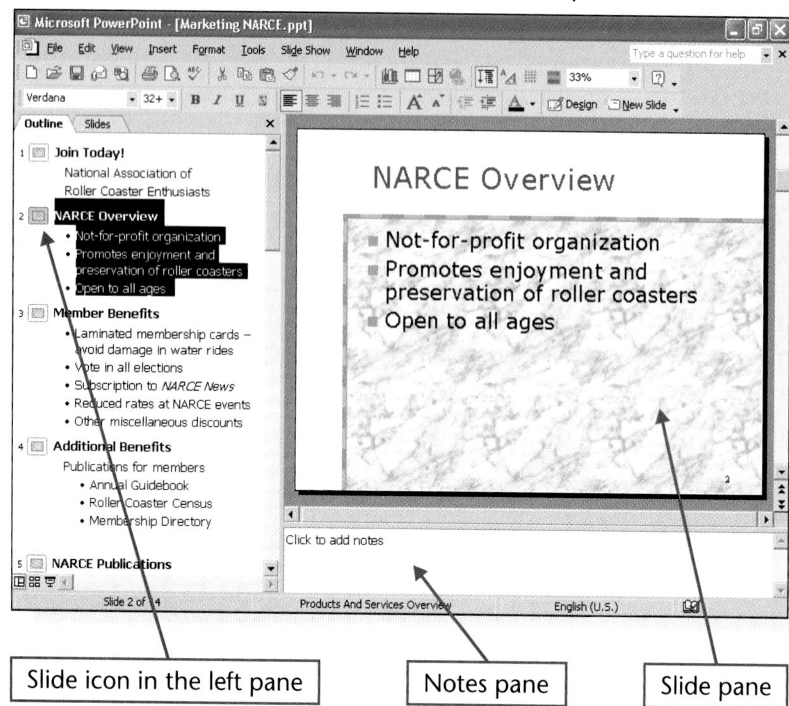

6 Go to slide 11. On the View toolbar, click Slide Sorter View to see thumbnails of all slides (see Figure 1.4).

7 Click Normal View. The last slide selected is in the slide pane. Resize the panes as needed.

8 Switch to slide sorter view, and select slide 1. Press End to go to slide 14. In normal view, press Home to return to slide 1. Click Slide Show and click the mouse to view each slide. Click to return to normal view.

Figure 1.4 Slide sorter view

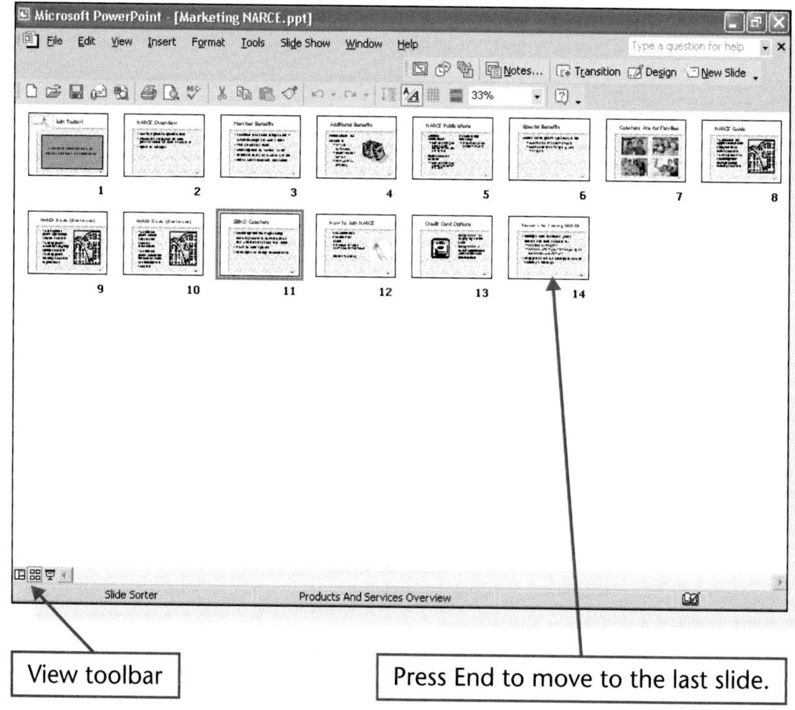

Parts of a Presentation

The first slide in a presentation is called the **title slide**. It displays the main topic of the presentation. The main topic of any slide is displayed in the **title**. Any text that follows the title and gives more detail about the title is called a **subtitle**. The slides in a presentation may include **objects**, which are nontext elements such as charts, tables, clip art, pictures, photos, movie clips, or other types of information.

A **placeholder** is a preset location reserving space for a slide element. There are three types of placeholders. The **title area** is a placeholder for the slide's title; the **text area** is a placeholder for a subtitle or a numbered or bulleted list; and the **object area** is reserved for objects. An instruction such as *Click to add text* is often included inside a placeholder.

The status bar shows the number of the slide that is currently displayed in the slide pane and the total number of slides in the presentation. Scroll bars help you move vertically or horizontally in the pane. You can adjust the display size of a slide on the Slides tab or in the slide pane. You can also adjust the size of a pane by using the Zoom box on the Standard toolbar.

In the following exercise, you will navigate the marketing presentation and practice adjusting the sizes of its panes.

Type: zoom

Figure 1.5 Navigating a presentation

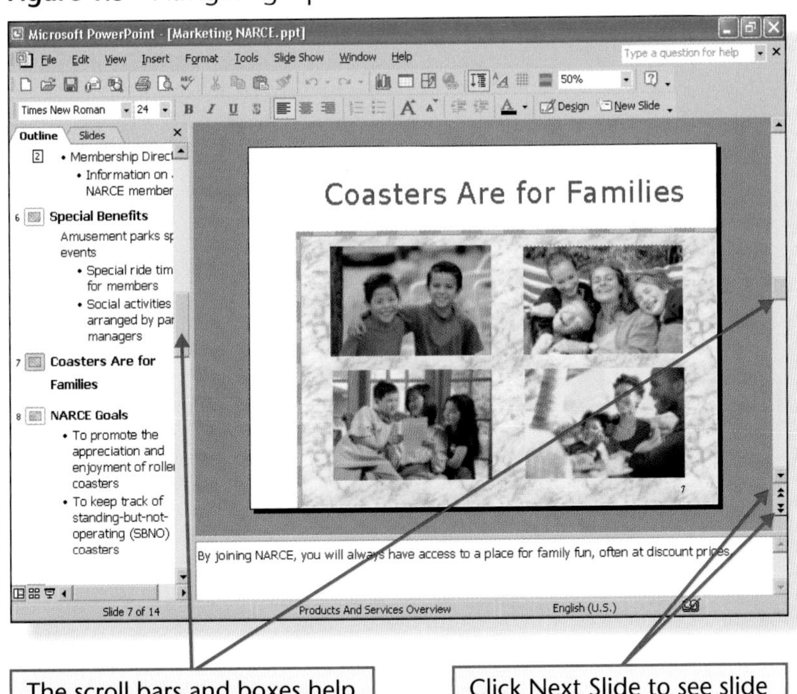

The scroll bars and boxes help you navigate a presentation in normal view.

Click Next Slide to see slide 8; click Previous Slide to return to slide 7.

Step Through It™

Exercise 1B: Navigate a slide show

1. Go to slide 7 in *Marketing NARCE.ppt* (see Figure 1.5). Click Previous Slide. Then, click Next Slide.
2. Click the scroll bar or arrows to move quickly through the slides.
3. Press Page Up to see a previous slide. Press Page Down to see the next slide. Press Home, and then press End.

PowerPoint®

4. Click the Slides tab and move quickly through the thumbnails.

5. Double-click the slide 5 icon on the Outline tab to collapse the outline so that you can read only the title (see Figure 1.6). Double-click again to expand the outline.

6. Go to slide 10 on the Slides tab. On the Standard toolbar, click the Zoom down arrow and select 75% as the size of the thumbnails. Drag the left pane splitter bar to the right to increase the thumbnails to 100%.

Figure 1.6 Expanding and collapsing outlines

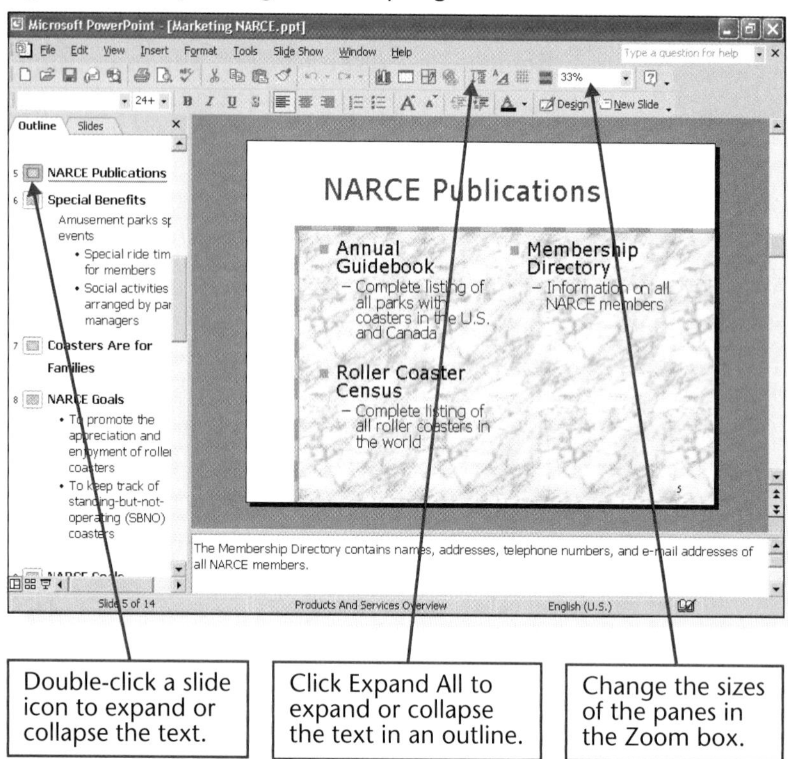

7. Click the slide pane and change the size to 100%, and then select *Fit* in the Zoom box. Click the slide 10 thumbnail again. Resize the left pane as desired.

8. In slide sorter view, adjust the size to 100% (see Figure 1.7). In normal view, drag the splitter bars to adjust the size of the slide pane.

9. Close the presentation without saving it.

Figure 1.7 Slide sorter view at 100% size

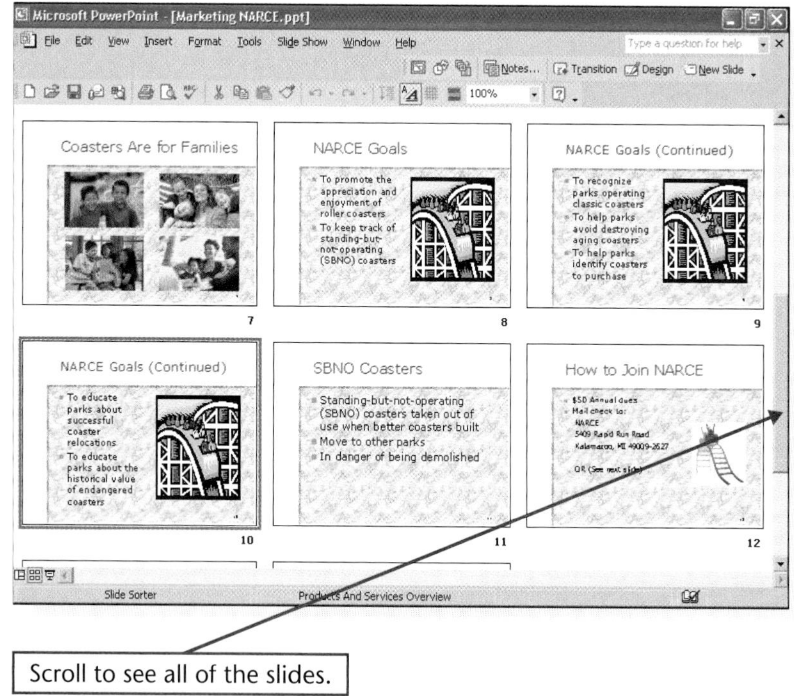

Exercise 2 Overview:
Manage Files and Folders

Microsoft Office Specialist PP2002 6.4, 7.3

Managing presentation files helps you locate and work with your presentations easily. You can save your presentation files in the same folder with the same name, in the same folder with a new name, in a new folder with the same name, or in a new folder with a new name. Practice using meaningful file and folder names so that you can remember them and locate your files easily.

You may need to save a presentation in the file format used by an earlier version of PowerPoint for someone who doesn't have the latest version to be able to view your presentation. You may also save a presentation in **Rich Text Format (RTF)**, a file format with the extension *.rtf* that enables text to be transferred and read by different applications, such as Word. Alternatively, you can import a presentation outline into Word using PowerPoint's Send To feature in order to read and revise it easily in Word. With both of these features, the Word document includes text only, omitting any graphics that are in the presentation.

In the following exercises, you will save a presentation in a new folder and in RTF format so you can review it in Word.

Figure 1.8 Saving a file in a newly created folder

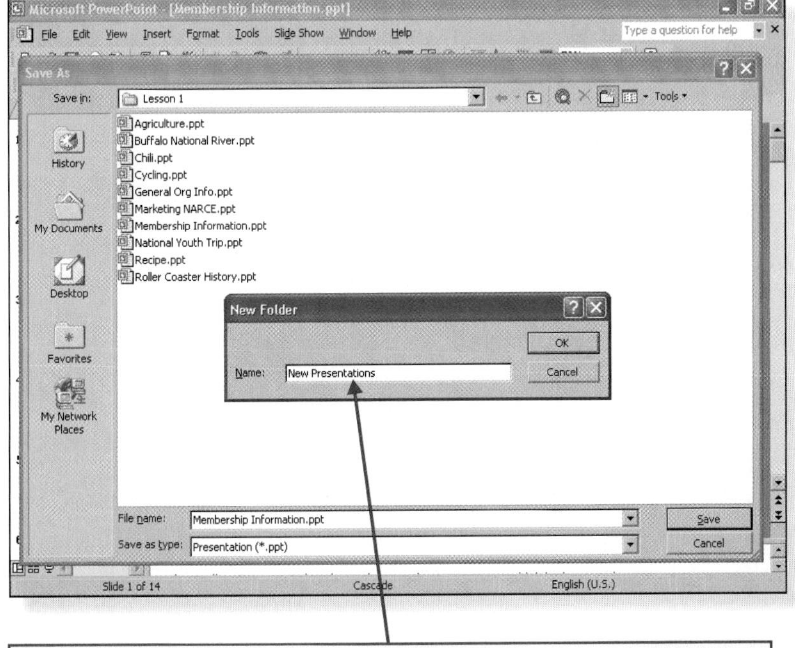

Use meaningful folder names so that you can locate files efficiently.

Step Through It™
Exercise 2A: Save a presentation in a new folder

1. Open *Membership Information.ppt*.
2. In the Save As dialog box, navigate to the *Lesson 1* subfolder within your *Unit 4* folder, and click Create New Folder.
3. Type New Presentations as the folder name (see Figure 1.8). Click OK.
4. Save the presentation as *xxx-Slide Show 1.ppt* in the new folder.

Step Through It™

Exercise 2B: Save as a different file type in a new location

1. Open the Save As dialog box. In the *Save in* box, navigate to the *New Presentations* folder you just created, if necessary.
2. In the *Save as type* list, click Outline/RTF.
3. Type xxx-Membership Information in the *File name* box (see Figure 1.9).
4. Click Save, and close the file.

Figure 1.9 Saving a presentation as an RTF file

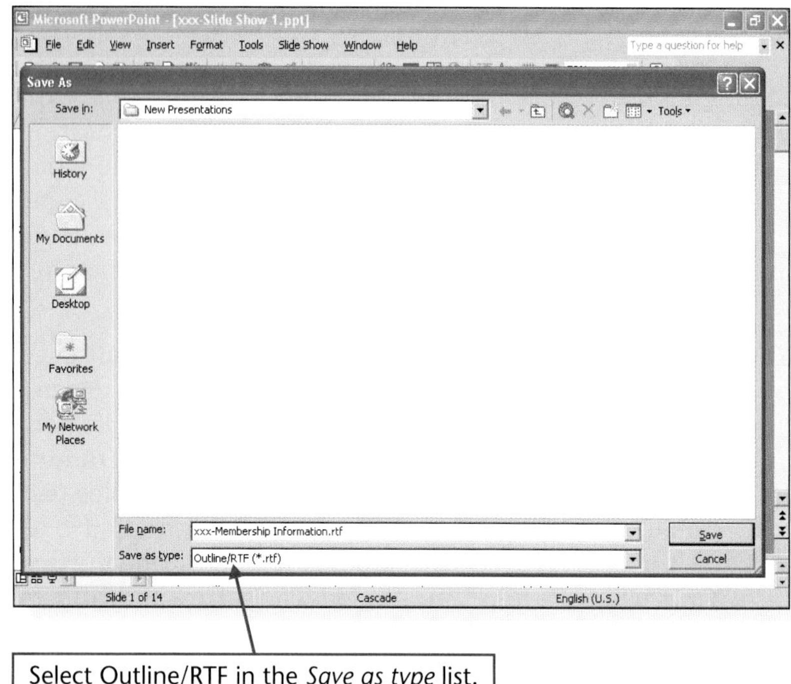

Select Outline/RTF in the *Save as type* list.

5. Open Word. In the Open dialog box, click the Rich Text Format file type. In the *New Presentations* folder, open and view *xxx-Membership Information.rtf*. Close the file and exit Word.
6. Open *Membership Information.ppt*. On the File menu, point to Send To, and select Microsoft Word. Click the *Outline only* option button (see Figure 1.10). Click OK to open the outline in Word.
7. Close all files without saving, and exit Word.

Figure 1.10 Sending a presentation to Word

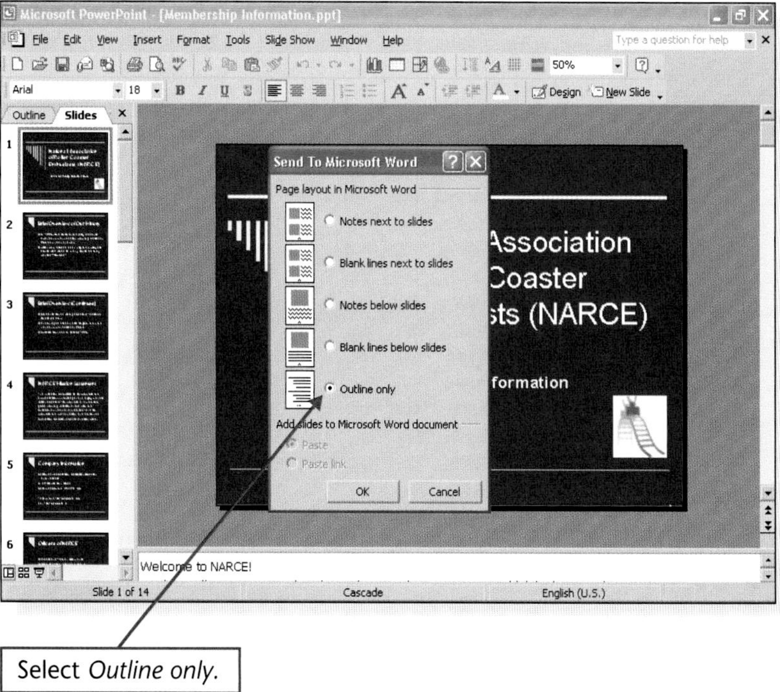

Select *Outline only.*

Tech Talk

Streaming Media

If you like to download tunes and watch movie trailers online, you're probably familiar with *streaming media*. This technology lets you see concerts or sports events live and listen to thousands of radio stations, from downtown New York to Down Under (in Australia!).

Streaming media is a way of encoding audio or video data for online transmission. Data in streaming media format are delivered to your computer in a continuous *stream* and placed in a buffer, a temporary storage area. Unlike traditional downloads, streaming media plays while it is being sent.

If you work for a large company, you may use streaming media on the job. Many big companies are using this technology for product launches, customer feedback, business-to-business collaboration, internal and public briefings, and employee recruitment and training.

For quality streaming without hesitations or stopping, higher bandwidths (data transmission speeds) are usually required. This can mean upgrading company intranets and switching to broadband (high-speed Internet access) for consumers.

CRITICAL THINKING

1. Is high-speed Internet access available in your community? Have you used it? Why do so few households have it?
2. Form a work team with two or three other students to investigate the cost of streaming media, locally, nationally, and internationally. Is it feasible for small as well as large companies? Present your findings in a PowerPoint presentation.

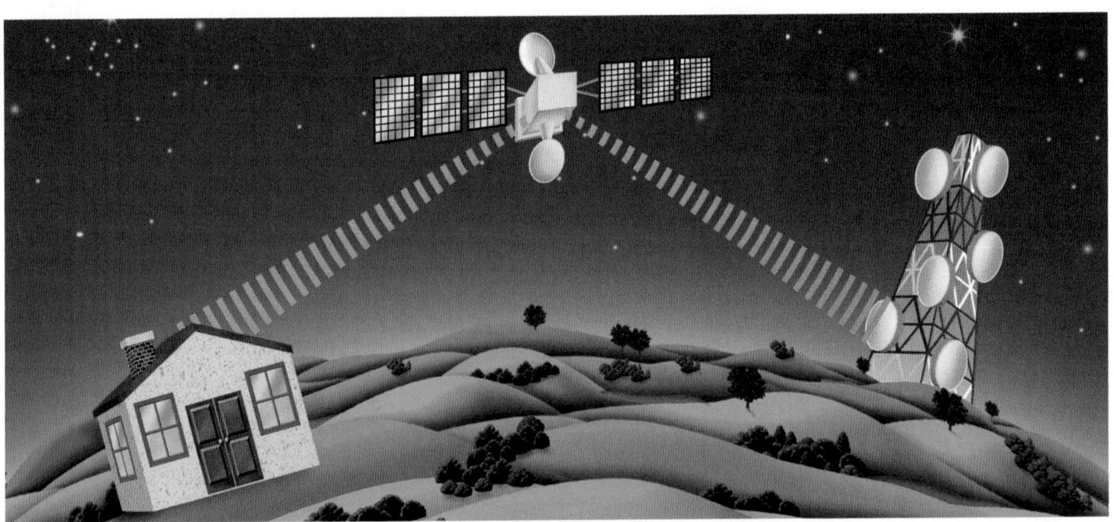

Microsoft Office Specialist PP2002 5.1

PowerPoint®

Exercise 3 Overview:
Preview and Print Presentation Components

As with other types of documents, you should always preview presentations before you print them. You have several options when printing a presentation: (1) You can print from one to nine slides per page. (2) You may print handouts for your audience. If you print three slides on each handout page, lines will appear next to each slide on which the audience members can write notes. (3) You can print notes pages, with each page consisting of one slide and its notes. (4) You can print comment pages along with the slides. (5) You can print the presentation outline.

PowerPoint has three different modes for printing slides: Color, Grayscale, and Pure Black and White. Grayscale mode is the default mode; it represents the slide colors in shades of gray. Pure Black and White mode prints in black and white only. To print slides in Color mode, you must set a color printer as your default printer first. In the following exercise, you will preview and print different components of a presentation that briefs new members on the structure of the NARCE organization.

Step Through It™
Exercise 3: Preview and print components of a presentation

1. Open *General Org Info.ppt* and click Print Preview on the Standard toolbar. Click the Print What down arrow (Print What: Slides) and select Slides.
2. Click anywhere on the slide to enlarge it; click again to return to the original size (see Figure 1.11). Click Print (Print...).

Figure 1.11 Previewing a slide

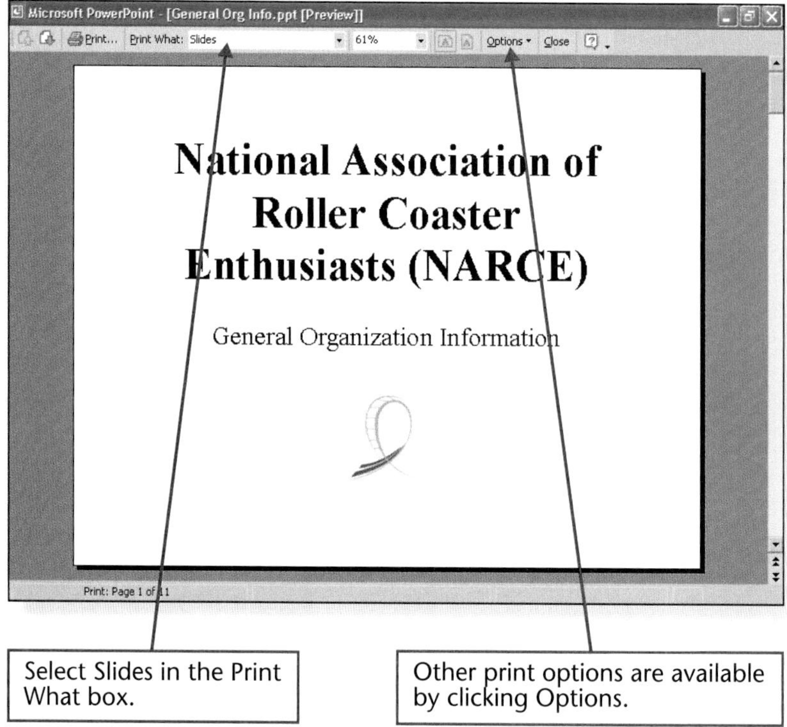

Figure 1.12 Previewing a slide containing a comment

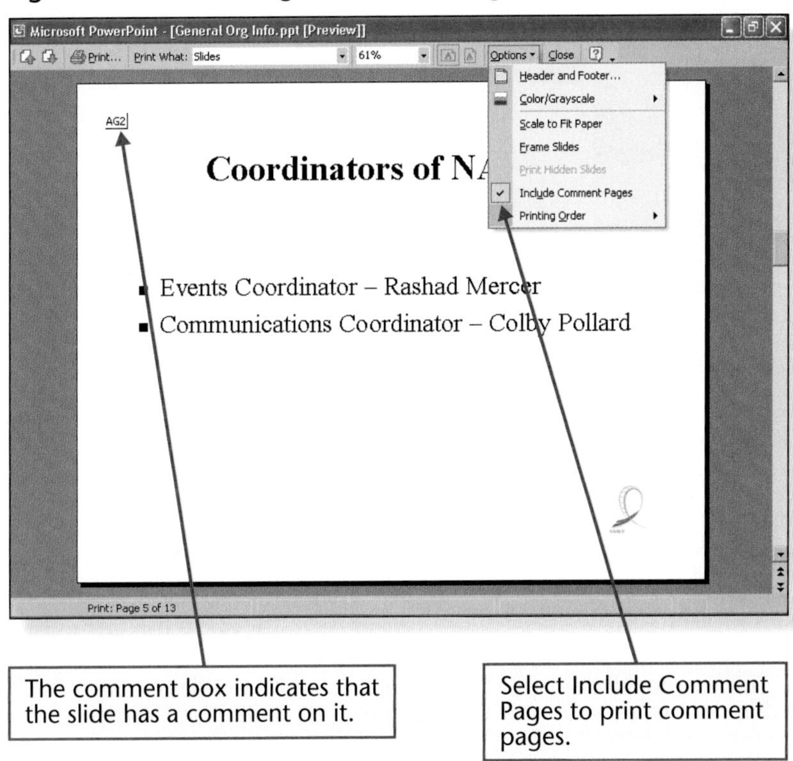

3. In the Print dialog box, verify that the All option button is selected, the *Print what* box is set to Slides, and the *Color/grayscale* box is set to Grayscale. Click OK to print the slides.
4. In the Print Preview window, click Next Page [icon] to navigate to slide 5.
5. Click Options and select Include Comment Pages (see Figure 1.12). Click Options, point to Color/Grayscale and select Pure Black and White.

PowerPoint®

Figure 1.13 Previewing a notes page

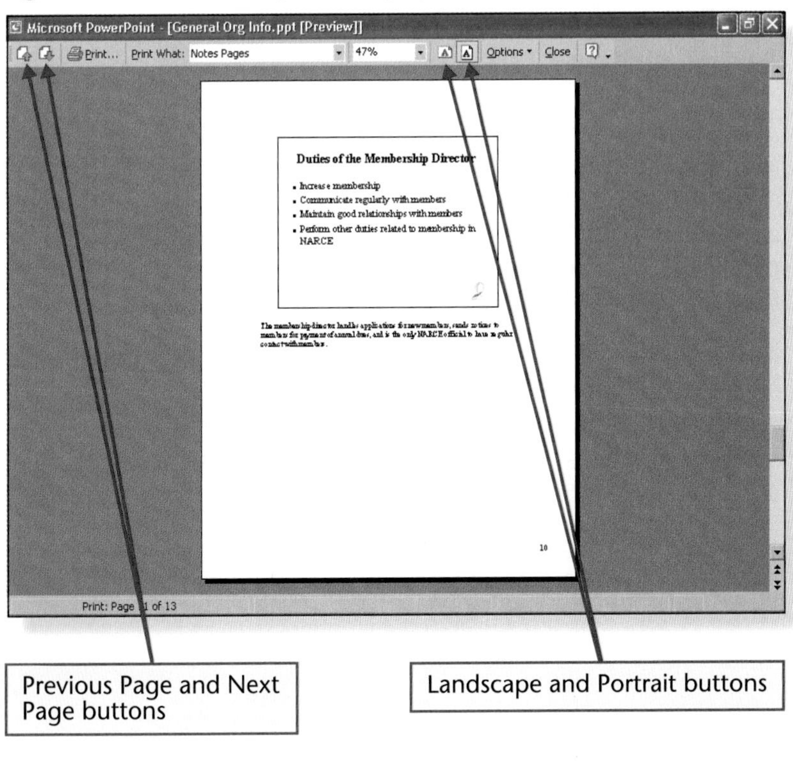

6. Keep clicking Next Page to navigate the slides and comment pages. Adjust the magnification, if necessary, to read the comments. Click Print, and then click OK.
7. In the Print Preview window, select Notes Pages in the Print What box. Click Next Page [icon] or Previous Page [icon] to see each slide and its notes (see Figure 1.13). Click Portrait [icon] if necessary.
8. Deselect Include Comment Pages. Click Print, and then click OK.

9 In the Print Preview window, select *Handouts (6 slides per page)* in the Print What box, and click Print. In the *Handouts* section of the Print dialog box, select Vertical and then Horizontal. Note how the thumbnail layout changes each time. Select *Frame Slides* (see Figure 1.14). Click OK to print.

10 In the Print Preview window, select Outline View in the Print What box, and preview the presentation's outline. Click Close Preview Close and close the presentation.

Figure 1.14 Previewing and printing handouts

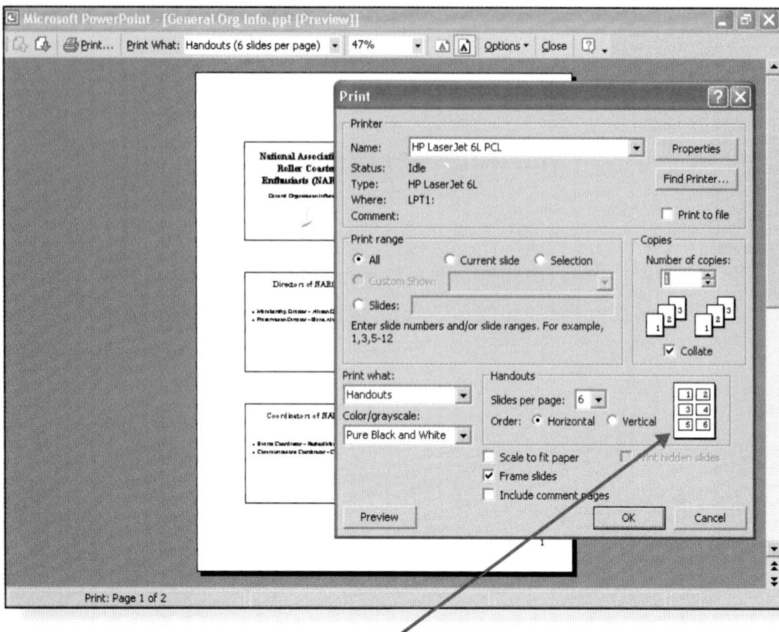

This thumbnail displays a horizontal layout of the slides on each handout page; you can choose between Horizontal and Vertical.

Microsoft Office Specialist PP2002 1.1, 2.2

Exercise 4 Overview: Create a Presentation Using the AutoContent Wizard

The **AutoContent Wizard** is a tool to help you create a presentation easily with preprogrammed layouts, design, and text. You select the type of presentation you want, such as General or Sales/Marketing, and your slides will be prepared automatically using **boilerplate text**, standard text which is appropriate for that type of presentation.

You may customize the boilerplate text and add other elements to your presentation after clicking the appropriate placeholders. For example, the AutoContent Wizard may include subtitles you need to delete. You may insert a table, a bar chart, an organization chart, or another image.

In the following exercise, you will use the AutoContent Wizard to create a presentation for orienting new NARCE employees.

Figure 1.15 The AutoContent Wizard

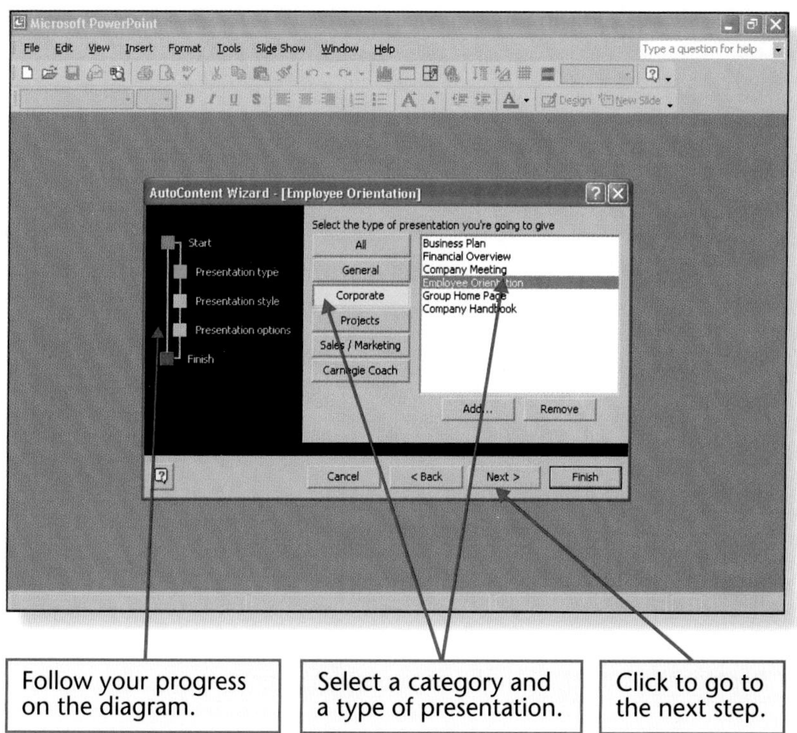

Step Through It™

Exercise 4: Use the AutoContent Wizard

1. Select New on the File menu to open the New Presentation task pane.
2. Select From AutoContent Wizard to open the AutoContent Wizard dialog box. (***Note:*** If the Office Assistant appears asking if you would like help, click No.) Click Next.
3. Select the Corporate category, and then select the Employee Orientation template (see Figure 1.15). Click Next.

Figure 1.16 Selecting presentation options

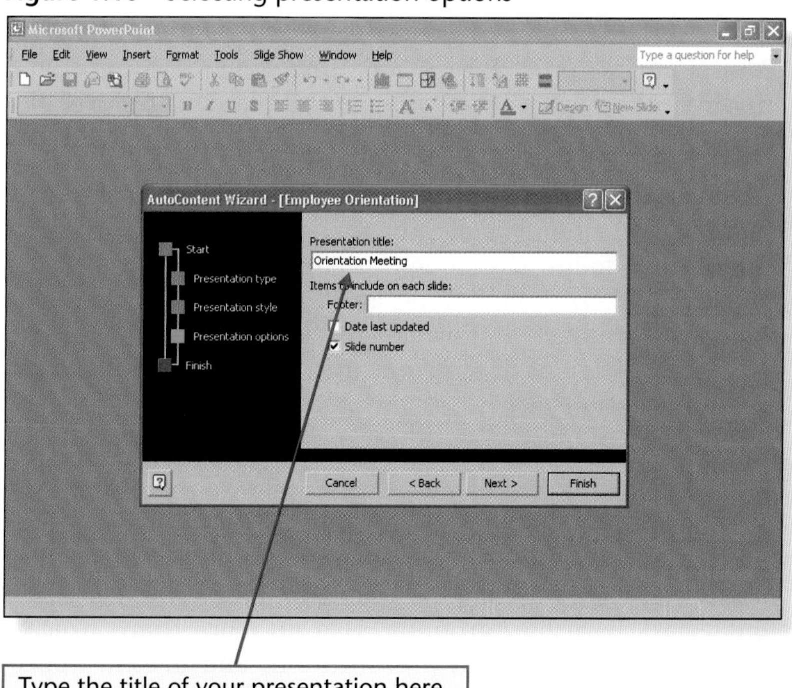

4. Select *On-screen presentation* as your presentation's output, and click Next. Type Orientation Meeting as the presentation's title.
5. Deselect the *Date last updated* check box. Select the *Slide number* check box, if necessary (see Figure 1.16). Click Next, and then click Finish.

6 On slide 1 in the newly created presentation, click the subtitle. Then, select the subtitle text, and type National Association of Roller Coaster Enthusiasts (see Figure 1.17).

7 Scroll through the remaining slides. Save the presentation as *xxx-New Employee Orientation.ppt* in the *New Presentations* folder.

Figure 1.17 Customizing the presentation

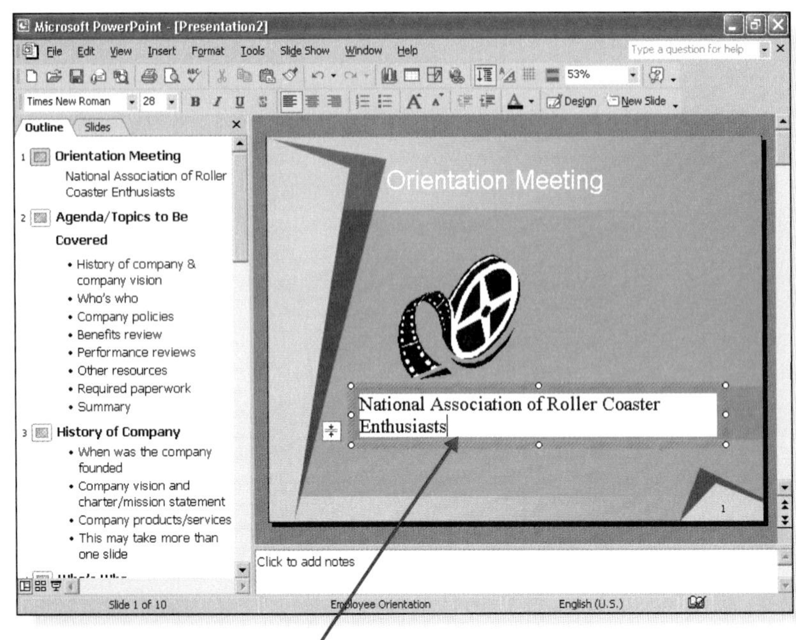

Replace the subtitle with the organization's name.

Microsoft Office Specialist PP2002 1.2, 2.2, 4.1

Exercise 5 Overview: Insert, Edit, and Modify Text

PowerPoint's procedures for inserting, editing, and modifying text are very similar to the Word procedures.

Adding, Deleting, and Modifying Text

To add text to a slide, you simply click in a placeholder, and begin typing when you see the insertion point. To delete or modify text, follow the same procedures as in Word. Word's Spelling and Grammar, Find and Replace, and Undo/Redo tools work similarly in PowerPoint. Use the Format Painter tool when you want to copy formatting of one element to one or more locations.

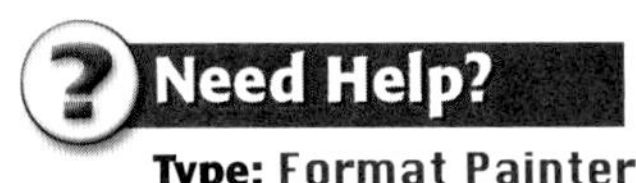

Type: Format Painter

Consider your presentation content and audience as you make consistent font choices (style, color, size, alignment). Choose serious fonts (like Times New Roman) for serious audiences and content; choose fun fonts (like Comic Sans MS) for less serious content. To ensure readability, contrast font colors with backgrounds. Use no more than three or four different fonts in a presentation; and use an appropriate font size for titles and subtitles.

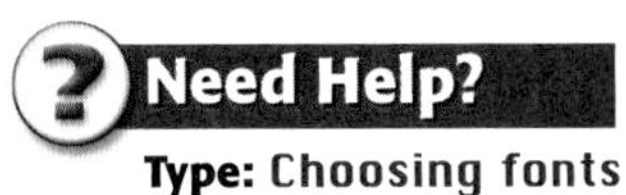

Type: Choosing fonts

In the following exercises, you will customize the *xxx-New Employee Orientation.ppt* presentation.

Figure 1.18 Inserting and editing text

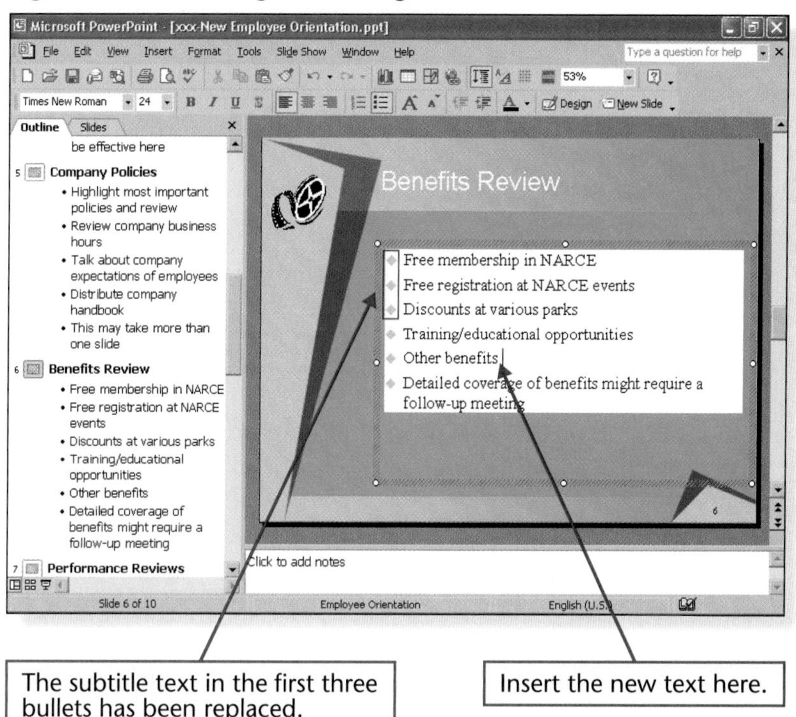

Step Through It™

Exercise 5A: Add and edit text

1. In *xxx-New Employee Orientation.ppt*, select the first three subtitles on slide 6. Type each of the following phrases as a separate bulleted item (with no punctuation): **Free membership in NARCE; Free registration at NARCE events; Discounts at various parks**.

2. Delete the fourth subtitle. Click at the end of the fifth subtitle (see Figure 1.18), press the spacebar, and type **based on years of service**.

Figure 1.19 Finding and replacing text

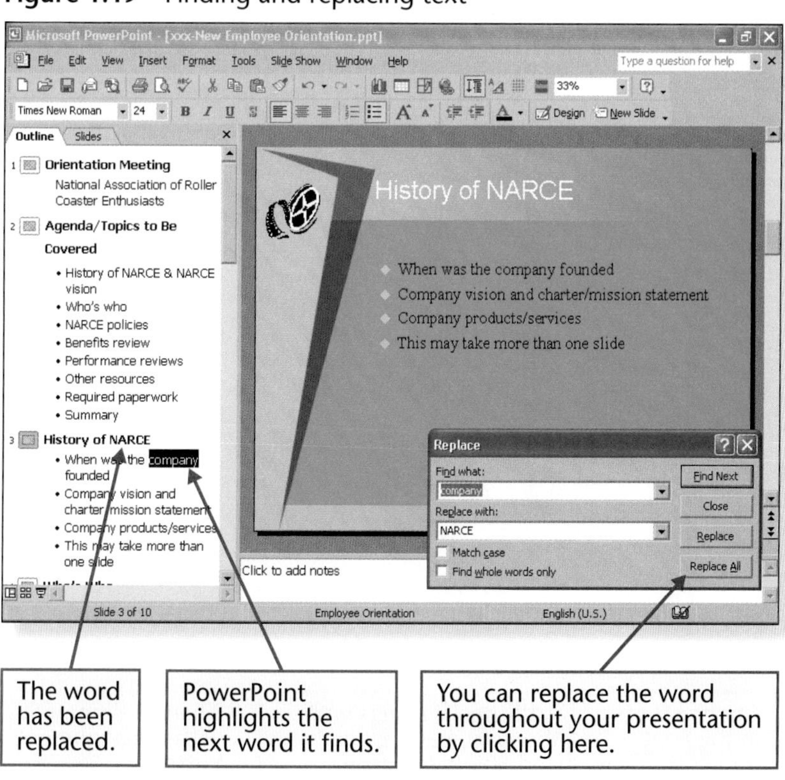

3. Go to slide 1 and click the Outline tab, if necessary. Replace all occurrences of the word *company* in the file with **NARCE**, except for the one in the first subtitle on slide 3 (see Figure 1.19).

4. On slide 3, delete *vision and charter/* from the second subtitle, and delete the last subtitle. On slide 5, delete the last subtitle, and then undo the deletion.

5. On slide 8, change *phone* to phone number in the last subtitle (see Figure 1.20).

6. Click the slide pane (*not* inside a placeholder), and press Home.

7. Check the spelling in the presentation. Then, save the presentation.

Figure 1.20 Inserting new text

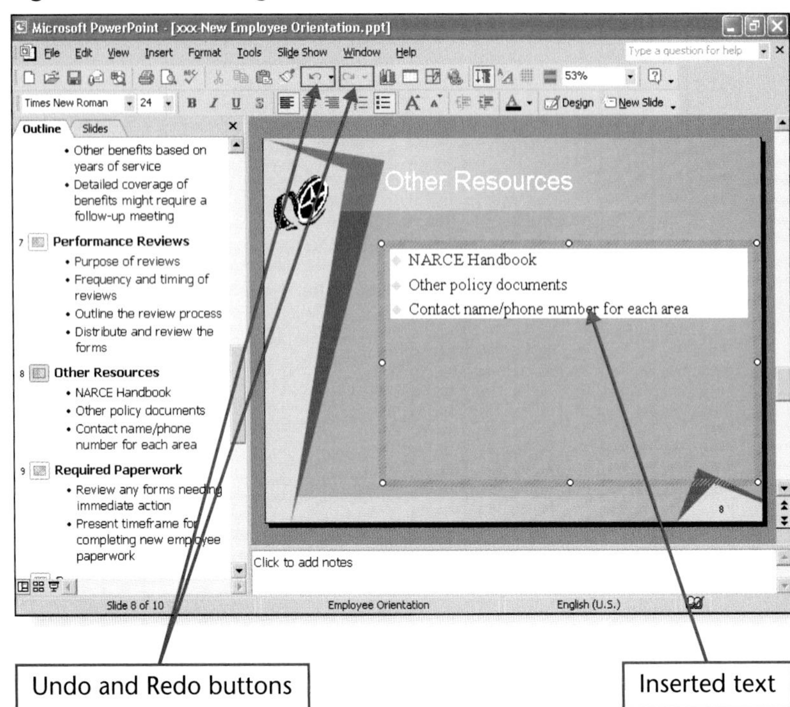

Step Through It™

Exercise 5B: Modify fonts and alignment

1. In *xxx-New Employee Orientation.ppt*, select the title of slide 1 and change the font to Verdana. ***Note:*** If you don't have this font, select another font. Add the Bold and Shadow special effects (see Figure 1.21).

2. Now change the subtitle font to Tahoma. Center and underline the subtitle.

Figure 1.21 Modifying fonts and adding special effects

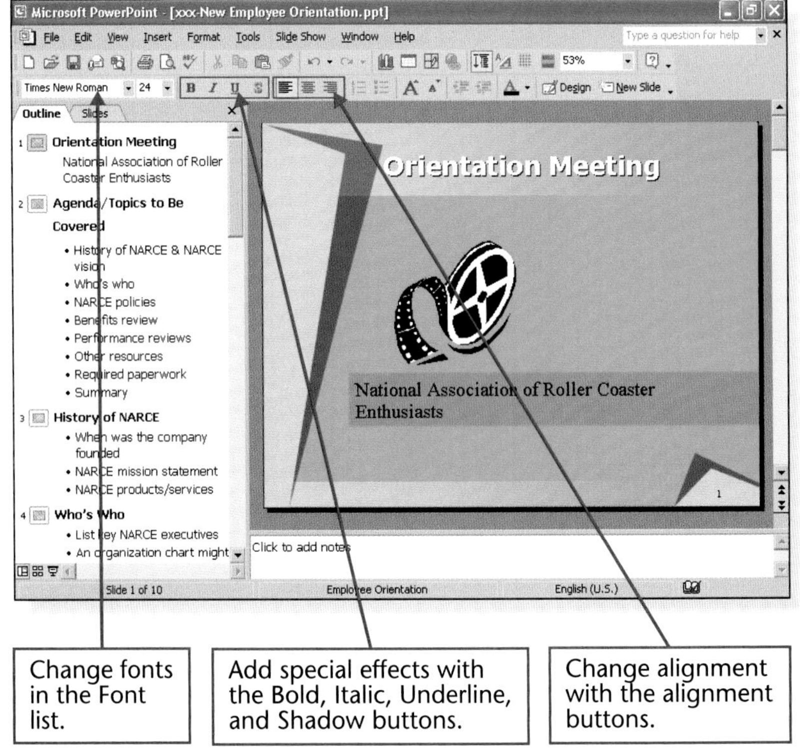

PowerPoint®

Figure 1.22 Using the Format Painter to change font size

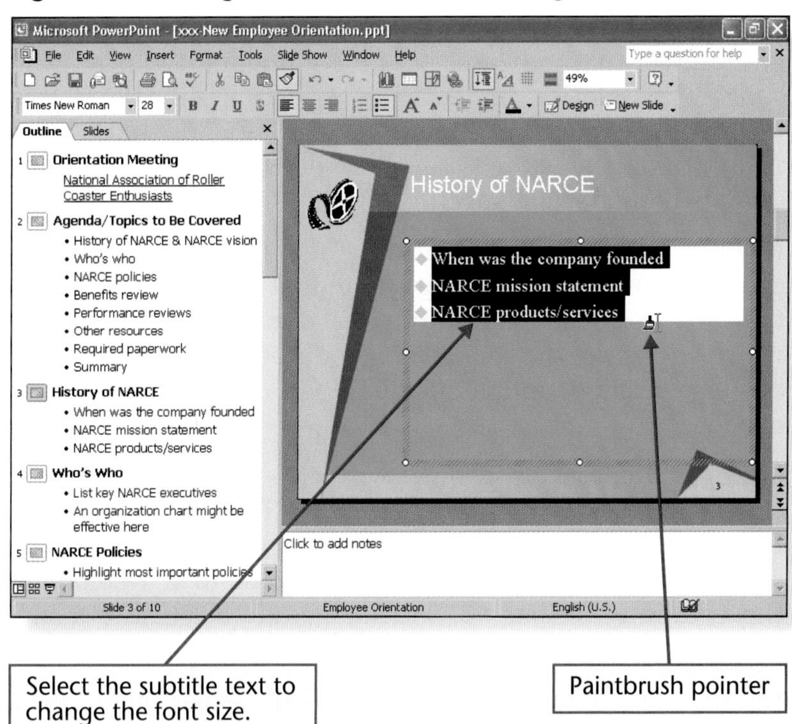

3. On slide 2, change the font size of all the subtitles to 28.
4. Use the Format Painter to change the formatting of the subtitles on slides 3 through 10 to match the subtitles on slide 2 (see Figure 1.22).
5. Change the last subtitle on each of slides 3, 4, 5, and 6 to italic.

PowerPoint®

Figure 1.23 Changing font colors

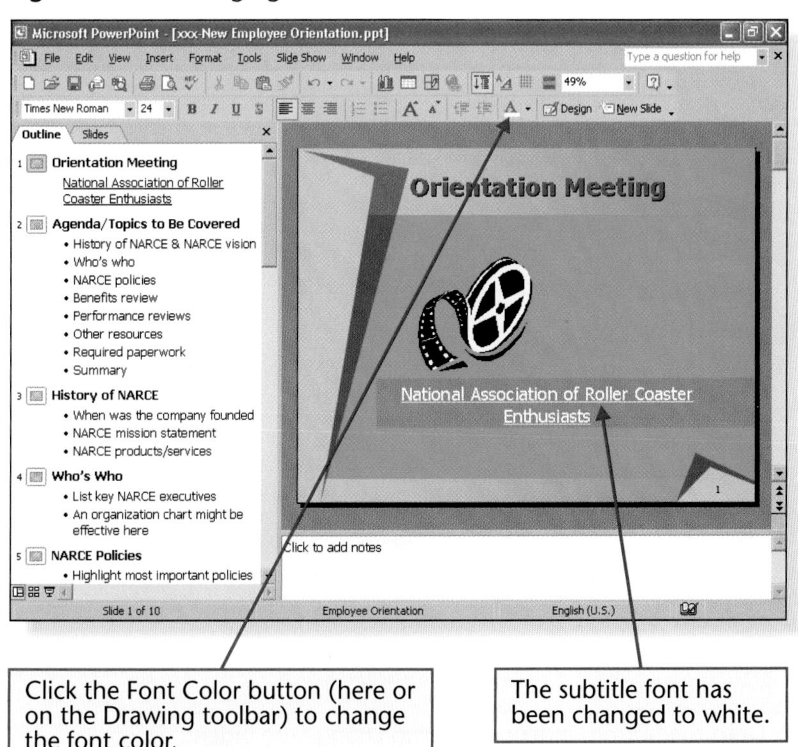

6. On slide 1, change the font color of the title to a shade of red. Change the subtitle color to white (see Figure 1.23).
7. Beginning with slide 1, view the slides in slide show view.
8. Save and close the presentation.

PowerPoint®

Working With Subtitles

Subtitles can have different indent levels. An **indent level** is a number that indicates the indent and importance of the subtitle in relation to the title. A level 2 subtitle is less important than a level 1 subtitle, which means that a level 2 subtitle has smaller type, a smaller bullet, and a larger indent than a level 1 subtitle.

If you want to move a subtitle to the next higher level, you can **promote** it, decreasing the indent and increasing the type size. You can also **demote** a subtitle to a lower level, which increases the indent and reduces the type size. You can also promote and demote individual bullets in a list as needed.

Type: change indent

Change indent levels in these ways: (1) On the Outline tab, click a subtitle, and press Tab or Shift + Tab or click Decrease Indent or Increase Indent. (2) On the Outline tab *or* in the slide pane, click a subtitle and click Promote or Demote on the Outlining toolbar. (3) To change all subtitles in a list, drag the indent marker below the ruler to the left or right.

In the following exercise, you will experiment with promoting and demoting subtitles in a presentation that outlines the history of U.S. roller coasters.

Step Through It™
Exercise 5C: Change the indent level of a subtitle

1. Open *Roller Coaster History.ppt*. Save the presentation as *xxx-Roller Coaster History.ppt*.Go to slide 3 in the slide pane. On the View menu, select Ruler, if necessary, and place the insertion point anywhere in the subtitle placeholder.

2. Drag the bottom indent marker to the right to number 1.5 (see Figure 1.24).

Figure 1.24 Ruler method for changing the indent level

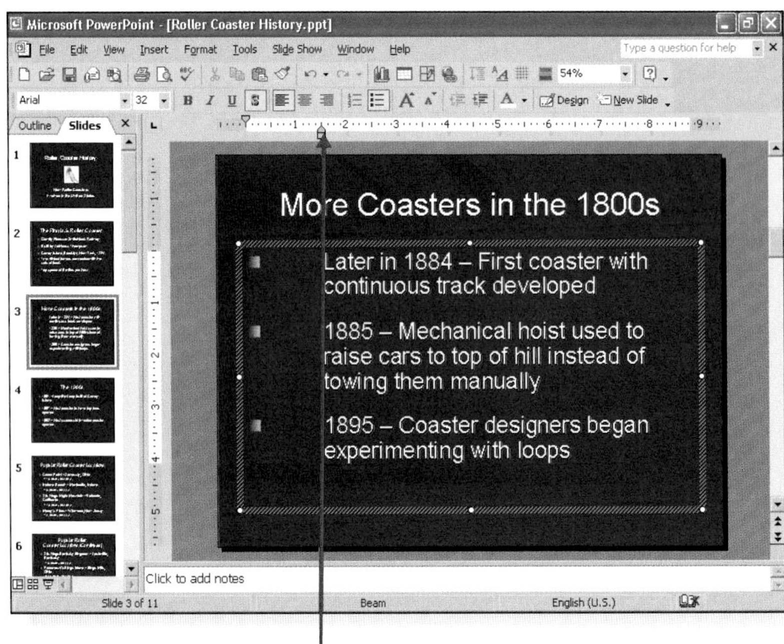

Drag the bottom indent marker to change the indent.

Figure 1.25 Promoting a subtitle

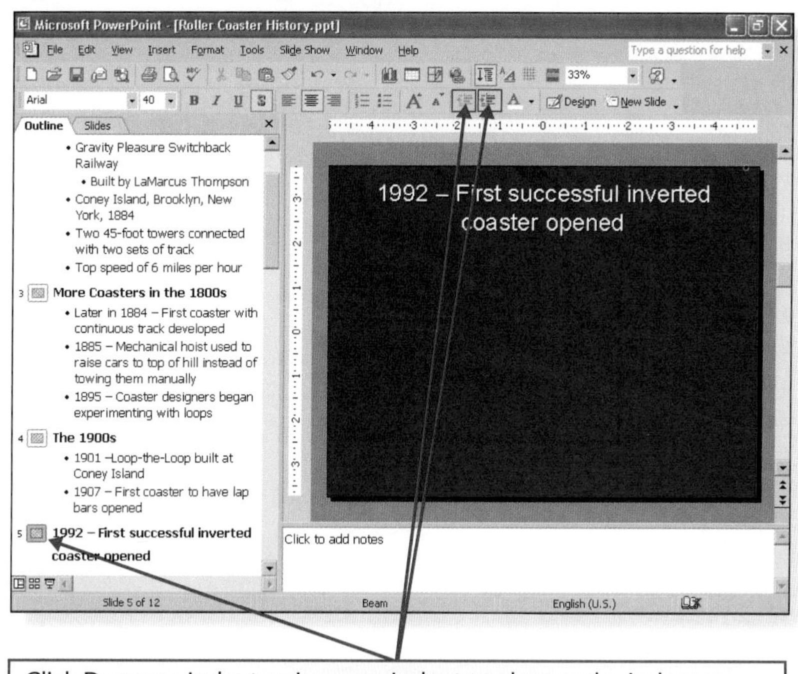

Click Decrease Indent or Increase Indent to change the indent, or change the indent on the Outline tab by pressing Tab or Shift + Tab.

3. On slide 2, click anywhere in the second subtitle, and click Increase Indent on the Formatting toolbar to demote the subtitle.

4. On slide 4, promote the last subtitle by clicking it on the Outline tab and then clicking Decrease Indent on the Formatting toolbar. The subtitle changes to a title, and a new slide 5 is inserted (see Figure 1.25).

Figure 1.26 Restoring the subtitle

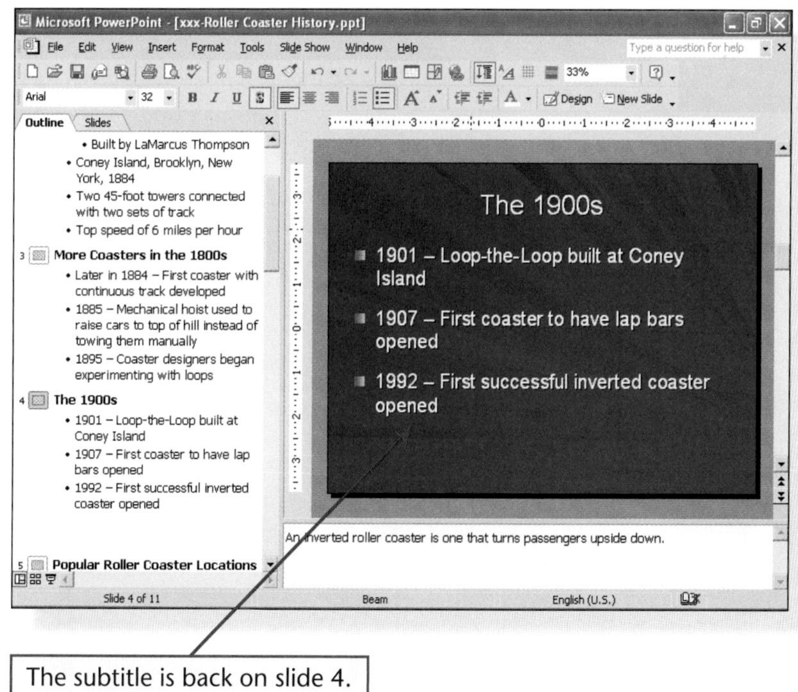

The subtitle is back on slide 4.

5. With the insertion point on the title of the new slide 5 on the Outline tab, press Tab, and the subtitle will return to slide 4 (see Figure 1.26). The new slide has been deleted.

6. View the presentation in slide show view. In normal view, save the presentation and close it.

APPLY IT! After finishing Exercises 1-5, you may test your skills by completing Apply It! Guided Activity 1, Modify, Preview, Print, and Save.

Business Connections

Using PowerPoint in Business

PowerPoint is a powerful tool that allows users to create professional-looking presentations for various business situations. For example, a chief executive officer (CEO) may use a PowerPoint presentation to give an annual overview to shareholders, or a sales representative may use PowerPoint to present a continuous-loop product advertisement at a kiosk. PowerPoint users may also create commonly used visual tools, including 35-mm slides, posters, and overhead transparencies.

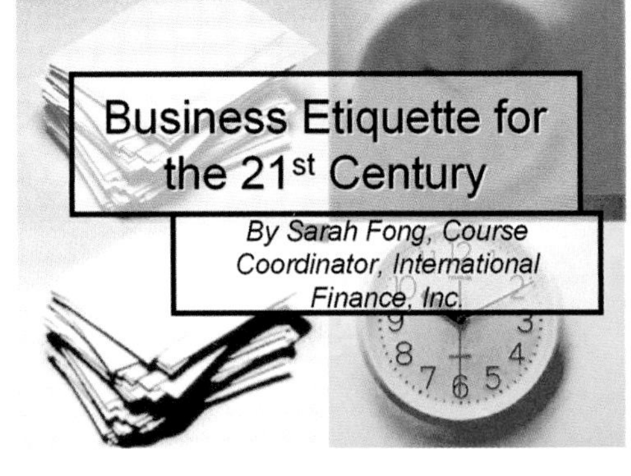

Additionally, PowerPoint presentations allow managers to communicate with employees in various forms:

- Broadcasts that employees may view from any location that has Internet access
- Training sessions at local and remote locations
- Online sales and marketing meetings
- Day-to-day communications
- Staff meetings with in-house and field employees

You can use various hardware and software with PowerPoint including, but not limited to, the following:

- desktop, portable, or laptop computers; liquid crystal display (LCD) projectors;
- small projectors for any size room;
- screens for large-audience viewing;
- video cameras and microphones for live broadcasts;
- kiosks for running continuous-loop presentations;
- PowerPoint Viewer (a free Microsoft download that enables users without PowerPoint software to view presentations); and
- Office Animation Runtime (a program that allows users who don't have Office XP to view a PowerPoint Web presentation that contains animations in Internet Explorer).

Sharing and viewing PowerPoint presentations on the Web is easier now than it ever was. You can use Microsoft Outlook to schedule PowerPoint broadcasts that others can view live or at a designated Web site. NetMeeting offers a means for real-time online collaboration in which a host and two or more participants can exchange information in real time. In addition, Producer (a free PowerPoint add-on) helps users capture, synchronize, and publish audio, video, slides, and images that they can view on demand in Internet Explorer and Windows.

CRITICAL THINKING

1. **Preparing Backups** Describe how you would start an online meeting in PowerPoint.
2. **Extending PowerPoint Features** Research the Producer add-on for PowerPoint at www.microsoft.com/office/powerpoint/producer. List three uses for Producer that are helpful for businesses. Provide a brief description of each use.

Microsoft Office Specialist
PP2002 1.1, 2.2, 4.8

Exercise 6 Overview: Manipulate Slides

You often need to add, copy, move, rearrange, and delete some slides to create your final presentation. You may also need to copy and paste slides from one presentation to another one, or duplicate slides in the same presentation.

Need Help?
Type: drag and drop

You can add a slide in many ways: (1) Decrease the indent to promote a subtitle. (2) Click New Slide on the Formatting toolbar. (3) Select New Slide on the Insert menu. (4) Click between two slides on the Slides tab or at the left edge of a title on the Outline tab, and press Enter. (5) In the Slide Layout task pane, select a slide layout, click its down arrow, and then select Insert New Slide.

You can delete a slide in these ways: (1) In the slide pane or on the Outline or Slides tab, select Delete Slide on the Edit menu. (2) Select a slide icon on the Outline tab or on the Slides tab, and press Delete. (3) In slide sorter view, select a slide and press Delete.

In the following two exercises, you will improve *General Org Info.ppt* by adding, deleting, duplicating, and rearranging slides. You will also move and copy slides from one presentation to another.

Step Through It™

Exercise 6A: Add and delete slides

1. Open *General Org Info.ppt*. Save the presentation as *xxx-General Org Info.ppt*. On the Formatting toolbar, click New Slide [New Slide]. Select the Title Only layout.
2. On slide 2, type **Company Information** in the title placeholder. Type the text in Figure 1.27 in the text area.

Figure 1.27 Text for slide 2

National Association of Roller Coaster Enthusiasts
5409 Rapid Run Road
Kalamazoo, MI 49009-2627

Telephone: (616) 555-7433
Fax: (616) 555-7474

PowerPoint®

Figure 1.28 Changing the formatting

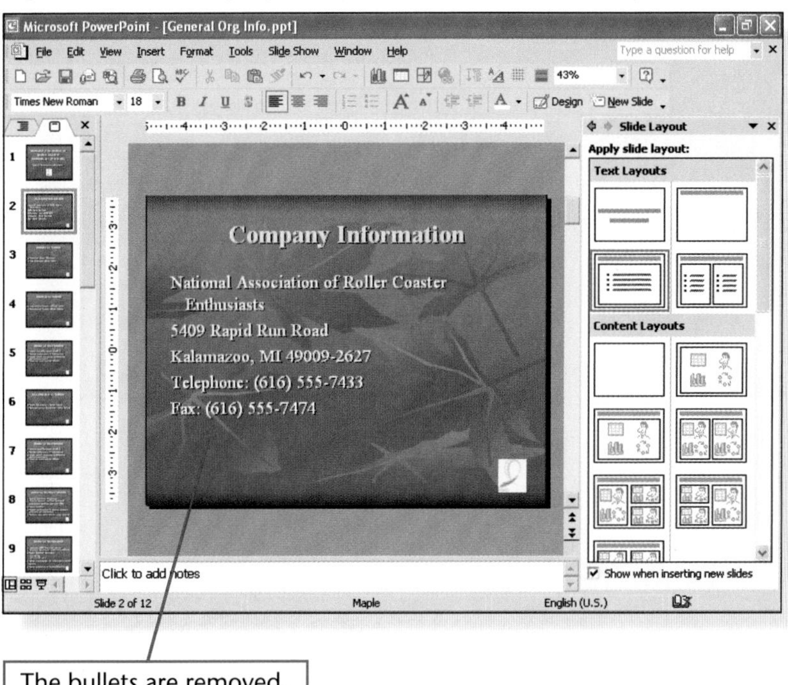

3. On slide 2, select all text in the text area and click Bullets to delete the bullets (see Figure 1.28). Close the task pane.

Figure 1.29 Deleting a slide

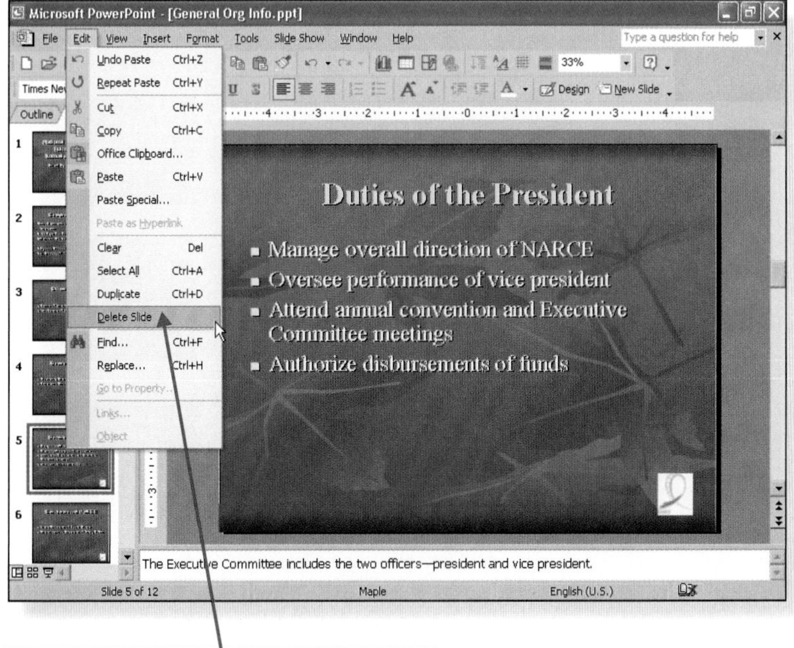

4. On slide 5, select Delete Slide on the Edit menu (see Figure 1.29). The slides will renumber.
5. Click slide 6 on the Slides tab, press and hold Shift, click slides 7 and 8, and then press Delete to remove the three slides.
6. In slide sorter view, delete slides 6, 7, and 8.
7. Save the presentation and close it.

PowerPoint®

Step Through It™

Exercise 6B: Copy, delete, duplicate, and rearrange slides

1. Open *xxx-Slide Show 1.ppt* in the *New Presentations* folder.

2. In slide sorter view, delete slides 6, 7, and 8. You now have 11 slides.

3. Click slide 10 (the organization chart), and drag it between slides 5 and 6; release slide 10 when the insertion point is between these two slides. The slides will be renumbered (see Figure 1.30).

Figure 1.30 Rearranging slides

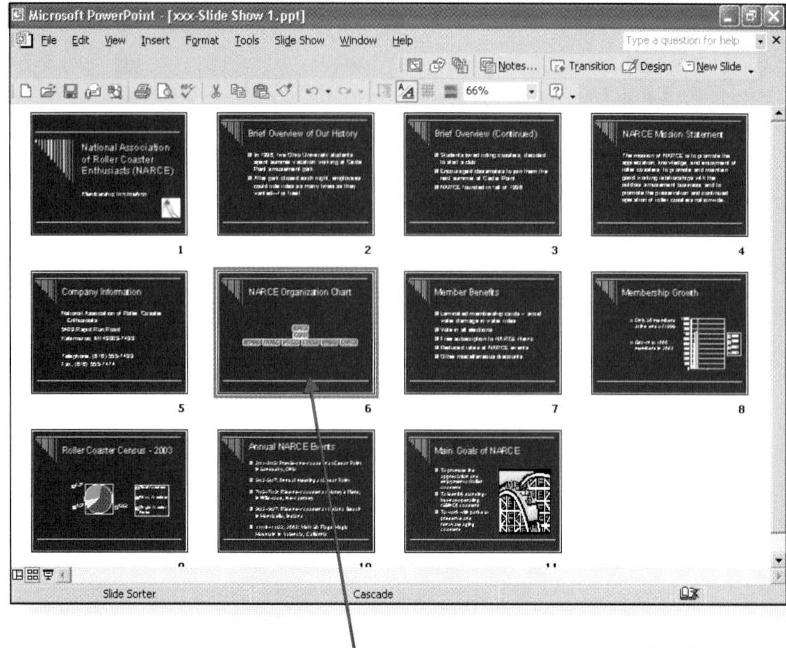

The organization chart has been moved, and the slides have been renumbered.

4. Go to slide 7 (*Member Benefits*). Right-click and select Copy. Move the insertion point between slides 8 and 9, right-click, and select Paste.

5. Select slide 12. On the Edit menu, select Duplicate to create another slide just like slide 12 (see Figure 1.31). Then, return to normal view and click the Slides tab.

Figure 1.31 Duplicating a slide

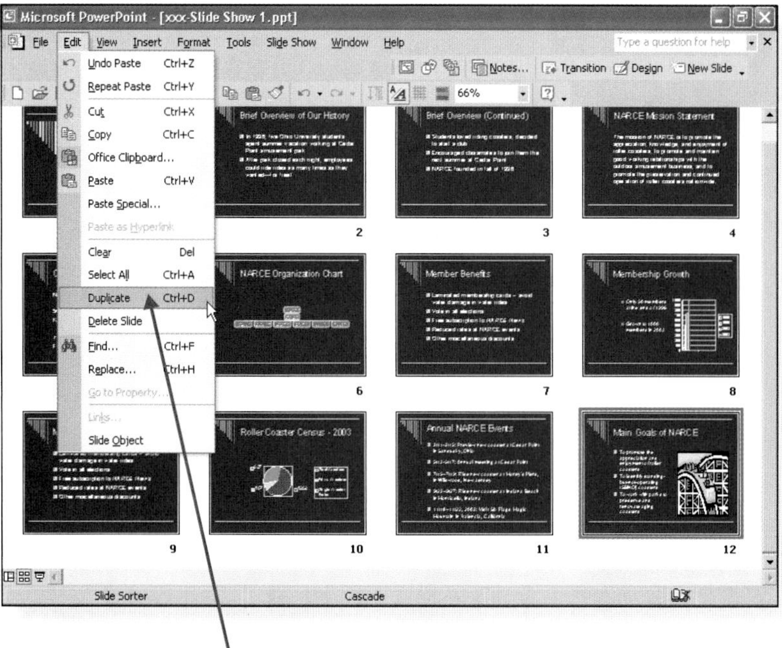

Select this option to duplicate slide 12.

Figure 1.32 Copying a slide

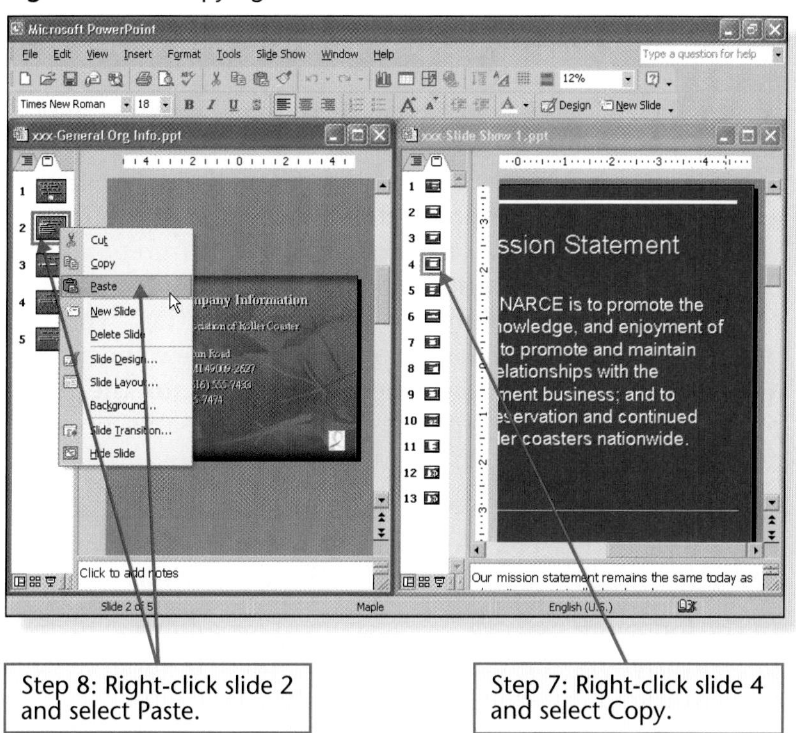

6. Open *xxx-General Org Info.ppt* and click the Slides tab. On the Window menu, select Arrange All to display both presentations side by side.

7. Adjust the size of the slides as desired. In *xxx-Slide Show 1.ppt*, click slide 4 on the Slides tab. Right-click and select Copy.

8. In *xxx-General Org Info.ppt*, right-click slide 2 and select Paste (see Figure 1.32).

Figure 1.33 Moving a slide to another presentation

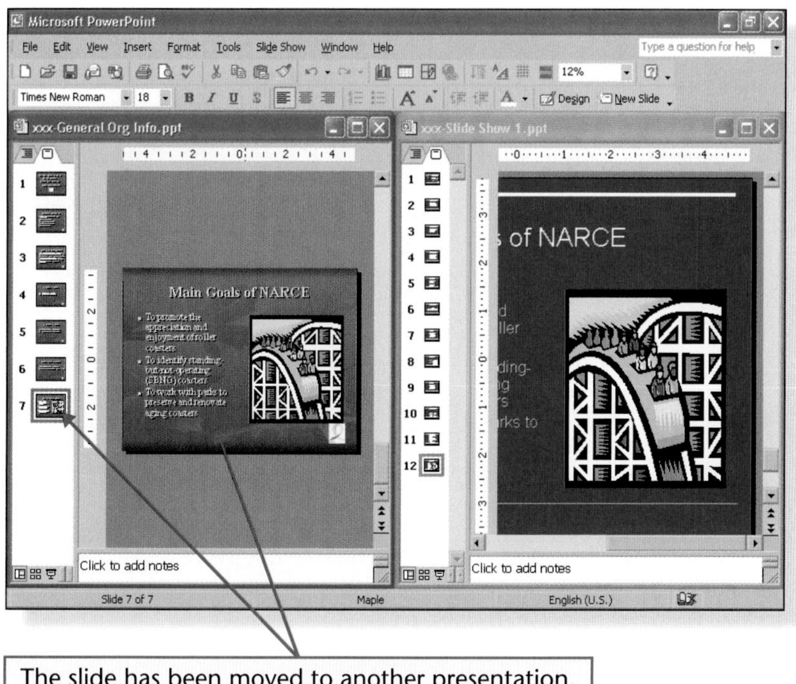

9. In *xxx-Slide Show 1.ppt*, right-click slide 12 and select Cut. Paste the slide after slide 6 in *xxx-General Org Info.ppt* (Figure 1.33).

10. In slide show view, view the slides in *xxx-General Org Info.ppt*.

11. On the Window menu, select Cascade and enlarge the presentation window.

12. Save and close both presentations.

PowerPoint®

Microsoft Office Specialist PP2002 4.10

Exercise 7 Overview:
Create Hyperlinks

In your PowerPoint presentations, you may create a hyperlink to another slide, to another presentation, or to a Web page. You may want to link together pages from two presentations that contain similar material. For example, you may want to present the *xxx-General Org Info.ppt* slides to new employees, using some of the *xxx-Roller Coaster History.ppt* slides to enhance your presentation. You can make one presentation longer by linking to a few slides from another presentation and then going back to the main presentation. Links to another slide in the same presentation or to a Web page are also helpful.

You can create all types of hyperlinks with the Insert Hyperlink dialog box. Although you create hyperlinks in normal view, they only "jump" in slide show view.

In the following two exercises, you will expand your history presentation by adding hyperlinks to another slide, to your presentation for new members, and to a Web site.

Step Through It™
Exercise 7A: Create a hyperlink to another slide or file

1) Open *xxx-Roller Coaster History.ppt*. On slide 5, select *Cedar Point* in the first subtitle (see Figure 1.34).

Figure 1.34 Selecting text to link

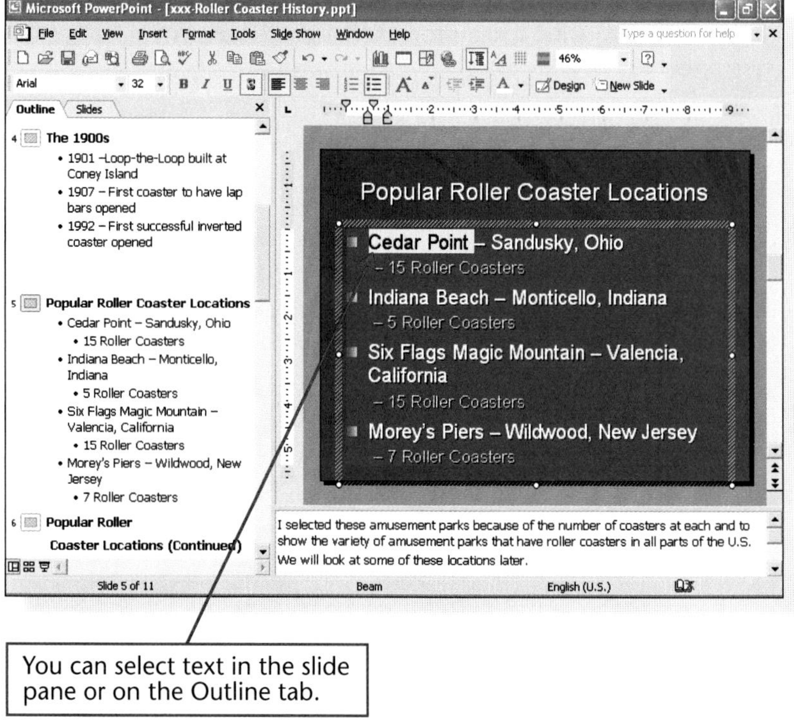

Figure 1.35 Creating a hyperlink to another slide

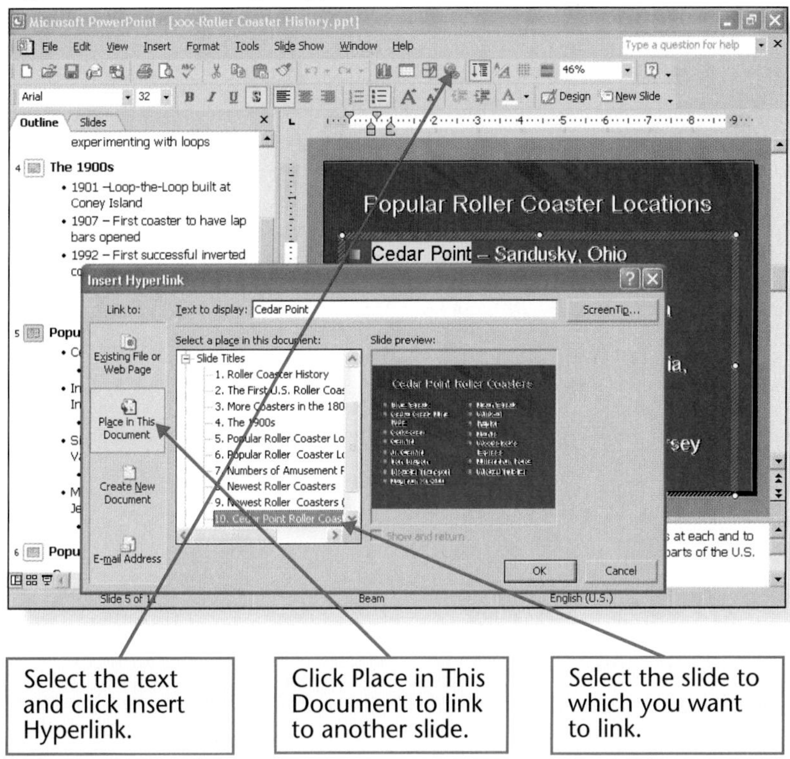

2. Click Insert Hyperlink on the Standard toolbar. Click Place in This Document in the *Link to* panel.
3. The *Select a place in this document* list box lists all slides in the presentation. Select slide 10 (see Figure 1.35). Click OK.

Figure 1.36 Slide show view of the slide 5 hyperlink

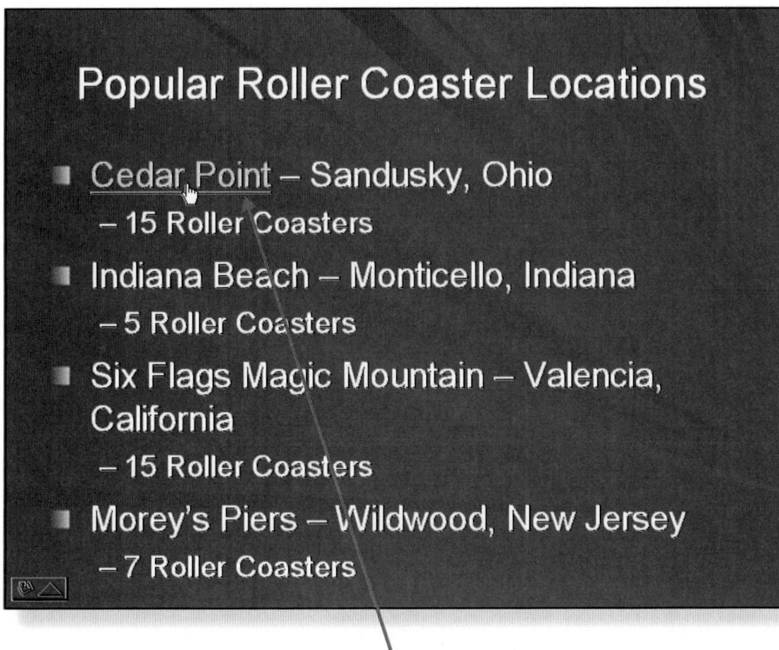

4. Click the slide pane. The words *Cedar Point* are now in a different color and underlined, indicating the hyperlink.
5. Switch to slide show view and point to *Cedar Point* (see Figure 1.36). Click the hyperlink, and slide 10 appears.
6. In normal view, note that the *Cedar Point* hyperlink on slide 5 changed color in the slide pane, indicating that you have followed the link.

7 On slide 10, select *Cedar Point* in the title and click Insert Hyperlink. Click Existing File or Web Page and select *Membership Information.ppt* (see Figure 1.37). Click OK.

8 Switch to slide show view and click *Cedar Point* in the title to open *Membership Information.ppt*. Press Esc twice.

9 On the Outline tab, right-click the hyperlink on slide 10, and select Remove Hyperlink.

10 Save the presentation.

Figure 1.37 Creating a hyperlink to another file

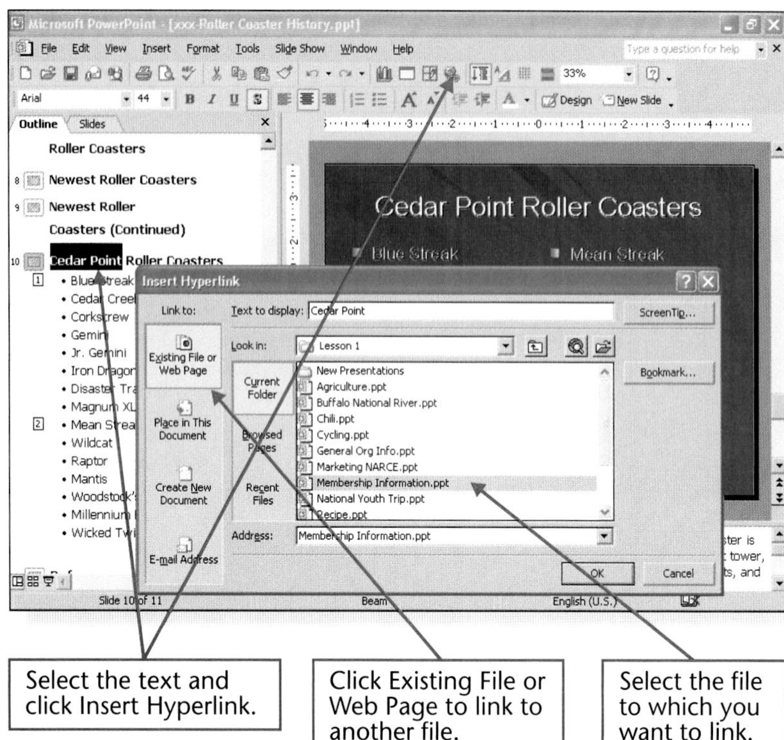

Step Through It™

Exercise 7B: Create a hyperlink to a Web site

1 On slide 1 of *xxx-Roller Coaster History.ppt*, select *Roller Coasters* in the subtitle, click Insert Hyperlink, and click Existing File or Web Page.

2 In the Address box, type www.coaster-world.com. Click ScreenTip. In the Set Hyperlink ScreenTip dialog box, type Coaster-World Web Site (see Figure 1.38); click OK. Click OK again. Deselect the text on slide 1.

Figure 1.38 Creating a hyperlink to a Web site

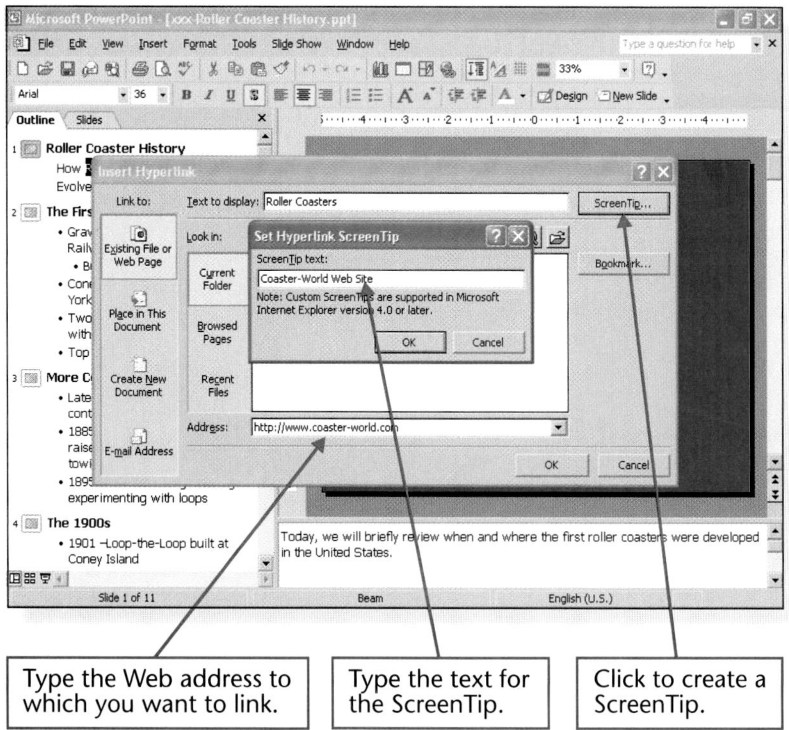

Type the Web address to which you want to link.
Type the text for the ScreenTip.
Click to create a ScreenTip.

Figure 1.39 Viewing the hyperlink ScreenTip

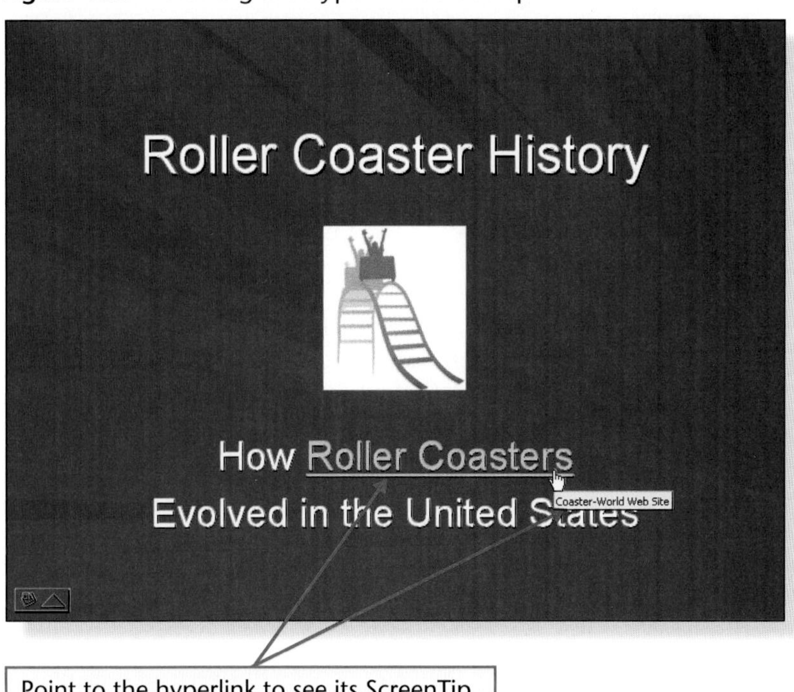

3. Connect to the Internet, if necessary. In slide show view, point to the hyperlink on slide 1, read the ScreenTip (see Figure 1.39), and click the hyperlink. When the Coaster-World home page appears, scan the page, click Back, and return to the presentation.

Figure 1.40 Returning to normal view

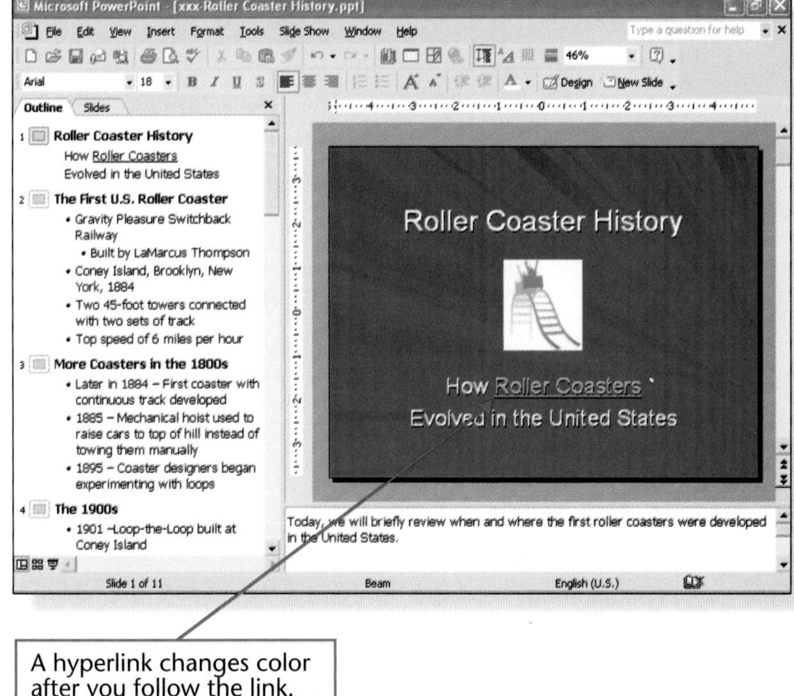

4. Press Esc to end the slide show and return to normal view (see Figure 1.40).

5. Save and close the file.

6. Exit PowerPoint. Close your browser and disconnect from the Internet, if necessary.

PowerPoint®

After finishing Exercises 6 and 7, you may test your skills by completing Apply It! Guided Activity 2, Manipulate Slides, Insert a Hyperlink, and Print a Comment.

Procedure Summary

Navigate Views

1. Click **View** . . . . Alt + V
2. Select **Normal** . . . . N
   OR
   Select **Slide Sorter** . . . . D
   OR
   Select **Slide Show** . . . . W
   OR
   Select **Notes Page**. . . . . P

OR

1. On the View toolbar, click **Normal View**.
   OR
   On the View toolbar, click **Slide Sorter View**.
   OR
   On the View toolbar, click **Slide Show**.

Navigate Panes in Normal View

1. Click the Slides tab in the left pane to see thumbnails of slides.
   OR
   Click the Outline tab in the left pane to see the outline of a presentation or add/edit text.
   OR
   Click the notes pane to type or see notes about a slide.
   OR
   Click the slide pane to add or edit text and graphics.

OR

1. Click **View** . . . . Alt + V
2. Select **Task Pane** to perform many common tasks . . . . K

Save a Presentation in a New Folder

1. Click **File** . . . . Alt + F
2. Select **Save As** . . . . A
3. In the Save As dialog box, click the **Save in** down arrow and navigate to the location where you wish to place the new folder . . . . Alt + I
4. Click **Create New Folder**.
5. In the New Folder dialog box, type a folder name and click OK.
6. In the **File name** box, type or edit the file name if desired. . . . . Alt + N
7. Click **Save**. Alt + S

Use Print Preview

1. Click **Print Preview**.
   OR
   Click **File** . . . . Alt + F
   Select **Print Preview** V
2. Click the slide to magnify it or restore it to its original size.
3. Click the down arrows on the toolbar and select options as desired.
4. Click **Close Preview**. . . . . Alt + C

Print Presentation Components

1. Click **Print Preview** .
   OR
   Click **File** . . . . **Alt + F**
   Select **Print Preview** . . . . **V**
2. Click the **Print What** down arrow and select one of the options. . . . . **Alt + P**
3. Click the down arrows on the toolbar and select options as desired.
4. Click **Print** , and select the print options as desired.
5. Click OK.

Use AutoContent Wizard

1. Click **File** . . . . **Alt + F**
2. Select **New** . . . . **N**
3. In the New Presentation task pane, click **From AutoContent Wizard**.
4. In the AutoContent Wizard dialog boxes, select the desired options and click Next to create a presentation.
5. Click **Finish**.

Modify Font, Size, and Color

1. In the slide pane or on the Outline tab, select the text to modify.
2. Click the **Font** down arrow Times New Roman.
3. Select a new font.
4. Click the **Font Size** down arrow 12.
5. Select a new font size.
6. Click the **Font Color** down arrow .
7. Select a new font color.

Add Text

1. In the slide pane or on the Outline tab, place the insertion point where you want to add text.
2. Type the new text.

Delete Text

1. In the slide pane or on the Outline tab, select the text to delete.
2. Press Delete.

OR

1. In the slide pane or on the Outline tab, place the insertion point to the right of text to be deleted.
2. Press Backspace as needed.

Procedure Summary

Change the Indent Level of a Subtitle

1. To change the indent of all subtitles in a list, open the ruler, if necessary.
2. Click anywhere in the subtitle placeholder.
3. Drag the bottom indent marker on the ruler to the right or left to the desired location.

OR

1. To change the indent of a particular subtitle, click anywhere in that subtitle.
2. Click **Increase Indent** to demote the subtitle.
   OR
   Click **Decrease Indent** to promote it.

Add Slides

1. In the slide pane, on the Outline tab, or on the Slides tab click where you want to add a slide.
2. Click **New Slide** .
   OR
   Click **Insert** . . . . Alt + I
   Select **New Slide** . . . . N

OR

1. On the Slides tab or at the left edge of a title on the Outline tab, place the insertion point between two slides.
2. Press **Enter** . . . . Enter

Copy Slides

1. On the Slides tab or in slide sorter view, select a slide to copy.
2. Click Copy .
   OR
   Right-click.
   Select **Copy** C
   OR
   Click **Edit** . . . . Alt + E
   Select **Copy** C
3. On the Slides tab or in slide sorter view, click where you want the slide to be located.
4. Click **Paste** .
   OR
   Right-click.
   Select **Paste** . . . . P
   OR
   Click **Edit** . . . . Alt + E
   Select **Paste** . . . . P

Delete Slides

1. In the slide pane, in slide sorter view, or on the Outline tab or Slides tab, select a slide to be deleted.
2. Press Delete.
   OR
   Click **Edit** . . . . Alt + E
   Select **Delete Slide** . . . . D
   OR
   Right-click and select **Delete Slide** . . . . D, Enter

Duplicate Slides

1. In slide sorter view, on the Outline tab, or on the Slides tab, select a slide to duplicate.
2. Click **Edit** . . . . .Alt + E
3. Select **Duplicate** I

Rearrange Slides

1. In slide sorter view, on the Slides tab, or on the Outline tab, select a slide to move to a different location.
2. Click and drag to place the insertion point in a new location.
3. Release the mouse.

OR

1. Right-click and select **Cut** . . . . .T, Enter
2. Place the insertion point in a new location.
3. Right-click, and select **Paste** . . . . P

Create Hyperlinks

1. On the Outline tab or in the slide pane, select the text where you want to create a hyperlink.
2. Click **Insert Hyperlink** .
   OR
   Click **Insert** .Alt + I
   Select **Hyperlink** I
3. In the Insert Hyperlink dialog box, select **Place in This Document** to link to another slide in the same presentation . . . . . Alt + A
4. Select a slide title.

OR

1. In the Insert Hyperlink dialog box, select **Existing File or Web Page** to link to another file or a Web page . . . . Alt + X
2. Navigate to and select the file, or type the Web address in the Address box.
3. To add a ScreenTip, click **ScreenTip** . . . . Alt + P
4. Type the ScreenTip text.
5. Click **OK** to close the Set Hyperlink ScreenTip dialog box.
6. Click **OK**.

Lesson Review and Exercises

PowerPoint®

Summary Checklist

- ☑ Are you able to navigate a presentation easily?
- ☑ Have you created a folder with a name that is easy to remember?
- ☑ Can you preview all components of a presentation?
- ☑ Can you print all components of a presentation?
- ☑ Can you use the AutoContent Wizard to create a presentation?
- ☑ Can you add text in a presentation?
- ☑ Can you edit text in a presentation?
- ☑ Can you modify text in a presentation?
- ☑ Do you know several ways to change the indent level of a subtitle?
- ☑ Can you manipulate the slides in a presentation?
- ☑ Can you create hyperlinks to another slide, to another file, and to a Web site?

Key Terms

- AutoContent Wizard (p. 488)
- boilerplate text (p. 488)
- demote (p. 494)
- indent level (p. 494)
- object (p. 481)
- object area (p. 481)
- placeholder (p. 481)
- presentation (p. 478)
- promote (p. 494)
- Rich Text Format (RTF) (p. 483)
- splitter bar (p. 479)
- subtitle (p. 481)
- text area (p. 481)
- thumbnail (p. 479)
- title (p. 481)
- title area (p. 481)
- title slide (p. 481)

APPLY IT! Guided Activities

1. Modify, Preview, Print, and Save

You are a farm manager, and your local high school has invited you to present information about the agriculture industry at its upcoming Career Day. You want to experiment with font styles and colors in the *Agriculture.ppt* presentation to improve the appearance of the slides for your audience. You also want to edit text, and then navigate the presentation to check your work. Finally, you will preview and print the presentation and then save it in a new location.

Follow these steps to modify text, and then to navigate, preview, print, and save your presentation:

a. Open *Agriculture.ppt*. Navigate to the *Lesson 1* subfolder within your *Unit 4* folder, and create a new folder named *Career Day*. Save the file as *xxx-Agriculture.ppt* in this newly created folder.

b. On slide 1, select the presentation title and change the font to Arial and the font color to a shade of green. Change the subtitle font to Verdana, bright yellow.

c. Navigate to slide 9. Change all of the subtitle text to Times New Roman and a shade of green.

d. Go to slide 2 on the Outline tab. Change the title's font color to the same yellow as in the subtitle on slide 1. Use Format Painter to change the font color for the titles on all remaining slides to the same yellow. In the third subtitle, delete the space before *workers* to change the subtitle to *Farmworkers*.

e. Click Print Preview, select Slides in the Print What box, and click Print. In the *Color/grayscale* section of the Print dialog box, choose Pure Black and White. In the *Print range* section, select Slides and type 1. Click OK to print the first slide.

f. In the Save As dialog box, select Outline/RTF in the *Save as type* list box **(see Figure 1.41)**, and save the file as *xxx-Agriculture Outline.rtf* in the newly created folder.

g. Close the presentation.

PowerPoint®

Figure 1.41 Selecting Outline/RTF format

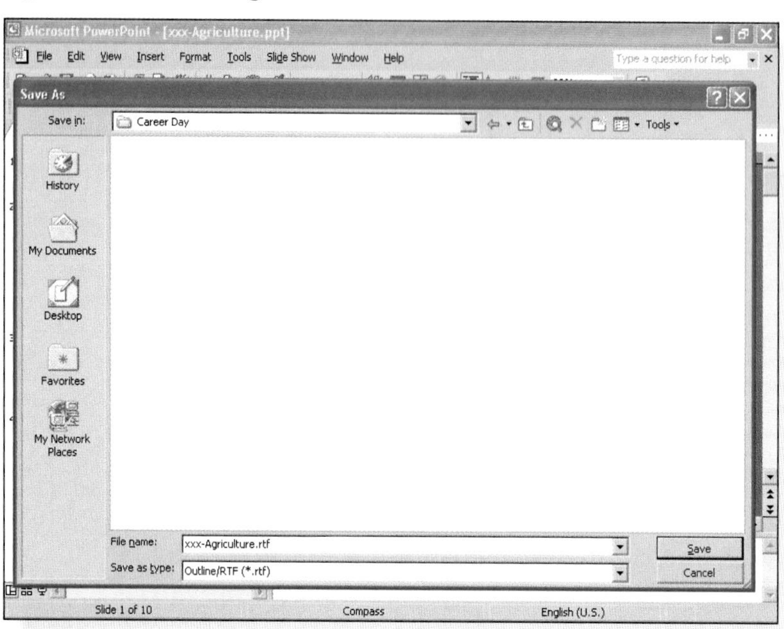

2. Manipulate Slides, Insert a Hyperlink, and Print a Comment

As the Safety and Education Director for your local cycling association, you will soon be giving a presentation regarding bicycle safety. You have the rough draft of your presentation, but you need to rearrange the slides. You also want to insert hyperlinks to jump to other slides within the presentation and link to a Web site.

Follow these steps to manipulate slides and create hyperlinks:

a. Open *Cycling.ppt* and switch to slide sorter view. Save the presentation as *xxx-Cycling.ppt*.

b. Move slide 5 between slides 2 and 3.

c. On slide 2 in normal view, select *Helmets* in the subtitle, and click Insert Hyperlink. In the *Link to* panel, click Place in This Document. In the *Select a place in this document* list box, select slide 3 and click OK.

d. Select the graphic on slide 1 **(see Figure 1.42)**, and insert a hyperlink to www.bhsi.org. Click ScreenTip and type Bicycle Helmet Safety Institute in the Set Hyperlink ScreenTip dialog box. Click OK to close the dialog boxes. Click outside the slide to deselect the text.

Figure 1.42 Selecting the graphic to be linked

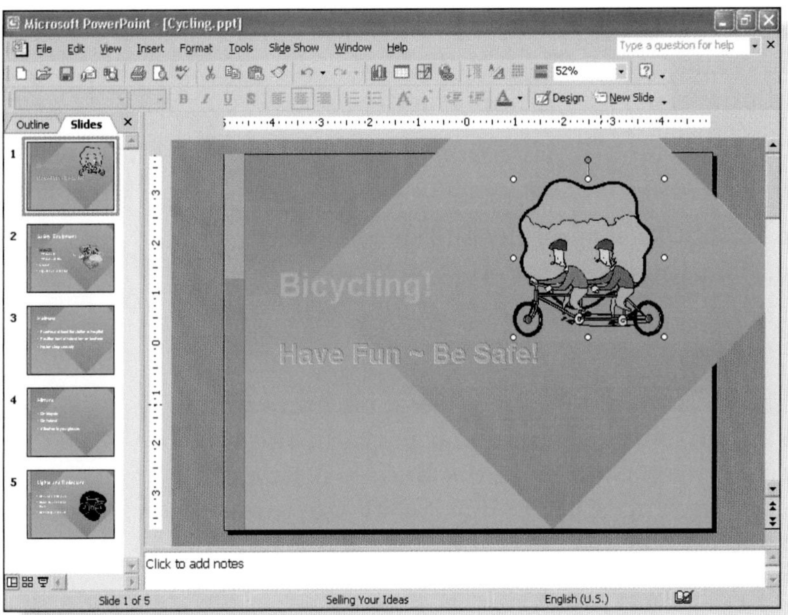

e. Log on to the Internet, if necessary. In slide show view, test the hyperlinks. (***Note:*** After you link to the BHSI Web site, click Back to return to your presentation.)

f. Click Print Preview and navigate to slide 3. Click Options and select Include Comment Pages. Click Print, and print only slide 3.

g. Save the presentation and close the presentation. Close your browser, and disconnect from the Internet, if necessary.

Do It Yourself

1. Create a Presentation to Introduce a Speaker

As the Public Relations Director at Home Market Realty, you will be introducing the speaker at the next monthly meeting. You want to create a presentation for this purpose.

To create your presentation to introduce the speaker, do the following:

a. Use the AutoContent Wizard to create your presentation. Select the Carnegie Coach type of presentation for introducing a speaker. Create an on-screen presentation.

b. Title your presentation appropriately for your audience.

c. Insert the company name as the subtitle on slide 1. On slide 2, replace the boilerplate text in the subtitles with your speaker's name and appropriate biographical information about your speaker.

d. Modify the font color and font size on slide 1.

e. Proofread your presentation carefully and save it as *xxx-Speaker Intro.ppt*. Then, close the presentation.

2. Add and Delete Slides

As a park ranger with the National Park Service, you try to influence others to appreciate and preserve the national parks in the U.S. You are currently preparing a presentation on the Buffalo National River Park for an upcoming meeting with a Boy Scout troop and their parents. You need to add and modify text, and you may need to delete some slides.

To add and delete slides and to modify text, do the following:

a. Open and view *Buffalo National River.ppt*. Save the presentation as *xxx-Buffalo National River.ppt*.

b. Insert new slides as desired to include the following information:
Additional Park Activities:
Auto touring
Backpacking
Bird watching
Horseback riding
Nature walks
Stargazing
Wilderness workshops
Wildlife viewing

Regularly Scheduled Special Programs (offered by park rangers Memorial Day through Labor Day):
Guided hikes
Float trips
Junior ranger programs
Music programs
Evening programs

Contact information for Buffalo National River Park:
402 N. Walnut, Suite 136
Harrison, AR 72601-3841
E-mail: buff_information@nps.gov

c. Don't include too much information on any slide; use an appropriate font size that your entire audience can read easily. Add other appropriate text to the slides, and create level 2 subtitles as needed. Change the formatting on some or all of the slides attractively **(see Figure 1.43)**. Use Format Painter to copy formatting.

Figure 1.43 Changing the formatting

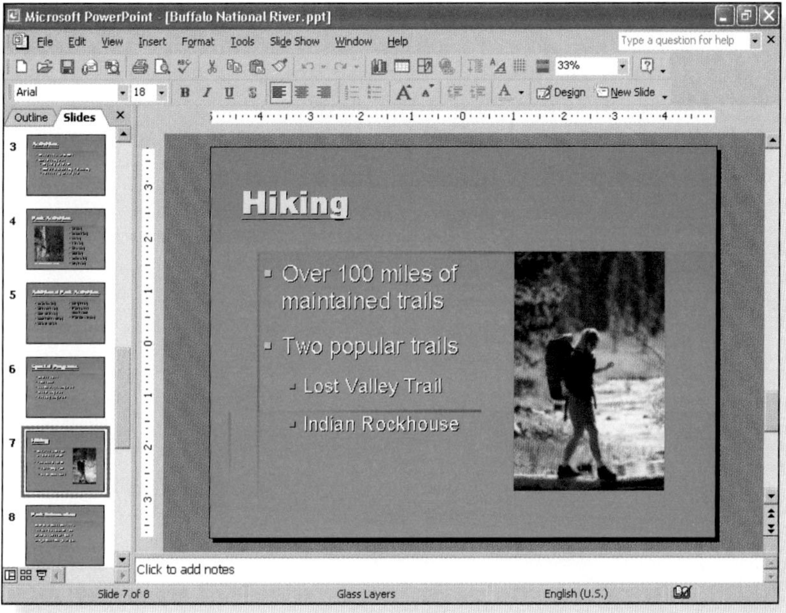

d. Delete slides that seem inappropriate. Rearrange the slides as desired.

e. View the entire presentation in slide show view, and correct any errors. When you are satisfied with your presentation, save it and close it.

3. Duplicate and Edit Slides

As Administrative Assistant of a national youth organization, you recently attended a meeting where you saw a presentation about the Buffalo National River Park. The presentation captured your interest, and you are now eager to arrange a youth group trip to Buffalo National River Park next summer. On the trip, you would like the group to enjoy the outdoors, take long walks, participate in water activities, and see part of the country they may never have seen. To interest your director in this trip, you have been creating a PowerPoint presentation named *National Youth Trip.ppt*. You have already included most of the information that was contained in the Buffalo National River Park presentation, and you want to add camping information and other details about the park that will create enthusiasm for the trip.

To duplicate and edit slides, do the following:

a. Open *National Youth Trip.ppt*. Save the presentation as *xxx-National Youth Trip.ppt* in a new folder named *Camping Trip*. Duplicate slide 5.

b. Make the following changes to the new slide 6: Replace the title with Camping, replace the first level 1 subtitle with Buffalo Point, replace the second level 1 subtitle with Carver, and replace the two level 2 subtitles with the following six subtitles: Erbie, Hasty, Kyles Landing, Lost Valley, Ozark, and Steel Creek **(see Figure 1.44)**.

c. Open *xxx-Buffalo National River.ppt*. Position the two presentations side by side on the screen.

Figure 1.44 Duplicating a slide

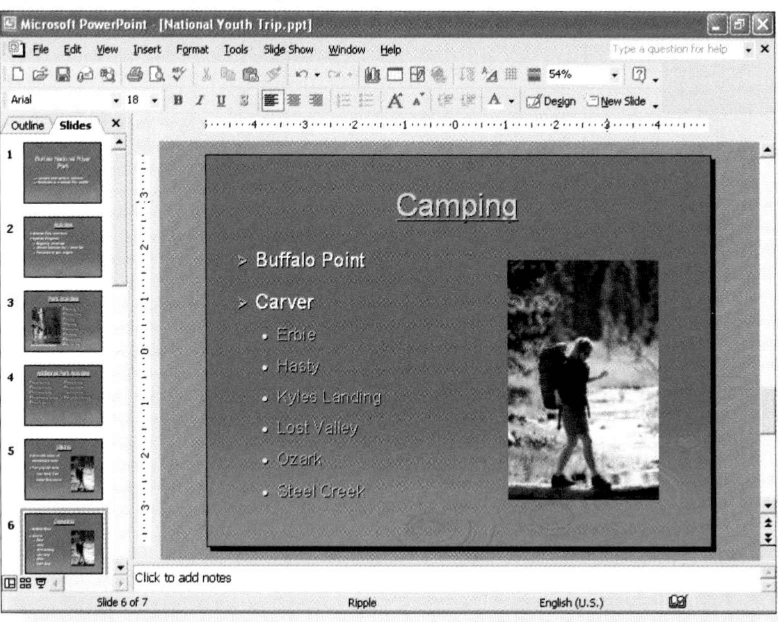

d. In *xxx-Buffalo National River.ppt*, copy slide 5, and paste it between slides 6 and 7 in *xxx-National Youth Trip.ppt*.

e. Select Cascade on the Window menu, and maximize *National Youth Trip.ppt*. View the revised presentation in slide show view; make any desired changes to finalize the presentation.

f. Preview and print the presentation as handouts (3 per page).

g. Close *xxx-Buffalo National River.ppt* without saving. Save the other presentation. Save the presentation again in the same folder with the same file name, but with an extension of *.rtf*. Then, close the presentation.

4. Create a Presentation With Hyperlinks

You have been working at a local chili parlor for nearly a year. Since you have more experience than the other restaurant associates and you are learning how to use PowerPoint, your manager asked you to create a presentation to orient new employees to the restaurant.

To create a presentation for new employees that will include hyperlinks, do the following:

a. Open *Chili.ppt*. Save the presentation as *xxx-Chili.ppt*.

b. View the presentation in slide show view.

c. In normal view, go to slide 3. Type Optional ingredients as the fourth level 1 subtitle. On slide 5, demote the last two subtitles to level 2 **(see Figure 1.45)**.

Figure 1.45 New level 2 subtitles

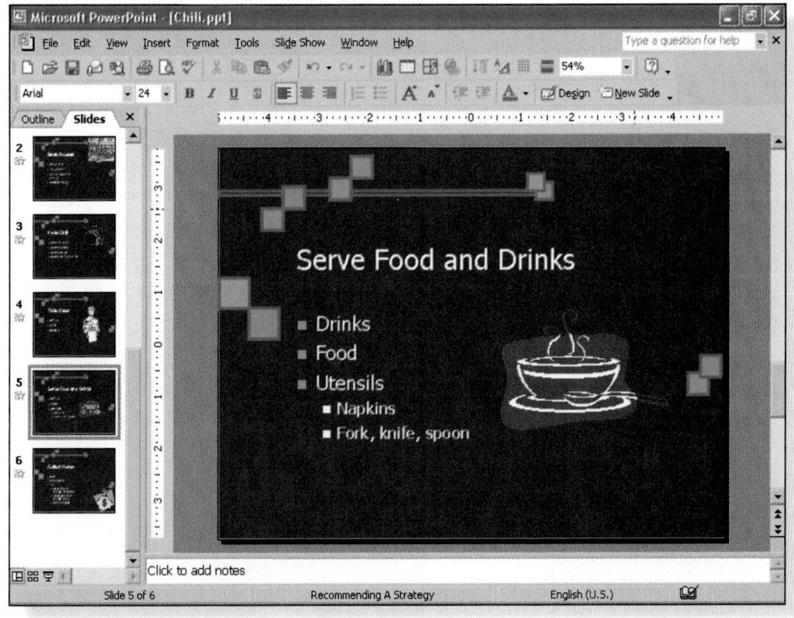

d. On the last slide, change the third level 1 subtitle to Tips. Promote the last level 2 subtitle to level 1.

e. On slide 2, insert a hyperlink in each of the four subtitles, linking each one to an appropriate slide in this presentation. (For example, link the first subtitle on slide 2 to slide 3.)

f. On slide 3, insert a hyperlink to *Recipe.ppt* and insert an appropriate ScreenTip. Test all hyperlinks in slide show view. (***Note:*** Since this presentation will include numerous hyperlinks, press Esc to stop the slide show after you test each hyperlink. Then, restart the slide show to check the remaining hyperlinks.)

g. Preview and print the notes pages. Save the presentation. Close all open files.

Challenge Yourself

Create a Travel Presentation

Assume that you own and operate a travel agency named Anytime Travel Group, Inc. You must present information about traveling to the Caribbean Islands to a group of prospective clients.

Before you can create your presentation, you must search the Internet to locate appropriate information about the Caribbean Islands.

You want to include information on the following:

- Interesting sites on St. Lucia and Barbados
- The weather for the current month
- The clothing for the current month
- Other facts that might intrigue prospective clients

Use the AutoContent Wizard to create an on-screen presentation. Choose a General, Generic presentation. Create an appropriate title slide. Instead of replacing the boilerplate information, delete all slides except the first one. Then, list in outline form—either directly on the new slides or on the Outline tab—information about the Caribbean Islands.

Your final travel presentation should include at least six slides **(see Figure 1.46)**. Remember to use Increase Indent and Decrease Indent to create different levels of subtitles. Add, delete, and rearrange slides as appropriate. Modify the font, font size, and font color on two or more slides. Include at least two hyperlinks in your presentation.

Figure 1.46 A travel presentation

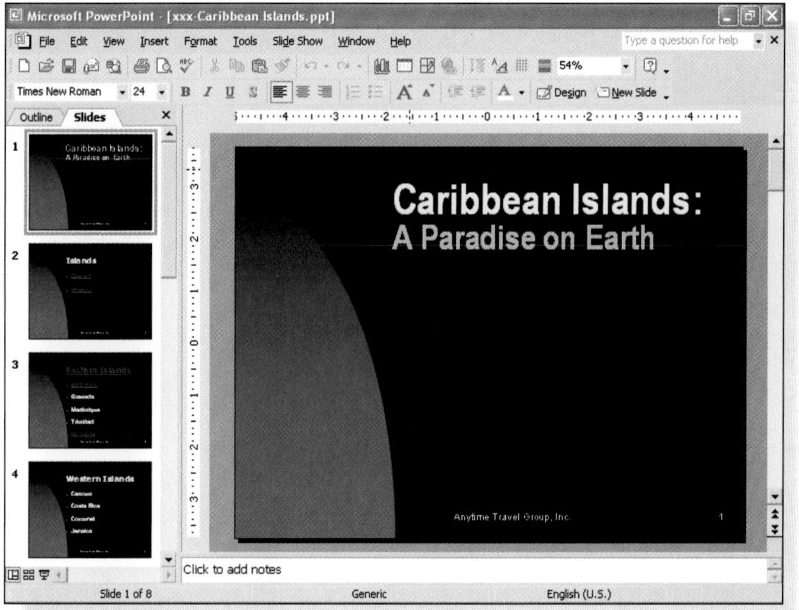

When you are satisfied with your presentation, view it in slide show view. Then, preview and print handouts (3 slides per page).

Save the presentation as *xxx-Caribbean Islands.ppt* in a new folder called *Travel Presentations*. Then, change the file type to Outline/RTF and save the presentation as *xxx-Caribbean Islands.rtf* in the *Travel Presentations* folder.

Share your presentation with a classmate. Critique each other's presentations to determine whether all slides are easy to read and whether each of you has included appropriate information to capture your classmate's interest.

Lesson 2

Designing a Presentation

Lesson Exercise Objectives

After completing this lesson, you'll be able to do the following tasks:

1. Create a presentation using a design template
2. Customize a design template and a slide layout
3. Create a presentation from a blank presentation
4. Import text from Word to create a presentation

Key Terms

- color scheme (p. 525)
- design template (p. 522)
- slide layout (p. 524)

Microsoft Office Specialist Activities

PP2002: 1.1, 2.1, 4.1, 4.4, 4.5, 4.9

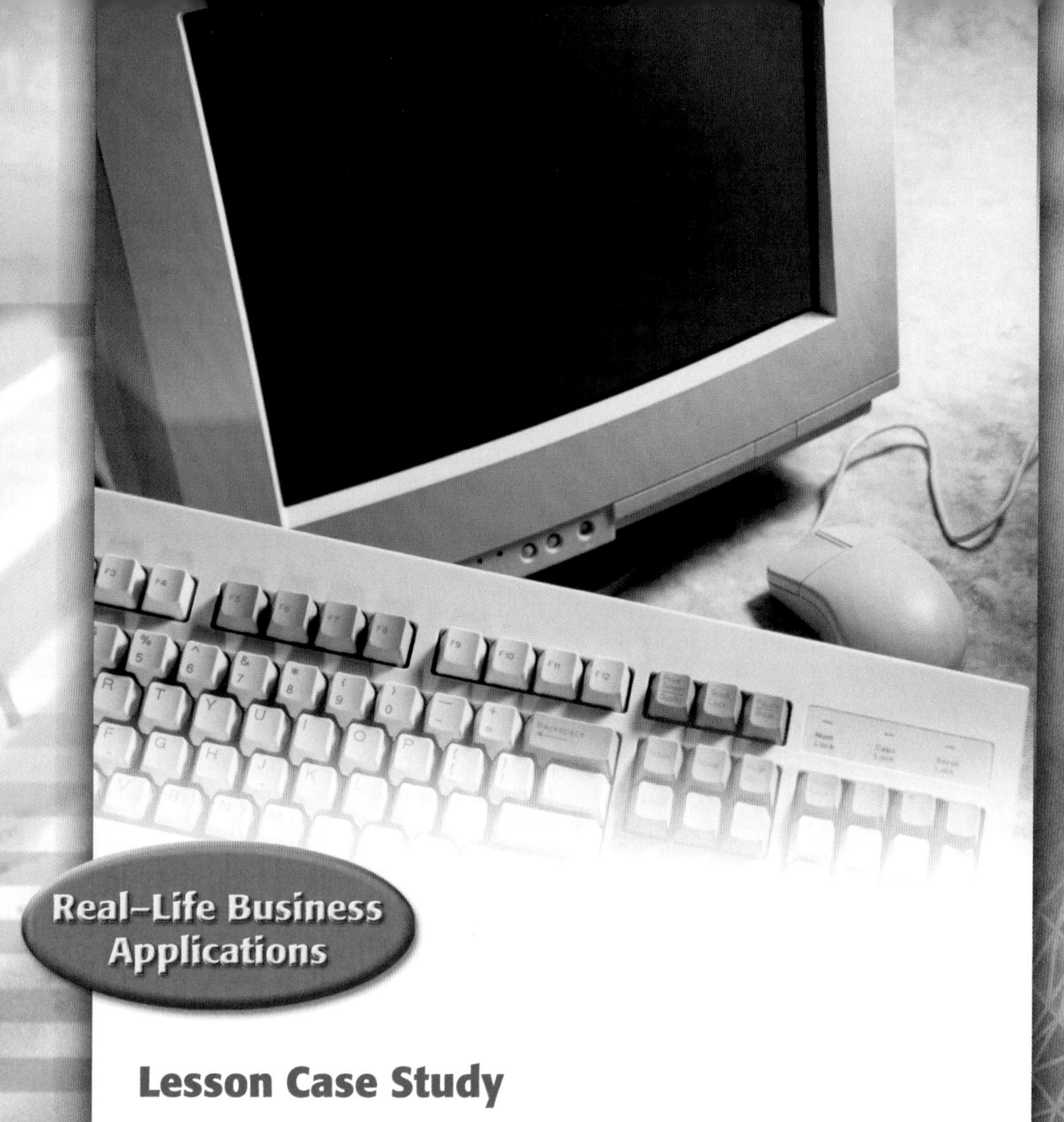

Real-Life Business Applications

Lesson Case Study

In this lesson, you will play the role of the Events Coordinator for the National Association of Roller Coaster Enthusiasts. Keep the following information in mind as you work through the lesson exercises.

- **Job responsibilities and goals.** As the Events Coordinator, you are responsible for organizing and publicizing NARCE events. One such event is the annual trip NARCE members take to an amusement park that is within driving distance of Kalamazoo. Other events include trips to parks in states farther away, as well as a meeting to kick off the summer roller coaster season. One of your goals is to create an attractive presentation about these events to use when addressing current and potential NARCE members as well as members of other roller coaster enthusiast clubs.
- **The project.** You are preparing a series of presentations to use when publicizing NARCE trips and annual meetings.
- **The challenge ahead.** You want to be sure your presentations are audience appropriate, professional, and eye-catching.

Microsoft Office Specialist PP2002 1.1, 4.1

Exercise 1 Overview:
Create a Presentation Using a Design Template

You can use a design template to create a polished presentation. A **design template** is a file that contains the preprogrammed formatting available for a presentation, such as colors, background design, fonts, and bullets. You can select a design template as you create a presentation, or you can add a design template to an existing presentation.

You can apply design templates to one slide, several slides, or all the slides in a presentation. You can also use more than one design template in a presentation, although you should remember to maintain consistency throughout the presentation.

You can preview and select design templates in the Slide Design task pane. With a slide displayed in the slide pane, the Slide Design task pane (see figure 2.1) displays the slide design currently in use, the designs that you have used recently, and all the designs that are available.

In the following exercises, you will begin creating a presentation to publicize the next NARCE annual trip, first using one design template, and then applying multiple design templates to the presentation.

Figure 2.1 Use the Slide Design task pane

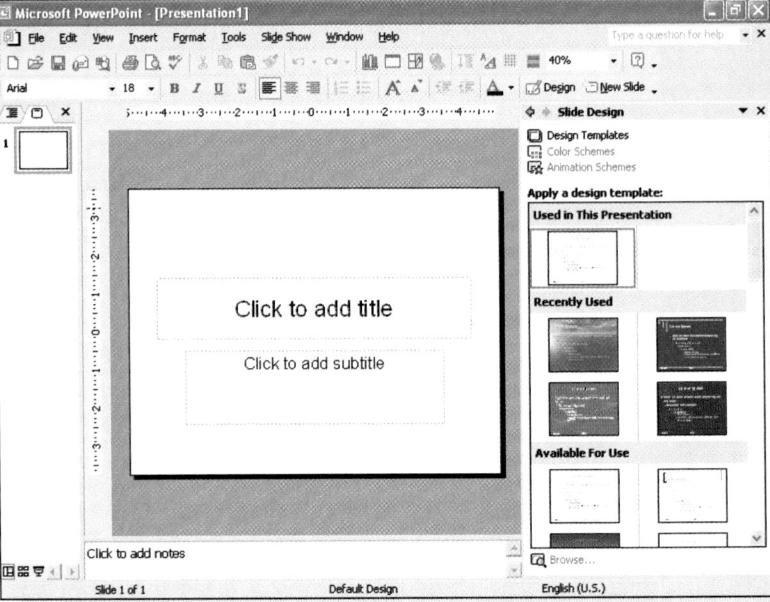

Figure 2.2 New Presentation task pane

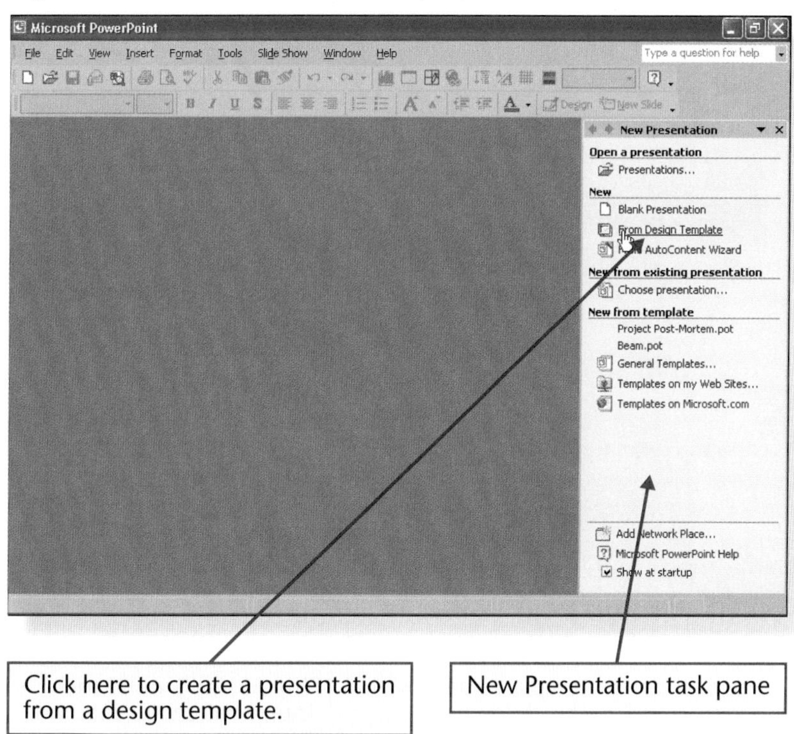

Step Through It™

Exercise 1A: Use a design template

1. Select New on the File menu if the task pane is not open.
2. Select From Design Template in the task pane (see Figure 2.2).
3. Scroll down to view the alphabetical list of available design templates. Next, point to the Beam template and click its down arrow.

PowerPoint®

Figure 2.3 Selecting a design template

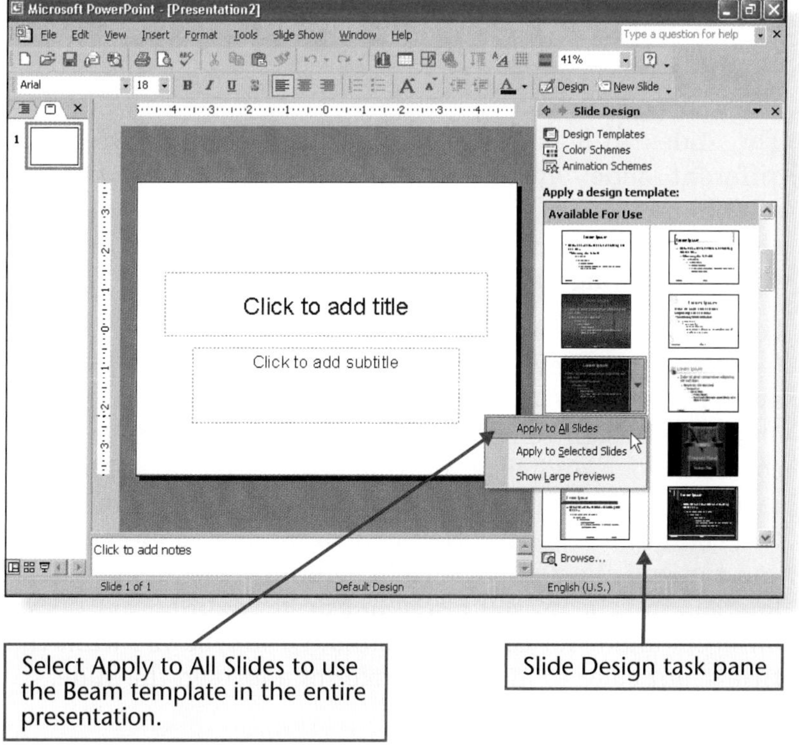

4. Select Apply to All Slides (see Figure 2.3).
5. Type NARCE Annual Trip as the title and June 24–25 as the subtitle. Then, insert a second slide.
6. On slide 2, type Amusement Parks We'll Visit as the title. For the three subtitles, type Six Flags Kentucky Kingdom, Paramount's Kings Island, and Cedar Point.
7. Save the presentation as *xxx-Annual Trip.ppt*.

Step Through It™
Exercise 1B: Change a slide design template

1. Save *xxx-Annual Trip.ppt* as *xxx-Annual Trip Revised.ppt* and display the first slide.
2. Select Design Templates in the Slide Design task pane.
3. Point to the Textured template, click its down arrow, and select Apply to Selected Slides.
4. Apply the Cliff design template to slide 2 only (see Figure 2.4). Save and close the presentation.

Figure 2.4 Applying a design template

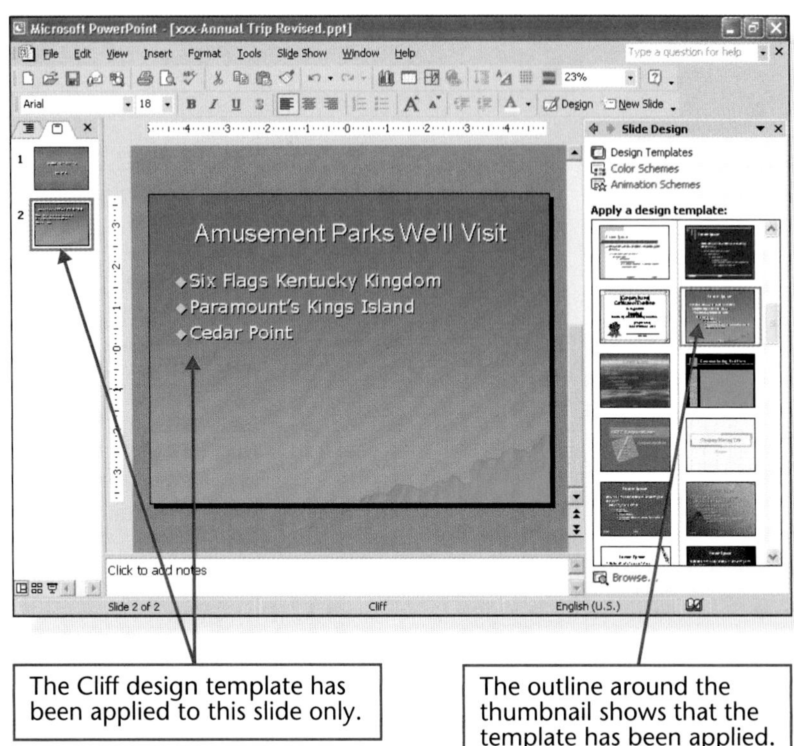

Microsoft Office Specialist
PP2002 4.1, 4.4, 4.5, 4.9

Exercise 2 Overview:
Customize a Design Template and a Slide Layout

The slides in a PowerPoint presentation can have many different slide layouts. A **slide layout** is a particular combination of placeholders for text and/or graphical elements. You can choose a slide layout for a particular slide by opening the Slide Layout task pane.

Once you have created a presentation using a design template, you may realize you could improve the presentation by making some changes to one or more slide layouts, or to the design template, to better fit your presentation content, your audience, or your own personal taste. For instance, you might want to change from one-column text to two-column text, or position text in the left column only so you can add clip art in the right column. You might like the font color in the presentation, but prefer a different color or different shade for the background. Or maybe you want the title's font color to match the color of a logo on the slide.

One way to customize a design template is by changing its color scheme. A **color scheme** consists of the eight colors used in the design of the slide—colors for background, fonts, hyperlinks, and so on. A presentation's color scheme varies depending on the design template used in the presentation.

PowerPoint provides nine preset color schemes that allow you to use specific color settings for various parts of your presentation, or you can edit a color scheme to achieve different results (see Figure 2.5). Once you have customized a design template, you can save it with a new name so that you can use it in other presentations. However, always be sure you have permission from your instructor or the computer's owner before you save a customized template.

Type: modify a color scheme

Figure 2.5 The Edit Color Scheme dialog box

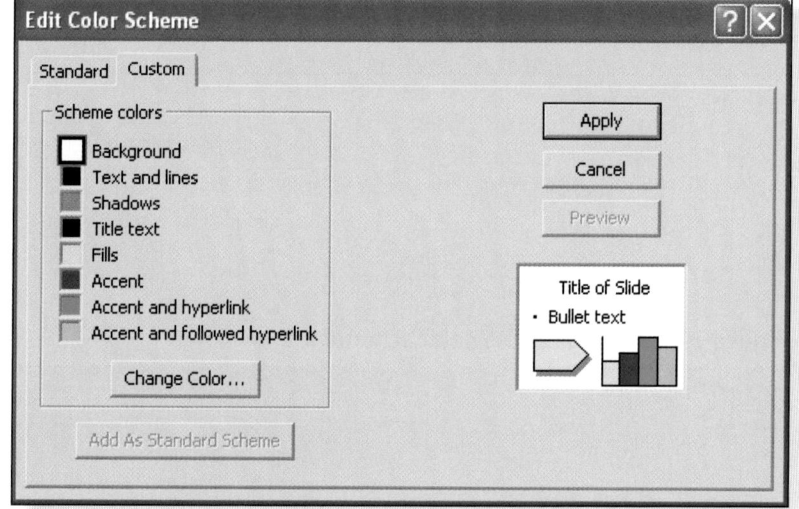

In addition to customizing a design template, you may customize one or several slides in a presentation. You already know how to *choose* a slide layout; now you will learn how to *customize* one. For instance, you might want to increase the font size on a slide for more emphasis or improved readability, change the bullet style, or change the color of an object.

In the following exercises, you will work on the *Roller Coaster Roundup.ppt* presentation, which advertises an upcoming NARCE event. You will customize the design template by editing the color scheme, and then you will change the layout on one of the slides.

Step Through It™

Exercise 2A: Customize a design template

1. Open *Roller Coaster Roundup.ppt* and save it as *xxx-Roundup Color.ppt*. Display the Slide Design task pane.
2. Select Color Schemes and view the available color schemes (see Figure 2.6).
3. With slide 1 in the slide pane, point to the second dark blue color scheme, and apply it to the selected slide.

Figure 2.6 Color schemes

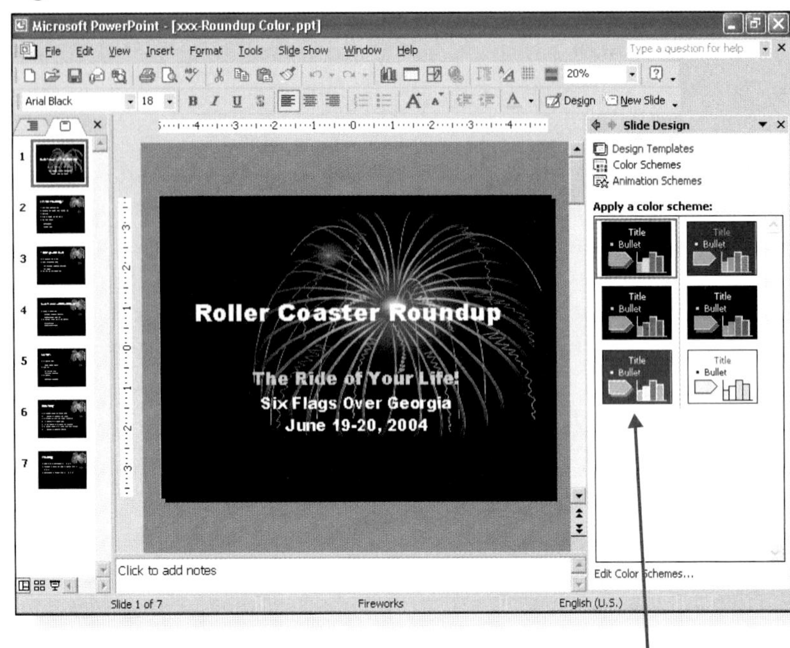

4. Point to the same dark blue color scheme again and apply it to all slides in the presentation (see Figure 2.7).
5. Select Edit Color Schemes at the bottom of the task pane.
6. In the Edit Color Scheme dialog box, click Background, if necessary, and then click Change Color.

Figure 2.7 Changing the color scheme

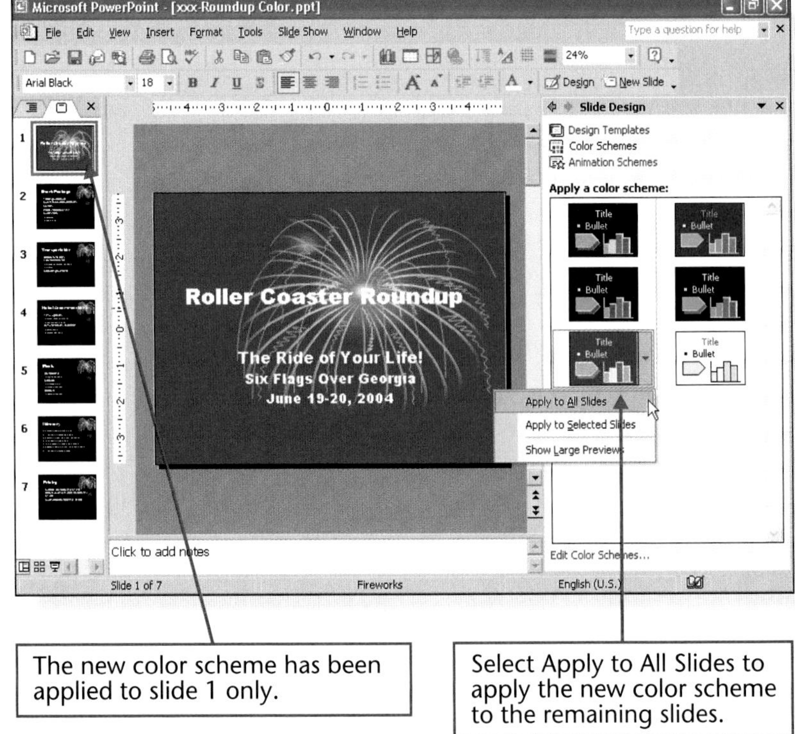

Figure 2.8 Changing the background color

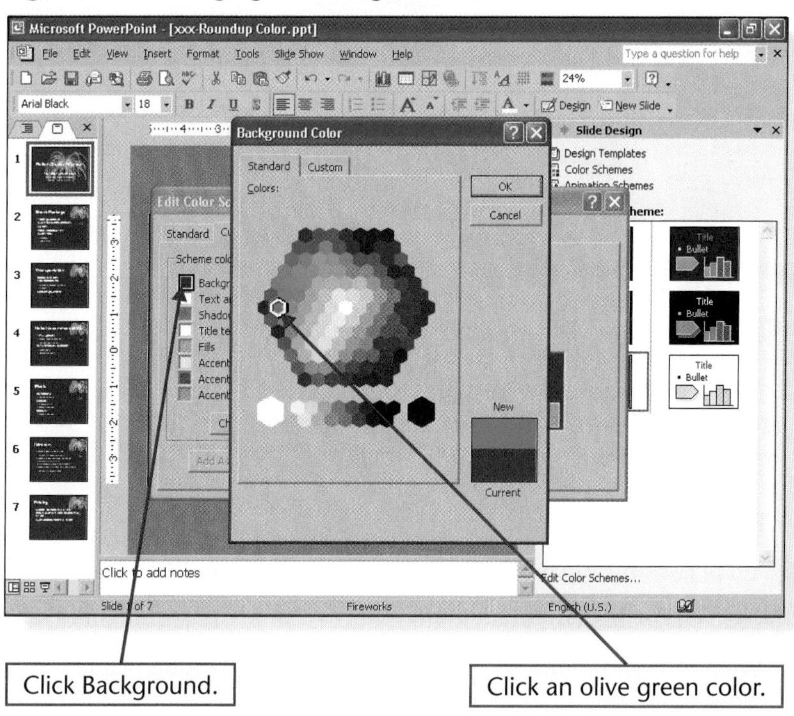

7. Click an olive green color (see Figure 2.8), click OK, and then click Apply.
8. Look at the new background color on the slides.
9. Save and close the presentation.

PowerPoint®

Figure 2.9 Selecting the Title and 2-Column Text layout

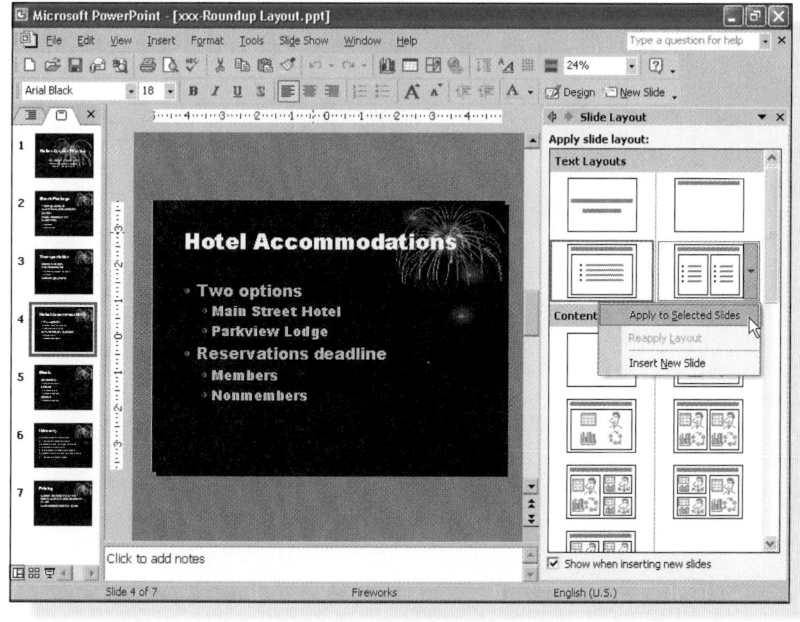

Step Through It™

Exercise 2B: Change a slide layout

1. Open *Roller Coaster Roundup.ppt* and save it as *xxx-Roundup Layout.ppt*. Display slide 4 and select Slide Layout on the Format menu.
2. In the Slide Layout task pane, apply the Title and 2-Column Text layout to slide 4 only (see Figure 2.9).
3. Move *Reservations deadline* and its subitems to column 2.
4. Save and close the presentation.

After finishing Exercises 1 and 2, you may test your skills by completing Apply It! Guided Activity 1, Create a Presentation.

Business Connections

Planning a Presentation That Makes a Difference

Effective presentations don't just happen. They require detailed planning. So, before you create the first slide in every presentation, always ask and answer these critical questions:

- Why are you making the presentation?
- Who is the specific audience for your presentation?
- What materials will you use to enhance your presentation?
- When will you make the presentation, and how much time will you have?
- Where (in what type of room) will you make your presentation?
- How will you deliver your presentation—will it be live, self-running, or online?

Remember that every detail of your presentation's design will either work with or against your purpose. Apply the following guidelines to develop professional presentations:

- Use brief lists with no more than six lines per slide and six words per line. This allows you to use larger fonts (at least 36 points on titles and at least 24 points on bulleted items), which results in improved readability and immediate impact.
- Limit each slide to one topic, and use transitions and animations appropriately.
- Use a consistent color scheme throughout a presentation, and limit the number of colors per slide to four or five at most.
- Choose background colors, fonts, and font colors that work well together. As a general rule, use dark colors for backgrounds and bright colors for text.
- Incorporate appropriate graphics that support the topic and attract interest.

CRITICAL THINKING

1. **Customizing Templates** Assume that you are making a motivational presentation to a college football team. Select an appropriate design template. Evaluate its fonts and color scheme. How would you customize the design template to be more appropriate for your audience?
2. **Creating Effective Presentations** With an assigned partner, explore the Web for guidelines on effective presentations, and develop a presentation that focuses on these guidelines. Exchange your presentation with another team, and provide constructive criticism based on the guidelines.

PowerPoint®

Microsoft Office Specialist
PP2002 1.1

Exercise 3 Overview:
Create a Presentation From a Blank Presentation

You know how to create a presentation from a design template and by using the AutoContent Wizard, but the quickest way to create a presentation is to start from a blank slide—also known as starting from a blank presentation or "starting from scratch."

You simply start PowerPoint and begin typing text. When you do this, your slides will initially appear with black text on a white background. Creating a presentation in this way, with no preset formatting and no preset color schemes, gives you the opportunity to format and customize the slides as you prefer.

In the following exercise, you will create a presentation that you will use at a summer meeting for NARCE members. You will start from scratch and then add slides, apply formatting, and add design templates.

Step Through It™
Exercise 3: Create a presentation from a blank presentation

1. Select New on the File menu and select Blank Presentation.
2. On the title slide, type NARCE Summer Kickoff as the title and May 21 as the subtitle (see Figure 2.10).
3. Add a new slide and type Member Meeting as the title.

Figure 2.10 Creating the title slide

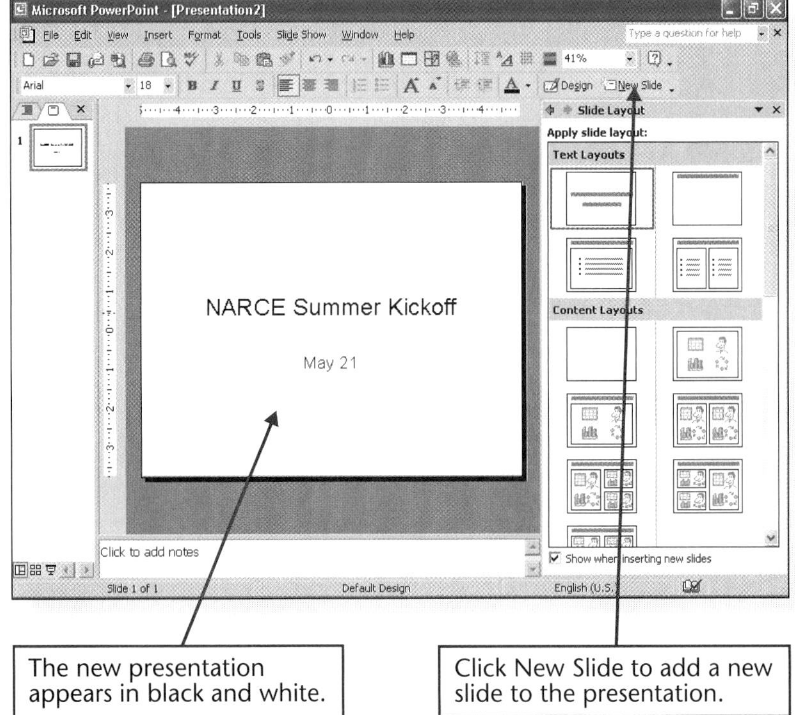

Figure 2.11 New bullet design for slide 2

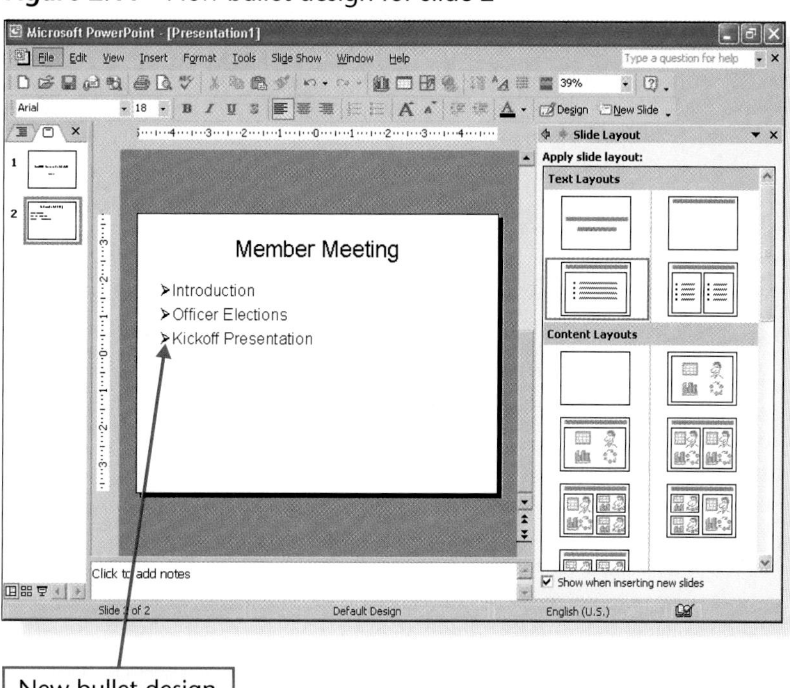

4. Type these subtitles:
   - Introduction
   - Officer Elections
   - Kickoff Presentation
5. Highlight the bulleted text, and change the bullets to arrowheads (see Figure 2.11).
6. On slide 2, change the title to 54 pt. bold, and change the subtitle font size to 40 pt. with 1.5 line spacing.
7. Apply the Pixel design template to the entire presentation.

Figure 2.12 Customizing the presentation

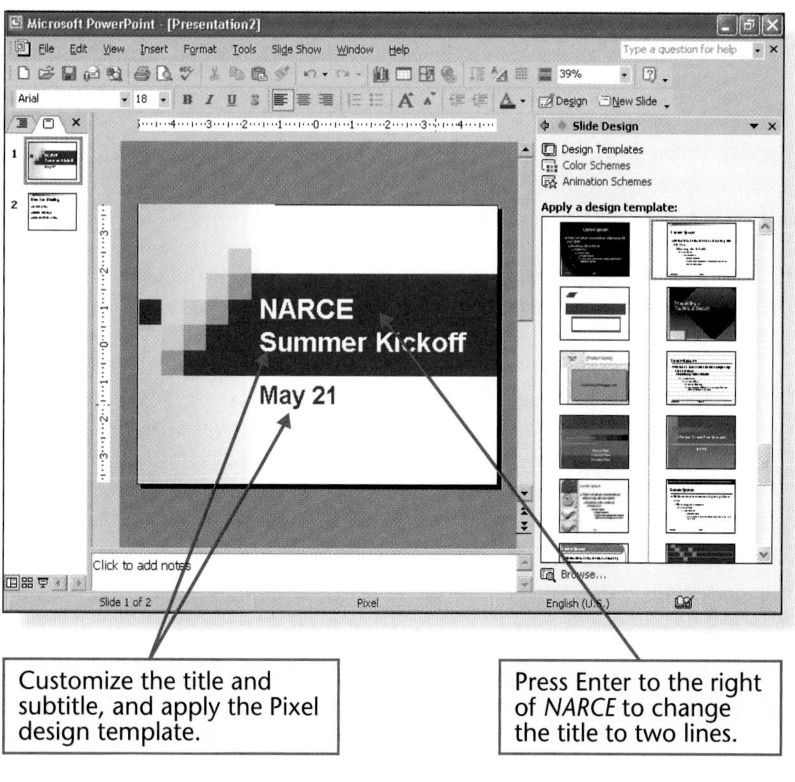

8. On the first slide, change the title font to 54 pt. bold, and change the subtitle font to 48 pt. bold, dark blue. Adjust the title so that *NARCE* appears on a line by itself (see Figure 2.12).
9. Edit the color scheme so that the entire presentation has a light blue background.
10. View the presentation, save it as *xxx-Kickoff.ppt*, and close the file.

Technology@School

Using PowerPoint in Class Presentations

In this unit, you are learning how to use PowerPoint in business, but how about using it in your everyday life? Can PowerPoint be as useful to students as it is to business professionals? In a word, yes. Whether you are giving an oral report, leading a group discussion, or running for class president, a well-designed presentation can help.

If your history teacher asks you to prepare an oral report on the effects of the Great Depression on America, PowerPoint can support your presentation in several ways:

- You can use bulleted lists to detail main points.
- You can display old photos from the Great Depression.
- You can prepare charts of statistics on the impact of the Great Depression.

✓CRITICAL THINKING

1. Think of assignments that you have coming up in school. Brainstorm a list of the ways you could use PowerPoint in some or all of these assignments.
2. Create a presentation for one of the assignments you listed. Continue to modify your presentation as you learn more about PowerPoint features in this unit.

Class	How You Can Use PowerPoint
Art	For an art report, you can download graphic files of works of art from the Web, scan your own artwork and display it on slides, or publish a gallery of your art on the Internet.
Science	Experiments are often performed as a series of steps. You can create a simple numbered list for the class to follow. You can make presentations of science projects with audience handouts.
Math	Formulas can be long and complex. With PowerPoint, however, you can easily create a formula and animate its parts so that each part appears on the screen as you are ready to discuss it.
English	You can display quotations, photos of authors, or an outline of a book's plot. Using PowerPoint's support for audio, you can play a recording of a literary reading as a slide appears
Social Studies	A PowerPoint presentation can enhance almost any social studies project. Historical photos, audio and video files, and even narration by your own recorded voice can make your presentation stand out.

Exercise 4 Overview:
Import Text From Word to Create a Presentation

Microsoft Office Specialist PP2002 2.1

You know how to create presentations by typing new text into placeholders; now you will learn how to create a presentation by importing text from a Microsoft Word document.

You can import either a Word outline or a Word document. Outlines imported into PowerPoint are based on heading level styles in Word. If you import a Word document, PowerPoint uses the styles in the document to create an outline structure. For instance, a Heading 1 style in Word displays as the slide title in PowerPoint; a Heading 2 style displays as a level 1 subtitle; and a Heading 3 style displays as a level 2 subtitle. It's easiest if you import an outline that was created in Word's Outline View, as shown in the Word document (see Figure 2.13), since it automatically contains styles.

Figure 2.13 Use Word's Outline view

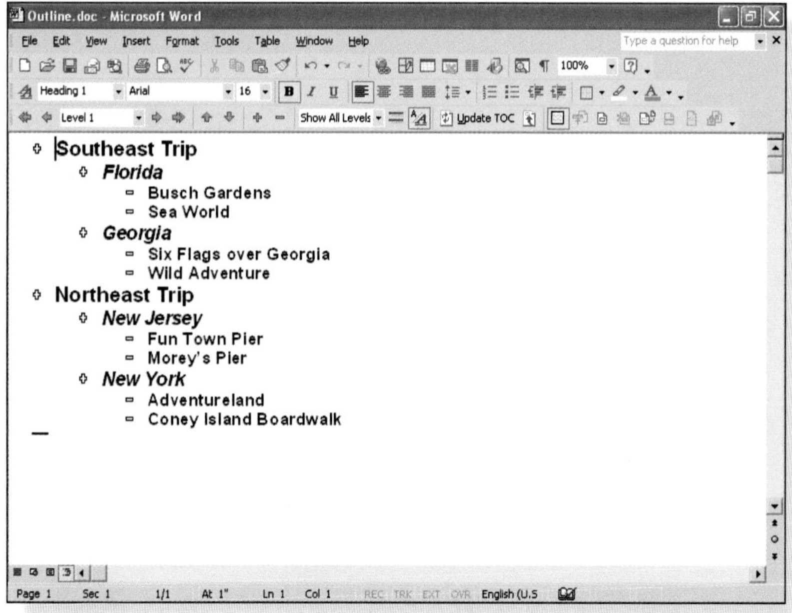

In the following exercise, you will import a Word outline to create a PowerPoint presentation on future NARCE trips to amusement parks. You will then make some formatting and design changes to the presentation so that it is more appropriate for your audience.

Step Through It™

Exercise 4: Use a Word outline to create a presentation

1 In PowerPoint, open *Outline.doc* (see Figure 2.14). (***Note:*** In the Open dialog box, select All Outlines or All Files in the *Files of type* box to display the Word documents.)

Figure 2.14 Imported Word outline

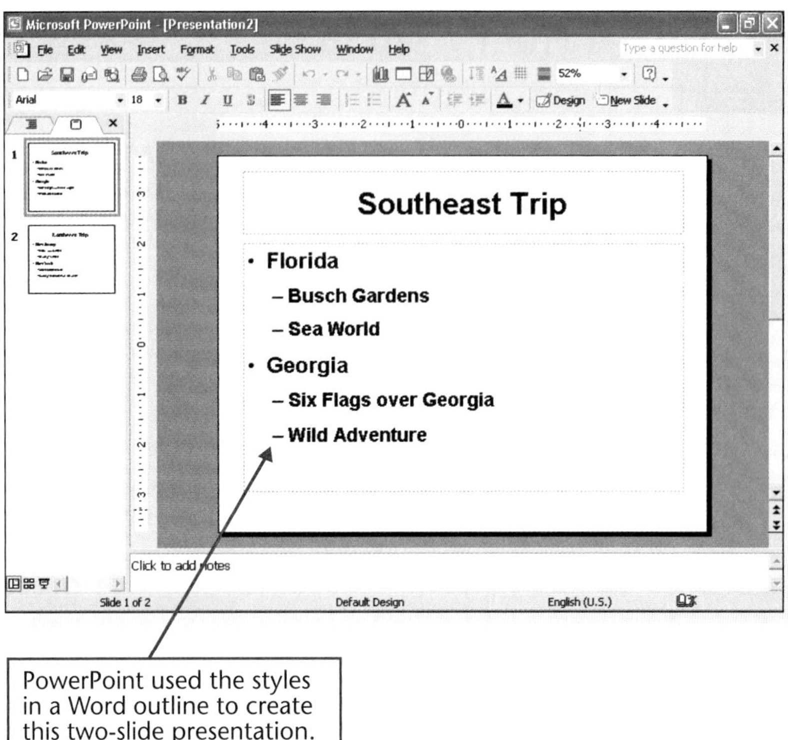

2 Save the presentation as *xxx-Upcoming Trips.ppt*. Insert a new slide as slide 1.

3 Change the layout of slide 1 to Title Only, and type Upcoming Trips as the title.

4 Apply the Ocean design template to all slides, and then center the slide 1 title vertically and horizontally on the slide (see Figure 2.15).

Figure 2.15 New slide layout and design template

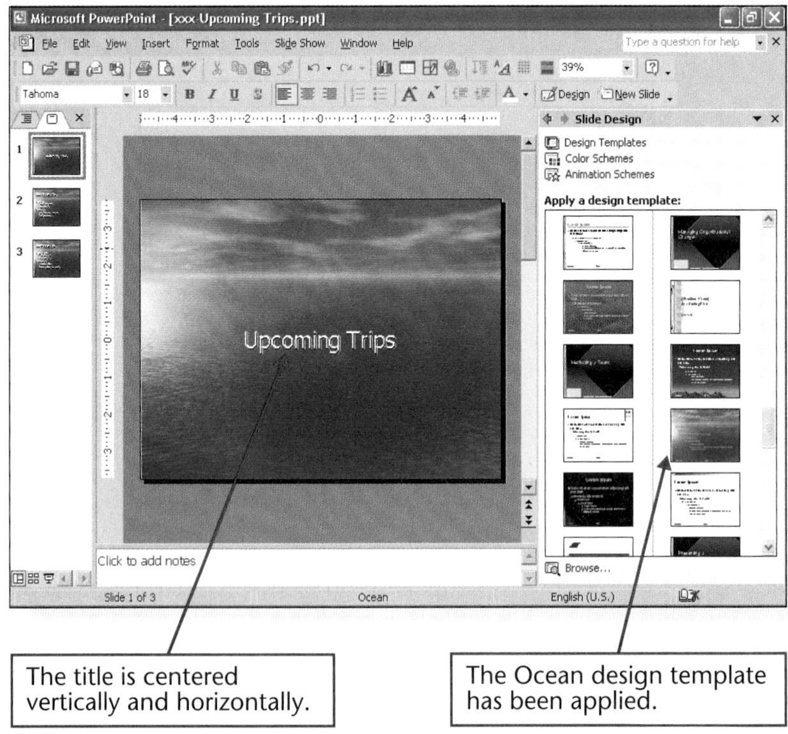

PowerPoint®

Figure 2.16 Customized Presentation

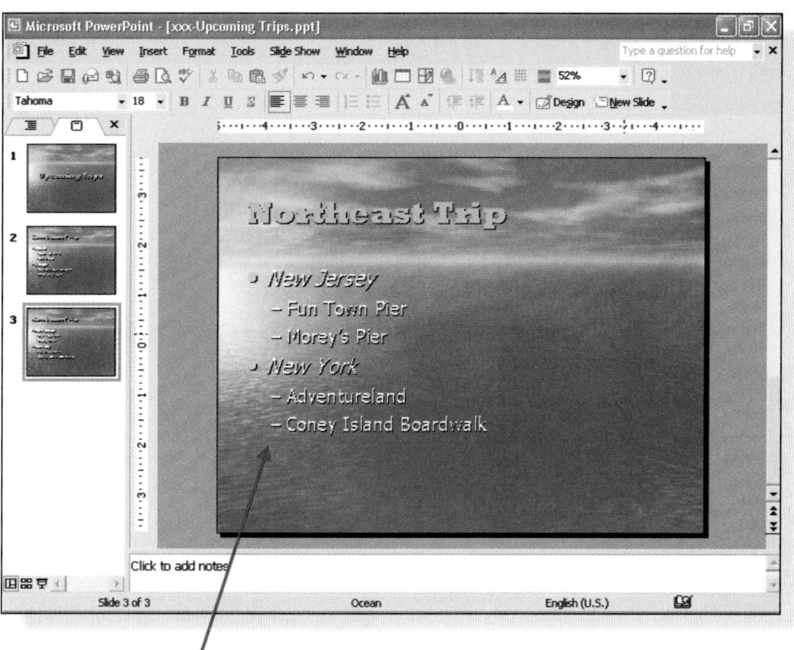

You customized the presentation by applying a design template and editing the color scheme.

5. On slide 1, change the title font to 54 pt. Rockwell Extra Bold (or another font of your choice).
6. Change the titles on slides 2 and 3 to match the font style on slide 1.
7. Edit the color scheme to make all titles appear in a mint green color (see Figure 2.16).

Figure 2.17 Edited color scheme

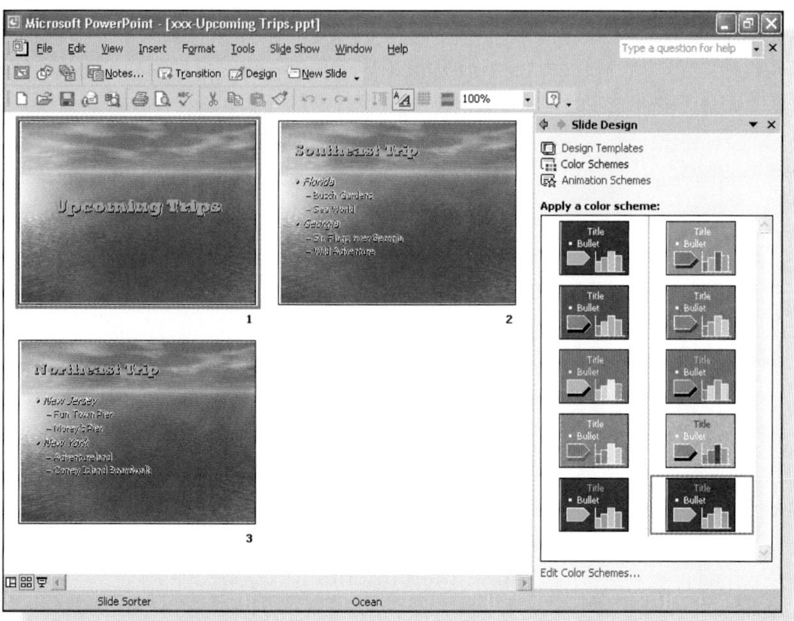

8. In slide sorter view, increase the Zoom percentage and look at all the slides (see Figure 2.17). Save and close the presentation.

APPLY IT! After finishing Exercises 3 and 4, you may test your skills by completing Apply It! Guided Activity 2, Create Presentations from a Blank Slide and From a Word Outline.

Procedure Summary

Create a Presentation Using a Design Template

1. Click **File** . . . . .Alt + F
2. Select **New** . . . . N
3. In the *New* section in the New Presentation task pane, select **From Design Template.**
   OR
   Click **New** button . . . . Ctrl + N
   Click **Slide Design** button Design . . Alt + S
   OR
   Click **Format** . . . . Alt + O
   Select **Slide Design** . . . . D
4. If you want to apply a design template to selected slides, select the slides in the Slides tab.
5. In the *Apply a design template* section in the Slide Design task pane, point to the desired design template. . . . . . . **Arrow keys, Enter**
6. Click the design template down arrow.
7. Select **Apply to All slides** . . . . .A
   OR
   Select **Apply to Selected Slides** . . . . .S
8. Replace placeholder information in the title slide.
9. Insert new slides and format as desired.

Change the Slide Design Template

1. Open the presentation.
2. Click **Slide Design** button Design . . Alt + S
   OR
   Click **Format** . . . . Alt + O
   Select **Slide Design** . . . . D
3. If you want to change the design template for selected slides, select the slide(s) to change in the Slides tab.
4. In the *Apply a design template* section in the Slide Design task pane, point to the desired design template . . **Up or Down arrow key, Enter**
5. Click the design template down arrow. **Enter**
6. Select **Apply to All Slides** . . . . A
   OR
   Select **Apply to Selected Slides**. . . . . S

Customize the Slide Design Template

1. Open the presentation.
2. Click **Slide Design** button Design . . . Alt + S
3. If you want to change the design template for selected slides, select the slide(s) to change in the Slides tab.
4. In the Slide Design task pane, select **Color Schemes**.
5. In the *Apply a color scheme* section, point to the desired color scheme option.
6. Click the desired color scheme down arrow.
7. Select **Apply to All Slides** . . . . A
   OR
   Select **Apply to Selected Slides**. . . . . S

OR

1. Select **Edit Color Schemes**.
2. In the Edit Color Scheme dialog box, click the **Custom** tab.
3. In the Scheme colors section, select the **Scheme colors** option to change. . . . . **Up or Down arrow key**
4. Click **Change Color**.
5. In the Color dialog box, click a color on the Standard or Custom tab . . . . **Alt + C, arrow keys**
6. Click OK. Enter
7. Click **Apply**.

Apply a New Color Scheme

1. Open the presentation.
2. Click **Slide Design** button Design . . . Alt + S
   OR
   Click **Format** . . . . .Alt + O
   Select **Slide Design** . . . . D

3. If you want to apply a new color scheme to selected slides, select the slide(s) to change in the Slides tab.
4. In the Slide Design task pane, select **Color Schemes**.
5. In the *Apply a color scheme* section, point to the desired color scheme option.
6. Click the desired color scheme down arrow.
7. Select **Apply to All Slides** . . . . A
   OR
   Select **Apply to Selected Slides** . . . . S

Edit the Color Scheme

1. Open the presentation.
2. Click **Slide Design** button [Design] . . . **Alt + S**
   OR
   Click **Format**. . . . . **Alt + O**
   Select **Slide Design**. . . . .**D**
3. In the Slide Design task pane, select **Color Schemes**.
4. Select **Edit Color Schemes**.
5. In the Edit Color Scheme dialog box, click the **Custom** tab.
6. Select an option to change in the *Scheme colors* section. . . . . **Up or Down arrow key**
7. Click **Change Color**.
8. Choose the desired color on the Standard or Custom tab of the Color dialog box. . . . .**Alt + C, arrow keys**
9. Click OK . . . . **Enter**
10. Click **Apply**.

Change a Slide Layout

1. Open the presentation.
2. If you want to change the slide layout for selected slides, select the slide(s) to change in the Slides tab.
3. Click **Format**. . . . . **Alt + O**
4. Select **Slide Layout**. . . . . **L**
5. In the *Apply slide layout* section in the Slide Layout task pane, point to desired slide layout . . . .**Arrow keys**
6. Click the desired slide layout down arrow.
7. Select **Apply to Selected Slides** . . . .**S**
   OR
   Select **Insert New Slide**. . . . . **N**

Create a Presentation From a Blank Presentation (From Scratch)

1. Click **New** button . . . . **Ctrl + N**
   OR
   Click **File** . . . . **Alt + F**
   Select **New** . . . . **N**
   In the New Presentation task pane, select **Blank Presentation**.
2. Replace the placeholder information.
3. Insert new slides as desired.
4. Format all slides appropriately.

Use a Word Outline to Create a Presentation

1. Click **Open** button . . . . **Ctrl + O**
   OR
   Click **File**. . . . . **Alt + F**
   Select **Open**. . . . . **O**
2. In the Open dialog box, click the *Files of type* down arrow.
3. Select **All Outlines**.
4. In the **Look in** box, navigate to the location of the Word outline document.
   . . . **Alt + I, Up or Down arrow keys, Enter**
5. Select the desired file. . . . . **Enter**
6. Click **Open** . . . . **Alt + O**
7. Format all slides as desired.

Lesson Review and Exercises

Summary Checklist

- ☑ Can you create a presentation using a design template?
- ☑ Can you apply a design template to an existing presentation?
- ☑ Can you use multiple design templates in a single presentation?
- ☑ Do you feel comfortable with customizing a design template?
- ☑ Can you apply a new color scheme to a presentation?
- ☑ Can you edit a color scheme?
- ☑ Can you change a slide layout?
- ☑ Can you create a presentation from a blank presentation?
- ☑ Do you know how to format presentations that have been created from scratch?
- ☑ Can you import a Word outline to create a PowerPoint presentation?

Key Terms

- color scheme (p. 525)
- design template (p. 522)
- slide layout (p. 524)

APPLY IT! Guided Activities

1. Create a Presentation

You are working as a public relations associate at the Hurricane Relief Fund (HRF), a local charitable organization. One of your jobs is to create a presentation to promote an upcoming fund-raising carnival. You will give the presentation to local schools in an effort to attract carnival attendees and, therefore, funds for the charity.

Follow these steps to create a new presentation from a design template, and then customize the design template and slides.

a. Select New on the File menu. Select From Design Template in the task pane. Point to the Ripple template and click its down arrow. Select Apply to All Slides.

b. Type Summer Fun as the title, and then type Come to the HRF Carnival! as the first subtitle. Type Reyes Park, June 10–12 on the line below.

c. Insert a second slide. Type the title, Carnival Schedule. Next, type the following subtitles:
Friday, June 10, 6 p.m.–11 p.m.
Saturday, June 11, 10 a.m.–11 p.m.
Sunday, June 12, 12 noon– 6 p.m.

d. Insert another slide. Type Important Details as the title, and type the following subtitles:
12 Rides!
16 Game Booths!
9 Food Booths!
HRF Raffle!

e. Select all four subtitles, and select Line Spacing on the Format menu. Type 2 in the *Line spacing* box.

f. Select Slide Layout on the Format menu. Click the Title and 2-Column Text down arrow and select Apply to Selected Slides.

g. Select the last two bulleted items in the left column and click Cut. Click in the right column placeholder and click Paste.

h. Add a final slide and select the Title Slide layout. Type Where Will the Money Go? as the title. Type this paragraph in the subtitle placeholder:
All proceeds from the HRF Carnival will go to the Hurricane Relief Fund, which provides much-needed food, clothing, shelter, and emotional counseling to victims of hurricanes all over the state. Your support is much appreciated!

i. Click Slide Design, and while still in normal view, hold Ctrl and click slides 2 and 3 on the Slides tab. (***Note:*** Slide 4 should already be selected.)

j. Point to the Watermark design template, click its down arrow, and select Apply to Selected Slides **(see Figure 2.18)**.

Figure 2.18 Presentation with two design templates

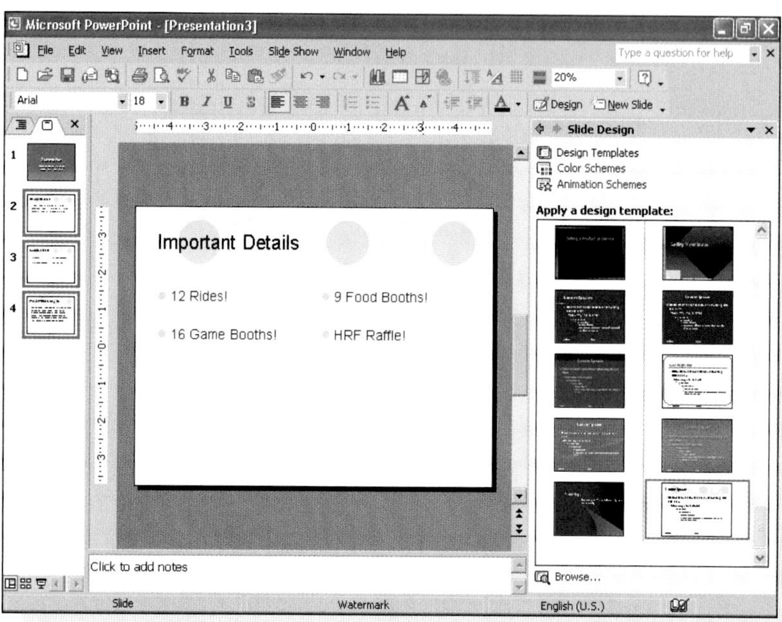

k. On the title slide, change the title to 66 pt. Lucida Sans, bold. Change the subtitles to 36 pt. Lucida Sans, bold, lime green. On slide 4, change the title size to 40 pt. and the subtitle size to 28 pt.

l. Display slide 2, select Color Schemes in the task pane, select Edit Color Schemes, and then click Fills. Click Change Color, choose a lime green color, click OK, and then click Apply. Then, follow the same steps to change the Accent color to lime green. (***Note:*** The two lime green colors may not match *exactly* because you must choose one in the Accent Color dialog box, and you choose the other in the Fill Color dialog box.)

m. View the presentation, save it as *xxx-Carnival.ppt,* and close the file.

2. Create Presentations From a Blank Slide and From a Word Outline

As a human resources assistant at a large law firm, you are creating a presentation to publicize an upcoming medical fair, which will be held on-site for company employees. Health personnel, insurance companies, and fitness clubs will set up booths for employees to visit. The employees can gather information on health issues and have blood pressure, cholesterol, and other tests performed.

Follow these steps to create a presentation from scratch, to create another related presentation by importing a Word outline, and to format both presentations attractively.

a. Select New on the File menu and select Blank Presentation. Type Annual Medical Fair as the title, and type Company Atrium November 5–6 as the subtitle on two lines.

b. Add a new slide and type Visiting Sponsors as the title. Type the following subtitles:
Health Clubs
Insurance Companies
Medical Groups

c. Select the bulleted text, and change the line spacing to 2. Change the title to 54 pt. bold, red; change the subtitle text to 36 pt., green.

d. Use Format Painter to change the formatting of the slide 1 title to match the slide 2 title, and again to change the formatting of the slide 1 subtitle to match the slide 2 subtitle. (***Note:*** Using Format Painter ensures that the red and green colors on the two slides will match.) Now change the subtitle on slide 1 to 48 pt., bold.

e. Apply the Radial design template to the entire presentation, and then edit the color scheme so that the background is pale yellow.

f. View the presentation, save it as *xxx-Medical Fair.ppt*, and close the file.

h. Change the title on all slides to 54 pt. bold, italic, and change the subtitles to 40 pt. Apply the teal color scheme, and then edit it so the text and lines appear in a light blue color instead of white **(see Figure 2.19)**.

i. View the presentation, and save and close the file.

Figure 2.19 Presentation imported from Word

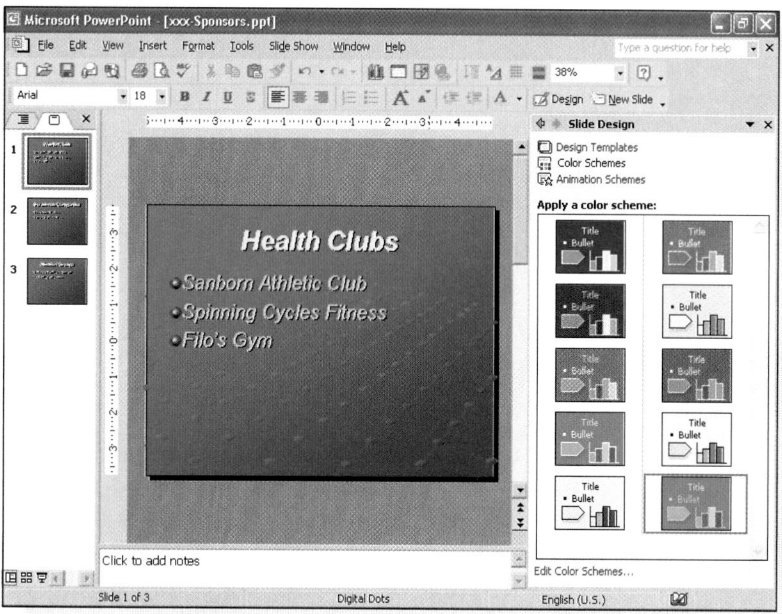

Do It Yourself

1. Use a Design Template

As a manufacturing associate at a sporting goods company, you have been asked to research transportation and distribution methods for your products and then give a presentation to the manufacturing director displaying your research.

Figure 2.20 Information for the manufacturing presentation

Transportation Options
- Air
  - Very quick
  - Expensive
  - Fairly flexible
- Boat
  - Slowest method
  - Inexpensive
  - Not very flexible
- Road
  - Slower than air
  - Quicker than boat or train
  - Much less expensive than air
  - Flexible
- Train
  - Slower than air or road
  - Somewhat inexpensive
  - Not very flexible

a. Create a presentation from a design template. Include an appropriate title slide, and incorporate other slides for the information in **Figure 2.20**. (In reality, you would want to include financial data with your research, but for now, your presentation will include only the transportation/distribution options available, as well as the advantages and disadvantages of each option.)

b. Format the presentation to look professional. Consider the presentation content and your audience when choosing a design template and formatting the presentation. Be consistent in style and appearance.

c. Save your presentation as *xxx-Manufacturing.ppt* **(see Figure 2.21)** and close it.

Figure 2.21 Manufacturing presentation

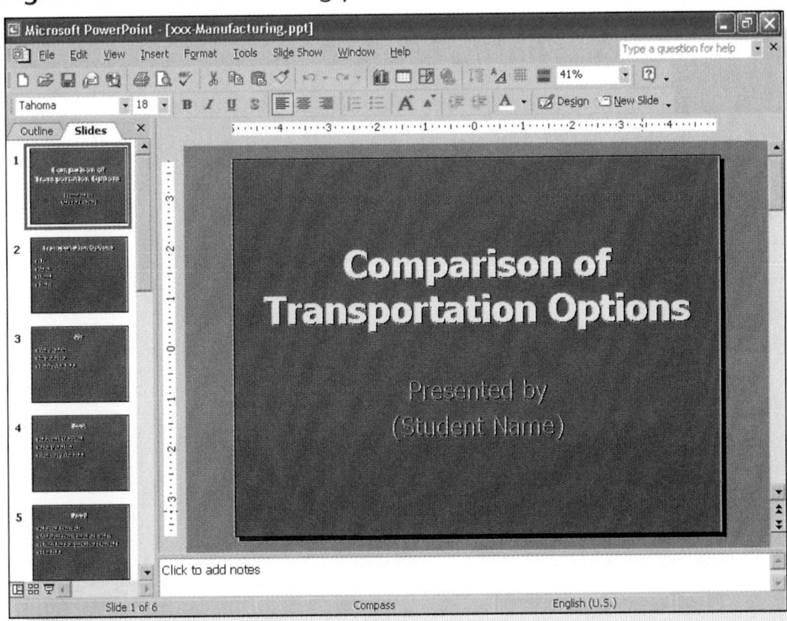

PowerPoint®

PowerPoint®

2. Work With Multiple Design Templates and Slide Layouts

You are an executive assistant in charge of scheduling the fall semester classes for the math department at a university. You need to create a presentation showing the fall schedule that will be used during a meeting with other members of the department. Do the following:

a. Use the data provided in **Figure 2.22** to create the presentation. You may organize the slides in any manner—by class, by days of the week, by times, or by instructor. You may use tables in your presentation if you wish.

b. Create the presentation from a design template, and then apply at least one different design template to one or more slides in the presentation. Customize one or more of the templates.

c. Include an appropriate title slide. Save your file as *xxx-Math.ppt*.

d. View the presentation. Do you need a larger type size, a different color scheme, or a modified slide layout? If so, make the necessary modifications.

e. Save and close the presentation.

Figure 2.22 Information for the math presentation

Level 100 Math Courses: Fall Semester
- Algebra
  - Prof. Gorbea—8:00–8:45 Tuesdays and Thursdays; 3:30–4:15 Mondays and Wednesdays
  - Mr. Taylor—8:30–9:15 Tuesdays and Thursdays; 9:30–10:15 Tuesdays and Thursdays
- Calculus
  - Mrs. Diaz—11:00–11:45 Mondays and Wednesdays; 2:00–3:30 Fridays
  - Mr. Fry—12:15–1:00 Mondays and Wednesdays; 1:30–2:15 Tuesdays and Thursdays
- Finite Math
  - Ms. Iwasaki—10:00–10:45 Tuesdays and Thursdays; 2:00–2:45 Tuesdays and Thursdays
  - Prof. Stilwell—9:00–9:45 Tuesdays and Thursdays; 9:00–10:30 Fridays

3. Create and Format a Presentation

You are a social worker at a YMCA youth center in a troubled neighborhood. Your manager has asked you to create a presentation that will give the teenagers who come to the center constructive ideas for their summer plans, including work opportunities, vacation, and personal goals.

Create a three- to five-slide presentation that will show the teenagers how they can become responsible members of society and caring citizens while having fun this summer. Include details, but keep your bulleted items brief. Follow these steps:

a. Create your presentation from scratch, but then format it attractively. Consider applying a design template, applying a color scheme, editing a color scheme, or just formatting text and backgrounds as you go.

b. Verify that the text is large enough to be seen by the people sitting in the back of the room.

c. Save your presentation as *xxx-Summer.ppt* **(see Figure 2.23)** and close it.

Figure 2.23 Summer plans presentation

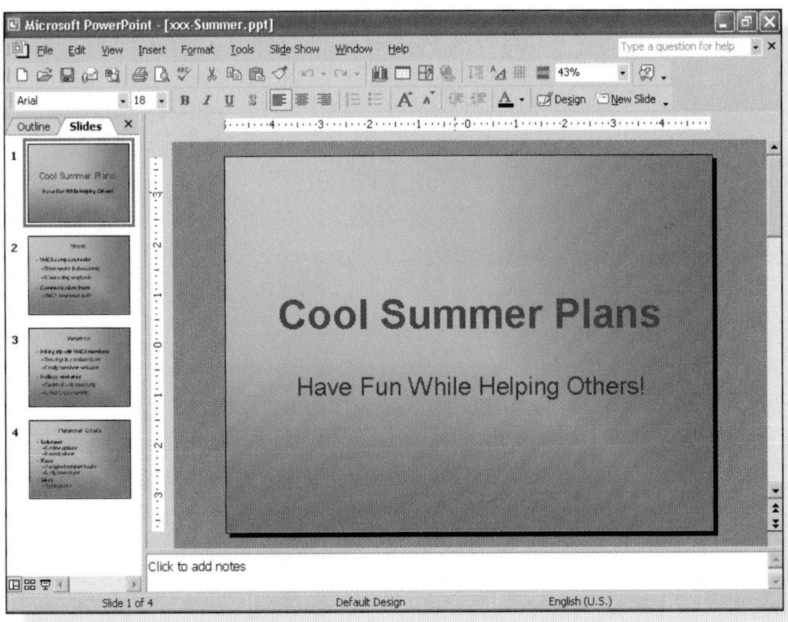

4. Import a Word Outline

As the Corporate Real Estate Manager at Rafferty & Updike Insurance, you are responsible for new construction and all work space renovation in the company. Several department managers have come to you requesting more work space due to their expanding departments. There is no unused space available in the building, so in order to accommodate them you must reduce the size of the existing workstations. You need to compare costs and numbers to see if the renovation is feasible, and then present your information to the company officers. Follow these steps:

a. Import the Word outline *Work Space.doc* into PowerPoint. Save the file as *xxx-Work Space.ppt* **(see Figure 2.24)**. Read the outline and add a title slide.

b. Move information around if you think the presentation will flow better. For example, would the presentation look better if you spread it out on more slides?

c. Format the presentation attractively.

d. Consider using abbreviations to make the slides more attractive and less cluttered. Think about using *RSF* in place of *Rentable Square Footage* or *WS* in place of *Workstation*.

e. Save and close your final presentation.

Figure 2.24 Imported Word Outline

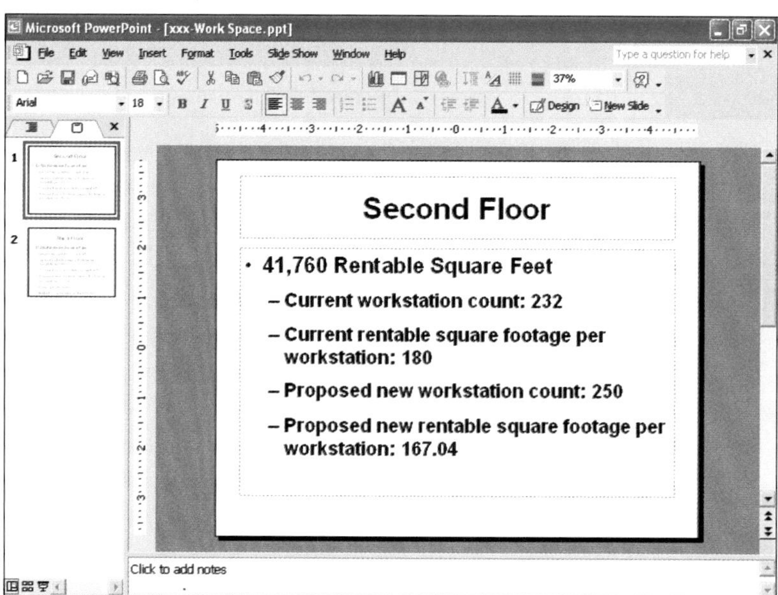

Challenge Yourself

Create a Financial Presentation

You are a high school accounting teacher. Your principal has asked you to give a presentation at an assembly for juniors and seniors. Your goal is to give them useful information on saving money wisely to prepare them for life after high school.

Search the Internet to find advice on this from experts in the field. A good way to find sites is to use a search engine. Be sure to document the source(s) of your information. You can include this information directly on the slide, or you can add it in the notes pane. If you need help in creating notes, search Help for *about notes*.

Create a presentation either from a design template or from a blank slide. Then, change the formatting to make it unique for your presentation, including changing the slide layout. Consider using more than one design template in the presentation, if appropriate, and/or applying a new color scheme.

Explore Help as needed for instructions on adding clip art or a photo to a presentation. Using the Help information and your skills learned in other Office applications, add clip art or a photo to this presentation **(see Figure 2.25)**.

Save the presentation as *xxx-Save Money.ppt* and close it.

Figure 2.25 Financial presentation

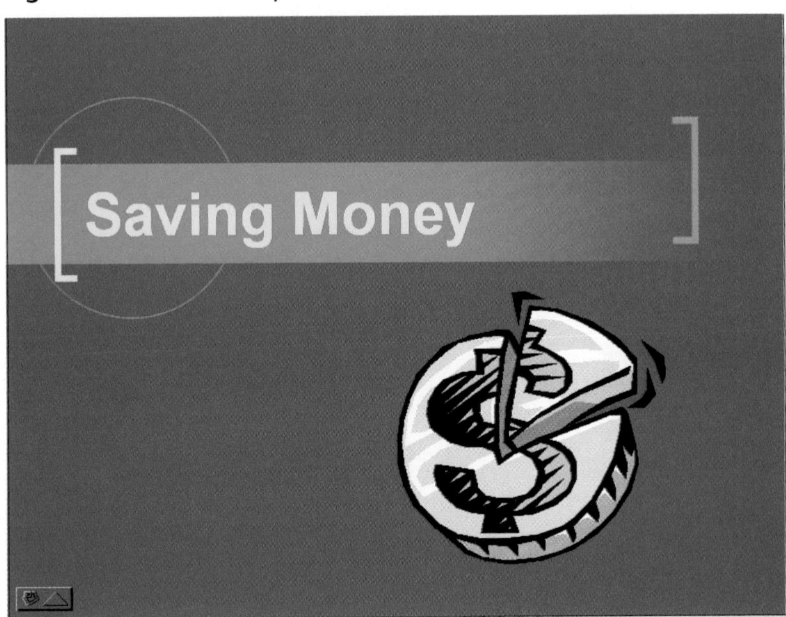

Lesson 3

Enhancing A Presentation

Lesson Exercise Objectives

After completing this lesson, you'll be able to do the following tasks:

1. Insert and modify clip art
2. Insert a bit-mapped image
3. Create and customize a table
4. Create a chart
5. Create OfficeArt elements
6. Insert sound effects and movies
7. Manage slide masters
8. Animate your presentation

Key Terms

- animated object (p. 576)
- animated text (p. 576)
- animation (p. 576)
- bit-mapped image (bitmap) (p. 552)
- embed (p. 556)
- footer (p. 570)
- header (p. 570)
- link (p. 556)
- slide master (p. 570)
- title master (p. 570)
- transition (p. 576)

Microsoft Office Specialist Activities

PP2002: 1.1, 1.3, 2.2, 3.1–3.4, 4.1–4.6, 4.9, 6.1–6.3

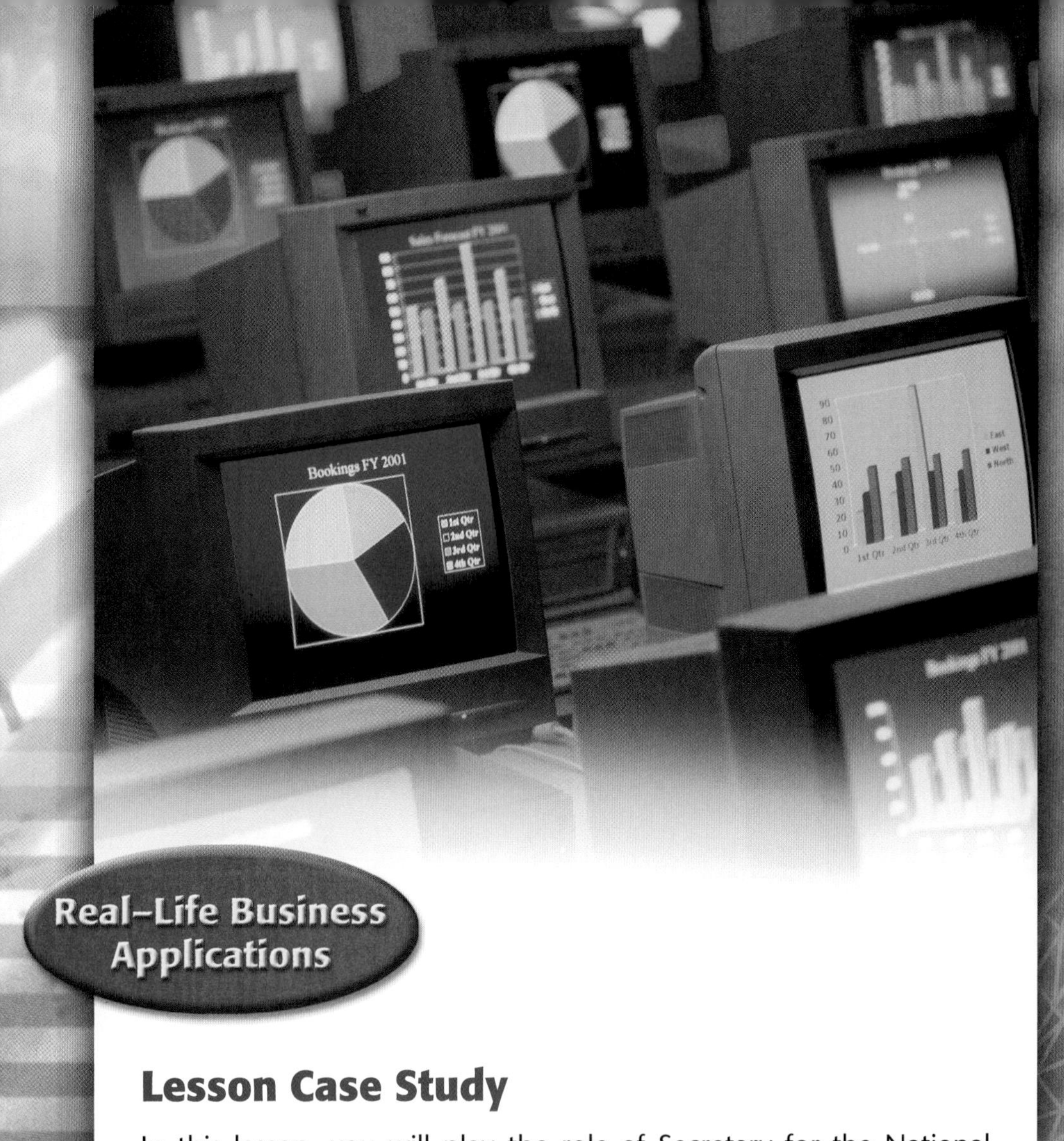

Real-Life Business Applications

Lesson Case Study

In this lesson, you will play the role of Secretary for the National Association of Roller Coaster Enthusiasts. Keep the following information in mind as you work through the lesson exercises.

- **Job responsibilities and goals.** You support the President and Vice President of NARCE by recording the minutes of meetings and creating different types of documents. The President and Vice President have asked for your help in creating presentations for the annual NARCE meeting.
- **The project.** You need to create presentations on numerous topics, including the meeting agenda, club awards, and miscellaneous news and announcements. Since elections will take place, you will also need to create a presentation to present your skills and qualifications to other club members if you decide to run for Secretary again.
- **The challenge ahead.** You need to review your presentations to be sure they contain accurate information and they are presented in a pleasing manner.

Microsoft Office Specialist
PP2002 3.1, 4.9

Exercise 1 Overview:
Insert and Modify Clip Art

You can use clip art images to enhance your presentations. Clips may include drawings, photos, sound effects, music, videos, and all other media files.

Make sure that clips relate well to your presentation content, add appropriate visual appeal, and are large enough to be seen by your audience. Also keep in mind that effective presentations do not overuse clips. Consistent, simple use of clips is more effective than having too many in a presentation.

You can insert clip art in PowerPoint by choosing one of the many slide layouts in the Slide Layout task pane that contain a graphic image (see Figure 3.1).

Figure 3.1 Slide layout with content placeholder

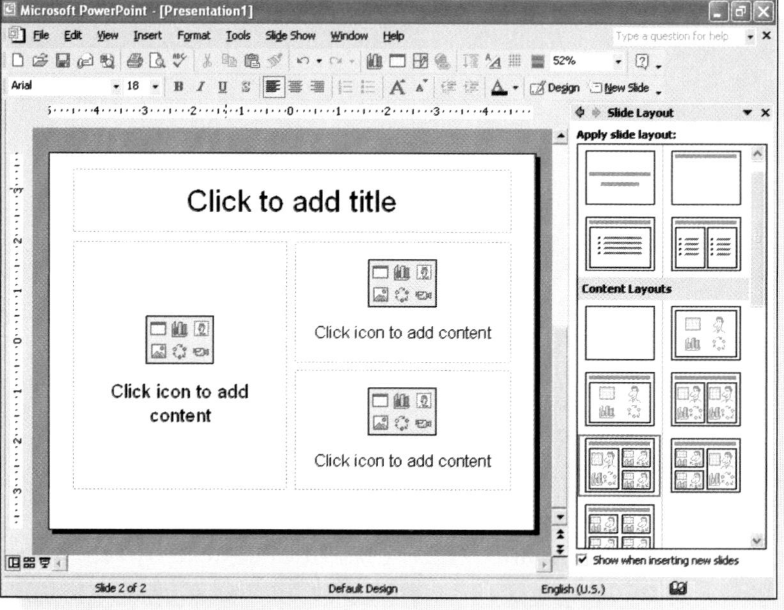

Each of these slide layouts allows you to insert an object in the content placeholder. To insert clip art, you simply click the Insert Clip Art icon in the content placeholder. You can also insert clip art *without* a placeholder by using the Insert menu, just as you would in a Word document. After you insert a clip art image, you can move and resize it.

Type: find a clip

In the following exercises, you will create a presentation for the president to show to NARCE members at the year-end meeting. You will insert clip art and then resize and move the image.

Figure 3.2 Select Picture dialog box

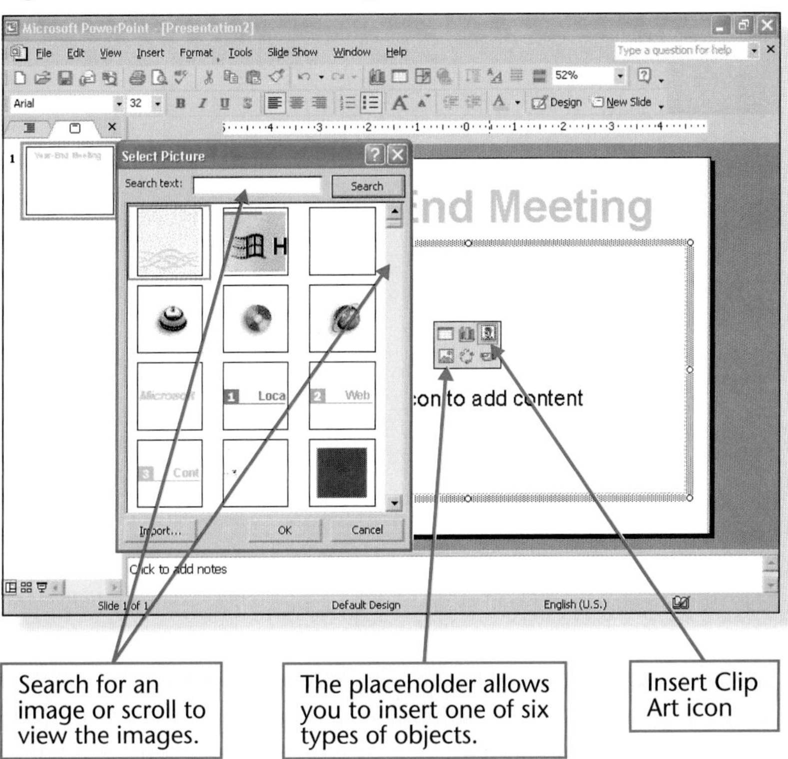

Figure 3.3 Slide 1 with clip art inserted

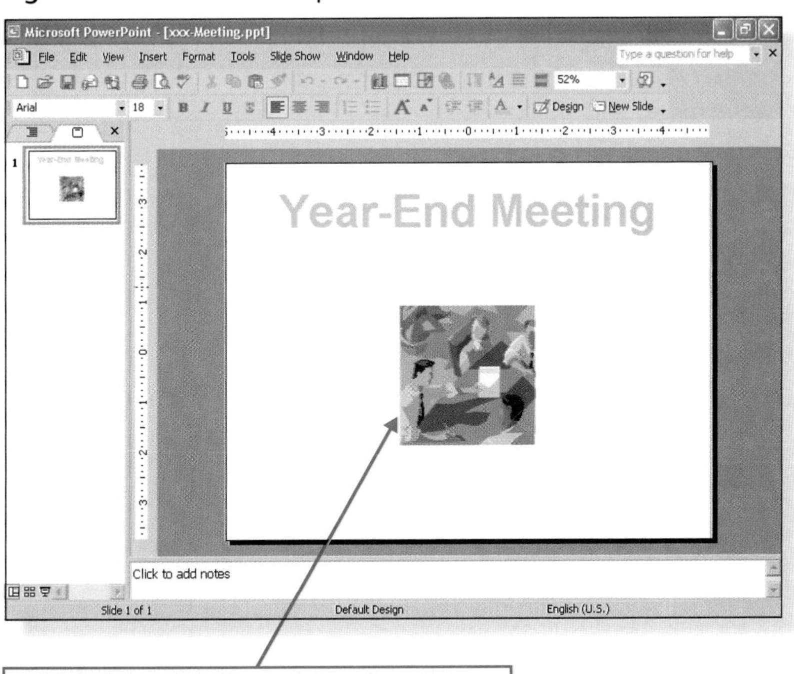

Step Through It™

Exercise 1A: Insert clip art

1. Create a presentation from a blank presentation.
2. Select the Title and Content layout.
3. Type Year-End Meeting as the title and format it in 66 pt., lime green, bold.
4. Click the Insert Clip Art icon in the content placeholder (see Figure 3.2).
5. Scroll down to view the images, type meeting in the Search text box, and click Search.
6. Select an image that shows several people working together at a table, and then click OK. Deselect the clip.
7. Save the presentation as *xxx-Meeting.ppt* (see Figure 3.3).

Step Through It™
Exercise 1B: Move and resize clip art

1. Save *xxx-Meeting.ppt* as *xxx-Meeting Revised.ppt.*
2. Click the clip art image and drag the bottom right corner diagonally down to the right to resize it.
3. Move the image back to the center of the slide (see Figure 3.4).
4. Save and close your presentation.

Figure 3.4 Resized clip art

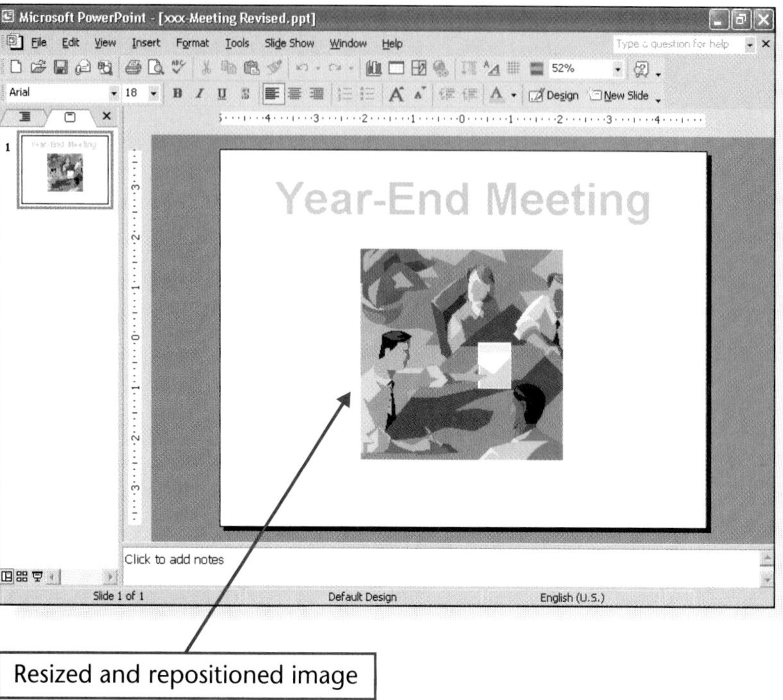

Microsoft Office Specialist PP2002 3.1

Exercise 2 Overview:
Insert a Bit-Mapped Image

You can also import an image file into a presentation. PowerPoint allows you to insert bitmaps. **Bit-mapped images (bitmaps)** are made from a series of small dots and may have a *.bmp, .png, .jpg*, or *.gif* file extension. You may have downloaded images from the Internet or purchased a software package that provides image files. Or perhaps you have a photograph from a digital camera, or one that you have scanned. All scanned graphics and photographs are bit-mapped images.

Just as with clip art, you can insert a bit-mapped image in a placeholder or in a random location on the slide. Afterward, you can resize or reposition the image as appropriate.

Type: add a picture

In the following exercise, you will insert a bit-mapped image into an awards presentation that will be shown during the NARCE year-end meeting.

Figure 3.5 Insert Picture dialog box

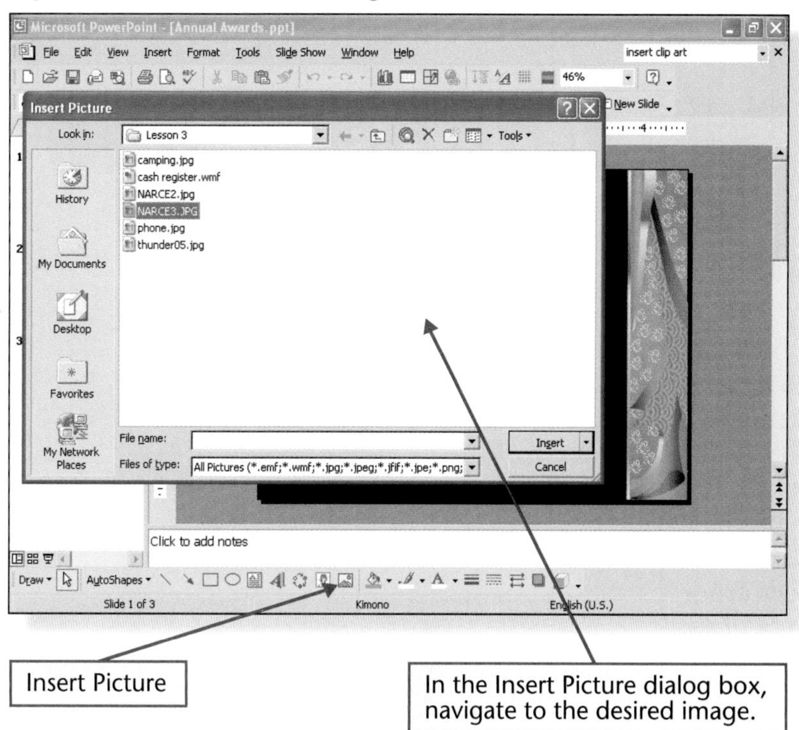
Insert Picture
In the Insert Picture dialog box, navigate to the desired image.

Step Through It™

Exercise 2: Import a bit-mapped image

1. Open *Annual Awards.ppt*, and save it as *xxx-Annual Awards Bitmap.ppt.*

2. On the first slide, click Insert Picture on the Drawing toolbar (see Figure 3.5).

3. Select *narce3.jpg* and click Insert (see Figure 3.6).

4. Save and close your presentation.

Figure 3.6 Bit-mapped image inserted

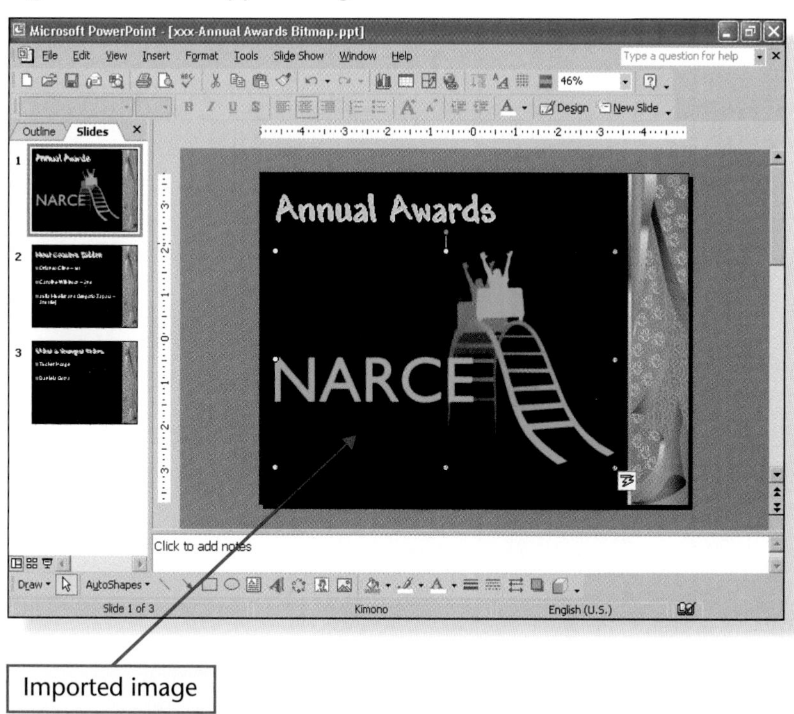
Imported image

PowerPoint®

Business Connections

Presenting Legally

Enhancing your presentations with visual appeal is one of the best ways to connect with your audience and to create a successful presentation. At times, however, finding just the right visual (whether it is a clip, table, graph, drawing, photograph, sound, video, or other media file) for your presentation content may be quite challenging. Remember that copyright laws exist to protect creators' rights for their literary and artistic works.

Copyright Laws

- Just about anything you see when you access the Internet is protected by copyright laws. According to the U.S. Copyright Office, copyright protection exists the moment a work of any kind is created—on the Internet or elsewhere—with or without a copyright notice!
- Even if you do not see a copyright notice (with the three standard elements: ©, the publication year, and the owner's name) on a Web site that you visit, you must assume that all information on the entire site is copyright protected.
- Although copyright laws no longer require a copyright notice, such notice may be beneficial. A creator may apply for a copyright notice through the U.S. Copyright Office.

Getting Permission

- If you find the perfect text or media file to enhance your presentation, what should you do?

1. Contact the owner of the printed material, the CD, or the Web site. Find out who owns the copyright on the material you want to use in your presentation.
2. Secure written permission from the copyright owner. Be sure to reference the specific information and its location for which you want permission.
3. If you secure written permission, include the appropriate credit line or footnote in your presentation so that you will legally acknowledge the copyright owner properly.

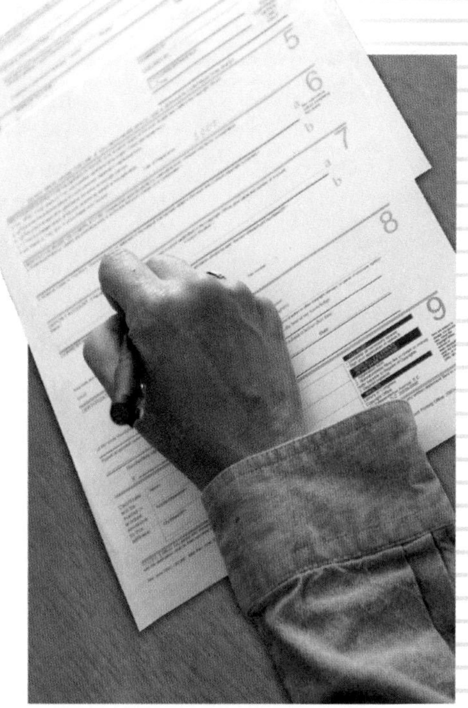

Credit Where Credit is Due

- If you are found guilty of *copyright infringement* (using material from a copyrighted source without permission to do so), you can be sued for failure to obtain permission, and you may be required to pay the owner's legal fees in addition to paying damages.
- No matter what, avoid the temptation to *plagiarize* (to use another person's information as your own).

CRITICAL THINKING

1. **Finding Copyright Information** Search the Internet for information on copyright law. Look also for copyright notices. In your own words, write a summary of copyright information.
2. **Investigating Copyright Lawsuits** Search the Internet or print material for information about recent copyright lawsuits arising from the use of the Internet. Write a brief summary of one of the lawsuits.

Microsoft Office Specialist PP2002 3.1, 3.4, 6.3

Exercise 3 Overview: Create and Customize a Table

You can easily insert a table on a slide by using a slide layout that has a content placeholder for a table. You can also insert a table on a slide *without* using a content placeholder by clicking Insert Table on the Standard toolbar.

Need Help?
Type: tables

As you create tables in PowerPoint, you want the font large enough to be seen by your audience. You should generally use 18 point type or larger, have three or four rows, and have two or three columns, and include column and row headings as appropriate. To ensure readability, no table should contain more than four columns or five rows. And as you learned in other Office XP applications, you can customize a table by changing fonts, adding table borders, using a fill color, changing alignment, and so on.

You can also import a Word table on a slide by embedding or linking it. After you **embed** a Word table, any changes made to the Word source file are *not* shown in the PowerPoint destination file. However, when you **link** a table, any changes made to the source file *are* reflected in the destination file.

In the following exercises, you will create tables in the awards presentation for the NARCE year-end meeting, customize those tables, and then embed a Word table.

Step Through It™
Exercise 3A: Create a table

1. Open *xxx-Annual Awards Bitmap.ppt*, and save it as *xxx-Annual Awards Table.ppt*.
2. Insert a new slide 3 with the Title and Content layout. Click the Insert Table icon, and specify 3 columns and 5 rows (see Figure 3.7).
3. Type Most Coasters Ridden (Continued) as the title. Use Format Painter to match this title to the title font on slide 2; change the font to 40 pt.

Figure 3.7 Inserting a table

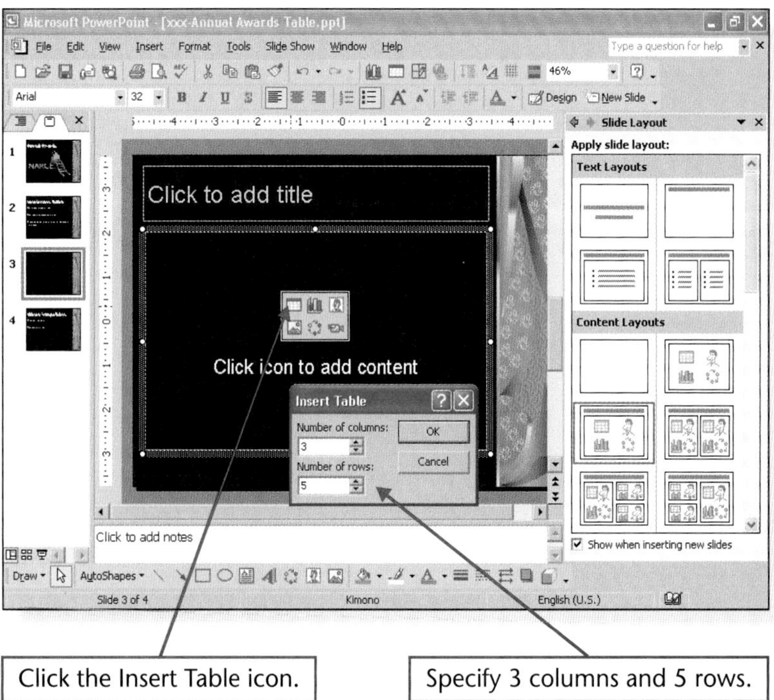

Table 3.1

Name	Coasters Ridden	Time Frame
Orlando Cline	27	8 months
Caroline Wilkinson	24	8 months
Julia Mueller	23	7 months
Gregorio Zapata	23	7 months

4. Type the information in Table 3.1.

Figure 3.8 Creating a table

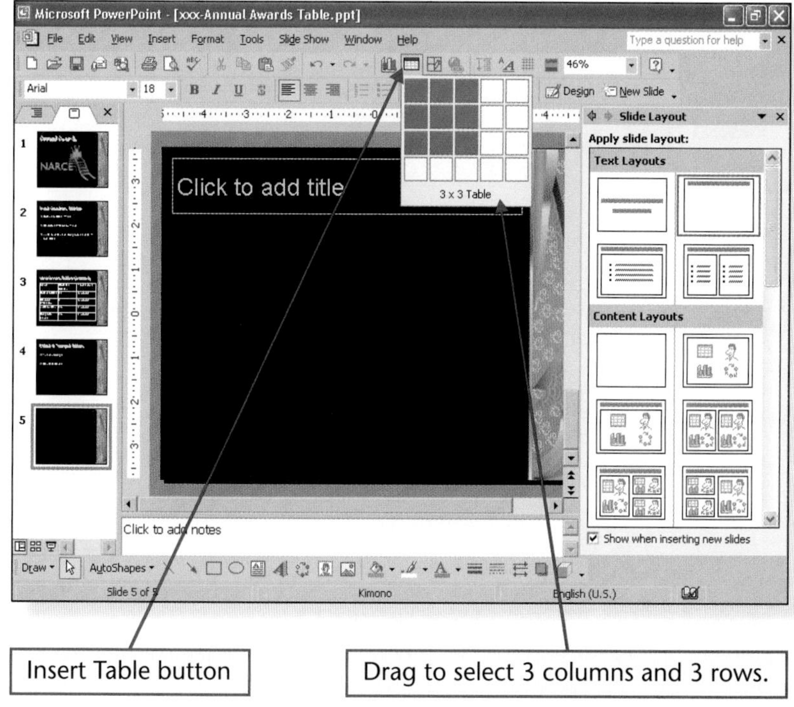

Insert Table button

Drag to select 3 columns and 3 rows.

5. Insert a new slide 5 with the Title Only layout.
6. Click Insert Table on the Standard toolbar, and select 3 columns and 3 rows (see Figure 3.8).
7. Type Oldest & Youngest Riders (Continued) as the title. Use Format Painter to match the title font on slide 3.

PowerPoint®

Quick Tip

Use Format Painter to copy formatting quickly.

8 Type the information in Table 3.2.

9 Save your presentation.

Table 3.2

Name	Age	Coasters Ridden in Lifetime
Tucker Hodges	78	703
Daniela Garza	4	11

Step Through It™

Exercise 3B: Apply custom formats to a table

1 Save *xxx-Annual Awards Table.ppt* as *xxx-Annual Awards Table Customized.ppt*.

2 Display slide 3 and open the Tables and Borders toolbar. Click in the table. Click the Border Width down arrow 1 pt and select 3 pt.

3 Click Border Color and select a dark green color. Click all borders in the table with the pencil (see Figure 3.9).

Figure 3.9 Changing borders

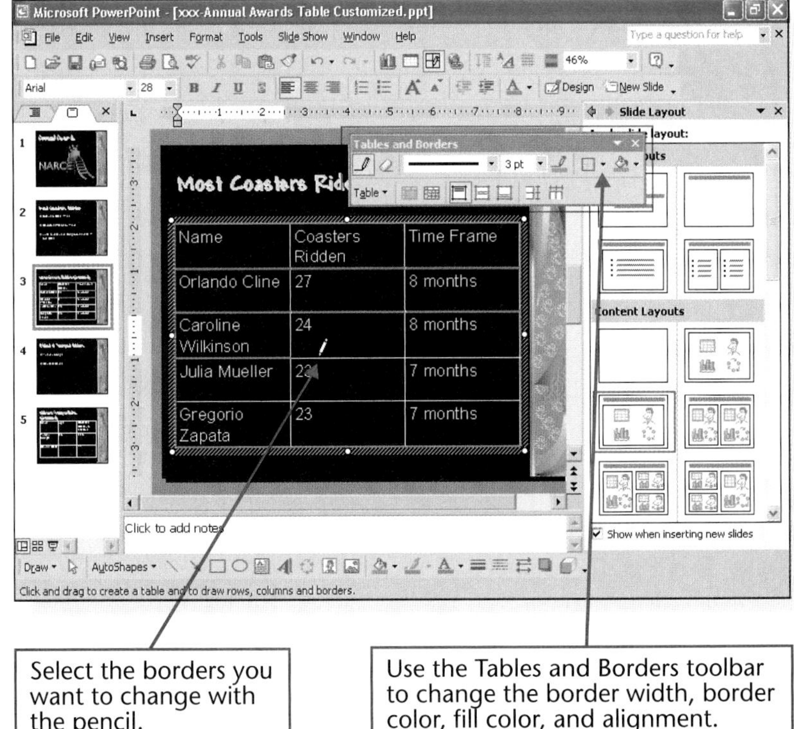

Select the borders you want to change with the pencil.

Use the Tables and Borders toolbar to change the border width, border color, fill color, and alignment.

To widen a column in a table, drag the divider between that column and the one next to it.

Figure 3.10 Customized table on slide 3

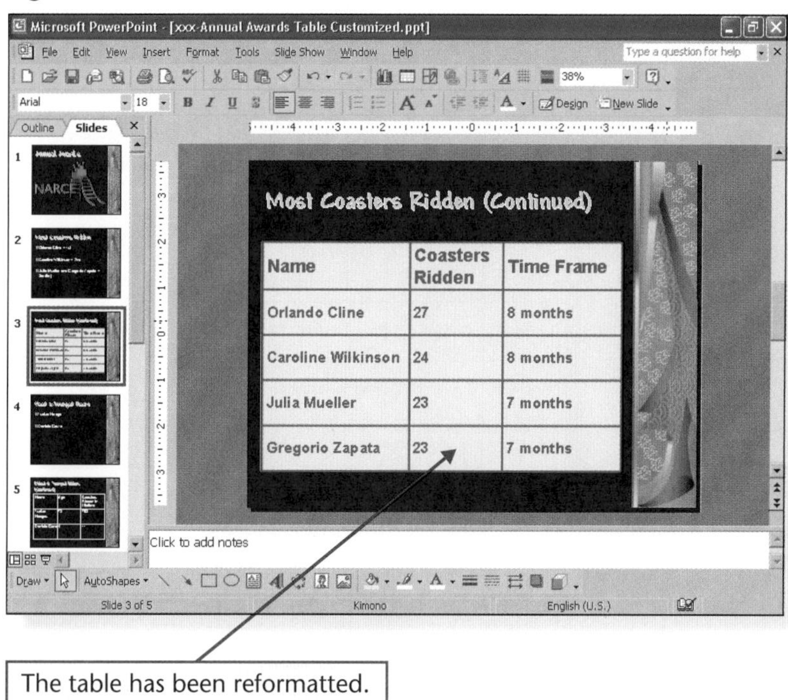

4. Select the entire table and click the Fill Color down arrow; select a light yellow color. Click Center Vertically.

5. Change all text in the table to the same green color you used for the borders, and make it bold. Bold the text in the first row.

6. Change all text but the title row to 24 pt. Widen column 1 until Caroline Wilkinson's name fits on one line (see Figure 3.10).

7. Customize slide 5 in the same way, and then save your changes.

Figure 3.11 New slide with formatted title

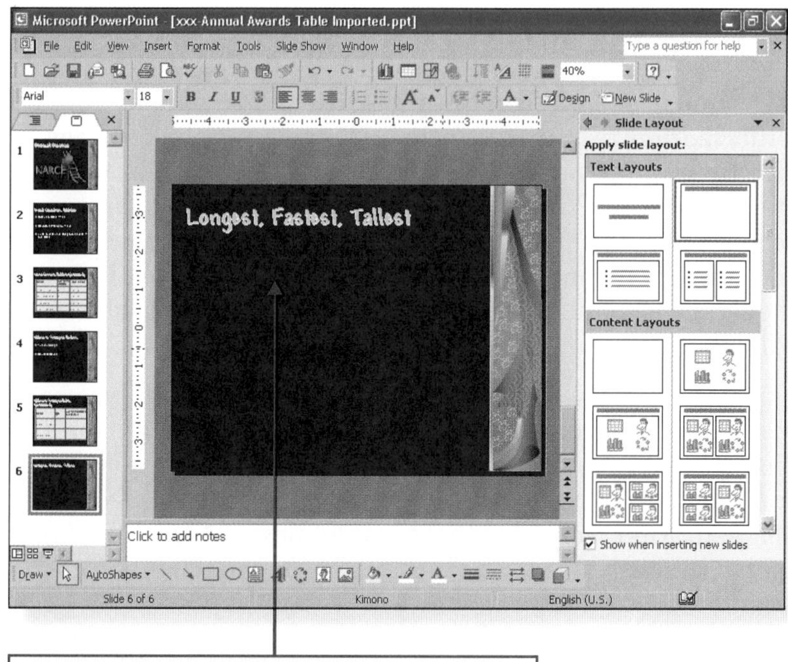

Step Through It™
Exercise 3C: Insert a Word table

1. Save *xxx-Annual Awards Table Customized.ppt* as *xxx-Annual Awards Table Imported.ppt*.

2. Insert a new slide 6 with a Title Only layout. Type **Longest, Fastest, Tallest** as its title. Use Format Painter to match the title to the slide 4 title (see Figure 3.9).

3. On the Insert menu, select Object, click *Create from file*, and browse to locate *Awards Table.doc*. Click OK twice.

PowerPoint®

4 Resize and reposition the table, similar to the tables on slides 3 and 5 (see Figure 3.12).

5 Save and close your presentation.

Figure 3.12 Imported Word table

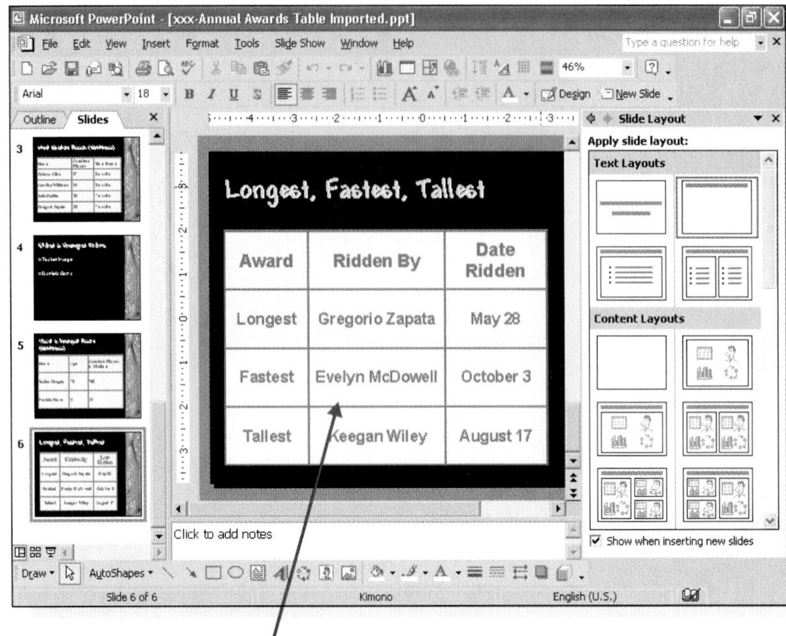

The table has been resized and repositioned.

Microsoft Office Specialist PP2002 3.1, 6.1

Exercise 4 Overview: Create a Chart

At times, a chart or graph is the best way to display information in a presentation. Charts may make it easier for your audience to see comparisons, patterns, or data trends. PowerPoint offers several standard chart types: column chart, bar chart, line chart, pie chart, and organization chart. Each of the main chart types includes several chart subtypes (including 3-D variations), which are alternative formats of the main chart types.

If you want to use a chart on a slide, carefully analyze your data to determine the most effective chart type for the information you want to display in your presentation. Then, as you decide upon the appropriate chart type for your presentation, consider these guidelines: (1) Use a *column chart* to show data changes over time or comparisons among items. (2) Use a *bar chart* to show comparisons of individual items. (3) Use a *line chart* to show trends in data at equal intervals. (4) Use a *pie chart* to show the relationship of parts to a whole. (5) Use an *organization chart* to show the levels of authority within a work group or company.

As with clip art or tables, you can insert a chart by using a slide layout that contains a placeholder reserving space for a chart. In addition to using any of the layouts that contain content placeholders, you can also choose among several layouts that have chart placeholders. These are in the Other Layouts section of the Slide Layout task pane. However, just as with other objects, you can insert a chart on a slide *without* using a placeholder by using the Insert Chart button on the Standard toolbar.

You can create a chart directly on a PowerPoint slide by using the datasheet that will appear on screen. You can also import an Excel chart by embedding or linking it. Embedded and linked charts are similar to embedded and linked tables.

Whether you create or import a chart, you can reformat it by changing borders, colors, or fonts, and you can resize and reposition it, just as you resize and reposition other objects.

In the following exercises, you will create a chart for a presentation on club merchandise that will be shown during the NARCE year-end meeting, and then you will import an Excel chart into that presentation.

PowerPoint®

Figure 3.13 Clearing a datasheet column

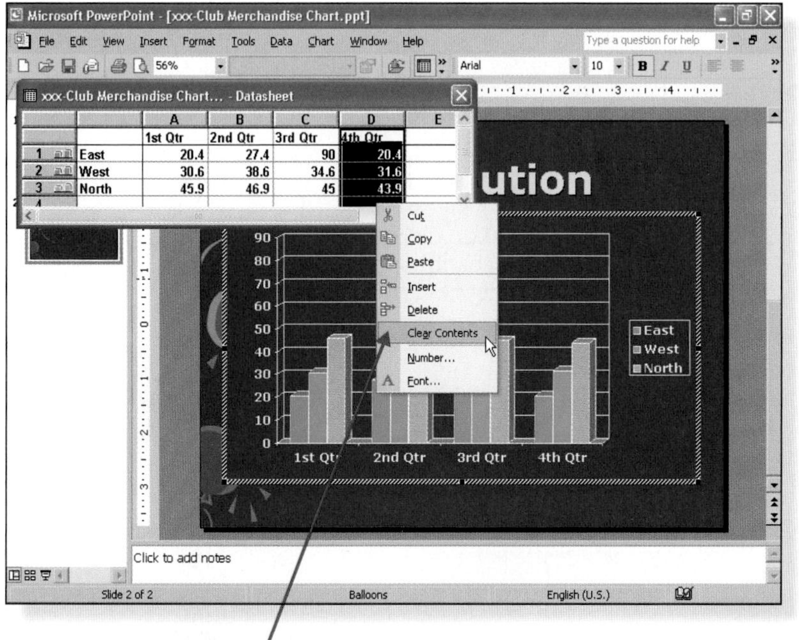

Click to clear the selected column's contents.

Step Through It™

Exercise 4A: Create a chart

1. Open *Club Merchandise.ppt* and save it as *xxx-Club Merchandise Chart.ppt.* Display slide 2.
2. Click the Insert Chart icon on the slide.
3. In the datasheet, select all of column D, right-click, and select Clear Contents (see Figure 3.13).

4 Replace the remaining information in the datasheet with the information shown in Table 3.3.

Table 3.3

	A	B	C
	Members	Nonmembers	Freebies
Tote bags	325	215	125
T-shirts	750	410	100
Water bottles	800	350	250

5 Close the datasheet.

6 Change the chart type from a column chart to a bar chart (see Figure 3.14).

7 Save and close your presentation.

Figure 3.14 Bar chart on slide 2

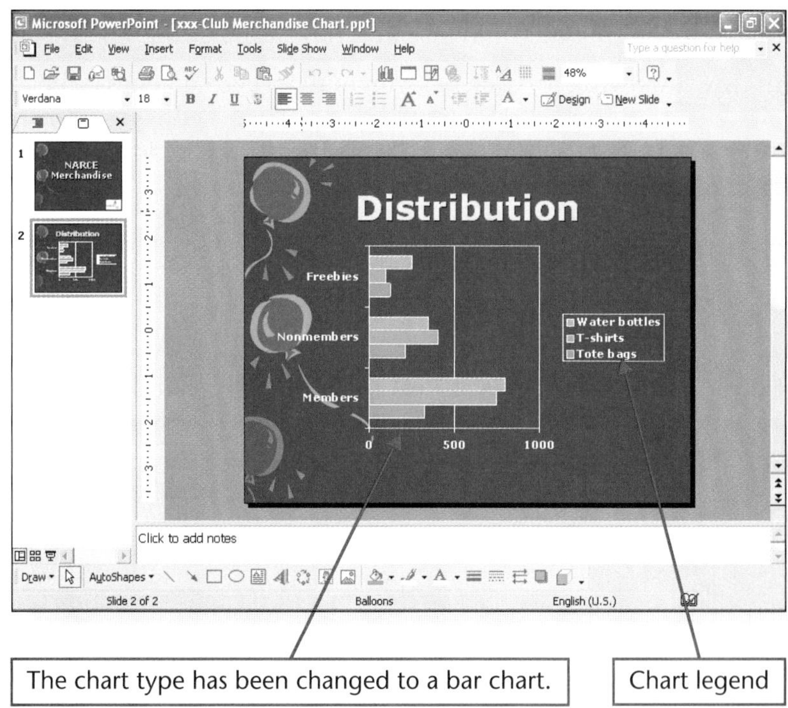

To replace information in a datasheet, click a cell and begin typing.

Figure 3.15 Linking an object

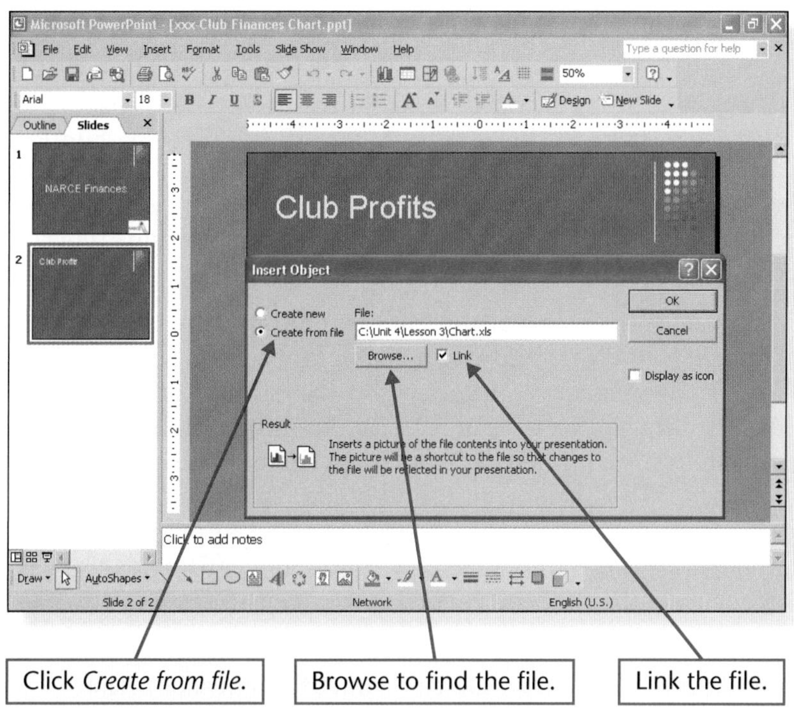
Click *Create from file.*
Browse to find the file.
Link the file.

Step Through It™

Exercise 4B: Insert an Excel chart

1. Open *Club Finances.ppt* and save it as *xxx-Club Finances Chart.ppt*. Display slide 2.
2. Select Object on the Insert menu, and then click *Create from file* in the Insert Object dialog box.
3. Click Browse, and then locate and select *Chart.xls*. Click OK.
4. Click Link (see Figure 3.15), and then click OK.
5. Increase the size of the chart and then recenter it on the slide (see Figure 3.16).
6. Save and close your presentation.

Figure 3.16 Linked column chart

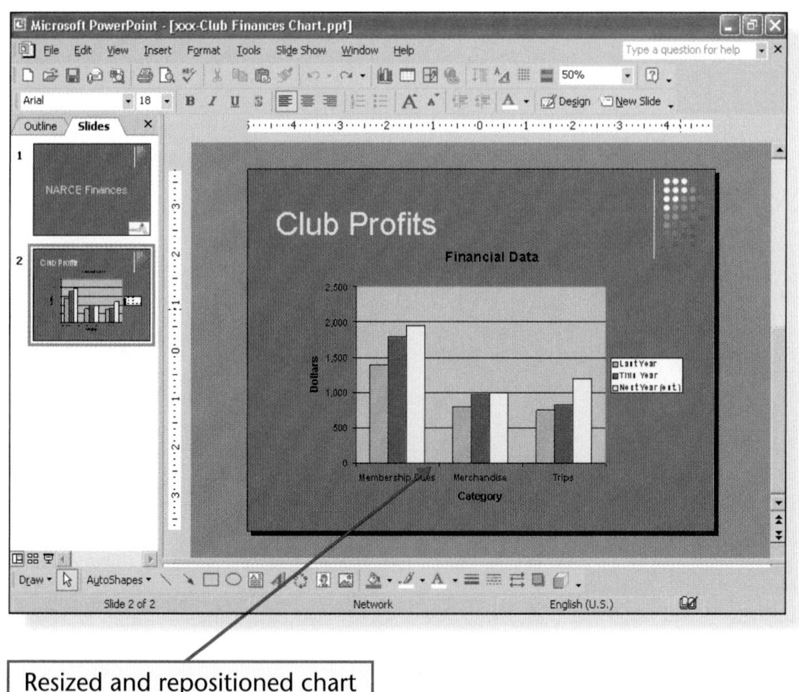
Resized and repositioned chart

PowerPoint®

APPLY IT! After finishing Exercises 1–4, you may test your skills by completing Apply It! Guided Activity 1, Customize a Presentation.

Microsoft Office Specialist
PP2002 2.2, 3.3

PowerPoint®

Exercise 5 Overview: Create OfficeArt Elements

At times you may want to create an object yourself. The Drawing toolbar allows you to create and format shapes, drawings, diagrams, and organization charts. In addition, you can manipulate objects—change a shape, add a fill color, change the line size, and so on—using various tools on the Drawing toolbar.

Need Help?
Type: about organization charts

As you create an organization chart, remember these general guidelines: (1) Use a consistent font (style, size, and color) to ensure readability for the entire audience. (2) Abbreviate job titles if necessary to allow for larger boxes and fonts. (3) Make wise color choices (for fonts, box borders, fills, background, and so on) to ensure readability and appropriate contrasts. (4) Choose an appropriate chart layout for the information to display. (5) Clearly and accurately display the reporting relationships.

In the following exercise, you will use drawing tools to create a NARCE organization chart for a presentation to be shown during the NARCE year-end meeting just before the annual elections.

Step Through It™
Exercise 5: Create an organization chart

1. Open *Organization.ppt* and save it as *xxx-Organization Chart.ppt*. Display slide 2.
2. Click Insert Diagram or Organization Chart on the Drawing toolbar.
3. Click Organization Chart in the Diagram Gallery dialog box, click OK, and type President in the top box (see Figure 3.17).

Figure 3.17 Creating an organization chart

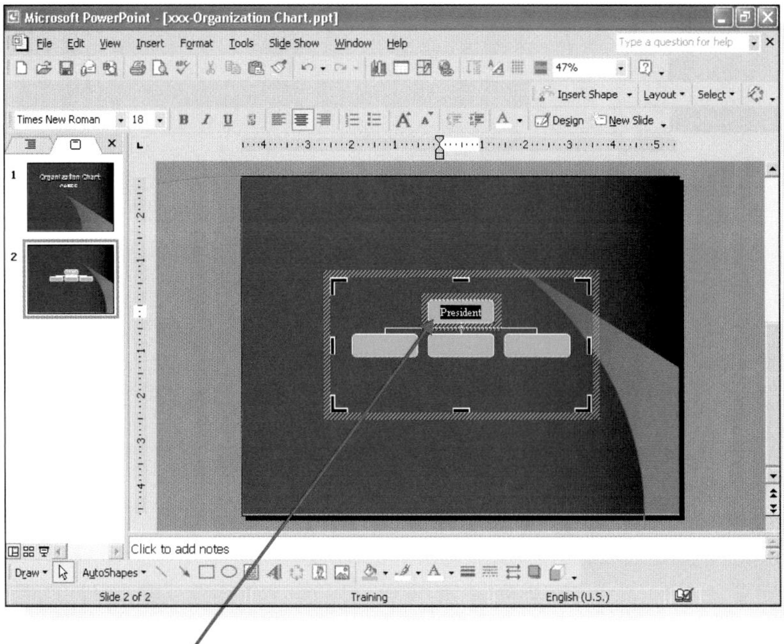

Type **President** in the top box.

Figure 3.18 Organization chart with three levels

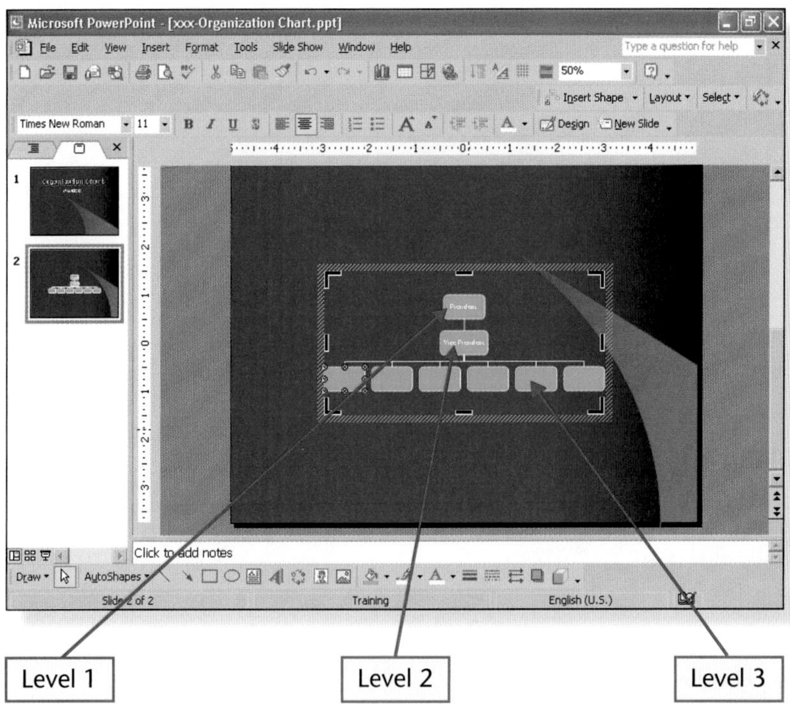

4. For two of the three subordinate boxes below the president's box, right-click the edge of the box until you see selection handles, and then select Delete. Then, type Vice President in the remaining box.

5. With the second-level box still selected, right-click the edge, and select Subordinate.

6. Click the third-level box, right-click the edge, and select Coworker. Repeat this four times until you have six boxes displayed (see Figure 3.18).

Figure 3.19 Selecting a level for formatting

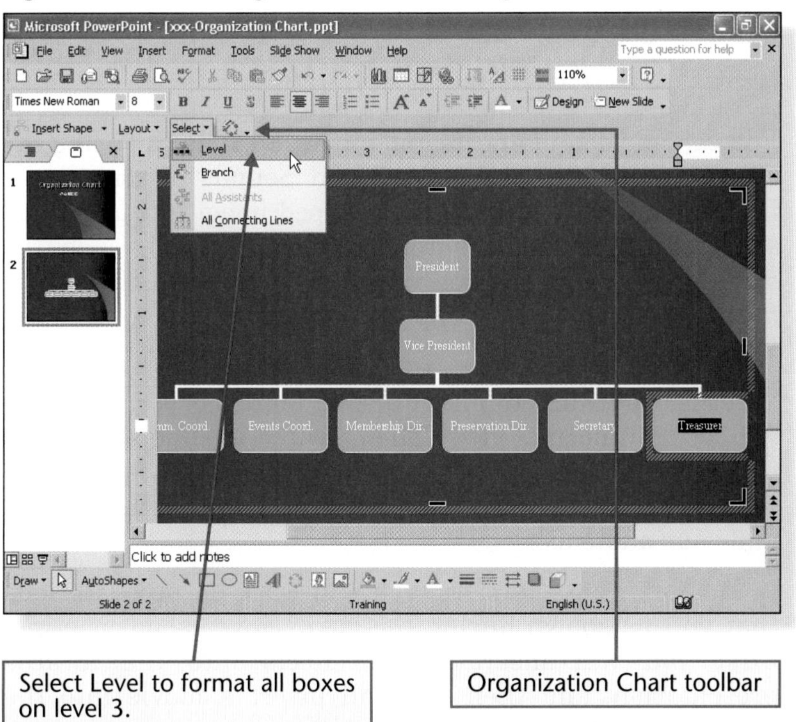

7. Type the following job titles in the six empty boxes:
   Comm. Coord.
   Events Coord.
   Membership Dir.
   Preservation Dir.
   Secretary
   Treasurer

8. With your insertion point still on the third level, click Select on the Organization Chart toolbar, and click Level (see Figure 3.19).

PowerPoint®

9. Click the Fill Color down arrow on the Drawing toolbar, and click the yellow-gold color.

10. Select the *President* box and choose the red fill color. Click Select and then Branch. Change the text in all boxes to 9 pt., bold, dark blue to match the background.

11. Resize and reposition the entire chart, if necessary (see Figure 3.20).

12. Save and close your presentation.

Figure 3.20 Formatted organization chart

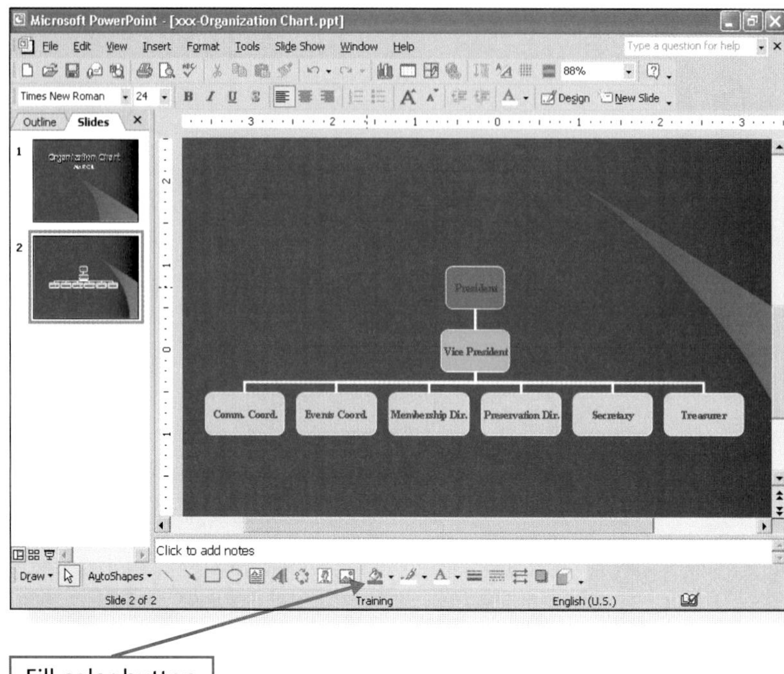

Fill color button

PowerPoint®

Microsoft Office Specialist PP2002 6.2

Exercise 6 Overview: Insert Sound Effects and Movies

You can add sound effects and movies to slides by using the Clip Organizer or the Movies and Sounds option on the Insert menu. Just as with bit-mapped images, you can add sound effects and movies from other sources, too—such as a sound you already have on your computer, a song from your favorite CD, or a movie clip you have downloaded from the Internet.

Type: add music or sound effects

Whether you want to insert a sound effect or a movie, you will work in normal view. Then, switch to slide show view to test your choices. Always remember to choose sound effects and movies based on appropriateness for the content and your audience.

In the following exercises, you will work on presentations that will be shown during the NARCE year-end meeting. First you will insert sound effects into the awards presentation, and then you will insert a movie into the presentation on NARCE finances.

Figure 3.21 Searching for a sound clip

Figure 3.22 Slide 1 in slide show view

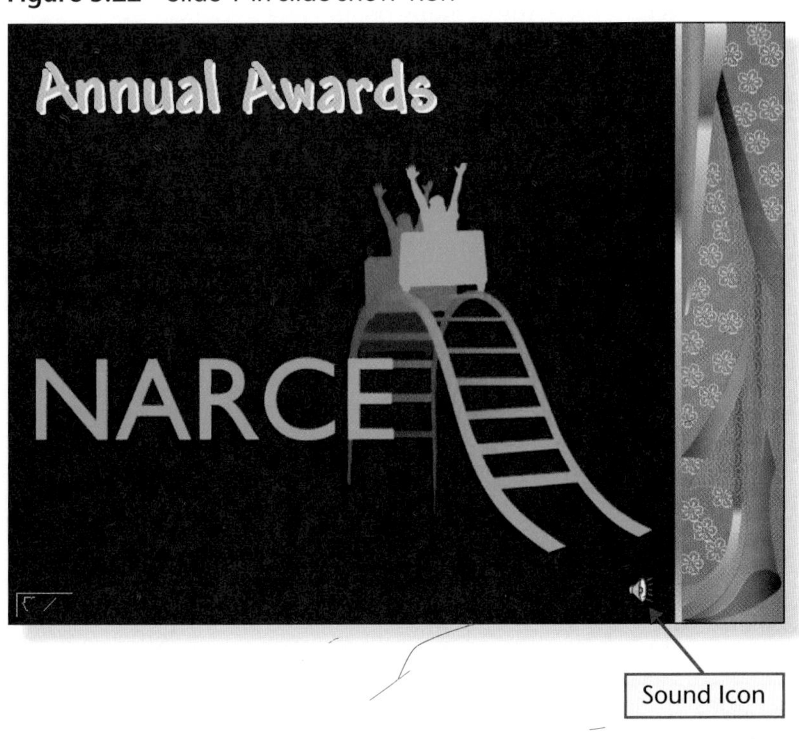

Step Through It™

Exercise 6A: Insert sound effects

1. Open *xxx-Annual Awards Table Imported.ppt* and save it as *xxx-Annual Awards Sound.ppt.*
2. On slide 1, point to Movies and Sounds on the Insert menu, and then select Sound from Clip Organizer.
3. View the sound clips displayed in the Insert Clip Art task pane, and then click Modify (see Figure 3.21).
4. Type applause in the *Search text* box, select Sounds in the *Results should be* box, and click Search.
5. Click Applause Loop, and then click Yes.
6. Move the sound icon to the bottom right corner of the black portion of the slide.
7. Click Slide Show, and listen to the sound that plays on slide 1 (see Figure 3.22).
8. Press Esc to end the slide show, and then save and close the file.

PowerPoint®

Step Through It™

Exercise 6B: Insert a movie

1. Open *xxx-Club Finances Chart.ppt* and save it as *xxx-Club Finances Movie.ppt*.
2. On slide 1, point to Movies and Sounds on the Insert menu, and then select Movie from Clip Organizer.
3. Scroll to locate the movie that shows a person on top of a large dollar sign (see Figure 3.23), and click it.

Figure 3.23 Selecting a movie

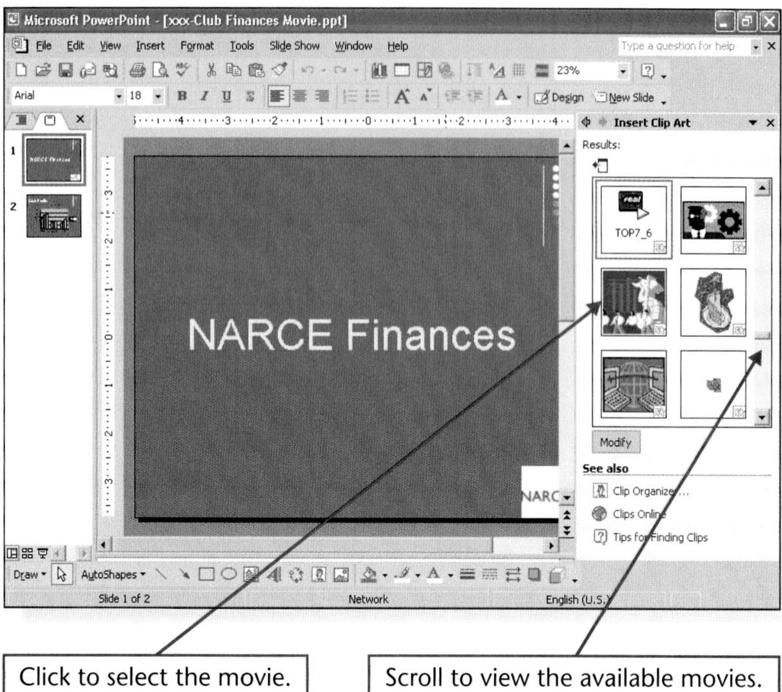

4. Click Yes to play automatically in the slide show. (***Note:*** You may need to resize and reposition the NARCE logo and the slide title.)
5. Move the movie clip icon to the upper-left corner of the slide and increase its size (see Figure 3.24).
6. Click Slide Show and notice the movie that plays on the slide.
7. Press Esc to end the slide show. Then, save and close your presentation.

Figure 3.24 Slide 1 with the movie inserted

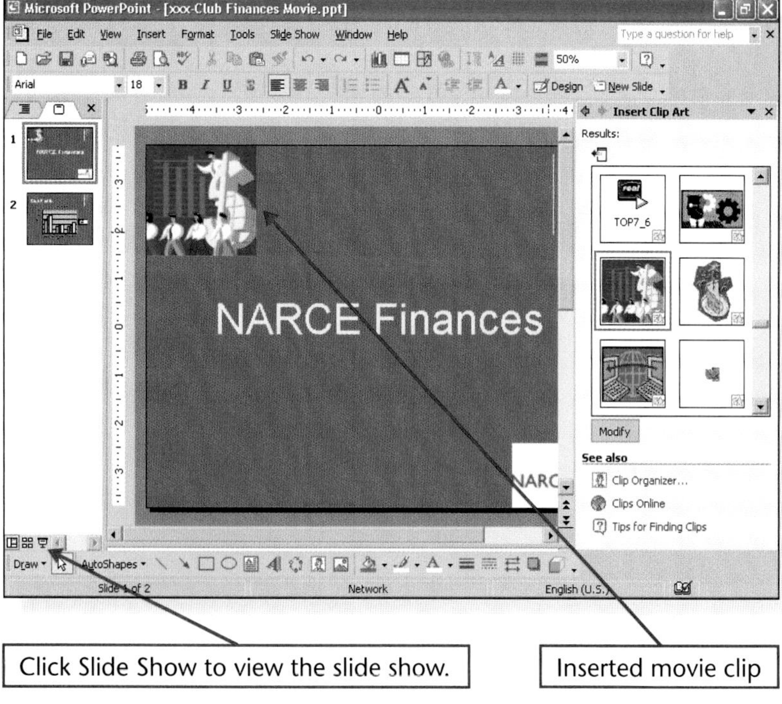

Career Corner

Lights, Camera, Computer!

Do you catch yourself doodling on your papers or your book covers? If you're interested in drawing, and you enjoy working with computers, you may want to consider a career in computer animation.

Computer animators use special 3D computer animation software to draw the key frames of an animation—what happens every half-second or so. Then the program fills in what happens in between. Animators also manipulate images scanned from models to look or act the way they want.

Animators combine their work with scenes, background, sound effects, and music. The result is the amazing characters, settings, and "special fx" we see in movies, TV shows, commercials, computer games, and Web pages. Given all this coordination that must take place, you can see why computer animators must be able to communicate and work well with others.

There are also many opportunities in related careers such as computer-aided design (CAD)—people with CAD backgrounds are in demand in many design-related fields, such as architecture, engineering, and interior design.

Some people are hired as animators right after high school. But, to get really good, you should take additional courses or earn a college degree. Two-year programs offer instruction in areas like computer character design, gaming design, and 3D. Some animators hold degrees in computer science or fine arts. You can also learn on the job as a trainee or an intern. Or, you can combine work and school. Regardless of the path you take, you must enjoy learning, because computer animation is a rapidly changing field.

You can explore computer animation by taking classes in art, broadcast technologies, and computers. Find opportunities to draw, paint, design, and make computer graphics by designing scenery or costumes for a school production or by creating your own anime or manga characters at home.

CRITICAL THINKING

1. Consider movies you have seen with computer animation. What were some of the best effects? How do you think they were done?
2. Create a storyboard for a cartoon, commercial, or music video.

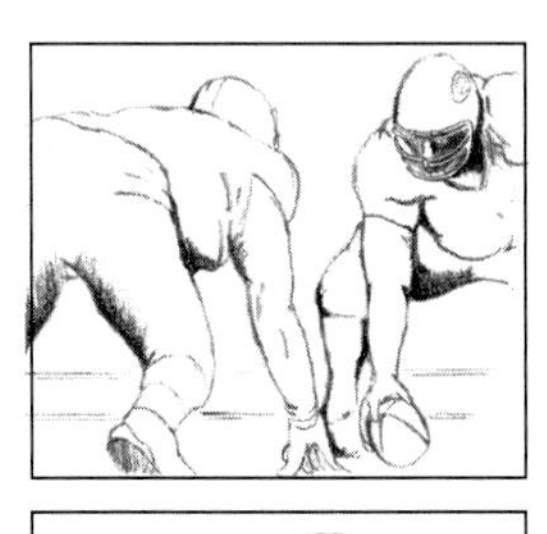

Microsoft Office Specialist PP2002 1.3, 2.2, 3.2, 4.1, 4.4, 4.5, 4.6, 4.9

PowerPoint®

Exercise 7 Overview: Manage Slide Masters

You can make changes to all slides at one time (which are referred to as global changes) by using the slide master. A **slide master** is a hidden slide in every presentation that stores design template specifications—such as placeholder sizes and positions, bullet styles, font styles and sizes, and background color—for all slides but the title slide. The **title master** stores specifications for any slide that uses the Title Slide layout.

When you edit the slide master, that change is reflected on every slide except the title slide when you return to normal view. For example, you may want to add headers or footers to a presentation. A **footer** is text that repeats at the bottom of each slide. A footer contains three placeholders: a date area, a footer area, and a slide number area (see Figure 3.25).

Figure 3.25 Footer area in slide master view

A **header** is text that repeats at the top of each notes page or handout. Likewise, you may decide that you prefer to use a different bullet style than the one used by the design template. Or perhaps you want to manipulate the font by changing its type, size, or color. You might want a specific picture, text box, or other object to repeat on each slide.

Each presentation that uses a design template contains four masters: a slide master, a title master, a handout master, and a notes master.

You can view the slide, handout, and notes masters using the View menu. In slide master view, you can access the slide master or the title master. Just as with the slide master, any changes you make to the title master are reflected on the title slide when you return to normal view.

In some instances, you might want to make a change to only one slide. In that case, you can override the slide master by editing that particular slide.

In the following exercises, you will make a variety of changes to the slide master in the presentation you have created in your efforts to run for secretary of NARCE. Then, you will edit the title master in the presentation.

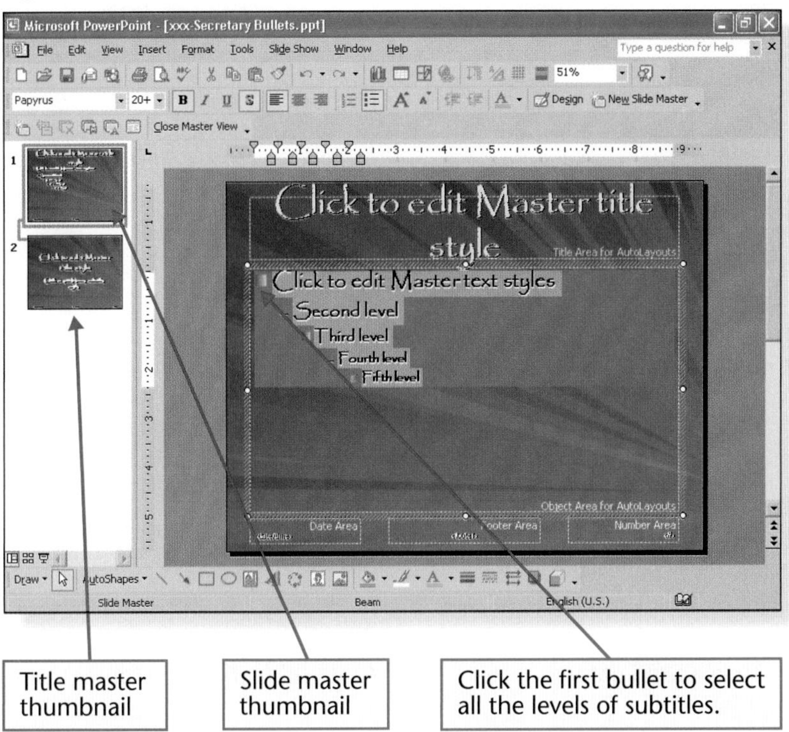

Figure 3.26 Changing the font on the slide master

Step Through It™

Exercise 7A: Change font attributes and bullets

1. Open *Secretary.ppt* and save it as *xxx-Secretary Bullets.ppt*.
2. On slide 2, hold Shift and click Slide Master View.
3. Click *Click to edit Master title style*, and change the font to 54 pt. Papyrus (or another font), bold.
4. Select all text in the text placeholder, and change the font to Papyrus (or another font), bold (see Figure 3.26).

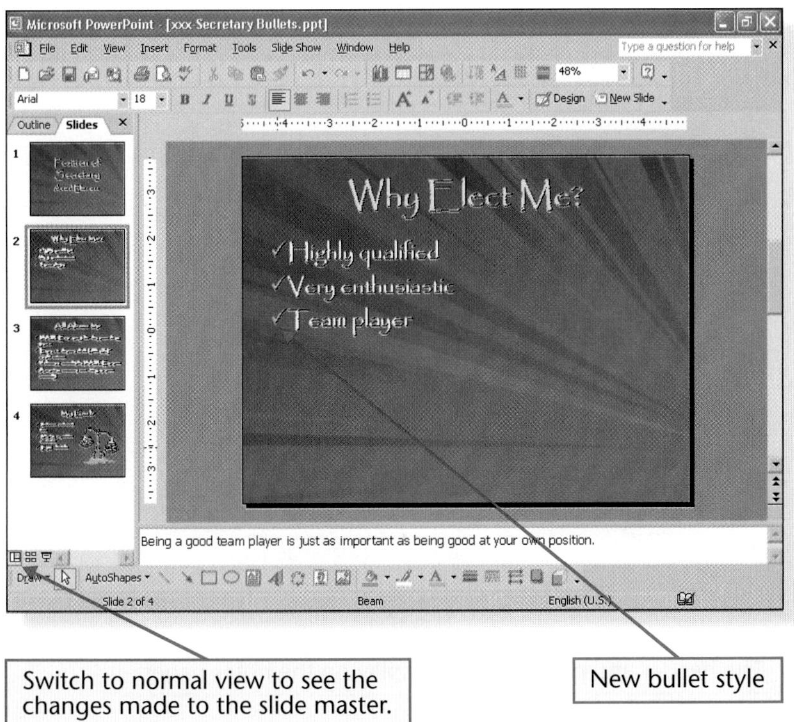

Figure 3.27 Font and bullet changes

5. Click *Click to edit Master text styles*, and change the font size to 36.
6. Select all five levels of the text placeholder again, and select Bullets and Numbering on the Format menu.
7. Click the check mark bullet style, and click OK. ***Note:*** The bullet for each subtitle level is changed and sized appropriately.
8. Click Normal View to see the changes (see Figure 3.27), and then save the presentation.

PowerPoint®

Step Through It™

Exercise 7B: Work with headers and footers

1. Save *xxx-Secretary Bullets.ppt* as *xxx-Secretary Header-Footer.ppt*.
2. On slide 2, switch to slide master view.
3. On the slide master, click *<date/time>* in the Date Area placeholder and type today's date.
4. In the Footer Area placeholder, click *<footer>* and type Annual Elections (see Figure 3.28).

Figure 3.28 Adding a date and a footer

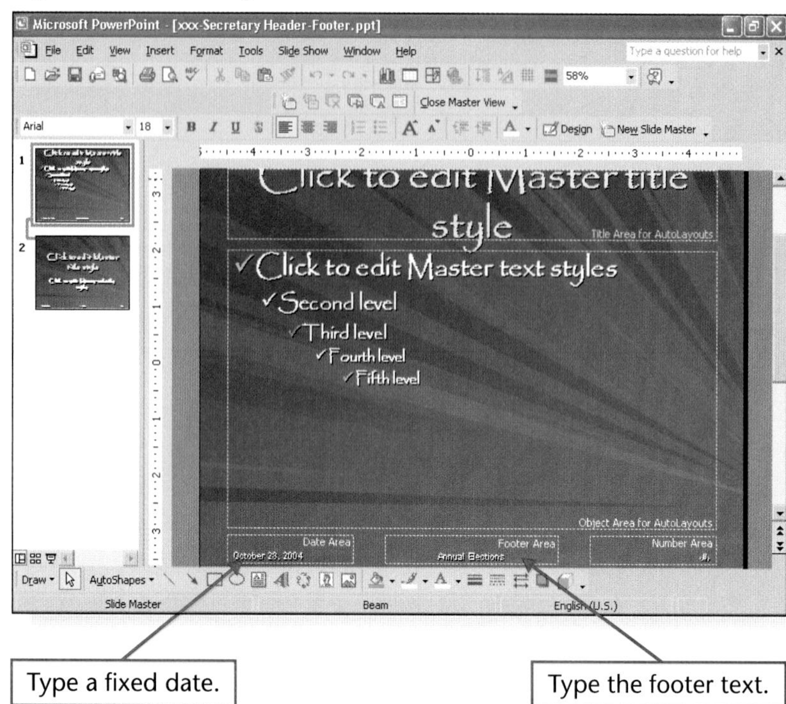

5. Select Header and Footer on the View menu, click *Slide number*, and click *Don't show on title slide.*
6. On the Notes and Handouts tab, click Header, if necessary. Type Annual Elections-Secretary in the Header box.
7. Click Apply to All; click Notes Page on the View menu to see the changes (see Figure 3.29).
8. Return to normal view and save your changes.

Figure 3.29 Notes page view

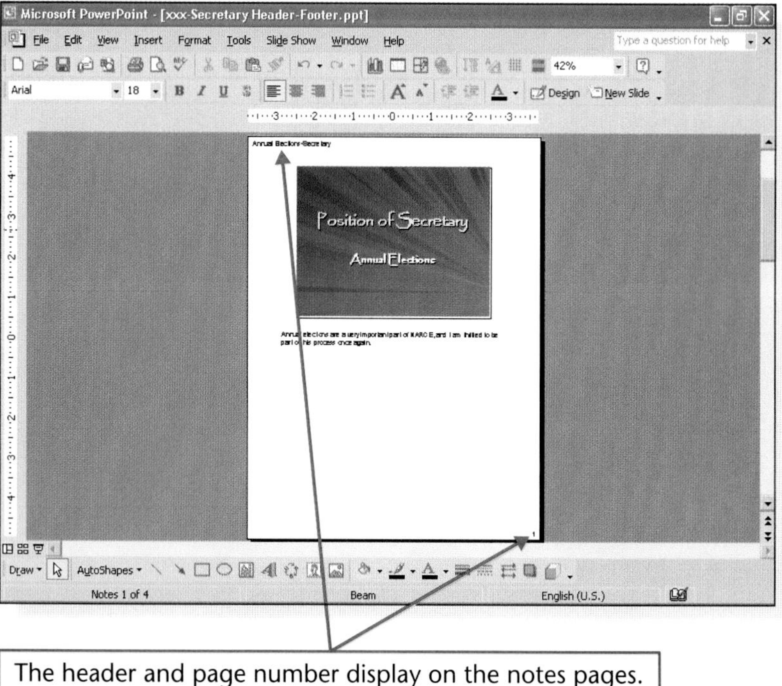

Figure 3.30 Inserting an object

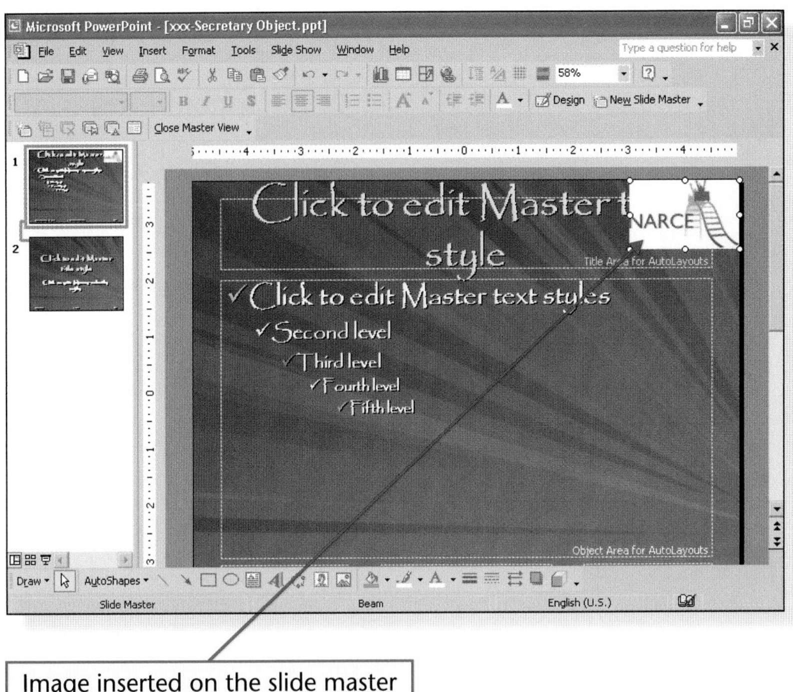

Image inserted on the slide master

Step Through It™
Exercise 7C: Add a repeating object

1. Save *xxx-Secretary Header-Footer.ppt* as *xxx-Secretary Object.ppt*.
2. Display slide 2 in normal view. Display the slide master. Insert *narce2.jpg*.
3. Resize the image to a width of about 2 inches, and move it to the upper-right corner of the slide master (see Figure 3.30).

Figure 3.31 Slide 4 of the presentation

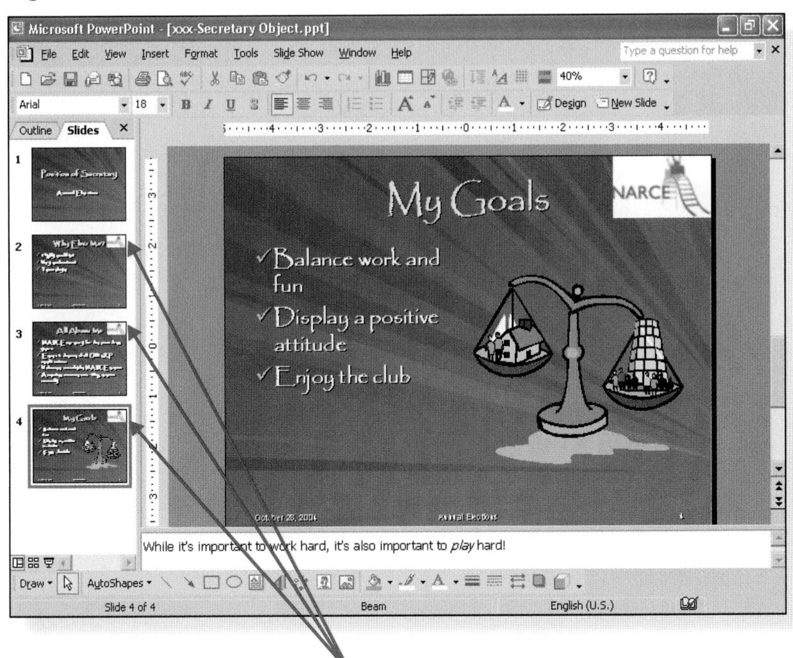

The NARCE logo appears on all slides except the title slide.

4. Switch to normal view.
5. View slides 2, 3, and 4, noticing the image on each slide (see Figure 3.31).
6. Save your presentation.

PowerPoint®

Step Through It™

Exercise 7D: Add a text box on the slide master

1. Save *xxx-Secretary Object.ppt* as *xxx-Secretary Text Box.ppt*.
2. Display slide 2 in normal view. In slide master view, select Text Box on the Insert menu.
3. When you see the text box crosshair, click the blank area near the bottom of the slide (see Figure 3.32).

Figure 3.32 Inserting a text box

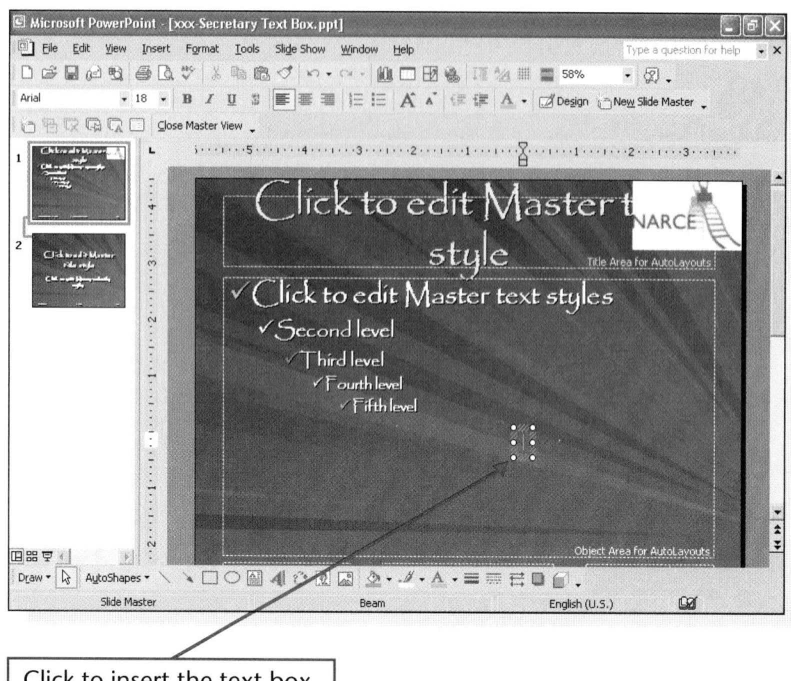

4. With the cursor blinking in the text box, type Your Name, using your actual name.
5. Reformat your name in 18 pt. bold, bright green, and then reposition the text box until it is just below the NARCE logo.
6. Switch to slide sorter view and increase the zoom percentage to see the text boxes you have inserted (see Figure 3.33).
7. Return to normal view and save your file.

Figure 3.33 Viewing the inserted text

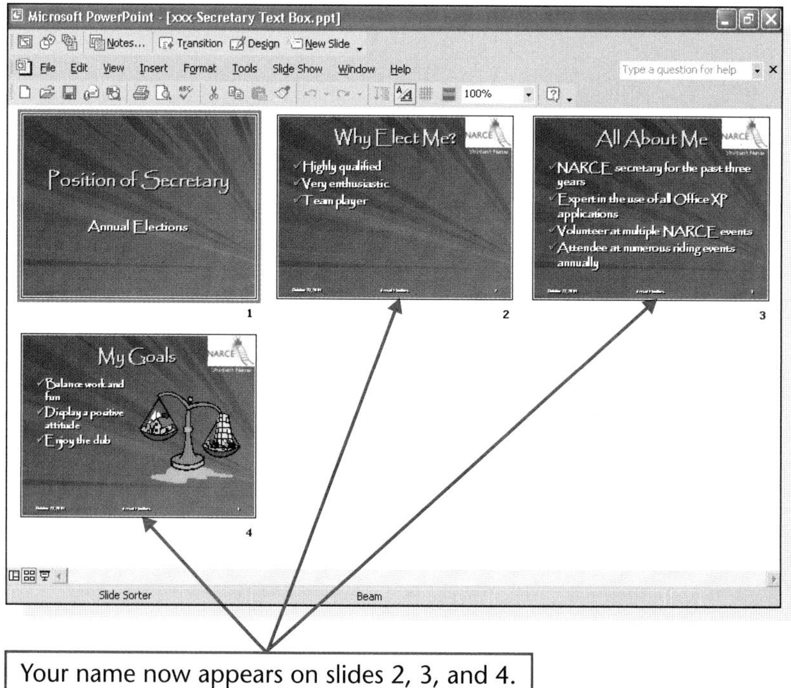

Figure 3.34 Changing bullets to numbers

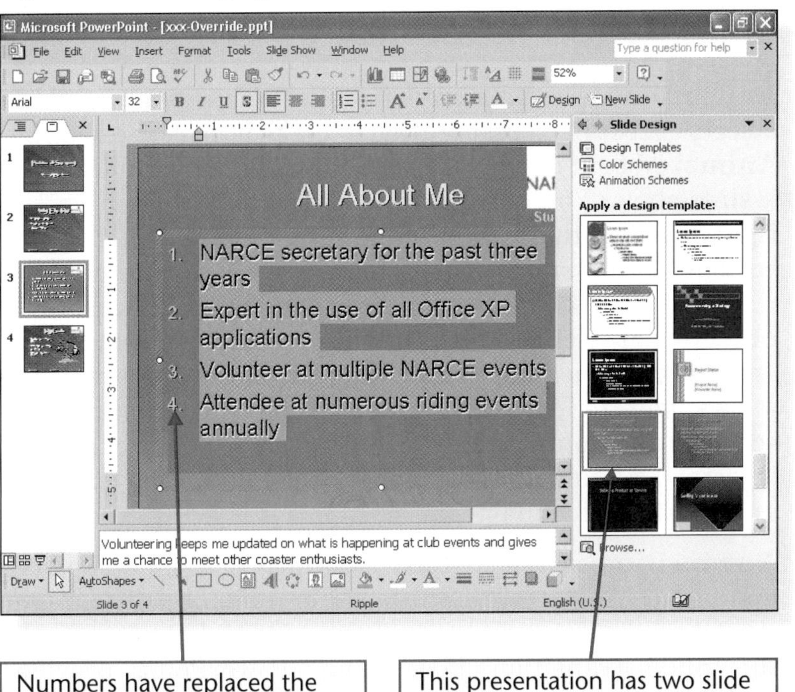

Numbers have replaced the bullets, overriding the Ripple design template's slide master.

This presentation has two slide masters—one for each design template.

Step Through It™

Exercise 7E: Override a slide master

1. Save *xxx-Secretary Text Box.ppt* as *xxx-Override.ppt*.
2. Apply the Ripple design template to slide 3 only, select its subtitles, and click Numbering (see Figure 3.34).
3. On the new slide master, add the footer and date. Format the date, footer, and slide number in 12 point.
4. View the changes, save your file, and close the task pane.

Figure 3.35 Reformatting the subtitle

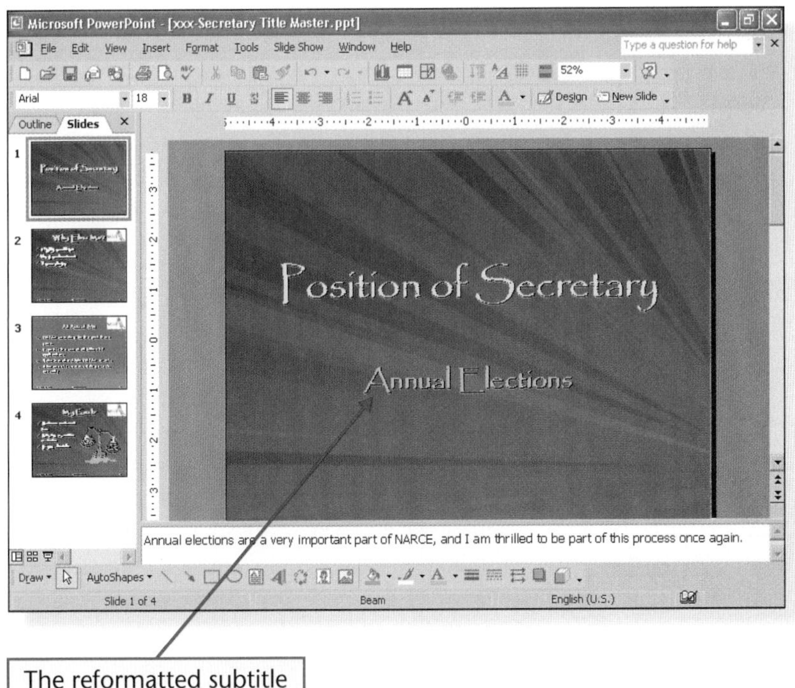

The reformatted subtitle

Step Through It™

Exercise 7F: Work with the title master

1. Save *xxx-Override.ppt* as *xxx-Secretary Title Master.ppt*.
2. Display slide 1, and then switch to slide master view to display the title master.
3. Click the subtitle placeholder, and change it to 48 pt., bright green.
4. In normal view, view your changes (see Figure 3.35), and then save and close the presentation.

Microsoft Office Specialist PP2002 4.2, 4.3

Exercise 8 Overview:
Animate Your Presentation

Animations are sound or visual effects that you can add to objects or text in a presentation to make it more interesting. **Animated text** displays on a slide one line at a time during a slide show. You can animate a title to "fly" in from the right side, and then animate the subtitle to "fly" in from the bottom, while a *swoosh* sound plays. Or you can animate the bulleted items to appear on-screen one by one. **Animated objects** are pictures, text boxes, or other graphics that appear one at a time rather than all at once. PowerPoint allows you to choose between using preset animation schemes and applying custom animation to specific text and objects. You can animate slides individually, or you can animate the slide master.

A **transition** is the method by which one slide replaces another during a presentation. For instance, you might want one slide to fade out and the next slide to fade in. In the Slide transition task pane, PowerPoint provides multiple transition effects from which you can choose (see Figure 3.30).

Figure 3.36 Slide Transition task pane

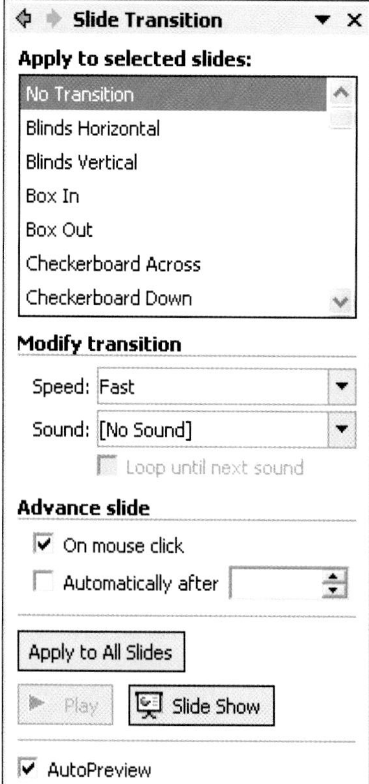

You can apply transition effects by adding them in slide sorter view. Once you apply a transition effect to a slide, a transition icon appears below that slide in slide sorter view. However, to see the actual transitions and animations you have added to a presentation, you must switch to slide show view.

You can set both animations and transitions to take place either after a specified amount of time, or only when you click the mouse. As with any PowerPoint feature, use your best judgment in applying special effects.

Don't overuse animations and transitions; you don't want them to draw too much attention away from the presentation content. And remember that consistent use of animations and transitions is critical for an effective presentation.

In the following three exercises, you will first apply slide transitions to the awards presentation that will be shown during the NARCE year-end meeting, and then you will animate both text and objects.

Figure 3.37 Slide Transition task pane

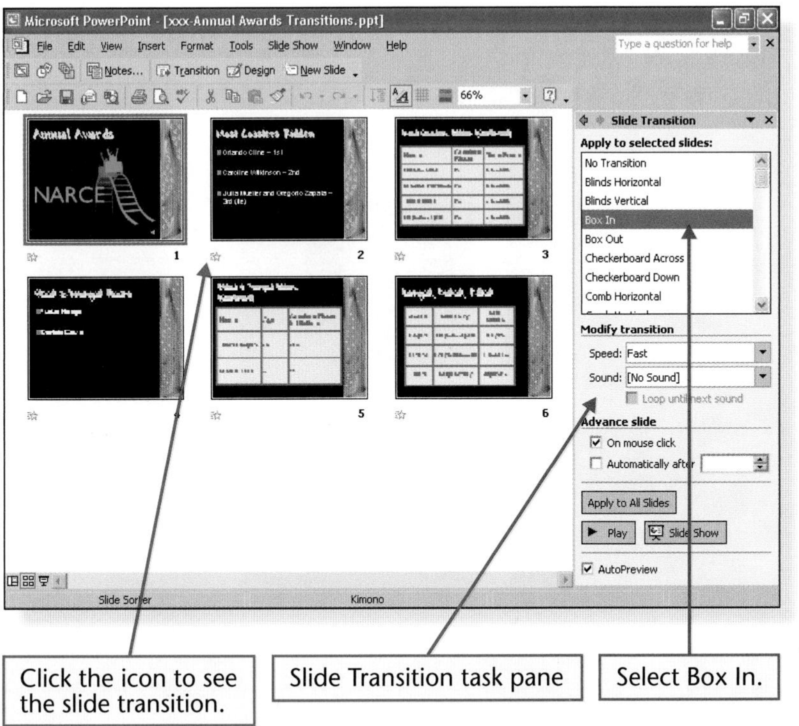

Step Through It™

Exercise 8A: Apply slide transitions

1. Open *xxx-Annual Awards Sound.ppt* and save it as *xxx-Annual Awards Transitions.ppt.*
2. Switch to slide sorter view and click slide 2.
3. Click Slide Transition [Transition] on the Slide Sorter toolbar, and click Box In in the *Apply to selected slides* list box (see Figure 3.37).

4. Click the slide transition icon below slide 2 to see the transition effect. With Box In still selected, click Apply to All Slides.

5. Hold Control and click slides 3, 5, and 6. Then select Blinds Vertical.

6. In the Speed box, select Medium (see Figure 3.38).

7. Click slide 1. View the slide show. Then, in normal view, save and close the file.

Figure 3.38 Modifying slide transitions

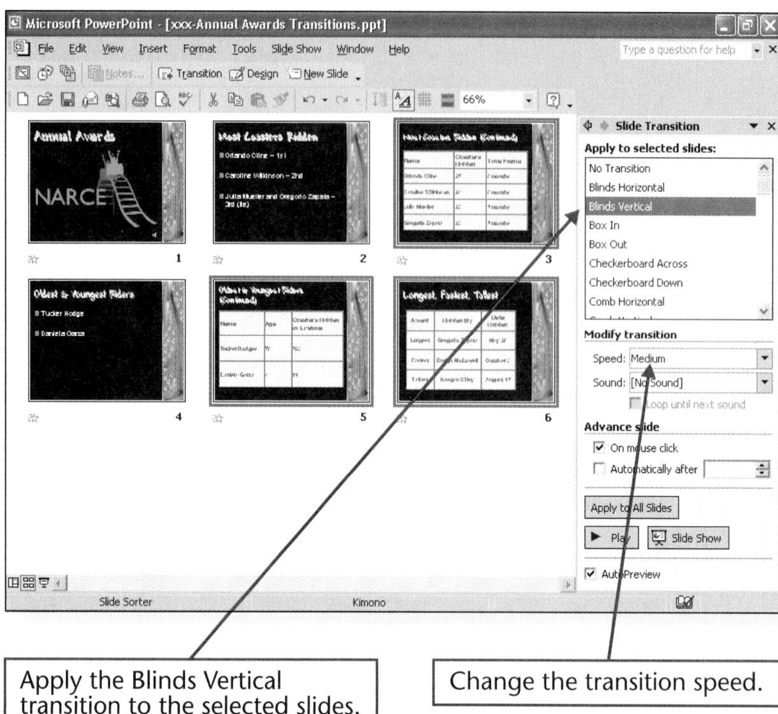

Step Through It™
Exercise 8B: Animate text

1. Open *xxx-Secretary Title Master.ppt* and save it as *xxx-Secretary Text.ppt*. In slide sorter view, select Animation Schemes on the Slide Show menu.

2. In the Moderate section of the *Apply to selected slides* box, select *Rise up* and click Apply to All Slides (see Figure 3.39). Click the icons below the slides one at a time.

3. Close the task pane. In normal view, save and close the presentation.

Figure 3.39 Animating text

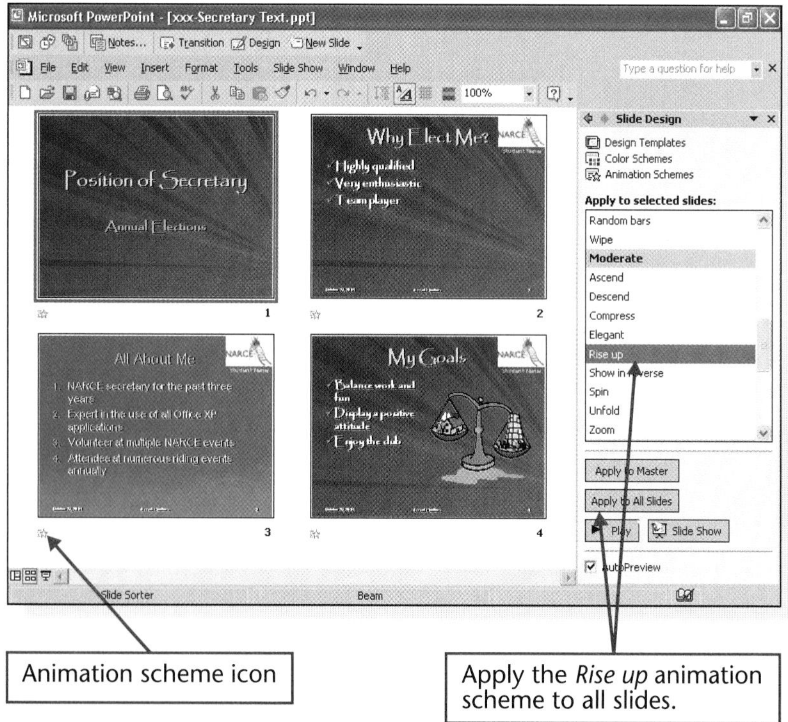

Figure 3.40 Custom Animation option

Use custom animations to enhance your presentations.

Figure 3.41 Animating an object

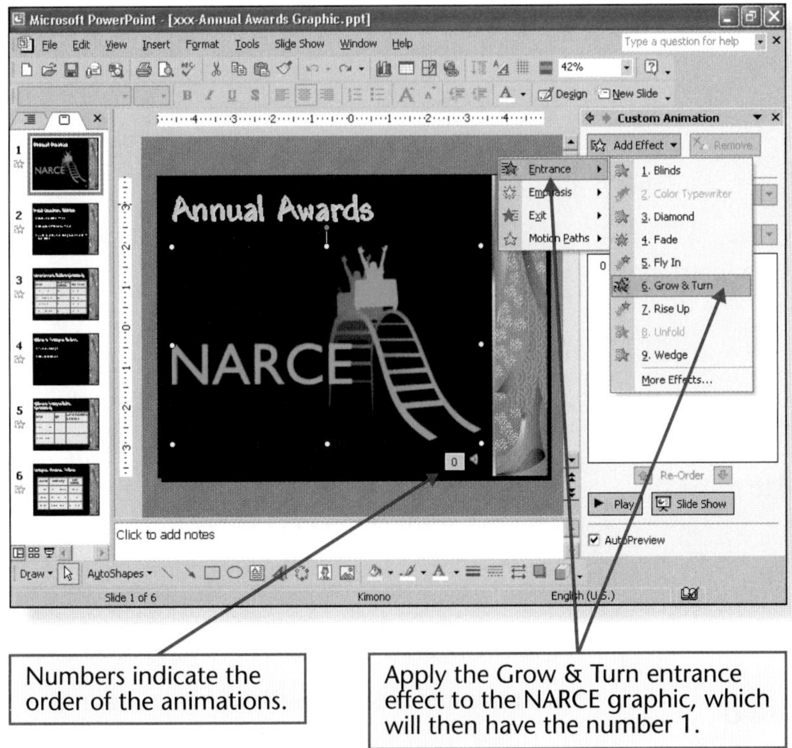

Numbers indicate the order of the animations.

Apply the Grow & Turn entrance effect to the NARCE graphic, which will then have the number 1.

Step Through It™

Exercise 8C: Animate objects

1. Open *xxx-Annual Awards Transitions.ppt* and save it as *xxx-Annual Awards Graphic.ppt*.
2. Display slide 1 in normal view, select the graphic that appears, and select Custom Animation on the Slide Show menu (see Figure 3.40).
3. Click Add Effect, point to Entrance, and select Grow & Turn (see Figure 3.41). Save your changes.
4. View the slide show, and then close the file.

PowerPoint®

APPLY IT! After finishing Exercises 5–8, you may test your skills by completing Apply It! Guided Activity 2, Animate a Presentation.

Procedure Summary

PowerPoint® Procedure Summary

Insert Clip Art

1. Click the Insert Clip Art icon in a content placeholder.
2. In the *Search text* box of the Select Picture dialog box, type a term describing the image you want.
3. Click **Search**.
4. In the search results, select a clip to insert into your presentation.
5. Click OK.

OR

1. Select a slide on which you want to insert clip art.
2. Click **Insert Clip Art** on the Drawing toolbar.
   OR
   Click **Insert** . . . . Alt + I
   Point to **Picture** . . . . P
   Select **Clip Art** C
3. In the *Search text* box on the Insert Clip Art task pane, type a term that describes the image you want.
4. Set the search options.
5. Click **Search**.
6. In the search results, click a clip to insert into your presentation.

Resize Clip Art

1. Select the clip art to resize.
2. Drag a corner selection handle to resize the image proportionally.

OR

1. Double-click the clip art to resize.
   OR
   Right-click the clip art to resize.
   Select **Format Picture** I
2. In the Format Picture dialog box, click the **Size** tab.
3. Select **Lock aspect ratio** . . . . Alt + A
4. Set the **Height** as desired. . . . . Alt + E
   OR
   Set the **Width** as desired . . . . Alt + D
5. Click OK.

Move Clip Art

1. Select the clip art to move.
2. Drag the clip art to the desired position.

OR

1. Right-click the clip art to move.
2. Click **Format Picture** I
3. In the Format Picture dialog box, click the **Position** tab.
4. Set the **Horizontal** and **From** positions . . . . Alt + H; Alt + F
   OR
   Set the **Vertical** and **From** positions . . . . Alt + V; Alt + R
5. Click OK.

Import a Bit-Mapped Image

1. Select the slide on which you want to insert a bit-mapped image.
2. Click the Insert Picture icon in a content placeholder.
   OR
   Click **Insert Picture** on the Drawing toolbar.
   OR
   Click **Insert** . . . . Alt + I
   Point to **Picture** . . . . P
   Select **From File** . . . . F
3. In the Insert Picture dialog box, navigate to and select the desired image.
4. Click **Insert** . . . . Alt + S
5. Resize and reposition the image as desired.

Create a Table

1. Select the slide on which you want to add a table.
2. Click **Insert Table** .
3. Drag to select the number of columns and rows.
4. Enter the text for the table.
5. Format the text as desired.

OR

1. Select the slide on which you want to add a table.
2. Click the Insert Table icon in the content placeholder.
   OR
   Click **Insert** . . . . **Alt + I**
   Select **Table** . . . . **B**
3. Enter the number of columns and rows.
4. Click OK.
5. Enter the text for the table.
6. Format the text as desired.

Customize a Table

1. Select a table to customize.
2. Right-click the table.
3. Click Borders and Fills.
4. In the Format Table dialog box, click the **Borders** or **Fill** tab and format as desired.
5. Click OK.

Import a Word Table

1. Click **Insert** . . . . **Alt + I**
2. Point to **Object** . . . . **O**
3. In the Insert Object dialog box, click **Create from file** . . . . **Alt + F**
4. Click **Browse** . . . . **B**
5. Navigate to and select the Word file.
6. Click OK.
7. Click **Link** if you want to link the file . . . . . **L**
8. Click OK.
9. Format, resize, and reposition the table as desired.

Create a Chart

1. Select the slide on which you want to add a chart.
2. Click **Insert Chart**.
   OR
   Click the Insert Chart icon in a content placeholder.
   OR
   Click **Insert** . . . . **Alt + I**
   Click **Chart** . . . . **H**
3. As needed, replace the information in the datasheet.
4. Close the datasheet.
5. Format, resize, and reposition the chart as desired.

Import an Excel Chart

1. Click **Insert** . . . . **Alt + I**
2. Point to **Object** . . . . **O**
3. In the Insert Object dialog box, click **Create from file** . . . . **Alt + F**
4. Click **Browse**. . . . . **B**
5. Navigate to and select the Excel file.
6. Click OK.
7. Click **Link** if you want to link the file . . . . . **L**
8. Click OK.
9. Format, resize, and reposition the chart as desired.

Procedure Summary

Create an Organization Chart

1. Click Insert Diagram or Organization Chart on the Drawing toolbar.

   OR
   Click the Insert Diagram or Organization Chart icon in a content placeholder.
   OR
   Click **Insert** . . . . Alt + I
   Click **Diagram** . . . . G
2. In the Diagram Gallery dialog box, click Organization Chart.
3. Click OK.
4. As needed, select a shape to which you want to insert other shapes.
5. Click **Insert Shape** down arrow on the Organization Chart toolbar.
6. As appropriate, select **Subordinate**, **Coworker**, or **Assistant** . . . . **S, C, or A**
7. Click in each shape and type the desired text.
8. Select the text in each shape and format as desired.
9. To reformat the organization chart, click the organization chart.
10. Right-click the chart.
11. Select **Format Organization Chart** . . . . . . **F**
12. In the Format Organization dialog box, click the **Colors and Lines, Size**, or **Position** tabs and format as desired.

Insert a Sound Effect

1. Click **Insert** . . . . Alt + I
2. Point to **Movies and Sounds**. V
3. Select **Sound from Clip Organizer** . . . . . . S
   OR
   Select **Sound from File** . . . . N
4. In the results in the Insert Clip Art task pane, click the desired sound effect down arrow.
5. To preview the sound file, click **Preview/ Properties** . . . . .W
6. Close the Preview/Properties dialog box . . . . Alt + C
7. To insert the sound effect, click the desired sound effect and click **Insert** I
8. Click **Yes** or **No** to automatically play the sound in the slide show. . . . .**Y OR N**
9. Resize and reposition the sound icon as desired.
10. View the slide in slide show view.

Insert a Movie

1. Click **Insert** .Alt + I
2. Point to **Movies and Sounds**. V
3. Select **Movie from Clip Organizer** . . . . . M
   OR
   Select **Movie from File** . . . . .F
4. In the results in the Insert Clip Art task pane, click the desired movie down arrow.
5. To preview the movie, click **Preview/ Properties** . . . . .W
6. Close the Preview/Properties dialog box . . . . Alt + C
7. To insert the movie, click the desired movie file, and click Insert.
8. Click **Yes** or **No** to automatically play the movie in the slide show . . . .**Y OR N**
9. Resize and reposition the movie icon as desired.
10. View the slide in slide show view.

Edit a Slide Master

1. Press Shift + **Slide Master View**.
   OR
   Click **View** . . . . Alt + V

Point to Master. M
Select Slide Master. . . . . S

2. Select the slide master.
3. Edit as desired.
4. To see the changes, click **Normal View**.
   OR
   Click **View**. **Alt + V**
   Select **Normal**. **N**

Edit a Title Master

1. Press Shift + **Slide Master View**.
   OR
   Click **View**. **Alt + V**
   Point to **Master**. **M**
   Select **Slide Master**. . . . . **S**
2. Select the title master.
3. Edit as desired.
4. To see the changes, click **Normal View**.
   OR
   Click **View**. **Alt + V**
   Select **Normal**. **N**

Add a Repeating Object on the Slide Master

1. Display the slide master view.
2. Click the master on which you want to add the repeating object.
3. Insert the object where desired.
4. Format the object as desired.
5. Switch to normal view to view the presentation.

Apply Slide Transitions

1. In slide sorter view, select the slide(s) to which you want to apply a transition.
2. Click **Slide Transition** Transition . . . . **Alt + R**
   OR
   Click **Slide Show**. . . . . **Alt + D**
   Click **Slide Transition** . . . . **T**
3. In the Slide Transition task pane, select a transition.
4. Select other options as desired.
5. To view the transition, click the icon below the slide(s).

Apply Preset Animation Schemes

1. In slide sorter view, select the slide(s) to which you want to apply a preset animation scheme.
2. Click **Slide Show**. . . . . **Alt + D**
3. Click **Animation Schemes**. . . . . **C**
4. In the Slide Design task pane, select an animation scheme.
5. Select other options as desired.
6. To view the animation, click Play or Slide Show in the Slide Design task pane.
   OR
   Click the animation scheme icon below the slide(s).

Apply Custom Animation

1. In normal view, select text or an object to animate.
2. Click **Slide Show**. . . . . **Alt + D**
3. Click **Custom Animation**. . . . . **M**
4. In the Custom Animation task pane, click **Add Effect**.
5. Select an effect.
6. Select other options as desired.
7. To view the animation, click Play or Slide Show in the Custom Animation task pane.

Lesson Review and Exercises

Summary Checklist

- ☑ Can you insert, move, and resize clip art?
- ☑ Can you import a bit-mapped image?
- ☑ Can you create and customize a table?
- ☑ Can you insert a Word table?
- ☑ Can you insert an Excel chart?
- ☑ Can you create a chart?
- ☑ Can you insert sound effects and movies?
- ☑ Can you change font attributes and bullets?
- ☑ Can you use the slide master and title master to make changes to a presentation?
- ☑ Can you override the slide master?
- ☑ Can you apply slide transitions?
- ☑ Can you animate text and objects?

Key Terms

- animated object (p. 576)
- animated text (p. 576)
- animation (p. 576)
- bit-mapped image (bitmap) (p. 552)
- embed (p. 556)
- footer (p. 570)
- header (p. 570)
- link (p. 556)
- slide master (p. 570)
- title master (p. 570)
- transition (p. 576)

APPLY IT! Guided Activities

1. Customize a Presentation

You are working as a trainer in the circulation department of a large newspaper's call center. The newspaper has a circulation of approximately 400,000.

In your role of training new customer service representatives (CSRs), you need to create an informative, yet entertaining, presentation that outlines the role of a CSR.

Follow these steps to customize a presentation, inserting clip art images, images from files, and charts.

a. Open *Newspaper.ppt* and save it as *xxx-Newspaper Training.ppt*. Display slide 2. Click the Insert Clip Art icon in the content placeholder.

b. Type telephone in the *Search text* box and click Search. Click the image that shows a telephone hooked up to a computer, click OK, and then resize and reposition the image on the slide **(see Figure 3.42)**.

Figure 3.42 Clip art inserted on slide 2

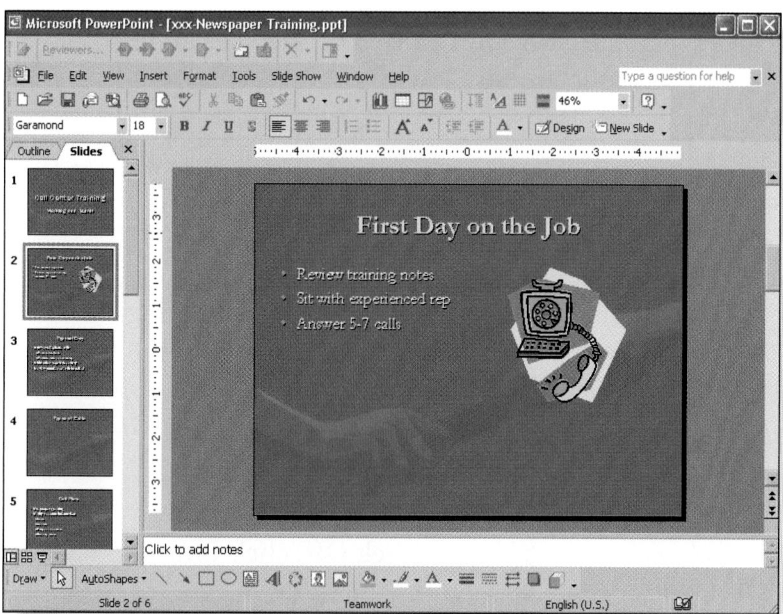

PowerPoint®

c. Display slide 5, point to Picture on the Insert menu, and select From File. Locate and insert the file *phone.jpg*, and position it near the lower-right corner of the screen.

d. Display slide 4 and click the Insert Chart icon. Replace the information in the datasheet with the information in **Table 3.4**.

Table 3.4

	A	B	C	D
	1st Qtr	2nd Qtr	3rd Qtr	4th Qtr
New Subscriptions	11,500	9,000	10,000	13,000
Cancellations	8,000	9,500	9,500	7,500
Vacation Holds	2,000	2,300	3,500	2,500
Complaints	275	200	250	300

e. Select Chart Type on the Chart menu, and select Bar to change to a bar chart. Click OK. Click twice in the area outside the slide to remove the datasheet and the chart handles. Save and close the presentation.

2. Animate a Presentation

As a landscape designer, you are putting together a presentation to publicize the products and services you offer. Since this presentation will be used to attract new customers, you want it to be an eye-catching presentation. Follow these steps to animate a presentation, create a table, use a slide master, and override a slide master.

a. Open *Landscape.ppt* and save it as *xxx-Landscape Animation.ppt*. Display slide 3. Select Object on the Insert menu, and then click *Create from file*.

b. Locate the data file *Landscape Table.doc*, click OK, click Link, and then click OK again. Resize and center the table.

c. Click View, point to Master, and select Slide Master. Select *Click to edit Master title style* and change the font to dark green, and then switch to normal view to see your changes **(see Figure 3.43)**.

Figure 3.43 Changes displayed in normal view

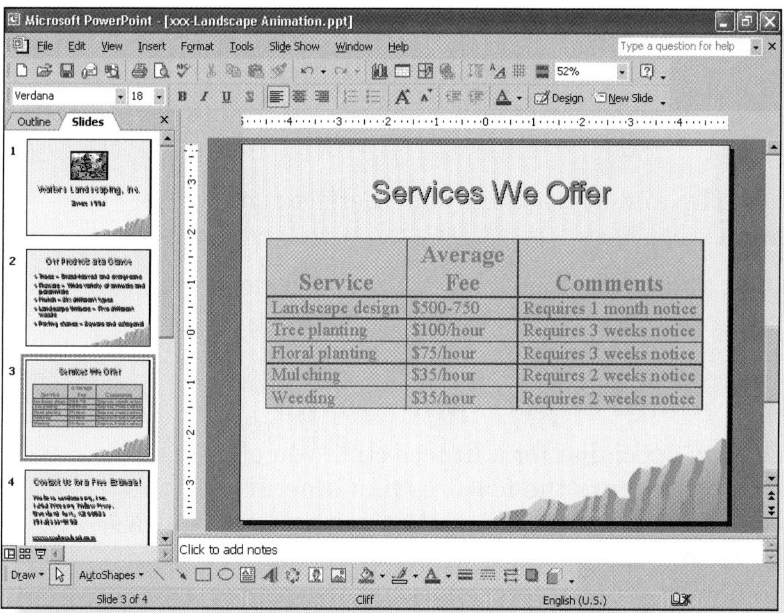

d. With slide 3 still displayed, select Animation Schemes on the Slide Show menu, and then select Spin in the Moderate section of the *Apply to selected slides* box. Then, click slide 2 on the Slides tab and hold Ctrl while clicking slide 4. Select Elegant in the Moderate section of the *Apply to selected slides* box.

e. Display slide 3 again. Select the table graphic, and select Custom Animation on the Slide Show menu. In the Custom Animation task pane, click Add Effect, point to Entrance, and select Blinds.

f. Save your changes, view the slide show, and close the presentation.

Do It Yourself

1. Use Images, Animation, and Sound

As a group director of wilderness trips designed to help rehabilitate troubled youths, you have been asked to give a presentation to a local civic club, discussing these outings. You have created a rough draft of your presentation, but you want to "jazz up" your presentation with sound and graphics.

PowerPoint®

Follow these steps:

a. Open *Wilderness.ppt* and save it as *xxx-Wilderness Challenge.ppt*.

b. Insert the bit-mapped image *camping.jpg* in an appropriate place.

c. Insert at least one clip and at least one sound effect somewhere in the presentation.

d. Animate some text and at least one object. Save and close your presentation.

2. Work With Tables, Sound Effects, and Movies

In your role as a marketing specialist for a fitness club, you often have to create presentations that discuss the features and amenities of the club. You are working on a new presentation that you will show at a meeting for potential new members next month. Follow these steps to add tables, sound, and a movie to your presentation:

a. Open *Fitness.ppt* and save it as *xxx-Fitness Membership.ppt*.

b. Insert an appropriate movie on slide 1, repositioning the title and subtitle if necessary.

c. Add a relevant sound effect on slide 2 and reposition it. Insert *Equipment Table.doc* on slide 3. Move and resize the table if necessary.

d. Use the information provided in **Table 3.5** to create a table on slide 4. Edit the table as needed, and format it attractively.

Table 3.5

Level	Monthly Price	Comments
Single	$59	
Single plus one	$99	
Family	$135	
Senior	$49	55 and older

e. View your presentation in slide sorter view, and then save and close it.

3. Import and Create a Chart

You are drumming up new business for Residential Cleaning, a cleaning business that you founded four years ago. You plan to give a presentation at a gathering of the residents in your neighborhood, and you want to show them how successful your business has been. Follow these steps:

a. Create the presentation using an appropriate design template.

b. Using the following information, add an organization chart on slide 2 to show residents the structure of your company:
Level 1: Owner
Level 2: Managers (3 total)
Level 3: Associates (4 for each manager)

c. On slide 3, import the Excel file *cleaning.xls*, a chart that shows the increase in the number of your clients during the past four years. Then, on slide 4, create a chart showing your profits during the past four years, using the following data:
Profit
1st year: $27,000
2nd year: $39,000
3rd year: $55,000
4th year: $73,000

d. Now apply a different design template to slides 3 and 4, choosing a template and colors that compliment your original template. Make changes to these two slides using the appropriate slide master.

e. Include appropriate footers on the slides. Make sure the footers on the two templates match as well as possible. Include headers on the notes and handout pages.

f. Override one of the slide masters to make whatever changes you would like. Indicate in the notes panes of the slides the changes you made to the title and slide master(s).

g. Insert a relevant image on the title slide **(see Figure 3.44)**. (***Note:*** Your presentation does not have to match **Figure 3.44**. Choose your own design templates and image.)

h. Save your presentation as *xxx-Cleaning.ppt*.

Figure 3.44 Sample cleaning presentation

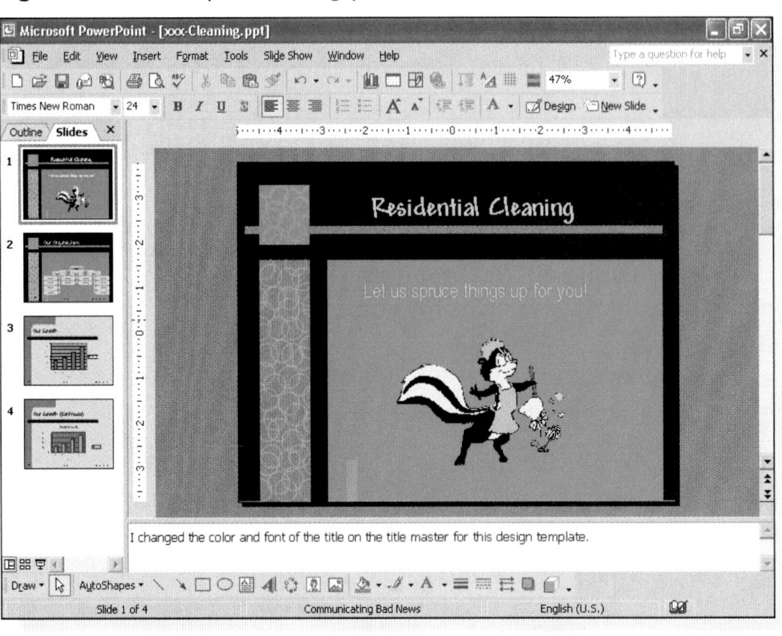

4. Use and Override the Slide Master

In your role as an assistant in a home building company, you periodically need to give a presentation to your bank showing the status of the company's projects. You are creating your next quarterly report presentation for the bank, and you want to include interesting visuals and sound effects to hold their attention.

Follow these steps to use and override the slide master:

a. Open *Builder.ppt*. Display slide 2 and switch to slide master view.

b. Insert a repeating image on the slide master.

c. Insert an appropriate sound on one of the slides in the presentation.

d. Next, create eye-catching slide transitions and animations for the presentation.

e. Save your final presentation as *xxx-Builder Report.ppt*.

Challenge Yourself

Create an Informative Presentation

As the regional manager for a department store, you need to create a presentation for the regional personnel that displays general sales information. In the presentation, you will create and insert charts and tables, and then add a bit-mapped or clip art image and a sound effect. Insert a movie if you think it is appropriate for the presentation. Format the charts and tables attractively, and resize and reposition the images as appropriate. You will begin with *Sales.ppt*. Other data files you will need for the presentation are *Sales Chart.xls* (for slide 4) and *Top Departments.doc* (for slide 6). The information you will need for slide 3 is shown in **Table 3.6**.

Table 3.6

	1st Qtr	2nd Qtr	3rd Qtr
Northeast	117,245	115,739	114,039
Southwest	113,304	101,194	109,985
Midwest	114,548	119,438	113,821

The information you will need for slide 5 is shown in **Table 3.7**.

Table 3.7

	Northeast	Southwest	Midwest
Housewares	12%	9%	13%
Men's Shoes	18%	12%	15%
Juniors	21%	17%	13%

In addition, you should make changes to the title master and override the slide master in a variety of ways. Include footers for slides, as well as headers for printed handouts and notes pages. Animate your presentation, using both preset animation schemes as well as custom animation, and then apply transition effects. Explore Help to learn more about creating shapes with the Drawing toolbar, and then try to insert a text box inside a shape on one of the slides. Save your final presentation as *xxx-Sales.ppt*.

Lesson 4

Managing and Delivering a Presentation

Lesson Exercise Objectives

After completing this lesson, you'll be able to do the following tasks:

1. Set up a presentation for delivery
2. Deliver a presentation
3. Prepare a presentation for delivery on another computer
4. Set up a review cycle
5. Manage a reviewed presentation
6. Publish presentations to the Web
7. Set up and schedule an online broadcast

Key Terms

- change marker (p. 602)
- comment marker (p. 602)
- comment (p. 602)
- embedded font (p. 598)
- liquid crystal display (LCD) projector (p. 594)
- online broadcast (p. 615)
- publish (p. 612)

Microsoft Office Specialist Activities

PP2002: 1.3, 4.7, 5.1, 7.1–7.6, 8.1–8.4

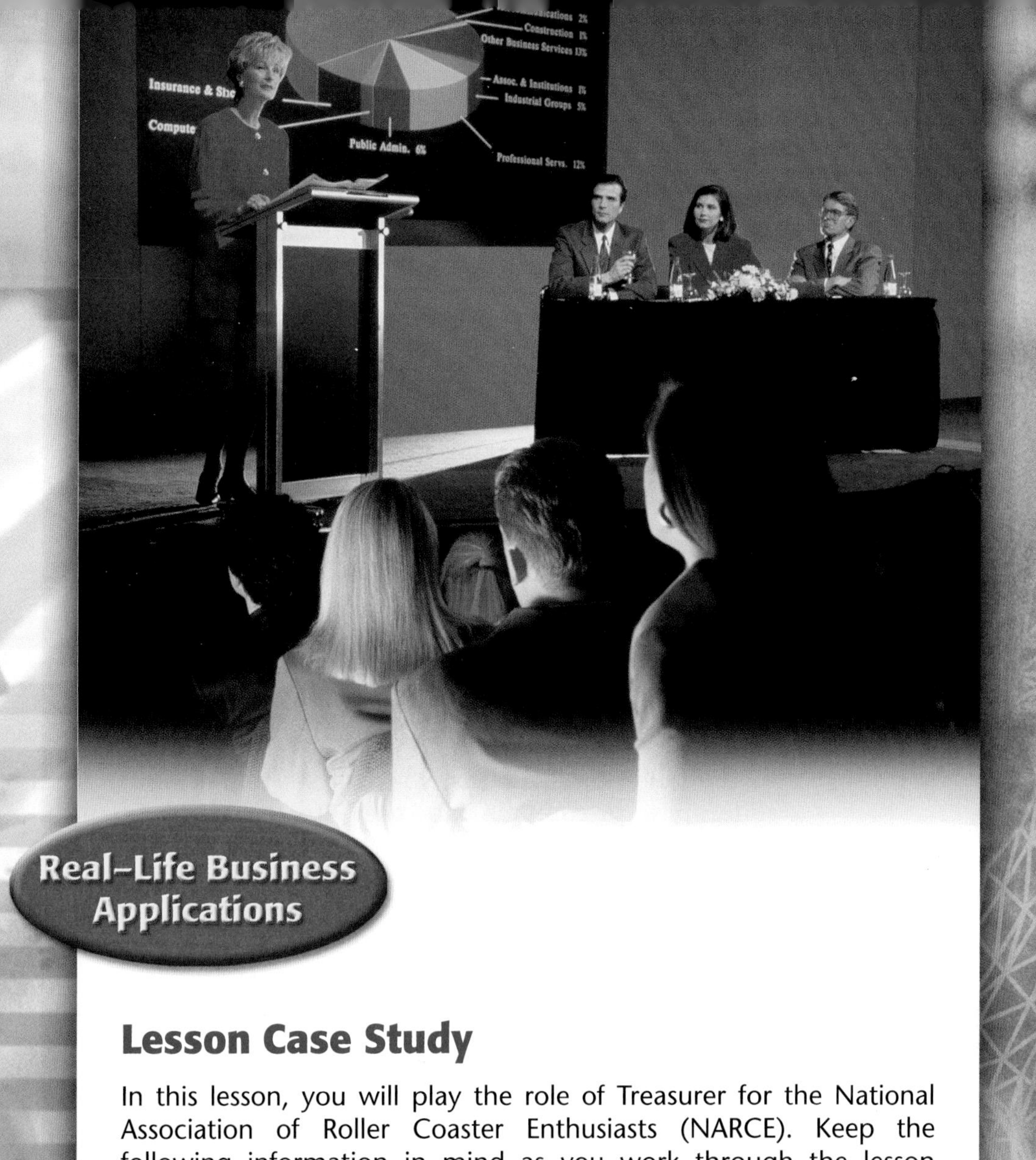

Real-Life Business Applications

Lesson Case Study

In this lesson, you will play the role of Treasurer for the National Association of Roller Coaster Enthusiasts (NARCE). Keep the following information in mind as you work through the lesson exercises.

- `Job responsibilities and goals.` As Treasurer, you report all financial aspects of the organization to NARCE members. You also send presentations to other roller coaster enthusiast clubs to brief them on how your organization survives financially.
- `The project.` You are preparing a presentation to use when communicating financial figures on NARCE-sponsored trips.
- `The challenge ahead.` You must review your presentation to be sure that it is appropriate for your audiences. You want your presentation to be professional, eye-catching, and informative. To help with this, others will review your presentation. Additionally, you must prepare the presentation to run on another computer, even if that other computer does not have PowerPoint installed.

Microsoft Office Specialist
PP2002 4.7, 5.1, 7.1, 7.2

Exercise 1 Overview:
Set Up a Presentation for Delivery

To deliver a presentation efficiently, you should know your presentation thoroughly, and you should know how to operate your equipment. You can deliver a PowerPoint presentation in these ways: (1) from your computer in slide show view, (2) using a **liquid crystal display (LCD) projector**, which allows you to project the slides in slide show view from your computer onto a blank wall or large video screen, or (3) viewing the presentation in normal view on one monitor while displaying it in slide show view on a larger monitor or LCD projector.

Before you deliver a presentation, you must adjust various settings in the Set Up Show dialog box. You must specify whether you want the slides to advance automatically or only when you click the mouse, whether you will be using multiple monitors, and whether you will be delivering the presentation or using the self-running mode.

In the following exercises, you will set up and rehearse a slide show to communicate the latest NARCE financial figures to NARCE members and other roller coaster clubs.

Step Through It™
Exercise 1A: Set up the slide show

1. Open *Trip Finances.ppt* and save it as *xxx-Trip Finances.ppt*.
2. View the presentation in normal view and read the notes in the notes pane, which are there to help you deliver the presentation.
3. On slide 1, select Set Up Show on the Slide Show menu (see Figure 4.1).

Figure 4.1 Setting up the slide show

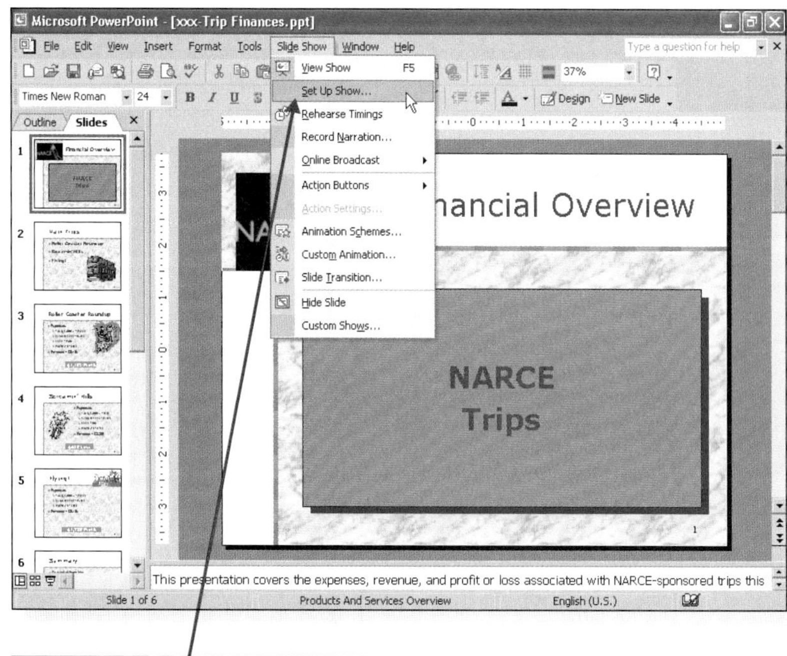

Click to set up the slide show.

Figure 4.2 Set Up Show dialog box

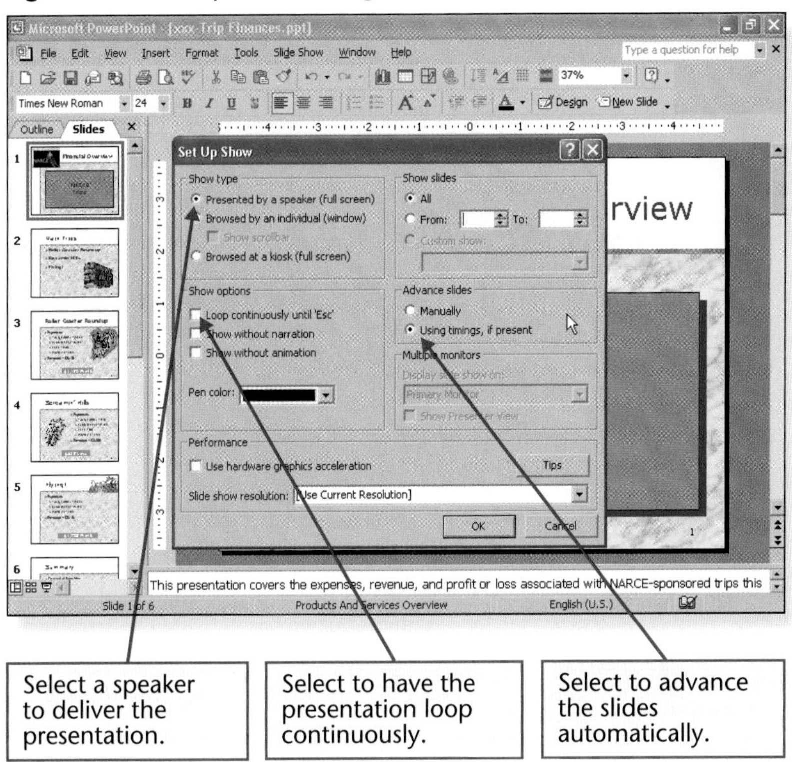

Select a speaker to deliver the presentation.
Select to have the presentation loop continuously.
Select to advance the slides automatically.

4. In the *Show type* section of the Set Up Show dialog box, verify that *Presented by a speaker (full screen)* is selected (see Figure 4.2).

5. Verify that All is selected in the *Show slides* section and that *Using timings, if present* is selected in the *Advance slides* section.

6. Click OK.

PowerPoint®

Figure 4.3 Rehearsing timings

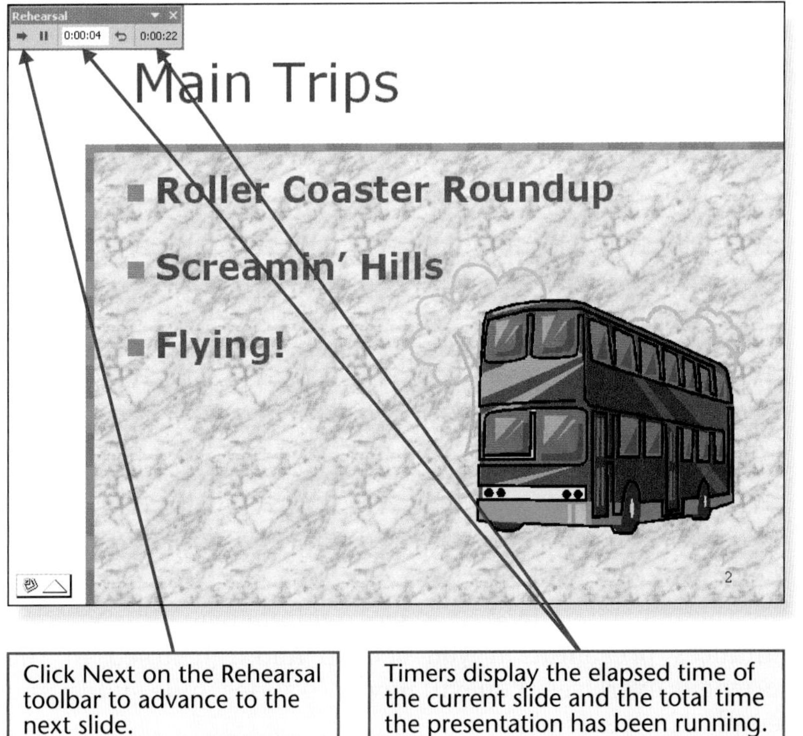

Timers display the elapsed time of the current slide and the total time the presentation has been running.

Step Through It™

Exercise 1B: Set and rehearse the timing

1. If necessary, print the notes pages for *xxx-Trip Finances.ppt* for reference during your presentation. Then select Rehearse Timings on the Slide Show menu.

2. Practice giving the presentation, making any necessary comments. Click Next on the Rehearsal toolbar to move from one slide to the next (see Figure 4.3).

3. After you finish rehearsing the last slide, click Close. Click Yes to save your timings. Notice your timings indicated below each slide (see Figure 4.4 for examples).

4. Select slide 4. In the Slide Transition task pane, change the number in the *Automatically after* box to 15 seconds.

5. Run the slide show two more times—first advancing slides manually and then automatically. Make any timing adjustments, return to normal view, and save your changes.

Figure 4.4 Timings shown in slide sorter view

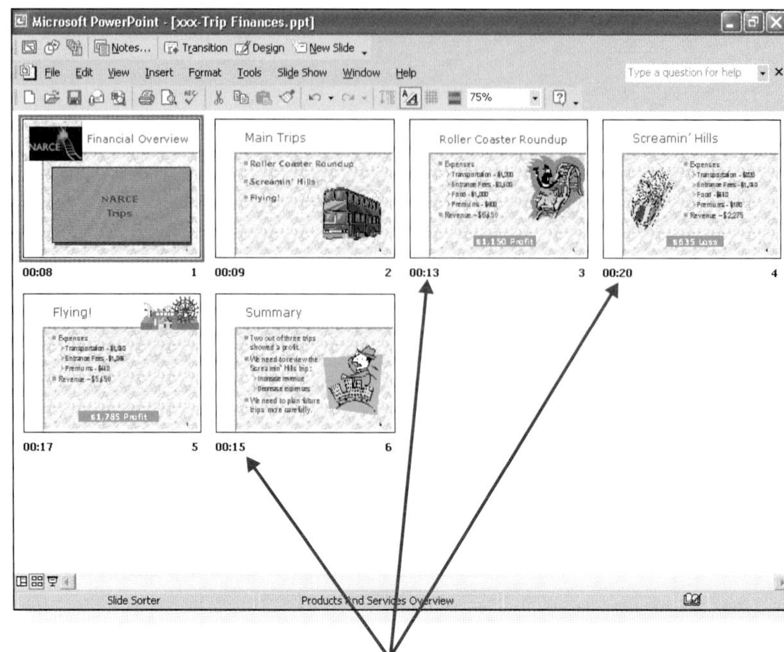

The timings indicate the number of seconds each slide will display during the presentation.

Microsoft Office Specialist PP2002 7.2

Exercise 2 Overview: Deliver a Presentation

To deliver a presentation effectively, you need to know how to navigate a presentation in slide show view so that you can jump quickly between slides, if necessary, to make a point.

You may find that some slides in a presentation are appropriate for one audience but not for another. In cases such as this, you can hide particular slides so that they will not display when you run your presentation in slide show view for a particular audience. These slides will continue to display in normal and slide sorter views, however.

During a presentation, you can use the mouse pointer to emphasize parts of the presentation. You can move the pointer over words on the slides, and you can even change the pointer to a "pen," underlining or circling words and phrases for emphasis.

In the following exercise, you will deliver the NARCE finances presentation you set up and rehearsed in the previous exercises. You will navigate slides, hide slides, and emphasize parts of slides.

Figure 4.5 Setting automatic slide advancement

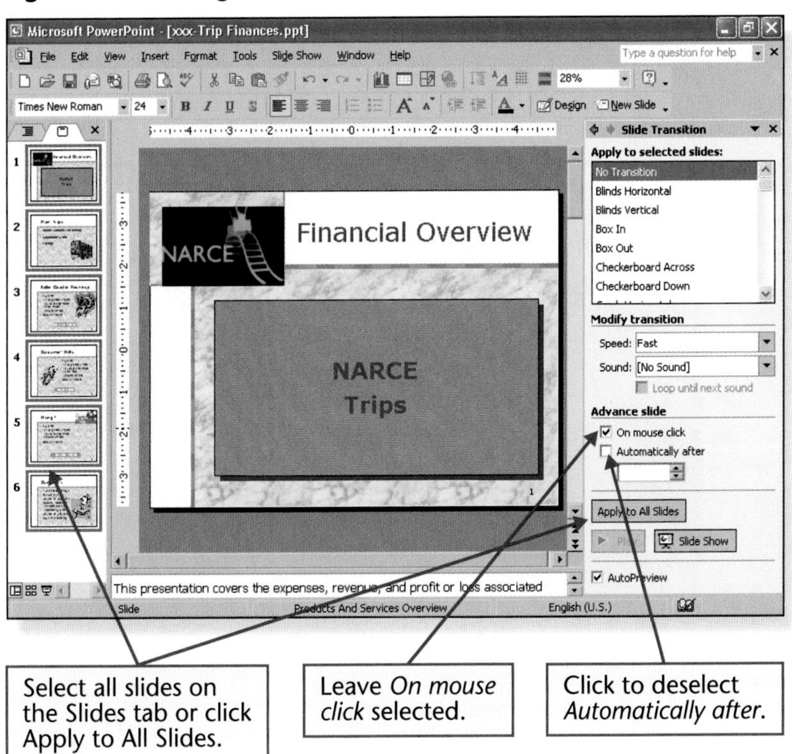

Step Through It™

Exercise 2: Run the slide show

1. With *xxx-Trip Finances.ppt* open, select Slide Transition on the Slide Show menu.
2. Select all six slides. If necessary, click to deselect *Automatically after* in the Slide Transition task pane (see Figure 4.5), click Apply to All Slides, and close the task pane.
3. Run the slide show again, clicking to advance each slide. Right-click slide 6, point to Go, point to By Title, and select slide 4.

Figure 4.6 Hidden slide

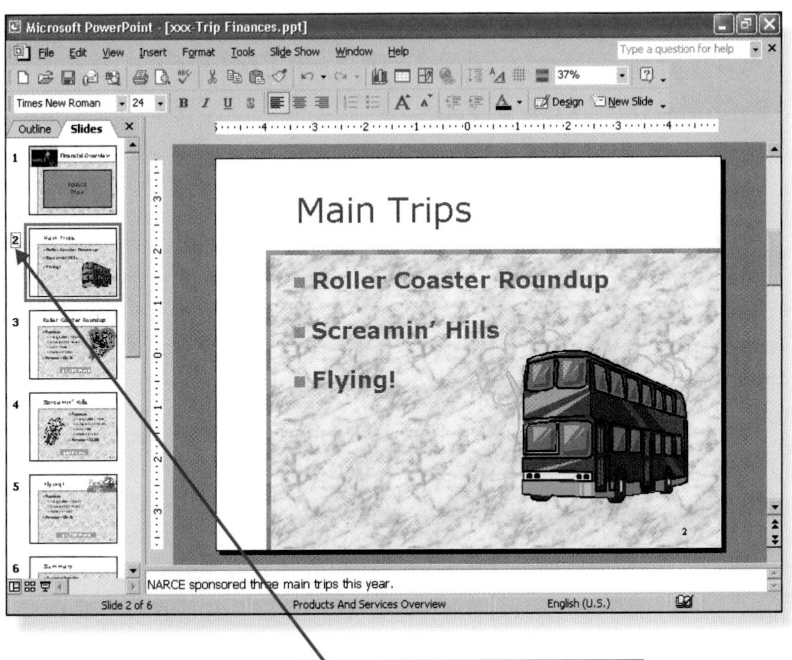

4. Right-click again, navigate to slide 6, and then press Esc to end the presentation.
5. In normal view, click slide 2, and select Hide Slide on the Slide Show menu. Notice the diagonal line through slide 2's number on the Slides tab (see Figure 4.6).
6. Return to slide 1 and run the slide show. Note that slide 2 does not appear.

7. When you get to slide 6 in slide show view, right-click, point to Pointer Options, and select Pen.
8. Using the pen pointer, first draw an arrow pointing to the first subtitle, and then circle the last subtitle (see Figure 4.7).
9. Return to normal view, and select slide 2 on the Slides tab. Right-click and select Hide Slide to unhide the slide.
10. Save the presentation.

Figure 4.7 Slide 6 showing pen marks

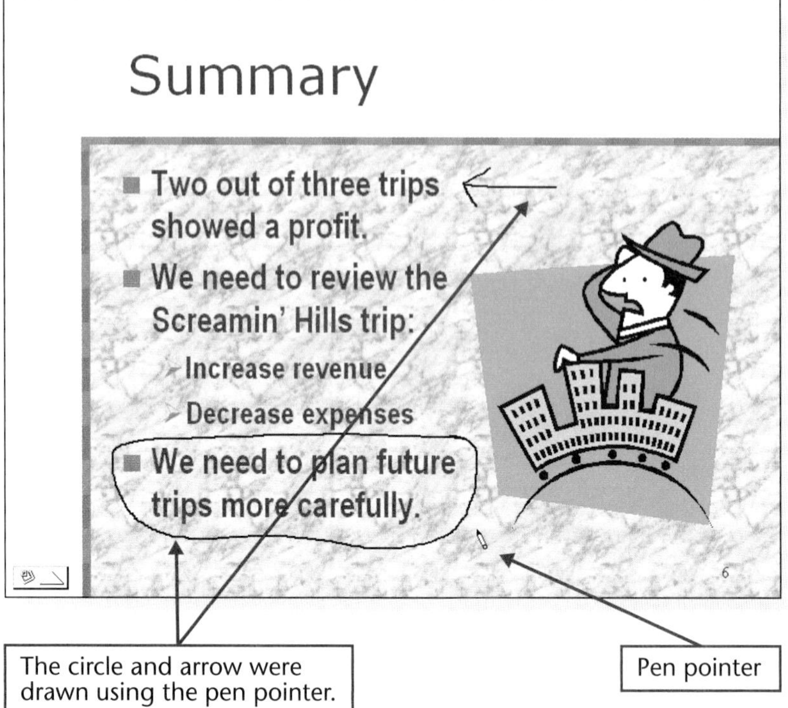

PowerPoint®

Microsoft Office Specialist PP2002 7.2, 7.4, 7.6

Exercise 3 Overview: Prepare a Presentation for Delivery on Another Computer

One of the easiest ways to ensure that the fonts in your presentation will appear the same on the presentation computer is to embed TrueType fonts. An **embedded font** is a TrueType font that will always appear the same, even if the presentation is shown on another computer. If you do *not* embed the fonts, the other computer will have to substitute fonts if it does not have the same fonts you used.

You can embed TrueType fonts when you use Pack and Go, a PowerPoint feature that stores a presentation as a special file, enabling it to be displayed on another computer. When you package a presentation using Pack and Go, you can include PowerPoint Viewer, a special program that allows the presentation to be shown even on computers that don't have PowerPoint installed.

In the following exercises, you will prepare the trip finances presentation to be shown on another computer, embedding TrueType fonts and using Pack and Go.

Figure 4.8 Save Options dialog box

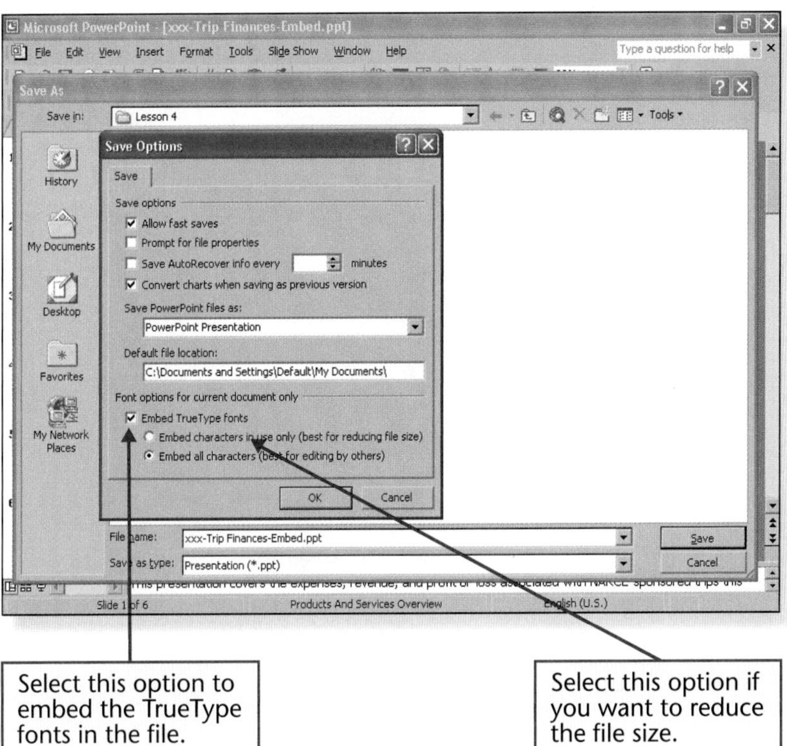

Step Through It™

Exercise 3A: Embed fonts in a presentation

1. Save *xxx-Trip Finances.ppt* as *xxx-Trip Finances-Embed.ppt*.
2. In the Save As dialog box, click the Tools down arrow and select Save Options.
3. Select *Embed TrueType fonts*, and select *Embed all characters (best for editing by others)*, if necessary (see Figure 4.8).
4. Click OK, click Save, and save your changes.

Figure 4.9 Pack and Go Wizard

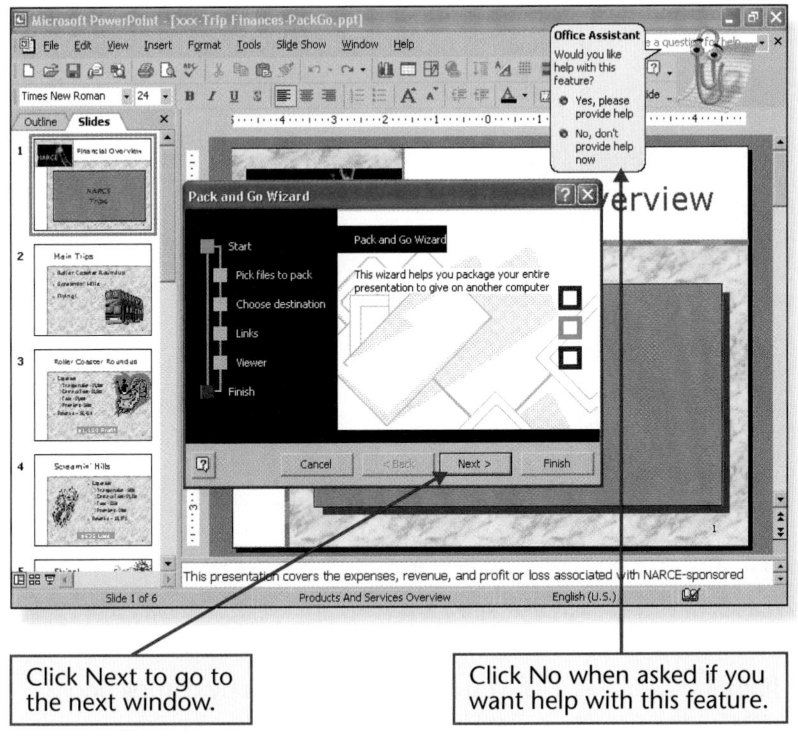

Step Through It™

Exercise 3B: Use Pack and Go

1. Save *xxx-Trip Finances-Embed.ppt* as *xxx-Trip Finances-PackGo.ppt*.
2. Select Pack and Go on the File menu to open the Pack and Go Wizard. (***Note:*** If the Office Assistant asks if you would like help, click No.) Click Next (see Figure 4.9).
3. In the second window, choose Active Presentation, if necessary. Click Next.

4. In the third window, click *Choose destination.* Browse to locate the *Lesson 4* folder within your *Unit 4* folder. Create a new subfolder named *Packed Presentation* within your *Lesson 4* folder. Click Select, and click Next.

5. Choose both options in the fourth window (see Figure 4.10). Click Next.

6. In the fifth window, select Viewer for Microsoft Windows. (***Note:*** If the viewer is not available, see your teacher.) Click Next, and then click Finish.

Figure 4.10 Fourth window in the Wizard

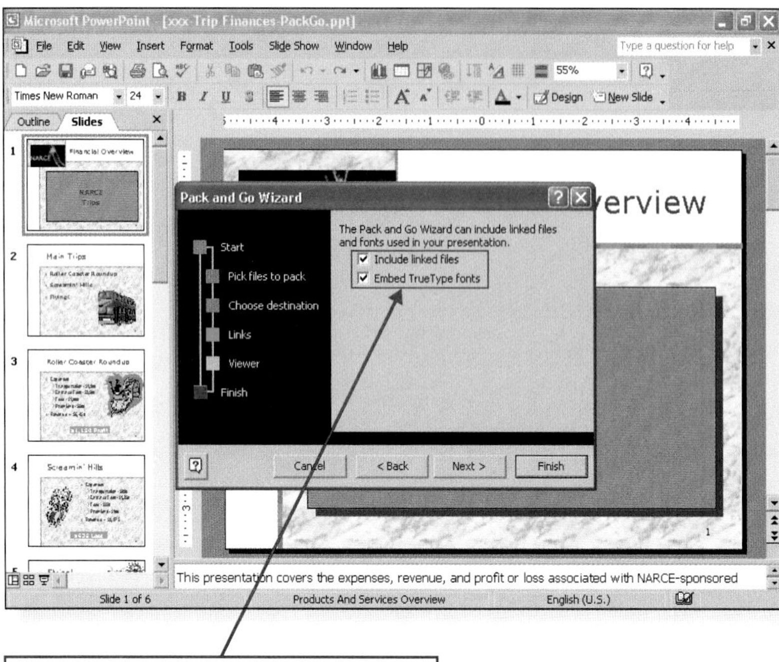

7. Save and close the presentation.

8. In Windows Explorer, navigate to the *Packed Presentation* folder and double-click *PNGSETUP.EXE* (see Figure 4.11).

9. Click OK to extract the presentation in the *Packed Presentation* folder, click Yes to unpack the presentation, and click Yes to run the slide show.

10. After running the slide show, close Windows Explorer.

Figure 4.11 Contents of the *Packed Presentation* folder

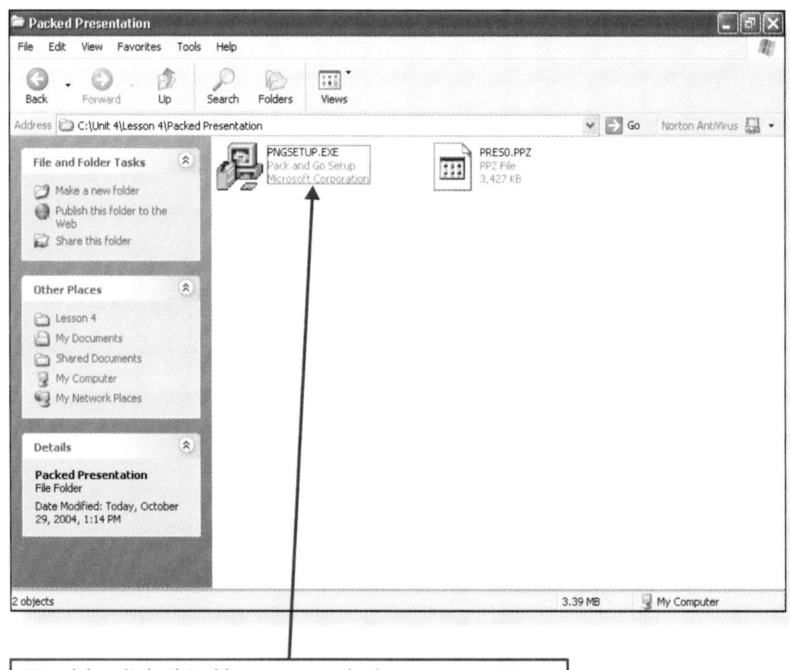

APPLY IT! After finishing Exercises 1–3, you may test your skills by completing Apply It! Guided Activity 1, Set Up, Deliver, and Package a Presentation.

Tech Talk

Delivering Presentations

How can you deliver a presentation to a large number of people at the same time? One method is online broadcasts, which you'll learn about in this lesson. This Tech Talk discusses several other options.

Projection systems hook up to a desktop or laptop computer and display the slides on a screen or blank wall. Sophisticated systems include a remote control that works as a remote mouse and a laser pointer. With such a system, a presenter can stand in front of the audience while running a slide show as if sitting in front of a PC. Developing wireless technology enables a speaker to run a presentation from a notebook or even from a personal digital assistant without cables.

You can also connect your computer to a large-screen monitor or "smart" white-board. Still another alternative is a large-screen TV, with a special PC-to-TV device or video card.

Increasingly, kiosks are being used in stores, conventions, trade shows, and conferences as tools for selling products or services or providing information. Kiosk presentations are often set up to be self-running. Action buttons and animation allow visitors to navigate with a mouse or keyboard or, more commonly, by touching the screen. A kiosk option in PowerPoint loops the presentation to the first slide if the user has reached the last or restarts the show if it has been idle for five minutes.

CRITICAL THINKING

1. Suppose you had to give a PowerPoint presentation using a laptop and large-screen monitor or projection system. Work with a partner to develop a checklist of equipment-related items that will help ensure your presentation is a success.
2. Kiosk uses range from selling swimming pools to educating voters to listing job vacancies to selling airline tickets. Find an article on how kiosks are used. Create a presentation that could be shown in a kiosk.

Microsoft Office Specialist
PP2002 1.3, 8.1, 8.2

Exercise 4 Overview: Set Up a Review Cycle

In the work environment, people often need to review each other's presentations—adding comments, suggesting edits, and making changes to improve the presentation. A **comment** is a special text box in which a reviewer has inserted a note about the presentation. The comment can be deleted, copied, or moved to another location on the slide. A **comment marker** is a small icon that looks like a sticky note and points out the comment on that slide. To read the comment, just click the comment marker.

While reviewing your presentation, a reviewer can also make any desired changes directly on the slides—changing formatting, text, design template, slide layout, slide and title masters, and so on—rather than just suggesting those changes in the form of comments. A **change marker** is an icon indicating that a reviewer has made a change (see Figure 4.12). You can accept or reject each change in a reviewed presentation by clicking options on the Reviewing toolbar. Likewise, you can combine all reviewed copies of the presentation with the original file, accepting or rejecting all changes to each slide at one time.

Figure 4.12 Change marker in reviewed presentation

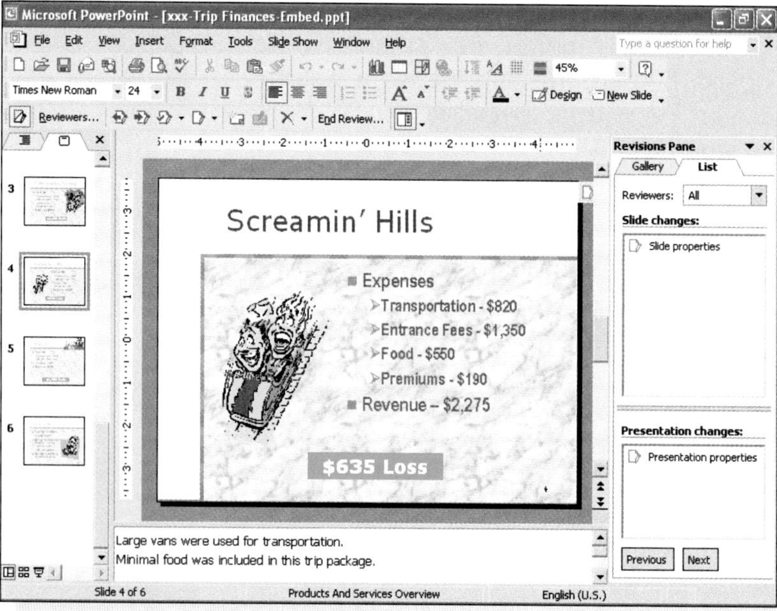

PowerPoint®

The following table illustrates some of the commonly used buttons on the Reviewing toolbar.

Reviewing Toolbar

Button		Purpose
	Previous Item	Finds and selects the previous change
	Next Item	Finds and selects the next change
	Apply	Accepts the change that is selected
	Unapply	Rejects the change that is selected
	Insert Comment	Inserts a comment box

In the following exercises, you will set up and send your trip finances presentation for review and review a presentation. (***Note:*** PowerPoint allows you to send a presentation for review to as many people as you want.)

Figure 4.13 Sending a file for review

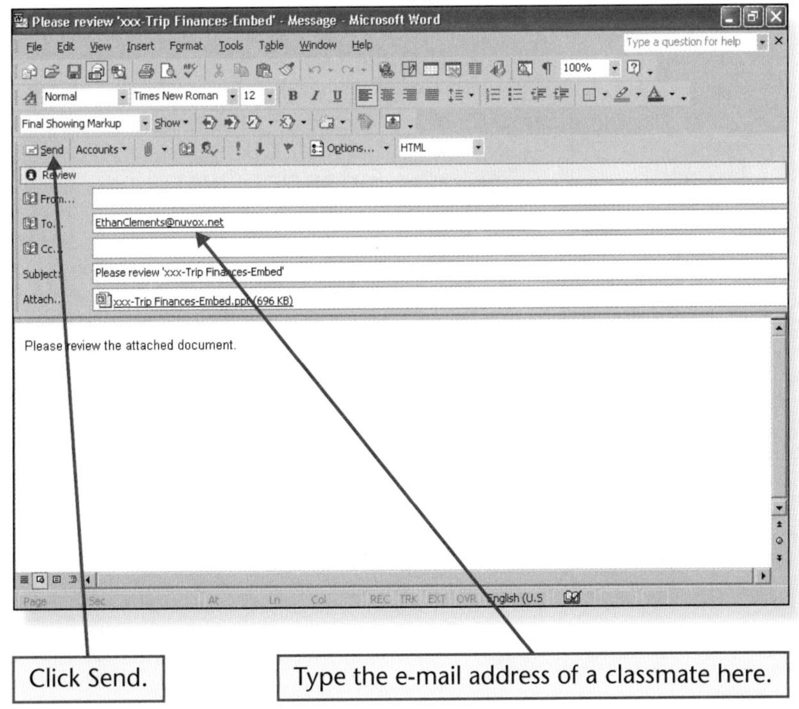

Step Through It™

Exercise 4A: Send a presentation for review

1. Connect to the Internet, if necessary.
2. Open *xxx-Trip Finances-Embed.ppt.* Point to Send To on the File menu and select Mail Recipient (for Review).
3. In the To box, type the e-mail address of a classmate and click Send (see Figure 4.13). *Note:* Your teacher will provide you with the e-mail address or addresses to use.

4 Close the presentation and Launch Microsoft Outlook.

5 In Outlook, point to Go To on the View menu, and select Inbox, if necessary.

6 Click the *Outbox* folder to see the message you created, and then point to Send/Receive on the Tools menu and select Send and Receive All (see Figure 4.14).

Figure 4.14 Sending a file from Outlook's *Outbox* folder

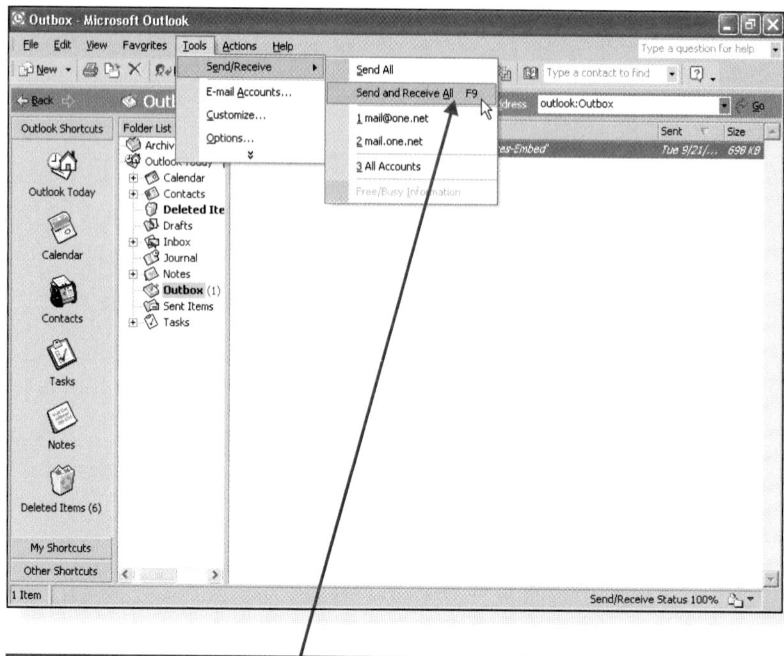

Step Through It™

Exercise 4B: Review and return a presentation

1 In Outlook, find and open a message in the *Inbox* folder from another student asking you to review a presentation.

2 Right-click the presentation icon, select Save As, and save the presentation in your *Lesson 4* folder. Close the message.

3 Open the presentation. In normal view, display the Reviewing toolbar, if necessary (see Figure 4.15).

Figure 4.15 Reviewing toolbar

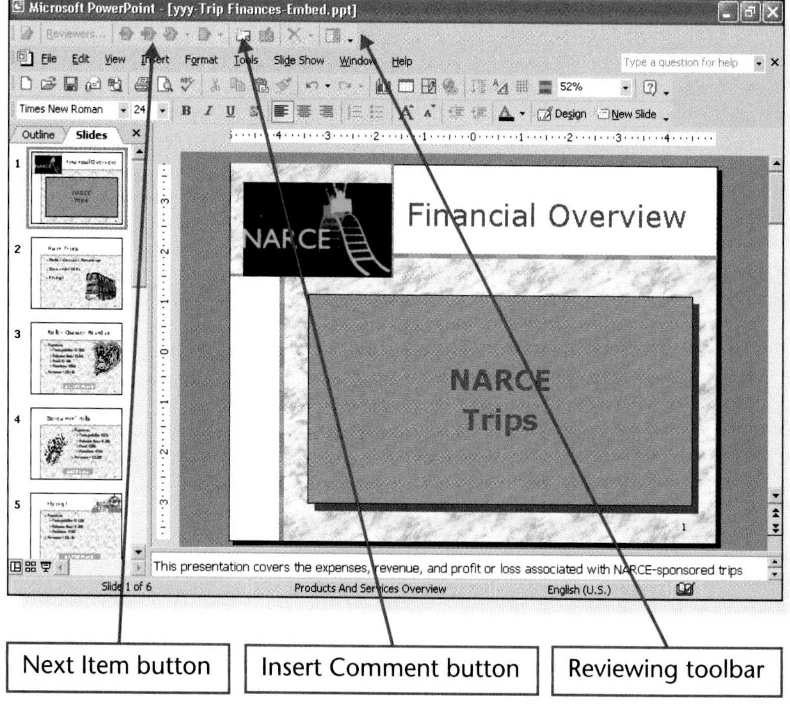

Figure 4.16 Comment box and comment marker

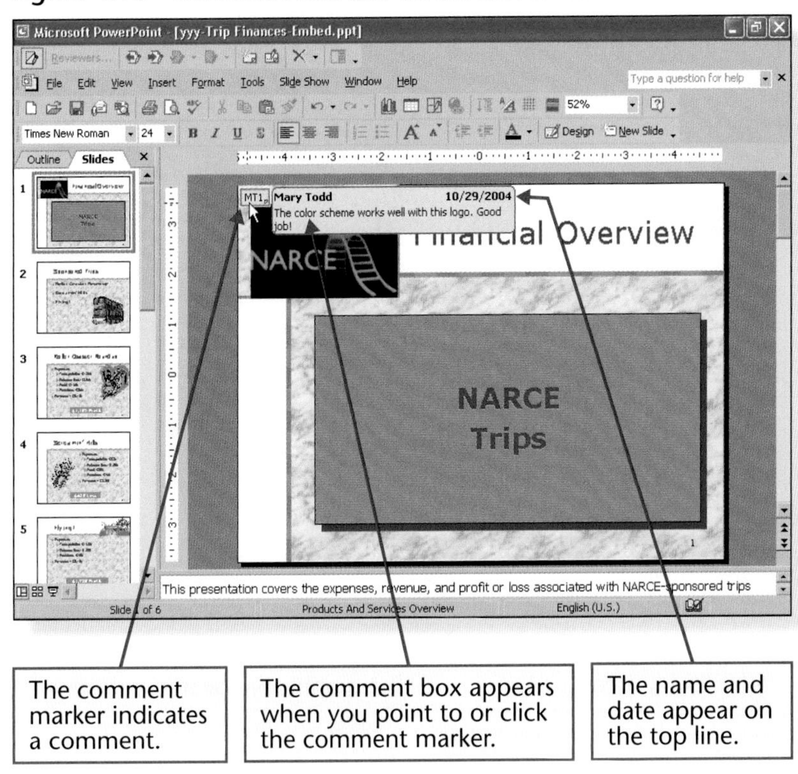

4. On slide 1, click Insert Comment on the Reviewing toolbar.

5. In the comment box that appears, type the following: **The color scheme works well with this logo. Good job!**

6. Click outside the comment box, and then point to the comment marker in the upper-left corner of the slide to read the comment you just typed (see Figure 4.16).

Figure 4.17 Edited presentation

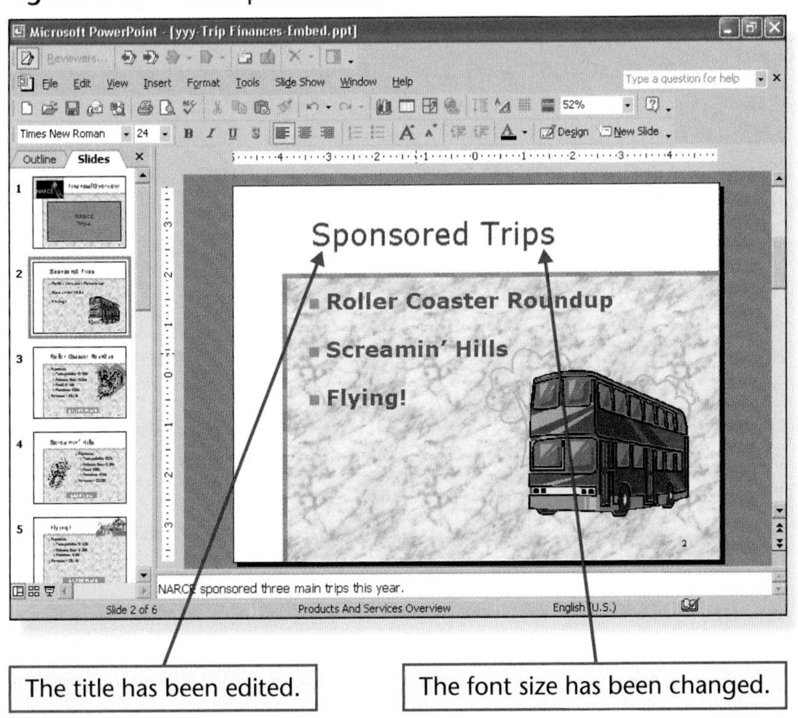

7. Insert another comment on slide 1, and type the following text: **What do you think about switching the positions of the title and subtitle on this slide?**

8. Drag the second comment marker to the upper-right corner of slide 1, near the title.

9. On slide 2, change the title from *Main Trips* to **Sponsored Trips** and change the font size to 44 pt. (see Figure 4.17).

PowerPoint®

10 Using the Header and Footer dialog box, add NARCE Trips as a footer on all slides except the title slide. Click Apply to All.

11 On slide 5, move the graphic down so that it appears to the right of the bulleted text (see Figure 4.18).

12 Resave the file, point to Send To on the File menu, and select Original Sender.

13 Type a message to your classmate, if desired. Click Send and close the file. In Outlook, click Send/Receive.

Figure 4.18 Repositioned graphic

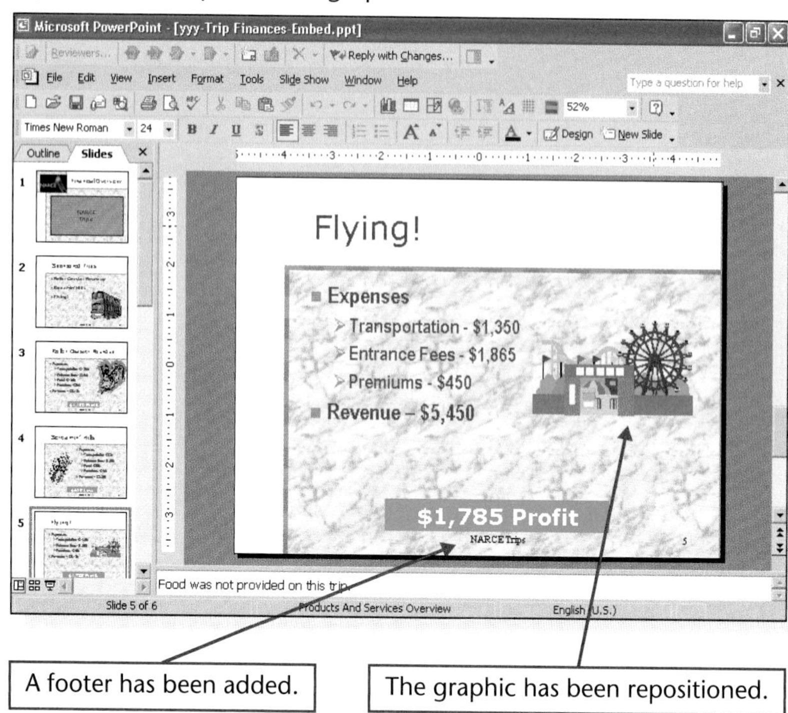

Microsoft Office Specialist PP2002 5.1, 8.2

Exercise 5 Overview:
Manage a Reviewed Presentation

When you receive a presentation back from a reviewer, you can use the buttons on the Reviewing toolbar to view each change individually and either accept or reject it. In the same way, you can view each comment individually and decide whether you want to make any changes based on the comment. You can also print reviewer comments.

Type: print reviewer comments

The Revisions Pane is a special toolbar with a List tab and a Gallery tab that helps you manage a reviewed presentation. The List tab presents the reviewer's comments for each slide in list form. The Gallery tab shows a thumbnail image of how each slide would appear if you accepted the changes suggested by the reviewer. The Revisions Pane also reports changes that have been made to the slide or title master, and it informs you if no comments or changes have been made on a slide.

In the following exercises, you will work with the trip finances presentation you set up and sent for review in Exercise 4A. You will merge the reviewed copy or copies (depending on how many reviewers you sent it to) with your original presentation and then accept and reject various changes, incorporating reviewer comments along the way.

Figure 4.19 Reviewed presentation returned

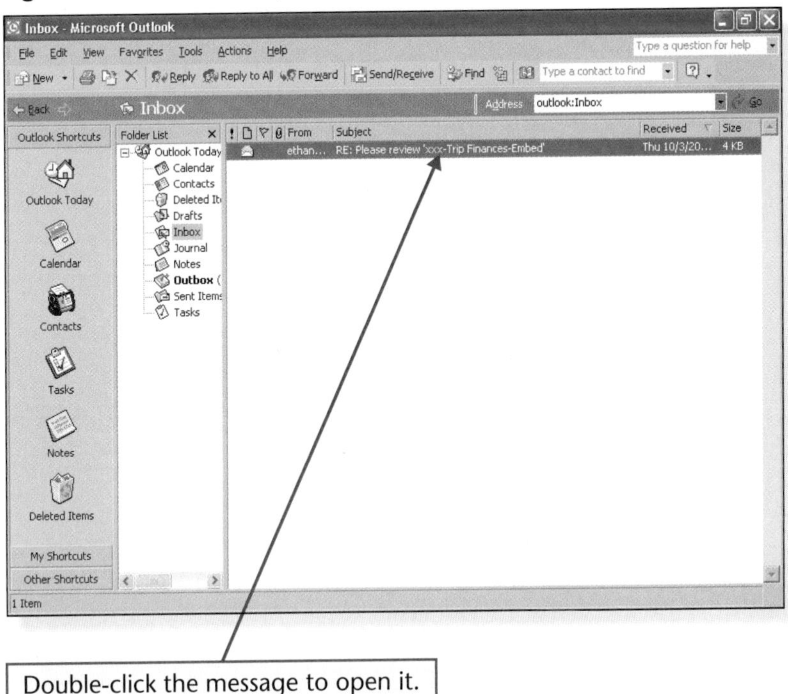
Double-click the message to open it.

Figure 4.20 Merging changes into a presentation

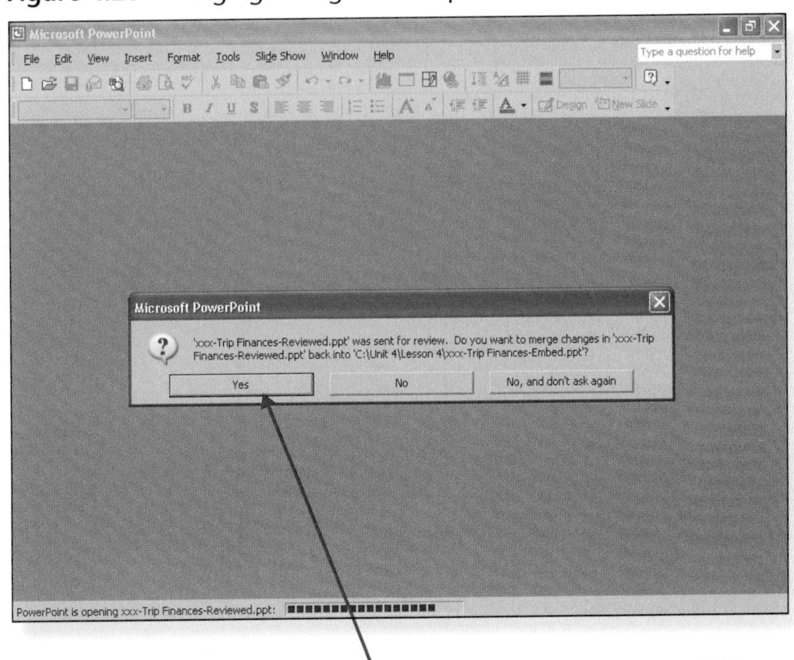
Click Yes to merge the reviewed presentation with your original presentation.

Step Through It™

Exercise 5A: Consolidate an edited presentation with the original

1. In Outlook, go to your *Inbox* folder. Use the Send/Receive command to receive any incoming messages and to send any messages in your *Outbox* folder.
2. In the *Inbox* folder, double-click the message your classmate sent to you with the reviewed copy of your presentation attached (see Figure 4.19).
3. Right-click the presentation icon, select Save As, and save the presentation in your *Lesson 4* folder as *xxx-Trip Finances-Reviewed.ppt*.
4. Close the message and Outlook. Open the presentation. When asked if you want to merge the changes from the reviewed presentation into your original copy, click Yes (see Figure 4.20).

PowerPoint®

Step Through It™

Exercise 5B: Accept and reject reviewer changes

1. Display the Reviewing toolbar and the Revisions Pane if they do not appear. If desired, print the reviewer comments.

2. Click the comment marker in the top left corner of slide 1, and read the comment (see Figure 4.21). Click Next Item on the Reviewing toolbar.

Figure 4.21 Displayed comments

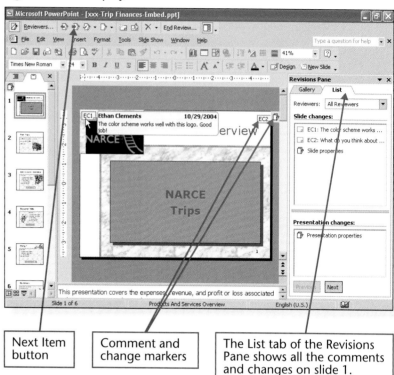

Next Item button

Comment and change markers

The List tab of the Revisions Pane shows all the comments and changes on slide 1.

3. Click Previous Item to go back to the first comment, and then click Delete Comment.

4. Click Next Item again, and delete the second comment after reading it. (*Note:* You have decided not to switch the title and subtitle.)

5. On slide 2, click the Gallery tab in the Revisions Pane. Enlarge the Revisions Pane, if necessary, and view the reviewer's changes (see Figure 4.22).

Figure 4.22 Gallery tab

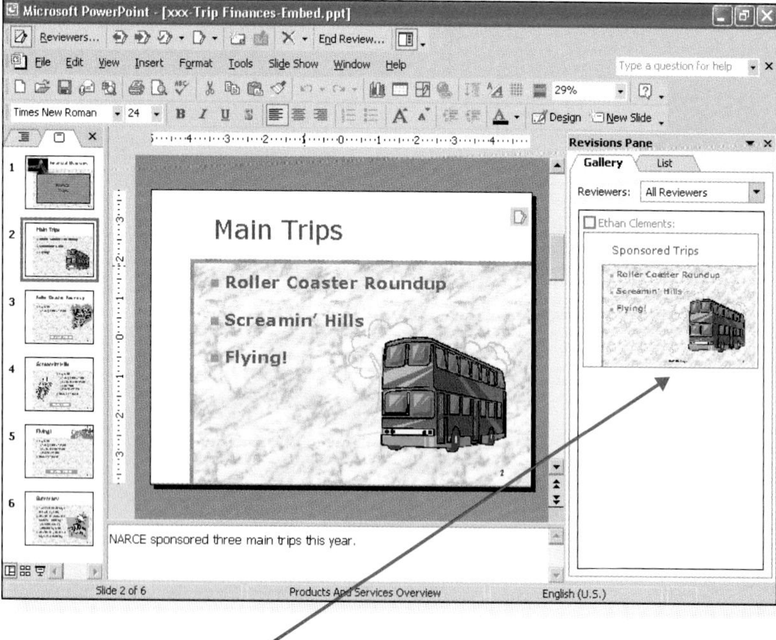

Suggested changes appear on the Gallery tab.

PowerPoint®

Figure 4.23 Change marker

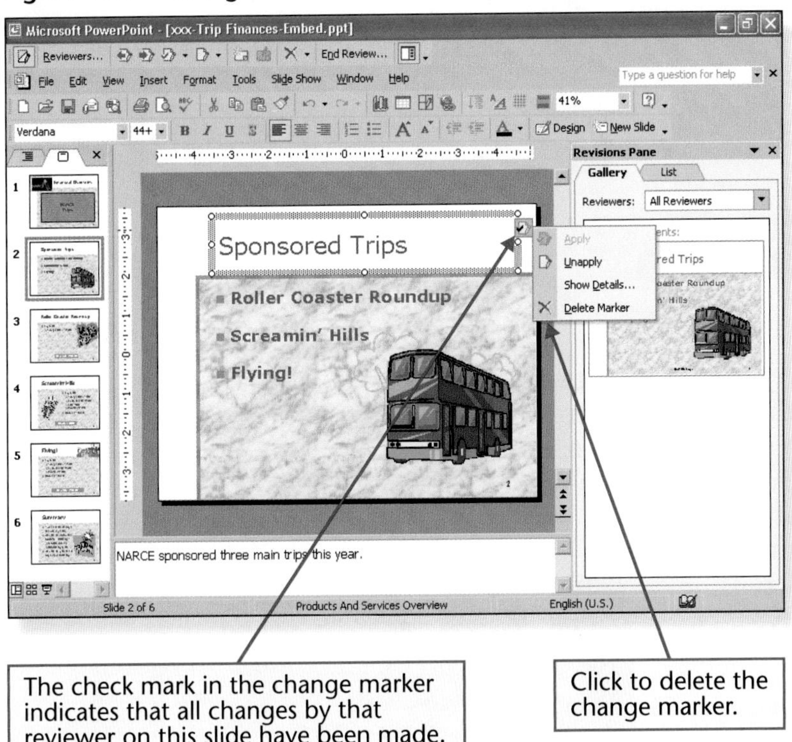

The check mark in the change marker indicates that all changes by that reviewer on this slide have been made.
Click to delete the change marker.

6. Click the Apply down arrow and select Apply All Changes to the Current Slide.
7. Right-click the change marker on slide 2 (see Figure 4.23), and select Delete Marker.
8. Go to slide 5, click the change marker, and click to insert a check mark in the small box that appears in the screen tip. Click Unapply.

Figure 4.24 Selecting the header and footer changes

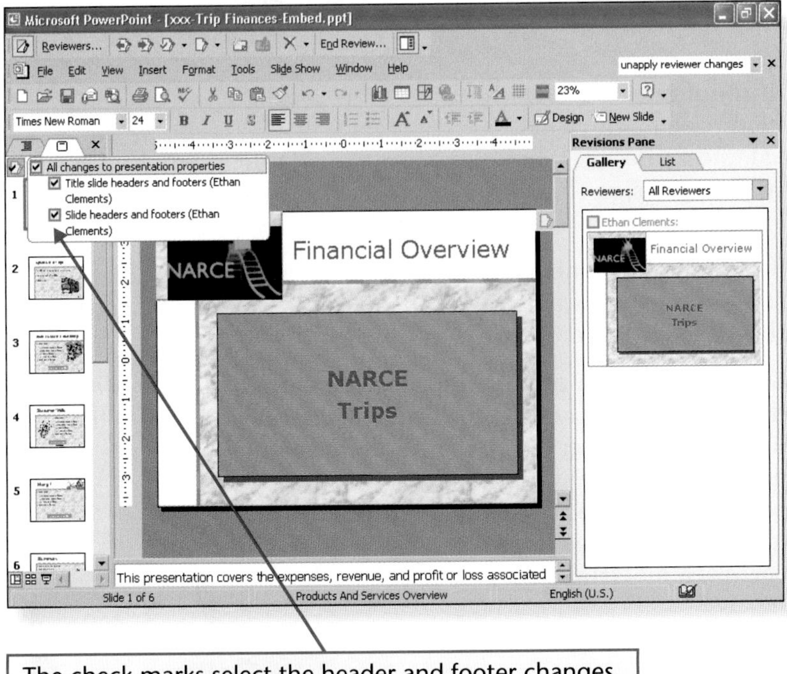

9. Click the change marker at the top of the Slides tab. Insert a check mark in the small box to the left of *All changes to presentation properties* (see Figure 4.24). Click Unapply to reject the headers and footers change.
10. Click End Review End Review... . Click Yes when PowerPoint warns you that this will end the review.
11. Save the presentation as *xxx-Trip Finances-Final.ppt*, and then close the presentation.

PowerPoint®

APPLY IT! After finishing Exercises 4 and 5, you may test your skills by completing Apply It! Guided Activity 2, Review a Presentation.

Business Connections

Analyzing Multimedia Presentations

When you watch a movie, play a computer game, or surf the 'Net, you are experiencing a multimedia presentation. A *multimedia presentation* integrates text, graphics, video, and sound. By following these simple rules, you can use PowerPoint tools to create an engaging multimedia presentation that holds your audience's attention and communicates effectively:

1. **Focus on the purpose of your presentation.** Make sure that every slide element (from the slide title to each subtitle and each embedded media file) reinforces the purpose and helps the audience to remember the presentation content.

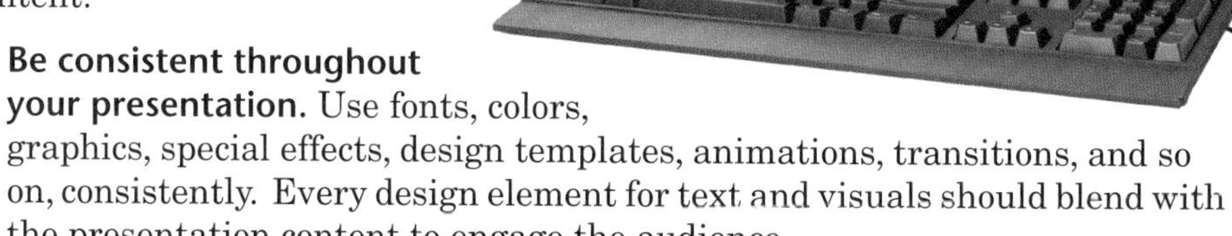

2. **Be consistent throughout your presentation.** Use fonts, colors, graphics, special effects, design templates, animations, transitions, and so on, consistently. Every design element for text and visuals should blend with the presentation content to engage the audience.

3. **Be simple.** Remember that less is more; clean, uncluttered slides are more interesting than slides that are so packed that they lose visual interest.

4. **Borrow only with permission and give credit where credit is due.** Explore for the best media files (whether clip art, sound files, or full-motion video) to include in your multimedia presentation. Always get permission to use copyrighted material, and provide source lines for borrowed material.

5. **Use animations and transitions with care and consistency.** Verify that animations and transitions truly help to achieve the professional look you want. Use animations to highlight text or objects. Use transitions to reveal information in the correct sequence and at the right time and to provide a smooth flow of information from one slide to the next.

6. **Include navigation tools.** If your presentation is interactive, include appropriate navigation tools to guide the audience from one slide, object, or hyperlink to the next, and then back to the right place in the presentation.

7. **Choose the most effective delivery methods.** Determine exactly where and how the presentation will be delivered and what equipment is needed. Also consider whether to supplement a presentation with handouts, a pointer, transparencies, and so on.

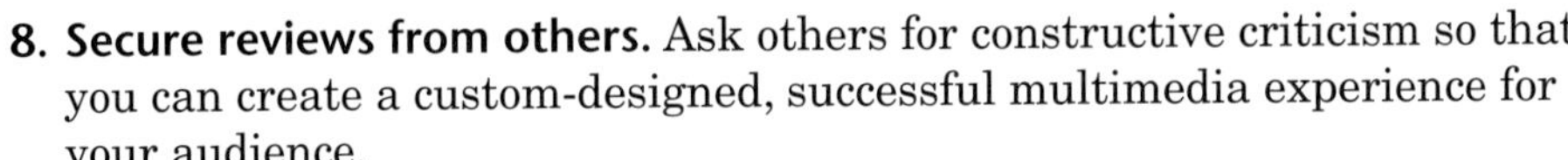

8. **Secure reviews from others.** Ask others for constructive criticism so that you can create a custom-designed, successful multimedia experience for your audience.

9. **Rehearse and revise the multimedia presentation.** Ensure that you set just the right amount of display time for every slide element. Confirm that the presentation achieves all that you desire, and remember that you want to appeal to (rather than overload) your audience's senses.

CRITICAL THINKING

1. **Finding Multimedia Online** Explore the Internet to discover ways in which businesses are using multimedia presentations. Find a Web site that has a multimedia presentation, and critically analyze the presentation.

2. **Using Multimedia in Business** With a partner and specific directions from your teacher, select a local business that interests you. Arrange to interview someone regarding how the company is using multimedia presentations to achieve company goals.

Microsoft Office Specialist PP2002 7.5, 8.4

Exercise 6 Overview:
Publish Presentations to the Web

Once you have created a presentation, you can publish it to the Web, allowing others to view the presentation online. In Unit 1, you learned how to save documents as Web pages. When you **publish** a PowerPoint presentation, you save it as a set of Web pages on an intranet or a Web server, allowing others to open and navigate the presentation using their Web browsers (see Figure 4.25).

Figure 4.25 A published presentation

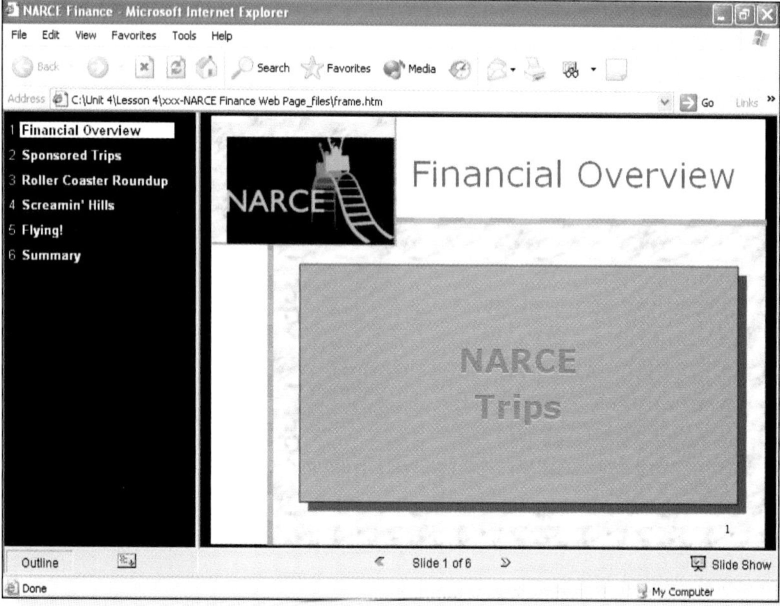

You can save PowerPoint presentations as Web pages in two different ways. You can use the Save as Web Page command on the File menu to simply save the presentation as a Web page on your computer's hard drive or a network drive. Or you can use the Publish command to select options that will let others view your presentation in their Web browsers. This second method allows you choose such options as only including certain slides in the presentation or letting viewers see notes pages.

In the following exercise, you will publish the trip finances presentation to the Web.

Figure 4.26 Maximized browser window

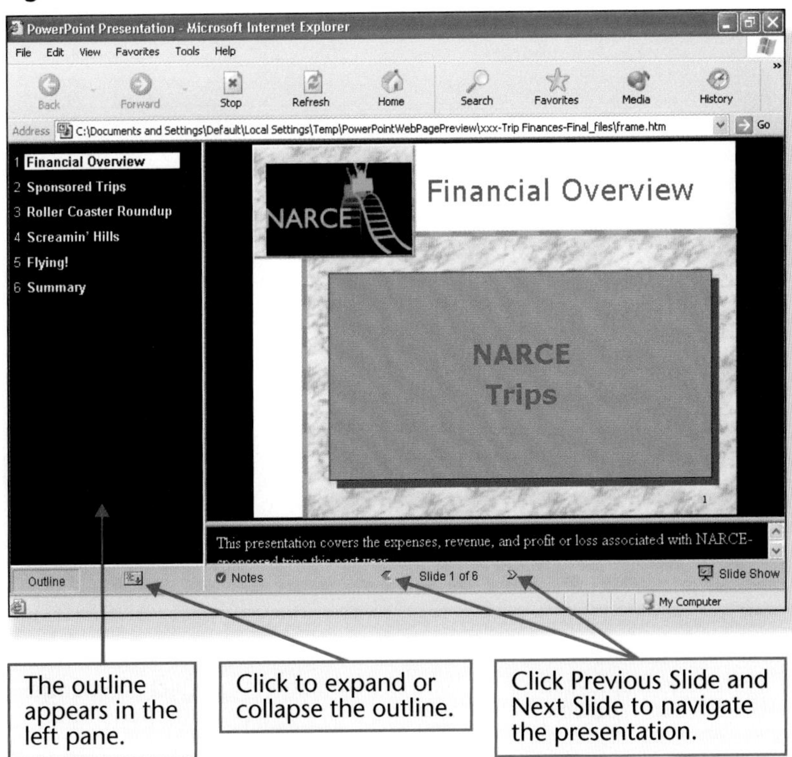

Figure 4.27 Expanded outline

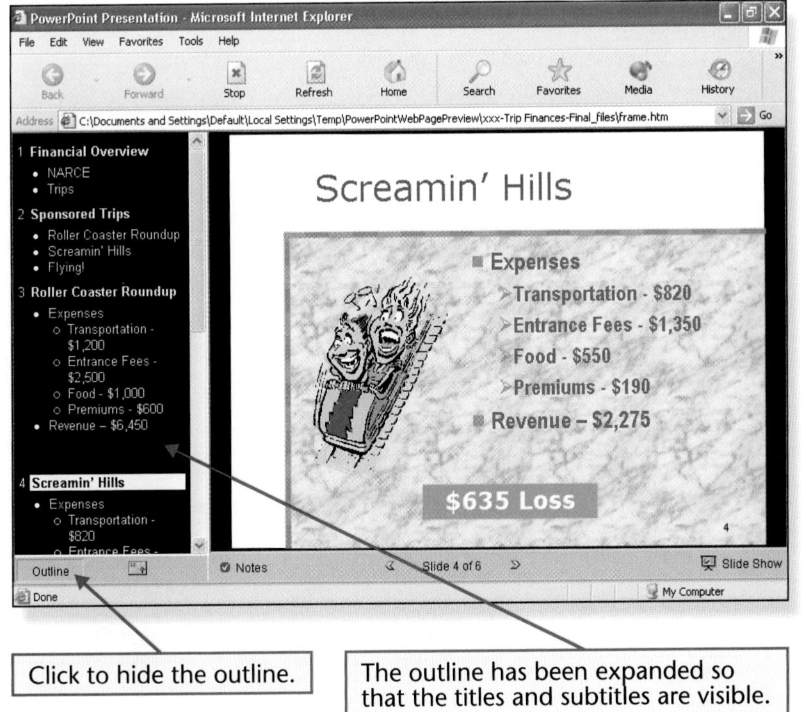

Step Through It™

Exercise 6: Publish a presentation

1. Open *xxx-Trip Finances-Final.ppt*, select Web Page Preview on the File menu, and maximize the browser window (see Figure 4.26).
2. Click Next Slide [»] to move to slide 2.
3. In the Outline pane, click the *Summary* hyperlink to jump to slide 6.
4. Click Previous Slide [«] twice to move to slide 4, and then click Full Screen Slide Show [Slide Show].
5. Click once to advance to slide 5, and then press Esc to end the slide show.
6. Click Show/Hide Notes [Notes] to hide the notes pane.
7. Click Expand/Collapse Outline [icon] (see Figure 4.27) and then click Show/Hide Outline [Outline].

PowerPoint®

PowerPoint®

8. Close your browser. In PowerPoint, select Save as Web Page on the File menu.

9. Type xxx-NARCE Finance Web Page as the file name (see Figure 4.28).

10. Click Change Title, type NARCE Finance as the page title, and click OK.

11. Click Publish, and then click *Complete presentation*, if necessary.

12. Click to deselect *Display speaker notes.*

Figure 4.28 Saving a presentation as a Web page

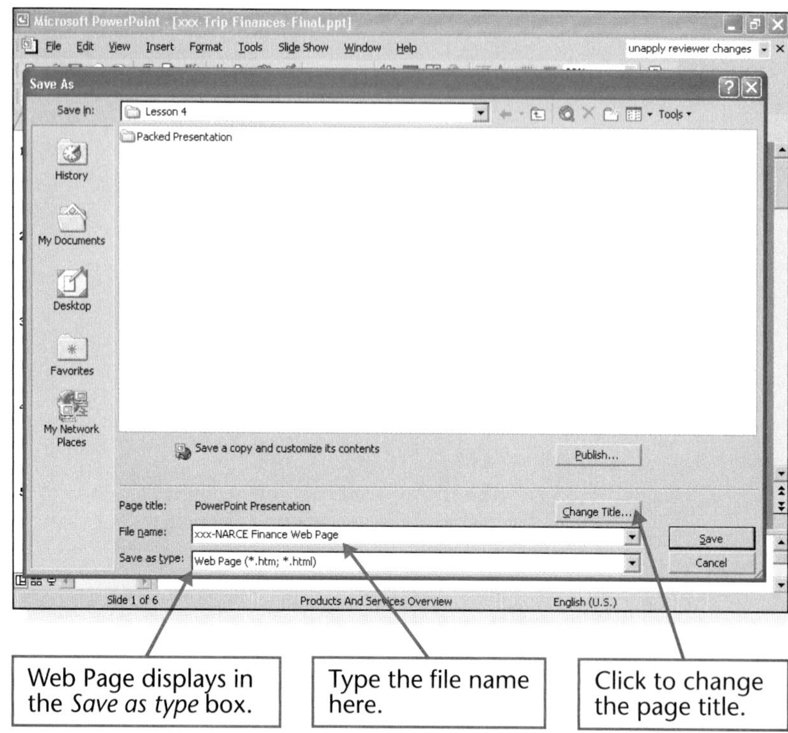

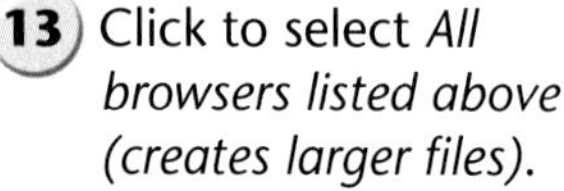

13. Click to select *All browsers listed above (creates larger files).*

14. Click to select *Open published Web page in browser* (see Figure 4.29), if necessary, and then click Publish.

15. Navigate the slides in your browser, and then close the browser.

16. Close the presentation without saving it.

Figure 4.29 Publish as Web Page dialog box

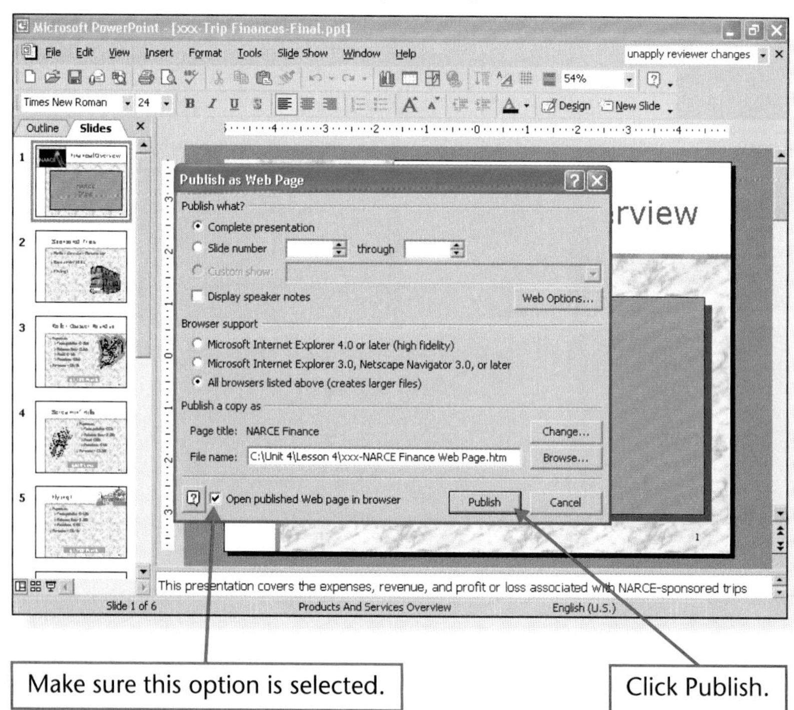

Exercise 7 Overview: Set Up and Schedule an Online Broadcast

Microsoft Office Specialist PP2002 8.3

You can use PowerPoint's broadcasting feature to give a presentation to an audience whose members are in different locations. When you use the **online broadcast** feature, members of the audience view the presentation on their own computers, using a Web browser.

You can set up a broadcast in a variety of ways. You can schedule a broadcast (see Figure 4.30) and invite attendees, using Outlook or another e-mail program. Then, audience members can click a hyperlink in their invitations to take them directly to the presentation. Or you can record a broadcast and save it to shared network server that audience members can access using the Internet or an intranet. Attendees use a set of navigation tools in their browsers to navigate the presentation on their individual computers. You can use your computer's microphone to include narration, and if you have a video camera with your computer, you can include live video with the presentation.

Figure 4.30 Schedule Presentation Broadcast dialog box

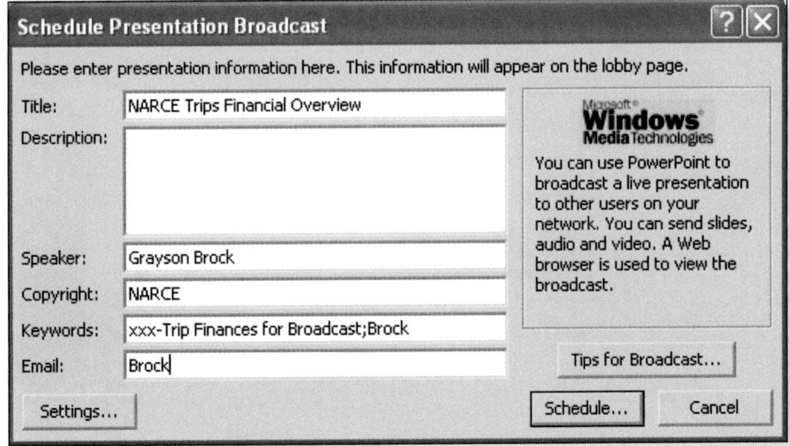

In the following exercise, you will set up the trip finances presentation for a live broadcast and use Outlook to invite attendees.

PowerPoint®

Step Through It™

Exercise 7: Set up the live presentation broadcast

PowerPoint®

1. Open *xxx-Trip Finances-Final.ppt* and save it as *xxx-Trip Finances for Broadcast.ppt* in a shared location, as directed by your teacher.

2. Point to Online Broadcast on the Slide Show menu and select Schedule a Live Broadcast.

3. Type NARCE Trips Financial Overview as the title (see Figure 4.31).

4. Type your name in the Speaker box, if necessary, and leave all other options unchanged. Click Settings.

5. On the Presenter tab, select the audio and video settings that match your computer. ***Note:*** Ask your teacher if you need help.

6. Click to deselect *Display speaker notes with the presentation*, if necessary.

7. Select Resizable Screen in the *Slide show mode* box (see Figure 4.32).

Figure 4.31 Schedule Presentation Broadcast dialog box

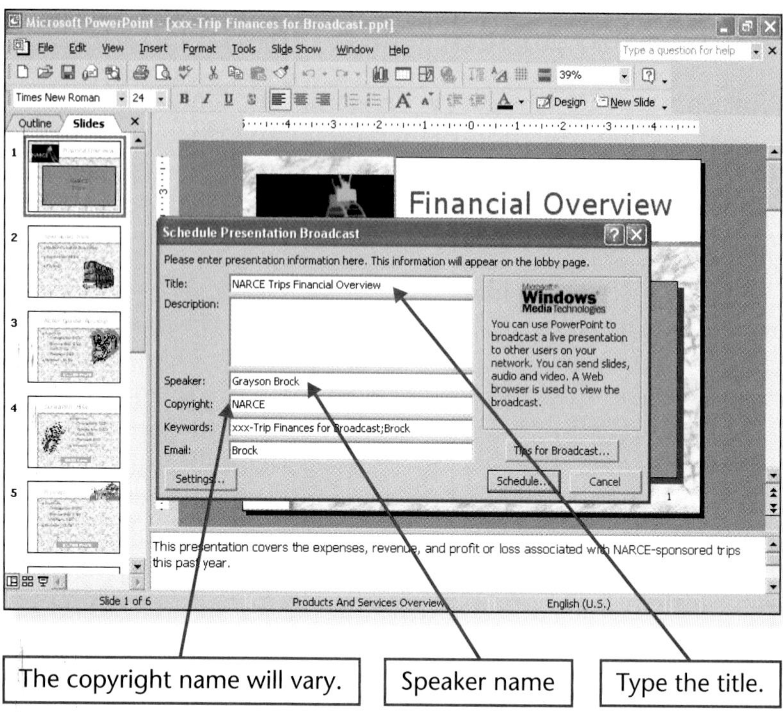

Figure 4.32 Broadcast Settings dialog box

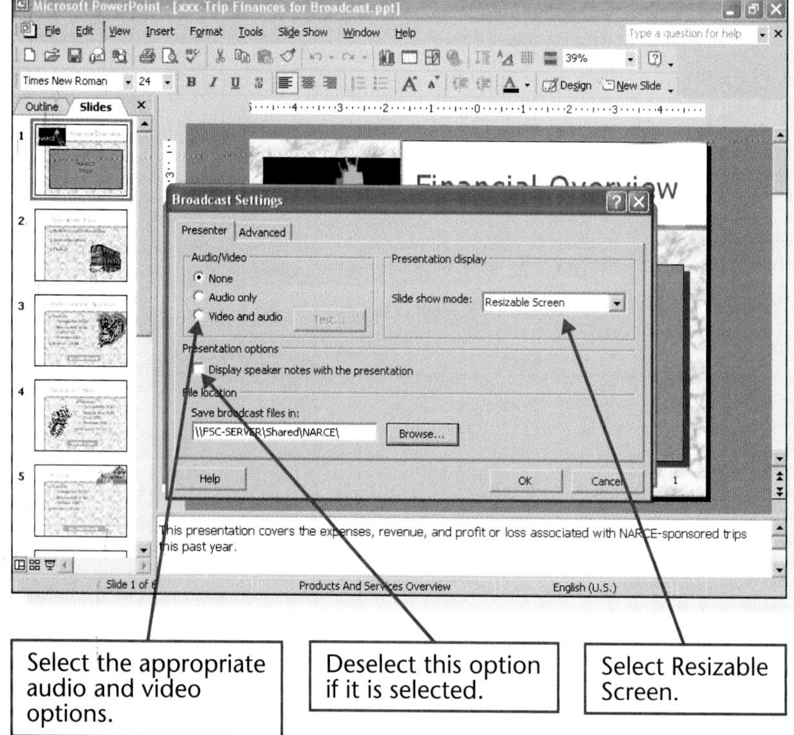

Figure 4.33 Inviting attendees

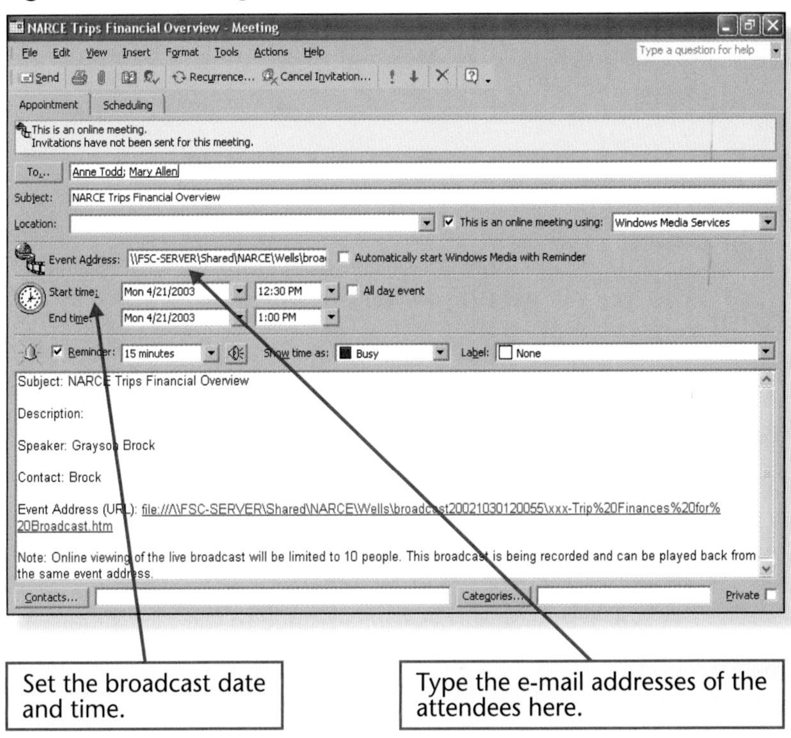

8. Click Browse, and then navigate to and select the shared folder, if necessary. Click Select and click OK.
9. Click Schedule.
10. In Outlook (or another e-mail program that opens), maximize the window.
11. In the To box, type the e-mail addresses of other students, as directed by your teacher (see Figure 4.33).

Figure 4.34 PowerPoint message

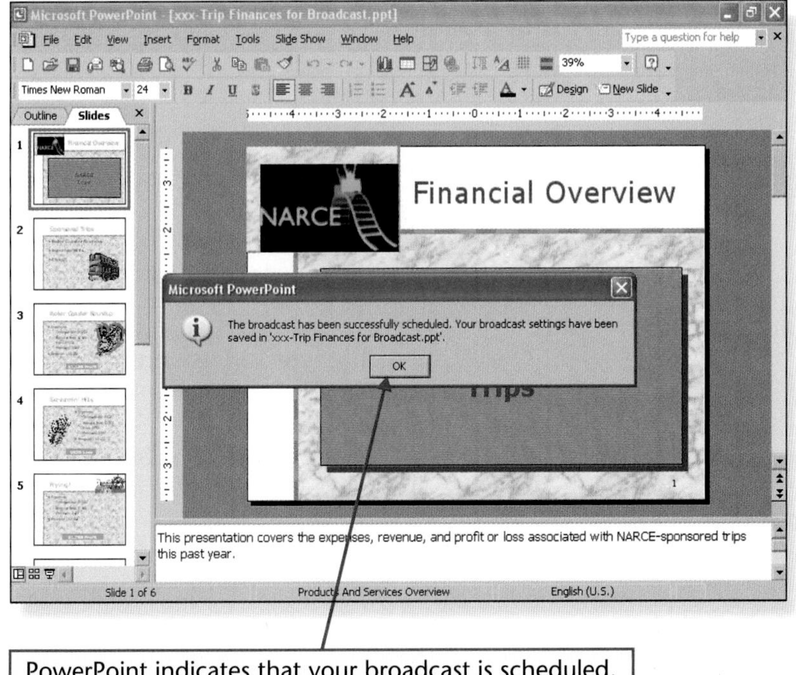

12. In the *Start time* area, select a date for the broadcast and set the time for 12:30 PM.
13. Click Send.
14. When you see a message telling you that the broadcast has been successfully scheduled, click OK (see Figure 4.34).
15. Close the presentation.

APPLY IT! After finishing Exercises 6 and 7, you may test your skills by completing Apply It! Guided Activity 3, Publish and Broadcast a Presentation.

Procedure Summary

Set up Presentation for Delivery

1. Click **Slide Show** . . . . Alt + D
2. Select **Set Up Show** . . . . S
3. In the Set Up Show dialog box, select appropriate options.
4. Click OK.

Set and Rehearse Timings

1. Click **Slide Show** . . . . Alt + D
2. Select **Rehearse Timings** . . . . R
3. Click **Advance** when you are ready to go to the next slide.
4. Click **Yes** to save the timings.

Change Timings

1. In slide sorter view, select the slide on which you want to change the timing.
2. Click **Slide Transition** [Transition].
   OR
   Click **Slide Show** . . . . Alt + D
   Select **Slide Transition** . . . . T
3. Adjust the time in the **Automatically after** box.

Hide or Unhide a Slide

1. In the left pane or in slide sorter view, select the slide you want to hide or unhide.
2. Click **Slide Show** . . . . Alt + D
3. Select **Hide Slide** . . . . H
   OR
1. In the left pane or in slide sorter view, right-click the slide you want to hide or unhide.
2. Select **Hide Slide** . . . . H

"Write" With a Pen on Slides

1. Switch to slide show view . . . . . Alt + V, W
2. During the slide show, right-click the slide on which you want to write.
3. Point to **Pointer Options** . . . . O
4. Select **Pen** . . . . P
5. Use the pen to write or draw on slides.

Erase Pen Annotations on Slides

In slide show view, advance to the next slide.
OR
Press E . . . . .E

Embed True Type Fonts

1. Click **File** . . . . Alt + F
2. Select **Save As** . . . . A
3. In the Save As dialog box, click the **Tools** down arrow . . . . Alt + L
4. Select **Save Options** . . . . S
5. In the Save Options dialog box, click **Embed True Type fonts** . . . . .E
6. Click **Embed characters in use only (best for reducing file size)**. . . . . U
   OR
   Click **Embed all characters (best for editing by others)** . . . . A
7. Click **OK**.
8. Click **Save** . . . . Alt + S

Package a Presentation

1. Click **File** . . . . Alt + F
2. Select **Pack and Go**. . . . . K
3. In the Pack and Go Wizard dialog boxes, follow the instructions and select appropriate options.

Unpackage a Presentation

1. In Windows Explorer, navigate to the folder that contains your packaged presentation.
2. Double-click the file *PGNSETUP.EXE.*
3. In the Pack and Go Setup dialog box, navigate to the folder where you want to place the extracted presentation.
4. Click **OK**.
5. Click **Yes** to run the unpackaged slide show.

Send a Presentation for Review Using Outlook

1. Open the presentation you want to send for review.
2. Click **File** . . . . .Alt + F
3. Point to **Send To**. . . . . .D
4. Select **Mail Recipient (for Review)**. C
5. In Outlook, enter the e-mail address of the recipient in the To box.
6. Click **Send** [Send].
7. Launch Microsoft Outlook.
8. Go to the Inbox. . . . . Ctrl + Shift + I
   OR
   Click **View**. . . . . Alt + V
   Point to **Go To** .G
   Click **Inbox** I
9. Click **Tools**. . . . . Alt + T
10. Point to **Send/Receive** . . . . E
11. Select **Send and Receive All** . . . . A

Receive a Presentation for Review and Receive a Reviewed Presentation Using Outlook

1. Launch Microsoft Outlook.
2. Go to the Inbox. . . . . Ctrl + Shift + I
   OR
   Click **View** . . . . Alt + V
   Point to **Go To**. G
   Click **Inbox** I
3. Click **Tools**. . . . . Alt + T
4. Point to **Send/Receive** . . . . E
5. Select **Send and Receive All** . . . . A
6. Double-click the new message.
7. Right-click the presentation attachment icon.
8. Select **Save As** . . . . S
9. Navigate to the folder in which you want to save the presentation.
10. Click **Save** . . . . Alt + S
11. If you have received a reviewed presentation, click Yes to merge the reviewed presentation into your original file.
12. Close the e-mail message.
13. Close Outlook.

Procedure Summary

Insert a Comment in a Presentation

1. Verify that the Reviewing toolbar is displayed . . . . **Alt + V; T**
2. Click the slide on which you want to comment.
3. Click **Insert Comment** .
   OR
   Click **Insert** . . . . **Alt + I**
   Select **Comment** . . . . **M**
4. Type a comment in the comment box.
5. Click outside the comment box.

Review and Return a Presentation Using Outlook

1. Verify that the Reviewing toolbar is displayed . . . . **Alt + V; T**
2. Edit the presentation and insert comments, as necessary.
3. When you are finished reviewing the file, save it . . . . **Ctrl + S**
4. Click **File**. . . . . **Alt + F**
5. Point to **Send To** . . . . **D**
6. Select **Original Sender**.
7. Click **Send** Send .
8. Launch Microsoft Outlook.
9. Click **Tools** . . . . **Alt + T**
10. Point to **Send/Receive** . . . . **E**
11. Select **Send and Receive All** . . . . **A**

Manage a Reviewed Presentation

1. Verify that the Reviewing toolbar and the Revisions Pane are displayed.
2. Click **Next Item** to move to each edit or comment.
3. Click **Apply** or **Unapply** to accept (apply) or reject (unapply) edits.
4. To delete a comment marker, click the comment and click **Delete** .
5. To delete a change marker, right-click the change marker and select Delete Marker.
6. Click **End Review** End Review... to end the review.
7. Click **Yes** when PowerPoint warns you that this will end the review.
8. Save the presentation. . . . . **Alt + F; S**

Publish a Presentation to the Web

1. Click **File** . . . . Alt + F
2. Select **Web Page Preview**. . . . . B
3. Navigate through the presentation in the browser.
4. Close the browser.
5. Click **File** . . . . .Alt + F
6. Select **Save As Web Page** . . . . .G
7. In the File name box, type or edit the file name if desired . . . . Alt + N
8. Click **Change Title** . . . . Alt + C
9. In the Set Page Title dialog box, type or edit the page title if desired.
10. Click **OK**.
11. Click **Publish**. . . . . .Alt + P
12. In the Publish As Web Page dialog box, select appropriate options.
13. Click **Publish**.

Set Up and Schedule an Online Broadcast

1. Open the presentation you want to broadcast.
2. Save the presentation to broadcast in a shared location.
3. Click **Slide Show**. . . . . Alt + D
4. Point to **Online Broadcast**. . . . . O
5. Select **Schedule a Live Broadcast** . . . . . . .S
6. In the Schedule Presentation Broadcast dialog box, type or change information, as necessary.
7. Click **Settings** . . . . Alt + G
8. In the Broadcast Settings dialog box, select options and type or change information, as necessary.
9. Click **OK**.
10. Click **Schedule** . . . . Alt + S
11. In Outlook, type the e-mail addresses of the attendees in the To box.
12. Select a date and time for the broadcast in the *Start time* area.
13. Click Send.
14. When you see a message telling you that the broadcast has been successfully scheduled, click **OK**.
15. Close the presentation.

Lesson Review and Exercises

Summary Checklist

- ☑ Can you set up a presentation for delivery?
- ☑ Can you deliver a presentation?
- ☑ Can you prepare a presentation for delivery on another computer?
- ☑ Can you set up a review cycle?
- ☑ Can you send a presentation for review?
- ☑ Can you manage a reviewed presentation?
- ☑ Can you publish a presentation to the Web?
- ☑ Can you set up and schedule an online broadcast?

Key Terms

- change marker (p. 602)
- comment marker (p. 602)
- comment (p. 602)
- embedded font (p. 598)
- liquid crystal display (LCD) projector (p. 594)
- online broadcast (p. 615)
- publish (p. 612)

APPLY IT! Guided Activities

1. Set Up, Deliver, and Package a Presentation

You are the curator of the Merrill Car Museum, a museum dedicated to classic cars. You want to create a presentation giving information about classic cars and about the museum itself and then send it to tour group directors. You want to set up the slide show, rehearse timings, experiment with hiding and unhiding slides, deliver the presentation, and then package the presentation so that it can be delivered on another computer.

Follow these steps to set up, rehearse, and package the presentation:

a. Open *Cars.ppt* and resave it as *xxx-Cars.ppt*. On slide 1, select Set Up Show on the Slide Show menu. Select *Presented by speaker (full screen)*. Next, select All in the *Show slides* section and select *Using timings, if present* in the *Advance slides* section. Click OK. Select Rehearse Timings on the Slide Show menu and rehearse the presentation. Select Next to move from one slide to the next. Save your timings at the end of the rehearsal.

b. In slide sorter view, select slide 4, and in the Slide Transition task pane, change the number in the Automatically after box to 18 seconds. Then deliver the presentation again, letting the slides advance automatically. Make any necessary timing adjustments and save your changes.

c. With the Slide Transition task pane displayed, select all slides on the Slides tab, click to deselect *Automatically after* in the Slide Transition task pane, and close the task pane. Click outside the slide in the slide pane to deselect all but slide 1. Then deliver the presentation again, clicking to advance each slide. When you get to slide 4, right-click, point to Go, point to By Title, and select slide 2. Right-click again, navigate to slide 7, and then press Esc to end the presentation.

d. In normal view, click slide 3, and select Hide Slide on the Slide Show menu. Return to slide 1, switch to slide show view, and advance slides manually, noting that slide 3 does not appear. When you get to slide 4, *Vehicles*, right-click, point to Pointer Options, and select Pen. Use the pen pointer to underline the title and circle both level 2 subtitles **(see Figure 4.35)**.

Figure 4.35 Using the pen pointer

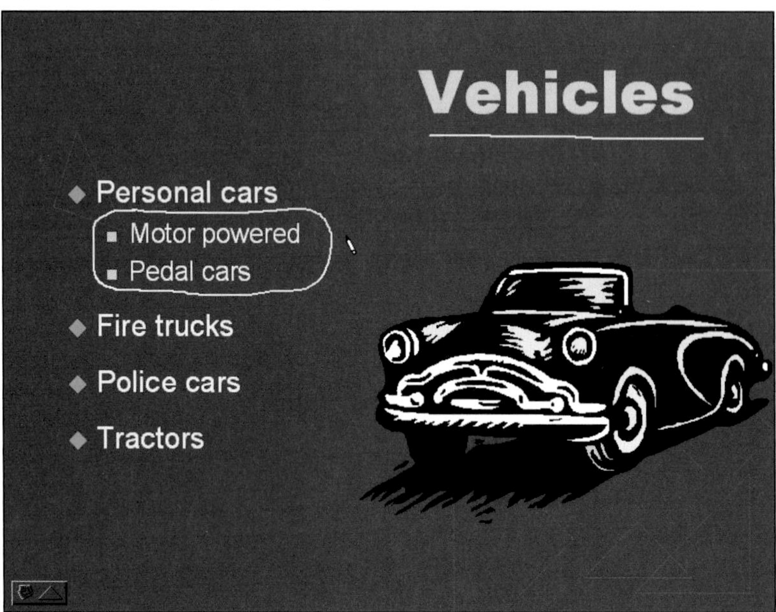

e. Return to normal view and select slide 3 on the Slides tab. Right-click and select Hide Slide to unhide the slide. Save the presentation, and then save it again as *xxx-Cars-Embed.ppt*. In the Save As dialog box, click the Tools down arrow and select Save Options. Select *Embed TrueType fonts* and *Embed all characters (best for editing by others)*. Click OK, and then click Save.

f. Save the presentation as *xxx-Cars-PackGo.ppt*, and then select Pack and Go on the File menu. Follow the directions in the Pack and Go Wizard to package the presentation: In the second window, choose Active presentation; in the third window, create a new folder named *Car Presentation* in your *Unit 4, Lesson 4* folder; and in the fourth window, choose both options. Include the PowerPoint Viewer with the presentation.

g. Save and close the presentation. In Windows Explorer, navigate to the *Car Presentation* folder and double-click *PNGSETUP.EXE*. Extract the presentation in the *Car Presentation* folder, and then click Yes to run the slide show. After running the slide show, close Windows Explorer.

2. Review a Presentation

As a high school accounting teacher, you did research and created a presentation for the school's juniors and seniors about how to save money. Now you will ask at least one student to exchange presentations with you for reviewing. Then you will work with the reviewed presentation, incorporating and rejecting the reviewer comments and edits.

Follow these steps to set up a review cycle, review a presentation, and work with a reviewed presentation:

a. Connect to the Internet, if necessary, and open *Save Money-PackGo.ppt* in the *Money Presentation* subfolder of the *Lesson 4* folder. Save it as *xxx-Save Money-PackGo.ppt* in the *Lesson 4* folder. Next, point to Send To on the File menu and select Mail Recipient (for Review). In the To box, type the e-mail address of one or more classmates and click Send. ***Note:*** Your teacher will provide you with the e-mail address(es) to use. Launch Microsoft Outlook.

b. In Outlook, point to Go To on the View menu, and select Inbox, if necessary. Click the *Outbox* folder to see the message you created, and then point to Send/Receive on the Tools menu and select Send and Receive All. Return to the *Inbox* folder, if necessary, and find a message from another student asking you to review a presentation. Double-click to open the message. Right-click the presentation icon, select Save As, and save the presentation in your *Lesson 4* folder. Close the message and close Outlook.

c. Open the presentation in PowerPoint. In normal view, display the Reviewing toolbar, if necessary. On slide 1, change the title to 60 pt. Verdana, white. Then click Insert Comment and type the following in the comment box: What do you think about changing the title to How to Save Money? Click outside the comment box, and then point to the comment marker to read the comment. Drag the comment marker to position it closer to the title.

d. On slide 2, change each bullet to a check mark in a box **(see Figure 4.36)**. Use Format Painter to copy the format to the bullets on the remaining slides. On slide 4, change the title from *Dine and Save* to Review Dining Habits. Resave the file, point to Send To on the File menu, and select Original Sender. Click Send and close the presentation.

PowerPoint®

Figure 4.36 Customized bullets on slide 2

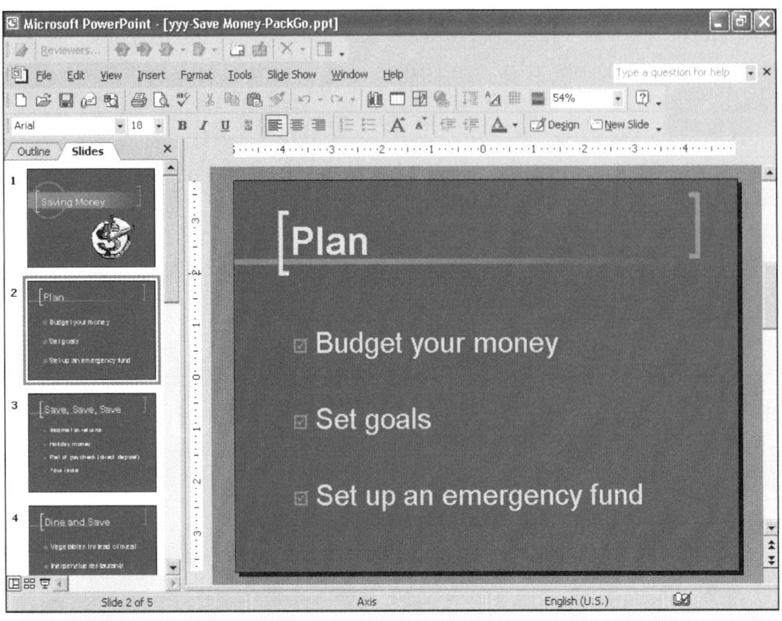

e. In Outlook, go to your *Inbox* folder. Use the Send/Receive command to receive any incoming messages and to send any messages in your *Outbox* folder. In the *Inbox* folder, double-click the message your classmate sent to you with the reviewed presentation attached. Right-click the presentation icon, select Save As, and save the presentation as *xxx-Save Money-PackGo-Reviewed.ppt.* Close the message, and open the presentation in PowerPoint. Click Yes when you are asked if you want to merge the changes from the reviewed presentation into your original copy. Close Outlook and maximize the presentation.

f. Point to Toolbars on the View menu, and select the Reviewing toolbar and the Revisions Pane if they are not displayed. If desired, print the reviewer comments. Click the comment marker at the top of slide 1, read the comment, and then click Delete Comment. Click Next Item. Right-click the change marker and select Delete Marker.

g. On slide 2, click the change marker, and click to insert check marks in the boxes that appear in the screen tip. Click Apply. Repeat these steps on the remaining slides in the presentation to accept the changes. On slide 4, click the change marker, click to insert a check mark in the screen tip, and click Unapply. Click End Review and click Yes when PowerPoint warns you that this will end the review for all reviewers. Save the presentation as *xxx-Save Money-PackGo-Final.ppt*.

3. Publish and Schedule an Online Broadcast

As a high school accounting teacher, you did research and created a presentation for the school's juniors and seniors about how to save money. Now you will publish the presentation and schedule it for broadcast.

Follow these steps:

a. Open *xxx-SaveMoney-PackGo-Final.ppt*. Select Web Page Preview on the File menu and maximize the browser window. Click Next Slide twice to move to slide 3. In the Outline pane, click the *Haggle Over Prices* hyperlink to jump to slide 5. Click Previous Slide twice to move to slide 3, and then click Slide Show. Click once to advance to slide 4 and then press Esc to end the slide show.

b. Click Show/Hide Notes to hide the notes pane, click Expand/Collapse Outline, click Show/Hide Outline, and then close your browser. In PowerPoint, select Save as Web Page on the File menu. Type xxx-Save Money Web Page as the file name. Click Change Title, type Save Money as the page title **(see Figure 4.37)**, and click OK.

Figure 4.37 Set Page Title dialog box

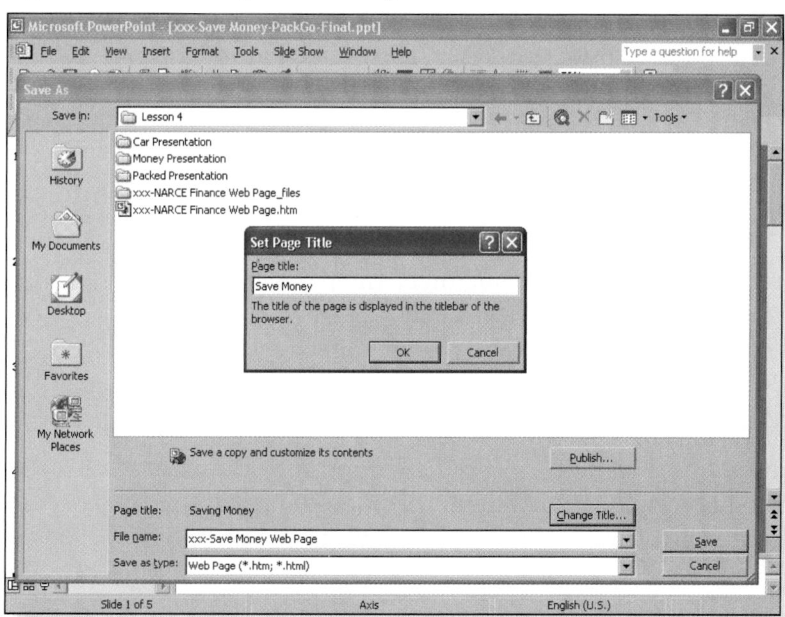

c. Click Publish, and then click to select *Complete presentation*, if necessary. Click to deselect *Display speaker notes*. Click to select *All browsers listed above (creates larger files)*. Click to select *Open published Web page in browser*, if necessary, and then click Publish. Navigate the slides in your browser, and then close the browser.

d. Save *xxx-SaveMoney-PackGo-Final.ppt* as *xxx-SaveMoney-Broadcast* in a shared location, as directed by your teacher. Point to Online Broadcast on the Slide Show menu and select Schedule a Live Broadcast. Type Save Money as the title. Type your name in the Speaker box, if necessary, and leave all other options unchanged.

e. Click Settings. On the Presenter tab, select the audio and video settings that match your computer. Click to deselect *Display speaker notes with the presentation*, if necessary, and then select Resizable Screen in the *Slide show mode* box. Click Browse and then navigate to and select the shared folder. Click Select, click OK, and then click Schedule.

f. In Outlook (or another e-mail program that opens), maximize the window. In the To box, type the e-mail addresses of other students, as directed by your teacher. Select a date and time for the broadcast in the *Start time* area. Click Send.

g. When you see a message telling you that the broadcast has been successfully scheduled, click OK, and then close the presentation.

Do It Yourself

1. Set Up and Deliver a Presentation

As the training coordinator at Rolcie Insurance, Inc., you have been asked to set up and deliver a presentation for the new employees introducing automobile insurance and briefly covering the other types of insurance your company offers. To set up and deliver your presentation, do the following:

a. Open *Insurance.ppt* and save it as *xxx-Insurance.ppt*. View the presentation and add any notes in the notes panes that will help you deliver the presentation. Print a copy of the notes pages, if necessary.

b. Use the Set Up Show option on the Slide Show menu to set up the presentation. Select all of the appropriate options, and then rehearse the timings as you deliver the presentation. Practice navigating to various slides **(see Figure 4.38)**, and save your timings.

Figure 4.38 Navigating during a slide show

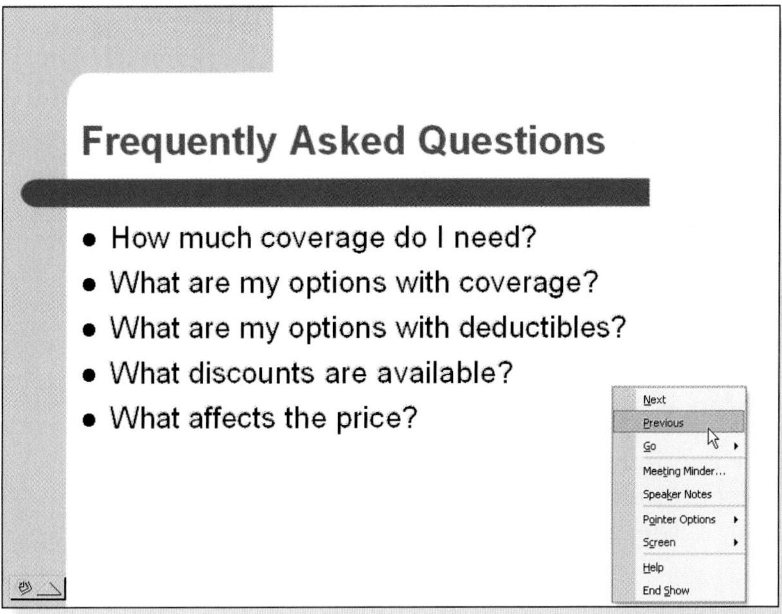

c. Hide the last two slides in the presentation and deliver the slide show again. In the Slide Transition task pane, increase the timing for each slide by 3 seconds. Then deliver the presentation again, letting the slides advance automatically. Make any timing adjustments and save your changes.

d. Clear all of the timings and deliver the presentation again, first in slide order, and then navigating to several different slides. End the presentation.

e. Unhide slides 7 and 8, and then switch to slide show view. On slide 2, underline *Contract* in the first level 2 subtitle and draw an arrow pointing to the last level 2 subtitle. Return to normal view. Save and close the presentation.

2. Prepare a Presentation for Delivery on Another Computer

As the training coordinator at Rolcie Insurance, Inc., you have been asked to prepare your insurance introduction presentation so that it can be shown at many locations across the country, even on computers that do not have PowerPoint installed. You also need to make sure that the fonts you have chosen will display correctly during the slide show.

To embed TrueType fonts and package your presentation for delivery on other computers, do the following:

a. Open *xxx-Insurance.ppt*. In the Save As dialog box, use the Save Options command to embed TrueType fonts, including the entire character set in the presentation.

b. Save the presentation as *xxx-Insurance-PackGo.ppt*, and then use the Pack and Go Wizard to package this as an active presentation in a new *Insurance Presentation* folder. Be sure to include embedded fonts and the PowerPoint Viewer.

c. Save and close the presentation, and use Windows Explorer to extract the presentation in the *Insurance Presentation* folder. Run the slide show, and then close Windows Explorer.

3. Work With Reviewed Presentations

In your role as a library and information services specialist, you have been asked to give a presentation on the Dewey Decimal Classification system. You have created the presentation, but you want another person to review it.

To set up a review cycle, review another student's presentation, and then work with a reviewed presentation, do the following:

a. Connect to the Internet, if necessary, and open *Dewey Decimal.ppt*. Save it as *xxx-Dewey Decimal.ppt* in your *Lesson 4* folder. View the presentation to become familiar with it, and then use Outlook or another e-mail program to send it to another classmate for review.

b. In Outlook, go to your Inbox, find the message you created in the *Outbox* folder, and then use the Send/Receive command to send and receive all messages. Next, find a message from another student in your Inbox asking you to review a presentation. Save that student's presentation in your *Lesson 4* folder. Open the presentation, making sure the Reviewing toolbar is displayed.

c. Insert comments, make formatting changes, and make appropriate text edits. When you have finished reviewing the presentation, save your changes, and send the presentation back to the original sender.

d. In Outlook, use the Send/Receive command again to receive any incoming messages and to send any messages in your *Outbox* folder. In the *Inbox* folder, find the message your classmate has sent to you with your reviewed presentation attached. Save that presentation to your *Lesson 4* folder. Open the reviewed presentation, merging the changes from the reviewed presentation into your original copy. If desired, print the reviewer comments.

e. Use the Reviewing toolbar and the Revisions Pane to accept and reject edits as appropriate, and then delete the change markers. Read all comments, act on them if necessary, and delete the comments **(see Figure 4.39)**. Save the final presentation as *xxx-Dewey Decimal-Final.ppt*.

Figure 4.39 Deleting a comment

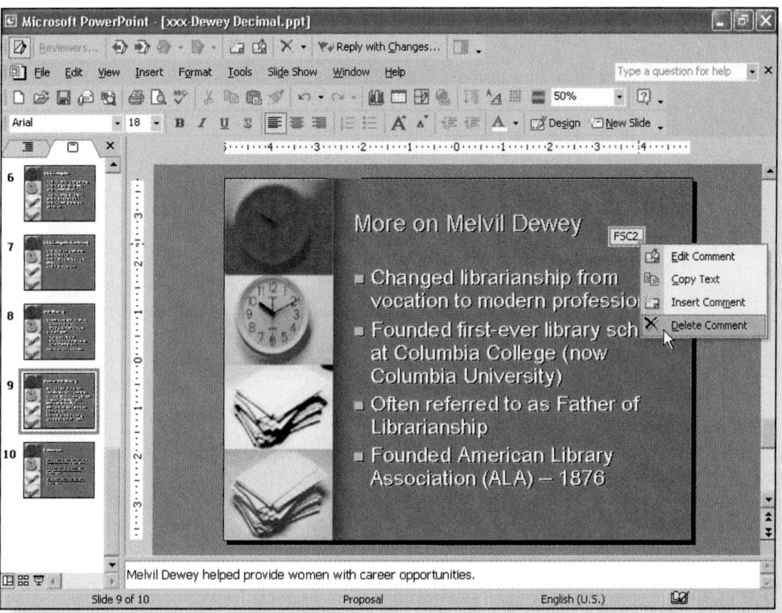

4. Save as a Web Page and Schedule a Broadcast

In your role as a library and information services specialist, you want to publish and broadcast your Dewey Decimal Classification presentation so that library and information services specialists across the country will have access to it.

To publish your presentation and schedule it for broadcast, do the following:

a. Open *xxx-Dewey Decimal-Final.ppt*. Use the Web Page Preview command to view the presentation in your browser; maximize the browser window **(see Figure 4.40)**. Use Next Slide, Previous Slide, and the hyperlinks in the Outline pane to navigate the presentation. Practice hiding and unhiding the notes pane, and practice expanding and collapsing the outline.

Figure 4.40 Dewey Decimal presentation in browser

b. Close your browser. In PowerPoint, save the presentation as a Web page with the file name *xxx-Dewey Decimal Web Page*. Type Dewey Decimal Classification as the page title.

c. Publish the complete presentation, selecting options so that speaker notes are not displayed, the presentation will display in all browsers, and the published Web page will open in a browser. View the slides in your browser, and then close your browser.

d. Save *xxx-Dewey Decimal-Final.ppt* as *xxx-Dewey Decimal-Broadcast.ppt* in a shared location, as directed by your teacher. Use the Online Broadcast command to schedule a live broadcast, using Dewey Decimal Classification as the title. Use your name as the speaker.

e. Select audio and video settings that match your computer, make sure that speaker notes are not displayed with the presentation, and select the Resizable Screen option. Next, schedule the presentation for broadcast using a shared folder.

f. In Outlook (or another e-mail program that opens), send the presentation to another student, after selecting a date and time for the broadcast. Once the broadcast has been successfully scheduled, close the presentation.

Challenge Yourself

Create a Telecommunications Presentation

Assume that you are a teacher and that you must present basic information about telecommunications to your class as part of the curriculum. You want to create a presentation titled *xxx-Telecommunications.ppt*.

Before you can create your presentation, you must search the Internet to locate basic information about the telecommunications industry. You want to include information on the following:

- Definition of telecommunications
- Benefits of telecommunications
- Primary components of the telecommunications industry
- Relative costs of different types of media

Working with a partner (assigned by your teacher), incorporate all of the skills you have learned in Lesson 4 as well as many you learned in previous lessons. First, research the topic, and then create the presentation, using slide transitions, animations, and sound or clip art.

Next, set up the presentation for delivery, and then take turns with your partner delivering it, hiding and unhiding slides as you practice giving the presentation for various audiences, rehearsing your timings **(see Figure 4.39)**. Use the Pack and Go Wizard to prepare the presentation for delivery on another computer, remembering to embed TrueType fonts.

Set up a review cycle for your presentation using another team of classmates, as assigned by your teacher. Exchange presentations with the other team. Make reviewer comments and changes on the other team's presentation, and then merge their review of your presentation with your original presentation, print the reviewer comments if desired, and accept or reject their comments and changes. Finally, publish your presentation to the Web, and set up and schedule an online broadcast.

Unit 4 Applications and Projects

Apply Your Knowledge

Complete the following exercises in order, as directed by your teacher. As you work through these projects, you will use PowerPoint to create multiple presentations in a variety of ways. You will create one presentation to introduce your waste and recycling company to consumers and another presentation to deliver pricing information to others in your company. Your presentations must be attractive and professional, and each one should be created with your target audience in mind. Save all files in the *Unit Applications and Projects* subfolder within your *Unit 4* folder.

1. Create a Presentation to Introduce Your Products and Services

a. Use the AutoContent Wizard to create an on-screen presentation. Select the Sales/Marketing category and the Product/Services Overview presentation type. Type your company name, Katz Waste & Recycling, as the presentation title, and include the slide number in the footer. Choose a new color scheme that includes blue instead of brown.

b. On slide 1, replace the subtitle with Our Services. Format all text attractively, and then insert the image *Katz Logo.wmf*, your company's logo. Resize and position the logo in the upper-left corner of the slide. Add a small text box somewhere on the slide that says Since 1965. Format it with a color and font style of your choice. *Optional:* Try using the AutoShapes button on the Drawing toolbar to create an Explosion star shape. Then, click and drag the text box into the shape, changing the order of the objects so that the text displays in the star. Finally, position the shape and text box attractively on the slide **(see Figure 1)**.

Figure 1 Slide 1 of the Katz presentation

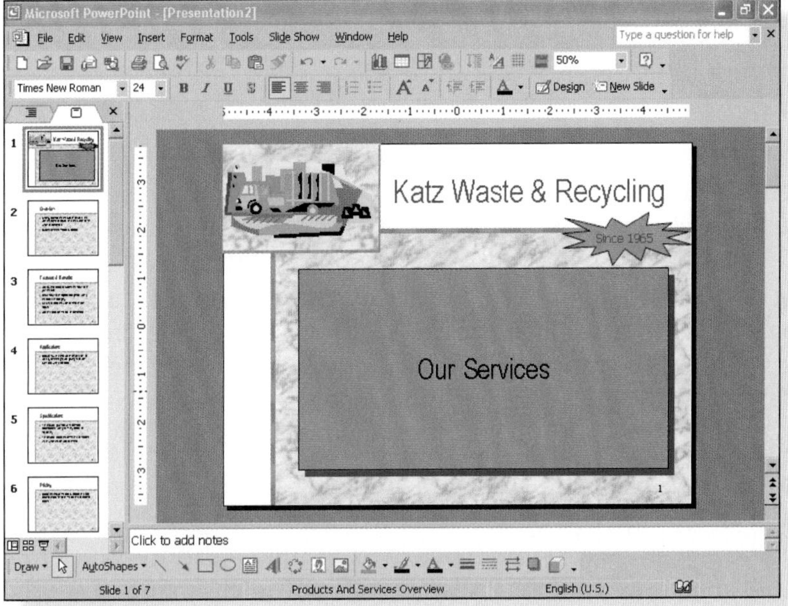

c. Delete the remaining slides in the presentation, and then add as many new slides as necessary to include the following information in the presentation. (***Note:*** The *Internal Office Staff* information should appear as an organization chart.)

Services We Offer
Commercial trash pickup
Residential trash pickup
Residential recycling

What We Recycle
Aluminum cans
Steel cans
Glass bottles
Glass jars
Magazines
Newspapers
No. 1 and No. 2 plastic containers

Internal Office Staff (does not include the field employees—the waste and recycling associates)
Level 1: President
Level 2: Vice President
Level 3: Four regional managers and one office manager
The president, vice president, and office manager all have assistants reporting to them.

Contact Information
8400 Guion Road
Brownsburg, IN 46112
317-555-0122
info@katz.com

d. Include at least one hyperlink to another part of the presentation. Present the company's contact information as the last slide. Don't include too much information on any slide, and create level 2 subtitles as needed. Change font attributes and line spacing as desired. In addition to the information shown in step c, import the Word table *Residential Trash Prices.doc* on one slide as a linked or embedded object. Resize and reposition the table attractively on the slide, adding an appropriate title.

e. In addition to the company logo you inserted on slide 1, include clip art on one or more of the slides. Size and position the clip art attractively. Change the bullet style used for each level of subtitles to another style of your choice. Next, apply a different design template only to the slide that contains the company's contact information, but edit its color scheme, if necessary, to more closely match the rest of the presentation.

f. View the presentation in the Print Preview window, and then print the first and last slides. Add any notes in the notes panes that will help you to deliver the presentation. Then, view the presentation in the Print Preview window again, and print notes pages. Save your presentation as *xxx-Katz Intro.ppt* and close the file.

2. Create a Presentation to Discuss Company Finances

a. Create a presentation from a design template, and incorporate the company name and the subtitle Financial Meeting on the title slide. Then open the Word file *Katz Outline.doc* in PowerPoint, and copy the slide from that presentation to the second slide in your Financial Meeting presentation. Close the presentation you converted from Word to PowerPoint without saving it.

b. Change the formatting of one or both slides to make it unique for your presentation, including changing the slide layout and changing font attributes (such as font style, point size, and formatting). Change to a different color scheme, and then edit the new color scheme, changing at least one color.

c. Insert a new slide, select the Title and Content layout, and create a table that shows the current and proposed new residential monthly trash pickup prices shown in **Table 1**. Use the Format Table dialog box to customize the format of the table in an attractive style. Include an appropriate title for the slide.

Table 1

Available Plans	Current Prices	Proposed New Prices
1 can or bag	$7.50	$9.50
2 cans or bags	$9.00	$11.50
3-6 cans or bags	$11.00	$14.50

d. On another slide, import the Excel file *Trash Chart.xls*. Include an appropriate title, and format the chart attractively. Then, edit the title master to include the company logo on the title slide. Include the slide number in the footer area of each slide except the first one, and include today's date (fixed) and Financial Meeting in the header area of each handout page. Save the file as *xxx-Katz Finances.ppt*.

e. Preview and print the presentation as handouts (2 per page), as shown in **Figure 2**.

f. Next, create a new folder named *Financial Presentations* and save the presentation in that folder in Outline/RTF format. Close the presentation.

Figure 2 Print preview of a handout page

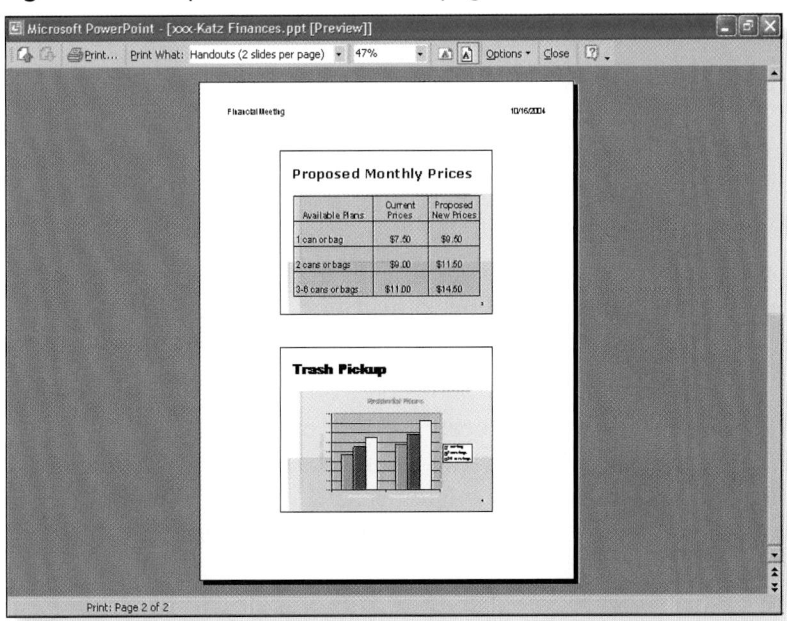

PowerPoint®

3. Add Animation, a Movie, and Sound to a Presentation

a. Open *xxx-Katz Intro.ppt* and save it as *xxx-Katz Animated.ppt*. Delete the company logo on slide 1 and replace it with a movie from the Clip Organizer.

b. Add a sound effect of your choice, also from the Clip Organizer, to the title slide, and then reposition the organization chart slide as slide 2.

c. Somewhere in the presentation, include at least one hyperlink to a Web site that discusses waste removal or recycling efforts.

d. Add slide transitions for each slide and animate text and objects, using a combination of preset animation schemes and custom animation.

e. Save your presentation.

4. Prepare and Send a Presentation for Review

a. Save *xxx-Katz Animated.ppt* as *xxx-Katz Rehearsed.ppt*. Set up and deliver the presentation, rehearsing your timings. Save your rehearsed timings, and then manually change the timing, increasing it by five seconds for two of the slides.

b. Deliver your presentation again, clicking to advance each slide. Hide the organization chart slide, and deliver the presentation one more time, this time letting all slides advance automatically. When you arrive at any slide that contains a hyperlink, click the hyperlink at the appropriate time. Unhide the organization chart slide, and save the presentation.

c. Save the presentation again as *xxx-Katz PackGo.ppt*. Use the Pack and Go Wizard to embed the TrueType fonts in the presentation and prepare it for delivery on another computer that has PowerPoint installed, saving the presentation in a new folder named *Timed Presentation*.

d. Using Outlook or another e-mail program, set up a review cycle, and send your *xxx-Katz Rehearsed* presentation for review to at least one student (as assigned by your teacher). One or more students will send a presentation to you for review.

e. Review the presentations you receive from other students, making edits and inserting comments as necessary **(see Figure 3)**. When you are finished, save each presentation, and use Outlook or another e-mail program to return each presentation to the original sender.

f. When you receive your reviewed presentation from other assigned student(s), read each comment and notice each edit, applying and unapplying changes as appropriate. Print the comments pages, and then delete each comment. Save your final presentation as *xxx-Katz Reviewed.ppt*.

Figure 3 Inserted comment

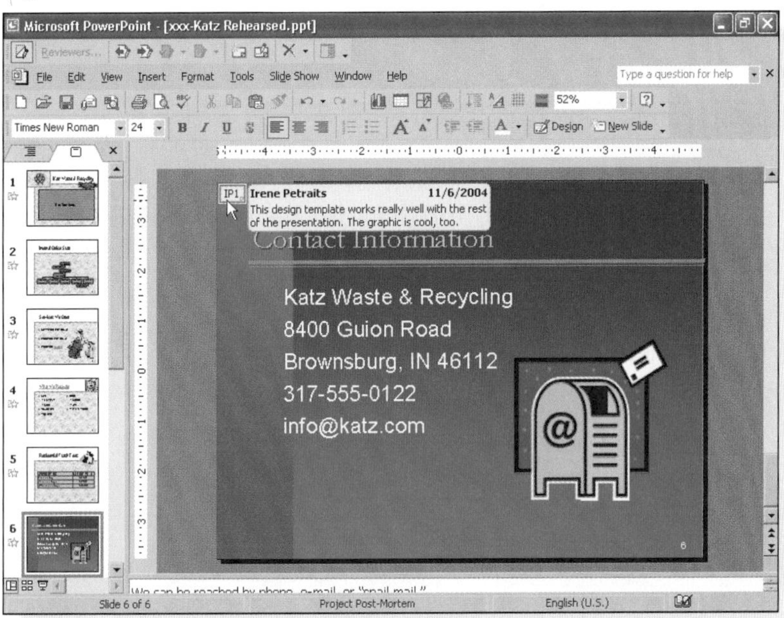

5. Publish a Presentation to the Web and Schedule an Online Broadcast

a. In *xxx-Katz Reviewed.ppt*, use the Web Page Preview command to view the presentation in your browser. Navigate the presentation.

b. In PowerPoint, save the presentation as a Web page with the file name *xxx-Katz Web Page.htm*. Type Katz Intro as the page title.

c. Publish the complete presentation, selecting options so that speaker notes are not displayed, the presentation will display in all browsers, and the published Web page will open in a browser. View the slides in your browser.

d. Save *xxx-Katz Reviewed.ppt* as *xxx-Katz Broadcast.ppt* in a shared location, as directed by your instructor. Use the Online Broadcast command to schedule a live broadcast, using Katz Intro as the title. Use your name as the speaker.

e. Select audio and video settings that match your computer, make sure that speaker notes are not displayed with the presentation, and select the Resizable Screen option. Next, schedule the presentation for broadcast using a shared folder.

f. In Outlook (or other e-mail program that opens), send the presentation to another student, after selecting a date and time for the broadcast. Once the broadcast has been successfully scheduled, close the presentation.

What's Wrong With This Picture?

Using your knowledge of effective presentation design, identify the seven errors in the slide shown in **Figure 4**, and describe how you would fix each error using PowerPoint's tools.

Figure 4 This slide has many flaws. How many can you name?

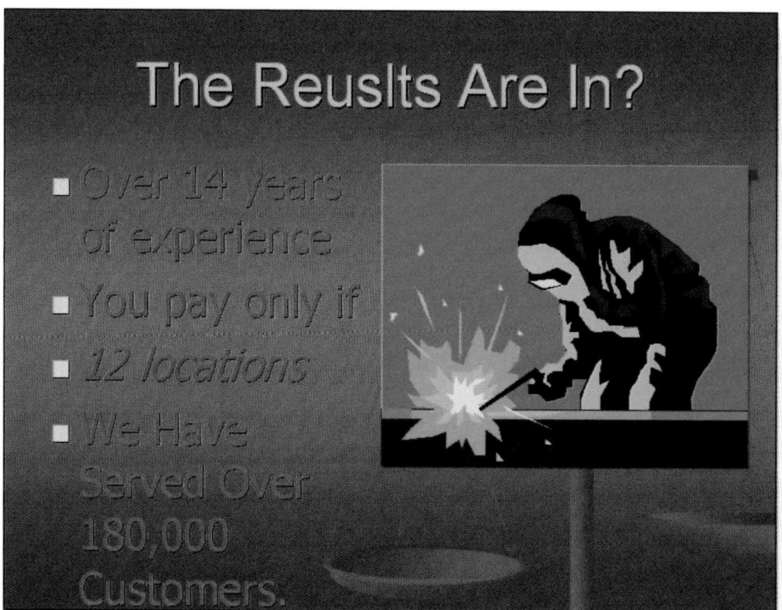

Cross-Curriculum Project

Assume that your English teacher has asked you to create a presentation to teach others about verb tenses. With your assigned team members, conduct appropriate research to learn more about verb tenses, such as perfect tense, present tense, past perfect tense, and so on. In addition to any research you do online, be sure to check with local resources. For example, your school library or local public library may have books that discuss verb tenses in depth.

Using the results of your research, develop a presentation named *xxx-Verb Tenses.ppt* that includes the following features:

- Multiple slide layouts
- Multiple design templates
- Different color schemes
- Edited color scheme
- Hyperlinks (at least one)
- Clip art
- Movie
- Sound
- Animations
- Slide transitions

Your teacher may ask you to include endnotes or a bibliography on a slide. If so, ask your teacher how to properly format these items.

Two team members should create a first draft of the presentation. Then, using Outlook or another e-mail program, the two team members should send the presentation to their other team members for review. Each team member should make edits and add comments, and then return the presentation to the original sender. Working together, the team should study all edits and comments in order to finalize the presentation, adding and deleting slides and making changes as appropriate. Next, rehearse the presentation, saving the rehearsed timings.

Use the Print Preview window to check your slides, notes, handouts, and comment pages before printing each of these.

Once your team has finalized the presentation, save it with the same name, and then save it again in Outline/RTF form in a newly created folder named *Cross-Curriculum Project* in the *Unit Applications and Projects* folder. Open the *xxx-Verb Tenses.ppt* presentation, and use the Pack and Go Wizard to embed TrueType fonts and prepare the presentation for delivery on another computer that has PowerPoint installed. Then, save the presentation again as a Web page, view it in your browser, publish it to the Web, and set up and schedule an online broadcast.

Business Telecommunications

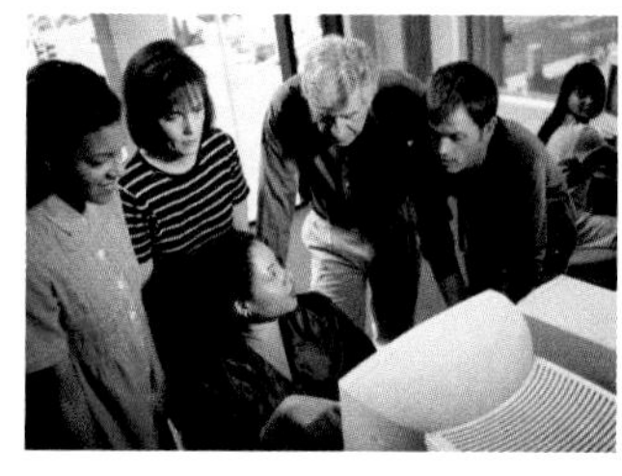

Unit Contents

Unit Objectives

1. Get started with Outlook.
2. Explore the Outlook window.
3. Send and receive electronic mail.
4. Customize views.
5. Organize and locate messages.
6. Modify message settings and delivery options.
7. Archive and save messages.
8. Create and edit contact information.
9. Manage contact information.
10. Schedule appointments.
11. Schedule meetings and respond to meeting requests
12. Manage the Outlook Calendar.
13. Create and update tasks.
14. Work with task requests.
15. Create and manage notes.

Lesson 1

Managing Messages

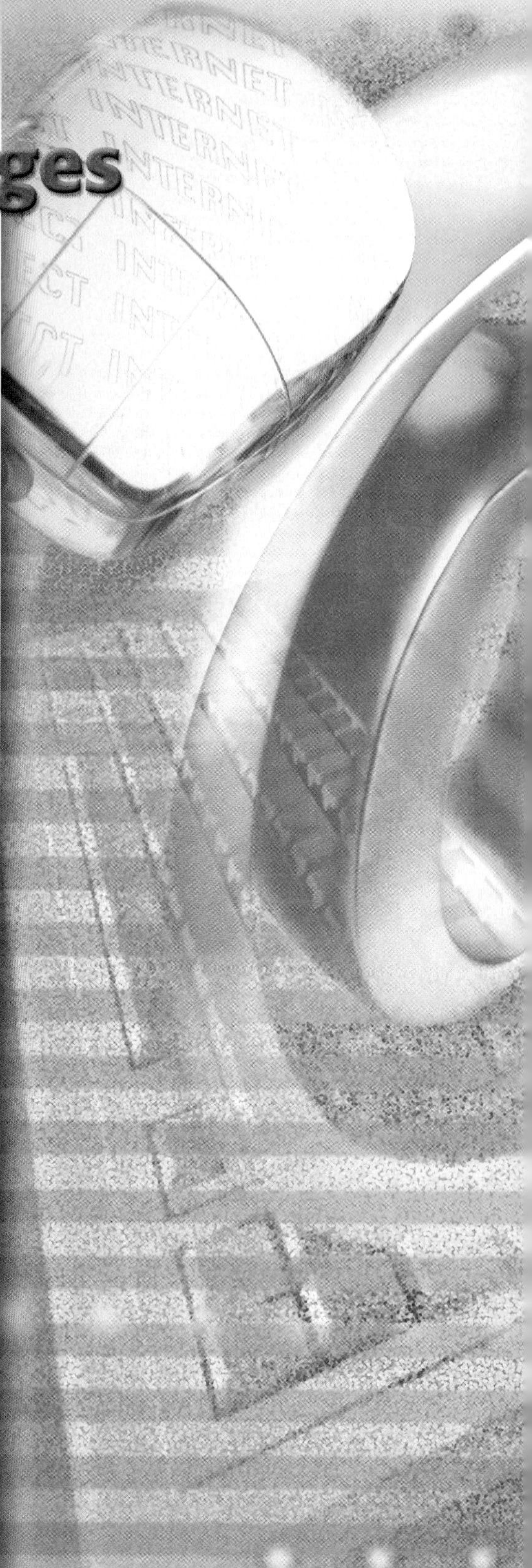

Lesson Exercise Objectives

After completing this lesson, you'll be able to do the following tasks:

1. Get started with Outlook
2. Explore the Outlook window
3. Send and receive electronic mail
4. Customize views
5. Organize and locate messages
6. Modify message settings and delivery options
7. Archive and save messages

Key Terms

- archiving (p. 675)
- attachment (p. 661)
- AutoArchive (p. 675)
- category (p. 668)
- delivery options (p. 671)
- download (p. 652)
- e-mail (p. 646)
- Find and Advanced Find (p. 668)
- Folder List (p. 648)
- Forward (p. 654)
- HTML format (p. 676)
- Importance level (p. 671)
- Inbox (p. 648)
- nethics (p. 664)
- netiquette (p. 664)
- Outlook Bar (p. 648)
- Outlook Rich Text format (p. 676)
- Outlook Today (p. 646)
- Preview Pane (p. 648)
- Reply (p. 654)
- Reply to All (p. 654)
- Sensitivity level (p. 671)
- Signature Picker (p. 657)
- signatures (p. 657)
- stationery (p. 659)
- Text Only format (p. 676)
- upload (p. 654)
- views (p. 651)

Microsoft Office Specialist Activities

OL2002: 1.1–1.4, 3.1–3.5

Real-Life Business Applications

Lesson Case Study

In this lesson, you will play the role of project leader for *Maehr Park Clean & Green Up*, your Sophomore class community project. Keep the following information in mind as you work through the lesson exercises.

- **Job responsibilities and goals.** As project leader, your mission is to coordinate the cleanup of a neighborhood park. You will communicate with subcommittee team leaders, the Project Advisor, and local businesses to determine who will participate in the project by volunteering time and talents, services, funding, and other donations.
- **The project.** As the project swings into high gear, you will use Outlook as your primary communication tool to manage the project efficiently.
- **The challenge ahead.** Using Outlook, you will create a "project" signature to use on e-mail correspondence. You'll also send several messages and organize the Inbox by customizing views, setting options, and organizing messages in folders.

Exercise 1 Overview: Get Started With Outlook

Have you ever had to deal with information overload? Are there days when you have too many appointments to keep, too many assignments due, and not enough time to get it all done? Outlook is a personal information management program—designed to manage your personal and business messages (telephone and electronic), contacts, tasks, and appointments all from one location, which will greatly increase your productivity and communication efficiency.

Your journey through Outlook will begin by using **e-mail** (electronic messages) to communicate with others about your Sophomore class community project—*Maehr Park Clean & Green Up*. In order to send and receive e-mail, you will need an account on an e-mail server, a computer or program that forwards, retrieves, and stores messages on your behalf. This server can be located on a local area network or may be located at an Internet Service Provider. (You will learn more about local area networks and Internet Service Providers in Unit 6.) Your teacher will provide any e-mail informa-tion or accounts you need in order to complete the exercises in this unit.

When you launch Outlook, you will recognize the title bar, toolbar, and menu bar from other Microsoft applications. **Outlook Today,** a page that may appear when you launch Outlook, shows a summary of your current appointments, any tasks on your "to-do" list, and how many new e-mail messages are waiting in the Inbox. You can jump to various Outlook items to update, add, or delete information. In the following exercise, you will launch Outlook, examine the elements on the screen, and navigate between several Outlook items.

Figure 1.1 Outlook Today

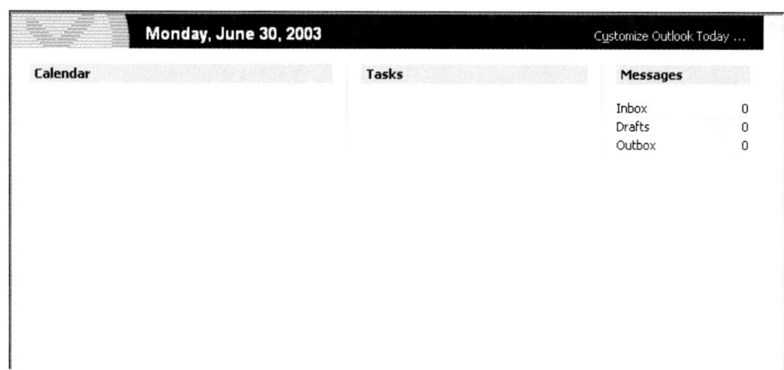

Figure 1.2 Outlook Today page

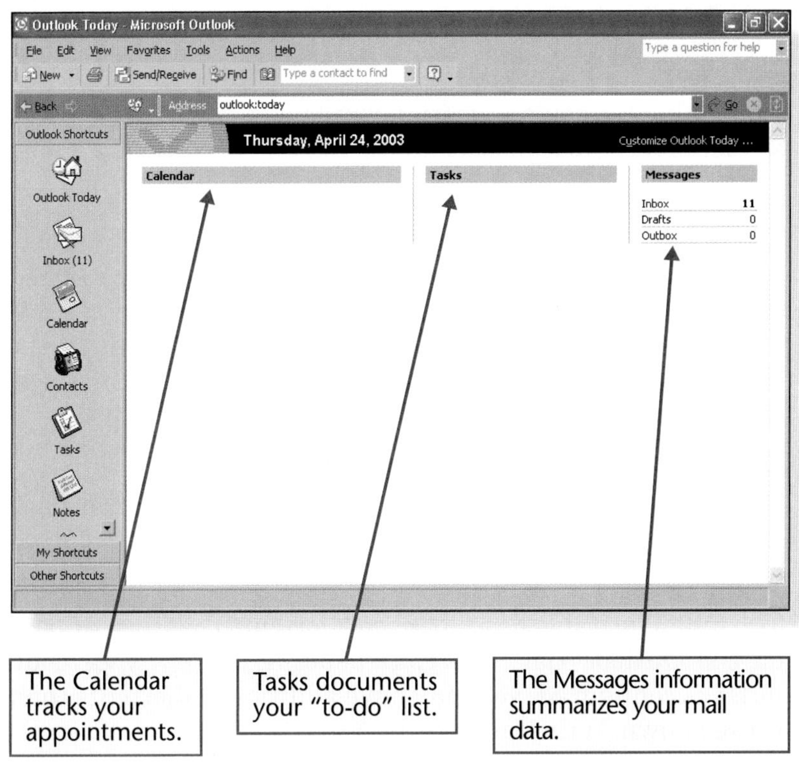

The Calendar tracks your appointments.

Step Through It™

Exercise 1: Launch the Outlook program

1. Launch Microsoft Outlook. Maximize the Outlook window, if necessary.
2. The Outlook Today page appears (see Figure 1.2). (***Note:*** If you don't see the Outlook Today page, select Go To on the View menu; then click Outlook Today.)
3. Click Tasks on the Outlook Today page. You are taken to your task list.

Figure 1.3 The main Outlook application window

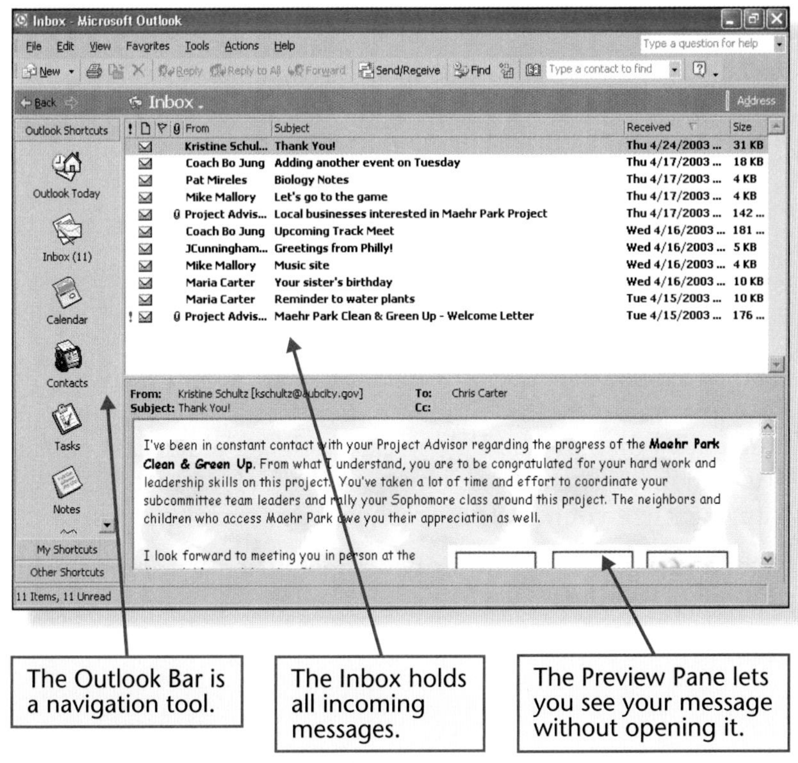

The Outlook Bar is a navigation tool.
The Inbox holds all incoming messages.
The Preview Pane lets you see your message without opening it.

4. On the View menu, select Go To and then select Inbox. You are now in the main application window (see Figure 1.3).

Microsoft Office Specialist
OL2002 1.4

Outlook®

Exercise 2 Overview: Explore the Outlook Window

The main Outlook application window is divided into three sections: the Outlook Bar, the Inbox, and the Preview Pane.

Inbox and Preview Pane

The **Inbox** is where you will receive, store, and organize your e-mail messages. Messages in the Inbox are sorted chronologically by the received date. The selected, or highlighted, message appears in the **Preview Pane** at the bottom of your screen where you can read the message without actually opening it.

Outlook Bar and Folder List

The **Outlook Bar**, which includes groups such as Outlook Shortcuts or Other Shortcuts, is a navigation tool that enables you to link to other items within Outlook.

The following table describes the shortcuts that may appear on the Outlook Bar. (***Note:*** Depending on how your computer is configured, you may have additional shortcuts than those shown in the table.)

Outlook Bar shortcuts

Shortcut	Description
Outlook Shortcuts	Links to Outlook Today, Inbox, Calendar, Contacts, Tasks, Notes, and Deleted Items
My Shortcuts	Links to Drafts, Outbox, Sent Items, Journal, and Outlook Updates
Other Shortcuts	Links to My Computer, My Documents, and Favorites

You can also use the **Folder List** (a list of folders available in your mailbox) to navigate between various Outlook items. (To display the Folder List, select Folder List on the View menu.) Each of the items on the Folder List will help you organize your personal, school, and social events.

The following table describes the Outlook items on the Folder List and Outlook Bar.

Need Help?

Type: folder list in the Ask a Question box at the right end of the menu bar

Items on the Outlook Folder List and Outlook Bar

Folder List	Outlook Bar Icon	Description
Outlook Today	Outlook Today	A snapshot of your day including your upcoming calendar events, Tasks list, and a summary of your messages.
Calendar	Calendar	A daily, weekly, or monthly view of your scheduled appointments, meetings, events, and tasks.
Contacts	Contacts	An electronic address book in which you may enter names, addresses, phone numbers, and e-mail addresses.
Deleted Items	Deleted Items	Items that you deleted from the Inbox.
Drafts	Drafts	Items that you created and saved but have not yet sent.
Inbox	Inbox	A folder which allows you to read, compose, send, and store e-mail messages. New items appear in bold. Read items appear un-bolded. Important items will be flagged with an exclamation point.
Journal	Journal	A record of actions you select, displayed in a timeline view.
Notes	Notes	Electronic notes you use as reminders or other information for later use.
Outbox	Not on Outlook Bar	Items that you created and are waiting to be sent to your server.
Sent Items	Not on Outlook Bar	A copy of items sent from your Outbox.
Tasks	Tasks	An electronic to-do list.

In the next exercise, you will use the Outlook Bar and Folder List to navigate between several Outlook items.

Outlook®

Step Through It™

Exercise 2A: Explore the Outlook Bar and Folder List

1. Click Calendar on the Outlook Bar (see Figure 1.4). ***Note:*** Your screen will reflect today's date.

2. Click Inbox on the Outlook Bar.

3. On the View menu, select Folder List. The Folder List appears to the right of the Outlook Bar.

4. On the View menu, select Outlook Bar. The Outlook Bar is closed and the Folder List remains (see Figure 1.5).

5. Click each of the following folders in the Folder List in the order indicated and notice how the screen changes with each item: Outlook Today, Contacts, Tasks, Notes, Inbox.

Figure 1.4 Outlook's daily Calendar

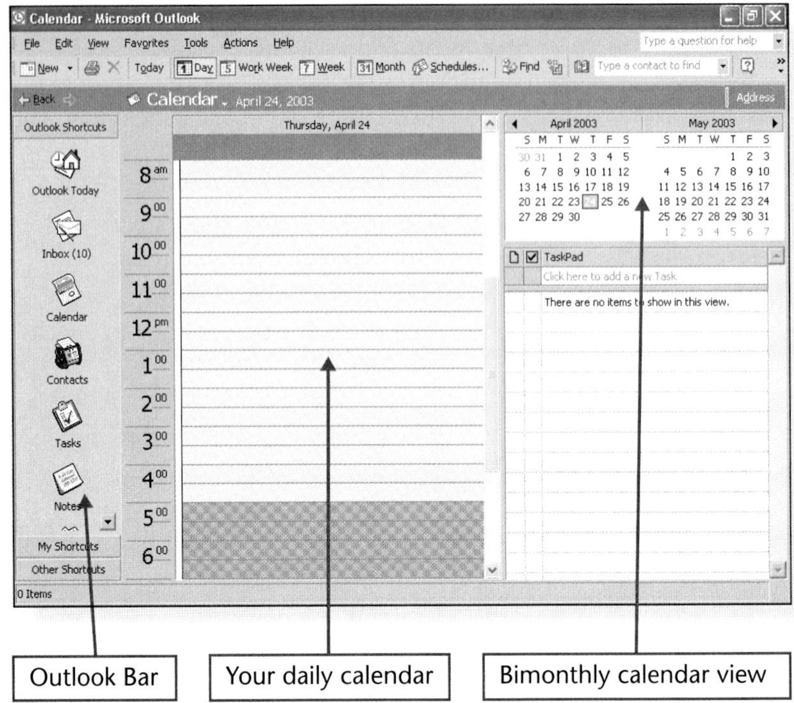

Figure 1.5 Outlook's Folder List

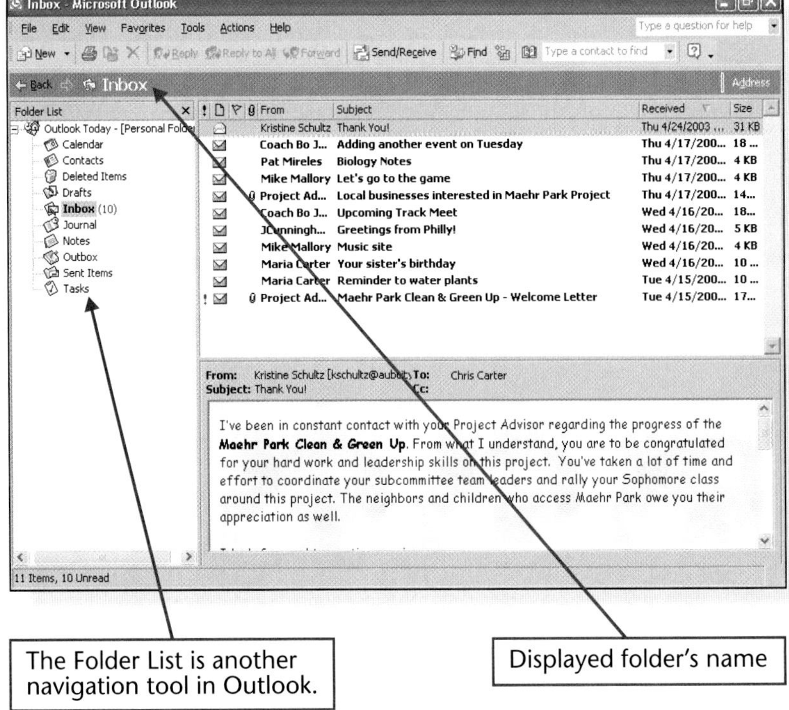

Outlook Views

You can easily navigate using the Outlook Bar, the Folder List, the links in Outlook Today, or the Go To feature. In addition to the many navigation choices, Outlook includes numerous **views**, or window displays, from which to choose.

When you click an item or a folder, Outlook will display your messages in a default view. For example, by default, messages are displayed in the Inbox chronologically by received date. Additionally, the Inbox will include the following default column headings on the Sort By bar: Importance icon, Message icon, Flag icon, Attachment icon, From, Subject, Received, and Size.

You can customize this view depending on your work style. For example, you may wish to see a preview of the messages in the Inbox or sort messages by sender, conversation topic, or other sort options, rather than by received date. You can also reduce or enlarge parts of the window to help you quickly locate information.

In the next exercise, you'll try a few different views.

Figure 1.6 Messages displayed with AutoPreview

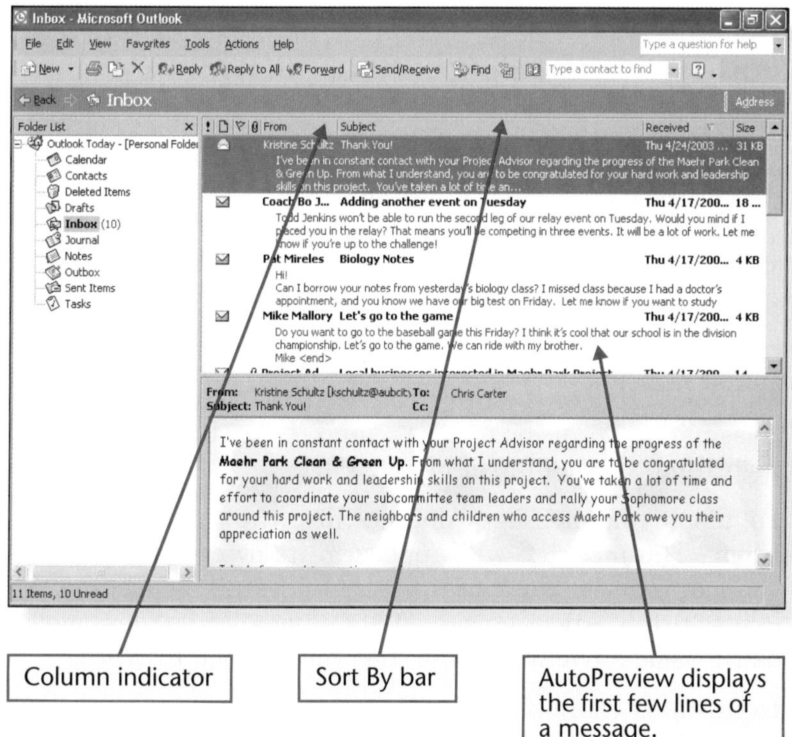

Step Through It™
Exercise 2B: Work with various views

1. In the Inbox, click From on the Sort By bar. Messages are sorted alphabetically in ascending order by sender. Click From again. Messages are now sorted in descending order.
2. Click Received. Messages are sorted chronologically in descending order by received date.
3. On the View menu, select AutoPreview (see Figure 1.6).

4 Point to the column indicator to the right of From on the Sort By bar. A double-sided arrow appears. Drag the column indicator to the right until the entire From column is visible (see Figure 1.7).

5 On the View menu, select AutoPreview. The AutoPreview is removed.

Figure 1.7 AutoPreview with *From* column widened

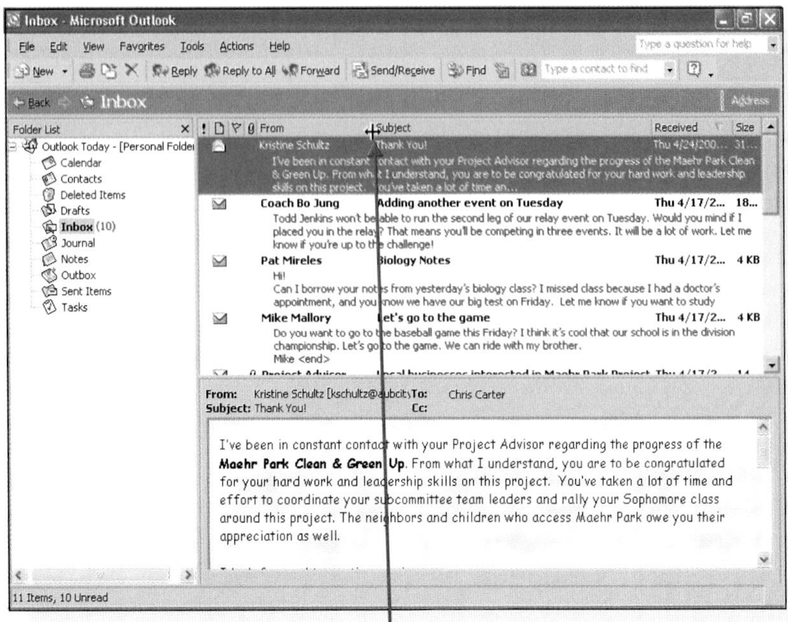

The double-headed arrow allows you to resize any column heading on the Sort By bar.

Microsoft Office Specialist OL2002 1.1, 1.2, 1.3

Exercise 3 Overview: Send and Receive Electronic Mail

Each time you log on to your computer and open Outlook, new messages will **download** from your e-mail server to the Inbox. You can also manually download your messages at any time by clicking Send/Receive on the Outlook toolbar. New messages appear in the Inbox in bold type with a closed envelope icon.

Display and Print a Message

As project leader, you are required to communicate with classmates, local businesses, and your Project Advisor regarding the cleanup of Maehr Park.

To display a message, double-click the message in the Inbox. The message will appear in its own window where you can read it. You can print the message by clicking the Print button. And, you can easily navigate in a message by using basic navigation tools that you learned in Word.

In this next exercise, you will open, read, and respond to an e-mail message sent to you from your Project Advisor.

Figure 1.8 Message displayed in the message window

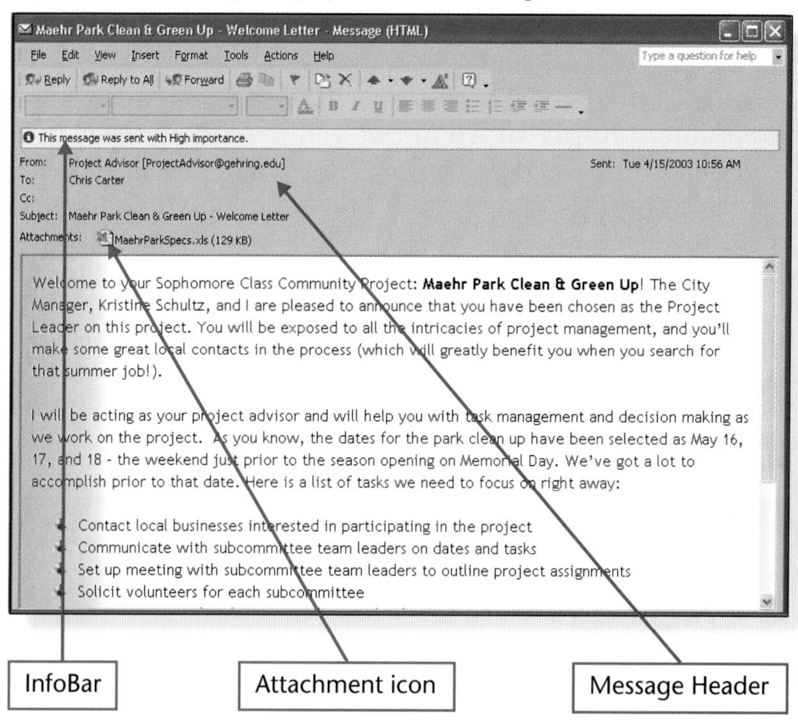

Step Through It™

Exercise 3A: Display and print a message and an attachment

1. Double-click the *Maehr Park Clean & Green Up – Welcome Letter* message in the Inbox. The message appears in its own window (see Figure 1.8). Verify that the Standard and Formatting toolbars are displayed.
2. Examine the Message Header and InfoBar.
3. Click Print.

Figure 1.9 Outlook opens the e-mail attachment in Excel

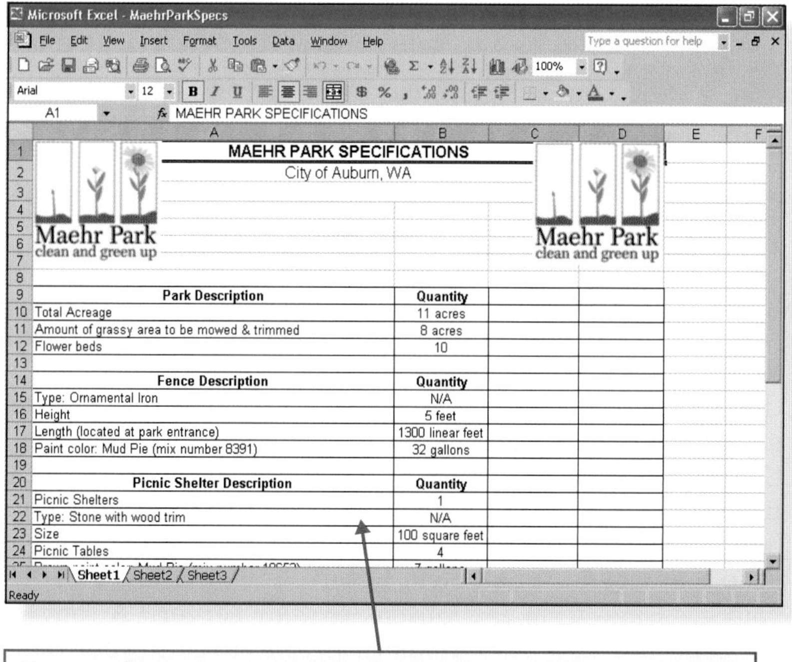

You can choose to open an attachment from within your message window or save the attachment to another location to open later.

4. Double-click the Excel worksheet attachment icon. Click *Open it* in the Opening Mail Attachment dialog box, and click OK. Outlook will launch Microsoft Excel and open the worksheet (see Figure 1.9). ***Note:*** Maximize the window, if necessary.
5. Preview the worksheet and save it as *xxx-MaehrParkSpec.xls* (replacing *xxx* with your initials).
6. Print and close the worksheet, and then exit Excel.

Message Replies

You have several options available for replying to messages: Reply, Reply to All, and Forward. **Reply** allows you to send a response to the message sender (the person listed on the *From* line). **Reply to All** allows you to send a response to everyone who received a copy of the original message (those listed on the *To, Cc*, and *From* lines). **Forward** allows you to send the message to anyone. With each of these options, a copy of the original message automatically appears in the message window. However, if an attachment was sent with the original message, it will only be included in a forwarded message.

Figure 1.10 Options for replying to messages

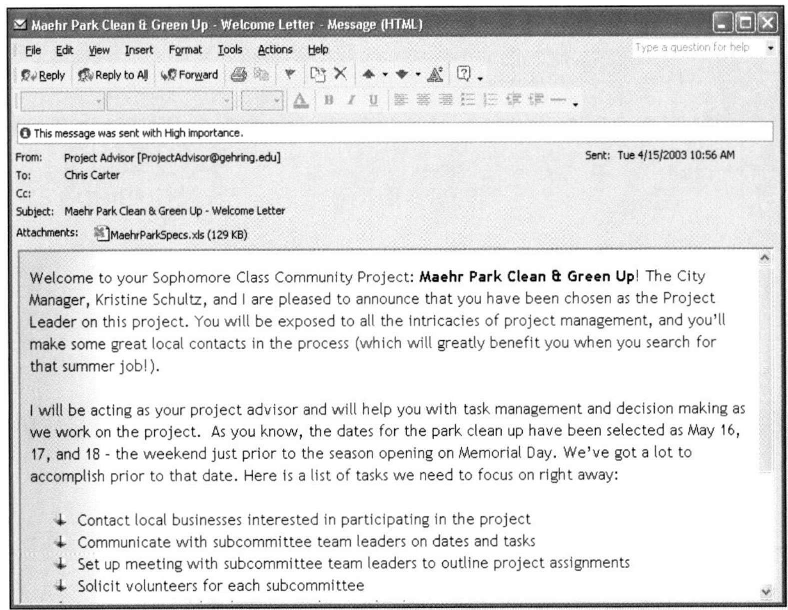

After typing a reply to your Project Advisor, you will send the message. You will know the message has been sent by the yellow InfoBar that appears across the top of your message header indicating the date and time of your reply. Completed messages wait in your Outbox until Outlook **uploads** (or transfers) them to your server, which will happen based on the variables defined on your computer. (You may need to click Send/Receive to manually transfer your message from the Outbox to your server.) A copy of the sent message will automatically be saved to your Sent Items folder. You will reply to the Project Advisor's e-mail in the following exercise.

The following table illustrates some of the commonly used buttons on the Standard toolbar.

Standard Toolbar

Button		Purpose
New	New Mail Message	Create a new message
Reply	Reply	Reply to a message
Reply to All	Reply to All	Reply to everyone on *To* and *Cc* lines
Forward	Forward	Forward a message
Send/Receive	Send/ Receive	Send and receive messages
Find	Find	Find a message

The following table illustrates some of the commonly used buttons on the Message toolbar.

Message Toolbar

Button		Purpose
Send	Send	Send a message
	Insert File	Insert a file to a message
!	Importance: High	Mark a message with high importance
	Importance: Low	Mark a message with low importance
Options	Options	Using message options

Outlook®

Step Through It™

Exercise 3B: Send a message reply

Outlook®

1. With the *Welcome Letter* message displayed, click Reply on the Standard toolbar. A new message window opens (see Figure 1.11).

2. Type the following in the message window: I'll be happy to meet with you tomorrow at noon. I'll come to your office.

Figure 1.11 Reply message window

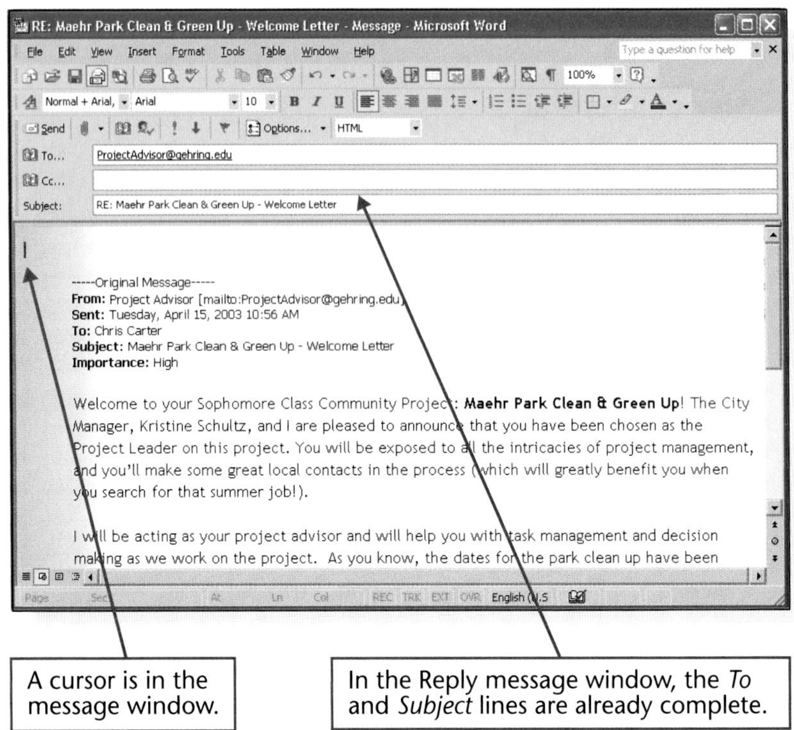

3. Add two blank lines and then type the following on separate lines: *Your Name, Project Leader* Maehr Park Clean & Green Up (***Note:*** Insert your name as the project leader.)

4. Click Send on the Message toolbar. The message has been sent as indicated on the InfoBar (see Figure 1.12). Close the message window.

Figure 1.12 InfoBar provides message information

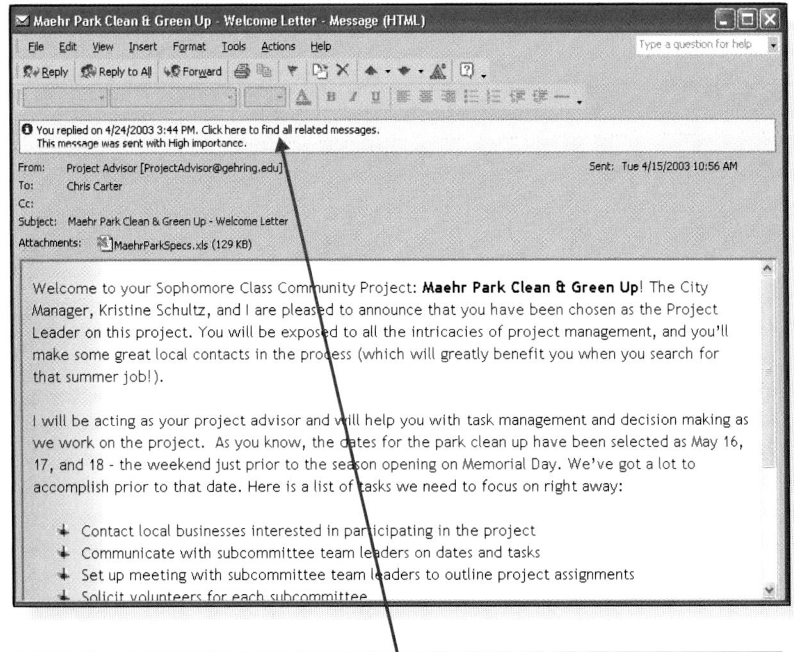

Customizing Your Messages

Outlook provides various options that allow you to customize the look of your messages. You can add personalized signatures and apply stationery themes to your messages.

You can save time and energy by creating a stored **signature** (stored information such as your name, title, and phone number) that will be automatically added to your next message. This will allow you to quickly customize information for different audiences.

If multiple users are on a computer, or if you are composing message to different audiences, you can create and store multiple signatures. You can then select different signatures from the **Signature Picker**, a list within Outlook where the signatures are stored. To switch from the default signature, right-click the signature in the message window and select the correct signature, or select E-mail Signature to create and store a new signature.

Type: signature

In the next exercise, you'll create a signature to use on all future *Maehr Park Clean & Green Up* project messages.

Outlook®

Figure 1.13 Mail Format dialog box

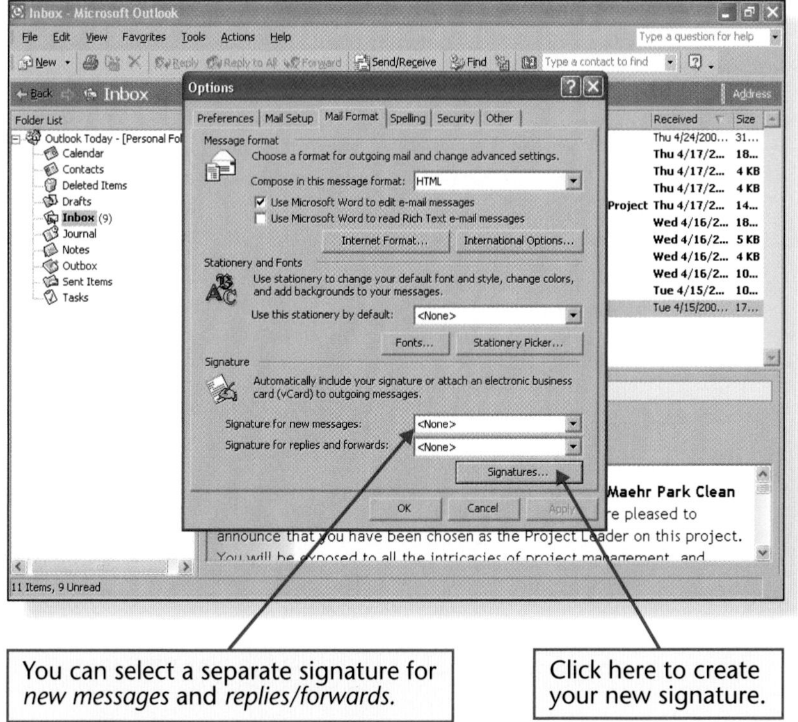

Step Through It™

Exercise 3C: Create a signature

1. On the Tools menu, select Options. On the Mail Format tab, click Signatures (see Figure 1.13), and click New.
2. Type Maehr Park Clean & Green Up as the name, and click Next.
3. Type the signature:
   Line 1: Maehr Park Clean & Green Up
   Line 2: Sophomore Class Community Project
   Line 3: *Your Name,* Project Leader

4. Select the first line of the signature. Use the Font and Paragraph buttons to format as follows: SnapITC font, 14 point, green color, align center. (***Note:*** If the font is not available, choose an alternative.)

5. Select the second and third lines of the signature. Format as follows: Arial font, 10 point, green color, align center (see Figure 1.14).

Figure 1.14 Edit Signature dialog box

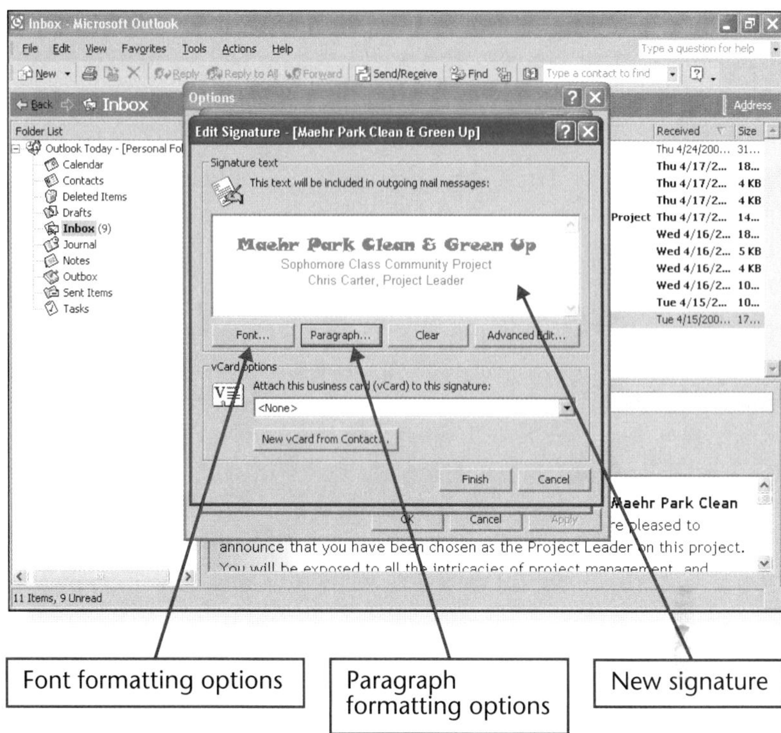

6. In the Edit Signature dialog box, click Finish. Then, click OK. Your new signature has been added to the *Signature for new messages* box. Click OK to close the Options dialog box.

7. Click New Mail Message New. Your new signature has automatically been added to your message (see Figure 1.15).

Figure 1.15 Maehr Park Clean & Green Up signature

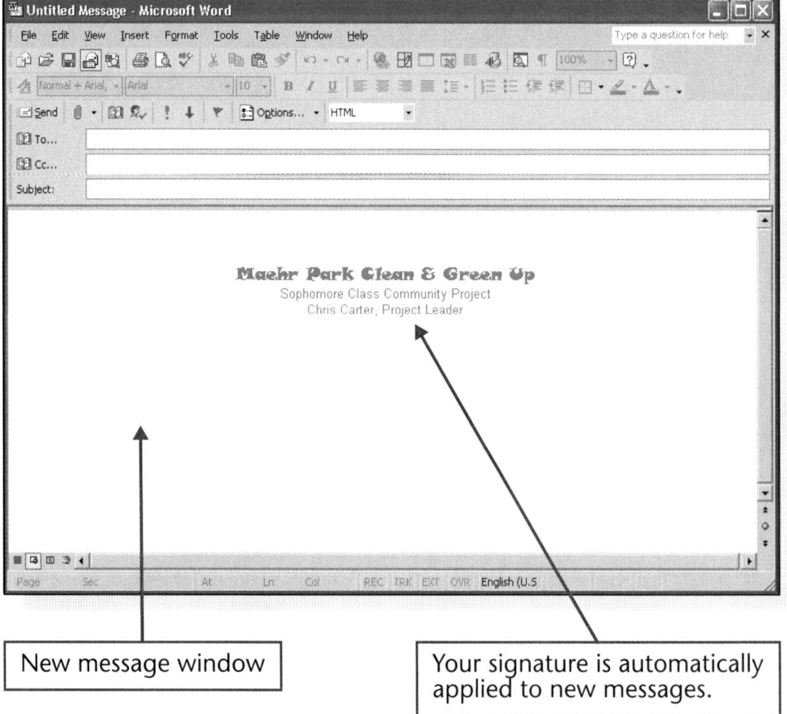

Compose a Message

When you compose an e-mail message, Outlook opens Microsoft Word as your default e-mail editor. This feature allows you to take advantage of all the tools Word has to offer, such as the Spelling and Grammar tool, formatting options, table features, and so on. When you open a new message window, or when you click Reply to respond to a message, the Word Standard and Formatting toolbars will automatically appear on your screen.

Figure 1.16 New message window in Word

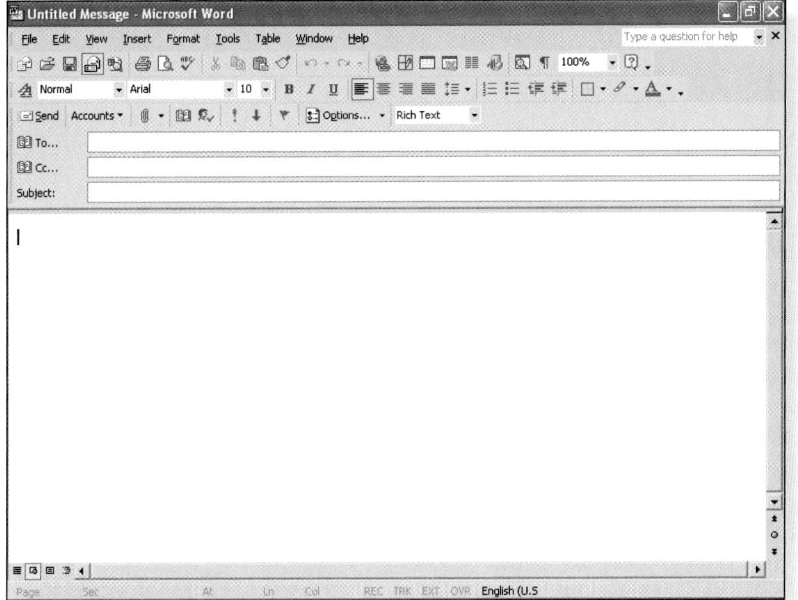

If you use HTML as your message format, you can add pizzazz to your messages by using stationery. **Stationery** will apply a set of design elements, such as fonts, bullets, background color, and images to your messages. You can apply one stationery theme to all outgoing messages or apply separate themes to individual messages as you compose them. You can choose from Outlook's stationery options or modify existing stationery options. You can also create new stationery or download stationery from the Web.

In the next exercise, you will compose a new message to your subcommittee team leaders to inform them of their project assignments. Then, you will add a stationery theme to the e-mail message.

Step Through It™

Exercise 3D: Compose a message

1. On the *To* line of the open new message, type the following addresses exactly (unless your teacher provides other addresses): **Amaghathe@gehring.edu; MJpalmisano@gehring.edu; Jsamuels@gehring.edu; Hkemper@gehring.edu.**

2. On the *Cc* line, enter the e-mail address of your Project Advisor. (See Figure 1.17.)

Figure 1.17 New Message window

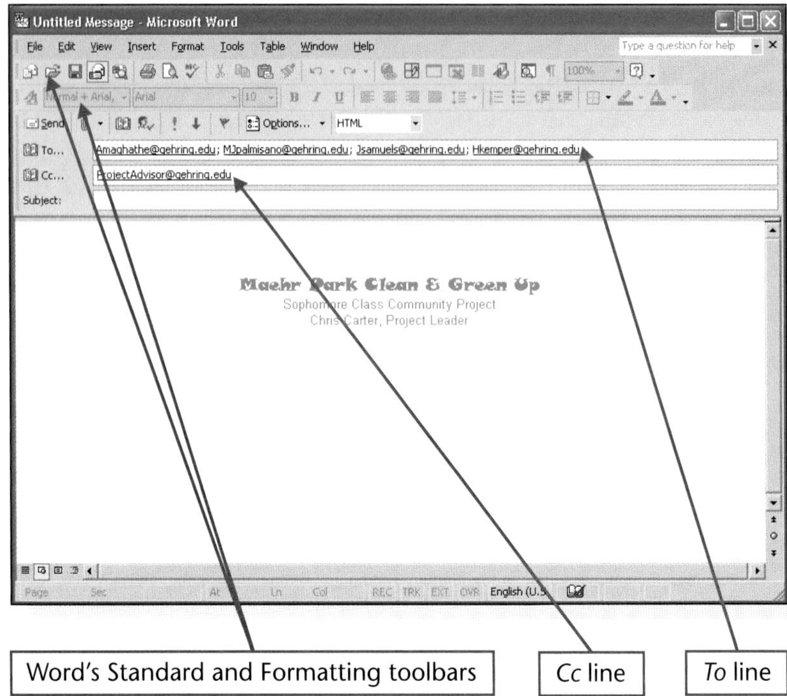

3. On the *Subject* line, type the following: **Maehr Park Clean & Green Up - Subcommittee Assignments**.

4. Type the content displayed in Figure 1.18 in the message window–positioned above the signature. Use Word's Table feature to enter the information in the table.

Figure 1.18 E-mail message

Hello Subcommittee Team Leaders

Congratulations! You have been chosen to act as a team leader on our Sophomore class community project: Maehr Park Clean & Green Up. An attachment is included to give more detail about the park. Please see your subcommittee assignment below.

Maehr Park Clean & Green Up - Subcommittee Assignments		
Team Leader	Subcommittee Name	Subcommittee Duties
Azmi Maghathe	Mowing	Mowing and flower bed preparation
Mary Jane Palmisano	Landscaping	Landscaping (planting flowers and bushes, mulching beds)
Jermaine Samuels	Painting/power washing	Power washing of playground equipment and picnic shelter, painting of picnic shelter, fences, and playground equipment
Heather Kemper	Waste removal	Trash pickup and debris removal

We have only one month to plan the park clean up, and there is still a lot to do. Let's plan to meet during lunch on Thursdays to talk about what needs to be done. Our advisor has volunteered to buy pizza! Please let me know if you can make it to our first meeting this Thursday.

Figure 1.19 Stationery theme applied to composed message

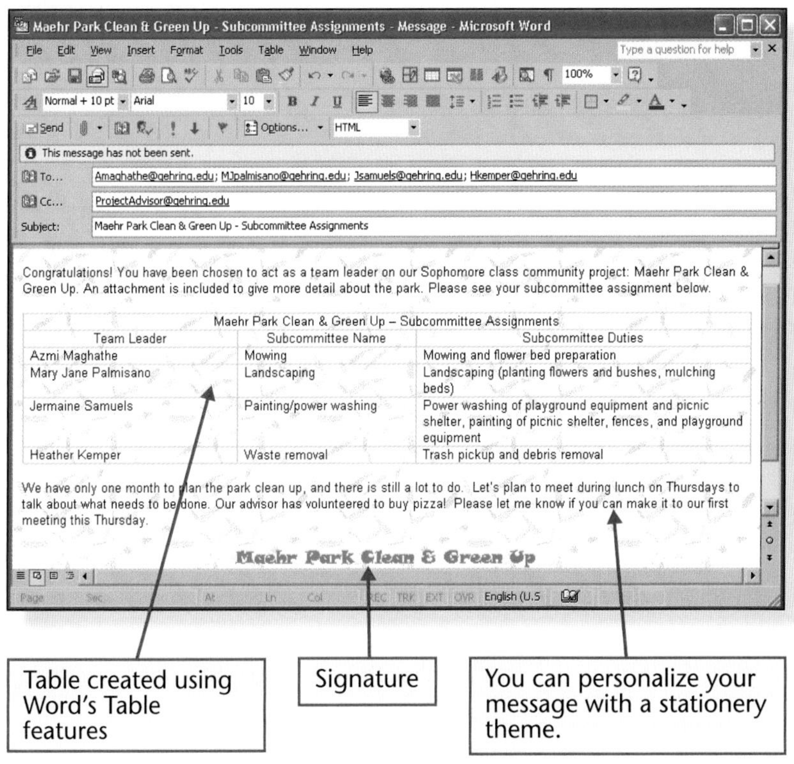

5. Proofread your message and correct any errors.
6. Select Theme on the Word Format menu.
7. Explore several theme choices, and then click Citrus Punch. Click OK to apply a stationery theme to your document (see Figure 1.19).

Outlook®

Insert an Attachment

Outlook allows you to include **attachments** (or files) with your messages. You can send attachments in any file format, such as Word, Excel, PowerPoint, Access, or other Outlook items. The only limitations are the size of the attachment and the ability of the receiver to open the file. In order for the recipient to open the file attachment, the receipient must have the correct version of the software that was used to create the file. Also, since large or multiple files take a long time to download, it is best not to send multiple files in one message. Before forwarding an attachment, you can make changes to it; however, the original file stays intact.

Type: attachment

To insert an attachment, simply click the Insert File button. Then, in the Insert File dialog box, navigate to and select the file you want to attach to your message and click Insert. You will then see an Attachment line in the message header along with the file icon for the attached file. If you accidentally attach the wrong file to a message, simply select the attachment and press Delete.

In the next exercise, you will add an attachment to your message to each subcommittee team leader.

Step Through It™

Exercise 3E: Insert an attachment

1 With the message still open, click Insert File .

2 Navigate to *xxx-MaehrParkSpecs.xls* in your *Lesson 1* folder, select it, and click Insert. Outlook will automatically add an Attachment line and the file icon in the message header (see Figure 1.20).

3 Double-click the attachment. Select Open it, and click OK to open the Excel worksheet.

Figure 1.20 Adding a file attachment to a document

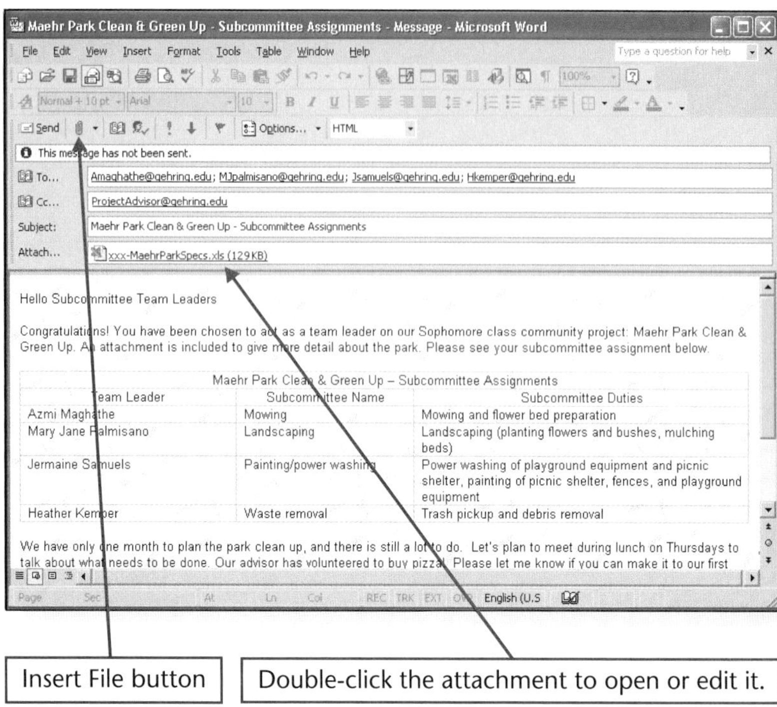

4 In cell A3, type today's date (see Figure 1.21).

5 Save the document and close Excel. The message window reappears, and the edited file is still attached.

Figure 1.21 Attachment opened in Excel

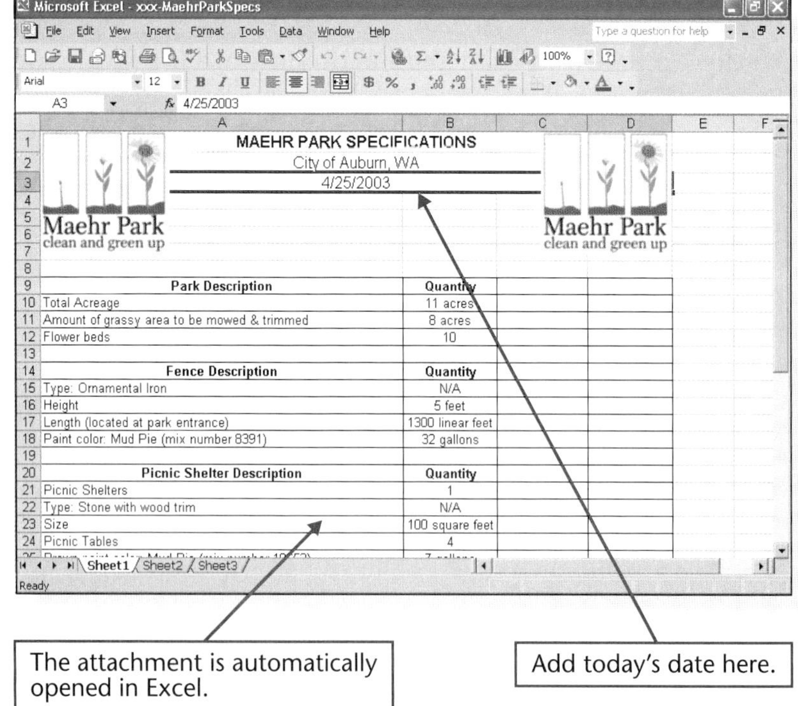

Send a Message

You are now ready to send your message. During the previous exercises you accomplished these steps: you created a signature to be automatically applied to your new messages, you entered the recipient's names and the message subject in the message header, you composed your message and read through it for grammatical and spelling errors, you applied a stationery theme, and you attached a file to send with your message. The only step left is to actually send your message.

Depending on how Outlook is set up on your computer, you may need to click Send in your message window and then Send/Receive on your Outlook toolbar. When you click Send, Outlook will either automatically upload the message to your server, or it will temporarily store the message in your Outbox until the next scheduled Send/Receive, depending on your settings.

In the next exercise, you'll send the e-mail message to the subcommittee team leaders and then look at the Sent Items folder to see a copy of the saved message.

Figure 1.22 Sent Items folder

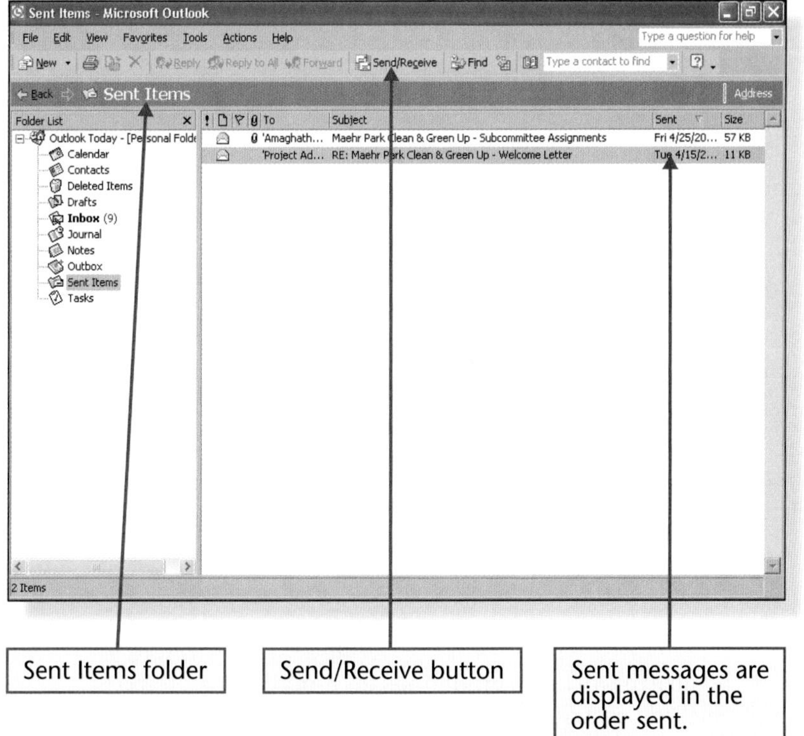

Step Through It™
Exercise 3F: Send a message

1. Click Send on the Message toolbar.
2. If necessary, click Send/Receive Send/Receive to upload the message to your server. (***Note:*** If the Outbox is empty, your message has been sent.)
3. Click the Sent Items folder. You will see the two messages you sent during Exercises 3B and 3F (see Figure 1.22). Return to the Inbox.

Outlook®

Business Connections

Netiquette, Nethics, Privacy, and the Law

E-mail rules exist to create a safe environment for everyone using e-mail. Some rules are implied while others are written policies established for the workplace or schools. State and federal agencies also establish e-mail laws.

Netiquette (e-mail etiquette) and **nethics** (e-mail ethics) are ways of communicating via e-mail using clear language, being respectful and sensitive to possible misinterpretations, and applying the "golden rule"—e-mail others as you would like to be e-mailed. To ensure that you are *netiquette* and *nethics* savvy in your e-mail messages, follow these guidelines for each e-mail message:

- Always include a short, descriptive subject.
- Keep the message brief.
- Never use all uppercase letters; it implies yelling and is difficult to read.
- Use correct spelling and grammar.
- Use a signature.
- Be courteous in the tone of your message.
- Respect others' privacy.
- Forward personal information *only* if you have the sender's approval.
- Never gossip.
- Use emoticons, if desired, where appropriate (see the Emoticons table).
- Know your school and employer's (if you are working) guidelines for e-mail usage on the premises, which may include restrictions.

Emoticons

:)	smiley face	:*	kissing face
;)	winking face	:|	indifferent face
:(	unhappy face	:o	shocked face
:D	laughing face	:O	yelling face

Spam, which is like electronic junk mail, is an unsolicited e-mail message sent to many recipients at one time, or simultaneously posted to several newsgroups. Sending spam is a misuse of the Internet. On March 14, 2001, Congress signed the **Anti-Spamming Act of 2001** to prohibit unsolicited e-mail.

Another law, the **Netizens Protection Act of 1997**, makes it illegal to send an unsolicited advertisement to an e-mail address without providing a date and time of the message, the name of the sender, and the sender's return e-mail address. If you receive unwanted or unsolicited e-mail, don't respond to it — just delete the message. Responding to the message may add your name and e-mail address to a distribution list. New software programs (such as Mailshell.com) are now available to protect you from unwanted e-mail.

CRITICAL THINKING

1. **Assess E-mail Policy** Research your school's e-mail policy. Are there restrictions to using e-mail at your school? Do you agree with the school's policy? Why or why not?
2. **Comparing Software Options** With your teacher's permission, use the Internet to research the various software packages and costs available to help block spam on your computer. What are the benefits to using such a package?

Microsoft Office Specialist OL2002 1.4

Exercise 4 Overview: Customize Views

Earlier in this lesson, you practiced changing your Outlook views by clicking on the Sort By bar. You can change how your messages are displayed by clicking on any column heading. Outlook provides other methods for customizing your views to simplify your message management.

Suppose you are involved in several school groups, such as the Prom committee, a foreign language club, or a sports team, in addition to the *Maehr Park Clean & Green Up* project. If you receive several messages from each group weekly, those messages, along with messages from friends and family, would add up quickly.

Learn to organize your messages in order to conveniently locate the information you need. Outlook allows you to customize your view based on what you think is important. In the next exercise, you'll examine several different views.

Step Through It™

Exercise 4: Customize your Inbox

1. Click Inbox, if necessary. Then, on the View menu, select Current View and select Unread Messages. (***Note:*** If you have read all of your messages, the Inbox will appear empty.)

2. On the View menu, select Current View and then select By Sender. Click the plus sign next to Coach Bo Jung. Two messages will be displayed (see Figure 1.23).

Figure 1.23 View Sorted by Sender

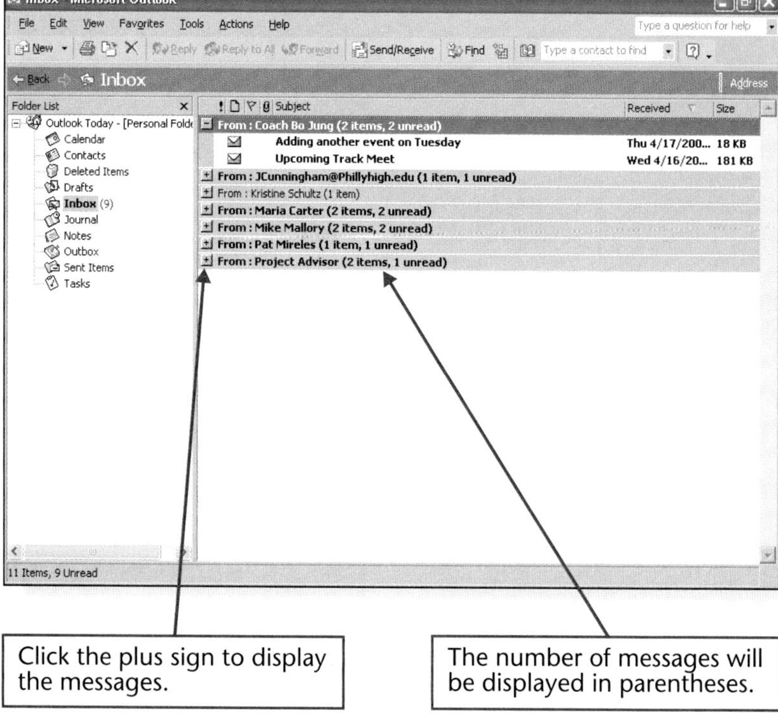

APPLY IT! After finishing Exercises 1-4, you may test your skills by completing Apply It! Guided Activity 1, Reply to a Message and Change a View.

Figure 1.24 *Ways to Organize Inbox* window pane

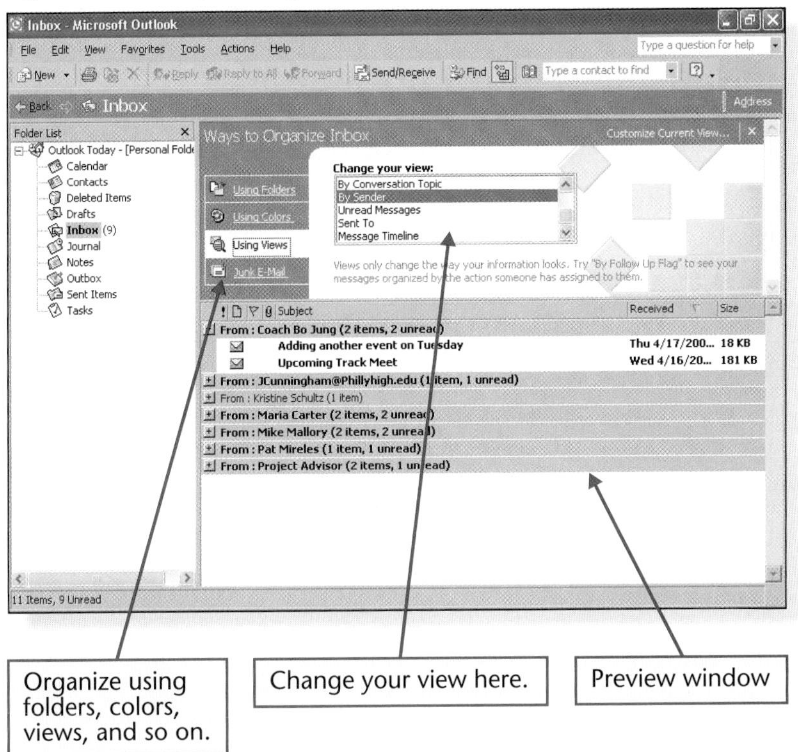

Organize using folders, colors, views, and so on.
Change your view here.
Preview window

3. On the Tools menu, select Organize. Click the Using Views link on the left side of the *Ways to Organize Inbox* window pane (see Figure 1.24).

4. Preview each of the views. Select Messages and close the *Ways to Organize Inbox* window pane.

Figure 1.25 View Summary dialog box

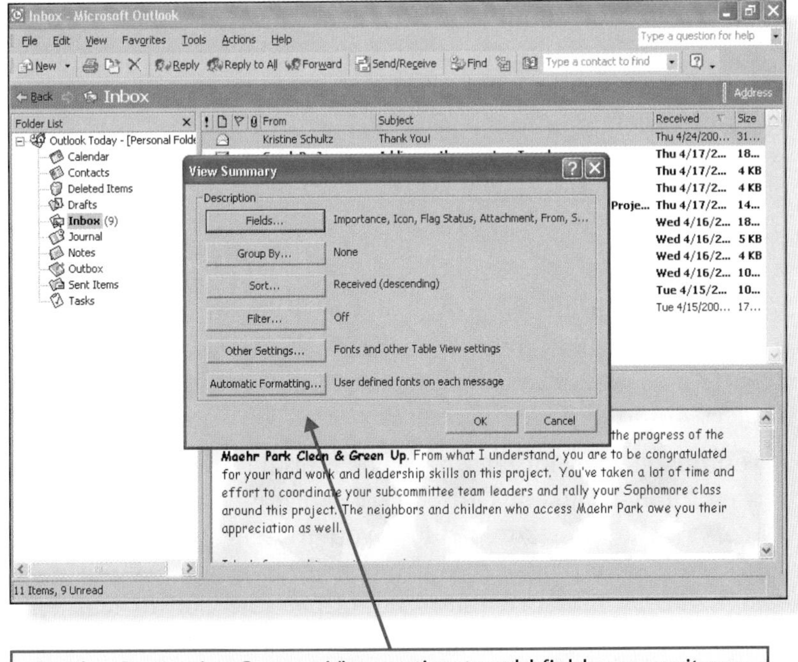

Use the Customize Current View option to add fields, group items, sort or filter messages, and format the look of your window.

5. On the View menu, select Current View and then select Customize Current View (see Figure 1.25).

6. Click Fields to see a list of all available fields in the current Outlook view. In the *Show these fields in this order box*, click and drag *From* to the top of the list, using the red arrows as guides. Click OK to close the Show Fields dialog box.

7. Click Other Settings. Under Column Headings, click Font. Change the *Column heading* font to System and click OK.

8. Change the *Grid Line Style* to Solid and *Grid Line Color* to lime green. Click OK.

9. Click OK to close the dialog box. Examine your changes (see Figure 1.26).

10. To reset the column heading order, drag *From* on the Sort By bar and position the red arrows to the left of *Subject*.

Figure 1.26 Inbox with customized view

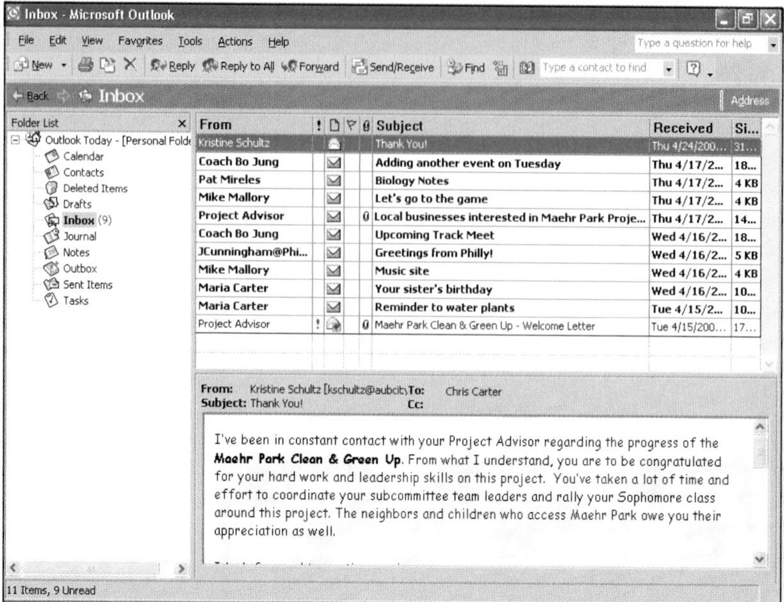

Microsoft Office Specialist OL2002 3.1, 3.2, 3.4

Exercise 5 Overview:
Organize and Locate Messages

After you receive and read e-mail messages, you'll want to keep or delete them. If you keep messages for future reference, you should organize them into folders and keep your general Inbox folder for newly received messages. For example, you can create a folder to store all messages related to the *Maehr Park Clean & Green Up* project and delete unimportant messages.

Another way to organize your messages is to assign categories. A **category** is a keyword or phrase that enables you to find, sort, filter, or group items. Assigning a category is like giving a message a code—messages from friends would be coded *friend*, messages from others working on the Maehr Park Project would be coded *Maehr Park Project*, and so on.

Type: category

If you misplace or forget where you stored a message, you can search for it by using Outlook's **Find** and **Advanced Find** features. These features allow you to search for messages containing a word or phrase, from or to a specific person, or by assigned categories, read/unread, importance, or attachment. In the next few exercises, you'll create some folders for the Maehr Park Project, then move messages, assign categories, and search for messages using Find and Advanced Find.

Figure 1.27 Create New Folder dialog box

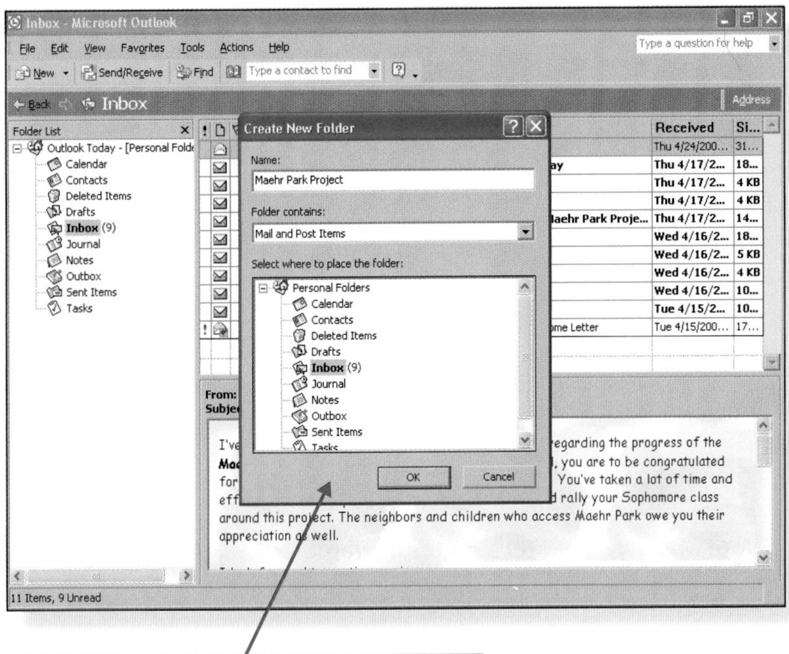

Use the Create New Folder dialog box to add new folders to your list.

Step Through It™

Exercise 5A: Move messages between folders

1. Right-click the Inbox folder and select New Folder.
2. In the Name box, type Maehr Park Project and click OK (see Figure 1.27).
3. Select and drag the two messages from your Project Advisor to the new folder.
4. Open the *Maehr Park Project* folder. The two messages are now located in the new folder.

Figure 1.28 Categories dialog box

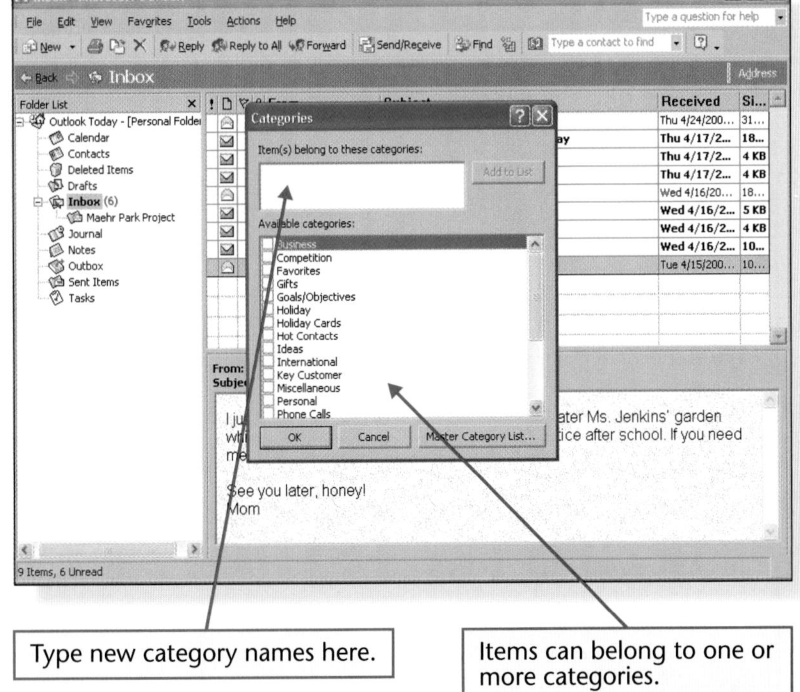

Type new category names here.
Items can belong to one or more categories.

Step Through It™

Exercise 5B: Assign categories to messages

1. Click Inbox, right-click the *Reminder to Water Plants* message from Maria Carter, and click Categories on the shortcut menu (see Figure 1.28).
2. Assign the message from Maria Carter to *Personal*. Click OK.

Outlook®

APPLY IT!

After finishing Exercises 5A-5C, you may test your skills by completing Apply It! Guided Activity 2, Search for, Categorize, and Move Messages.

3. Using Table 1.1, continue to assign categories to the remaining items in the folders. (***Note:*** To create a new category, type the category name in the box at the top of the Categories dialog box, and then click Add to List.)

Table 1.1 Assign categories to your messages

From	Subject	Category
Coach Bo Jung	Adding another event on Tuesday	Track
Coach Bo Jung	Upcoming Track Meet	Track
J Cunningham	Greetings from Philly	Friends
Kristine Schultz	Thank You!	Maehr Park Project
Maria Carter	Your sister's birthday	Personal
Mike Mallory	Music site	Friends
Mike Mallory	Let's go to the game	Friends
Pat Mireles	Biology Notes	School/ Homework
Project Advisor	Local businesses interested in Maehr Park Project	Maehr Park Project
Project Advisor	Maehr Park Clean & Green Up – Welcome Letter	Maehr Park Project

Step Through It™

Exercise 5C: Search for messages

1. Click Inbox. Click Find Find.
2. To search for messages related to Maehr Park Project tasks, type task in the *Look for* Look for: box.
3. Click the Search In down arrow Search In ▾. Click *Mail I Received* and click Find Now Find Now (see Figure 1.29).
4. Review the found messages, and then click Clear Clear.

Figure 1.29 Searching messages for the word *task*

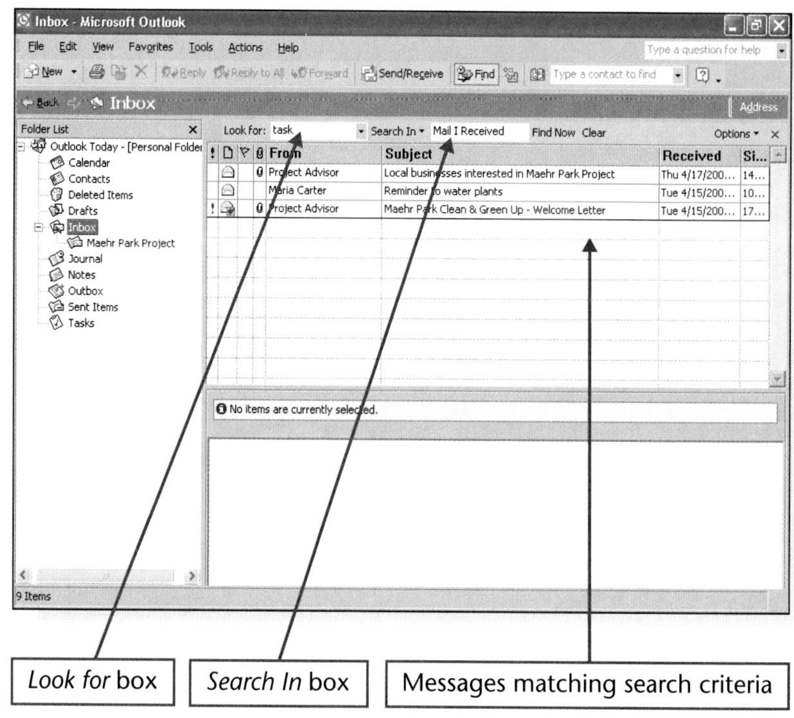

Figure 1.30 Using the Advanced Find feature

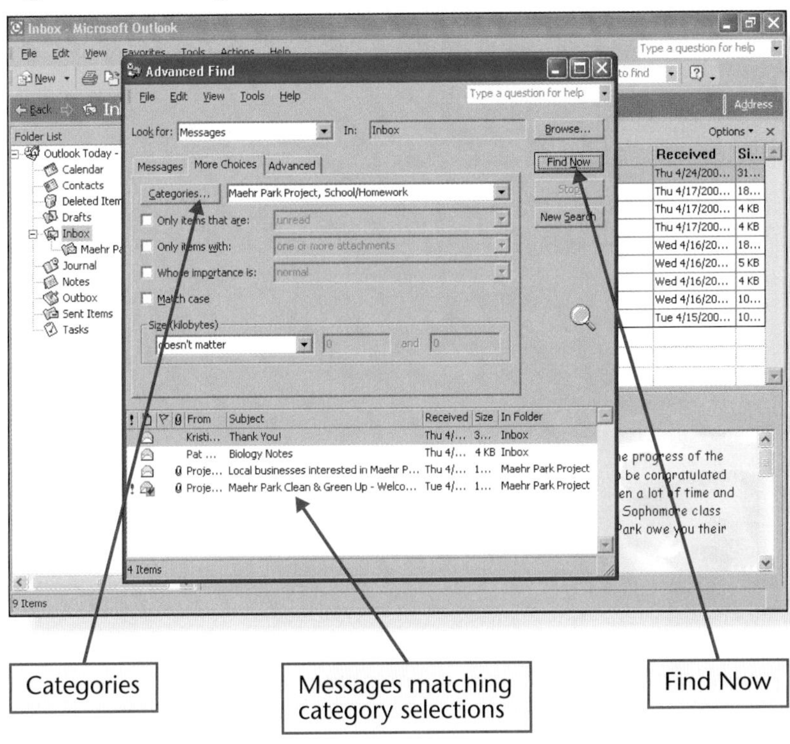

5 On the Find bar, click Options. Click Advanced Find.

6 Click the More Choices tab, and then click Categories. Select the *Maehr Park Project* and *School/Homework* categories, and click OK.

7 Click Find Now. All messages that match your category selections are listed (see Figure 1.30). Close the Advanced Find window and close the Find bar.

Outlook®

Exercise 6 Overview:
Modify Message Settings and Delivery Options

Microsoft Office Specialist OL2002 3.5

Outlook provides message settings and delivery options to help you better manage your messages. Two convenient message settings are the importance levels and sensitivity levels of outgoing messages. The **Importance level** indicates the urgency of the message. High importance is indicated with a red exclamation point in the Importance column. Normal importance contains no icon, and Low importance is indicated with a blue downward arrow. The importance level helps recipients know how quickly they must act on a received message. **Sensitivity level** options, which include Normal, Personal, Private, or Confidential, indicate the sensitivity of the message content. A note such as "Please treat this as private" will appear on the InfoBar of the sent message.

Delivery options provide additional convenience features that you can attach to individual messages.

In the next exercise, you'll create a new message and practice setting the Importance level and delivery options.

Type: importance

Step Through It™

Exercise 6: Modify message settings and delivery options

Outlook®

1. In Windows Explorer, open the data file *Maehr Park Clean & Green Up-Schedule of Events.msg*.

2. Include the following information in the message header (see Figure 1.31):
   To:
   Amaghathe@gehring.edu;
   MJpalmisano@gehring.edu;
   Jsamuels@gehring.edu;
   Hkemper@gehring.edu
   Cc:
   YourName@YourSchool;
   ProjectAdvisor@YourSchool

3. Click Options .

4. In the Message settings section, click the Importance down arrow and click High (see Figure 1.32).

5. In the Delivery options section, click Browse. If necessary, expand the folders. Select the *Maehr Park Project* folder, click OK, and close the Message Options dialog box. Notice the Importance: High button ! is active.

Figure 1.31 Modifying a message

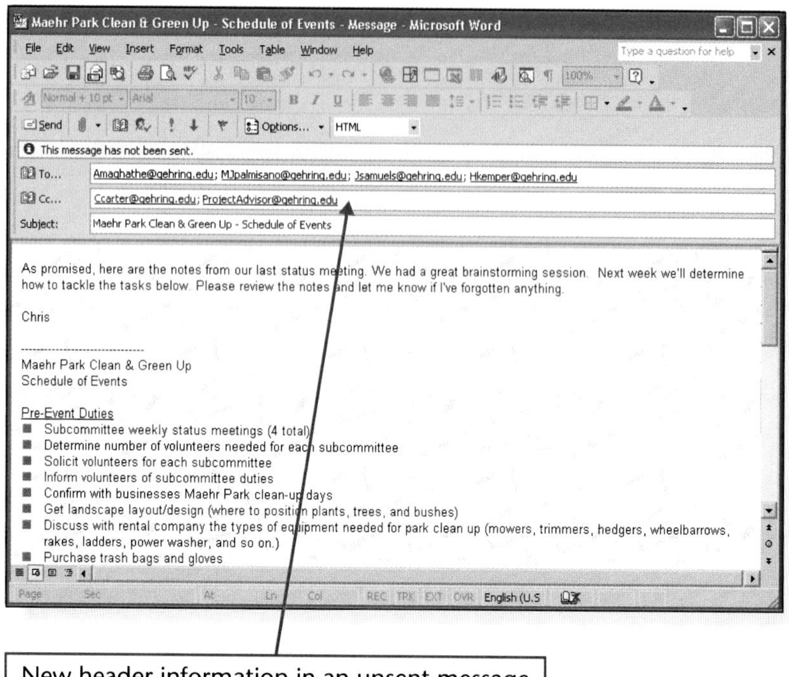

Figure 1.32 The Message Options dialog box

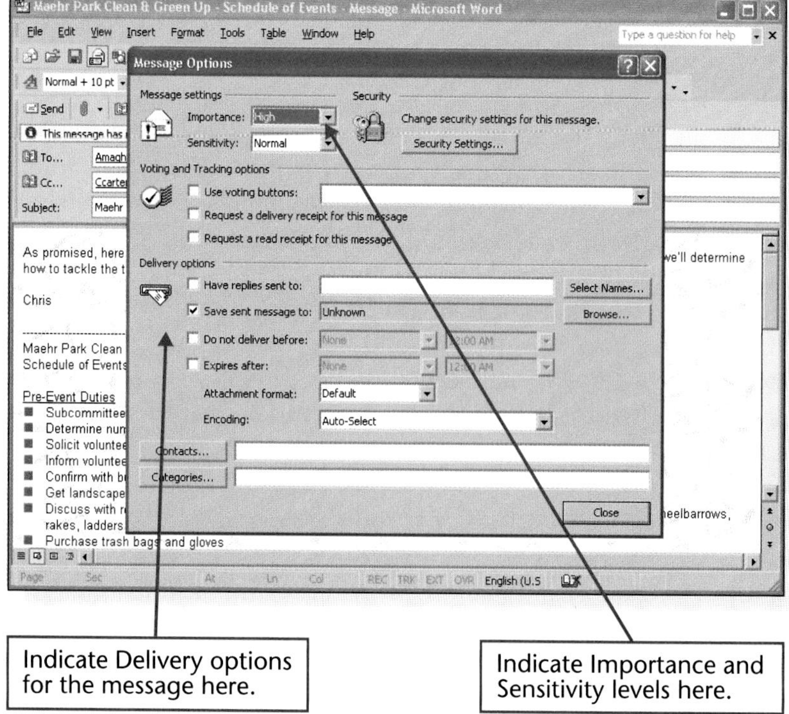

Figure 1.33 A new message with different settings

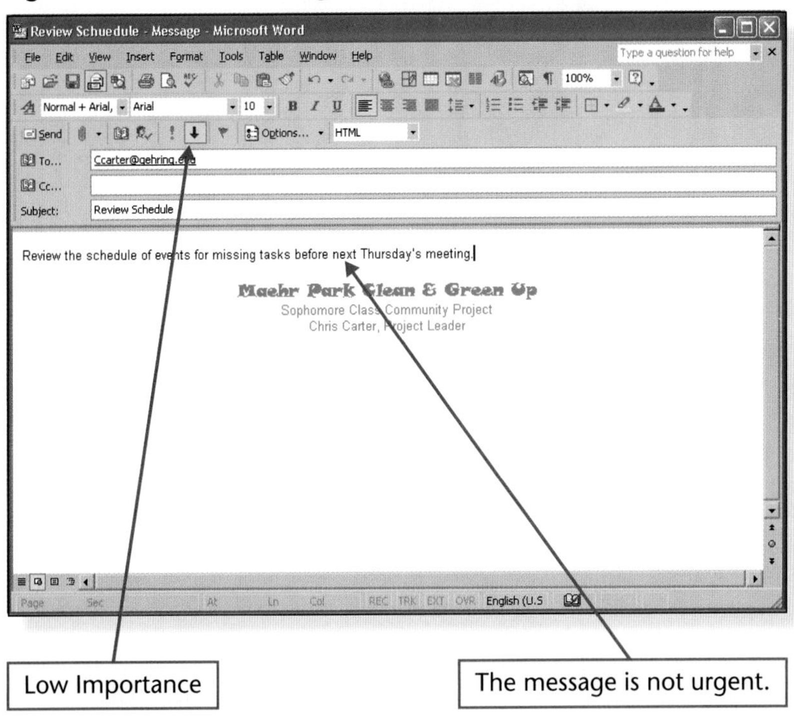

6 Click Send to send the message.

7 Create a new message, using the following information (see Figure 1.33):
To: *Your Name*
Subject: Review Schedule
Message: Review the schedule of events for missing tasks before next Thursday's meeting.
Message Settings: Importance - Low
Delivery Options: Save sent messages to *Maehr Park Project* folder.

Outlook®

Figure 1.34 *Maehr Park Project* folder

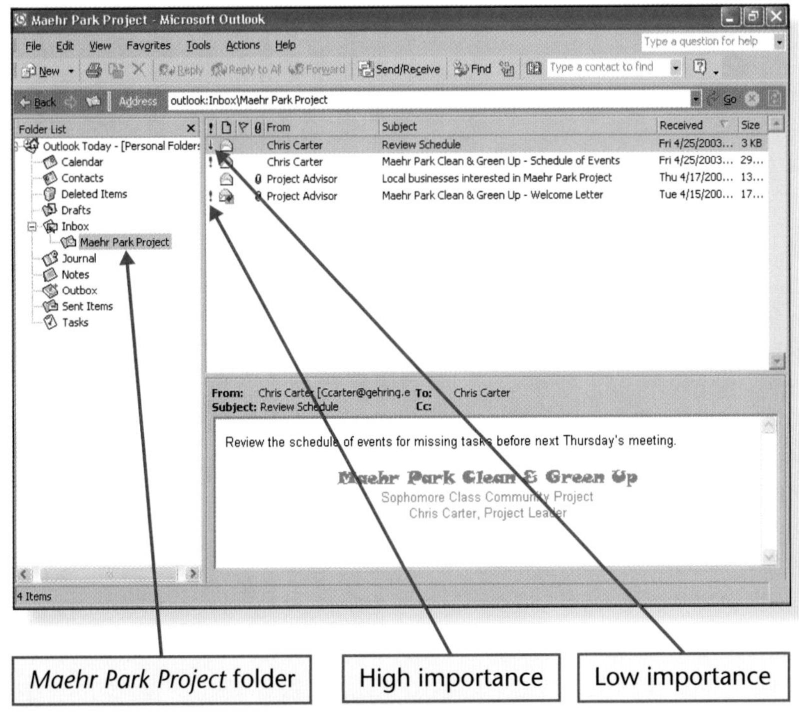

8 Send the message. Then, click Send/Receive. Click the *Maehr Park Project* folder to see the copies of the sent messages (see Figure 1.34).

9 Click Inbox. Delete the received copies of the *Maehr Park Clean & Green Up – Schedule of Events* and *Review Schedule* messages by selecting each message and clicking Delete. (If necessary, click Send/Receive to download the messages.)

Career Corner

Wired America

Everywhere you look, there's someone on a cell. Advances in telecommunications and more affordable options are radically changing how many people do their jobs—especially those jobs that traditionally require people to be "out of the office."

Take the real estate broker or agent for example. Helping people buy and sell property involves a lot of phone calls, appointments, and travel. You can imagine how laptops, cell phones, and PDAs—with software like Outlook on them—make this work easier. How about real estate listings posted on the Web (with digital photos)? Or software that allows a sale to be tracked in real time on a secure, personal Web site?

Real estate is a good career for people who like working on their own. Brokers and agents must be high school graduates, be at least 18 years old, and pass a written test. They may also need to take a brief class on real estate topics.

Do you like to shop and travel? Buyers choose the products a store will carry, often traveling extensively, sometimes to foreign countries, to visit trade shows and wholesalers. They also surf the Net and scour catalogs to find the products at the lowest prices. And, of course, they must communicate immediately with "the home office" in order to get the product to the marketplace before their competition does!

Buyers can advance to a variety of managerial positions and typically earn from $25,000 to $80,000. For this job and many other jobs in retail, hard work, sales ability, and enthusiasm can take you far, fast.

A part-time job at a retail store is a good way to learn about working in sales. Check into it to see if it's right for you. And don't forget your laptop, PDA, and cell phone!

CRITICAL THINKING

1. Examine the pros, cons, and costs (locally, nationally, and internationally) of using telecommunications tools such as e-mail, cell phones, pagers, and PDAs.
2. Shadow someone who works in one of the career areas described above. Find out how this person uses computers and telecommunications technology. Use Outlook to send an e-mail to your teacher describing what you learned.

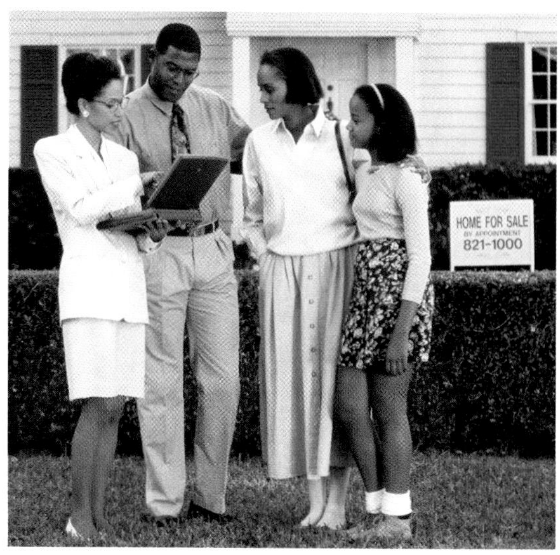

Exercise 7 Overview: Archive and Save Messages

Microsoft Office Specialist OL2002 3.3, 3.5

Archiving messages allows you to move messages to an alternate location (your hard drive or another drive on your network) for storage while still being able to access the messages from Outlook. Outlook will **AutoArchive** old messages after a set number of days by default. However, you can also manually archive your messages by setting options in the Archive dialog box (see Figure 1.35).

Figure 1.35 Archive dialog box

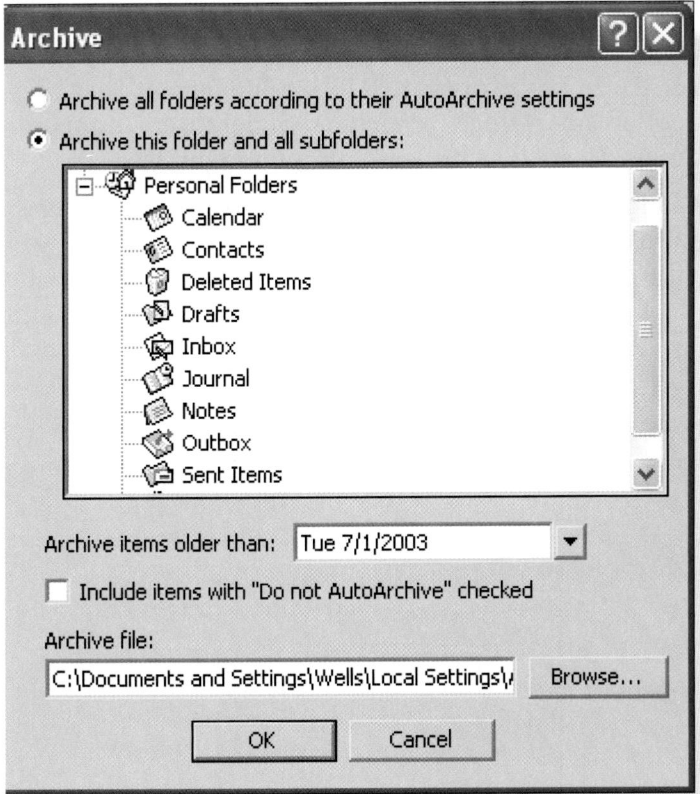

When you archive a message, Outlook will automatically create an Archive folder and will copy the archived messages along with any subfolders to your Folder List. Then, when you need to access an archived message, you can search your Archive folders.

With Outlook, you can also save messages to your hard drive in several file formats. The most used formats are Text Only, HTML, or Outlook Rich Text.

Text Only format, a format that all e-mail programs understand, will save your message content but will not retain the message formatting. Files saved as Text Only can be viewed in Microsoft Word or Notepad and will consume the least amount of space because the message content has no formatting codes.

HTML format (Hypertext Markup Language), the same language used to create Web pages, will save the message content as well as message formatting (such as fonts, numbering, bullets, alignment, and signatures) and can be viewed using your Web browser.

Outlook Rich Text format (RTF), a file format that only certain Microsoft Office programs understand, supports text formatting such as bullets and alignment.

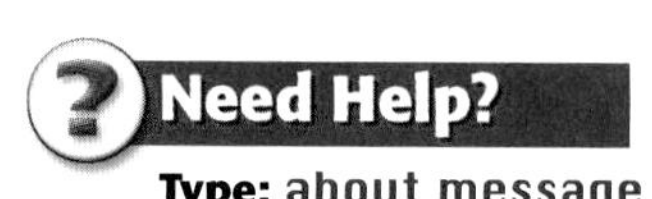

Type: about message formats

In the following exercises, you'll practice manually archiving messages and saving messages as both text files and HTML files.

Step Through It™

Exercise 7A: Archive messages

1. In the *Maehr Park Project* folder, note the received date for the *Welcome Letter*.
2. On the File menu, select Archive and click Inbox.
3. Click the *Archive items older than* down arrow, and select the day ***after*** the date you received the *Welcome Letter* (see Figure 1.36). Click OK to run the archive process. Then, note the new folder called Archive Folders in the Folder List.

Figure 1.36 Archive dialog box

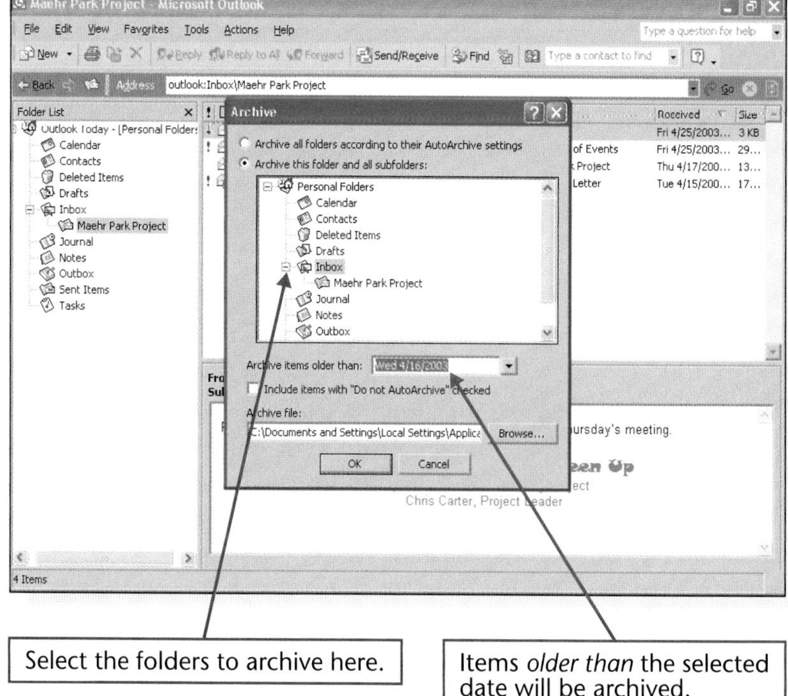

Figure 1.37 Saving a message as an HTML file

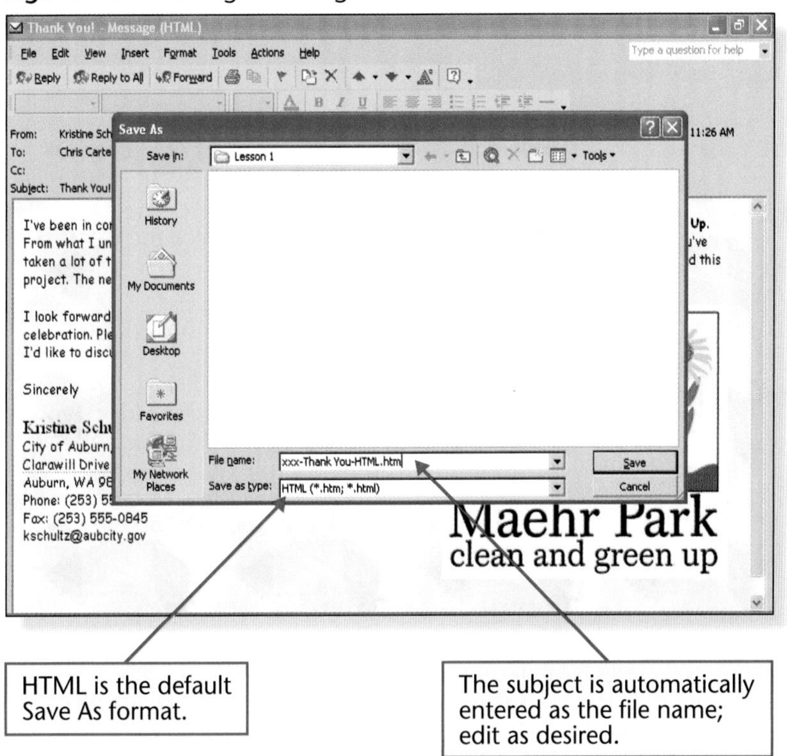

Figure 1.38 Saving a message as a text file

Step Through It™

Exercise 7B: Save messages as text and HTML files

1. Read the *Thank You!* message in the Inbox. On the File menu, select Save As.
2. Save the file as *xxx-Thank You-HTML.htm* (see Figure 1.37).
3. Select Save As again. Change the save as file type to *Text Only* and save the file as *xxx-Thank You-Text Only.txt* (see Figure 1.38).
4. Close the message.

Procedure Summary

Open and Close the Outlook Bar

1. Click **View** . . . . Alt + V
2. Select **Outlook Bar** . . . . O

Open and Close the Folder List

1. Click **View** . . . . Alt + V
2. Select **Folder List** . . . . E

Display and Print a Message

1. In the Folder list, click the **Inbox** folder . . . . Ctrl + Shift + I
   OR
   Click **View** . . . . Alt + V
   Point to **Go To** . . . . G
   Select **Inbox** I
   OR
   Click **Inbox** on the Outlook Bar.
2. Double-click the message to open.
   OR
   Right-click the message to open.
   Select **Open** . . . . O
3. In the Message window, click **Print** . . . . Ctrl + P
   OR
   Click **File** . . . . Alt + F
   Select **Print** . . . . P
4. Click OK.

Send a Message Reply

1. Display the message in which to reply.
2. Click **Reply** . . . . . Alt + R OR Ctrl + R
   OR
   In the Inbox, right-click the message to which to reply.
   Select **Reply** . . . . R
3. Type your message response.
4. Click **Send** . . . . Alt + S

Create a Signature

1. Click **Tools** . . . . Alt + T
2. Select **Options** . . . . O
3. In the *Options* dialog box, click the Mail Format tab.
4. Click **Signatures** . . . . Alt + G
5. In the *Create Signature* dialog box, click **New** . . . . Alt + N
6. In the *Create a New Signature* dialog box, enter a name for your new signature.
7. Click Next.
8. In the *Edit Signature* dialog box, type the text for your signature and format as desired . . . . Alt + O, Alt + P
9. Click **Finish** . . . . Alt + F
10. In the *Create Signature* dialog box, click OK.
11. In the *Options* dialog box, click OK.

OR

1. In a new Message window, click the **Options** down arrow.
2. Select **E-mail Signature** . . . . E
3. In the *E-mail Options* dialog box, type the name of your new signature.
4. Press Tab.
5. In the *Create your e-mail signature* box, type and format your signature. . . . . Alt + C
6. Apply your signature to new and/or replies and forwards. . . . . Alt + M or Alt + F; Up and Down arrow keys
7. Click OK.

Compose and Send a Message With an Attachment

1. In the Folder list, click the **Inbox** folder. . . . . Ctrl + Shift + I
   OR
   Click **Inbox** on the Outlook Bar.
2. Click **New Mail Message** . . . . Ctrl + N
   OR
   Click **New Mail Message** down arrow . . . . Alt + N
   Select **Mail Message** . . . . M
   OR
   Click **File** . . . . Alt + F
   Point to **New**. . . . . W
   Select **Mail Message** . . . . M
3. Click in the *To* box, type the address(es) of the recipient(s).
4. Click in the *Subject* box, and type the message subject.
5. Click in the message box, and type your message.
6. With the Message window still open, click **Insert File**.
7. In the *Insert File* dialog box, navigate to the location of the file.
   OR
   Click in the *FileName* box, type the file name. Alt + N
8. Click **Insert** . . . . Alt + S
9. Click **Send** . . . . Alt + S

Create a New Folder — Ctrl + Shift + E

1. Click **File** . . . . Alt + F
2. Point to **Folder** . . . . F
3. Select **New Folder** . . . . N
4. In the *Create New Folder* dialog box, type a name for the folder . . . . Alt + N

5. Select where to place the folder.
6. Click OK.

OR

1. Click the **New Mail Message** down arrow . . . . Alt + N
2. Select **Folder**. . . . . E
3. In the *Create New Folder* dialog box, type a name for the folder . . . . Alt + N
4. Select where to place the folder.
5. Click OK.

Move Messages Between Folders

1. Select the message to move.
2. Click **Move to Folder** . . Ctrl + Shift + V
   OR
   Click **Edit** . . . . .Alt + E
   Select **Move to Folder** . . . . M
   OR
   Right-click the message to move.
   Select **Move to Folder** . . . . M
3. In the *Move Items* dialog box, select the desired folder.
4. Click OK.

OR

1. Select the message to move.
2. Drag the message to the desired folder in the Inbox.

OR

1. Select the message to move.
2. Click **Organize** .
   OR
   Click **Tools** .Alt + T
   Click **Organize** . . . . .Z
3. In the Ways to Organize Inbox, select **Using Folders**.
4. In the *Move message selected below to* box, select the desired folder.
5. Click **Move**.

Assign Categories to Messages

1. Select the message you wish to assign a category.
2. Click **Edit** . . . . Alt + E
3. Select **Categories** I
   OR
   Right-click the message you wish to assign a category.
   Select **Categories** I
4. In the Available categories list in the *Categories* dialog box, select the desired categories . . . . **Up or Down arrow key; Spacebar**
5. Click OK.

Search for Messages

1. In the Inbox folder, click **Find** . . . . Alt + I
2. In the *Look for* box, type a word or phrase for your search.
3. Click the *Search In* down arrow and select the folders or items to search.
4. Click **Find Now**.
5. Click **Clear**.

OR

1. In the Inbox folder, click **Find** .. Alt + I
2. Click **Options** on the Find bar.
3. Select **Advanced Find** . . . . D
4. Select the More Choices tab.
5. Click **Categories** . . . . Alt + C
6. In the Available categories list in the *Categories* dialog box, select the desired categories . . . . **Up or Down arrow key; Spacebar**
7. Click OK.
8. Click **FindNow**. . . . . Alt + N
9. Close the Find bar.

Modify Message Settings and Delivery Options

1. In the new Message window, click **Options** . . . . Alt + P
2. Under Message settings, select the appropriate setting options (**Importance** and **Sensitivity**). . . . . Alt + P, Alt + Y
3. Under Delivery options, select the desired delivery options (such as *Save sent message to*) . . . . Alt + N
4. Click **Close**.

OR

1. In the new Message window, click **Importance High** or **Importance Low** .

Manually Archive Messages

1. Click **File** . . . . Alt + F
2. Select **Archive** . . . . .R
3. In the *Archive* dialog box, select the folders in which there are messages you wish to archive.
4. In the *Archive items older than box*, select the archive date. . . . . Alt + O
5. Click OK.

Save Message as Text Only or HTML Files

1. Select the message to save.
2. Click **File** . . . . Alt + F
3. Select **Save As** . . . . A
4. In the *Save As* dialog box, navigate to the location you wish to save the message.
5. In the *File name* box, enter a name for the saved message. . . . . Alt + N
6. In the *Save as type* box, select the format type. . . . . Alt + T
7. Click **Save** . . . . Alt + S

Outlook® Procedure Summary

Lesson Review and Exercises

Summary Checklist

- ☑ Can you explore the Outlook window and navigate between various items?
- ☑ Can you receive, open, and respond to e-mail messages?
- ☑ Can you create e-mail messages and utilize Word's editing tools?
- ☑ Can you customize the Inbox views using a variety of methods?
- ☑ Can you modify message settings and delivery options to enhance the convenience of electronic messaging?
- ☑ Have you practiced archiving and saving messages?
- ☑ Have you modeled acceptable e-mail ethics and etiquette in your messages?

Key Terms

- archiving (p. 675)
- attachment (p. 661)
- AutoArchive (p. 675)
- category (p. 668)
- delivery options (p. 671)
- download (p. 652)
- e-mail (p. 646)
- Find and Advanced Find (p. 668)
- Folder List (p. 648)
- Forward (p. 654)
- HTML format (p. 676)
- Importance level (p. 671)
- Inbox (p. 648)
- nethics (p. 664)
- netiquette (p. 664)
- Outlook Bar (p. 648)
- Outlook Rich Text format (p. 676)
- Outlook Today (p. 646)
- Preview Pane (p. 648)
- Reply (p. 654)
- Reply to All (p. 654)
- Sensitivity level (p. 671)
- Signature Picker (p. 657)
- signatures (p. 657)
- stationery (p. 659)
- Text Only format (p. 676)
- upload (p. 654)
- views (p. 651)

APPLY IT! Guided Activities

1. Reply to a Message and Change a View

As a computer education trainer at the Columbus Local Library, you are required to take classes on new software products that are being taught through your library. Whenever new training classes are offered, you receive an e-mail message from Karyn Jackson, your training supervisor, requesting the time and day you wish to take the training class. You'll open the message and forward your class request to your teacher.

a. Using Windows Explorer, drag and drop the data file *New Training Courses.msg* to the Inbox. (***Note:*** Do not copy and paste your data file to the Inbox.) Point to Current View on the View menu and select By Sender.

b. Open, read, and print the message from Karyn Jackson; then click Forward.

c. Include your teacher's e-mail address on the *To* line. Then, in the message window, type these sentences: Please enroll me in the Microsoft Outlook course on Friday, May 23. Thank you.

d. Type the following information as a signature on three lines at the end of the message **(see Figure 1.39)**: *Your Name,* Computer Education Trainer, Columbus Local Library. Then, send the message, and return your Current View to *Messages*.

Figure 1.39 Compose a message

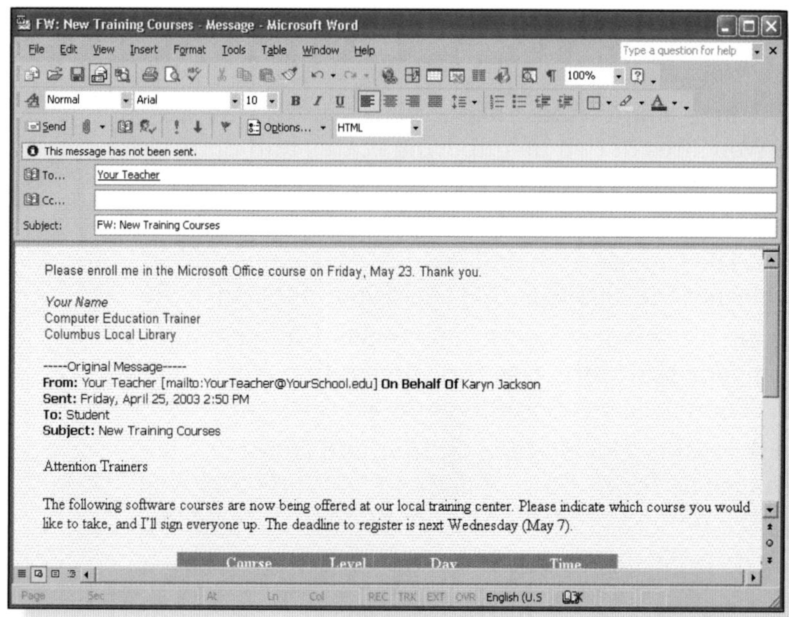

Outlook®

2. Search for, Categorize, and Move Messages

Several days after sending the message to your supervisor regarding Microsoft Outlook training, you realize you forgot to make note of the time and day of your upcoming training course. Conduct a search to find the message you sent regarding your course.

a. Click Find and type Outlook course in the *Look for* box. Click the Search In down arrow and select *Mail I Sent*. Click Find Now. The message matching your search will appear.

b. Categorize the message as *Training*. (***Note:*** You will need to create a new category.)

c. Create a new folder called *Columbus Local Library* and move your response (found in the search) and the original message (from the Inbox) to the folder. Close the Find bar.

Do It Yourself

1. Create a Message With a Personal Signature

As a marketing consultant to your state's Hospitality and Tourism division, you are required to develop ideas to improve your state's Web site. You decide to compare your state's Web site with those of neighboring states. The Hospitality and Tourism marketing director sent you a message with instructions on how to access your state's online information services.

a. Open Windows Explorer; then, drag and drop the data file *Accessing Online Information.msg* to your Inbox. Open, read, print, and then close the message. With your teacher's permission, visit your state's Web site as described in the message.

b. Note the three things you like best about your state's Web site. Then, visit the Web sites of two neighboring states and note three things that compare or contrast to your state's Web site.

c. Create a personal signature that will be added to *new messages* and *replies/forwards*. The signature should include your name and street address. Format the signature to reflect your personal style.

d. Compose and send a new message to your teacher describing your findings on your state site. Use the subject line *Notes on Our State Site*. (The message should include your signature.)

e. Categorize the *Accessing Online Information* and *Notes on Our State Site* messages as *Ideas*. Save *Notes on Our State Site* as a Text File using the name *xxx-Notes on Our State Site-Text Only*.

f. Create a new *State Information* folder and move the messages to the new folder.

Challenge Yourself

Learning Company Policies

As a new employee at HealthCare Claims Corporation, you must respond to an e-mail from the Human Resources (HR) department.

- Use Windows Explorer to drag and drop the data file *New Employee Information.msg* to the Inbox. (Do not use the Copy command.) Open, read, and print the message. Save the message as an HTML file named *xxx-New Employee Information-HTML*.
- Create a new *HealthCare HR* folder and move *New Employee Information.msg* to it. Open *New Employee Information.msg*. Open and read the *Internet Usage Policy* attachment. On the last page of the attachment (page 3), type your name, phone number, today's date, and your teacher's name next to *Supervisor Name* **(see Figure 1.40)**. On the signature line within the paragraph, replace the underscore with your name. Change the font of your name to underlined Lucida Handwriting (or another script font). Save the attachment changes. Then, save a copy of the attachment for yourself.

Figure 1.40 Internet Usage Policy Acceptance Letter

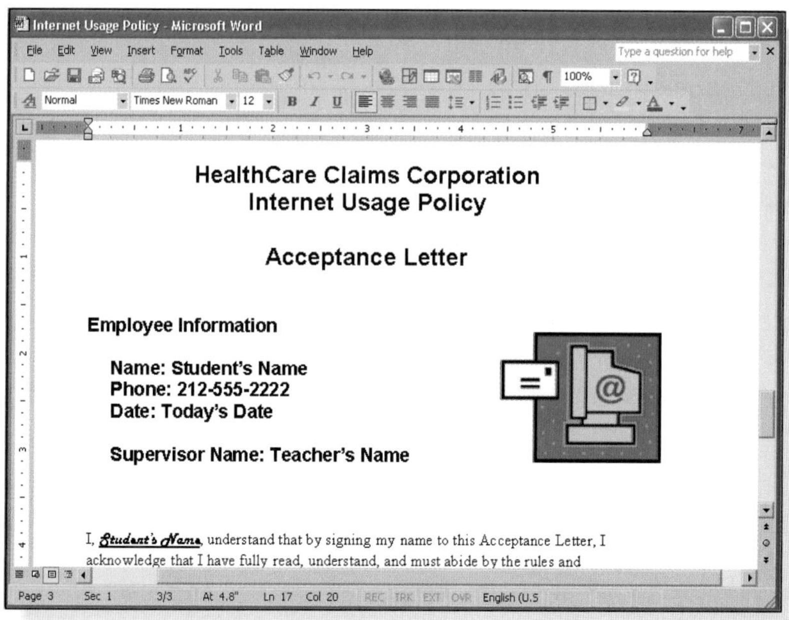

- Forward the message to your teacher. Include two attachments (Internet Usage Policy with changes and your resume) and your signature with the message. In the body of the message, indicate that you are sending a copy of the signed Internet Usage Policy and your resume. Mark the message with High Importance and use the delivery options to save the sent message to your *HealthCare HR* folder.

Lesson 2

Using the Contacts Folder and the Calendar

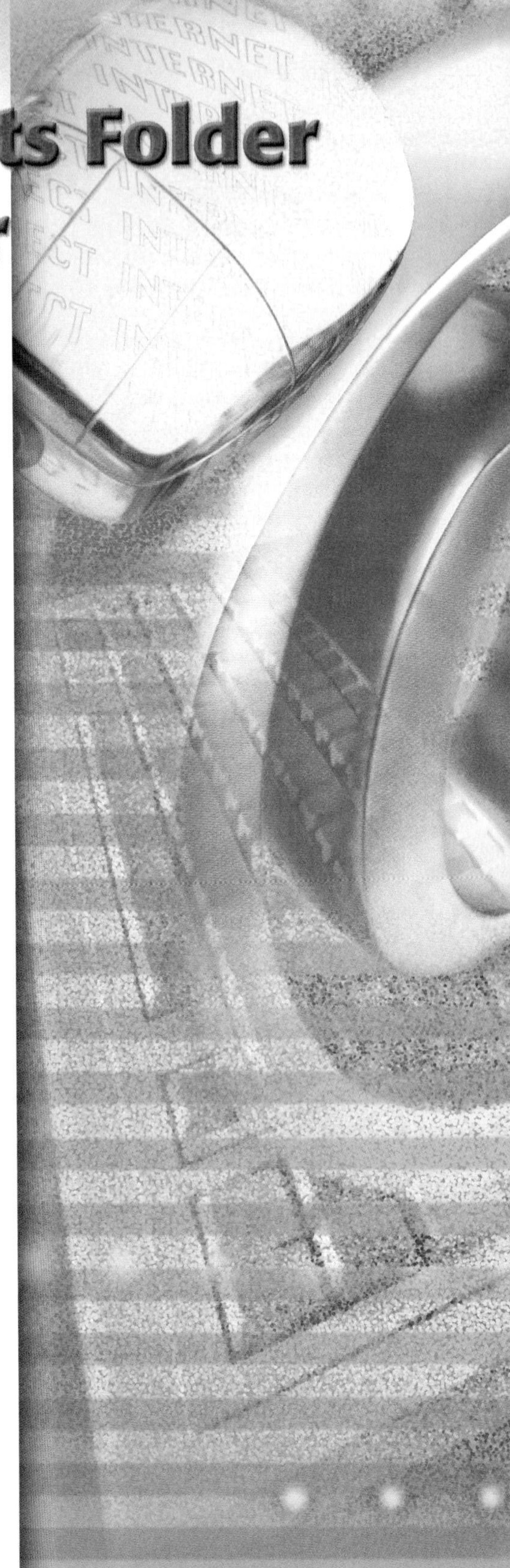

Lesson Exercise Objectives

After completing this lesson, you'll be able to do the following tasks:

1. Create and edit contact information
2. Manage contact information
3. Schedule appointments
4. Schedule meetings and respond to meeting requests
5. Manage the Outlook Calendar

Key Terms

- accept (p. 697)
- Address Card view (p. 689)
- appointment (p. 694)
- Calendar (p. 694)
- contact information (p. 686)
- Contacts (p. 686)
- Contacts list (p. 687)
- Day/Week/Month view (p. 704)
- decline (p. 697)
- Detailed Address Cards (p. 689)
- event (p. 694)
- free/busy time (p. 697)
- Global Address List (p. 686)
- Journal (p. 689)
- meeting request (p. 697)
- Outlook Address Book (p. 686)
- Personal Address Book (p. 687)
- propose new time (p. 697)
- recurring (p. 694)
- resource (p. 697)
- timeline (p. 689)
- time management (p. 702)

Microsoft Office Specialist Activities

OL2002: 1.4, 2.1–2.5, 4.1–4.3

Real-Life Business Applications

Lesson Case Study

In this lesson, you will play the role of Project Leader on your Sophomore Class community project—*Maehr Park Clean & Green Up*. Keep the following information in mind as you work through the lesson exercises.

- **Job responsibilities and goals.** In order for the project to be successful, you need to communicate effectively with everyone on the team. You're responsible for ensuring that everyone has appropriate information to fulfill his or her role on the project.
- **The project.** Although you've accomplished a lot on the Maehr Park Project, you are searching for ways to work more efficiently. Several Outlook tools will help you organize everything and keep everyone informed.
- **The challenge ahead.** The *Maehr Park Clean & Green Up* is well under way. You've already lined up the subcommittee team leaders, held several weekly status meetings, and communicated to team leaders and your Project Advisor via e-mail. Next, you'll use Outlook to create, edit, organize, and sort contacts as well as add appointments and meetings to the Calendar.

Microsoft Office Specialist OL2002 4.1

Exercise 1 Overview:
Create and Edit Contact Information

Your work on the *Maehr Park Clean & Green Up* has already provided you with **contact information**, including names, e-mail addresses, phone numbers, and other essential information associated with those on the project. Currently, the information for these contacts is stored in various locations—within e-mail messages, e-mail attachments, your personal address book, or your memory. Managing all the contact information is crucial to staying organized.

Type: about contacts

With Outlook, you can store contact information in one convenient place. In the **Contacts** folder, you can store the contact's name; company and job title; business and home address; business, home, mobile, and fax numbers; e-mailaddresses; and other personal or professional details (see Figure 2.1). You can create a new contact based on an existing contact; share contact information with others through e-mail; track your inter-actions with contacts; and view, sort, and print contact information to fit your needs.

Figure 2.1 Untitled Contact window

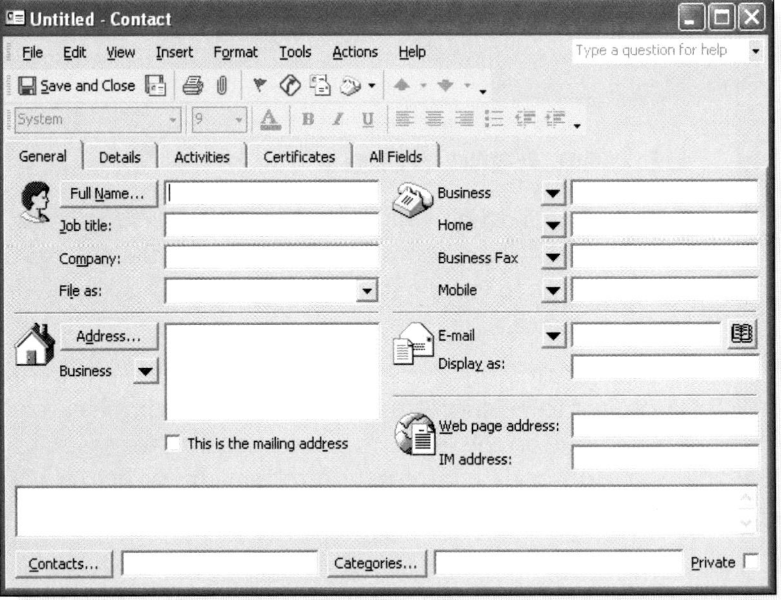

The **Outlook Address Book** provides several options for storing contact information. A **Global Address List** is a list of e-mail addresses available within an organization using Microsoft Exchange Server. A network administrator maintains these addresses, and network users can view them. The **Contacts list** contains information about everyone you have added to *your* Contacts folder. Another installable option for Outlook is the **Personal Address Book**, a place to store personal contacts and distribution lists to keep them separate from business-related contacts.

The following table illustrates some of the commonly used buttons on the Contacts toolbar.

Contacts toolbar

Button		Purpose
New	New Contact	Create a new contact
×	Delete	Delete a contact
Save and Close	Save and Close	Save a contact and close the Contact window
	Save and New	Save a contact and enter a new contact

In the following exercises, you will use the Contacts folder to add new contacts based on an existing company name, edit contact information, and delete a contact in your Contacts list.

Figure 2.2 The Contact window

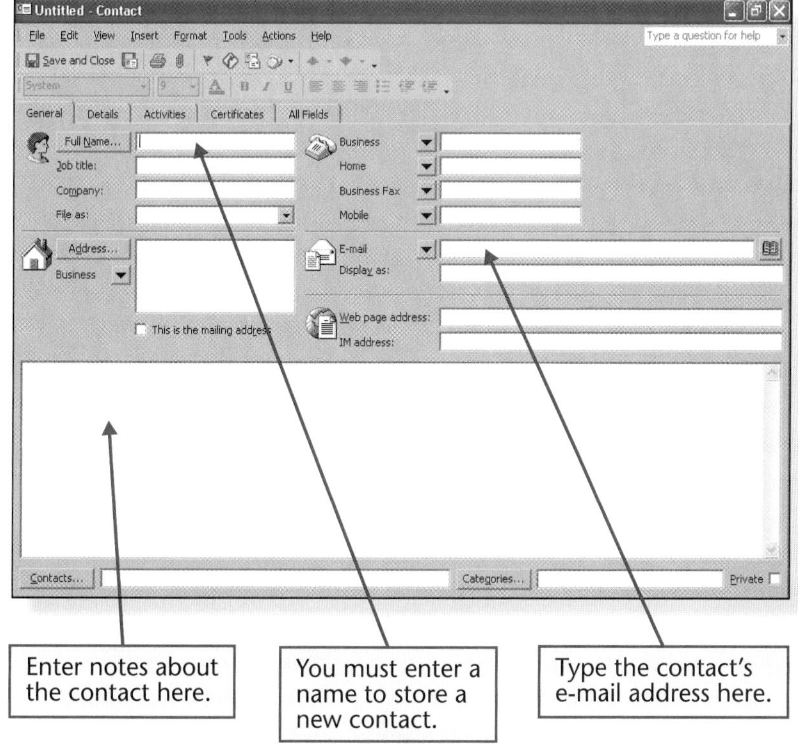

Untitled - Contact
Enter notes about the contact here.
You must enter a name to store a new contact.
Type the contact's e-mail address here.

Step Through It™

Exercise 1A: Add contacts

1. Start Outlook and click the Contacts folder. Your Contacts folder is displayed, but the list will be empty.
2. Click New Contact New; maximize the window if necessary. The Contact window appears (see Figure 2.2).

Outlook®

3. Type the information for Kristine Schultz as shown in Table 2.1. Click Save and New to save the data and open a new Contact window.

4. Type your Project Advisor's information. Then, click Save and Close **Save and Close**.

5. In your Contacts list, click the title bar for your Project Advisor. On the Actions menu, select New Contact from Same Company.

Table 2.1

	Contact 1	Contact 2 (Example)
Full Name	Kristine Schultz	Your Teacher
Job Title	City Manager	Project Advisor
Company	City of Auburn, WA	Gehring High School
Business Phone	253-555-7040	253-555-8500
Business Address	6810 Clarawill Drive North Auburn, WA 98071-3116	3447 Timberbrook Court Auburn, WA 98092-7049
E-mail Address	kschultz@aubcity.gov	YourTeacher@gehring.edu

6. Enter and save all contact data in Table 2.2. Use New Contact from Same Company for each contact (as in Step 5).

7. In the *Maehr Park Project* folder in the Inbox, open the Excel attachment to the *Local businesses interested in Maehr Park Project* message. Enter contact information for the four businesses participating in the Maehr Park Project.

8. Close the Excel worksheet.

Table 2.2

	Contact 1	Contact 2
Full Name	Mary Jane Palmisano	Azmi Maghathe
Home Phone	253-555-0142	253-555-2592
Mobile Phone	253-555-1812	253-555-8352
E-mail Address	MJpalmisano@gehring.edu	Amaghathe@gehring.edu
Notes	*Maehr Park Clean & Green Up* Landscaping Team Leader	*Maehr Park Clean & Green Up* Mowing Team Leader
	Contact 3	**Contact 4**
Full Name	Jermaine Samuels	Heather Kemper
Home Phone	253-555-2194	253-555-8719
Mobile Phone	253-555-9490	253-555-4316
E-mail Address	Jsamuels@gehring.edu	Hkemper@gehring.edu
Notes	*Maehr Park Clean & Green Up* Painting/Power Washing Team Leader	*Maehr Park Clean & Green Up* Waste Removal Team Leader

Table 2.3

Contact Name	Home Address
Mary Jane Palmisano	6105 Spruce Creek Drive Auburn, WA 98002-8447
Azmi Maghathe	121 Highland Avenue Auburn, WA 98001-1502
Jermaine Samuels	10899 Riddles Run Road Auburn, WA 98071-1327
Heather Kemper	56 Princeton Square West Auburn, WA 98092-4672

Step Through It™
Exercise 1B: Edit contacts

1. In your Contacts list, double-click *Mary Jane Palmisano.*
2. Click the Address down arrow and select Home on the shortcut menu.
3. Add Mary Jane's home address as shown in Table 2.3. Then, add the home address for the other contacts in Table 2.3.

Outlook®

Exercise 2 Overview: Manage Contact Information

Microsoft Office Specialist OL2002 1.4, 4.2, 4.3

As your Contacts list grows, you need to effectively manage your contacts. One way to manage your contacts is to change the view of your Contacts list. By default, Outlook displays contacts in **Address Card view**, which presents information in a business card format. **Detailed Address Cards** present contact information in a business card format but include additional fields such as job title and company name. You can also choose from the following columnar views, each of which can be sorted or customized to be useful to you: Phone List, By Category, By Company, By Location, and By Follow-up Flag.

An additional way to manage your contacts is to assign categories and to track contact activity. In Lesson 1, you practiced assigning categories to e-mail messages. Similarly, assigning categories to contacts will enable you to organize, sort, and search for contacts using categories. When you track contact activity, you link all e-mail messages, notes, events, and so on, directly to the appropriate contact. The **Journal** automatically records contact activities and places the actions in a **timeline** (a view type that displays items on a time scale).

Type: tracking items

In the following exercises, you will assign categories to your contacts, organize your contacts by category, sort contacts using various views, and track contact activity.

Step Through It™

Exercise 2A: Assign categories and organize contacts

1. Drag these contacts from your *Lesson 2* folder to your Contacts folder: Mallory, Carter, Jung, Cunningham, and Mireles.
2. Open Alice Mosley's contact information; click Categories at the bottom of the window. Select *Maehr Park Project*, click OK, and click Save and Close.
3. Assign categories for each contact as shown in Table 2.4.

Table 2.4

Contact Name	Categories
Carter, Maria	Personal
Cunningham, Jeremy	Friends
Eichler, Margie	Maehr Park Project
Hahn, Gerald	Maehr Park Project
Jung, Coach Bo	Track
Kemper, Heather	Friends, Maehr Park Project, School/Homework
Maghathe, Azmi	Friends, Maehr Park Project, School/Homework
Mallory, Mike	Friends, School/Homework
Mireles, Pat	Friends, School/Homework
Palmisano, Mary Jane	Friends, Maehr Park Project, School/Homework
Pederson, Wendell	Maehr Park Project
Project Advisor (Your Teacher)	Maehr Park Project, School/ Homework
Samuels, Jermaine	Friends, Maehr Park Project, School/Homework
Schultz, Kristine	Hot Contacts , Maehr Park Project

4. On the View menu, select Current View and then select By Category.
5. Expand the information in the Friends and Maehr Park Project categories (see Figure 2.3).

Figure 2.3 Organizing contacts by category

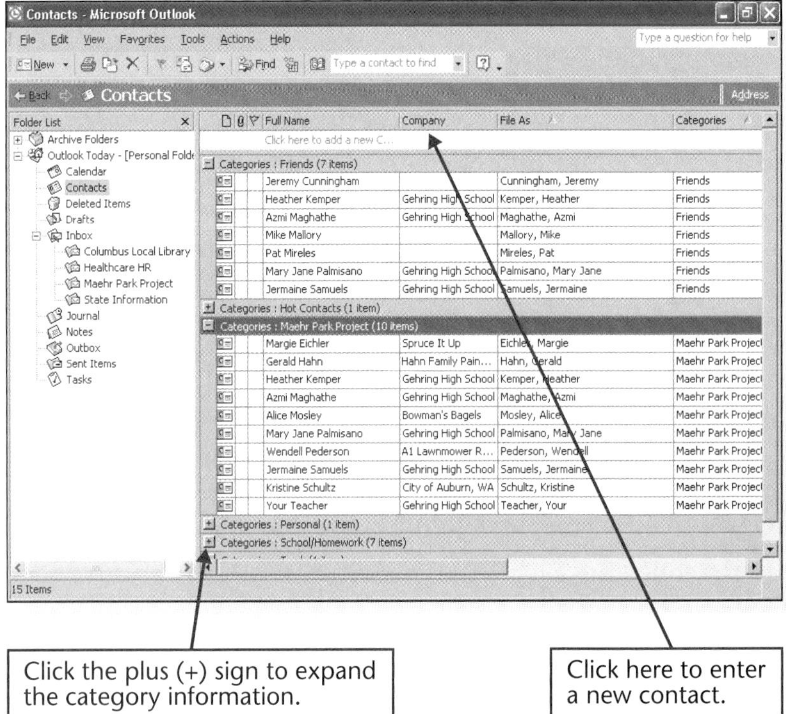

Click the plus (+) sign to expand the category information.
Click here to enter a new contact.

Figure 2.4 Contacts sorted by company in Phone List view

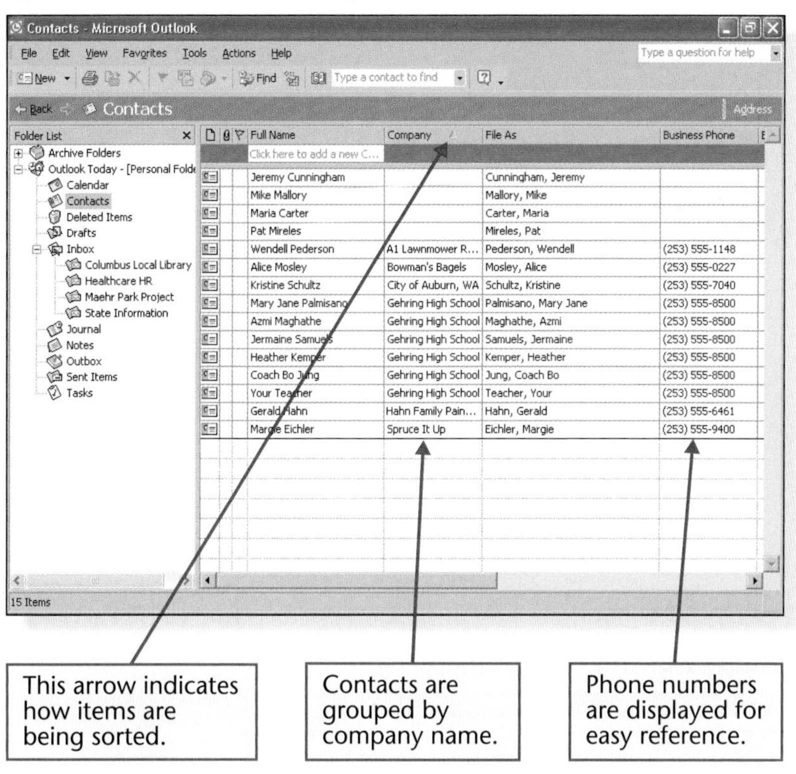

This arrow indicates how items are being sorted.
Contacts are grouped by company name.
Phone numbers are displayed for easy reference.

Step Through It™
Exercise 2B: Sort contacts

1. Click Full Name on the Sort By bar to change the sort order.
2. Click File As on the Sort By bar to sort by last name first in descending order.
3. On the View menu, select Current View and then select Phone List. Outlook sorts the entries by the File As column.
4. Click Company on the Sort By bar (see Figure 2.4).

Figure 2.5 The Journal Entry window

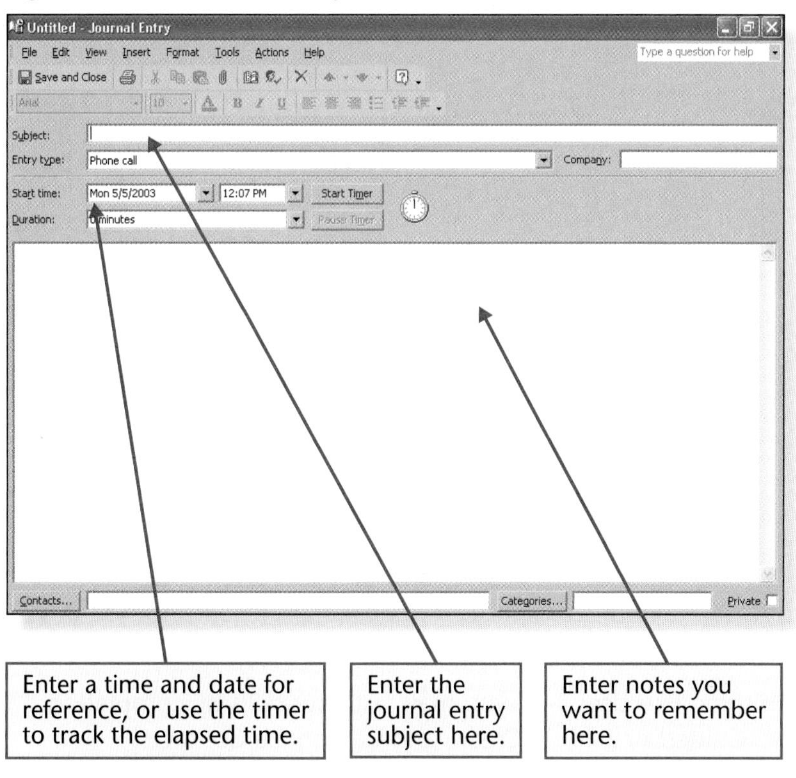

Enter a time and date for reference, or use the timer to track the elapsed time.
Enter the journal entry subject here.
Enter notes you want to remember here.

Step Through It™
Exercise 2C: Track contact activity

1. Click the Journal folder on the Folder List. Click No in the dialog box asking if you want to turn on the Journal feature.
2. On the Actions menu, select New Journal Entry. Maximize the window (see Figure 2.5).

3. Enter the information shown in Table 2.5. Click the down arrows to examine the entry types and to enter a start time.

Table 2.5

Subject	Permission to post flyers
Entry type	Phone call
Start time	5/06/200x 3:30 PM
Notes	We are authorized to post flyers to recruit volunteers for the subcommittees. We will post the flyers outside the cafeteria.
Contacts	Project Advisor
Categories	Maehr Park Project

4. Click Save and Close. The new journal entry will appear on the timeline. Expand the entry (see Figure 2.6). (***Note:*** If you don't see the journal entry, click the Date down arrow in the title bar and select the correct date.)

5. In the Contacts list, open the Project Advisor contact information.

6. Click the Activities tab. All items (e-mail and journal entries) associated with the Project Advisor are displayed.

7. Click Save and Close.

Figure 2.6 The New Journal entry

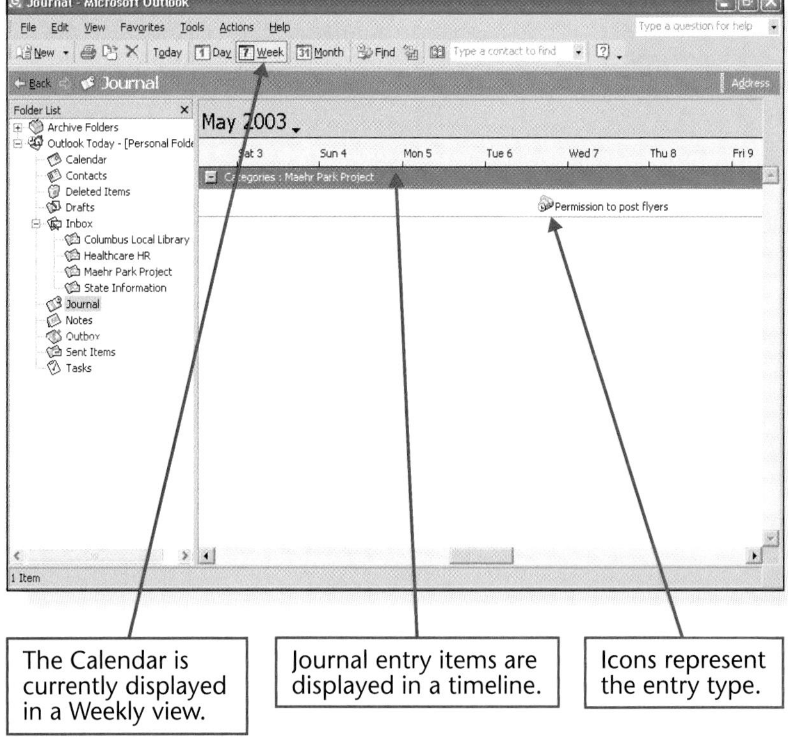
Journal - Microsoft Outlook
May 2003
Permission to post flyers
The Calendar is currently displayed in a Weekly view.
Journal entry items are displayed in a timeline.
Icons represent the entry type.

APPLY IT!

After finishing Exercises 1–2, you may test your skills by completing Apply It! Guided Activity 1, Create and Categorize Contacts.

Tech Talk

Understanding Instant Messaging

Instant messaging (IM) lets you "talk" with people in real time by exchanging text messages over the Internet. Popularized by ICQ (*I Seek You*) and AOL Instant Messenger (AIM), instant messaging is offered in one form or another by many Internet companies.

Each IM user sets up a contact or buddy list. When you log on, you can see the status of the people on your list—who is online and who is offline. You can start a conversation with anyone who is online.

When you send an instant message, a window containing the message opens on the receiver's computer. That person can type a response. The exchange continues until one of you decides to stop. For most IM tools, you must be using the same messaging software.

Instant messaging is rapidly becoming popular at work. It lets employees multitask and collaborate efficiently—no missed phone calls or waiting for e-mail. Retailers like Lands' End offer IM customer support. Corporations are increasingly adopting wireless IM, via PDAs and other mobile devices.

Because instant messages move across public networks and servers, security is an important issue. Many organizations are addressing security issues by setting up proprietary systems or buying encryption software.

CRITICAL THINKING

1. Instant messaging uses both emoticons and special abbreviations, such as BTW (*by the way*) and IMHO (*in my humble opinion*). Pair up with another student and create a list of these abbreviations. Send your partner an e-mail using both IM abbreviations and emoticons.
2. What does IM cost businesses compared to telephoning? Form a team with two or three other students and find out. Consider local, national, and international contacts. Use Word or Excel to create a table of your results.

Microsoft Office Specialist
OL2002 2.1, 2.2

Exercise 3 Overview:
Schedule Appointments

With everything you are doing on the *Maehr Park Clean & Green Up*, in addition to other unrelated events, you may be having a hard time managing all your activities. The **Calendar** lets you manage your daily schedule (such as meetings, appointments, and events) so you can stay organized and avoid over-committing.

Type: about calendar

Outlook's Calendar enables you to track **appointments** (activities with specific start times that do not involve other people) and **events** (activities which last 24 or more hours or have no specific start time). You can designate appointments and events as **recurring**, indicating that they occur more than once at set intervals (such as weekly status meetings for the *Maehr Park Clean & Green Up*).

To enter a Calendar item, you indicate the subject, location, and start and end times of an appointment or event. Appointments will appear on your calendar as a block of time, while events appear as a banner that spans the designated days.

You can set reminder notices; schedule your time as free, tentative, busy, or out of office; assign contacts and categories; and apply a label (or color code) to items on your Calendar. You can also set a conditional format so that appointments that meet certain requirements are marked (color coded) for easy identification.

Need Help?

Type: color appointments automatically

The following table ilustrates two of the commonly used buttons on the New Appointment toolbar.

New Appointment toolbar

Button		Purpose
New	New Appointment	Create a new appointment
Recurrence...	Recurrence	Make a recurring appointment

In the following exercises, you will add three new items to your Calendar and set conditional formatting for all Maehr Park events and appointments.

Figure 2.7 The New Appointment window

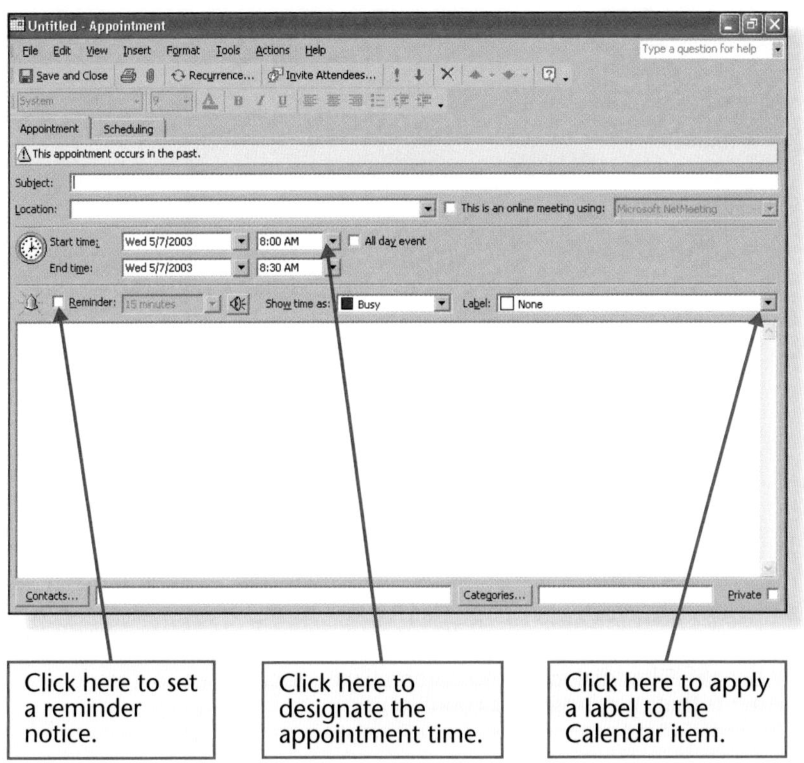

Click here to set a reminder notice.
Click here to designate the appointment time.
Click here to apply a label to the Calendar item.

Step Through It™

Exercise 3A: Add appointments

1. Click the Calendar folder. The Daily Calendar will open.
2. Click New Appointment New. Maximize the window if necessary (see Figure 2.7).
3. Create three new Calendar items, typing or selecting the information as shown in Table 2.6. After entering each item, click Save and Close.
4. On the View menu, point to Go To and select Go To Date. Type **5/23/200x**. Click the *Show in* down arrow and select Day Calendar. Click OK. The event is displayed as a banner at the top of the Calendar.

Table 2.6

	Calendar Item 1	Calendar Item 2	Calendar Item 3
Subject	**Meeting with Alice Mosley**	**Mom's birthday**	**Maehr Park Clean & Green Up**
Location	**Bowman's Bagels**		**Maehr Park**
Start Time	**5/08/200x 3:00 PM**	**5/23/200x**	**5/16/200x**
End Time	**5/08/200x 4:00 PM**	**5/23/200x**	**5/18/200x**
All Day Event		✔	✔
Reminder	✔ **1 hour**	✔ **1 day**	✔ **1 day**
Show time as	***Busy***	***Free***	***Out of Office***
Label	***None***	***Birthday***	***None***
Notes	**Discuss food and refreshments for Maehr Park Project.**		**Refer to the Schedule of Events message.**

Outlook®

Step Through It™

Exercise 3B: Apply conditional format to appointments

1. Right-click the Calendar grid, and select Automatic Formatting on the shortcut menu.
2. Click Add. In the Name box, type Maehr Park appointments.
3. Click Condition (see Figure 2.8).

Figure 2.8 The Filter dialog box

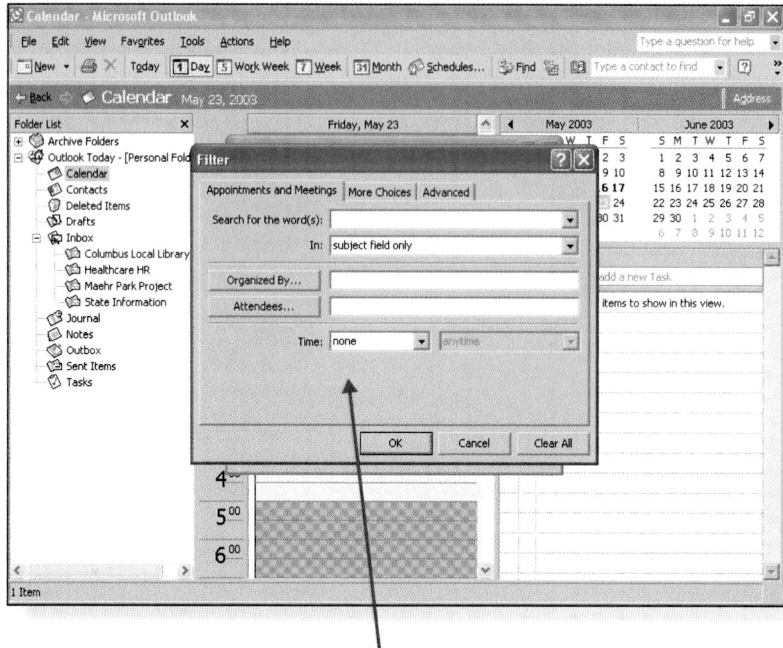

Use the Filter dialog box to automatically apply labels to Calendar items that match specific conditions.

4. In the *Search for the word(s)* text box, type Maehr Park.
5. Click the In down arrow and select *subject and notes fields*. Click OK.
6. Click the Label down arrow and select Important. Click OK.
7. One-by-one, click the following dates on the Date Navigator: May 8, 16, 17, and 18. Notice the new label has automatically been applied to each item (see Figure 2.9).

Figure 2.9 Appointments meeting conditions

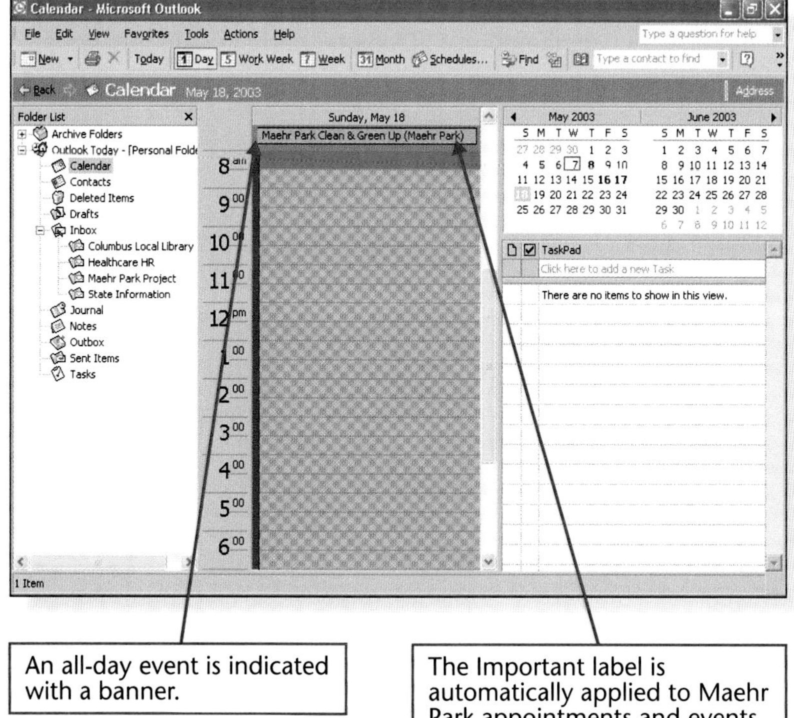

An all-day event is indicated with a banner.

The Important label is automatically applied to Maehr Park appointments and events.

Exercise 4 Overview: Schedule Meetings and Respond to Meeting Requests

Microsoft Office Specialist OL2002 2.1, 2.3

Outlook®

Now that you've entered appointments and events on your Calendar, it is time to use Outlook to schedule meetings for the *Maehr Park Clean & Green Up*. Within Outlook, you can easily schedule meetings, invite attendees, and schedule available resources.

When you create a **meeting request**, you invite the required and optional attendees, schedule **resources** (such as a conference room, computer, or equipment), and enter the meeting specifics. The meeting request will be sent to the attendees, and the meeting will be entered on your Calendar.

Type: schedule a meeting or resources

When you receive a meeting request, you have three response options. Meetings you **accept** are automatically entered into your Calendar. Those you **decline** are not entered into your Calendar. If a meeting conflicts with your schedule, you can select **propose new time** and choose another time. With this option, the original meeting time is entered into your Calendar as tentative.

The following table illustrates some of the commonly used buttons on the Meeting Request toolbar.

Meeting Request toolbar

Button		Purpose
✓ Accept	Accept	Accept a meeting request
? Tentative	Tentative	Tentatively accept a meeting request
✕ Decline	Decline	Decline a meeting request
Propose New Time	Propose New Time	Propose a new time for a meeting
Calendar...	Calendar	Check your Calendar before accepting a meeting

An organization that uses Outlook on Microsoft Exchange Server can track employees' and resources' **free/busy time** by examining their calendar events. An employee will make his or her Calendar available over the company intranet (or externally over the Internet), and others will be able to plan a meeting based on the attendees free time. Free and busy times are displayed in colors and patterns in the Calendar.

The same principle applies to tracking resources. Each resource is given a mailbox that is monitored by an administrator. You can schedule a resource while creating a new meeting request or add it to an existing meeting. (To schedule a resource, open the meeting and click the Scheduling tab; click Add Others and select Add from Address Book; select the resource from the Global Address List, click OK, and then click Send or Send Update.) When the resource is booked, the Calendar will show the resource as busy. Tracking the availability of attendees and resources before scheduling a meeting can save valuable time and energy.

Need Help?

Type: others' free/busy time

In the following exercises, you will schedule a meeting and invite attendees, accept and decline meeting requests, and propose alternative meeting times.

Step Through It™

Exercise 4A: Schedule meetings and invite attendees

1. Click the Calendar folder. On the Actions menu, select New Meeting Request and maximize the window.
2. Click To. The *Select Attendees and Resources* dialog box appears.
3. Using the Name list, double-click these names to add them to the *Required* list: Maghathe, Kemper, Samuels, and Palmisano (see Figure 2.10).

Figure 2.10 Select Attendees and Resources dialog box

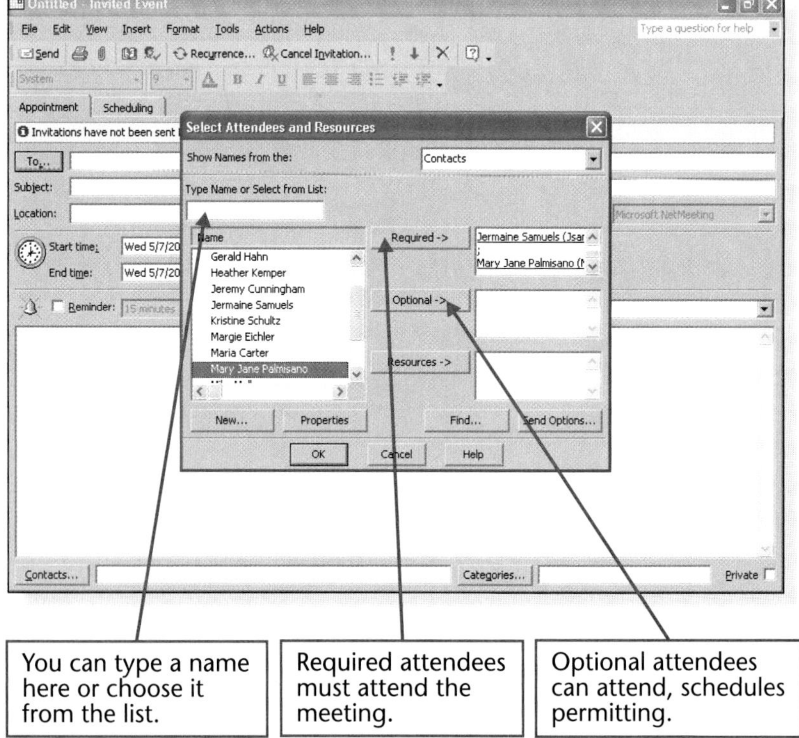

Table 2.7

Subject	**Maehr Park Project – Weekly Status Meeting**
Location	**Project Advisor's Office**
Start Time	**5/08/200x 12:00 PM**
End Time	**5/08/200x 1:00 PM**
Reminder	☑ **1 hour**
Show time as	***Busy***
Label	***None***
Notes	**Pizza will be provided.**

4. Select the Project Advisor's name, click Optional, and click OK.

5. Enter the meeting information as shown in Table 2.7. (***Note:*** An important label will automatically be applied.)

Figure 2.11 Meeting request on your Calendar

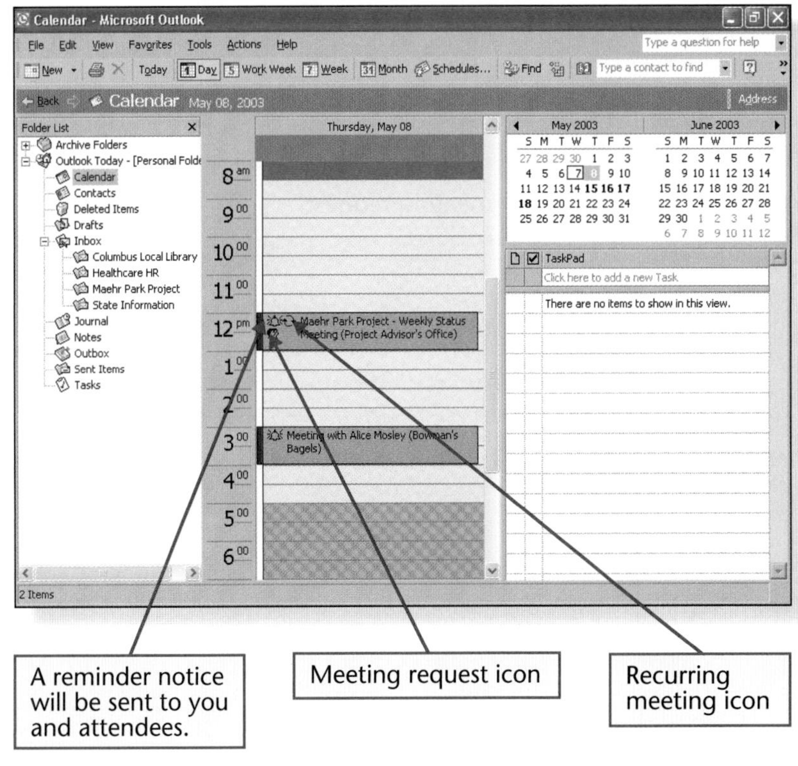

6. Click Recurrence [Recurrence...]. Verify that the correct Start and End times are entered, and the Recurrence pattern is *Weekly*. In the *Range of recurrence* section, click End After and type **2**.

7. Click OK. Click Send.

8. Click May 8 on the Date Navigator (see Figure 2.11).

Outlook®

Another Way

To schedule a meeting, click the New down arrow and select Meeting Request, or press Ctrl + Shift + Q.

Step Through It™

Exercise 4B: Accept and decline meeting requests

Outlook®

1. Click Inbox. Open and read *Landscaping Plans*. The Meeting Request form will open in a separate window (see Figure 2.12).
2. Click Calendar Calendar... . Your Calendar will appear with the meeting request displayed. Click Close.
3. Click Accept ✓ Accept . Click OK to accept the *Send the response now* option.

Figure 2.12 The Meeting request

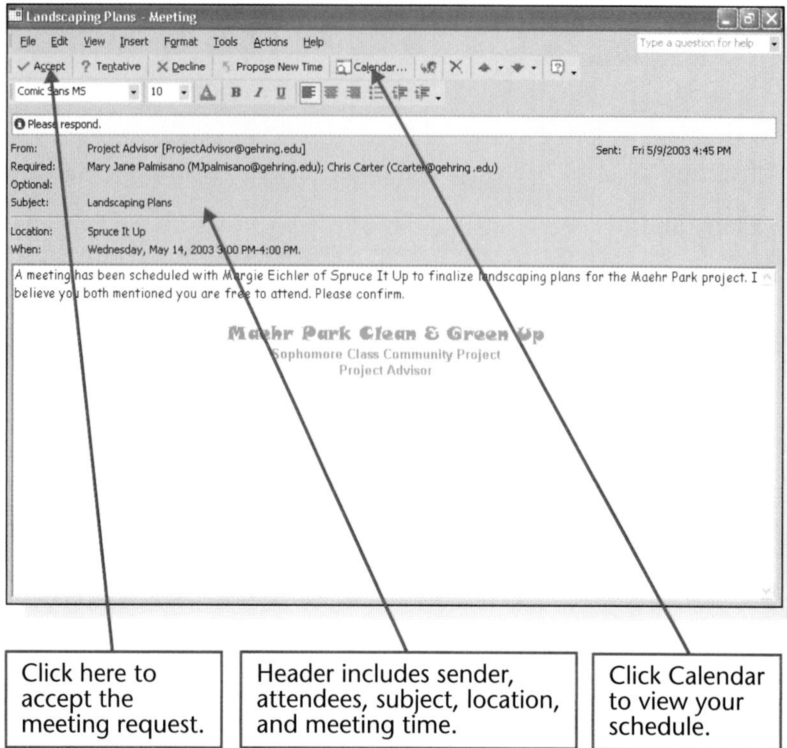

4. Open and read *Meeting with A1 Lawnmower Rental*. Click Decline ✕ Decline .
5. Select *Edit the response before sending*.
6. Maximize the Meeting Response window and type the following note: I'm sorry I won't be able to go. I have an exam scheduled at that time. (See Figure 2.13.)
7. Click Send. Your response is sent and the meeting is not placed in your Calendar.

Figure 2.13 Declining a meeting request

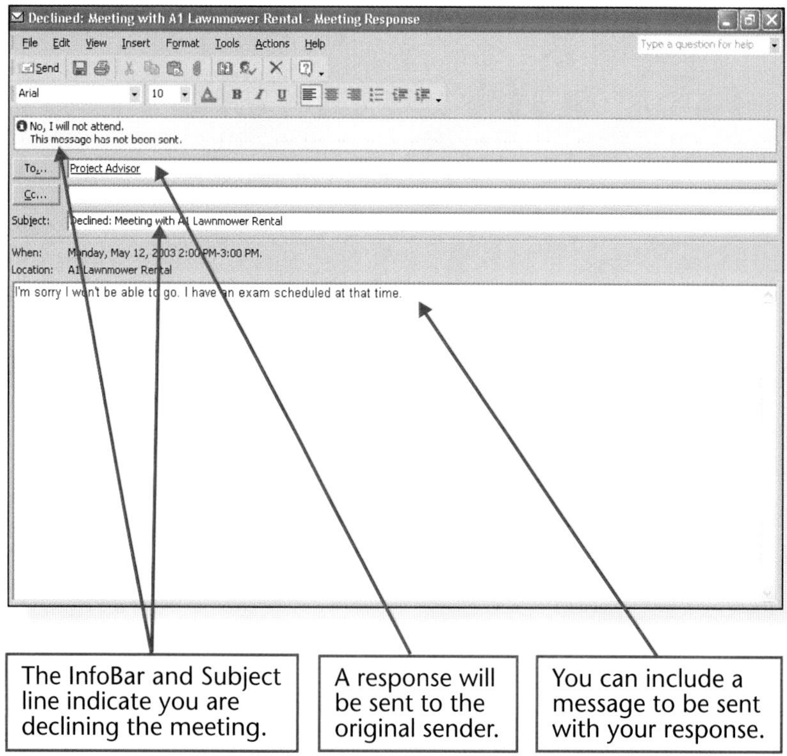

Figure 2.14 Proposing a new meeting time

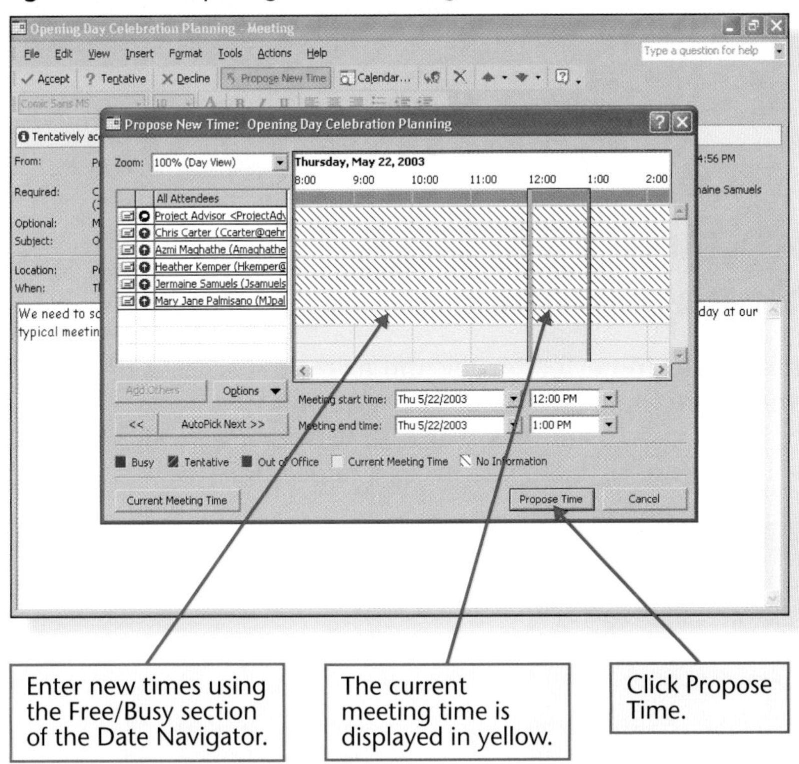

Figure 2.15 Meeting response for proposed time

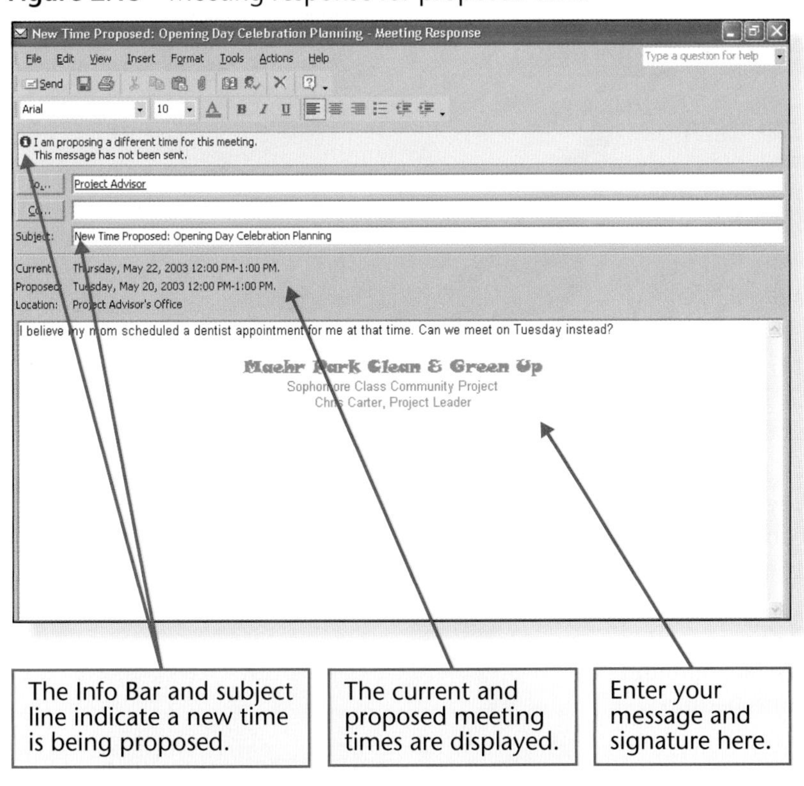

Step Through It™

Exercise 4C: Propose alternative meeting times

1. Open and read *Opening Day Celebration Planning*. Click Propose New Time (see Figure 2.14). (***Note:*** If you receive a dialog box prompting you to join the Microsoft Office Internet Free/Busy service, click Cancel.)

2. Click the *Meeting start time* down arrow and click 5/20/200x. Verify the time is set for 12:00 PM – 1:00 PM.

3. Click Propose Time and type the following text in the Meeting Response window: **I believe my mom scheduled a dentist appointment for me at that time. Can we meet on Tuesday instead?**

4. Add your signature to the message (see Figure 2.15) and click Send. Your message will be sent and the original meeting request will appear on your Calendar as tentative.

Maximizing Productivity Through Effective Time Management

Some people seem to have their lives in perfect order and are experts at balancing work and home life while others have poor organizational skills and are an overstressed mess. Fortunately, most of us fall someplace in the middle of these two groups of people.

Time management, the ability to organize, prioritize, and effectively perform responsibilities with a positive attitude, is the key to balancing your life. But time management skills take practice. Here are some of the tools to help us get our business and personal lives in order:

- **"To-do" lists** offer a tried and true method of writing tasks to do and crossing them off when completed. At times, we may lose or need to rewrite the list.
- **Personal address books** provide a place to record names, addresses, and phone numbers of personal, school, and business contacts.
- **Daily planners** are portable calendars in which to write daily tasks and appointments. Many planners have an address section and daily and monthly calendars to schedule and prioritize tasks.

- **Personal information management programs**, such as Outlook, allow you to send and receive e-mail, update contact information, and track daily tasks, notes, meetings, events, and appointments conveniently and efficiently.
- **Personal digital assistants (PDAs)** allow you to send and receive e-mail, download and modify your calendar, access contact information, and take meeting notes—all on a hand-held device. You can then download or upload information to or from Outlook so that you have the most up-to-date information at your fingertips.

Successfully completing a project, big or small, for work or at home, is an accomplishment to be proud of. Using time management tools such as Outlook can increase your chance of success by maximizing your organizational and planning skills, ensuring your dependability and punctuality, and enabling you to take pride in your accomplishments.

CRITICAL THINKING

1. **Predicting Use** Think about your own daily tasks. What Outlook tools could help you organize your day?
2. **Completing Projects** Explain how you felt the last time you successfully completed a project, an assignment, or a personal goal. What time management tools did you use? Are there any Outlook tools that could have helped you?

Microsoft Office Specialist OL2002 1.4, 2.1, 2.4, 2.5

Outlook®

Exercise 5 Overview:
Manage the Outlook Calendar

As your schedule begins to fill, you'll need the versatility of Outlook to help you stay organized. Outlook provides various options for managing the way information is displayed in your Calendar. For example, you may wish to display a list of all appointments associated with the *Maehr Park Clean & Green Up*. Outlook enables you to organize your schedule, change your view, and print your Calendar based on what is important to you.

By default, Outlook displays your calendar as a single day in the **Day/Week/Month view**. Within this view, you can display your Calendar as a single day, a five-day work week, a seven-day week, or an entire month. You can also change your Calendar to display the Day/Week/Month view with an AutoPreview. Or, you can choose to display and print Calendar items by active appointments, events, annual events, recurring appointments, or by category.

Need Help?

Type: change the look of your Calendar

In the following exercises, you'll assign categories to various appointments, change your Calendar background color, and examine and print the Calendar in several views.

Step Through It™
Exercise 5A: Assign categories to appointments

1. Go to May 12, 200x. Create an appointment with the data in Table 2.8.
2. Click Categories. Select School/Homework, click OK, and click Save and Close.

Table 2.8

Subject	Geometry Exam
Location	Room 203
Start time	2:00 PM
End time	3:00 PM
Reminder	1 day
Show time as	*Busy*
Label	*Needs Preparation*

Table 2.9

Subject	**Dentist Appointment**
Location	**Family Dentistry**
Start time	**12:00 PM**
End time	**12:30 PM**
Reminder	**2 hours**
Show time as	***Busy***
Label	***Personal***
Categories	***Personal***

3 Go to May 22, 200x and create a new appointment as shown in Table 2.9. (***Note:*** Remember, another meeting is tentatively scheduled for that time.)

Table 2.10

Calendar Item	Calendar Date	Categories
Meeting with Alice Mosley	May 8, 200x	Maehr Park Project
Landscaping Plans	May 14, 200x	Maehr Park Project
Maehr Park Project – Weekly Status Meeting	May 15, 200x	Maehr Park Project
Maehr Park Clean & Green Up	May 16 – 18, 200x	Maehr Park Project
Opening Day Celebration Planning	May 22, 200x	Maehr Park Project
Mom's birthday	May 23, 200x	Personal

4 Assign Categories to the Calendar items as shown in Table 2.10.

Step Through It™

Exercise 5B: Change and print Calendar views

1. On the View menu, select Current View and then select By Category.
2. Expand the *Maehr Park Project* and *Personal* categories (see Figure 2.16).
3. On the View menu, select Current View and then select Day/Week/Month. The Calendar is displayed in the default single day view.
4. On the Tools menu, select Options and then select Calendar Options. In the Background color list, choose the color you wish. Click OK twice.
5. Click May 12, 200x on the Date Navigator.
6. Click Work Week [5 Work Week] on the toolbar. Your calendar will display for five work days (Monday through Friday).
7. Reduce the size of the Date Navigator to display only one month (see Figure 2.17).

Figure 2.16 Viewing the Calendar by category

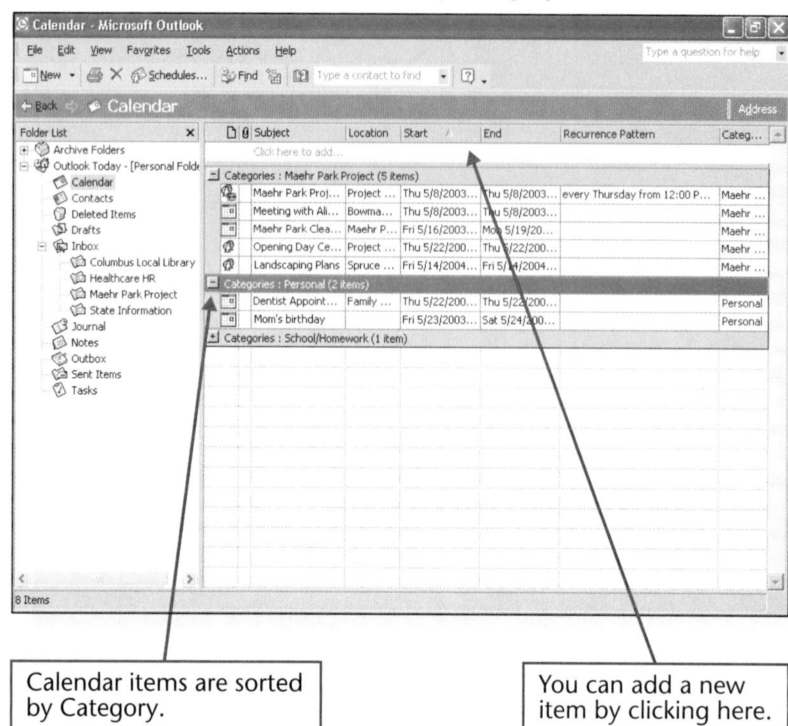

Calendar items are sorted by Category.
You can add a new item by clicking here.

Figure 2.17 The Work Week display of the Day/Week/Month view

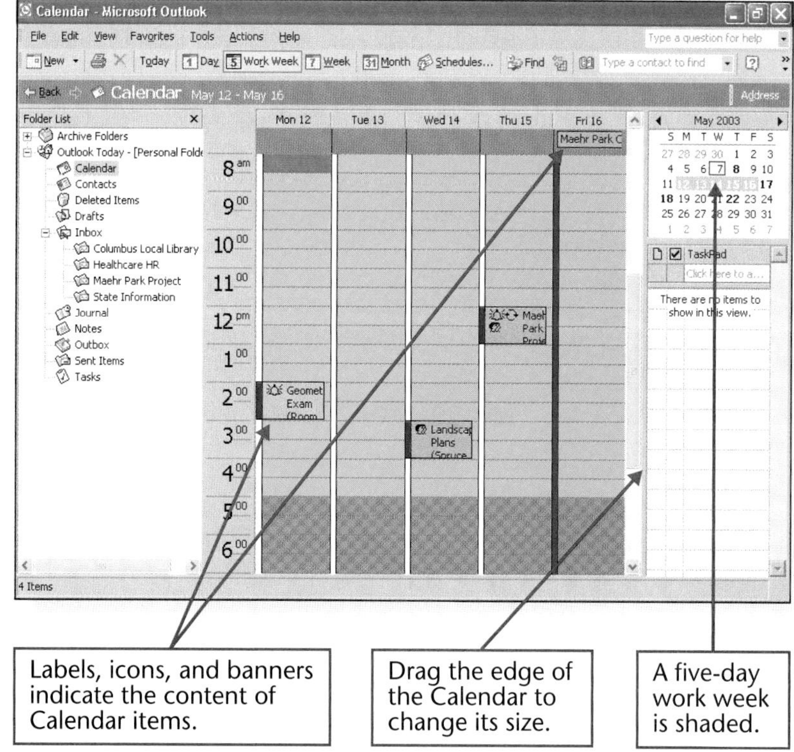

Labels, icons, and banners indicate the content of Calendar items.
Drag the edge of the Calendar to change its size.
A five-day work week is shaded.

Figure 2.18 Printing the Calendar with a Week view

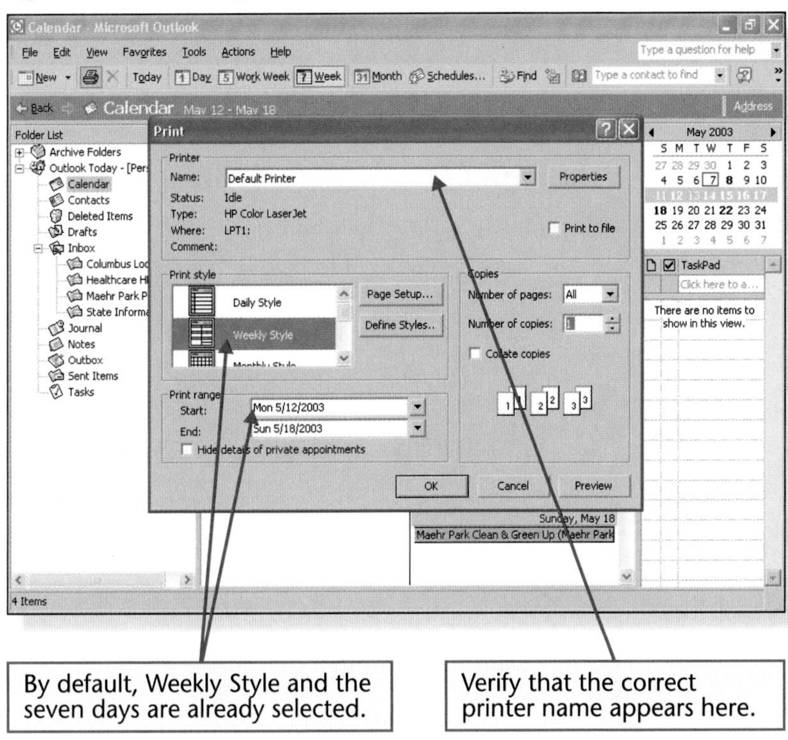

By default, Weekly Style and the seven days are already selected.
Verify that the correct printer name appears here.

8. Click Week. You will see Calendar items in a Week view.
9. Click Print. The Print dialog box appears (see Figure 2.18).
10. Click OK. Your Calendar will print in Week view.

Outlook®

Figure 2.19 Previewing the calendar with a Month view

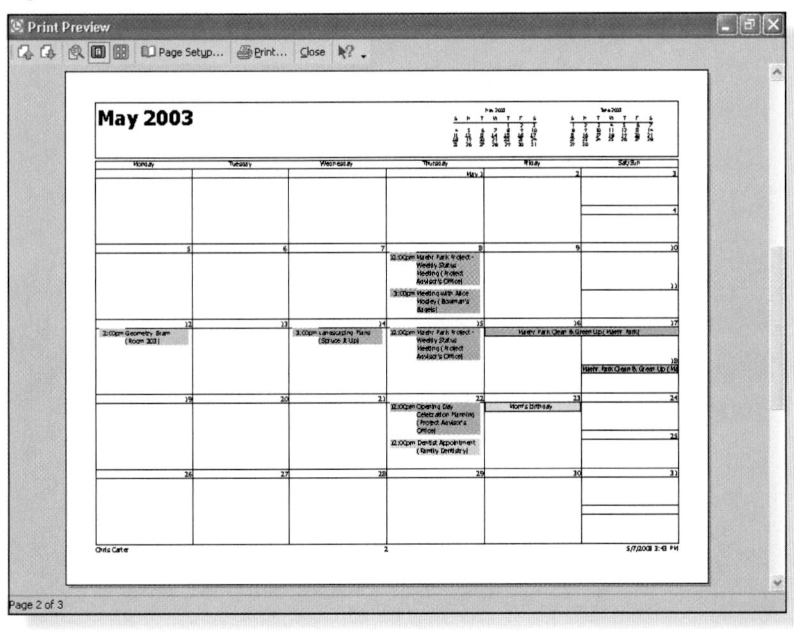

11. Click Month.
12. On the File menu, select Print. The Print dialog box displays in Monthly Style with the month Calendar dates entered by default.
13. Click Preview and click Page Down to view May 200x (see Figure 2.19). Click Print and click OK. Your Calendar will print with a Month view. Return your Calendar to Day view.

After finishing Exercises 1–5, you may test your skills by completing Apply It! Guided Activity 2, Print Calendars.

Procedure Summary

Add a Contact Ctrl + Shift + C

1. In the Folder List, click the **Contacts** folder.
   OR
   Click **View**. Alt + V
   Point to **Go To** . . . . G
   Select **Contacts**. O
   OR
   Click **Contacts** on the Outlook Bar.
2. Click **New Contact** . . . . . . Ctrl + N
   OR
   Click **Actions**. . . . . Alt + A
   Select **New Contact** . . . . N
   OR
   Click **File**. . . . . Alt + F
   Point to **New** . . . . W
   Select **Contact** C
   OR
   Click the **New** down arrow . . . . Alt + N
   Select **Contact** C
3. Enter the contact information.
4. Click **Save and Close** . . . Alt + S

Edit a Contact

1. In the Contacts folder, open the contact to edit.
2. In the Contact window, make changes as desired.
3. Click **Save and Close** . . . Alt + S

Assign Categories to Contacts

1. In the Contacts folder, select the contact.
2. Click **Edit**. . . . . Alt + E
3. Click **Categories** I
4. In the *Available categories* list in the Categories dialog box, click the check boxes next to the desired categories. . . . .**Up or Down arrow key, Spacebar**
5. Click OK.

OR

1. In the Contacts folder, open the contact you want to assign to a category.
2. Click **Categories** . . . . Alt + G
3. In the *Available categories* list in the Categories dialog box, click the check boxes next to the desired categories. . . . .**Up or Down arrow key, Spacebar**
4. Click OK.
5. Click **Save and Close** . . . Alt + S

OR

1. In the Contacts folder, right-click the contact you want to assign to a category.
2. Select **Categories** I
3. In the *Available categories* list in the Categories dialog box, click the check boxes next to the desired categories. . . . .**Up or Down arrow key, Spacebar**
4. Click OK.

Sort Contacts by Category

1. In the Contacts folder, click View . . . . Alt + V
2. Point to **Current View** V
3. Select **By Category** . . . . **Up or Down arrow key, Enter**

Track Contact Activity

1. In the Contacts folder, open the contact.
2. Click the Activities tab.
3. Examine items linked to the contact.
4. Close the contact.

Add Appointments With Conditional Formats to the Calendar Ctrl + Shift + A

1. In the Folder List, click the **Calendar** folder.
   OR
   Click **View** . . . . Alt + V
   Point to **Go To** . . . . .G
   Select **Calendar** .C
   OR
   Click **Calendar** on the Outlook Bar.
2. Click **New Appointment** . . . Ctrl + N
   OR
   Click **Actions** . . . . Alt + A
   Select **New Appointment** . . . . O
   OR
   Click **File** . . . . Alt + F
   Point to **New** . . . . W
   Select **Appointment** . . . . A
   OR
   Click the **New** down arrow . . . . Alt + N
   Select **Appointment** . . . . A
3. On the Appointment tab, click in the **Subject** field, and type the appointment name . . . . .Alt + J
4. Click in the **Location** field, and type the location. . . . . Alt + L
5. Click the **Start time:** down arrow, and set the date and time . . . . **Alt + Shift + :**
6. Select the **End time** down arrow, and set the date and time . . . . Alt + M
7. Select a **Label**, if desired. . . . .**Alt + B; Up or Down arrow key**
8. If desired, click **Categories**, select a category, and click OK. . . . . Alt + G; **Up or Down arrow key, Spacebar**
9. If desired, click in the Notes area, and type a note.
10. Click **Save and Close** Save and Close . . . Alt + S

Schedule Meetings and Invite Attendees and Resources Ctrl + Shift + A

1. In the Calendar folder, click **Actions** . . . . Alt + A
2. Select **New Meeting Request** . . . . Q
   OR
   Click **File** . . . . Alt + F
   Point to **New** . . . . .W
   Select **Meeting Request** . . . . Q

Procedure Summary

OR
Click the New down arrow . . . . Alt + N
Select **Meeting Request** . . . . Q

3. On the Appointment tab in the Meeting window, click **To.** . . . . Alt + .
   OR
   Click the Scheduling tab.
   Click **Add Others** . . . . Alt + D
   Select Add from **Address Book**. . . . . .A
4. In the Select Attendees and Resources dialog box, select the desired names and click **Required, Optional**, or **Resources**.
5. Click OK.
6. On the Appointment tab, click in the **Subject** box and type the meeting name . . . . Alt + J
7. Click in the **Location box**, and type the meeting location . . . . Alt + L
8. Click the **Start time:** down arrow, and set the date and time . . . . Alt + Shift + :
9. Click in the **End time** down arrow, and set the date and time . . . . Alt + M
10. Select a **Label**, if desired . . . Alt + B; Up or Down arrow key
11. If desired, click **Categories**, select a category, and click OK . . . . .Alt + G; Up or Down arrow key; Spacebar
12. If desired, click in the Notes area, and type a note.
13. Click **Send** Send . . . . Alt + S

Accept and Decline Meeting Requests

1. In the Inbox folder, open the meeting request.
2. Click **Accept** ✓ Accept or **Decline** ✕ Decline . . . . Alt + C OR Alt + D
   OR
   In the Inbox, right-click the meeting request.
   Select **Accept** or **Decline** . . . . C OR E
   OR
   In the Inbox, select the meeting request.
   Click **Actions** . . . . Alt + A
   Select **Accept** or **Decline** . . . . C OR E
   OR
   In the Inbox, select the meeting request.
   Click **Accept** ✓ Accept or **Decline** ✕ Decline in the Preview Pane.
3. Select how you want to respond (with or without response).
4. Click OK.
5. If desired, type a message response.
6. Click **Send** Send. . . . . Alt + S

Propose Alternative Meeting Times

1. In the Inbox folder, open the meeting request.
2. Click **Propose New Time** Propose New Time . . . . Alt + S
   OR
   In the Inbox, right-click the meeting request.
   Select **Propose New Time** . . . . S
   OR
   In the Inbox, select the meeting request.
   Click **Actions** . . . . Alt + A
   Select **Propose New Time** . . . . S
   OR

In the Inbox, select the meeting request.
Click **Propose New Time** button Propose New Time in the Preview Pane.

3. Enter the new meeting time.
4. Click **Propose Time**.
5. If desired, type a message response.
6. Click **Send** Send . . . . **Alt + S**

Assign Categories to Appointments

1. In the Calendar folder, select the appointment.
2. Click **Edit** . . . . **Alt + E**
3. Select **Categories** . . . . **I**

OR

In the Calendar folder, open the appointment.
Click **Categories** . . . . **Alt + G**

OR

In the Calendar folder, right-click the appointment.
Select **Categories** . . . . **I**

4. In the *Available categories* list in the Categories dialog box, click the check boxes next to the desired categories.. . . . . . . **Up or Down arrow key, Spacebar**
5. Click OK.

Change and Print Calendar Views

1. In the Calendar folder, click **Day** Day. . . . . **Alt + Y**

OR

Click **View** . . . . **Alt + V**
Select **Day**. . . . . **Y**

OR

In the Calendar folder, click **Work Week** Work Week. . . . . **Alt + R**

OR

Click **View** . . . . **Alt + V**
Select **Work Week**. . . . . **R**

OR

In the Calendar folder, click **Week** Week. . . . . **Alt + W**

OR

Click **View** . . . . **Alt + V**
Select **Week**. . . . . **W**

OR

In the Calendar folder, click **Month** Month. . . . . **Alt + M**

OR

Click **View** . . . . **Alt + V**
Select **Month** . . . . **M**

OR

2. Click **Print** . . . . **Ctrl + P**

OR

Click **File** . . . . **Alt + F**
Select **Print** . . . . **P**

3. In the *Print style* section of the Print dialog box, select the desired style . . . . **Alt + Y, Up or Down arrow key**
4. In the *Print range* section, set the **Start** date . . . . **Alt + S**
5. In the *Print range* section, set the **End** date . . . . **Alt + E**
6. In the *Copies* section, set the **Number of copies** . . . **Alt + C, Up or Down arrow key**
7. Click **Preview** . . . . **Alt + V**
8. Click **Print** . . . . **Alt + P**

Lesson Review and Exercises

Summary Checklist

- ☑ Can you create, edit, and organize contact information to demonstrate productive work habits?
- ☑ Can you add appointments to the Calendar and label the items in a logical and understandable manner?
- ☑ Can you add events to the Calendar and label the items in a logical and understandable manner?
- ☑ Can you schedule meeting requests?
- ☑ Can you invite attendees to a meeting while modeling acceptable e-mail etiquette?
- ☑ Can you accept and decline meeting request?
- ☑ Can you propose alternative meeting times using available and convenient e-mail features?
- ☑ Can you organize your Calendar items using categories, changing views, and printing the Calendar to meet your needs?

Key Terms

- accept (p. 697)
- Address Card view (p. 689)
- appointment (p. 694)
- Calendar (p. 694)
- contact information (p. 686)
- Contacts (p. 686)
- Contacts list (p. 687)
- Day/Week/Month view (p. 704)
- decline (p. 697)
- Detailed Address Cards (p. 689)
- event (p. 694)
- free/busy time (p. 697)
- Global Address List (p. 686)
- Journal (p. 689)
- meeting request (p. 697)
- Outlook Address Book (p. 686)
- Personal Address Book (p. 687)
- propose new time (p. 697)
- recurring (p. 694)
- resource (p. 697)
- timeline (p. 689)
- time management (p. 702)

APPLY IT! **Guided Activities**

1. Create and Categorize Contacts

You are going to utilize your newly learned Outlook skills to set up a study group for you and three of your classmates. In this exercise, you'll use Outlook to create, edit, categorize, organize, and sort contacts and track contact activity.

a. Decide upon the class for which you want to set up a study group. In your Contacts folder, add or verify contact information for three classmates in your class. Be sure to include valid e-mail addresses.

b. Edit one of the contacts to include a nickname on the Details tab of the Contact form.

c. Create a custom category for the class and add the three classmates to the new category (see the History Study Group category in **Figure 2.20**).

d. On the View menu, point to Current view and select By Category. Open the custom category. Click File As on the Sort By bar to sort the contacts.

e. Send a test message to one of the three classmates. Then open the Contact for that classmate and click the Activities tab. The test message will appear in the list.

Figure 2.20 Set up a new category

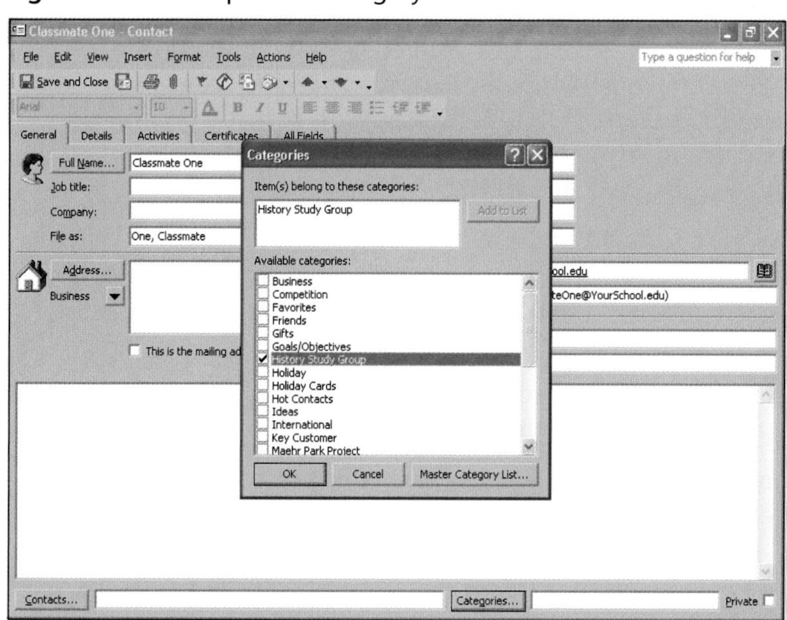

Outlook®

Outlook®

2. Print Calendars

For maximum efficiency, you want two printed views of your Calendar—one for the month and one for the week.

a. Click the Calendar folder. On the File menu, select Print. In the *Print Style* section of the Print dialog box, select Monthly Style. Set the *Start* date as 3/1/200x, and the *End* date as 3/31 of the same year. Click OK.

b. On the File menu, select Print. In the *Print style* section of the Print dialog box, select Tri-fold Style. Set the start date as the first Monday in March of the current year and the end date as the following Monday of the same year.

c. Click Define Styles and click Edit. In the *Options* section of the Page Setup Tri-fold Style dialog box, select Weekly Calendar in the left section, TaskPad in the middle section, and Notes (Blank) in the right section. Click OK and click Close. Then, click Preview to see the tri-fold and print one copy of the calendar.

Do It Yourself

Schedule a Meeting

You are now ready to schedule study meetings. Assume your class has a quiz every two weeks throughout the spring term (January 15 through May 15), and your study group wants to meet the day before each quiz.

a. In your Calendar folder, schedule a recurring quiz (every two weeks throughout the spring term) for your class on Wednesdays from 11 a.m.–12 p.m. The schedule a recurring meeting from 7–8 p.m. on the evening before each quiz. In the Subject box, type Study Group. Send the meeting request to your three study group contacts identified in Guided Activity 1.

b. Right-click the Calendar grid and apply a conditional format so that the appointments or meeting requests on your calendar will have a *Must Attend* (orange) label if they contain the word *study*.

c. Assign the custom study group category to each study group appointment (see Step c of Guided Activity 1). (***Hint:*** Open the "series" for the recurring appointment.)

d. If you receive meeting invitations from your classmates, accept one, decline one, and propose a new time of 6 p.m. for one.

e. Open one of your study group contacts and examine the Activities tab.

Challenge Yourself

Manage Your Calendar

As a newly hired summer intern at the mayor's office in your city, you are eager to make a good impression by being organized and demonstrating productive work habits. Your first week on the job is incredibly busy and you'll use Outlook as your primary organizational tool during your internship (June 1 – August 15).

Enter the items in **Table 2.11** into your Calendar. Use Kristine Schultz's contact information to create a *New Contact from Same Company* for the mayor (EdmondJones@aubcity.gov) and the mayor's assistant (your teacher will provide you an e-mail address). Categorize each contact as Business and VIP. View the contacts by Phone List and sort by Company. Then, invite the assistant to a recurring bi-weekly meeting to help you prioritize upcoming assignments. After you receive a reply, confirm the meeting time and view your Calendar by Recurring Appointments. Create a conditional format so that all Assignment Meetings appear in blue (*Business*) and City Council Meetings appear in mustard (*Needs Preparation*) on the Calendar. Print the Calendar in Weekly style (for the second week of June) and Monthly style (for June) and view the Contact activity for the assistant.

Table 2.11

	Calendar Item 1	Calendar Item 2	Calendar Item 3	Calendar Item 4
Subject	Weekly Staff Meeting	Fundraiser Event	City Council Meeting	Assignment Meeting
Location	Conference Room 1	Convention Center	City Hall	Assistant's Office
Time	Friday 12:00-1:00 PM	First Saturday in June - All Day Event	Tuesday 2:00-5:00 PM	Monday and Wednesday 9:00-9:30 AM
Recurrence	Weekly	None	Weekly	Weekly
Show time as	Busy	Out of Office	Busy	Busy
Reminder	15 minutes	18 hours	15 minutes	15 minutes
Label	None	Important	None	None
Notes	Lunch is provided.		Prepare agenda.	
Contacts	Mayor, Assistant	Mayor, Assistant	Mayor, Assistant	Assistant
Categories	Status	VIP Event	Business	Status

Lesson 3

Using Tasks and Notes

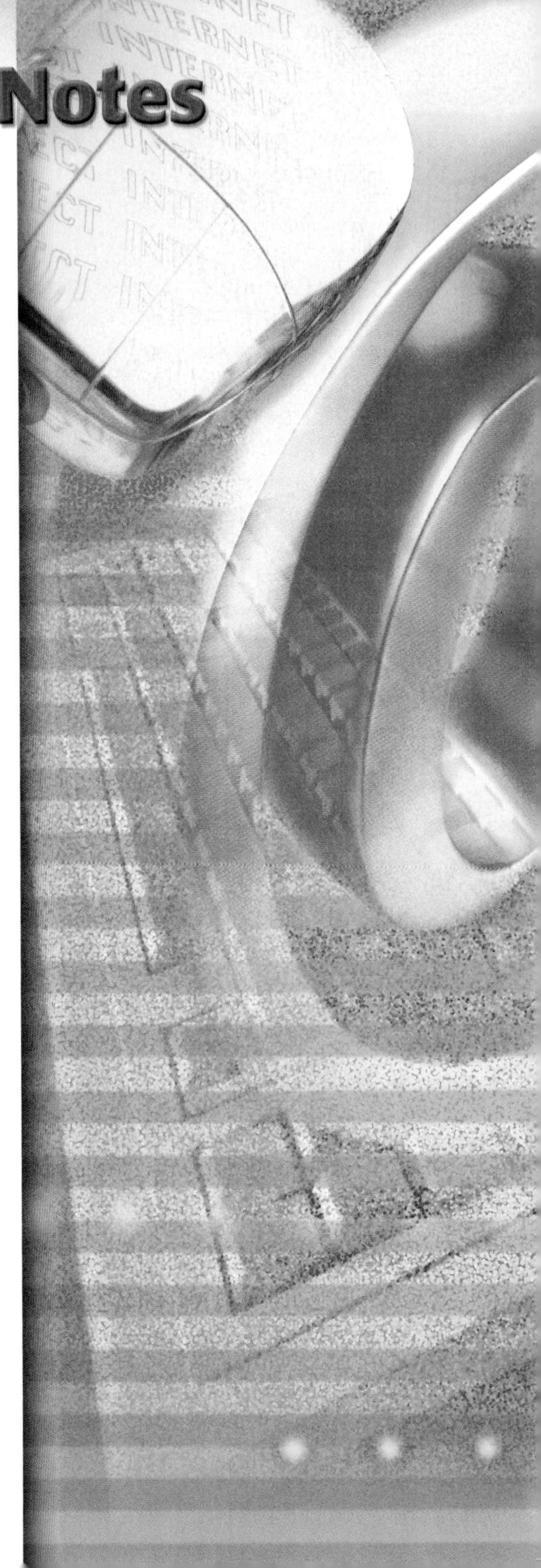

Lesson Exercise Objectives

After completing this lesson, you'll be able to do the following tasks:

1. Create and update tasks
2. Work with task requests
3. Create and manage notes

Key Terms

- note (p. 728)
- Notes (p. 728)
- task (p. 718)
- task list (p. 718)
- task owner (p. 722)
- TaskPad (p. 718)
- task request (p. 722)
- Tasks (p. 718)

Microsoft Office Specialist Activities

OL2002: 5.1–5.5

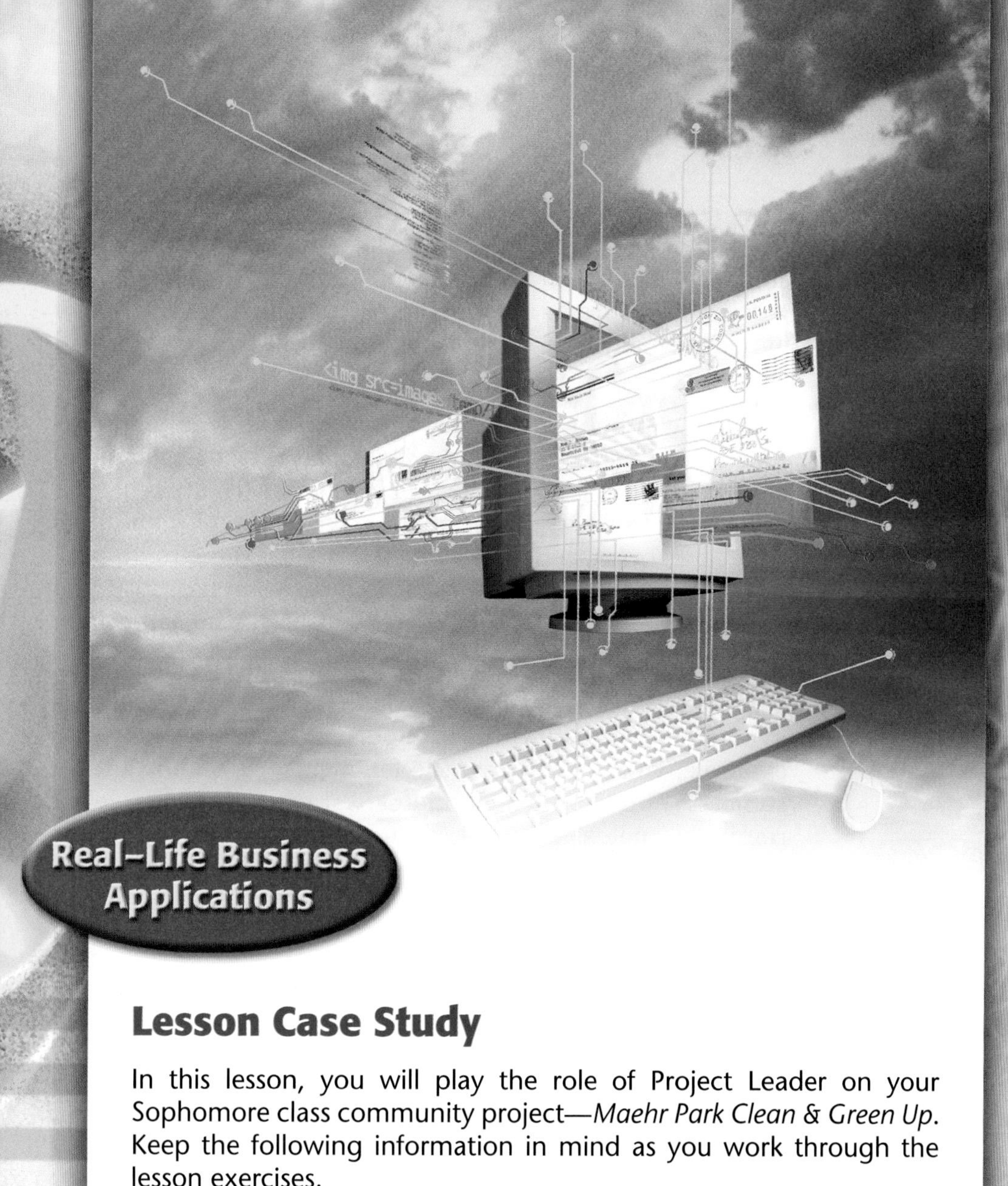

Lesson Case Study

In this lesson, you will play the role of Project Leader on your Sophomore class community project—*Maehr Park Clean & Green Up*. Keep the following information in mind as you work through the lesson exercises.

- `Job responsibilities and goals.` There is only one week to go until the *Maehr Park Clean & Green Up*. You and the other team leaders will need to make sure all subcommittee volunteers know their assignments for the clean-up days.
- `The project.` The success of the Maehr Park Project depends on everyone knowing their role and nothing slipping through the cracks.
- `The challenge ahead.` In a continued effort to be as organized as possible, you'll use Outlook's Tasks and Notes to help with last-minute project details.

Microsoft Office Specialist
OL2002 5.1, 5.2, 5.5

Exercise 1 Overview: Create and Update Tasks

Does it ever seem that on certain days there is too much to remember? Do you have trouble keeping all of your responsibilities straight? Many people create "to-do" lists by writing down items they need to accomplish on a piece of paper or on a calendar. However, lists tend to get misplaced or forgotten.

Outlook can help you track your **tasks** (personal or work-related chores that you can track until they are complete) electronically on a **task list**. You can view the task list on the Outlook Today page, on the **TaskPad** of your daily Calendar, or in the **Tasks** folder (an electronic to-do list). And best of all, a task will remain on your list until you mark it complete—no more rewriting items or potentially misplacing your list.

Outlook's Tasks feature uses many of the same options available in other Outlook items (see Figure 3.1). For example, you can indicate the following criteria for a task: subject, start and end dates, status, priority level, reminder, notes, contacts, and categories. On the Tasks toolbar, the New Task button is the most commonly used button.

Type: create a task

Figure 3.1 Sample task

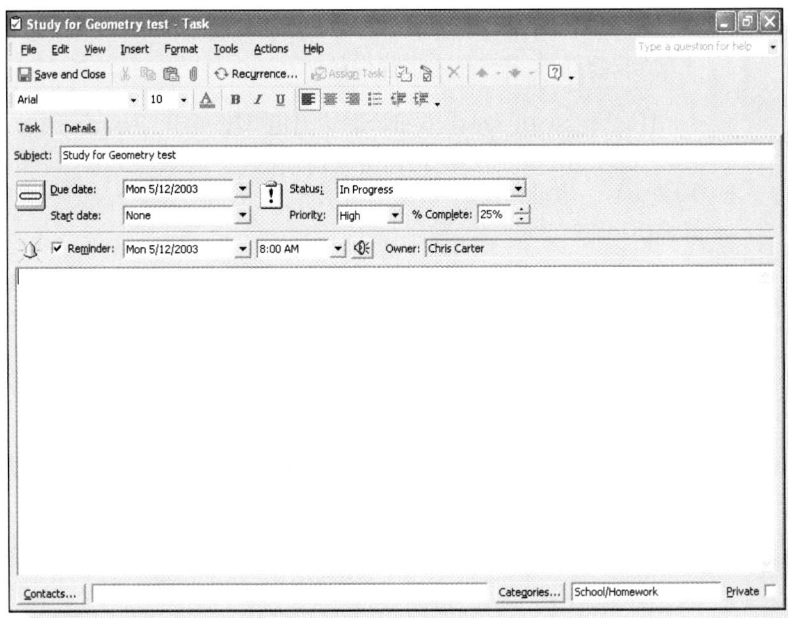

In the following exercises, you will add several tasks to your task update a task, and change the Task view.

Figure 3.2 The Task form

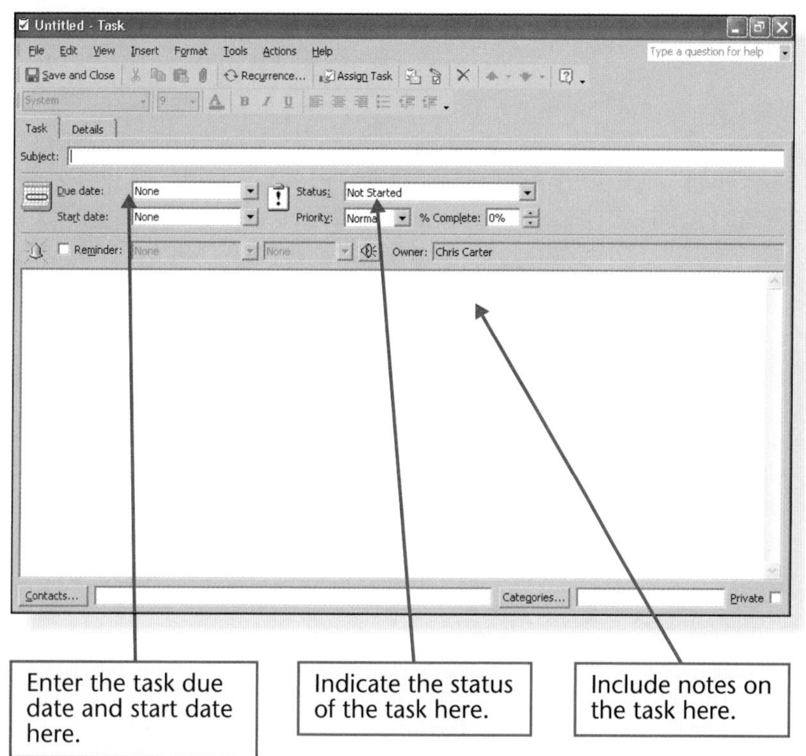

Step Through It™

Exercise 1A: Create a task

1. Click the Tasks folder. You will see the task list displayed in Simple List view.
2. Click New Task [New] on the Standard toolbar. The Task form will open. Maximize the window (see Figure 3.2).

Table 3.1

	Task 1	Task 2	Task 3
Subject	Take down volunteer sign-up sheets	Study for Geometry test	Get card for Mom's birthday
Due date	5/12/200x	5/12/200x	5/23/200x
Start date	None	None	None
Status	Not Started	In Progress	Not Started
Priority	High	High	Normal
% Complete	0%	25%	0%
Reminder	5/12/200x 8:00 AM	5/12/200x 8:00 AM	5/23/200x 8:00 AM
Categories	Maehr Park Project	School/ Homework	Personal

3. Enter the information for Task 1 as shown in Table 3.1. (***Note:*** Use a future date for this exercise.)
4. Click Save and Close. Your task will now be displayed in the task list.
5. Add Tasks 2 and 3 as shown in Table 3.1. Click Save and Close after you have entered each task.

Step Through It™
Exercise 1B: Update a task

1. Click the Calendar folder and select May 12.
2. Click Day on the Standard toolbar, if necessary.
3. Expand the TaskPad by dragging the frame to the left. Your TaskPad will display your current tasks (see Figure 3.3).
4. Double-click the *Take down volunteer sign-up sheets* item.

Figure 3.3 Viewing tasks on the TaskPad

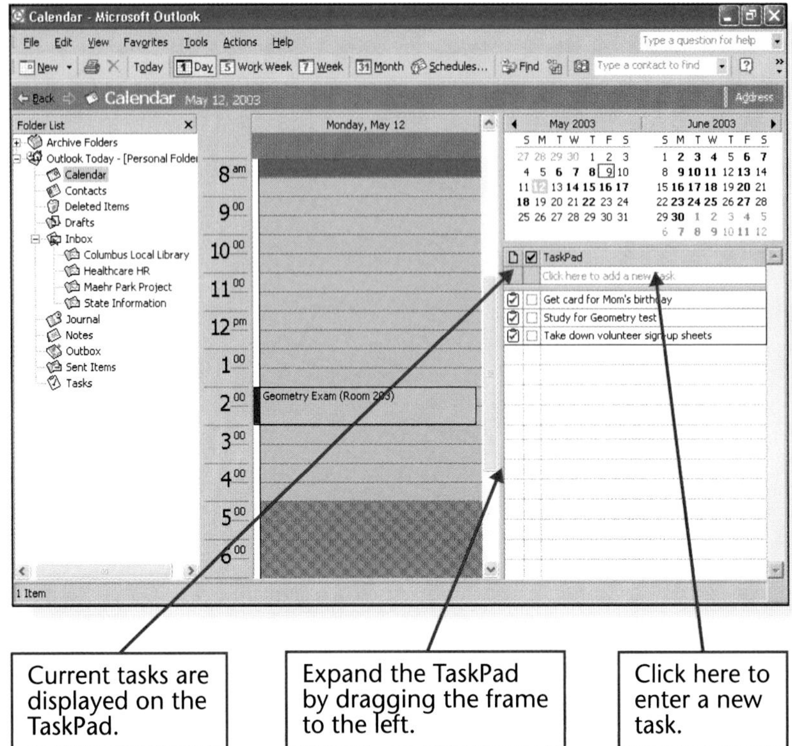
Current tasks are displayed on the TaskPad.
Expand the TaskPad by dragging the frame to the left.
Click here to enter a new task.

5. Update the task to reflect the following information (see Figure 3.4):
   Due date: May 13
   Status: In Progress
   Notes: Distribute lists to subcommittee team leaders.
6. Click Save and Close.

Figure 3.4 Updating a task

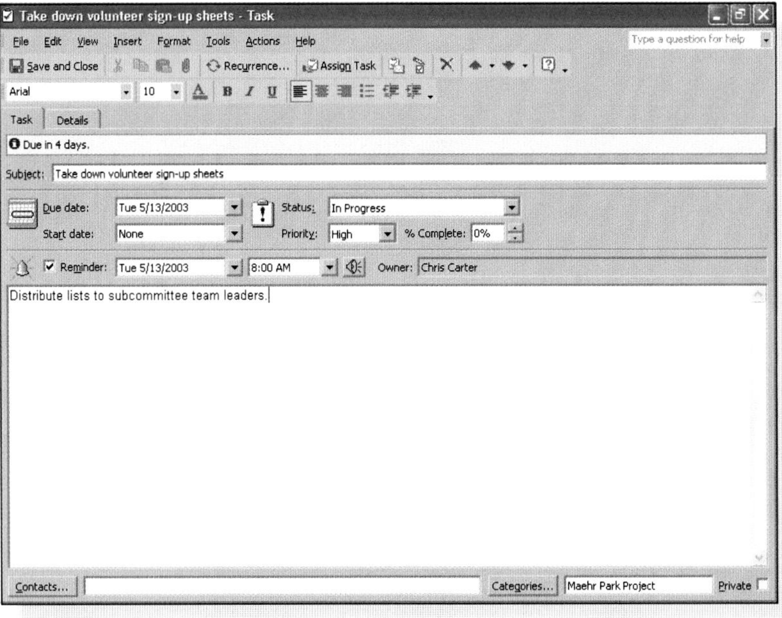

Outlook®

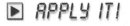

APPLY IT! After finishing Exercises 1A–1B, you may test your skills by completing Apply It! Guided Activity 1, Create and Update Tasks.

Technology@School

Schools on the Web

Practically every organization has a Web site, and your school is probably no exception. Many educational institutions have created Web sites to communicate with their students, parents, and community.

Your school's Web site is a great place to find out all sorts of general information about your school, from the football team's schedule and statistics to the time and place of the next school board meeting. By using a password, you (and your parents!) may also be able to find out specific information about your grades, homework assignments, and graduation requirements. Here are just a few things that you may be able to do on your school's Web site:

- Check your grades and upcoming homework assignments.
- E-mail your teacher.
- Create your own personal Web page.
- Find out more about a club or team that interests you.

Feature	Description
Menus	What's for lunch? Many schools post their cafeteria menus online.
Calendar	When's your next day off? Your school calendar may be just a click away.
Library	Need to do some research? Your school library may be online and accessible through your school's Web site.
Classes	Check your class Web site to find homework assignments, an overview of what the class covers, schedules, study hints, and helpful links.
Publications	Read your school newspaper and other publications online.

CRITICAL THINKING

1. Pair up with another student and review your school's Web site. What features does it offer? Is it easy to navigate? What, if anything, should be added to the Web site? If your school doesn't have a Web site, write an opinion column on why it should. Include a list of suggested features for the Web site.
2. Form a team with other students. Design (or redesign) a Web page for your class. Use Outlook to organize and communicate about your work. Present your Web site plan to your class.

Microsoft Office Specialist OL2002 5.2, 5.3

Exercise 2 Overview:
Work With Task Requests

As you can see, creating tasks is another way to utilize Outlook to keep organized and manage your duties on the *Maehr Park Clean & Green Up*. In addition to creating and managing your own task list, you can send **task requests** to others.

When you create a task request, you may keep a copy of the task on your task list as well as receive a status report when the task is complete.

When you receive a task request, you have the option to accept, decline, or assign the task to someone else. If you accept the task, the task is added to your task list and you become the **task owner**. (Only the task owner can make changes or updates to a task.) If you decline the task request, the task is not added to your task list. If you assign the task to someone else and he/she accepts it, the new recipient becomes the task owner and the task is added to his/her task list. In each case, the task requester will receive a message indicating if the task was accepted, declined, or delegated.

Type: about tasks and task assignments

The following table illustrates some of the commonly used buttons on the Tasks toolbar.

Tasks toolbar

Button		Purpose
✓ Accept	Accept	Accept a task request
✕ Decline	Decline	Decline a task request
Assign Task	Assign Task	Assign or delegate a task to someone else

In the following exercises, you will send a task request, change your task view, accept and decline a task request, and delegate a task to someone else.

Figure 3.5 The Task Request form

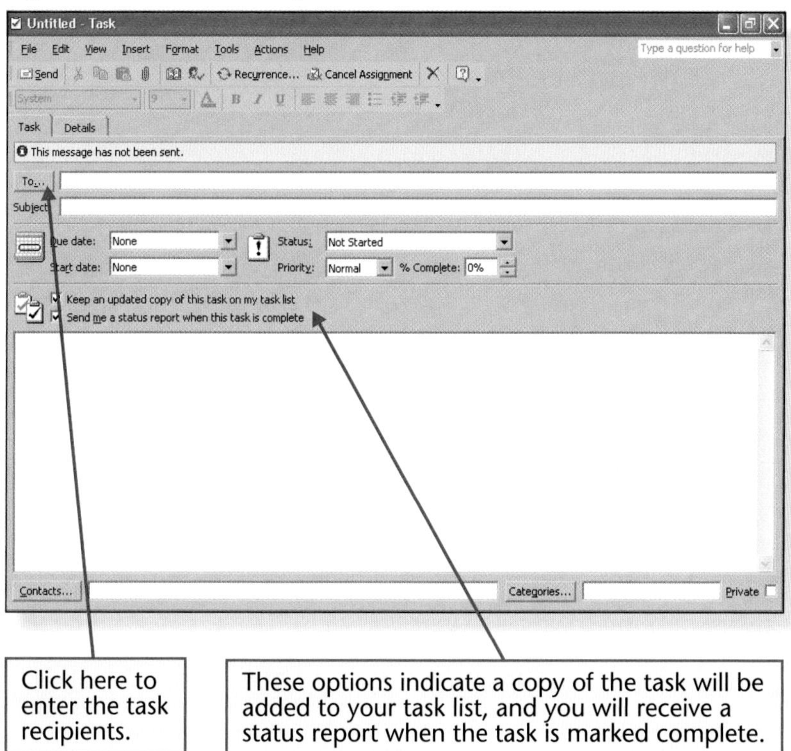

Click here to enter the task recipients.
These options indicate a copy of the task will be added to your task list, and you will receive a status report when the task is marked complete.

Step Through It™

Exercise 2A: Send a task request

1. Click the Tasks folder.
2. On the Actions menu, select New Task Request. The Task Request form appears. Maximize the window, if necessary (see Figure 3.5).

Table 3.2

To	**Azmi Maghathe; Heather Kemper; Jermaine Samuels; Mary Jane Palmisano; Project Advisor**
Subject	**Update volunteers**
Due date	**5/14/200x**
Start date	**None**
Notes	**Please verify that all volunteers on your subcommittee know when to arrive at Maehr Park for their assignments.**
Categories	**Maehr Park Project**

3. Enter the information as shown in Table 3.2.
4. Click Send; then click OK in the message box indicating that your task will not be updated. The task request will be sent, and a copy of the task will appear in your task list. (***Note:*** If you open the task, the InfoBar will indicate that task updates will not be tracked.)

Quick Tip

You can easily organize your tasks by clicking the Organize button and using the *Ways to Organize Tasks* window pane.

Step Through It™

Exercise 2B: Accept and decline a task request

1. In the Inbox folder, open and read *Task Request: Pick Up Bowman's Bagels* (see Figure 3.6).
2. Click Accept. (If necessary, click OK to send the response now.) The request will be moved to your task list. (***Note:*** If another item opens, close it.)
3. Open and read the *Task Request: Opening Day Celebration Signs*. Click Close without taking action.
4. Open and read *Task Request: Trash bags and gloves*. Click Close.
5. Click the Tasks folder. On the View menu, point to Current View and then click Detailed List (see Figure 3.7).
6. Open *Trash bags and gloves* and click Decline. (If necessary, click OK to send the response now.) The task will disappear from your list.

Figure 3.6 Accept a task

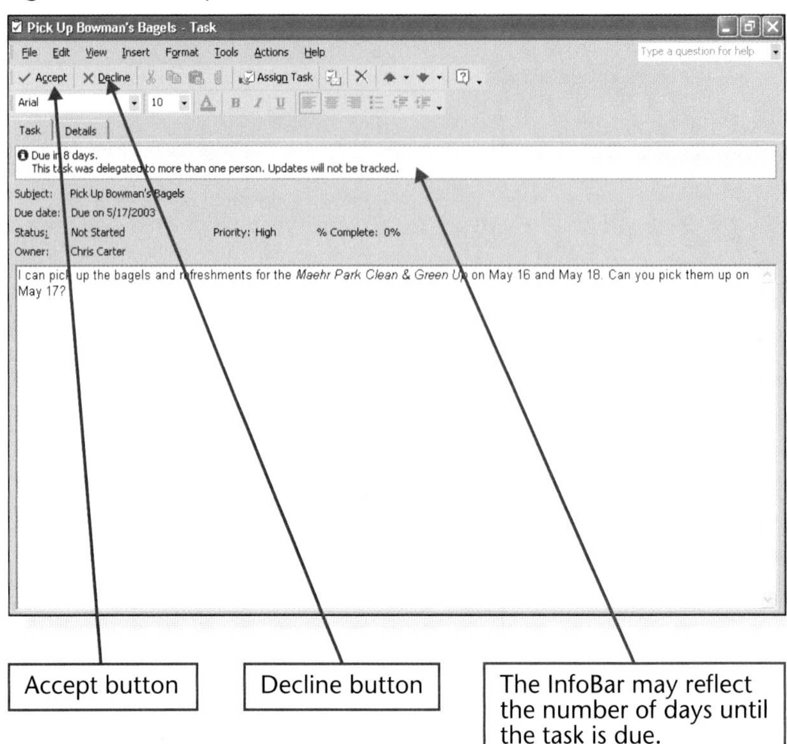

Figure 3.7 Displaying tasks in Detailed List view

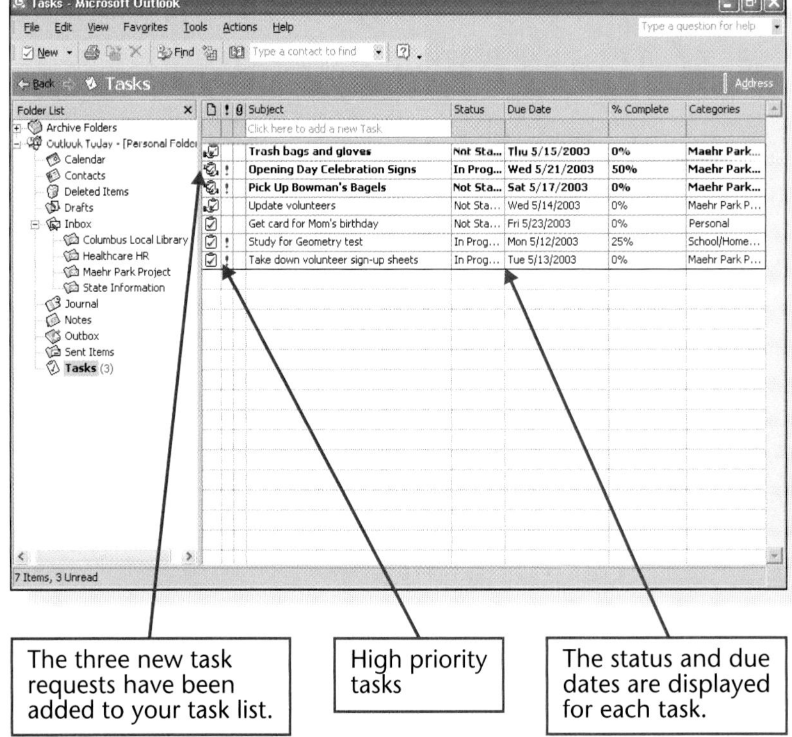

Figure 3.8 Delegate a task

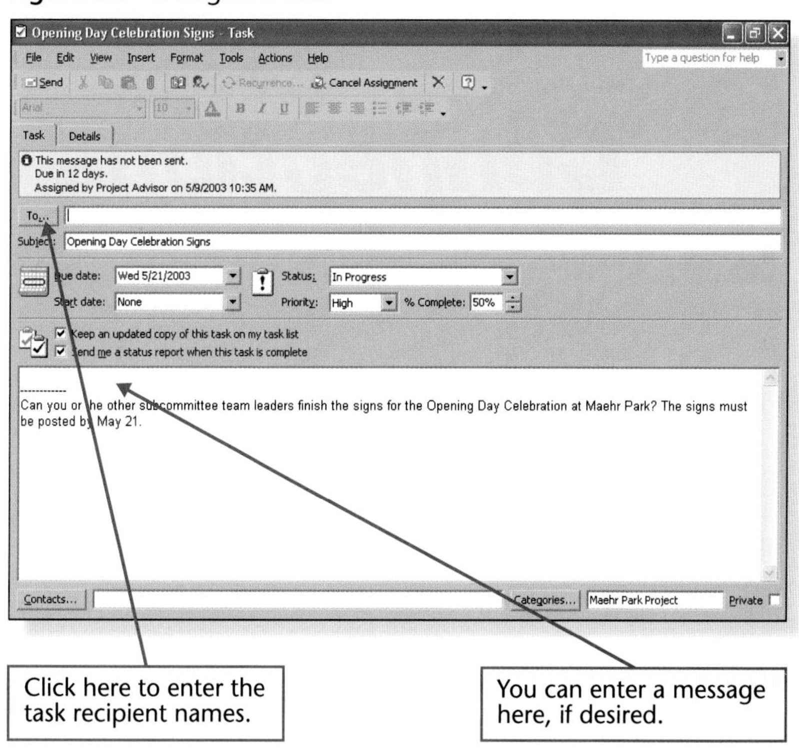

Step Through It™

Exercise 2C: Delegate a task request

1. From the task list, open *Opening Day Celebration Signs*.
2. Click Assign Task Assign Task (see Figure 3.8).
3. Click To. The Select Task Recipient dialog box appears.

Figure 3.9 The Select Task Recipient dialog box

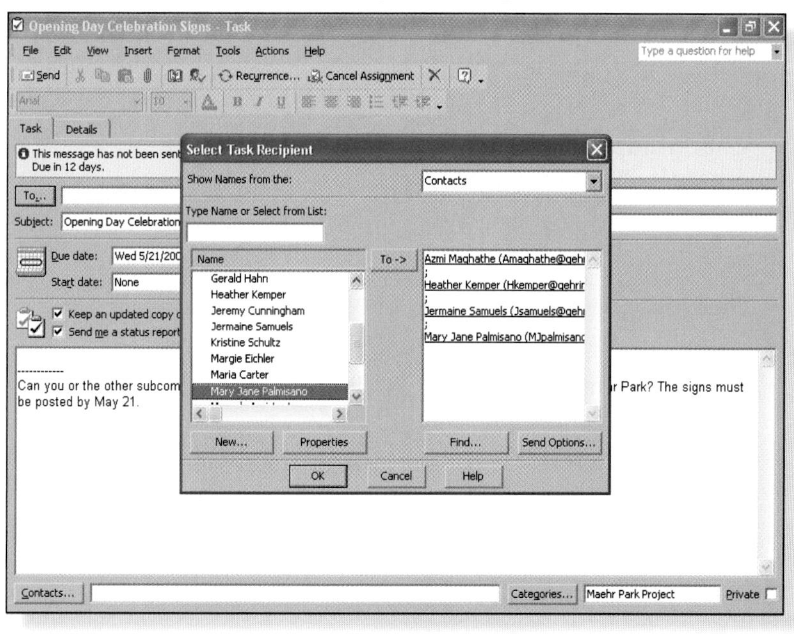

4. Double-click the following names: Azmi Maghathe, Heather Kemper, Jermaine Samuels, and Mary Jane Palmisano (see Figure 3.9). Click OK.
5. Click Send. (If necessary, click OK.) The task will be forwarded to each of the recipients, and a copy of the task will remain on your task list.
6. If necessary, open and close any "unread" (bold) task requests.

After finishing Exercises 2A–2C, you may test your skills by completing Apply It! Guided Activity 2, Assign Tasks to Others.

Business Connections

Communicating in a Digital World

In the pony express days, it took a message 10 days to travel 1,800 miles from St. Joseph, Missouri to Sacramento, California. Today, while connected to the Internet, we can send and receive instant messages and hold international real-time desktop video conferences. We also have many ways to send, receive, and research information electronically:

- **Bulletin boards and newsgroups** for participation in public discussions on particular subjects.
- **E-mail** for exchanging messages and files via the Internet.
- **Organized information services** (such as America Online) for searching digital information (news, weather, city information, and so on).
- **Chat groups** for communicating in real-time with others having similar interests.
- **Instant messaging** for exchanging information instantly in an online conversation.
- **Desktop video conferencing or NetMeeting** for teleconferences held over the Internet.
- **Wireless communication** for surfing the 'Net, reading e-mail, and using small hand-held devices (such as cell phones and PDAs).

Online Security

Increased digital communication results in the need for increased security measures. Companies must protect their information and data transfer from electronic abuse by ensuring:

- authentication (using passwords),
- authorization (allowing access only to authorized information),
- auditing (monitoring the security solution for abuse),
- using e-mail virus protection software, and
- installing firewalls.

Additionally, some companies are using Virtual Private Networks or VPNs (which allows communication across the Web to companies in a secure environment) and data encryption (sending an encrypted message to a recipient who decrypts the message with a secret "key") to ensure data security.

Total Access

Today, global connectivity is a reality. Digital access from anywhere to anyone at any time is expected by a company's employees, partners, and consumers.

CRITICAL THINKING

1. **Compare Internet Access Service** Research the difference between high-speed cable and high-speed phone line (ADSL) Internet access. What are the pros, cons, and cost considerations of each?
2. **Examine Security Risks** What vulnerability does a user have when no firewall or anti-virus software exists on a personal computer?

Microsoft Office Specialist
OL2002 5.4, 5.5

Outlook®

Exercise 3 Overview:
Create and Manage Notes

How many times have you relied on a sticky note to remember a task or an idea? Outlook's **Notes** folder is an electronic version of sticky notes. You can use **notes** to record information about a phone call, reminders about an upcoming meeting, ideas about a report, or anything that you would ordinarily write on paper.

As with other Outlook items, you can assign categories, contacts, and colors to notes. You can view notes by large or small icons, list, last seven days, category, or color.

If you are working on a project with someone else, you can forward a note to them for reference. And because notes can remain on your screen while you work, you can conveniently jot down information from within any Outlook item. The New Note button is a commonly used button on the Notes toolbar.

Type: notes

In the following exercises, you will create and update a note; assign contacts, categories, and colors to notes; and view notes by list, color, and category.

Step Through It™
Exercise 3A: Create and edit notes

1. Click the Notes folder. The empty Notes window will appear.
2. Click New Note New. A Note form appears with the current date and time displayed at the bottom of the window.
3. Type Meet with Kristine Schultz, press Enter twice, and type Maehr Park Opening Day Celebration. (See Figure 3.10.)

Figure 3.10 Create a note

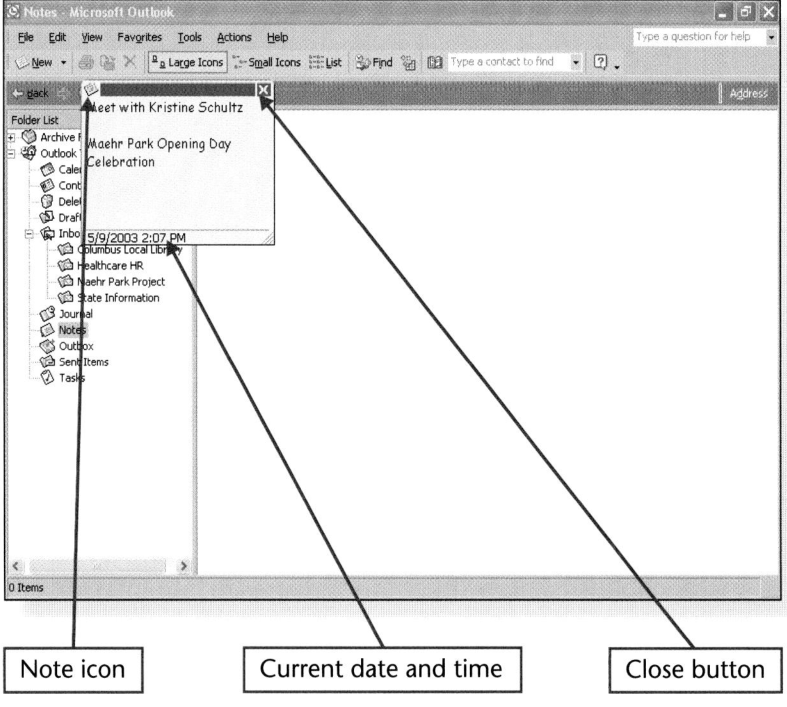

Table 3.3

Note 1	Note 2	Note 3
Call A1 Lawnmower Rental about debris removal pick-up times.	**Get Biology notes for Friday's class.** **Class Final is 5/30/200x.**	**Send thank you notes to subcommittee team leaders.**

4. Click Close to save and close your note. You are returned to the Notes folder, and the new note will appear in the window in Icons view.

5. Create three new notes by typing the information as shown in Table 3.3. Close each note when finished.

Figure 3.11 Notes displayed in Notes List view

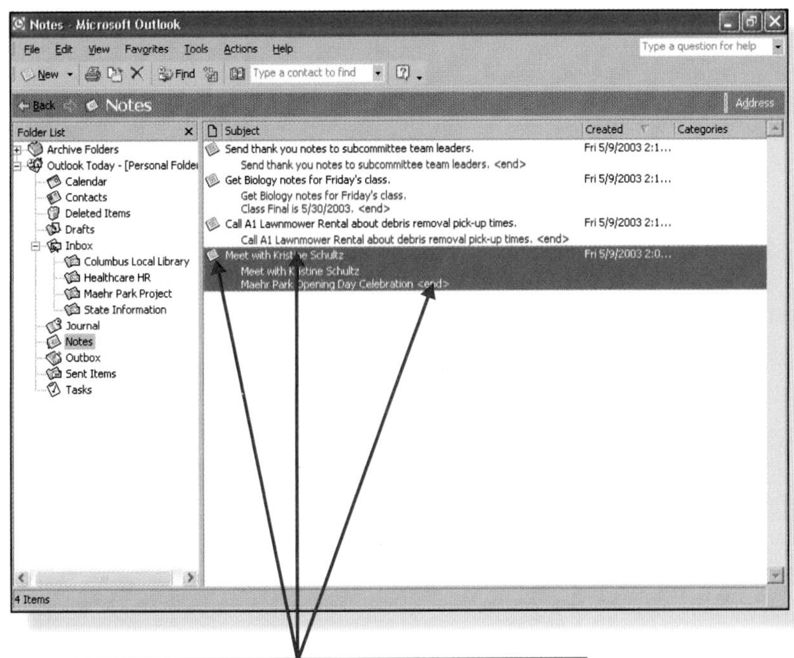

6. On the View menu, point to Current View and then select Notes List. The notes are displayed (see Figure 3.11).

7. Double-click the *Meet with Kristine Schultz* note.

8. Place your cursor at the end of the note and press Enter twice. Then, type the following: **Thank her for reference letter**.

9. Close the note.

Quick Tip

You can delete a note at any time. Simply click the note and then click Delete.

Outlook®

Step Through It™

Exercise 3B: Assign contacts and categories to notes

1. Open the *Meet with Kristine Schultz* note and drag it to the center of the window.
2. Click the Note icon in the upper-left corner of the Note window (see Figure 3.12).
3. Select Categories, click *Maehr Park Project*, and click OK.
4. Click the Note icon again and select Contacts.

Figure 3.12 The Note icon menu

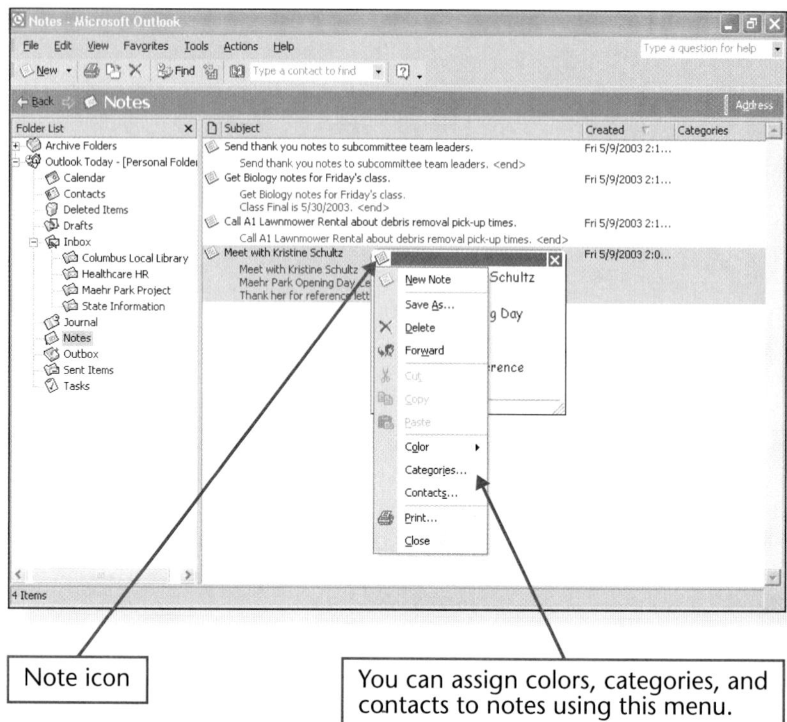

Note icon
You can assign colors, categories, and contacts to notes using this menu.

5. Click the Contacts button. The *Select Contacts* dialog box appears (see Figure 3.13).
6. Scroll down the Items list and select Kristine Schultz. Click OK.
7. Close the Contacts for Note dialog box.

Figure 3.13 The Select Contacts dialog box

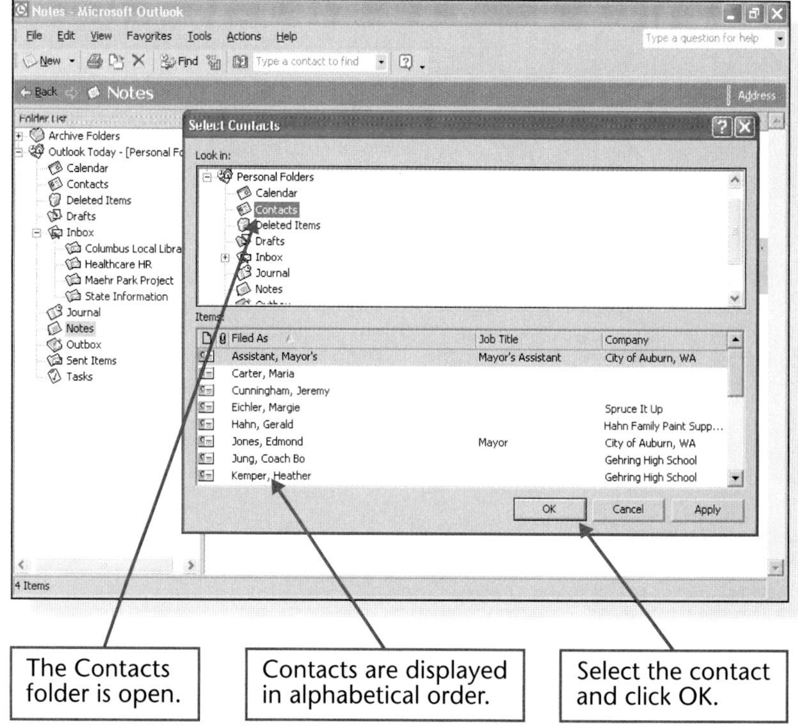

Outlook®

Table 3.4

Note	Call A1 Lawnmower Rental about debris removal pick-up times.	Get Biology notes for Friday's class.	Send thank you notes to subcommittee team leaders.
Category	**Maehr Park Project**	**School/ Homework**	**Maehr Park Project**
Contact	**Wendell Pederson**	**Pat Mireles**	**Azmi Maghathe, Heather Kemper, Jermaine Samuels, Mary Jane Palmisano**
Color	**Blue**	**Green**	**Blue**

8. Click the Note icon, point to Color and then select Blue. Close the note.
9. Assign categories, contacts, and colors to the remaining notes as shown in Table 3.4.

Figure 3.14 Notes displayed by color

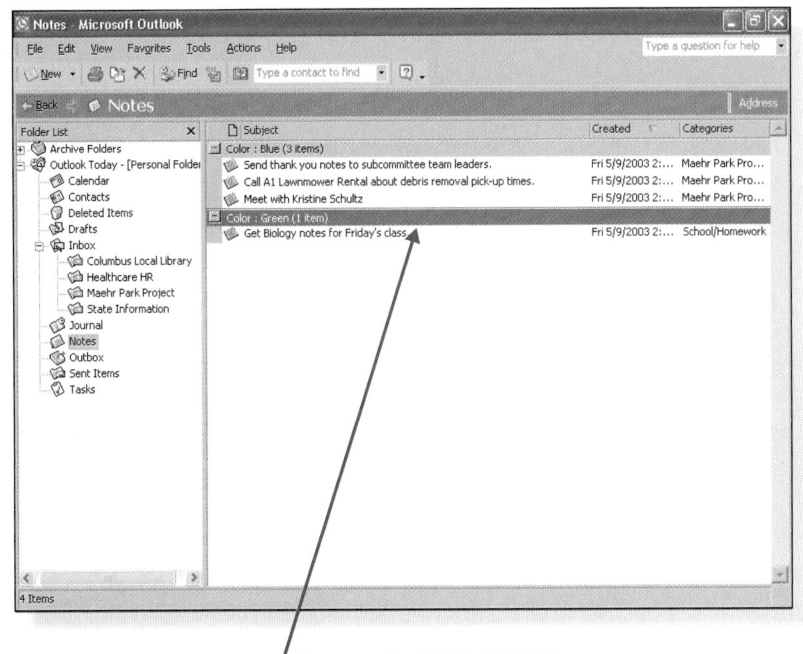

By Color view displays notes grouped by color, subject line, date created, and categories.

10. On the View menu, point to Current View and then select By Category.
11. Expand the categories so the notes are displayed.
12. On the View menu, point to Current View and then select By Color. Expand the colors (see Figure 3.14).

Procedure Summary

Outlook® Procedure Summary

Create a Task — Ctrl + Shift + K

1. In the Folder list, click the Tasks folder.
   OR
   Click **View** . . . . Alt + V
   Point to **Go To** . . . . G
   Select **Tasks** . . . . T
   OR
   Click **Tasks** on the Outlook Bar.
2. Click **New Task** . . . . Ctrl + N
   OR
   Click **Actions** . . . . Alt + A
   Select **New Task** . . . . A
   OR
   Click **File** . . . . Alt + F
   Point to **New** . . . . W
   Select **Task** . . . . T
   OR
   Click the **New** down arrow . . . . Alt + N
   Select **Task** . . . . T
3. Enter the task information.
4. Click **Save and Close** . . . . Alt + S

Update a Task

1. In the Folder list, click the Tasks folder.
   OR
   Click **View** . . . . Alt + V
   Point to **Go To** . . . . G
   Select **Tasks** . . . . T
   OR
   Click **Tasks** on the Outlook Bar.
2. Click in the Status column (available in the following views: Detailed List, Active Tasks, Next Seven Days, Overdue Tasks, By Category, Assignment, or By Person Responsible).
3. In the drop-down list, select Not Started, In Progress, Completed, Waiting on someone else, or Deferred.
4. Click in the % Complete column and edit as necessary.

OR

1. In the Folder list, click the Tasks folder.
   OR
   Click **View** . . . . Alt + V
   Point to **Go To** . . . . G
   Select **Tasks** . . . . T
   OR
   Click **Tasks** on the Outlook Bar.
2. Double-click the task to be updated.
3. Update the **Status:** and **% Complete** boxes . . . . Alt + :, Alt + L
4. Click **Save and Close** . . . . Alt + S

Send a Task Request — Ctrl + Shift + U

1. In the Tasks folder, click **Actions** . . . . Alt + A
2. Select **New Task Request** . . . . Q
   OR
   Click **File** . . . . Alt + F
   Point to **New** . . . . W
   Select **Task Request** . . . . R
   OR
   Click the **New** down arrow . . . . Alt + N
   Select **Task Request** . . . . Q
3. On the Task tab in the Task Request window, click **To.** . . . . Alt + .
4. In the Select Task Recipient dialog box, double-click the desired names . . . **Up and Down arrow key; Enter**
5. Click OK.
6. On the Task tab, click the **Subject** box and type the task name. . . . . Alt + J
7. Click the **Due date** down arrow, and set the due date . . . . Alt + D
8. Click the **Start date** down arrow, and set the start date . . . . Alt + R
9. If desired, click in the **Notes** area, and type a note.
10. If desired, click **Contacts**, select contacts from list, click Apply, and click OK . . . . Alt + C; Alt + I; **Up or Down arrow key; Alt + A**
11. If desired, click **Categories**, select a category, and click OK . . . . Alt + G; **Up or Down arrow key; Spacebar**
12. Click **Send** . . . . Alt + S

Accept and Decline Task Requests

1. In the Inbox folder, open the task request.
2. Click **Accept** or **Decline** .... **Alt + C OR Alt + D**
   OR
   In the Inbox, right-click the task request.
   Select **Accept** or **Decline**......... **C OR E**
   OR
   In the Inbox, select the task request.
   Click **Accept** or **Decline** in the Preview Pane.
   OR
   In the task list, open the task request.
   Click **Accept**
   or **Decline** ..... **Alt + C OR Alt + D**
   OR
   In the task list, right-click the task.
   Select **Accept** or **Decline**......... **C OR E**
3. If necessary, select how you want to respond (with or without a response), and click OK.
4. If desired, type a message response.
5. Click **Send** .... **Alt + S**

Delegate a Task Request

1. In the Inbox folder, open the task request.
2. Click **Assign Task** .... **Alt + N**
   OR
   In the task list, right-click the task.
   Select **Assign Task**.................. **N**
   OR
   In the task list, open the task request.
   Click **Assign Task** .... **Alt + N**
3. On the Task tab in the Task Request window, click **To.** .... **Alt + .**
4. In the Select Task Recipient dialog box, double-click the desired names.
5. Click OK.
6. Click **Send** .... **Alt + S**

Create a Note **Ctrl + Shift + N**

1. In the Folder list, click the Notes folder.
   OR
   Click **Notes** on the Outlook Bar.
2. Click **New Note** .... **Ctrl + N**
   OR
   Click **Actions**.................. **Alt + A**
   Select **New Note**.................. **N**
   OR
   Click **File** .... **Alt + F**
   Point to **New**.................... **W**
   Select **Note** .... **N**
   OR
   Click the **New** down arrow ...... **Alt + N**
   Select **Note** .... **N**
3. Enter the note content.
4. Close the note.

Assign Contacts to a Note

1. In the Notes folder, open the note.
2. Click the Note icon.
3. Select **Contacts** from the list .... **S**
4. Click the **Contacts** button .... **Alt + C**
5. Select the desired contact from the **Items** list . .**Alt + I; Up OR Down arrow key**
6. Click **Apply** (repeat steps 5 and 6 for each desired contact)................ **Alt + A**
7. Click OK.
8. Click **Close** .... **Alt + C**
9. Close the note.

Assign Categories to Notes

1. In the Notes folder, select the note.
2. Click **Edit**..................... **Alt + E**
3. Select **Categories** .... **I**
   OR
   In the Notes folder, open the note.
   Click the Note icon.
   Select **Categories** .... **I**
   OR
   In the Notes folder, right-click the note.
   Select **Categories** .... **I**
4. In the *Available categories* list in the Categories dialog box, select the desired categories ....**Up or Down arrow key, Spacebar**
5. Click OK.

Outlook® Procedure Summary

Lesson Review and Exercises

Summary Checklist

- ☑ Can you create tasks to help you stay organized?
- ☑ Can you update tasks to help you stay organized?
- ☑ Can you display tasks in several different views?
- ☑ Can you assign contacts and categories to your tasks?
- ☑ Can you utilize Outlook tools to accept and decline tasks appropriately?
- ☑ Can you utilize Outlook tools to delegate tasks appropriately?
- ☑ Can you create and edit your notes?
- ☑ Can you organize your notes?
- ☑ Can you assign contacts to your notes?
- ☑ Can you assign categories to your notes?

Key Terms

- note (p. 728)
- Notes (p. 728)
- task (p. 718)
- task list (p. 718)
- TaskPad (p. 718)
- task owner (p. 722)
- task request (p. 722)
- Tasks (p. 718)

APPLY IT! Guided Activities

1. Create and Update Tasks

You are currently working as an office assistant in a legal office. Your latest assignment is to inventory the office supplies in the main supply room.

For this project, which is expected to take at least a few days, you will create a task, and then update the task as you complete the assignment.

a. Create a new task using the information in **Table 3.5**.

Table 3.5

Subject	Inventory office supplies in main supply room
Due date	8/12/200x
Start date	8/5/200x
Status	Not Started
Priority	High
% Complete	0%
Categories	Business

b. Two days after the start date, you estimate that the task is 50% complete. Open the task and update the *Status* and *% Complete* entries **(see Figure 3.15)**.

c. Four days after the start date, you complete the assignment. Open the task and update the *% Complete* entry to 100%.

Outlook®

Figure 3.15 Updated task

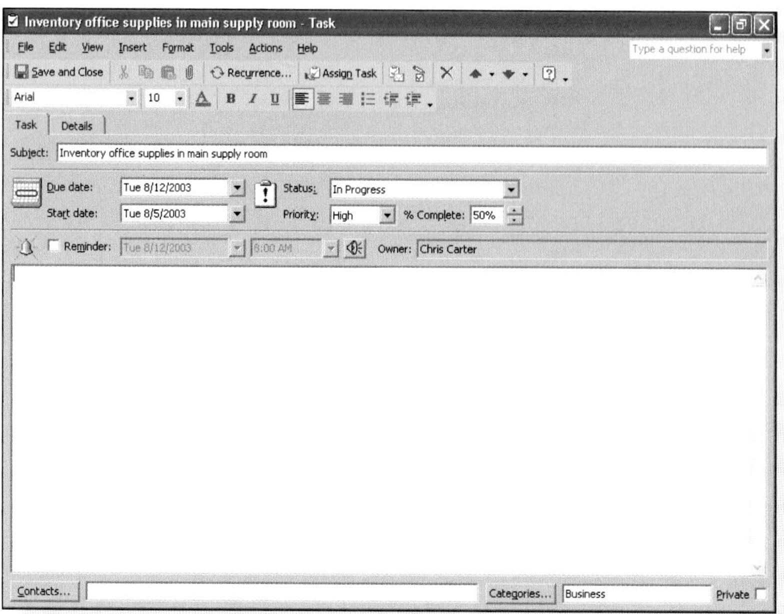

2. Assign Tasks to Others

Part of your role as the Office Assistant in a legal office is to coordinate meeting agendas and meeting refreshments. In preparation for the next staff meeting, you'll create and assign two tasks to two co-workers to help you get ready for the upcoming meeting.

a. Using the information in **Table 3.6**, create two tasks.

Table 3.6

	Agenda Task	Refreshments Task
Subject	Set up and publish agenda	Bring meeting refreshments
Due date	8/20/200x	8/20/200x
Start date	None	None
Priority	High	High
Reminder	8/19/200x 8:00 AM	8/19/200x 8:00 AM
Notes area	Check with Mr. Powers for important items - 555-4646.	Doughnuts, lattes from Perky's Coffee, no bear claws (food allergies)
Categories	Business	Business

b. Right-click the Tasks page and select Show Fields. Double-click Notes in the Available fields list to add it to the list. Position Notes beneath the Subject field in the list. Widen the new Notes column in the Task List view so that you can read most of the words).

c. Assign each task to one of your classmates (as instructed by your teacher).

d. When you receive the task assignments from the other students, accept one and decline the other. Then, update the accepted task to mark it complete.

Do It Yourself

1. Create and Work With Notes

You want to use keyboard shortcuts in Outlook, but you have a hard time remembering them. You'll create a note that contains the shortcuts you want to use, and assign the Help category to the note so that you can find it easily. Finally, you'll assign contacts to the note so that you can help co-workers who often ask you questions about keyboard shortcuts.

a. Type keyboard shortcuts in the Ask a Question box of the Outlook window. Select the Keyboard Shortcuts topic and explore *for basic navigation* information related to Outlook shortcuts.

b. In Outlook Help, select the shortcuts text for the note and drag the selected text to the Notes folder.

c. Drag a corner of the note to make it large enough to read all the text **(see Figure 3.16)**. Then type Outlook Shortcuts at the top of the note.

Figure 3.16 Create a note

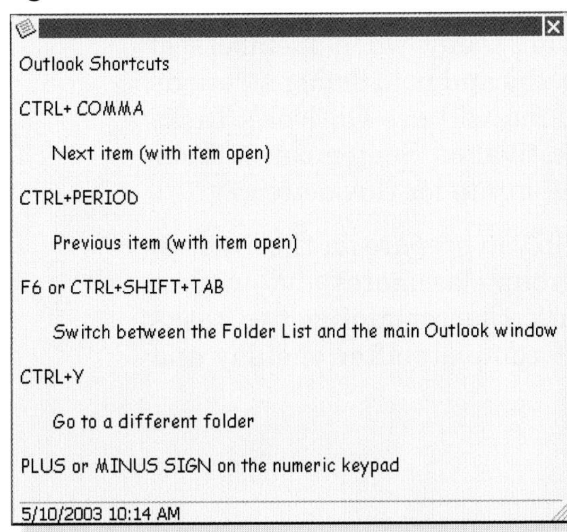

Outlook Shortcuts
CTRL+ COMMA
Next item (with item open)
CTRL+PERIOD
Previous item (with item open)
F6 or CTRL+SHIFT+TAB
Switch between the Folder List and the main Outlook window
CTRL+Y
Go to a different folder
PLUS or MINUS SIGN on the numeric keypad
5/10/2003 10:14 AM

Outlook®

d. Assign the color pink and the custom category *Help* to the note. Assign two of your contacts to the note. Close the note and close Outlook Help.

e. Switch the Notes folder view to *By Category* **(see Figure 3.17)**.

Figure 3.17 The By Category view of the Notes folder

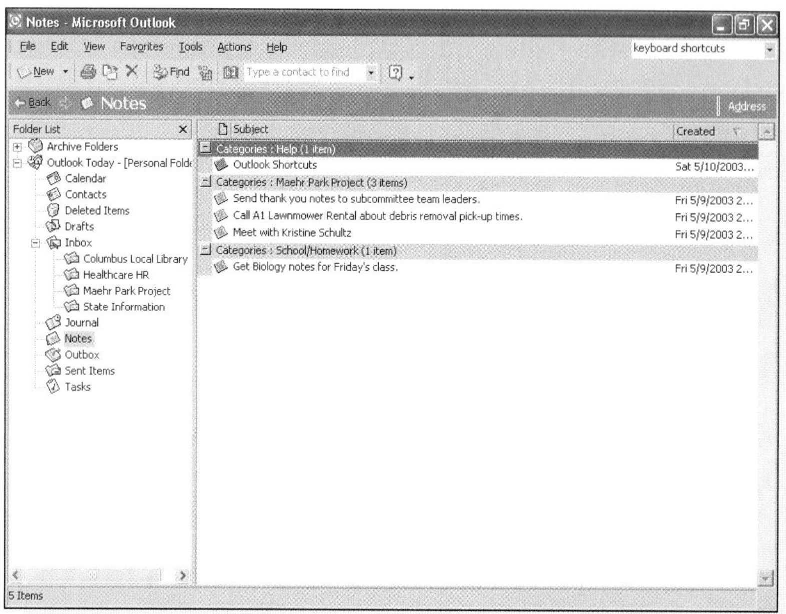

Challenge Yourself

Using Tasks and Notes to Prepare for a Meeting

As Outreach Coordinator in your local community, you are actively preparing for the next Outreach festival, a day when members of various human services groups set up booths and hold demonstrations in order to solicit funds and volunteers. You will use Outlook's Tasks and Notes to help you prepare for the festival on September 8. (Your teacher will assign you to work in a small group for this activity.)

Use **Table 3.7** to create a list of tasks to help you prepare for the festival. Assign one of the tasks to one of your group classmates and another task to a second group classmate. Track the remaining two tasks through completion (mark the task 50% complete after one day and 100% complete after two days).

Create three notes to remind you to (1) visit booths and sign up to volunteer, (2) pass out exhibitor evaluation forms, and (3) talk to attendees regarding needs for future festivals. Assign your group classmates as contacts to the notes and categorize each note as *Outreach*.

If you receive task requests from your classmates, accept one and decline another. After several days, mark the task complete and send a status report that includes your signature.

Table 3.7

	Task 1	Task 2	Task 3	Task 4
Subject	Confirm table needs	Verify delivery of tables and chairs	Festival set up	Pick up refresh-ments for exhibitors
Due date	9/05/200x	9/06/200x	9/07/200x	9/08/200x
Start date	9/04/200x	9/05/200x	9/07/200x	9/08/200x
Status	Not Started	Not Started	Not Started	Not Started
Priority	Normal	High	High	Normal
Reminder	9/05/200x 8:00 AM	9/06/200x 8:00 AM	9/06/200x 8:00 AM	9/08/200x 7:00 AM
Notes area	Call exhibitors to confirm number of tables needed.	Call rental company to confirm delivery time.	Set up tables and chairs for exhibitors.	Pick up coffee, juice, water, and doughnuts for exhibitors.
Contacts	Classmates	Classmates	Classmates	Classmates
Categories	Outreach	Outreach	Outreach	Outreach

Outlook®

Unit 5 Applications and Projects

Apply Your Knowledge

Complete the following exercises in order, as directed by your teacher. As you work through these projects, you will be winding up the successful completion of the *Maehr Park Clean & Green Up*.

You will communicate by e-mail with the Project Advisor to provide your critique of the *Maehr Park Clean & Green Up* and to ask permission to plan a celebration party.

You will then schedule a party-planning meeting with the Maehr Park Project team leaders, create and assign tasks for the party, create a note for yourself, respond to a meeting request, organize and locate messages, and archive and save files.

1. Read, Print, Compose, and Send an E-mail Message

a. In your Inbox, open, read, and print the *Request for Critiques* message from your Project Advisor.

b. Create a new message to the Project Advisor (your teacher). Include an appropriate subject line for your message, and include the personal signature that you created in the Lesson 1 Do It Yourself exercise. Apply a theme, if desired.

c. Attach *MaehrParkParty.xls* to your message for your Project Advisor to review.

d. In your message, include a brief evaluation of the Maehr Park Project by answering the questions in the *Request for Critiques* message **(see Figure 1)**. Ask whether you may schedule a team leaders' meeting on the first Tuesday in June at 7 p.m. to plan a celebration party. Mention that you are attaching a proposed budget for the party for the Project Advisor's review.

e. Mark the message with High Importance. Use the delivery options to save the sent message to your *Maehr Park Project* folder. Then, send the message.

Figure 1 Maehr Park Project Critique message

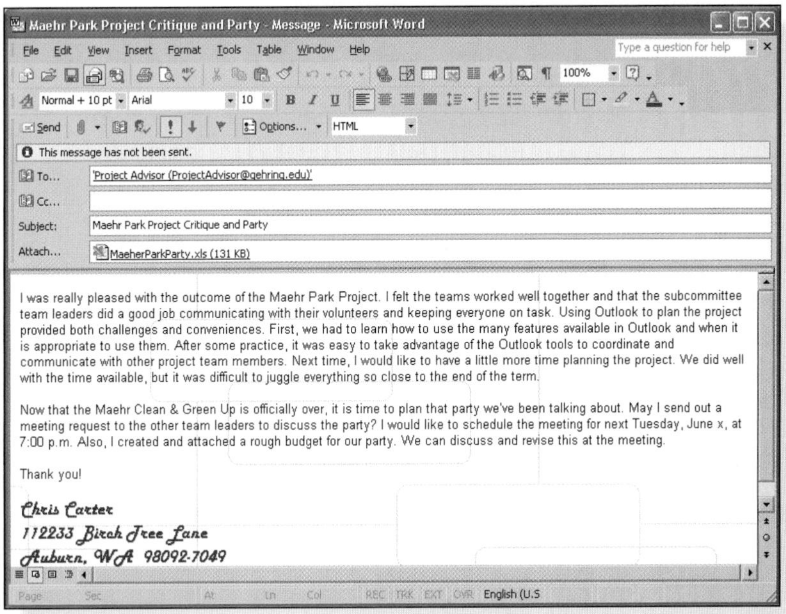
Maehr Park Project Critique and Party - Message - Microsoft Word
File Edit View Insert Format Tools Table Window Help
Type a question for help
Normal + 10 pt
Arial
10
100%
Send
Options...
HTML
This message has not been sent.
To...
'Project Advisor (ProjectAdvisor@gehring.edu)'
Cc...
Subject:
Maehr Park Project Critique and Party
Attach...
MaeherParkParty.xls (131 KB)
I was really pleased with the outcome of the Maehr Park Project. I felt the teams worked well together and that the subcommittee team leaders did a good job communicating with their volunteers and keeping everyone on task. Using Outlook to plan the project provided both challenges and conveniences. First, we had to learn how to use the many features available in Outlook and when it is appropriate to use them. After some practice, it was easy to take advantage of the Outlook tools to coordinate and communicate with other project team members. Next time, I would like to have a little more time planning the project. We did well with the time available, but it was difficult to juggle everything so close to the end of the term.
Now that the Maehr Clean & Green Up is officially over, it is time to plan that party we've been talking about. May I send out a meeting request to the other team leaders to discuss the party? I would like to schedule the meeting for next Tuesday, June x, at 7:00 p.m. Also, I created and attached a rough budget for our party. We can discuss and revise this at the meeting.
Thank you!
Chris Carter
112233 Birch Tree Lane
Auburn, WA 98092-7049
English (U.S

2. Schedule a Meeting, Invite Attendees, and Manage Your Calendar

a. Assume that your Project Advisor gave you the approval to schedule the party-planning meeting. In your Calendar, schedule the meeting for the first Tuesday in June at 7 p.m. in the Project Advisor's office; set a reminder for 5 hours before the meeting. Then, send a meeting request to invite the project team leaders to the scheduled meeting.

b. Assign all four team leaders as contacts to the party-planning meeting.

c. Add an event called *MP Project Party* to your calendar on the last Saturday of June. Indicate the School Gymnasium is the location, and use the default reminder notice.

d. Apply a conditional format to all calendar items that contain the word *party* so that they will be displayed in the color green.

e. Add the custom category *Party* to each party item in the calendar.

f. Display and print a monthly view of the calendar. (***Note:*** Be sure that the date of your planning meeting and the date of the party are displayed.) Then, display and print a daily view of the calendar for the date of the party; make sure that you will be able to write notes about things to do that day.

3. Create, Assign, and Update Tasks

a. Create a task request *Order party food and beverages* to assign to Azmi Maghathe. Create another task request *Hire party DJ* to assign to Jermaine Samuels. Both task requests are due the third Friday in June. Create a task *Plan party cleanup* for you to handle (due the day after the party).

b. Assign the custom category *Party* to your contacts for Azmi Maghathe and Jermaine Samuels, and assign the *Party* category to each of the three tasks.

c. Open and read the task *Next Year's Project*. Assign it to one of your classmates (as instructed by your teacher).

d. When you receive a task assignment from a classmate, either accept or decline it. Track the task status by examining the Details tab in the Task Request window.

e. Update your *Plan party cleanup* task to 50% complete **(see Figure 2)**. Then, change your Tasks view to show only unfinished (Active) tasks.

Figure 2 Plan party cleanup task

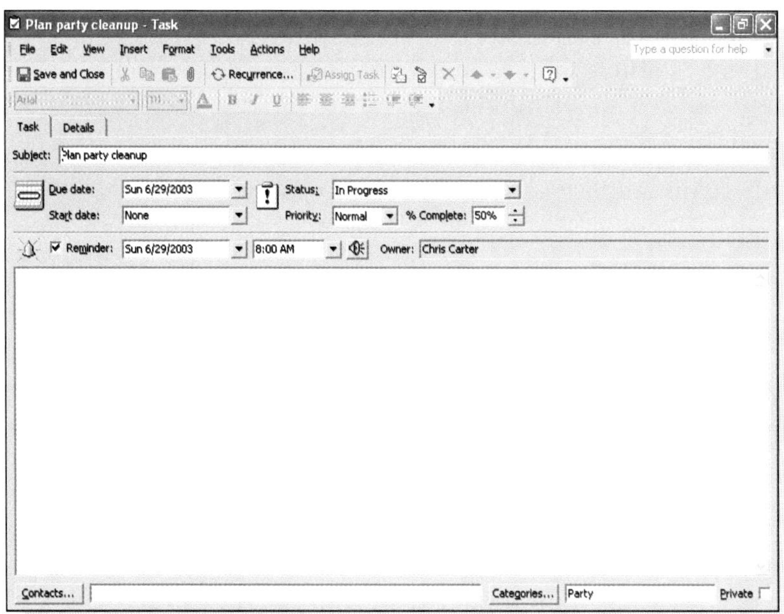

4. Create a Note

a. Create a note that reads: Tell Jermaine about the disc jockey I heard last weekend. Should we use him for the party?

b. Assign the *Party* category to the note, and assign Jermaine to the note (so that you can pass the information along to him).

5. Respond to a Meeting Request and Manage Your Messages

a. In your Inbox, open and read the *Party plan approval* message. Propose a new time for the meeting.

b. In your Inbox, search for all messages that are related to *Maehr Park*. Move the messages into the *Maehr Park Project* folder.

c. Assign the *Party* category to the party-planning message.

d. Select the message you sent to your Project Advisor with your critique and save it as both an HTML file (named xxx-*Subject*-html) and as a text file (named xxx-*Subject*-text). (***Note***: Replace *Subject* with the subject of your message and *xxx* with your initials.)

e. In your Inbox, archive all messages prior to today's date or the date provided by your teacher **(see Figure 3)**.

Figure 3 Archive dialog box

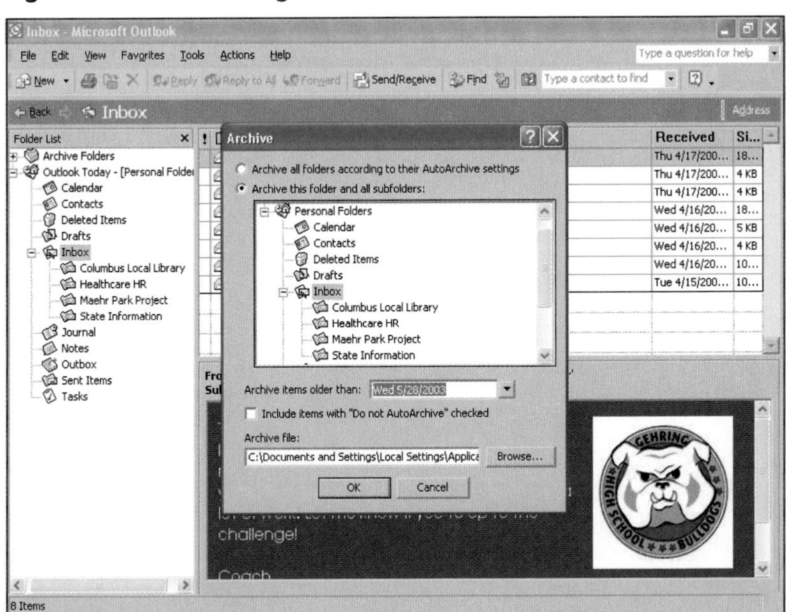

Cross-Curriculum Project

During this school term (January 15, 200x through May 15, 200x), you have decided to use Outlook to help you organize your school work and to communicate with your friends. You will share class notes and other documents as attachments, set up study dates with meeting requests, and keep detailed contact information.

a. Add contact information for two new study contacts as shown in the **Table 1**.

Table 1

Contact	Home Phone	Category
Mia Rodgers	(253) 555-3140	School/Homework
Tad Schwartz	(253) 555-3978	School/Homework

b. Edit Mia Rodgers' contact information to change her phone number to (253) 555-3141.

c. Group your contacts by category, and sort the contacts by Full Name within categories.

d. In the Calendar, enter all the exams and quizzes in the schedule in **Table 2** as recurring appointments. Then, apply a conditional format to each of the exam and quiz appointments so that they display with the specified color.

e. Print the Calendar for the month of April.

Table 2

Subject	Time	Schedule	Contacts	Color
Business Communi-cations Quiz	10–11 AM	Every Wednesday, beginning the second week through the end of the term	Azmi Maghathe, Heather Kemper	Blue (Business)
Biology Quiz	9–10 AM	Every other Thursday, beginning the third week through the end of the term	Heather Kemper, Jermaine Samuels, Pat Mireles	Pink (Important)
Geometry Quiz	2–3 PM	Every Monday, beginning the second week through the end of the term	Azmi Maghathe, Mary Jane Palmisano	Yellow-Green (Needs Preparation)
Chemistry Quiz	1–2 PM	Every other Tuesday, beginning the third week through the end of the term	Mary Jane Palmisano, Heather Kemper, Jermaine Samuels	Orange (Must Attend)
Art Midterm Art Final	8–9 AM	Midterm on Friday of the 9th week; Final on Friday of the 17th week	Jermaine Samuels, Mia Rodgers, Tad Schwartz	Yellow (Phone Call)

f. For each subject appointment, assign the contacts.

g. Track all the activities for Jermaine Samuels.

Unit 6 Operating Systems, Utilities, and Networks

Unit Contents

Unit Objectives

1. Identify the various types of computer systems.
2. Identify hardware components.
3. Understand operating systems.
4. Work with utility programs.
5. Understand application software.
6. Understand the basics of telecommunications and Internet services.
7. Increase productivity by using a network.
8. Understand the components of a network.

Systems

Lesson 1

What Makes Your Computer Go?

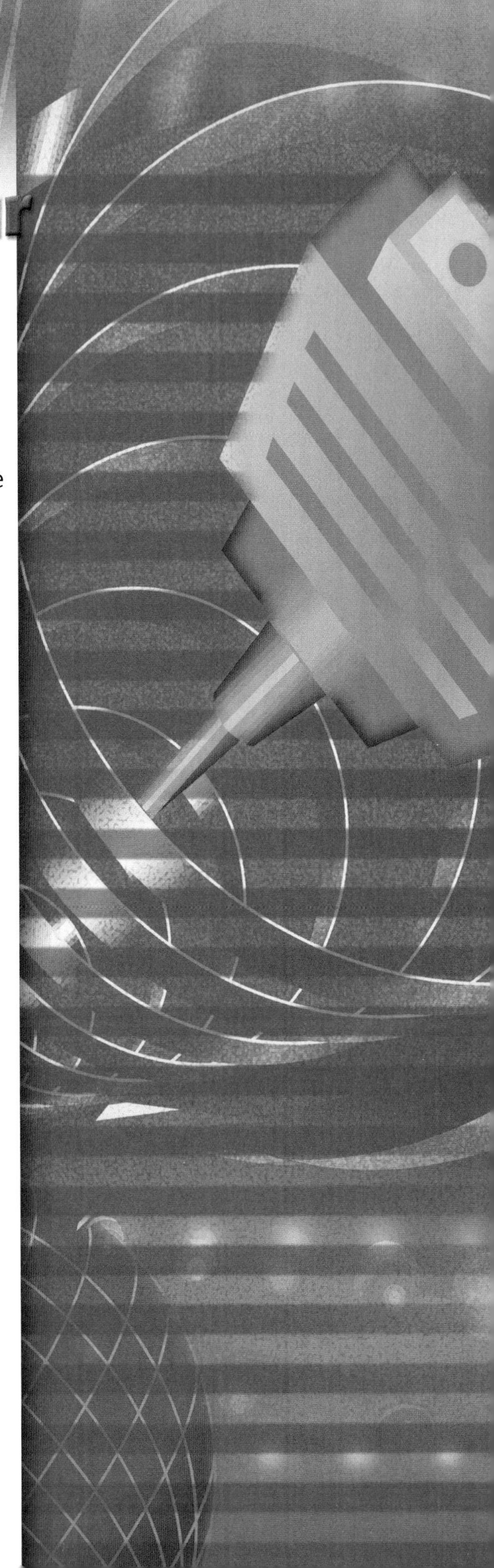

Lesson Exercise Objectives

After completing this lesson, you'll be able to do the following tasks:

1. Identify the various types of computer systems
2. Know your hardware components
3. Understand operating systems
4. Work with utility programs

Microsoft Office Specialist Activities

W2002: 1.1, 1.2, 3.4, 3.5, 4.3

EX2002: 1.2, 2.3, 3.6, 3.7

PP2002: 1.1, 1.2, 2.2, 4.1

Real-Life Business Applications

Key Terms

- central processing unit (CPU) (p. 754)
- expansion slots (p. 755)
- flash memory (p. 760)
- graphical user interface (GUI) (p. 765)
- hard drive (p. 758)
- hardware (p. 754)
- input device (p. 755)
- Linux (p. 769)
- MacOS (p. 768)
- mainframe (p. 750)
- minicomputer (p. 751)
- motherboard (p. 754)
- operating system (OS) (p. 764)
- output device (p. 758)
- platform (p. 764)
- professional workstation (p. 751)
- random access memory (RAM) (p. 755)
- read-only memory (ROM) (p. 755)
- supercomputer (p. 750)
- syntax (p. 765)
- system software (p. 764)
- system unit (p. 754)
- user interface (p. 764)
- utility program (p. 771)
- virus (p. 774)
- Windows (p. 767)

Microsoft Office Specialist W2002 1.1, 4.3

Systems

Exercise 1 Overview: Identify the Various Types of Computer Systems

Usually when you think of a computer system, you think of the personal computer that is sitting on your desk. However, many businesses require computer systems that can serve hundreds of people and handle specialized tasks. While all computers have the same basic components, they differ greatly in size, cost, and performance.

Multiuser Computers and Professional Workstations

Mainframes perform multiple tasks for many users simultaneously—usually for large corporations or organizations. They typically are housed in special, climate-controlled rooms. Users hook up to mainframes either through personal computers or terminals, which are remote monitors and keyboards that have little or no processing capabilities of their own.

Employees can use terminals (top photo) to send and receive information to and from a single mainframe computer (bottom photo).

Mainframes were the first type of computer used by businesses and government agencies. Today, their use is limited to companies such as nationwide car-rental agencies (in which tens of thousands of terminals are linked to huge databases) or government agencies like the Social Security Administration. Possessing an enormous processing capacity, mainframes enable thousands of employees to request and update data from a central location, with response time similar to a personal computer. However, mainframes may cost hundreds of thousands or even millions of dollars.

While experts once predicted that mainframes would eventually be replaced by personal computers, many large corporations have been reluctant to relinquish the power and reliability of their mainframes and the investment in software they have put into them.

In rare instances, the need for processing power and speed is so great that even a mainframe computer is not enough. **Supercomputers** meet this need by processing trillions of calculations per second.

Some academic institutions use supercomputers for academic research. Large government agencies use supercomputers to forecast the weather or simulate car crash testing. Supercomputers can cost almost $100 million.

Smaller multiuser systems called **minicomputers** were common in the 1970s and 1980s. Because minicomputers were cheaper than mainframes and took up less room, they were popular for small to medium-sized businesses and organizations, such as schools and single-office companies with less than 100 users. Although they usually cost less than $100,000, the popularity of minicomputers has faded as personal computers have become just as powerful but less expensive.

The **professional workstation** meets the needs of users requiring more computing power than a personal computer, yet less than a minicomputer. Scientists, graphics designers, financial analysts, and architects, for example, choose these single-user workstations because of their rapid processing abilities at a relatively low cost—usually only a few thousand dollars. As personal computers become increasingly more powerful, the day may come when the distinction between personal computers and workstations is erased.

Undoubtedly the trend toward miniaturization and increased speed and capacity will continue for all types of computers. New technologies may even replace the electronics-based computers of today. It is believed that, some day, computer memory and processing may be based on three-dimensional molecular structures.

A supercomputer can perform trillions of operations per second.

A minicomputer

Personal Computers

The explosion in the use of personal computers in the late 1980s and early 1990s had an immediate impact on society. Within only a few years, word processing, spreadsheet software, and database management programs became available to millions of office and home users. Despite the initially high cost of personal computers (an early complete system could easily run over $3,000), an increasing number of consumers found so many uses for them that many homes and virtually all businesses owned at least one personal computer by the beginning of the 21st century.

In the early days of personal computers, many different types were manufactured. Today, all but two have disappeared from general use. We know these two survivors as the IBM PC and its compatibles and the Apple family of computers.

IBM and IBM-Compatible Computers. When IBM's personal computer hit the market in 1981, it was readily accepted by most people in the business world because of

Quick Tip

Moore's Law, a trend defined by Intel Corporation's Gordon Moore in 1965, states that approximately every two years, the processing power of new CPU chips is doubled, due to advances in chip-making technology and miniaturization.

Systems

IBM's reputation as a quality manufacturer of mainframe computers. Thus, the IBM personal computer became the individual computer of choice in offices in the U.S. and in much of the rest of the world. Most of the components of the IBM personal computer were not manufactured by IBM, however. Soon other companies purchased the same basic components and manufactured personal computers that were functionally identical to those made by IBM. These computers became known as IBM-compatibles, or clones. The IBM personal computer and compatibles are commonly referred to as *PCs*.

As PCs become cheaper and more powerful, their uses will continue to become more varied. In business offices, properly equipped PCs rival high-powered workstations in the fields of computer-aided design and computer-aided manufacturing (CAD/CAM). On the other hand, low-end PCs function as little more than terminals, accessing databases and printing receipts. Most PCs fall in between these two extremes, running productivity software (such as word processing, spreadsheet, and database management), communicating with other users over company networks, researching data over the Internet, and sending and receiving e-mail.

Undoubtedly, PCs will become even more powerful in the future. As processing speeds and storage capacities grow, the space needed to house them will decrease. In other words, small, extraordinarily powerful computers will increasingly be included in cell phones and other hand-held devices, TVs, DVD players, and household appliances.

An IBM personal computer

Apple Computers. Unlike IBM, Apple Corporation started out as a personal computer manufacturing company. Steve Wozniak and Steve Jobs created and marketed the Apple I computer from Jobs' garage in 1976. In 1977, before the IBM PC was even available, the Apple II was being sold successfully to businesses, schools, and home users.

Although the IBM PC and compatibles soon took over dominance in the business world, the release of the user-friendly Macintosh line (including the iMac, eMac, Power Mac, iBook, and PowerBook computers) solidified Apple's market share, especially in the areas of education, design, publishing, music, and other artistic fields.

Tomorrow's Apple computers are likely to retain their emphasis on user-friendliness, graphics, and multimedia. The latest iMac hints at the ergonomically sound and innovatively designed computers Apple will produce in the future. Like the PCs, these computers will be faster and more compact, and will hold huge amounts of data.

In the following exercise, you will recommend the appropriate type of computer system for a variety of work scenarios.

Quick Tip

Before you begin Exercise 1, check with your teacher regarding where your data files are located and where you should save your solutions.

Figure 1.1 *Computer Systems.doc* document

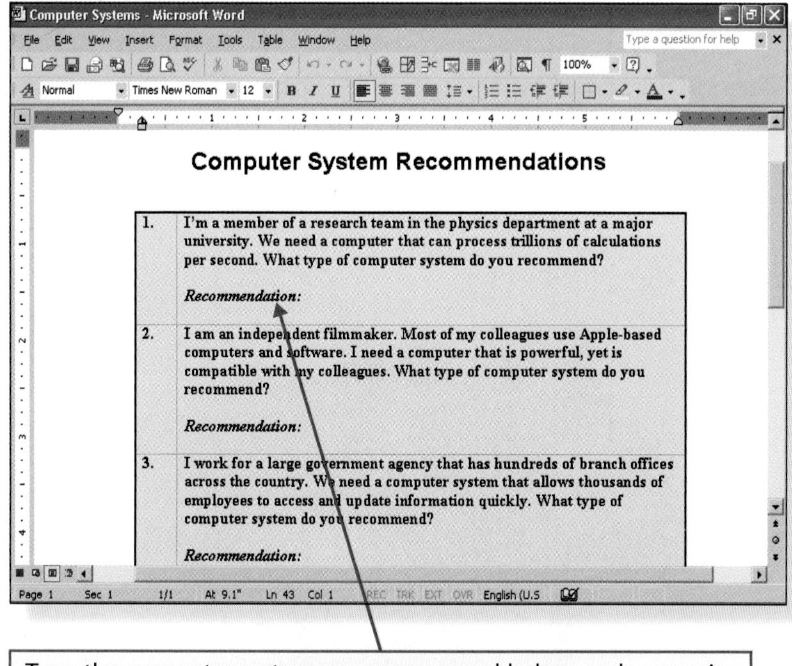

Computer Systems - Microsoft Word

Computer System Recommendations

1.	I'm a member of a research team in the physics department at a major university. We need a computer that can process trillions of calculations per second. What type of computer system do you recommend? *Recommendation:*
2.	I am an independent filmmaker. Most of my colleagues use Apple-based computers and software. I need a computer that is powerful, yet is compatible with my colleagues. What type of computer system do you recommend? *Recommendation:*
3.	I work for a large government agency that has hundreds of branch offices across the country. We need a computer system that allows thousands of employees to access and update information quickly. What type of computer system do you recommend? *Recommendation:*

Type the computer system you recommend below each scenario.

Step Through It™

Exercise 1: Choose the right system for the job

1. Open the file *Computer Systems.doc* located in the *Lesson 1* subfolder of your *Unit 6* folder.
2. Read each of the scenarios described in the document, and type your recommended computer system(s) below each scenario (see Figure 1.1).
3. Save the document as *xxx-Computer Systems.doc*, replacing *xxx* with your initials. Then close the file and exit Word.

Microsoft Office Specialist W2002 1.1, 1.2, 3.4, 4.3

Systems

Exercise 2 Overview:

Know Your Hardware Components

Hardware encompasses all the physical components of a computer system. All of the devices you touch, plug in, turn on, and view are computer hardware. Some hardware components process information, some display or print data, some let you type or command the computer to perform a desired action, while others store information for a later date. Circuit boards, disk drives, displays, and printers are all considered computer hardware.

Every computer contains the same basic types of hardware components. Laptop or notebook computers include all of the devices in one rectangular box. Many Apple computers combine several of the components in what looks like the display unit. Most IBM PC and IBM-compatible computers physically separate the devices as described below. Regardless of their location, however, all computers contain the following devices.

The System Unit

In a personal computer, the **system unit** is the case that houses the computer's internal processing circuitry—including the motherboard, disk drives, power supply, plug-in boards, and internal speaker.

All computer circuitry is connected to the main circuit board, or **motherboard.** Residing on the motherboard is the **central processing unit (CPU).** Although no more than a few inches square, the CPU is responsible for performing all of the arithmetic and logical instructions that the computer can do. It is known as the basic brain of the system.

A typical PC motherboard

Other self-contained circuits, or chips, hold information. **Read-only memory (ROM)** chips have instructions and data built into them. This information can be used by the computer at any time and is maintained even when the power is turned off. Some of these ROM chips contain the program that is responsible for starting the computer when it is turned on. **Random access memory (RAM)** chips store data only temporarily; all information is erased when the computer is turned off.

The motherboard also contains **expansion slots,** connections that let you install expansion boards (also called adapter cards)—circuit boards that allow you to attach additional devices to your computer system.

Input Devices

Before any computer processing can take place, you must first get the data you want to have processed into the system unit. Most **input devices** are external to the system unit and are attached to it using specific connectors and ports.

Examples of input devices are described in Table 1.1.

Devices that are external to the system unit, such as keyboards and printers, are often referred to as *peripheral devices.*

Table 1.1

Input Device	Description
Keyboard	The most common input device. It consists of letter, number, symbol, and special computer keys.
Mouse	The most popular pointing device. As you move the mouse on a flat surface, a pointer moves in a corresponding manner on the computer monitor.
Trackball	Similar to an upside-down mouse, in which a ball is moved directly with the fingers instead of being moved by the mouse. Trackballs are especially useful when desktop space is limited, since the device itself does not need to be moved.
Pointing stick	A small rod located near the middle of the keyboard that can be pushed in any direction to move the onscreen pointer. Many portable computers have pointing sticks.
Touchpad	A rectangular surface located below a keyboard. Moving your finger over the surface moves the pointer.
Touch screen	An input device placed on or within a computer monitor. By touching the screen where the images appear, the user selects the functions they represent.
Graphics tablet	An electronically sensitive tablet upon which you can draw using a pen-shaped instrument called a stylus.
Scanner	Converts photographs, magazine articles, or almost any kind of paper image into a digital form that can be stored and displayed on the computer.
Digital camera	Translates light into digital form. When a digital camera is connected to the system unit, the images can be stored and displayed on the computer.

There are several other types of input devices available, depending on the data you want to get into your computer. For example, to include narration in a PowerPoint presentation requires a microphone for voice input. Microphone headsets are also required in conjunction with speech recognition software to enable the user to dictate text and/or commands to the computer. Musicians connect MIDI-compliant (Musical Instrument Digital Interface) musical keyboards, mixers, etc. to create music using the computer.

The newer versions of many of the input devices described above employ wireless technology. The freedom to move around without entangling cables is becoming increasingly popular. The future of input device technology promises to offer more hands-free methods. Sensors are already able to acquire information from the environment, such as light, temperature, and motion. As sensor technology evolves, computers will use sensors to better "see," "hear," "smell," and "touch" events in the outside world.

In the following exercise, you will determine the properties of your computer system and the input devices connected to it.

Step Through It™

Exercise 2A: Determine system properties and input devices

1. Select Control Panel from the Start menu and select Switch to Classic View (if necessary) in the left pane of the Control Panel window (see Figure 1.2).

2. Double-click the System icon in the right pane of the Control Panel window to open the System Properties dialog box.

Figure 1.2 The Windows XP Control Panel

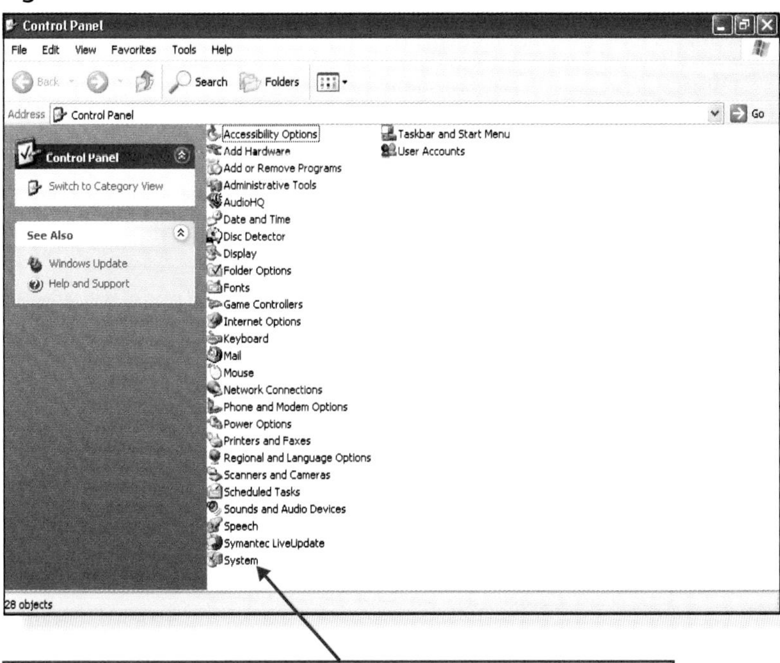

Double-click the System icon in the Control Panel window.

Figure 1.3 The Device Manager window

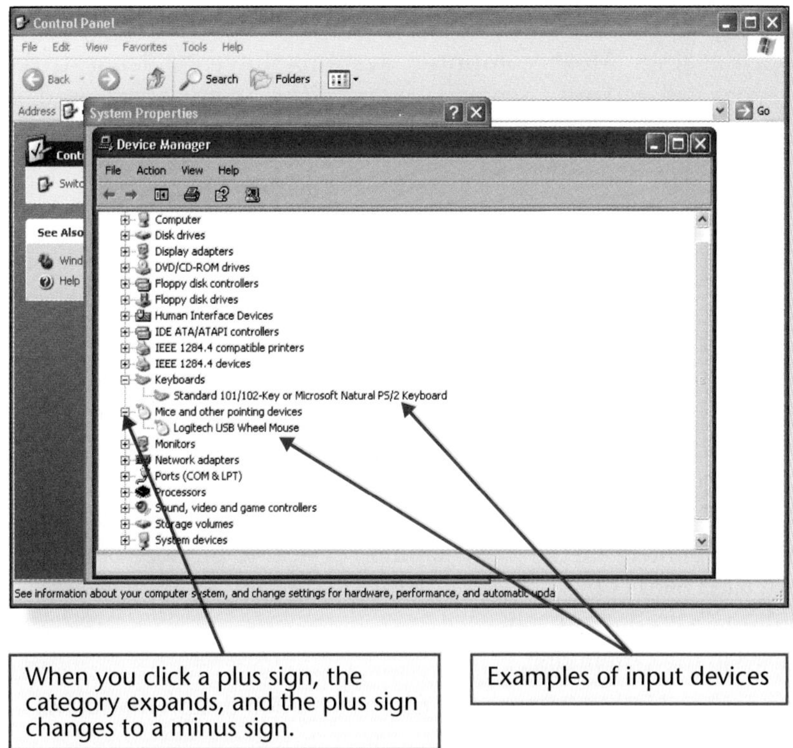

Figure 1.4 Example Word document

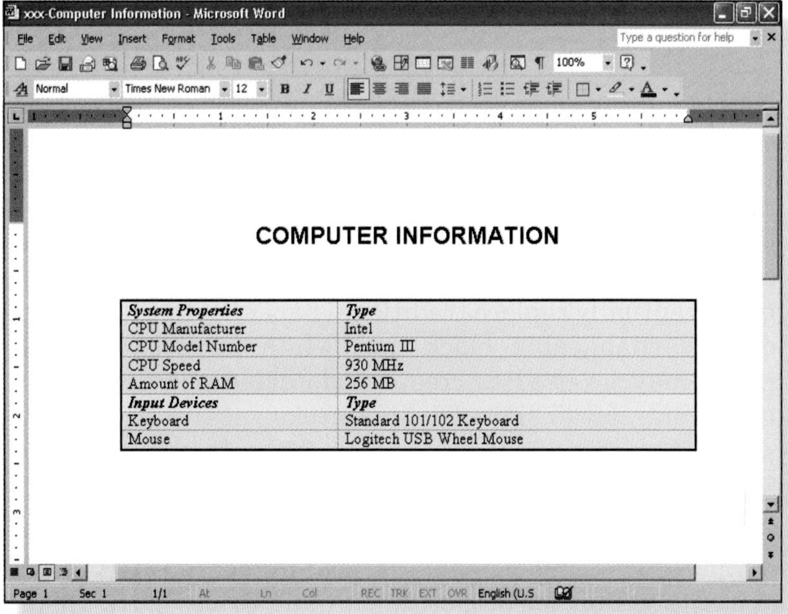

COMPUTER INFORMATION

System Properties	***Type***
CPU Manufacturer	Intel
CPU Model Number	Pentium III
CPU Speed	930 MHz
Amount of RAM	256 MB
Input Devices	***Type***
Keyboard	Standard 101/102 Keyboard
Mouse	Logitech USB Wheel Mouse

Quick Tip

Refer to Lesson 3 in Unit 1 if you need help creating a table.

3. From information displayed on the General tab, write down the CPU manufacturer and model number, the speed of your CPU, and the amount of RAM on your computer.
4. Click the Hardware tab, and then click the Device Manager button.
5. In the Device Manager window, click the plus signs to display the names of input devices attached to your system (see Figure 1.3). Write down the names of the input devices.
6. Create a new Word document. Type the heading COMPUTER INFORMATION.
7. Insert a 2-column table below the heading, and type the column headings System Properties and Type in row 1. Then type the information you recorded in step 3.
8. In the next blank row, type the column headings Input Devices and Type. Then type the information you recorded in step 5.
9. Format the document attractively, and save it as *xxx-Computer Information* (see the example in Figure 1.4).
10. Close all open windows.

Systems

Output Devices

Output devices show you the results of the computer's processing. Most computer systems have at least three types of output devices—a monitor, a printer, and a speaker. Examples of some common output devices are described in Table 1.2.

Table 1.2

Output Device	Description
Monitor	Computer monitors provide visual output, and typically measure from 15 to 19 inches diagonally. The quality of the screen display depends on the quality of the monitor itself as well as the quality of the video adapter card in the system unit to which it connects.
Printer	Inkjet and laser printers are the most common devices to produce output on paper (called hard copy).
Speakers or headphones	Audio output comes through either speakers or headphones connected to a sound card in the system unit.
Plotter	Output device used in architecture and computer-aided design that draws line art on large paper.
Projection unit	Output device that projects data onto a large screen.

New, improved output devices are constantly being developed. Flat-panel displays take up little desk space, and with their lower costs and high resolution, they have become increasingly popular. Display units built into goggles or beamed directly onto the user's eye may eventually replace computer monitors totally. In some cases, electronic paper may eventually replace traditional paper. With the ability to display changeable black and white images, electronic paper may be used to create updateable newspapers and magazines, retail signs, and textbooks.

A hard drive is usually encased within the system unit.

Storage Devices

The **hard drive** is the storage device at the heart of most computer systems. Capable of holding over 40 GB of data magnetically on one or more disks, hard drives per-manently store software programs and data files. Read/write heads move back and forth across rapidly spinning disks, either placing (*writing*) magnetic spots on the surface in patterns representing letters, numbers, symbols, and program instructions, or interpreting those patterns (*reading*). Because they are usually encased within the system unit, hard drives are also called fixed, or non-removable, storage devices.

In addition to the hard drive, most computer systems have some type of secondary storage device, such as a floppy disk drive, a Zip drive, or a CD-ROM drive. These secondary storage devices are used in conjunction with some type of removable storage medium, such as a floppy disk, a Zip cartridge, or a CD-ROM disc. You can easily remove the medium and transport it or store it in another location. There are several types of secondary storage devices/media in use today. Table 1.3 describes some common secondary storage media.

Table 1.3

Secondary Storage Media	Description
Floppy disk	A magnetic storage media, floppy disks were once the main form of inexpensive, portable storage. They have become increasingly obsolete due to theavailability of greater capacity media (the capacity of a floppy disk is only approximately 1.44 megabytes) and their sensitivity to heat, cold, and other environmental factors.
Zip cartridge	Also a magnetic storage media, Zip cartridges can store 100–250 megabytes of data, considerably more than floppy disks.
CD-ROM disc	CD-ROM is an acronym for compact disc-read only memory. A CD-ROM is a common form of optical storage media. CD-ROMs hold up to 650 MB of data and can be inserted into either CD or DVD drives. CD-ROMs are generally used to hold software, multimedia files, or large databases. You can read data from a CD-ROM; however, you cannot write data to a CD-ROM, nor can you change the data it contains.
DVD-ROM disc	Often simply called DVDs, DVD-ROM (digital versatile disc-read only memory) discs are another form of optical storage media. DVD-ROMs store up to 17 GB of data and can only be used in DVD drives. Just as with CD-ROMs, you can read data from a DVD-ROM; however, you cannot write data to a DVD-ROM, nor can you change the data it contains.
CD-R disc	With a recordable CD drive, you can record data one time onto special CD-R discs. However, once written, the data cannot be edited.
CD-RW disc	Using a CD-RW (compact disk-rewritable) drive, you can record, delete, and alter data stored on CD-RW discs an unlimited number of times.

One 128 MB Memory Stick can hold as much data as 88 floppy disks.

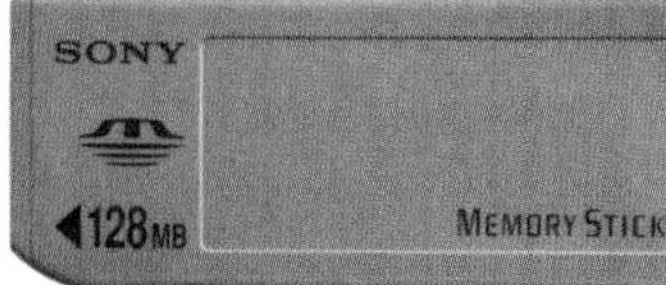

The explosion of small, handheld devices such as digital cameras, digital music players, and other portable devices has created a need for small, removable storage devices. SmartMedia and CompactFlash cards store megabytes of data on small, thin, rectangular cards using a type of chip known as **flash memory.** For example, Sony's Memory Stick holds up to 128 MB of data on a device about the size of a stick of chewing gum.

It is certain that in the future, storage devices will follow the same trend as in the past—much higher capacity along with much cheaper cost per unit of storage. Recordable DVD devices will surely become very popular as soon as the cost drops near the price of CD-RW drives. A new form of optical storage, FMD-ROM (fluorescent multilayer disc-read only memory), which uses a technology that reflects a special light through many layers of discs, promises to store up to 100 times more data than CD-ROMs.

In the following exercise, you will continue to analyze your computer system by identifying its output devices and storage devices.

Step Through It™

Exercise 2B: Identify output devices and storage devices

1. Select Control Panel from the Start menu and select Switch to Classic View (if necessary) in the left pane of the Control Panel window.
2. Double-click the System icon in the right pane of the Control Panel window to open the System Properties dialog box.
3. Click the Hardware tab in the System Properties dialog box, and then click the Device Manager button (see Figure 1.5).

Figure 1.5 The Hardware tab of the System Properties dialog box

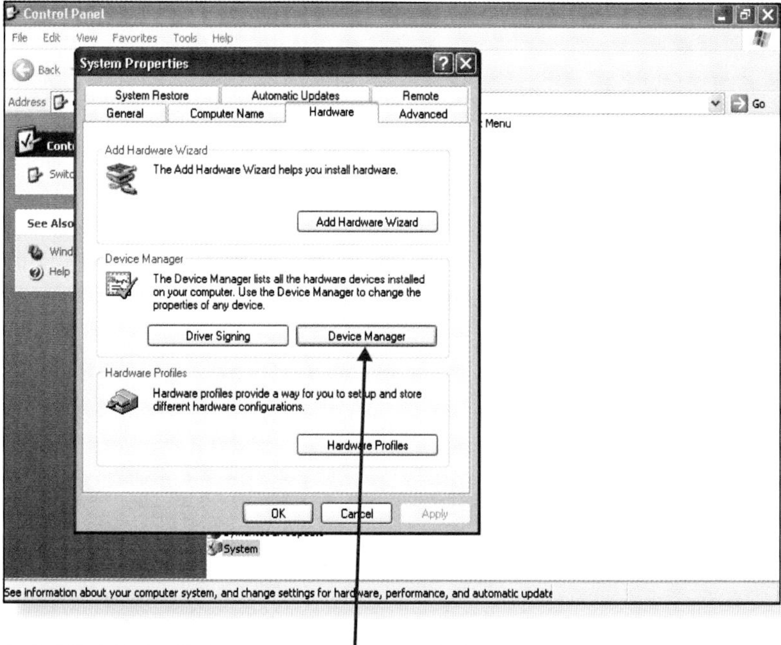

Click the Device Manager button to display a list of hardware devices attached to your computer.

Figure 1.6 The Device Manager window

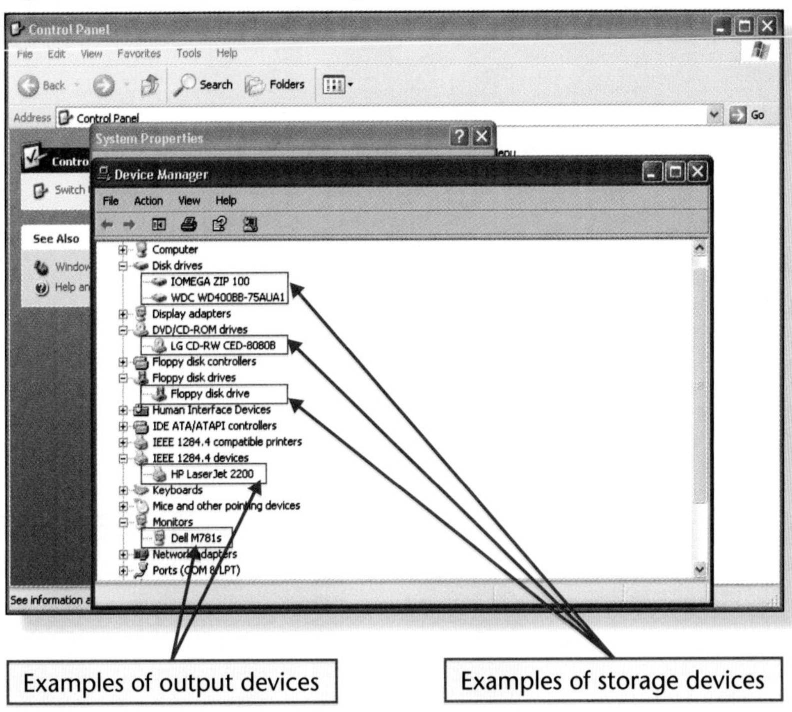

4. In the Device Manager window, click the plus signs to display the names of output devices attached to your system.

5. Now click the plus signs to display the names of the storage devices that are part of your system (see Figure 1.6).

6. Write down the names of the output devices and storage devices.

Systems

Figure 1.7 Example Word document

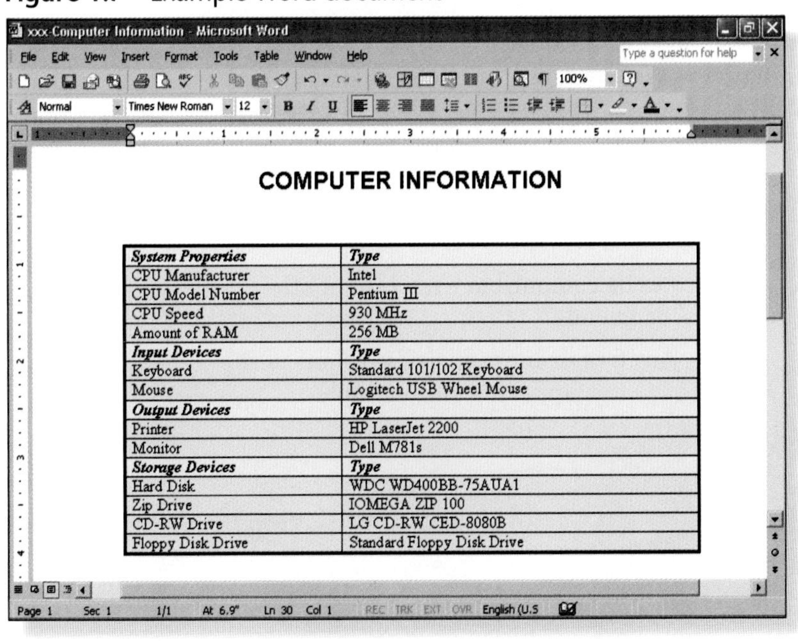

COMPUTER INFORMATION

System Properties	***Type***
CPU Manufacturer	Intel
CPU Model Number	Pentium III
CPU Speed	930 MHz
Amount of RAM	256 MB
Input Devices	***Type***
Keyboard	Standard 101/102 Keyboard
Mouse	Logitech USB Wheel Mouse
Output Devices	***Type***
Printer	HP LaserJet 2200
Monitor	Dell M781s
Storage Devices	***Type***
Hard Disk	WDC WD400BB-75AUA1
Zip Drive	IOMEGA ZIP 100
CD-RW Drive	LG CD-RW CED-8080B
Floppy Disk Drive	Standard Floppy Disk Drive

7. Open the *xxx-Computer Information.doc* file you created and saved in Exercise 2A. Type the information you recorded in step 6 into the table, adding appropriate column headings as necessary. (See the example in Figure 1.7.)

8. Save your document and print it. Then close all open windows.

APPLY IT! After finishing Exercise 2, you may test your skills by completing Apply It! Guided Activity 1, Compare Storage Devices.

Business Connections

Making Wise Computer Choices

Every day, you probably see ads for computers on TV or in newspapers and magazines. Computer prices have dropped drastically since the first PCs were introduced over 20 years ago, which makes them affordable for almost everyone.

Analyzing Your Software Needs

There's more to a computer than just its hardware. Before you purchase a computer system for either your personal or business use, you must first determine the system's primary use.

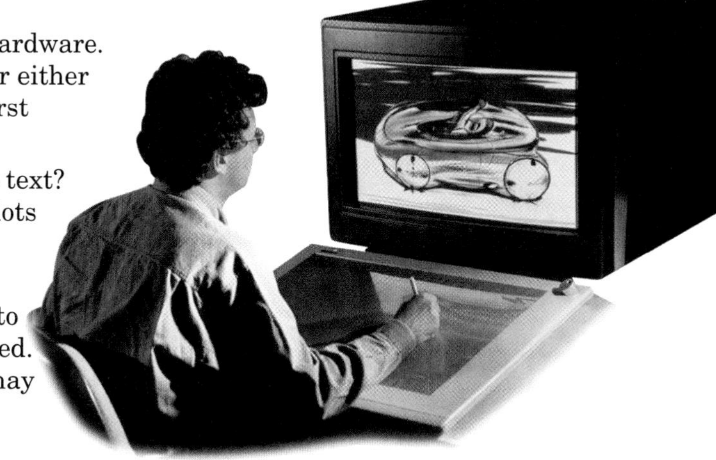

Will the system mainly be used to prepare text? Crunch numbers? Manage and maintain lots of data? Create artwork? Create graphs, charts, and technical drawings?

Your answers to these questions will help to determine the application software you need. You may discover that a cheap computer may not be a bargain if you can't run the applications you need to use.

- Are some (or all) of the applications you need included with the hardware?
- Do you need your software to be compatible with that of other students, workers, or friends?
- Are free or inexpensive versions of the applications available?

SOFTWARE

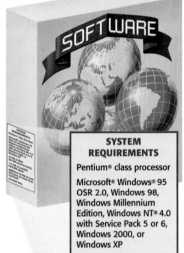

SYSTEM REQUIREMENTS

Pentium® class processor

Microsoft® Windows® 95 OSR 2.0, Windows 98, Windows Millennium Edition, Windows NT® 4.0 with Service Pack 5 or 6, Windows 2000, or Windows XP

32 MB of RAM (64 MB recommended)

115 MB of available hard-disk space

Additional 70 MB of hard-disk space for Asian fonts (optional)

CD-ROM drive

Assessing Your Hardware Needs

Once you have your software requirements figured out, you need to consider your hardware requirements. Here are some questions you should consider when choosing your hardware:

- How many megabytes of RAM are needed? What is recommended to run your application programs?
- How much hard disk space is needed? What type of secondary storage devices do you need? Do you need a floppy disk drive? A CD-ROM or DVD-ROM drive? A CD-R or CD-RW drive?
- In addition to a keyboard and a mouse, what other types of input devices are needed? Do you need a scanner, camera, or microphone?
- What about output devices? What size of monitor do you need? What kind of printer? Any special speakers?

Make sure the hardware you want to buy can run the software you need to use. Not every program runs on every platform. For example, programs designed to run on an IBM-compatible computer usually won't run on a Macintosh computer. You can easily find the compatible platform for your software by checking the requirements on the side of the application software box or on the manufacturer's Web site.

CRITICAL THINKING

1. **Forecasting Computer Needs** Think about the ways you use a computer now, and how you would like to use a computer in the future. Then create a table that contains the components of your ideal computer system.
2. **Hardware Needs Assessment** Research the hardware components required to run software for the following types of applications: CAD, multimedia authoring, and a business (Office suite). Contrast and compare the hardware requirements for the three types of applications.

Microsoft Office Specialist
EX2002 1.2, 2.3, 3.6, 3.7

Systems

Exercise 3 Overview: Understand Operating Systems

When you turn on, or boot, your computer, a small program located on a ROM chip goes to a storage device (usually your hard drive) and copies special files into RAM memory. These files are part of the **operating system (OS)**—the software program that oversees and controls everything that happens while your computer is turned on. Without an operating system, a computer is nothing more than an expensive piece of furniture. With an operating system, a computer can do the following:

- Pass data to and from memory and the peripheral devices
- Run programs
- Maintain the filing system on your storage devices
- Display the **user interface**—the way in which the user interacts with the computer

Your computer runs two types of software—system software and application software. **System software** includes the operating system and utility programs that help to operate and maintain your computer's data management tasks—usually automatically without any action on your part. (You'll learn more about application software in Lesson 2. Microsoft Office, the software you've been using throughout this textbook, is a popular application software package.)

The combination of a specific type of computer system and a specific version of operating system is called a **platform,** or computer environment. Application software is designed for specific platforms. For example, Microsoft Office XP is designed to run on IBM PCs or compatibles, using an Intel or compatible CPU, and running a version of the Microsoft Windows operating system. Such a platform is referred to as an Intel-based Windows PC. Other popular platforms include Apple Corporation's Macintosh computer running a version of MacOS or IBM PCs or compatibles running a version of the Unix operating system.

Quick Tip

The most popular operating systems for personal computers are Microsoft Windows (for IBM PC or compatible computers) and MacOS (for Macintosh computers).

The Evolution of Operating Systems

The first PCs used operating systems that seem primitive by today's standards. As computer hardware grew more sophisticated and a larger proportion of people became computer users, the operating systems evolved into easier, more powerful user interfaces.

Unix System. Bell Laboratories developed the Unix operating system in the early 1970s, long before the introduction of the PC. It is still widely used today, mainly in multiuser environments. Unix defined what operating systems should do and how they should perform. Innovative Unix features include the following:

- Multitasking, in which a computer can run more than one program at a time
- Secure, centrally administrated computer networking capabilities
- Multiprocessing, in which different portions of a program can be executed at the same time by a high-powered computer that has more than one CPU
- File management, where files are stored and accessed within directories or folders
- Client/server networking, in which program processing is shared between your computer and a larger, central network computer

The Unix operating system is very powerful, but it is not very user-friendly. Unix was created with a command-line, character-based user interface. This means that, in order to communicate with the system, the user must type commands using particular keywords, punctuation symbols, and other rigidly enforced rules, collectively known as **syntax.** In recent years, several user-friendly, graphical user interfaces have been developed for Unix, which has increased its popularity in personal computer systems.

Another factor that prevents Unix from becoming a more popular operating system for the PC is that Unix is not a single, standardized operating system. Instead, there are many different variations, or flavors. Despite these drawbacks, Unix is still a viable operating system for PCs, particularly those involved in academic and government research and computers tied to and managing the Internet.

Xerox's PARC Research. In the early 1970s, researchers at Xerox Corporation's Palo Alto Research Center (PARC) built the Alto computer, the first computer system to use a **graphical user interface (GUI)** instead of the command line, character-based interface. The GUI lets users point and click on recognizable, intuitive, and consistent objects, eliminating the need to memorize complex commands and syntax. By the mid- to late 1970s, the PARC GUI included all of the elements most users recognize today—icons, sizable screen fonts, windows, and pull-down lists, all on a

Systems

background or desktop—and is recognized as the forerunner of how operating systems should "look and feel."

MS-DOS. In 1981, Microsoft Corporation developed MS-DOS (Microsoft Disk Operating System), the operating system used in the first IBM-compatible PCs. MS-DOS is the foundation of Microsoft Windows (discussed later in this lesson), and is still used today.

Similar to the Unix operating system, MS-DOS uses a command-line, character-based interface. Table 1.4 contains a few of the more common MS-DOS commands.

Table 1.4

MS-DOS Command	Purpose
CD	Changes the default directory
COPY	Duplicates a file in another location
DATE	Displays the current date and lets you change the system date
DEL	Deletes a file from the disk
DIR	Displays the contents of a folder or directory
MD	Makes a new directory
RD	Removes a directory (must be empty)
REN	Changes the name of a file
VER	Displays the version number of the operating system

Microsoft developed a virtually identical version of MS-DOS called PC-DOS for use by IBM when they first started marketing the IBM personal computer in the early 1980s.

Even though MS-DOS was used extensively in the 1980s and early 1990s (and is still in use today), it had limitations that frustrated its users. First of all, its command-line interface was non-intuitive, confusing, and complex. Secondly, the OS could not take advantage of hardware advancements, including increased memory, storage capacity, and monitor technology.

In the following activity, you will access MS-DOS from Windows XP and issue some operating system commands.

Figure 1.8 The Command Prompt window in Windows XP

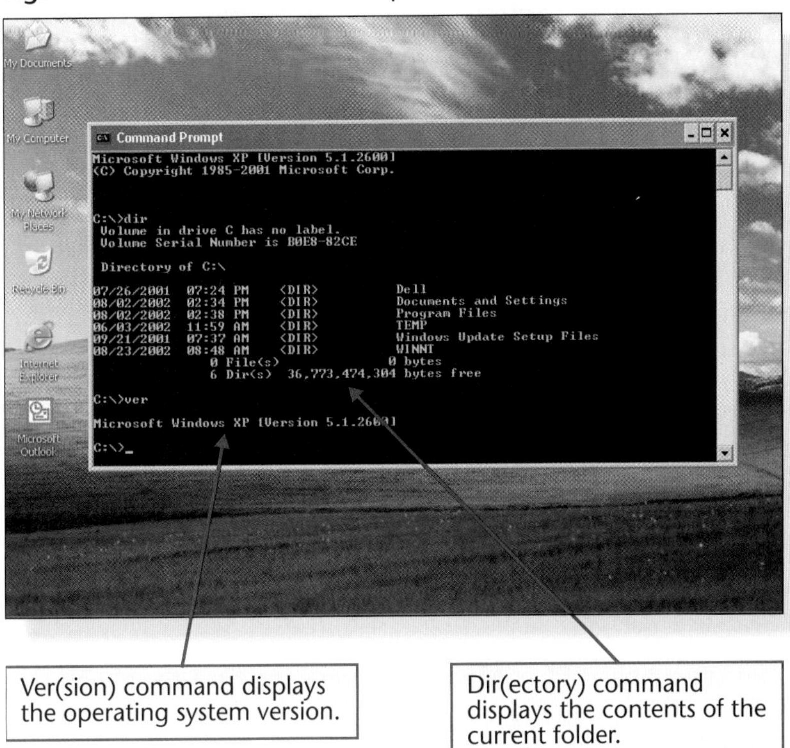

Step Through It™

Exercise 3A: Use operating system commands

1. Point to All Programs on the Start menu. Then point to Accessories and click Command Prompt.
2. In the Command Prompt window, type dir and press Enter to list the contents of the folder or drive.
3. Type ver and press Enter to display the version of Windows you are using (see Figure 1.8).
4. Type exit and press Enter to close the Command Prompt window.

Systems

Current Operating Systems

Most of today's IBM PCs and compatibles run a version of the Windows operating system, while the Apple family of computers runs a version of MacOS. Each of these operating systems has evolved over the last 20-plus years before reaching its current form.

Microsoft Windows. In 1985, Microsoft Corporation introduced its own graphical user interface called **Windows.** Early versions of Windows were really not operating systems at all—they were merely graphical shells that overlaid MS-DOS and made it easier to use. However, because of underlying MS-DOS limitations, it became apparent that a radically new version of Windows was needed.

In 1995, Microsoft introduced Windows 95 as a true GUI operating system for IBM-PCs and compatibles. Windows 95 was capable of true multitasking and was able to take advantage of improvements in hardware technology, such as increased memory, larger storage devices, and higher resolution monitors. Further improvements in the Windows 9*x* family (Windows 98, Windows 98 SE, and Windows ME) added a more stable environment, compatibility with new standards for peripherals, and tighter integration with the Internet.

Later, Microsoft introduced a different line of Windows—Windows NT and Windows 2000—that offered some of the Windows 9*x* features to companies running networked computers. Unfortunately, these operating systems forced users to sacrifice some hardware and software compatibility for increased stability and security.

Microsoft ended this two-tracked approach with the release of Windows XP in 2001. Although there are several versions of Windows XP, all are based on the same essential OS. With the release of Windows XP, Microsoft added new features, including messaging and CD-burning capabilities, and provided a means to help users install minor updates to the OS with little or no effort.

Mac OS. Apple Computer was the first to bring a GUI to personal computer users in the early 1980s. Originally called System for versions 1–7, Macintosh's operating system was later renamed **Mac OS** beginning with version 8. Closely resembling the GUI developed by Xerox's PARC researchers, the Mac provided a sharp contrast to the character-based PCs. Mac users were the first to rely on the mouse and to depend on WYSIWYG (what you see is what you get) screen fonts and graphics.

Mac OS versions through 9.2 improved on the older versions, but many users felt that the Mac OS had slipped behind the Windows operating systems. With the release of Mac OS X in 2000, Macs now have a stable, secure operating system based on Unix with a striking, animated, user-friendly interface rivaling that of Windows.

An Apple iMac

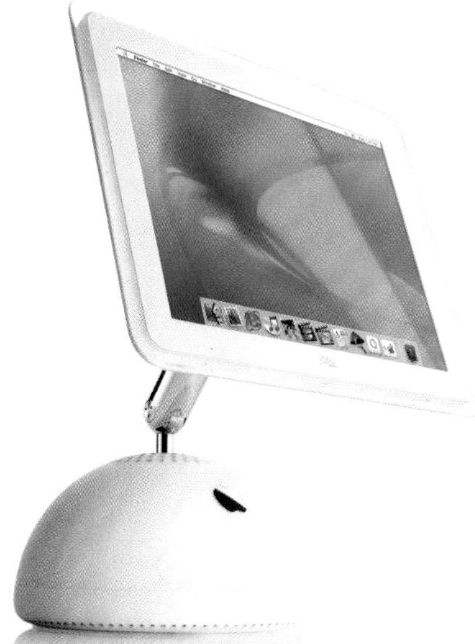

Quick Tip

Microsoft has also developed another version of Windows, Windows CE, for use with small computing devices, such as personal digital assistants. Windows CE has fewer features than other Windows operating systems.

Up-and-Coming Operating Systems

While Windows and MacOS systems dominate the market today, other operating systems have their share of users. **Linux** is a powerful operating system for PCs based on Unix. Linus Torvalds, a Finnish student, created Linux in 1991 and immediately made the program code available over the Internet. Since then, thousands of programmers have improved on the code to make Linux the fastest growing OS for Intel-based PCs. Many versions now exist for other platforms as well.

Future operating systems may include natural language interfaces, in which you can write or speak commands just as you would if you were talking to a person. And, as artificial intelligence technology improves, operating systems may move to include agents—programs that manage our computer systems automatically based on individual preferences and needs.

In the following exercise, you will research three different operating systems and present your findings in an Excel worksheet.

Figure 1.9 *OS Comparisons* Excel file

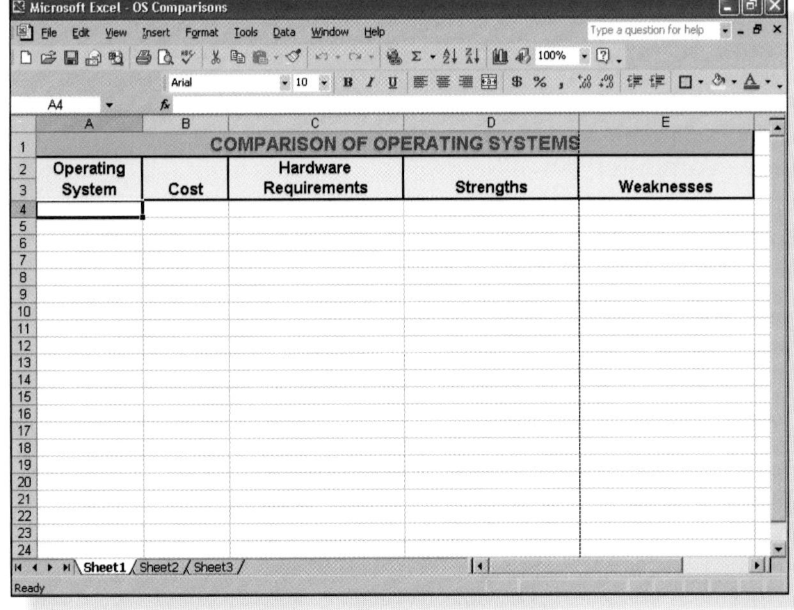

COMPARISON OF OPERATING SYSTEMS				
Operating System	Cost	Hardware Requirements	Strengths	Weaknesses

Step Through It™

Exercise 3B: Compare different operating systems

1. Open the file *OS Comparisons.xls* in the *Lesson 1* subfolder of your *Unit 6* folder (see Figure 1.9).
2. Research the following operating systems: MacOS X, Windows XP, and Red Hat Linux 7.3, a popular version of the Linux operating system. Type the information into your Excel worksheet.
3. Print the worksheet, positioned attractively on one page in landscape orientation.
4. Save the worksheet as *xxx-OS Comparisons*, close the file, and exit Excel.

Career Corner

All Systems Go

Do you like to work with computers? How about a high-paying job in one of the fastest growing occupations in the country—one with many new jobs and plenty of opportunities for advancement?

Computer support specialists provide technical support for hardware, software, and systems. They are the ones who keep our computers running day after day. When you think of how much our society relies on computers, you will realize how vital computer support specialists can be.

These workers install and maintain hardware and software. They assess software, write manuals, and train users. In 2001, the starting pay ranged from $30,500 to $61,000.

Computer support specialists often advance into more responsible positions. Related occupations include computer software engineers, systems analysts, systems or network administrators, and computer scientists.

There are many ways to become a computer support specialist. Certification programs, two- and four-year degrees, and practical experience can all lead to a permanent job in this field. A work-study program or an internship through a local college could also be your ticket to success.

Computer support specialists need good analytical, problem-solving, and communication skills. Patience and experience in working with customers—in retail sales, for example—can also be very helpful.

Because new computer technologies are replacing current ones at an explosive rate, computer support specialists are always learning—on the job, in professional development seminars, in continuing education programs, and on their own.

CRITICAL THINKING

1. A growing number of high school students are getting summer jobs working with computers. They might answer questions at a help desk or evaluate Web sites. Pair up with another student to investigate this trend. Give an oral report on what you learn.
2. How are computers used in an occupation that interests you? Write a paragraph that answers this question.

Exercise 4 Overview:
Work With Utility Programs

Utility programs, the other part of the system software, perform "behind the scenes" duties that are important but not essential to the basic operation of the system. Some utility programs are designed to work so flawlessly with the OS that the user may be unaware of their presence.

In the early days of the PC, most utility programs were distributed by third party vendors—companies other than those that manufactured the hardware or operating system. Over time, however, many of the functions of these utility programs have been included in the system software.

File Management Utility Programs

A computer's main function is to manipulate and move data. File management utility programs perform important "housekeeping duties" to help maintain data integrity, arrange data for quick access, and compress and store data. The following list describes some of the more common file management utilities.

- *Cleaners.* These utilities remove unneeded files, and thus create more free space on the hard drive. The Windows utility Disk Cleanup removes temporary Internet files, temporary files created by the operating system, and files in the Recycle Bin.
- *Error checking.* When you suspect that the disk filing system of your operating system has become corrupted, you can run an error-checking utility to locate corrupted files or bad sectors on the hard drive.
- *Defragmentation.* File fragmentation occurs when a large file is saved in pieces all over the hard drive. A defragmentation utility reassembles these pieces into a continuous file that can be opened quickly.
- *File compression.* File compression utilities can significantly reduce the size of a file. Compressed files take up less disk storage space and can be transmitted faster over a network or the Internet than uncompressed files. The same utility program can also decompress compressed files so that they can be opened.
- *Backup.* To store data offline and to safeguard against data loss, you can use backup utilities to compress and store data on magnetic tape, floppy disks, or CD-R discs.

Disk Cleanup utility

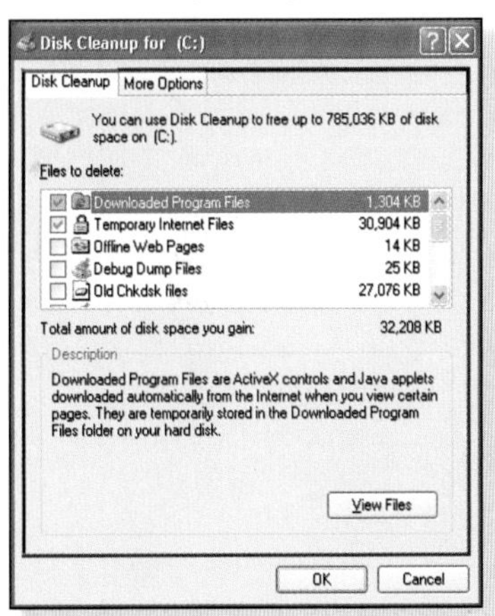

Programs such as WinZip, PKZIP, and StuffIt are common third-party file compression utilities.

Systems

Accessibility Utility Programs

Accessibility programs assist users who have visual, hearing, movement, or learning disabilities to more easily use their computers. Third-party vendors produce many accessibility programs. Most versions of Windows include accessibility utilities as part of the system software. The following list describes various types of accessibility programs.

- *Screen magnifier.* These programs enlarge the portion of the screen where the pointer is located. Users simply move their pointing device to get a magnified view of any object on the screen.
- *Screen reader.* For people with visual or reading disabilities, these programs convert the screen text to sound using speech synthesizer utilities, sound cards, and speakers or headphones. Screen readers enable users to view and surf the Web, as well as read documents and screen prompts.
- *Onscreen keyboard.* These utilities display an image of a keyboard on the screen. People with mobility impairments or disabilities can use a variety of pointing devices to select the letters, numbers, symbols, or special keys by clicking on the screen.
- *Speech recognition.* Speech recognition software is a utility program that is often used by people with mobility, visual, or learning disabilities. Users speak into a microphone or microphone/headset and the software either translates their words into text or acts on the spoken command. Before using the software, users must spend some time "training" the software to correctly interpret their speech patterns and accent.

Communication and Entertainment Utility Programs

Many of today's computer users are connected to networks and the Internet whenever they either boot up their computers or open their Web browsers. Communication utility programs ensure that data can be accurately sent and received for a wide variety of communication needs. Some types of communications utilities are described below.

- *Remote control.* Programs such as Symantec's pcAnywhere allow a user to view the screen or take over the operation of another computer. These utilities are especially useful to specialists who need to help less experienced users fix problems with their computers. Users

Windows XP includes a remote control utility called Remote Assistance.

who work on one computer at work and a different computer at home can use remote control utilities to run programs, access files, or log on to a network from either computer.

- *Small office, home office (SOHO) network setup.* Many small offices and homes contain more than one computer that are connected together by network cards and cables or wireless technology. You can use SOHO network setup utilities to configure each computer to share files, printers, and an Internet connection. Network hardware and third party vendors supply SOHO networking utilities. Recent versions of Windows include networking wizards that let you configure each computer in minutes.
- *Internet setup.* Connecting a computer to the Internet used to be a matter of multiple telephone calls to a technical expert and considerable "tinkering" with settings. Then providers of Internet services (discussed in the next lesson) began supplying subscribers with program disks to automate the Internet setup process. Today's system software usually includes an Internet setup utility that allows users to connect by responding to a few prompts.

Today's computers have multimedia capabilities that few even dreamed about just a few years ago. System software now includes utility programs to handle the audio, video, and still image files that users can create and share over the Internet. The following list describes some of these "entertainment" utilities.

A professional workstation

- *Sound recorder.* With a microphone and a sound card, users can save narration as sound files. Windows XP includes the Sound Recorder, a utility you can use to record, mix, play, and edit sounds.
- *Audio/video file players.* Utility programs that allow you to play audio and video files are part of most system software or are available over the Internet. Windows Media Player is regularly updated by Microsoft, and plays most of the popular audio and video file types. Apple Corporation offers a free basic version of its media player, QuickTime, and sells a professional version for users who want to develop their own multimedia files. RealNetworks markets two versions of RealOne Player—one that's free and one that includes radio and additional media content for a fee.

Many people use their computers to listen to music or watch video clips or movies.

Systems

Security Utility Programs

With a stand-alone (non-networked) computer, security is a matter of preventing anyone from booting the system and reading, copying, or deleting files from the hard drive. In this case, passwords can be assigned to individual files or to the computer itself.

Today, however, many computers are networked, either to other computers in the office or home, or over the Internet. Unfortunately, because many individuals are intent on invading or destroying computer systems, most users must rely on security utilities to safeguard their systems. The following list describes a few types of security utilities.

- *Antivirus.* **Viruses** are small pieces of unauthorized program code written to invade hard drives. Some viruses are relatively harmless, while others can wipe out an entire disk.

  Antivirus programs load into RAM when the computer starts up, scanning files for suspicious activity. Some programs, such as Norton Anti-virus and McAfee VirusScan, also examine incoming e-mail for viruses. Since new viruses are invented daily, antivirus programs need to be updated frequently.

- *Firewall.* Network and cable modem users sometimes leave their computers online twenty-four hours a day. Some malicious individuals scan networks and the Internet looking for "connected" computers they can access to erase files or cause other damage.

  As wireless technology becomes more widespread, the number of easily accessible computers will increase. Firewall programs, along with firewall hardware devices, protect computers from all but authorized access.

- *Data encryption.* Sensitive information is constantly moving through networks and over the Internet. Data encryption programs scramble the information when it is sent or saved and unscramble the data when it needs to be opened by authorized users.

- *File wiping.* Many people believe that when they delete a file from the hard drive, the file is permanently erased. Actually, the file is *not* erased; instead, the operating system simply marks the disk space as available. When another file is saved in that space, the old file is overwritten, but if another file is not saved in that space, the old file (that you thought you deleted) is still there. Unauthorized users can run special programs to read the supposedly erased data. File wiping utilities write over deleted files several times, ensuring that the data is not accessible.

In the following exercise, you will explore Windows Media Player, an audio and video player utility that is included in the Windows XP operating system.

Figure 1.10 Using Windows Media Player

Step Through It™

Exercise 4: Use a utility program

1. Click Start, point to All Programs, and click Windows Media Player (see Figure 1.10).
2. In the Windows Media Player window, click Open on the File menu.
3. Navigate to the *Sample Music* subfolder in the *My Documents* folder. Double-click a file and listen to its content. ***Note:*** If you cannot find the *Sample Music* folder, ask your teacher for assistance.
4. Close Windows Media Player.

After finishing Exercise 4, you may test your skills by completing Apply It! Guided Activity 2, Compare Utility Programs.

Lesson Review and Exercises

Summary Checklist

- ☑ Can you describe the different types of computers and do you know in which environment each is used?
- ☑ Can you distinguish between the two main types of personal computers in use today?
- ☑ Can you identify the main components located within the system unit?
- ☑ Do you understand the difference between an input device and an output device?
- ☑ Can you identify various types of input devices and output devices?
- ☑ Do you understand the difference between a hard drive and secondary storage devices?
- ☑ Can you identify various types of secondary storage devices/media?
- ☑ Can you describe the purpose of an operating system and compare the distinguishing features and history of the major operating systems?
- ☑ Can you explain the main types of utility programs and give examples of each type?

Key Terms

- central processing unit (CPU) (p. 754)
- expansion slots (p. 755)
- flash memory (p. 760)
- graphical user interface (GUI) (p. 765)
- hard drive (p. 758)
- hardware (p. 754)
- input device (p. 755)
- Linux (p. 769)
- MacOS (p. 768)
- mainframe (p. 750)
- minicomputer (p. 751)
- motherboard (p. 754)
- operating system (OS) (p. 764)
- output device (p. 758)
- platform (p. 764)
- professional workstation (p. 751)
- random access memory (RAM) (p. 755)
- read-only memory (ROM) (p. 755)
- supercomputer (p. 750)
- syntax (p. 765)
- system software (p. 764)
- system unit (p. 754)
- user interface (p. 764)
- utility program (p. 771)
- virus (p. 774)
- Windows (p. 767)

APPLY IT! **Guided Activities**

1. Compare Storage Devices

The computer you use at work no longer has the storage capacity you need to perform your job efficiently; however, your company has not budgeted to replace your computer for another two years. You decide to submit a request to purchase a secondary storage device; however, you must first determine what type of storage device you need. Follow these steps to research secondary storage devices and present your findings:

a. Create a new Word document named *xxx-Storage Device Comparison*. (Substitute your initials for *xxx*.)

b. Type the heading Comparison of Storage Devices and format it attractively.

c. Insert a table into the document, and type the following column headings: Device Name, Device Cost, Media Name, Media Cost, and Media Capacity **(see Figure 1.11).**

Figure 1.11 *xxx-Storage Device Comparison* sample document

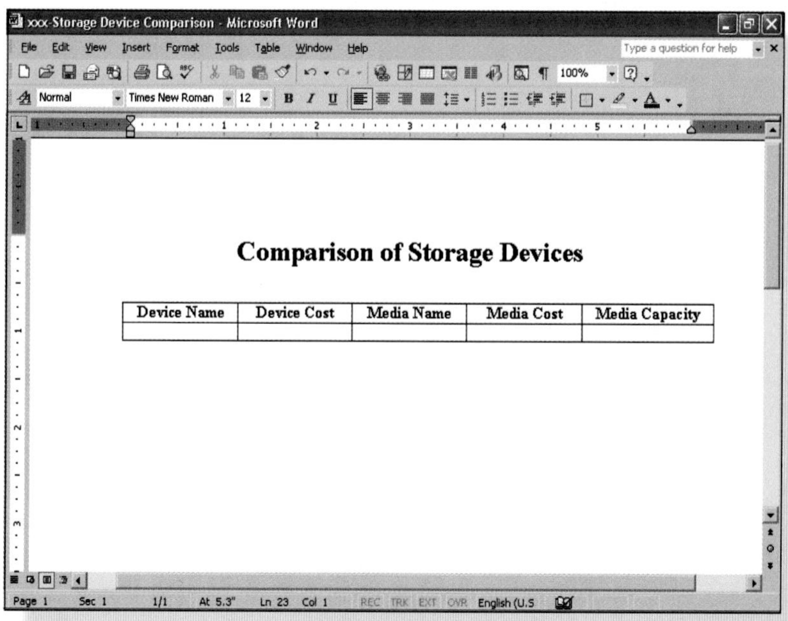

d. Research at least five different types of storage devices. (To conduct your research, you can visit a local computer store, review a computer equipment sales catalog, or search for information on the Internet.)

e. Type your findings into your Word table and format the table attractively.

f. Print and save your document. Then close the file and exit Word.

2. Compare Utility Programs

You have read recently about a new commercial utility program that you would like to purchase and install on your computer. However, before doing so, you want to determine if a similar utility program is already included in your operating system, or if there are freeware utility programs that perform the same task. Prepare a Word document that compares the features of the commercial utility product with the utility program included in your OS (if applicable), and at least one freeware program. Follow these steps:

a. Choose a utility program from one of the categories presented in the lesson. Suggestions include a backup utility, defragmentation utility, file compression utility, antivirus utility, or multimedia player.

b. Use the Windows online Help feature to determine if a similar utility is already included in your operating system. (Click Help and Support on the Start menu, and then enter an appropriate keyword(s) in the Search text box. **See Figure 1.12.**)

Figure 1.12 Windows Help feature

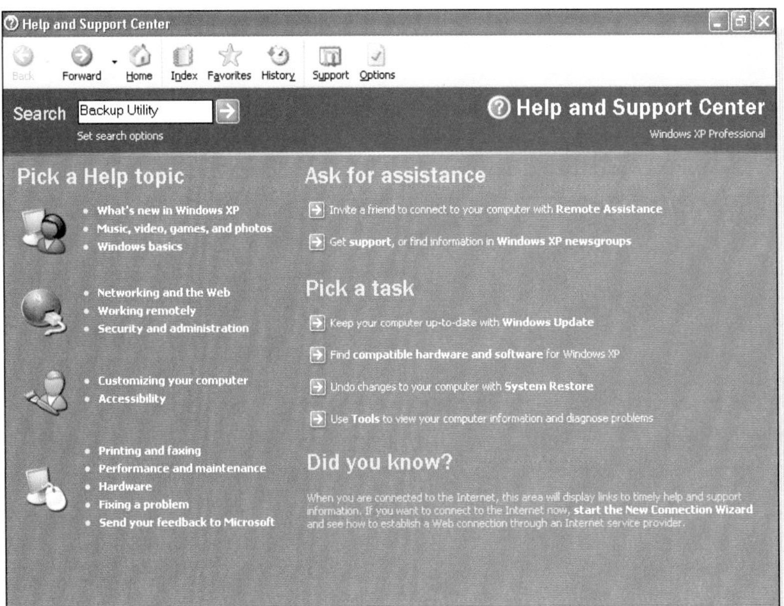

c. Research information on both a commercial and a freeware version of the same type of utility program. ***Note***: Use a Web site such as **www.download.com** to find freeware software; however, do *not* download any software without your teacher's permission.

d. Present your findings in a Word document. An example is shown in **Figure 1.13**.

Figure 1.13 *xxx-Utility Program Comparison* sample document

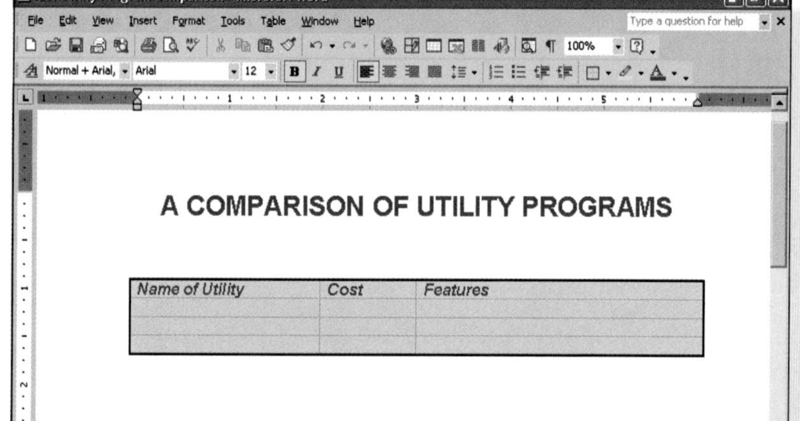

e. Format the document attractively and print it.

f. Save the document as *xxx-Utility Program Comparison.doc*; then close the file and exit Word.

Do It Yourself

1. What Technology Do They Use?

Suppose you are considering a career as a computer support specialist. Before applying for a job, you decide to look at various openings to see what kinds of computer hardware and software companies expect job applicants to have knowledge of.

a. Use the Internet to search for jobs in this field. (***Hint:*** Explore Web sites such as **www.monster.com**, **www.careerbuilder.com**, or

www.flipdog.com.) Find at least three companies that have openings for a computer support specialist. Determine the types of computer hardware and software the companies use and with which the applicant is expected to be familiar.

b. Using Microsoft Word, prepare a report describing the hardware and software used by the organizations you identified in your research.

c. Format the report attractively and print it. Save the document as *xxx-Computer Support Specialist.doc;* then close the file and exit Word.

2. What's in an Upgrade?

Operating system software undergoes revisions at least once every 1 to 2 years. However, it is a good idea to compare the new features of the upgraded software with the features of your current software to determine if you need or want to invest in the upgrade. Research the new features of Windows XP, and create a PowerPoint presentation that describes some of those new features.

a. Use the Windows online Help feature to locate information on the new features of Windows XP. (Click Help and Support on the Start menu, click *What's new in Windows XP*, click *What's new topics*, and then follow the appropriate links. **See Figure 1.14.**) ***Note:*** If you are not running Windows XP, find information on the Internet.

Figure 1.14 Search for new Windows XP features

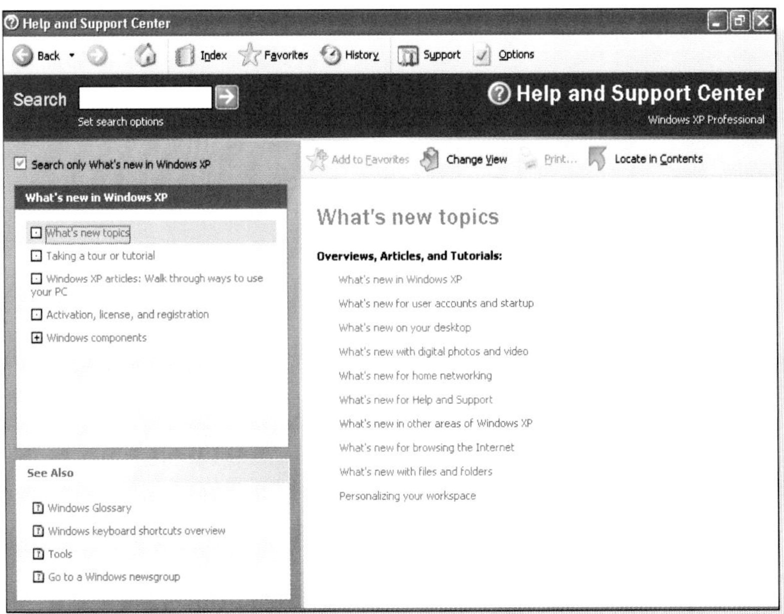

b. Prepare a PowerPoint presentation describing the new features. Include a title slide and at least three additional slides.

c. Format the presentation attractively, and save it as *xxx-New Features of Windows XP.ppt*.

d. Review your presentation in Slide Show view, and then present it to the class.

e. Save and close the presentation.

Challenge Yourself

Choose a Computer System

Assume you work in the print advertising department of a large company, preparing large graphic files for advertising mock-ups, brochures, and magazine ads.

Your company has asked you to submit a proposal for a new personal computer system that would help you perform your work more quickly and efficiently.

- Determine the various components of your system. Be sure to include information about the following:
    - CPU
    - the amount of RAM (at least 256 MB)
    - the hard drive
    - an appropriate secondary storage device
    - a monitor (at least 17 inches)
    - a printer
- Determine the type of operating system and utility programs you want for your computer. Include costs where applicable.
- Do research on the Web and find at least two systems that meet your needs.
- Consider commercial sites such as **www.dell.com**, **www.hp.com**, **www.ibm.com**, or **www.apple.com**. Each of these Web sites lets you configure your own system and calculates the total price.
- Prepare a Word document that lists your findings and justifies the system you would like to purchase.

Lesson 2

Putting the Computer To Work

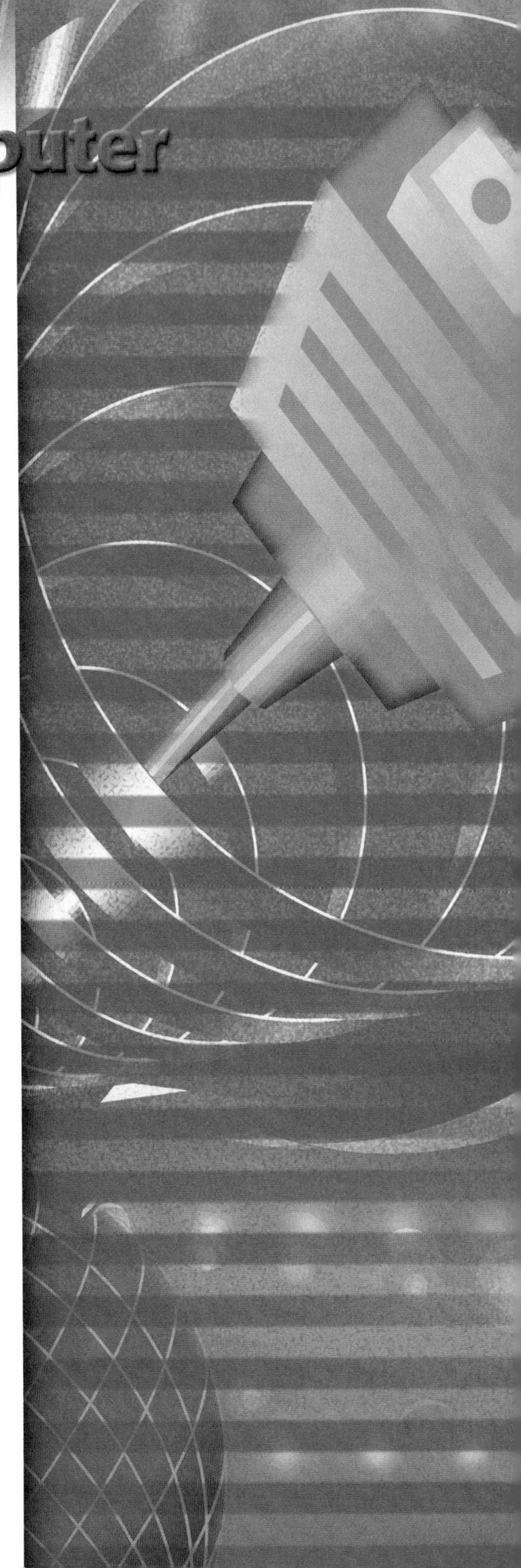

Lesson Exercise Objectives

After completing this lesson, you'll be able to do the following tasks:

1. Understand application software
2. Understand the basics of telecommunications and Internet services
3. Increase productivity by using a network
4. Understand the components of a network

Microsoft Office Specialist Activities

W2002: 1.1, 2.1

EX2002: 1.2, 1.5, 3.1, 5.1, 6.1

PP2002: 1.1, 1.2, 4.1, 4.2, 4.3

Real-Life Business Applications

Key Terms

- application software (p. 784)
- bits per second (bps) (p. 789)
- bus topology (p. 797)
- commercial software (p. 784)
- custom software (proprietary software) (p. 784)
- draw program (p. 786)
- e-mail client (p. 787)
- Ethernet (p. 800)
- Fast Ethernet (p. 800)
- file server (p. 796)
- freeware (p. 785)
- horizontal application software (p. 785)
- integrated program (p. 785)
- Internet Service Provider (ISP) (p. 791)
- local area network (LAN) (p. 793)
- LocalTalk (p. 800)
- metropolitan area network (MAN) (p. 794)
- modem (p. 788)
- network interface card (NIC) (p. 797)
- network operating system (NOS) (p. 797)
- node (p. 796)
- online services (p. 791)
- paint program (p. 786)
- physical media (p. 796)
- program suite (p. 786)
- protocols (p. 799)
- ring topology (p. 798)
- shareware (p. 784)
- star topology (p. 798)
- telecommunications (p. 788)
- Token Ring (p. 800)
- vertical application software (p. 785)
- Web browser (p. 787)
- wide area network (WAN) (p. 794)

Microsoft Office Specialist
PP2002 1.1, 4.2, 4.3

Exercise 1 Overview:
Understand Application Software

In Lesson 1 you learned that operating system software makes the computer work. However, it is **application software** that helps people use their computers to perform their work (or play!) more effectively. Application software includes all of the programs that allow users to write reports and memos, inventory business supplies and products, prepare and print monthly budgets, draw diagrams, design company logos, play games, and more. In other words, while you *need* operating system software to actually run your computer, you *want* application software to actually use your computer.

Application software is often categorized in two ways—by the way it is acquired and by the way it is used. First let's take a look at how application software can be acquired.

People usually buy **commercial software** in retail stores, on Web sites, or "bundled" with a new computer system. Because the cost of developing, marketing, and maintaining support for commercial software involves the investment of a lot of money, large computer companies such as Microsoft, Apple, Corel, Adobe, Lotus, and IBM dominate the commercial software field.

But what if the right application is not available "off the shelf"? In those cases, businesses or individuals can purchase **custom (or proprietary) software**. This can be very expensive, because custom software must be developed by professional programmers. However, a custom software application can do exactly what a user wants because it is tailored to the user's exact specifications.

Some programmers write application programs and sell them on their own or in small groups as **shareware**. Typically, people download shareware over the Internet and use the program at no charge for a specified time period. After that trial period expires, the user is expected to send money to the developer. If no money is sent, the program may stop working or display messages encouraging the user to pay for the software. In other cases, shareware programs may not initially perform all features, such as printing or saving. Then after the user pays, the shareware developer provides a special code that "unlocks" the program and allows access to all operations.

Freeware is application software that is distributed without cost. Freeware programs have been copyrighted by their developers and made available to the public without charge. Because freeware programs are copyrighted, they cannot be resold by the user for profit.

Application software is also categorized by the way it is used. **Horizontal application software** is designed to be used for a wide variety of purposes. For example, the same word processing software that is used by an office assistant in an accounting firm to send a memo to his boss can also be used by a restaurant manager to create a menu. Or, the same graphics program that is used to design a letterhead for office stationery can also be used to make a poster for a rock concert.

Vertical application software, on the other hand, is highly specialized and is used for very specific purposes. For example, a school may use a special program to track students' attendance, grades, and transcripts. Such a program would be of no use to a company manufacturing restaurant supplies. Many entertainment and educational software programs, such as games and typing programs, are classified as vertical application software—they do exactly what they are designed to do—nothing more and nothing less.

Due to its nature, horizontal application software is more prevalent than vertical application software. Some common types of horizontal application software are general productivity programs, graphics programs, and browser and e-mail programs. Each of these types is discussed in the following sections.

General Productivity Programs

Users from a wide variety of fields, careers, and interests need general productivity programs to write documents, manage finances, keep track of inventory, convince an audience, and manage address books, to-do lists, and appointments. Common general productivity programs include word processing programs, spreadsheet programs, database management programs, presentation graphics programs, and personal information management programs.

Many commercial software developers package their general productivity programs as standalone products, as integrated programs, or as program suites. An **integrated program** combines the functionality of two or more programs, such as word processing functions, spreadsheet functions, and database management functions, into one program. Microsoft Works and AppleWorks are examples of integrated programs.

Quick Tip

Many operating systems include *applets*—small programs with limited features that perform specific functions. However, most users need a full range of features that are available only in application software. An example of a word processing applet in Windows XP is WordPad.

On the other hand, a **program suite** is actually a package of standalone programs that can be used independently of one another, yet allows the user to move data effectively among the programs. In general, program suites are more popular with users than integrated programs because program suites offer more features and advanced functionality.

Program suites often contain four or more individual programs, and it is usually more cost effective to purchase a program suite than it is to purchase the individual programs. A typical general productivity program suite contains a word processing program, a spreadsheet program, a database management program, and a presentation graphics program. Microsoft Office, Corel WordPerfect Office, Lotus SmartSuite, and StarOffice (freeware by Sun Microsystems) are examples of program suites.

Graphics Programs

Figure 2.1 Microsoft Paint program

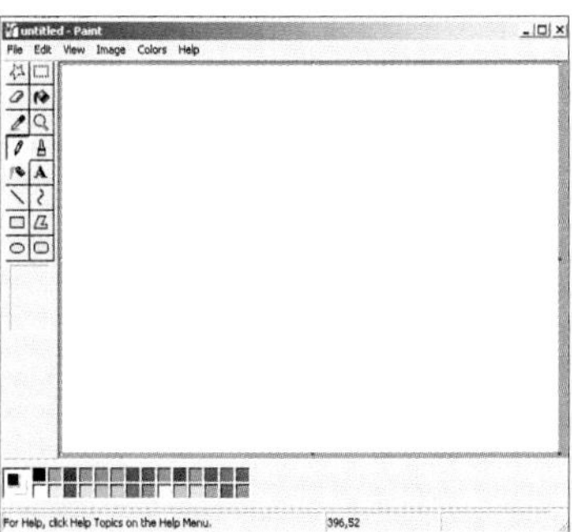

Two very different types of programs can be used to produce illustrations, although the resulting graphics may look very similar. **Paint programs** provide tools with which you can "paint" each individual dot, or pixel, on the computer screen. Paint programs produce bit-mapped graphics (also called raster graphics), which are basically a collection of dots (pixels) arranged to form an image. The advantages of a paint program are that it is simple to use, and it saves the image as a relatively small file. A major disadvantage is its inability to enlarge an image without sacrificing its resolution. Popular paint programs include Fractal Design Painter and Adobe PhotoShop.

Draw programs, on the other hand, store the lines and shapes of an image as mathematical formulas instead of a collection of dots. Since these image components exist mathematically, changing the size of the image does not adversely affect its resolution. Images created with draw programs are called object-oriented graphics (also called vector graphics), because the program stores the shapes and lines of the image (the objects) as mathematical formulas, instead of storing a collection of dots. Draw programs create files that are significantly larger than paint programs, and they are usually more difficult to use. However, many professional illustrators prefer draw programs because the images are easier to edit than bit-mapped images. Popular draw programs include Adobe Illustrator and Macromedia Freehand.

Other graphics software exists for more specialized purposes, such as photo-editing programs, 3-D modeling software, computer-aided drawing and manufacturing programs (CAD/CAM), and animation programs.

Browser and E-mail Programs

Special application software is required to access the many services available over the Internet. To view Web pages online, you need a **Web browser**—an application program that allows you to surf the Web and display Web pages.

Web pages contain special codes called HyperText Markup Language (HTML). The Web browser converts the HTML code into formatting features such as font characteristics, margins, tables, and graphics. Embedded into most Web pages are hyperlinks (also known as links). The Web browser lets you access Web pages by clicking on these links, by typing in the Web page's Internet address or Uniform Resource Locator (URL), or by selecting saved Web page addresses from a favorites or bookmark list. Microsoft Internet Explorer and Netscape Navigator currently dominate the Web browser market.

To send and receive e-mail messages over the Internet, you need an application program called an **e-mail client**. Both Internet Explorer and Netscape Navigator include basic e-mail clients (Outlook Express and Netscape Communicator, respectively). Microsoft Outlook and Qualcomm's Eudora are examples of more advanced e-mail clients. In addition to handling messages, e-mail clients can manage address books, set up distribution lists to send one message to more than one recipient, and include files, called attachments, with the message.

In the following exercise, you will prepare a PowerPoint presentation that compares four popular program suites.

Figure 2.2 Research points for Exercise 1

Consider the following points as you conduct your research on each program suite:

- Name of program suite
- Basic programs contained in program suite
- Additional programs contained in program suite (if available)
- System requirements
- Cost
- Advantages
- Disadvantages

Need Help?

Refer to Appendix A for information on using Internet Explorer, the Web browser that is part of the Windows operating system.

Systems

Step Through It™

Exercise 1: Compare program suites

1. Conduct research on each of the following program suites: Microsoft Office, Corel WordPerfect Office, Lotus SmartSuite, and Sun StarOffice. Use the information provided in Figure 2.2 as the basis for your research.
2. Create a PowerPoint presentation that compares the program suites. Format the presentation attractively and add animations and transitions as appropriate. Save your presentation as *xxx-Program Suites Comparison.ppt.*

After finishing Exercise 1, you may test your skills by completing Apply It! Guided Activity 1, Identify Application Software.

Microsoft Office Specialist
EX2002 1.2, 6.1

Systems

Exercise 2 Overview: Understand the Basics of Telecommunications and Internet Services

Since *tele* means "over a distance," **telecommunications** is the technology of long-distance electronic communication. The television, telephone, telegraph, and facsimile machine are all examples of everyday telecommunications devices. This exercise concentrates on telecommunications as it applies to computers and the Internet.

Figure 2.3 illustrates one way in which computers telecommunicate. The user sends a command or request for information by typing at the keyboard or clicking with the mouse. The request is encoded by the user's software and is then sent to a device that transmits the information over telephone lines, cables, or other means. At the receiving end, the information is captured and decoded so that it can be viewed on the other computer.

Figure 2.3 An example of telecommunications over telephone lines

Establish a Connection

To send and receive data from your computer through standard analog telephone lines, you must have a **modem** (short for modulator/demodulator). Figure 2.4 illustrates both an external and an internal modem. A modem attaches to your computer on one end and the telephone jack at the other end. The modem converts the digital signals your computer understands into an analog signal, or sound wave, that can be sent over the telephone wires. The receiving computer must have a modem as well, in order to turn the analog signal back into a digital signal. Since the 1990s, some telephone companies have offered Integrated Services Digital Network (ISDN), which is a digital, instead of analog, telephone service. With ISDN, you connect your computer to regular telephone lines using an ISDN adapter instead of a modem.

Figure 2.4 An external modem (top) and an internal modem (bottom)

While virtually anyone can access the Internet using a regular telephone line connection, many other types of connections are only available in certain areas. For example, Digital Subscriber Lines (DSL) use special twisted pair telephone lines to transmit data at very high speeds, and also require special DSL modems. However, DSL service cannot extend beyond a couple of miles from telephone switching stations. Therefore, this service is usually unavailable in rural areas.

Cable TV companies are capable of using their cables to transmit data. To make use of this service, your computer must have a network interface card (discussed later in this lesson), a cable modem, and a connection to the cable network. Also, wireless connections can be made using radio wave signals or satellite dishes.

Cost and availability are two important factors that will influence your choice of connection type. Another major factor is data transmission speed (measured in **bits per**

second (bps)) which varies widely among the connection types. High-speed connections deliver enough data to allow for audio and video exchange and make it possible for large files to be downloaded quickly. Table 2.1 compares some common types of telecommunications connections used by individuals and small businesses.

Table 2.1

Connection Type	Typical Cost	Availability	Typical Data Transmission Speed
Analog phone line	$10 – $25/mo.	Almost everywhere	42 – 56 Kbps
ISDN	$100 and up/mo.	Only where offered	64 – 128 Kbps
DSL	$50 and up/mo.	Mostly in metropolitan areas	512 Kbps – 1.544 Mbps
Cable	$40 – $60/mo.	Where offered by cable TV companies	1.5 – 3 Mbps
Satellite	$70 and up/mo.	Where offered by satellite dish TV services	150 Kbps – 1000 Kbps

Connection Type	Convenience	Usability
Analog phone line	Plug into phone jack/most modems already in computer	Dial-up
ISDN	Uses regular telephone lines/requires ISDN adapter	Dial-up
DSL	Uses special telephone lines/requires DSL modem	Always on
Cable	Requires cable TV access, special modem, and network card	Always on
Satellite	Requires satellite dish installation; (also requires regular phone line and modem to upload files)	Always on

The Role of the Internet Service Providers (ISPs) and Online Services

In a typical Internet telecommunications session, the user boots the computer and launches the telecommunications software, such as a Web browser, which establishes a connection to an Internet service provider. **Internet Service Providers (ISPs)** are companies that provide access to the Internet for users who subscribe to them. Some ISPs such as Earthlink and MSN are available nationwide, while others serve only local areas.

For a monthly fee, ISPs provide their subscribers with a variety of Internet services, such as Web access, e-mail, file transfers, and newsgroups. ISPs may also offer free Web hosting services, giving their subscribers space to display their own Web pages over the Internet.

Online services provide direct access to information that is maintained outside of the Internet, such as chat rooms, online shopping malls, and stock quotes. America Online (AOL), CompuServe, MSN, and Prodigy are popular, general online service companies. Other online services provide in-depth, specialized information targeted to specific markets. For example, LexisNexis is a well-known online service that provides information to the legal, academic, and corporate markets.

Types of Internet Services

Many people mistakenly refer to the Internet as the World Wide Web (or simply the Web), but in reality, the Web is only one of the many ways data can be exchanged on the Internet. Table 2.2 describes some of the other ways data can be exchanged on the Internet.

Quick Tip

Discount ISPs may display advertising as a way to lower their costs to subscribers and/or increase their company's revenue.

Table 2.2

Service	Description
File Transfer Protocol (FTP)	Remote computers, acting as FTP servers, store files. Users can download files to their computers or upload files they wish to share with others.
Internet Relay Chat (IRC)	Users "meet" in chat rooms where they can type and read messages in online group conversations.
Instant Messaging (IM)	Users can send and receive messages instantly whenever anyone on their "buddies list" is also online.
Newsgroups	Newsgroups (also called *forums*) are online discussion groups that are organized into specific topics covering almost any hobby or interest. Users send (or post) articles to groups to which they belong. Follow-ups by other users are collected into a series of articles called threads. Users need a newsreader, a software program for reading and posting articles, in order to access a newsgroup.
Electronic commerce (e-commerce)	Companies wishing to sell products or services can use the Internet for business-to-business (B2B) or business-to-customer (B2C) transactions.
Bulletin board system (BBS)	A bulletin board system is similar to a newsgroup; however, users don't need a newsreader to access a BBS. Most BBSs are very small—they're often created by individual hobbyists, and are usually based on only one PC that is accessed by modem through one or two phone lines.
Internet telephony	Using special hardware and software, users can transmit voice or fax data using the Internet instead of a regular telephone. Local, long distance, and international calls made using Internet telephony can be very cost effective, depending on the cost of Internet access (which for many users is a fixed price per month).
Video conferencing	Two or more users at different locations can use the Internet to transmit both video and audio data, and thus participate in a "real-time" meeting. Each participant must have a video camera, a microphone, and speakers attached to his or her computer, in addition to special conferencing software.

In the following exercise, you will prepare an Excel chart that compares the monthly costs of various Internet service providers.

Figure 2.5 Example Excel chart comparing ISPs

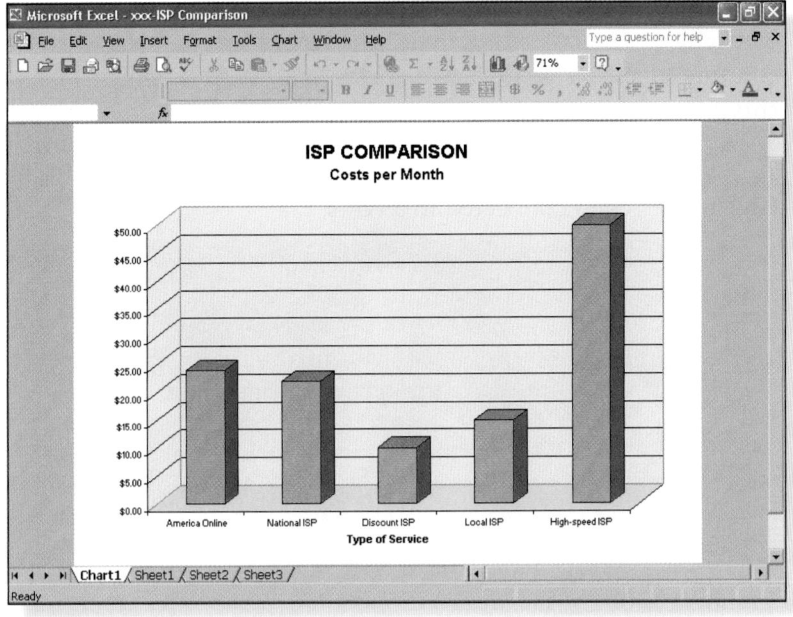

Step Through It™

Exercise 2: Compare available ISPs

1. Research the monthly costs to subscribe to the following ISPs in your area: America Online (AOL), one national ISP, one discount ISP (such as Juno or NetZero), one local ISP, and one high-speed ISP (cable, DSL, or satellite).
2. Enter your research results in an Excel worksheet, and then create a column chart comparing ISPs and their monthly costs. (See the example in Figure 2.5.)
3. Save the worksheet as *xxx-ISP Comparison.xls*.

Exercise 3 Overview: Increase Productivity by Using a Network

A network is, essentially, two or more computers linked to each other by some type of cabling or other data transmission media, and is used to exchange data. Usually when people use the term *network*, they are referring to a local area network. A **local area network (LAN)** connects computers within a home, an office, or a building. LANs can also be used to connect computers in separate buildings that are physically close together.

Companies and other organizations set up LANs in order for their employees to access and exchange information quickly and efficiently. In addition, users connected via a LAN can share hardware, such as printers and other devices, which reduces costs. Software costs can be reduced as well when companies purchase network software licenses instead of buying individual licenses for each machine.

Organizations with offices located within a small region can connect their separate LANs to a **metropolitan area network (MAN)** using telephone or telecommunications company services. In turn, all LANs or MANs can be connected into a **wide area network (WAN)** regardless of the distances separating them (see Figure 2.6).

Figure 2.6 LANs connected to a WAN

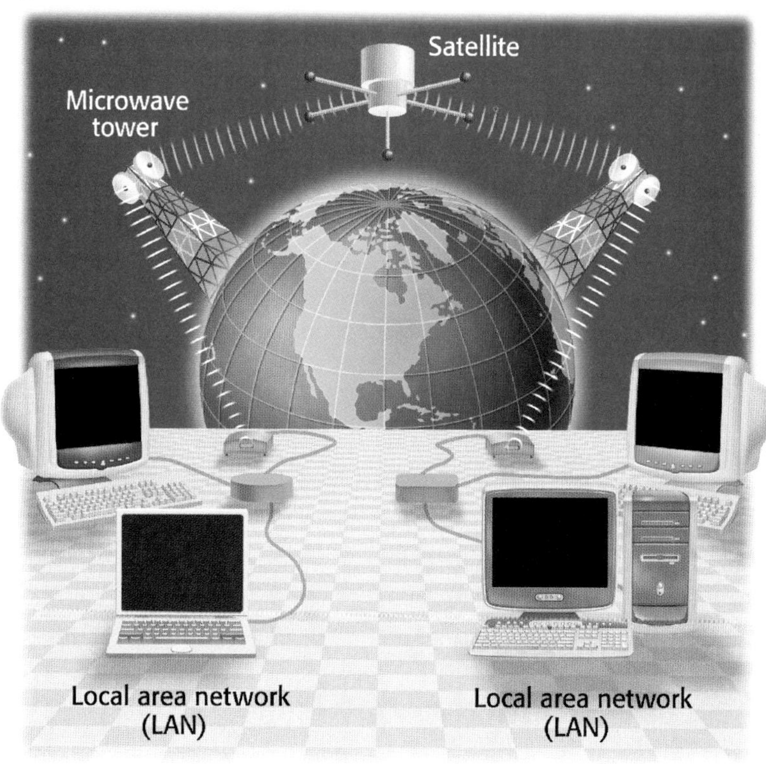

In reality, the Internet is one huge WAN. However, because the Internet is not totally secure, many companies use WANs other than the Internet to transmit financial data and other sensitive information.

Once people are connected to a network, the way they are able work with others changes dramatically. Groupware software le workgroups coordinate appointments and calendars, exchan data files, and send internal e-mail. (Internal e-mail differs fro external e-mail in that it travels only on an organization's LA it does not travel over the Internet.) Programs such as Lot Notes and Microsoft Exchange are examples of groupwa applications.

Besides exchanging document files, network users can also view and make changes to documents using collaborative writing tools. Once requiring special software, today's general productivity programs, such as Microsoft Word, allow each user to make comments, additions, deletions, and changes without directly affecting the original document. Multiple users can see the edits, identify the person making the changes, and make suggestions of their own. Once everyone is in agreement, the finished document reflects the efforts of the group.

A network administrator is in charge of coordinating the setup, maintenance, and access to an organization's network. To limit and control access, the network administrator assigns user names and initial passwords to employees. Since not all employees should be allowed access to all network resources, network administrators may assign users to workgroups that give them user rights to only certain hardware devices, folders, and files. For example, sales personnel might be assigned to a sales workgroup that gives them access to a company's products database but not to its accounting database.

In the following exercise, you will display the devices connected to your computer via your network.

Systems

Figure 2.7 Window showing devices on your network

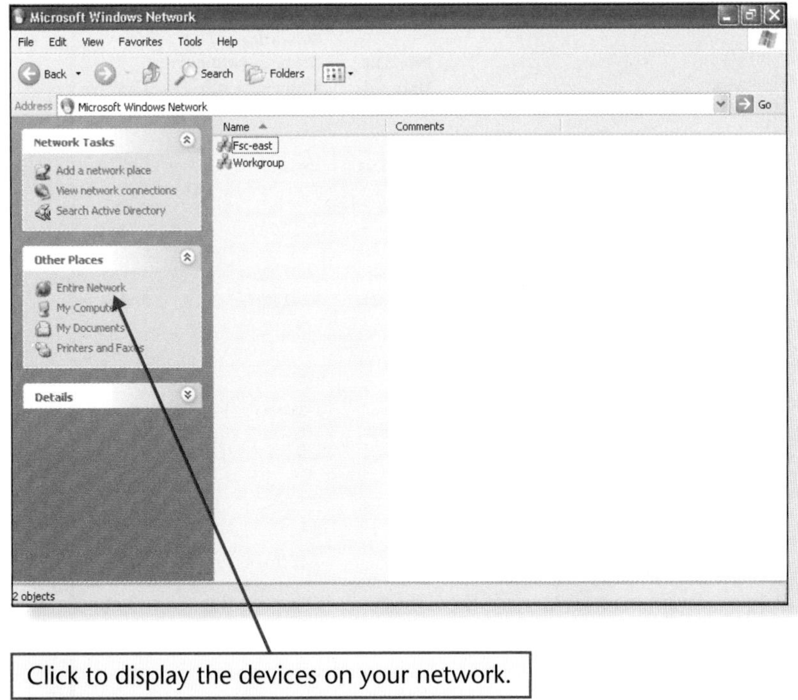

Step Through It™

Exercise 3: Explore My Network Places

1. Select My Network Places from the Start menu.
2. Click Views on the Standard Buttons toolbar, and choose the Details option.
3. Click Entire Network in the left pane of the My Network Places window to display the devices on your network (see Figure 2.7).
4. Close the window to return to the Windows desktop.

Systems

Exercise 4 Overview:
Understand the Components of a Network

Each device on a local area network, such as a computer or a printer, is referred to as a **node**. Each of these nodes is connected to one or more **file servers**—high-speed computers with large hard drives that are used to store large amounts of data.

Each node on the network that has been granted the appropriate rights by the network administrator can access the data on the file servers. Collecting and centralizing data on a network file server provides two important benefits: (1) it gives users access to the most up-to-date data and (2) it eliminates the problem of the same data being duplicated on each user's computer, which not only wastes storage space, but also increases the likelihood of people using outdated data.

All of the nodes and file servers on a network are connected by **physical media**—the cables or wireless connections that transmit the data on a network. Many different types of physical media can be used in computer networks (see Figure 2.8).

Figure 2.8 Types of physical media

NETWORKS ARE BUILT ON PHYSICAL MEDIA

Type	Principal Uses	Maximum Operating Distance (without amplification)	Cost
Twisted pair	Small LANS	300 feet	Low
Coaxial cable	Large LANS	600–2,500 feet	Medium
Fiber optic	Network backbones; WANS	1–25 miles	High
Wireless/infrared	LANS	3–1,000 feet (line of sight)	Medium
Wireless/radio	Connecting things that move	Varies considerably	High

You connect a computer to a network cable through a **network interface card (NIC)**. Most NICs are designed to connect to a particular type of cable, although some work with more than one type. The NIC is responsible for controlling the flow of data between the computer's RAM and the network cable.

Most LANs used in businesses and other organizations are client/server networks. In a client/server network, one or more file servers store most of the shared data and run the network operating system. A **network operating system (NOS)** manages the LAN by establishing and maintaining the connections between the nodes and the file server. All of the other computers on the network are clients and depend on the file servers for all network functions. The most common network operating systems are Microsoft's Windows NT or XP Servers and Novell Corporation's NetWare.

Network Topology

Network topology is the physical arrangement of computers on a network. The topology of a network determines how the flow of data is handled when two computers try to transmit data across the network at the same time. The three most common LAN topologies are bus topology, star topology, and ring topology.

The simplest topology is a **bus topology**, in which a single cable runs the length of the network (see Figure 2.9). Each node (computer or peripheral device) connects to this one cable. Although this is an inexpensive network arrangement, a break in the cable may cause the entire network to "crash." A bus-topology network employs special data management techniques to handle the flow of data when two computers transmit data simultaneously.

Figure 2.9 A bus topology

With a **star topology**, each node connects to a hub, or switch, through which data travels to the file server and/or other computers (see Figure 2.10). Star topologies use more cable than a bus topology, but a single broken cable will not "crash" the network. Like the bus topology, a star-topology network also employs special data management techniques to handle the flow of data when two computers transmit data simultaneously.

Figure 2.10 A star topology

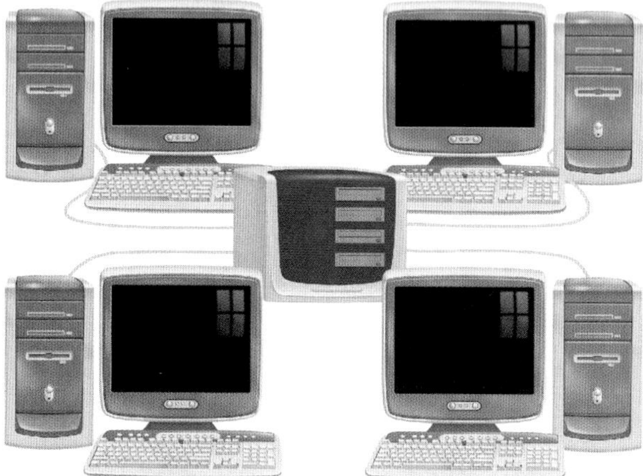

In a **ring topology**, each node connects to the next in a circular arrangement. A special set of data, called a token, travels from one computer to the next around the circle (see Figure 2.11). If a computer needs to send or receive data, it must wait until the token gets to it. Thus, this configuration eliminates the problem of two computers transmitting data at the same time. Like the bus topology, however, a single break in the ring can ruin the network.

Figure 2.11 A ring topology

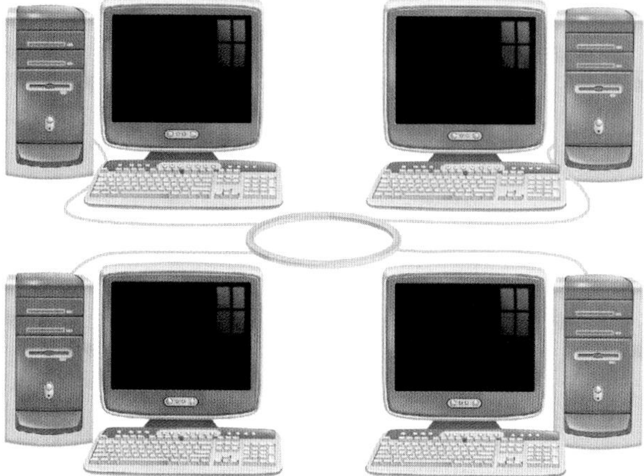

Network Protocols

There's more involved with transmitting data over a network than simply hooking up the network's physical components. Differences in data format, in various hardware devices, and in software applications require the need for protocols. **Protocols** are standards that describe how the different devices on a network communicate with each other. One network could use literally dozens of protocols to specify how data should be "presented" and handled in order to transmit it efficiently and accurately across the network.

When data is transmitted from a sending computer, it must travel through layers before it actually reaches the physical media. Similarly, on the other end, data must travel through layers from the physical media before it can reach the receiving computer. Each layer performs a specific function and has its own set of protocols that define exactly how data must pass from one layer to the next. A protocol stack is the series of layers through which data moves (see Figure 2.12).

Figure 2.12 Data moving through a protocol stack

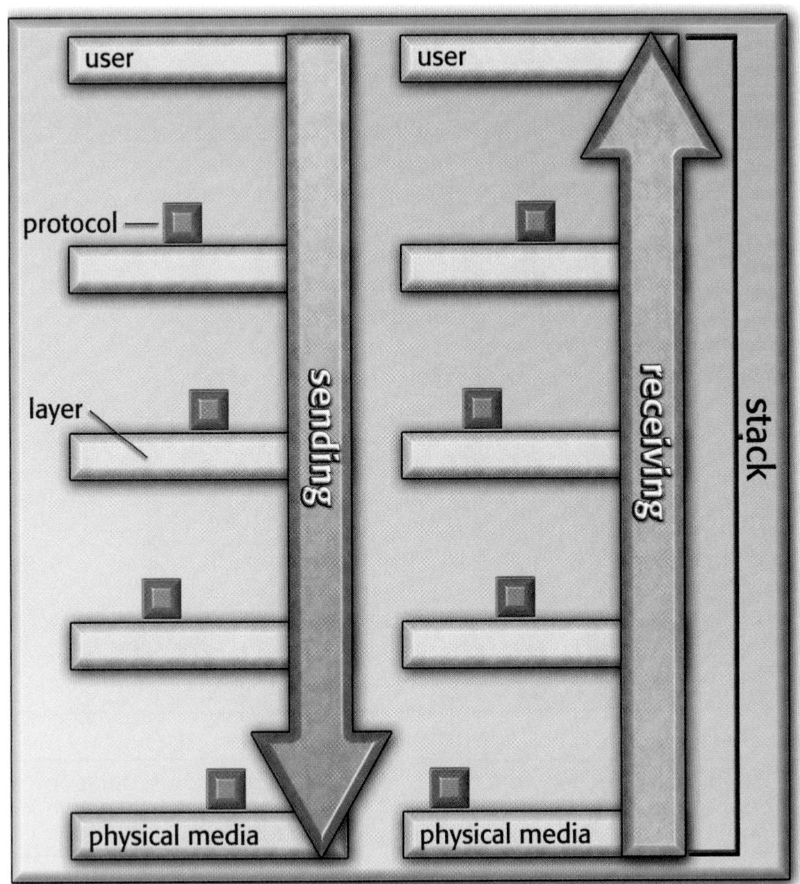

Systems

LAN Standards

All of these various network elements, from network interface cards and physical media to protocols and topologies, are usually viewed together as a set of LAN standards, or specifications. One of the most widely implemented LAN standards is **Ethernet**. Ethernet is used with bus and star topologies, twisted-pair or fiber optic cables, and an Ethernet-compatible network interface card (NIC).

Ethernet can transmit data at 10 Mbps (10 million bits per second). However, a newer standard called **Fast Ethernet** can support data transfer rates of up to 100 Mbps (100 million bits per second).

The second most widely used LAN standard is the **Token Ring**. This standard uses a ring topology and transfers data at either 4 or 16 Mbps.

Probably the simplest LAN standard is **LocalTalk**, the system that Macintosh uses, in which ordinary phone cables are arranged in a bus topology. However, the data transfer rate on a LocalTalk network is only 230 Kbps, or 230 thousand bits per second—which is much slower than the transfer rate on an Ethernet or Token Ring network.

Step Through It™

Exercise 4: Display network connection status

1. Select Control Panel on the Start menu, and then double-click Network Connections in the right pane of the Control Panel window.
2. In the right pane of the Network Connections window, double-click the network connection option (see Figure 2.13).
3. Click the General tab of the Status dialog box (if necessary), and note the status, duration, and speed of your network.
4. Close the Status dialog box and the Network Connections window.

Figure 2.13 Network connection status viewed in Windows XP

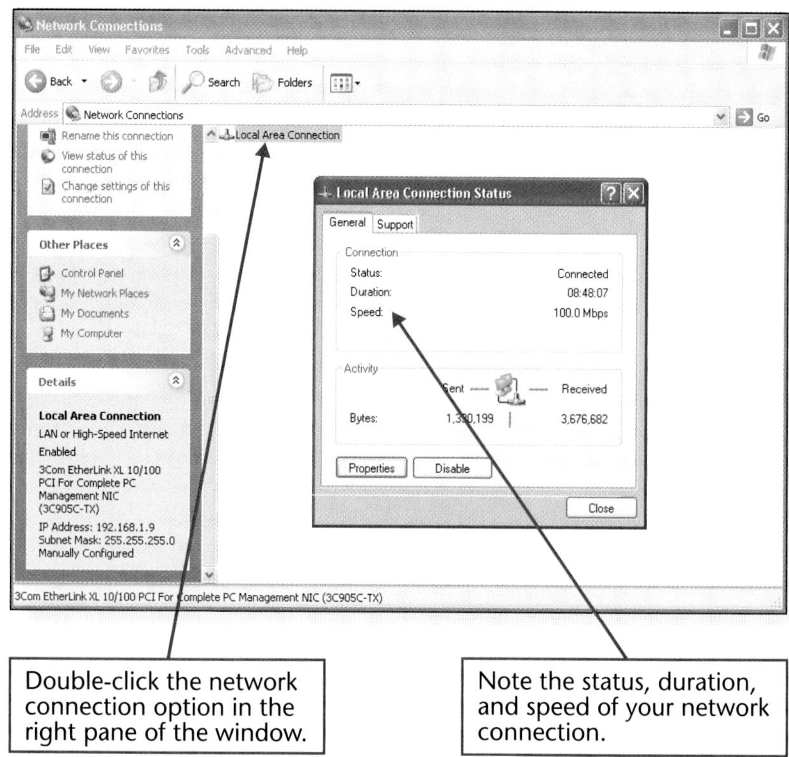

Tech Talk

Personal Area Networks– A Look Into the Future

Experts predict that networking in the future will encompass not only desktop computers, but a myriad of other electronic devices. Integration of cell phones, personal digital assistants (PDAs), and laptops will provide people with a personal area network (PAN)—a network of their own computer-based appliances that communicate to each other and the outside world through ever-improving satellite and wireless technologies.

Think of a PAN as a personal bubble of connectivity: You get a page on your pager, and the number is automatically uploaded to your cell phone. Your PDA "unlocks" your workstation, car, or home security system. You walk through a mall, and your mobile phone or pager delivers special offers to you.

PANs permit ad hoc networking—the creation of informal networks whenever two or more PAN-enabled devices are within range of each other (generally 10 meters or less). Many PAN-enabled devices seek and connect to others automatically.

Three technologies are being explored for developing PANs: short-range radio applications such as Bluetooth, infrared, and magnetic field.

Here are a few of the many other things that PANs could let you do:

- Synchronize Outlook contacts on a cell phone
- Send a presentation to an audience's laptops
- Use a pay phone without entering a calling card number or PIN

CRITICAL THINKING

1. PANs can eliminate redundancy in electronic devices. Explain how.
2. Form a team with two or three other students. Investigate one of the PAN technologies described above. Report to the class on how it works and how it might be used. If possible, include information on cost, convenience, and availability.

Business Connections

Networking—Getting Connected

Most businesses today use computer networks—sophisticated combinations of hardware, software, and communication media—in order to share and exchange data between two or more computers (and other devices). Not only are networks an essential tool in the business world today, they are also becoming more prevalent in homes as people's need to link multiple personal devices grows.

There are several factors to consider when selecting a network. Not only is it important to select the type of network that suits your needs, such as a wired network or a wireless network; you must also consider other factors, such as cost and data transmission speed.

Wired Networks

Most networks used today are connected by cables. The installation of cables is usually done by networking professionals and can be expensive. Depending on the number of computers, their distance from each other, and how they are connected, today's networks generally consist of the following:

- One cable for each computer
- A network interface card (NIC) for each computer
- A firewall to protect the network from unauthorized access
- Network operating system software
- Antivirus software

The cost to set up a wired network can vary greatly depending on the number of users and the amount of security desired. You must also consider the cost of file servers to store shared data and the cost of network or site licensing agreements for application software, network operating system software, and antivirus software.

Wireless Networks

Wireless networks are a relatively new networking technology, and are improving rapidly as the wireless technology evolves. Wireless networks transmit data using either radio or infrared technology instead of cables. Each computer on a wireless network contains either an infrared or a radio transmitter to send and receive data and a wireless network interface card. Wireless networks provide portability but are more costly to install and pose greater security risks than wired networks. Many organizations maintain a wired network but add wireless capabilities where practical, such as providing network access to laptop users so they can connect to the network without cables.

When selecting a networking system, you must also consider your "need for speed"—data transmission speed, that is. Any speed is good enough to send e-mail, but a high-speed network is necessary if large files, such as video and audio, must be transmitted. For the most part, wireless networks are significantly slower than wired networks; however, wireless transmission speed is likely to improve as wireless technology evolves.

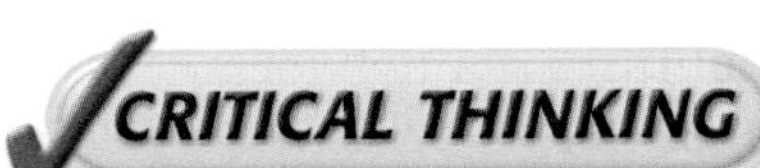

1. **Assessing Network Security** Why do you think a wireless network poses a greater data security risk than a wired network?

2. **Ranking Network Needs** Many people today are networking multiple computers and peripheral devices in their homes. Conduct Web research on both wired and wireless networks for the home. Ask your classmates which of the following factors do they think would be most important to someone considering a home network: data transmission speed, cost, or security? Show your results as an Excel pie chart.

Lesson Review and Exercises

Summary Checklist

- ☑ Do you understand the difference between commercial software, custom software, shareware, and freeware?
- ☑ Can you explain the difference between horizontal application software and vertical application software?
- ☑ Can you explain the difference between an integrated program and a program suite, and give an example of each?
- ☑ Can you compare and contrast paint and draw programs?
- ☑ Can you give examples of various types of telecommunications connections?
- ☑ Can you describe some of the Internet services available besides accessing the Web?
- ☑ Can you describe how networks can improve productivity?
- ☑ Can you describe the main components of a network?
- ☑ Can you compare and contrast the three most common LAN topologies?

Key Terms

- application software (p. 784)
- bits per second (bps) (p. 789)
- bus topology (p. 797)
- commercial software (p. 784)
- custom software (proprietary software) (p. 784)
- draw program (p. 786)
- e-mail client (p. 787)
- Ethernet (p. 800)
- Fast Ethernet (p. 800)
- file server (p. 796)
- freeware (p. 785)
- horizontal application software (p. 785)
- integrated program (p. 785)
- Internet Service Provider (ISP) (p. 791)
- local area network (LAN) (p. 793)
- LocalTalk (p. 800)
- metropolitan area network (MAN) (p. 794)
- modem (p. 788)
- network interface card (NIC) (p. 797)
- network operating system (NOS) (p. 797)
- node (p. 796)
- online services (p. 791)
- paint program (p. 786)
- physical media (p. 796)

Key Terms—continued

- program suite (p. 786)
- protocols (p. 799)
- ring topology (p. 798)
- shareware (p. 784)
- star topology (p. 798)
- telecommunications (p. 788)
- Token Ring (p. 800)
- vertical application software (p. 785)
- Web browser (p. 787)
- wide area network (WAN) (p. 794)

APPLY IT! Guided Activities

1. Identify Application Software

Assume you work as an information systems (IS) support specialist for a large manufacturing company. In addition to the IS department, your company also has several other departments, such as the accounting department, the advertising department, the cost estimating department, and the mechanical engineering department, to name a few. One of your tasks is to identify and catalog all the application programs currently being used in the company. Follow these steps to complete your task:

a. Open the *Company Applications Programs.xls* worksheet **(see Figure 2.14)**. Place an "X" in all the categories to which a particular program belongs.

b. Filter the worksheet to find answers to the following questions. Record your answers as complete sentences in a Microsoft Word document.

   1. How many different application programs are used in the company?
   2. Does the company use any integrated programs? If so, identify them.
   3. What program suites does the company use?
   4. How many graphics programs does the company use? Identify them and indicate whether they are draw programs or paint programs.

c. In your Word document, list all the programs that you placed in the *Other* category and indicate what type of programs they are.

Hint: Use Windows Help and/or conduct research on the Web to identify the programs.

d. Save your Excel worksheet as *xxx-Company Applications Programs.xls* and your Word document as *xxx-Application Programs Report.doc.*

Figure 2.14 The *Company Applications Programs.xls* worksheet

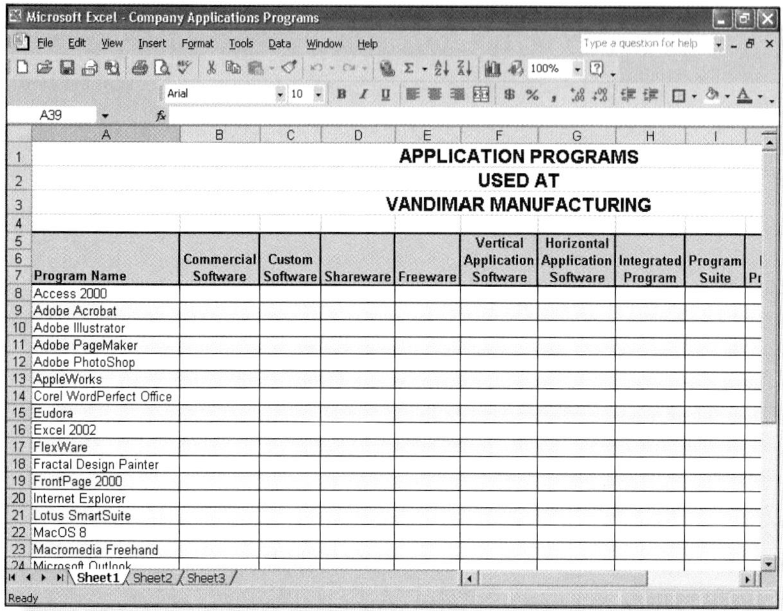

Microsoft Excel - Company Applications Programs

APPLICATION PROGRAMS
USED AT
VANDIMAR MANUFACTURING

Program Name	Commercial Software	Custom Software	Shareware	Freeware	Vertical Application Software	Horizontal Application Software	Integrated Program	Program Suite	Pr
Access 2000									
Adobe Acrobat									
Adobe Illustrator									
Adobe PageMaker									
Adobe PhotoShop									
AppleWorks									
Corel WordPerfect Office									
Eudora									
Excel 2002									
FlexWare									
Fractal Design Painter									
FrontPage 2000									
Internet Explorer									
Lotus SmartSuite									
MacOS 8									
Macromedia Freehand									
Microsoft Outlook									

2. Investigate a Newsgroup or BBS

Because technology changes so rapidly, one of the major issues facing IT (Information Technology) professionals is the ability to stay up to date with new information in their field. Use the Search feature of your Web browser to identify one newsgroup or one bulletin board service that deals with any topic in the information technology field. Record the name of the newsgroup or BBS, its Internet site address, and a brief summary of its purpose. With your teacher's permission, join the discussion group and follow some of the threads.

Do It Yourself

1. Prepare a Networking Proposal

Assume you work for NetPro, a network consulting company. You receive a call from Chris Schott, the owner of Schott Realty, a small, but growing, real estate company. Chris Schott is considering installing a small network at Schott Realty, which currently has four computers (one for each employee) and two printers. Using Microsoft Word, do the following to prepare a preliminary proposal for your client:

a. Prepare a brief paragraph detailing the benefits of installing a client/server network using a star topology.

b. Using the drawing tools in Word, draw and label a simple schematic of a star-topology network that incorporates the client's four computers and two printers and any other additional equipment that must be represented.

c. Format the proposal attractively and save it as *xxx-Network Proposal.doc*.

d. Using the information in **Table 2.3**, prepare an Excel worksheet that contains projected component costs to network the client's six devices. Calculate a total cost.

Table 2.3

Network Component	Typical Cost
Physical media (cables)	$45
Network interface card	$120
Network operating system	$980
File server	$1500
Hub	$60

e. Format the worksheet attractively and save it as *xxx-Proposal Costs.xls*.

Challenge Yourself

Research Peer-to-Peer Networks

Unlike a client/server network, a peer-to-peer network is a network that does not use a file server, and each computer on the network is considered equal. In order to share files, each user on the network decides which files or devices (such as a printer) he/she wishes to share with other users. Peer-to-peer networks are relatively easy to set up, and are often used in Small Office/Home Office (SoHo) environments. Conduct research on peer-to-peer networking. Prepare a Word document or PowerPoint presentation that compares and contrasts peer-to-peer and client/server networks.

Systems

Unit 6 Applications and Projects

Apply Your Knowledge

Complete the following exercises in order, as directed by your teacher. As you work through these projects you will design a computer system for DesignWeb, a small, high-tech firm specializing in Web design. DesignWeb needs a small local area network, computers, other hardware devices, and software. You will create three documents for DesignWeb: (1) a business report that describes the firm's system needs, (2) an Excel workbook that contains hardware and software specifications, along with related cost and inventory information, and (3) a PowerPoint presentation addressing the firm's software requirements. You must proofread your documents carefully, edit them as necessary, and format them attractively. Save all files in the *Unit Applications and Projects* subfolder within your *Unit 6* folder.

1. Create a System Needs Analysis Report

a. Launch Microsoft Word and write a report describing the computer hardware and software needs for DesignWeb. Conduct research as appropriate to determine the specifications for relatively high-end hardware and appropriate software. Include *at least* the following:

- Four personal computers (Be sure to include specifications for the CPU, the amount of RAM, the hard drive, a secondary storage device, and a monitor.)
- One laser printer
- One inkjet printer
- Operating system software
- Utility software
- Application software (Some examples of application programs used for Web design are: Dreamweaver®, FrontPage, Macromedia® Flash™, and Photoshop®.)
- LAN hardware and software (Assume you will be installing a client/server network using a bus topology.)

b. Design a letterhead with the company name, and insert it at the beginning of your report. Find a clip art image to use as the company's logo.

c. Print the report. Save the report as *xxx-System Needs Analysis.doc* and exit Word.

2. Prepare a Cost Estimate

a. Conduct research (either by searching the Web, reviewing computer equipment catalogs, or visiting a local computer retail store) to determine the cost and specifications of the hardware and software you identified in your System Needs Analysis report. Record your findings in an Excel worksheet. Include the following column headings in the worksheet:

- Item Description
- Manufacturer
- Model/Version Number
- Cost
- Additional Information

b. Total the Cost column, and name the worksheet tab *Costs*.

c. Save the workbook as *xxx-System Information.xls*.

3. Prepare an Inventory List

a. On a new worksheet in your *xxx-System Information.xls* workbook, enter inventory information about the hardware and software you identified in the previous exercise. Include the following column headings in the worksheet. (Since you have not yet actually purchased the hardware and software, do not enter any data in the last three columns.)

- Item Description
- Manufacturer
- Model/Version Number
- Cost
- Date Purchased
- Purchased From
- Warranty Information

b. Name the worksheet tab *Inventory*, and print both worksheets.

c. Save and close the workbook, and then exit Excel.

4. Create a Presentation on Software Requirements

a. Use Microsoft PowerPoint to create a presentation that identifies specific software requirements for DesignWeb's computer system. Your presentation should include at least three slides, with related text and graphics that support the topics as appropriate. Create and organize your presentation as desired. The title slide should be DesignWeb Software Needs **(see Figure 1)**. Include these slides in your presentation: System Software Needs and Application Software Needs. On the appropriate slides, include a bulleted list of the specific software programs you identified earlier.

Figure 1 Title slide for presentation

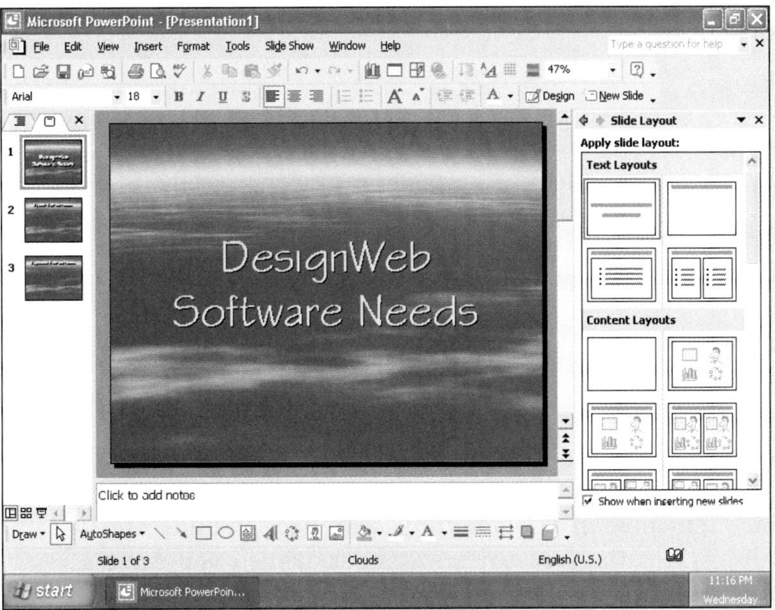

b. Choose an appropriate design template for your presentation. Then customize the design template. Remember to use consistent color schemes throughout your presentation.

c. Format each slide to present the content in an interesting manner. Remember to apply the guidelines for using graphics, fonts, and special effects.

d. Apply animations and transitions to enhance your presentation. Insert hyperlinks if desired.

e. Set up the presentation for delivery to an audience. Include slide show timings and speaker notes. View the presentation in slide show view.

f. Preview and print the presentation as handouts (3 per page). Then save the presentation as *xxx-Software Requirements.ppt* and exit PowerPoint.

Cross-Curriculum Project

To fulfill your community involvement high school graduation requirement, you plan to design a computer network for a nonprofit community center. Conduct Internet and/or print media research or visit a local community center to learn more about community centers and their computer needs. You may also want to ask classmates, teachers, friends, and family members whether they have any firsthand experience with community centers.

Typical nonprofit centers have few, if any, computers, and those they have may be obsolete. However, for this project, assume that the community center has three fairly new personal computers, but no printer or other peripheral devices.

Use appropriate Office XP software applications to do the following:

- Prepare a report that contains:
    - an overview of the results of your research on community centers and their computer needs
    - a section on the benefits of setting up a computer network
    - your recommendations regarding the network topology, the purchase of any additional equipment, the type of physical media, and acceptable data transmission speeds
    - a schematic of the network topology
- Develop a budget to set up the network. Be sure to include estimated costs for:
    - additional hardware
    - physical media
    - network operating system software

Exercise 1 Overview: Start the Computer

What happens when you turn on a computer? A built-in program called the **POST (power-on self test)** checks to make sure the computer hardware is working properly. Then the computer loads the **operating system.** This program oversees everything that is done on the computer until it is turned off. Turning on the computer, running the POST, and loading the operating system is called performing a **system boot** or simply **booting** the computer.

In a large computer system or network, you may need to **log on.** This tells the system or network who you are and what programs and files you are allowed to use. It usually means typing your **user name** and **password**. The user name is the name you are known by on the system or network. The password is a series of characters known only to you. User names and passwords protect a computer system or network from unauthorized use.

When the computer is up and running, the screen it displays is the **desktop,** your main work area. The desktop includes **icons,** small pictures representing programs and other items; a Start button, which opens a **menu** of commands; and a **taskbar** listing current programs, files, and features.

Step Through It™

Exercise 1: Boot the system and log on

1. Turn on the computer and monitor. Wait while the computer goes through the POST and loads the Windows operating system.
2. If a Log On screen appears, type your user name and password in the appropriate boxes.
3. The Windows XP desktop should appear (see Figure A.1).

Figure A.1 The Windows XP desktop

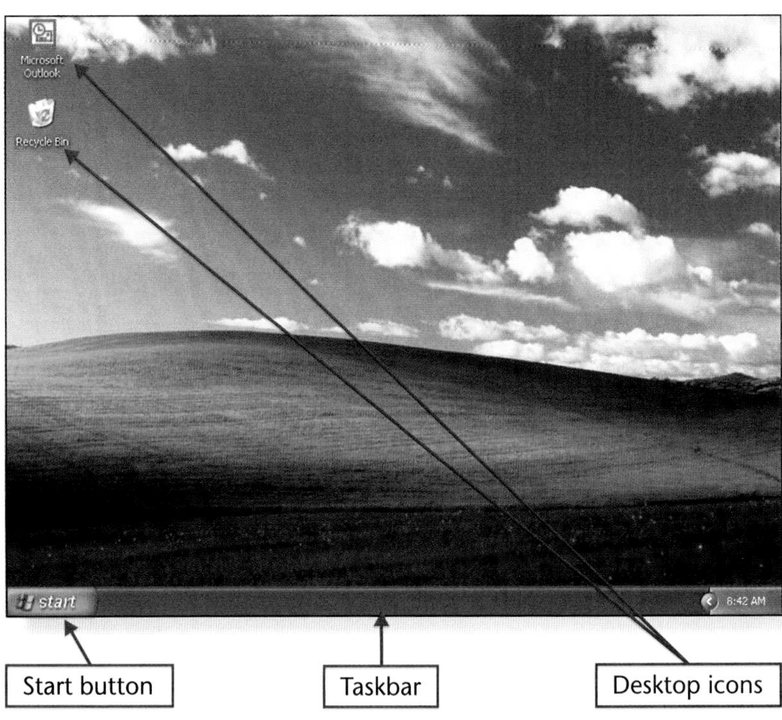

Exercise 2 Overview: Communicate Effectively With Your Computer

When you want to command the computer to do something, you use an **input device**. The most common input devices are the keyboard and mouse. Some computers have a trackball, joystick, or touchpad instead of a mouse. You can find out more about these and other input devices in Unit 6.

The mouse controls the movement of the **pointer**, the arrow on the screen. You can use the mouse to start programs, choose commands, move icons, and perform many other tasks. What you can do with a mouse varies with the program, but the basic mouse actions are generally the same:

- **Point.** Move the mouse to position the pointer on an object.
- **Click.** Press and release the left mouse button. Clicking opens menus and chooses, or **selects,** commands. Clicking also selects an object or text, singling it out so you can work with it.
- **Double-click.** Click the left mouse button twice rapidly. Double-clicking opens a desktop icon or document.
- **Drag.** Press and hold the left mouse button and move the mouse. Dragging moves or copies items.
- **Right-click.** Click the right mouse button. This calls up a shortcut menu containing the most commonly used commands for an item. The menu changes depending on what you are doing.

Figure A.2 Right-clicking on text in Word

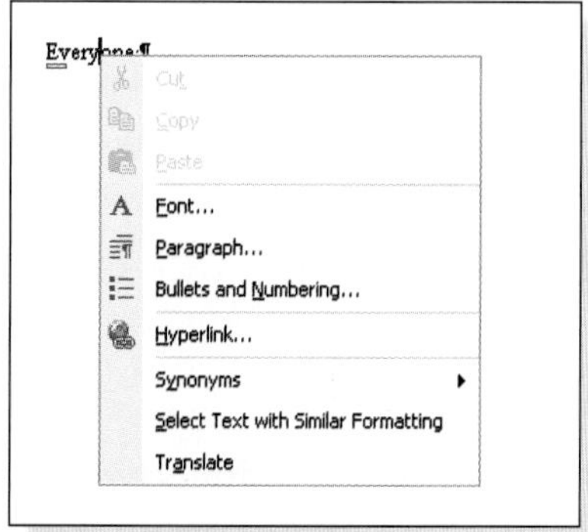

- **Right-drag.** Press and hold the right mouse button and move the mouse. This displays a shortcut menu of options for dragging an item.

Appendix A

The keyboard is used for typing text and as another way of entering commands. Keyboard commands, or shortcuts, vary across programs, but for basic tasks they are often the same. For example, in all the Office programs, the keyboard shortcut Ctrl + S saves a document. Keyboard shortcuts are sometimes quicker than using the mouse.

Step Through It™
Exercise 2: Use the mouse

1. Move the pointer around the screen.
2. Practice clicking different desktop icons.
3. Practice dragging icons to empty areas of the screen and back.
4. Right-click a blank area to display a shortcut menu. Point to Arrange Icons By. If Auto Arrange is not checked, select it. Repeat for Align to Grid (see Figure A.3).

Figure A.3 Working with icons

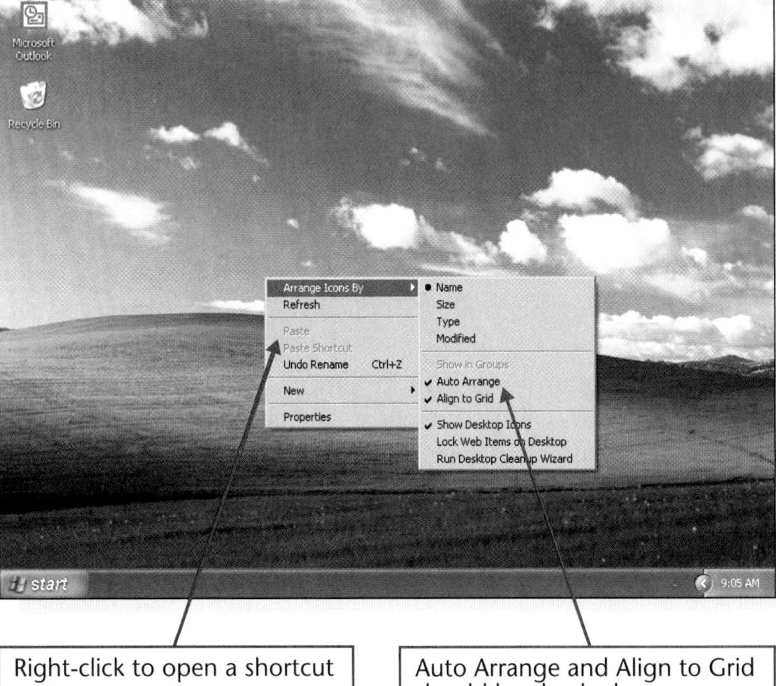

Exercise 3 Overview: Work With Windows

In Microsoft Windows, programs, files, folders, and other features are displayed on the computer screen in rectangular frames called **windows.** All windows have the same basic parts and work the same way.

At the top of a window, the **title bar** lists the title of the open program or feature.

The right side of the title bar has three buttons:

- The **Minimize button** makes the window inactive, removing it from the screen. Minimizing gives you an easy way to switch between programs and files as you work.
- The **Maximize button** enlarges the window. This gives you more space so you can work in the window more

easily. After you have maximized a window, the Maximize button changes to the **Restore Down button.** Clicking this button restores the window to the size it was before you maximized it.

- The **Close button** closes the window.

When there is more information in a window than can be displayed at one time, the window includes one or more **scroll bars**. You can click these bars to bring information into view. You can also click the **scroll arrows** or drag the **scroll boxes** to bring the information into view. Windows are sometimes divided into sections, or **panes.**

Below the window title bar is a **menu bar** listing the names of menus. Below the menu bar are one or more **toolbars** with buttons you can click to perform common tasks. You'll learn more about menus and toolbars in later exercises.

To move a window, you drag it by its title bar. To resize it, you drag a side or corner. Dragging a side resizes the window horizontally or vertically. Dragging a corner resizes it both ways at the same time.

Figure A.4 Parts of the Word Window

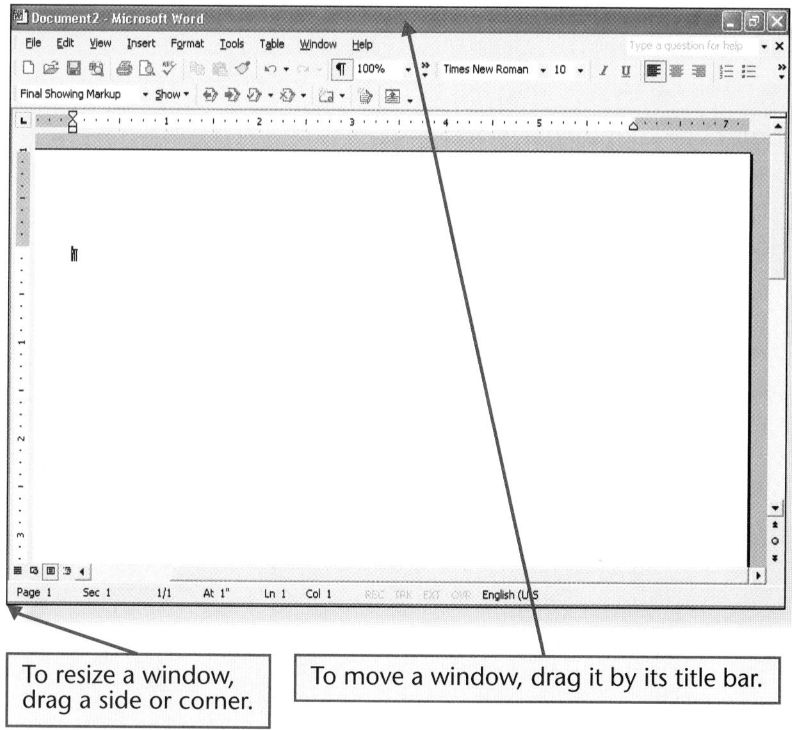

Some mouse devices have a wheel that you can use to scroll.

Step Through It™
Exercise 3: Manipulate Windows

1. Double-click the Recycle Bin icon to open the Recycle Bin window (see Figure A.5).
2. Click the Minimize button to minimize the window.
3. Click the Recycle Bin button on the taskbar to make the Recycle Bin window active.
4. Click the Maximize button to maximize the window.

Figure A.5 The Recycle Bin window

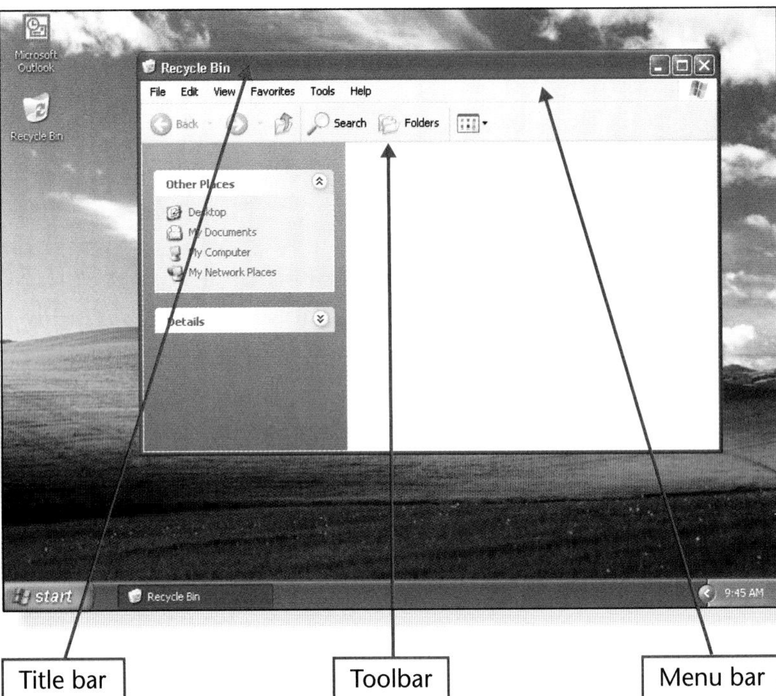

5. Click the Restore Down button to restore the window to its previous size.
6. Practice dragging the window by its title bar.
7. Practice scrolling. If there is no scroll bar, drag the bottom of the window up until one appears.
8. Practice resizing the window (see Figure A.6). Then resize it to its original size.
9. Click the Close button to close the window.

Figure A.6 Resizing a window

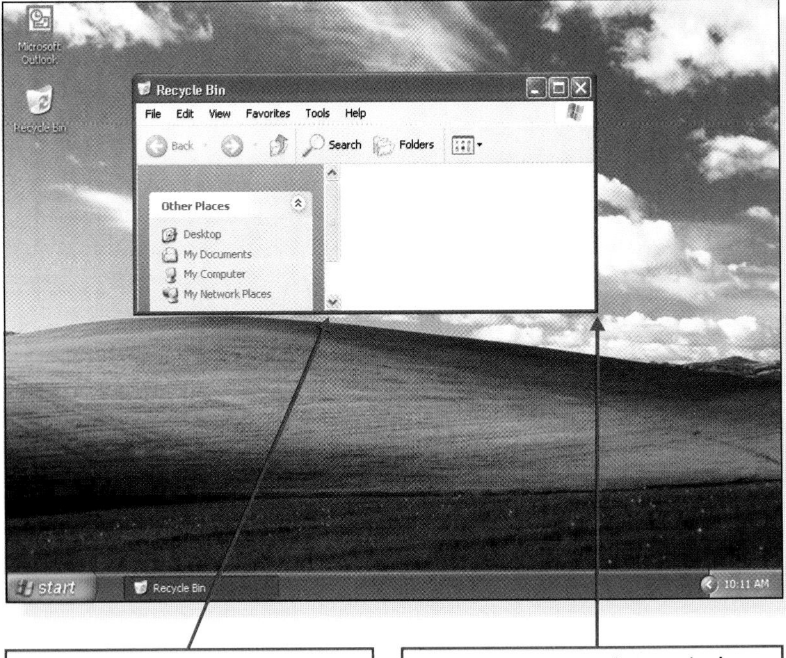

Exercise 4 Overview:
Use Windows Explorer to Work With Folders and Files

Computers can hold thousands of files. A **file** is a collection of data or information stored under a name. Some files contain the documents you create in application programs. These are called *document* or *data files*. Others control the computer or its devices, like the printer. These include program files, executable files, and device drivers. **Windows Explorer** is a tool you can use to navigate your computer's file system and locate and organize files.

Files are stored on hard disks, floppy disks, CD-ROMs, and so on, and can be accessed through drives. Windows assigns a unique letter to each drive on your system. For example, the computer's internal hard drive is usually labeled the C drive. The drive for 3.5-inch, or floppy, disks is usually the A drive.

Within each disk are one or more **folders,** each capable of holding files and subfolders. Windows XP and other programs create their own folders and subfolders. You may create additional folders to organize your document files.

All these files and folders are organized in a **hierarchy.** At the top of each drive are "parent" folders. The folders in the next level are "children" of the parent folders, or subfolders. These subfolders, in turn, may be "parents" of other folders, and so on. Figure A.7 shows a hierarchical folder structure.

Figure A.7 Hierarchical folder structure

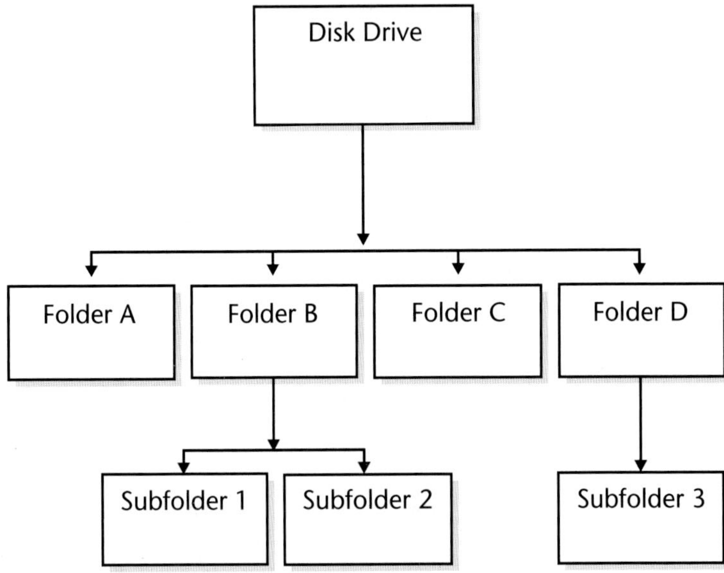

Appendix A

Windows Explorer displays a window consisting of two panes. On the left, the Folders pane shows the hierarchy of your computer system. At the top is the *Desktop* folder with its subfolders, such as *My Documents* and *My Computer*. Within *My Computer* are the disk drives for your computer.

A plus or minus sign beside a folder means that it is a parent folder containing at least one subfolder. The right pane displays the contents of a folder—files, subfolders, or both.

Step Through It™

Exercise 4A: Navigate the file system

1. Click Start, point to All Programs, point to Accessories, and select Windows Explorer.
2. In the Folders pane, click the plus sign (+) by several folders to display their subfolders below them. Click the minus sign (–) to collapse a folder.
3. In the Folders pane, click an *item's name* to display its subfolders below it and its contents in the right pane (see Figure A.8).

Figure A.8 Working With Windows Explorer

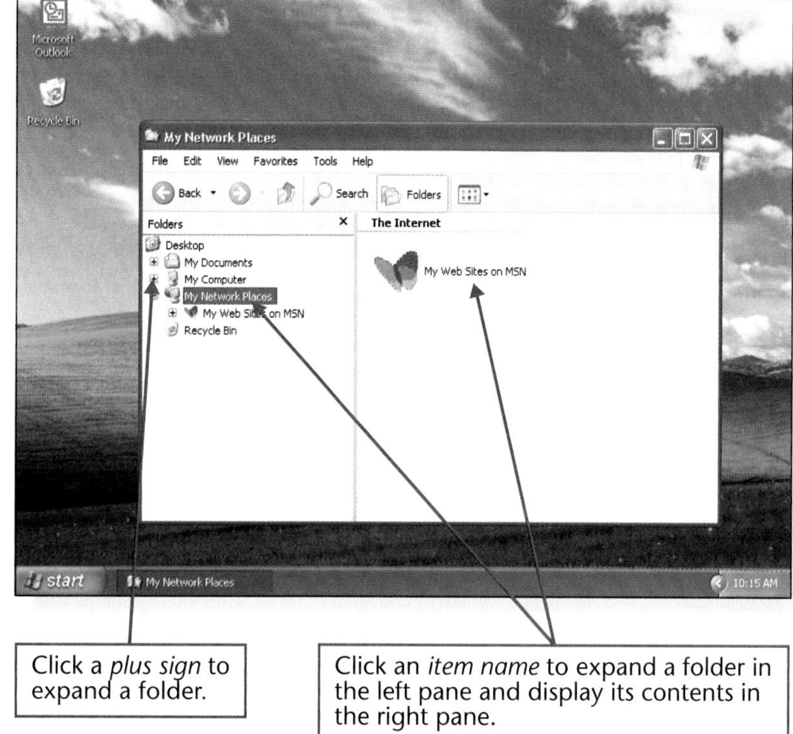

Figure A.9 Creating a new folder

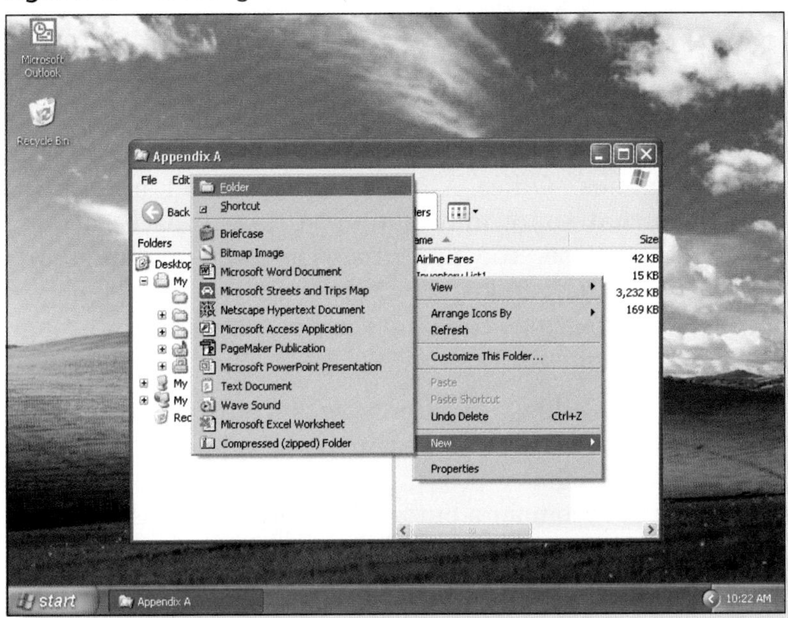

Step Through It™

Exercise 4B: Work With folders

1. Navigate to the *Appendix A* folder.
2. Click *Appendix A* (the item name), right-click a blank area in the right pane, point to New, and select Folder (see Figure A.9).
3. Type Letters and press Enter to name the folder.
4. Create another folder called Reports.

Figure A.10 Deleting a folder

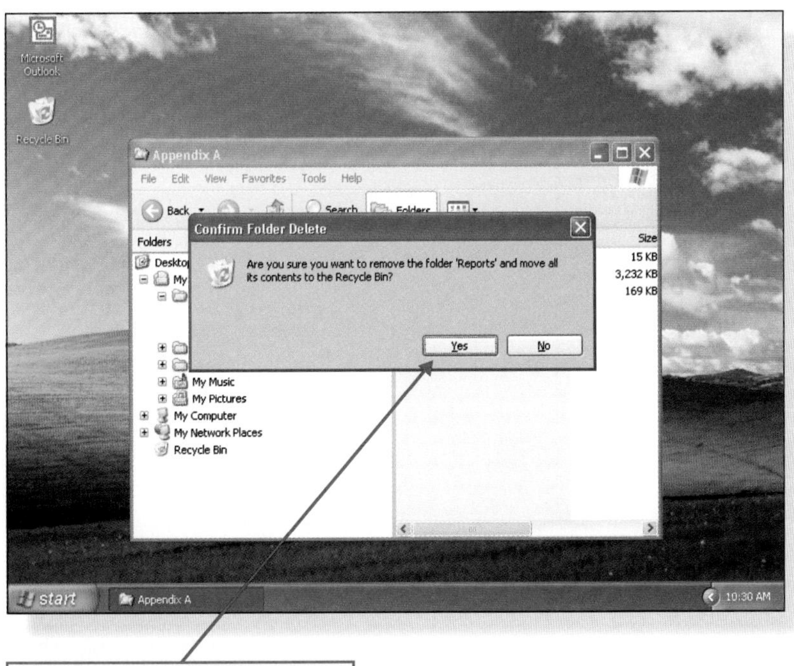

Click Yes to delete the folder.

5. Move *Airline Fares* into the *Letters* folder by dragging it on top of the folder.
6. Right-click the *Letters* folder and click Rename. Type Memos and press Enter.
7. Select (click) the *Reports* folder and press Delete. In the warning box, click Yes to remove the folder (see Figure A.10).
8. Close Windows Explorer.

Appendix A

Exercise 5 Overview: Start Application Programs

Application programs are used for specific tasks, like typing reports, creating worksheets and slide shows, and playing games. Office XP is a collection of application programs that share information. Although each serves a different purpose, the programs look and operate quite similarly, which makes working with them easier. All application programs can be started the same way, through the Start menu.

Windows XP allows you to have several programs and documents open at the same time. Each appears in its own window, and each is represented by a button on the taskbar. If there is not room for a button for every file, all the files for an application will be grouped under one button.

Although you can have several items open, you can only work with one at a time. Clicking the button for an inactive program or document brings up its window so you can work with it.

Step Through It™

Exercise 5: Start the Office applications

1. Click Start, point to All Programs, and select Microsoft Word.
2. Repeat the process to open Excel, PowerPoint, Access, and Outlook (see Figure A.11).
3. Click the taskbar button for each inactive program to make it active.

Figure A.11 Managing applications with the taskbar

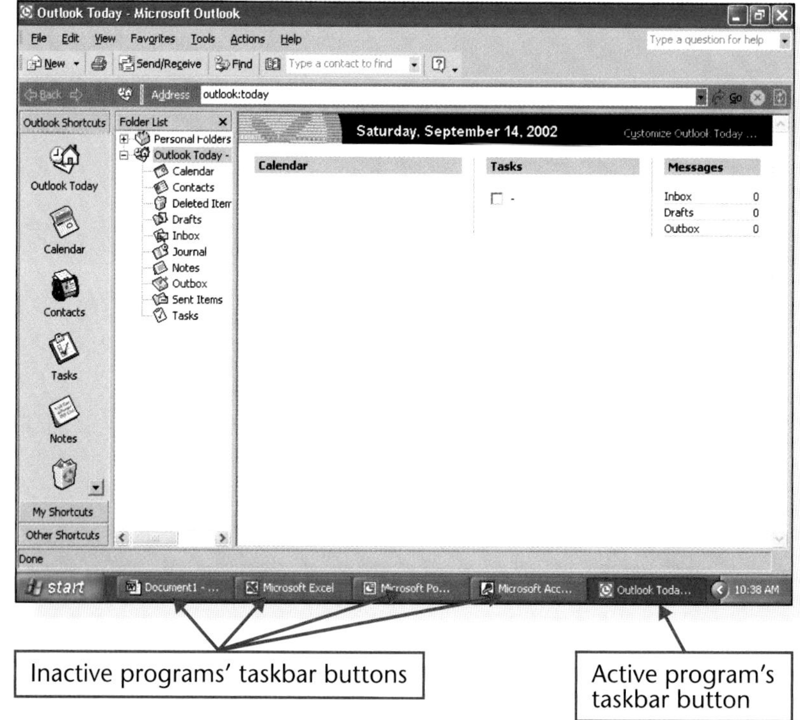

Exercise 6 Overview:
Explore Application Windows

In the last exercise, you probably noticed some familiar items in the Office application windows. Each contains a title bar, a menu bar (which is similar across all the programs), and one or more toolbars. Each window also has a **status bar,** and most have a **task pane.** Some of these items may be turned off to display more of the screen.

The status bar appears at the bottom. It tells you what the program is currently doing, such as printing or spell checking. It also tells you where you are in a document and gives you other information, depending on the program.

On the right side of the window (except in Outlook), you will see a task pane, with a list of actions grouped into categories. This task pane appears each time you start a program or a new document. Some task panes are common to all Office applications (except Outlook, which has only the Clipboard task pane). Others are unique to a particular application. Clicking the down arrow in a task pane lists all the task panes that the application has.

Figure A.12 Task panes available in Word

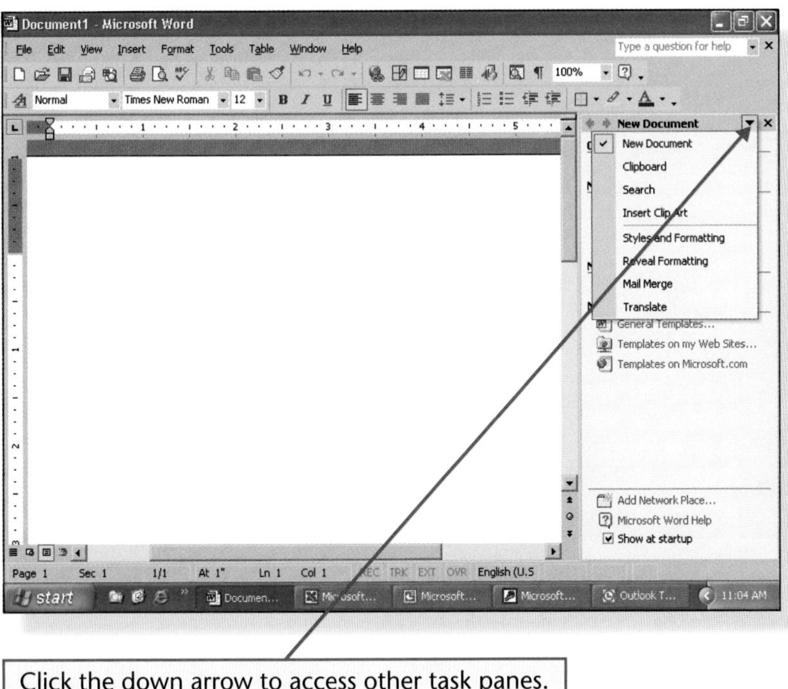

Step Through It™
Exercise 6: Work with task panes

1. Bring Word up from the taskbar, if it is not active already. Close the task pane.
2. On the View menu, select Task Pane to reopen the task pane.
3. Click the down arrow on the task pane to access other task panes (but not Insert Clip Art). See Figure A.12.
4. Explore task panes in the other Office applications.

Exercise 7 Overview: Work With Menus

A menu bar organizes commands by type. For example, the Edit menu includes commands you might use in editing a document. You can open, or display, a menu by clicking the menu name. Through the menu bar, you can access every command available in the program.

When you open a menu, you generally see a list of the most commonly used options and those you have used recently. If you leave the menu open for a moment, it expands to show all the options.

For many menu commands, selecting the command executes it at once. When you select a command followed by three dots (an *ellipsis*), a **dialog box** or task pane usually opens. Here you choose options or supply information. A third type of menu option has a right-pointing arrow. When you point to one of these options, a submenu appears with more commands from which to choose.

Some menu commands are on/off. You select them to turn them on and select them again (or **deselect** them) to turn them off. These commands have a check mark when active.

Step Through It™
Exercise 7: Using menus and dialog boxes

1. Make Excel active. Open and expand the Edit menu (see Figure A.13).
2. Point to menu items that have a right arrow to see the options available.
3. Point to the Tools menu and select Options. Click the Help (question mark) button on the Options dialog box title bar and click an item. Excel will display additional information about the item.
4. Click Cancel to close the dialog box without making any changes.

Figure A.13 Menu options

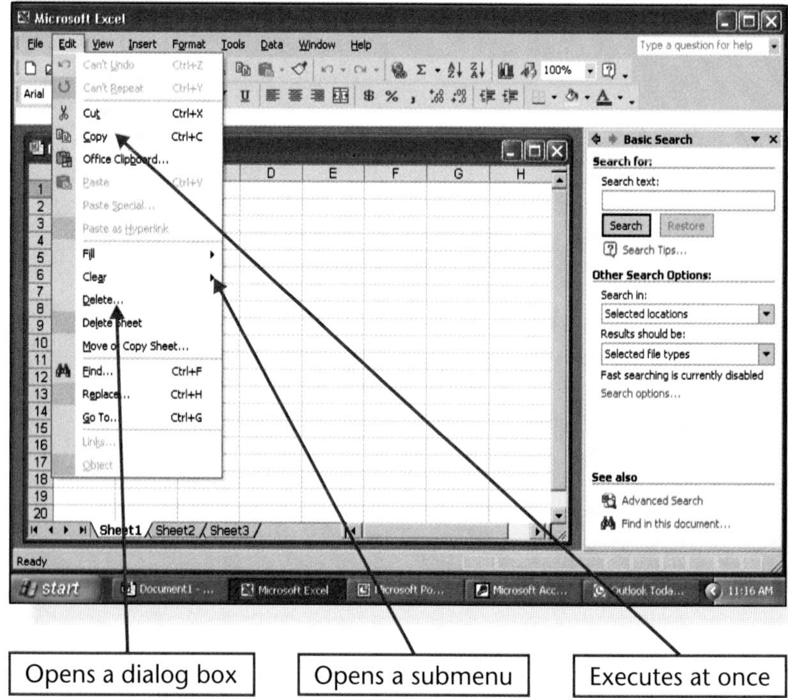

Exercise 8 Overview:
Work With Toolbars

Toolbars offer a quick and easy way to choose frequently used commands. All Office XP applications have a Standard toolbar with buttons for common tasks. All except Outlook have a Formatting toolbar for changing the appearance of text. Some toolbars are similar across most applications. Others are unique to a particular application.

To display a toolbar, open the View menu, select Toolbars, and select the toolbar. You can turn off a toolbar the same way.

Pointing to a toolbar button and waiting displays a **ScreenTip** that identifies the button.

Remember, you can access every command in the program through the menus. Toolbars, task panes, and keyboard shortcuts are simply different ways of choosing some of these commands. As you work with the programs, you will find the methods that work best for you.

Figure A.14 Excel toolbars

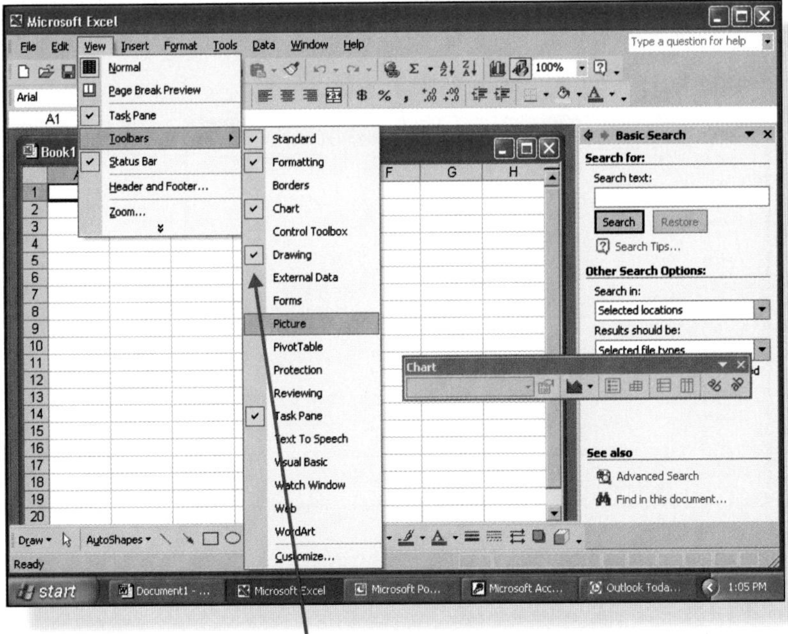

An active toolbar has a check mark next to its name.

Step Through It™
Exercise 8: Use toolbars

1. On the View menu in Excel, select Toolbars. Select several different toolbars (see Figure A.14).
2. Point to some toolbar buttons and read the ScreenTips that appear.
3. Repeat step 1 to turn off (deselect) all toolbars except the Standard, Formatting, and Task Pane toolbars.

Quick Tip

Toolbars can be customized to suit your needs.

Appendix A

Appendix A

Exercise 9 Overview:
Open and Close Files

You will often want to open existing files to work with them. You can use any of these methods to open a file in Word, Access, Excel, and PowerPoint:

Recently Used Files

- Select the file from the New Document task pane (the exact name of the pane varies among applications).
- Open the File menu and select the file from the bottom.
- Open the Start menu, point to My Recent Documents, and select the file.

Any File

- Click Open on the Standard toolbar.
- Press Ctrl + O.
- On the File menu, select Open.

The last three methods take you to the Open dialog box. Clicking History in the box displays a list of recently accessed files and folders. You can also navigate to find a file, similar to the way you did in Windows Explorer, by clicking the *Look in* down arrow.

Figure A.15 Open dialog box in Word

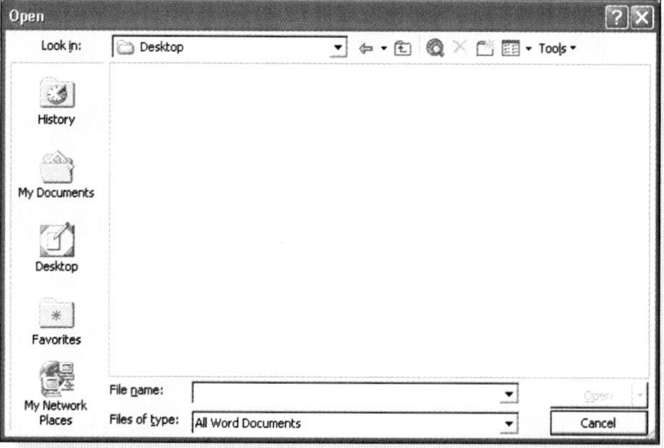

When you are done with a file, you will close it. There are a variety of ways to close a file:

- Click Close, if available, on the Standard toolbar.
- On the File menu, select Close.
- Press Alt + F, C.
- Click the Close Window button at the right of the menu bar, if available (not the Close button on the title bar, unless you have more than one document open).

Figure A.16 Opening a file

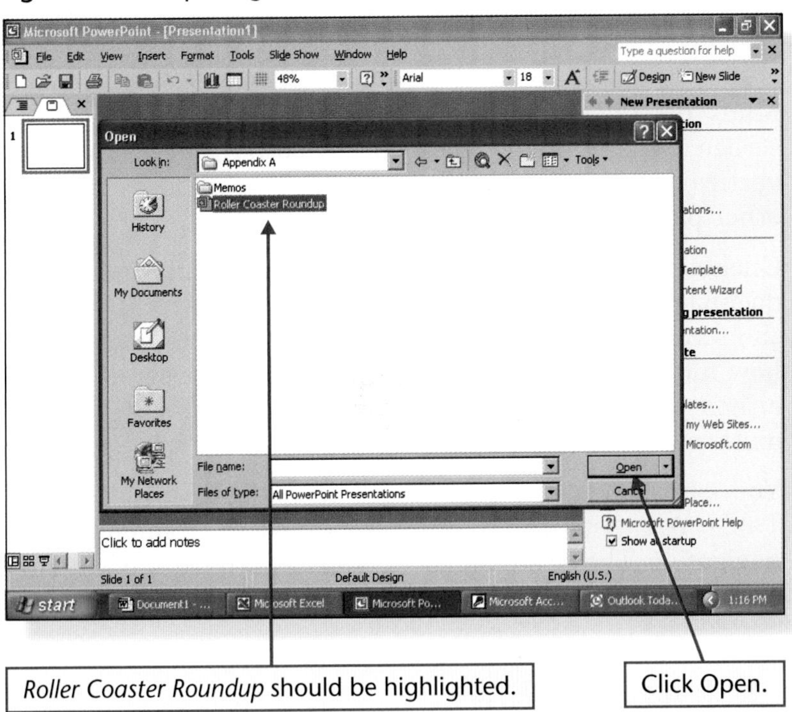

Roller Coaster Roundup should be highlighted.
Click Open.

Step Through It™

Exercise 9: Retrieve files

1. Bring PowerPoint up from the taskbar.
2. Click Open on the Standard toolbar. The Open dialog box appears.
3. Click the *Look in* down arrow. Navigate to the *Appendix A* folder.
4. Select the folder and click Open. Select *Roller Coaster Roundup.ppt*, if necessary, and click Open (see Figure A.16).

Figure A.17 Closing a file

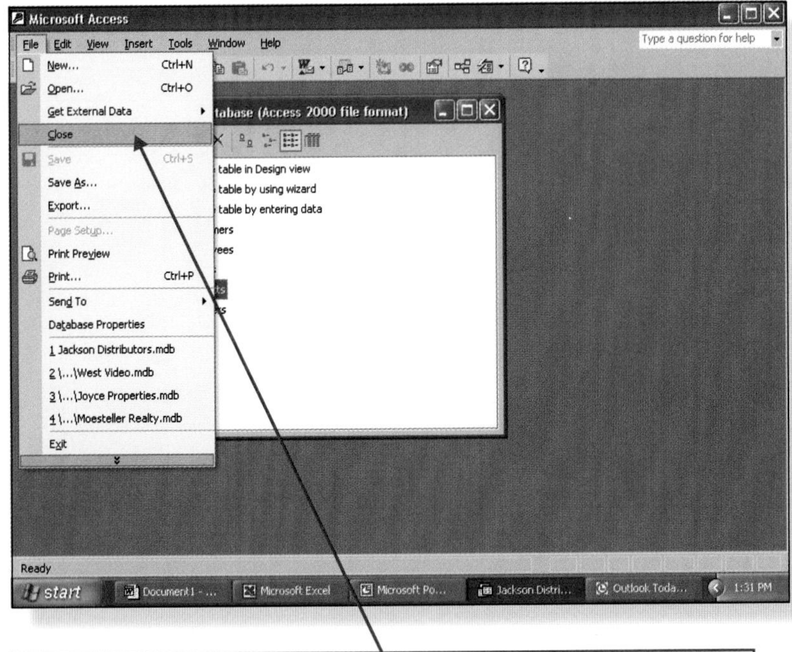

5. Bring Excel up from the taskbar.
6. On the File menu, select Open. Navigate to the *Appendix A* folder and open *Inventory List1.xls*.
7. Open *Jackson Distributors.mdb* (Access) in the *Appendix A* folder and *Airline Fares.doc* (Word) in the *Memos* subfolder of the *Appendix A* folder.
8. Close all the files you just opened except *Airline Fares.doc* (see Figure A.17).

Exercise 10 Overview:
Navigate and Edit a Document

Many documents are too long or too wide to see on the screen in their entirety. You can use both the horizontal and vertical scroll bars, scroll arrows, and scroll boxes to bring other parts of a document into view.

Clicking a scroll arrow at an end of a scroll bar moves the document up, down, left, or right a little at a time. Dragging the scroll box in the center of a scroll bar lets you control how much the document moves. Clicking the scroll bar on either side of the scroll box moves the document a larger distance either forward or backward.

You can also use the keyboard to navigate a document. Table A.1 lists some common keyboard commands for navigating. These commands work in most Office applications.

Table A.1

To Go	Press
Up one line, row, etc.	↑
Down one line, row, etc.	↓
Left one character or cell	←
Right one character or cell	→
To the top	Ctrl + Home
To the end	Ctrl + End
To the left edge	Home
To the right edge	End
Up one screen	Page Up
Down one screen	Page Down

The status bar in Word provides information about where you are in a document, such as the page and line number and the distance from the top of the page.

As soon as you open most Office documents, you are ready to **edit,** or make changes to, them. To add text, you move the **insertion point** (the blinking vertical line) where you want to work and start typing. As you type the new text, the old text is pushed to the right.

To replace text, you can select, or drag over, it and type the new text. In Word, you can also choose **Overtype mode** and type over the existing text. In Excel worksheets, you must double-click or press F2 if you want to add or make changes to the existing text rather than replace it.

Each Office application gives you many tools that make editing easier. These tools are discussed in the different units of this text.

Appendix A

Figure A.18 Using scroll bars

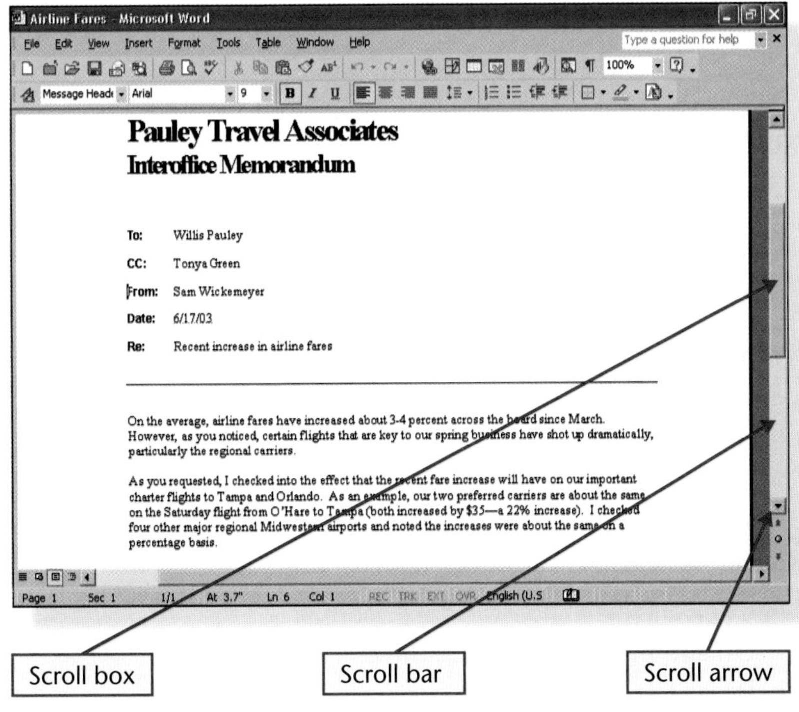

Step Through It™

Exercise 10A: Move around in a document

1. Experiment with using both the vertical and horizontal scroll arrows, scroll boxes, and scroll bars (see Figure A.18).
2. Try each keyboard command listed in Table A.1.

Step Through It™
Exercise 10B: Edit a document

1. In the *To* line, drag to select *Willis Pauley*. Type Tom Mehlen in its place.
2. Move the insertion point to the bottom of the page, just before the initials *jpl*. Press Insert to enter Overtype mode. Type your initials (see Figure A.19).
3. Press Insert again to return to Insert mode.

Figure A.19 Replacing text

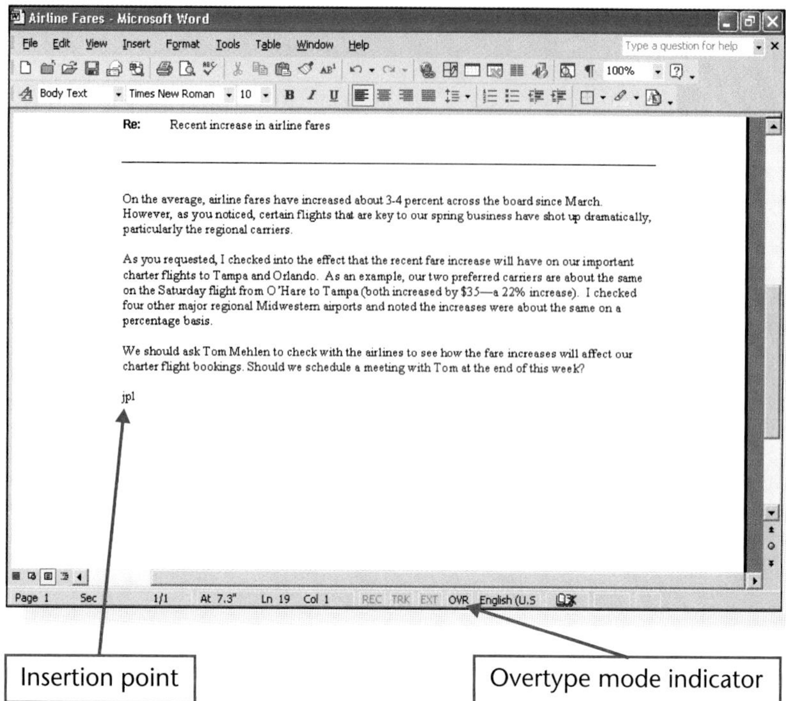

Exercise 11 Overview: Save a File

When you create a new document, it exists in the computer's temporary memory. If you turn off the computer, the document will be erased. To keep your work, you will need to save your document.

Saving a document stores it on a computer hard disk, a floppy or Zip disk, or some other storage device. The file is permanent unless you change or delete it.

You can use any of the following commands to save documents in Word, Excel, Access, and PowerPoint:

- Click Save on the Standard toolbar.
- On the File menu, select Save.
- Press Ctrl + S.

When you save a document for the first time, you must decide on a name and a location. The location consists of the drive and folder, if any, where you will store the document.

Whenever you make changes to a document, you must resave the document if you want the changes to be permanent. You have probably heard stories of people who worked for hours revising a document, only to have a power outage or a computer problem and lose all their changes.

Resaving is easy and quick. It uses the same commands as saving. Frequent computer users get in the habit of pressing Ctrl + S every few minutes as they go along. How often should you save? How much can you afford to lose?

Sometimes you will want to open a document, make changes to it, and save the edited version without replacing the original document. For example, you may want to use a first-quarter budget worksheet as a model for the second-quarter budget. You can use the Save As command on the File menu to save a copy of the document under a new name, leaving the original intact.

Figure A.20 Save As dialog box in Excel

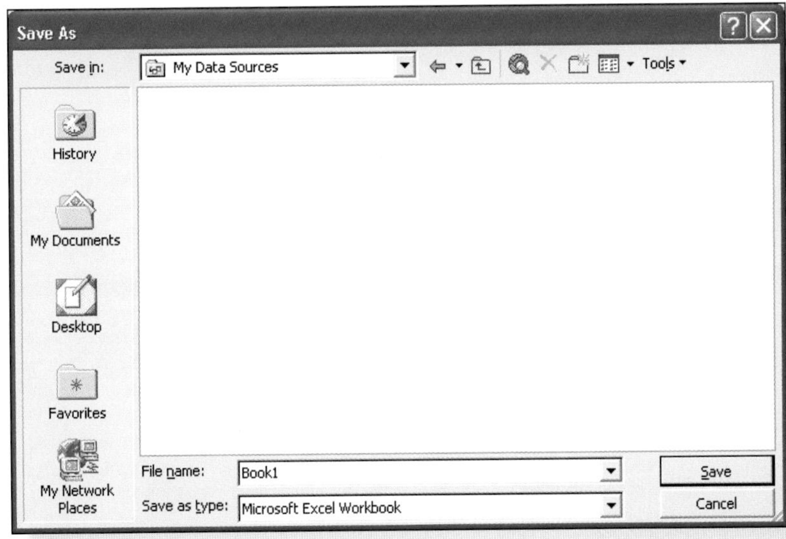

In the next two exercises, you will save a copy of the memo to Willis Pauley to use as a basis for a memo to Tom Mehlen. You will also begin making revisions to the memo.

Warning

Use the Save As command as early as possible in your editing session. That way, you will be less likely to resave by mistake as you work and make unintentional changes to your original file.

Step Through It™

Exercise 11A: Save a copy of the current file

1. On the File menu, select Save As to open the Save As dialog box.
2. In the *File name* box, select the file's current name, and type xxx-Airline Fares replacing *xxx* with your initials (see Figure A.21). Click Save.

Figure A.21 Save As dialog box

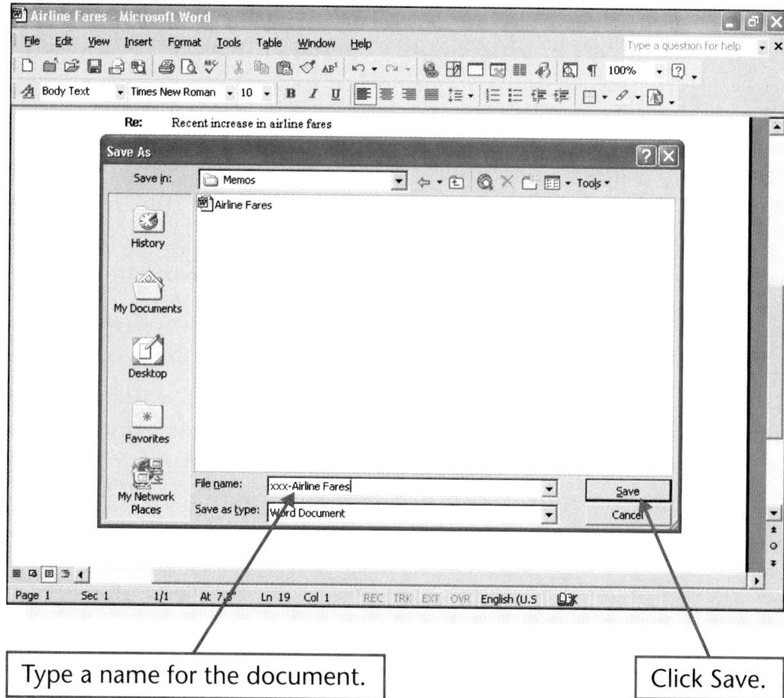

Step Through It™

Exercise 11B: Resaving a file

1. In your *xxx-Airline Fares* document file, type —meeting at the end of the *Re*: line.
2. In the first paragraph, select the phrase *as you noticed*, and press Delete (see Figure A.22).
3. Click Save on the Standard toolbar to save these changes.
4. Delete the next paragraph.
5. Press Ctrl + S.

Figure A.22 Revising and resaving a memo

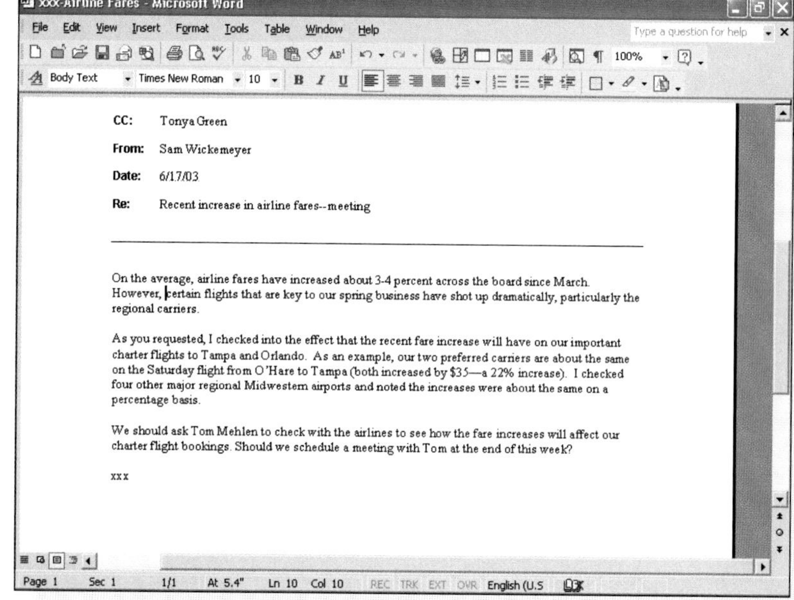

Exercise 12 Overview:
Access Online Help

Got a question? Need information? There are many kinds of online help available to you. Some are on the screen. You can access others through the Help menu or the Help button on the Standard toolbar.

The Ask a Question box appears on the right side of the menu bar. Type a question in this box for immediate help.

Selecting the Office Assistant command places a cartoon character (the Assistant) in the document window. Clicking the Assistant produces a box for typing questions.

Figure A.23 Office Assistant in Word

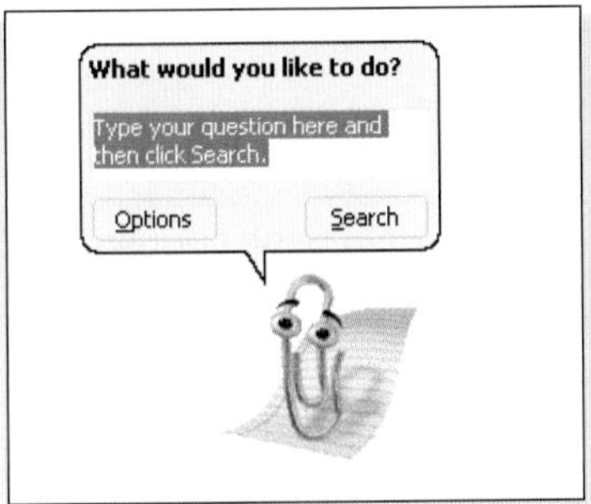

ScreenTips, which you used in earlier exercises, explain items you see on the screen. Pointing to a toolbar button and waiting gives you its name. Selecting *What's This?* from the Help menu and clicking an item provides a description and sometimes instructions. In dialog boxes, you can get the same kind of help by clicking the question mark in the top right corner.

The Help window provides three features, organized by tabs. You can type questions in the Answer Wizard tab. It works like the Office Assistant or Ask a Question box but gives you more possible answers.

The Index tab lets you search for topics by keyword. You can type a keyword or choose one from a list. The result will be a list of all topics that contain the keyword.

The Contents tab provides an extensive list of Help topics, arranged into books that you can navigate similarly to Windows Explorer. Clicking a plus sign opens a book, showing its subtopics. Clicking a page displays its text.

If you are using the Office Assistant, you will need to turn it off to display the main Help window. Click the Assistant, click Options, and deselect *Use the Office Assistant.*

Step Through It™
Exercise 12A: Use the Ask a Question box

1. In the *Ask a Question* box, type how do I start a new document and press Enter.
2. Click *Create a document.* The Microsoft Word Help window opens, with instructions on creating a document displayed in the right pane (see Figure A.24).
3. Read the page. In the right pane, click *templates* and read the definition.

Figure A.24 The Microsoft Word Help window

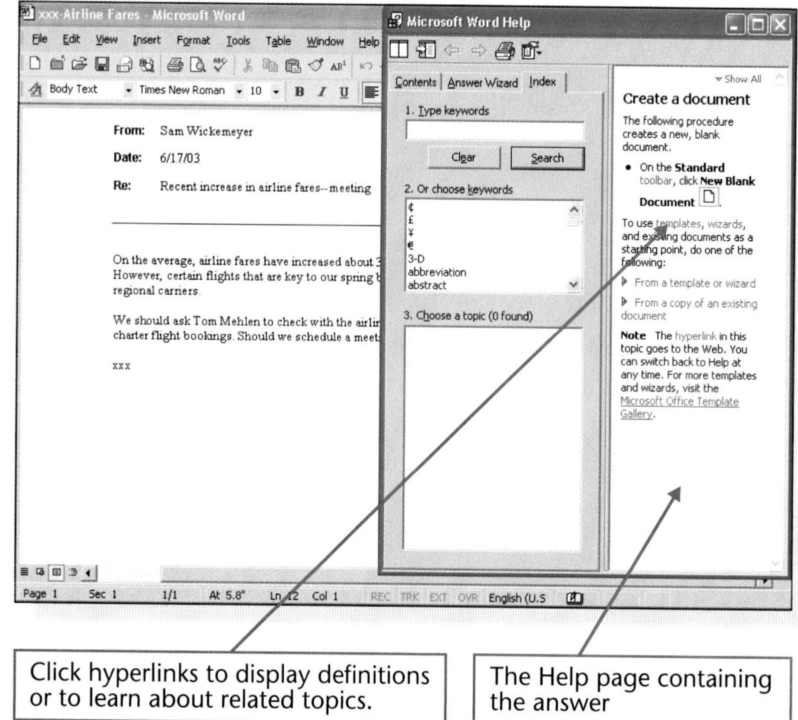

Click hyperlinks to display definitions or to learn about related topics.
The Help page containing the answer

Step Through It™
Exercise 12B: Use the Contents

1. Click the Contents tab.
2. Click the plus signs to expand *Microsoft Word Help* and *Getting Started with Microsoft Word,* if necessary.
3. Click the *What's new in Microsoft Word* help page. Its contents appear in the right pane (see Figure A.25).
4. Close the Microsoft Word Help window.

Figure A.25 Help window with Contents tab active

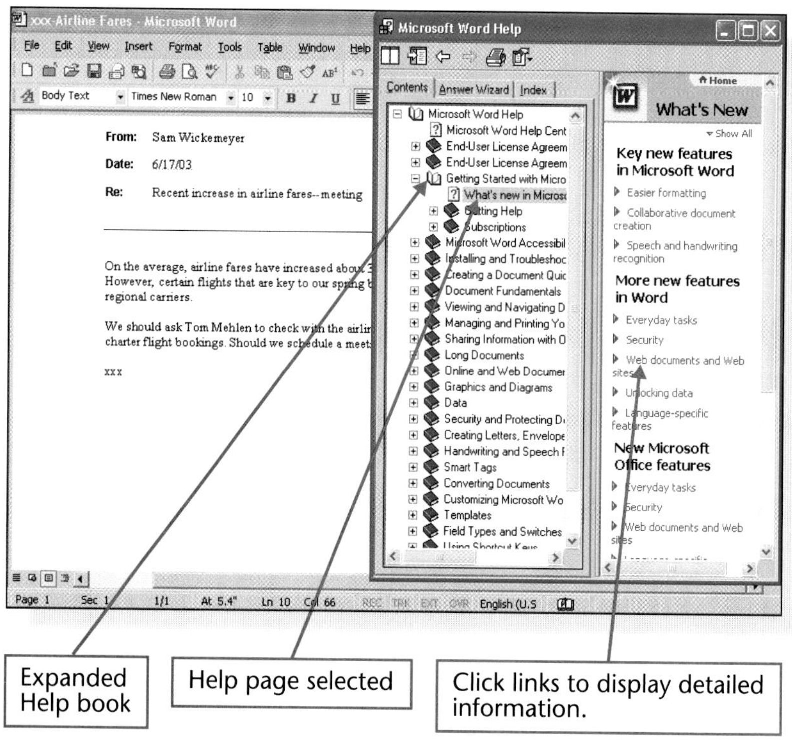

Expanded Help book
Help page selected
Click links to display detailed information.

Figure A.26 Microsoft Office Tools on the Web page

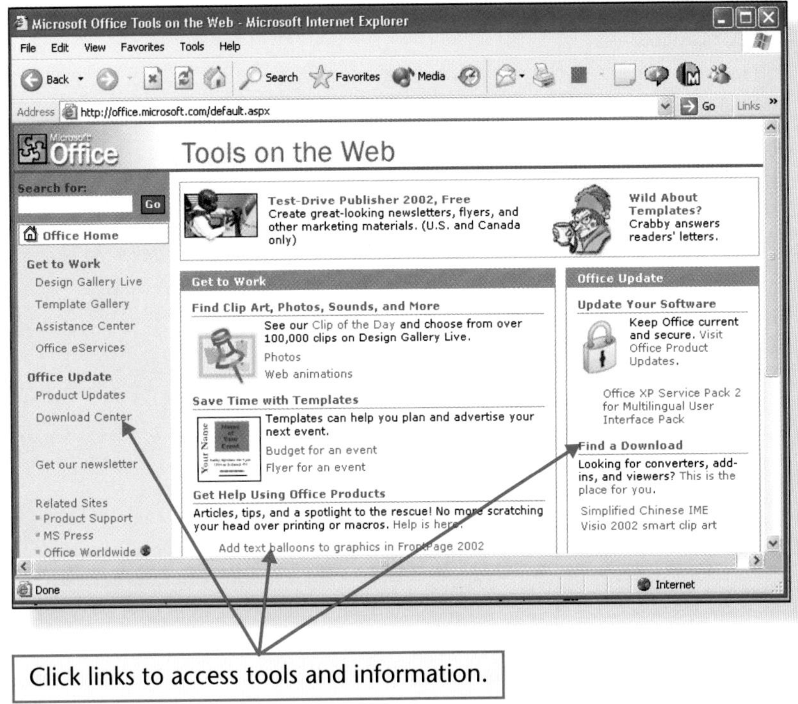

Step Through It™

Exercise 12C: Use the Office Web site

1. On the Help menu, select Office on the Web. If a map appears, click *United States*. The Office Assistance Center Web page opens. (***Note:*** The Web site may no longer match the illustration in the book, but the content should be the same.)
2. In the Assistance By Product center, click Excel. Scan this page.
3. Click Back to go back a page. Click Office Home (see Figure A.26). Examine this page.
4. Close the window.

Exercise 13 Overview: Use Internet Explorer

The **Internet** is a worldwide network linking millions of computers. People use the Internet to correspond (**e-mail**) and to get information on just about any topic. They shop, download music, play games, and take classes. These are just a few of the many things people can do on the Internet.

The **World Wide Web** is a network within the Internet. When you "surf the Web," you type a **Web address**, which takes you to a **Web site**—a location on the Web maintained by a company, organization, or individual. Web sites are made up of pages (**Web pages**). These pages can include text, pictures, video, sound, and **hyperlinks** (*links* for short) to other pages or sites.

People usually connect to the Internet through an **Internet service provider (ISP),** a company that provides Internet connection services and manages your Internet connection. To surf the Web and view Web pages, you need a **Web browser,** such as Internet Explorer.

Did you know that, in the last exercise, you were on the Internet? You connected through an ISP, launched a Web browser, and visited a site on the World Wide Web.

Step Through It™

Exercise 13A: Navigate the Web

1. Follow your teacher's directions to connect to the Internet and launch Internet Explorer.
2. In the Address box, replace the address with www.nps.gov and press Enter. The National Park Service Web site appears (see Figure A.27).
3. Click Visit Your Parks. Use hyperlinks and the Back and Forward buttons to find information on a place that interests you. Print a page about it.

Figure A.27 National Park Service Web site

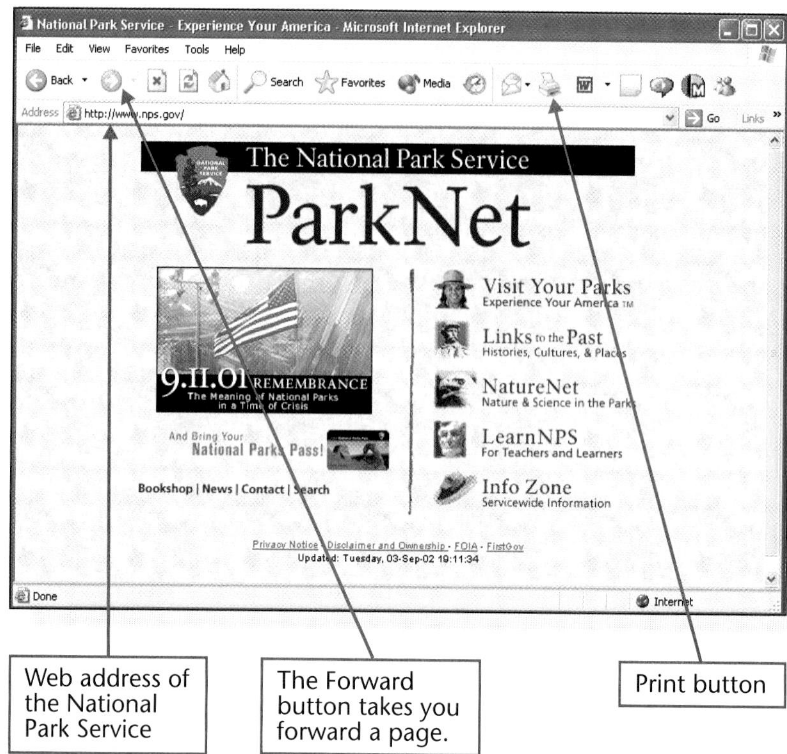

4. Type www.howstuffworks.com to visit the HowStuffWorks Web site.
5. Click Home to return to your home page.
6. Type www.students.gov to visit the Students.gov Web site (see Figure A.28).

Figure A.28 Students.gov Web site

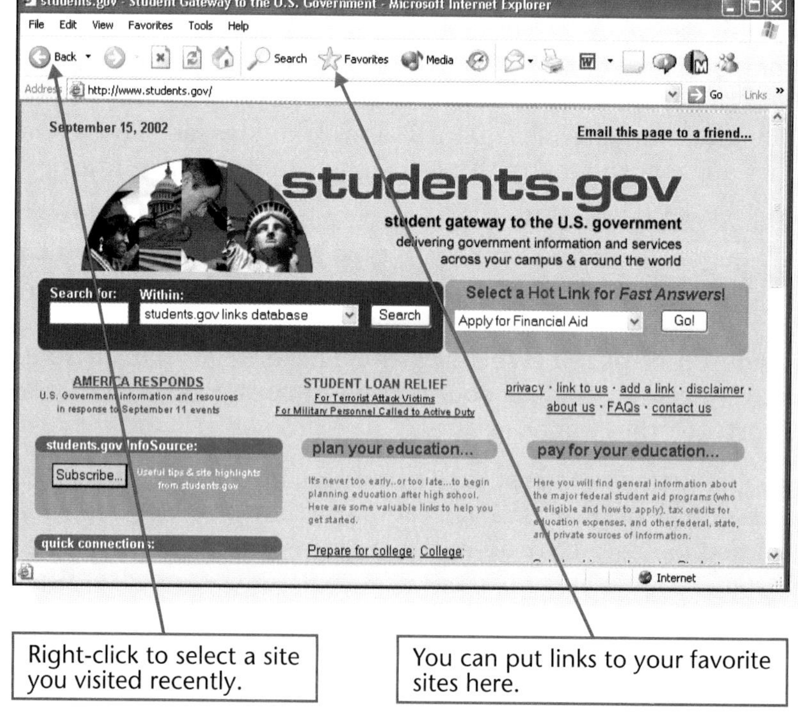

Figure A.29 Search Companion pane

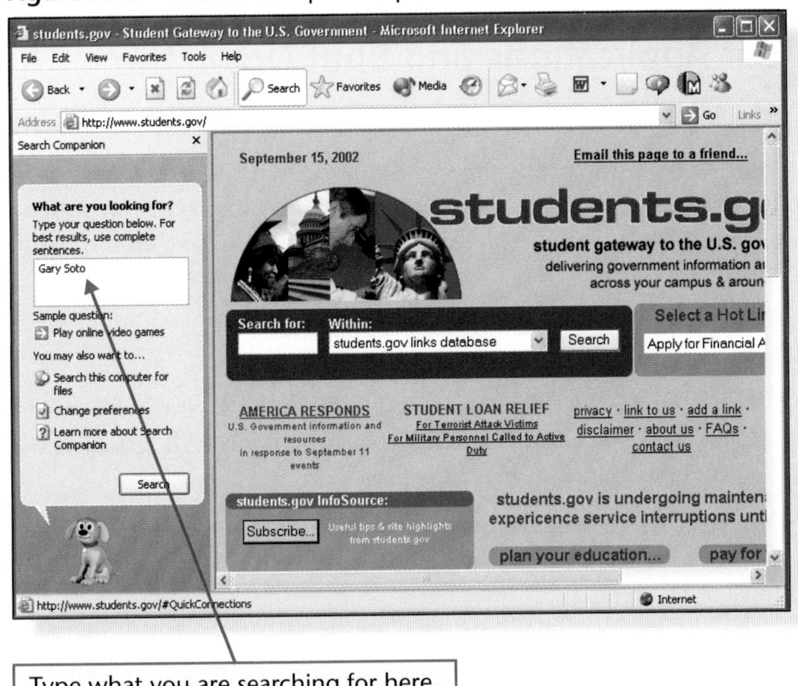

Step Through It™
Exercise 13B: Use the Search Companion pane

1. Click Search on the Web toolbar [Search] to open the Search Companion pane.
2. In the box, type **Gary Soto** and press Enter (see Figure A.29).
3. Use the search results to find a short biography of Gary Soto, one of his poems, or a review of a book that you might like. Print your findings.

Figure A.30 Finding information on the Web

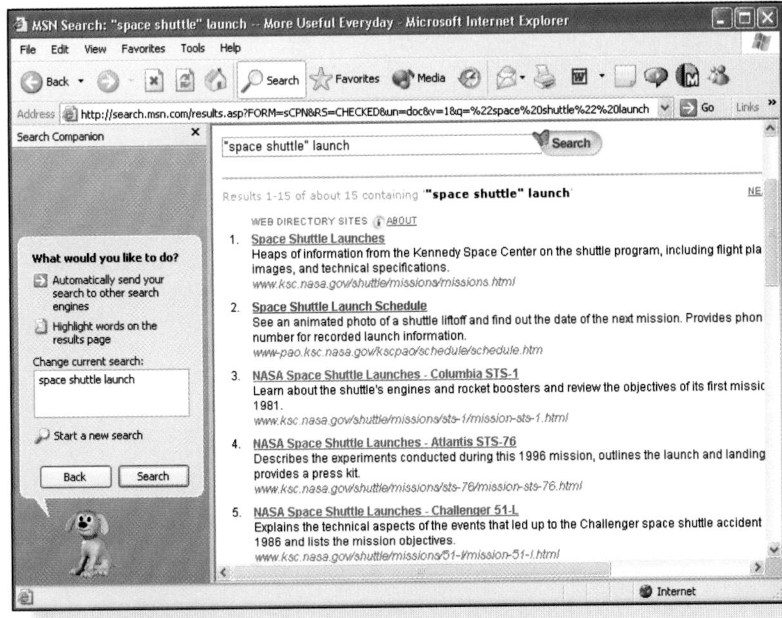

4. Click *Start a new search.* You may need to scroll down to display this option.
5. Type **space shuttle launch**. Find the date of the next launch. Write it down (see Figure A.30).
6. Find a site where you can get homework help. Write down the address.
7. Close the Search Companion pane and Internet Explorer. Then disconnect from the Internet, if your teacher instructs you to do so.

Appendix A

Exercise 14 Overview:
Exit Applications and Shut Down the Computer

At the end of a computer session, you will need to close any documents you have been working on, exit your applications, and shut down the computer (or log off). You can quit an Office application in any of the following ways:

- Open the File menu and select Exit.
- Press Alt + F4.
- Click Close in each window's title bar. If you have more than one document open, the application will close when you close the last window.

During this process, you will be asked if you want to save changes for any documents that were edited since they were last saved.

Your teacher will tell you whether you should log off or shut down the computer and what procedures you should follow. Both the Log Off and Shut Down options are on the Start menu. If you are turning off the computer, you may also need to turn off the CPU or keyboard and monitor.

Figure A.31 Turn off computer dialog box

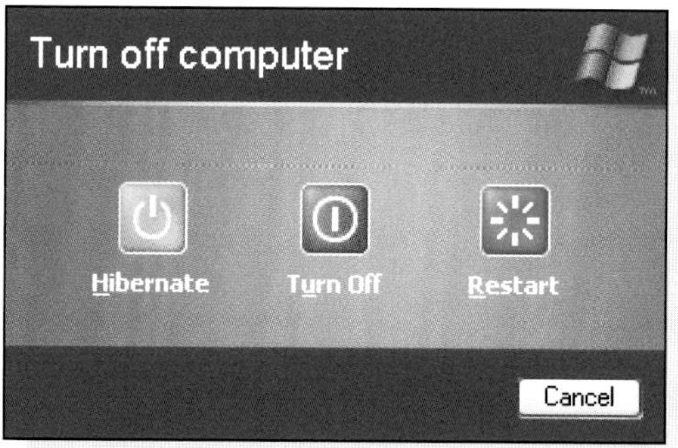

Figure A.32 Exiting an application

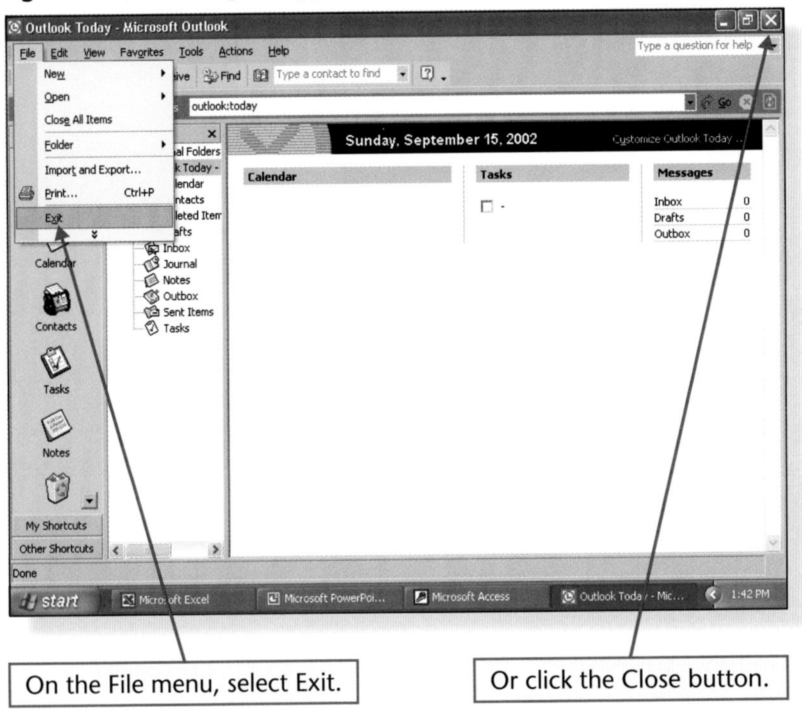

Step Through It™

Exercise 14: End your computing session

1. Exit the Office programs, trying each method presented in the Overview on page 836 (see Figure A.32).
2. If you are prompted to save changes to any documents, click No.

Figure A.33 Click No to disgard changes to a document

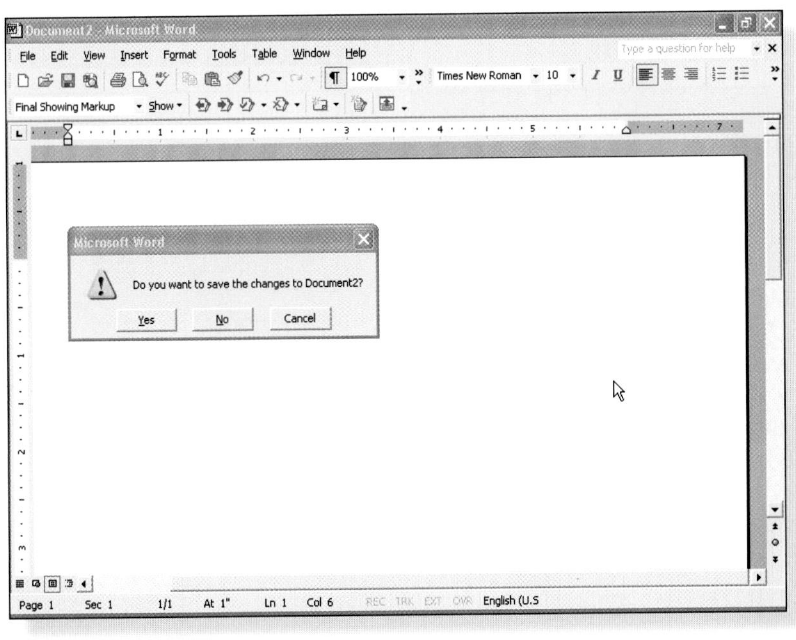

3. Remove any media (like CDs) from the drives, if necessary.
4. On the Start menu, select Log Off or Shut Down (follow your teacher's directions).
5. In the dialog box that appears, select the appropriate option (follow your teacher's directions).

Appendix B

Microsoft Word 2002 Core Level

Code	Skills Being Measured	Text Reference
W2002.1	**Inserting and Modifying Text**	
W2002.1.1	Insert, modify, and move text and symbols	U1–L1, U1–L3, U6–L1, U6–L2
W2002.1.2	Apply and modify text formats	U1–L2, U6–L1
W2002.1.3	Correct spelling and grammar usage	U1–L1
W2002.1.4	Apply font and text effects	U1–L3
W2002.1.5	Enter and format Date and Time	U1–L4
W2002.1.6	Apply character styles	U1–L2
W2002.2	**Creating and Modifying Paragraphs**	
W2002.2.1	Modify paragraph formats	U1–L2, U6–L2
W2002.2.2	Set and modify tabs	U1–L2
W2002.2.3	Apply bullet, outline, and numbering format to paragraphs	U1–L2
W2002.2.4	Apply paragraph styles	U1–L2
W2002.3	**Formatting Documents**	
W2002.3.1	Create and modify a header and footer	U1–L2
W2002.3.2	Apply and modify column settings	U1–L3
W2002.3.3	Modify document layout and Page Setup options	U1–L2, U1–L3
W2002.3.4	Create and modify tables	U1–L3, U6–L1
W2002.3.5	Preview and Print documents, envelopes, and labels	U1–L1, U1–L3, U6–L1
W2002.4	**Managing Documents**	
W2002.4.1	Manage files and folders for documents	U1–L1
W2002.4.2	Create documents using templates	U1–L1
W2002.4.3	Save documents using different names and file formats	U1–L1, U6–L1
W2002.5	**Working with Graphics**	
W2002.5.1	Insert images and graphics	U1–L3
W2002.5.2	Create and modify diagrams and charts	U1–L3
W2002.6	**Workgroup Collaboration**	
W2002.6.1	Compare and Merge documents	U1–L4
W2002.6.2	Insert, view, and edit comments	U1–L4
W2002.6.3	Convert documents into Web pages	U1–L4

Microsoft Excel 2002 Core Level

Code	Skills Being Measured	Text Reference
EX2002.1	**Working with Cells and Cell Data**	
EX2002.1.1	Insert, delete, and move cells	U2–L1, U2–L4
EX2002.1.2	Enter and edit cell data, including text, numbers, and formulas	U2–L1, U2–L3, U6–L1, U6–L2
EX2002.1.3	Check spelling	U2–L1
EX2002.1.4	Find and replace cell data and formats	U2–L1
EX2002.1.5	Work with a subset of data by filtering lists	U2–L3, U6–L2
EX2002.2	**Managing Workbooks**	
EX2002.2.1	Manage workbook files and folders	U2–L1
EX2002.2.2	Create workbooks using templates	U2–L3
EX2002.2.3	Save workbooks using different names and file formats	U2–L1, U6–L1
EX2002.3	**Formatting and Printing Worksheets**	
EX2002.3.1	Apply and modify cell formats	U2–L2, U6–L2
EX2002.3.2	Modify row and column settings	U2–L2
EX2002.3.3	Modify row and column formats	U2–L2
EX2002.3.4	Apply styles	U2–L2
EX2002.3.5	Use automated tools to format worksheets	U2–L2
EX2002.3.6	Modify Page Setup options for worksheets	U2–L2, U6–L1
EX2002.3.7	Preview and print worksheets and workbooks	U2–L2, U2–L4, U6–L1, U6–L2
EX2002.4	**Modifying Workbooks**	
EX2002.4.1	Insert and delete worksheets	U2–L4
EX2002.4.2	Modify worksheet names and positions	U2–L4
EX2002.4.3	Use 3-D references	U2–L4
EX2002.5	**Creating and Revising Formulas**	
EX2002.5.1	Create and revise formulas	U2–L3, U6–L2
EX2002.5.2	Use statistical, date and time, financial, and logical functions in formulas	U2–L3
EX2002.6	**Creating and Modifying Graphics**	
EX2002.6.1	Create, modify, position, and print charts	U2–L3, U6–L2
EX2002.6.2	Create, modify, and position graphics	U2–L3
EX2002.7	**Workgroup Collaboration**	
EX2002.7.1	Convert worksheets into Web pages	U2–L3
EX2002.7.2	Create hyperlinks	U2–L4
EX2002.7.3	View and edit comments	U2–L3

Microsoft Access 2002 Core Level

Code	Skills Being Measured	Text Reference
AC2002.1	**Creating and Using Databases**	
AC2002.1.1	Create Access databases	U3–L1
AC2002.1.2	Open database objects in multiple views	U3–L1
AC2002.1.3	Move among records	U3–L1
AC2002.1.4	Format datasheets	U3–L3
AC2002.2	**Creating and Modifying Tables**	
AC2002.2.1	Create and modify tables	U3–L2
AC2002.2.2	Add a predefined input mask to a field	U3–L2
AC2002.2.3	Create Lookup fields	U3–L2
AC2002.2.4	Modify field properties	U3–L2
AC2002.3	**Creating and Modifying Queries**	
AC2002.3.1	Create and modify Select queries	U3–L3
AC2002.3.2	Add calculated fields to Select queries	U3–L3
AC2002.4	**Creating and Modifying Forms**	
AC2002.4.1	Create and display forms	U3–L4
AC2002.4.2	Modify form properties	U3–L4
AC2002.5	**Viewing and Organizing Information**	
AC2002.5.1	Enter, edit, and delete records	U3–L1
AC2002.5.2	Create queries	U3–L3
AC2002.5.3	Sort records	U3–L3
AC2002.5.4	Filter records	U3–L3
AC2002.6	**Defining Relationships**	
AC2002.6.1	Create one-to-many relationships	U3–L2
AC2002.6.2	Enforce referential integrity	U3–L2
AC2002.7	**Producing Reports**	
AC2002.7.1	Create and format reports	U3–L4
AC2002.7.2	Add calculated controls to reports	U3–L4
AC2002.7.3	Preview and print reports	U3–L1
AC2002.8	**Integrating with Other Applications**	
AC2002.8.1	Import data to Access	U3–L2
AC2002.8.2	Export data from Access	U3–L2
AC2002.8.3	Create a simple data access page	U3–L4

Microsoft PowerPoint 2002 Comprehensive

Code	Skills Being Measured	Text Reference
PP2002.1	**Creating Presentations**	
PP2002.1.1	Create presentations (manually and using automated tools)	U4–L1, U4–L2, U4–L3, U6–L1
PP2002.1.2	Add slides to and delete slides from presentations	U4–L1, U6–L1
PP2002.1.3	Modify headers and footers in the Slide Master	U4–L3
PP2002.2	**Inserting and Modifying Text**	
PP2002.2.1	Import text from Word	U4–L2
PP2002.2.2	Insert, format, and modify text	U4–L1, U4–L3, U6–L1
PP2002.3	**Inserting and Modifying Visual Elements**	
PP2002.3.1	Add tables, charts, clip art, and bitmap images to slides	U4–L3
PP2002.3.2	Customize slide backgrounds	U4–L3
PP2002.3.3	Add OfficeArt elements to slides	U4–L3
PP2002.3.4	Apply custom formats to tables	U4–L3
PP2002.4	**Modifying Presentation Formats**	
PP2002.4.1	Apply formats to presentations	U4–L1, U4–L2, U4–L3, U6–L1
PP2002.4.2	Apply animation schemes	U4–L3
PP2002.4.3	Apply slide transitions	U4–L3
PP2002.4.4	Customize slide formats	U4–L2, U4–L3
PP2002.4.5	Customize slide templates	U4–L2, U4–L3
PP2002.4.6	Manage a Slide Master	U4–L3
PP2002.4.7	Rehearse timing	U4–L4
PP2002.4.8	Rearrange slides	U4–L1
PP2002.4.9	Modify slide layout	U4–L2, U4–L3
PP2002.4.10	Add links to a presentation	U4–L1
PP2002.5	**Printing Presentations**	
PP2002.5.1	Preview and print slides, outlines, handouts, and speaker notes	U4–L1
PP2002.6	**Working with Data from Other Sources**	
PP2002.6.1	Import Excel charts to slides	U4–L3
PP2002.6.2	Add sound and video to slides	U4–L3
PP2002.6.3	Insert Word tables on slides	U4–L3
PP2002.6.4	Export a presentation as an outline	U4–L1
PP2002.7	**Managing and Delivering Presentations**	
PP2002.7.1	Set up slide shows	U4–L4
PP2002.7.2	Deliver presentations	U4–L4
PP2002.7.3	Manage files and folders for presentations	U4–L1
PP2002.7.4	Work with embedded fonts	U4–L4
PP2002.7.5	Publish presentations to the Web	U4–L4
PP2002.7.6	Use Pack and Go	U4–L4
PP2002.8	**Workgroup Collaboration**	
PP2002.8.1	Set up a review cycle	U4–L4
PP2002.8.2	Review presentation comments	U4–L4
PP2002.8.3	Schedule and deliver presentation broadcasts	U4–L4
PP2002.8.4	Publish presentations to the Web	U4–L4

Appendix B

Microsoft Outlook 2002 Core Level

Code	Skills Being Measured	Text Reference
OL2002.1	**Creating and Viewing Messages**	
OL2002.1.1	Display and print messages	U5–L1
OL2002.1.2	Compose and send messages to corporate/workgroup and Internet addresses	U5–L1
OL2002.1.3	Insert signatures and attachments	U5–L1
OL2002.1.4	Customize views	U5–L1, U5–L3
OL2002.2	**Scheduling**	
OL2002.2.1	Add appointments, meetings, and events to the Outlook calendar	U5–L2
OL2002.2.2	Apply conditional formats to the Outlook calendar	U5–L2
OL2002.2.3	Respond to meeting requests	U5–L2
OL2002.2.4	Use categories to manage appointments	U5–L2
OL2002.2.5	Print calendars	U5–L2
OL2002.3	**Managing Messages**	
OL2002.3.1	Move messages between folders	U5–L1
OL2002.3.2	Search for messages	U5–L1
OL2002.3.3	Save messages in alternate file formats	U5–L1
OL2002.3.4	Use categories to manage messages	U5–L1
OL2002.3.5	Set message options	U5–L1
OL2002.4	**Creating and Managing Contacts**	
OL2002.4.1	Create and edit contacts	U5–L2
OL2002.4.2	Organize and sort contacts	U5–L2
OL2002.4.3	Link contacts to activities and journal entries	U5–L2
OL2002.5	**Creating and Managing Tasks and Notes**	
OL2002.5.1	Create and update tasks	U5–L3
OL2002.5.2	Modify task organization and task view	U5–L3
OL2002.5.3	Accept, decline, or delegate tasks	U5–L3
OL2002.5.4	Create and modify notes	U5–L3
OL2002.5.5	Use categories to manage tasks and notes	U5–L3

Figure C.1 Block Style Letter

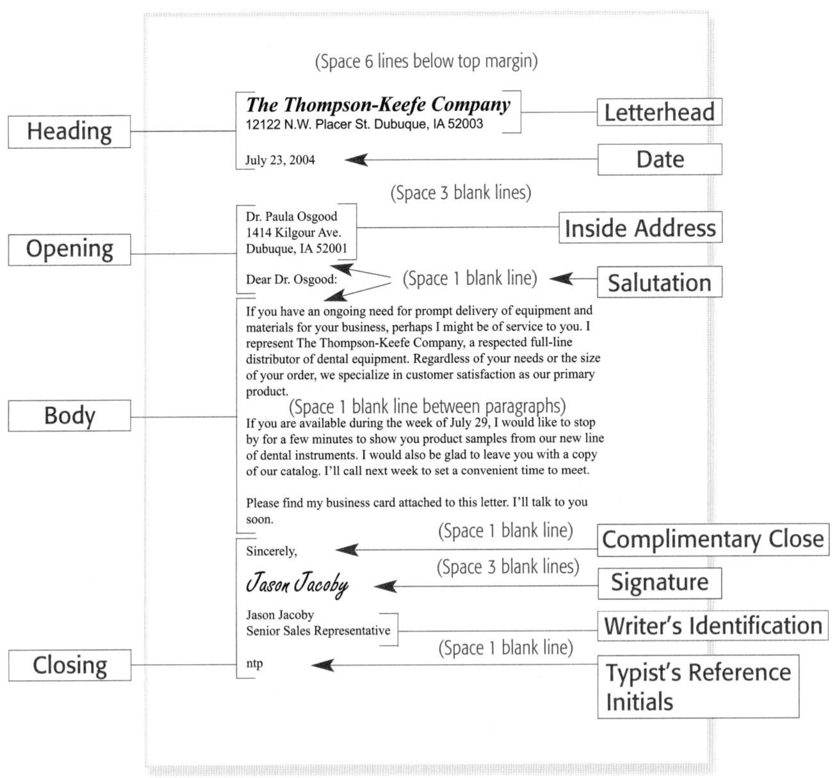

The Thompson-Keefe Company
12122 N.W. Placer St. Dubuque, IA 52003

July 23, 2004

Dr. Paula Osgood
1414 Kilgour Ave.
Dubuque, IA 52001

Dear Dr. Osgood:

If you have an ongoing need for prompt delivery of equipment and materials for your business, perhaps I might be of service to you. I represent The Thompson-Keefe Company, a respected full-line distributor of dental equipment. Regardless of your needs or the size of your order, we specialize in customer satisfaction as our primary product.

If you are available during the week of July 29, I would like to stop by for a few minutes to show you product samples from our new line of dental instruments. I would also be glad to leave you with a copy of our catalog. I'll call next week to set a convenient time to meet.

Please find my business card attached to this letter. I'll talk to you soon.

Sincerely,

Jason Jacoby

Jason Jacoby
Senior Sales Representative

ntp

Figure C.2 Modified Block Style Letter

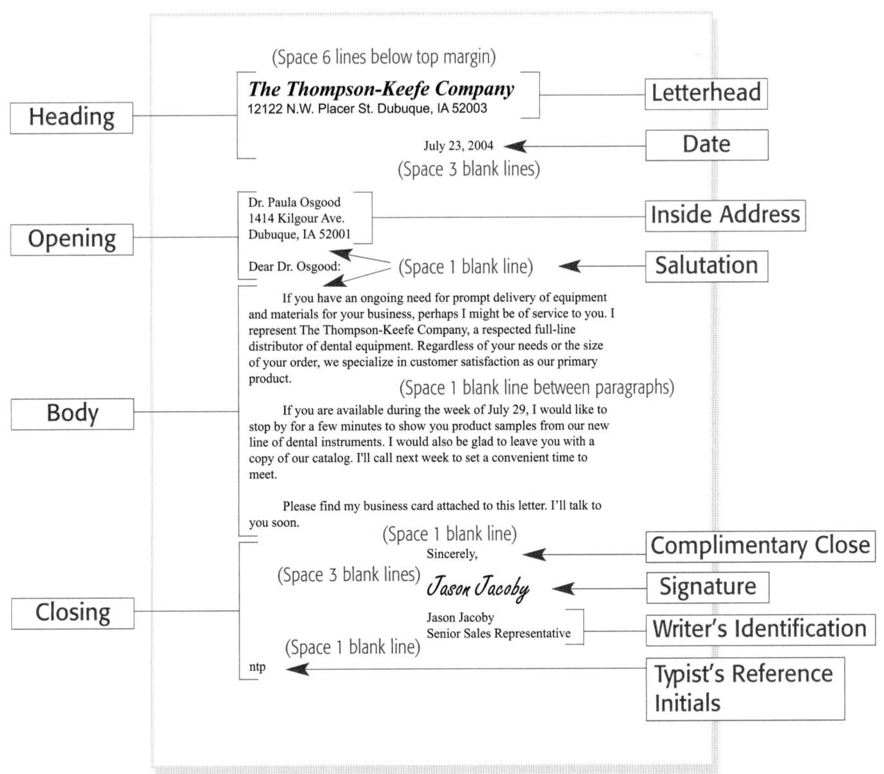

The Thompson-Keefe Company
12122 N.W. Placer St. Dubuque, IA 52003

July 23, 2004

Dr. Paula Osgood
1414 Kilgour Ave.
Dubuque, IA 52001

Dear Dr. Osgood:

If you have an ongoing need for prompt delivery of equipment and materials for your business, perhaps I might be of service to you. I represent The Thompson-Keefe Company, a respected full-line distributor of dental equipment. Regardless of your needs or the size of your order, we specialize in customer satisfaction as our primary product.

If you are available during the week of July 29, I would like to stop by for a few minutes to show you product samples from our new line of dental instruments. I would also be glad to leave you with a copy of our catalog. I'll call next week to set a convenient time to meet.

Please find my business card attached to this letter. I'll talk to you soon.

Sincerely,

Jason Jacoby

Jason Jacoby
Senior Sales Representative

ntp

Figure C.3 Chronological Resume

1231 Pin Oak Lane
Batavia, OH 45103
Jason Anders

Phone: 513.555.3535
Jason_Anders@myemail.com

Objective Seeking Vice President, Sales position that would utilize my successful sales management background and extensive sales experience.

Employment **1997–2002 Leland Products Leland, SC**

National Sales Manager

- Increased *Plastics* division sales by 350% to $44 million
- Expanded sales territories from 12 to 32 states
- Advised on 43 new products that increased sales by $12 million
- Developed "Ideas for Tomorrow," a new product advisory team composed of representatives from the functional areas of Sales, Marketing, Manufacturing, and Finance
- Helped negotiate successful union settlement, 2001

1993–1997 Kelsey Manufacturing Cypress, LA

Sales Representative

- Developed new south-central sales territory, which increased sales by 170% in two years
- Received *Superseller* award (1994) for reaching $2 million sales goal
- Responsible for training 12 new sales representatives

Education **1988–1993 Northwest State University Nigel, OH**

- B.A., Business Administration
- Graduated *magna cum laude*
- Editor-in-chief of school newspaper, *The Titan*
- President, American history club

Interests Jogging, gardening, carpentry, travel

References Upon request

Figure C.4 Achievements-Oriented Resume

Jason Anders
1231 Pin Oak Lane
Batavia, OH 45103

Phone: 513.555.3535
Jason_Anders@myemail.com

OBJECTIVE

Seeking Vice President, Sales position that would utilize my successful sales management background and extensive sales experience.

SKILLS

- Well-rounded background in sales, accounting, and business management
- Excellent human relations skills developed through diverse work experience in both manufacturing and sales
- High degree of both management and technical skill to help ensure sound business decisions

ACHIEVEMENTS

National Sales Manager, Leland Products, Leland, SC, 1997-2002

- Increased Plastics division sales by 350% to $44 million
- Expanded sales territories from 12 to 32 states
- Advised on 43 new products that increased sales by $12 million
- President of the Southwestern Plastics Manufacturing Association, 2001-2002
- Lifetime member of National Management Association
  Helped negotiate successful union settlement, 2001

Sales Representative, Kelsey Manufacturing, Cypress, LA, 1993-1997

- Developed new south-central sales territory which increasd sales by 170% in two years
- Responsible for training 12 new sales representatives

EDUCATION

B.A., Business Administration, Northwest State University, Nigel, Ohio, 1988-1993

Graduated magna cum laude. Editor-in-chief of school newspaper, the Titan. Star performer on track team, 400-meter relay. President of American history club.

REFERENCES

Upon request, I can provide excellent references from a number of industry professionals in both the sales and manufacturing areas.

Figure C.5 Common Memorandum

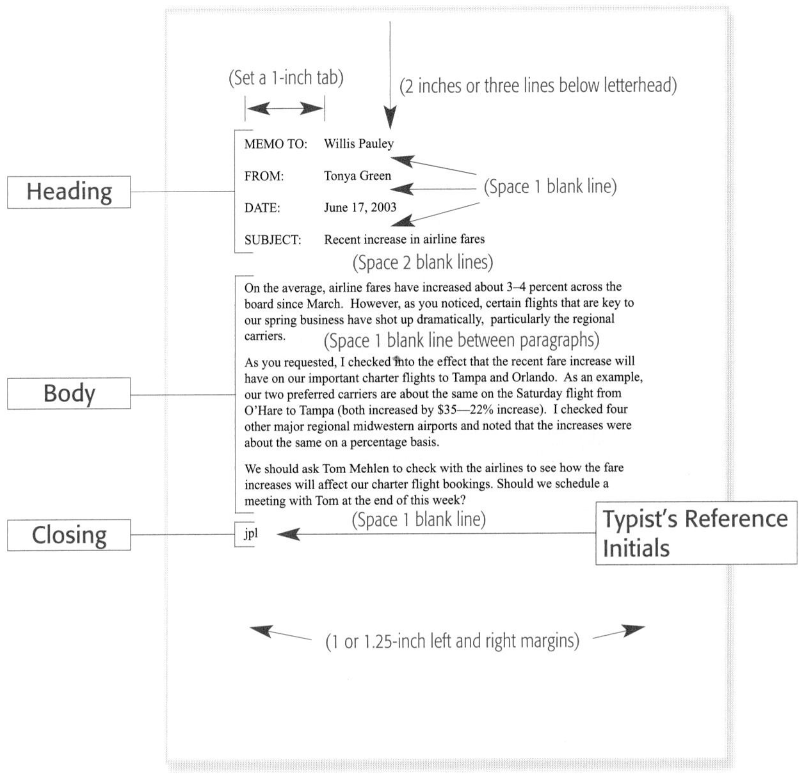

Figure C.6 Organizational Memorandum

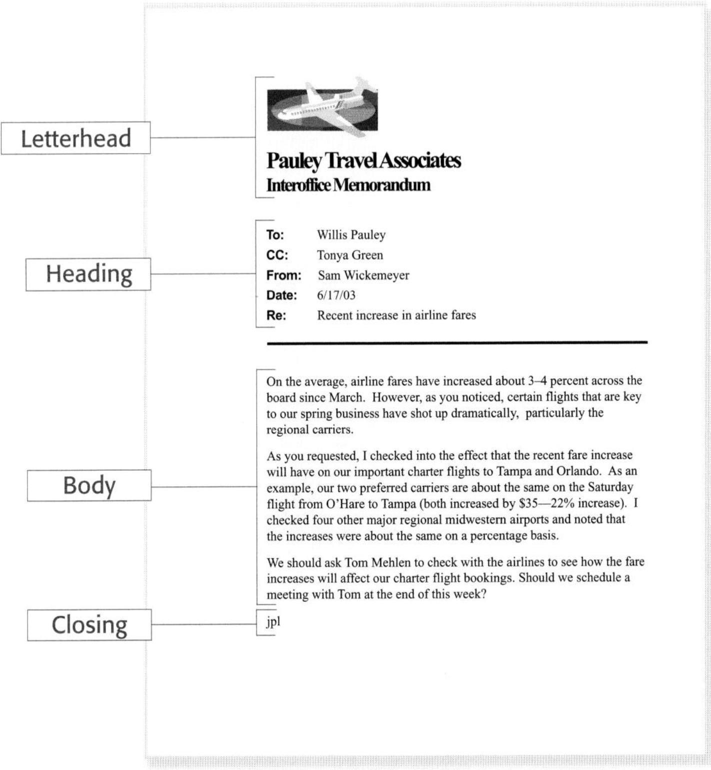

Figure C.7 Research paper

The Industrial Revolution: Who Paid?

by

Leonard Wang

While it has been concluded that the Industrial Revolution was a major turning point of modern world history, the question remains whether that period of unprecedented scientific and industrial advancement actually improved living conditions of the Western European-particularly the British-masses.

Text or reference book definitions of the Industrial Revolution commonly describe the period as one of social, economic, and cultural change, initially taking place in Great Britain in the latter half of the eighteenth century. The period was characterized by an increase in the output of industrial goods—many of which had previously been unavailable to the public—and the coinciding acceleration of the use of power-driven machinery to produce these goods.

The century preceding the Industrial Revolution in England was characterized by a new and expanding trade market, which was hard pressed to keep up with the growing demand for diverse commodities on an international level.

An important tool in understanding the lifestyle of working-class England in the eighteenth century is the knowledge of how many working-class citizens were living in the period of the Industrial Revolution. There are several unofficial population estimates of England and Wales made by a group of demographers contemporary to the period. These figures show a combined population of England and Wales in 1700 of some 5.7 million.[1] The overall figures seem to climb steadily through the beginning of the Industrial Revolution and into the early nineteenth century as follows:

- 5.8 million in 1730
- 6.2 million in 1750
- 7.6 million in 1780
- 8.3 million in 1790

At this point, more reliable information becomes available with the beginning of census-taking in England. Following a broader time frame, we see the British population quadruple during the nineteenth century, with a

The Industrial Revolution: Who Paid? Page 1

reported 8.8 million British citizens counted in 1801, 17.9 million in 1851, and 32.5 million in 1901.[2]

Thus, the sheer number of working people in England before the Industrial Revolution is a major clue to the common lifestyle. Long prior to the period, large shifts among the laboring population became noticeable as farmlands were "enclosed," or shut off from private cultivation or livestock raising by the government or large corporations. Examples of this are traced back to the seventeenth century, as the high price and demand for wool caused much land to be taken over for the pasturing of sheep:

> ***Sheep drove out men in consequence, for only a few shepherds were needed to run the farms, and the labourers were forced into the towns. . . . It was strongest in England, where the highways swarmed with beggars, and the outskirts of towns with cheap labour.***[3]

This shift became much more pronounced in the following century, as new technological advances narrowed the demand for hand labor, both in manufacturing and agriculture. Achievements such as the steam engine, the spinning jenney, and the "fire engine for plowing" brought about unprecedented advances in the mining, transportation, textile and agriculture markets—and squeezed thousands of heretofore manual laborers out of their traditional job markets, forcing mass migrations to more industrialized villages and cities. These towns, many springing up in the path of industrialism, "ate up men, women, and children."[4]

A vicious cycle of squalor and overpopulation is evident as many new cities sprang up in the wake of mechanization. As populations grew, living standards in these rising townships declined accordingly. For instance, the small town of Bradford, one of many which developed along with the country's newly expanding railroad lines, grew astonishingly, from a population of 8,800 in 1760 (the official start of the Industrial Revolution), to 66,715 in 1841.[5] It is noted that the quality of life did not necessarily rise in relation to population in such towns.

Life does not appear to have been much better in some of Britain's existing cities, which grew rapidly. In the period between 1801 and 1831, the population of Birmingham, "undoubtedly England's most versatile industrial city," grew from 70,000 to 130,000 residents.[6]

The Industrial Revolution: Who Paid? Page 2

Endnotes

[1]D. V. Glass, "Population and Population Movements in England and Wales, 1700 to 1850," in *Population and History*, eds. D. V. Glass and D. E. C. Eversley (London: Edward Arnold Publishers Ltd., 1965), p. 240.

[2]B. R. Mitchell, *European Historical Statistics* (New York: Columbia University Press, 1975), p. 163.

[3]Renard and Weulersse, p. 16.

[4]J. H. Plumb, "England in the Eighteenth Century," in *The Pelican History of England*, no. 7 (Aylesbury: Hunt Barnard Printing Limited, 1963), p. 11.

[5]Asa Briggs, *Iron Bridge to Crystal Palace* (London: Thames and Hudson Ltd., 1979), p. 68.

[6]Briggs, p. 68.

[7]H. Smithers, quoted by Briggs, pp. 67–68.

[8]Plumb, p. 150.

The Industrial Revolution: Who Paid? Page 3

Bibliography

Renard, G. and Weulersse, G. *Life and Work in Modern Europe*. New York: Barnes and Noble, Inc., 1968.

Briggs, Asa. *Iron Bridge to Crystal Palace*. London: Thames and Hudson Ltd., 1979.

Plumb, J. H. "England in the Eighteenth Century." In *The Pelican History of England*, no. 7. Aylesbury: Hunt Barnard Printing Ltd., 1963.

Glass, D. V. "Population and Population Movements in England and Wales, 1700 to 1850." In *Population and History*, edited by D. V. Glass and D. E. C. Eversley. London: Edward Arnold Publishers Ltd., 1965.

Mitchell, B. R. *European Historical Statistics*. New York: Columbia University Press, 1975.

The Industrial Revolution: Who Paid? Page 4

Figure C.8 Newsletter

The Inside Line

An exclusive quarterly report for *Sun and Sea* agency subscribers

Issue 3 Fall, 2003

MORE DISCOUNTS AHEAD

A recent survey by the *Sun and Sea* staff reveals that cruise operators plan to continue the current price war. This means deeper discounts than ever for passengers and more opportunities than ever for travel agents.

Icelandic Cruise Lines, for example, is preparing to announce its lowest fares ever for round-trip fights to Reykjavik, its primary departure point. Special offers include 50% off first-class fares and buy-one-get-one-free fares for economy class tickets.

Meanwhile, CruisArctic has already announced lowest-ever fares on its most popular 7- and 9-day packages. A typical passenger can save as much as 30% compared to fares available at the beginning of the year.

ISSUES, ISSUES,ISSUES

Don't forget us! Subscribing agents are invited to give a free copy of *Sun & Sea* to your cruise customers. You can give away either the current issue or any back issue—whichever will help your customers the most. Running out of copies? Call our Subscriber Service Line to request more.

A BOON FOR AGENTS

The International Cruise Operators Association (ICOA) has announced plans to boost commissions to travel agents.

"This move is unprecedented in the travel industry," said Franz Gaumann, ICOA President. He cited a five-year trend in lowering commissions, largely due to travelers' use of the Internet to book their own tickets.

"It is clear that cruise lines need help from professional travel agents," said Gaumann. "Booking a cruise is not like renting a car or reserving a hotel room. There are too many options for most consumers to deal with. They need advice, and the operators must be prepared to subsidize agents who send customers our way."

Although some operators seemed reluctant to resume paying commissions at their 1995 levels, most agreed the plan will give agents incentives to book more cruises for their customers.

A SPECIAL "THANK YOU"

Do you give away lots of copies of *Sun and Sea*? Do you encourage your customers to subscribe? If so, you can be a winner!

If any new subscriber lists you as a reference on his or her subscription form, you'll be entered in our annual "Sun & Sea Spectacular" drawing.

CAYMAN IS NOW GRANDER

Send many of your customers to the Caymans? Well, now there's one more reason for cruise passengers to visit this wonderful destination—to get married!

Cayman Getaways LLC has just announced a new program for cruise passengers. Disembark on Grand Cayman and get married on the island.

Options include ceremonies:

- Underwater, using scuba gear or a submarine
- At Stingray City
- At the Blowholes
- At Rum Pointe

Contact Cayman Getaways or any cruise operator for more information.

NEXT TIME

Our next edition will feature the latest information on cruises to the South Pacific.

Figure C.9 Business Report

New Homes Division Marketing Plan

Feldman's Best Opportunity to Dominate the Industry in 2004 2005

Performance Summary, 2002-2003

To have a sense of where we are going we must know where we are today. Our Midwest region includes the six states of Michigan, Wisconsin, Ohio, Illinois, Indiana, and West Virginia. Our 2002-2003 sales data are contrasted with the previous year in the table and chart below.

Midwest Region New Home Sales (in thousands)

Item (per unit)	2002-2003	2001-2002	Percentage Increase
New Home sales	325	187	73%
Average selling price	290	240	20%
Average gross profit	44	32	37%

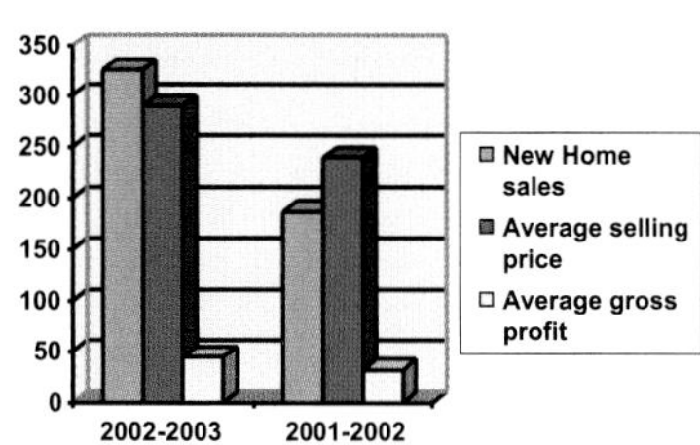

Feldman New Homes Division Marketing Plan 1

Figure C.10 Profit and Loss Statement

Jensen Investment Services
Profit and Loss Statement
January through December, 2004

	Jan. - Dec. 2004
Revenue	
Northeast division	$ 2,473,429
Midwest division	6,908,977
Southwest division	5,873,120
Other divisions	920,985
Total Revenue	$16,176,511
Cost of Sales	
Northeast division	$40,192
Midwest division	91,678
Southwest division	72,367
Other divisions	16,923
Total Cost of Sales	$ 221,160
GROSS PROFIT	$15,955,351
Expenses	
Payroll expenses	$ 2,103,457
Outside services	7,823
Supplies	23,054
Repairs and maintenance	145,098
Advertising	372,154
Travel	20,913
Accounting and legal	24,698
Rent	32,185
Telephone	4,592
Utilities	587,129
Insurance	432,052
Taxes (real estate, etc.)	159,376
Interest	12,053
Depreciation	79,032
Total Expenses	$ 4,003,616
NET PROFIT	$11,951,735

Figure C.11 Balance Sheet

Ellingson Enterprises
Balance Sheet
Calendar year ending 12/31/03

Assets	
Current assets:	
Cash	$ 253,093.00
Investments	1,249,830.00
Accounts receivable	128,734.00
Prepaid expenses	259,870.00
Other current assets	54,018.00
Total current assets:	$ 1,945,545.00
Fixed assets:	
Property and equipment	$ 5,598,271.00
Leasehold improvements	156,874.00
Equity and other investments	329,012.00
Less accumulated depreciation	(109,652.00)
Net fixed assets	$ 5,974,505.00
TOTAL ASSETS	$ 7,920,050.00
Liabilities and Owner's Equity	
Current liabilities:	
Accounts payable	$ 78,450.00
Income taxes payable	301,289.00
Unearned revenue	120,947.00
Other	32,017.00
Total current liabilities	$ 532,703.00
Long-term liabilities	
Mortgage payable	$ 340,956.00
Total long-term liabilities	$ 340,956.00
Owner's equity	
Investment capital	$ 6,321,788.00
Accumulated retained earnings	724,603.00
Total owner's equity	$ 7,046,391.00
TOTAL LIABILITIES AND STOCKHOLDERS' EQUITY	$7,920,050.00

3-D cell reference A reference to a cell in another Excel worksheet within a workbook that includes the sheet name as part of the reference.

A

Absolute reference A cell reference in an Excel formula that doesn't change when you copy the formula to another cell or range. See also *relative reference*.

Accept In Outlook, an option when responding to a meeting request. A meeting request you accept is automatically entered into your Calendar. Contrast with *decline* and propose new time. See also *meeting request*.

Active cell In Excel, the cell that is currently selected.

Address Card view In Outlook's Contacts, the default view that presents information in a business card format.

Alignment The placement of text in relationship to the right and left margins of a page.

Animated object An object such as a picture, text box, or other graphic that appears by itself during a PowerPoint presentation. Compare with *animated text*. See also *animation*.

Animated text Text that displays on a PowerPoint slide one line or bulleted point at a time. Compare with animated object. See also *animation*.

Animation A sound or visual effect added to a PowerPoint presentation to make the presentation more interesting. See also *animated object* and *animated text*.

Application software (application program) Programs that allow the user to perform activities on the computer such as word processing, surfing the Web, and playing games.

Appointment In Outlook's Calendar, an activity with specific start times that does not involve other people. Contrast with *event*.

Archiving In Outlook, to move messages to an alternate location (your hard drive or another drive on your network) for storage while still being able to access the messages.

Arguments Inputs such as numbers, text, cell references, or logical values that are used in Excel functions to perform calculations.

Ascending sort A sort order that sorts text values from A to Z and number values from 1 to 10.

Attachment A file created in another program (such as Word, Excel, PowerPoint, Access, or other Outlook items) that has been attached to an e-mail message.

AutoArchive Outlook's automatic archiving feature, which will archive old messages after a set number of days. See also *archiving*.

AutoContent Wizard A tool to help PowerPoint users create a presentation easily by using a set of preprogrammed slide layouts, a design template, and boilerplate text.

AutoCorrect A Microsoft Office feature that can replace one set of typed characters with another. This feature can be used to correct typographical errors or to insert special characters automatically as you type.

AutoFilter An Excel feature that enables you to apply a filter to a list in order to display a subset of data.

Autoform An Access form that is created automatically by the Form Wizard with no user input.

B

Bandwidth The amount of data that can be transmitted through a communication medium at a given time; often defined as data transmission speed. See also *broadband*.

Bit-mapped image (bitmap) An image made from a series of small dots; it may have a *.bmp*, *.png*, *.jpg*, or *.gif* file extension.

Bits per second (bps) A measure of data transmission speed.

Boilerplate text Standard text that is appropriate for the type of presentation selected when using PowerPoint's AutoContent Wizard.

Border A line placed around a paragraph or group of paragraphs.

Bound control A control that is tied to a specific underlying field in an Access query or table to display the data in that field.

Broadband A type of Internet connection that offers higher bandwidth and therefore faster Internet access than standard modem connections. See *bandwidth*.

Buffer A temporary storage area used for storing streaming media. See *streaming media*.

Bullet A graphic (such as a dot or picture) used to introduce each item in a bulleted list.

Bus topology A networking arrangement in which all computers connect to a single cable.

C

Calculated control An unbound control (usually a text box) that contains an expression that calculates the values in other controls in an Access form or report.

Calculated field A field in an Access query, form, or report in which the displayed values are the result of calculations performed on other fields.

Calendar One of the default folders in Outlook; the folder or tool which allows you to manage your daily schedule (such as meetings, appointments, and events) so you can stay organized. See also *Inbox*, *Contacts*, *Journal*, *Notes*, and *Tasks*.

Category In Outlook, a keyword or phrase that enables you to find, sort, filter, or group items.

Cell The intersection of a row and a column in a table or worksheet. A cell contains information such as text, numbers, or graphics.

Central processing unit (CPU) The part of the computer that executes instructions, controls the flow of data, and performs the arithmetic and logic decisions.

Change marker An icon in a PowerPoint presentation indicating that a reviewer has made a change. Compare with *comment marker*.

Character effect A special effect that can be applied to individual characters of text. Examples of character effects include superscript, subscript, and strikethrough. Character effects can be viewed in a printed document as well as on screen. See also *text effect*.

Character style A named set of formatting characteristics that can be applied to individual characters, such as a word or a letter.

Chart A type of graphic that visually presents numerical data. See also *diagram*.

Click To press and release the left mouse button.

Clip art An image (also called a *clip*) that is ready to add to a document.

Clipboard An area of the computer's memory reserved by Windows to temporarily store text and other objects that have been cut or copied from a file.

Close button Button at the upper right of a window that closes it.

Color scheme The eight colors used in the design of a PowerPoint presentation—colors for background, fonts, hyperlinks, etc. A presentation's color scheme varies depending on the design template used in the presentation.

Column A vertical line of cells identified by an alphabetic label at the top of the column.

Comment

1. In Word, small balloons in the margin of a document that hold remarks or suggestions.

2. In PowerPoint, a special text box in a presentation in which a reviewer inserts a note. The comment includes the date the reviewer wrote the comment along with the name of the registered user of the reviewer's computer. See also *comment marker*.

Comment marker An icon in a PowerPoint presentation that looks similar to a sticky note, indicating that a reviewer has made a comment. Compare with *change marker*. See also *comment*.

Commercial software Programs sold at retail stores, Web sites, or bundled with new computer systems, usually manufactured by large computer companies.

Concatenation In Access, joining two values to display them as a single value; for example, if you concatenate a FirstName field to a LastName field, as in [FirstName]&[LastName], the two names are displayed as a full name in a single field.

Contact information Names, e-mail addresses, phone numbers, and other essential information associated with the individuals and businesses with whom you communicate. See also *Contacts* and *Contacts list*.

Contacts One of the default folders in Outlook; the folder or tool that stores business and personal contact information. See also *Inbox*, *Calendar*, *Journal*, *Notes*, *Tasks*, and *Contacts list*.

Contacts list Contains information about individuals and businesses included in your Contacts folder. See also *Contact information* and *Contacts*.

Control An object on an Access form or report that displays data, performs an action, or adds graphics to the form or report (examples are text boxes, image controls, option buttons, labels, command buttons, and subform controls).

Copy A command that duplicates selected data or an object and temporarily stores it on the Clipboard. The item may be pasted into the same file or a different file.

Criteria A limiting condition, such as "Arizona" or ">100" used in Access queries and filters to show a limited set of records.

Custom software (proprietary software) Programs created by professional programmers to serve a company's or individual's specific needs.

Cut A command that removes selected data or an object from a document and temporarily stores it on the Clipboard. The item may be pasted into the same file or a different file.

D

Data type In Access, a field property that determines what type of data the field can contain (for example: Number, Text, Date/Time, or Yes/No).

Database A collection of data related to a particular topic. An Access database is a single file that contains all the tables, queries, forms, and reports for that collection of information.

Database object Tables, queries, reports, forms, and other objects that are the functional parts of an Access database.

Database window The window that appears when you first open an Access database. The Database window gives you access to all the objects in a database.

Datasheet In Access, data displayed in a row-and-column format in a table, query, or form.

Datasheet view In Access, an object view that displays records in a row-and-column format similar to a spreadsheet. Datasheet view allows you to see many records at the same time.

Day/Week/Month view Outlook's default Calendar view that allows you to display your Calendar as a single day, a five-day work week, a seven-day week, or an entire month.

Decline In Outlook, an option when responding to a meeting request. A meeting request that you decline is not entered into your Calendar. Contrast with *accept* and *propose new time*. See also *meeting request*.

Delivery options In Outlook, convenience features, such as having message replies sent to someone else, delaying message delivery, or setting a message expiration date which you can attach to an e-mail message.

Demote In PowerPoint, to lower the level of a subtitle so that it has a larger indent and a smaller type size. Contrast with *promote*.

Descending sort A sort order that sorts text values from Z to A and number values from 10 to 1.

Deselect To make an object or text inactive by clicking away from it or, for checked menu commands, by selecting them again so they are unchecked.

Design template A file that contains the preprogrammed formatting available for a PowerPoint presentation, such as colors, background design, fonts, and bullets.

Design view In Access, an object view that allows you to design and change tables, queries, forms, reports, and other objects.

Desktop The main work area on a computer.

Detailed Address Cards In Outlook, a Contact view that presents information in a business card format and includes fields such as job title and company name.

Diagram A type of graphic that visually presents conceptual information rather than numerical data. See also *chart*.

Dialog box Box opened by some menu commands in which you must choose options or supply information to execute the command.

Discussion comments Comments that are displayed with an Excel workbook but stored on a discussion server. See also *discussion server* and *thread*.

Discussion server A computer that stores discussion comments. See also *discussion comments*.

Document In Word, a file of any length that contains text and/or other objects. Letters, resumes, memos, and reports are examples of common documents.

Double-click To click the left mouse button twice rapidly.

Download To transfer a file from a remote computer to your computer. In Outlook, to retrieve data or messages from your server to your Inbox. See *upload*.

Drag To press and hold the left mouse button and move the mouse.

Draw program Graphics software that uses mathematical formulas to determine the size and appearance of lines and images, rather than dots. See also *paint program*.

E

Edit To make changes to a document.

E-mail A system for exchanging written, voice, and video messages and computer files via the Internet or a network. Abbreviation for electronic mail.

E-mail client Software that allows users to send and receive electronic mail over the Internet.

Embed To insert a source file into a destination file; any changes made later to the source file are not reflected in the destination file. Contrast with *link*.

Embedded font A font inserted in a PowerPoint presentation in such a way that the font will always appear the same, even if the presentation is shown on another computer.

Ethernet A local area network (LAN) standard running at 10 Mbps. Used with bus and star topologies, twisted-pair or fiber optic cables, and an Ethernet-compatible network interface card.

Event In Outlook's Calendar, an activity which lasts 24 or more hours or has no specific start time. Contrast with *appointment*.

Expansion slots A part of the motherboard that allows the connection of circuit boards with additional ports. These ports let the user attach additional devices to the computer.

Export The process of copying data from an Access table or query to another database or to another type of file, such as an Excel worksheet.

Expression A formula that calculates a value or defines criteria; in Access, you can use an expression to calculate new values or to specify which records should be displayed.

F

Fast Ethernet A local area network (LAN) standard running at 100 Mbps. Used with bus and star topologies, twisted-pair or fiber optic cables, and an Ethernet-compatible network interface card.

Field

1. In Word, a special placeholder for changeable information such as the date or time.

2. In Access, a field is displayed as a column in Datasheet view. See also *field code*.

Field code In Word, the underlying code that enables information in a field to change. See also *field*.

Field list A list of all the fields in an underlying Access table or query.

Field name The name by which Access recognizes a data field.

Field property A specific attribute of an Access data field, such as name, caption, field size, or input mask.

File A collection of data or information saved and stored under a name.

File format See *file type*.

File server A computer on a network that stores data that is shared by other computers on the network.

File type The program standards that are used to store data on a disk. The file type is identified by the three-letter file extension. Examples of various file types include Word Document (.doc) and Rich Text Format (.rtf). Also called *file format*.

Fill handle In Excel, the small, black square located in the lower-right corner of a selected cell or range that you can use to copy a value or formula to adjacent cells.

Filter

1. In Excel, a feature that allows you to display a subset of data in a list on a worksheet. See also *AutoFilter*.

2. In Access, one or more criterion that you can apply to a datasheet to display a subset of records. Those records that do not meet the criterion are "filtered out" and are not displayed in the subset of records. See also *Filter By Selection* and *Filter By Form*.

Filter By Form In Access, a filtering technique in which you can type the values for which you want to filter using a form that contains all the fields in the datasheet.

Filter By Selection In Access, a filtering technique in which you select a value or partial value for which you want to filter using the Filter By Selection button.

Find A command that searches for specified text and/or formatting in a document. See also *Replace*.

Find and Advanced Find In Outlook, features that allow you to search for messages containing a word or phrase, from or to a specific person, or by assigned categories, read/unread, importance, or attachment.

Flash memory A type of removable memory commonly used in small hand-held devices, such as cell phones, digital cameras, and digital music players.

Folder A location on the computer in which files and other folders can be stored.

Folder List In Outlook, a list of folders available in your mailbox; a tool used to navigate between various Outlook items.

Font A complete set of alphabetical characters, including letters, numbers, punctuation marks, and symbols, based on the same, unique design.

Font style A special effect that can be applied to text characters. Examples of font styles are bold, italic, and underline.

Footer A line of text that appears at the bottom of each page in a file, containing information such as the document's name, a page number, or the date. See also *header*.

Form An Access database object that holds controls for entering, editing, and displaying data from an underlying table or query.

Form view In Access, an object view that usually displays data one record at a time, with added graphical elements for easier reading. This view is convenient for entering and editing data in tables.

Formatting Making changes to a document's appearance.

Formula In Excel, a cell entry that performs calculations.

Formula Bar The long white bar above the column headings in an Excel worksheet that you can use to enter or edit cell data. The Formula Bar displays the contents of the active cell.

Forward In Outlook, to send a copy of a received e-mail message to someone else.

Free/busy time In Outlook's Calendar, blocks of time marked as available (indicated as *free*) or unavailable (indicated as *busy*) for individuals who make their Calendar available on a shared location so that others will be able to plan a meeting based on the attendees' free time. Outlook displays free and busy times in colors and patterns in the Calendar. This feature requires Microsoft Exchange Server or the Microsoft Office Internet Free/Busy service.

Freeware Software that has been copyrighted by its developers and made available to the public without charge.

Freeze panes An Excel feature that enables you to freeze rows and columns that are above and to the left of the selected cell so that they remain fixed while scrolling the worksheet.

Function A predefined formula in Excel that performs a specific, built-in operation.

G

Global Address List In Outlook, a list of e-mail addresses available within an organization using Microsoft Exchange Server or the Microsoft Office Internet Free/Busy service. A network administrator maintains these addresses, and network users can view them. See also *Outlook Address Book* and *Personal Address Book*.

Grammar checker An editing tool that reviews the grammar used in a file, highlights possible errors, and suggests one or more ways to fix the errors. See also *spelling checker*.

Graphical user interface (GUI) A design for the part of an operating system in which the user typically operates a mouse to point and click on graphic icons representing files, folders, disks, and programs.

H

Hard drive A nonremovable storage device used to hold software and data on a computer system.

Hardware The physical parts of a computer system including input, output, storage, and other devices.

Header A line of text that appears at the top of each page in a file containing information such as the document's name, a page number, or the date. See also footer.

Hierarchy A system organized by rank, or level. On a computer, the system of organizing files in folders, beginning with a root folder at the top of a disk drive.

Highlight A colored background applied to selected text.

Horizontal application software Software designed to be used for a wide variety of purposes, such as word processing or graphics programs.

HTML format In Outlook, the default message format that uses the same language used to create Web pages. HTML format supports all message formatting (such as fonts, numbering, bullets, alignment, signatures, and graphics) and allows you to view the message using your Web browser. Compare with *Outlook Rich Text format* and *Text Only format*.

Hyperlink A specially formatted text or graphic that, when clicked, connects you to another location (usually a Web page or Web site). In application software Help features, text hyperlinks provide additional information. Also called links.

Hypertext Markup Language (HTML) The underlying code that determines how Web documents look and behave when viewed in a Web browser.

I

Icon Small pictures representing programs and other items.

Import The process of copying data from another source, such as a database or spreadsheet, into an open Access database.

Importance level

In Outlook, message options (such as High, Low, and Normal) that indicate the urgency of the message.

Inbox One of the default folders in Outlook; allows you to receive, read, compose, send, store, and organize your e-mail messages. See also *Calendar*, *Contacts*, *Journal*, *Notes*, and *Tasks*.

Indent The amount of space between a paragraph and the right or left margin.

Indent level In PowerPoint, a number that indicates the indent and importance of a subtitle in relation to the title.

Input device Any device that accepts data from the user, such as a keyboard or mouse.

Input mask In Access, a field property that determines display format and limits the type of data that can be entered; makes data entry faster and more precise.

Insert mode A method of inserting text into a file by pushing existing characters to the right instead of overwriting them. See also Overtype mode.

Insertion point A blinking vertical line that shows your current position in a document.

Integrated program Software that combines the functionality of two or more programs, such as word processing functions, spreadsheet functions, and database management functions, into one program.

Internet A worldwide system that connects thousands of individual networks together. These connections allow a computer on one network to communicate with virtually any other computer on any other network.

Internet service provider (ISP) A company that provides Internet access to individuals and companies, usually for a fee.

Intranet A small, private network that enables users to communicate and access files as though they were using the Internet.

J

Journal One of the default folders in Outlook; the folder or tool that automatically tracks the activities related to a contact and displays them in a timeline. See also *Inbox*, *Calendar*, *Contacts*, *Notes*, and *Tasks*.

Junction table In Access, a table that provides a link between two tables that have a many-to-many relationship; the junction table has a one-to-many relationship with each of the two tables it links.

L

Label A text entry in an Excel worksheet.

Landscape orientation A page orientation in which text is printed across the wider dimension of the page. See also *portrait orientation*.

Line spacing The amount of vertical space between the lines within a paragraph. See also *paragraph spacing*.

Link The connection between a source file and a destination file, or between two tables; any changes made later to the source file are reflected in the destination file. Contrast with *embed*. See also *hyperlink*.

Linux An operating system based on Unix that permits any programmer to improve upon it and is available as freeware.

Liquid crystal display (LCD) projector Equipment that allows you to project the slides in a PowerPoint presentation in slide show view from your computer onto a blank wall or large video screen.

Local area network (LAN) A system in which nearby computers are connected to each other so they can share printers, data, and other resources.

LocalTalk A LAN standard used to connect Apple computers.

Log on The process of identifying yourself to a computer system or network, usually by typing your user name and password. Tells the system or network who you are and what programs and files you are allowed to use.

Lookup field In Access, a field that looks up a list of values in another table or in a static list, and presents the list of values for data entry selection.

M

MacOS The operating system of the Macintosh line of computer systems.

Main form In Access, the large form in a main/subform, which contains the primary table of data and displays a single record.

Main/subform In Access, a form that combines two forms, one for the primary table of data and a nested form for the related table of data.

Mainframe A computer system used by large organizations that can support many users and large databases.

Many-to-many relationship In Access, a relationship between two tables in which each table can have many related records in the other table.

Margin Blank space along the edge of a page where text is not printed. All documents have a top, bottom, right, and left margin which can have the same or different widths.

Maximize button Button at the upper right of a window that enlarges the window.

Meeting request In Outlook, a Calendar activity to which you invite people and/or resources. See also *accept* and *decline*.

Menu A list of commands organized under a common heading.

Menu bar A bar, usually appearing below a window title bar, that lists menus by name and provides access to them.

Merge In Excel, an action that combines selected cells into a single cell. See also *split*.

Metropolitan area network (MAN) A networking system in which two or more LANs within a single region are connected using telephone or telecommunications company services.

Minicomputer A computer system smaller and less powerful than a mainframe but capable of supporting multiple users for a small to medium-sized organization.

Minimize button Button at the upper right of a window that shrinks the window and makes it inactive.

Modem An input/output device that converts the digital signals from a computer into analog signals that can be sent over telephone lines and back again.

Motherboard The main circuit board containing a computer's central processing unit (CPU), memory, and expansion slots.

N

Nethics Network and e-mail ethics. Compare with *netiquette*.

Netiquette Network and e-mail etiquette; a set of rules that include communicating using clear language, being respectful and sensitive to possible misinterpretations, and applying the "golden rule"—e-mail others as you would like to be e-mailed. Compare with *nethics*.

Network interface card (NIC) A device that controls the flow of data between a computer's RAM and a network cable.

Network operating system (NOS) Systems software that manages a LAN by establishing and maintaining the connections between the nodes and the file server.

Node A device attached to a network, such as a computer or a printer.

Note In Outlook, a tool which allows you to record information about a phone call, reminders about an upcoming meeting, ideas about a report, or anything that you would ordinarily write on paper. See also *Notes*.

Notes One of the default folders in Outlook; the folder which allows you to create electronic notes that you use as reminders or other information for later use. See also *Calendar, Contacts, Inbox, Journal*, and *Tasks*.

O

Object In PowerPoint, a nontext element such as a chart, table, clip art image, picture, photo, movie clip, or another type of information.

Object area A placeholder on a PowerPoint slide that is reserving space for objects such as tables, charts, or graphic images. Compare with *text area* and *title area*.

One-to-many relationship In Access, a relationship between two tables in which only one table (the primary table) can have many related records in the other table (the related table).

One-to-one relationship In Access, a relationship between two tables in which each table has only one related record in the other table.

Online broadcast A PowerPoint feature that allows audience members to view a presentation on their own computers using their Web browsers.

Online services Companies that provide direct access to information that is maintained outside of the Internet, such as chat rooms, online shopping malls, and stock quotes.

Operating system (OS) The software program that oversees and controls everything that happens while a computer is turned on, such as running the application software, managing the hardware, and maintaining file storage.

Organization chart A diagram that visually presents the structure of departments or personnel in an organization.

Orphan In Access, records in a related table (on the "many" side of a relationship) that are left unrelated if their related record in the primary table (on the "one" side of the relationship) is deleted or changed so that the relationship is broken.

Outlook Address Book A place to store contact information. The Outlook Address Book can include a Global Address List, a Contacts list, and a Personal Address Book. See also *Global Address List* and *Personal Address Book*.

Outlook Bar A navigation tool that includes groups such as Outlook Shortcuts or Other Shortcuts and enables you to link to other items within Outlook.

Outlook Rich Text format A file format that only certain Microsoft Office programs understand and which supports text formatting such as bullets and alignment. Compare with *HTML format* and *Text Only format*.

Outlook Today A page that shows a summary of your appointments for the day, your complete task list, and how many new e-mail messages are waiting in the Inbox. If desired, you can set Outlook Today as the default page in Outlook.

Output device A part of the computer system that displays information to the user, such as a monitor or a printer.

Overtype mode A method of inserting text into a file by overwriting existing characters with new ones. See also *Insert mode*.

P

Page break A marker that indicates the end of one page and the start of a new one.

Paint program Graphics software that creates images as dots rather than mathematical formulas. See also *draw program*.

Pane A section of a window.

Paragraph Any text that is followed by a paragraph mark (¶).

Paragraph spacing The amount of vertical space between paragraphs. See also *line spacing*.

Paragraph style A named set of formatting characteristics that can be applied to one or more entire paragraphs.

Password A series of characters known only to you, which, along with a user name, protects a computer system or network from unauthorized use.

Paste A command that inserts text or an object from the Clipboard into a document. See also *Cut* and *Copy*.

Personal Address Book In Outlook, a place to store personal contacts and distribution lists to keep them separate from business contacts. See also *Global Address List* and *Outlook Address Book*.

Physical media The cables or wireless connections that transmit data on a network.

Placeholder

1. In Word, formatted text within a template file that you can replace with your own text. See also *template*.

2. In PowerPoint, a preset location reserving space for a slide element.

Platform The combination of hardware and operating system that defines the types of programs and devices your computer will support.

Point

1. A unit of measure applied to fonts and paragraph spacing. One point equals 1/72 inch.

2. To move the mouse to position the pointer on an object.

Pointer The arrow icon on a computer screen.

Portrait orientation A page orientation in which text is printed across the shorter dimension of the page. See also *landscape orientation*.

POST (Power-On Self Test) A built-in program that checks to make sure the computer hardware is working properly.

Presentation A formal or an informal report, usually given orally, which is sometimes referred to as a "talk" or a "speech."

Preview Pane In Outlook, a pane that allows you to read a selected message, open attachments, and respond to meeting requests without actually opening the message.

Primary key In Access, one or more fields in a table whose values uniquely identify each record.

Primary table In Access, the table on the "one" side of a one-to-many relationship.

Print Preview A document view that shows how your document will look when it is printed.

Print titles Repeated row or column labels that appear on each page of a printed Excel worksheet.

Professional workstation A computer system smaller than a minicomputer but more powerful than most personal computers.

Program suite A package of standalone application programs designed to work independently yet share data easily.

Promote In PowerPoint, to raise the level of a subtitle so that it has a smaller indent (or no indent at all) and a larger type size. Contrast with *demote*.

Propose new time In Outlook, an option when responding to a meeting request. If a meeting conflicts with your schedule, you can select Propose New Time and choose another time. With this option, the original meeting time is entered into your Calendar as tentative. Contrast with *accept* and *decline*. See also *meeting request*.

Protocols A set of rules used to describe how different devices on a network communicate with each other.

Publish To save a PowerPoint presentation as a set of Web pages on an intranet or Web server, allowing others to open and navigate the presentation using their Web browsers.

Q

Query In Access, a database object that shows specific data you want to work with. The data may be drawn from multiple related tables, may have several filters applied, and may include calculated expressions.

R

Random access memory (RAM) A computer's primary working memory that temporarily stores information while the computer is turned on. The central processing unit (CPU) works with information stored in RAM.

Range A cell or group of cells that can be selected in an Excel worksheet.

Read-only memory (ROM) The part of a computer's primary storage that permanently stores information, even when the computer is turned off.

Record In Access, a set of information that belongs together, such as a customer's name and address information, or details about a product.

Record selector In Access, the gray box at the left side of each record in Datasheet view or in Form view. Click the record selector to select the entire record.

Recurring In Outlook, Calendar appointments or events that occur more than once at set intervals.

Referential integrity A system of rules that Access uses to ensure that relationships between records in related tables are valid, and that you don't accidentally delete or change related data.

Related table In Access, the table on the "many" side of a one-to-many relationship.

Relational database A type of database in which information is stored in separate but related tables, which allows for nonredundant, more efficient data storage and retrieval.

Relationship In Access, the association between two tables that share a field with matching values; the matching fields allow the tables to be joined, so that a query can select data from both tables.

Relative reference In Excel, a cell reference in a formula that automatically adjusts to the new location when you copy the formula to another cell or range. See also *absolute reference*.

Replace A command that searches for specified text and/or formatting in a document and replaces it with new text and/or formatting that you specify. See also *Find*.

Reply To send a message response to the message sender (the person listed on the From line).

Reply to All To send a message response to everyone who received a copy of the original message (those listed on the original To, Cc, and From lines).

Report In Access, a database object that presents data organized and formatted to your specifications.

Resource A conference room, a computer, or other equipment that Outlook users can schedule for a meeting. To schedule resources, Outlook must be used with Microsoft Exchange Server or the Microsoft Office Internet Free/Busy service.

Restore Down button Button at the upper right of a window that restores the window to its size before maximizing.

Rich Text Format (RTF) A file format with the extension *.rtf* that enables the text in the file to be transferred and read by different applications; most word processing programs can read RTF.

Right-click To click the right mouse button.

Right-drag To press and hold the right mouse button and move the mouse.

Ring topology A networking arrangement in which computers connect in a circle, passing a special set of data, or token, from one computer to the next to determine who can transmit data.

Row In Excel, a horizontal line of cells identified by a row number at the left end of the row.

S

Save To store a document on a disk as a named file.

ScreenTip Help feature that provides information about elements on the screen.

Scroll arrow Arrow at an end of a scroll bar that can be clicked to move a document up, down, left, or right by small increments.

Scroll bars Bars, usually at the right and bottom of a window, used for navigating the window's contents.

Scroll box Box in the center of a scroll bar that can be dragged to move a document as much as you want.

Sections A part of an Access form or report that contains a specific type of data, such as a header, footer, or detail section.

Select To choose a menu, command, or other item; to single out an object or text in order to work with it.

Select query The most common type of query in Access, the select query retrieves specific data from one or more tables and displays the results in a datasheet; however, it does not alter the data in the table(s). You can sort and summarize the results of a select query, and you can perform calculations on the fields in a select query.

Sensitivity level In Outlook, options (such as Normal, Personal, Private, or Confidential) that indicate the sensitivity of the message content.

Shading A gray or colored background that can be placed behind a paragraph or group of paragraphs.

Shareware Software typically distributed over the Internet that users can try out for free; however, they are expected to pay the developer if they intend to use the software or want its extra features.

Signature Picker A list within Outlook where signatures are stored.

Signature In Outlook, stored information (such as your name, title, and phone number) used to identify you in an e-mail message.

Slide layout A particular combination of placeholders on a PowerPoint slide, reserving space for text and/or graphical elements.

Slide master A hidden slide in every PowerPoint presentation that stores design template specifications—such as placeholder sizes and positions, bullet styles, font styles and sizes, and background color—for all slides but the title slide. The slide master can be used to make changes to an entire presentation. Compare with *title master*.

Spelling checker An editing tool that reviews the spelling in a file, highlights possible misspelled words, and suggests one or more replacements. See also *grammar checker*.

Split

1. In Word, an action that divides a single table cell into two or more smaller cells.

2. In Excel, an action that returns a merged cell back into individual cells. See also *merge*.

Splitter bar In PowerPoint, one of the narrow bars that separate the left, slide, and notes panes in normal view.

Star topology A networking arrangement in which each node connects to a hub or switch through which data travels to a file server and/or other computers.

Stationery In Outlook, a set of design elements, such as fonts, bullets, background color, and images that you can apply to your messages.

Status bar Bar at the bottom of an application window that tells you what a program is currently doing. It also tells you where you are in a document and provides other information, depending on the program.

Streaming media An Internet delivery technology that allows you to see video data and/or hear audio data as a continuous stream almost immediately.

Style A named set of formatting characteristics. See also *paragraph style* and *character style*.

Subdatasheet In Access, a datasheet that is nested within another datasheet and contains records related to the records in the datasheet in which it is nested.

Subform In Access, the nested form in a main/subform combination that displays a table of several related records.

Subtitle In PowerPoint, any text in one or two columns, or a bulleted item in a list, that follows the title and gives more detail about the title. Compare with *title*.

Supercomputer A computer that is faster and more powerful than a mainframe. Supercomputers are used by large research facilities or government agencies needing a lot of processing ability.

Syntax The structure for entering functions and commands, including spelling, punctuation, and acceptable keywords.

System boot (booting) Turning on the computer, running the POST, and loading the operating system.

System software The software necessary to operate and maintain a computer system, including operating systems and utility programs.

System unit The case that holds the main, internal circuitry of a computer including the motherboard, disk drives, and power supply.

T

Tab An amount of space by which text is indented from the left margin. In Word, tabs are set on the horizontal ruler.

Tab order In Access, the order in which the focus moves from control to control on a form when you press the Tab key.

Tab scrolling buttons In Excel, the buttons that display to the left of the sheet tabs that enable you to move to the first, previous, next, or last worksheet in a workbook.

Tab split bar In Excel, the gray vertical bar just left of the horizontal scroll bar that you can drag to the right to view hidden sheet tabs.

Table

1. In Word, a grid made up of horizontal rows and vertical columns that is used to order certain types of information.

2. In Access, a collection of data with the same subject or topic. Data are stored in records (rows) and fields (columns).

Task In Outlook, a personal or work-related chore that you can track in an electronic to-do list until it is complete. See *Tasks*.

Taskbar A toolbar, usually displayed at the bottom of the desktop, listing current programs, files, and features.

TaskPad A list of tasks that are displayed on the Outlook Calendar. See *Tasks* and *task list*.

Tasks One of the default folders in Outlook; the folder which allows you to create an electronic to-do list. See also *Calendar, Contacts, Inbox, Journal*, and *Notes*.

Task list In Outlook, a place where you can track your to-do list electronically. The list appears in the Tasks folder and in the TaskPad on the Calendar. See also *Tasks* and *TaskPad*.

Task owner In Outlook, when you receive and accept a task request, the task is added to your task list and you become the task owner. Only the task owner can make changes or updates to a task. See *task, task list, task request*, and *Tasks*.

Task pane Pane in an Office application containing a list of commands.

Task request In Outlook, a task that you create and send to someone else through e-mail. When you create a task request, you may keep a copy of the task on your task list as well as receive a status report when the task is complete.

Telecommunications The technology of long-distance electronic communication.

Template A file that contains basic formatting, text, and/or formulas that you can customize to create a new file. See also *placeholder*.

Text area In PowerPoint, a placeholder that reserves space for a subtitle or a numbered or bulleted list. Compare with *object area* and *title area*.

Text effect A special effect that can be applied to one or more characters of text. Examples of text effects include shimmering or sparkling text. Text effects can be viewed on screen but do not appear in a printed document. See also *character effect*.

Text Only format In Outlook, a file format that all e-mail programs understand and that will save your message content but will not retain the message formatting. Compare with *HTML format* and *Outlook Rich Text format*.

Thesaurus In Word, a language tool that provides definitions and a list of synonyms for a selected word.

Thread A set of discussion comments and responses that are grouped and displayed in hierarchical order. See also *discussion comments*.

Thumbnail A small-size view of a slide in a PowerPoint presentation. Thumbnails appear on the Slides tab, in slide sorter view, and in various task panes.

Time management The ability to organize, prioritize, and effectively perform responsibilities with a positive attitude.

Timeline In Outlook's Journal, a view type that displays items in relation to time.

Title In PowerPoint, the main topic of a presentation or slide; the first line of text on a slide. Compare with *subtitle*. See also *title slide*.

Title area In PowerPoint, a placeholder that reserves space for a slide's title. Compare with *object area* and *text area*.

Title bar Bar at the top of a window that lists the title of the document.

Title master A hidden slide in every PowerPoint presentation that stores design template specifications—such as placeholder sizes and positions, font styles and sizes, and background color—for any slide that uses the Title Slide layout. Compare with *slide master*.

Title slide The first slide in a PowerPoint presentation that displays the main topic of the presentation. See also *title*.

Token Ring A LAN standard that uses a ring topology and transfers data at 4 or 16 Mbps.

Toolbar Bar containing icons (buttons) for frequently used commands.

Toolbox In Access, the floating toolbar that contains the buttons for creating controls in form or report Design view; also called the *Controls Toolbox*.

Transition The way in which one slide replaces another during a PowerPoint presentation.

U

Unbound control In Access, a control that is not tied to a specific field in a query or table; used to display general information or to perform calculations on the values in other controls in a form or report.

Upload

1. To transfer a file from your computer to a remote computer.
2. In Outlook, to send data or messages from your Outbox to your server.

User interface The visual portion of the operating system software that determines the manner in which users interact with the computer.

User name The name you are known by on the system or network, which, along with a password, protects a computer system or network from unauthorized use.

Utility program A program that assists the user in maintaining and improving the operating system. Some utility programs are supplied by the operating system while others are sold by third-party vendors.

V

Value A numeric entry in Excel.

Vertical application software Software designed for a specific purpose, such as programs written for particular types of businesses, games, and educational software.

Views Window displays which allow you to look at data in different ways.

Virus A program designed as a prank that replicates itself from one computer to another. Viruses can be harmless but annoying to users or they can affect software performance and destroy information.

W

Web browser A type of application program used to display Web pages and surf the Internet.

Web page A document that is formatted in Hypertext Markup Language (HTML) so that it can be published on the World Wide Web. Web pages can contain text, pictures, video, sound, and hyperlinks to other pages or sites.

Web site A location on the Web maintained by a company, organization, or individual, consisting of one or more Web pages.

Wide area network (WAN) A system of interconnected LANs and WANs able to transfer data between computers regardless of the distance between them.

Windows The common name of the family of operating systems with graphical user interfaces, manufactured by Microsoft Corp.

Windows Explorer A tool you can use to navigate your computer's file system and locate and organize files.

Wizard An automated tool that helps you perform a task by presenting step-by-step content and organization choices.

Workbook An Excel file that can contain up to 256 worksheets.

Worksheet A page in an Excel workbook.

World Wide Web A network within the Internet whose computers use the same language to communicate, in which information is presented in the form of Web pages.

3-D cell reference/referencia de celda 3D Referencia a una celda de otra hoja de trabajo de Excel dentro de un libro de trabajo, que incluye el nombre de la hoja como parte de la referencia.

A

Absolute reference/Referencia absoluta Referencia de celda en una fórmula de Excel que no cambia cuando se copia la fórmula a otra celda o intervalo. Ver también *relative reference*.

Accept/Aceptar En Outlook, opción que se tiene al responder a una solicitud de reunión. Una solicitud de reunión aceptada se incluye automáticamente en el Calendario. Comparar con *decline* y *propose new time*. Ver también *meeting request*.

Active cell/Celda activa En Excel, la celda seleccionada en ese momento.

Address Card view/Vista de Tarjeta de dirección En Contactos de Outlook, la presentación predeterminada que muestra la información en un formato de tarjeta de presentación.

Alignment/Alineación Colocación del texto respecto a los márgenes derecho e izquierdo de una página.

Animated object/Objeto animado Objeto, como una imagen, cuadro de texto u otro gráfico, que aparece por sí solo durante una presentación de PowerPoint. Comparar con *animated text*. Ver también *animation*.

Animated text/Texto animado Texto que exhibe, en una diapositiva de PowerPoint, una línea o punto elevado a la vez. Comparar con *animated object*. Ver también *animation*.

Animation/Animación Sonido o efecto visual que se agrega a una presentación de PowerPoint para hacerla más interesante. Ver también *animated object* y *animated text*.

Application software (application program)/Software de aplicación (programa de aplicación) Programa que permite al usuario realizar actividades en la computadora, como procesar texto, navegar por Internet y jugar juegos.

Appointment/Cita En el Calendario de Outlook, actividad con hora de inicio específica en la que no participan otras personas. Comparar con *events*.

Archiving/Archivar En Outlook, trasladar mensajes a otro lugar (del disco duro u otra unidad de la red) para almacenarlos, conservando la posibilidad de tener acceso a los mensajes.

Arguments/Argumentos Entradas como números, texto, referencias de celda o valores lógicos, que se usan en funciones de Excel para efectuar cálculos.

Ascending sort/Ordenamiento ascendente Orden de clasificación que organiza los valores de texto de la A a la Z y los valores numéricos del 1 al 10.

Attachment/Archivo adjunto Archivo creado en otro programa (como Word, Excel, PowerPoint, Access u otros elementos de Outlook) que ha sido anexado a un mensaje de correo electrónico.

AutoArchive/Autoarchivar Recurso de archivado automático de Outlook, que archiva los mensajes antiguos al cabo de un número determinado de días. Ver también *archiving*.

AutoContent Wizard/Asistente de autocontenido Herramienta que ayuda a los usuarios de PowerPoint a crear una presentación de manera sencilla por medio de un conjunto de diseños de diapositiva, una plantilla de diseño y textos fijos.

AutoCorrect/Autocorrección Recurso de Office de Microsoft que sustituye un conjunto de caracteres escritos por otro. Este recurso sirve para corregir errores tipográficos o para insertar caracteres especiales de forma automática a medida que se escribe.

AutoFilter/Autofiltro Recurso de Excel que permite aplicar un filtro a una lista para mostrar un subconjunto de datos.

Autoform/Autoformulario Formulario de Access que el Asistente de formularios crea automáticamente sin que el usuario aporte entradas.

B

Bandwidth/Ancho de banda Cantidad de datos que se pueden transmitir por un medio de una comunicación en un lapso determinado; suele definirse como rapidez de transmisión de datos. Ver también *broadband*.

Bit-mapped image (bitmap)/Imagen de mapa de bits Imagen formada a partir de una serie de pequeños puntos; puede tener como extensión de archivo .bmp, .png, .jpg o .gif.

Bits per second (bps)/Bits por segundo Una medida de la rapidez de transmisión de datos.

Boilerplate text/Texto fijo Texto estándar que es apropiado para el tipo de presentación elegida al usar el Asistente de autocontenido de PowerPoint.

Border/Borde Línea que se coloca alrededor de un párrafo o grupo de párrafos.

Bound control/Control ligado Control que está ligado a un campo subyacente específico en una consulta o tabla de Access para mostrar los datos de ese campo.

Broadband/Banda ancha Tipo de conexión a Internet que ofrece mayor ancho de banda y, por tanto, acceso más rápido a Internet que las conexiones ordinarias por módem. Ver *bandwidth*.

Buffer/Almacenamiento temporal Área de almacenamiento temporal para almacenar un flujo de datos de diferentes medios. Ver *streaming media*.

Bullet/Punto elevado Gráfico (como un punto o una imagen) que sirve para introducir cada elemento en una lista con puntos elevados.

Bus topology/Topología de canal Organización de redes en la que todas las computadoras se conectan a un solo cable.

C

Calculated control/Control calculado Control no limitado (por lo regular un cuadro de texto) que contiene una expresión que calcula los valores de otros controles en un formulario o informe de Access.

Calculated field/Campo calculado Campo de una consulta, formulario o informe de Access en el que los valores que se muestran son el resultado de cálculos efectuados en otros campos.

Calendar/Calendario Una de las carpetas predeterminadas de Outlook; la carpeta o herramienta que permite manejar el calendario diario (como reuniones, citas y eventos) para mantener organizadas las actividades. Ver también *Inbox, Contacts, Journal, Notes* y *Tasks*.

Category/Categoría En Outlook, palabra clave o frase que permite buscar, ordenar, filtrar o agrupar elementos.

Cell/Celda Intersección de una fila y una columna en una tabla u hoja de trabajo. Una celda contiene información, como texto, números o gráficos.

Central processing unit (CPU)/ Unidad central de procesamiento Parte de la computadora que ejecuta instrucciones, regula el flujo de datos y ejecuta las decisiones aritméticas y lógicas.

Change marker/Marcador de cambio Icono de una presentación de PowerPoint que indica que un revisor ha realizado un cambio. Comparar con *comment marker*.

Character effect/Efectos de carácter Efecto especial aplicable a caracteres individuales de un texto. Son ejemplos de efectos de carácter el supraíndice, el subíndice y el tachado. Los efectos de carácter pueden verse en un documento impreso y también en la pantalla. Ver también text effect.

Character style/Estilo de fuente Conjunto con nombre de características de formato aplicables a caracteres individuales, como a una palabra o una letra.

Chart/Gráfica Tipo de gráfica que presenta datos numéricos en forma visual. Ver también *diagram*.

Click/Hacer clic Oprimir y soltar el botón izquierdo del ratón.

Clip art/Arte prediseñado Imagen (también llamada recorte) lista para agregarse a un documento.

Clipboard/Portapapeles Área de la memoria de la computadora reservada para que Windows almacene temporalmente en ella texto y otros objetos que han sido cortados o copiados de un archivo.

Close button/Botón de cierre Botón situado en la parte superior derecha de una ventana, que la cierra.

Color scheme/Combinación de colores Los ocho colores que se usan en el diseño de una presentación de PowerPoint: colores para el fondo, fuentes, hipervínculos, etc. La combinación de colores de una presentación varía según la plantilla de diseño que se use en la presentación.

Column/Columna Hilera vertical de celdas identificada mediante un rótulo alfabético situado en la parte superior de la columna.

Comment/Comentario
1. En Word, pequeños globos que aparecen al margen de un documento y que contienen observaciones o sugerencias.
2. En PowerPoint, cuadro de texto especial de una presentación en el que el revisor inserta una nota. El comentario incluye la fecha en que el revisor escribió el comentario, así como el nombre del usuario registrado de la computadora del revisor. Ver también *comment marker*.

Comment marker/Marcador de comentario Icono de una presentación de PowerPoint que se parece a una nota adhesiva, e indica que el revisor ha hecho un comentario. Comparar con *change marker*. Ver también *comment*.

Commercial software/Software comercial Programas que se venden en tiendas y sitios de Internet, o que vienen incluidos en los sistemas de computadora nuevos, fabricados normalmente por las grandes compañías de computadoras.

Concatenation/Concatenación Unión de dos valores para mostrarlos como uno solo, por ejemplo, si concatenas un campo de Nombre con un campo de Apellido, como en [Nombre]&[Apellido], los dos nombres se muestran como un nombre completo en un solo campo.

Contact information/Información de contactos Nombres, direcciones de correo electrónico, números de teléfono y otra información básica asociada con las personas y empresas con las que se comunica el usuario. Ver también *Contacts* y *Contacts list*.

Contacts/Contactos Una de las carpetas predeterminadas de Outlook; es la carpeta o herramienta que guarda información de contacto con empresas y personas. Ver también *Inbox, Calendar, Journal, Notes, Tasks* y *Contacts list*.

Contacts list/Lista de contactos Contiene información acerca de las personas y empresas incluidas en la carpeta de Contactos. Ver también *Contacts information* y *Contacts*.

Control/Control Objeto de un formulario o informe de Access que presenta datos, ejecuta una acción o agrega gráficos al formulario o informe (por ejemplo: cuadros de texto, controles de imagen, botones de opción, rótulos, botones de comandos y controles de subformularios).

Copy/Copiar Comando que duplica datos seleccionados o un objeto y los guarda temporalmente en el Portapapeles. El elemento se puede pegar en el mismo archivo o en otro.

Criteria/Criterios Condición limitante, como "Arizona" o ">100", por ejemplo, que se usa en consultas y filtros de Access para mostrar un conjunto limitado de registros.

Custom software (proprietary software)/Software personalizado (software patentado) Programas creados por programadores profesionales para satisfacer las necesidades específicas de una compañía o persona.

Cut/Cortar Comando que quita datos seleccionados o un objeto de un documento y los guarda temporalmente en el Portapapeles. El elemento se puede pegar en el mismo archivo o en otro.

D

Data type/Tipo del dato En Access, propiedad de campo que determina el tipo de datos que el campo puede contener (por ejemplo: Número, Texto, Fecha/Hora o Sí/No).

Database/Base de datos Conjunto de datos relacionados con un tema en particular. Una base de datos de Access es un archivo individual que contiene todas las tablas, consultas, formularios e informes que tienen que ver con ese conjunto de información.

Database object/Objeto de base de datos Tablas, consultas, informes, formularios y otros objetos que son las partes funcionales de una base de datos de Access.

Database window/Ventana de base de datos Ventana que aparece cuando se abre inicialmente una base de datos de Access. La ventana de base de datos ofrece acceso a todos los objetos de una base de datos.

Datasheet/Hoja de datos En Access, datos que se muestran con un formato de filas y columnas en una tabla, consulta o formulario.

Datasheet view/Presentación de hoja de datos En Access, presentación de un objeto que exhibe registros con un formato de filas y columnas semejante al de una hoja de cálculo. La presentación de hoja de datos permite ver muchos registros al mismo tiempo.

Day/Week/Month view/Presentación de Día/Semana/Mes Presentación predeterminada del Calendario de Outlook que permite mostrar el Calendario como día individual, semana laboral de cinco días, semana de siete días o todo un mes.

Decline/Rechazar En Outlook, opción de respuesta a una solicitud de reunión. La solicitud de reunión que se rechaza no se asienta en el Calendario. Contrastar con *accept* y *pro-pose new time*. Ver también *meeting request*.

Delivery options/Opciones de envío En Outlook, recursos de comodidad, como hacer que las respuestas a los mensajes se envíen a otra persona, retasar el envío de mensajes o fijar una fecha de caducidad de mensaje que se puede adjuntar a un mensaje de correo electrónico.

Demote/Degradar En PowerPoint, reducir el nivel de un subtítulo para que tenga una sangría más grande y un tipo de letra más pequeño. Contrastar con *promote*.

Descending sort/Ordenamiento descendente Orden de clasificación que organiza los valores de texto de la Z a la A y los valores numéricos del 10 al 1.

Deselect/Deseleccionar Hacer inactivo un objeto o texto haciendo clic con el botón del ratón o, en el caso de comandos de menú marcados, volver a seleccionarlos para eliminar la marca.

Design template/Plantilla de diseño Archivo que contiene el formato previamente programado disponible para una presentación de PowerPoint, como colores, diseño del fondo, fuentes y puntos elevados.

Design view/Presentación de diseño En Access, presentación de un objeto que permite diseñar y modificar tablas, consultas, formularios, informes y otros objetos.

Desktop/Escritorio Área principal de trabajo en una computadora.

Detailed Address Cards/Tarjetas de dirección en detalle En Outlook, presentación de Contacto que muestra la información en un formato de tarjeta de presentación e incluye campos tales como el título del puesto y el nombre de la compañía.

Diagram/Diagrama Tipo de gráfico que presenta visualmente información conceptual en vez de datos numéricos. Ver también *chart*.

Dialog box/Cuadro de diálogo Cuadro que se abre mediante ciertos comandos de menú, en el que debes elegir opciones o suministrar información para que se ejecute la orden.

Discussion comments/Comentarios de debate Comentarios que se muestran junto con un libro de trabajo de Excel pero se guardan en un servidor de debate. Ver también *discussion server* y *thread*.

Discussion server/Servidor de debate Computadora que guarda comentarios de debate. Ver también *discussion comments*.

Document/Documento En Word, archivo de cualquier longitud que contiene texto u otros objetos. Cartas, historiales, memorandos e informes son ejemplos de documentos comunes.

Double-click/Hacer doble clic Hacer clic rápidamente dos veces con el botón izquierdo del ratón.

Download/Descargar Transferir un archivo de una computadora remota a la computadora personal. En Outlook, recuperar datos o mensajes del servidor hacia la Bandeja de entrada. Ver *upload*.

Drag/Arrastrar Oprimir y mantener oprimido el botón izquierdo del ratón y desplazar el ratón.

Draw program/Programa de dibujo Software de gráficos que usa fórmulas matemáticas para determinar el tamaño y la apariencia de líneas e imágenes, en vez de puntos. Ver también *paint program*.

E

Edit/Editar Hacer cambios a un documento.

E-mail/Correo electrónico Sistema de intercambio de mensajes escritos, orales y visuales, y archivos de computadora, por medio de Internet o de una red. En inglés, e-mail es la abreviación de electronic mail (correo electrónico).

E-mail client/Cliente de correo electrónico Software que permite al usuario enviar y recibir correo electrónico por medio de Internet.

Embed/Insertar Introducir un archivo fuente en un archivo de destino; los cambios que se hagan posteriormente al archivo fuente no se reflejarán en el archivo de destino. Contrastar con *link*.

Embedded font/Fuente insertada Fuente introducida en una presentación de PowerPoint de tal manera que la fuente siempre tendrá la misma apariencia, incluso cuando la presentación se muestre en otra computadora.

Ethernet/Ethernet Red local (LAN, por sus siglas en inglés) estándar que funciona a 10 Mbps. Se usa con topologías de canal y de estrella, cables de par trenzado o de fibra óptica, y una tarjeta de interfaz de red compatible con Ethernet.

Event/Eventos En el Calendario de Outlook, actividad con duración de 24 horas o más o que no tiene hora de inicio específica. Contrastar con *appointment*.

Expansion slots/Ranuras de expansión Parte de la tarjeta madre que permite conectar tarjetas de circuitos con más puertos. Estos puertos permiten al usuario agregar más dispositivos a la computadora.

Export/Exportar Procedimiento que consiste en copiar datos de una tabla o consulta de Access a otra base de datos o un archivo de otro tipo, como una hoja de trabajo de Excel.

Expression/Expresión Fórmula que calcula un valor o define criterios; en Access, una expresión permite calcular valores nuevos o especificar los registros que deberán exhibirse.

F

Fast Ethernet/Ethernet rápida Red local (LAN, por sus siglas en inglés) estándar que funciona a 100 Mbps. Se usa con topologías de canal y de estrella, cables de par trenzado o de fibra óptica, y una tarjeta de interfaz de red compatible con Ethernet.

Field/Campo

1. En Word, separador especial para información cambiante, como la fecha o la hora.

2. En Access, un campo se muestra como una columna en presentación de hoja de datos. Ver también *field code*.

Field code/Código de campo Código subyacente que permite cambiar la información de un campo. Ver también *field*.

Field list/Lista de campos Lista de todos los campos de una tabla o consulta de Access subyacente.

Field name/Nombre de campo Nombre por el que Access reconoce un campo de datos.

Field property/Propiedad de campo Atributo específico de un campo de datos de Access, como nombre, leyenda, tamaño de campo o máscara de entradas.

File/Archivo Conjunto de datos o información que se guarda y se almacena bajo un nombre.

File format/Formato de archivo Ver *file type*.

File server/Servidor de archivos Computadora de una red que guarda datos que se comparten con otras computadoras de la red.

File type/Tipo de archivo Patrones de programa que se usan para guardar datos en un disco. El tipo de archivo se identifica mediante una extensión de archivo de tres letras. Dos ejemplos de tipos de archivo son documento de Word (.doc) y formato de texto enriquecido (.rtf). También se conoce como *file format* o formato de archivo.

Fill handle/Controlador de relleno En Excel, pequeño cuadrado negro situado en la esquina inferior derecha de una celda o intervalo seleccionado, que sirve para copiar un valor o fórmula en celdas adyacentes.

Filter/Filtrar

1. En Excel, recurso que permite mostrar un subconjunto de datos en una lista de hoja de trabajo. Ver también *AutoFilter*.

2. En Access, uno o más criterios aplicables a una hoja de datos para mostrar un subconjunto de registros. Los registros que no satisfacen el criterio se "eliminan por filtrado" y no se muestran en el subconjunto de registros. Ver también *Filter By Selection* y *Filter By Form*.

Filter By Form/Filtrar por formulario En Access, técnica de filtrado en la que se incorporan los valores que se desea filtrar mediante un formulario que contiene todos los campos de la hoja de datos.

Filter By Selection/Filtrar por selección En Access, técnica de filtrado en la que se selecciona un valor o valor parcial que se desea filtrar mediante el botón de Filtrar por selección.

Find/Buscar Comando que busca un texto o formato específico en un documento. Ver también *Replace*.

Find and Advanced Find/Buscar y Búsqueda avanzada En Outlook, recursos que permiten buscar mensajes que contengan una palabra o frase, de o para una persona específica, o por categorías asignadas, leídos/no leídos, importancia o archivos adjuntos.

Flash memory/Memoria instantánea Tipo de memoria desmontable, de uso común en aparatos de mano pequeños, como teléfonos celulares, cámaras digitales y reproductores digitales de música.

Folder/Carpeta Lugar de la computadora donde se guardan archivos y otras carpetas.

Folder List/Lista de carpetas En Outlook, lista de las carpetas disponibles en el buzón; herramienta que sirve para navegar entre diversos elementos de Outlook.

Font/Fuente Conjunto completo de caracteres alfabéticos que incluye letras, números, signos de puntuación y símbolos, y que se basa en un mismo diseño peculiar.

Font style/Estilo de fuente Efecto especial aplicable a caracteres de texto. Son ejemplos de estilos de fuente las negritas, las cursivas y el subrayado.

Footer/Pie de página Renglón de texto que aparece al final de cada una de las páginas de un archivo y que contiene información como el nombre del documento, un número de página o la fecha. Ver también *header*.

Form/Formulario Objeto de base de datos de Access que contiene controles para incorporar, editar y mostrar datos tomados de una tabla o consulta subyacente.

Form view/Presentación de formulario En Access, presentación de objetos, que por lo general muestra un registro a la vez, con elementos gráficos adicionales que facilitan la lectura. Esta presentación es conveniente para incorporar y editar datos en tablas.

Formatting/Dar formato Hacer cambios a la apariencia de un documento.

Formula/Fórmula En Excel, entrada de celda que realiza cálculos.

Formula Bar/Barra de fórmulas Barra blanca larga situada encima de los encabezados de las columnas de una hoja de trabajo de Excel, que sirve para incorporar o editar datos de celda. La Barra de fórmulas muestra el contenido de la celda activa.

Forward/Reenviar En Outlook, enviar a otra persona una copia de un mensaje de correo electrónico recibido.

Free/busy time/Tiempo libre/ocupado En el Calendario de Outlook, segmentos de tiempo, marcados como disponibles (indicados como libres) o no disponibles (indicados como ocupados), de personas que ponen su Calendario a disposición en un lugar compartido, a fin de que otras personas puedan organizar reuniones sobre la base del tiempo libre de los asistentes. Outlook muestra en el Calendario las horas libres y ocupadas en colores y con dibujos. Para usar este recurso se necesita el Servidor de Intercambio de Microsoft o el servicio de Libre/Ocupado en Internet de Office de Microsoft.

Freeware/Freeware Software cuyos creadores han registrado sus derechos de autor y lo ponen a disposición del público gratuitamente.

Freeze panes/Inmovilizar paneles Recurso de Excel que permite inmovilizar filas y columnas situadas encima y a la izquierda de la celda seleccionada para que permanezcan fijas mientras se desplaza la hoja de trabajo.

Function/Función Fórmula previamente definida en Excel que ejecuta una operación específica integrada.

Global Address List/Lista general de direcciones En Outlook, lista de direcciones de correo electrónico disponibles dentro de una organización cuando se usa el Servidor de Intercambio de Microsoft o el servicio de Libre/Ocupado en Internet de Office de Microsoft. Un administrador de red se encarga del mantenimiento de estas direcciones, y los usuarios de la red pueden verlas. Ver también *Outlook Address Book* y *Personal Address Book*.

Grammar checker/Revisor de gramática Herramienta de edición que revisa la gramática usada en un archivo, resalta los posibles errores y sugiere una o varias formas de corregir los errores. Ver también *spelling checker*.

Graphical user interface (GUI)/Interfaz gráfica con el usuario Diseño de la parte de un sistema operativo en la que el usuario usa típicamente un ratón para apuntar y hacer clic sobre iconos gráficos que representan archivos, carpetas, discos y programas.

H

Hard drive/Disco duro Dispositivo de almacenamiento no desmontable que sirve para guardar software y datos en un sistema de computadora.

Hardware/Hardware Partes físicas de un sistema de computadora; incluyen dispositivos de entrada, salida, almacenamiento y de otros tipos.

Header/Encabezado Renglón de texto que aparece en la parte superior de cada una de las páginas de un archivo y que contiene información como el nombre del documento, un número de página o la fecha. Ver también *footer*.

Hierarchy/Jerarquía Sistema organizado por rango o nivel. En una computadora, es el sistema de organización de archivos en carpetas que se inicia con una carpeta raíz situada en la parte superior de una unidad de disco.

Highlight/Resaltado Fondo colorido que se aplica al texto seleccionado.

Horizontal application software/Software de aplicación horizontal Software proyectado para diversos propósitos, como programas de procesamiento de texto o gráficos.

HTML format/Formato HTML En Outlook, es el formato de mensajes predeterminado que usa el mismo lenguaje con el que se crean páginas de Internet. El formato HTML admite todos los formatos de mensaje (como fuentes, numeración, puntos elevados, alineación, firmas y gráficos), y permite ver el mensaje con el explorador de Internet. Comparar con *Outlook Rich Text Format* y *Text Only Format*.

Hyperlink/Hipervínculo Texto o gráfico con formato especial que, cuando se hace clic sobre él, conecta con otro lugar (habitualmente una página o sitio de Internet). En los recursos de ayuda de las aplicaciones, los hipervínculos de texto suministran información adicional. También se les llama links o vínculos.

Hypertext Markup Language (HTML)/Lenguaje de marcado de hipertexto Código subyacente que determina la apariencia y el comportamiento de los documentos de Internet cuando son vistos con un explorador de Internet.

I

Icon/Icono Imagen pequeña que representa programas u otros elementos.

Import/Importar Procedimiento que consiste en copiar datos de otra fuente, como una base de datos o una hoja de cálculo, en una base de datos abierta de Access.

Importance level/Nivel de importancia En Outlook, opciones de mensaje (como Alta, Baja y Normal) que indican la prioridad del mensaje.

Inbox/Bandeja de entrada Una de las carpetas predeterminada de Outlook; permite recibir, leer, redactar, enviar, guardar y organizar los mensajes de correo electrónico. Ver también *Calendar, Contacts, Journal, Notes* y *Tasks*.

Indent/Sangría Espacio que se deja entre un párrafo y el margen derecho o izquierdo.

Indent level/Nivel de sangría En PowerPoint, número que indica la sangría y la importancia de un subtítulo respecto al título.

Input device/Dispositivo de entrada Todo dispositivo que acepta datos del usuario, como un teclado o un ratón.

Input mask/Máscara de entradas En Access, propiedad de campo que determina el formato de exhibición y limita el tipo de datos que se pueden incorporar; permite incorporar datos con más rapidez y precisión.

Insert mode/Modo de inserción Método de inserción de texto en un archivo por el que se desplazan los caracteres ya existentes a la derecha en vez de escribir sobre ellos. Ver también *overtype mode*.

Insertion point/Punto de inserción Línea vertical parpadeante que muestra la posición actual en un documento.

Integrated program/Programa integrado Software que combina las funciones de dos o más programas, como funciones de procesamiento de texto, funciones de hoja de cálculo y funciones de gestión de base de datos, en un solo programa.

Internet/Internet Sistema de alcance mundial que conecta entre sí miles de redes individuales. Estas conexiones permiten que una computadora de una red se comunique con prácticamente cualquier otra computadora de la red que sea.

Internet service provider (ISP)/Proveedor de servicios de Internet Compañía que proporciona acceso a Internet a personas y compañías, por lo general a cambio de una cuota.

Intranet/Intranet Red privada pequeña que permite a los usuarios comunicarse y tener acceso a archivos como si estuviesen usando Internet.

J

Journal/Diario Una de las carpetas predeterminadas de Outlook; es la carpeta o herramienta que busca automáticamente las actividades relacionadas con un contacto y las exhibe en una línea cronológica. Ver también *Inbox, Calendar, Contacts, Notes* y *Tasks*.

Junction table/Tabla de unión En Access, tabla que suministra un vínculo entre dos tablas que tienen entre sí una relación de muchos a muchos; la tabla de unión tiene una relación de uno a muchos con cada una de las tablas que vincula.

L

Label/Rótulo Entrada de texto en una hoja de trabajo de Excel.

Landscape orientation/Orientación horizontal Orientación de página en la que el texto se imprime a lo largo de la dimensión más ancha de la página. Ver también *portrait orientation*.

Line spacing/Interlineado Cantidad de espacio vertical que separa los renglones de un párrafo. Ver también *paragraph spacing*.

Link/Vínculo Conexión que se establece entre un archivo fuente y un archivo de destino o entre dos tablas; los cambios efectuados posteriormente al archivo fuente se reflejan en el archivo de destino. Contrastar con *embeded*. Ver también *hyperlink*.

Linux/Linux Sistema operativo basado en Unix que permite a cualquier programador hacerle mejoras, y que está disponible como freeware.

Liquid crystal display (LCD) projector/Proyector de pantalla de cristal líquido Equipo que permite proyectar las diapositivas de una presentación de PowerPoint en la modalidad de presentación desde la computadora, sobre una pared o una pantalla grande de video.

Local area network (LAN)/Red de área local Sistema en el que computadoras próximas entre sí se conectan unas con otras para compartir impresoras, datos y otros recursos.

LocalTalk/LocalTalk Patrón de red local (LAN, por sus siglas en inglés) que se usa para conectar computadoras Apple.

Log on/Identificación Procedimiento por el que el usuario se identifica ante un sistema de computadora o red, por lo general tecleando el nombre y la contraseña. Le indica al sistema o red quién es el usuario y qué programas o archivos está autorizado a usar.

Lookup field/Campo de búsqueda En Access, campo que examina una lista de valores en otra tabla o en una lista estática, y presenta la lista de valores para que el usuario seleccione los datos a ingresar.

M

MacOS/MacOS Sistema operativo de la línea de sistemas de computadoras Macintosh.

Main form/Formulario principal En Access, el formulario grande de un formulario principal/subformulario, que contiene la tabla de datos primaria y exhibe un registro individual.

Main/subform/Formulario principal/subformulario En Access, el formulario en el que se combinan dos formularios: uno para la tabla de datos primaria y otra, insertada, para la tabla de datos relacionada.

Mainframe/Computadora central Sistema de computadora que usan las grandes organizaciones, que admite muchos usuarios y bases de datos grandes.

Many-to-many relationship/Relación de muchos a muchos En Access, relación entre dos tablas en la que cada tabla puede tener muchos registros relacionados en la otra tabla.

Margin/Margen Espacio en blanco a lo largo del borde de una página donde no se imprime texto. Todos los documentos tienen un margen superior, uno inferior, uno derecho y uno izquierdo, los cuales pueden ser de igual o diferente anchura.

Maximize button/Botón de maximizar Botón de la esquina superior derecha de una ventana que agranda la ventana.

Meeting request/Solicitud de reunión En Outlook, actividad del Calendario a la que se invita a personas y/o recursos. Ver también *accept* y *decline*.

Menu/Menú Lista de comandos organizados bajo un encabezado común.

Menu bar/Barra de menús Barra, que habitualmente aparece debajo de la barra de título de una ventana, que presenta una lista de menús por su nombre y ofrece acceso a ellos.

Merge/Unir En Excel, acción que combina las celdas seleccionadas en una sola celda. Ver también *split*.

Metropolitan area network (MAN)/Red metropolitana Sistema de formación de redes en el que se conectan dos o más redes locales (LANs, por sus siglas en inglés) de una misma región mediante los servicios de compañías telefónicas o de telecomunicaciones.

Minicomputer/Minicomputadora Sistema de computadora más pequeño y menos poderoso que una computadora central, pero capaz de admitir varios usuarios de una organización pequeña o mediana.

Minimize button/Botón de minimizar Botón en la esquina superior derecha de una ventana que reduce la ventana y la inactiva.

Modem/Módem Dispositivo de entrada/salida que convierte las señales digitales provenientes de una computadora en señales analógicas, las cuales se pueden transmitir de ida y vuelta por líneas telefónicas.

Motherboard/Tarjeta madre Circuito principal que contiene la unidad central de procesamiento (CPU, por sus siglas en inglés), la memoria y las ranuras de expansión de una computadora.

N

Nethics/Nética Ética que debe regir en las redes y en el correo electrónico. Comparar con *netiquette*.

Netiquette/Netiqueta Etiqueta que debe regir en las redes y en el correo electrónico; conjunto de reglas que incluyen comunicarse con un lenguaje claro, ser respetuoso y sensible ante posibles malas interpretaciones, y aplicar la "regla de oro": envía mensajes de correo electrónico como los que quieres que te envíen a ti. Comparar con *nethics*.

Network interface card (NIC)/Tarjeta de interfaz de red Dispositivo que regula el flujo de datos entre la memoria de acceso aleatorio (RAM, por sus siglas en inglés) de una computadora y un cable de red.

Network operating system (NOS)/Sistema operativo de red Software de sistemas que administra una red local estableciendo y manteniendo las conexiones entre los nodos y el servidor de archivos.

Node/Nodo Dispositivo acoplado a una red, como una computadora o una impresora.

Note/Nota En Outlook, herramienta que le permite al usuario registrar información acerca de una llamada telefónica, recordatorios de una próxima reunión, ideas acerca de un informe, o cualquier cosa que normalmente anotaría en papel. Ver también *Notes*.

Notes/Notas Una de las carpetas predeterminadas de Outlook; es la carpeta que permite elaborar notas electrónicas que sirven como recordatorios u otra información para uso posterior. Ver también *Calendar, Contacts, Inbox, Journal* y *Tasks*.

O

Object/Objeto En PowerPoint, elemento que no es texto, como una gráfica, tabla, imagen de arte prediseñado, dibujo, fotografía, video clip u otro tipo de información.

Object area/Área de objeto Separador de una diapositiva de PowerPoint que reserva espacio para objetos como tablas, gráficas o imágenes gráficas. Comparar con *text area* y *title area*.

One-to-many relationship/Relación de uno a muchos En Access, relación entre dos tablas en la que una de ellas (la tabla primaria) puede tener muchos registros relacionados en la otra tabla (la tabla relacionada).

One-to-one relationship/Relación de uno a uno En Access, relación entre dos tablas en la que cada una tiene un solo registro relacionado en la otra tabla.

Online broadcast/Difusión en línea Herramienta de PowerPoint que permite a los integrantes del público ver una presentación en sus respectivas computadoras usando sus exploradores de Internet.

Online services/Servicios en línea Compañías que brindan acceso directo a información que se mantiene fuera de Internet, como "salas de conferencias", almacenes de compras en línea y cotizaciones de acciones.

Operating system (OS)/Sistema operativo Programa de software que supervisa y regula todo lo que ocurre mientras una computadora permanece encendida, como ejecutar las aplicaciones, administrar el hardware y dar mantenimiento al almacenamiento de archivos.

Organization chart/Diagrama de organización Diagrama que presenta de forma visual la estructura de los departamentos o del personal de una organización.

Orphan/Huérfanos En Access, registros de una tabla relacionada (del lado de los "muchos" de una relación) que quedan sin relación si su registro relacionado de la tabla primaria (del lado del "uno" de la relación) se borra o se modifica de modo que la relación se rompa.

Outlook Address Book/Libreta de direcciones de Outlook Lugar donde se guarda información sobre contactos. La Libreta de direcciones de Outlook puede incluir una lista general de direcciones, una lista de contactos y una libreta de direcciones personal. Ver además *Global Address List* y *Personal Address List.*

Outlook Bar/Barra de Outlook Herramienta de navegación que incluye grupos como funciones rápidas de Outlook u otras funciones rápidas, y que permite al usuario vincularse con otros elementos dentro de Outlook.

Outlook Rich Text Format/Formato de texto enriquecido de Outlook Formato de archivo que sólo ciertos programas de Office de Microsoft entienden, y que admite formatos de texto como puntos elevados y alineación. Comparar con *HTML format* y *Text Only format.*

Outlook Today/Outlook hoy Página que muestra un resumen de las citas del día, la lista de tareas completa y cuántos mensajes de correo electrónico nuevos aguardan en la Bandeja de entrada. Si se desea, se puede fijar Outlook hoy como página predeterminada de Outlook.

Output device/Dispositivo de salida Parte del sistema de computadora que muestra información al usuario, como un monitor o una impresora.

Overtype mode/Modo de sobreescritura Método para insertar texto en un archivo escribiendo nuevos caracteres sobre los ya existentes. Ver también *insert mode.*

P

Page break/Salto de página Marcador que indica el final de una página y el comienzo de otra.

Paint program/Programa de pintura Software de gráficos que crea imágenes con puntos en vez de fórmulas matemáticas. Ver también *draw program.*

Pane/Panel Sección de una ventana.

Paragraph/Párrafo Todo texto que va seguido de una marca de párrafo (¶).

Paragraph spacing/Espacio entre párrafos Cantidad de espacio vertical entre párrafos. Ver también *line spacing.*

Paragraph style/Estilo de párrafo Conjunto de características de formato, con nombre, aplicable a uno o más párrafos en su totalidad.

Password/Contraseña Serie de caracteres conocidos sólo por el usuario y que, junto con su nombre, protege un sistema de computadora o red contra uso no autorizado.

Paste/Pegar Comando que inserta texto o un objeto del Portapapeles en un documento. Ver también *Cut* y *Copy.*

Personal Address Book/Libreta de direcciones personal En Outlook, lugar donde se guardan los contactos y las listas de distribución personales para mantenerlas separadas de los contactos de negocios. Ver también *Global Address Book* y *Outlook Address Book.*

Physical media/Medios físicos Cables o conexiones inalámbricas que transmiten datos en una red.

Placeholder/Separador

1. En Word, texto con formato dentro de un archivo de plantilla que se puede sustituir por otro propio texto. Ver también *template.*

2. En PowerPoint, lugar fijado previamente que reserva espacio para un elemento de diapositiva.

Platform/Plataforma Combinación de hardware y sistema operativo que define los tipos de programas y dispositivos que admite la computadora.

Point/1. Punto; 2. Apuntar

1. Unidad de medida que se aplica a las fuentes y al espacio entre pá-rrafos. Un punto es igual a 1/72 de pulgada.

2. Desplazar el ratón para situar el puntero sobre un objeto.

Pointer/Apuntador Icono con forma de flecha que aparece en la pantalla de una computadora.

Portrait orientation/Orientación vertical Orientación de página en la que el texto se imprime a lo largo de la dimensión más corta de la página. Ver también *landscape orientation.*

POST (Power-On Self Test)/POST (Autoprueba con corriente) Programa integrado que comprueba que el hardware de la computadora esté funcionando correctamente.

Presentation/Presentación Informe formal o informal que por lo general se expone oralmente y al que se suele llamar “presentación” o “discurso”.

Preview Pane/Panel de vista previa En Outlook, panel que permite leer un mensaje seleccionado, abrir datos adjuntos y responder a solicitudes de reunión sin abrir propiamente el mensaje.

Primary key/Clave primaria En Access, uno o más campos de una tabla cuyos valores identifican de forma individual cada registro.

Primary table/Tabla primaria En Access, la tabla que está en el lado del "uno" de una relación de uno a muchos.

Print Preview/Vista preliminar de impresión Visualización de un documento que muestra cómo se verá éste una vez impreso.

Print titles/Títulos de impresión Rótulos de fila o columna repetidos que aparecen en todas las páginas de una hoja de trabajo de Excel.

Professional workstation/Estación de trabajo profesional Sistema de computación más pequeño que una minicomputadora pero más poderoso que la mayoría de las computadoras personales.

Program suite/Suite de programas Paquete de programas de aplicación autónoma diseñado para trabajar de forma independiente, pero capaces de compartir datos con facilidad.

Promote/Promover En PowerPoint, elevar el nivel de un subtítulo para que tenga una sangría más pequeña (o no la tenga) y un tipo de letra más grande. Contrastar con *demote*.

Propose new time/Proponer otra hora En Outlook, opción que se tiene al responder a una solicitud de reunión. Si una reunión no es compatible con el programa de actividades, se puede seleccionar Proponer otra hora y elegir una nueva hora. Con esta opción, la hora original de la reunión se incluye en el Calendario como tentativa. Contrastar con *accept* y *decline*. Ver también *meeting request*.

Protocols/Protocolos Conjunto de reglas que describen cómo se comunican unos con otros los diversos dispositivos de una red.

Publish/Publicar Guardar una presentación de PowerPoint como un conjunto de páginas de Internet en un servidor de Intranet o de Internet, lo que permite a otras personas abrir la presentación y navegar en ella con sus exploradores de Internet.

Q

Query/Consulta En Access, objeto de la base de datos que muestra los datos específicos con los que deseas trabajar. Los datos pueden tomarse de tablas relacionadas de forma múltiple, se les puede aplicar varios filtros y pueden incluir expresiones calculadas.

R

Random access memory (RAM)/ Memoria de acceso aleatorio Memoria de trabajo primaria de una computadora que guarda información de forma temporal mientras la computadora está encendida. La unidad central de procesamiento (CPU, por sus siglas en inglés) trabaja con información que se guarda en la Memoria de acceso aleatorio (RAM, por sus siglas en inglés).

Range/Intervalo Celda o grupo de celdas que se seleccionan en una hoja de trabajo de Excel.

Read-only memory (ROM)/Memoria sólo de lectura Parte del almacenamiento primario de una computadora que guarda información de forma permanente, incluso cuando la computadora está apagada.

Record/Registro En Access, conjunto de información relacionada, como información sobre el nombre y domicilio de un cliente, o detalles acerca de un producto.

Record selector/Seleccionador de registros En Access, el cuadro gris que aparece al lado izquierdo de cada registro en la presentación de Hoja de datos o de Formulario. Se hace clic con el ratón en el seleccionador de registros para seleccionar todo el registro.

Recurring/Recurrentes En Outlook, citas o eventos de Calendario que se presentan más de una vez a intervalos fijos.

Referential integrity/Integridad referencial Sistema de reglas que Access aplica para asegurar que las relaciones entre registros de tablas relacionadas sean válidas, y que el usuario no borre o modifique accidentalmente datos relacionados.

Related table/Tabla relacionada En Access, la tabla del lado de los "muchos" de una relación de uno a muchos.

Relational database/Base de datos relacional Tipo de base de datos en la que la información se guarda en tablas separadas pero relacionadas, lo que permite un almacenamiento y recuperación de datos más eficiente y no redundante.

Relationship/Relación En Access, asociación entre dos tablas que comparten un campo con valores concordantes; los campos concordantes permiten unir las tablas de modo que una consulta pueda seleccionar datos de ambas tablas.

Relative reference/Referencia relativa En Excel, referencia de celda en una fórmula que se ajusta automáticamente a la nueva ubicación cuando se copia la fórmula en otra celda o intervalo. Ver también *absolute reference*.

Replace/Reemplazar Comando que busca un texto o formato específico en un documento y lo sustituye por un nuevo texto o formato especificado por el usuario. Ver también *Find*.

Reply/Responder Enviar un mensaje de respuesta al remitente del mensaje (la persona indicada en el renglón From o De).

Reply to All/Responder a todos Enviar un mensaje de respuesta al remitente y a todos los que recibieron una copia del mensaje original (las personas indicadas en los renglones To o Para, CC y From o De).

Report/Informe En Access, objeto de la base de datos que presenta datos organizados y con formato de acuerdo con las especificaciones del usuario.

Resource/Recurso Sala de conferencias, computadora u otro equipo que los usuarios de Outlook pueden programar para una reunión. Para programar recursos es necesario que Outlook se utilice con el Servidor de intercambio de Microsoft o el servicio de Libre/Ocupado en Internet de Office de Microsoft.

Restore Down button/Botón de restaurar Botón situado en la esquina superior derecha de una ventana, que devuelve a la ventana el tamaño que tenía antes de ser maximizada.

Rich Text Format (RTF)/Formato de texto enriquecido Formato de archivo que lleva la extensión .rtf y que permite que el texto del archivo sea transferido y leído por diferentes aplicaciones; casi todos los programas de procesamiento de texto pueden leer el RTF.

Right-click/Hacer clic con el botón derecho Hacer clic con el botón derecho del ratón.

Right-drag/Derecho-arrastrar Oprimir y mantener oprimido el botón derecho del ratón mientras se desplaza el ratón.

Ring topology/Topología de anillo Organización de red en la que las computadoras se conectan en círculo, haciendo pasar un conjunto especial de datos, o señal, de una computadora a la siguiente para establecer quién puede transmitir datos.

Row/Fila En Excel, hilera horizontal de celdas identificada mediante un número de fila que aparece en el extremo izquierdo de la fila.

S

Save/Guardar Almacenar un documento en un disco como archivo con nombre.

ScreenTip/Consejo de pantalla Recurso de ayuda que proporciona información acerca de elementos que aparecen en la pantalla.

Scroll arrow/Flecha de desplazamiento Flecha situada en el extremo de una barra de desplazamiento, sobre la que se puede hacer clic para mover el documento hacia arriba, abajo, a la izquierda o a la derecha en pequeños incrementos.

Scroll bars/Barras de desplazamiento Barras que habitualmente aparecen a la derecha y en la parte inferior de una ventana y que sirven para navegar por el contenido de la ventana.

Scroll box/Cuadro de desplazamiento Cuadro que aparece en el centro de una barra de desplazamiento y que se puede arrastrar para mover el documento tanto como el usuario desee.

Sections/Secciones Parte de un formulario o informe de Access que contiene un tipo de datos específico, como un encabezado, un pie de página o una sección de detalles.

Select/Seleccionar Elegir un menú, un comando u otro elemento; señalar un objeto o texto a fin de trabajar con él.

Select query/Consulta de selección Es el tipo más común de consulta en Access; la consulta de selección recupera datos específicos de una o más tablas y muestra los resultados en una hoja de datos; sin embargo, no altera los datos de la tabla o tablas. Se pueden ordenar y resumir los resultados de una consulta de selección, así como realizar cálculos en los campos de una consulta de este tipo.

Sensitivity level/Nivel de sensibilidad En Outlook, opciones (como Normal, Personal, Privado o Confidencial) que indican la sensibilidad del contenido del mensaje.

Shading/Sombreado Fondo gris o de color que se puede colocar detrás de un párrafo o un grupo de párrafos.

Shareware/Shareware Software que normalmente se distribuye por medio de Internet y que los usuarios pueden probar gratuitamente; sin embargo, se espera que paguen a su autor si se proponen usar el software o desean sus recursos adicionales.

Signature Picker/Firmas Lista de Outlook donde se guardan las firmas.

Signature/Firma En Outlook, información almacenada (como el nombre, título y número telefónico) que sirve para identificar al usuario en un mensaje de correo electrónico.

Slide layout/Distribución de diapositiva Combinación específica de separadores en una diapositiva de PowerPoint, que reservan espacio para texto y/o elementos gráficos.

Slide master/Patrón de diapositivas Diapositiva oculta en toda presentación de PowerPoint que guarda las especificaciones de la plantilla de diseño —como tamaño y posición de los separadores, estilos de puntos elevados, estilos y tamaños de fuentes y color de fondo— de todas las diapositivas salvo la de título. El patrón de diapositivas permite hacer cambios a toda la presentación. Comparar con *title master*.

Spelling checker/Ortografía Herramienta de edición que revisa la ortografía de un archivo, resalta las palabras que podrían estar mal escritas y sugiere una o más sustituciones. Ver también *grammar checker*.

Split/Dividir
1. En Word, acción que divide una celda de tabla individual en dos o más celdas más pequeñas.
2. En Excel, acción que convierte de nuevo una celda unida en celdas individuales. Ver también *merge*.

Splitter bar/Barra divisoria En PowerPoint, una de las barras angostas que separan los paneles izquierdo, de diapositiva y de notas en la visualización normal.

Star topology/Topología de estrella Organización de red en la que cada uno de los nodos se conecta a un centro o conmutador, a través del cual los datos viajan hacia un servidor de archivos y a otras computadoras.

Stationery/Papelería En Outlook, conjunto de elementos de diseño, como fuentes, puntos elevados, color de fondo e imágenes que se pueden aplicar a los mensajes.

Status bar/Barra de estado Barra que aparece en la parte inferior de una ventana de aplicación y que indica lo que el programa está haciendo en ese momento. También indica en qué parte del documento se trabaja y da información adicional, según el programa del que se trate.

Streaming media/Flujo de medios Tecnología de envío por Internet que permite ver datos de video y oír datos de audio como flujo continuo y casi de inmediato.

Style/Estilo Conjunto de características de formato con nombre. Ver también *paragraph style* y *character style*.

Subdatasheet/Subhoja de datos En Access, hoja de datos anidada dentro de otra hoja de datos; contiene registros relacionados con los registros de la hoja de datos en la que está insertada.

Subform/Subformulario En Access, formulario insertado en una combinación de formulario principal/subformulario que muestra una tabla de varios registros relacionados.

Subtitle/Subtítulo En PowerPoint, todo texto en una o dos columnas, o elemento de lista con puntos elevados, que sigue al título y proporciona más detalles acerca del título. Comparar con *title*.

Supercomputer/Supercomputadora Computadora más rápida y poderosa que una mainframe o computadora central. Las grandes instituciones de investigación o los organismos gubernamentales que necesitan gran capacidad de procesamiento usan supercomputadoras.

Syntax/Sintaxis Estructura para capturar funciones y comandos; incluye ortografía, puntuación y palabras clave aceptables.

System boot (booting)/Carga inicial del sistema (secuencia de arranque) Encender la computadora, ejecutar el POST y cargar el sistema operativo.

System software/Software de sistema Software necesario para el funcionamiento y mantenimiento de un sistema de computadora; incluye los sistemas operativos y programas utilitarios.

System unit/Unidad de sistema Caja que contiene los circuitos internos principales de una computadora, como la tarjeta madre, las unidades de disco y la fuente de energía.

T

Tab/Tabulador Espacio con el que se sangra un texto respecto al margen izquierdo. En Word, los tabuladores se fijan en la regla horizontal.

Tab order/Orden de tabulador En Access, orden en el que el foco se desplaza de un control a otro en un formulario cuando se oprime la tecla de tabulador.

Tab scrolling buttons/Botones de desplazamiento de ceja En Excel, botones que aparecen a la izquierda de las cejas de hoja y que permiten desplazarse a la hoja de trabajo previa, siguiente o última de un libro de trabajo.

Tab split bar/Barra de división de cejas En Excel, barra vertical gris, inmediatamente a la izquierda de la barra de desplazamiento horizontal, que se arrastra hacia la derecha para ver las cejas de hoja ocultas.

Table/Tabla

1. En Word, cuadrícula formada por filas horizontales y columnas verticales, que sirve para ordenar información de ciertos tipos.

2. En Access, conjunto de datos del mismo asunto o tema. Los datos se guardan en registros (filas) y campos (columnas).

Task/Tarea En Outlook, quehacer personal o relacionado con el trabajo que puedes seguir en una lista electrónica de pendientes hasta completarlo. Ver *Tasks*.

Taskbar/Barra de tareas Barra de herramientas que normalmente se muestra en la parte inferior del escritorio, y que indica los programas, archivos y recursos en uso.

TaskPad/Cuaderno de tareas Lista de tareas que se muestra en el Calendario de Outlook. Ver *Tasks* y *Task list*.

Tasks/Tareas Una de las carpetas predeterminadas de Outlook; es la carpeta que permite elaborar una lista electrónica de pendientes. Ver también *Inbox, Calendar, Contacts, Journal* y *Notes*.

Task list/Lista de tareas En Outlook, lugar donde se puede seguir electrónicamente la lista de pendientes. La lista aparece en la carpeta de Tareas y en el Cuaderno de tareas del Calendario. Ver también *Tasks* y *Task Pad*.

Task owner/Propietario de tarea En Outlook, cuando se recibe y acepta una solicitud de tarea, la tarea se incorpora a la lista de tareas y el usuario se convierte en el propietario de la tarea. Sólo el propietario de la tarea puede hacer cambios o actualizaciones en esa tarea. Ver *Task, Task list, Task request* y *Tasks*.

Task pane/Panel de tareas Panel de una aplicación de Office que contiene una lista de comandos.

Task request/Solicitud de tarea En Outlook, tarea que se crea y envía a otra persona por medio del correo electrónico. Cuando se crea una solicitud de tarea, se puede guardar una copia de la tarea en la lista de tareas y también se puede recibir un informe de estado cuando la tarea está terminada.

Telecommunications/Telecomunicaciones Tecnología de comunicación electrónica a larga distancia.

Template/Plantilla Archivo que contiene formatos, texto o fórmulas básicas y que se puede ajustar a la medida de las necesidades para crear un archivo nuevo. Ver también *place holder*.

Text area/Área de texto En PowerPoint, un separador que reserva espacio para un subtítulo o una lista numerada o con puntos elevados. Comparar con *object area* y *title area*.

Text effect/Efecto de texto Efecto especial que se aplica a uno o más caracteres de un texto. Dos ejemplos de efectos de texto son el texto brillante y el texto chispeante. Los efectos de texto se ven en la pantalla pero no aparecen en el documento impreso. Ver también *character effect*.

Text Only format/Formato de sólo texto En Outlook, formato de archivo que todos los programas de correo electrónico entienden y que guarda el contenido de un mensaje pero no conserva su formato. Comparar con HTML format y Outlook Rich Text Format.

Thesaurus/Sinónimos En Word, herramienta de idioma que suministra definiciones y una lista de sinónimos de la palabra seleccionada.

Thread/Hilo Conjunto de comentarios y respuestas de una discusión, agrupados y mostrados en orden jerárquico. Ver también *discussion comments*.

Thumbnail/Miniatura Visualización de tamaño reducido de una diapositiva de presentación de PowerPoint. Las miniaturas aparecen en la ceja de Diapositivas, en la visualización de ordenamiento de diapositivas y en diversos paneles de tareas.

Time management/Administración del tiempo Capacidad para organizar, asignar prioridades y desempeñar responsabilidades eficazmente con una actitud positiva.

Timeline/Orden cronológico En el Diario de Outlook, tipo de visualización que presenta los elementos en relación con el tiempo.

Title/Título En PowerPoint, tema principal de una presentación o diapositiva; es el primer renglón de texto en una diapositiva. Comparar con *subtitle*. Ver también *title slide*.

Title area/Área de título En PowerPoint, separador que reserva espacio para el título de una diapositiva. Comparar con *object area* y *text area*.

Title bar/Barra de título Barra que aparece en la parte superior de una ventana y que muestra el título del documento.

Title master/Patrón de título Diapositiva oculta en toda presentación de PowerPoint que guarda especificaciones de la plantilla de diseño —como tamaño y posición de los separadores, estilos de viñetas, estilos y tamaños de fuentes y color de fondo— de todas las diapositivas que usan la distribución de Diapositiva de título. Comparar con *slide master*.

Title slide/Diapositiva de título Primera diapositiva de una presentación de PowerPoint que muestra el tema principal de la presentación. Ver también *title*.

Token Ring/Estafeta en anillo Patrón de red local que usa una topología de anillo y transfiere datos a razón de 4 a 16 Mbps.

Toolbar/Barra de herramientas Barra que contiene iconos (botones) de comandos de uso frecuente.

Toolbox/Caja de herramientas En Access, la barra de herramientas flotante que contiene los botones para crear controles en la visualización de Diseño de formularios o informes; también se llama Controls Toolbox o Caja de herramientas de controles.

Transition/Transición Forma de sustitución de una diapositiva por otra durante una presentación de PowerPoint.

U

Unbound control/Control no ligado En Access, control que no está ligado a un campo específico de una consulta o tabla; sirve para mostrar información general o para efectuar cálculos con los valores de otros controles en un formulario o informe.

Upload/Cargar
1. Transferir un archivo de una computadora a una computadora lejana.
2. En Outlook, enviar datos o mensajes de la Bandeja de salida al servidor.

User interface/Interfaz con el usuario Parte visual del software de sistema operativo que determina cómo interactúan los usuarios con la computadora.

User name/Nombre de usuario Nombre por el que el sistema o red identifica al usuario y que, junto con una contraseña, protege el sistema de computadora o red contra el uso no autorizado.

Utility program/Programa utilitario Programa que ayuda al usuario a dar mantenimiento al sistema operativo y a mejorarlo. El sistema operativo suministra ciertos programas utilitarios, en tanto que otros se compran de proveedores externos.

V

Value/Valor Entrada numérica en Excel.

Vertical application software/Software de aplicación vertical Software diseñado para diversos propósitos; por ejemplo, programas escritos para tipos específicos de empresas, juegos y software educativo.

Views/Vistas Exhibiciones en ventana que permiten mirar los datos de diferentes modos.

Virus/Virus Programa ideado maliciosamente, que se reproduce de una computadora a otra. Los virus pueden ser inocuos pero molestos para los usuarios, o bien afectar el comportamiento del software y destruir información.

W

Web browser/Explorador de Internet Tipo de aplicación que sirve para mostrar páginas de Internet y navegar por ella.

Web page/Página de Internet Documento al que se da formato de Lenguaje de marcado de hipertexto (HTML, por sus siglas en inglés) para poder publicarlo en Internet. Las páginas de Internet pueden contener texto, imágenes, video, sonido e hipervínculos con otras páginas o sitios.

Web site/Sitio de Internet Lugar de Internet cuyo mantenimiento está a cargo de una compañía, organización o persona, y que se compone de una o más páginas de Internet.

Wide area network (WAN)/Red de área extensa Sistema de redes locales y extensas interconectadas capaz de transferir datos entre computadoras sin que importe la distancia que las separa.

Windows/Windows Nombre común de la familia de sistemas operativos con interfaces gráficas con el usuario, fabricados por Microsoft Corp.

Windows Explorer/Explorador de Windows Herramienta con la que puedes navegar en el sistema de archivos de la computadora, y localizar y organizar archivos.

Wizard/Asistente Herramienta automatizada que ayuda a llevar a cabo una tarea presentando, paso a paso, opciones de contenido y de organización.

Workbook/Libro de trabajo Archivo de Excel que puede contener hasta 256 hojas de trabajo.

Worksheet/Hoja de trabajo Página de un libro de trabajo de Excel.

World Wide Web/World Wide Web Red comprendida dentro de Internet y cuyas computadoras usan el mismo lenguaje para comunicarse; la información se presenta en ella en la forma de páginas de Internet.

Index

Index

Credits

Staff Credits

The people who made up the PRENTICE HALL ***BUSINESS COMPUTER INFORMATION SYSTEMS*** team—representing design services, editorial, editorial services, electronic publishing technology, manufacturing & inventory planning, market research, marketing services, online services & multimedia development, planning & budgeting, product planning, production services, project office, publishing processes, and rights & permissions—are listed below. Bold type denotes the core team members.

Dori Amtmann, **Sarah M. Carroll**, Lois Ann Freier, **Jennifer Frew**, **Martha Heller**, Carol Lavis, **Vickie Menanteaux**, Matthew J. Raycroft, **Laura Ross**, Gerry Schrenk, Annette Simmons, Jan Singh, Monica Stipanov, Kathy Wanamaker

Additional Credits

Diane Alemina, Gregory Abrom, Ernest Albanese, Penny Baker, Rui Camarinha, John Carle, Martha Conway, Kathy Gavilanes, Beth Hyslip, Jennifer Keezer, John Kingston, Vicki Lamb, Sue Langan, Art Mkrtchyan, Kenneth Myett, Kim Ortell, Raymond Parenteau, Linda Punskovsky, Rachel Ross, Mildred Schulte, Melissa Shustyk

Art Credits

Charts, Graphs and Tables: Albanese, Ernest and Studio A

Albanese, Ernest: 55, 284, 395, 451

HRS Interactive: 569

Mkrtchyan, Art: 799

Schuster, Robert: 81, 131, 199, 285, 309, 321, 353, 409, 485, 727, 763, 788, 794, 797, 798, 802

Photo Credits

Special Features and Borders, Corbis, PhotoDisc/ Getty Images, Eyewire/Getty Images

Cover. ©Boden/Ledingham/Masterfile Stock Image Library **iii.** ©Richard Cummins/CORBIS **v.** ©Richard Cummins/CORBIS **2** *l.* Jiang Jin/SuperStock **2** *m.* Bob Daemmrich/Stock, Boston **2** *r* ©Lisa Loucks Christenson **3** *l.* Bob Daemmrich/Stock, Boston **3** *bkg.* PhotoDisc/ Getty Images **3** *m.* PhotoDisc/ Getty Images **3** *r.* Getty Images **4** *bkg.* PhotoDisc/ Getty Images **4** *bkg.* PhotoDisc/ Getty Images **5** *t.* PhotoDisc/ Getty Images **18** PhotoDisc/Getty Images **19** ©2001Image State. Inc. **23** ©Tony Savino/The Image Works **40** *bkg.* PhotoDisc/ Getty Images **41** *m.* ©Digital Vision **54** ©Wonderfile **55** *t.* ©Digital Vision/Wonderfile **80** *bkg.* PhotoDisc/ Getty Images **94** *r.* Walt and Company Communications **94** *b.* PhotoDisc/ Getty Images, Inc. **95** *t.* Getty Images **122** *bkg.* PhotoDisc/ Getty Images **123** *t.* John Henley/CORBIS **130** *b.* ©Masterfile **130** *t.l.* ©Digital Vision **131** *t.l.* ©Pierre Tremblay/Masterfile **136** Honda's ASIMO Humanoid Robot-courtesy of American Honda Motor Company Inc. **158** *l.* PhotoDisc/ Getty Images **158** *m.* Bob Daemmrich/Stock, Boston **158** *r.* ©Lisa Loucks Christenson **159** *m.* Jiang Jin/SuperStock **159** *l.* Bob Daemmrich/Stock, Boston **159** *r.* Getty Images **159** *bkg.* Jiang Jin/SuperStock **160** *bkg.* SuperStock **161** *m.t.* Powerstock/SuperStock **168** *l.* ©1992 Stephen Frisch/Stock, Boston **168** *r.* PhotoDisc/ Getty Images **169** ©Guy Grenier/Masterfile Stock Image Library **173** Tony Freeman/PhotoEdit **188** *bkg.* SuperStock **189** *t.* ©Bill Frymire/Masterfile Stock Image Library **198** *b.* PhotoDisc/ Getty Images **198** *t.* ©Neal & Molly Jansen/SuperStock **199** *t.* ©Josh Mitchell/ Index Stock Imagery/PictureQuest **209** Jon Feingersh/ CORBIS **224** *bkg.* SuperStock **225** *m.* Getty Images **228** H. Prinz/CORBIS **242** *t.l.* Mauritius/Index Stock **242** *b.l.* ©Pearson Education **242** *b.l.* ©Pearson Education **243** *t.r.* Francisco Cruz/SuperStock **268** *bkg.* SuperStock **269** *m.* PhotoDisc/ Getty Images **284** *b.* PhotoDisc/ Getty Images **285** ©Matthew Wiley/Masterfile **302** *m.* Jiang Jin/SuperStock **302** *r.* ©Lisa Loucks Christenson **303** *l.* Bob Daemmrich/Stock, Boston **303** *r.* Getty Images **303** *bkg.* Bob Daemmrich/Stock, Boston **303** *m.* Bob Daemmrich/Stock, Boston **304** *bkg.* ©Denis Scott/CORBIS **305** *m.* Getty Images **320** *b.* Bob Daemmrich/Stock, Boston **321** *t.* ©Network Productions/Rainbow **338** *bkg.* ©Denis Scott/corbisstockmarket **339** *m.* ©George B. Diebold/CORBIS **352** ©Doug Martin/Photo Researchers, Inc. **353** ©Michael Newman/PhotoEdit **360** *t.l.* ©David M. Grossman/Phototake **384** *bkg.* ©Denis Scott/CORBIS **385** *m.* Letraset Phototone **394** *t.* Getty Images **394** *b.* ©MTPA Stock//Masterfile **395** *t.l.* ©MTPA Stock/Masterfile **424** *bkg.* ©Denis Scott/corbisstockmarket **425** *m.* ©H. Prinz/CORBIS **450** *t.* ©Jim Karageorge/Masterfile **450** *b.* Getty Images **451** *t.* Getty Images **474** *l.* PhotoDisc/ Getty Images **474** *m.* Jiang Jin/SuperStock **474** *r.* Bob Daemmrich/Stock, Boston **475** *m.* ©Lisa Loucks Christenson **475** *l.* Bob Daemmrich/Stock, Boston **475** *r.* Getty Images **475** *bkg.* ©Lisa Loucks Christenson **476** *bkg.* Eyewire/Getty Images **477** *m.* ©Bill Frymire/Masterfile **496** *b.* ©Mtpa Stock/Masterfile Stock Image Library **497** *t.l.* PhotoDisc/ Getty Images **497** *t.r.* Walt & Company Communications **497** *m.* Associated Press,AP **497** *b.* Getty Images **520** *bkg.* Eyewire/Getty Images **521** *m.* PhotoDisc/ Getty Images **528** *b* ©José L. Pelaez/CORBIS **529** *t.* Getty Images **529** *b.* Comstock, Inc. **548** *bkg.* Eyewire/Getty Images **549** *m.* ©Royalty-Free/CORBIS **554** *t.* Pearson Education **554** *b.* ©David Frazier/Photo Researchers, Inc. **555** *r.* ©Michael Newman/PhotoEdit **555** *l.* PhotoDisc/Getty Images **592** *bkg.* Eyewire/Getty Images **593** *m.* Getty Images **601** Bob Daemmrich/Stock,Boston **610** *t.* Courtesy of International Business Machine **610** *m.b.* Courtesy of Sony ElectronicsInc. **610** Courtesy Walt & Company Comunication **610** *b.l.* Courtesy of Logitech,Inc. **610** *m.* ©Guy Grenier/Masterfile Stock Image Library **611** ©Doug Martin /Photo Researchers, Inc. **642** *l.* PhotoDisc/ Getty Images **642** *m.* Jiang Jin/SuperStock **642** *r.* Bob Daemmrich/Stock, Boston **643** *l.* ©Lisa Loucks Christenson **643** *m.* Bob Daemmrich/Stock, Boston **643** *r.* Getty Images **643** *bkg.* Bob Daemmrich/Stock, Boston **644** *bkg.* ©George B. Biebold/CORBIS **645** *m.* ©Simon DesRochers/Masterfile **664** *r.* Getty Images **664** *l.* Silver Burdett Ginn **665** *t.* ©Rick Fischer/Masterfile **665** *b.* ©Jon Feingersh/CORBIS **674** Corbis/Stock Market **648** *bkg.* ©George B. Biebold/CORBIS **685** *m.* ©M.G. Perrelli/CORBIS **693** Donna Day/Imagastate **702** *l.* ©Mtpa Stock/Masterfile Stock Image Library **702** *r.* PhotoDisc/ Getty Images **703** *m.* ©Lawrence Manning/CORBIS **703** *t.* Palm, Inc. **703** *b.* Jiang Jin/SuperStock **716** *bkg.* ©George B. Biebold/Corbisstockmarket **717** *m.* Ron Brown/Index Stock Photography, Inc. **726** *t.* PhotoDisc/ Getty Images **726** *b.* ©Wonderfile **746** *m.* Jiang Jin/SuperStock **746** *r.* Bob Daemmrich/Stock, Boston **746** *l.* PhotoDisc/ Getty Images **747** *m.* Getty Images **747** *l.* ©Lisa Loucks Christenson **747** *r.* Bob Daemmrich/Stock, Boston **747** *bkg.* Getty Images **748** *bkg.* Artville/Getty Images **749** *m.* ©Peter Saloutos/Corbisstockmarket **750** *t.* ©Christopher Bissell/Tony Stone Images **750** *b.* ©Steve Chenn/CORBIS **751** *t.* AP/Wide World Photos **751** *b.* Texas Instruments Incorporated **752** *t.l.* Courtesy of International Business Machines Corporation. Unauthorized use not permitted. **754** ASUS A7V8X courtesy of ASUS Computer International/www.asus.com **758** Courtesy Western Digital Corporation **760** Courtesy of Sony Electronics, Inc. **762** *b.* David Young-Wolt/PhotoEdit **762** *t.* Getty Images **763** *t.l.* Bill Aron/PhotoEdit **768** *t.l.* Courtesy of Apple **770** *t.l.* Francisco Cruz/SuperStock **773** Dan Nelken/Liaison Agency **774** Arlene Sandler/SuperStock **782** *bkg.* Artville/Getty Images **783** *m.* Eyewire/Getty Images **789** *b.* Courtesy of Zoom Telephonics Inc. **789** *t.* 3COM/U. S. Robatics **796** *t.* Champlain Cable Corporation **796** *m.1* Courtesy of Inmac **796** *m.2* Optical Cable Corporation **796** *m.3* Extended Systems **796** *b.* Proxim, Inc. **801** Getty Images **802** *t.l.* Photo courtesy of Linksys **803** Courtesy of Nokia. ©2002 Nokia. All rights reserved. Nokia and Nokia Connecting People are registered trademarks of Nokia Corporation. **Lesson Opener borders:** PhotoDisc/Getty Images **Special Features credits: Business Connections borders:** *t.* CORBIS, *r.* PhotoDisc/Getty Images. **Career & Technology borders:** (8) PhotoDisc/Getty Images. **Tech Talk borders:** (3) PhotoDisc/Getty Images **Technology @ School borders:** (2) *t, b,* PhotoDisc/Getty Images, *l.* Eyewire/Getty Images, *r.* CORBIS

Note: Every effort has been made to locate the copyright owner of material used in this textbook. Omissions brought to our attention will be corrected in subsequent editions.